Ordnance Survey

STREET ATLAS

Glasgow

and West Central Scotland

Contents

PHILIP'S

First edition published 1995
First colour edition published 1999 by

Ordnance Survey®   and   George Philip Ltd., a division of
Romsey Road   Octopus Publishing Group Ltd
Maybush   Michelin House
Southampton   81 Fulham Road
SO16 4GU   London SW3 6RB

ISBN 0-540-07648 1 (hardback)
ISBN 0-540-07649 X (spiral)

**The mapping between pages 1 and 241 (inclusive) in this atlas is
derived from Ordnance Survey® Large Scale and Landranger®
mapping, and revised using OSCAR® and Land-Line® data.**

Ordnance Survey, OSCAR, Land-line and Landranger are registered trade
marks of Ordnance Survey, the national mapping agency of Great Britain.

Printed and bound in Spain by Cayfosa

Digital Data

The exceptionally high-quality mapping
found in this book is available as digital
data in TIFF format, which is easily
convertible to other bit-mapped (raster)
image formats.

The index is also available in digital form
as a standard database table. It contains
all the details found in the printed index
together with the National Grid reference
for the map square in which each entry
is named and feature codes for places
of interest in eight categories such as
education and health.

For further information and to discuss
your requirements, please contact the
Ordnance Survey Solutions Centre on
01703 792929.

Symbol	Description
(22a)	Motorway (with junction number)
	Primary route (dual carriageway and single)
	A road (dual carriageway and single)
	B road (dual carriageway and single)
	Minor road (dual carriageway and single)
	Other minor road (dual carriageway and single)
	Road under construction
	Pedestrianised area
DY7	Postcode boundaries
	County and Unitary Authority boundaries
	Railway
	Tramway, miniature railway
	Rural track, private road or narrow road in urban area
	Gate or obstruction to traffic (restrictions may not apply at all times or to all vehicles)
	Path, bridleway, byway open to all traffic, road used as a public path
	The representation in this atlas of a road, track or path is no evidence of the existence of a right of way
126 94 164	Adjoining page indicators
	The map area within the pink band is shown at a larger scale on the page indicated by the red block and arrow

Abbr.		Abbr.	
Acad	Academy	Meml	Memorial
Crem	Crematorium	Mon	Monument
Cemy	Cemetery	Mus	Museum
C Ctr	Civic Centre	Obsy	Observatory
CH	Club House	Pal	Royal Palace
Coll	College	PH	Public House
Ent	Enterprise	Recn Gd	Recreation Ground
Ex H	Exhibition Hall	Resr	Reservoir
Ind Est	Industrial Estate	Ret Pk	Retail Park
Inst	Institute	Sch	School
Ct	Law Court	Sh Ctr	Shopping Centre
L Ctr	Leisure Centre	TH	Town Hall/House
LC	Level Crossing	Trad Est	Trading Estate
Liby	Library	Univ	University
Mkt	Market	YH	Youth Hostel

Symbol	Description
Walsall	Railway station
U	Glasgow Underground station
	Midland Metro
M	Metrolink station
	London Underground station
D	Docklands Light Railway station
M	Tyne and Wear Metro
	Private railway station
	Bus, coach station
	Ambulance station
	Coastguard station
	Fire station
	Police station
	Accident and Emergency entrance to hospital
H	Hospital
	Church, place of worship
i	Information Centre (open all year)
P P&R	Parking, Park and Ride
PO	Post Office
Prim Sch	Important buildings, schools, colleges, universities and hospitals
River Medway	Water name
	Stream
	River or canal (minor and major)
	Water
	Tidal water
	Woods
	Houses
House	Non-Roman antiquity
VILLA	Roman antiquity

■ The dark grey border on the inside edge of some pages indicates that the mapping does not continue onto the adjacent page ■ The small numbers around the edges of the maps identify the 1 kilometre National Grid lines

The scale of the maps is 5.52 cm to 1 km (3½ inches to 1 mile)

0 ¼ ½ ¾ 1 mile
0 250m 500m 750m 1 kilometre

The scale of the maps on pages numbered in red is 11.04 cm to 1 km (7 inches to 1 mile)

0 220 yards 440 yards 660 yards ½ mile
0 125m 250m 375m ½ kilometre

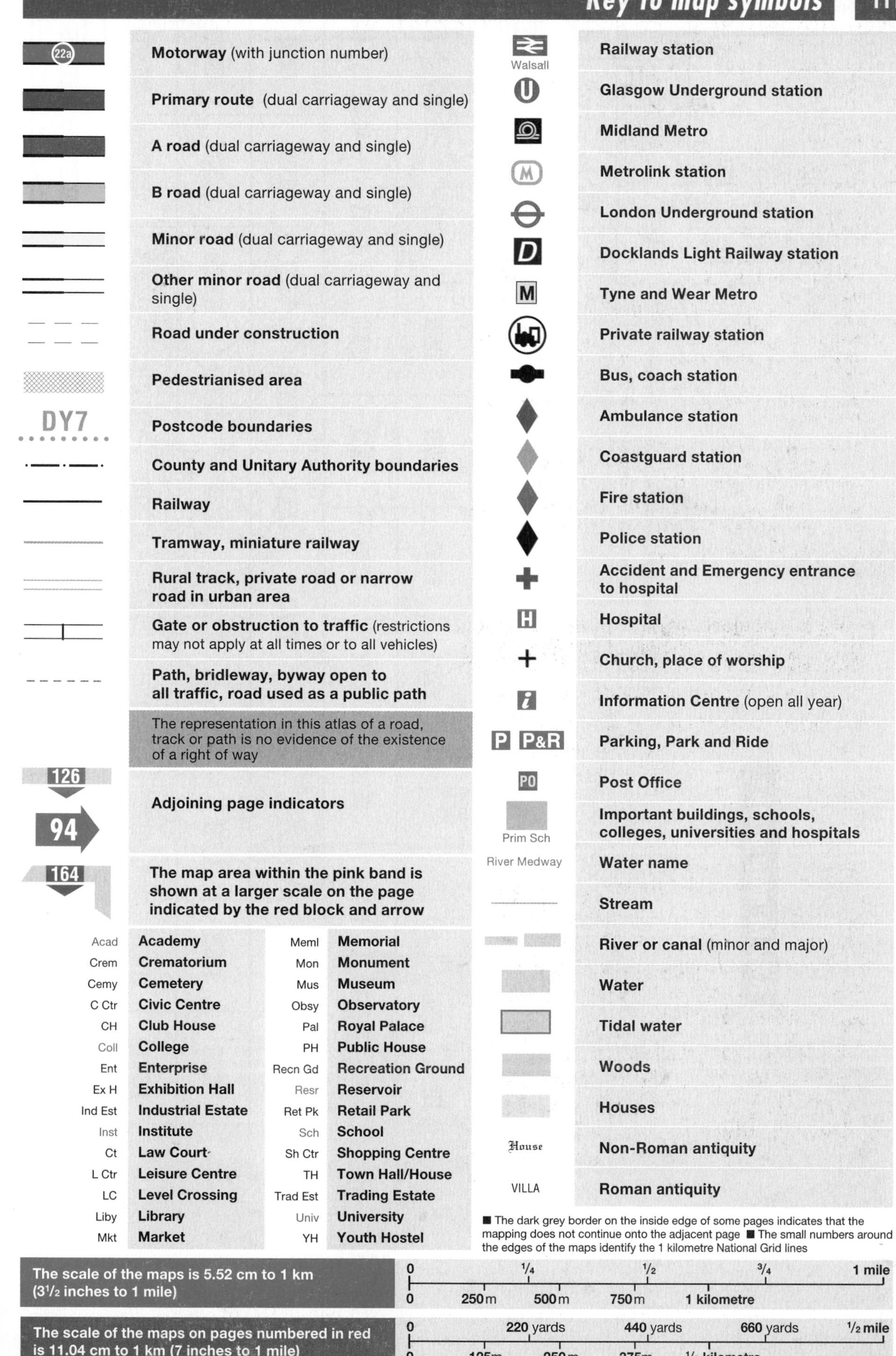

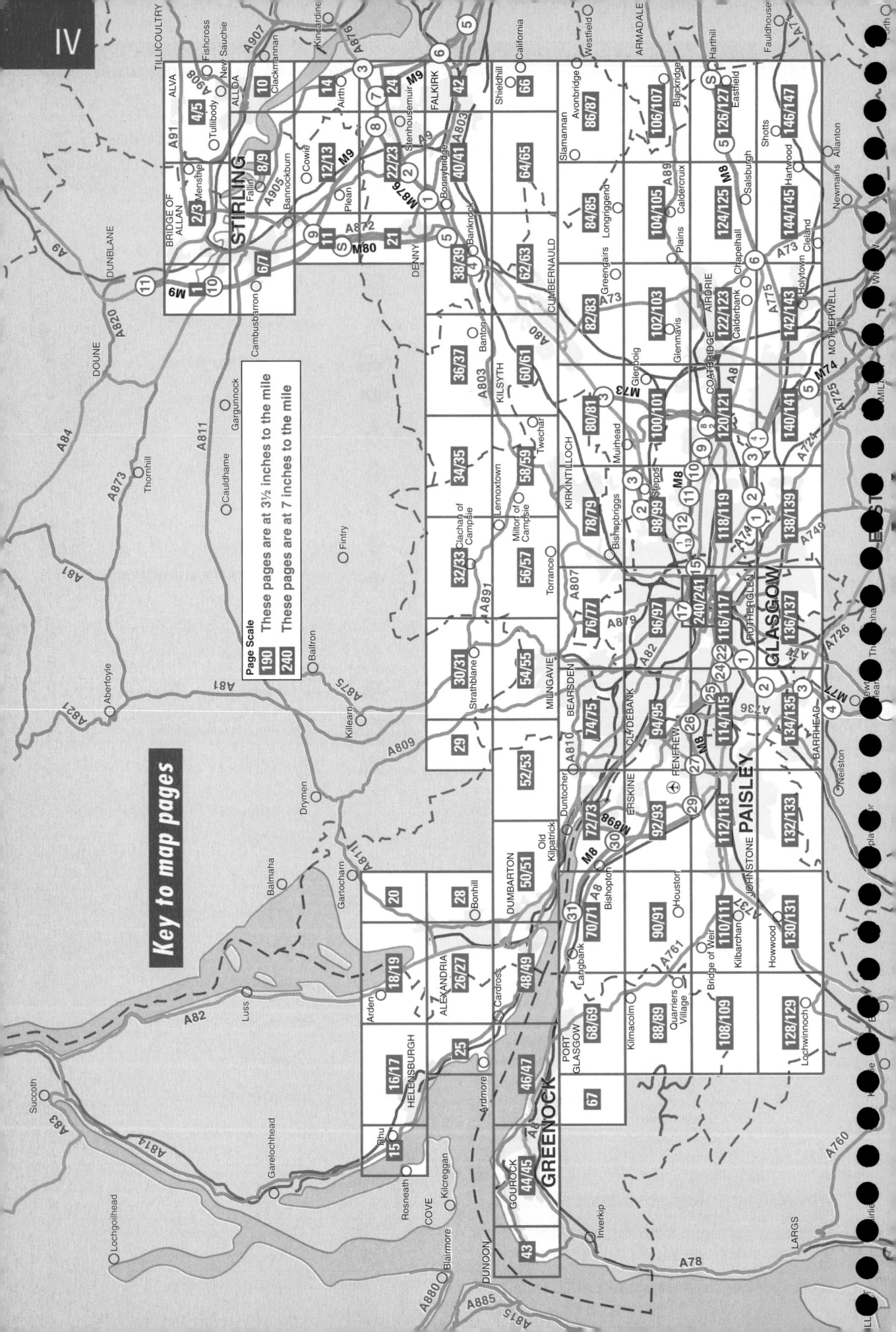

Key to map pages

Page Scale

190 These pages are at 3½ inches to the mile
240 These pages are at 7 inches to the mile

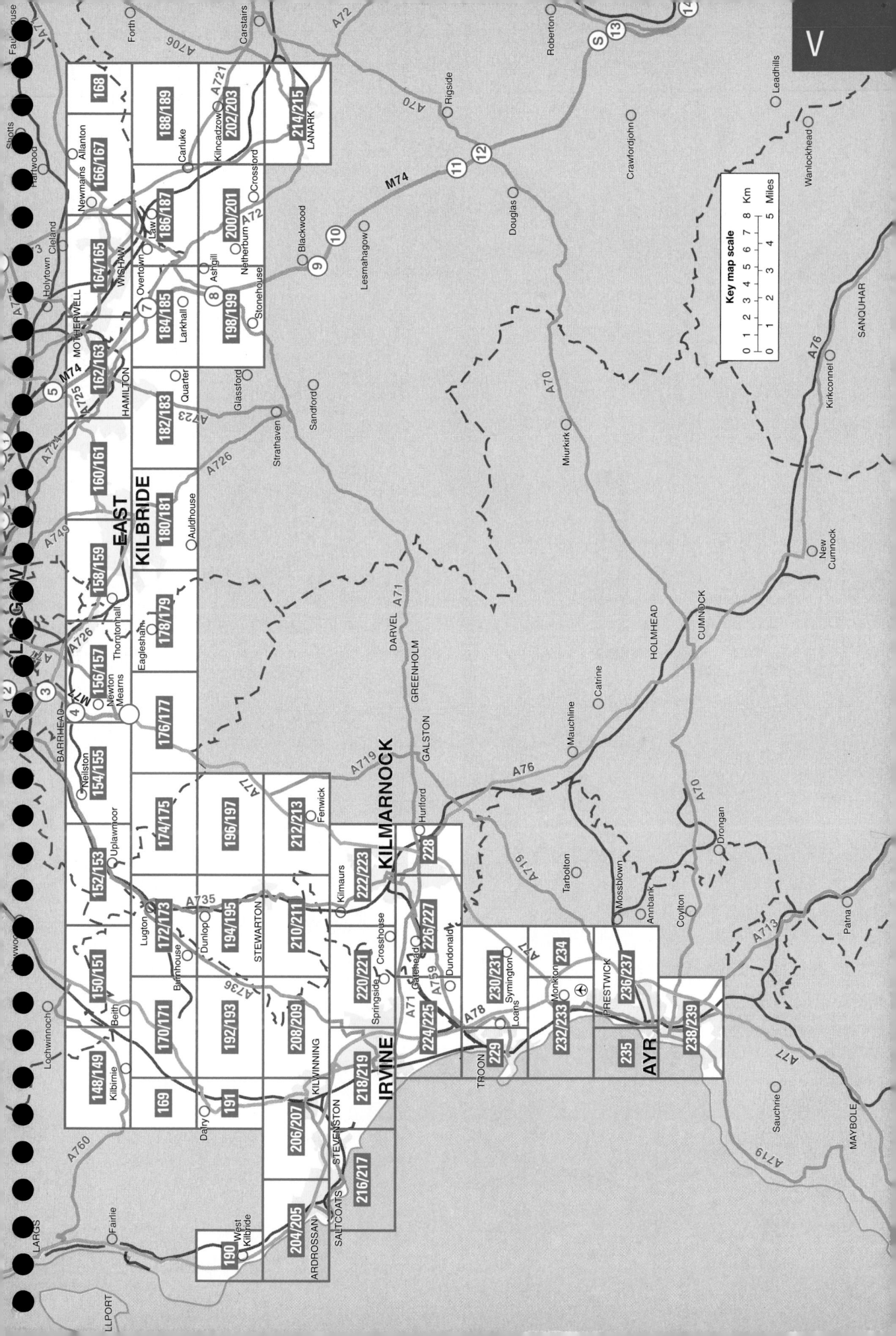

V
Key map scale
0 1 2 3 4 5 6 7 8 Km
0 1 2 3 4 5 Miles
GLASGOW
EAST KILBRIDE
KILMARNOCK
IRVINE
AYR
MOTHERWELL
HAMILTON
WISHAW
LANARK
BARRHEAD
STEWARTON
KILWINNING
STEVENSTON
SALTCOATS
ARDROSSAN
TROON
PRESTWICK
DARVEL
GREENHOLM
GALSTON
HOLMHEAD
CUMNOCK
SANQUHAR
MAYBOLE
LARGS
LLPORT
148/149
150/151
152/153
154/155
156/157
158/159
160/161
162/163
164/165
166/167
168
169
170/171
172/173
174/175
176/177
178/179
180/181
182/183
184/185
186/187
188/189
190
191
192/193
194/195
196/197
198/199
200/201
202/203
204/205
206/207
208/209
210/211
212/213
214/215
216/217
218/219
220/221
222/223
224/225
226/227
228
229
230/231
232/233
234
235
236/237
238/239
M74
M77
A71
A70
A72
A76
A77
A78
A719
A723
A724
A725
A726
A735
A736
A749
A759
A760
A706
A721
A713
Fairlie
Lochwinnoch
Kilbirnie
Beith
Uplawmoor
Neilston
Newton Mearns
Thorntonhall
Eaglesham
Auldhouse
Quarter
Lugton
Burnhouse
Dunlop
Dalry
West Kilbride
Fenwick
Kilmaurs
Springside
Crosshouse
Gatehead
Dundonald
Hurlford
Loans
Symington
Monkton
Tarbolton
Mauchline
Catrine
Mossblown
Annbank
Coylton
Drongan
Sauchrie
Patna
New Cumnock
Kirkconnel
Muirkirk
Holytown
Cleland
Newmains
Allanton
Harthill
Shotts
Overtown
Law
Larkhall
Carluke
Ashgill
Netherburn
Stonehouse
Crossford
Kilncadzow
Glassford
Strathaven
Sandford
Blackwood
Lesmahagow
Forth
Carstairs
Rigside
Douglas
Roberton
Crawfordjohn
Leadhills
Wanlockhead

VI
Route planning
QUEEN ELIZABETH FOREST PARK
LOCH ARD FOREST
BEN LOMOND
CAMPSIE FELLS
KILPATRICK HILLS
Carron Valley Forest
STIRLING
GLASGOW
GREENOCK
PAISLEY
HELENSBURGH
DUMBARTON
PORT GLASGOW
GOUROCK
DUNOON
CLYDEBANK
BEARSDEN
MILNGAVIE
KIRKINTILLOCH
CUMBERNAULD
COATBRIDGE
AIRDRIE
MOTHERWELL
RUTHERGLEN
BARRHEAD
JOHNSTONE
FALKIRK
GRANGEMOUTH
ALLOA
TILLICOULTRY
DUNBLANE
DOUNE
CALLANDER
KILSYTH
ALEXANDRIA
LARGS
Kilmacolm
Balfron
Aberfoyle
LOCH LOMOND

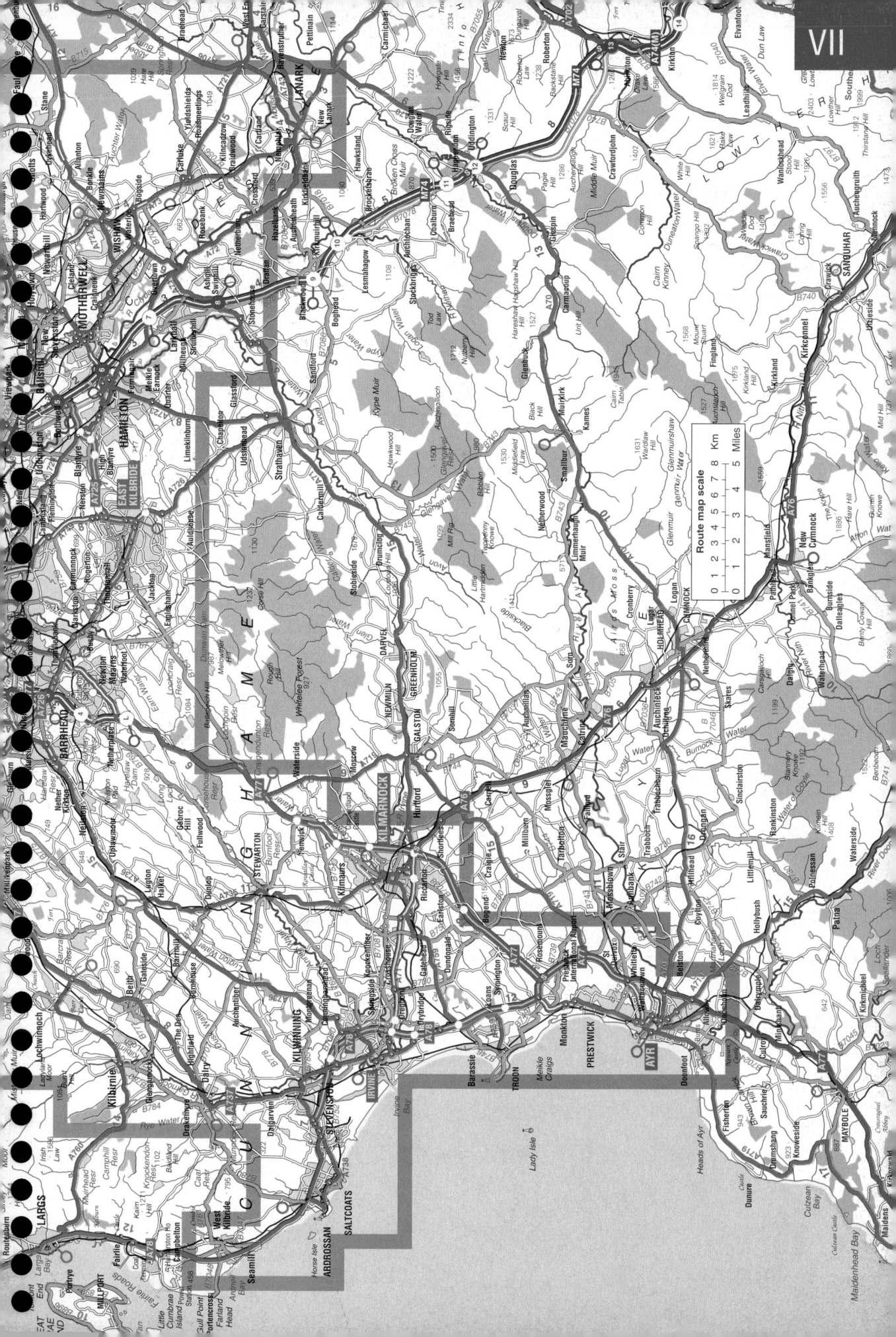
VII
Route map scale
0 1 2 3 4 5 6 7 8 Km
0 1 2 3 4 5 Miles
C U N N I N G H A M E
K Y L E
L O W T H E R
LARGS
MILLPORT
Kilbirnie
Lochwinnoch
BARRHEAD
MOTHERWELL
WISHAW
HAMILTON
EAST KILBRIDE
Carluke
LANARK
STEWARTON
KILWINNING
STEVENSTON
ARDROSSAN
SALTCOATS
IRVINE
KILMARNOCK
NEWMILN
DARVEL
GALSTON
GREENHOLM
Strathaven
Lesmahagow
Douglas
Muirkirk
Mauchline
Catrine
Auchinleck
CUMNOCK
New Cumnock
TROON
PRESTWICK
AYR
MAYBOLE
SANQUHAR
Leadhills
Wanlockhead
Dalry
West Kilbride
Seamill
Fairlie
Dunure
Patna
Whitelee Forest
Kype Muir
Airds Moss
Cairn Table
Lady Isle
Horse Isle
Heads of Ayr
Culzean Bay
Maidenhead Bay
Irvine Bay
Little Cumbrae Island

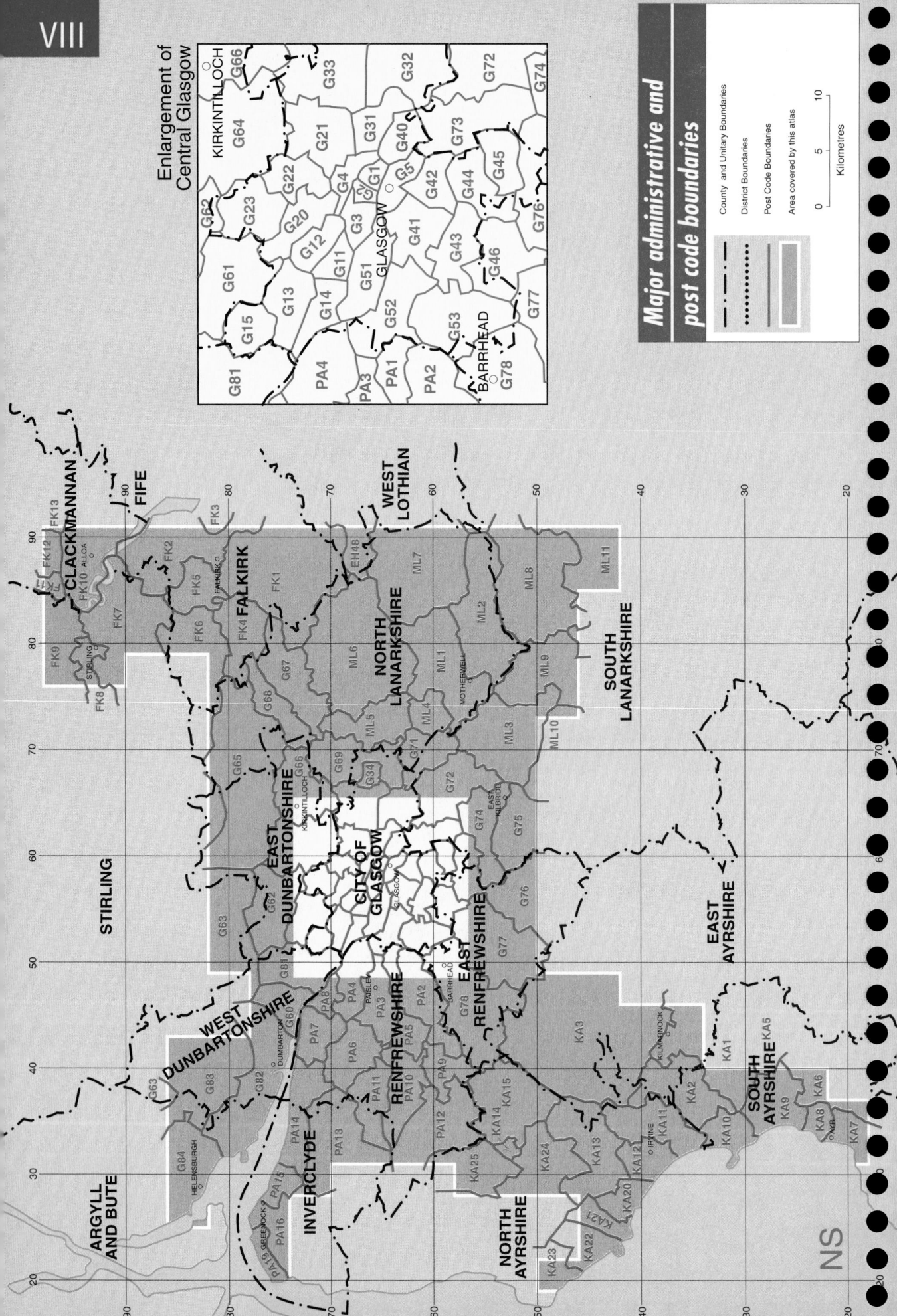

Enlargement of Central Glasgow

Major administrative and post code boundaries

County and Unitary Boundaries
District Boundaries
Post Code Boundaries
Area covered by this atlas

Kilometres
0   5   10

2

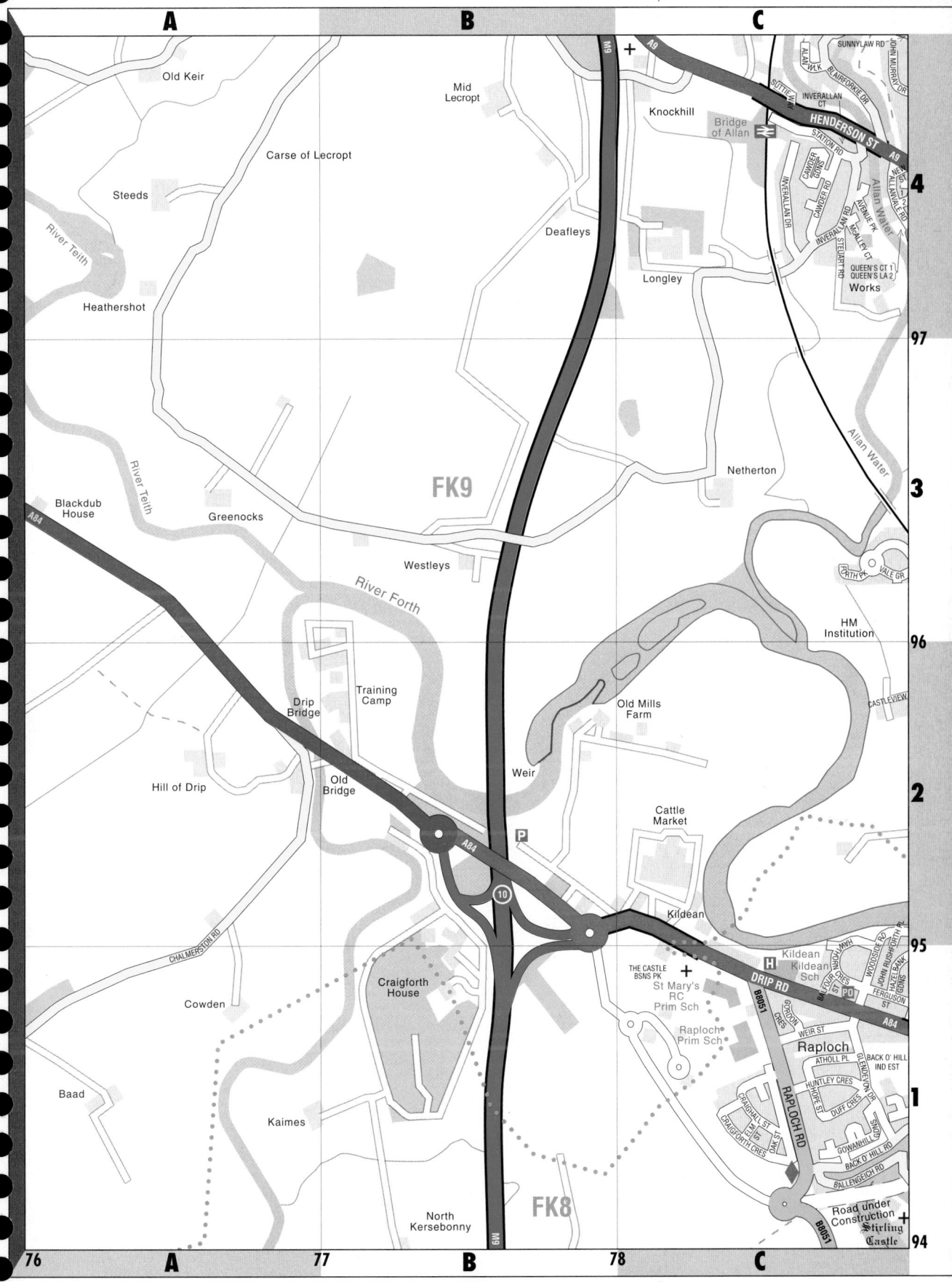

A
B
C
Old Keir
Mid Lecropt
Knockhill
Bridge of Allan
Carse of Lecropt
Steeds
River Teith
Deafleys
Longley
Heathershot
Works
HENDERSON ST
Allan Water
Netherton
FK9
River Teith
Blackdub House
Greenocks
Westleys
River Forth
HM Institution
Drip Bridge
Training Camp
Old Mills Farm
Hill of Drip
Old Bridge
Weir
Cattle Market
A84
A9
M9
Kildean
THE CASTLE BSNS PK
St Mary's RC Prim Sch
Kildean Sch
DRIP RD
B8051
Cowden
Craigforth House
Raploch Prim Sch
Raploch
RAPLOCH RD
Baad
Kaimes
FK8
North Kersebonny
Road under Construction
Stirling Castle
76
77
78
4
97
3
96
2
95
1
94

6
2

BRIDGE OF ALLAN

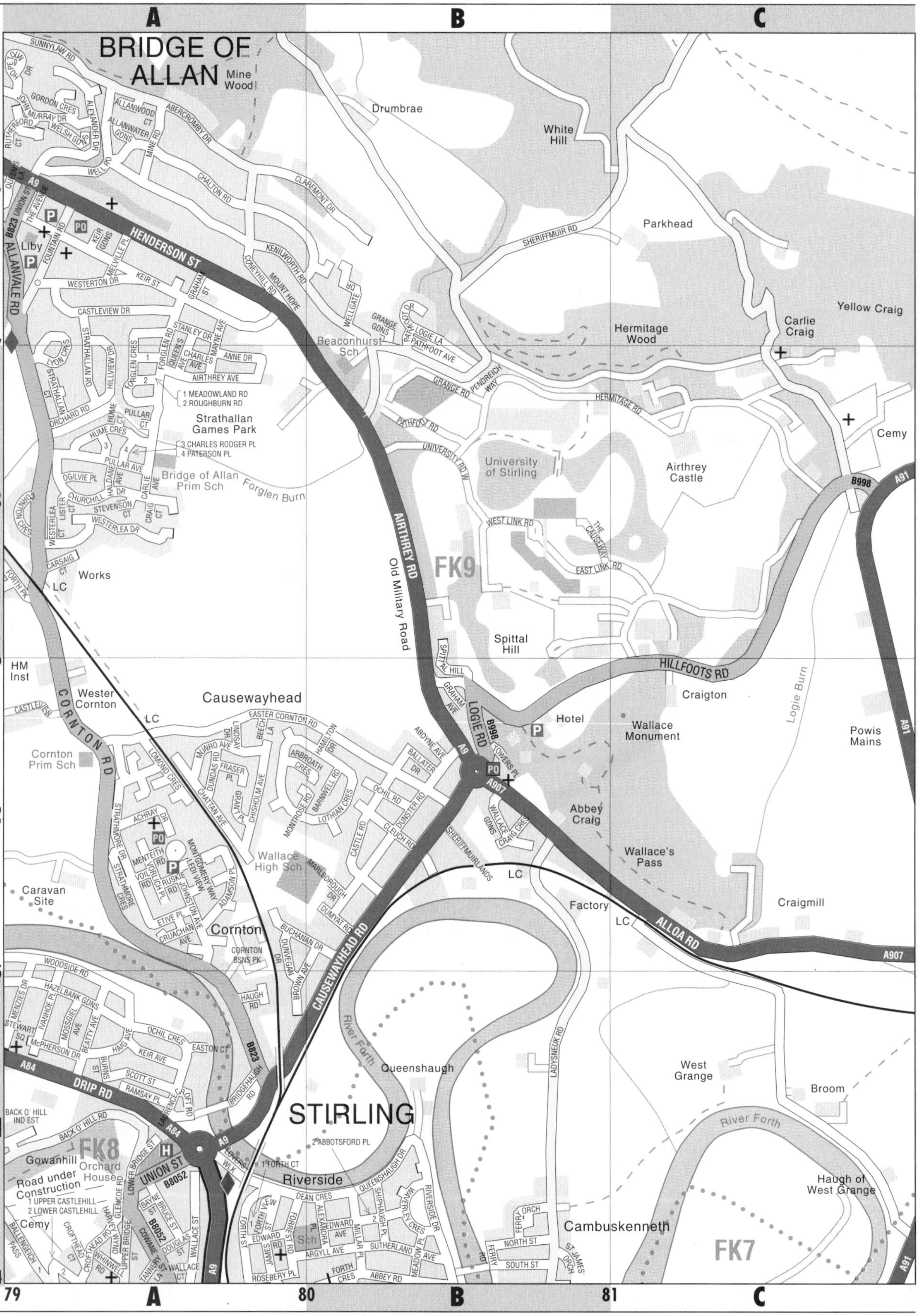

Mine Wood

Drumbrae

White Hill

Parkhead

Yellow Craig

Carlie Craig

SHERIFFMUIR RD

4

HENDERSON ST

Hermitage Wood

Cemy

Beaconhurst Sch

GRANGE GDNS

97

HERMITAGE RD

1 MEADOWLAND RD
2 ROUGHBURN RD

Strathallan Games Park

3 CHARLES RODGER PL
4 PATERSON PL

University of Stirling

Airthrey Castle

PATHFOOT RD

Bridge of Allan Prim Sch

Forglen Burn

UNIVERSITY RD

3

WEST LINK RD

FK9

EAST LINK RD

Works

LC

AIRTHREY RD

Old Military Road

Spittal Hill

96

HM Inst

Wester Cornton

Causewayhead

HILLFOOTS RD

Craigton

Logie Burn

Powis Mains

LC

Cornton Prim Sch

GRAHAM AVE

LOGIE RD

B998

P

Hotel

Wallace Monument

A91

2

PO

P

A907

PO

Abbey Craig

Wallace High Sch

Wallace's Pass

Caravan Site

Cornton

LC

CORNTON BSNS PK

Factory

LC

Craigmill

95

CAUSEWAYHEAD RD

ALLOA RD

A907

WOODSIDE RD

River Forth

Queenshaugh

West Grange

Broom

A84

DRIP RD

B823

STIRLING

River Forth

Haugh of West Grange

1

BACK O' HILL IND EST

FK8

Gowanhill

Orchard House

Road under Construction

UNION ST

H

Riverside

Cambuskenneth

FK7

1 UPPER CASTLEHILL
2 LOWER CASTLEHILL

Cemy

94

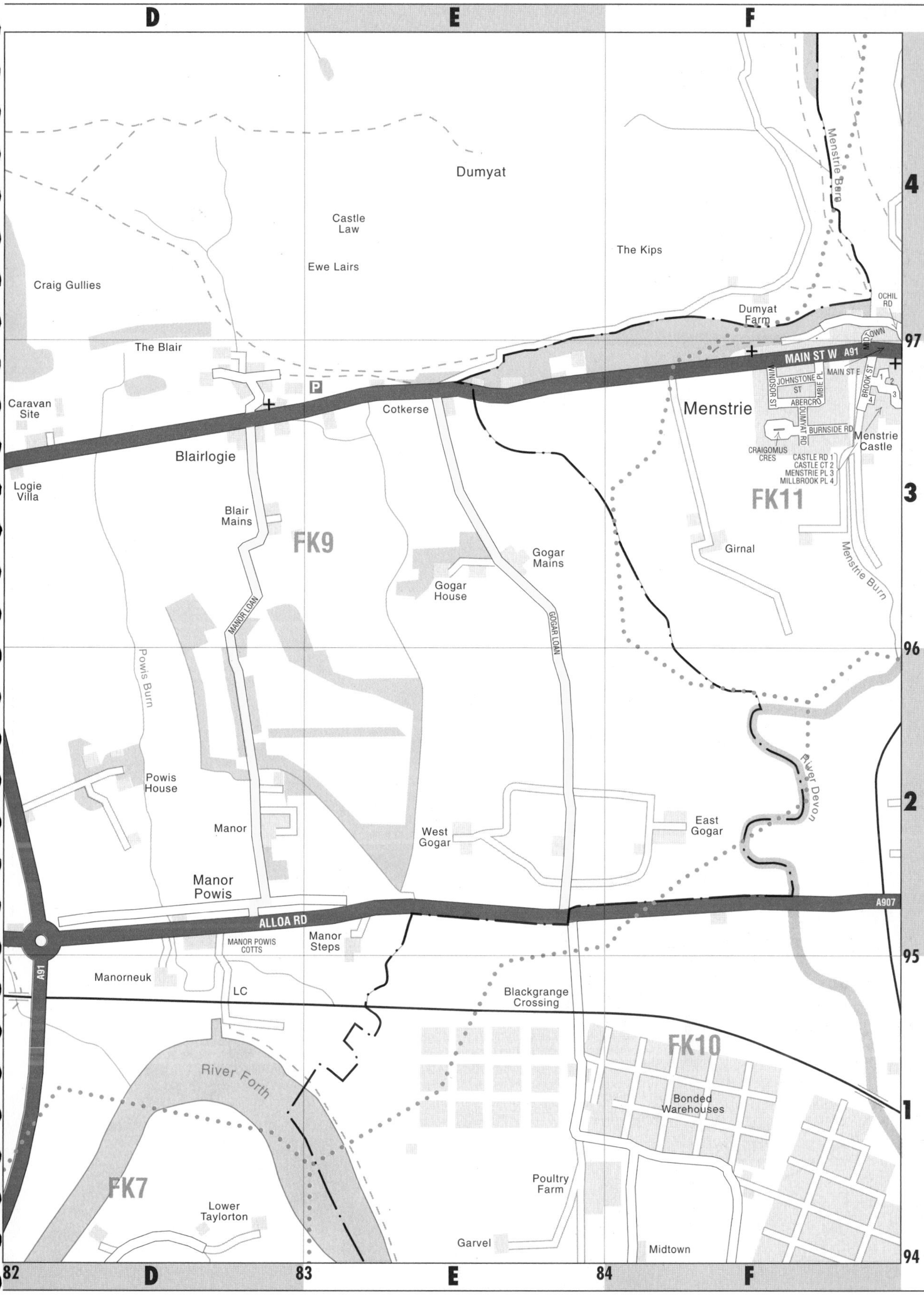

D   E   F

Dumyat

Castle
Law

Ewe Lairs

The Kips

Craig Gullies

Dumyat
Farm

OCHIL
RD

4

The Blair

MAIN ST W   A91

Caravan
Site

Cotkerse

Menstrie

JOHNSTONE ST

MAIN ST E

WINDSOR ST

ABERCRO

BROOK ST

97

Logie
Villa

Blairlogie

CRAIGOMUS
CRES

BURNSIDE RD

DUMYAT RD

Menstrie
Castle

Blair
Mains

FK9

Gogar
House

Gogar Mains

CASTLE RD 1
CASTLE CT 2
MENSTRIE PL 3
MILLBROOK PL 4

FK11

Girnal

Menstrie Burn

3

MANOR LOAN

GOGAR LOAN

96

Powis Burn

Powis
House

Manor

West
Gogar

East
Gogar

River Devon

2

Manor
Powis

ALLOA RD

A907

MANOR POWIS
COTTS

Manor
Steps

95

Manorneuk

LC

Blackgrange
Crossing

FK10

A91

River Forth

Bonded
Warehouses

1

FK7

Lower
Taylorton

Poultry
Farm

Garvel

Midtown

94

82   D   83   E   84   F

3

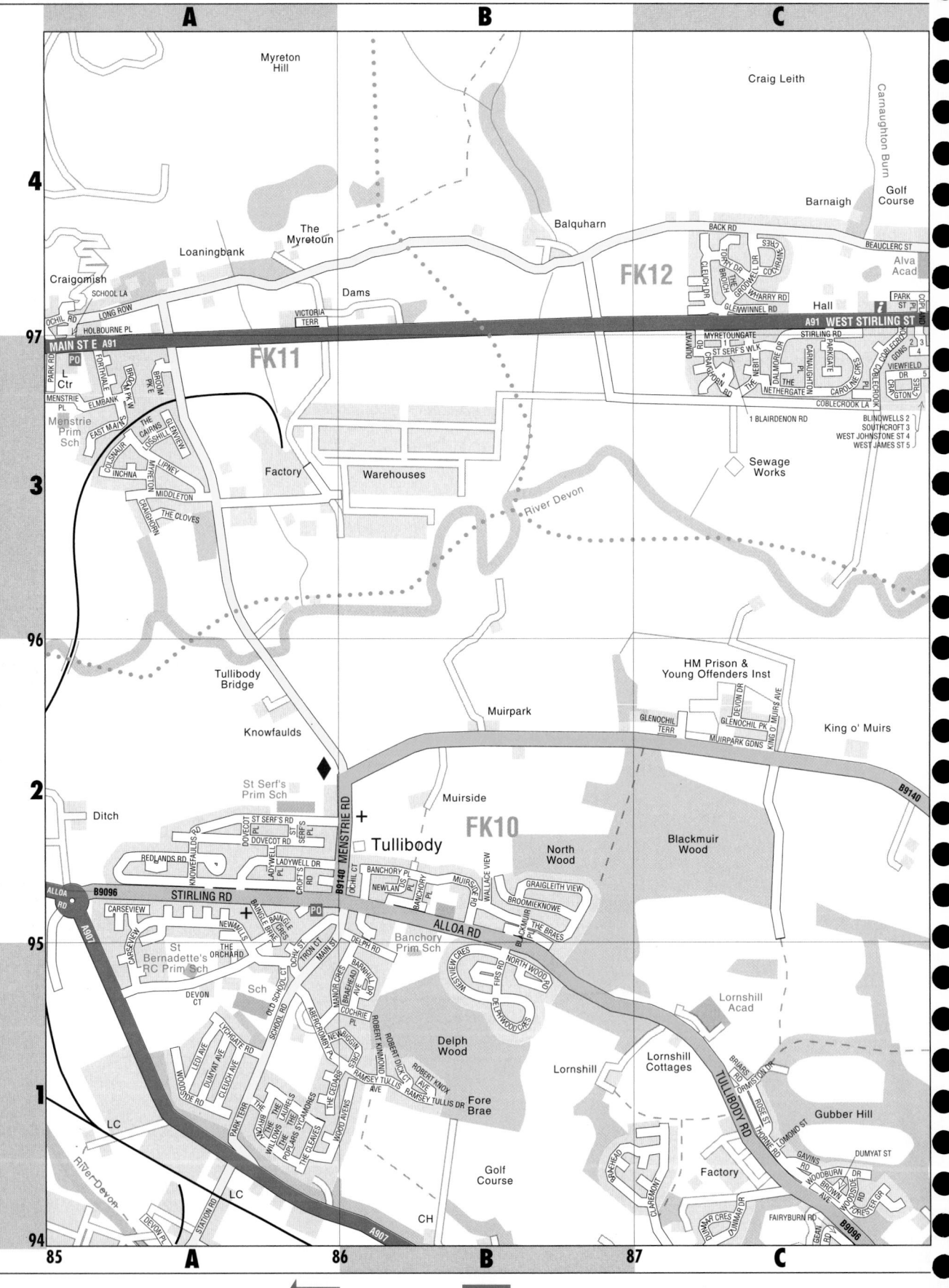

Myreton Hill
Craig Leith
Carnaughton Burn
Golf Course
Barnaigh
Balquharn
The Myretoun
Loaningbank
Craigomish
Dams
FK12
FK11
FK10
MAIN ST E A91
A91 WEST STIRLING ST
Hall
Alva Acad
Menstrie Prim Sch
Factory
Warehouses
Sewage Works
River Devon
Tullibody Bridge
HM Prison & Young Offenders Inst
Muirpark
Knowfaulds
King o' Muirs
St Serf's Prim Sch
Muirside
Ditch
Tullibody
North Wood
Blackmuir Wood
B9140
MENSTRIE RD
STIRLING RD
ALLOA RD
B9096
A907
St Bernadette's RC Prim Sch
Banchory Prim Sch
Sch
Lornshill Acad
Delph Wood
Lornshill
Lornshill Cottages
TULLIBODY RD
Fore Brae
Gubber Hill
Golf Course
Factory
LC
CH
River Devon

3
9

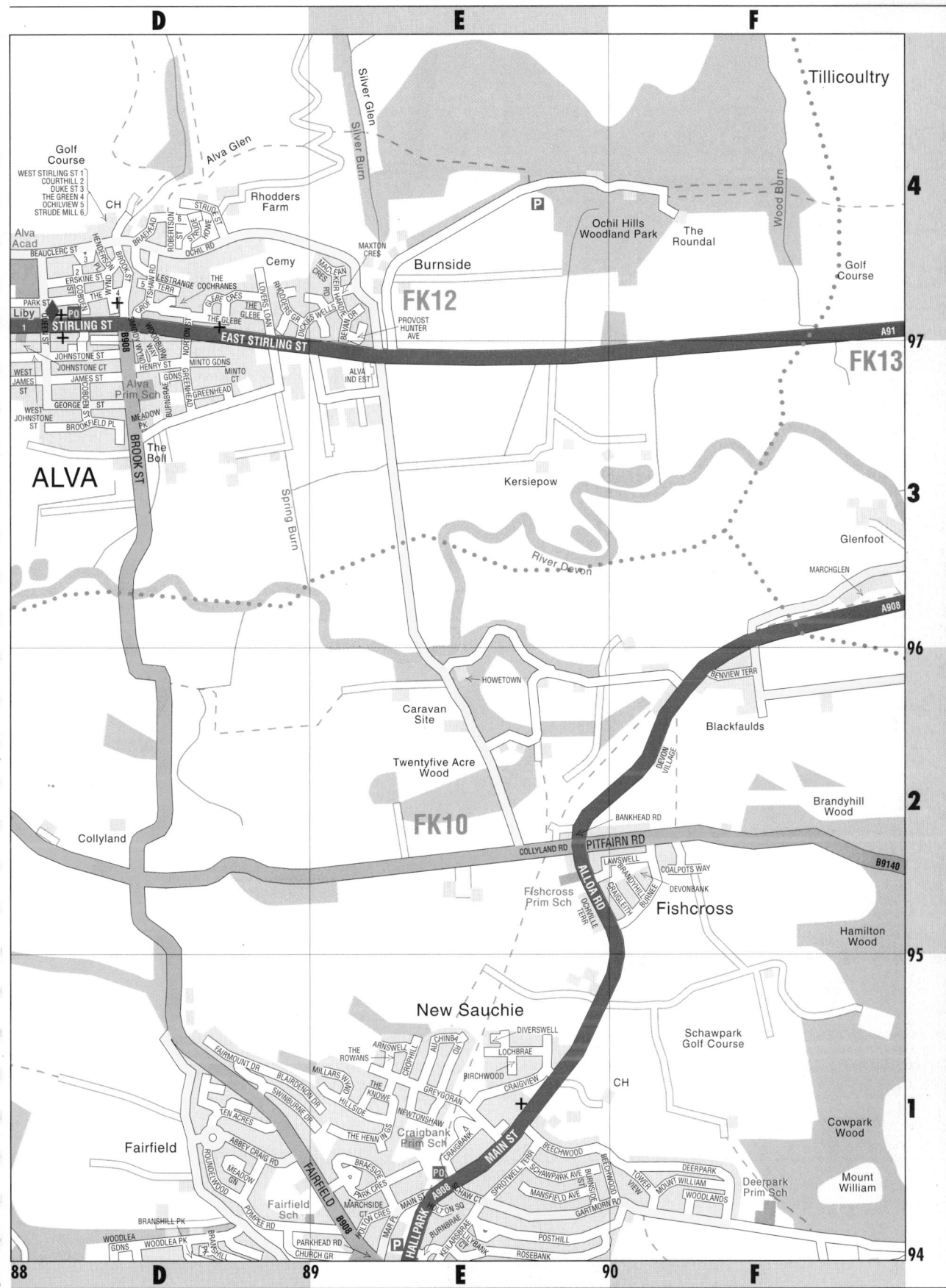

D
E
F
Tillicoultry
Silver Glen
Silver Burn
Alva Glen
Golf Course
WEST STIRLING ST 1
COURTHILL 2
DUKE ST 3
THE GREEN 4
OCHILVIEW 5
STRUDE MILL 6
CH
Rhodders Farm
Ochil Hills Woodland Park
The Roundal
Wood Burn
Alva Acad
BEAUCLERC ST
Cemy
Burnside
FK12
Golf Course
ERSKINE ST
THE COCHRANES
Liby
STIRLING ST
EAST STIRLING ST
PROVOST HUNTER AVE
A91
FK13
JOHNSTONE ST
JOHNSTONE CT
JAMES ST
ALVA IND EST
Alva Prim Sch
GREENHEAD
MINTO GDNS
MINTO CT
BROOKFIELD PL
The Boll
ALVA
BROOK ST
Spring Burn
Kersiepow
River Devon
Glenfoot
MARCHGLEN
A908
HOWETOWN
BENVIEW TERR
Caravan Site
Blackfaulds
Twentyfive Acre Wood
DEVON VILLAGE
FK10
Brandyhill Wood
Collyland
BANKHEAD RD
COLLYLAND RD
PITFAIRN RD
B9140
COALPOTS WAY
DEVONBANK
Fishcross Prim Sch
ALLOA RD
Fishcross
Hamilton Wood
New Sauchie
DIVERSWELL
LOCHBRAE
Schawpark Golf Course
BIRCHWOOD
CRAIGVIEW
CH
Cowpark Wood
Fairfield
Craigbank Prim Sch
MAIN ST
Deerpark Prim Sch
Mount William
Fairfield Sch
FAIRFIELD
HALLPARK
4
3
2
1
97
96
95
94
88
89
90

10

A   **B**   **C**

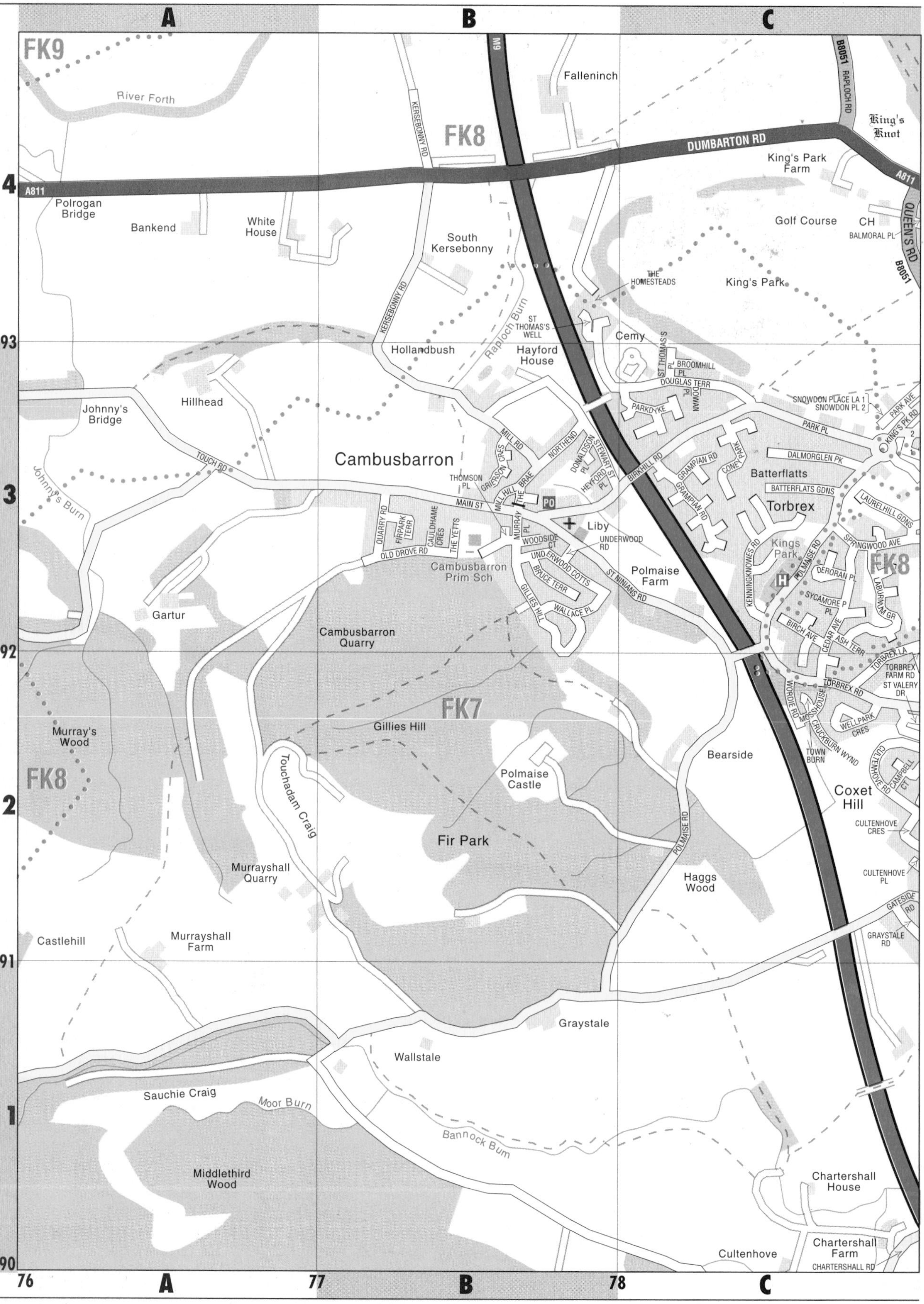

FK9

River Forth

FK8

Falleninch

DUMBARTON RD

King's Knot

A811

King's Park Farm

QUEEN'S RD

4

A811

Polrogan Bridge

Bankend

White House

South Kersebonny

Golf Course

CH

BALMORAL PL

King's Park

THE HOMESTEADS

93

Johnny's Bridge

Hillhead

Hollandbush

Hayford House

St Thomas's Well

Cemy

ST THOMAS S

BROOMHILL PL

DOUGLAS TERR

DOWAN

SNOWDON PLACE LA 1
SNOWDON PL 2

PARK AVE

KING'S PK RD

TOUCH RD

Cambusbarron

Raploch Burn

PARKD'YKE

PARK PL

DALMORGLEN PK

3

Johnny's Burn

THOMSON PL

GRIESSON CRES

MILL HILL

THE BRAE

MILL RD

NORTHEND

DONALDSON PL

STEWART ST

HEYFORD PL

BIRKHILL RD

GRAMPIAN RD

CONEY

GRAMPIAN RD

Batterflatts

BATTERFLATS GDNS

LAURELHILL GDNS

Torbrex

SPRINGWOOD AVE

FK8

QUARRY RD

FIRPARK TERR

CAULDHAME CRES

OLD DROVE RD

MAIN ST

THE YETTS

MURRAY

WOODSIDE CT

+

Liby

UNDERWOOD RD

Kings Park

POLMAISE RD

DEROARN PL

LABURNAM GR

PO

UNDERWOOD COTTS

BRUCE TERR

ST NINIANS RD

Polmaise Farm

H

SYCAMORE P PL

CEDAR AVE

ASH TERR

Gartur

Cambusbarron Prim Sch

GILLIES HILL

WALLACE PL

BIRCH AVE

TORBREX LA

92

Cambusbarron Quarry

TORBREX FARM RD

ST VALERY DR

TORBREX RD

MOSSHOUSE

FK7

Gillies Hill

WHORLE RD

WELL PARK CRES

CRUXBURN WYND

TOWN Burn

Coxet Hill

Murray's Wood

FK8

Polmaise Castle

Bearside

GATESIDE RD

CULTENHOVE CRES

CULTENHOVE PL

2

Fir Park

POLMAISE RD

Haggs Wood

Touchadam Craig

Murrayshall Quarry

GRAYSTALE RD

Castlehill

Murrayshall Farm

91

Graystale

Wallstale

Sauchie Craig

Moor Burn

Bannock Burn

Chartershall House

1

Middlethird Wood

Cultenhove

Chartershall Farm

CHARTERSHALL RD

90

76   **A**   77   **B**   78   **C**

2
8

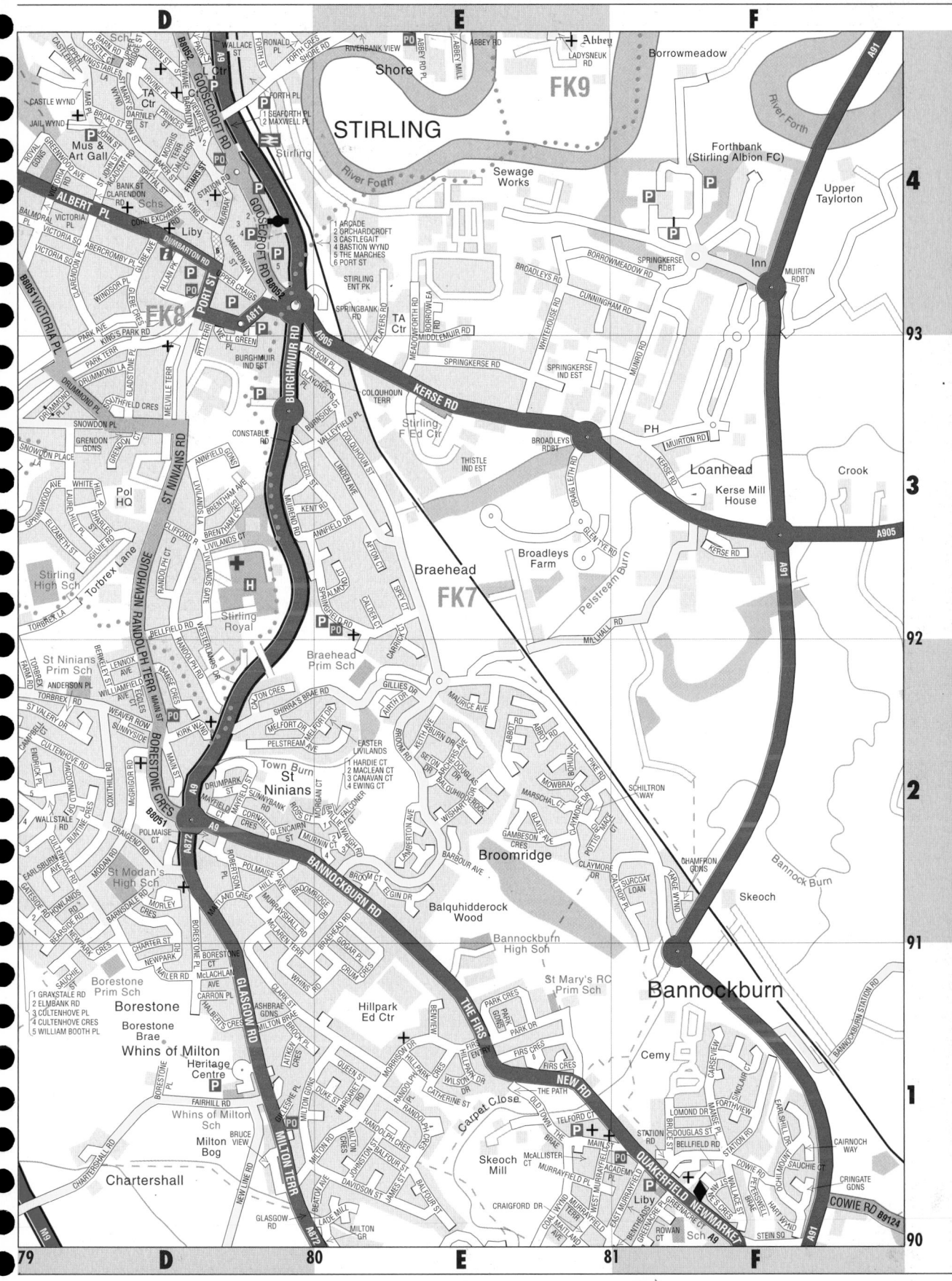
D
E
F
STIRLING
Shore
Abbey
Borrowmeadow
FK9
River Forth
Forthbank
(Stirling Albion FC)
Upper
Taylorton
Sewage
Works
Stirling
Mus &
Art Gall
TA
Ctr
Schs
Liby
FK8
ALBERT PL
DUMBARTON RD
PORT ST
GOOSECROFT RD
BURGHMUIR RD
KERSE RD
A905
A91
A811
A9
B8052
B8051
VICTORIA PL
1 ARCADE
2 ORCHARDCROFT
3 CASTLEGAIT
4 BASTION WYND
5 THE MARCHES
6 PORT ST
1 SEAFORTH PL
2 MAXWELL PL
STIRLING
ENT PK
TA
Ctr
SPRINGKERSE RD
BORROWMEADOW RD
SPRINGKERSE
RDBT
CUNNINGHAM RD
BROADLEYS RD
SPRINGKERSE
IND EST
MUIRTON
RDBT
Inn
PH
MUIRTON RD
BROADLEYS
RDBT
Loanhead
Kerse Mill
House
Crook
KERSE RD
BURGHMUIR
IND EST
Stirling
F Ed Ctr
THISTLE
IND EST
COLQUHOUN
TERR
Broadleys
Farm
Pelstream Burn
Braehead
FK7
MILLHALL RD
Pol
HQ
Stirling
High Sch
Torbrex Lane
ST NINIANS RD
NEWHOUSE
Stirling
Royal
H
Braehead
Prim Sch
St Ninians
Prim Sch
RANDOLPH TERR
BORESTONE CRES
St
Ninians
Town Burn
EASTER
LIVILANDS
1 HARDIE CT
2 MACLEAN CT
3 CANAVAN CT
4 EWING CT
PELSTREAM AVE
MAURICE AVE
Broomridge
SCHILTRON
WAY
Bannock Burn
Skeoch
CHAMFRON
GDNS
Balquhidderock
Wood
BANNOCKBURN RD
St Modan's
High Sch
A872
Bannockburn
High Sch
St Mary's RC
Prim Sch
Bannockburn
BANNOCKBURN STATION RD
Borestone
Prim Sch
Borestone
Borestone
Brae
Whins of Milton
Heritage
Centre
1 GRAYSTALE RD
2 ELMBANK RD
3 CULTENHOVE PL
4 CULTENHOVE CRES
5 WILLIAM BOOTH PL
GLASGOW RD
Hillpark
Ed Ctr
THE FIRS
NEW RD
Cemy
Carpet Close
Whins of Milton
Sch
Milton
Bog
Chartershall
MILTON TERR
Skeoch
Mill
QUAKERFIELD
NEWMARKET
Liby
Sch
COWIE RD
B9124
CAIRNOCH
WAY
CRINGATE
GDNS
M9
4
93
3
92
2
91
1
90
79
80
81

11
8

7
3

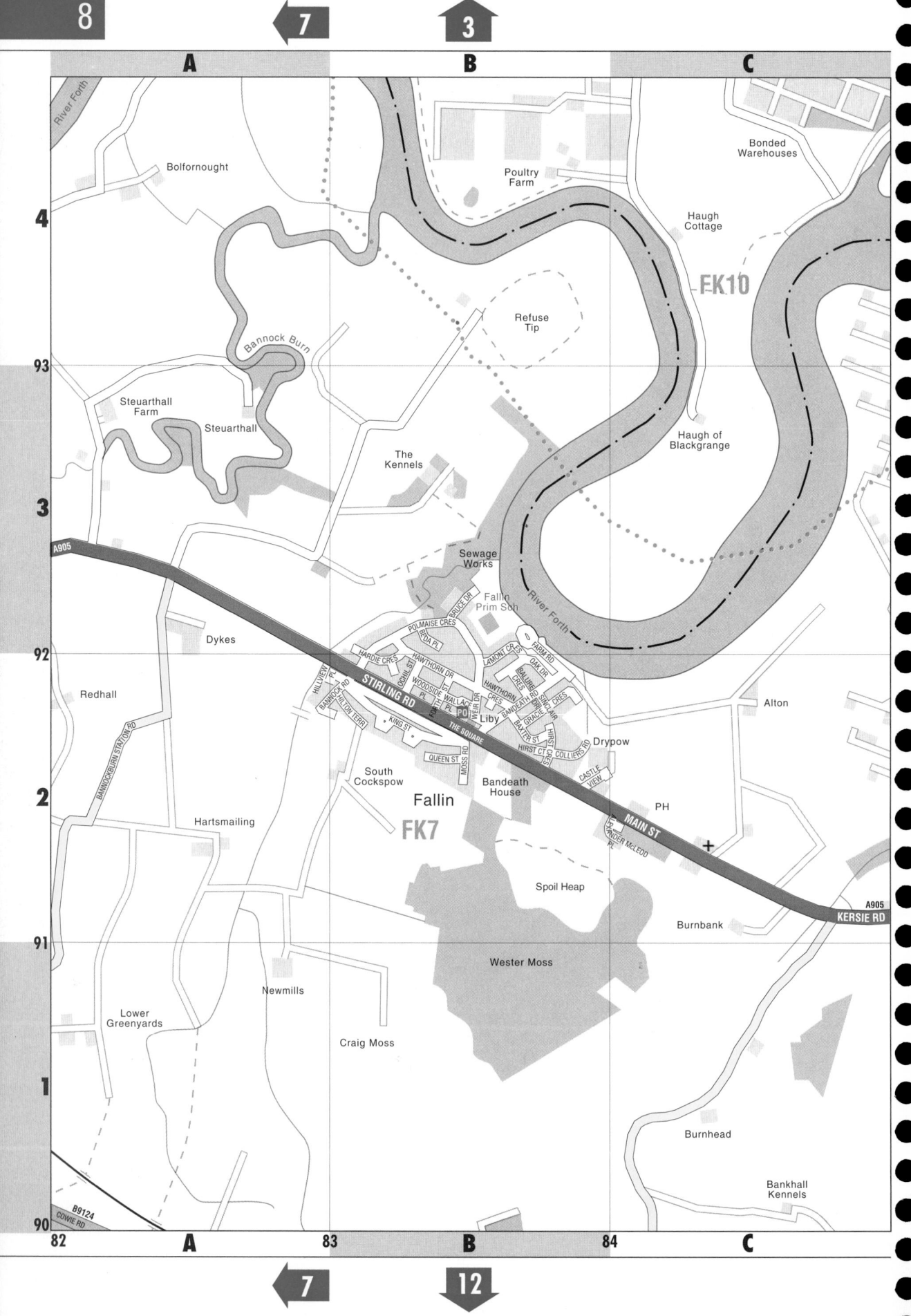
A
B
C
4
93
3
92
2
91
1
90
82
83
84
River Forth
Bolfornought
Poultry Farm
Bonded Warehouses
Haugh Cottage
FK10
Refuse Tip
Bannock Burn
Steuarthall Farm
Steuarthall
Haugh of Blackgrange
The Kennels
A905
Sewage Works
Fallin Prim Sch
River Forth
Dykes
Redhall
Alton
STIRLING RD
THE SQUARE
PO
Liby
Drypow
South Cockspow
Bandeath House
Fallin
FK7
Hartsmailing
MAIN ST
PH
Spoil Heap
A905
KERSIE RD
Burnbank
Wester Moss
Newmills
Lower Greenyards
Craig Moss
Burnhead
Bankhall Kennels
B9124
COWIE RD
BANNOCKBURN STATION RD
POLMAISE CRES
BRUCE DR
BEDA PL
HARDIE CRES
HAWTHORN DR
OCHIL ST
LAMONT CRES
FARM RD
OAK DR
HILLVIEW PL
BANNOCK RD
HILTON TERR
WOODSIDE PL
WALLACE
WEIR DR
HAWTHORN CRES
BALFOUR CRES
BANDEATH RD
SINCLAIR CRES
GRACIE
BAXTER ST
HIRST CRES
HIRST CT
COLLIERS RD
KING ST
QUEEN ST
MOSS RD
CASTLE VIEW
ALEXANDER McLEOD PL

A 83 B 84 C

7
12

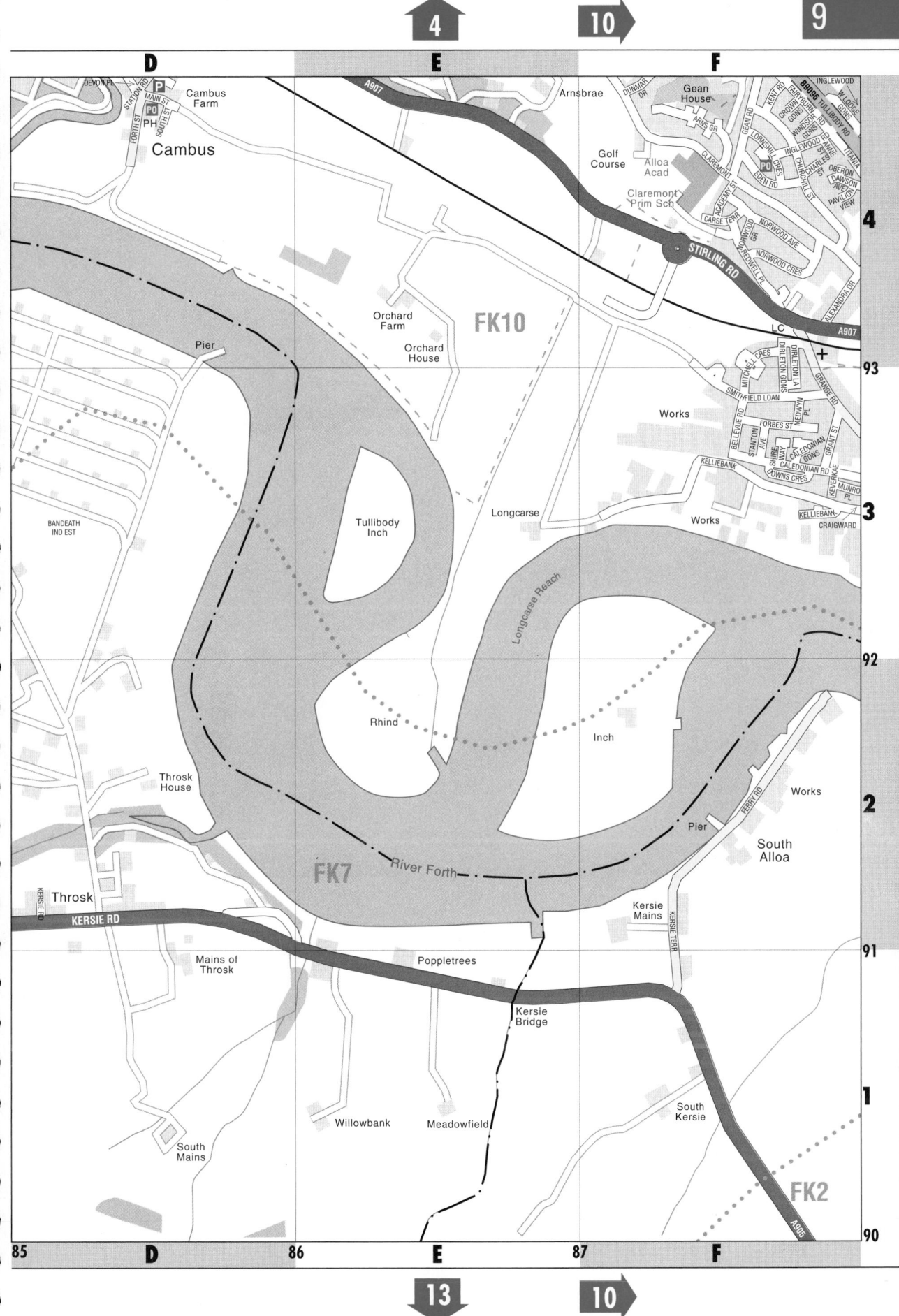
D
E
F
Cambus Farm
Cambus
Arnsbrae
Gean House
Golf Course
Alloa Acad
Claremont Prim Sch
STIRLING RD
A907
FK10
Orchard Farm
Orchard House
Pier
BANDEATH IND EST
Tullibody Inch
Longcarse
Works
Longcarse Reach
Rhind
Inch
Throsk House
Throsk
KERSIE RD
FK7
River Forth
Pier
South Alloa
Kersie Mains
Mains of Throsk
Poppletrees
Kersie Bridge
Willowbank
Meadowfield
South Kersie
South Mains
FK2
A905
4
93
3
92
2
91
1
90
85
86
87

9
5

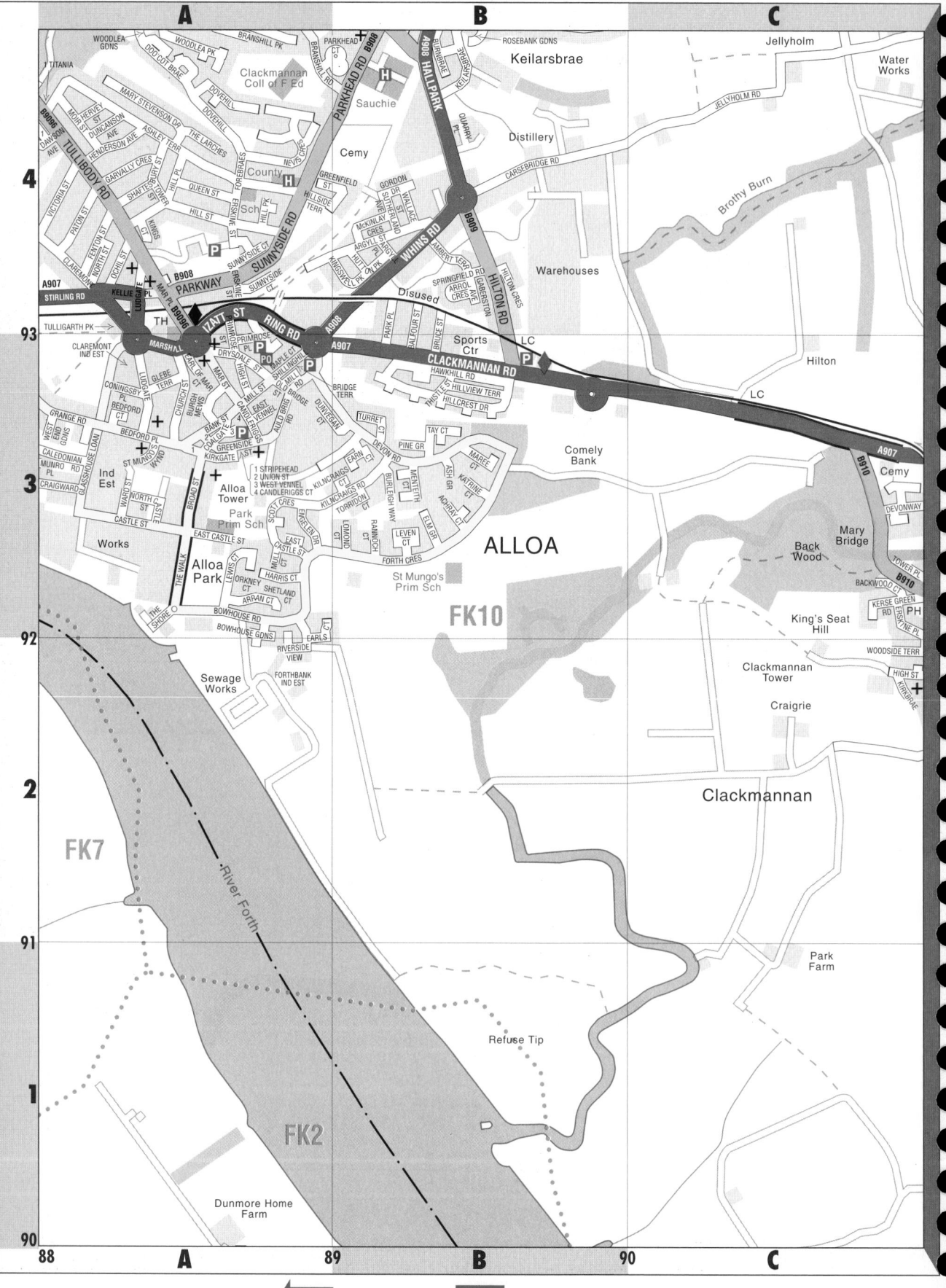
ALLOA
FK10
FK7
FK2
Clackmannan
Keilarsbrae
Jellyholm
Water Works
Distillery
Warehouses
Sauchie
Cemy
Clackmannan Coll of F Ed
Sports Ctr
Hilton
Comely Bank
Alloa Tower
Alloa Park
Works
Ind Est
Park Prim Sch
St Mungo's Prim Sch
Back Wood
Mary Bridge
King's Seat Hill
Clackmannan Tower
Craigrie
Sewage Works
Park Farm
Refuse Tip
Dunmore Home Farm
River Forth
Brothy Burn
Disused
CLACKMANNAN RD
TULLIBODY RD
SUNNYSIDE RD
PARKHEAD RD
HALLPARK
WHINS RD
HILTON RD
RING RD
IZATT ST
PARKWAY
STIRLING RD
A907
B909
B910
A908
B908
B9096
1 STRIPEHEAD
2 UNION ST
3 WEST VENNEL
4 CANDLERIGGS CT

9
14

7
12

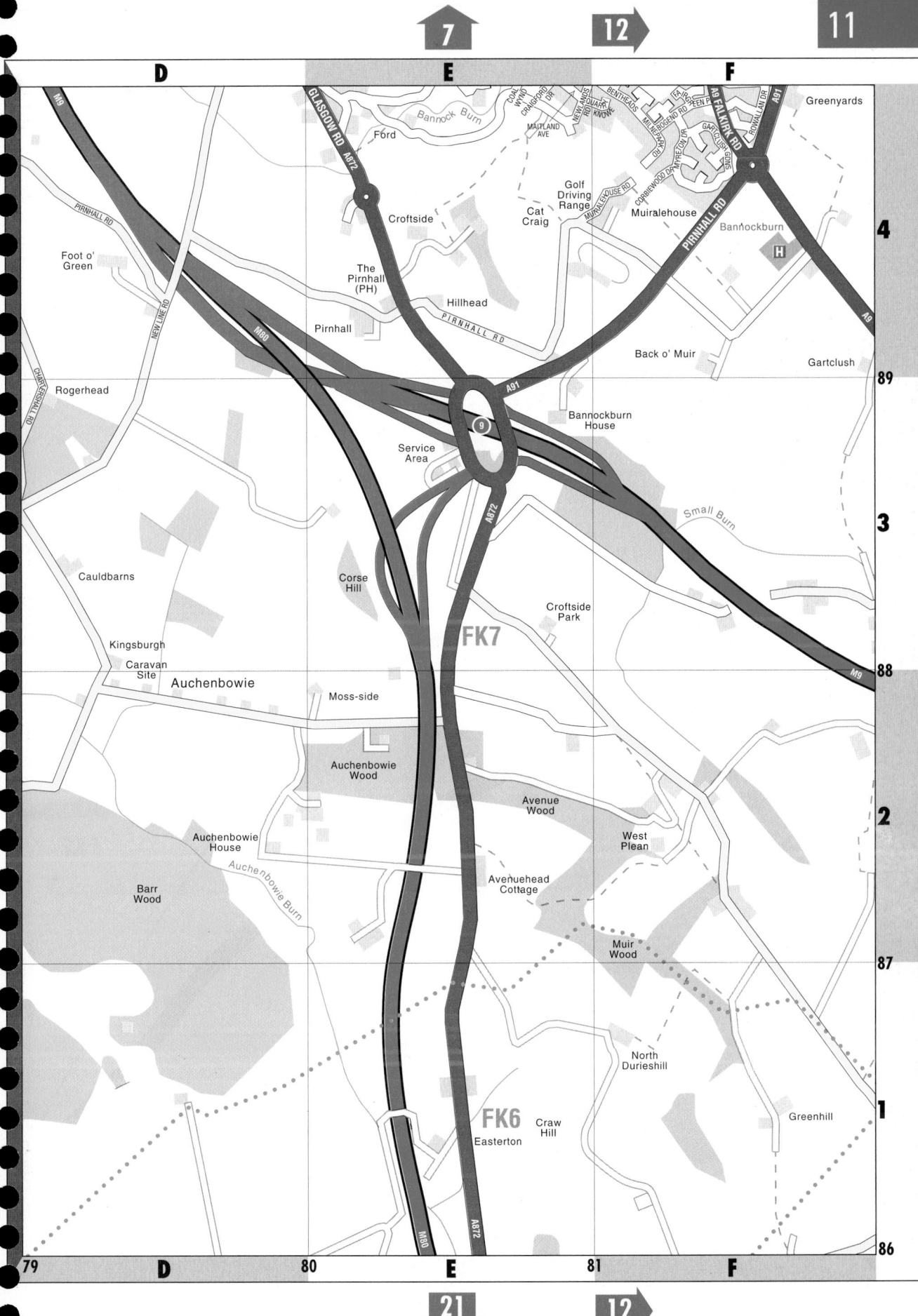
D
E
F
M9
GLASGOW RD
A872
Bannock Burn
Ford
COAL WYND
CRAIGFORD DR
MAITLAND AVE
NEWLANDS RD
QUARRY KNOWE
BENTHEADS
MILNEPARK RD
BOGEND RD
FAIRWAYS
GLENPARK
MYRETON DR
GARTCLUSH GDNS
A9 FALKIRK RD
ROWALLAN DR
A91
Greenyards
PIRNHALL RD
Foot o' Green
Croftside
Golf Driving Range
Cat Craig
MUIRALEHOUSE RD
CORBIEWOOD DR
Muiralehouse
Bannockburn
The Pirnhall (PH)
Hillhead
NEW LINE RD
M80
Pirnhall
Back o' Muir
Gartclush
A9
CHARTERSHALL RD
Rogerhead
Bannockburn House
Service Area
Small Burn
Cauldbarns
Corse Hill
Croftside Park
FK7
Kingsburgh
Caravan Site
Auchenbowie
Moss-side
Auchenbowie Wood
Avenue Wood
Auchenbowie House
West Plean
Auchenbowie Burn
Barr Wood
Avenuehead Cottage
Muir Wood
North Durieshill
FK6
Craw Hill
Easterton
Greenhill
4
3
2
1
89
88
87
86
79
80
81

21
12

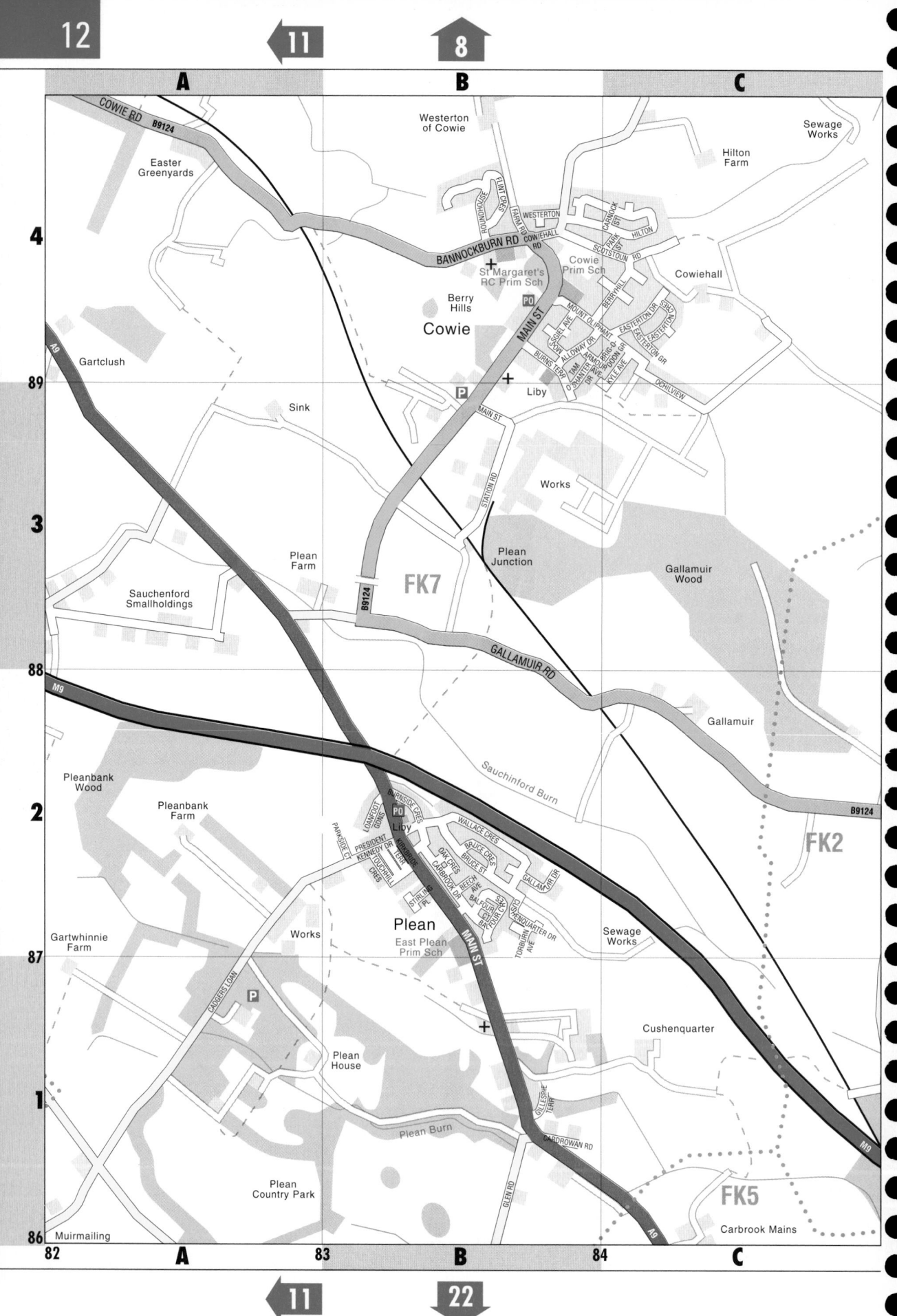

A B C

COWIE RD
B9124

Easter
Greenyards

Westerton
of Cowie

Hilton
Farm

Sewage
Works

4

ROUNDHOUSE
FLINT CRES
FARM RD
WESTERTON

BANNOCKBURN RD

COWIEHALL
RD

St Margaret's
RC Prim Sch

Berry
Hills

Cowie

PO

Cowie
Prim Sch

CARNOCK
PARK (ST)
HILTON

SCOTSTOUN RD

BERRYHILL

Cowiehall

Gartclush

A9

89

Liby

MOUNT OLIPHANT
SAUCHEL AVE
JOW
ALLOWAY DR
ARMOUR
DR
O SHANTER
AVE
TAM
BURNS TERR
KYLE AVE

EASTERTON DR
B927
EASTERTON GR

OCHILVIEW

Sink

P

MAIN ST

Works

Gallamuir
Wood

3

Plean
Farm

B9124

FK7

STATION RD

Plean
Junction

Sauchenford
Smallholdings

GALLAMUIR RD

88

M9

Gallamuir

Pleanbank
Wood

Sauchinford Burn

B9124

Pleanbank
Farm

BURNSIDE CRES

PO

2

FK2

Liby

LOANFOOT
GDNS

PARKSIDE CT

PRESIDENT
KENNEDY DR
KIRKSIDE
TERR
TOUCHILL
CRES

WALLACE CRES

BRUCE ST
BRUCE CRES

OAK CRES
CARBROOK DR

GALLAM UIR DR

Gartwhinnie
Farm

Works

BEECH
AVE
BAL
FOUR
CT

STIRLING
PL

BALFOUR CRES

TORBURN
AVE
CUSHENQUARTER DR

Sewage
Works

87

CADGERS LOAN

P

Plean

East Plean
Prim Sch

MAIN ST

GILLESHE
TERR

Cushenquarter

Plean
House

1

Plean Burn

GLEN RD

CARDROWAN RD

A9

M9

FK5

Plean
Country Park

Carbrook Mains

86

Muirmailing

82 A 83 B 84 C

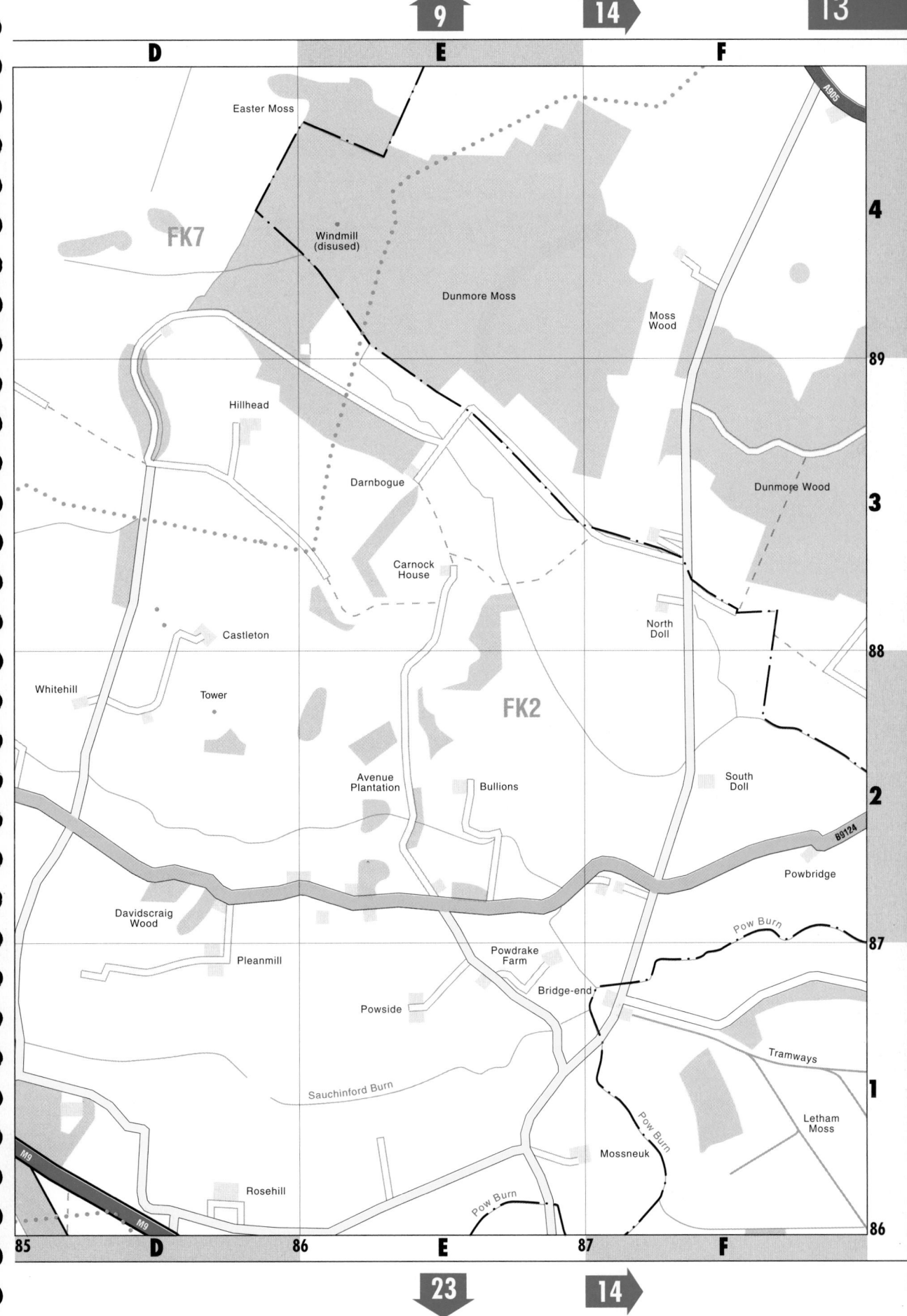

D   E   F

A905

Easter Moss

FK7

Windmill
(disused)

Dunmore Moss

Moss
Wood

4

89

Hillhead

Darnbogue

Dunmore Wood

3

Carnock
House

North
Doll

Castleton

88

Whitehill

Tower

FK2

South
Doll

2

Avenue
Plantation

Bullions

B9124

Powbridge

Pow Burn

Davidscraig
Wood

Pleanmill

Powdrake
Farm

87

Powside

Bridge-end

Tramways

Sauchinford Burn

1

M9

Pow Burn

Letham
Moss

M9

Mossneuk

Rosehill

Pow Burn

86

85   D   86   E   87   F

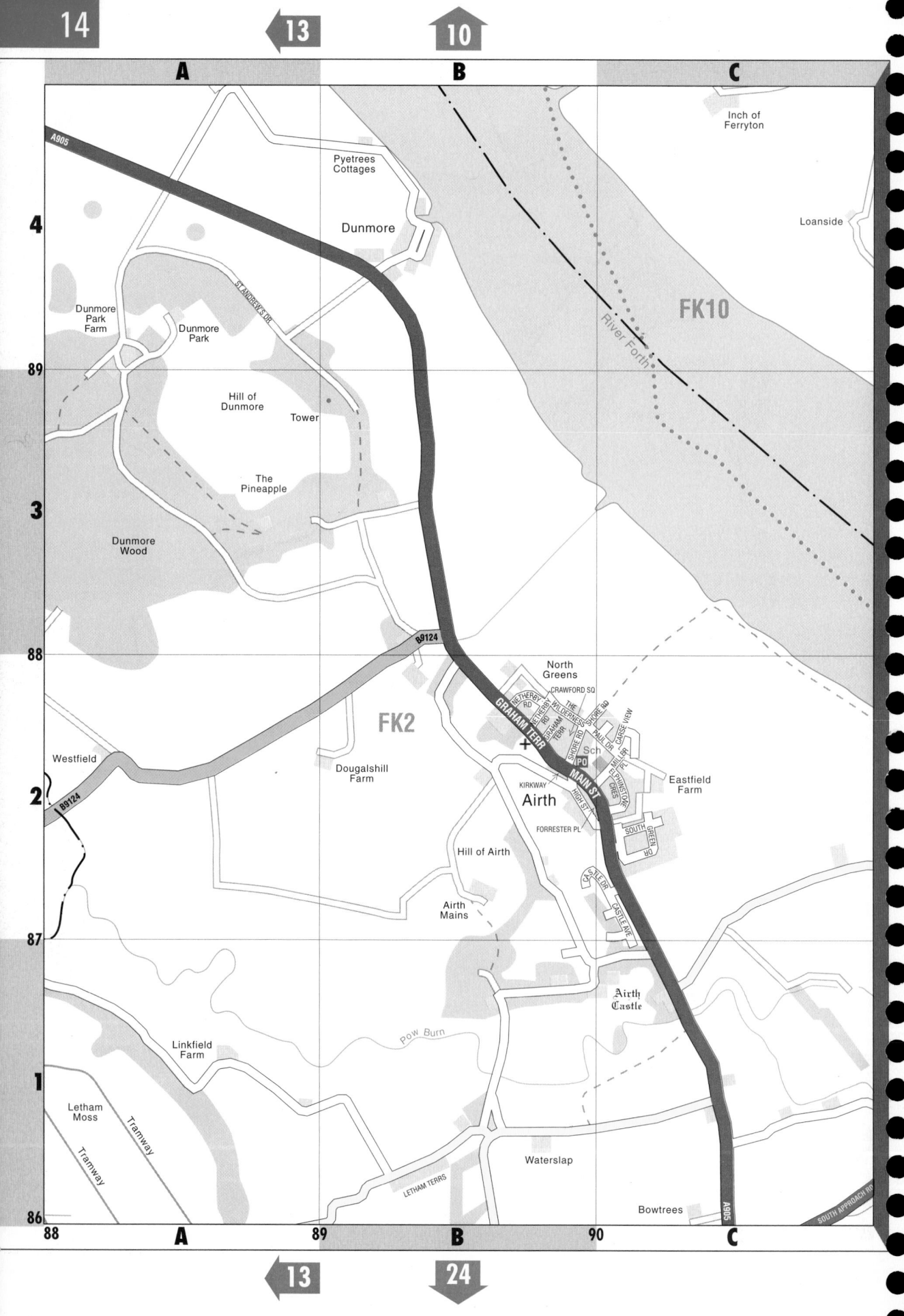

A   B   C

A905

Inch of
Ferryton

Pyetrees
Cottages

Loanside

Dunmore

4

FK10

River Forth

Dunmore
Park Farm

ST ANDREW'S DR

Dunmore
Park

89

Hill of
Dunmore

Tower

3

The
Pineapple

Dunmore
Wood

B9124

88

North
Greens

CRAWFORD SQ

FK2

NETHERBY RD

THE
WILDERNESS

NETHERBY RD

SHORE RD

CARSE VIEW

Westfield

GRAHAM TERR

SHORE RD

PAUL DR

Sch

ELPHINSTONE PL

Eastfield
Farm

B9124

Dougalshill
Farm

SIDHAM
TERR

PO

ELPHINSTONE
CRES

2

Airth

KIRKWAY

MAIN ST

HIGH ST

SOUTH
GREEN RD

FORRESTER PL

Hill of Airth

CASTLE TERR

Airth
Mains

CASTLE AVE

87

Airth
Castle

Pow Burn

Linkfield
Farm

1

Letham
Moss

Tramway

Tramway

Waterslap

Tramway

LETHAM TERRS

Bowtrees

A905

SOUTH APPROACH RD

86

88   A   89   B   90   C

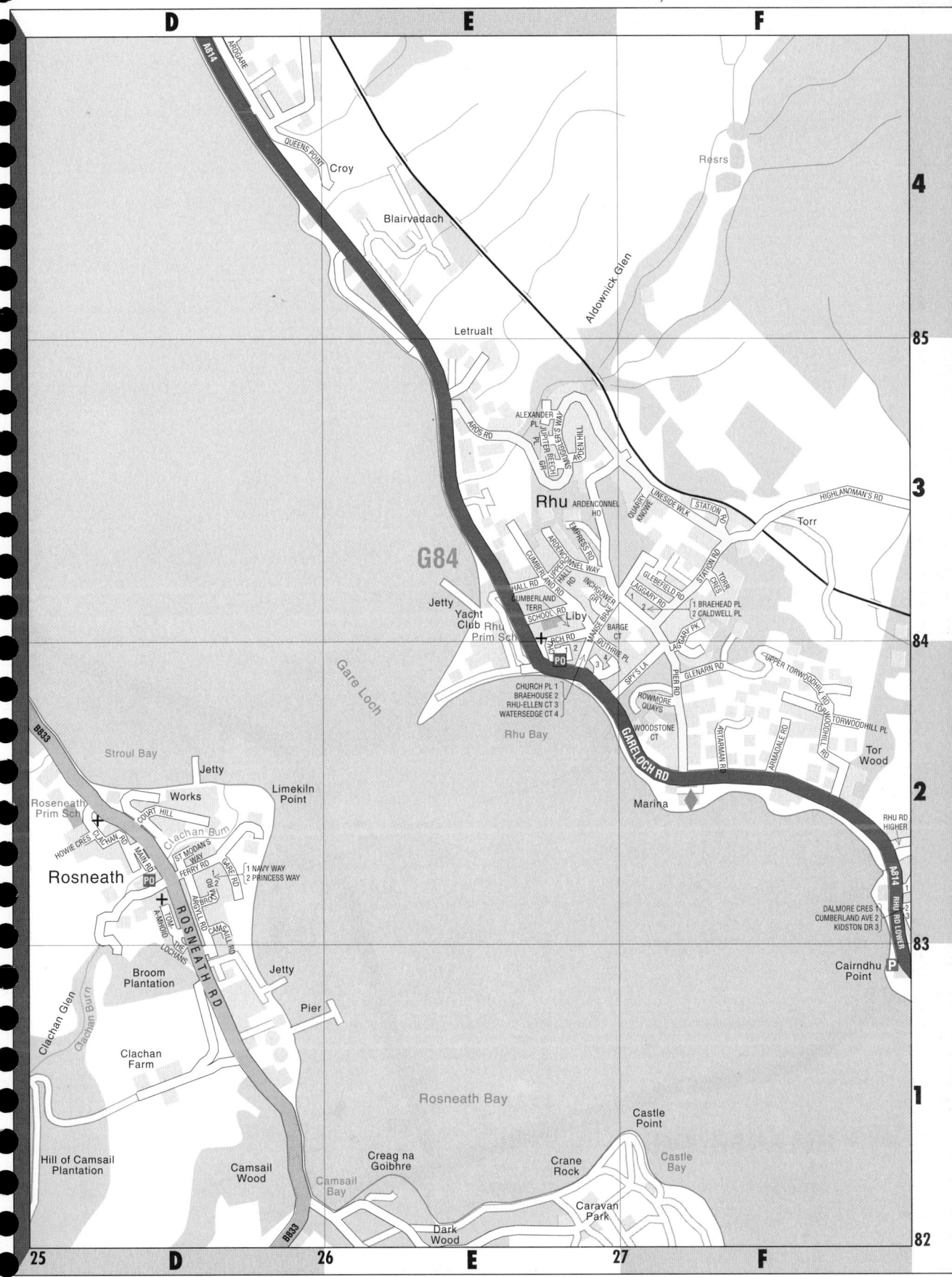

A814

Queens Point

Croy

Blairvadach

Resrs

4

Aldownick Glen

Letrualt

85

Alexander PL

Aros Rd

Jupiter Beech PL GR

ARDEN HILL

Rhu

G84

Ardenconnel HO

Lineside WLK

Highlandman's Rd

3

Quarry Knowe

Station Rd

Torr

Empress Rd

Ardenconnel Way

Glebefield Rd

Station Rd

York Cres

Jetty

Hall Rd

Inchgower Dr

Laggary Rd

1 Braehead PL

Yacht Club

Cumberland Terr

School Rd

Rhu Prim Sch

Liby

2 Caldwell PL

Barge CT

Guthrie PL

Laggary PK

84

Gare Loch

RCH Rd

PQ

Manse Brae

Spy's La

Glenarn Rd

Upper Torwoodhill Rd

CHURCH PL 1
BRAEHOUSE 2
RHU-ELLEN CT 3
WATERSEDGE CT 4

Rowmore Quays

Pier Rd

Woodstone CT

Ariarman Rd

Armadale Rd

Torwoodhill Rd

Torwoodhill PL

Rhu Bay

Garelloch Rd

Tor Wood

2

Stroul Bay

Jetty

Works

Court Hill

Limekiln Point

Marina

Rhu Rd Higher

Roseneath Prim Sch

Clachan Burn

St Modan's Way

Howie Cres

Main Rd

Gare Rd

A814

Rhu Rd Lower

Rosneath

PQ

Ferry Rd

1 Navy Way
2 Princess Way

Dalmore Cres 1
Cumberland Ave 2
Kidston Dr 3

Argyll Rd

Cam-Sail Rd

Rosneath Rd

83

The Lochans

Cairndhu Point

P

Broom Plantation

Jetty

Clachan Glen

Clachan Burn

Clachan Farm

Pier

Rosneath Bay

1

Castle Point

Hill of Camsail Plantation

Camsail Wood

Creag na Goibhre

Crane Rock

Castle Bay

Camsail Bay

Dark Wood

Caravan Park

82

15

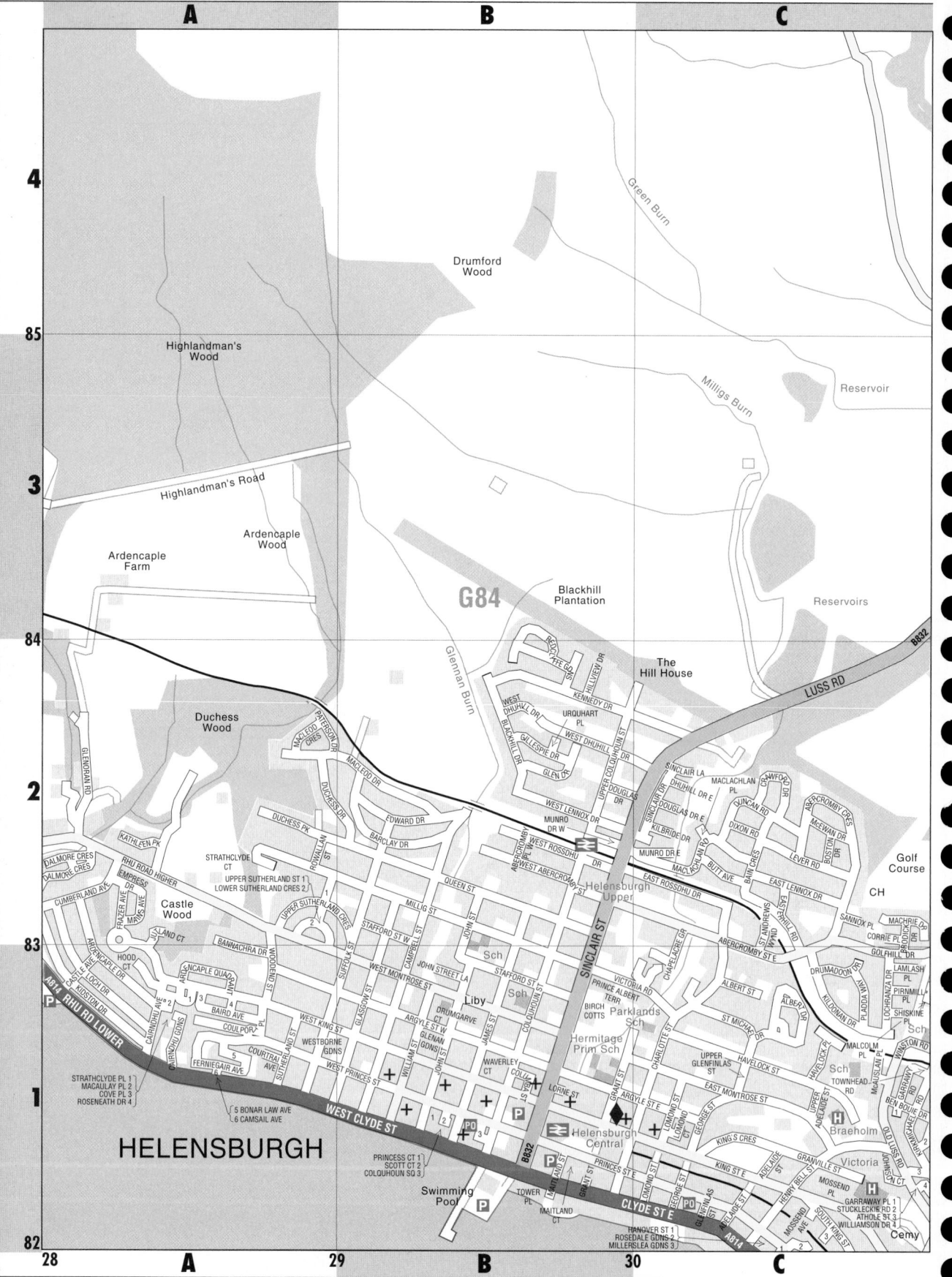

A
B
C
4
85
3
84
2
83
1
82
28
29
30
Drumford Wood
Green Burn
Highlandman's Wood
Milligs Burn
Reservoir
Highlandman's Road
Ardencaple Wood
Ardencaple Farm
G84
Blackhill Plantation
Reservoirs
Glennan Burn
The Hill House
B832
LUSS RD
Duchess Wood
Golf Course
CH
Castle Wood
Helensburgh Upper
SINCLAIR ST
Sch
Liby
Parklands Sch
Hermitage Prim Sch
Helensburgh Central
Braeholm
Victoria
Cemy
Swimming Pool
HELENSBURGH
WEST CLYDE ST
CLYDE ST E
A814 RHU RD LOWER
STRATHCLYDE PL 1
MACAULAY PL 2
COVE PL 3
ROSENEATH DR 4
5 BONAR LAW AVE
6 CAMSAIL AVE
PRINCESS CT 1
SCOTT CT 2
COLQUHOUN SQ 3
HANOVER ST 1
ROSEDALE GDNS 2
MILLERSLEA GDNS 3
GARRAWAY PL 1
STUCKLECKIE RD 2
ATHOLE ST 3
WILLIAMSON DR 4
STRATHCLYDE CT
UPPER SUTHERLAND ST 1
LOWER SUTHERLAND CRES 2

15

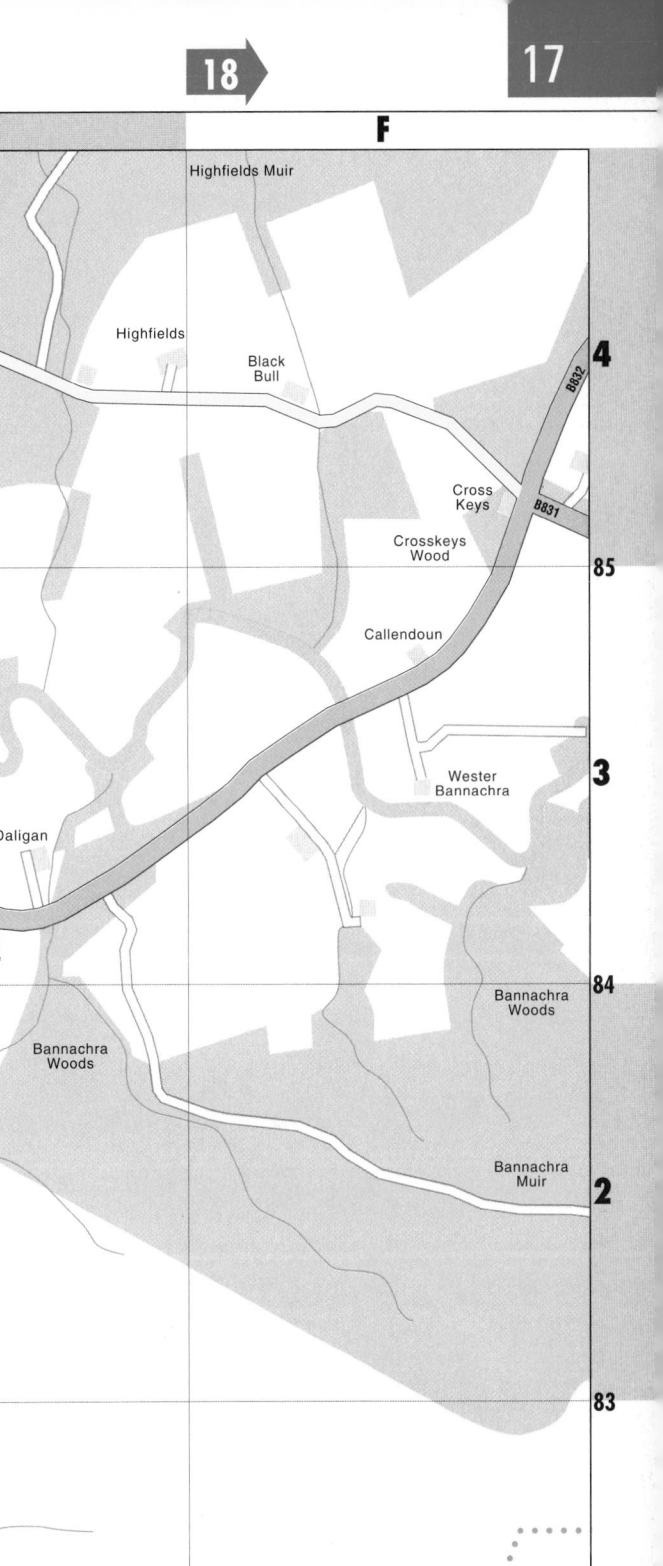

D E F

Highfields Muir

East
Kilbride

Highfields

Black
Bull

4

B832

Cross
Keys

B831

Crosskeys
Wood

85

Inverlauren

Callendoun

Drumfad

Inverlauren Wood

Fruin Water

Wester
Bannachra

3

Daligan

LUSS RD

G84

84

Bannachra
Woods

Old Luss Road

Bannachra
Woods

Golf
Course

Bannachra
Muir

2

Garrawy Glen

KENT DR

HORTON PL

GOLFHILL
DR

HARDY HILL

83

FISHER
PL

CAMPERDOWN CR

MALCOLM PL

PO

CHURCH

J. SQ

GOLF PL

Sch

GRAHAM

NE. PL

COLLINGWOOD PL

1 FROBISHER PL
2 RODNEY PL
3 COCHRANE PL
4 BEATTY PL
5 JERVIS PL

JELLICOE PL

WINSTON RD

Townhead

Black
Wood

1

TOWNHEAD
RD

Drumfork
Burn

G82

BEN BOUIE DR

BUCHANAN RD

STUCKLECKIE RD

6 WILLIAMSON DR
7 OLD LUSS RD

Colgrain Prim Sch

Quarry
Wood

Northfield
Wood

82

17

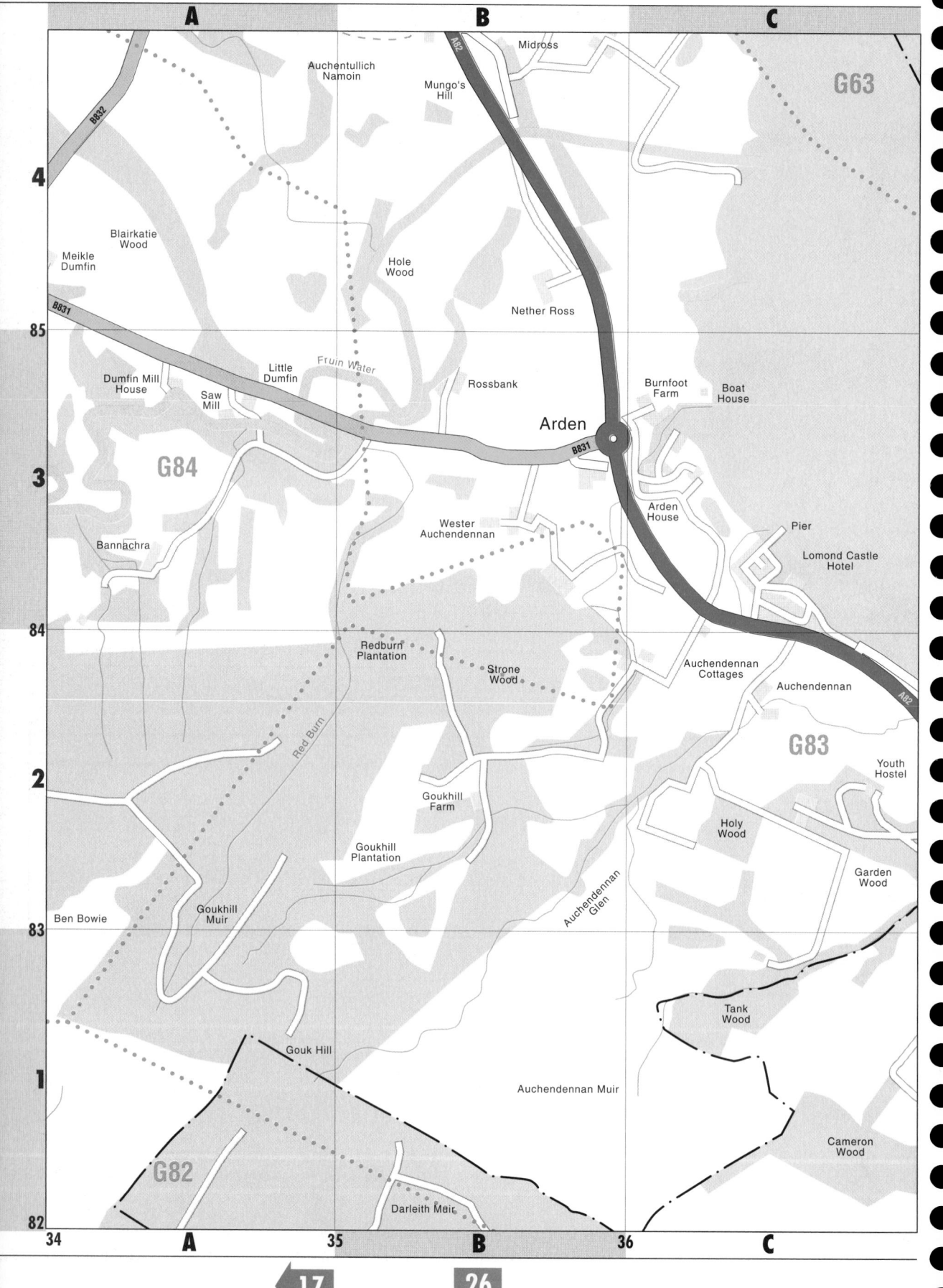
A
B
C
Midross
Auchentullich
Namoin
Mungo's
Hill
A82
B832
G63
4
Blairkatie
Wood
Meikle
Dumfin
Hole
Wood
B831
Nether Ross
85
Fruin Water
Little
Dumfin
Dumfin Mill
House
Saw
Mill
Rossbank
Burnfoot
Farm
Boat
House
Arden
B831
G84
3
Arden
House
Wester
Auchendennan
Pier
Lomond Castle
Hotel
Bannachra
84
Redburn
Plantation
Strone
Wood
Auchendennan
Cottages
Auchendennan
A82
Red Burn
G83
2
Youth
Hostel
Goukhill
Farm
Holy
Wood
Goukhill
Plantation
Garden
Wood
Auchendennan
Glen
Goukhill
Muir
Ben Bowie
83
Tank
Wood
Gouk Hill
1
Auchendennan Muir
Cameron
Wood
G82
Darleith Muir
82
34
A
35
B
36
C

17
26

D   E   F

G63

Loch Lomond

4

Knockour Wood

Lorn

Knockour Hill

Black Roundel

85

Boat Houses

Boturich Castle

3

Meikle Boturich

Whinny Hill

84

G83

Burn of Balloch

Ledrishmore Wood

Duck Bay

Over Balloch

2

Horsehouse Wood

Cameron Bay

Stable Wood

P

Cameron House

P

83

Balloch Castle

Cameron House Farm

Balloch Castle Country Park

Cameron Wildlife Park

Ledrishbeg

INCHFAD RD

CREINCH DR

1 McLEAN CRES
2 HARAN RD
3 SHANDON CRES
4 SHANDON BRAE
5 DUMBAIN RD
6 HALDANE TERR

1

Balloch Pier

P

Moss o' Balloch Plantations

INCHCONNACHAN AVE
TORRINCH DR
INCHMURRIN CRES
INCHLONAIG DR
MOLLANBOWIE RD
LEDRISH AVE
ENDRICK DR
LORN DR
PARK AVE
CASTLE AVE
CHURCH RD
LAWRENCE DR
DRYMEN RD
GALLACHER CRES
McKENZIE DR
BALLOCH RD
MAIN ST
LOMOND RD
MOSSBURN AVE
A811

River Leven

Balloch

PIER RD

P

P

1
2
6
5
3
4

OLD LUSS RD

A82

+

82

19

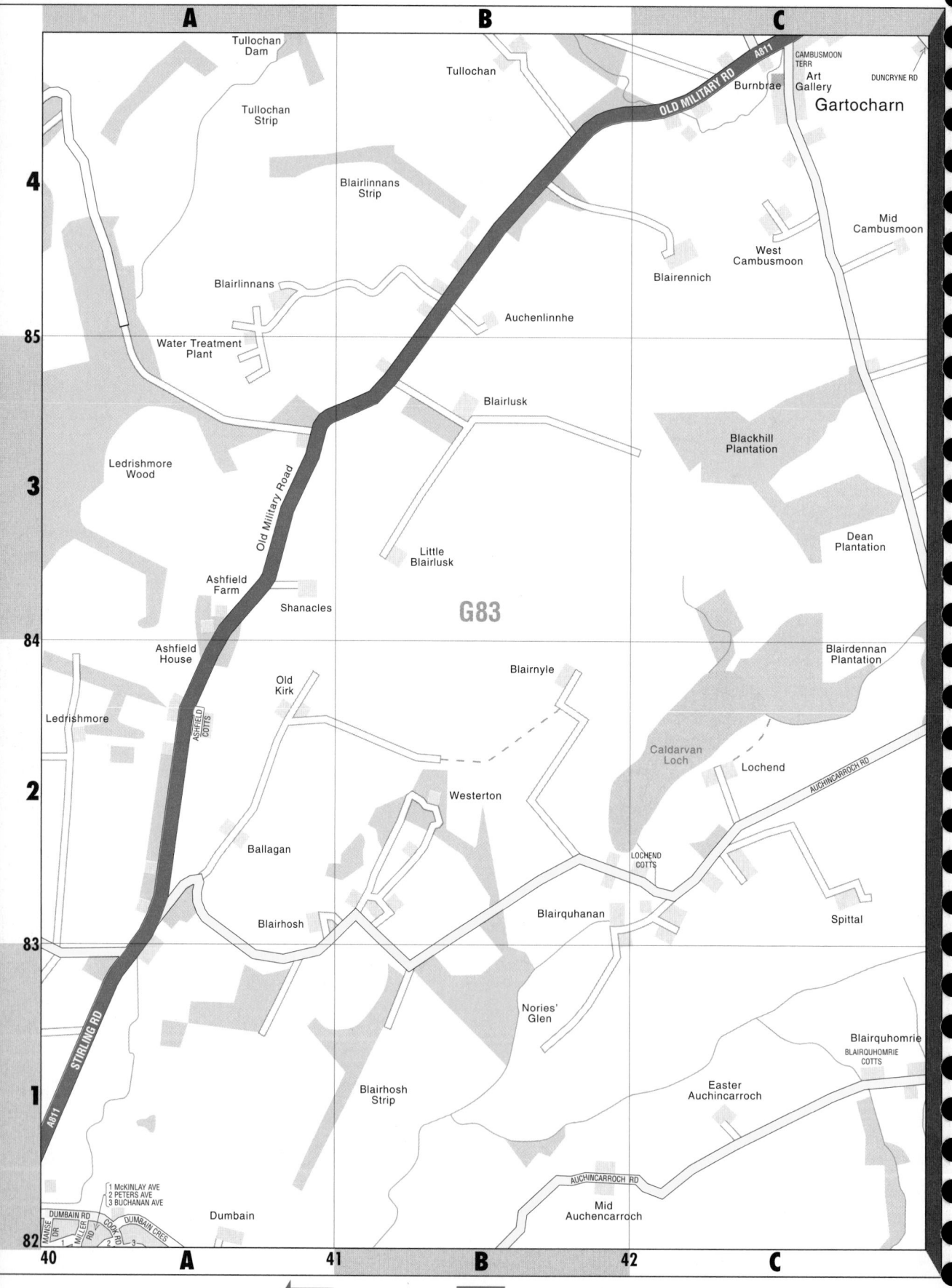
A
B
C
Tullochan Dam
Tullochan
Tullochan Strip
OLD MILITARY RD
A811
CAMBUSMOON TERR
Art Gallery
Burnbrae
DUNCRYNE RD
Gartocharn
4
Blairlinnans Strip
Mid Cambusmoon
West Cambusmoon
Blairennich
Blairlinnans
Auchenlinnhe
85
Water Treatment Plant
Blairlusk
Blackhill Plantation
Ledrishmore Wood
3
Old Military Road
Dean Plantation
Little Blairlusk
Ashfield Farm
Shanacles
G83
84
Ashfield House
Blairdennan Plantation
Blairnyle
Old Kirk
ASHFIELD COTTS
Ledrishmore
Caldarvan Loch
Lochend
AUCHINCARROCH RD
2
Westerton
Ballagan
LOCHEND COTTS
Blairquhanan
Blairhosh
Spittal
83
Nories' Glen
STIRLING RD
Blairquhomrie
BLAIRQUHOMRIE COTTS
1
Easter Auchincarroch
Blairhosh Strip
A811
1 McKINLAY AVE
2 PETERS AVE
3 BUCHANAN AVE
AUCHINCARROCH RD
DUMBAIN RD
Dumbain
Mid Auchencarroch
MANSE DR
MILLER RD
COOK RD
DUMBAIN CRES
82
40
A
41
B
42
C

19
28

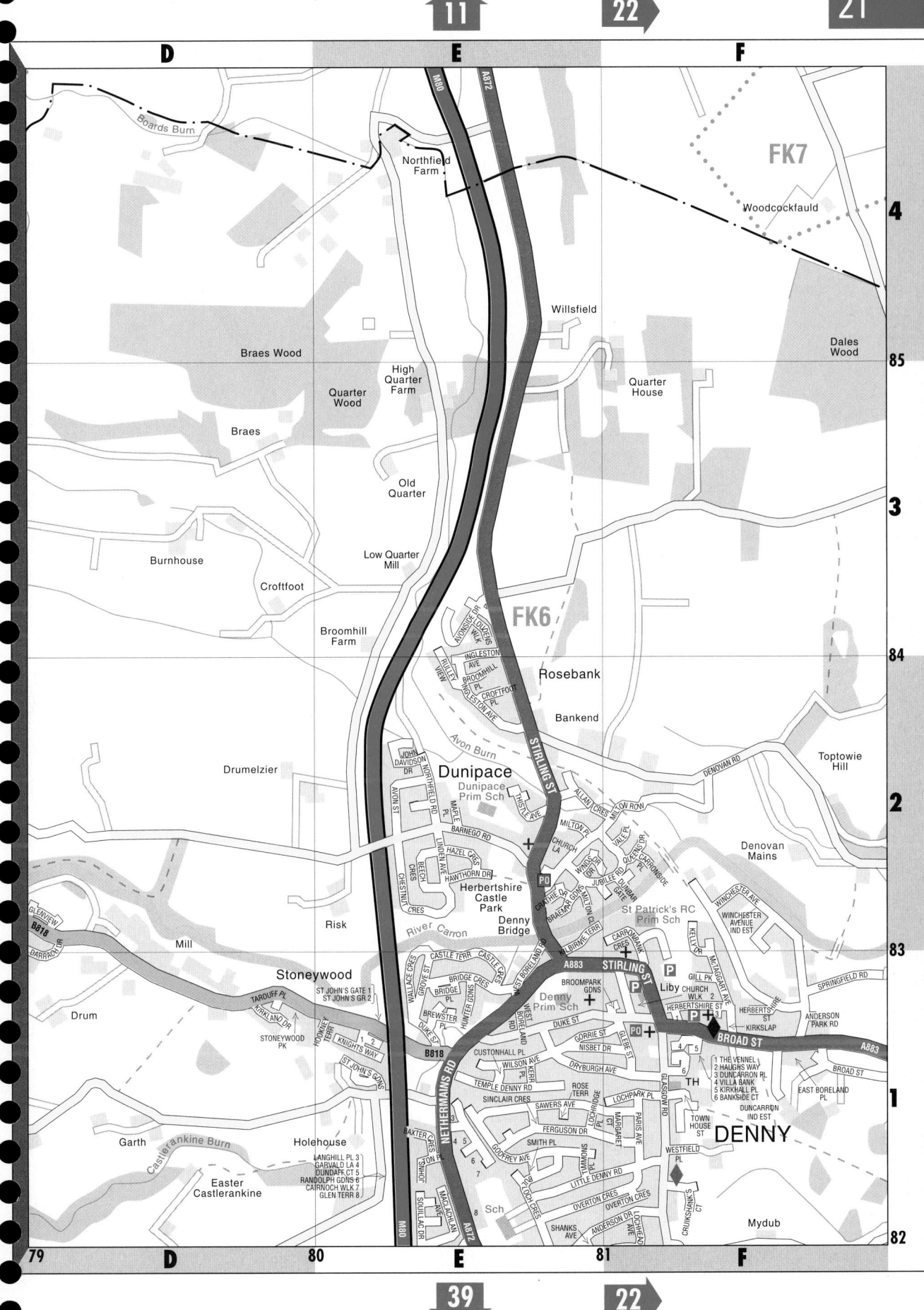

11
22
D
E
F
FK7
Woodcockfauld
Northfield Farm
Boards Burn
Willsfield
Braes Wood
Dales Wood
High Quarter Farm
Quarter Wood
Quarter House
Braes
Old Quarter
Burnhouse
Croftfoot
Low Quarter Mill
FK6
Broomhill Farm
Rosebank
Bankend
Drumelzier
Dunipace
Dunipace Prim Sch
Avon Burn
Toptowie Hill
Denovan Mains
Herbertshire Castle Park
St Patrick's RC Prim Sch
Risk
Mill
River Carron
Denny Bridge
Stoneywood
Drum
Denny Prim Sch
STIRLING ST
BROAD ST
DENNY
Garth
Holehouse
Castlerankine Burn
Easter Castlerankine
Mydub
Liby
TH
Sch
WINCHESTER AVENUE IND EST
DUNCARRON IND EST
1 THE VENNEL
2 HAUGHS WAY
3 DUNCARRON PL
4 VILLA BANK
5 KIRKHALL PL
6 BANKSIDE CT
LANGHILL PL 3
GARVALD LA 4
DUNDAFF CT 5
RANDOLPH GDNS 6
CAIRNOCH WLK 7
GLEN TERR 8
ST JOHN'S GATE 1
ST JOHN'S GR 2
M80
A872
A883
B818
85
84
83
82
4
3
2
1
79
80
81
39
22

FK7

Glenside

Tor Burn

GLEN RD

Hollings

BOGEND RD

A9

4

Langlands

GLEN RD

The Rocks

• Tappoch

85

Whinnie
Muir

Torwood

CASTLE CRES

Tor Wood

Torwood
Sch

3

FK6

FK5

Glenbervie
Golf Course

Torwoodhead

STIRLING RD

CH

84

Doghillock

Tod Hill

M876

Pamphellgoat
Wood

A9

2

STIRLING
RD

M876

2

OLD DENNY RD

Baxter
Wood

+

The Royal
Scottish
National

H

83

Oakbank
Wood

Sewage
Works

Big Wood

Kirkland

A883

Caravan
Park

1

BROAD
ST

Works

Household
Farm

Larbert
House

Cemy

DENNY RD

82

M876

A883

B905

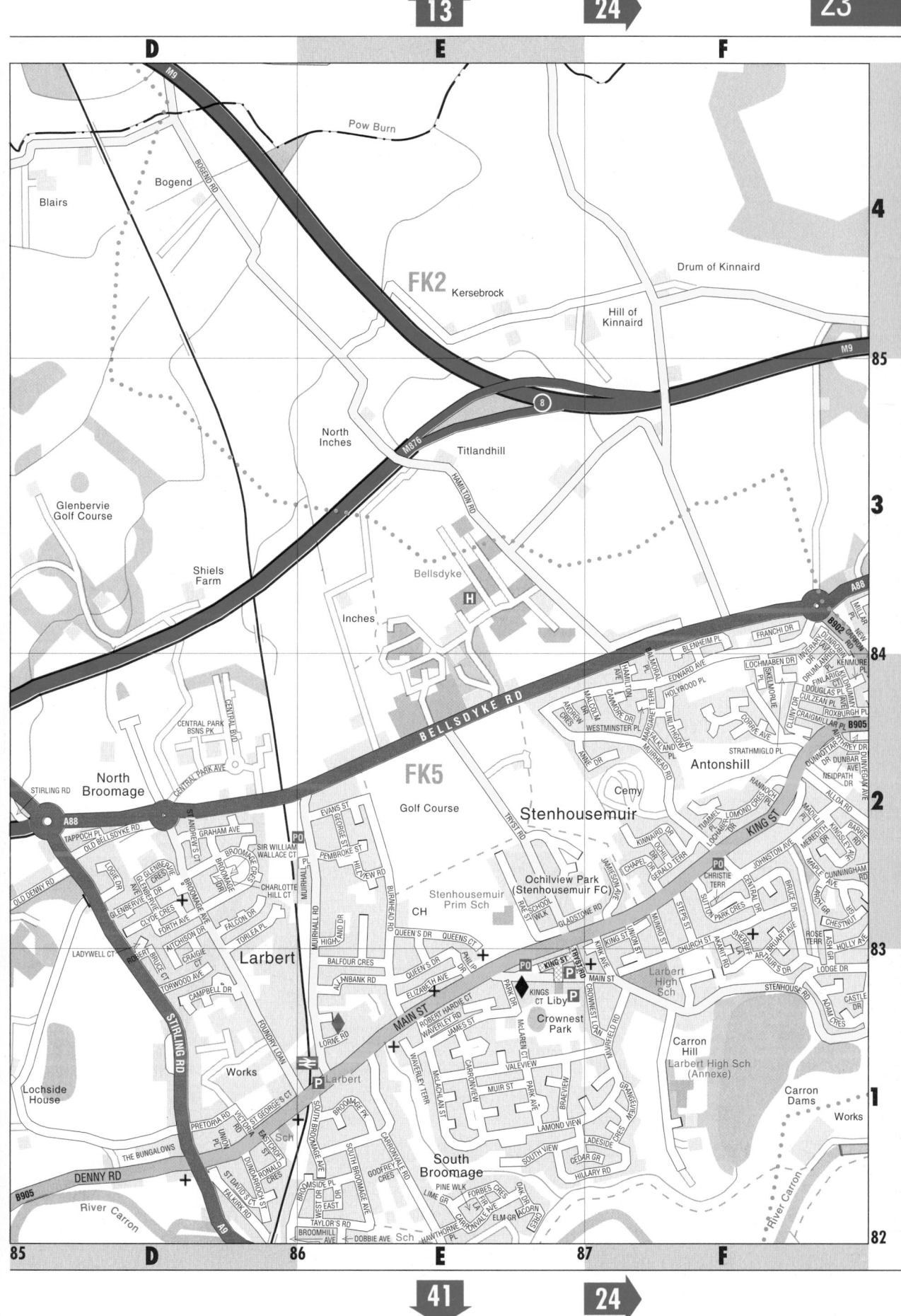
13
24
D
E
F
Pow Burn
M9
Bogend
BOGEND RD
Blairs
FK2
Kersebrock
Drum of Kinnaird
Hill of Kinnaird
85
North Inches
M876
Titlandhill
HAMILTON RD
Glenbervie Golf Course
3
Shiels Farm
Bellsdyke
Inches
A88
B902
84
BELLSDYKE RD
CENTRAL PARK BSNS PK
CENTRAL BVD
CENTRAL PARK AVE
North Broomage
STIRLING RD
FK5
Golf Course
Antonshill
Cemy
Stenhousemuir
2
Ochilview Park (Stenhousemuir FC)
Stenhousemuir Prim Sch
CH
Larbert
KING ST
MAIN ST
83
Larbert High Sch
Kings Ct
Liby
Crownest Park
Works
Larbert
Carron Hill
Larbert High Sch (Annexe)
Carron Dams
Works
1
Lochside House
DENNY RD
B905
River Carron
South Broomage
A9
Sch
82
85
86
87
41
24

23
14

A
B
C
Letham
Lochs of Airth
Tramways
Letham Farm
North Langdyke
LETHAM COTTS
M876
A905
SOUTH APPROACH RD
A876
Southfield
North Bellsdyke
M9
Kinnaird House
South Bellsdyke
BRACKENLEES RD
A88
BELLSDYKE RD
Muirdyke Burn
FK2
Bensfield
Kirkton
Howkerse
Carronshore Prim Sch
Roughlands
Carronshore
Westertown
BOTHKENNAR RD
Dutch Inn (PH)
Bothkennar Prim Sch
Skinflats
Backrow
NEW CARRON RD
B902
Carron Prim Sch
Carron House
FK5
Carron
River Carron
Yonderhaugh
FALKIRK
Langlees
Sewage Works
Dawson Park Sch
FK3
4
3
2
1
85
84
83
82
88
89
90

23
42

D
E
F

Colgrain
Prim Sch

BEECHGROVE PL

1 1 JEANIE DEANS DR
2 2 ABBOTSFORD DR

REDGAUNTLET RD

GUY MANNERING RD

Woodhead
Cottage

Drumfork
Farm

Camis Eskan
Farm

Quarry
Wood

Red Glen

Red Burn

Hermitage
Acad

TALISMAN CRES

A814

CAMPBELL DR

ARMSTRONG RD

ASHTON DR

COLLINS RD

AUBURN RD

WAVERLEY AVE

KENILWORTH AVE

DRUMFORK RD

Railway
Glen

CAMIS ESKAN
HOUSE

G84

Lawn
Wood

Manson's
Wood

4

LAWRENCE AVE

MARMION AVE

CARDROSS RD

DENNISTOUN CRES

MOORE DR

Craigendoran

81

Service's
Wood

16

Feddens
Wood

Moor
Cottage

STONEYMOLLAN RD

3

CLADDOCH
COTTS

Feddans
Cottage

C

82

QUEEN'S COURT

HANGINGSHAW PL

SOMERVILLE PL

CLYDE ST E

A814

SOUTH KING ST

OLD LUSS RD

TALISMAN CRES

Colgrain
Farm

High
Strip

80

G84

STATION RD

CRAIGENDORAN AVE

4

EASTWOOD LA 1
DRUMFORK CT 2
KING ST E 3
DIANA VERNON CT 4
ABBOTSFORD DR 5
MONAEBROOK PL 6
MIDDLETON LA 7

MIDDLETON DR

MOSS RD

LC

G82

Keppoch

Hillside
Cottage

RED RD

Craigendoran

Piers

Lyleston
Wood

Badyen
Farm

C

31

81

Lyleston

Knowehead

2

Drumhead

Lyleston
Farm

Crem

Cemy

79

LC

Ardmore
Crossing

Geilston Burn

Hill of
Ardmore

Ardmore
Farm

ARDARDAN
COTTS

Mollandhu

Geilston
House

1

Ardmore

Ardardan
House

Brooks
House

Moorpark

A814

78

31
D
32
E
33
F

A   B   C

4

Stoneymollan Muir
Stoneymollan Road

G83

Tullichewan Muir

Killoeter Burn

Blackthird

81

Auchinabreck

Darleith
House

Drumfairn

3

Gallston Burn

Lodge
Wood

80

Auchensail
Cottage

G82

Low
Auchensail

Cairniedrouth

Asker
Reservoir

Asker
Farm

2

High
Auchensail

Low
Slewan

High
Milndovan

Kilmahew Burn

79

Kilmahew
Farm

Low
Milndovan

Wallacetown Burn

CARDROSS RD

P +

Kirkton
House

1

Kilmahew
House

CAHMAN RD

KILMAHEW CT 1
KILMAHEW DR 2
KILMAHEW GR 3
NAPIER AVE 4

Cardross
Prim Sch

DARLEITH RD

MILL
RD

KIRKTON CRES

KIRKTON RD

BAHRS RD

KILMAHEW AVE
2 3
BARRS CT
4

HILLSIDE RD

78

34   35   36

A   B   C

19
28

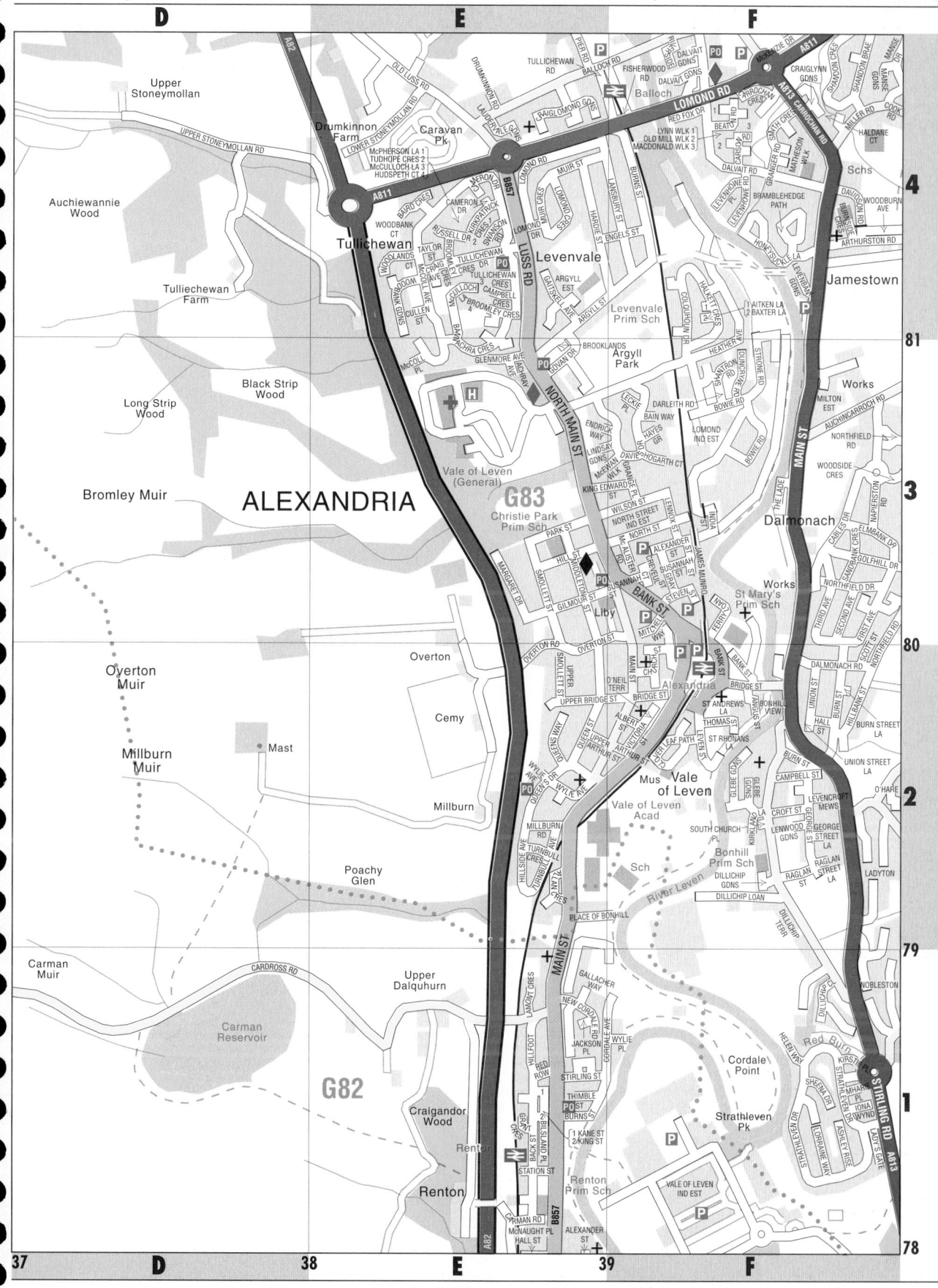
D
E
F
ALEXANDRIA
Upper Stoneymollan
UPPER STONEYMOLLAN RD
Auchiewannie Wood
Tulliechewan Farm
Long Strip Wood
Black Strip Wood
Bromley Muir
Overton Muir
Millburn Muir
Mast
Carman Muir
CARDROSS RD
Carman Reservoir
G82
G83
Poachy Glen
Upper Dalquhurn
Craigandor Wood
Renton
Millburn
Cemy
Overton
Vale of Leven (General)
H
Christie Park Prim Sch
Drumkinnon Farm
Caravan Pk
LOWER STONEYMOLLAN RD
OLD LUSS RD
DRUMKINNON RD
McPHERSON LA 1
TUDHOPE CRES 2
McCULLOCH LA 3
HUDSPETH CT 4
A82
A811
B857
Tullichewan
WOODBANK CT
WOODLANDS CT
WOODBANK GDNS
TAYLOR ST
McCOLL AVE
CULLEN ST
BARD CRES
CAMERON DR
RUSSELL DR
KIRKPATRICK CRES
SWANSON RD
BROMLEY CRES
TULLICHEWAN DR
TULLICHEWAN CRES
CAMPBELL CRES
BROMLEY CRES
McCULLOCH ST
ACHRA CRES
GLENMORE AVE
ACHRAY AVE
McCOLL PL
LUSS RD
LOMOND RD
MUIR ST
MUIR CRES
LOMOND CRES
LOMOND DR
Levenvale
ARGYLL EST
GAITSKELL AVE
ARGYLL ST
HARDIE ST
LANSBURY ST
ENGELS ST
BURNS ST
Levenvale Prim Sch
BROOKLANDS
GOVAN DR
Argyll Park
NORTH MAIN ST
TULLICHEWAN RD
PIER RD
BALLOCH RD
BAIGLOMOND GDNS
LAUDERVALE GDNS
FISHERWOOD RD
DALVAIT GDNS
Balloch
LOMOND RD
RED FOX DR
LYNN WLK 1
OLD MILL WLK 2
MACDONALD WLK 3
BEATON RD
CARSON RD
DALVAIT RD
McKENZIE DR
CARROCHAN RD
CARROCHAN CRES
SMITH CRES
GRANGER RD
MATHESON WLK
A813
LEVENHOWE PL
LEVENHOWE RD
BRAMBLEHEDGE PATH
HONEYSUCKLE LA
LEVENBANK GDNS
CRAIGLYNN GDNS
SHANDON CRES
SHANDON BRAE
MANSE GDNS
MANSE DR
MILLER RD
COOK RD
HALDANE CT
Schs
DAVIDSON RD
WOODBURN AVE
BURNSIDE CRES
ARTHURSTON RD
Jamestown
COLQUHOUN DR
HALKETT CRES
1 AITKEN LA
2 BAXTER LA
HEATHER AVE
SHANTRON RD
DUNCRYNE RD
STRONE RD
BOWIE RD
LOMOND IND EST
DARLEITH RD
BAIN WAY
LECKIE PL
ENDRICK WAY
HAYES GR
LINDSAY GDNS
McEWAN WLK
DAVIE DR
HOGARTH CT
GRANGE PL
KING EDWARD ST
WILSON ST
NORTH STREET IND EST
NORTH ST
LENNOX ST
INDIA ST
THE LADE
Works
MILTON EST
AUCHINCARROCH RD
NORTHFIELD RD
WOODSIDE CRES
NAPIERSTON RD
ELMBANK DR
Dalmonach
CABLES DR
SANDBANK CRES
GOLFHILL DR
NORTHFIELD DR
THIRD AVE
SECOND AVE
FIRST AVE
SCOTT ST
NORTHFIELD RD
MAIN ST
DALMONACH RD
UNION ST
BURN ST
HILLBANK ST
BURN STREET LA
HALL ST
UNION STREET LA
O'HARE
PARK ST
HILL ST
MIDDLETON ST
SMOLLETT ST
MARGARET DR
McALISTER RD
ALEXANDER ST
SUSANNAH ST
SUSANNAH CT
CREVEUL CT
GRAY ST
STEVEN ST
JAMES MUNRO
BANK ST
GILMOUR ST
Liby
MITCHELL WAY
St Mary's Prim Sch
FERRY LOAN
OVERTON RD
OVERTON ST
UPPER SMOLLETT ST
O'NEIL TERR
MAIN ST
CHURCH ST
BRIDGE ST
Alexandria
ST ANDREWS LA
BONHILL VIEW
ANGUS ST
THOMAS ST
ST RHONANS LA
UPPER BRIDGE ST
ALBERT ST
VICTORIA ST
QUEENS WAY
QUEEN ST
UPPER ARTHUR ST
ARTHUR ST
CLOVERLEAF PATH
LEVEN ST
GLEBE GDNS
GLEBE GDNS
Mus
Vale of Leven
WYLIE AVE
QUEEN'S DR
Vale of Leven Acad
KIRKLAND LA
CAMPBELL ST
LEVENCROFT MEWS
CROFT ST
GEORGE ST
GEORGE STREET LA
LENWOOD GDNS
SOUTH CHURCH PL
Bonhill Prim Sch
RAGLAN ST
RAGLAN STREET LA
LADYTON
DILLICHIP GDNS
DILLICHIP LOAN
DILLICHIP TERR
MILLBURN RD
HILLSIDE AVE
TURNBULL CRES
TURNBULL AVE
McLAN CRES
Sch
River Leven
PLACE OF BONHILL
LAMONT CRES
GALLACHER WAY
NEW CORDALE RD
CORDALE AVE
JACKSON PL
WYLIE PL
HILLFOOT
RED ROW
STIRLING ST
THIMBLE ST
BURNS ST
1 KANE ST
2 KING ST
GRANT CRES
BACK ST
BILSLAND PL
STATION ST
Renton Prim Sch
CARMAN RD
McNAUGHT PL
HALL ST
ALEXANDER ST
Cordale Point
Strathleven Pk
VALE OF LEVEN IND EST
DILLICHIP CL
NOBLESTON
HELEN WAY
Red Burn
KIRSTIE PL
SHEENA DR
STRATHLEVEN DR
MHAIRIE PL
IONA WYND
ASHLEY RISE
LORRAINE WAY
LADY'S GATE
STIRLING RD
81
80
79
78
4
3
2
1
37
38
39

49
28

27 20

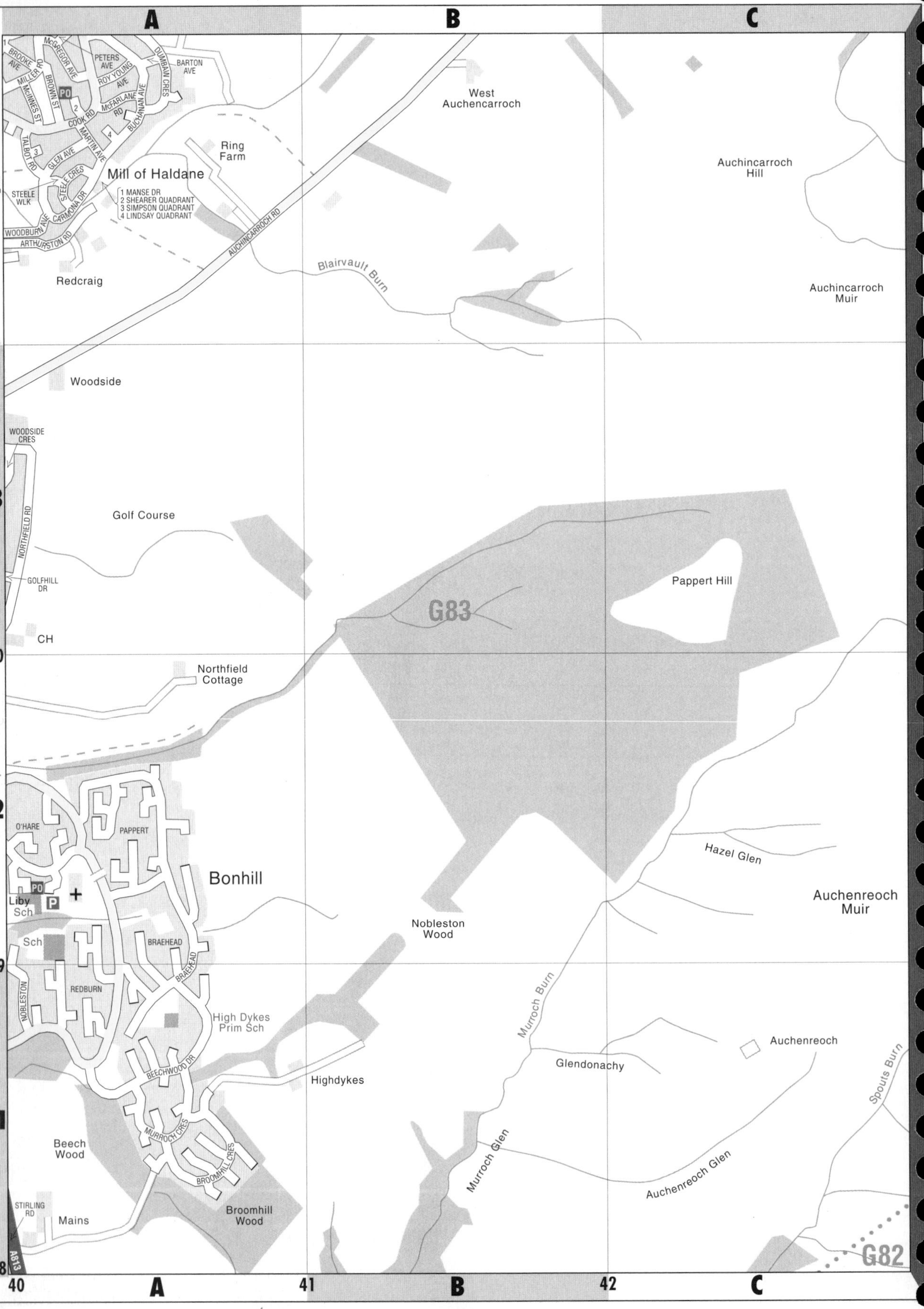

A B C

West
Auchencarroch

Auchincarroch
Hill

PETERS
AVE
ROY YOUNG
AVE
BARTON
AVE
McGREGOR AVE
BROOKE
AVE
MILLER
AVE
McINNES ST
BROWN ST
COOK RD
MARTIN AVE
McFARLANE
RD
BUCHANAN AVE
DUMBAIN CRES
PO
TALBOT RD
GLEN AVE
STEELE CRES
CARMONA DR
Ring
Farm
Mill of Haldane
STEELE
WLK
WOODBURN AVE
ARTHURSTON RD
1 MANSE DR
2 SHEARER QUADRANT
3 SIMPSON QUADRANT
4 LINDSAY QUADRANT
AUCHINCARROCH RD

4

Redcraig

Auchincarroch
Muir

Blairvault Burn

81

Woodside

WOODSIDE
CRES

NORTHFIELD RD

3

Golf Course

G83

Pappert Hill

GOLFHILL
DR

CH

80

Northfield
Cottage

O'HARE

PAPPERT

2

PO
Liby
Sch
P
+
Bonhill
Hazel Glen

Auchenreoch
Muir

Sch

BRAEHEAD

Nobleston
Wood

NOBLESTON

79

REDBURN

BRAEHEAD

High Dykes
Prim Sch

Murroch Burn

Auchenreoch

BEECHWOOD DR

Highdykes

Glendonachy

Spouts Burn

1

Beech
Wood

MURROCH CRES

BROOMHILL CRES

Murroch Glen

Auchenreoch Glen

STIRLING
RD

Mains

Broomhill
Wood

A813

G82

78

40 A 41 B 42 C

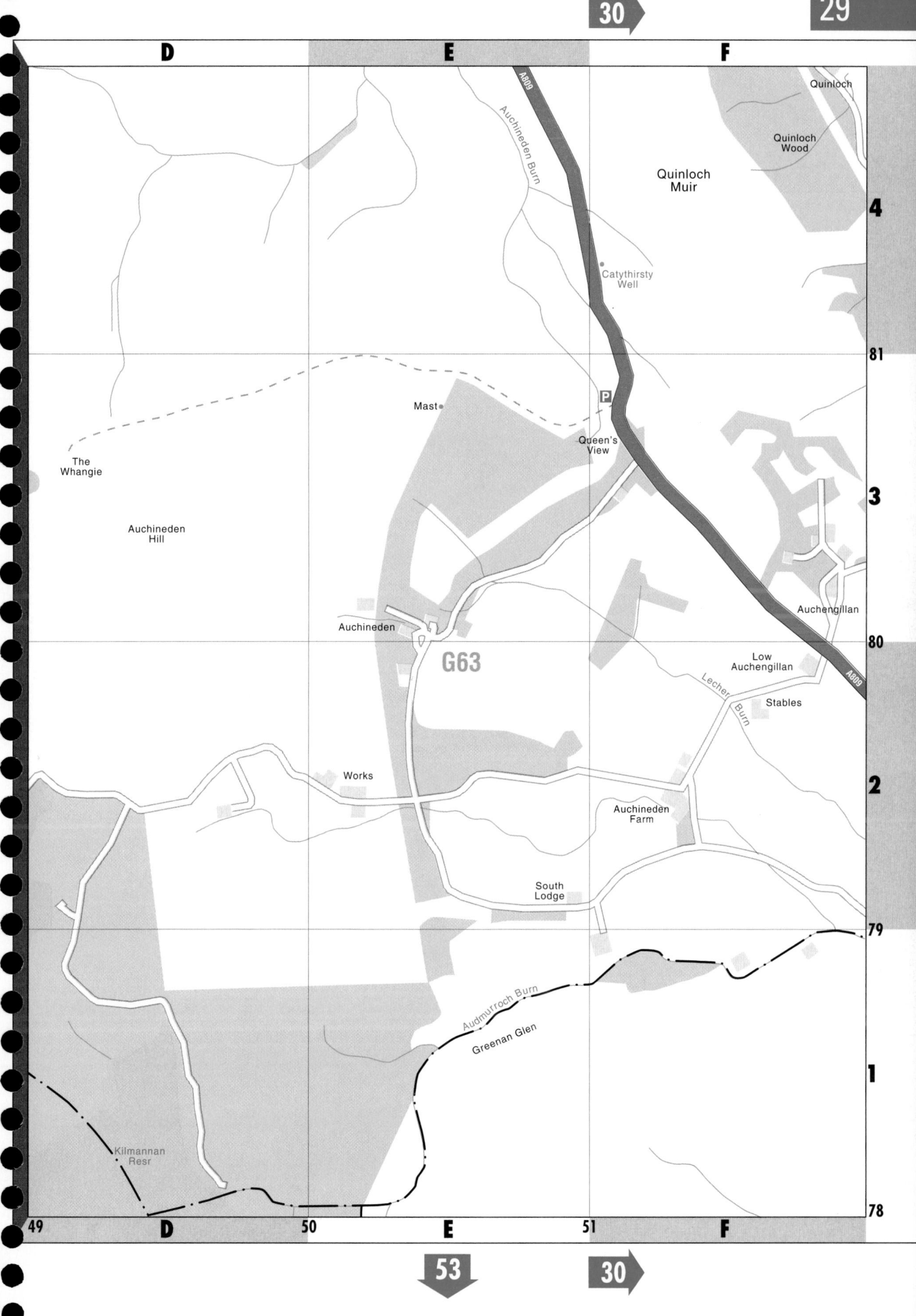

D   E   F

Quinloch

Quinloch
Wood

Quinloch
Muir

4

Catythirsty
Well

Auchineden Burn

A809

81

Mast

P

Queen's
View

The
Whangie

3

Auchineden
Hill

Auchengillan

Auchineden

80

G63

Low
Auchengillan

Lecher Burn

Stables

A809

Works

2

Auchineden
Farm

South
Lodge

79

Audmurroch Burn

Greenan Glen

1

Kilmannan
Resr

78

49   D   50   E   51   F

29

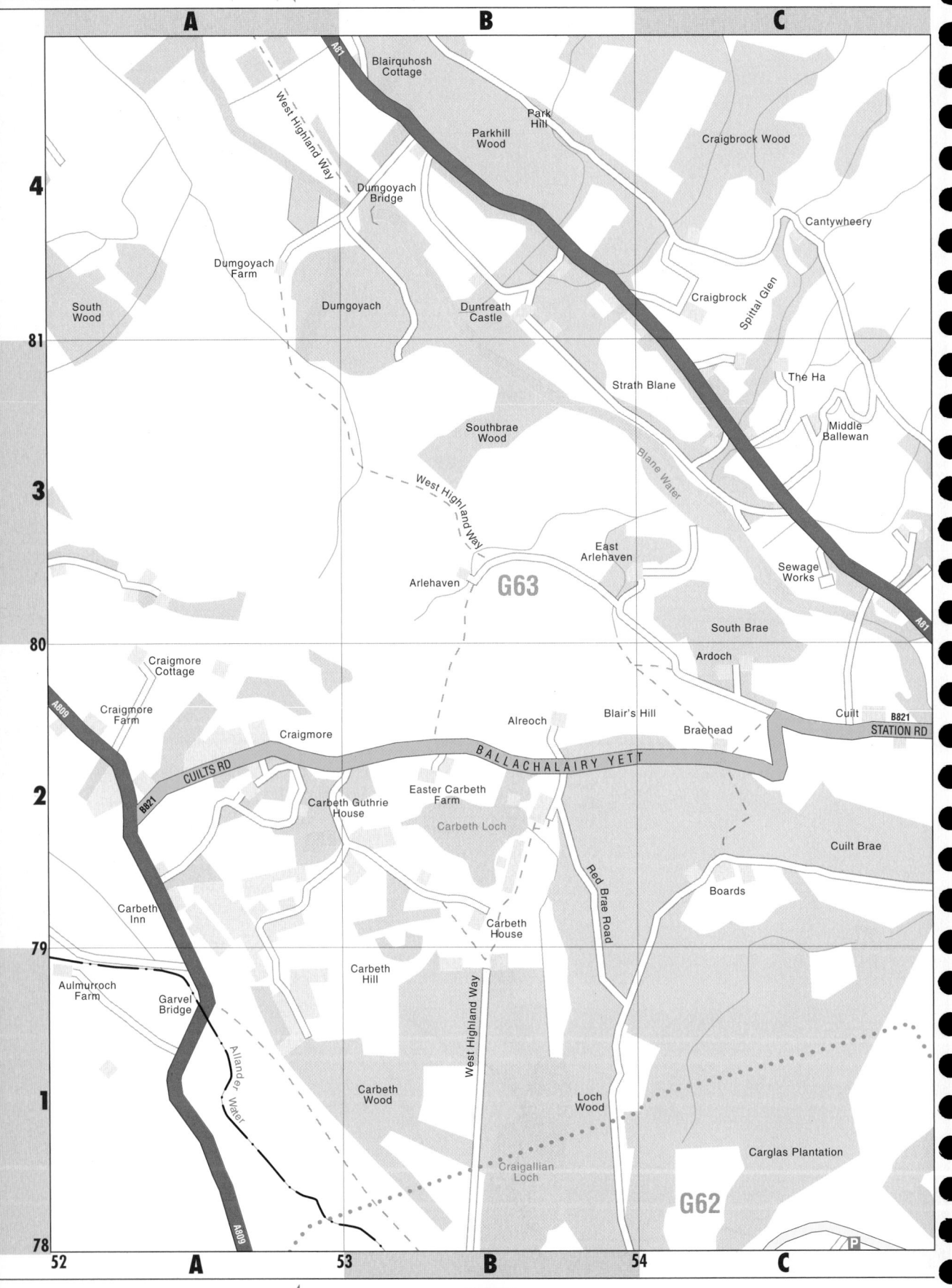
A
B
C
4
3
2
1
81
80
79
78
52
53
54
Blairquhosh Cottage
A81
West Highland Way
Park Hill
Parkhill Wood
Craigbrock Wood
Dumgoyach Bridge
Cantywheery
Dumgoyach Farm
South Wood
Dumgoyach
Duntreath Castle
Craigbrock
Spittal Glen
The Ha
Strath Blane
Southbrae Wood
Middle Ballewan
Blane Water
West Highland Way
East Arlehaven
Arlehaven
G63
Sewage Works
South Brae
Ardoch
Craigmore Cottage
Craigmore Farm
A809
Alreoch
Blair's Hill
Braehead
Cuilt
B821
STATION RD
Craigmore
CUILTS RD
BALLACHALAIRY YETT
B821
Easter Carbeth Farm
Carbeth Guthrie House
Carbeth Loch
Cuilt Brae
Red Brae Road
Boards
Carbeth Inn
Carbeth House
Carbeth Hill
Aulmurroch Farm
Garvel Bridge
West Highland Way
Allander Water
Carbeth Wood
Loch Wood
Carglas Plantation
Craigallian Loch
G62
A809
P

29
54

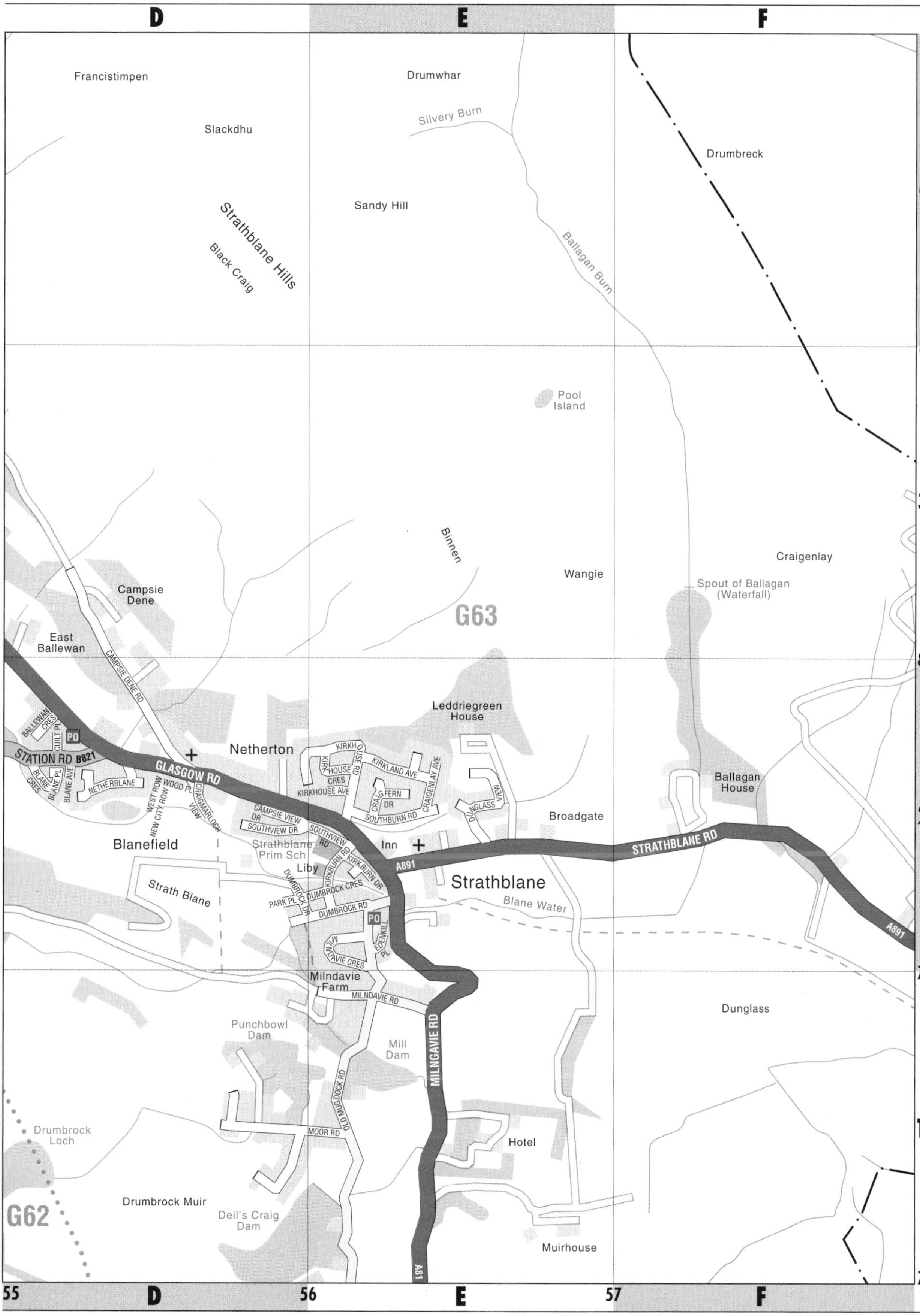

D E F

Francistimpen

Drumwhar

Slackdhu

Silvery Burn

Drumbreck

Strathblane Hills

Sandy Hill

4

Black Craig

Ballagan Burn

81

Pool Island

3

Binnen

Craigenlay

Wangie

Spout of Ballagan (Waterfall)

G63

Campsie Dene

80

East Ballewan

Leddriegreen House

Ballagan House

BALLEWAN CRES

PO

CAMPSIE DENE RD

Netherton

KIRKH

KIRKLAND AVE

CRAIGENLAY AVE

STATION RD

B821

BLANE PL

BLANE AVE

CULT PL

NETHERBLANE

NEW CITY ROW

WEST ROW

WOOD PL

CRAIGHARLOCH

GLASGOW RD

KIRKHOUSE CRES

KIRKHOUSE AVE

CRA

G-FERN DR

SOUTHBURN RD

DUNGLASS VIEW

Broadgate

2

BLANE CRES

CAMPSIE VIEW DR

SOUTHVIEW DR

SOUTHVIEW RD

KIRKHOUSE RD

Inn

STRATHBLANE RD

A891

Blanefield

Strathblane Prim Sch

Liby

KIRK BURN DR

A891

Strathblane

Strath Blane

PARK PL

DUMBROCK DR

DUMBROCK CRES

Blane Water

DUMBROCK RD

PO

BLUEBELL PL

Milndavie Farm

MILNDAVIE CRES

MILNDAVIE RD

79

Dunglass

Punchbowl Dam

Mill Dam

MILNGAVIE RD

OLD MUGDOCK RD

A81

Drumbrock Loch

MOOR RD

Hotel

1

G62

Drumbrock Muir

Deil's Craig Dam

Muirhouse

78

55 D 56 E 57 F

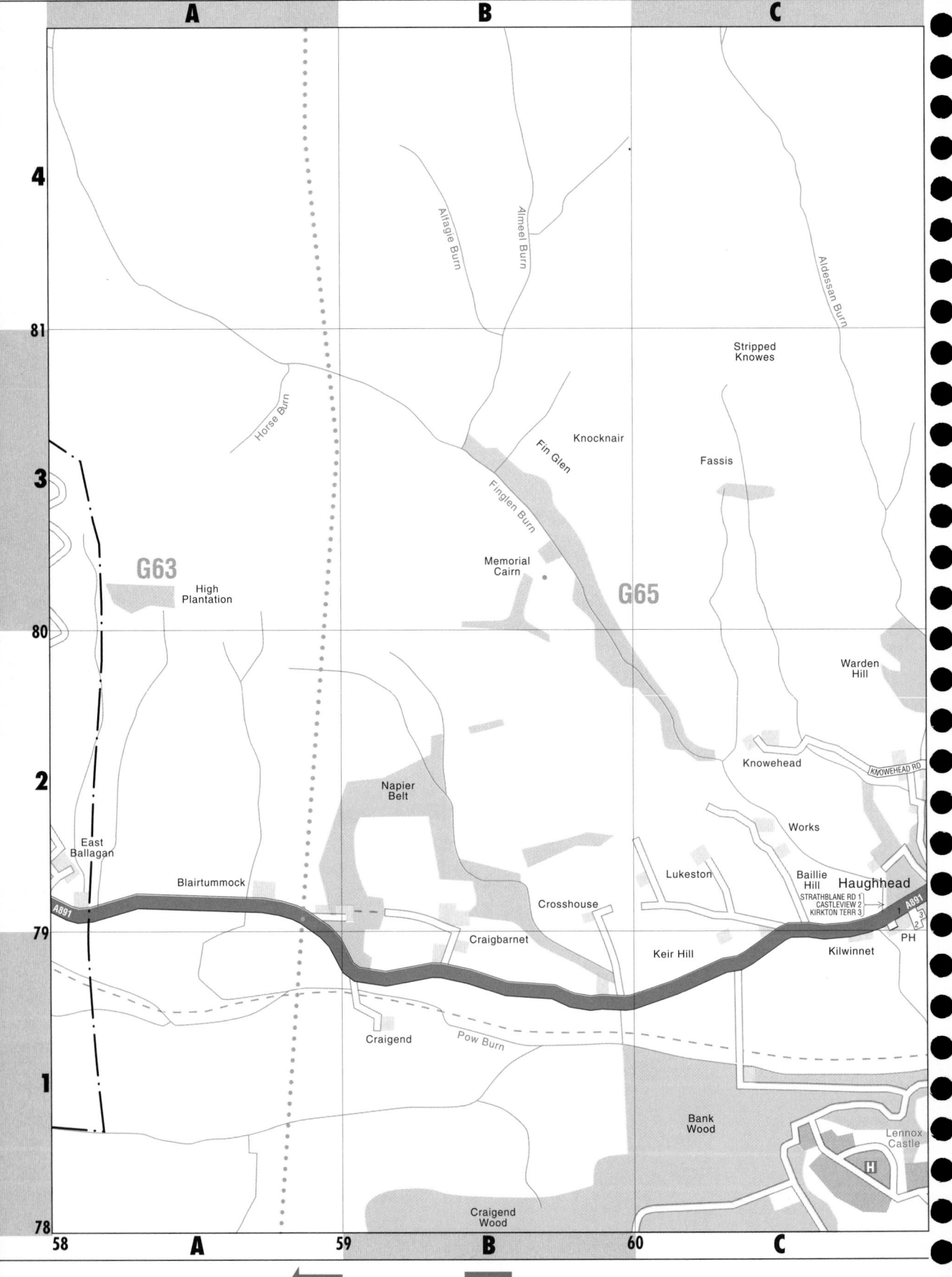

31

A B C

4

81

Alfagie Burn

Almeel Burn

Aldessan Burn

Stripped
Knowes

Horse Burn

Knocknair

Fin Glen

Fassis

3

Finglen Burn

G63

High
Plantation

Memorial
Cairn

G65

80

Warden
Hill

2

Napier
Belt

Knowehead

KNOWEHEAD RD

Works

East
Ballagan

Lukeston

Baillie
Hill

Haughhead

Blairtummock

STRATHBLANE RD 1
CASTLEVIEW 2
KIRKTON TERR 3

A891

A891

79

Craigbarnet

Crosshouse

Keir Hill

Kilwinnet

PH

Craigend

Pow Burn

1

Bank
Wood

Lennox
Castle

H

78

58 A 59 B 60 C

31 56

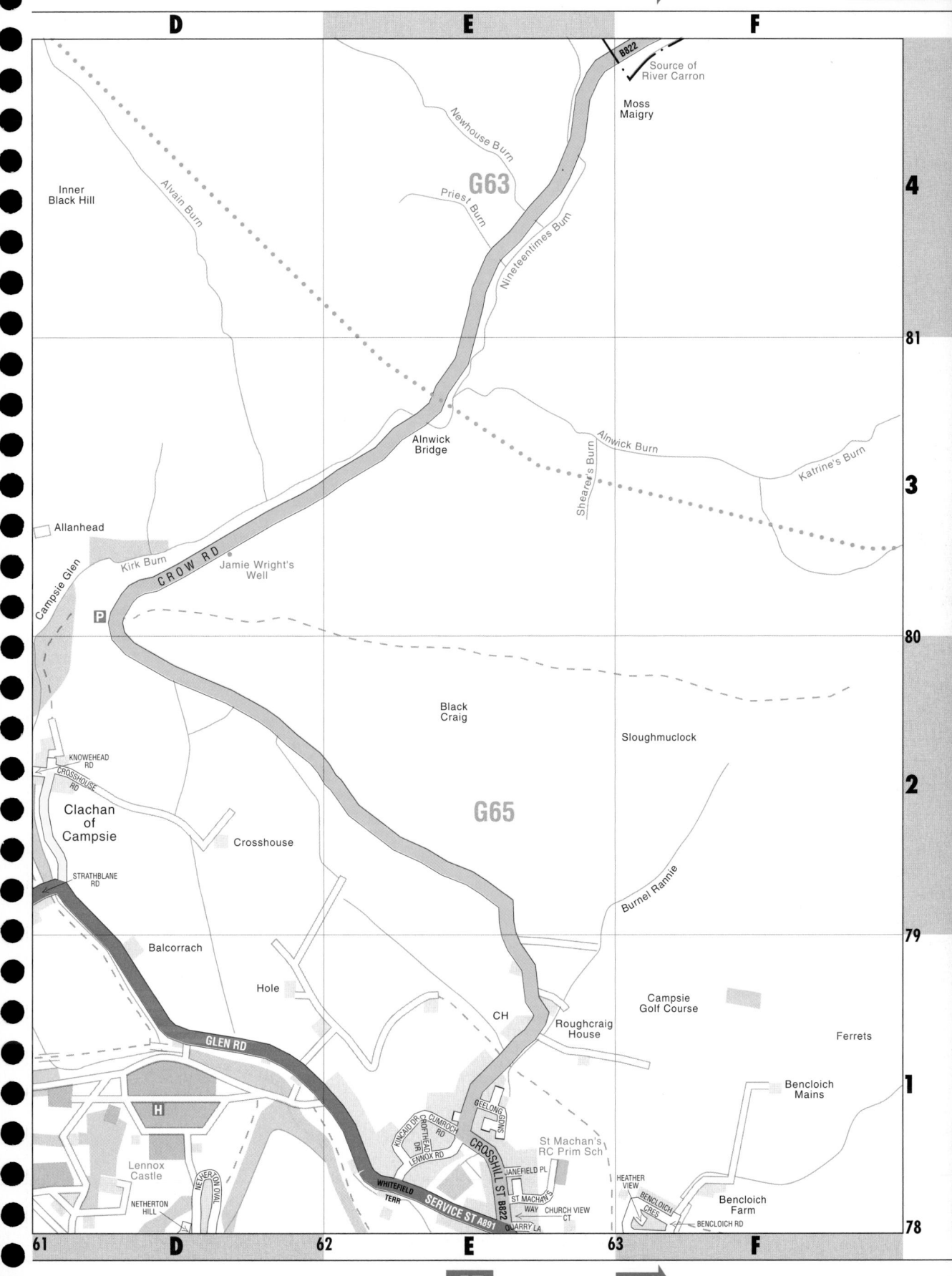

B822

Source of
River Carron

Moss
Maigry

Newhouse Burn

G63

Priest Burn

Nineteentimes Burn

4

Inner
Black Hill

Alvain Burn

81

Alnwick Burn

Shearer's Burn

Katrine's Burn

3

Alnwick
Bridge

Allanhead

CROW RD

Kirk Burn

Jamie Wright's
Well

Campsie Glen

P

80

Black
Craig

Sloughmuclock

KNOWEHEAD
RD

CROSSHOUSE
RD

G65

2

Clachan
of
Campsie

Crosshouse

STRATHBLANE
RD

Burnel Rannie

Balcorrach

79

Hole

Campsie
Golf Course

GLEN RD

CH

Roughcraig
House

Ferrets

H

GEELONG GDNS

Bencloich
Mains

1

KINCAID DR

CUMROCH
RD

CROFTHEAD
DR

LENNOX RD

CROSSHILL ST

St Machan's
RC Prim Sch

JANEFIELD PL

HEATHER
VIEW

BENCLOICH
CRES

Lennox
Castle

NETHERTON
OVAL

WHITEFIELD
TERR

ST MACHAN'S
WAY

CHURCH VIEW
CT

Bencloich
Farm

NETHERTON
HILL

SERVICE ST A891

B822

QUARRY LA

BENCLOICH RD

78

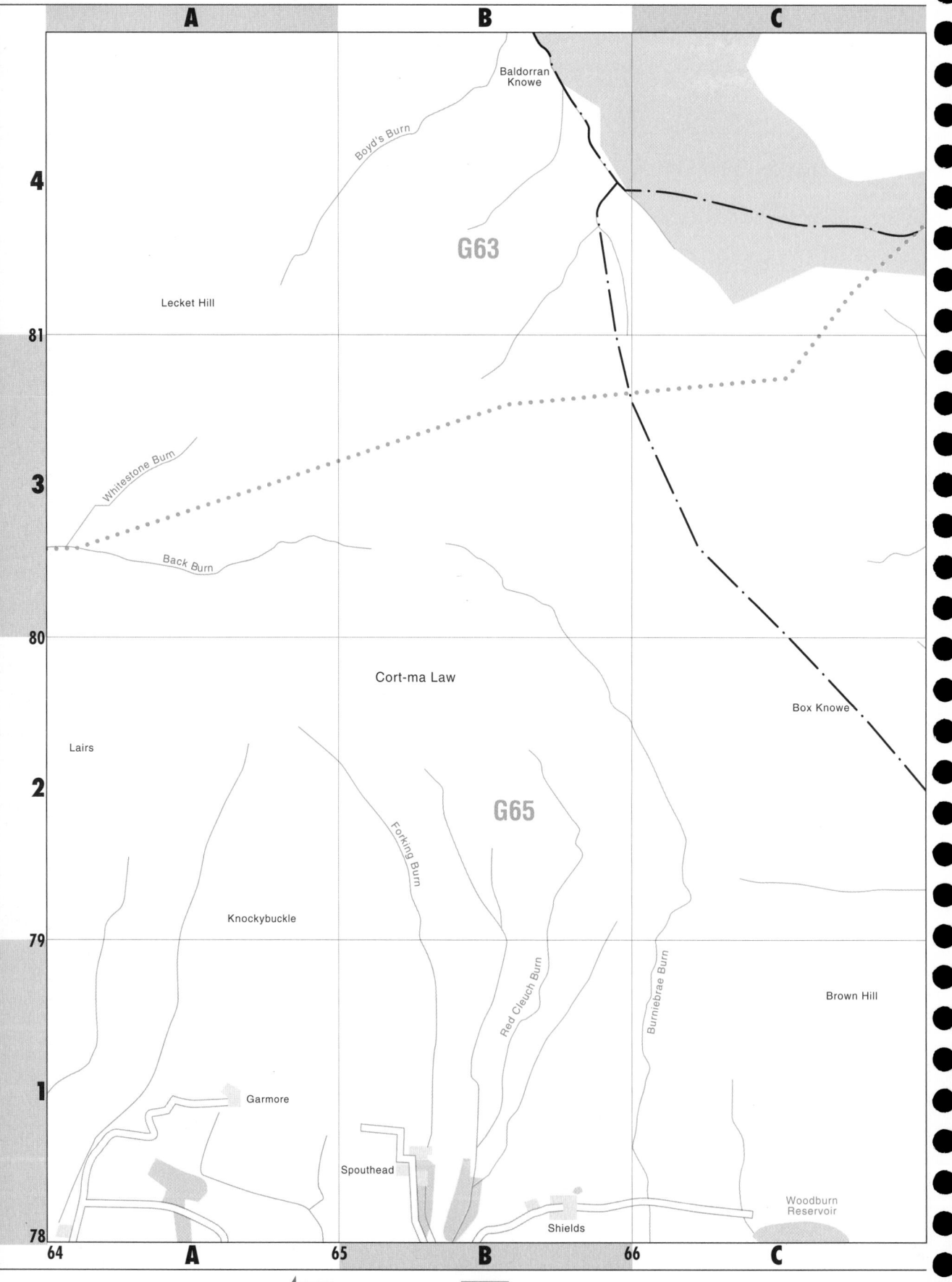

A   B   C

Baldorran
Knowe

Boyd's Burn

G63

Lecket Hill

4

81

Whitestone Burn

3

Back Burn

80

Cort-ma Law

Box Knowe

Lairs

2

G65

Forking Burn

Knockybuckle

Red Cleuch Burn

Burniebrae Burn

Brown Hill

79

1

Garmore

Spouthead

Woodburn
Reservoir

Shields

78

64   A   65   B   66   C

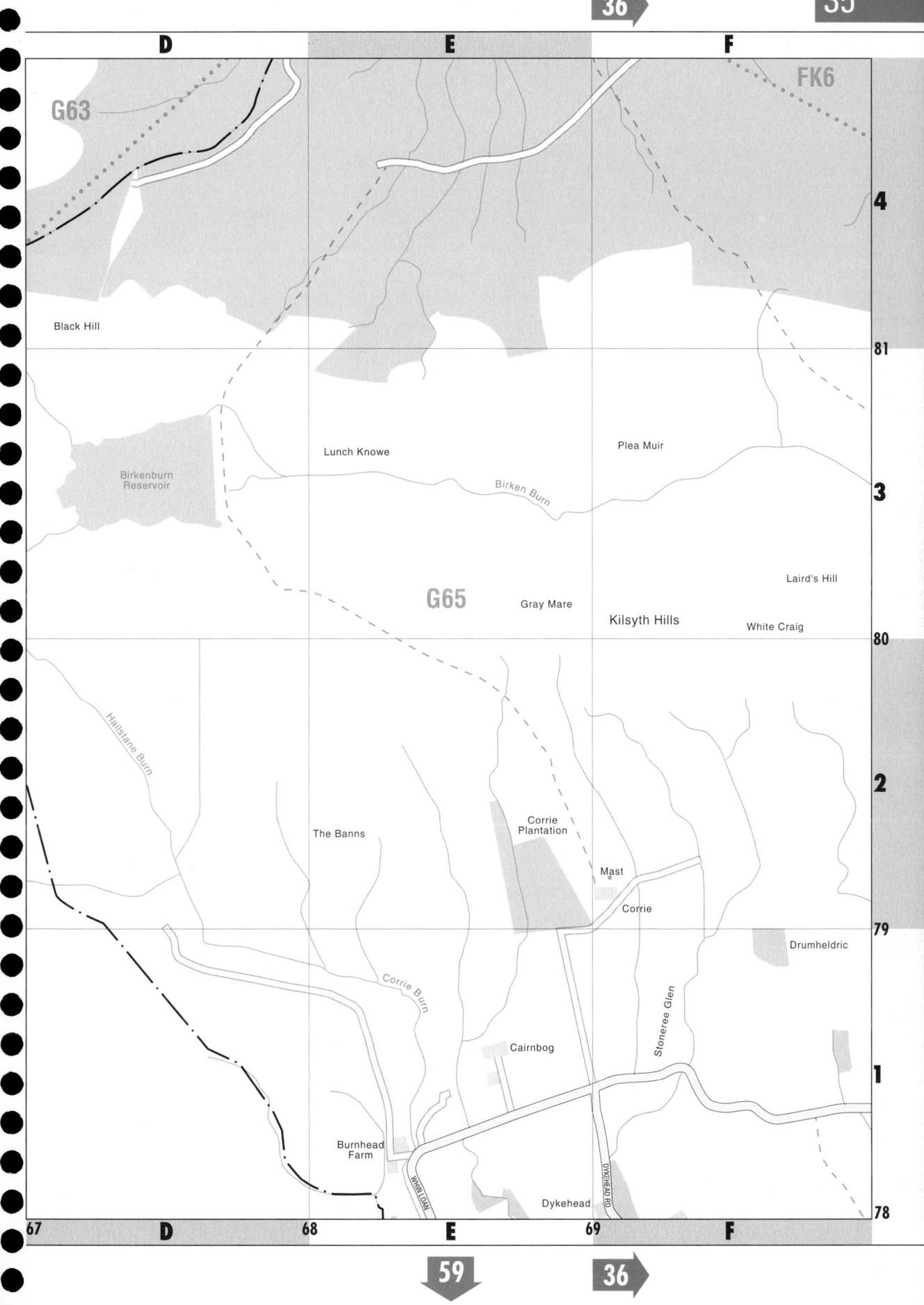

D E F

FK6

G63

Black Hill

4

81

Birkenburn Reservoir

Lunch Knowe

Birken Burn

Plea Muir

3

G65

Gray Mare

Laird's Hill

Kilsyth Hills

White Craig

80

Hailstane Burn

2

The Banns

Corrie Plantation

Mast

Corrie

Drumheldric

79

Corrie Burn

Stoneree Glen

Cairnbog

1

Burnhead Farm

WHIN LOAN

DYKEHEAD RD.

Dykehead

78

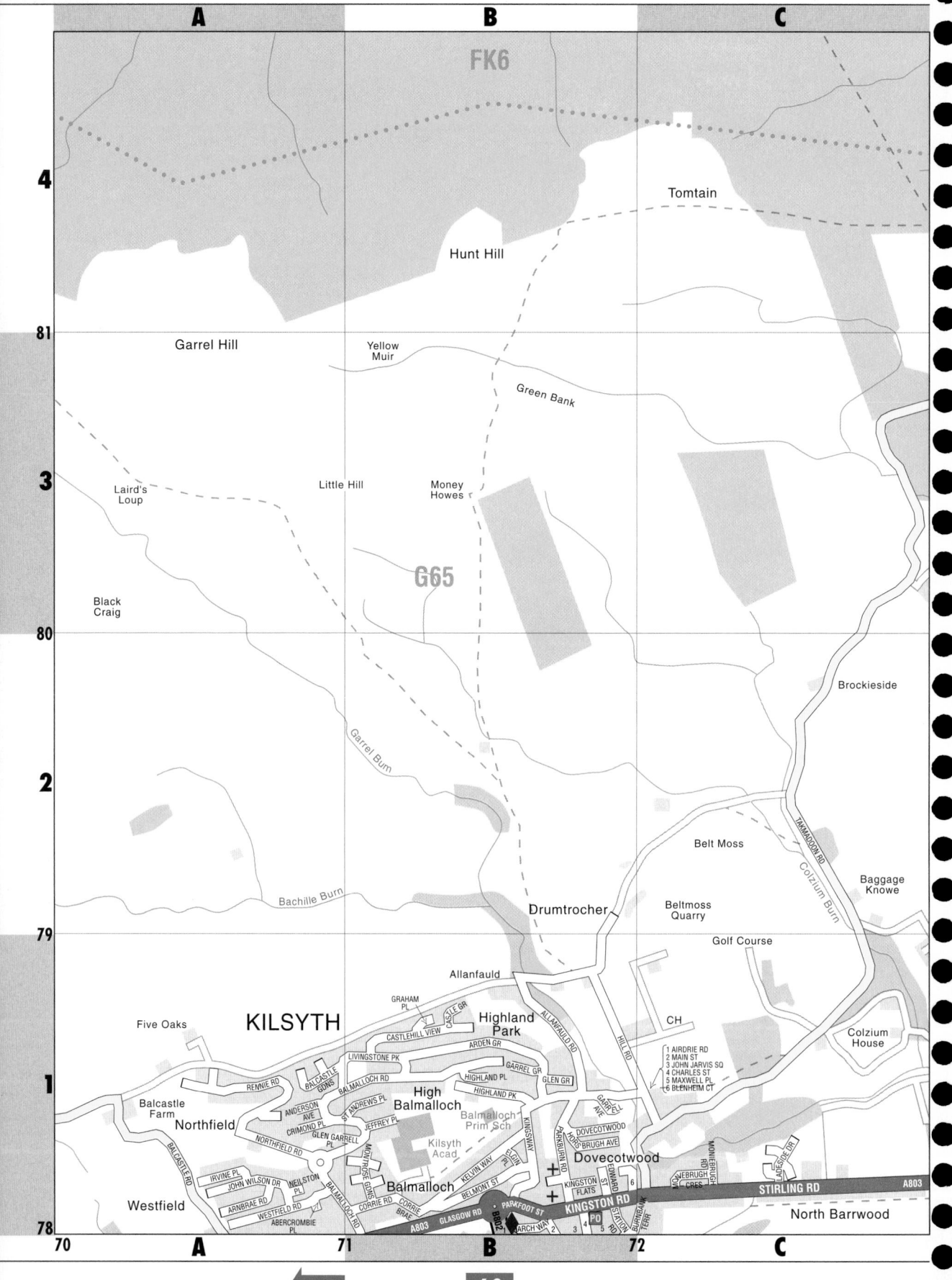

FK6

Tomtain

Hunt Hill

Garrel Hill

Yellow
Muir

Green Bank

Little Hill

Money
Howes

Laird's
Loup

G65

Black
Craig

Brockieside

Garrel Burn

Belt Moss

Baggage
Knowe

Colzium Burn

TAMMADOON RD

Bachille Burn

Drumtrocher

Beltmoss
Quarry

Golf Course

Allanfauld

Five Oaks

KILSYTH

GRAHAM
PL

CASTLE GR

Highland
Park

ALLANFAULD RD

CH

Colzium
House

CASTLEHILL VIEW

ARDEN GR

GARREL GR

HIGHLAND PL

GLEN GR

HILL RD

1 AIRDRIE RD
2 MAIN ST
3 JOHN JARVIS SQ
4 CHARLES ST
5 MAXWELL PL
6 BLENHEIM CT

LIVINGSTONE PK

REMNIE RD

BALCASTLE
GDNS

BALMALLOCH RD

HIGHLAND PK

High
Balmalloch

GARRELL AVE

Balcastle
Farm

ANDERSON
AVE

CRIMOND PL

ST ANDREWS PL

Balmalloch
Prim Sch

DOVECOTWOOD

Northfield

GLEN GARRELL PL

JEFFREY PL

KINGSWAY

PARKBURN RD

HORSBRUGH AVE

Dovecotwood

MONIEBRUGH
RD

MONIEBRUGH
CRES

BURNSIDE DR

LAKESIDE DR

BALCASTLE RD

IRVINE PL

JOHN WILSON DR

NEILSTON PL

MONTROSE GDNS

Kilsyth
Acad

KELVIN WAY

CLIN

6

STIRLING RD   A803

ARNBRAE RD

WESTFIELD RD

ABERCROMBIE
PL

BALMALLOCH RD

CORRIE RD

CORRIE
BRAE

Balmalloch

BELMONT ST

Kingston
Flats

KINGSTON
AVE

EDWARD
ST

MONIEBRUGH
TERR

Westfield

A803   GLASGOW RD

A803

PARKFOOT ST

MARCH WAY

2

KINGSTON RD

3   4   5

PO

KINGSTON
STATION

North Barrwood

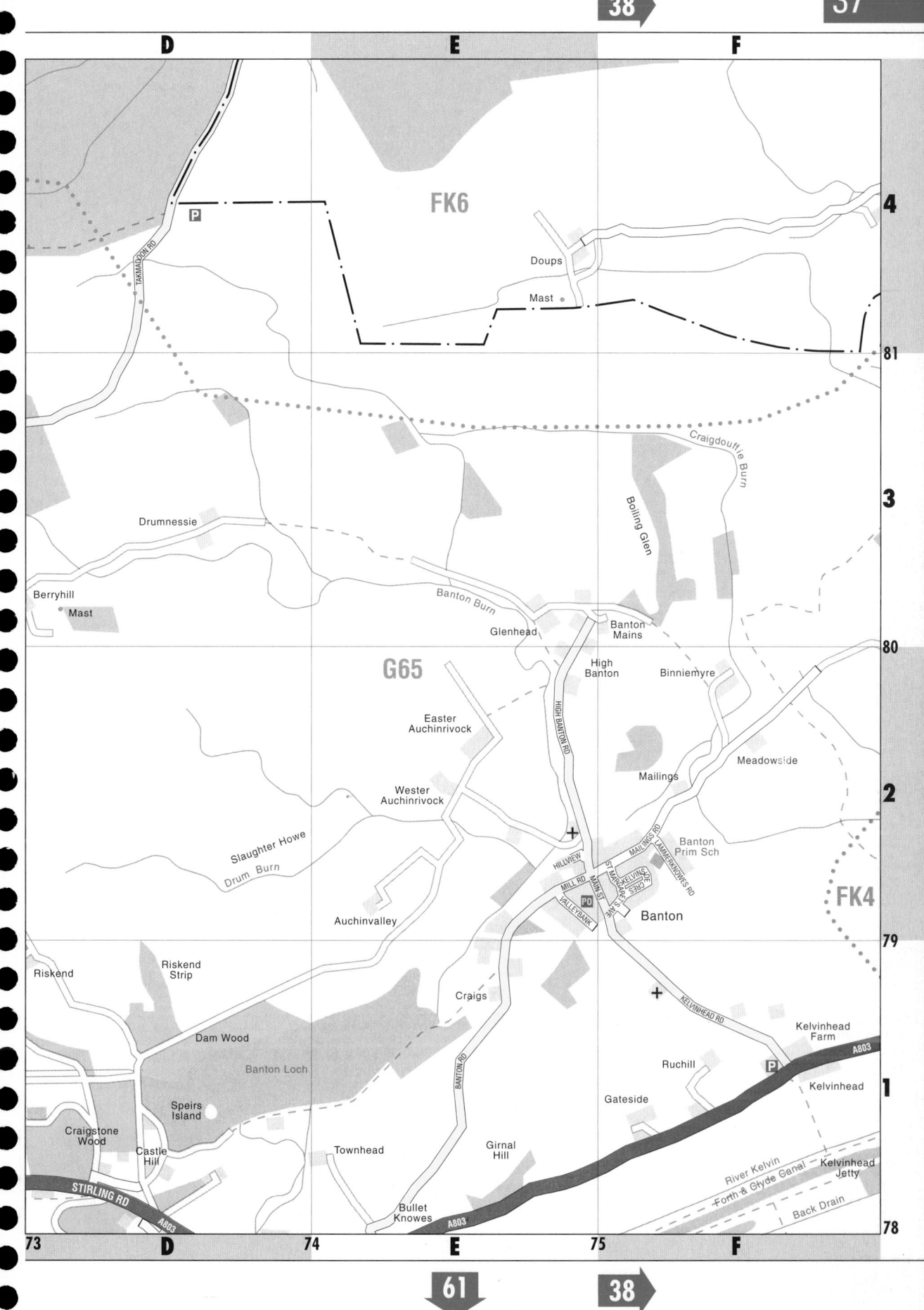

D   E   F

4

FK6

P

TARMACOON RD

Doups

Mast

81

Craigdouffie Burn

3

Boiling Glen

Drumnessie

Banton Burn

Banton
Mains

Berryhill

Mast

Glenhead

High
Banton

Binniemyre

80

G65

Easter
Auchinrivock

HIGH BANTON RD

Mailings

Meadowside

2

Wester
Auchinrivock

MAILINGS RD

Banton
Prim Sch

FK4

Slaughter Howe

Drum Burn

HILLVIEW
MILL RD
MAIN ST
ST MARY'S AVE
KELVIN CRES
LAMMERKNOWES RD

PO
VALLEYBANK

Banton

Auchinvalley

79

Riskend

Riskend
Strip

Craigs

KELVINHEAD RD

1

Dam Wood

Ruchill

Kelvinhead
Farm

P

A803

Banton Loch

BANTON RD

Gateside

Kelvinhead

Speirs
Island

Craigstone
Wood

Castle
Hill

Townhead

Girnal
Hill

River Kelvin

Kelvinhead
Jetty

STIRLING RD

A803

Bullet
Knowes

A803

Forth & Clyde Canal

Back Drain

78

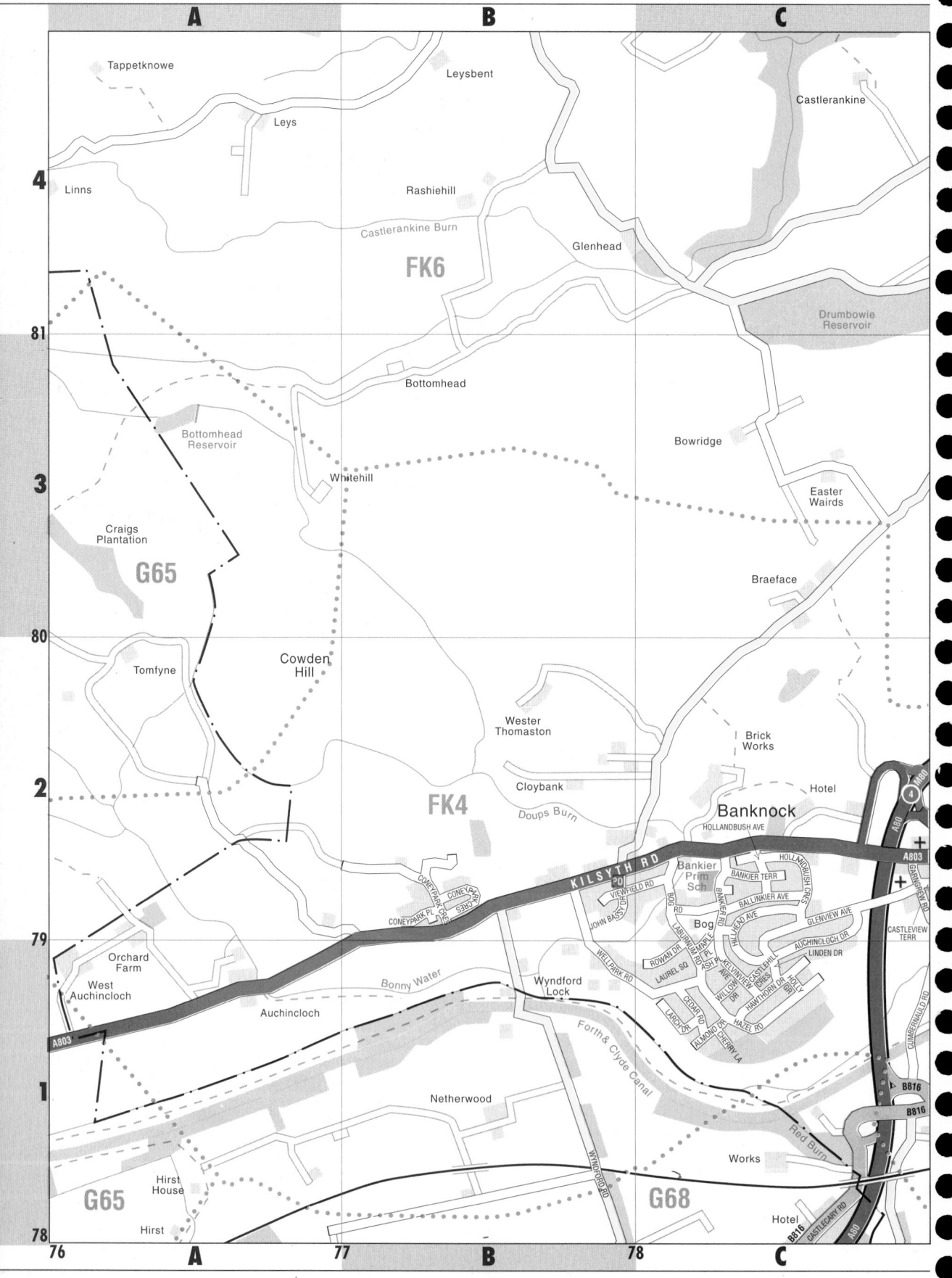

A   B   C

Tappetknowe

Leysbent

Castlerankine

Leys

Linns

Rashiehill

4

Castlerankine Burn

Glenhead

FK6

Drumbowie
Reservoir

81

Bottomhead

Bowridge

Bottomhead
Reservoir

Whitehill

3

Easter
Wairds

Craigs
Plantation

G65

Braeface

80

Tomfyne

Cowden
Hill

Wester
Thomaston

Brick
Works

Hotel

2

Cloybank

Banknock

FK4

Doups Burn

HOLLANDBUSH AVE

KILSYTH RD

Bankier
Prim
Sch

BANKIER CRES

HOLLANDBUSH RD

VIEWFIELD RD

BANKIER TERR

CONEYPARK PL

CONEY CRES

JOHN BASSY ORCHARD RD

BALLINKIER AVE

GLENVIEW AVE

BOG
RD

HILLHEAD AVE

AUCHINCLOCH DR

CASTLEVIEW
TERR

CONEYPARK PL

Bog

LINDEN DR

79

WELL PARK RD

ROWAN DR

MAPLE

ASH PL

CASTLEHILL

CUMBERNAULD RD

Orchard
Farm

LAUREL SQ

WILLOW
DR

HAWTHORN DR

West
Auchincloch

Wyndford
Lock

LABURNUM RD

CEDAR RD

ASH

HAZEL

Auchincloch

Bonny Water

LARCH DR

ALMOND DR

CHERRY LA

HAZEL RD

Forth & Clyde Canal

1

A803

Netherwood

WYNDFORD RD

Works

Red Burn

B816

B816

Hirst
House

Hotel

G65

G68

CASTLECARY RD

B816

Hirst

78

76   A   77   B   78   C

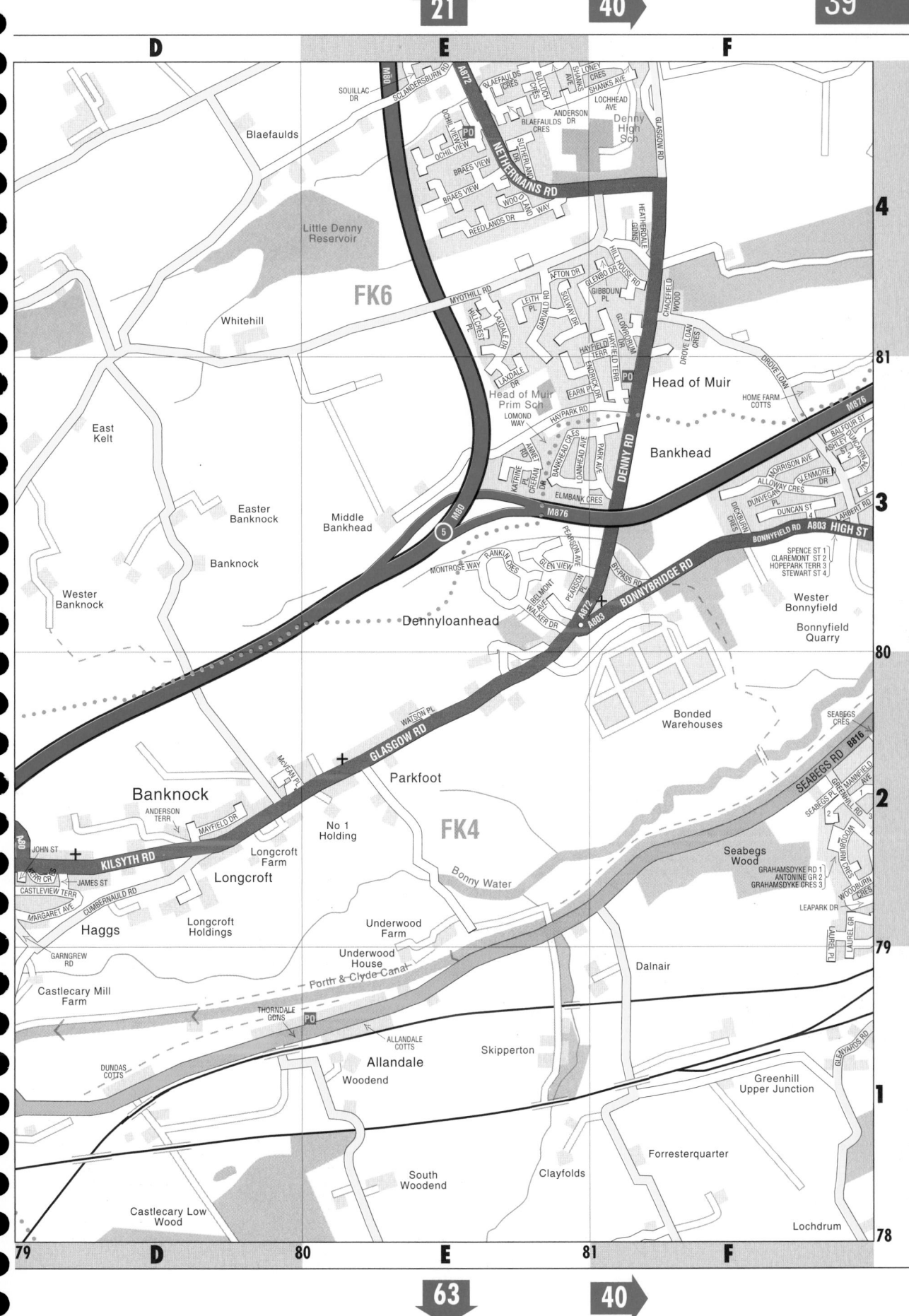
21
40
D
E
F
Blaefaulds
Little Denny Reservoir
FK6
Whitehill
MYOTHILL RD
M80
A872
NETHERMAINS RD
Denny High Sch
GLASGOW RD
Head of Muir
Head of Muir Prim Sch
HAYPARK RD
Bankhead
DENNY RD
East Kelt
Easter Banknock
Middle Bankhead
Banknock
Wester Banknock
M876
Dennyloanhead
A803
BONNYBRIDGE RD
HIGH ST
Wester Bonnyfield
Bonnyfield Quarry
Bonded Warehouses
GLASGOW RD
Parkfoot
Banknock
FK4
No 1 Holding
KILSYTH RD
Longcroft Farm
Longcroft
Bonny Water
Seabegs Wood
SEABEGS RD
B816
Haggs
Longcroft Holdings
Underwood Farm
Underwood House
Forth & Clyde Canal
Castlecary Mill Farm
Dalnair
Allandale
Woodend
Skipperton
Greenhill Upper Junction
Forresterquarter
South Woodend
Clayfolds
Castlecary Low Wood
Lochdrum
4
3
2
1
81
80
79
78

← 39
22 ↑

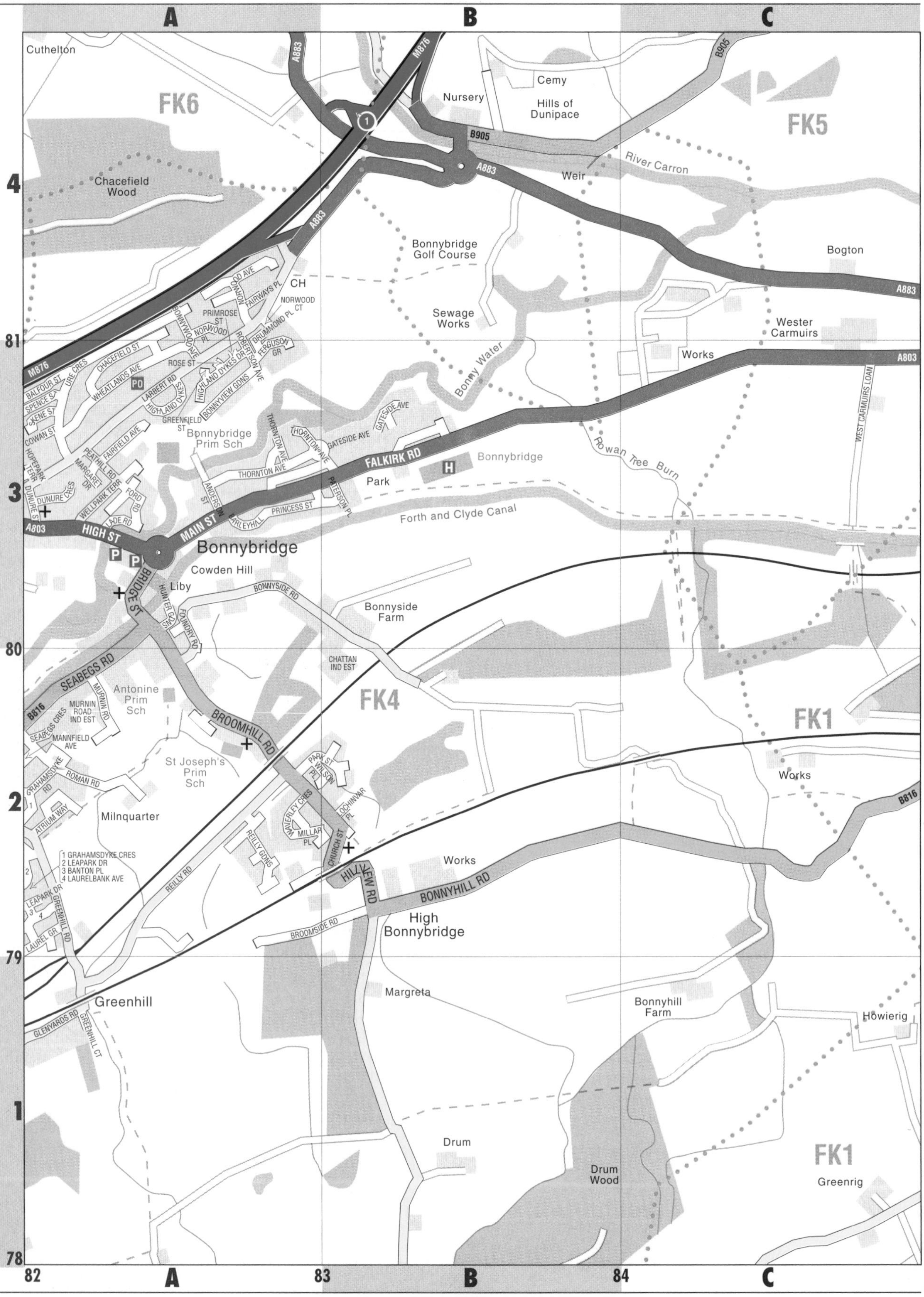

A   B   C

Cuthelton

FK6

M876

A883

4

Chacefield Wood

Nursery

Cemy

Hills of Dunipace

B905

FK5

River Carron

Weir

B905

Bogton

A883

Bonnybridge Golf Course

Sewage Works

Bonny Water

Wester Carmuirs

81

CH

NORWOOD CT

PRIMROSE ST

OLD AVE

FAIRWAYS PL

NORWOOD PL

BONNYWOOD AVE

DRUMMOND ST

ROBERTSON AVE

FERGUSON GR

Works

A803

M876

BALFOUR ST

SPENCE ST

SKENE ST

COWAN ST

NORPARK

LIME CRES

CHACEFIELD ST

WHEATLANDS AVE

LARBERT RD

HIGHLAND DYKES

P.O.

ROSE ST

GREENFIELD ST

HIGHLAND DYKES DR

BONNYVIEW GDNS

THORNTON AVE

THORNTON AVE

GATESIDE AVE

GATESIDE AVE

Bonnybridge Prim Sch

FAIRFIELD AVE

PEATHILL RD

MARGARET DR

WELLPARK TERR

FORD

PRIDE RD

THORNTON AVE

LANFERS PL

PATERSON PL

Rowan Tree Burn

A803

3

HIGH ST

MAIN ST

HARLEYHA

PRINCESS ST

FALKIRK RD

H

Bonnybridge

Park

DUNURE CRES

DUNURE ST

Forth and Clyde Canal

P P

Bonnybridge

Cowden Hill

BONNYSIDE RD

BRIDGE ST

HUNTER ST

COUNTRY RD

Liby

Bonnyside Farm

80

SEABEGS RD

CHATTAN IND EST

FK4

FK1

B816

SEABEGS CRES

GRAHAMSDYKE

MANNFIELD AVE

Antonine Prim Sch

MURNIN ROAD IND EST

BROOMHILL RD

Works

St Joseph's Prim Sch

PARK ST

WILSON

Works

B816

2

ATRIUM WAY

ROMAN RD

Milnquarter

WAVERLEY CRES

MILLAR PL

REILLY GDNS

LOCHINVAR PL

CHURCH ST

1 GRAHAMSDYKE CRES
2 LEAPARK DR
3 BANTON PL
4 LAURELBANK AVE

REILLY RD

REILLY RD

Works

LEAPARK DR

GREENHILL RD

LAUREL GR

HILLS

LEW RD

BONNYHILL RD

High Bonnybridge

79

BROOMSIDE RD

Margreta

Bonnyhill Farm

Howierig

Greenhill

GLENYARDS RD

GREENHILL CT

1

Drum

Drum Wood

FK1

Greenrig

78

82   A   83   B   84   C

← 39
64 ↓

23
42

D E F

Lochlands
LOCHLANDS IND EST
River Carron
BROOMHILL AVE
A9
FALKIRK RD
DOBBIE AVE
JONES AVE
Ladeside Prim Sch
CARRONVALE RD
WOODSIDE GR
Carronvale House
CHARLES DR
BEECH CRES
CALLANDER DR
LADE DR
TAIT DR
FK5
Mill
STIRLING RD
Dorrator
Longdales
Mungal Farm
River Carron
Crem
Golf Course
Picnic Area
FK2
Cauldhame
A883
A803
CH
Cemy
Camelon
MACADAM PLACE
Works
GLASGOW RD
ELIZABETH CRES
CARMUIRS DR
ST GILES WAY
ST GILES SQ
Sch
Rossvail Sch
WILSON GDNS
MARINER GDNS
CARMUIRS AVE
LAUREL CT
WATLING GDNS
HAMILTON RD
REDBRAE RD
ABERCROMBIE ST
AITKEN GDNS
SUNNYSIDE ST
MERCHISTON RD
KILNS PL
CARNEGIE DR
AITKEN RD
AITKEN TERR
SIMPSON ST
NAILER RD
ELFORD SQ
FLEMING GDNS
DORRATOR RD
ARBUTHNOT ST
HARRISON PL
PARDOVAN PL
Ed Ctr
GORDON PL
IRVING CT
COTTAGE CRES
PROSPECT ST
SUNNYSIDE RD
TOPHILL ENTRY
Carmuirs
Camelon
MARINER AVE
MARINER ST
MARINER DR
MARINER RD
WILSON DR
WILSON AVE
WATLING ST
WALL ST
WATLING AVE
WATLING DR
BROWN ST
ROMAN DR
CARMUIRS ST
MANSIONHOUSE RD
BAIRD ST
Ct
MAIN ST
PO
KENMUIR ST
GLENCAIRN ST
CLARINDA AVE
MOSSGIEL ST
OCHILTREE TERR
ANTONINE ST
ROSS CRES
ANTONINE GDNS
GLENFUIR ST
CARMUIRS AVE
FAIRLIE DR
FAIRLIE ST
FAIRLIE GDNS
STARK AVE
UNION RD
CLYDE ST
THE HEDGES
BURNSIDE TERR
COLLINGWOOD CT
CAMELON RD
ARNOTHILL CT
B816
ROSEBANK AVE
ROSEBANK PL
QUEEN'S CRES
MAGGIE WOOD'S LOAN
LOCK SIXTEEN
CANAL ST
RALEIGH CT
SPRINGFIELD DR
Forth and Clyde Canal
PORTDOWNIE
GLENFUIR RD
B8080
FROBISHER AVE
QUEENS DR
HOWARD ST
Tamfourhill
TAMFOURHILL IND EST
WHITEGATES PL
TAMFOURHILL AVE
STRACHAN ST
GILCHRIST DR
BEGG AVE
BLINKBONNY RD
ANSON AVE
Falkirk High Sch
WESTBURN AVE
TAMFOURHILL RD
Bantaskin
DERWENT AVE
BONNYHILL RD
LIME RD
HOWIE'S PL
BRODICK PL
KILMORY CT
CORRIE PL
SUMMERFORD
SUMMERFORD RD
TEVIOT ST
CONWAY CT
SHANNON DR
ROWAN CRES
KILBRENNAN DR
MACHRIE CT
CUMBRAE DR
ARRAN TERR
KINTYRE PL
CARRICK PL
DAVAAR PL
CARRADALE AVE
NURSERY RD
HAWTHORN DR
Bantaskin Prim Sch
ARNOTHILL LA
2 MAYFIELD MEWS
3 GREENVILLE CT
Univ
BANTASKINE RD
BANTASKINE DR
MARYFIELD PL
FK1
SUMMERFORD GDNS
Summerford
WINDSOR CRES
WINDSOR AVE
WINDSOR GDNS
WINDSOR DR
GREENBANK PL
WINDSOR RD
BANTASKINE GDNS
BALMORAL RD
BALMORAL ST
BANTASKINE ST
OSBORNE GDNS
OSBORNE ST
HURWORTH ST
GARTCOWS RD
Opencast Workings
Tamfourhill Wood
Union Canal
Greenbank
GREENBANK RD
GREENHORN'S WELL CRES 1
GREENHORN'S WELL DR 2
GREENHORN'S WELL AVE 3
GARTCOWS DR 1
GARTCOWS GDNS 2
GARTCOWS CRES 3
SOUTH BANTASKINE RD
Bantaskine Estate
Greenbank Farm
FK4
Mon
THOMSON CRES
DUMYAT DR
MYRETON WAY
SUNNYLAW PL
BLAIRDENON CRES
KINGSEAT PL
CRAIGLEITH AVE
CRAIGHORN DR
DRUMMOND PL
LENDRICK AVE
DUMYAT DR
LOCHGREEN RD
B803
SLAMANNAN RD
Canada Wood
Princes Park
SKYTHORN WAY 1
GLENTYE GDNS 2
MELLOCK GDNS 3
HILLCREST RD
HILLHEAD DR
Lochgreen
THORNDENE CT 1
SEAFIELD CT 2
CRAIGBURN CT 3
FORTHVIEW CT 4
PARKVIEW AVE
GLENVIEW DR
Greenrig Strip
NEWHOUSE DR
KILBEAN DR
GRAEME PL
SALMON DR
MITCHELL PL
GLENSHARRY CRES
GLENGARRY
LIONTHORN RD
ABBOTS MOSS DR
JAMES CROFT DR
Fox Covert
Craigburn Wood
Glen Burn
CLANRANALD PL 5
FARQUHARSON WAY 6
KEPPOCK PL 7
MACPHERSON PL 8
MACKENZIE PL 9
MACINTOSH PL 10
Seafield
Craigieburn
B803

4
81
3
80
2
79
1
78

85 D 86 E 87 F

65
42

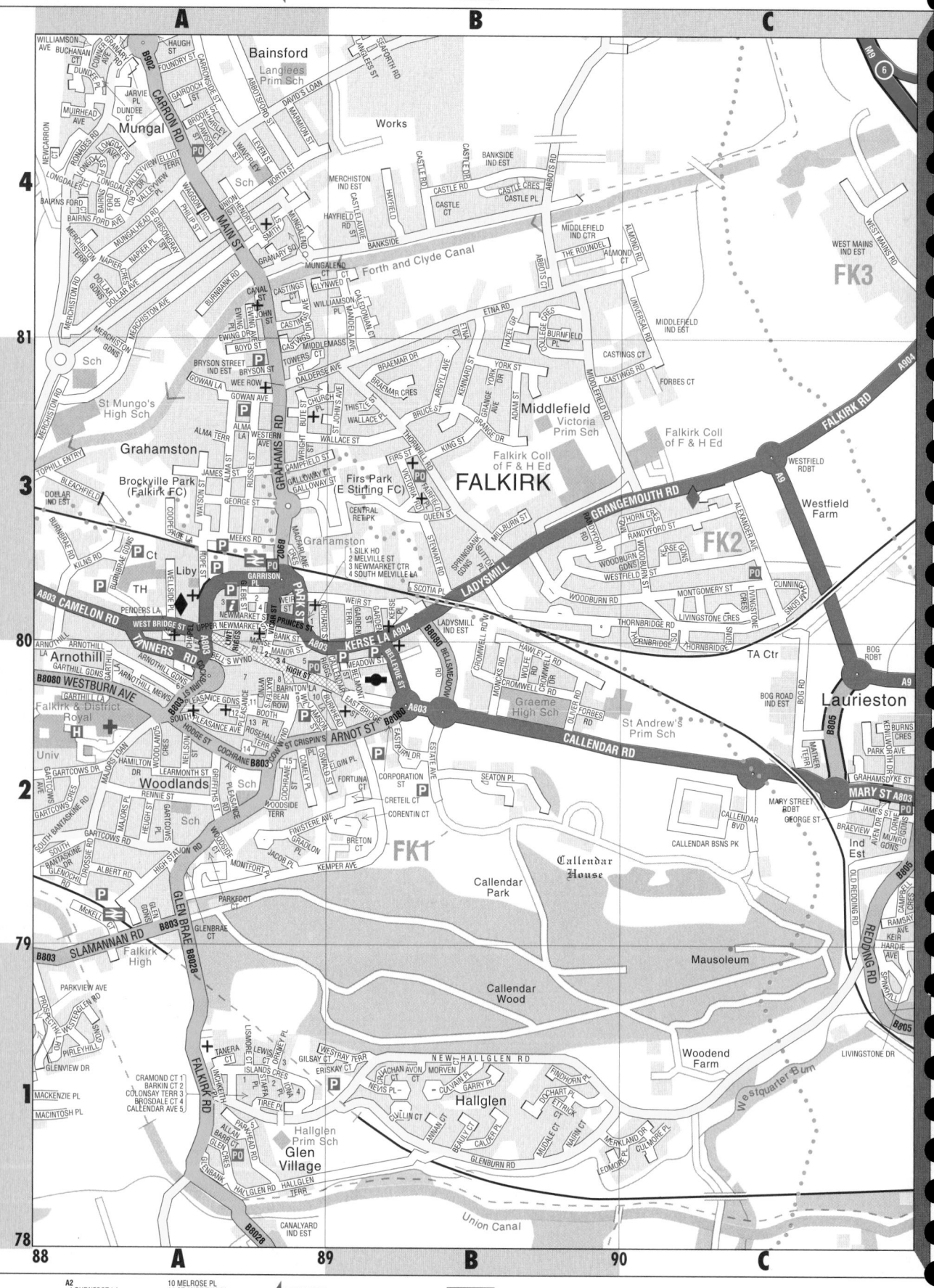

A2
1 BURNFOOT LA
2 KIRK WYND
3 TOLBOOTH ST
4 WOOER ST
5 CALLENDAR SQUARE SH CTR
6 ARNOTHILL BANK
7 HOWGATE SH CTR
8 KINGS CT
9 MISSION LA
10 MELROSE PL
11 ST ANDREWS PL
12 PLEASANCE SQ
13 PLEASANCE CT
14 ST MODANS CT
15 COMELY PARK TERR

D　　　　　　　E　　　　　　　F

4

77

McInroy's Point
P
A770

CLOCH RD

LEVANNE GDNS
LEVANNE PL
DUNVEGAN AVE
DUNROBIN DR
3
Hotel
BALMORAL PL
Hotel
STIRLING ST
BRODICK DR
CULZEAN DR
BLAIR GDNS
DOUNE AVE
TANTALLON GDNS
TAYMOUTH DR
EDINBURGH DR
URQUHART DR

Levan

Cloch Point
FAULDS PARK RD
Levan Burn
Works
Levan
Farm

76

Cloch
Lighthouse
Caravan
Park

Cloch
Plantation

Tannel Hill

PA19

2

Burneven Hill

Underheugh
Cottage

Underheugh

75

Clyde Muirshiel
Regional Park
P
North Knowe

PA16

1

Lunderston Bay

Curling
Pond

A770

Lunderston
74

19　　　　D　　　　20　　　E　　　21　　　F

43

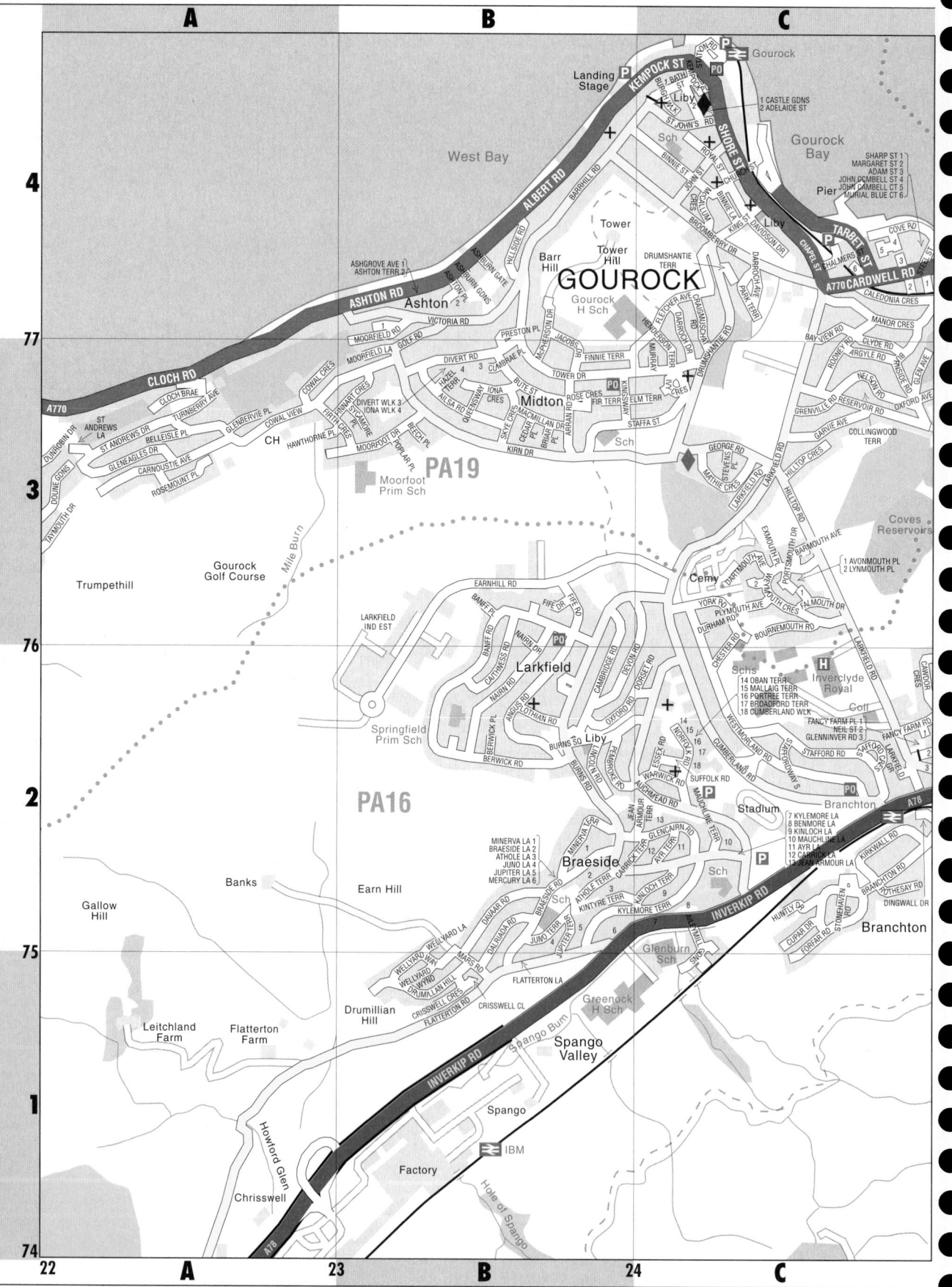

A
B
C
4
77
3
76
2
75
1
74
22
23
24
West Bay
Gourock Bay
Gourock
Landing Stage
KEMPOCK ST
SHORE ST
ALBERT RD
ASHTON RD
CLOCH RD
A770
Pier
TARBET ST
A770 CARDWELL RD
CALEDONIA CRES
1 CASTLE GDNS
2 ADELAIDE ST
SHARP ST 1
MARGARET ST 2
ADAM ST 3
JOHN CAMBELL ST 4
JOHN CAMBELL CT 5
MURIAL BLUE CT 6
ASHGROVE AVE 1
ASHTON TERR 2
GOUROCK
Tower
Tower Hill
Barr Hill
Gourock H Sch
Ashton
Midton
DRUMSHANTIE TERR
VICTORIA RD
MOORFIELD RD
MOORFIELD LA
GOLF RD
DIVERT RD
DIVERT WLK 3
IONA WLK 4
TOWER DR
FINNIE TERR
ROSE CRES
FIR TERR
ELM TERR
STAFFA ST
KIRN DR
COLLINGWOOD TERR
GARVIE AVE
RESERVOIR RD
GRENVILLE RD
HILLTOP CRES
GEORGE RD
ST ANDREWS LA
ST ANDREWS DR
BELLEISLE PL
GLENEAGLES DR
CARNOUSTIE AVE
ROSEMOUNT PL
COWAL VIEW
GLENBERVIE PL
TURNBERRY AVE
CLOCH BRAE
HAWTHORNE PL
MOORFOOT DR
CH
PA19
Moorfoot Prim Sch
Sch
Coves Reservoirs
1 AVONMOUTH PL
2 LYNMOUTH PL
Trumpethill
Gourock Golf Course
Mile Burn
EARNHILL RD
LARKFIELD IND EST
Larkfield
Cemy
Liby
Springfield Prim Sch
BERWICK RD
BURNS SQ
PLYMOUTH AVE
BOURNEMOUTH RD
Schs
Inverclyde Royal
14 OBAN TERR
15 MALLAIG TERR
16 PORTREE TERR
17 BROADFORD TERR
18 CUMBERLAND WLK
FANCY FARM PL 1
NEIL ST 2
GLENNINVER RD 3
STAFFORD RD
SUFFOLK RD
PA16
Stadium
Branchton
A78
7 KYLEMORE LA
8 BENMORE LA
9 KINLOCH LA
10 MAUCHLINE LA
11 AYR LA
12 CARRICK LA
13 JEAN ARMOUR LA
MINERVA LA 1
BRAESIDE LA 2
ATHOLE LA 3
JUNO LA 4
JUPITER LA 5
MERCURY LA 6
Braeside
KYLEMORE TERR
INVERKIP RD
Banks
Earn Hill
Gallow Hill
Glenburn Sch
Greenock H Sch
FLATTERTON LA
CRISSWELL CL
Drumillian Hill
Leitchland Farm
Flatterton Farm
Spango Valley
Spango Burn
Spango
IBM
Factory
Howford Glen
Chrisswell
Hole of Spango
DINGWALL DR

43

46

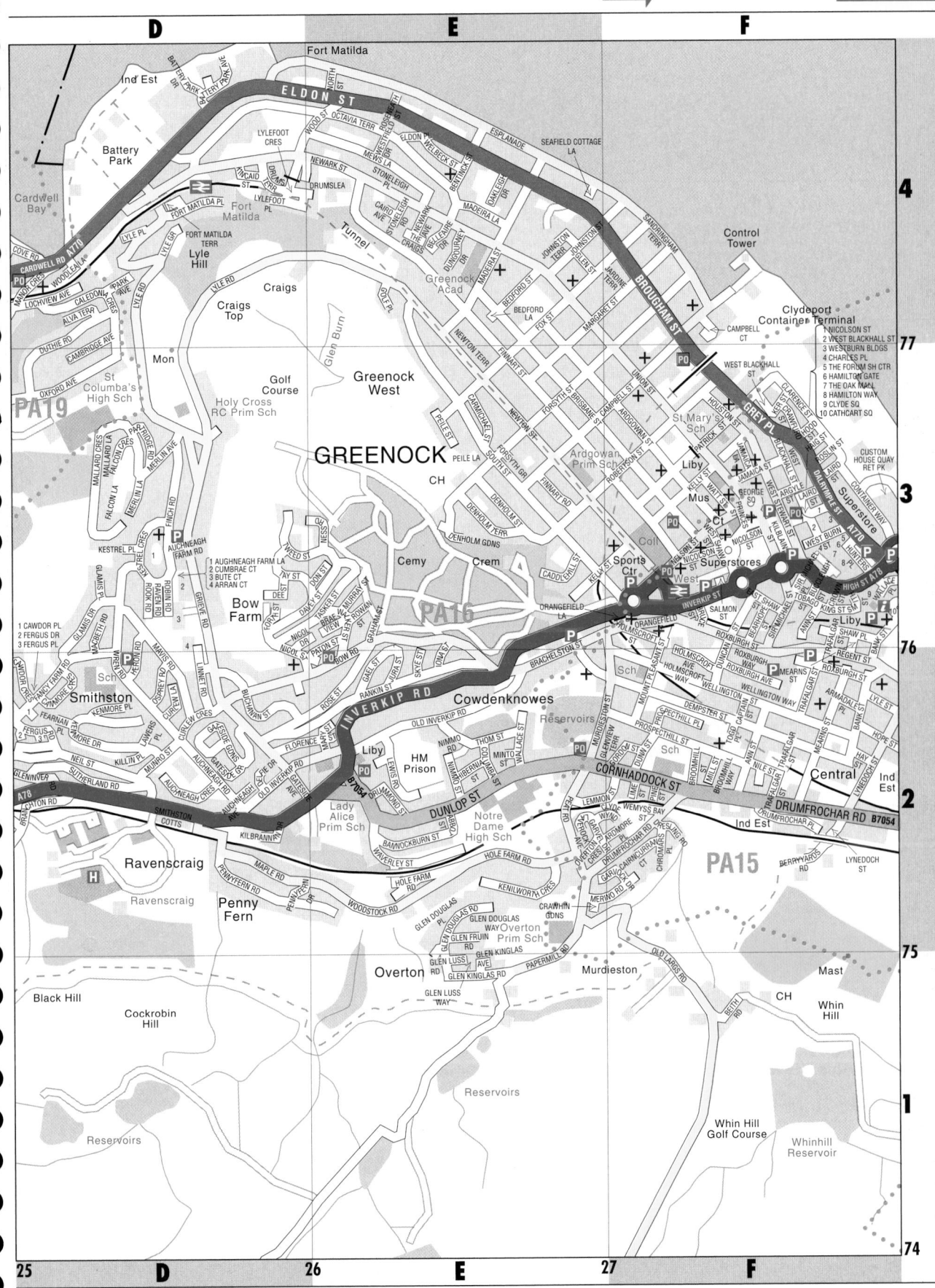
D
E
F
Fort Matilda
Ind Est
Battery Park
Cardwell Bay
ELDON ST
ESPLANADE
Fort Matilda
Lyle Hill
Tunnel
Craigs
Craigs Top
Mon
Golf Course
Greenock West
Greenock Acad
Control Tower
Clydeport Container Terminal
1 NICOLSON ST
2 WEST BLACKHALL ST
3 WESTBURN BLDGS
4 CHARLES PL
5 THE FORUM SH CTR
6 HAMILTON GATE
7 THE OAK MALL
8 HAMILTON WAY
9 CLYDE SQ
10 CATHCART SQ
BROUGHAM ST
GREY PL
St Columba's High Sch
PA19
Holy Cross RC Prim Sch
GREENOCK
St Mary's Sch
Ardgowan Prim Sch
Liby
Mus
Ct
Superstore
CUSTOM HOUSE QUAY RET PK
Cemy
Crem
Coll
Sports Ctr
Superstores
West
Bow Farm
PA16
1 AUGHNEAGH FARM LA
2 CUMBRAE CT
3 BUTE CT
4 ARRAN CT
1 CAWDOR PL
2 FERGUS DR
3 FERGUS PL
Smithston
Sch
INVERKIP RD
Cowdenknowes
Reservoirs
HM Prison
Liby
CORNHADDOCK ST
DRUMFROCHAR RD B7054
DUNLOP ST
Central
Ind Est
Lady Alice Prim Sch
Notre Dame High Sch
Ravenscraig
Penny Fern
PA15
Ind Est
Overton Prim Sch
Overton
Murdieston
Black Hill
Cockrobin Hill
Mast
CH
Whin Hill
Reservoirs
Reservoirs
Whin Hill Golf Course
Whinhill Reservoir
4
77
3
76
2
75
1
74
25
26
27

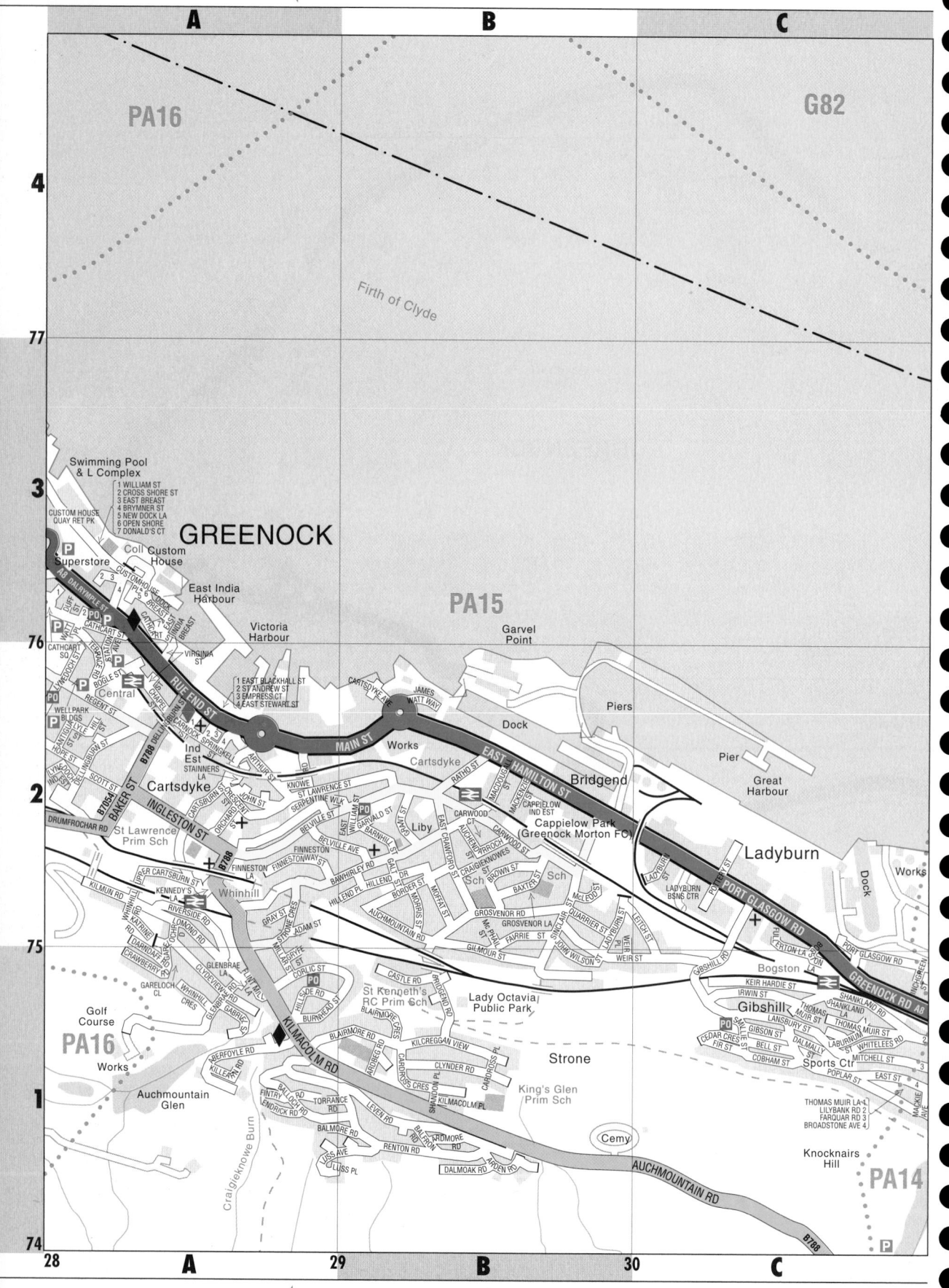

45

A   B   C

PA16

G82

4

Firth of Clyde

77

Swimming Pool
& L Complex

1 WILLIAM ST
2 CROSS SHORE ST
3 EAST BREAST
4 BRYMNER ST
5 NEW DOCK LA
6 OPEN SHORE
7 DONALD'S CT

3

CUSTOM HOUSE
QUAY RET PK

GREENOCK

Superstore   Coll   Custom
House

East India
Harbour

PA15

Victoria Harbour

Garvel
Point

76

CATHCART ST

VIRGINIA ST

1 EAST BLACKHALL ST
2 ST ANDREW ST
3 EMPRESS CT
4 EAST STEWART ST

CARTSDYKE AV

JAMES
WATT WAY

Piers

Central

RUE END ST

MAIN ST

Works

Cartsdyke

Dock

Pier

Great
Harbour

WELLPARK
BLDGS

Ind
Est

STAINNERS
LA

EAST HAMILTON ST

Bridgend

Ladyburn

PORT GLASGOW RD

Dock

Works

2

Cartsdyke

St Lawrence
Prim Sch

INGLESTON ST

Whinhill

ST LAWRENCE ST
SERPENTINE WLK

BELVILLE ST

Liby

Cappielow
Ind Est

Cappielow Park
(Greenock Morton FC)

LADYBURN
BSN6 CTR

DRUMFROCHAR RD

BAKER ST

FINNESTON LA

FINNESTONWAY

BELVILLE AVE

BARNHILL

CARWOOD ST

Sch

Sch

+

KILMUN RD

KENNEDY'S
LA

RIVERSIDE RD

GRAY ST

STONE CRES

BAWHIRLEY RD

HILLEND LA

HILLEND
DR

AUCHMOUNTAIN RD

CRAIGIEKNOWES

BROWN ST

McLEOD's

LADYBURN

POTTER ST

FULTERTON LA

Bogston

PORT GLASGOW RD

75

KATRINE
RD

LOMOND RD

DARNDAFF RD

CRAWBERRY RD

CLYDEVIEW RD

GLENBRAE
LA

STROVE

ADAM ST

CORLIC ST

CASTLE RD

GROSVENOR RD

GROSVENOR LA

QUARRIER ST

JOHN WILSON

LEITCH ST

WEIR ST

GIBSHILL RD

KEIR HARDIE ST

IRWIN ST

GREENOCK RD

Golf
Course

PA16

Works

GARELOCH
CL

WHINHILL RD

GABRIC
RD

CLYDESIDE RD

BURNHEAD RD

St Kenneth's
RC Prim Sch

BLAIRMORE CRES

Lady Octavia
Public Park

GILMOUR ST

FARRIE

Gibshill

Sports Ctl

THOMAS
MUIR ST

SHANKLAND

LANSBURY ST

GIBSON ST

CEDAR CRES

FIR ST

BELL ST

DALMALLY

LABURNUS

WHITELEES RD

MITCHELL ST

POPLAR ST

EAST ST

1

Auchmountain
Glen

KILMACOLM RD

BLAIRMORE RD

ARDGO RD

KILCREGGAN VIEW

CLYNDER RD

CARDROSS CRES

SHANDON PL

KILMACOLM PL

Strone

King's Glen
Prim Sch

COBHAM ST

THOMAS MUIR LA 1
LILYBANK RD 2
FARQUAR RD 3
BROADSTONE AVE 4

Knocknairs
Hill

PA14

FINTRY RD

BALLOCH RD

LENDRICK RD

BALMORE RD

TORRANCE
RD

LEVEN RD

BILFRUIN

ARDMORE
RD

RENTON RD

DALMOAK RD

TIGDEN RD

Cemy

AUCHMOUNTAIN RD

B7788

LISS AVE

LISS PL

Craigieknowe Burn

74

28   A   29   B   30   C

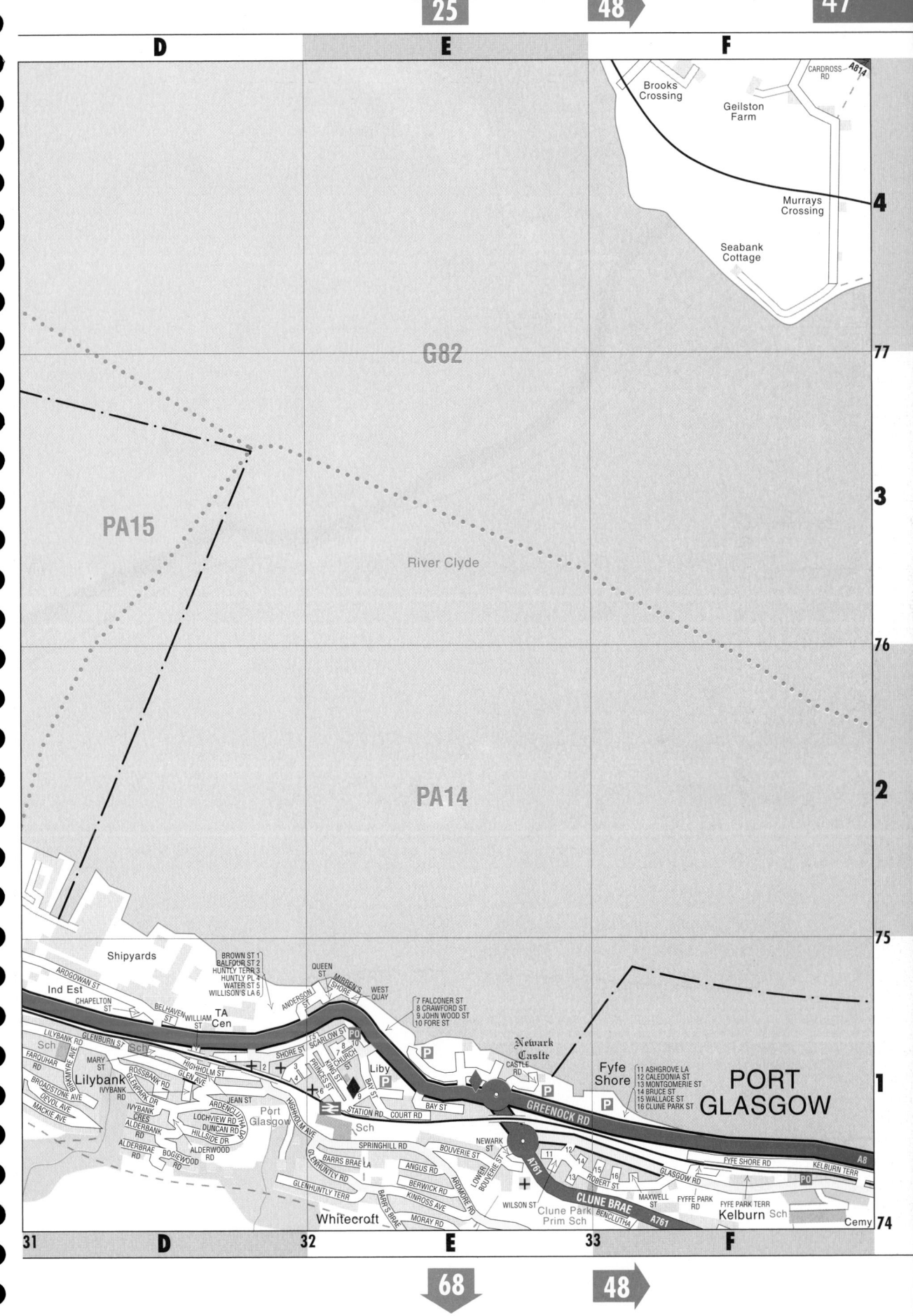

Brooks
Crossing

Geilston
Farm

CARDROSS
RD
A814

Murrays
Crossing

4

Seabank
Cottage

G82

77

PA15

River Clyde

3

76

PA14

2

Shipyards

BROWN ST 1
BALFOUR ST 2
HUNTLY TERR 3
HUNTLY PL 4
WATER ST 5
WILLISON'S LA 6

QUEEN
ST

MIRREN'S
SHORE

WEST
QUAY

75

ARDGOWAN ST

Ind Est

CHAPELTON
ST

BELHAVEN
ST

WILLIAM
ST

TA
Cen

ANDERSON
ST

SCARLOW ST

7 FALCONER ST
8 CRAWFORD ST
9 JOHN WOOD ST
10 FORE ST

Newark
Caslte

Fyfe
Shore

11 ASHGROVE LA
12 CALEDONIA ST
13 MONTGOMERIE ST
14 BRUCE ST
15 WALLACE ST
16 CLUNE PARK ST

PORT
GLASGOW

1

LILYBANK RD
Sch
FARQUHAR
RD
BIRKMYRE AVE
GLENBURN ST
MARY
ST
ROSSBANK
RD

HIGHHOLM ST

GLEN AVE

SHORE ST

PRINCES ST

CHURCH ST

Liby

BAY ST

CASTLE
RD

Lilybank

BROADSTONE AVE
DEVOL AVE
MACKIE AVE
IVYBANK
GLENPARK DR
IVYBANK
RD
CRES
ALDERBANK
RD
ALDERBRAE
RD
BOGLEWOOD
RD

JEAN ST
ARDENCLUTHA RD
LOCHVIEW RD
DUNCAN RD
HILLSIDE DR
ALDERWOOD
RD

Port
Glasgow

HIGHHOLM AVE

STATION RD

COURT RD

BAY ST

GREENOCK RD

Sch

P

P

P

Whitecroft

GLENHUNTLY RD

GLENHUNTLY TERR

BARR'S BRAE

SPRINGHILL RD

BERWICK RD

KINROSS AVE

ANGUS RD

ARDMORE RD

MORAY RD

BARRS BRAE LA

BOUVERIE RD

LOWER BOUVERIE ST

NEWARK ST

WILSON ST

A761

CLUNE BRAE

Clune Park
Prim Sch

BENCLUTHA

A761

11

12

13

14
15
16

ROBERT ST

MAXWELL
ST

GLASGOW RD

FYFFE PARK
RD

FYFE SHORE RD

A8

FYFE PARK TERR

KELBURN TERR

PO

Kelburn Sch

Cemy

PORT
GLASGOW

47
26

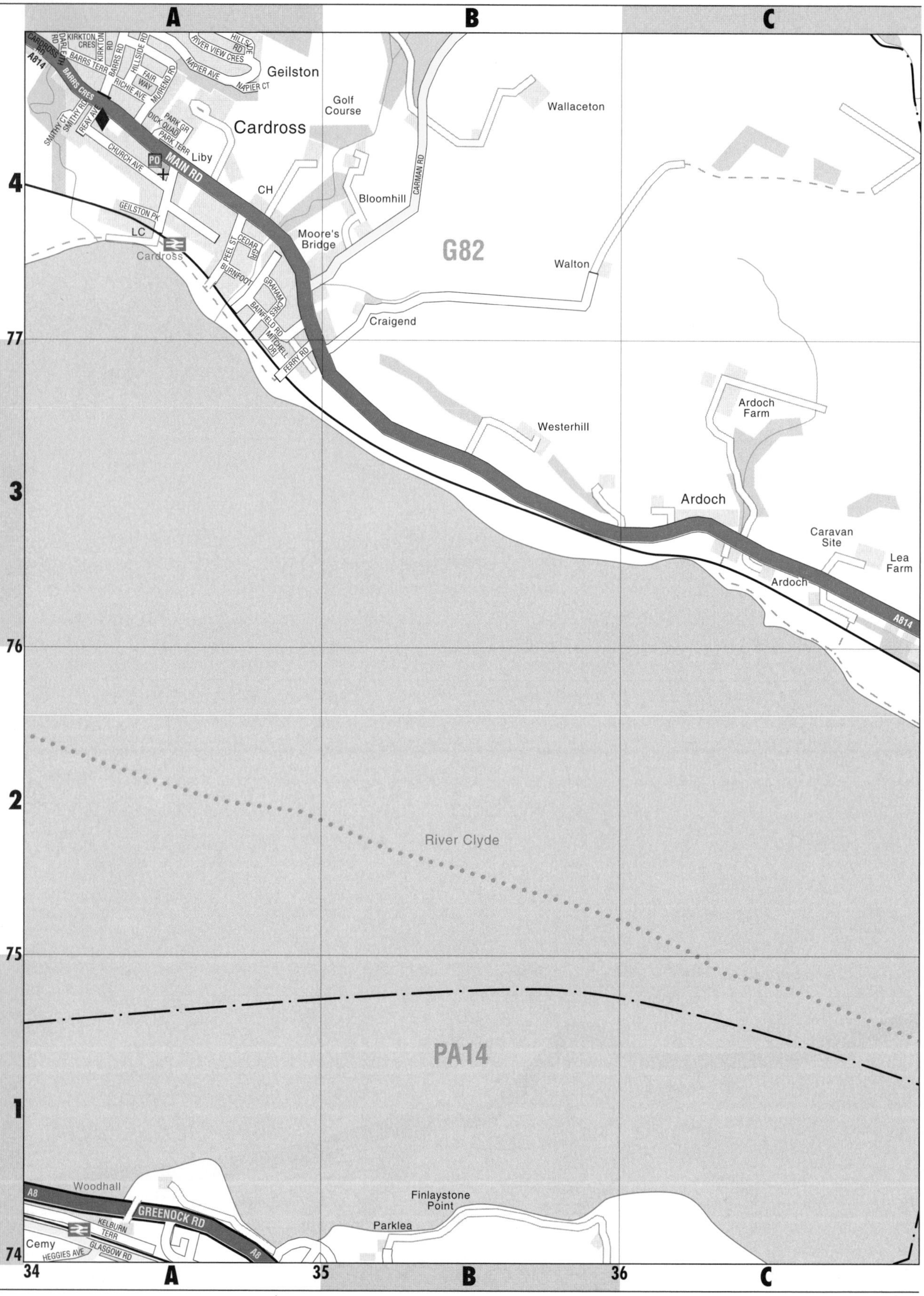

A B C

KIRKTON CRES
DARLEITH RD
BARRS TERR
HILLSIDE RD
HILLSIDE RD
RIVER VIEW CRES
NAPIER AVE
NAPIER CT
RICHIE AVE
FAIR WAY
MUIREND RD
PARK GR
Geilston
A814
CARDROSS RD
SMITHY CT
SMITHY RD
FRAN AVE
BARRS CRES
CHURCH AVE
GEILSTON PK
Cardross
Liby
DICK QUAD
PARK TERR
PARK QUAD
MAIN RD
PO
CH
CEDAR AVE
PEEL ST
GRAHAM CRT
BAINFIELD RD
MITCHELL DR
TERRY RD
BURNFOOT
LC
Cardross
Moore's Bridge

Golf Course
Bloomhill
Wallaceton
Carman Rd

G82

Walton
Craigend
Westerhill

Ardoch Farm

Ardoch

Caravan Site
Lea Farm
Ardoch
A814

4

77

3

76

2

River Clyde

75

PA14

1

Woodhall
A8
GREENOCK RD
KELBURN TERR
GLASGOW RD
Cemy
HEGGIES AVE
A8

Finlaystone Point
Parklea

74

34 A 35 B 36 C

47
69

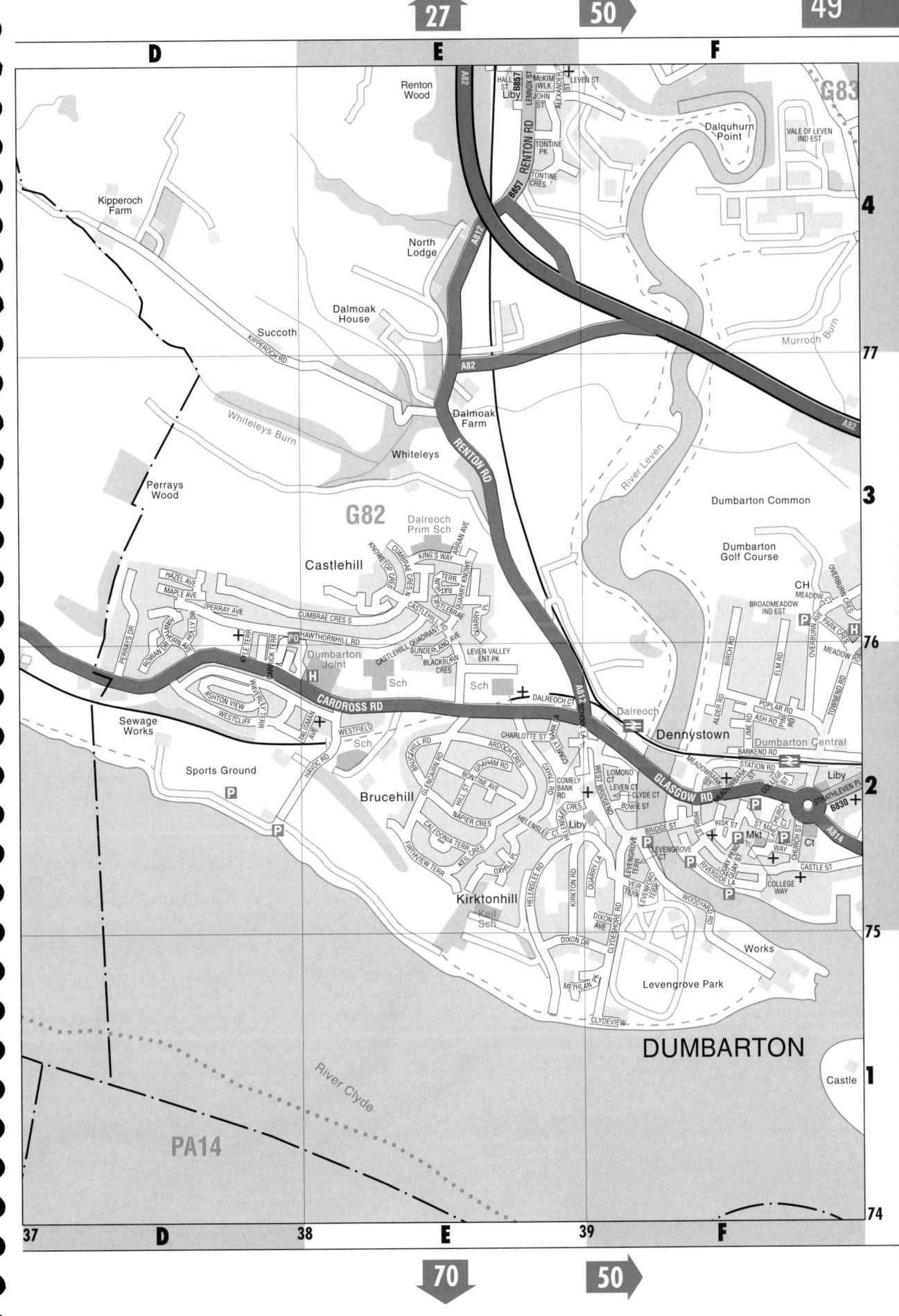

D
E
F

G83

4

Renton
Wood

A82

HALL
ST
McKIM
WLK
LEVEN ST
B857
Liby
LENNOX ST
JOHN ST
ALEXANDER

Dalquhurn
Point

VALE OF LEVEN
IND EST

RENTON RD

TONTINE
PK

TONTINE
CRES

North
Lodge

77

Murroch Burn

Succoth

KIPPEROCH RD

Kipperoch
Farm

Dalmoak
House

A82

A812

Dalmoak
Farm

A82

Whiteleys Burn

RENTON RD

Whiteleys

River Leven

3

Dumbarton Common

Perrays
Wood

G82

Dalreoch
Prim Sch

Dumbarton
Golf Course

Castlehill

KING'S WAY

ARRAN AVE

CH
MEADOW

OVERBURN CRES

BROADMEADOW
IND EST

PARK AVE

P

H

76

HAZEL AVE

KNOWETOP CRES

CUMBRAE CRES N

RAI

QUARRY KNOWE

QUARRY PL

MEADOW RD

MAPLE AVE

PERRAY AVE

CUMBRAE CRES S

CASTLEBRAE

CASTLEHILL RD

SUNDERLAND AVE

LEVEN VALLEY
ENT PK

BIRCH RD

ELM RD

OVERBURN AVE

TOWNEND RD

PERRAYS DR

ROWAN DR

HOLLY DR

KYLE TERR

PO

HAWTHORNHILL RD

CASTLEHILL QUADRANT

BLACKBURN
CRES

ALDER RD

POPLAR RD

CARRICK TERR

Dumbarton
Joint

H

Sch

Sch

ASH RD

LIME RD

DALREOCH CT

Dalreoch

Dennystown

Dumbarton Central

BANKEND RD

STATION RD

Liby

2

Sewage
Works

ASHTON VIEW

WATERLEY TERR

WESTCLIFF

TALISMAN AVE

CARDROSS RD

WESTFIELD

Sch

BRUCEHILL RD

GLENCAIRN RD

HILL ST

ARDOCH CRES

CHARLOTTE ST

BANK RD

OXHILL RD

COMELY
BANK
RD

WEST BRIDGEND

LOMOND RD

LEVEN CT

BOWIE ST

CLYDE CT

MEADOWBANK ST

HIGH ST

GLASGOW RD

STRATHLEVEN PL

B830

A814

HINOCK RD

P

Sports Ground

P

Brucehill

GRAHAM RD

BONTINE AVE

NAPIER CRES

CALEDONIA TERR

KEIL CRES

FIRTHVIEW TERR

HELENSLEE CT

HELENSLEE CRES

OXHILL PL

Liby

BRIDGE ST

LEVENGROVE
TERR

LEVENGROVE CT

QUAY PEND

RISK ST

ST MARY

CHURCH

Mkt

QUAY ST

RIVERSIDE LA

WAY

P

COLLEGE
WAY

Ct

CASTLE ST

Kirktonhill

HELENSLEE RD

KIRKTON RD

QUARRY LA

DIXON AVE

CLYDESHORE RD

VEIR TERR

WOODYARD RD

P

75

Keil
Sch

DIXON DR

METHLAN PK

Levengrove Park

Works

CLYDEVIEW

DUMBARTON

River Clyde

1

Castle

PA14

74

37
D
38
E
39
F

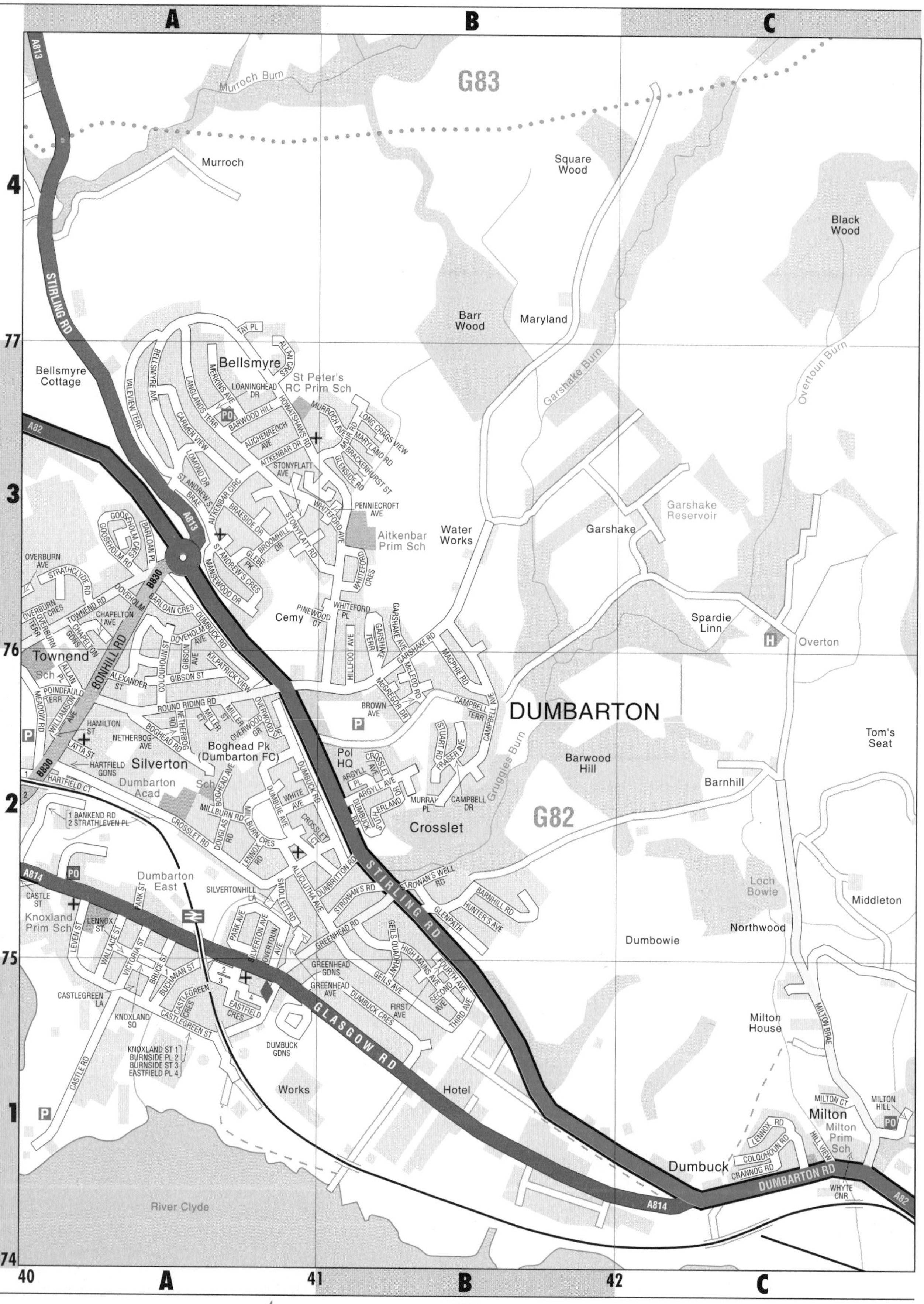

A   **B**   **C**

G83

Murroch Burn

Murroch

Square
Wood

Black
Wood

4

STIRLING RD

A813

Barr
Wood

Maryland

Garshake Burn

Overtoun Burn

77

Bellsmyre

St Peter's
RC Prim Sch

Bellsmyre
Cottage

A82

LOANINGHEAD DR

BARWOOD HILL

LONG CRAGS VIEW

PO

AUCHENREOCH AVE

AITKENBAR DR

LANGLANDS TERR

MERKINS AVE

HOWATSHAWS RD

BRACKENHURST ST

MURROCH AVE

MARYLAND DR

GLENSIDE RD

TAY PL

ALLAN CRES

BELLSMYRE AVE

VALEVIEW TERR

CARMEN VIEW

CARMEN VIEW

ORMOND DR

ST ANDREW'S BRAE

AITKENBAR CRES

BRAESIDE DR

BROOMHILL DR

GLEBE

STONYFLATT AVE

STONYFLATT ST

WHITEFORD AVE

PENNIECROFT
AVE

Garshake
Reservoir

3

A813

BARLOAN PL

GOOSEDUBS

GOOSEHOLM RD

ST ANDREW'S PK

MARSHWOOD DR

AITKENBAR
Prim Sch

Water
Works

Garshake

Cemy

Aitkenbar
Prim Sch

PINEWOOD CT

WHITEFORD CRES

HILLFOOT AVE

WHITEFORD PL

GARSHAKE TERR

GARSHAKE AVE

GARSHAKE RD

Spardie
Linn

H

Overton

76

OVERBURN
AVE

STRATHCLYDE RD

OVERBURN CRES

TOWNEND RD

CHAPELTON AVE

CHAPELTON GDNS

BONHILL RD

DOVEHOLM

BARLOAN CRES

DUMBUCK RD

COLQUHOUN AVE

KILPATRICK VIEW

NETHERBOG RD

GIBSON ST

ROUND RIDING RD

OVERWOOD DR

MILCROFT

BROWN
AVE

MACPHIE RD

CAMPBELL
TERR

STUART RD

MILTON
AVE

DUMBARTON

Townend
Sch

Tom's
Seat

Townend

Alexander
ST

HAMILTON
ST

MEADOW RD

WILLIAMSON ST

POINDFAULDS TERR

LATTA ST

GILBRAE

NETHERBOG
AVE

BOGHEAD RD

NETHERBOG RD

MILLER ST

Boghead Pk
(Dumbarton FC)

Pol
HQ

P

CAMPBELL AVE

FRASER AVE

Griggies Burn

Barwood
Hill

Barnhill

P

B830

HARTFIELD GDNS

HARTFIELD CT

Silverton

Dumbarton
Acad

Boghead
Sch

MILLBURN CRES

DOUGLAS

WHITE
AVE

DUMBUCK RD

CROSSLET RD

ARGYLL

ARGYLL AVE

MURRAY PL

ERLAND

CAMPBELL
DR

G82

2

1 BANKEND RD
2 STRATHLEVEN PL

CROSSLET RD

DUMBARTON RD

MCDOWN CRES

DUMBIE AVE

CROSSLET
PL

Crosslet

Loch
Bowie

Middleton

1

A814

PO

CASTLE
ST

Knoxland
Prim Sch

LEVEN ST

LENNOX
ST

PARK ST

PARK AVE

SILVERTONHILL LA

SILVERTON AVE

OVERTON RD

SMOLLETT RD

AUCHLITHA AVE

DUNBRITTON RD

STRODMAN'S RD

GREENHEAD RD

RONAN'S WELL
RD

GLENPATH

BARNHILL RD

HUNTER'S AVE

GELLS QUADRANT

HIGH MAINS AVE

FOURTH AVE

THIRD AVE

SECOND AVE

FIRST AVE

Dumbarton
East

Dumbowie

Northwood

MILTON BRAE

Milton
House

75

CASTLE RD

CASTLEGREEN
LA

WALLACE ST

VICTORIA ST

BRUCE ST

BUCHANAN ST

CASTLEGREEN ST

CASTLEGREEN CRES

KNOXLAND
SQ

EASTFIELD
CRES

2
3

GREENHEAD
GDNS

GREENHEAD
AVE

DUMBUCK CRES

GELLS AVE

GLASGOW RD

Hotel

Milton
Hill

MILTON CT

Milton

MILTON HILL

PO

Milton
Prim
Sch

LENNOX RD

COLQUHOUN RD

CRANNOG RD

HILLVIEW

KNOXLAND ST 1
BURNSIDE PL 2
BURNSIDE ST 3
EASTFIELD PL 4

DUMBUCK
GDNS

Works

Dumbuck

DUMBARTON RD

WHYTE
CNR

A814

A82

River Clyde

74

A 40   41   **B**   42   **C**

D

E

F

4

Meikle Soughen Brae

Roughting Burn

Doughnot Hill

Overtoun Burn

Fyn Loch

77

Black Linn Reservoir

Cairn of Fyn Loch

Lang Craigs

Darnycaip

3

Brown Hill

Greenland Reservoir No 1

G82

Greenland Reservoir No 2

Loch Humphrey (Reservoir)

76

Greenland Reservoir No 3

Craigarestie

2

Milton Burn

Middleton Wood

Rigangower

75

Auchentorlie Glen

Auchentorlie Burn

Greenland

Reservoir

G60

Glenarbuck

Craigunnock

MILTON HILL

Haw Craig

1

Auchentorlie Wood

Sheep Hill

Hill of Dun

DUMBARTON RD A82

Auchentorlie House

High Auchentorlie

74

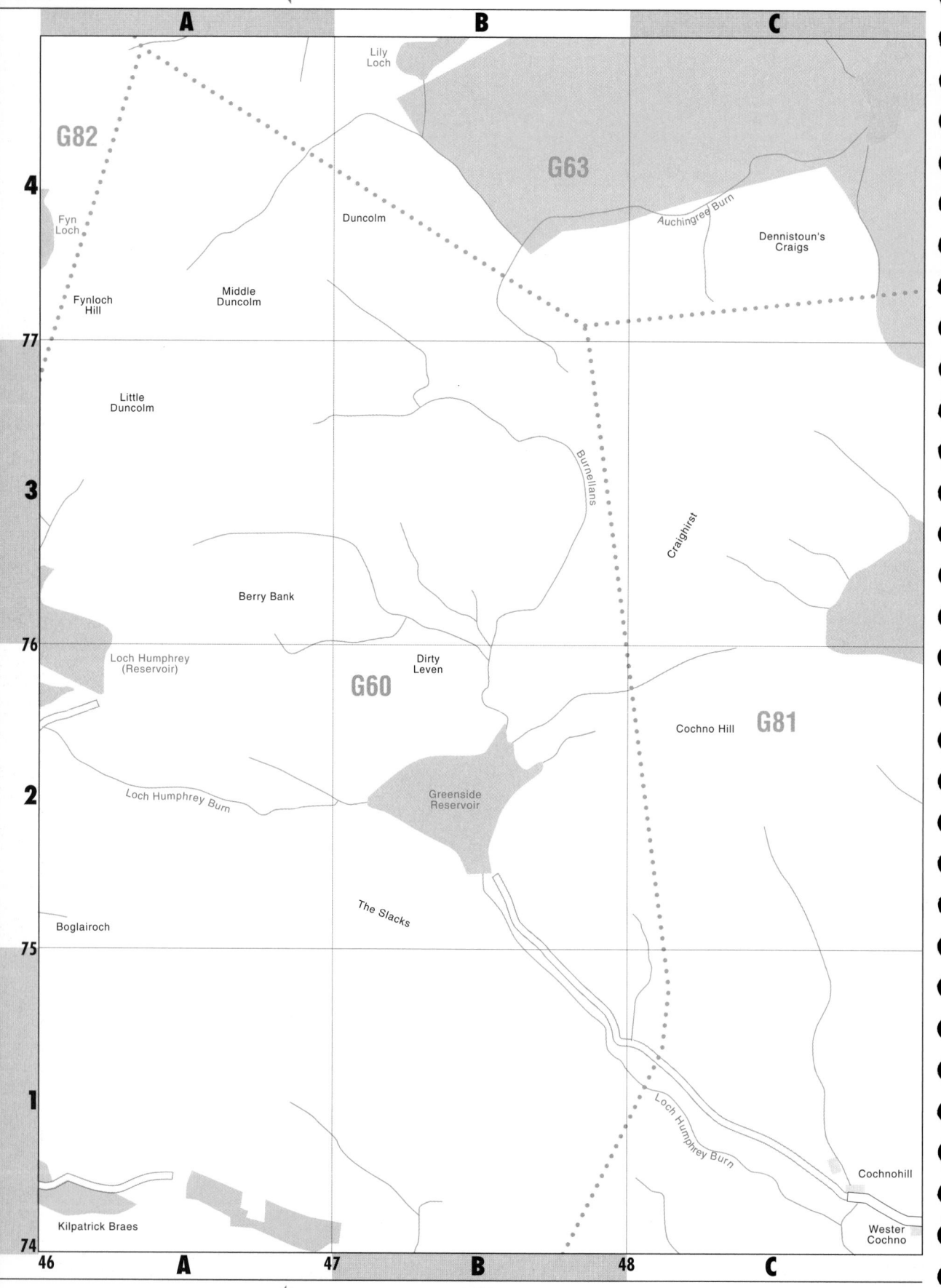

A
B
C

Lily Loch

G82

G63

Fyn Loch

Duncolm

Auchingree Burn

Dennistoun's Craigs

4

Fynloch Hill

Middle Duncolm

77

Little Duncolm

Burnellans

3

Craighirst

Berry Bank

76

Loch Humphrey (Reservoir)

Dirty Leven

G60

Cochno Hill

G81

2

Loch Humphrey Burn

Greenside Reservoir

The Slacks

75

Boglairoch

1

Loch Humphrey Burn

Cochnohill

Kilpatrick Braes

74

Wester Cochno

46
A
47
B
48
C

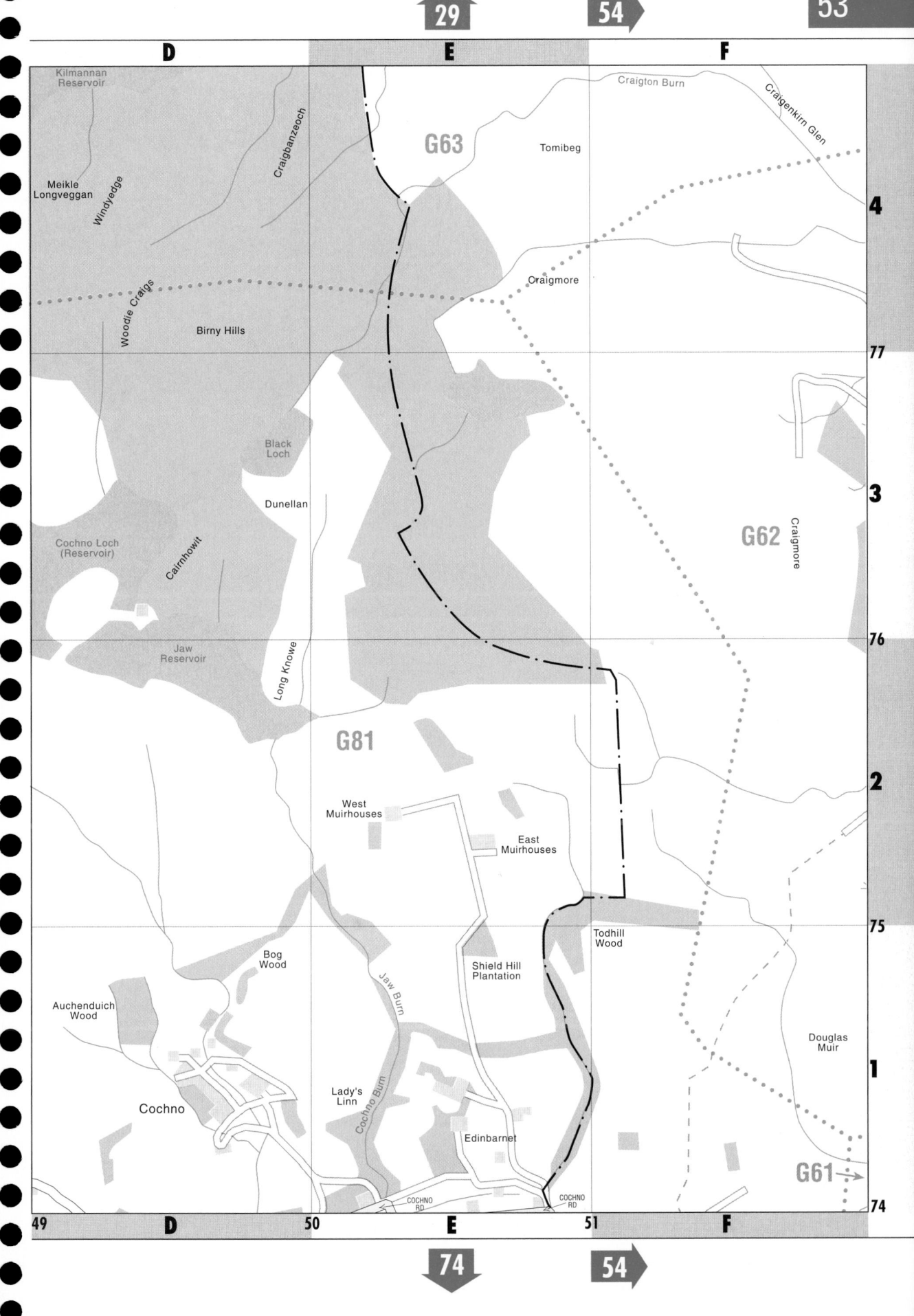
29
54
D
E
F
Kilmannan Reservoir
Craigton Burn
Craigenkirn Glen
Craigbanzeoch
G63
Tomibeg
Meikle Longveggan
Windyedge
4
Craigmore
Woodie Craigs
Birny Hills
77
Black Loch
Dunellan
3
Cochno Loch (Reservoir)
Cairnhowit
G62
Craigmore
Jaw Reservoir
76
Long Knowe
G81
2
West Muirhouses
East Muirhouses
75
Todhill Wood
Bog Wood
Shield Hill Plantation
Jaw Burn
Auchenduich Wood
Douglas Muir
1
Cochno
Lady's Linn
Cochno Burn
Edinbarnet
G61
COCHNO RD
COCHNO RD
74
49
D
50
E
51
F
74
54

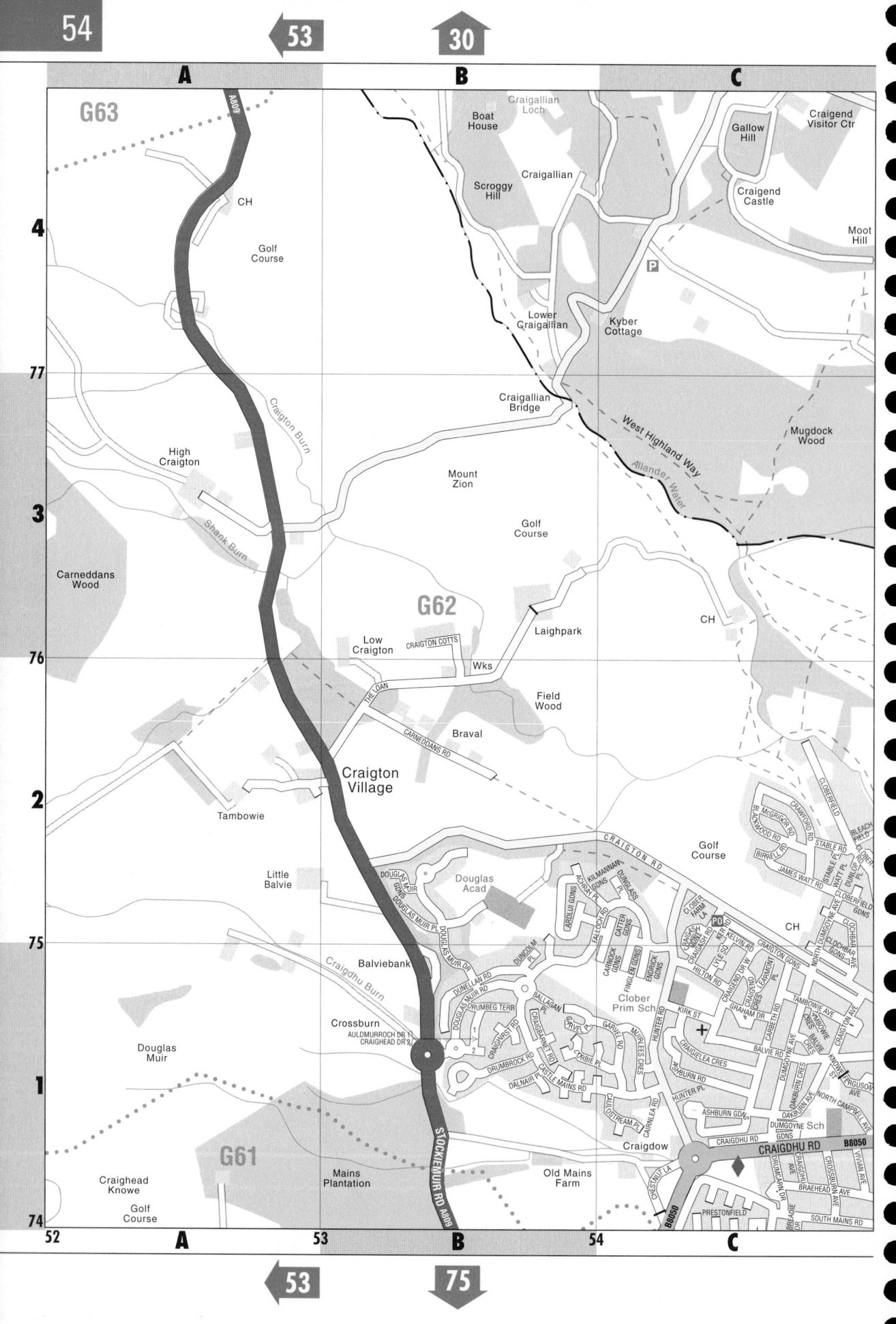

G63

A809

CH

Golf Course

Craigton Burn

Shank Burn

High Craigton

Carneddans Wood

G62

Low Craigton

CRAIGTON COTTS

THE LOAN

CARNEDDANS RD

Braval

Craigton Village

Tambowie

Little Balvie

Douglas Muir

Craighead Knowe

Golf Course

Craigdhu Burn

Balviebank

Crossburn
AULDMURROCH DR 1
CRAIGHEAD DR 2

DOUGLAS MUIR
DOUGLAS MUIR PL
DOUGLAS MUIR DR

DUNELLAN RD

DRUMBEG TERR

CRAIGHIRST RD

CRAIGBARNET RD

DRUMBROCK RD

DUNDONALD PL

BALLAGAN PL

DALNAIR PL

CASTLE MAINS RD

COLSTREAM PL

CAIRNLEA RD

G61

Mains Plantation

STOCKIEMUIR RD A809

Old Mains Farm

Boat House

Craigallian Loch

Scroggy Hill

Craigallian

Lower Craigallian

Craigallian Bridge

Mount Zion

Golf Course

Laighpark

Wks

Field Wood

Craigend Visitor Ctr

Gallow Hill

Craigend Castle

Moot Hill

P

Kyber Cottage

West Highland Way

Allander Water

Mugdock Wood

CH

Golf Course

CRAIGTON RD

McGRIGOR RD
CRAWFORD RD
BLACKWOOD RD
BLEACH FIELD
STABLE RD
BIRRELL
JAMES WATT RD
CLOBERFIELD
STABLE PL
WATT PL
DUN GT
CLOBERFIELD GDNS
CLOCHBAR GDNS

KILMANNAN
ACHRAY PL
DUNGLASS
DUNGLASS PL

CARDELL GDNS
FALLOCH RD

CLOBER RD
CRAIGFOOT RD
LYLE SQ
KELVIN RD
CRAIGTON GDNS
NORTH DUMGOYNE AVE

CARMICHAEL
FINGLEN GDNS
CARBETH GDNS
CRAIGEND DR W
HILTON RD
CRAIGDHU AVE
TAMBOWIE AVE

Douglas Acad

ENDRICK GDNS

DUNOLM PL

CATTER GDNS

MUIR-LEES CRES

GARVE RD
GARVE PL
CORRIE PL

PO

KIRK ST

Clober Prim Sch

+

GRAHAM DR

BALVIE RD

CRAIGIELEA CRES

HUNTER RD
HUNTER PL

ASHBURN CRES

ASHBURN GDNS

CH

CRAIGEND DR

CRAIGDHU RD

DUMGOYNE AVE

OAKBURN AVE

TAMBOWIE
KNOWE AVE

KNOWE RD

BALVIE AVE

FERGUSON ST

NORTH CAMPBELL AVE

DUMGOYNE Sch

Dumgoyne Sch

Craigdow

CRAIGDHU RD

CRAIGDHU RD B8050

CREST LN

B8050

PRESTONFIELD

CREST LN LA

VIVIAN AVE

CROSSBANK AVE

BRAEHEAD AVE

BRAE RD

DRUMCARN DR

SOUTH MAINS RD

CRAIGHILL
GDNS

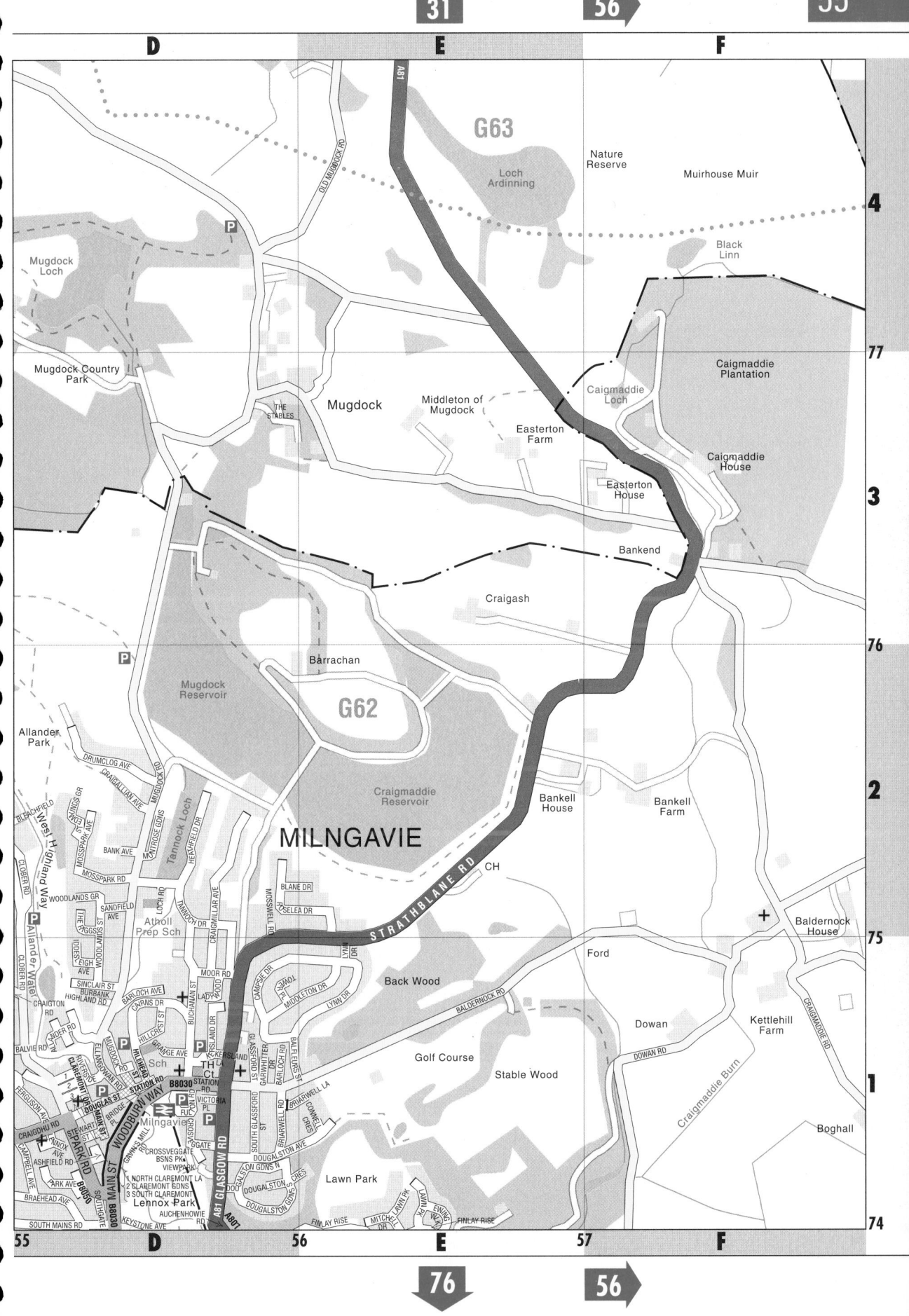
31
56
D
E
F
G63
Loch
Ardinning
Nature
Reserve
Muirhouse Muir
Black
Linn
Mugdock
Loch
Mugdock Country
Park
Mugdock
Middleton of
Mugdock
Easterton
Farm
Caigmaddie
Loch
Caigmaddie
Plantation
Caigmaddie
House
Easterton
House
Bankend
Craigash
Barrachan
G62
Mugdock
Reservoir
Allander
Park
Craigmaddie
Reservoir
Bankell
House
Bankell
Farm
MILNGAVIE
STRATHBLANE RD
CH
Baldernock
House
Ford
Back Wood
Dowan
Kettlehill
Farm
Golf Course
Stable Wood
Craigmaddie Burn
Boghall
Lawn Park
Milngavie
Lennox Park
Atholl
Prep Sch
West Highland Way
Allander Water
Tannock Loch
A81
A81 GLASGOW RD
A807
B8030
B8050
BALDERNOCK RD
DOWAN RD
CRAIGMADDIE RD
WOODBURN WAY
MAIN ST
PARK RD
STATION RD
DOUGALSTON AVE
FINLAY RISE
SOUTH MAINS RD
4
77
3
76
2
75
1
74
55
56
57
76
56

A **B** **C**

G63

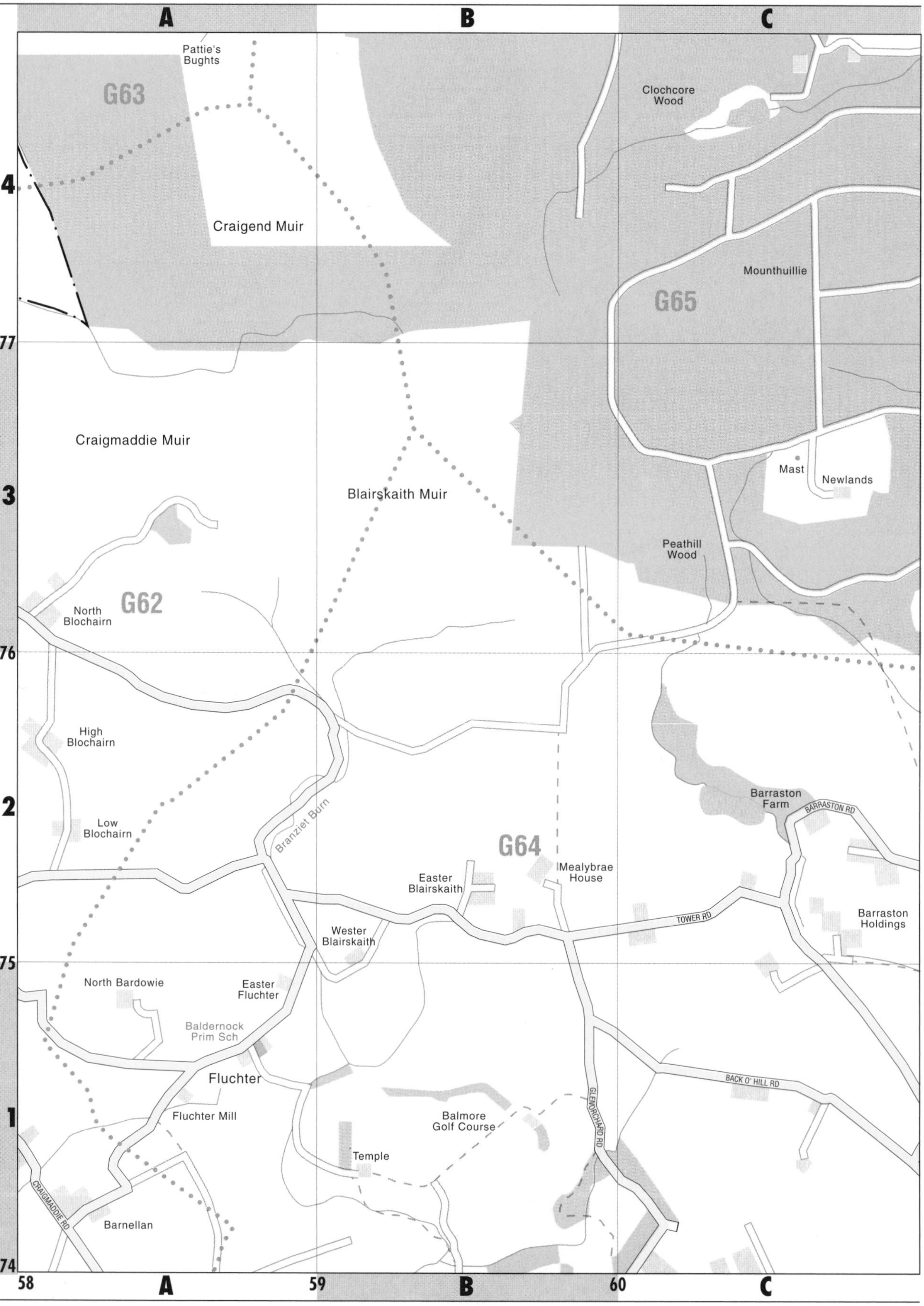

Pattie's Bughts

Craigend Muir

4

Clochcore Wood

Mounthuillie

G65

77

Craigmaddie Muir

Blairskaith Muir

Mast   Newlands

3

Peathill Wood

North Blochairn

G62

76

High Blochairn

Barraston Farm

BARRASTON RD

2

Low Blochairn

Branziet Burn

G64

Mealybrae House

Easter Blairskaith

TOWER RD

Barraston Holdings

Wester Blairskaith

75

North Bardowie

Easter Fluchter

Baldernock Prim Sch

BACK O' HILL RD

Fluchter

GLENORCHARD RD

1

Fluchter Mill

Balmore Golf Course

CRAIGMADDIE RD

Temple

Barnellan

74

58   **A**   59   **B**   60   **C**

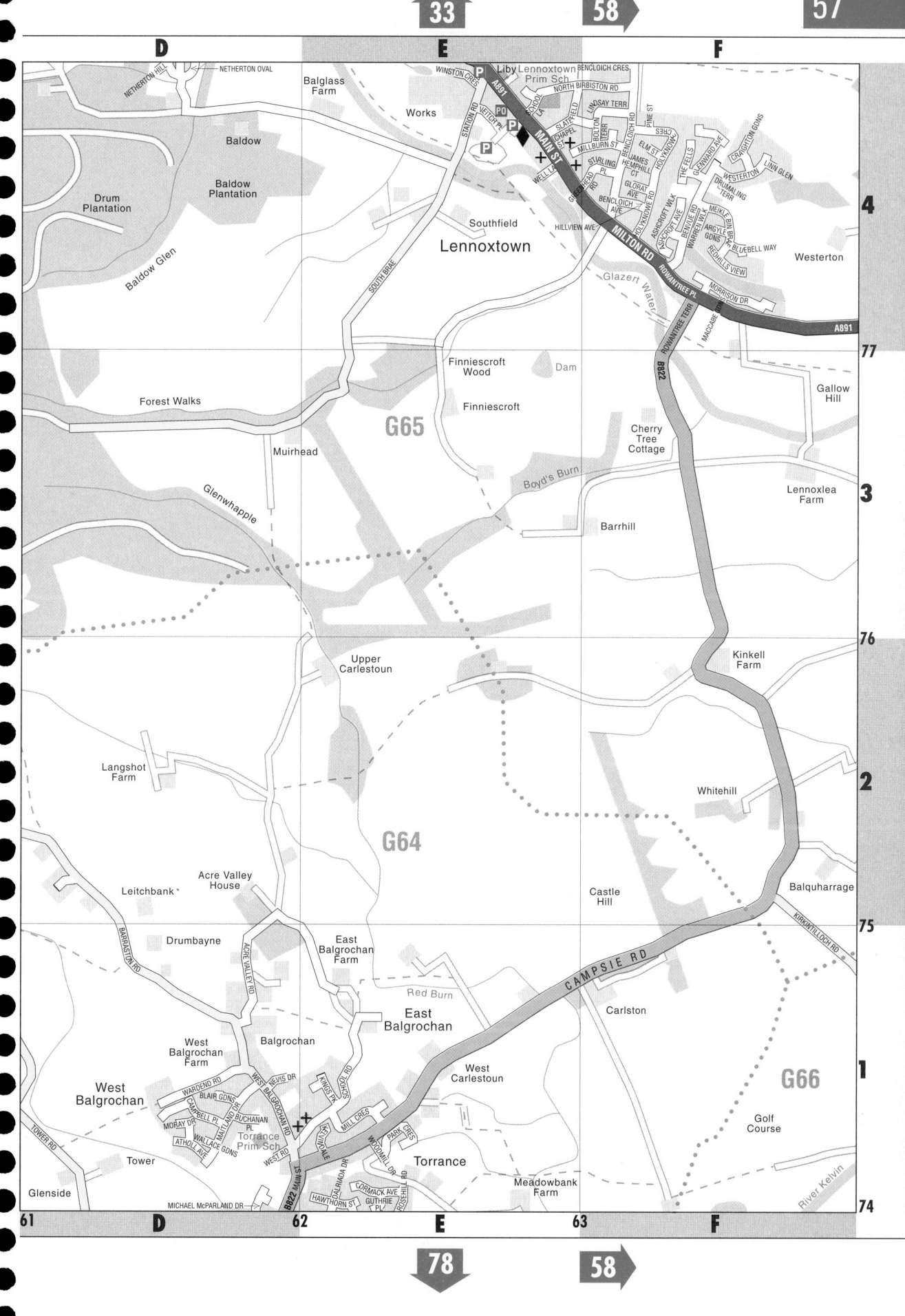
D
E
F
Netherton Hill
Netherton Oval
Balglass Farm
Works
Winston Cres
Liby
Lennoxtown Prim Sch
Bencloich Cres
North Birbiston Rd
Lindsay Terr
Station Rd
Veitch Pl
School La
Main St
A891
Slatefield
Chapel St
Millburn St
Bolton Terr
Bencloich Rd
Pine St
Elm St
James Hemphill Ct
Holyknowe Cres
The Fells
Glenward Ave
Craighton Gdns
Westerton
Linn Glen
Drumaling Terr
Well La
Stirling Pl
Greenhead Rd
Glorat Ave
Bencloich Ave
Holyknowe Rd
Ashcroft Wlk
Ashcroft Ave
Benview Rd
Warren Wlk
Meikle Bin Brae
Argyle Gdns
Bluebell Way
Redhills View
Hillview Ave
Milton Rd
Rowantree Pl
Morrison Dr
Rowantree Terr
Maccabe Gdns
Baldow
Baldow Plantation
Drum Plantation
Southfield
Lennoxtown
Westerton
Baldow Glen
South Brae
Glazert Water
4
77
Finniescroft Wood
Dam
Gallow Hill
B822
Forest Walks
Finniescroft
G65
Cherry Tree Cottage
Muirhead
Boyd's Burn
Glenwhapple
Lennoxlea Farm
3
Barrhill
76
Upper Carlestoun
Kinkell Farm
Langshot Farm
Whitehill
2
G64
Acre Valley House
Leitchbank
Castle Hill
Balquharrage
Kirkintilloch Rd
75
Barraston Rd
Drumbayne
Acre Valley Rd
East Balgrochan Farm
Campsie Rd
Red Burn
Carlston
East Balgrochan
West Balgrochan Farm
Balgrochan
West Carlestoun
1
G66
West Balgrochan
Wardend Rd
Nevis Dr
Blair Gdns
West Balgrochan Rd
Kings Pk
School Rd
Campbell Pl
Buchanan Pl
Maitland Dr
Moray Dr
Mill Cres
Golf Course
Tower Rd
Torrance Prim Sch
Wallace Gdns
Atholl Ave
Kelvinvale
Woodmill Dr
Park Cres
West Rd
Tower
Torrance
Dalriada Dr
Rosehill Rd
Meadowbank Farm
Glenside
B822 Main St
Cormack Ave
Hawthorn St
Guthrie Pl
River Kelvin
Michael McParland Dr
74
61
62
63

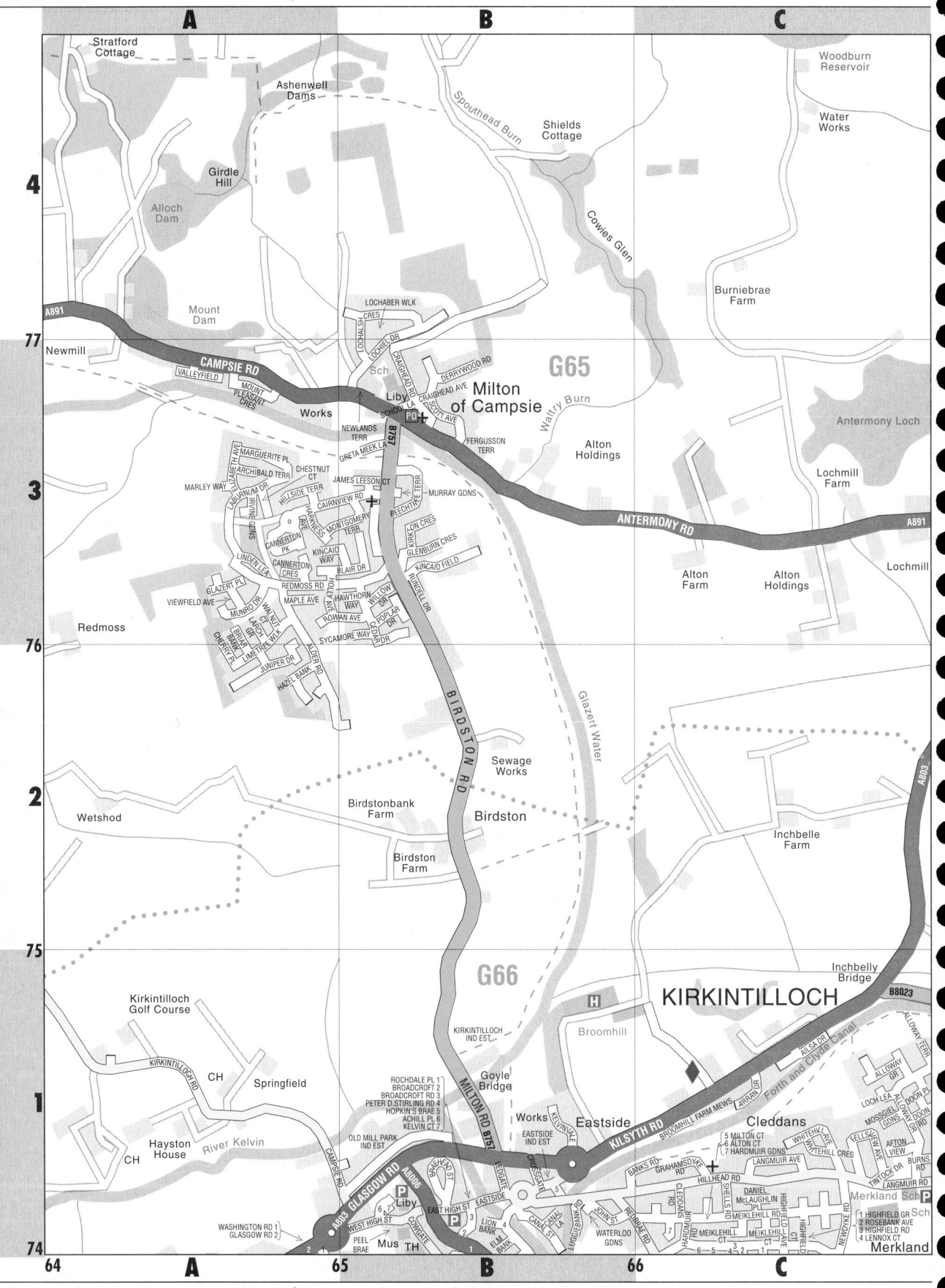

A   B   C

Stratford Cottage

Ashenwell Dams

Woodburn Reservoir

Water Works

4

Girdle Hill

Alloch Dam

Shields Cottage

Spouthead Burn

Cowies Glen

Burniebrae Farm

A891

Mount Dam

Newmill

CAMPSIE RD

Valleyfield

MOUNT PLEASANT CRES

Works

LOCHABER WLK

LOCHALSH CRES

LOCHIEL DR

CRAIGHEAD TERR

DERRYWOOD RD

Sch

Liby
PO

Milton of Campsie

G65

Antermony Loch

77

SCHOOL LA

B757

CRAIGHEAD ST

SCOTT AVE

NEWLANDS TERR

GRETA MEEK LA

FERGUSSON TERR

Alton Holdings

Watry Burn

Lochmill Farm

MARGUERITE PL

CHESTNUT CT

JAMES LEESON CT

MURRAY GDNS

LABURNUM DR

ARCHIBALD TERR

ELIZABETH AVE

MARLEY WAY

IRVING GDNS

HILLSIDE TERR

CAIRNVIEW RD

BEECHTREE TERR

KIRK LN CRES

ANTERMONY RD

A891

3

LINDEN LEA

CANNERTON PK

MONTGOMERY TERR

GLENBURN CRES

FAIFLEY

KINCAID WAY

KINCAID FIELD

Alton Farm

Alton Holdings

Lochmill

GLAZERT PL

CANNERTON CRES

BLAIR DR

REDMOSS RD

HAWTHORN WAY

WILLOW WAY

RUSHELL DR

VIEWFIELD AVE

MUNRO DR

LARCH PL

MAPLE AVE

ROWAN AVE

POPLAR DR

Redmoss

WALNUT GR

HOLLY LA

SYCAMORE WAY

CEDAR DR

76

BRIAR BANK PL

CHERRY PL

LIMETREE WLK

JUNIPER DR

ALDER RD

HAZEL BANK

Glazert Water

Inchbelle Farm

2

Wetshod

Birdstonbank Farm

BIRDSTON RD

Sewage Works

Birdston

Birdston Farm

A803

75

Kirkintilloch Golf Course

G66

Inchbelly Bridge

KIRKINTILLOCH

B8023

CH

Springfield

KIRKINTILLOCH IND EST

H

Broomhill

Forth and Clyde Canal

ALLOWAY TERR

ALLOWAY GR

KIRKINTILLOCH RD

Goyle Bridge

ARRAN DR

AILSA DR

LOCH LEA

MOSSGIEL AVE

ALLOWAY CT

DOON CT

1

Hayston House

River Kelvin

CAMPSIE RD

A806

ROCHDALE PL 1
BROADCROFT 2
BROADCROFT RD 3
PETER D.STIRLING RD 4
HOPKIN'S BRAE 5
ACHILL PL 6
KELVIN CT 7

MILTON RD

B757

Works

Eastside

KILSYTH RD

BROOMHILL FARM MEWS

Cleddans

5 MILTON CT
6 ALTON CT
7 HARDMUIR GDNS

WHITEHILL LA

WHITEHILL CRES

KELLS 2

AFTON VIEW

TINTOCK CT

BURNS RD

CH

OLD MILL PARK IND EST

EASTSIDE IND EST

KELVINDALE

BANKS RD

GRAHAMSDYKE RD

HILLHEAD RD

LANGMUIR AVE

Merkland Sch

P

GLASGOW RD

Liby

P

WEST HIGH ST

EAST HIGH ST

EASTSIDE

LION BANK

ELM BANK

CANAL ST

REINBANK RD

JOHN ST

SHELLS RD

CLEDDANS RD

BIRCH RD

Daniel McLaughlin PL

MEIKLEHILL RD

MEIKLEHILL AVE

HIGHFIELD CT

HIGHFIELD RD

NEWDYKE RD

LANGMUIR AVE

1 HIGHFIELD GR
2 ROSEBANK AVE
3 HIGHFIELD RD
4 LENNOX CT

WASHINGTON RD 1
GLASGOW RD 2

PEEL BRAE

Mus

TH

BRAEHEAD ST

CONGATE

LEDGATE

CROSSGATE

LUGGIEBANK RD

CANAL CT

WATERLOO GDNS

MEIKLEHILL RD

Merkland

74

64   A   65   B   66   C

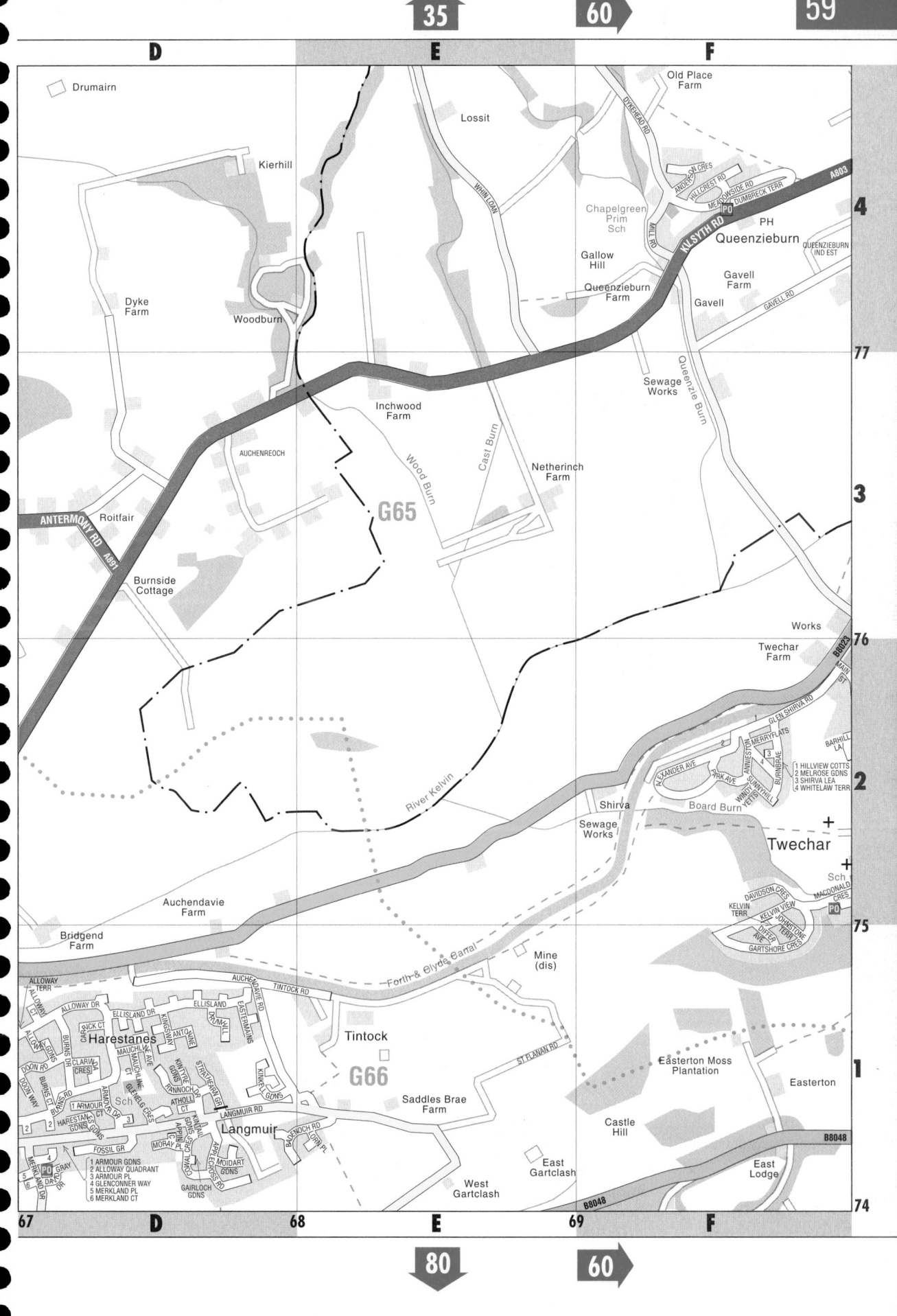

D | E | F

Drumairn

Lossit

Old Place Farm

Kierhill

DYKEHEAD RD

ANDERSON CRES

HILLCREST RD

MEADOWSIDE RD

DUMBRECK TERR

A803

4

Chapelgreen Prim Sch

Dyke Farm

MILL RD

PO

KILSYTH RD

PH

Queenzieburn

Woodburn

Gallow Hill

Queenzieburn Farm

Gavell Farm

Queenzieburn IND EST

Gavell

GAVELL RD

77

Inchwood Farm

Cast Burn

Sewage Works

Queenzie Burn

Wood Burn

Netherinch Farm

AUCHENREOCH

G65

3

ANTERMONY RD

Roitfair

A891

Burnside Cottage

Works

76

Twechar Farm

B8023

MAIN ST

GLEN SHIRVA RD

BARHILL LA

River Kelvin

Shirva

ALEXANDER AVE

PARK AVE

SUNNYHILL

YETTS

ANNIESTON

MERRYFLATS

BURNBRAE

1 HILLVIEW COTTS
2 MELROSE GDNS
3 SHIRVA LEA
4 WHITELAW TERR

2

Board Burn

Sewage Works

+

Twechar

+

Auchendavie Farm

DAVIDSON CRES

MACDONALD CRES

Sch

PO

Bridgend Farm

Forth & Clyde Canal

KELVIN TERR

KELVIN VIEW

JOHNSTONE TERR

DYER AVE

GARTSHORE CRES

75

ALLOWAY TERR

ALLOWAY DR

AUCHENDAVIE RD

TINTOCK RD

Mine (dis)

ELLISLAND DR

ELLISLAND

DRUMHILL

EASTERMAINS

ALLOWAY DR

Tintock

ST FLANAN RD

Easterton Moss Plantation

ALLOWAY

Harestanes

JACK CT

CLARK CRES

MAUCHLINE AVE

MAUCHLINE CT

ANNIE

KINGSWAY

KINTYRE DR

STRATHKELVIN

AUCHINLEA

G66

Easterton

1

BURNS DR

DOON RD

DOON WAY

BURNS RD

GLENELG CRES

HANNOCHAN

ATHOLL CT

KINPURNIE GDNS

APPIN DR

WARD

Saddles Brae Farm

Castle Hill

Sch

LANGMUIR RD

BADENOCH RD

OBAN PL

MOIDART GDNS

ARMOUR DR

MORAY PL

APPLECROSS RD

HARESTANES GDNS

FOSSIL GR

1 ARMOUR GDNS
2 ALLOWAY QUADRANT
3 ARMOUR PL
4 GLENCONNER WAY
5 MERKLAND PL
6 MERKLAND CT

Langmuir

GAIRLOCH GDNS

B8048

PO

GRAY

MERKLAND DR

East Gartclash

East Lodge

West Gartclash

B8048

B8048

74

67 | 68 | 69 |

D | E | F

59
36

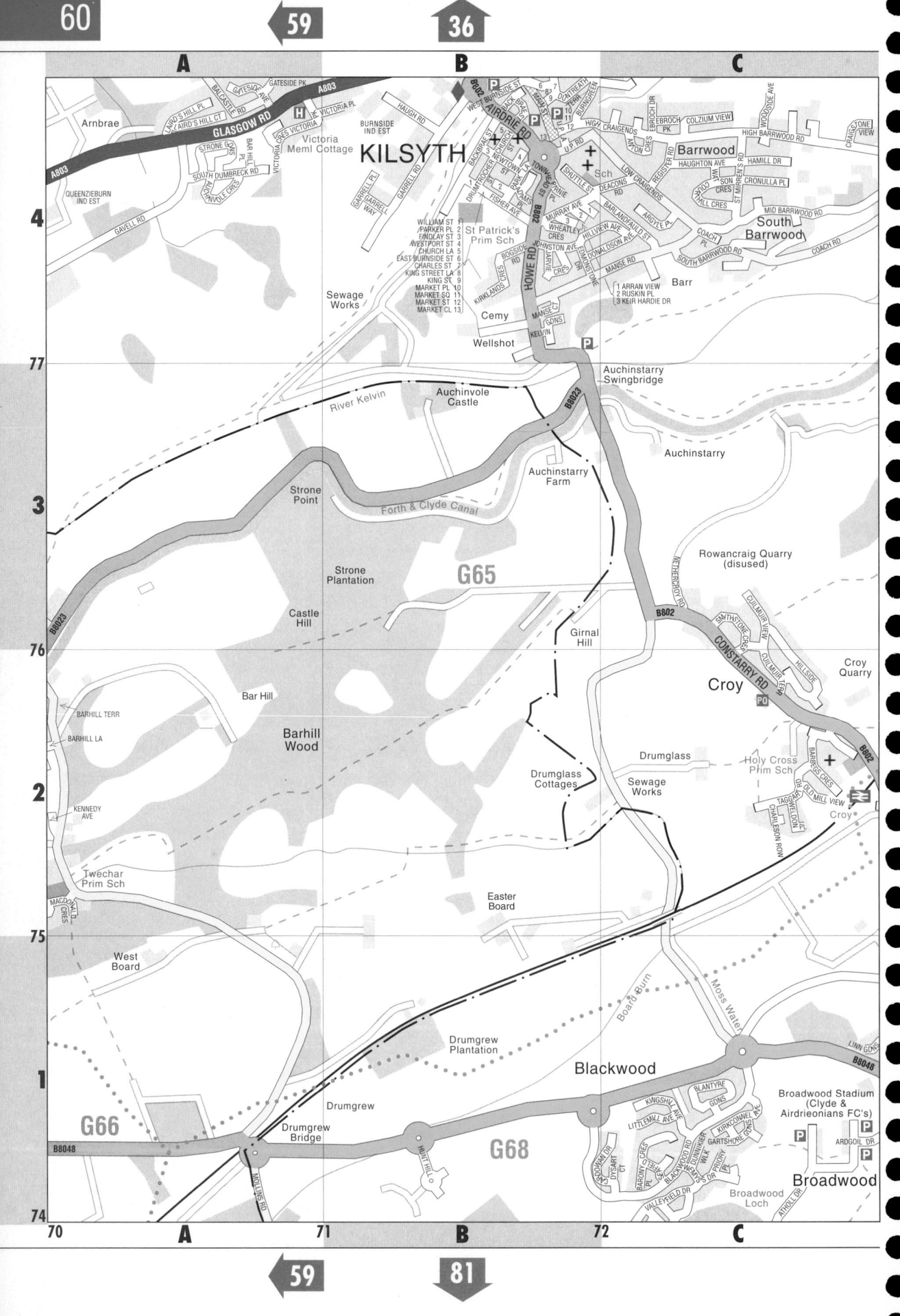
A
B
C
4
3
2
1
77
76
75
74
70
71
72
KILSYTH
Arnbrae
QUEENZIEBURN IND EST
GLASGOW RD
A803
GAVELL RD
STRONE GDNS
SOUTH DUMBRECK RD
AUCHINVOLE CRES
BAR HILL PL
VICTORIA CRES
VICTORIA PL
Victoria Meml Cottage
BURNSIDE IND EST
HAUGH RD
GARRELL PL
GARRELL WAY
GARRELL RD
B802
AIRDRIE RD
WEST BURNSIDE ST
BACKBRAE ST
NEWTOWN ST
FISHER AVE
TOWNHEAD
HIGH CRAIGENDS
EBROCH DR
EBROCH PK
COLZIUM VIEW
WOODSIDE AVE
HIGH BARRWOOD RD
CRAIGSTONE VIEW
Barrwood
HAUGHTON AVE
HAMILL DR
CRONULLA PL
ST MIRREN'S RD
MID BARRWOOD RD
South Barrwood
COACH RD
COACH PL
SOUTH BARRWOOD RD
LOW CRAIGENDS
SHUTTLE ST
DEACONS RD
MURRAY AVE
WHEATLEY CRES
HILLVIEW AVE
DONALDSON AVE
MANSE RD
JOHNSTON AVE
Sch
St Patrick's Prim Sch
WILLIAM ST 1
PARKER PL 2
FINDLAY ST 3
WESTPORT ST 4
CHURCH LA 5
EAST BURNSIDE ST 6
CHARLES ST 7
KING STREET LA 8
KING ST 9
MARKET PL 10
MARKET SQ 11
MARKET ST 12
MARKET CL 13
1 ARRAN VIEW
2 RUSKIN PL
3 KEIR HARDIE DR
Barr
HOWE RD
BOGSIDE RD
KIRKLANDS CRES
Sewage Works
Cemy
Wellshot
KELVIN
Auchinstarry Swingbridge
B8023
River Kelvin
Auchinvole Castle
Auchinstarry
Auchinstarry Farm
Strone Point
Forth & Clyde Canal
Strone Plantation
G65
Rowancraig Quarry (disused)
NETHERCROY RD
Castle Hill
Girnal Hill
B802
CONSTARRY RD
CULMUIR VIEW
SMITHSTONE CRES
HILLSIDE
Croy
Croy Quarry
Bar Hill
BARHILL TERR
BARHILL LA
Barhill Wood
Drumglass
Drumglass Cottages
Holy Cross Prim Sch
Sewage Works
BARBEGS CRES
OLD MILL VIEW
TAGGART RD
WELDON PL
CHARLESON ROW
Croy
KENNEDY AVE
Twechar Prim Sch
MACDONALD CRES
Easter Board
West Board
Board Burn
Moss Water
Drumgrew Plantation
Blackwood
LINN GDNS
B8048
Broadwood Stadium (Clyde & Airdrieonians FC's)
G66
Drumgrew
Drumgrew Bridge
B8048
MOLLINS RD
HUNT HILL
G68
BLANTYRE GDNS
KINGSHILL AVE
LITTLEMILL AVE
KIRKCONNEL AVE
GARTSHORE GDNS
DUNNIKIER WLK
BLACKWOOD RD
BARONY PL
DYSART CT
CARDOWAN DR
WEMYSS DR
PRIORY PL
VALLEYFIELD DR
ARDGOIL DR
ATHOLL DR
Broadwood Loch
Broadwood

59
81

37
62

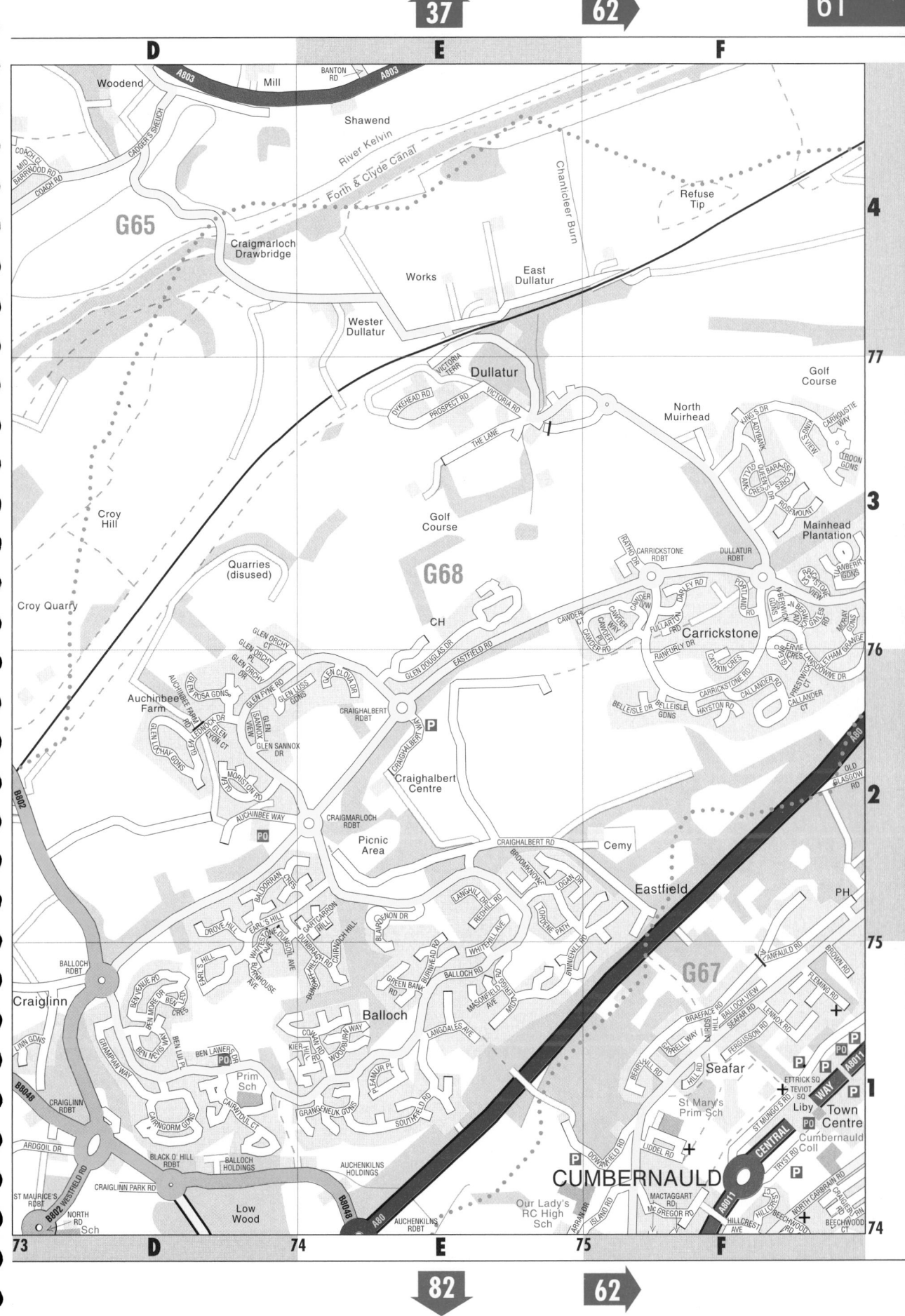
D
E
F
Woodend
Mill
BANTON RD
A803
Shawend
River Kelvin
Forth & Clyde Canal
CADGER'S SHEUCH
COACH CL
MID BARRWOOD RD
COACH RD
G65
Craigmarloch Drawbridge
Chanticleer Burn
Refuse Tip
Works
East Dullatur
Wester Dullatur
Dullatur
VICTORIA TERR
DYKEHEAD RD
PROSPECT RD
VICTORIA RD
THE LANE
North Muirhead
Golf Course
KING'S DR
LADYBANK
CARNOUSTIE WAY
TROON GDNS
ROSEMOUNT
Mainhead Plantation
Croy Hill
Golf Course
Quarries (disused)
G68
RATHO DR
CARRICKSTONE RDBT
DULLATUR RDBT
Croy Quarry
CH
CAWDER VW
DARLEY RD
PORTLAND RD
FULLARTON RD
Carrickstone
RANFURLY DR
CAWDER CT
CAWDER WAY
CAWDER PL
CAWDER RD
EASTFIELD RD
GLEN DOUGLAS DR
GLEN ORCHY CT
GLEN ORCHY PL
GLEN ORCHY DR
GLEN ROSA GDNS
GLEN FYNE RD
GLEN LUSS GDNS
GLEN CLOVA DR
Auchinbee Farm
AUCHINBEE FARM RD
GLEN LEDNOCK DR
GLEN LYON CT
GLEN SANNOX VIEW
GLEN SANNOX DR
GLEN LOCHAY GDNS
GLEN MORISTON RD
CRAIGHALBERT RDBT
CRAIGHALBERT WAY
CARRICKSTONE RD
CALLANDER RD
CALLANDER CT
LANSDOWNE DR
LETHAM GRANGE
PRESTWICK CT
BELLEISLE DR
BELLEISLE GDNS
HAYSTON RD
CATHKIN CRES
Craighalbert Centre
B802
AUCHINBEE WAY
CRAIGMARLOCH RDBT
Picnic Area
CRAIGHALBERT RD
Cemy
A80
OLD GLASGOW RD
Eastfield
PH
BROOMKNOWE
LOGAN DR
BALDORRAN CRES
LANGHILL DR
REDHILL RD
TORDENE PATH
DROVE HILL
EARL'S HILL
WHITESTONE AVE
DUNGOIL AVE
GARTCARRON HILL
CAIRNOCH HILL
BLAIRLINNON DR
WHITEHILL AVE
BINNIEHILL RD
BALLOCH RDBT
BURNHOUSE AVE
DUNBRACH RD
BURNHEAD RD
BALLOCH RD
GREEN BANK RD
MASONFIELD AVE
MIDDLERIGGS RD
G67
PANFAULD RD
BROWN RD
FLEMING RD
Craiglinn
BEN VENUE RD
BEN MORE DR
BEN LEDI CRES
Balloch
COLMAN RD
WOODBURN WAY
LANGDALES AVE
BRAEFACE RD
LAIRDS HILL
BALLOCH VIEW
SEAFAR RD
LENNOX RD
LINN GDNS
GRAMPIAN WAY
BEN NEVIS WAY
BEN LUI PL
BEN LAWERS DR
KIER HILL
GARRELL WAY
FERGUSSON RD
A8011
B8048
CRAIGLINN RDBT
Prim Sch
PLEAMUIR PL
BERRYHILL RD
HILL RD
Seafar
ETTRICK SQ
TEVIOT SQ
WAY
Liby
Town Centre
CAIRNGORM GDNS
CAIRNTOUL CT
GRANGENEUK GDNS
SOUTHFIELD RD
St Mary's Prim Sch
ST MUNGO'S RD
CENTRAL
Cumbernauld Coll
ARDGOIL DR
BLACK O' HILL RDBT
BALLOCH HOLDINGS
AUCHENKILNS HOLDINGS
DOWANFIELD RD
LIDDEL RD
TRYST RD
NORTH CARBRAIN RD
CRAIGLINN PARK RD
CUMBERNAULD
ST MAURICE'S RDBT
WESTFIELD RD
NORTH RD
Sch
Low Wood
AUCHENKILNS RDBT
Our Lady's RC High Sch
ARRAN DR
ISLAND RD
MACTAGGART RD
McGREGOR RD
HILLCREST AVE
BEECHWOOD RD
BEECHWOOD CT
4
77
3
76
2
75
1
74
73
74
75

82
62

A B C

4

77

76

3

76

2

75

1

74

G65

Westerwood

Airport

G68

Drumcap Plantation

Golf Course

Hotel

Mainhead Plantation

Cumbernauld Village

Wardpark

NAPIER PL
NAPIER CT
WYNFORD RD
WARDPARK EAST IND EST
TOLLPARK RD
TOLLPARK PL
DUNCAN McINTOSH RD
NAPIER RD
NAPIER WAY
WARDPARK NORTH IND EST

CASTLEVIEW
CASTLE CT
CASTLE GLEN
Castlecary
Dunn Wood
Castle Cary

FK4
Castlecray Cottage

GARSHALL FARM RD
B816
A80

CASTLECARY RD

Walton Burn

FOREST RD

DUNNS WOOD RD

Napier Pk

B816
OLD INNS RDBT
A8011

CUMBERNAULD

Crow Wood

WARDPARK SOUTH IND EST
WARDPARK RD
WARDPARK CT
WARDPARK PL
BROOM RD
ASH RD

WHITELEES RD
WHITELEES RD
BIRKENBURN RD
ROSEBURN PL
BRAESBURN PL
RAEBURN PL
REABURN PL
WHITELEES RDBT
Whitelees Prim Sch
LILAC AVE
LILAC PL
CHESTNUT CT
CHESTNUT CT
CHESTNUT
MAPLE RD
MAPLE CT
FOREST RD

Glenhead Prim Sch

St Lucy's Prim Sch

G67

Cumbernauld House

Vault Glen

Red Burn

Abronhill

Kildrum

DARROCH WAY
WOODLAND WAY
CAMPSIE VIEW
BRAEHEAD
AFTON RD
KILDRUM RD
Kildrum Prim Sch
PARK WAY
CASTLE WAY
MEADOW VIEW
FOREST VIEW
GLEN VIEW
MACLEHOSE RD
LOCHLEA RD
AINSLIE RD
BURN RD
ROWAN RD
HAZEL RD
CEDAR RD
REDWOOD RD
FOREST RD

Abronhill Prim Sch

Abronhill High Sch
LARCH RD
LARCH GR
LARCH CT
SPRUCE RD
PINE PL
PINE RD
PINE CT
PINE CRES
OAK RD
ELM RD
MOSS RD
GEAN CT
HAWTHORN RD
BIRCH RD
LIME CRES
BLACKTHORN RD

Liby

DRUMMOND HOUSE 1
SCOTT HOUSE 2
BLAIR HOUSE 3
SEAFAR RD
MITCHISON RD
BARKE RD
IHUME RD
Liby
MUIRHEAD BRAEHEAD RDBT
KYLE RD
TARBOLTON RD

Supermarket
LYE BRAE
CENTRAL WAY
A8011
B8054
SOUTH MUIRHEAD RD
BURNS RD

Sacred Heart Prim Sch
ELLISLAND RD
CLOUDEN RD
KENMORE RD
DOON SIDE
KENMUIR RD
CORBISTON WAY

GLENCAIRN RD
JAMIESON RD
KNOWE RD
MOSS-SIDE RD

Mid Forest

Palacerigg Country Park

Forest Plantation

Carbrain
TH
Ct
IRYST RD
BRUN WAY
GLENHOVE RD
NORTH CARBRAIN RD
TORBREX RD
MILLCROFT RD
GREENRIGG RD
GREENRIGG RD
SOUTH CARBRAIN RD
GLENCRYAN RD
CRAIGIEBURN RD
CRAIGIEBURN RD
STONELEA RD
KILBOWIE RD
BROOMLANDS RD

Cumbernauld High Sch
ALDER RD
LARBURN RD
LABURNUM RD

Prim Sch

TA Centre

KILDRUM SOUTH RDBT
CARBRAIN IND EST
B8054 LENZIEMILL RD
GREENYARDS INTERCHANGE

76 77 78

A B C

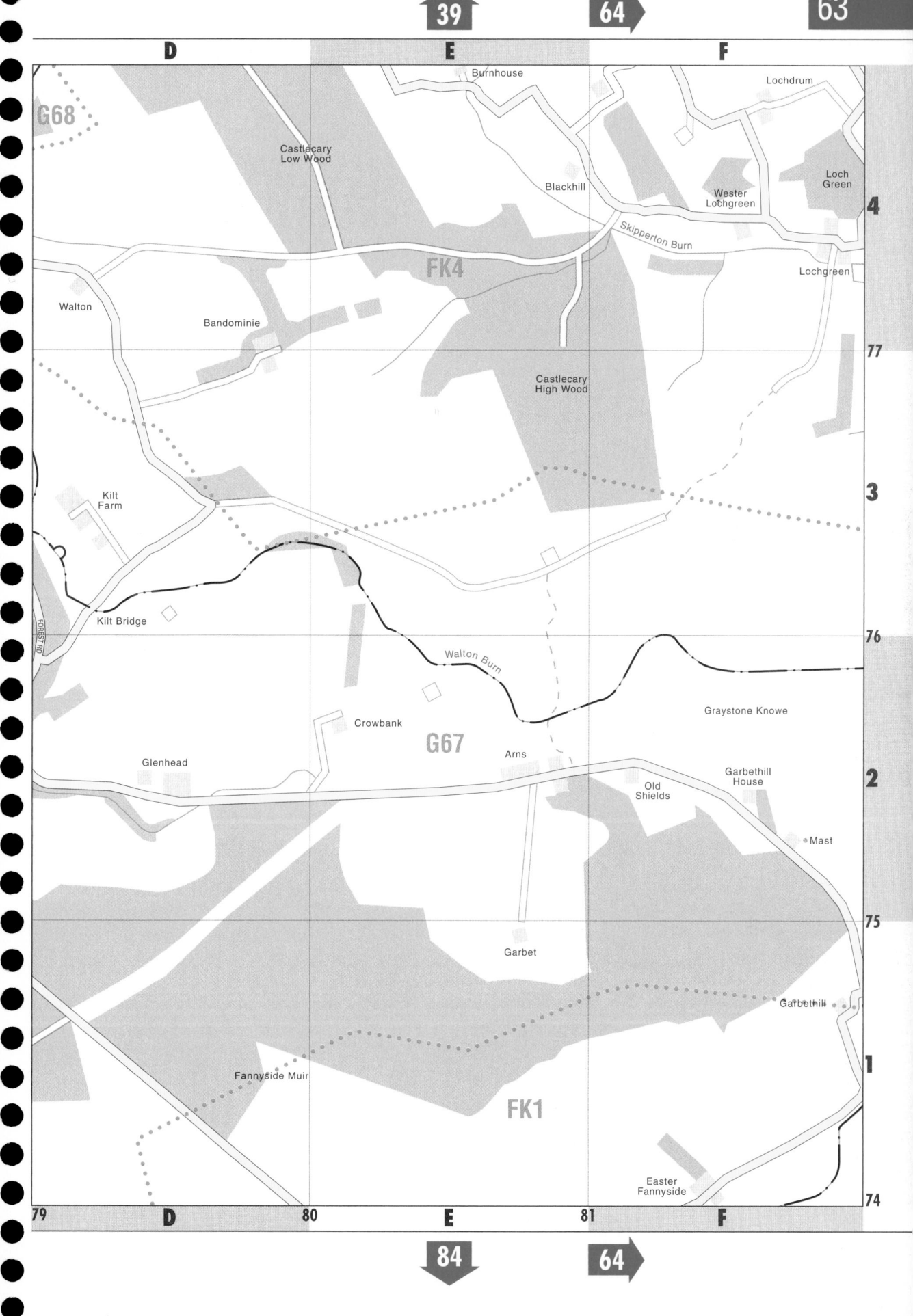

D
E
F

G68

Burnhouse

Lochdrum

Castlecary
Low Wood

Blackhill

Wester
Lochgreen

Loch
Green

Skipperton Burn

4

FK4

Lochgreen

Walton

Bandominie

77

Castlecary
High Wood

Kilt
Farm

3

FOREST RD

Kilt Bridge

76

Walton Burn

Graystone Knowe

Crowbank

G67

Glenhead

Arns

Old
Shields

Garbethill
House

2

Mast

75

Garbet

Garbethill

1

Fannyside Muir

FK1

Easter
Fannyside

74

79
D
80
E
81
F

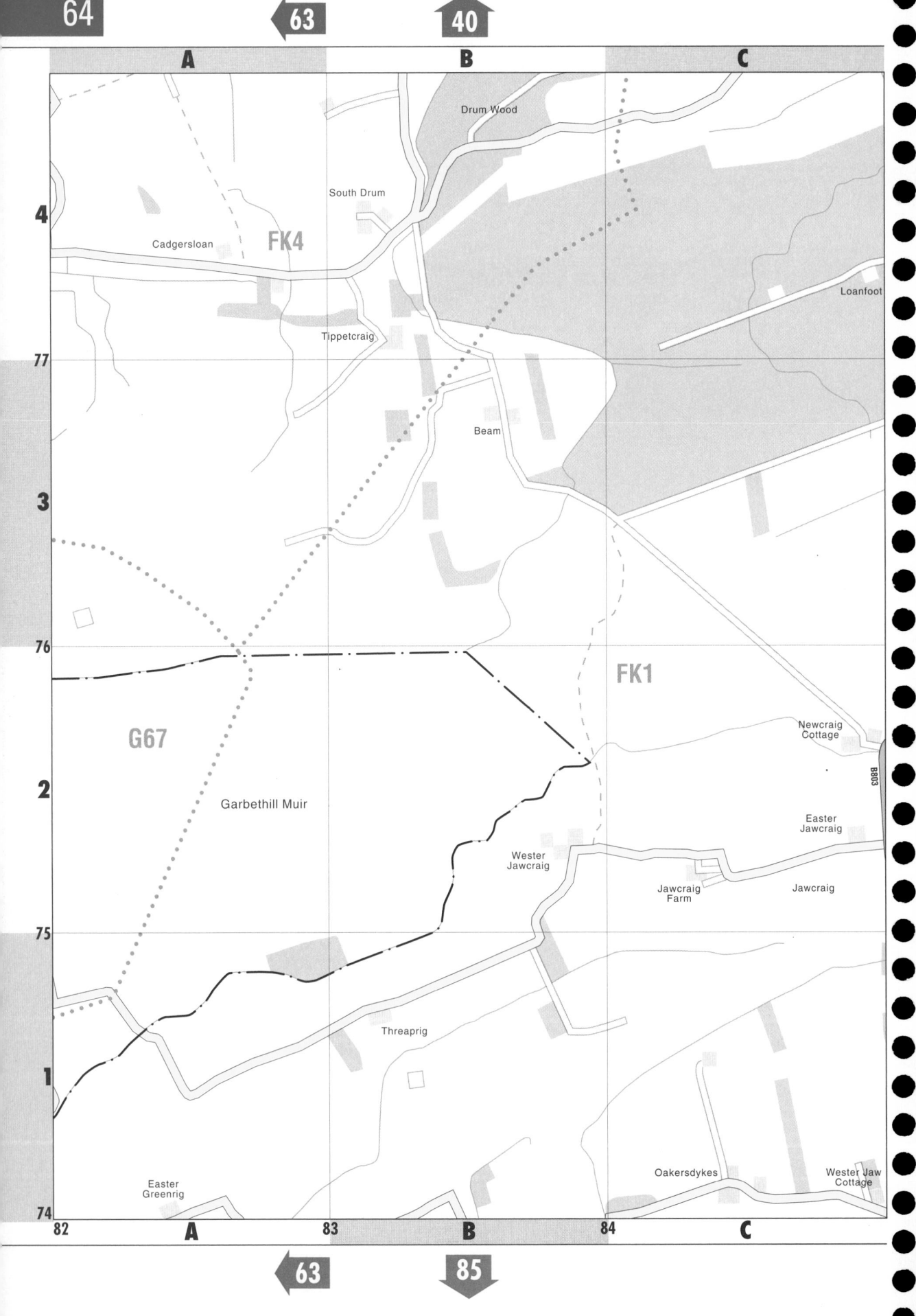

Drum Wood

South Drum

Cadgersloan

FK4

4

Loanfoot

Tippetcraig

77

Beam

3

76

G67

FK1

Newcraig
Cottage

2

Garbethill Muir

Easter
Jawcraig

Wester
Jawcraig

Jawcraig
Farm

Jawcraig

75

Threaprig

1

Easter
Greenrig

Oakersdykes

Wester Jaw
Cottage

74

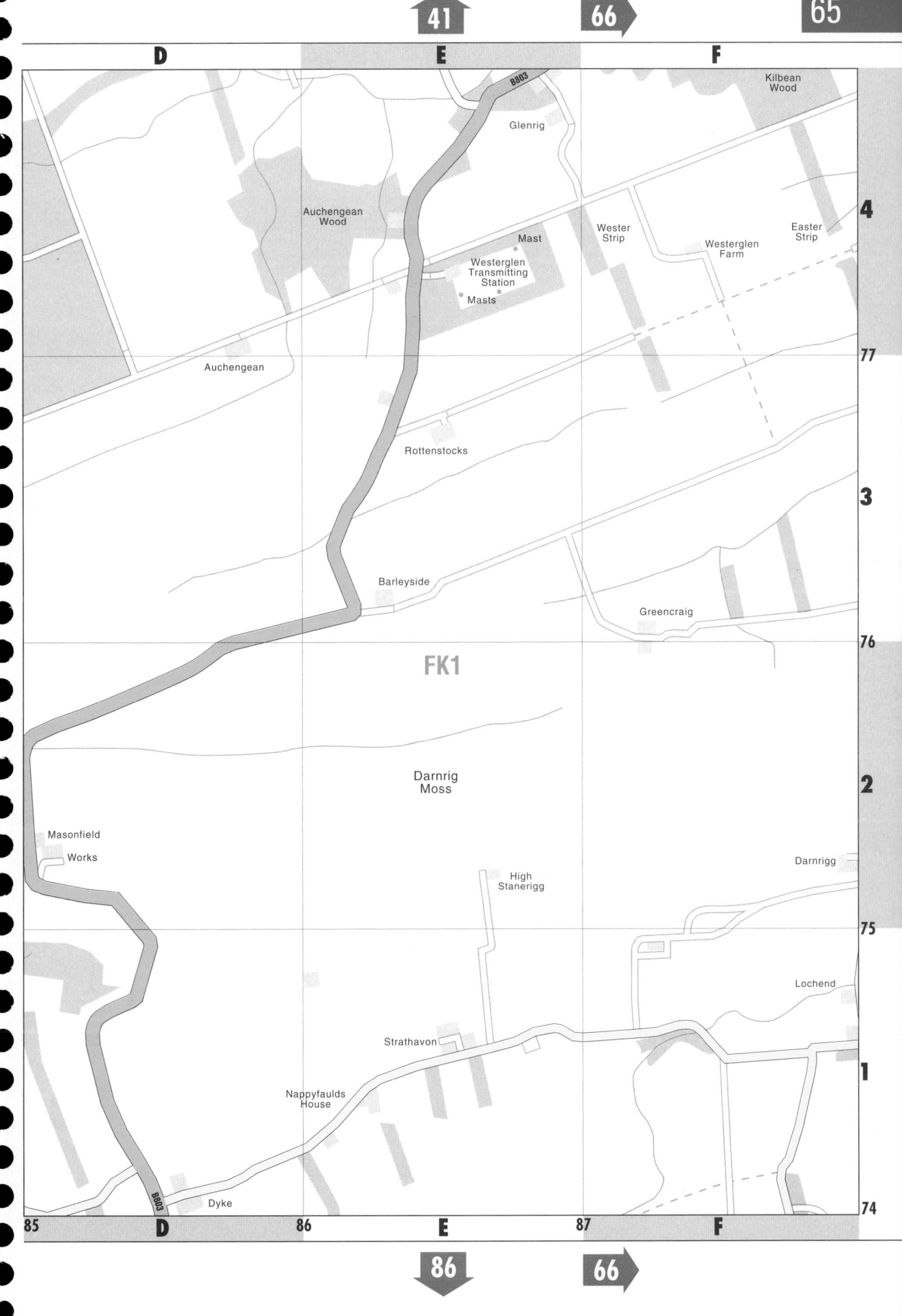

D E F

B803

Kilbean Wood

Glenrig

Auchengean Wood

Mast

Wester Strip

Westerglen Farm

Easter Strip

4

Westerglen Transmitting Station

Masts

Auchengean

77

Rottenstocks

3

Barleyside

Greencraig

76

FK1

Darnrig Moss

2

Masonfield

Works

High Stanerigg

Darnrigg

75

Lochend

Strathavon

1

Nappyfaulds House

85 86 87

D E F

B803

Dyke

74

65
42

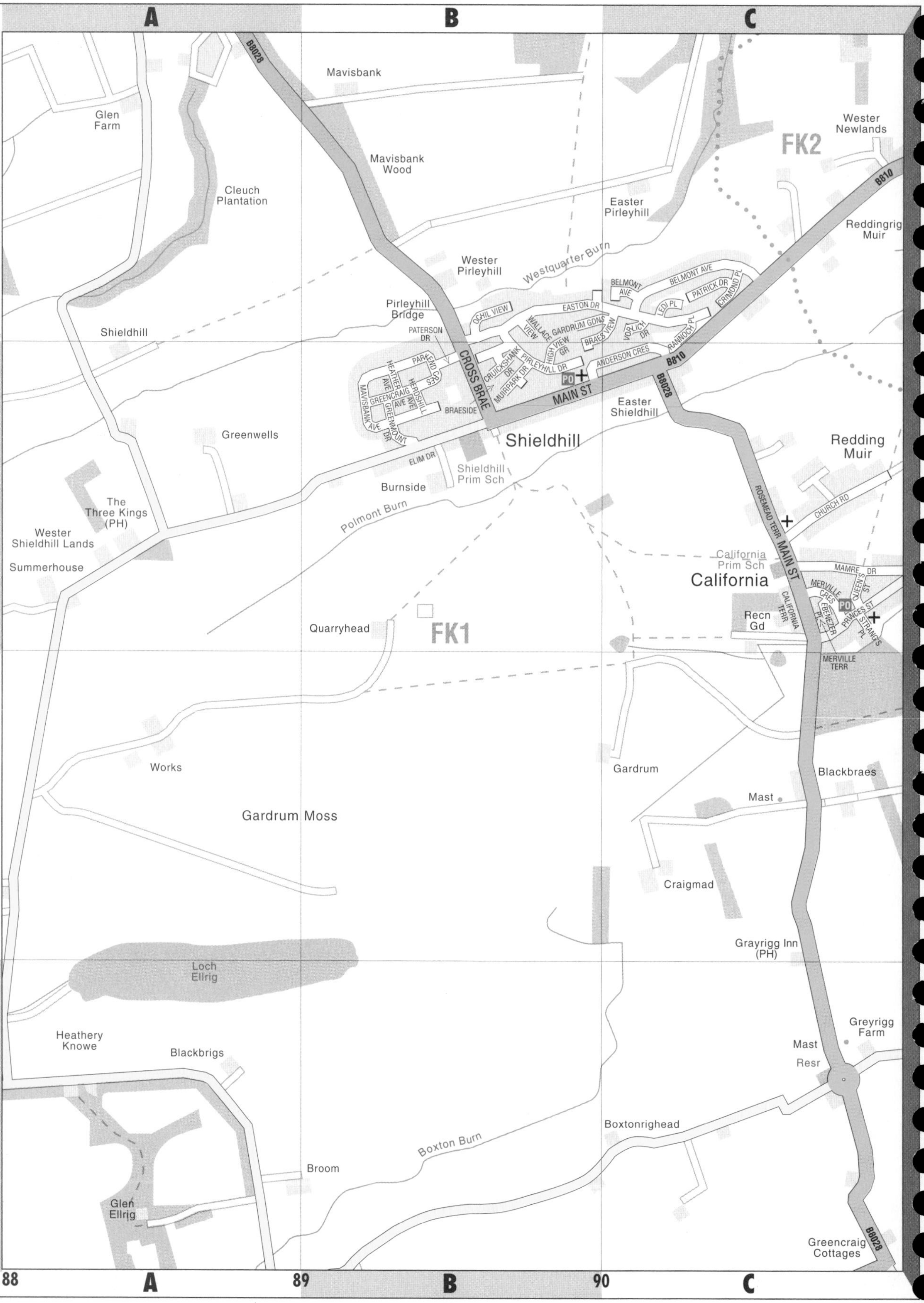

A   B   C

4

Mavisbank

Glen Farm

Mavisbank Wood

Cleuch Plantation

Wester Newlands

FK2

B810

Easter Pirleyhill

Reddingrig Muir

Westquarter Burn

Wester Pirleyhill

BELMONT AVE

Belmont Ave

PATRICK DR

77

Shieldhill

Pirleyhill Bridge

SCHIL VIEW

EASTON DR

EDI PL

ORMOND PL

PATERSON DR

WALLACE VIEW

GARDRUM GDNS

BRAES VIEW

RANNOCK PL

PARK DR

HIGH VIEW GR

MURPARK DR

PIRLEYHILL DR

ANDERSON CRES

B810

HEATHERCRAIG AVE

GREENWELL DR

CRUICKSHANK DR

PO

MAIN ST

Easter Shieldhill

MAVISBANK AVE

HERDSHILL AVE

GREENCRAIG UNK

BRAESIDE

Shieldhill

Redding Muir

Greenwells

ELIM DR

Shieldhill Prim Sch

CHURCH RD

3

The Three Kings (PH)

Burnside

ROSSHEAD TERR

MAIN ST

Wester Shieldhill Lands

Polmont Burn

California Prim Sch

MAMRE DR

Summerhouse

California

MERVILLE CRES

QUEEN'S ST

PRIMES ST

76

Quarryhead

FK1

Recn Gd

CALIFORNIA TERR

STRANGS

MERVILLE TERR

Gardrum

Blackbraes

Works

Mast

2

Gardrum Moss

Craigmad

Grayrigg Inn (PH)

75

Loch Ellrig

Heathery Knowe

Greyrigg Farm

Blackbrigs

Mast

Resr

1

Boxtonrighead

Boxton Burn

Broom

Glen Ellrig

Greencraig Cottages

B8028

88   A   89   B   90   C

74

65
87

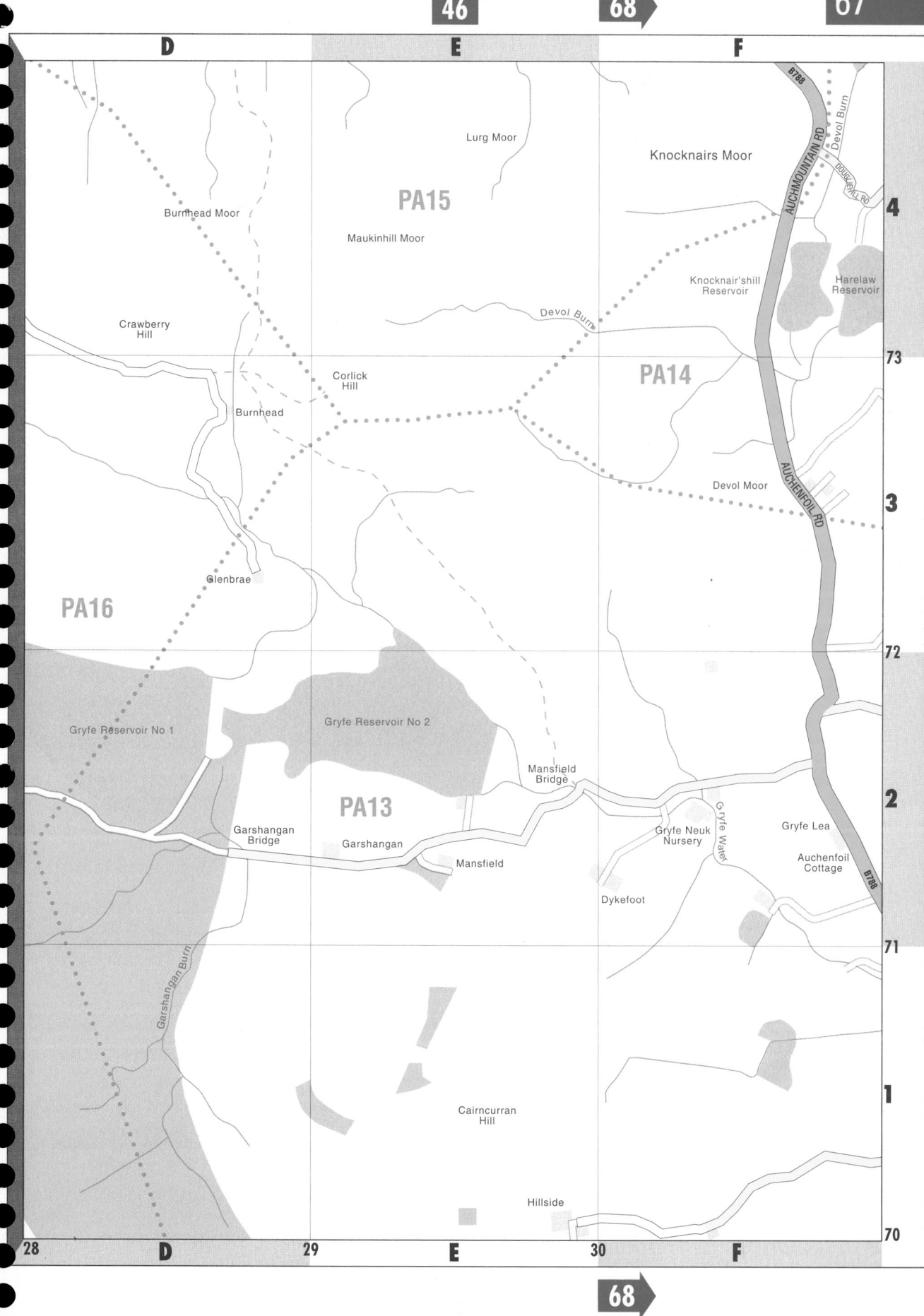

46
68
D
E
F
B788
Devol Burn
Lurg Moor
Knocknairs Moor
AUCHMOUNTAIN RD
DOUGLIEHILL RD
Burnhead Moor
PA15
Maukinhill Moor
4
Knocknair'shill Reservoir
Harelaw Reservoir
Crawberry Hill
Devol Burn
73
Corlick Hill
PA14
Burnhead
AUCHENFOIL RD
Devol Moor
3
Glenbrae
PA16
72
Gryfe Reservoir No 1
Gryfe Reservoir No 2
Mansfield Bridge
2
PA13
Gryfe Water
Gryfe Lea
Garshangan Bridge
Gryfe Neuk Nursery
Garshangan
Mansfield
Auchenfoil Cottage
B788
Dykefoot
71
Garshangan Burn
1
Cairncurran Hill
Hillside
70
28
29
30

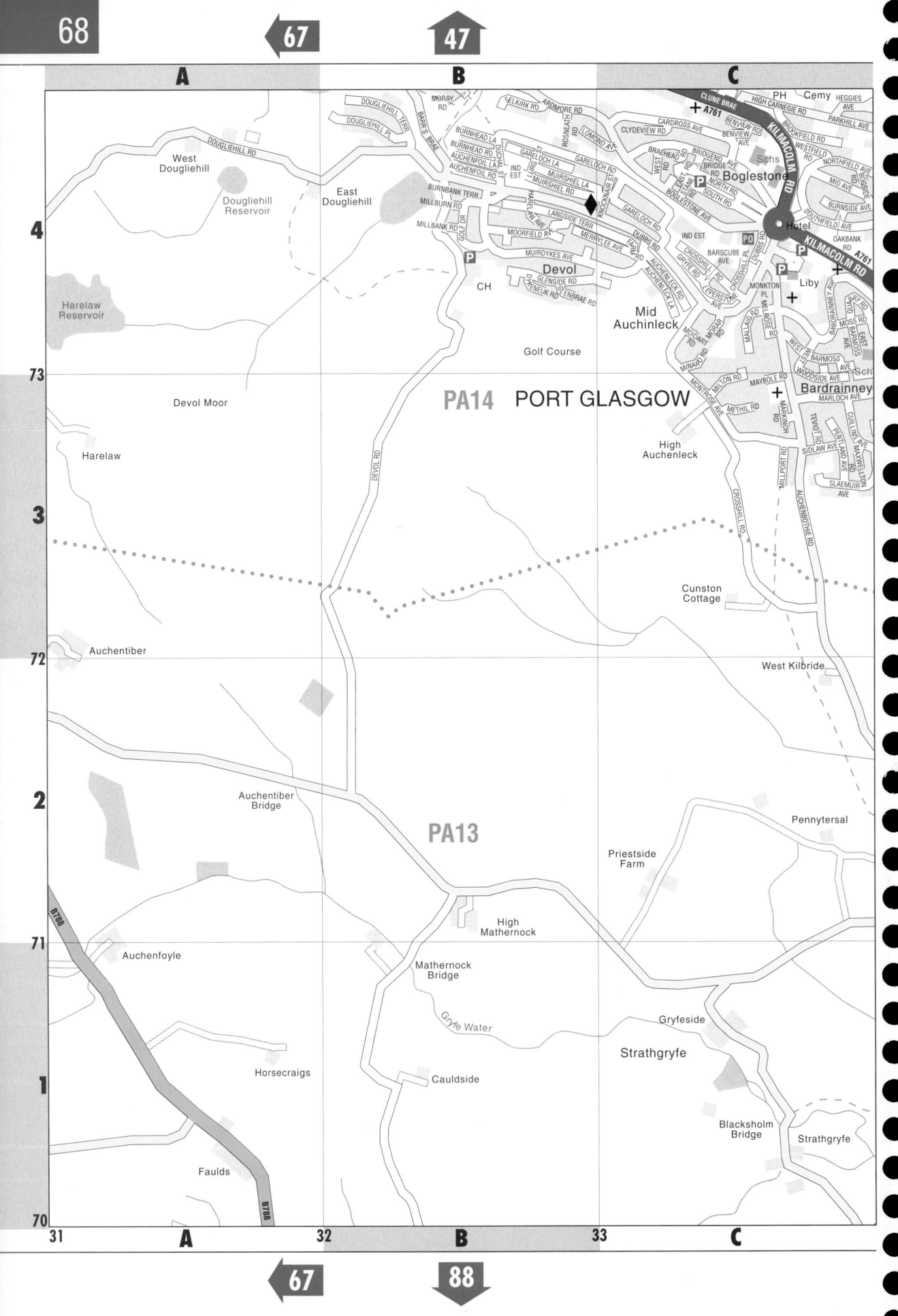

67
47

A

B

C

DOUGLIEHILL RD

West Dougliehill

Dougliehill Reservoir

East Dougliehill

MORAY RD

BARR'S BRAE

DOUGLIEHILL TERR

DOUGLIEHILL PL

SELKIRK RD

ARDMORE RD

DUDHAL ST

BURNHEAD LA

BURNHEAD RD

AUCHENFOIL LA

AUCHENFOIL RD

BURNBANK TERR

MILLBURN RD

MILLBANK RD

GOLF DR

MOORFIELD RD

MUIRDYKES AVE

ROSNEATH RD

LOMOND AVE

GARELOCH LA

GARELOCH RD

MUIRSHIEL RD

IND EST

HARELAW AVE

LANGSIDE TERR

MERRYLEE AVE

DURRS RD

KNOCKNAIR ST

GLENSIDE RD

GLENBRAE RD

ZENEUK RD

Devol

CH

CLUNE BRAE

A761

HIGH CARNEGIE RD

CLYDEVIEW RD

CARDROSS AVE

BRAEHEAD RD

WEST RD

EAST RD

BRIDGEND AVE

BRIDGE RD

NORTH RD

SOUTH RD

BOGLESTONE AVE

KILMACOLM RD

Cemy

HEGGIES AVE

PARKHILL AVE

BENVIEW RD

BENVIEW AVE

WESTFIELD RD

NORTHFIELD AVE

AVONSIDE RD

MID AVE

BURNSIDE AVE

SOUTHFIELD AVE

OAKBANK RD

Schs

Boglestone

P

PH

Hotel

PO

KILMACOLM RD A761

Liby

BARSCUBE AVE

AUCHENLECK RD

GRYFE RD

EPERSTON AVE

CROSSHILL PL

LDURRS RD

MELROSE AVE

MONKTON PL

MOULDART RD

MINARD RD

MORAIL RD

MALLARD RD

Mid Auchinleck

IND EST

P

P

Golf Course

PA14 **PORT GLASGOW**

High Auchenleck

MONTROSE AVE

MILTON RD

METHIL RD

MAYBOLE RD

WOODSIDE AVE

MARINDON RD

TEVIOT RD

SIDLAW AVE

PENTLAND AVE

WEST BARMOSS AVE

EAST BARMOSS AVE

MOSS RD

PHO

RD

CULLINS MAXWELTON AVE

SLAEMUIR AVE

Schs

Bardrainney

MARLOCH AVE

Devol Moor

DEVOL RD

Harelaw

Harelaw Reservoir

73

4

CROSSHILL RD

Cunston Cottage

AUCHENBOTHIE RD

West Kilbride

Auchentiber

72

Auchentiber Bridge

PA13

Priestside Farm

Pennytersal

2

High Mathernock

Mathernock Bridge

Gryfe Water

Gryfeside

Strathgryfe

71

Auchenfoyle

B788

Horsecraigs

Cauldside

Blacksholm Bridge

Strathgryfe

1

Faulds

B788

70

31   **A**   **32**   **B**   **33**   **C**

67
88

D   E   F

River Clyde

GREENOCK RD

A8

HEGGIES AVE
WOODHALL AVE
PLEASANTSIDE AVE
BRIGHTSIDE
MANSION AVE
GLASGOW RD
Woodhall
WOODHALL TERR
SUNNYSIDE AVE

Brackenhead
Plantation

Finlaystone
House
Finlaystone

Sch
Broadfield

PARKHILL AVE
BRACKEN
NORTHFIELD AVE
BROADFIELD AVE
COLL AVE
BUTE AVE
COLONSAY AVE

Parkhill

Larch
Strip

SOUTHFIELD AVE
BURNSIDE
AVE

St Stephen's
High Sch

CASTLE AVE
FINLAYSTONE RD
GALLAHILL AVE
CUMBRAE AVE
ERISKA AVE
HARRIS AVE
ARRAN AVE

OLD GREENOCK RD

Damhead
Plantation

MOSS
RD
Sch
IONA RD
NETHERTON
AVE
TIREE AVE
LISMORE AVE

PO

Midhill
Plantation

Burnside

73

MARLOCH AVE
SLAEMUIR
EASTSIDE

UIST AVE
MONACH AVE
STAFFA AVE
MULL AVE
PLADDA AVE
RONA AVE
SANDAY

Park Farm

PA14

Chapel
Hill

Port
Glasgow
High Sch

CROMDALE
RD
GRAMP. RD

STROMA AVE
WESTRAY AVE
ORONSAY AVE
SKYE RD

Castlehill
Plantation

Bogside Wood

Bogside

Slaemuir

KILMACOLM RD

Laigh
Castlehill

Finlaystone Burn
Finlaystone Glen

Slaemuir
Prim Sch

Auchendores
Cotts

3

High
Castlehill

Auchendores
Reservoir

Knockmountain

72

Craigmarloch
Wood

CLOAK RD

Cloak

Langside

Knockmountain

FINLAYSTONE RD

Knockmountain
Wood

Craigmarloch

Leperstone
Reservoir

PA13

2

South
Craigmarloch

Windmill
Wood

Kays
Wood

Migdale

Dargavel Burn

Cairnkibbuck
Knowe

AUCHENBOTHIE RD

Auchenbothie Burn

PORT GLASGOW RD

Auchenbothie
House

Old
Hall

LEPERSTONE AVE

LEPERSTONE
RD

71

Auchenbothie
Mains

Cemy
Planetreeyetts

QUARRY DR
SPRINGBOOR DR
WATERTETTS
YETTS
AVE
FINLAYSTONE
CR

Resr

1

Netherwood
Bridge

Gryfe Water

KNOCKBUCKLE RD

VICTORIA
GDNS
KNOCKBUCKLE
AVE
CASTLEHILL
CRES
NURSERY LA
NURSERY GR
VICTORIA GDNS
WHITELEA RD

HILLSIDE AVE
WOODROW AVE

1 GLENBURN LA
2 GLENBURN RD
3 GLENBURN DR
OLDHALL

A761
HIGH ST
BARRS BRAE

LANGBANK
WEST GLEN
LANGBANK
WEST GLEN RD
LODGE GDNS
OVERTON GDNS
OVERTON GR
LODGE PK
WEST GLEN RD

WHITELEA CRES
WHITELEA
CRES
ROSEBANK
TERR
GIBSON

70

34   D   35   E   36   F

69 49

A B C

G82

River Clyde

4

MARYPARK RD   MAIN RD B789

GREENOCK RD

A8

Langbank

LITHGOW AVE

MIDDLEPENNY RD

MIDDLEPENNY PL

DENNISTOUN RD

Sch

2 GLENCAIRN RD

1

PO

Langbank

SPRUCEBANK AVE

BEECHWOOD AVE

STATION RD

MAIN RD

A8

1 LEVEN RD
2 HELENSLEE RD

ELMBANK RD

ELM GR

DOUGLAS AVE

SEATH AVE

73

The Grange

Eastbank House

East Langbank

Ferryhill Plantation

OLD GREENOCK RD

Undercraig

Undercraig

Gleddoch House Hotel

CH

Gleddoch Burn

3

Golf Course

Netherton

Gleddoch Plantation

72

PA14

Ravenshaw

North Glen Farm

Barscube Hill

2

Gled Craig

Drums Cottage

71

Dargavel Burn

Barscube

Park Glen

PA13

PA6

Parkglen Wood

Whinny Hill

Mid Glen

1

WEST GLEN RD

Yetston

Craig Muir

West Glen Farm

Elphinstone Wood

Corsliehills Wood

Haddockston

70

37   A   38   B   39   C

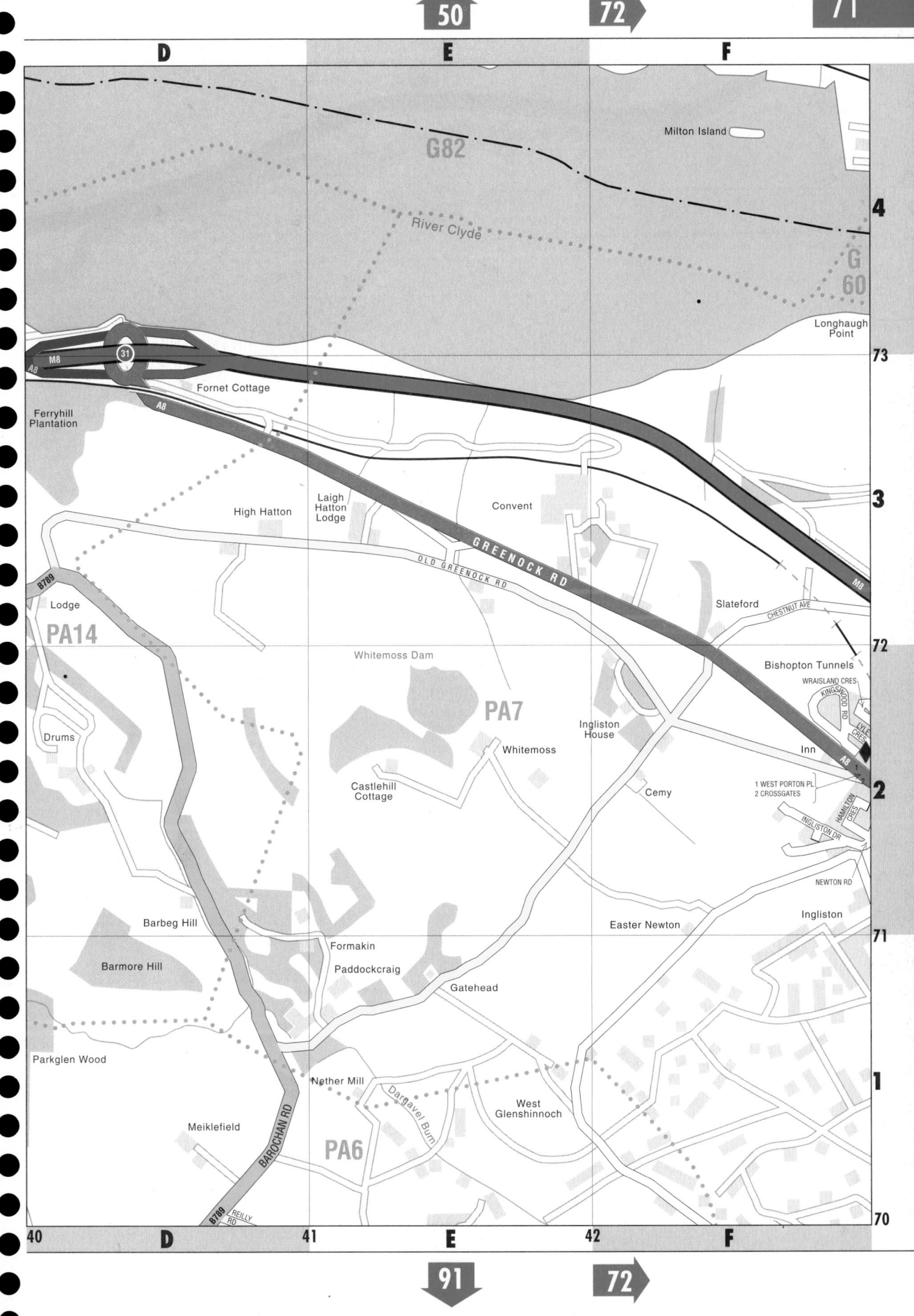

D
E
F

G82

Milton Island

River Clyde

4

G 60

Longhaugh Point

73

M8
31
A8

Fornet Cottage

Ferryhill Plantation

A8

Laigh Hatton Lodge

High Hatton

Convent

GREENOCK RD

OLD GREENOCK RD

3

M8

Slateford

CHESTNUT AVE

B789

Lodge

PA14

72

Bishopton Tunnels

WRAISLAND CRES

Whitemoss Dam

KINGSWOOD RD

LYLE CRES

Drums

PA7

Ingliston House

Inn

A8

Whitemoss

1 WEST PORTON PL
2 CROSSGATES

HAMILTON CRES

2

Castlehill Cottage

Cemy

INGLISTON DR

NEWTON RD

Barbeg Hill

Easter Newton

Ingliston

71

Barmore Hill

Formakin

Paddockcraig

Gatehead

Parkglen Wood

1

Nether Mill

Dargavel Burn

West Glenshinnoch

BAROCHAN RD

Meiklefield

PA6

B789
REILLY RD

70

40
D
41
E
42
F

71
51

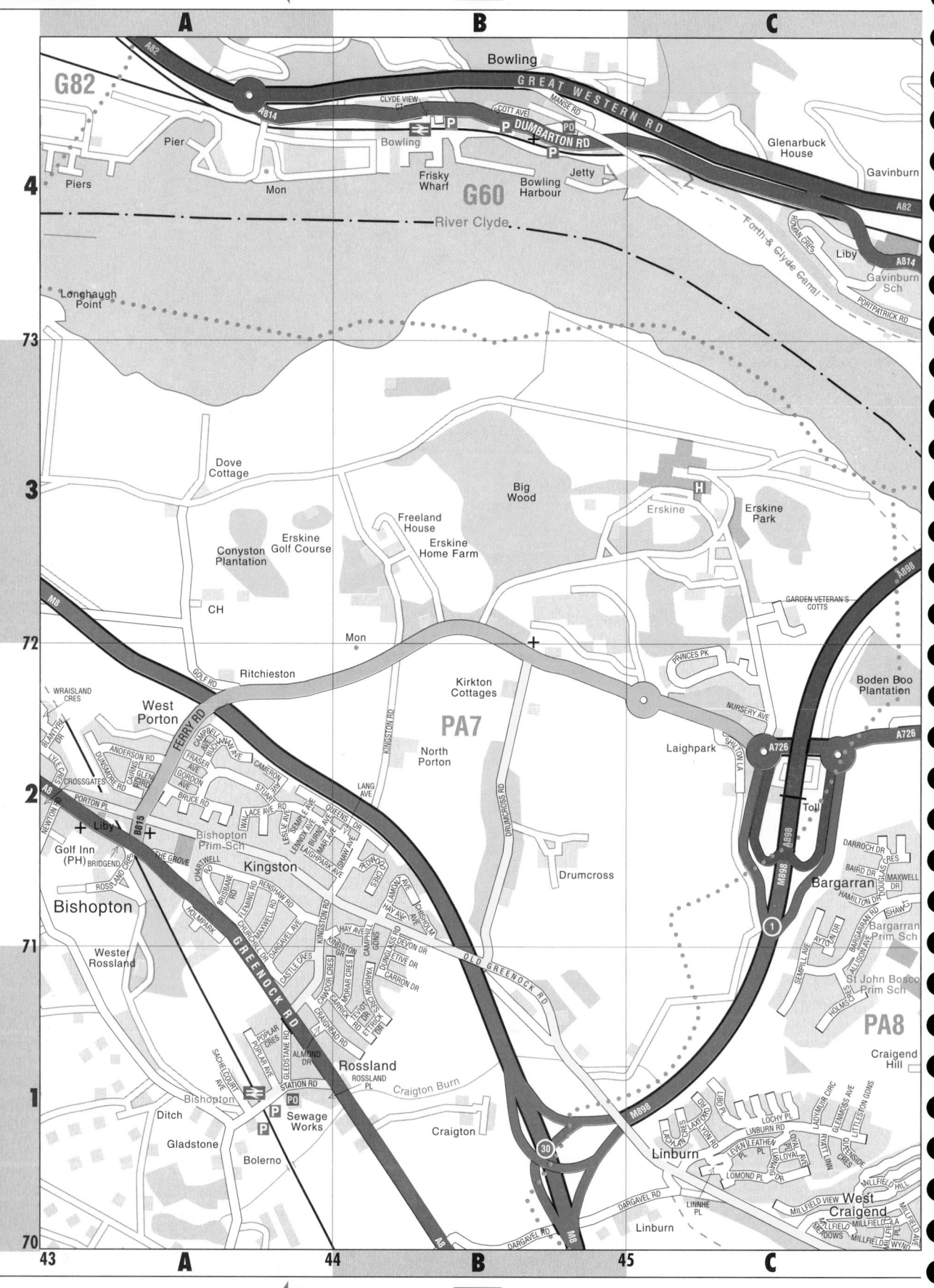
A
B
C
Bowling
GREAT WESTERN RD
G82
A82
A814
CLYDE VIEW CT
COTT AVE
MANSE RD
DUMBARTON RD
PO
Pier
Bowling
Glenarbuck House
Gavinburn
Piers
Mon
Frisky Wharf
G60
Bowling Harbour
Jetty
River Clyde
Forth & Clyde Canal
ROMAN CRES
Liby
Gavinburn Sch
PORTPATRICK RD
Longhaugh Point
Dove Cottage
Big Wood
Erskine
Erskine Park
Freeland House
Erskine Home Farm
Conyston Plantation
Erskine Golf Course
M8
A898
GARDEN VETERAN'S COTTS
CH
Mon
PRINCES PK
Boden Boo Plantation
GOLF RD
Ritchieston
Kirkton Cottages
WRAISLAND CRES
West Porton
PA7
NURSERY AVE
Laighpark
A726
SHILTON LA
FERRY RD
KINGSTON RD
North Porton
ANDERSON RD
CAMPBELL AVE
BUCHANAN AVE
CAMERON AVE
FRASER AVE
GLEN RD
GORDON AVE
CAIRNS RD
DUNSMORE RD
CROSSGATES
LYLE CRES
BLANTYRE DR
STUART DR
BRUCE RD
LANG AVE
DRUMCROSS RD
Toll
PORTON PL
NEWTON RD
Liby
B815
WALLACE AVE
LESLIE AVE
SEMPLE AVE
LENNOX AVE
BURNS AVE
MAR AVE
QUEENS DR
SHAW AVE
LAIGHPARK AVE
EDWARD CRES
Bishopton Prim Sch
THE GROVE
Kingston
Drumcross
DARROCH DR
BAIRD DR
DOUGLAS CRES
MAXWELL DR
Golf Inn (PH)
BRIDGEND
ROSS
LAND CRES
CHARTWELL RD
BRISBANE RD
FLEMING RD
RENSHAW RD
MAXWELL RD
LAMONT AVE
CHISHOLM AVE
HAY AVE
M898
Bargarran
HAMILTON DR
Bishopton
HOLMPARK
KINGSTON GR
CAMPHILL GDNS
DUNGLASS RD
DEVON DR
ETIVE DR
CARRON DR
CHURCHILL DR
DARGAVEL AVE
CASTLE CRES
BARGARRAN RD
AYTON DR
SHAW CRES
Bargarran Prim Sch
Wester Rossland
GREENOCK RD
OLD GREENOCK RD
SEMPILL AVE
ALLISON AVE
St John Bosco Prim Sch
HOLMS CRES
CAMOOR CRES
MORAR CRES
YARROW CRES
CARRICK RD
TEVIOT DR
ETTRICK DR
CRAIGHEAD RD
PA8
POPLAR CRES
POPLAR AVE
GLEDSTANE RD
ALMOND DR
Rossland
Craigend Hill
SACHELCOURT AVE
STATION RD
ROSSLAND PL
Craigton Burn
LIBO PL
LOCHY PL
LADYMUIR CIRC
GLENMOSS AVE
LITTLESTON GDNS
Bishopton
PO
Ditch
Sewage Works
Craigton
M898
LAGHAN CRES
LAXFORD RD
LYON RD
LINBURN RD
LEVEN PL
LEATHEN PL
LOYAL AVE
RYATT LINN
RISLEDE DR
FENSIDE CRES
Gladstone
Linburn
LOMOND PL
MILLFIELD HILL
Bolerno
DARGAVEL RD
LINNHE PL
MILLFIELD VIEW
West Craigend
MILLFIELD MEADOWS
MILLFIELD LA
MILLFIELD PL
MILLFIELD AVE
MILLFIELD WYND
Linburn
DARGAVEL RD
A8
4
73
3
72
2
71
1
70
43
44
45

71
92

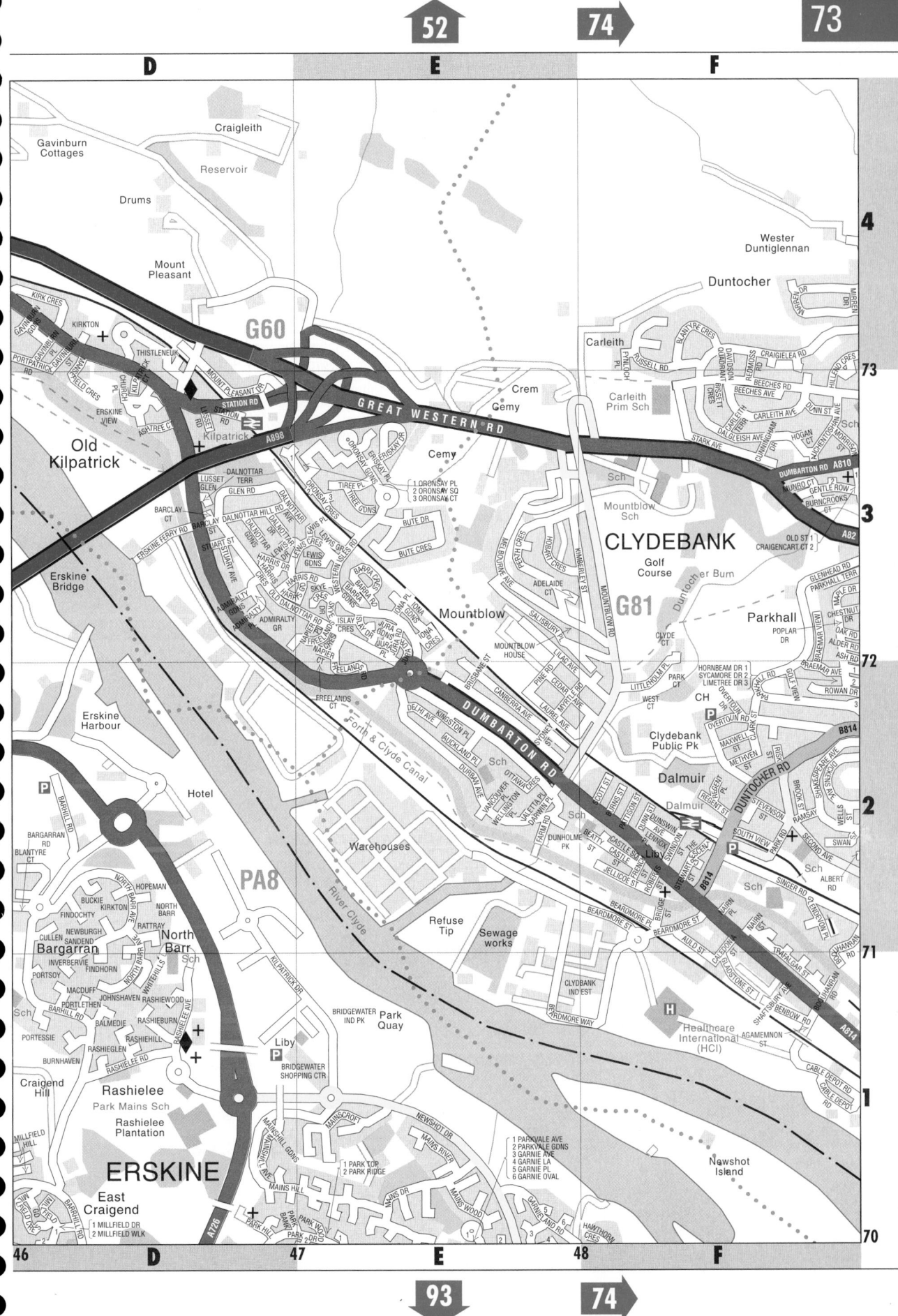
52
74
D
E
F
Craigleith
Gavinburn Cottages
Reservoir
Drums
Mount Pleasant
Wester Duntiglennan
Duntocher
G60
Carleith
Carleith Prim Sch
Crem
Cemy
GREAT WESTERN RD
Old Kilpatrick
Kilpatrick
KIRKTON
THISTLENEUK
ERSKINE VIEW
STATION RD
A898
Cemy
CLYDEBANK
Golf Course
Mountblow Sch
DUMBARTON RD
A810
A82
Erskine Bridge
Mountblow
G81
Parkhall
MOUNTBLOW HOUSE
Erskine Harbour
DUMBARTON RD
Forth & Clyde Canal
Clydebank Public Pk
Dalmuir
DUNTOCHER RD
B814
Hotel
Warehouses
PA8
River Clyde
Refuse Tip
Sewage works
Bargarran
North Barr
CLYDBANK IND EST
Healthcare International (HCI)
BRIDGEWATER IND PK
Park Quay
Liby
BRIDGEWATER SHOPPING CTR
Craigend Hill
Rashielee
Park Mains Sch
Rashielee Plantation
ERSKINE
East Craigend
Newshot Island
A726
A814
46
47
48
70
71
72
73
1
2
3
4
93
74

A B C

Cochno Filters
Whitehill
Law
Golf Course

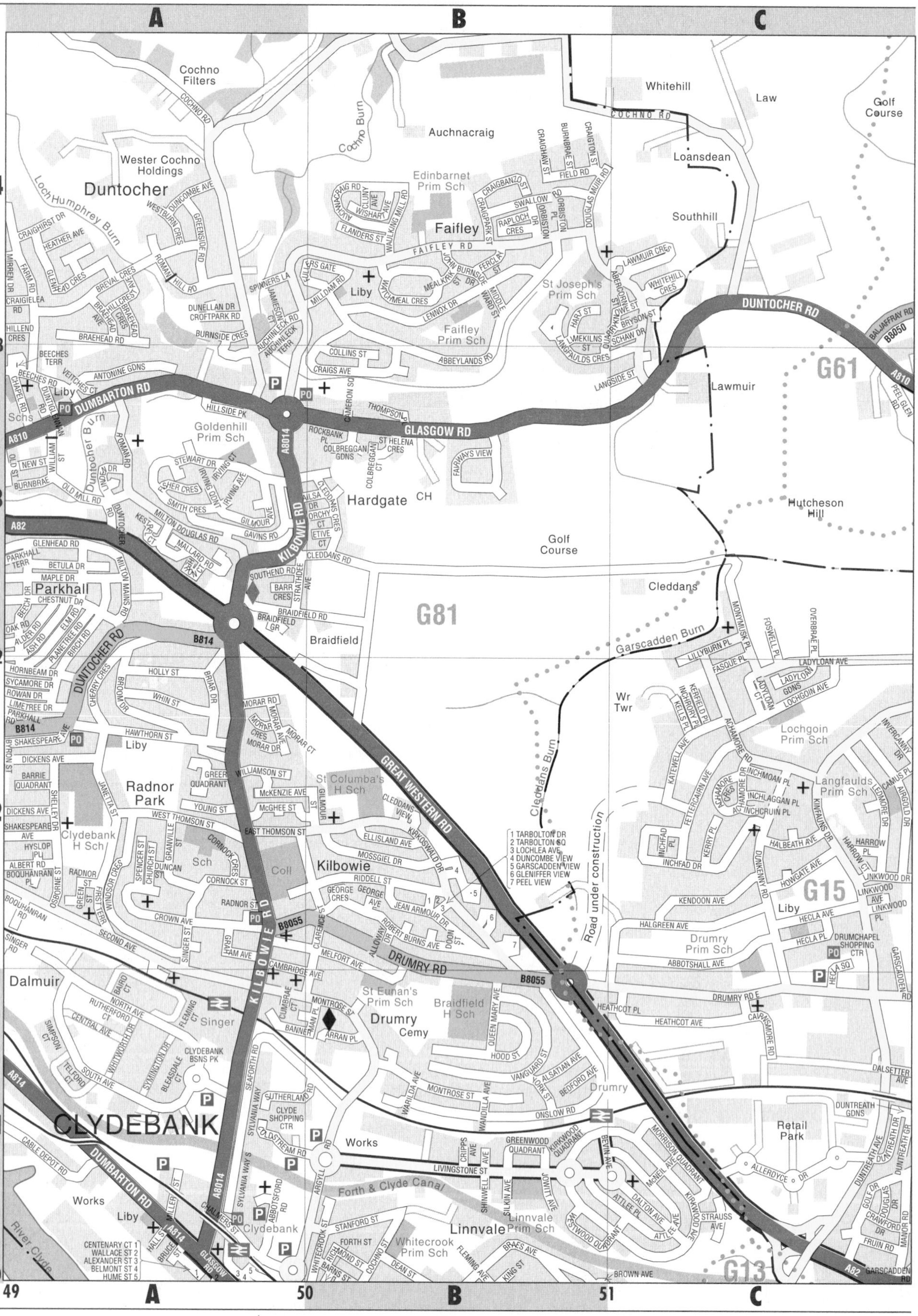

Wester Cochno Holdings
Duntocher
Auchnacraig
Edinbarnet Prim Sch
Faifley
Loansdean
Southhill

73

DUNTOCHER RD
G61

Liby
Schs
DUMBARTON RD
A810
St Joseph's Prim Sch
Lawmuir

Goldenhill Prim Sch
GLASGOW RD
Hardgate
CH
Golf Course
Hutcheson Hill

3

A82
Parkhall
KILBOWIE RD
Cleddans
G81
Garscadden Burn

72

DUNTOCHER RD
B814
Braidfield
Wr Twr
Lochgoin Prim Sch
Langfaulds Prim Sch

Radnor Park
Clydebank H Sch
St Columba's H Sch
Kilbowie
GREAT WESTERN RD

1 TARBOLTON DR
2 TARBOLTON SQ
3 LOCHLEA AVE
4 DUNCOMBE VIEW
5 GARSCADDEN VIEW
6 GLENIFFER VIEW
7 PEEL VIEW

G15
Liby
Drumry Prim Sch
DRUMCHAPEL SHOPPING CTR

2

DRUMRY RD
B8055
Drumry

71

Dalmuir
Singer
St Eunan's Prim Sch
Drumry Cemy
Braidfield H Sch
Drumry

A814
CLYDEBANK
CLYDEBANK BSNS PK
CLYDE SHOPPING CTR
Works
Retail Park

1

DUMBARTON RD
A814
Works
Liby
Clydebank
Forth & Clyde Canal
Linnvale
Whitecrook Prim Sch
Linnvale Prim Sch
G13
A82

CENTENARY CT 1
WALLACE ST 2
ALEXANDER ST 3
BELMONT ST 4
HUME ST 5

River Clyde

70

D E F

1 TORRIDON GDNS
2 KINNOUL GDNS
3 ALVA GDNS
4 CHEVIOT GDNS
5 LOUDON TERR
6 CAIRD TERR
7 THE POPLARS
8 MUIRHOUSE PK

Windyhill Golf Course
CH
Windyhill Cottage
FOREST DR
NASMYTH AVE
MOORFOOT WAY
ALSTON GDNS
MURRAY GR
GREENSIDE PL
RUTHERFORD AVE
CULLOCH RD
KILPATRICK DR
FINTRY GDNS
PATERSON PL
CROMALT CRES
A809
CRAIGDHU RD
B8050
PRESTONFIELD
Craigdhu Prim Sch
G62
KEYSTONE QUADRANT
BREADIE DR
Craigdhu Burn
DRUMLIN DR
GALBRAITH DR
ABERCROMBIE DR
BALJAFFRAY RD
Baljaffray Prim Sch
STOCKIEMUIR RD
LOCHNAGAR DR
CAIRNSMORE DR
LOYAL GDNS
CORREEN GDNS
FINNIEN GDNS
CLEISH AVE
KILBECK GDNS
MENTEITH GDNS
MERRICK GDNS
GRAMPIAN WAY
LOWTHER AVE
WYVIS AVE
LUBNAIG GDNS
ETTRICK DR
VORLICH GDNS
LAMMERMUIR GDNS
BURNCROOKS AVE
AUCHINEDEN CT
Hungry Hill
OCHIL RD
CRUACHAN RD
LEDI DR
PENTLAND PL
CRAIGMORE RD
NEVIS RD
SIDLAW RD
LAWERS DR
TINTO RD
BURNSIDE GATE
COLLEGE GATE
St Andrew's Coll
St Andrew's RC Prim Sch
CAIRNGORM CRES
BONNAUGHTON RD
KENILWORTH CRES
A810
DUNTOCHER RD
A809
COURTHILL
Court Hill
HEATHER AVE
DUMGOYNE DR
CAMPSIE DR
BAILIE DR
HAMILTON CRES
SUTHERLAND AVE
ATHOLL GDNS
ARGYLE RD
BRANDON DR
STOCKIEMUIR AVE
ROXBURGH DR
MONTROSE DR
TWEEDSMUIR CRES
QUEENSBERRY AVE
1 BUCCLEUCH DR
2 STOCKIEMUIR CT
3 AIRLIE AVE
4 HUNTLY DR
Mosshead Prim Sch
CROMARTY CRES
MAR DR
LOVAT AVE
ELGIN RD
SEAFIELD AVE
ROWAN DR
OAK AVE
MOSSHEAD RD
HAWTHORN AVE
NORTH GRANGE RD
KILMARDINNY DR
Kilmardinny Loch
MORVEN RD
EDGEHILL RD
SINCLAIR AVE
GARTCONNELL RD
ELM GDNS
ELM WLK
Bearsden Acad
KILMARDINNY GR
KILMARDINNY AVE
KILMARDINNY CRES
LENNOX DR
Castle Hill
CASTLEHILL RD
TIREE GDNS
LEWIS GDNS
IONA GDNS
SKYE GDNS
ROSSLYN RD
DRYBURGH RD
NITHSDALE CRES
WHITEHURST
Manse Burn
IAIN DR
IAIN RD
STIRLING DR
LAURENCE DR
SCHAW DR
SCHAW CT
GARTCONNELL DR
GARTCONNELL GDNS
RUSSELL DR
THOMSON DR
ANTONINE RD
ABBOTSFORD RD
NITHSDALE CRES
SCOTT DR
MILVERTON AVE
EAGLE CRES
FAIRWAY
PARK CRES
GOLFVIEW
SOUTHVIEW
WESTBOURNE CRES
G61
BALLAIG AVE
NORTH ERSKINE PK
SOUTH ERSKINE PK
BEARSDEN
RALSTON RD
Liby
JEDWORTH CT
KILMARDINNY GATE 1
HILLNEUK AVE 2
HILLFOOT AVE
HILLFOOT DR
HILLSIDE AVE
MANSE RD
CAMPBELL DR
Garscadden Burn
PEEL GLEN RD
Bearsden Golf Course
CH
WESTBOURNE DR
BAIRD DR
THORN DR
COLQUHOUN DR
KIRK RD
KIRK LA
KIRK PL
DOUGLAS PL
GRANGE RD
ROMAN RD
ROMAN AVE
MANSE AVE
UPPER GLENBURN RD
GLENBURN RD
NEW KIRK RD
ROMAN CT
A808
ROMAN RD
ROMAN DR
B8049
Garscadden Wood
Summerhill Prim Sch
THORN RD
Scotas Coll
DRYMEN RD
HORSESHOE RD
Fort
JUBILEE GDNS
DOUGLAS GDNS
BOCLAIR AVE
LADYLOAN AVE
KILCLOY AVE
SPRINGSIDE PL
BACKMUIR RD
SADDELL RD
Sch
DRUMMORE RD
SUMMERHILL RD
GROGARRY RD
BANKGLEN RD
SUMMERHILL PL
MANNOFIELD
CAMSTRADDEN DR W
CHESTERS RD
LEDCAMEROCH PK
WHITEHILL RD
COLLYLINN RD
LEDCAMEROCH RD
LEDCAMEROCH CRES
Sch
High Sch of Glasgow (Jun Sch)
Bearsden
ROSEVALE RD
WEST CHAPELTON CRES
GREENHEAD RD
WEST CHAPELTON DR
MILNGAVIE RD
INVERCANNY PL
G15
St Pius' Prim Sch
NORTHMUIR RD
Drummore Sch
STATION RD
CAMSTRADDEN DR E
ELLERGREEN RD
WEST CHAPELTON AVE
CHAPELTON GDNS
Drumchapel High Sch
INVERCANNY DR
1 ARDHU PL
CALLY AVE
BAYFIELD AVE
RYEDALE PL
RAYNE PL
SHERWOOD PL
PILTON RD
SUMMERHILL DR
PITMILLY RD
Pinewood Prim Sch
Colquhoun Park
ST GERMAINS
CHAPELTON LA
WEST CHAPELTON LA
HILLCREST RD
CARRICKARDEN RD
ENDRICK DR
FERGUSTON RD
LEVEN DR
SUMMERHILL GDNS
BARNKIRK AVE
BLACKCRAIG AVE
KINFAUNS DR
KINCLAVEN AVE
MERRYTON PL
MERRYTON AVE
JEDWORTH AVE
JEDWORTH RD
ROZELLE AVE
TALLANT TERR
TALLANT RD
GOYLE AVE
CONON AVE
TEITH DR
DOON CRES
TWEED DR
PENDICLE RD
PENDICLE CRES
LOCHEND CRES
LOCHEND RD
RUBISLAW DR
LOCHVIEW RD
St Germains Loch
LOCHSIDE
WHISTLEFIELD CT
NORWOOD PK
BEECHWOOD DR
BEECHWOOD LA
BEECHWOOD CT
A81
LINKWOOD DR
BAYFIELD TERR
INKWOOD CRES
Broadholm Prim Sch
Drumchapel
CAROLSIDE DR
ANNAN DR
LOCHEND DR
GRAY DR
MOORE DR
MILNGAVIE RD
SOUTHDEEN RD
SOUTHDEEN AVE
Colquhoun Park Prim Sch
CANNIESBURN RD
ELDERBANK
FERNLEA
Canniesburn
MACFARLANE RD 1
SECOND AVE 2
KILLERMONT RD 3
CANNIESBURN TOLL 4
A809
Garscadden Burn
CARRON CRES
ANNICK DR
FORTH RD
ESKDALE RD
ALLANDER RD
WHEATFIELD RD
DIRLETON GATE
DEEPDENE RD
HENDERLAND DR
Cairn Hill
MARYHILL RD
A739
SWITCHBACK RD
HOLLYMOUNT
GLENKIRK DR
Stonedyke Prim Sch
STONEDYKE GR
CLOAN AVE
KINGLAS RD
TEVIOT CRES
MONREITH AVE
STIRLING AVE
BRAEMAR CRES
LOMOND RD
BIRKHALL DR
BALLATER DR
CORONATION WAY
GARSCADDEN RD
BELSYDE AVE
ARCAN CRES
DIPPLE PL
ESSENSIDE AVE
FALLOCH RD
SPEY RD
DORNOCH RD
DEVERON RD
NORTH VIEW
Liby
WESTFIELD DR
BUTE CRES
DALSETTER AVE
BOON DR
DRUMCHAPEL GDNS
DRUMCHAPEL PL
DRUMCHAPEL RD
1 BLADNOCH DR
2 NORTH MORAINE LA
3 SOUTH MORAINE LA
Westerton Prim Sch
WESTFIELD CRES
ASCOG RD
DALSETTER PL
WHITEKIRK PL
Drumchapel
KIRKHOPE DR
STRAMRAER DR
MORAINE AVE
ALMOND RD
CRARAE AVE
KELVIN CRES
FIRDON CRES
KIRKVILLE
MONKTON DR
ROTHERWOOD LA
ORCHY CRES
MAXWELL AVE
CAIRNHILL RD
SWITCHBACK RD
GOLF DR
Drumchapel
ROTHERWOOD AVE
Forth & Clyde Canal
Westerton
MURRAYFIELD DR
RAVELSTON RD
SOMERFORD RD
GOWANLEA AVE
CRAWFORD DR
GARSCADDEN RD
SUNNYSIDE PL
SUNNYSIDE DR
KINIVER DR
MORAINE DR
MORAINE CIR
BANNER DR
BANNER RD
TOWERHILL RD
GLAIVE RD
CURFEW RD
CLOBERHILL RD
LARCHFIELD RD
WARDLAW RD
KINELLAN RD
MORAINE PL
GORGET PL
GORGET QUADRANT
Blairdardie Prim Sch
BLAIRDARDIE RD
GORGET AVE
G13
MACE RD
KNIGHTSWOOD RD
MONKSBRIDGE AVE
HERALD AVE
PALMER AVE
FRIARSCOURT AVE
BALDWIN AVE
CRUSADER AVE
MINSTREL RD
TEMPLAR AVE
ROWENA AVE
ROTHERWOOD AVE
WYVIL AVE
AVENEL RD
GLENDINNING RD
HENDERLAND RD
Old Drumchapel
BALVIE AVE
ROMAN AVE
KAYSTONE RD
KEARN PL
KEARN AVE
Blairdardie
GORGET QUADRANT
St Ninian's Prim Sch
TRINLEY RD
TURRET RD
ASHBY CRES
1 WAMBA AVE
A739
A82
GREAT WESTERN RD
A82

4
73
3
72
2
71
1
70

52 D 53 E 54 F

95
76

75
55

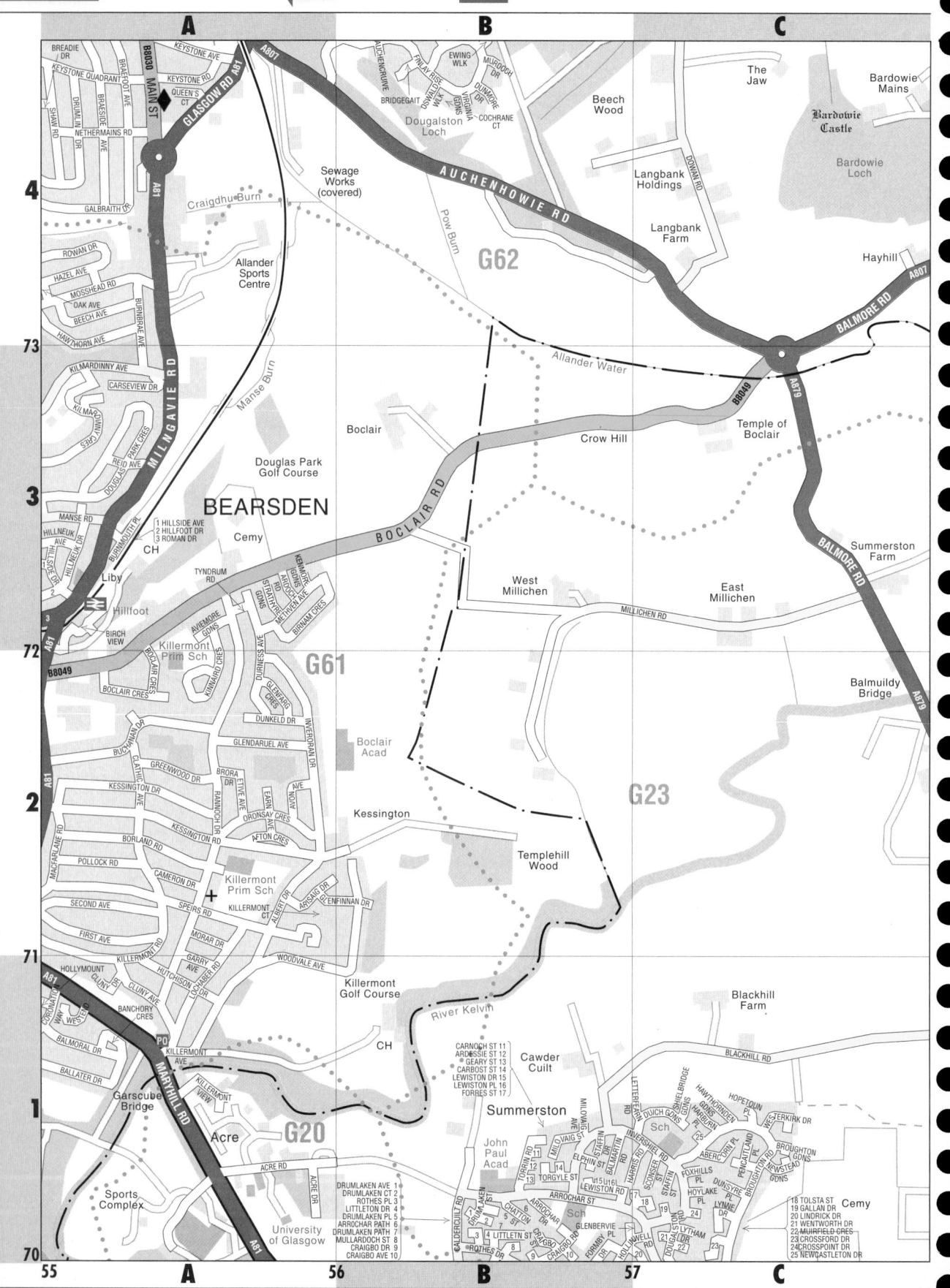
A
B
C
4
73
3
72
2
71
1
70
55
56
57
BEARSDEN
Summerston
Acre
G62
G61
G23
G20
A807
A81
B8030
MAIN ST
GLASGOW RD
MILNGAVIE RD
AUCHENHOWIE RD
BALMORE RD
A879
B8049
BOCLAIR RD
MILLICHEN RD
BLACKHILL RD
MARYHILL RD
ACRE RD
Dougalston Loch
Sewage Works (covered)
Beech Wood
The Jaw
Bardowie Mains
Bardowie Castle
Bardowie Loch
Langbank Holdings
Langbank Farm
Hayhill
Craigdhu Burn
Pow Burn
Allander Sports Centre
Allander Water
Manse Burn
Boclair
Crow Hill
Temple of Boclair
Douglas Park Golf Course
Cemy
CH
Liby
Hillfoot
West Millichen
East Millichen
Summerston Farm
Killermont Prim Sch
Balmuildy Bridge
Boclair Acad
Kessington
Templehill Wood
Killermont Golf Course
River Kelvin
Blackhill Farm
Cawder Cuilt
John Paul Acad
Sch
Garscube Bridge
Sports Complex
University of Glasgow
1 HILLSIDE AVE
2 HILLFOOT DR
3 ROMAN DR
CARNOCH ST 11
ARDESSIE ST 12
GEARY ST 13
CARBOST ST 14
LEWISTON DR 15
LEWISTON PL 16
FORRES ST 17
DRUMLAKEN AVE 1
DRUMLAKEN CT 2
ROTHES PL 3
LITTLETON DR 4
DRUMLAKEN PL 5
ARROCHAR PATH 6
DRUMLAKEN PATH 7
MULLARDOCH ST 8
CRAIGBO DR 9
CRAIGBO AVE 10
18 TOLSTA ST
19 GALLAN DR
20 LINDRICK DR
21 WENTWORTH DR
22 MUIRFIELD CRES
23 CROSSFORD DR
24 CROSSPOINT DR
25 NEWCASTLETON DR

75
96

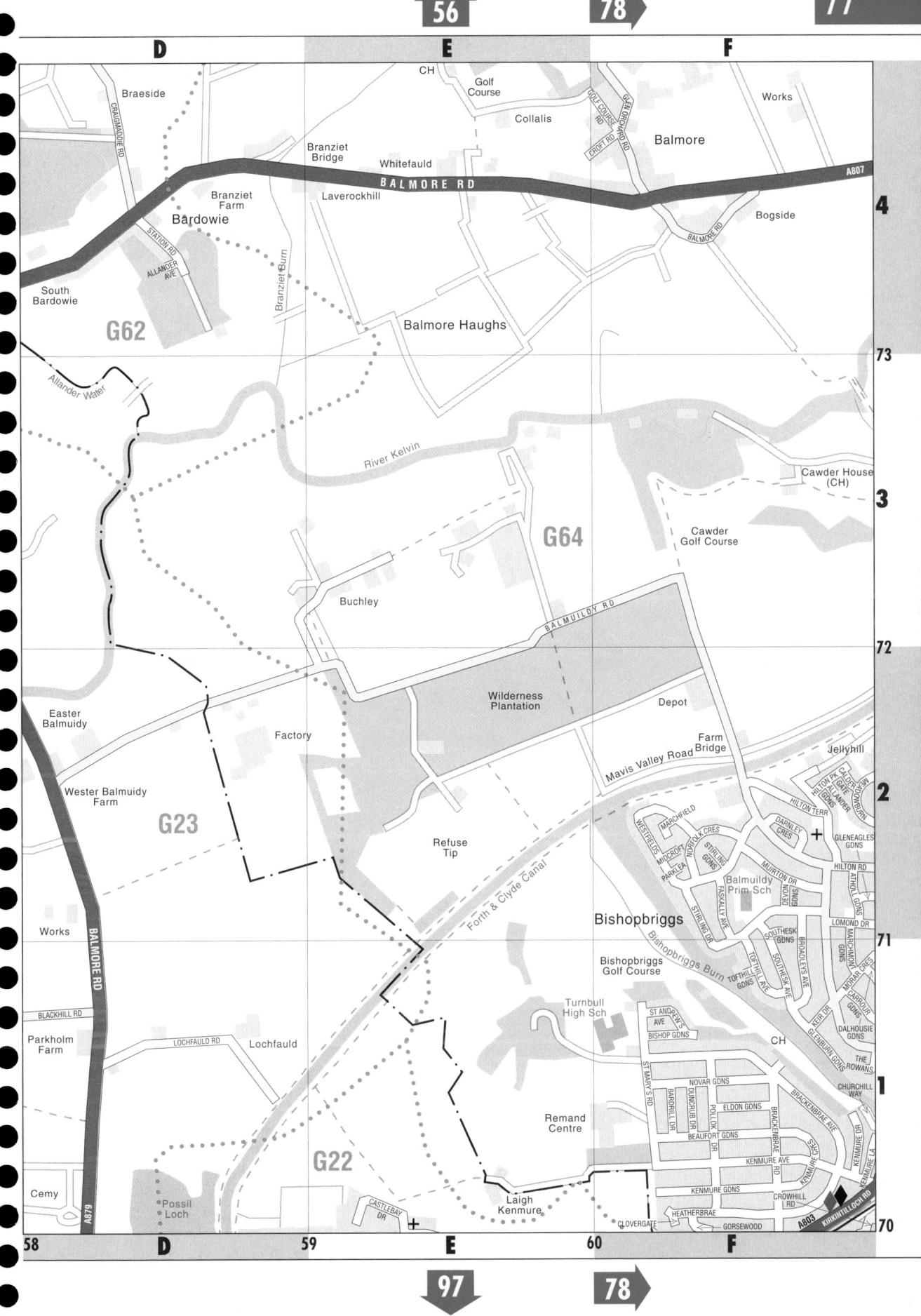

D
E
F

CH
Golf Course
Collalis
Works
Balmore
Braeside
Branziet Bridge
Whitefauld
BALMORE RD
A807
Branziet Farm
Laverockhill
Bardowie
Bogside
BALMORE RD
South Bardowie
4
ALLANDER AVE
STATION RD
CRAGMADDIE RD

G62
Branziet Burn
Balmore Haughs
73

Allander Water
River Kelvin
Cawder House (CH)
3

G64
Cawder Golf Course

Buchley
BALMUILDY RD
72

Wilderness Plantation
Depot
Easter Balmuidy
Factory
Farm Bridge
Jellyhill

Mavis Valley Road
HILTON PK
CALDER
GRAEME
HILTON
ALLANDER
COLQUHOUN
HILTON TERR
2
Wester Balmuidy Farm
MARGHFIELD
WESTFIELDS
MIDCROFT
PARKLEA
NORFOLK CRES
STIRLING GDNS
MURTON DR
DARNLEY CRES
GLENEAGLES GDNS
FASKALLY AVE
Balmuildy Prim Sch
HILTON RD
ATHOL GDNS

G23
Refuse Tip
SOUTHESK GDNS
STIRLING DR
BROADLEYS AVE
MORAR GDNS
LOMOND DR
MARCHMONT GDNS
CAERHUR GDNS
71
Works
Bishopbriggs
Bishopbriggs Burn
SOUTHESK AVE
TOFTHILL AVE
TOFTHILL GDNS
SOUTHESK AVE
KEIR DR
GLENBURN GDNS
MORAR CRES
DALHOUSIE GDNS
THE ROWANS
BLACKHILL RD
Bishopbriggs Golf Course
Turnbull High Sch
CH
Parkholm Farm
LOCHFAULD RD
Lochfauld
ST ANDREWS AVE
BISHOP GDNS
BRACKENBRAE AVE
CHURCHILL WAY
1
BALMORE RD
A879
Remand Centre
ST MARY'S RD
NOVAR GDNS
DUNCRUB DR
ELDON GDNS
POLLOK DR
BEAUFORT DR
BRACKENBRAE RD
KENMURE DR
BARDRILL DR

G22
Cemy
KENMURE AVE
CROWHILL RD
KENMURE LA
Possil Loch
CASTLEBAY DR
Laigh Kenmure
KENMURE GDNS
HEATHERBRAE
CLOVERGATE
GORSEWOOD
A803 KIRKINTILLOCH RD
70

Forth & Clyde Canal

58
D
59
E
60
F

Map Labels

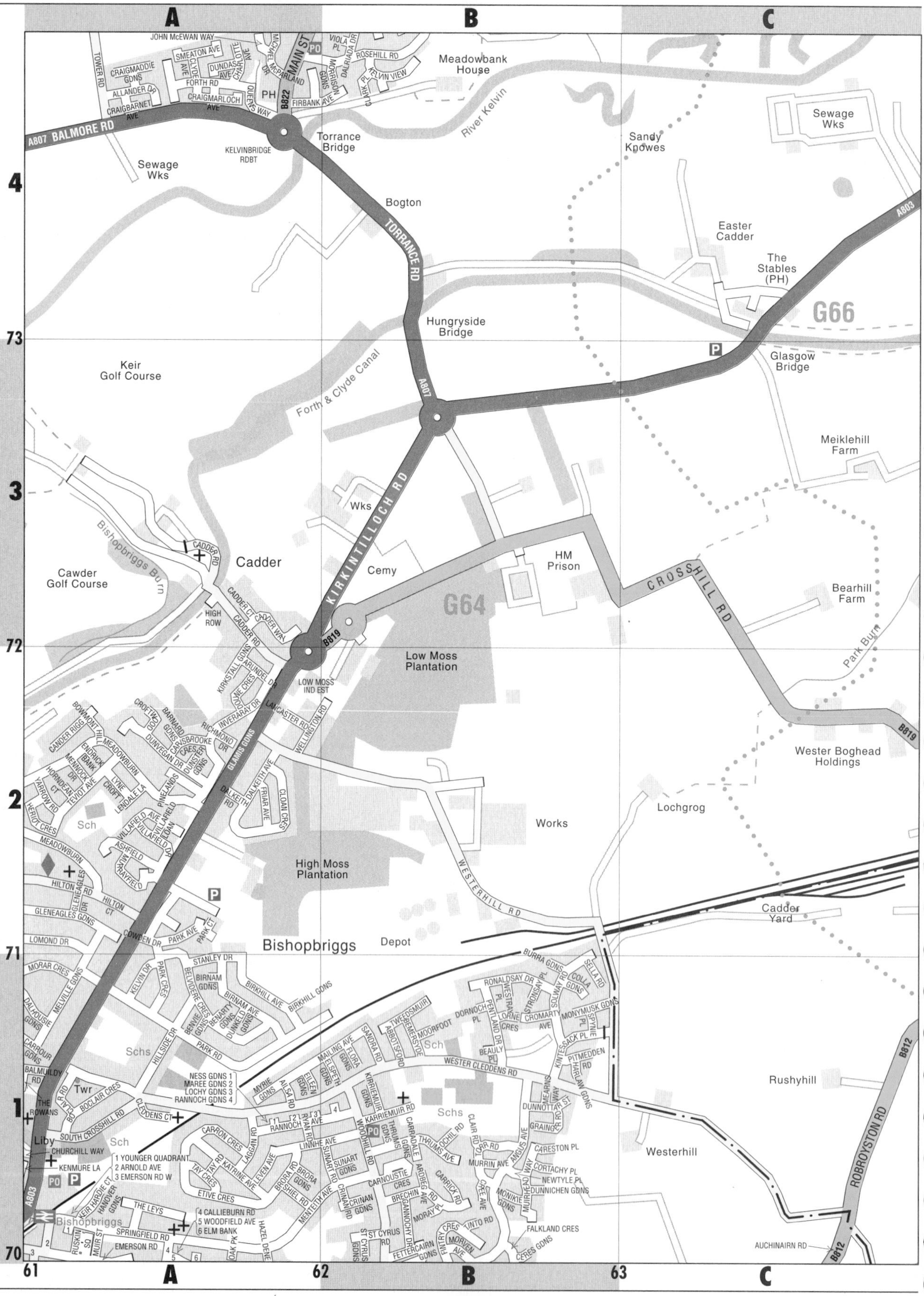

A   **B**   **C**

JOHN McEWAN WAY
SMEATON AVE
CRAIGMADDIE GDNS
TOWER RD
ALLANDER
CRAIGBARNET
CRAIGMARLOCH AVE
CLYDE AVE
DUNDASS AVE
FORTH RD
QUEEN'S WAY
MAIN ST
PO
VIOLA PL
ROSEHILL RD
KELVIN VIEW
FIRBANK AVE
PH
B822

A807 BALMORE RD
KELVINBRIDGE RDBT
Torrance Bridge
Torrance
Bridge

Sewage Wks

Meadowbank House

River Kelvin

Sandy Knowes

Sewage Wks

Bogton

TORRANCE RD

Easter Cadder

The Stables (PH)

A803

G66

4

Keir Golf Course

Hungryside Bridge

Forth & Clyde Canal

A807

P

Glasgow Bridge

73

Meiklehill Farm

Bishopbriggs Burn

Wks

KIRKINTILLOCH RD

Cawder Golf Course

Cadder

CADDER

Cemy

HM Prison

CROSS HILL RD

Bearhill Farm

Park Burn

3

HIGH ROW
CADDER CT
CADDER WYN
CADDER RD
KIRKSTALL GDNS
ARUNDEL DR
INVERARAY DR
LANCASTER RD
WELLINGTON RD
GLAMIS GDNS

G64

Low Moss Plantation

LOW MOSS IND EST

B819

72

B819

Wester Boghead Holdings

BOWMONT HILL
MEADOWBURN
CANDER RIGG
EMERICK
MENNOCK
HORNBEAL DR
CROFTWOOD GDNS
BARNARD GDNS
CRANSBROOKE CRES
DUNTIGLENNAN DR
RICHMOND DR
CROFT RD
LYLE
LENDALE LA
HILLSIDE
VILLAFIELD
DALKEITH RD
DALKEITH AVE
FRIAR AVE
CLONA CRES

Lochgrog

2

Sch
YARROW CT
HEROD CRES
PINE LEAS
PLAYFIEL
HILTON RD
HILTON CT
GLENEAGLES GDNS
LOMOND DR
COWDEN DR
PARK AVE
PARK CT

High Moss Plantation

WESTERHILL RD

Works

Cadder Yard

MORAR CRES
KELVIN DR
BELVIDERE CRES
STANLEY DR
BIRNAM
BIRKHILL AVE
BIRNAM AVE
BIRKHILL GDNS

Depot

BURRA GDNS
RONALDSAY DR
DORNOCH PL
WESTRAY CRES
PORTLAND PL
COLL A
SELLA RD
GIGHA
MONYMUSK GDNS

Bishopbriggs

Rushyhill

B812

ROBROYSTON RD

71

DALHOUSIE GDNS
MELVILLE GDNS
CARROUR GDNS
BALMULDY RD
PARK CRES
HILLSIDE DR
Schs
PARK RD

MAILING AVE
MYRIE GDNS
ALSA RD
EILEEN
LEITH
SANDRA RD
ABBOTSFORD
TWEEDSMUIR
LOCH
WESTER CLODDENS RD
CROMARTY
BEAULY
Sch

CLAIR RD
MEARNS
DUNNOTTAR ST
GRAINGE
PITMEDDEN RD
HARLAW GDNS
KINTESSACK PL
NEWTYLE PL

Westerhill

B812

1

THE ROWANS
BOCLAIR CRES
SOUTH CROSSHILL RD
CLODDENS CT
Sch

NESS GDNS 1
MAREE GDNS 2
LOCHY GDNS 3
RANNOCH GDNS 4

CARRON CRES
KATRINE AVE
LEVEN DR
TAY CRES
BRORA
BRISBIE RD
SUNART GDNS
LINNHE AVE
KIRRIEMUIR RD
WOODHILL RD

CARRADALE
THRUMS AVE
ARDBEG AVE
CARNOUSTIE CRES
MURRIN AVE
CORTACHY PL
CREE AVE
MOIKE RD
DUNNICHEN GDNS

CARESTON PL

FALKLAND CRES

A803

Liby
CHURCHILL WAY
KENMURE LA
PO

1 YOUNGER QUADRANT
2 ARNOLD AVE
3 EMERSON RD W

4 CALLIEBURN RD
5 WOODFIELD AVE
6 ELM BANK

THE LEYS
RUSKIN
MUIR ST
KEIR HARDIE CT
HANOVER
SPRINGFIELD RD
EMERSON RD
OAK PK
HAZEL DENE
MENTIETH AVE
ETIVE CRES
CRINAN GDNS
BRANNOCHY
ST CYRUS RD
MORAY PL
BRECHIN RD
CARRICK RD
CEYRES GDNS
FETTERCAIRN
FINTRY
MORVEN AVE
AUCHINAIRN RD

≋ Bishopbriggs

70

61   **A**   **62**   **B**   **63**   **C**

D
E
F

Hayston
Westermains
Townhead
Barleybank
Hillhead
Oxgang
Oxgang Bridge
KIRKINTILLOCH
The Greens
Holy Family Prim Sch
High Gallowhill
Lenzie Acad
Lenzie Moss Prim Sch
Lenzie
Lenzie Prim Sch
Langbrae Sch
Boghead
G66
Millersneuk
Claddens
Claddens Smallholdings
Woodilee
Cult Burn
Gadloch
Gadloch Farm
Lenzie Golf Course
Easter Auchinloch
Auchinloch
Parkhillhead
Wester Auchinloch
Auchinloch Prim Sch
North Broomknowes
South Broomknowes
Cardyke Plantation
G64
Forth & Clyde Canal
Works
Canal Feeder
CROSSHILL RD
ROBROYSTON RD
STEPPS RD
KIRKINTILLOCH RD
AUCHINLOCH RD
LENZIE RD
LINDSAYBEG RD
WATERSIDE RD
NEW LAIRDSLAND RD
GLASGOW RD

64 65 66
70 71 72 73

99
80

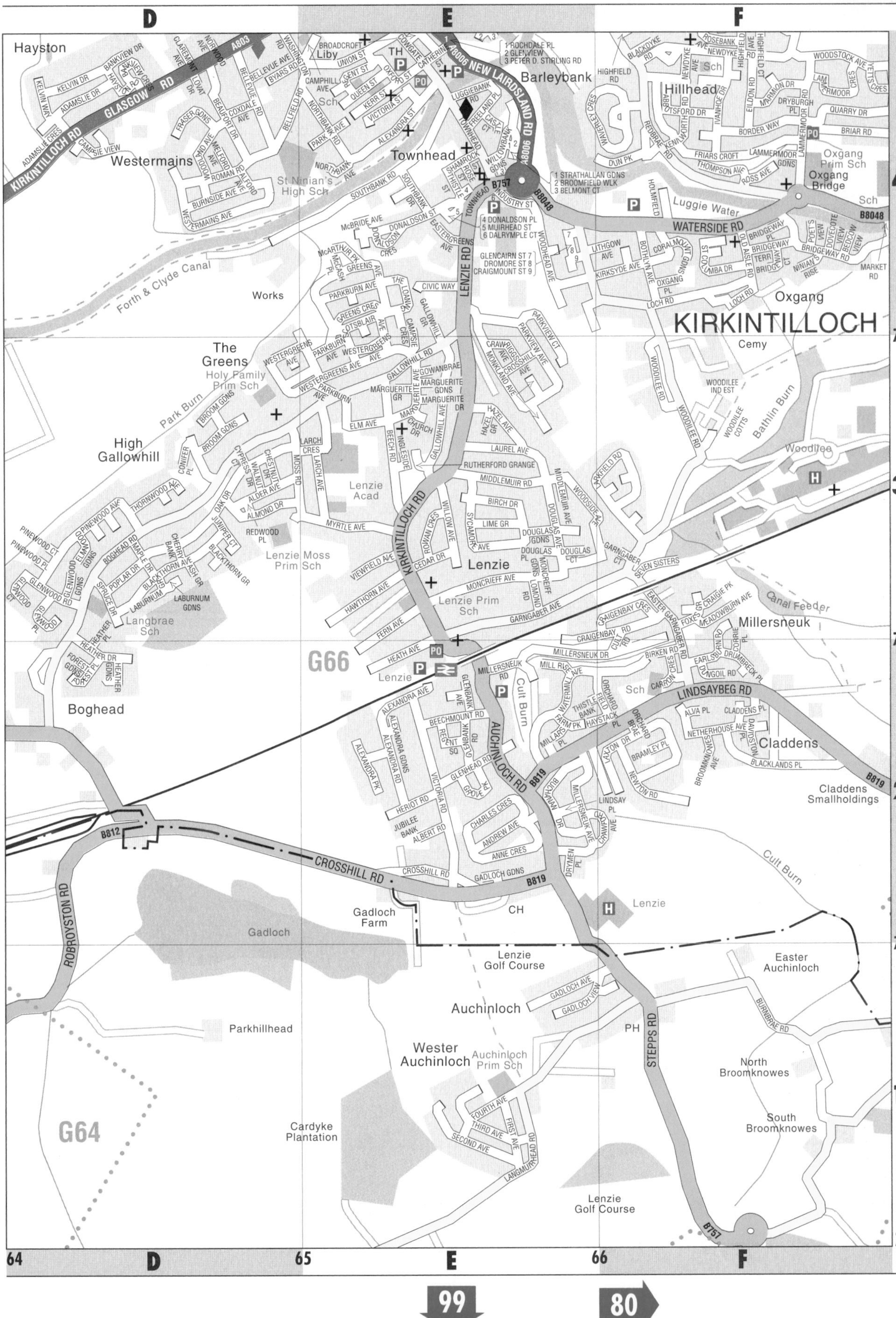

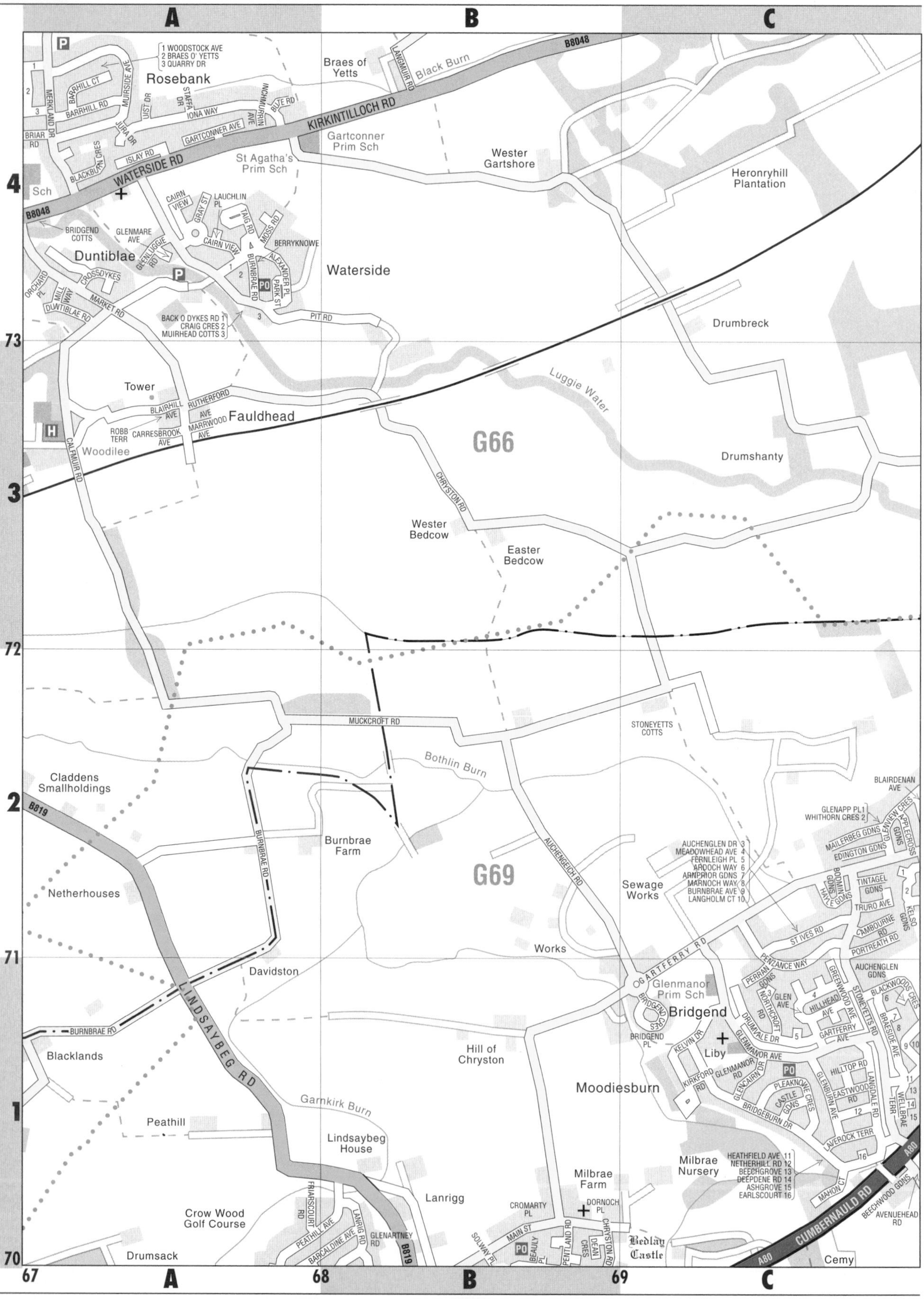

79 59

A **B** **C**

P

1 WOODSTOCK AVE
2 BRAES O' YETTS
3 QUARRY DR

Rosebank

Braes of Yetts

Black Burn

B8048

MUIRSIDE AVE
MERKLAND DR
BARRHILL CT
BARRHILL RD
BRIAR RD
BLACKBRAES CRES
JURA DR
IONA WAY
STAFFA DR
INCHMURRIN AVE
BUTE RD
GARTCONNER AVE
LANGMUIR RD
ISLAY RD

KIRKINTILLOCH RD

Gartconner
Prim Sch

Wester
Gartshore

Heronryhill
Plantation

4 WATERSIDE RD

Sch

B8048

St Agatha's
Prim Sch

CAIRN VIEW
GRAY ST
LAUCHLIN PL
TAIG RD
MOSS RD
Berryknowe

BRIDGEND
COTTS

GLENMARE
AVE

GEILLUGGIE RD

Duntiblae

CAIRN VIEW

Waterside

Drumbreck

ORCHARD PL
MILL WAY
DUNTIBLAE RD
CROSSOYKES
MARKET RD

P

BACK O DYKES RD 1
CRAIG CRES 2
MUIRHEAD COTTS 3

ALEXANDER PL
PARK ST
PO
BURNBRAE RD

PIT RD

73

Tower

BLAIRHILL AVE
RUTHERFORD AVE
MARRWOOD AVE
ROBB TERR
CARRESBROOK AVE

Fauldhead

Luggie Water

G66

Drumshanty

H

CALMUIR RD

Woodilee

CHRYSTON RD

3

Wester
Bedcow

Easter
Bedcow

72

MUCKCROFT RD

Bothlin Burn

STONEYETTS
COTTS

BLAIRDENAN
AVE

Claddens
Smallholdings

BURNBRAE RD

Burnbrae
Farm

AUCHENGLOCH RD

G69

Sewage
Works

GLENAPP PL 1
WHITHORN CRES 2

GLENVIEW CRES
APPLECROSS

MAILERBEG GDNS
EDINGTON GDNS

2 B819

Netherhouses

AUCHENGLEN DR 3
MEADOWHEAD AVE 4
FERNLEIGH PL 5
WARDOCH WAY 6
ARNPRIOR GDNS 7
MARNOCH WAY 8
BURNBRAE AVE 9
LANGHOLM CT 10

BODMIN GDNS
HAY GDNS
TINTAGEL GDNS
TRURO AVE

KELSO GDNS

CAMBOURNE AVE
PORTREATH RD
ST IVES RD

Works

Davidston

GARTFERRY RD

Glenmanor
Prim Sch

BRIDGEND RD
BRIDGEND PL

Bridgend

PENZANCE WAY
PERRAN GDNS
GLEN AVE
GREENWOOD DR
GREENHILL AVE
GARTFERRY AVE
NORTHCROFT RD
DRUMDALE DR
HILLHEAD AVE
MOUNTHERRICK DR

AUCHENGLEN
GDNS

BRAESIDE AVE
BLACKWOODS CRES
WELLBRAE TERR

71 LINDSAYBEG RD

BURNBRAE RD

Blacklands

Hill of
Chryston

Moodiesburn

KELVIN DR
KIRKFORD RD
GLENMANOR RD
GLENMANOR AVE
Liby
GLENCAIRN RD
CASTLE CRES
PLEAKNOWE CRES
BRIDGEBURN DR
PO
HILLTOP RD
EASTWOODGAIL RD
GLENBURN AVE
HILLTOP RD

1

Peathill

Garnkirk Burn

Lindsaybeg
House

Lanrigg

Milbrae
Farm

Milbrae
Nursery

LAVEROCK TERR

HEATHFIELD AVE 11
NETHERHILL RD 12
BEECHGROVE 13
DEEPDENE RD 14
ASHGROVE 15
EARLSCOURT 16

MAHON CT
CUMBERNAULD RD
BEECHWOOD GDNS
AVENUEHEAD RD

Crow Wood
Golf Course

FRIARSCOURT RD
PEATHILL AVE
BARCALDINE AVE
LANRIG RD
B819
GLENARTNEY RD

CROMARTY PL
DORNOCH PL
MAIN ST
SOLWAY PL
BEAULY PL
PENTLAND RD
CHRYSTON RD
DEAN CRES

Bedlay
Castle

A80

70 Drumsack

67 **A** **68** **B** **69** **C**

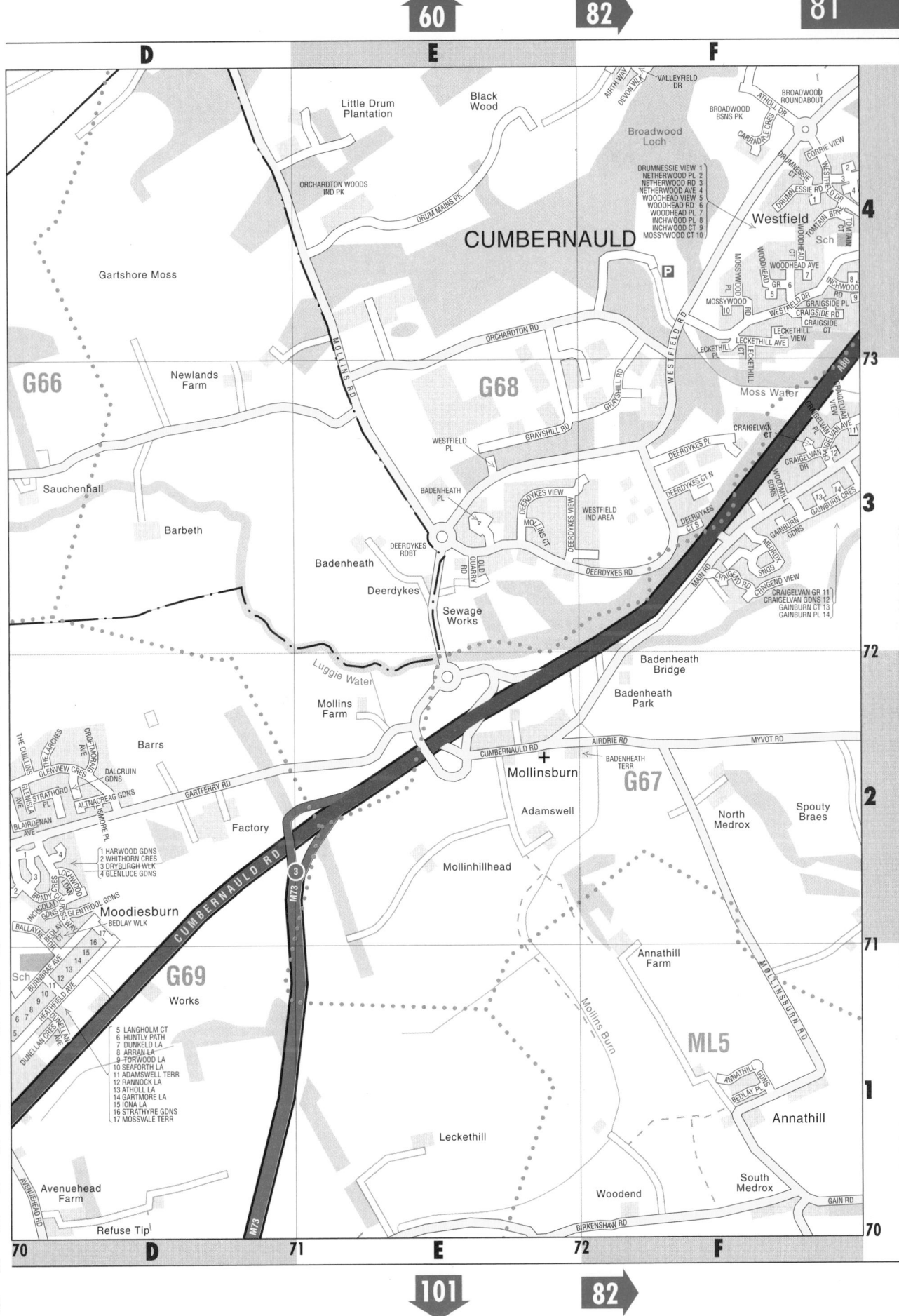

D   E   F

VALLEYFIELD DR
AIRTH WAY
DEVON WLK
BROADWOOD ROUNDABOUT
BROADWOOD BSNS PK
ATHOLL DR
CARTADALE CRES
CORRIE VIEW
Broadwood Loch
DRUMNESSIE RD
DRUMNESSIE DR
WESTFIELD DR
TOMTAIN BRAE
TOMTAIN CT

DRUMNESSIE VIEW 1
NETHERWOOD PL 2
NETHERWOOD RD 3
NETHERWOOD AVE 4
WOODHEAD VIEW 5
WOODHEAD RD 6
WOODHEAD PL 7
INCHWOOD PL 8
INCHWOOD CT 9
MOSSYWOOD CT 10

Little Drum Plantation

Black Wood

ORCHARDTON WOODS IND PK

DRUM MAIRS PK

CUMBERNAULD

Westfield Sch

MOSSYWOOD PL
MOSSYWOOD RD
WOODHEAD AVE
GR
WESTFIELD DR
GRAIGSIDE PL
CRAIGSIDE RD
CRAIGSIDE CT
LECKETHILL VIEW
INCHWOOD RD

4

P

ORCHARDTON RD

LECKETHILL PL
LECKETHILL AVE
LECKETHILL CT

G66   Gartshore Moss   Newlands Farm   G68   WESTFIELD RD   Moss Water   73

A80
CRAIGVALE VIEW

Sauchenhall   WESTFIELD PL   GRAYSHILL RD   DEERDYKES PL   CRAIGELVAN CT   CRAIGELVAN DR   CRAIGELVAN AVE

Barbeth   BADENHEATH PL   DEERDYKES VIEW   DEERDYKES VIEW   WESTFIELD IND AREA   MOLLINS CT   DEERDYKES CT N   CRAIGELVAN DR   WOODMILL GDNS   GAINBURN CRES   3

Badenheath   DEERDYKES RDBT   OLD QUARRY RD   DEERDYKES CT S   MAIN RD   CRAIGEND RD   MCGREGOR RD   GAINBURN GDNS   73 74

Deerdykes   DEERDYKES RD   CRAIGEND RD   CRYNGEND VIEW
CRAIGELVAN GR 11
CRAIGELVAN GDNS 12
GAINBURN CT 13
GAINBURN PL 14

Sewage Works

Luggie Water   Badenheath Bridge   72

Mollins Farm   Badenheath Park

The Challins   Barrs   MYVOT RD
CROFTMORAIG AVE
GLENVIEW CRES
DALCRUIN GDNS   CUMBERNAULD RD   AIRDRIE RD   BADENHEATH TERR   G67   Spouty Braes   2
GLENSLICA AVE
STRATHORD PL
ALTNACREAG GDNS   GARTFERRY RD   Mollinsburn   North Medrox
BLAIRDENAN AVE

BLAIRDENAN AVE   Factory   Adamswell
1 HARWOOD GDNS
2 WHITHORN CRES
3 DRYBURGH WLK
4 GLENLUCE GDNS
BRADY CRES
INCHCOLM PL
GLENTROOL GDNS   CUMBERNAULD RD   MT3   Mollinhillhead
LOCH LOMOND CRES   3
BALLAYNE

Moodiesburn
BEDLAY WLK   71
Sch
BURNBRAE AVE
HEATHFIELD AVE   G69   Annathill Farm
DUNELLAN CRES
DUNELLAN AVE   Works   5 LANGHOLM CT
6 HUNTLY PATH
7 DUNKELD LA
8 ARRAN LA
9 TORWOOD LA
10 SEAFORTH LA
11 ADAMSWELL TERR
12 RANNOCK LA
13 ATHOLL LA
14 GARTMORE LA
15 IONA LA
16 STRATHYRE GDNS
17 MOSSVALE TERR   Mollins Burn   ML5
BEDLAY PL   1

Leckethill   Annathill

Avenuehead Farm   South Medrox
AVENUEHEAD RD   Woodend   GAIN RD
Refuse Tip   BIRKENSHAW RD   70

70   D   71   E   72   F

81
61

A
B
C
CUMBERNAULD
St Maurices High Sch
G68
Low Wood
NORTH RD
GLASGOW RD
CONDORRAT INTERCHANGE
AUCHENKILNS ROUNDABOUT
St Francis of Assisi Prim Sch
Condorrat Prim Sch
Greenfields High Sch
Ravenswood Prim Sch
Melrose Prim Sch
St Helen's Prim Sch
Liby
MAIN RD
Condorrat
CONDORRAT RING RD
Dalshannan
Nursery
Auchenkilns Holdings
North Myvot
Luggie Water
Greenfaulds
LANGLANDS-SEAFAR INTERCHANGE
JANE'S BRAE
JANE'S BRAE INTERCHANGE
Garngibboch House
Wester Blairlinn
BLAIRLINN IND EST
G67
MYVOT RD
Madgiscroft Quarry
Milncroft
SPAIRDRUM RD
South Myvot
Craigend Nursery
Wester Myvot
WESTER MYVOT RD
North Bellstane Plantation
Hallbrae
Gain Burn
Loanhead
SUMMERHILL AND GARNGIBBOCH RD
CONDORRAT RD
Summerhill
Summerhill Strips
Shank Burn
ML6
Shank Bridge
Bellstane
Summerfield
Mossywood
GAIN AND SHANKBURN RD
The Grain
CULLOCHRIG RD
South Bellstane Plantation
ML5
Gain Farm
Cleddans
Douglas Glen
Douglas Plantation
GAIN RD
ML6
73
74
75
4
3
2
1
70
72
71

81
102

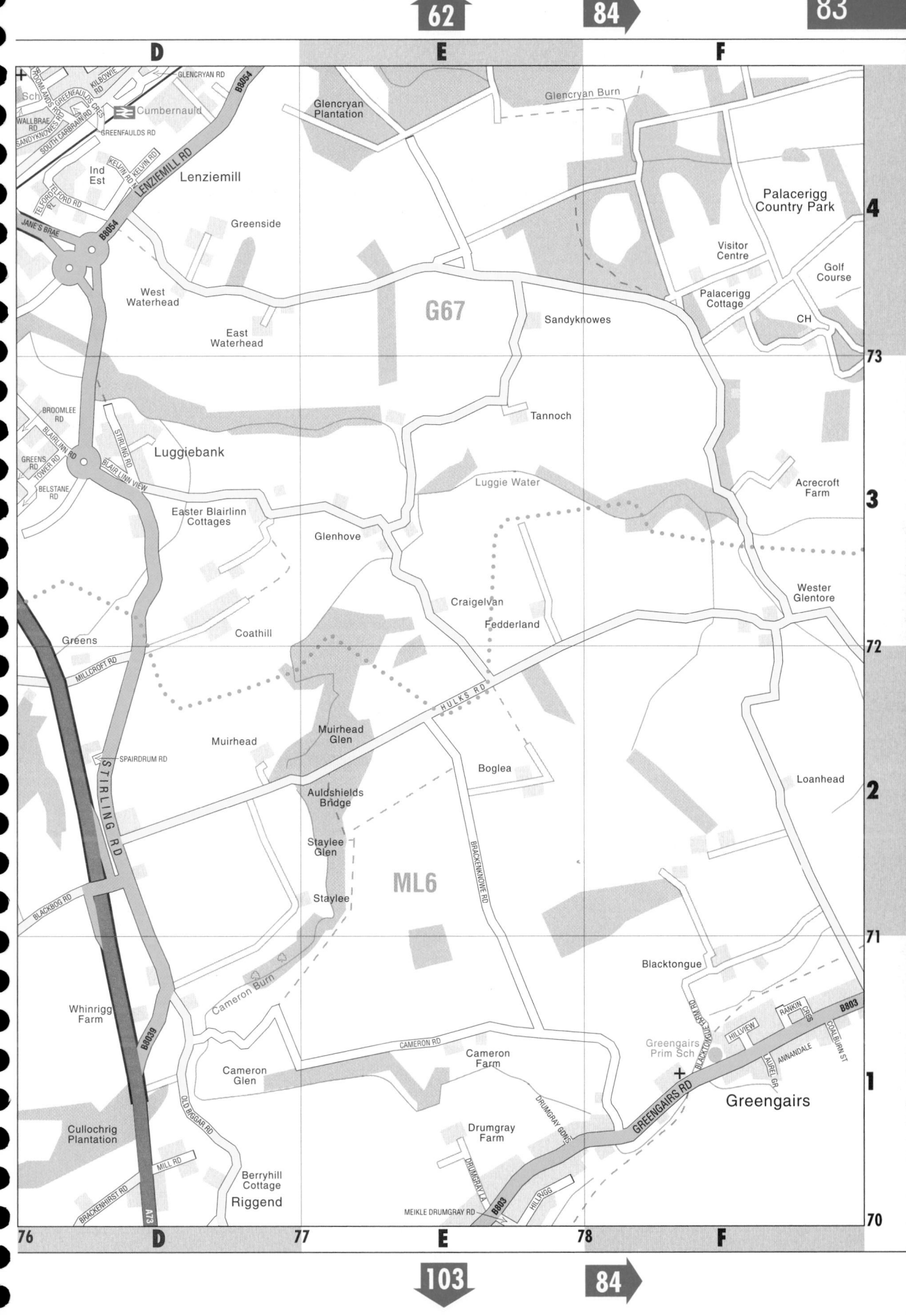

62
84
D
E
F
Glencryan Plantation
Glencryan Burn
Cumbernauld
GLENCRYAN RD
B8054
GREENFAULDS RD
LENZIEMILL RD
Lenziemill
Ind Est
Greenside
Palacerigg Country Park
Visitor Centre
Golf Course
Palacerigg Cottage
CH
West Waterhead
East Waterhead
G67
Sandyknowes
Tannoch
Luggiebank
STIRLING RD
BLAIR LINN VIEW
Luggie Water
Acrecroft Farm
Easter Blairlinn Cottages
Glenhove
Wester Glentore
Craigelvan
Fedderland
Coathill
Greens
MILLCROFT RD
HULKS RD
Muirhead
Muirhead Glen
SPAIRDRUM RD
Boglea
Loanhead
Auldshields Bridge
Staylee Glen
ML6
BRACKENKNOWE RD
Staylee
BLACKBOG RD
Blacktongue
Cameron Burn
Whinrigg Farm
B8039
CAMERON RD
Cameron Farm
Cameron Glen
Greengairs Prim Sch
GREENGAIRS RD
B803
Greengairs
Cullochrig Plantation
OLD BIGGAR RD
DRUMGRAY GDNS
Drumgray Farm
MILL RD
Berryhill Cottage
Riggend
BRACKENHIRST RD
A73
MEIKLE DRUMGRAY RD
76
77
78
4
73
3
72
2
71
1
70
103
84

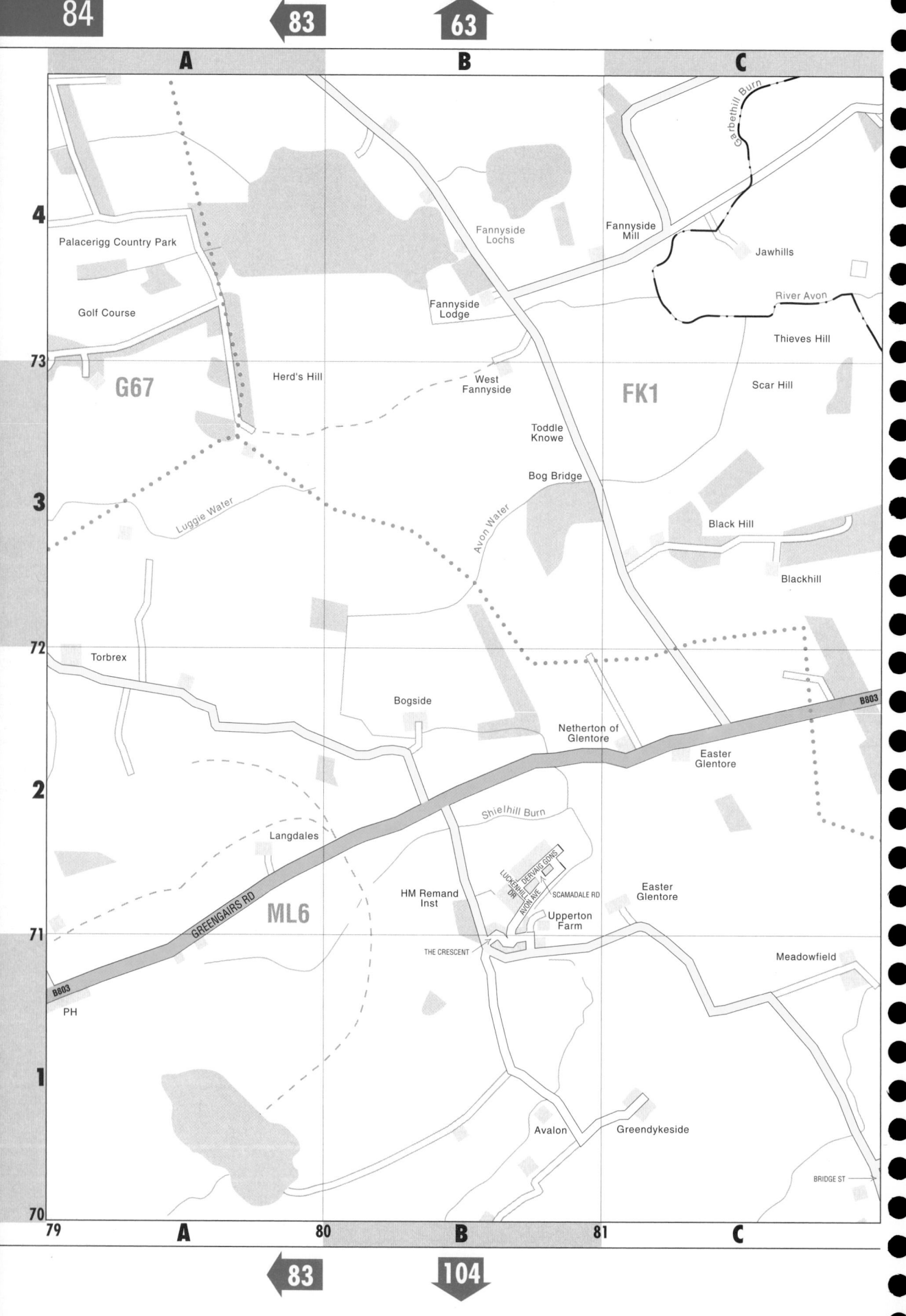

A
B
C

4

Palacerigg Country Park

Fannyside Lochs

Fannyside Mill

Jawhills

River Avon

Golf Course

Fannyside Lodge

Thieves Hill

73

G67

Herd's Hill

West Fannyside

FK1

Scar Hill

Toddle Knowe

Bog Bridge

3

Luggie Water

Avon Water

Black Hill

Blackhill

72

Torbrex

Bogside

Netherton of Glentore

Easter Glentore

B803

2

Shielhill Burn

DERVAIG GDNS

LUCKENHILL DR

AVON AVE

SCAMADALE RD

Easter Glentore

Langdales

HM Remand Inst

Upperton Farm

GREENGAIRS RD

ML6

71

B803

THE CRESCENT

Meadowfield

PH

1

Avalon

Greendykeside

BRIDGE ST

70

79
A
80
B
81
C

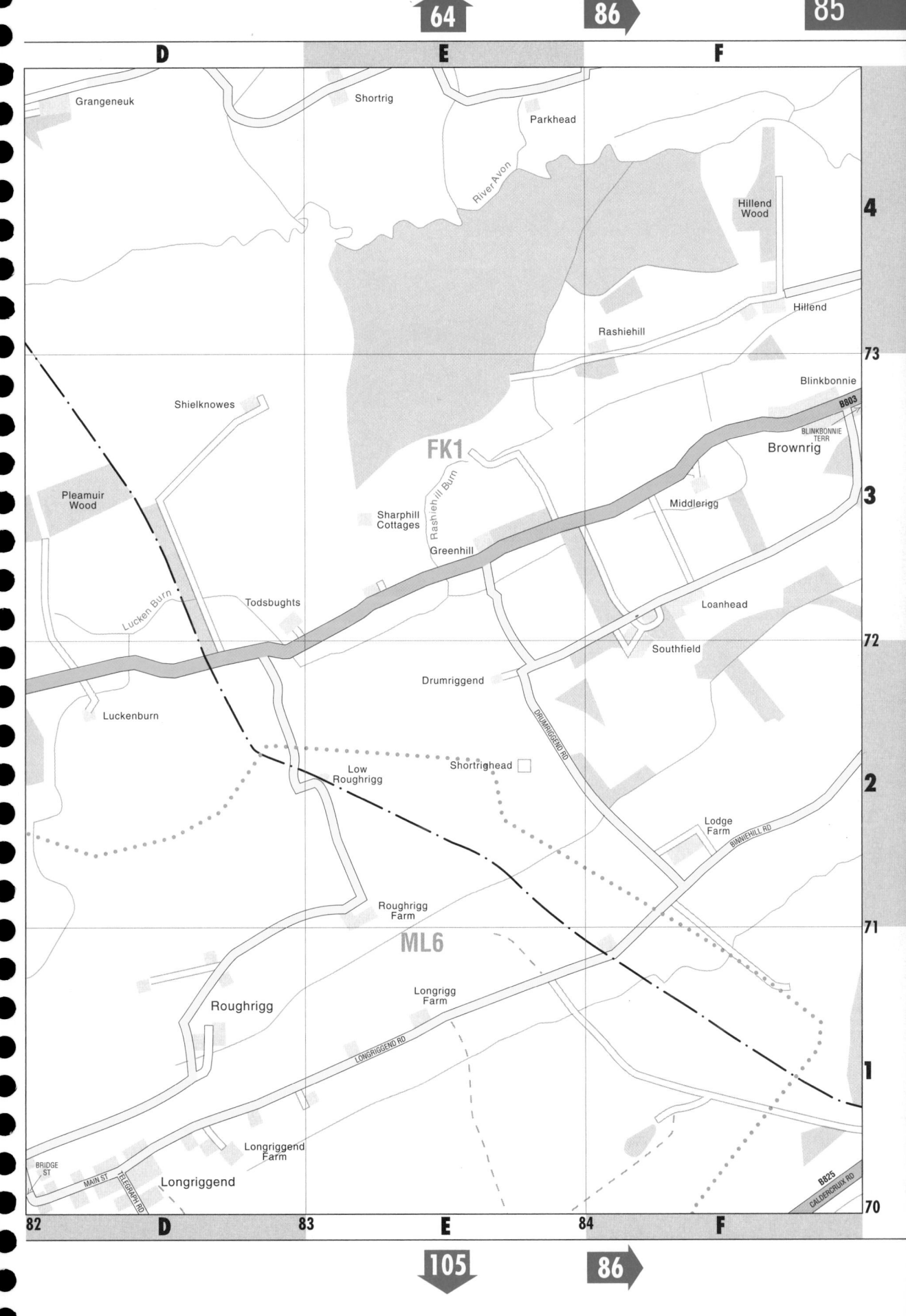
64
86
D
E
F
Grangeneuk
Shortrig
Parkhead
River Avon
Hillend Wood
Hillend
Rashiehill
Blinkbonnie
B803
BLINKBONNIE TERR
Brownrig
Shielknowes
FK1
Rashiehill Burn
Middlerigg
Pleamuir Wood
Sharphill Cottages
Greenhill
Lucken Burn
Todsbughts
Loanhead
Southfield
Drumriggend
Luckenburn
DRUMRIGGEND RD
Low Roughrigg
Shortrighead
Lodge Farm
BINNIEHILL RD
Roughrigg Farm
ML6
Roughrigg
Longrigg Farm
LONGRIGGEND RD
Longriggend Farm
BRIDGE ST
MAIN ST
TELEGRAPH RD
Longriggend
B825
CALDERCRUIX RD
4
73
3
72
2
71
1
70
82
83
84
105
86

85
65

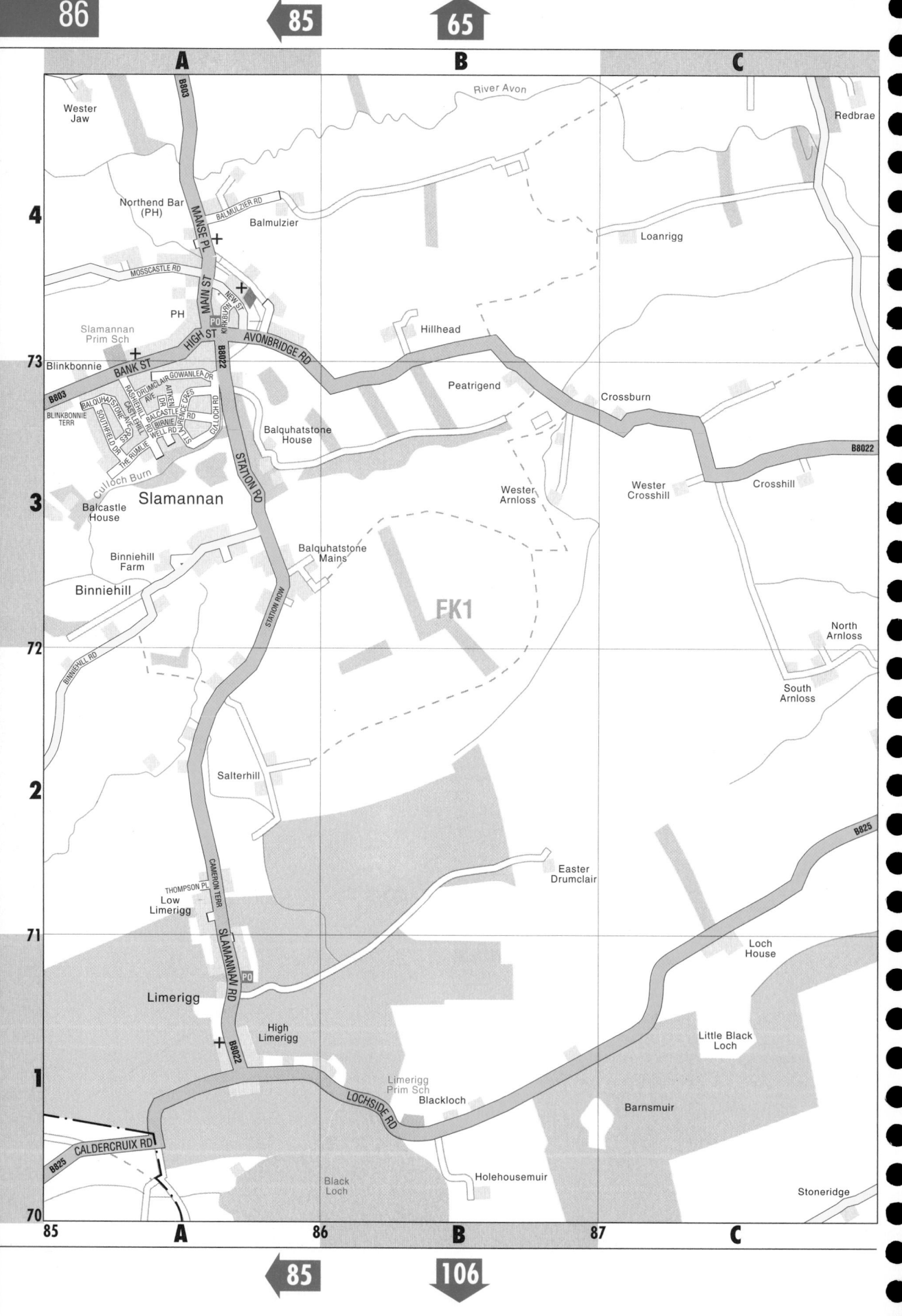
A
B
C
4
73
72
3
2
71
1
70
85
86
87
Wester Jaw
River Avon
Redbrae
B803
Northend Bar (PH)
MANSE PL
BALMULZIER RD
Balmulzier
Loanrigg
MOSSCASTLE RD
MAIN ST
NEW ST
KIRKBURN
PH
PO
Slamannan Prim Sch
HIGH ST
AVONBRIDGE RD
Hillhead
Blinkbonnie
BANK ST
B8022
GOWANLEA DR
DRUMCLAIR AVE
Peatrigend
Crossburn
BLINKBONNIE TERR
BALQUHATSTONE CRES
SOUTHFIELD DR
CASTLEHILL AVE
RASHIEHILL RD
AITKEN DR
BALCASTLE RD
BIRNIE
WELL RD
ST LAURENCE CRES
CULLOCH RD
THE RUMLIE
Balquhatstone House
B8022
Culloch Burn
STATION RD
Wester Arnloss
Wester Crosshill
Crosshill
Slamannan
Balcastle House
Binniehill Farm
Balquhatstone Mains
Binniehill
STATION ROW
FK1
North Arnloss
BINNIEHILL RD
South Arnloss
Salterhill
B825
Easter Drumclair
THOMPSON PL
CAMERON TERR
Low Limerigg
SLAMANNAN RD
PO
Loch House
Limerigg
High Limerigg
B8022
Little Black Loch
Limerigg Prim Sch
Blackloch
LOCHSIDE RD
Barnsmuir
CALDERCRUIX RD
B825
Holehousemuir
Black Loch
Stoneridge

85
106

66

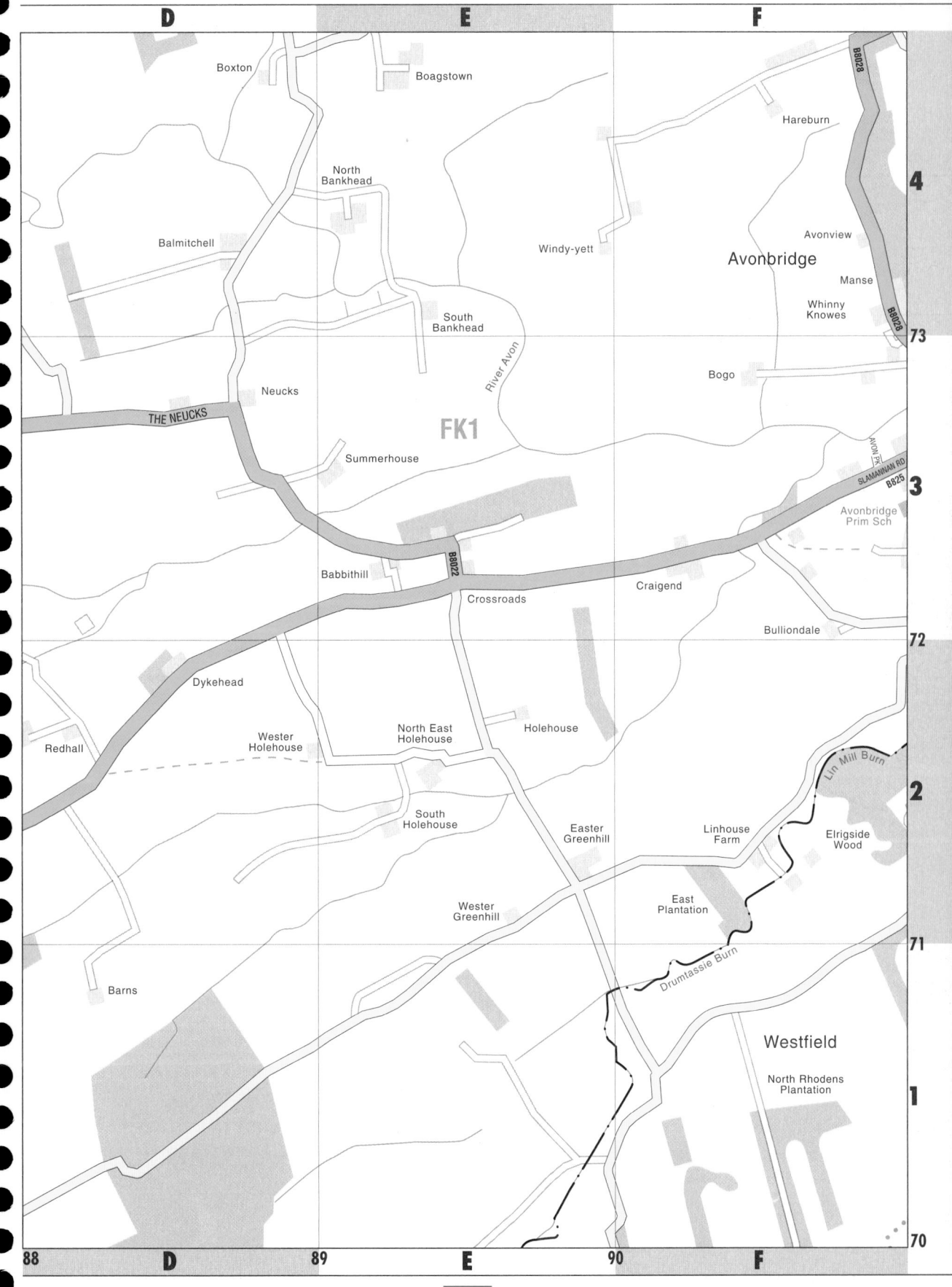
D
E
F
Boxton
Boagstown
Hareburn
B8028
North
Bankhead
Balmitchell
Windy-yett
Avonview
Avonbridge
Manse
Whinny
Knowes
South
Bankhead
River Avon
Bogo
Neucks
THE NEUCKS
FK1
Summerhouse
AVON PK
SLAMANNAN RD
B825
Avonbridge
Prim Sch
B8022
Babbithill
Crossroads
Craigend
Bulliondale
Dykehead
Holehouse
North East
Holehouse
Wester
Holehouse
Redhall
Lin Mill Burn
South
Holehouse
Easter
Greenhill
Linhouse
Farm
Elrigside
Wood
East
Plantation
Wester
Greenhill
Drumtassie Burn
Barns
Westfield
North Rhodens
Plantation
4
73
3
72
2
71
1
70
88
89
90
D
E
F

107

68

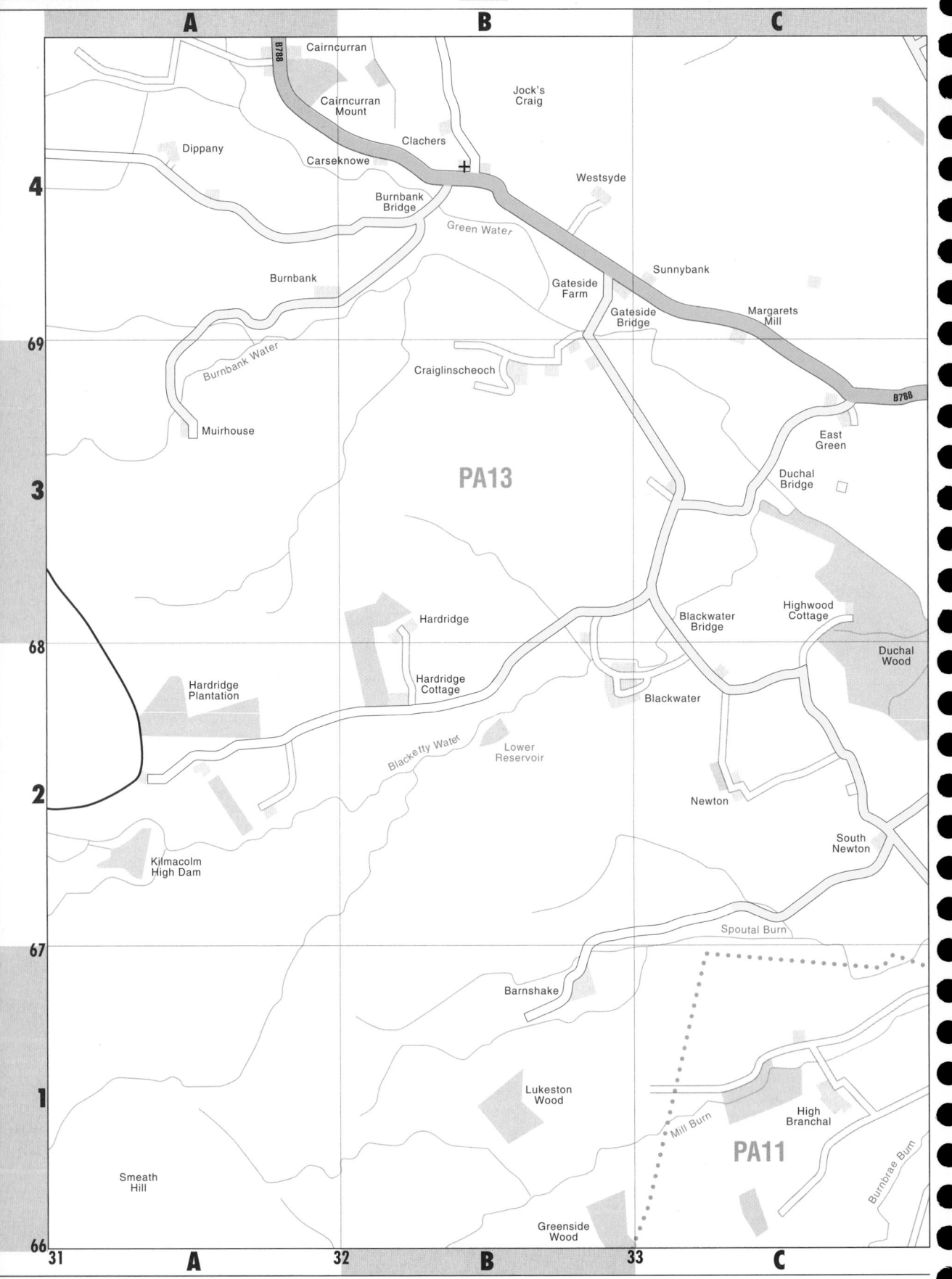

A
B
C
Cairncurran
B788
Jock's Craig
Cairncurran Mount
Dippany
Clachers
Carseknowe
Westsyde
4
Burnbank Bridge
Green Water
Burnbank
Sunnybank
Gateside Farm
Gateside Bridge
Margarets Mill
69
Burnbank Water
Craiglinscheoch
B788
Muirhouse
East Green
PA13
3
Duchal Bridge
Hardridge
Blackwater Bridge
Highwood Cottage
68
Duchal Wood
Hardridge Plantation
Hardridge Cottage
Blackwater
Blacketty Water
Lower Reservoir
2
Newton
South Newton
Kilmacolm High Dam
Spoutal Burn
67
Barnshake
1
Lukeston Wood
High Branchal
Mill Burn
PA11
Burnbrae Burn
Smeath Hill
Greenside Wood
66
31
A
32
B
33
C

108

69
90

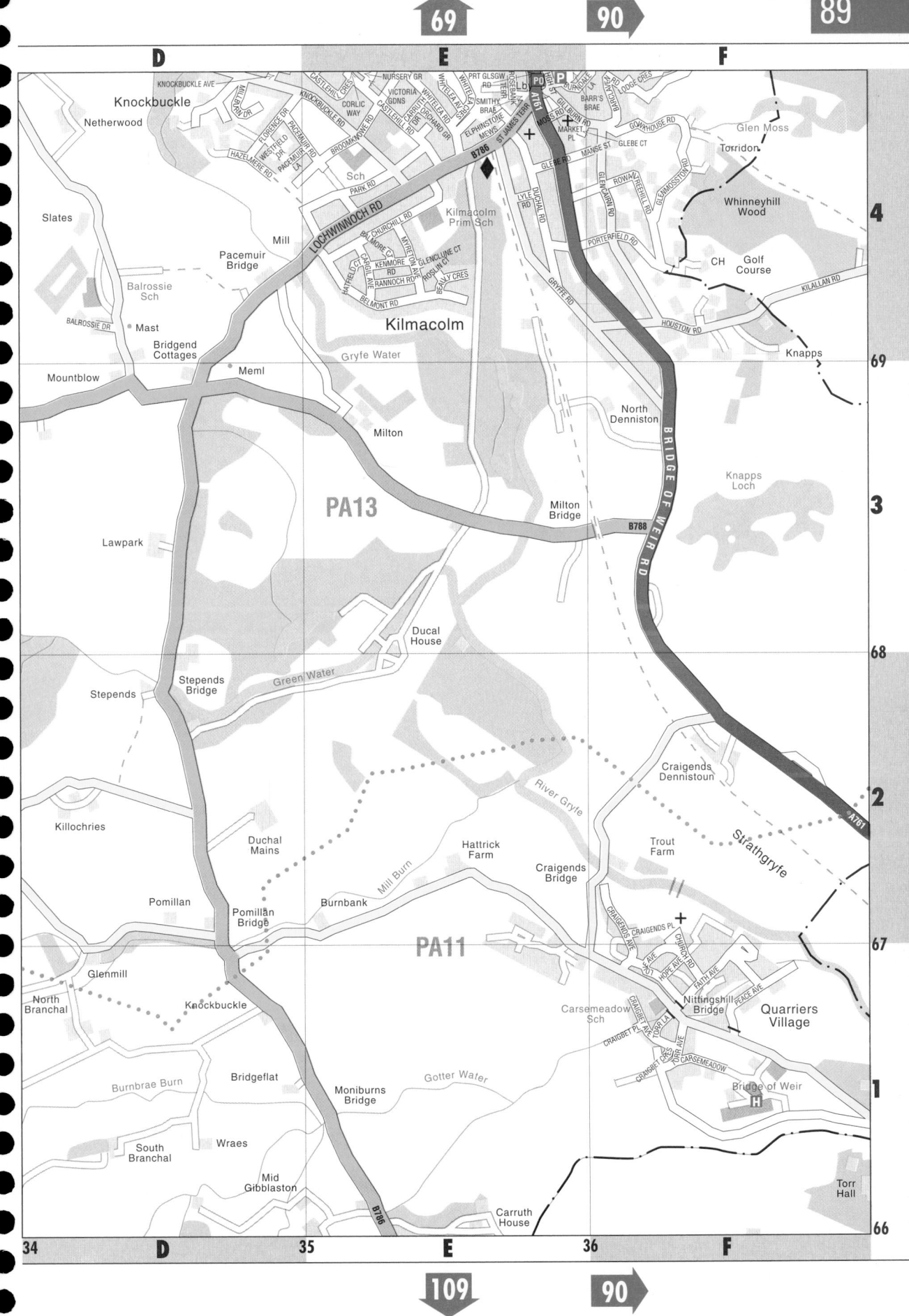
D
E
F
Knockbuckle
Netherwood
Slates
Kilmacolm
Kilmacolm Prim Sch
Sch
Mill
Pacemuir Bridge
Balrossie Sch
Mast
Bridgend Cottages
Meml
Mountblow
Gryfe Water
Milton
PA13
Lawpark
Milton Bridge
North Denniston
BRIDGE OF WEIR RD
Glen Moss
Torridon
Whinneyhill Wood
CH
Golf Course
Knapps
Knapps Loch
Ducal House
Green Water
Stepends Bridge
Stepends
Killochries
Duchal Mains
Hattrick Farm
River Gryfe
Craigends Dennistoun
Trout Farm
Strathgryfe
Craigends Bridge
Pomillan
Pomillan Bridge
Burnbank
Mill Burn
PA11
Glenmill
North Branchal
Knockbuckle
Carsemeadow Sch
Nittingshill Bridge
Quarriers Village
Bridge of Weir
Bridgeflat
Burnbrae Burn
Moniburns Bridge
Gotter Water
South Branchal
Wraes
Mid Gibblaston
Carruth House
Torr Hall
LOCHWINNOCH RD
B786
B788
A761
KILALLAN RD
HOUSTON RD
GRYFFE RD
PORTERFIELD RD
GOWKHOUSE RD
GLEBE CT
MANSE ST
GLEBE RD
4
69
3
68
2
67
1
66
34
35
36

109
90

89
70

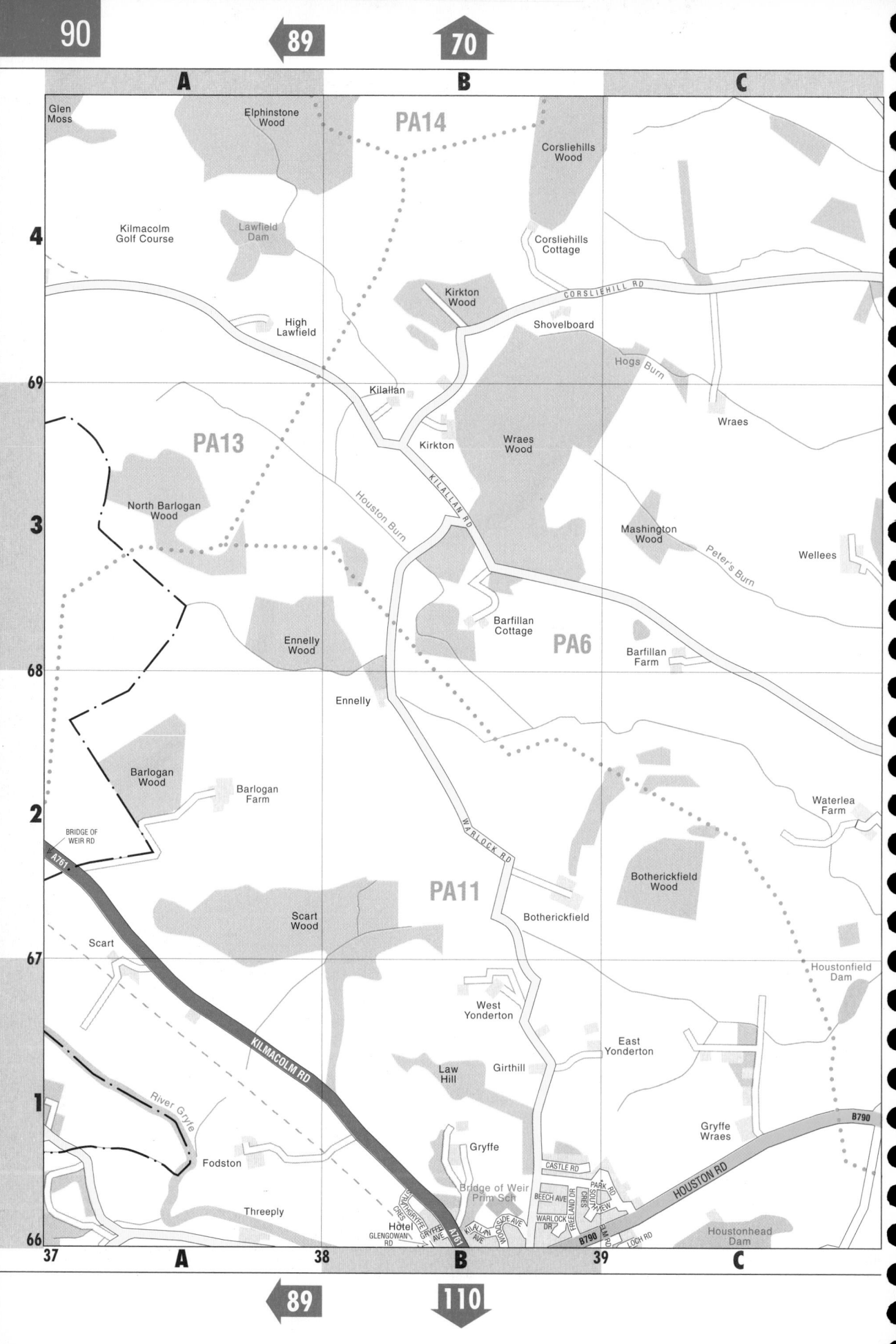
A
B
C
Glen Moss
Elphinstone Wood
PA14
Corsliehills Wood
Kilmacolm Golf Course
Lawfield Dam
Corsliehills Cottage
4
Kirkton Wood
CORSLIEHILL RD
High Lawfield
Shovelboard
Hogs Burn
69
Kilallan
Wraes
PA13
Kirkton
Wraes Wood
KILALLAN RD
Houston Burn
North Barlogan Wood
3
Mashington Wood
Peter's Burn
Wellees
Barfillan Cottage
PA6
Ennelly Wood
Barfillan Farm
68
Ennelly
Barlogan Wood
Barlogan Farm
Waterlea Farm
2
BRIDGE OF WEIR RD
A761
WARLOCK RD
Botherickfield Wood
PA11
Scart Wood
Botherickfield
Scart
67
Houstonfield Dam
West Yonderton
KILMACOLM RD
East Yonderton
Law Hill
Girthill
River Gryfe
1
B790
Gryffe Wraes
Gryffe
Fodston
CASTLE RD
HOUSTON RD
Bridge of Weir Prim Sch
PARK RD
BEECH AVE
SOUTHVIEW CRES
FREELAND DR
Threeply
STRATHGRYFFE CRES
WOODSIDE AVE
WARLOCK DR
Hotel
GRYFFE AVE
KILALLAN AVE
GLENGOWAN RD
B790
ELM RD
LOCH RD
Houstonhead Dam
66
37
38
39

89
110

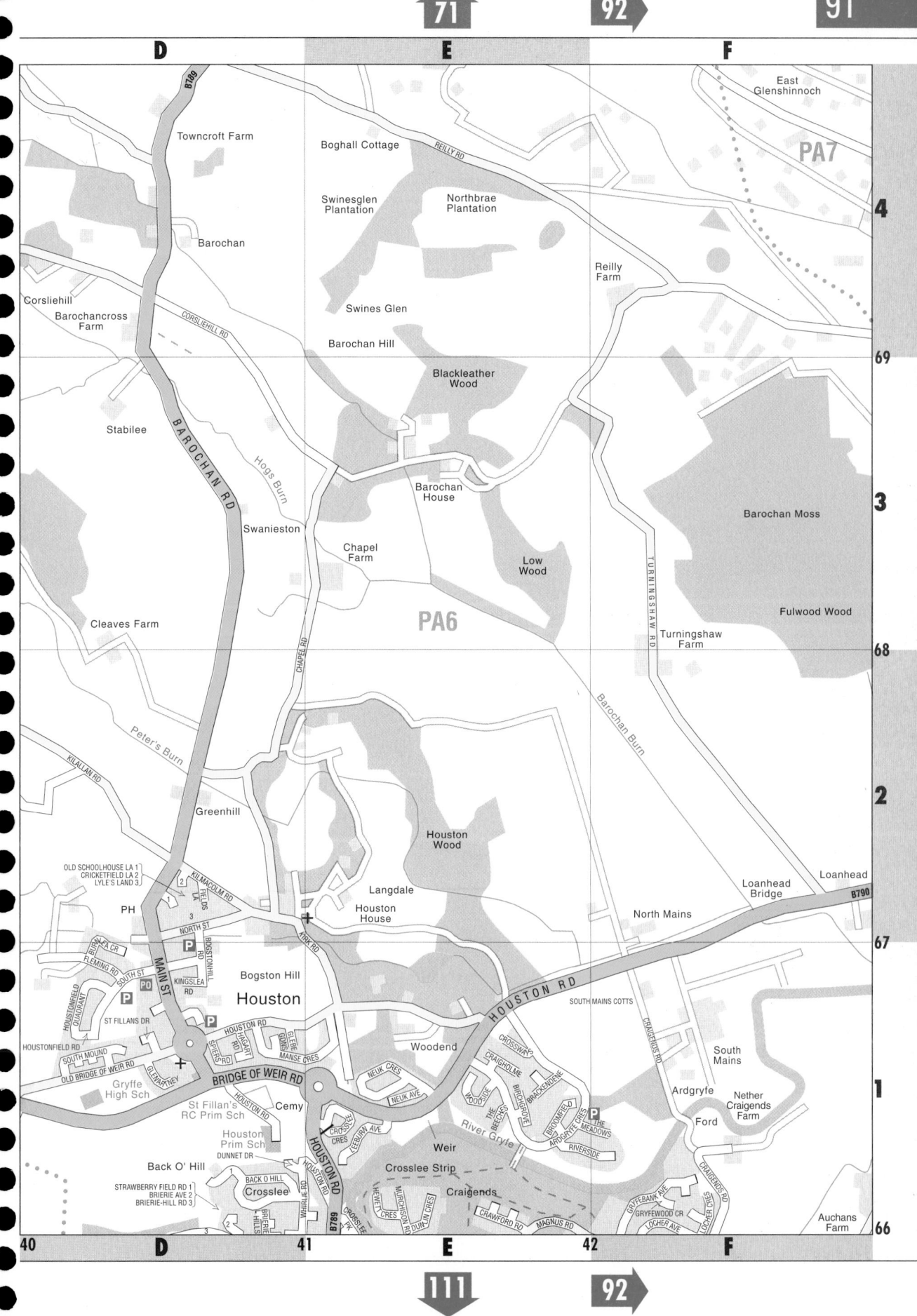
D
E
F
East Glenshinnoch
PA7
Towncroft Farm
Boghall Cottage
REILLY RD
Swinesglen Plantation
Northbrae Plantation
Barochan
Reilly Farm
Corsliehill
Barochancross Farm
CORSLIEHILL RD
Swines Glen
Barochan Hill
Blackleather Wood
Stabilee
BAROCHAN RD
Hogs Burn
Barochan House
Swanieston
Chapel Farm
Low Wood
Barochan Moss
TURNINGSHAW RD
PA6
Fulwood Wood
Cleaves Farm
Turningshaw Farm
CHAPEL RD
Barochan Burn
Peter's Burn
KILALLAN RD
Greenhill
Houston Wood
OLD SCHOOLHOUSE LA 1
CRICKETFIELD LA 2
LYLE'S LAND 3
KILMACOLM RD
FIELDS LA
Langdale
Loanhead Bridge
Loanhead
B790
PH
Houston House
North Mains
NORTH ST
BOGSTONHILL RD
KIRK RD
MAIN ST
FLEMING RD
SOUTH ST
Bogston Hill
KINGSLEA RD
HOUSTON RD
SOUTH MAINS COTTS
Houston
HOUSTONFIELD QUADRANT
ST FILLANS DR
HOUSTON RD
HAGART RD
GLEBE GDNS
MANSE CRES
Woodend
CROSSWAY
CRAIGHOLME
South Mains
HOUSTONFIELD RD
SOUTH MOUND
OLD BRIDGE OF WEIR RD
SPIERS RD
BRIDGE OF WEIR RD
NEUK CRES
NEUK AVE
BRACKENDENE
BIRCHGROVE
THE BEECHES
WOODSIDE
CRAIGENDS RD
Ardgryfe
Nether Craigends Farm
Gryffe High Sch
GLENAPNEY
St Fillan's RC Prim Sch
HOUSTON RD
Cemy
CROSSLEE CRES
EEBURN AVE
River Gryfe
BROOMFIELD
ARDGRYFE CRES
THE MEADOWS
RIVERSIDE
Ford
Houston Prim Sch
DUNNET DR
HOUSTON RD
Weir
Back O' Hill
BACK O HILL
Crosslee Strip
STRAWBERRY FIELD RD 1
BRIERIE AVE 2
BRIERIE-HILL RD 3
Crosslee
WHIRLIE RD
HEWETT CRES
MURCHISON RD
DUNLIN CRES
Craigends
CRAWFORD RD
MAGNUS RD
GRYFEBANK AVE
GRYFEWOOD CR
LOCHER AVE
LOCHER CRES
CRAIGENDS RD
Auchans Farm
B789
CROSSLEE PK
BRIERIE HILLS
4
69
3
68
2
67
1
66
40
41
42

91
72

A
B
C
4
3
2
1
69
68
67
66
43
44
45
DARGAVEL RD
A8
M8
OLD GREENOCK RD
Barrangary
Craigmuir
PA8
Linburn
Plantation
Southbar
Southbar House
GREENOCK RD
PA7
Dargavel House
Nether Southbar
Dargavel Burn
North
Commonside
PA4
Lin Burn
Fulwood Moss
East
Fulwood
PA6
Dargavel Burn
Barnhill
HOUSTON RD
Netherfield
B790
River Gryfe
Fulwood
Selvieland
Wester
Fulwood
Birkenhead
PA3
MOSS RD
AUCHANS RD
Knowes
Locher Water
Blackstoun
Mains
Blackstoun
Black Cart Water
Linwoodmoss
Wood
Moss
Cottage
Auchans

91
112

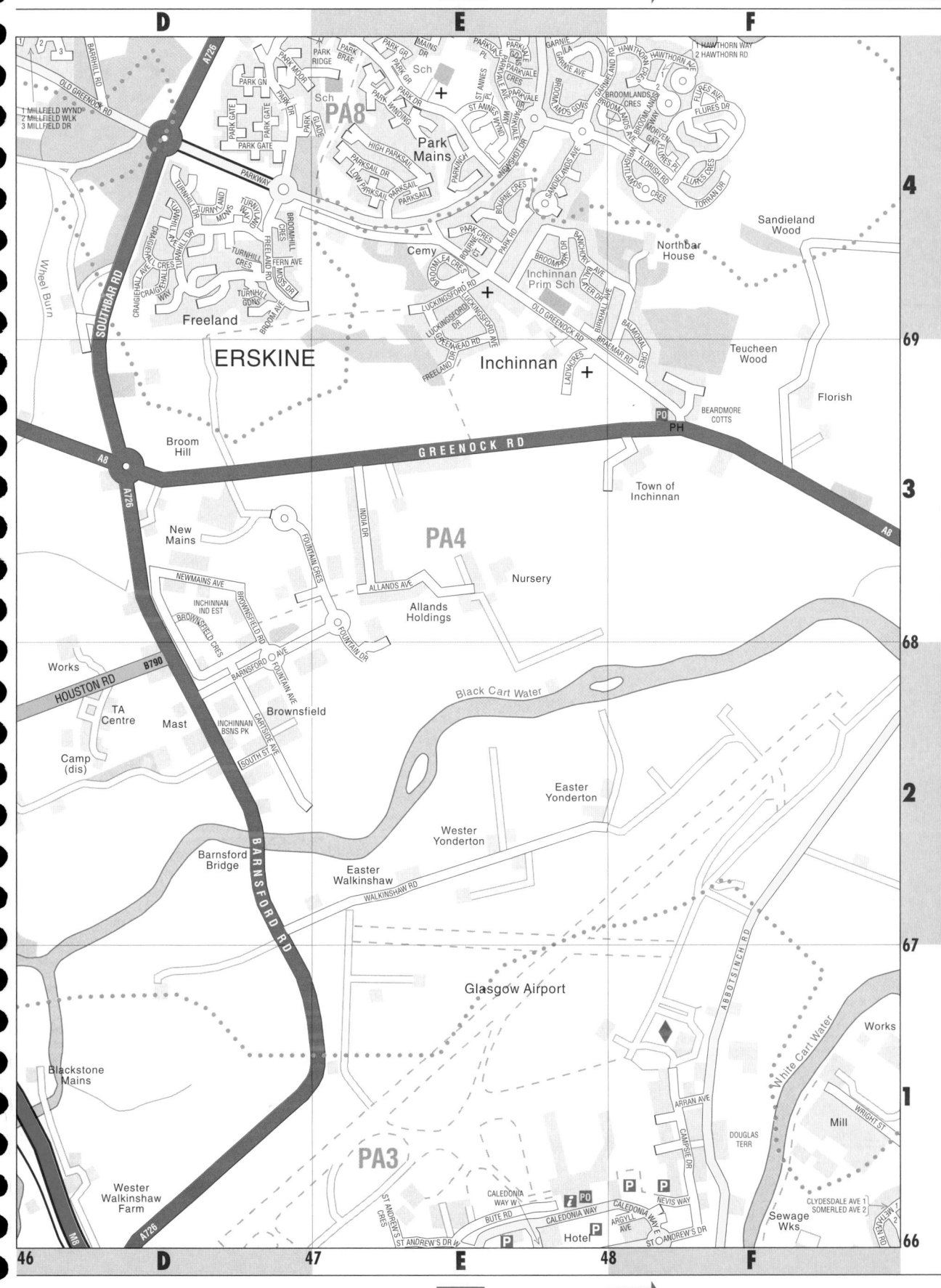

D E F

4
69
3
68
2
67
1
66

PA8

1 MILLFIELD WYND
2 MILLFIELD WLK
3 MILLFIELD DR

OLD GREENOCK RD
BARRHILL RD
A726

Sch
Park Mains

PARK MOOR
PARK RIDGE
PARK GN
PARK GATE
PARK GATE
PARK GATE
PARK DR
HIGH PARKSAIL
PARKSAIL DR
LOW PARKSAIL
PARKSAIL
PARK LANDING
PARK CRES
PARK RD

MAINS DR
PARK BRAE
ST ANNES
ST ANNES WYND
PARKVALE AVE
PARKVALE PL
PARKVALE WYND

GARNIE AVE
GARNIE LA
BROOMLANDS GDNS
1 HAWTHORN WAY
2 HAWTHORN RD
HAWTHORN AVE
BROOMLANDS CRES
BROOMLANDS WAY
GARNIEHILL RD
BROOMLANDS GATE
MORTEN GDNS
FLORISH RD
FLURES AVE
FLURES DR
ALDO CRES
FLURES CRES
TORRAN DR

PARKWAY
TURNHILL DR
TURNHILL AVE
TURNLAW
TURNLAND MDWS
TURNHILL WLK
TURNHILL CRES
TURNHILL GDNS
FERN AVE
MOSS DR
BROOM AVE
BROOMHILL
CRAIGIEHALL AVE
CRAIGIEHALL WAY
FREELAND RD

Freeland

SOUTHBAR RD
A726

ERSKINE

Cemy
LUCKINGSFORD CRES
LUCKINGSFORD DR
LUCKINGSFORD AVE
GREENLEA RD
FREELAND RD

BOURNE CRES
LOW ROMANLEA CRES
LADYACRES

Inchinnan Prim Sch

BROOM RD
BANCHORY AVE
LATER AVE
BIRKHALL AVE
BRAEMAR RD
BALMORAL CRES

Northbar House

Sandieland Wood

Teucheen Wood

Florish

Inchinnan

OLD GREENOCK RD

PO
PH
BEARDMORE COTTS

Broom Hill

A8

GREENOCK RD

Town of Inchinnan

A8

Wheel Burn

New Mains

PA4

NEWMAINS AVE
INCHINNAN IND EST
BROWNSFIELD CRES
BROWNSFIELD RD
INDIA DR
FOUNTAIN CRES
ALLANDS AVE
FOUNTAIN DR
FOUNTAIN AVE
BARNSFORD AVE
CARTSIDE AVE
SOUTH ST
INCHINNAN BSNS PK

Allands Holdings

Nursery

Works

HOUSTON RD
B790

TA Centre

Mast

Brownsfield

Camp (dis)

Black Cart Water

Barnsford Bridge

BARNSFORD RD

Easter Walkinshaw

WALKINSHAW RD

Wester Yonderton

Easter Yonderton

ABBOTSINCH RD

White Cart Water

Works

Blackstone Mains

Glasgow Airport

M8

A726

Wester Walkinshaw Farm

PA3

ST ANDREW'S CRES
CALEDONIA WAY W
BUTE RD
CALEDONIA WAY
ST ANDREW'S DR W

i
PO
P
P
Hotel
NEVIS WAY
CALEDONIA WAY E
ARGYLL AVE
ST ANDREW'S DR
P

ARRAN AVE
CAMPSIE DR
DOUGLAS TERR

Mill
WRIGHT ST

CLYDESDALE AVE 1
SOMERLED AVE 2

Sewage Wks

A | B | C

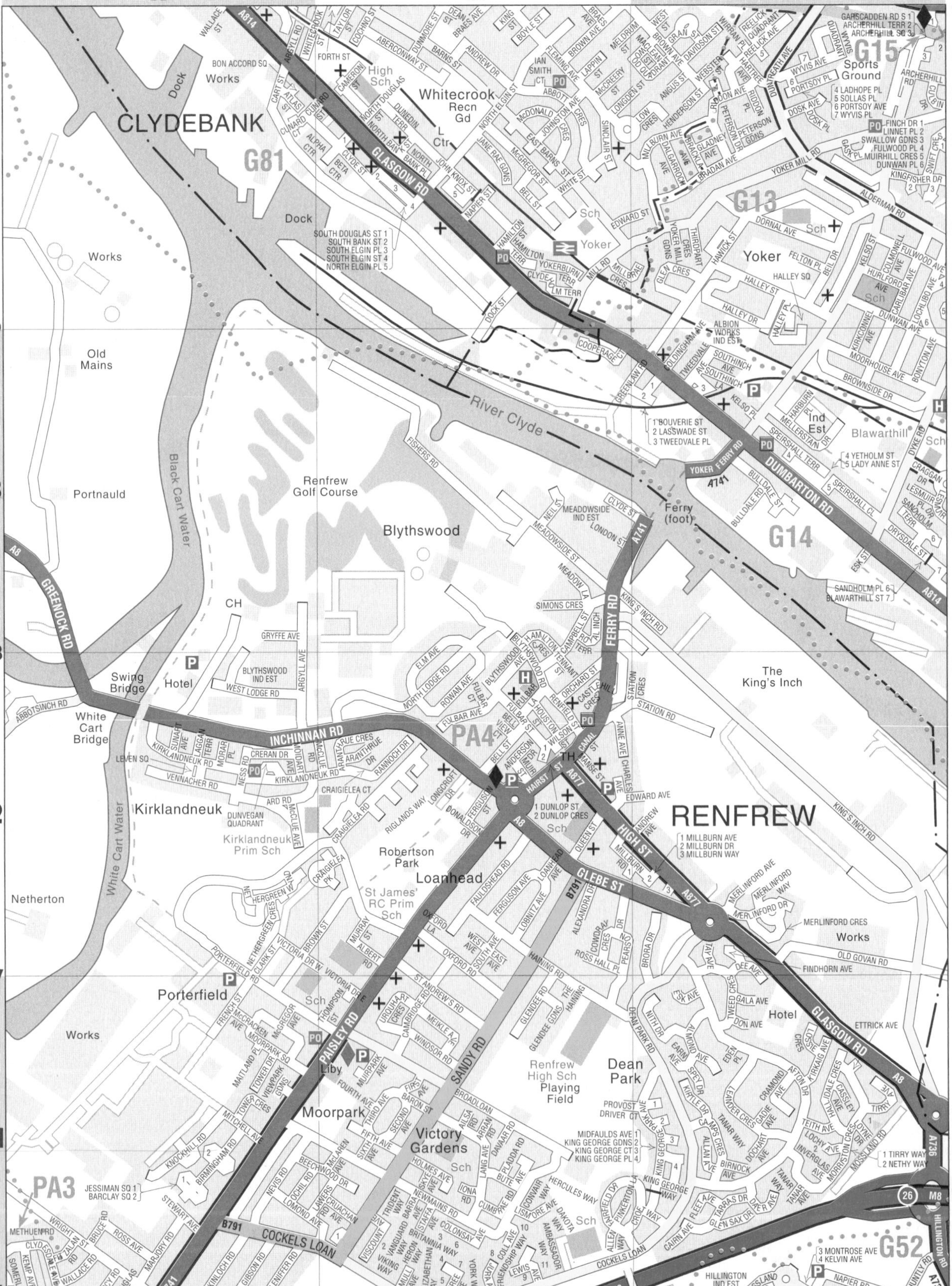

CLYDEBANK
G81

Whitecrook

Yoker

G13

G15 Sports Ground

Yoker

G14

Blawarthill

River Clyde

Renfrew Golf Course

Blythswood

Portnauld

Old Mains

Black Cart Water

White Cart Water

Swing Bridge

White Cart Bridge

Kirklandneuk

Netherton

Robertson Park

Loanhead

The King's Inch

PA4

RENFREW

Porterfield

Moorpark

Victory Gardens

Dean Park

Renfrew High Sch Playing Field

PA3

G52

Works

GLASGOW RD

GREENOCK RD

DUMBARTON RD

PAISLEY RD

SANDY RD

GLEBE ST

HIGH ST

FERRY RD

INCHINNAN RD

COCKELS LOAN

4 | 69 | 3 | 68 | 2 | 67 | 1 | 66

49 | A | 50 | B | 51 | C

B1
1 CLAIRINCH GDNS
2 HERALD WAY
3 ARGOSY WAY
4 LANCASTER WAY
5 WELLINGTON WAY
6 ANSON WAY
7 HALIFAX WAY
8 STIRLING WAY
9 LYSANDER WAY
10 CARAVELLE WAY
11 HAMPDEN WAY

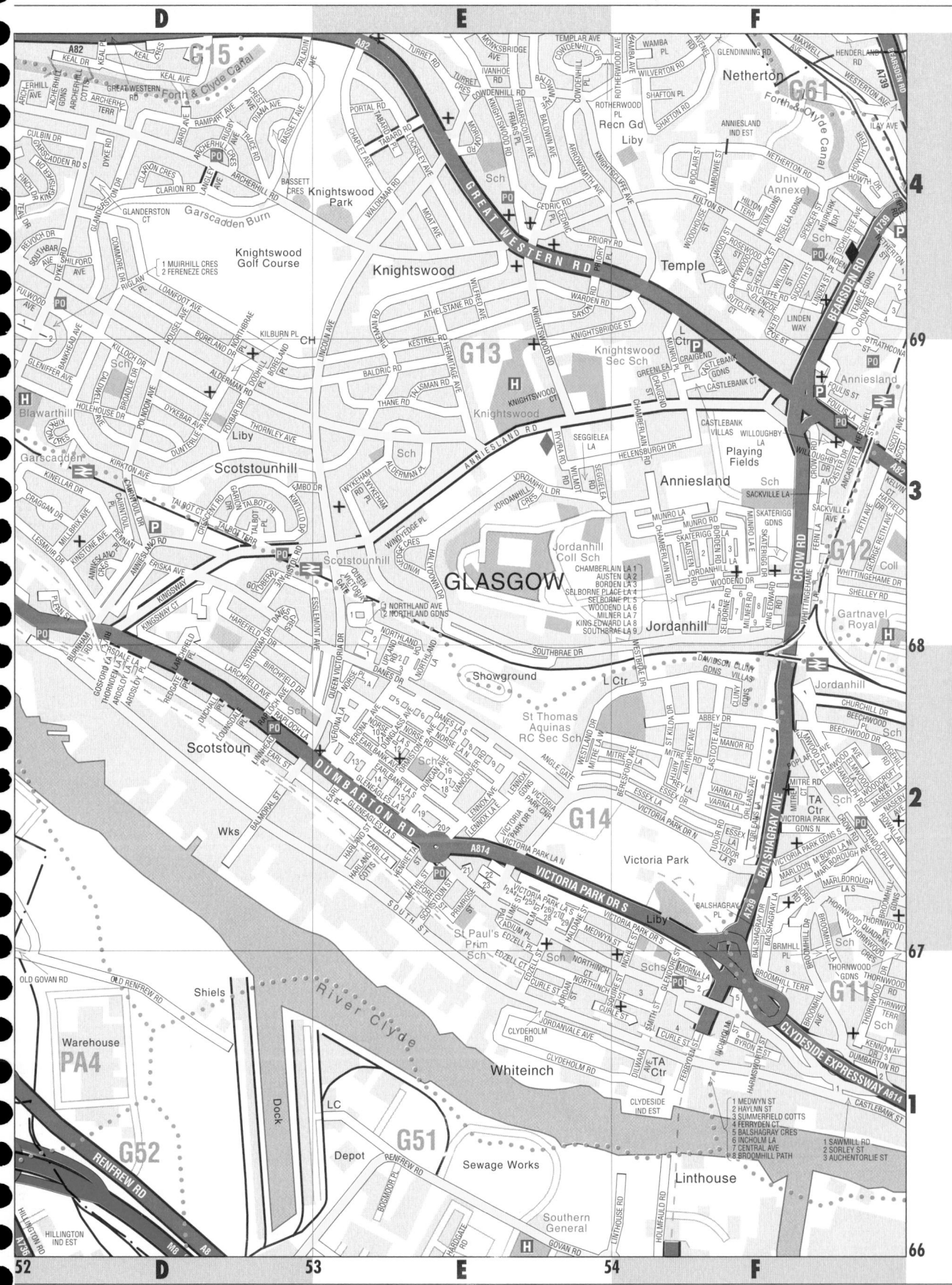

D
E
F
GLASGOW
G15
G61
G13
G14
G12
G11
G51
G52
PA4
Knightswood
Knightswood Park
Knightswood Golf Course
Netherton
Temple
Anniesland
Scotstounhill
Scotstoun
Jordanhill
Whiteinch
Linthouse
Victoria Park
Gartnavel Royal
Blawarthill
Garscadden
Showground
Jordanhill Coll Sch
Knightswood Sec Sch
St Thomas Aquinas RC Sec Sch
Southern General
Sewage Works
Warehouse
Shiels
Dock
Depot
Wks
River Clyde
Forth & Clyde Canal
Garscadden Burn
GREAT WESTERN RD
DUMBARTON RD
VICTORIA PARK DR S
CLYDESIDE EXPRESSWAY A814
BALSHAGRAY AVE
CROW RD
ANNIESLAND RD
SOUTHBRAE DR
RENFREW RD
BEARSDEN RD
1 MUIRHILL CRES
2 FERENEZE CRES
1 NORTHLAND AVE
2 NORTHLAND GDNS
CHAMBERLAIN LA 1
AUSTEN LA 2
BORDEN LA 3
SELBORNE PLACE LA 4
SELBORNE PL 5
WOODEND LA 6
MILNER LA 7
KING EDWARD LA 8
SOUTHBRAE LA 9
1 MEDWYN ST
2 HAYLNN ST
3 SUMMERFIELD COTTS
4 FERRYDEN CT
5 BALSHAGRAY CRES
6 INCHOLM LA
7 CENTRAL AVE
8 BROOMHILL PATH
1 SAWMILL RD
2 SORLEY ST
3 AUCHENTORLIE ST
4
3
2
1
69
68
67
66
52
53
54

96

A2
1 DEVONSHIRE GDNS
2 DEVONSHIRE GDNS LA
3 WESTBOURNE TERR LA S
4 KINGSBOROUGH GATE
5 TURNBERRY AVE
6 LANE GDNS
7 MONKSCROFT AVE
8 KIRKMICHAEL GDNS
9 KIRKMICHAEL AVE
10 THORNWOOD DR
11 BLAIRATHOLL GDNS
12 TIBBERMORE RD

95

B3
1 THORNBRIDGE AVE
2 BELLSHAUGH PL
3 GARRIOCH CRES
4 GARRIOCH QUADRANT
5 WYNDFORD PL
6 DUNBEITH PL

76

B3
7 LATHERTON DR
8 INVERSHIN DR
9 CARRBRIDGE DR
10 TOWIE PL
11 KELVINDALE PL
12 GLENFINNAN PL
13 STRATHY PL
14 BEAULY PL
15 STRATHCARRON PL
16 KIRKHILL PL
17 GARRIOCH GATE

For full street detail of the highlighted area see page 240.

Map area covering Maryhill, Kelvindale, Kelvinside, Hyndland, Partick, Partickhill, Kelvingrove, Kelvinhaugh, North Kelvin, Gilshochill, Cadder and surrounding districts of Glasgow (grid squares G11, G12, G13, G20, G22, G23, G3, G4, G51, G61). Features include University Veterinary Hosp (Univ of Glasgow), Dawsholm Park, River Kelvin, Forth & Clyde Canal, Great Western Rd, Maryhill Rd, Byres Rd, Clydeside Expressway, River Clyde, Glasgow Bot Gdns, Kelvingrove Park, Kelvin Hall, Kelvingrove Mus & Art Gall, Gartnavel Royal, Gartnavel General, Ruchill Park, Western Necropolis, Golf Course.

B2
1 KERSLAND LA
2 SANDRINGHAM LA
3 VINICOMBE LA
4 BURGH LA
5 CRESSWELL ST
6 GREAT GEORGE LA
7 DOWANSIDE LA
8 RUTHVEN LA
9 SALTOUN LA
10 GROSVENOR CRES
11 OBSERVATORY LA
12 GROSVENOR CRES LA
13 GROSVENOR TERR
14 MARCHMONT TERR
15 BOWMONT GDNS
16 VICTORIA CRES PL
17 BEAUMONT GATE
18 FOREMOUNT TERR LA
19 CROWN CIR
20 PRINCE'S PL
21 KENSINGTON GATE
22 KENSINGTON GATE LA
23 KENSINGTON RD
24 LORRAINE RD
25 LORRAINE GDNS LA
26 WESTBOURNE GDNS LA
27 WESTBOURNE GDNS N
28 WESTBOURNE GDNS W
29 WESTBOURNE TERR LA N
30 LANCASTER TERR LA
31 LANCASTER TERR
32 GREAT WESTERN TERR LA
33 GREAT WESTERN TERR
34 REDLANDS TERR
35 LOWTHER TERR
36 BELHAVEN TERR W
37 BELHAVEN TERR W LA
38 ROSSLYN TERR
39 BELHAVEN TERR LA

B2
40 BELHAVEN TERR
41 KIRKLEE TERR RD
42 KIRKLEE QUADRANT
43 REDLANDS RD
44 REDLANDS TERR LA
C1
1 SOUTHPARK LA
2 OAKFIELD LA
3 ETON LA
4 BOTHWELL LA
5 CALEDONIAN CRES
6 WEST PRINCE'S ST
7 WESTBANK CT
8 WILLOWBANK CRES
9 HOLYROOD QUADRANT
10 NAPIERSHALL PL
11 PARK TERR LA
12 LA BELLE PL
13 LA BELLE ALLEE
14 N CLAREMONT ST
15 KELVINGROVE ST
16 PARKGROVE TERR LA
17 CRAIGMADDIE TERR LA
C2
1 YARROW GDNS LA
2 JEDBURGH GDNS
3 LOTHIAN GDNS
4 CLOUSTON CT
5 OBAN CT
6 QUEEN MARGARET CT
7 KELVINSIDE GDNS LA
8 KELVINSIDE TERR W
9 KELVINSIDE TERR S
10 DOUNE QUADRANT
11 ALFRED LA
12 COLEBROOKE ST

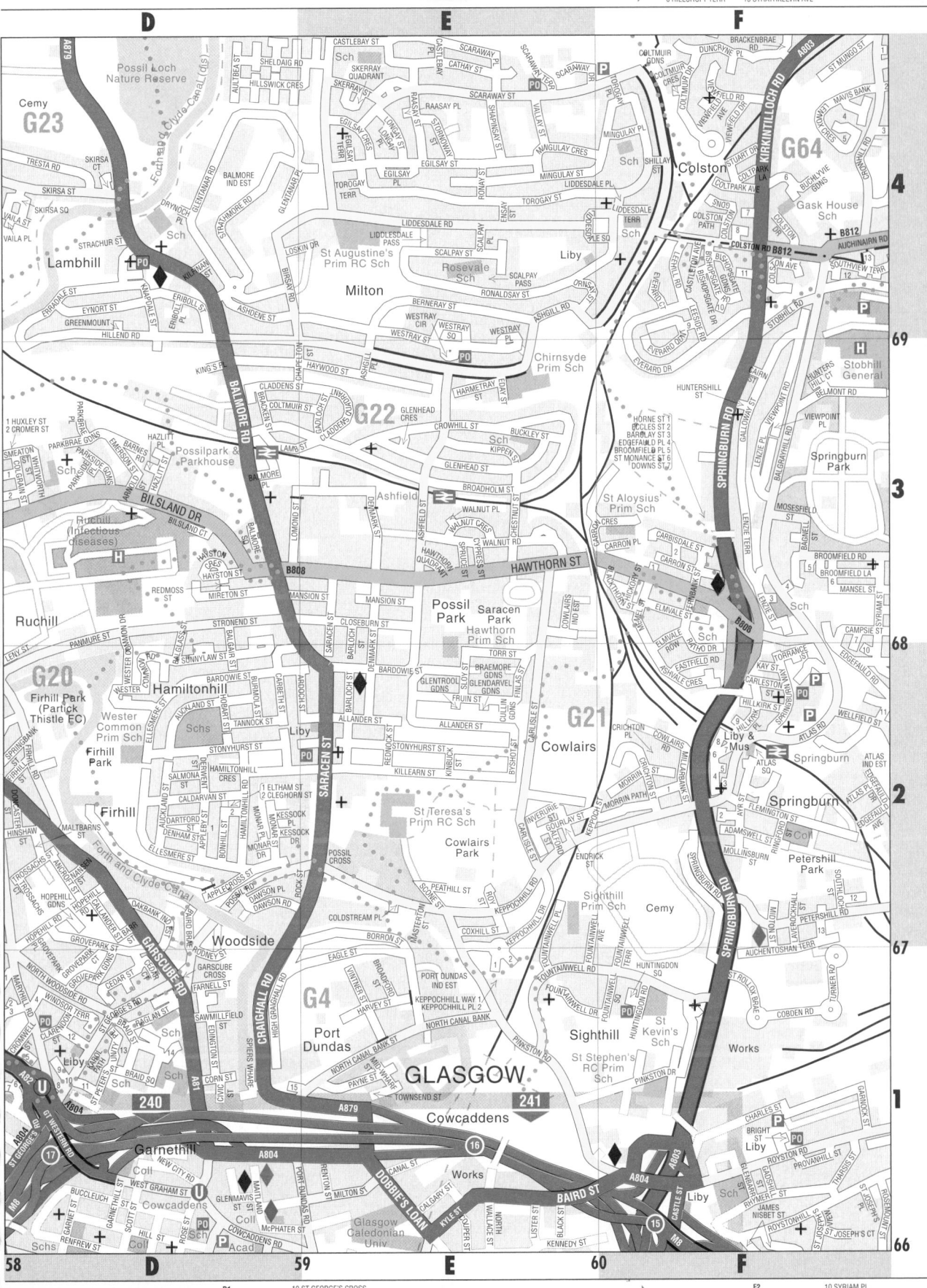

77

98

97

F4
1 FORRESTER CT
2 MUIRPARK TERR
3 HUNTERSHILL RD
4 FULMAR CT
5 RAVENS CT
6 HILLCROFT TERR
7 MILTON DR
8 COLSTON PL
9 EVERARD PL
10 BISHOPSGATE PL
11 NEWBOLD AVE
12 SOUTHVIEW CT
13 STRATHKELVIN AVE

For full street detail of the highlighted area see pages 240 and 241.

D1
1 SEAMORE ST
2 BURNBANK PL
3 BURNBANK TERR
4 WINDSOR ST
5 CROMWELL LA
6 MELROSE ST
7 QUEEN'S CRES
8 ST GEORGE'S PL
9 CLARENDON PL
10 ST GEORGE'S CROSS
11 GLADSTONE ST
12 GLENFARG ST
13 ST PETER'S PATH
14 MANRESA PL
15 DUNDASHILL

F2
1 GOURLAY ST
2 VALLEYFIELD ST
3 PALERMO ST
4 SPRINGBURN WAY
5 VULCAN ST
6 COWLAIRS RD
7 ANGUS ST
8 KEMP ST
9 SPRINGVALE TERR
10 SYRIAM PL
11 CROFTBANK ST
12 SOUTHLOCH GDNS
13 AUCHINLOCH ST

97
78

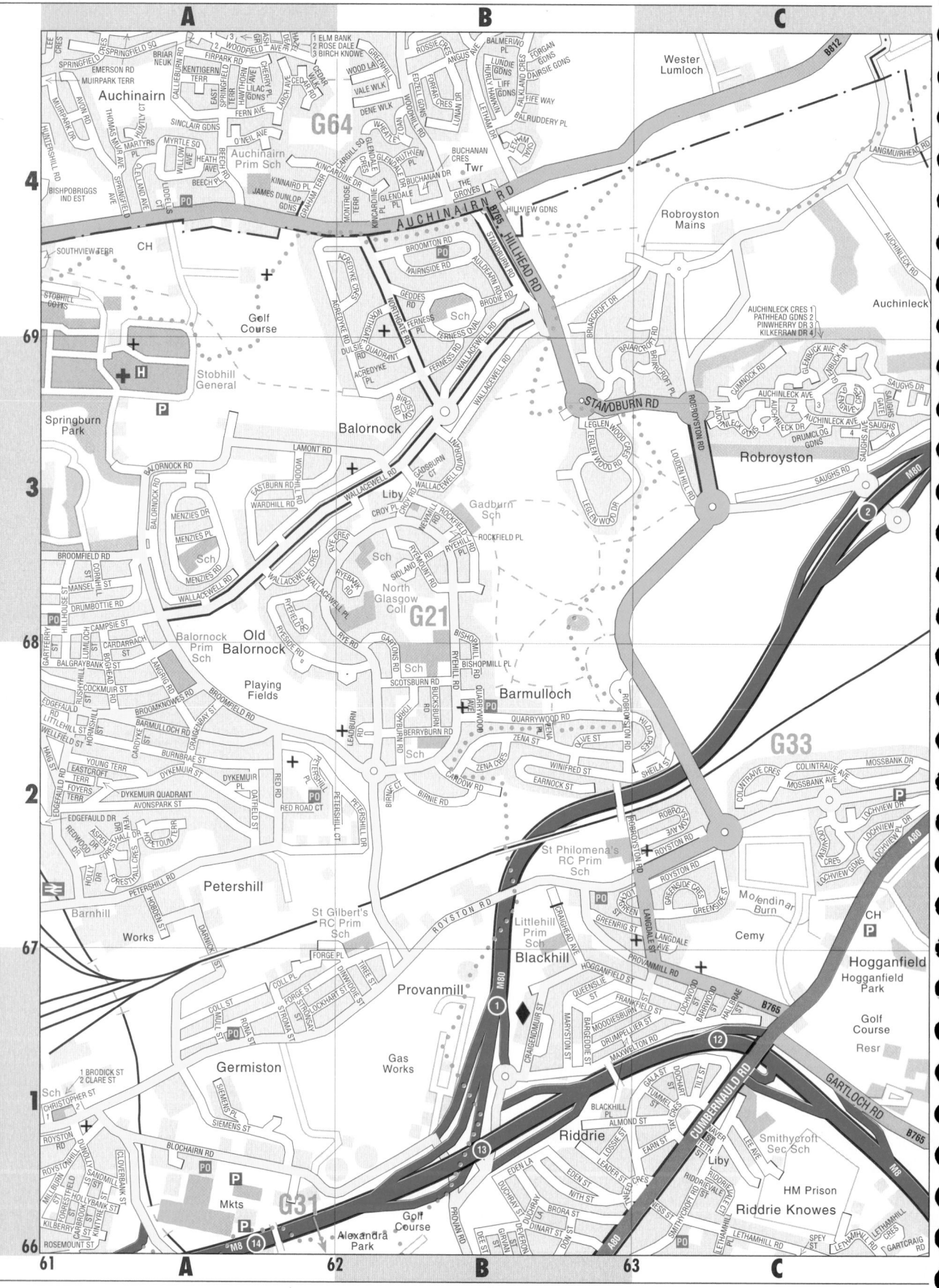
A
B
C
4
69
3
68
2
67
1
66
61
62
63
Auchinairn
G64
Auchinairn Prim Sch
AUCHINAIRN RD
Wester Lumloch
B812
Robroyston Mains
Auchinleck
AUCHINLECK CRES 1
PATHHEAD GDNS 2
PINWHERRY DR 3
KILKERRAN DR 4
Golf Course
Stobhill General
Springburn Park
Balornock
STANDBURN RD
ROBROYSTON RD
Robroyston
M80
Gadburn Sch
North Glasgow Coll
G21
Old Balornock
Balornock Prim Sch
Playing Fields
Barmulloch
G33
St Philomena's RC Prim Sch
Petershill
Barnhill
Works
St Gilbert's RC Prim Sch
ROYSTON RD
Littlehill Prim Sch
Blackhill
Molendinar Burn
Cemy
Hogganfield
Hogganfield Park
Golf Course
Resr
Provanmill
Gas Works
Germiston
Riddrie
Smithycroft Sec Sch
HM Prison
Riddrie Knowes
Mkts
G31
Alexandra Park
CUMBERNAULD RD
GARTLOCH RD
B765
M8
A80
1 BRODICK ST
2 CLARE ST
1 ELM BANK
2 ROSE DALE
3 BIRCH KNOWE

97
118

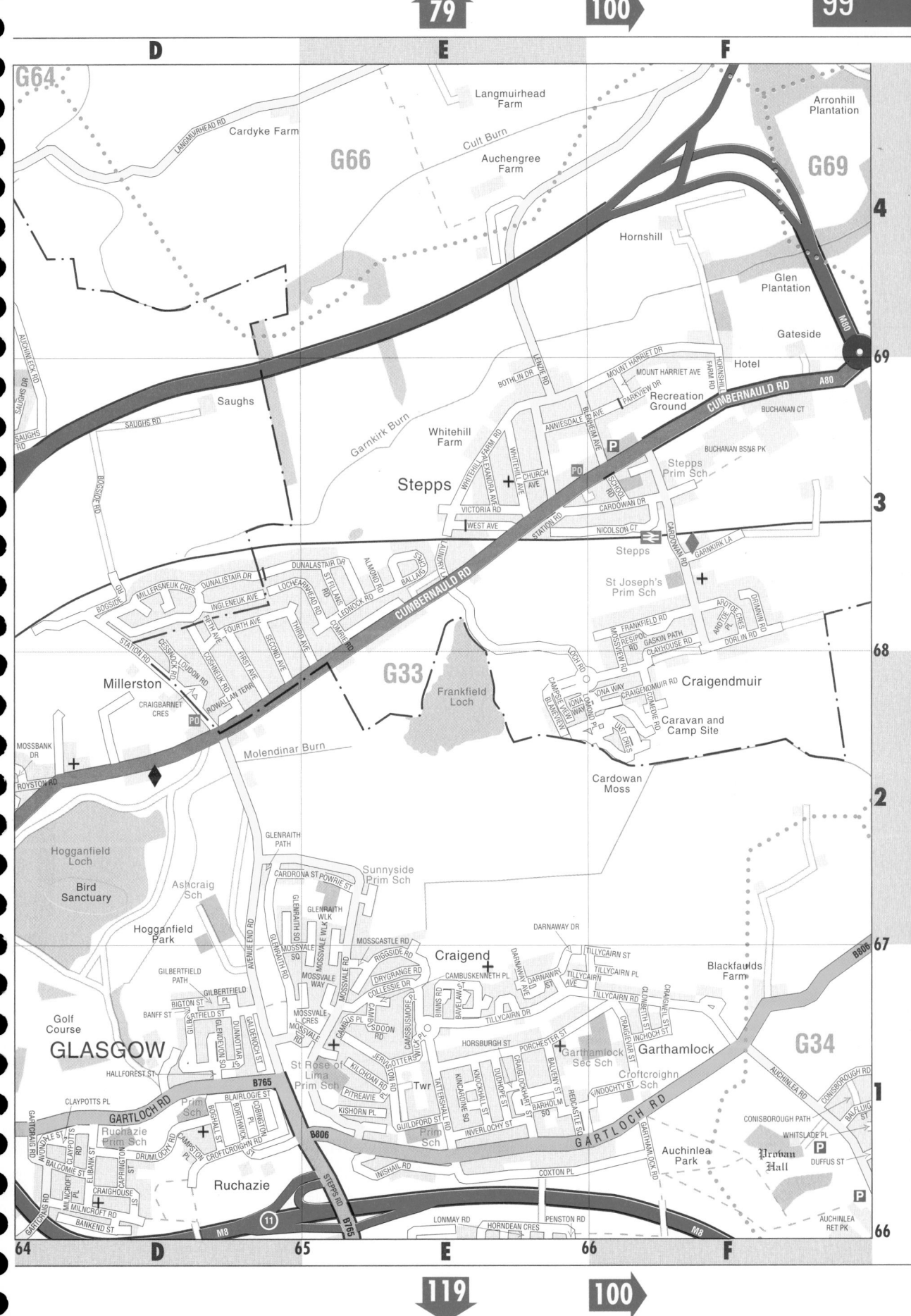
79
100
D
E
F
G64
G66
G69
G33
G34
Langmuirhead Farm
Cardyke Farm
Cult Burn
Auchengree Farm
Arronhill Plantation
Hornshill
Glen Plantation
Gateside
Hotel
Saughs
Recreation Ground
Whitehill Farm
Garnkirk Burn
Stepps
Stepps Prim Sch
Stepps
St Joseph's Prim Sch
CUMBERNAULD RD
A80
M80
Millerston
Frankfield Loch
Craigendmuir
Caravan and Camp Site
Cardowan Moss
Molendinar Burn
Hogganfield Loch
Bird Sanctuary
Ashcraig Sch
Hogganfield Park
Sunnyside Prim Sch
Craigend
Blackfaulds Farm
Golf Course
GLASGOW
Garthamlock
Garthamlock Sec Sch
Croftcroighn Sch
St Rose of Lima Prim Sch
Twr
Prim Sch
Ruchazie Prim Sch
Ruchazie
Auchinlea Park
Provan Hall
GARTLOCH RD
B765
B806
M8
4
3
2
1
69
68
67
66
64
65
66
D
E
F
119
100

99 80

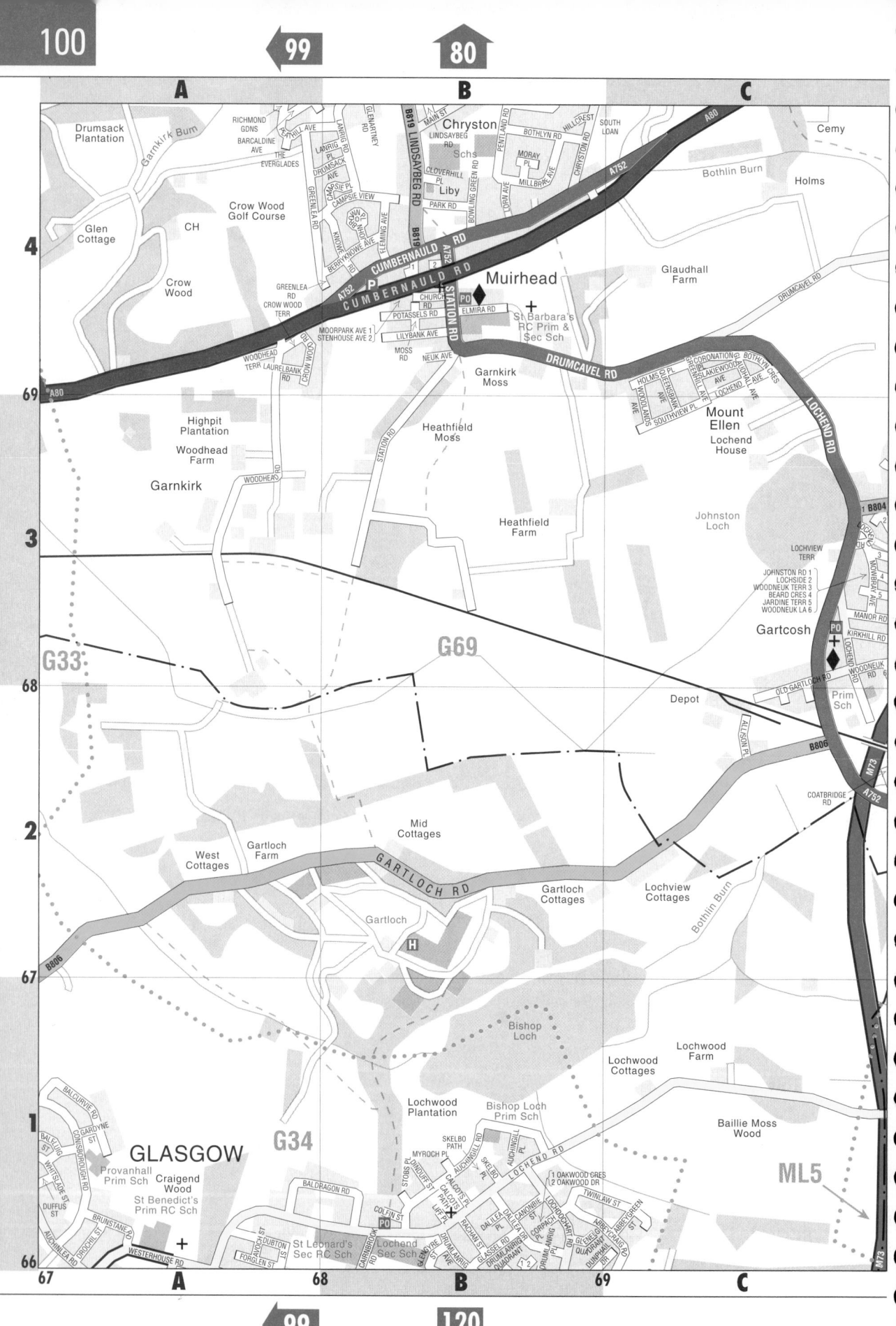
Drumsack Plantation
Garnkirk Burn
Glen Cottage
CH
Crow Wood Golf Course
Crow Wood
Chryston
Muirhead
CUMBERNAULD RD
STATION RD
DRUMCAVEL RD
Garnkirk Moss
St Barbara's RC Prim & Sec Sch
Glaudhall Farm
Bothlin Burn
Holms
Cemy
Highpit Plantation
Woodhead Farm
Garnkirk
Heathfield Moss
Heathfield Farm
Mount Ellen
Lochend House
LOCHEND RD
Johnston Loch
Gartcosh
G33
G69
Depot
Prim Sch
Mid Cottages
West Cottages
Gartloch Farm
GARTLOCH RD
Gartloch
Gartloch Cottages
Lochview Cottages
Bishop Loch
Lochwood Cottages
Lochwood Farm
Lochwood Plantation
Bishop Loch Prim Sch
Baillie Moss Wood
GLASGOW
Provanhall Prim Sch
Craigend Wood
St Benedict's Prim RC Sch
G34
St Leonard's Sec RC Sch
Lochend Sec Sch
ML5
LOCHEND RD
A B C
67 68 69
4 3 2 1

99 120

81
102

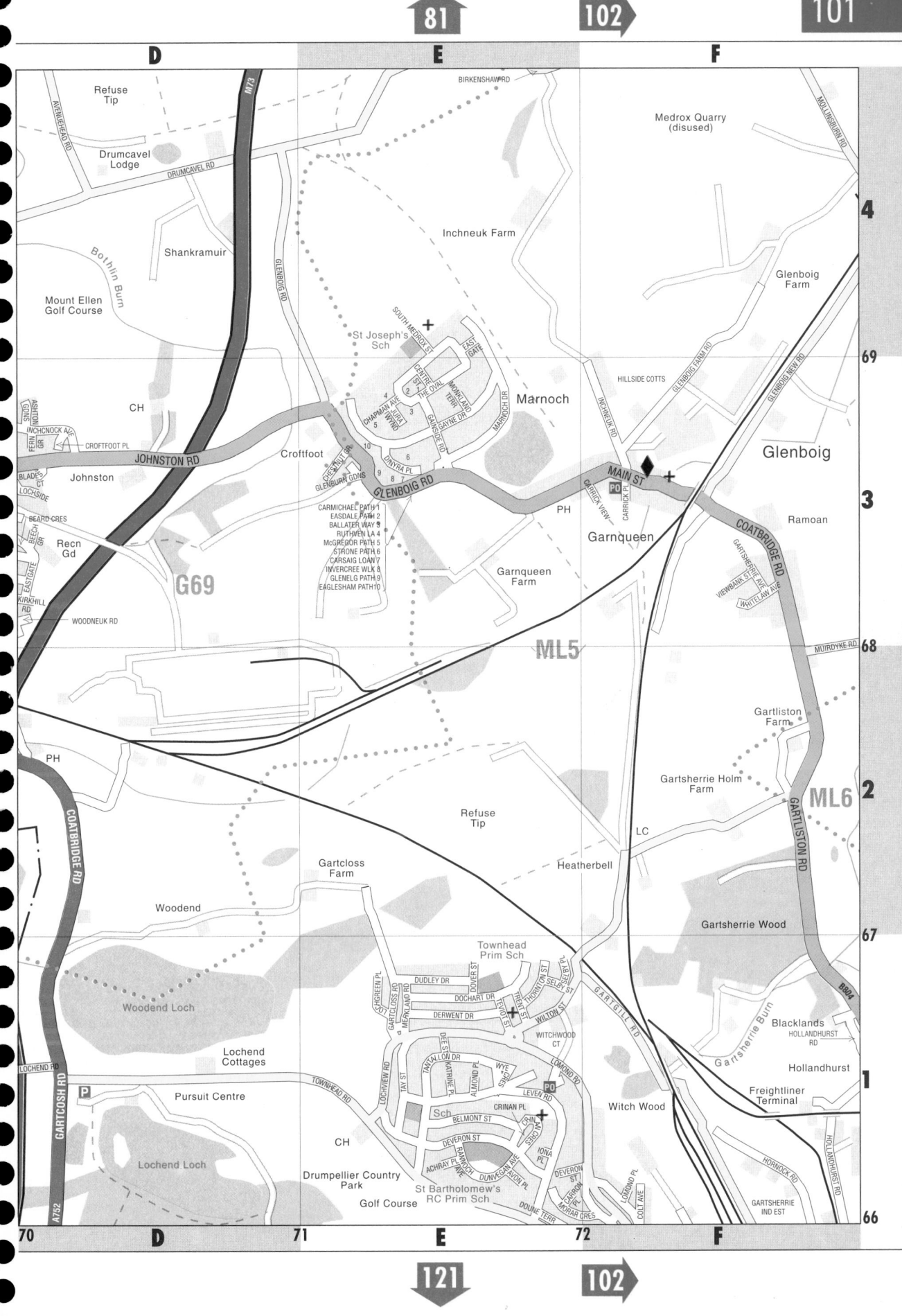
D
E
F
Refuse Tip
M73
BIRKENSHAW RD
Medrox Quarry (disused)
MOLLINSBURN RD
AVENUEHEAD RD
Drumcavel Lodge
DRUMCAVEL RD
Inchneuk Farm
Bothlin Burn
Shankramuir
GLENBOIG RD
Glenboig Farm
Mount Ellen Golf Course
SOUTH MEDROX ST
St Joseph's Sch
EAST GATE
CENTRE ST
THE OVAL
MONKLAND TERR
CHAPMAN AVE
JURA WYND
GAYNE DR
GAINSIDE RD
MARNOCH DR
Marnoch
HILLSIDE COTTS
GLENBOIG FARM RD
GLENBOIG NEW RD
INCHNEUK RD
CH
ASHTON GDNS
INCHNCOCK AVE
FERN GR
CROFTFOOT PL
JOHNSTON RD
Croftfoot
CHESTNUT GR
GLENBURN GDNS
DINYRA PL
GLENBOIG RD
MAIN ST
PO
CARRICK PL
CARRICK VIEW
Glenboig
BLADES CT
Johnston
LOCHSIDE
CARMICHAEL PATH 1
EASDALE PATH 2
BALLATER WAY 3
RUTHVEN LA 4
McGREGOR PATH 5
STRONE PATH 6
CARSAIG LOAN 7
INVERCREE WLK 8
GLENELG PATH 9
EAGLESHAM PATH 10
PH
Garnqueen
Ramoan
COATBRIDGE RD
BEARD CRES
BEECH GR
Recn Gd
EASTGATE
G69
Garnqueen Farm
GARTSHERRIE AVE
VIEWBANK ST
WHITELAW AVE
KIRKHILL RD
WOODNEUK RD
ML5
MUIRDYKE RD
Gartliston Farm
PH
Gartsherrie Holm Farm
COATBRIDGE RD
Refuse Tip
ML6
GARTLISTON RD
LC
Gartcloss Farm
Heatherbell
Woodend
Gartsherrie Wood
Townhead Prim Sch
DUDLEY DR
DOVER ST
THORNTON ST
SELBY ST
DOCHART DR
TRENT ST
TEVIOT ST
DERWENT DR
WILTON ST
GARTGILL RD
Woodend Loch
GARTCLOSS RD
MERKLAND RD
WITCHWOOD CT
Blacklands
HOLLANDHURST RD
Gartsherrie Burn
B804
Lochend Cottages
TANTALLON DR
DEE ST
KATRINE PL
ALMOND PL
WYE CRES
LOMOND RD
Hollandhurst
LOCHEND RD
GARTCOSH RD
TOWNHEAD RD
LOCHVIEW RD
TAY ST
LEVEN RD
Freightliner Terminal
P
Pursuit Centre
Sch
BELMONT ST
CRINAN PL
Witch Wood
CH
DEVERON ST
IONA PL
HORNOCK RD
HOLLANDHURST RD
Lochend Loch
ACHRAY PL
RANNOCH AVE
DUNVEGAN AVE
AVON PL
DEVERON ST
Drumpellier Country Park
St Bartholomew's RC Prim Sch
CARRON PL
LOMOND PL
COLT AVE
Golf Course
DOUNE TERR
MORAR CRES
GARTSHERRIE IND EST
A752
70
71
72
4
69
3
68
2
67
1
66

121
102

101
82

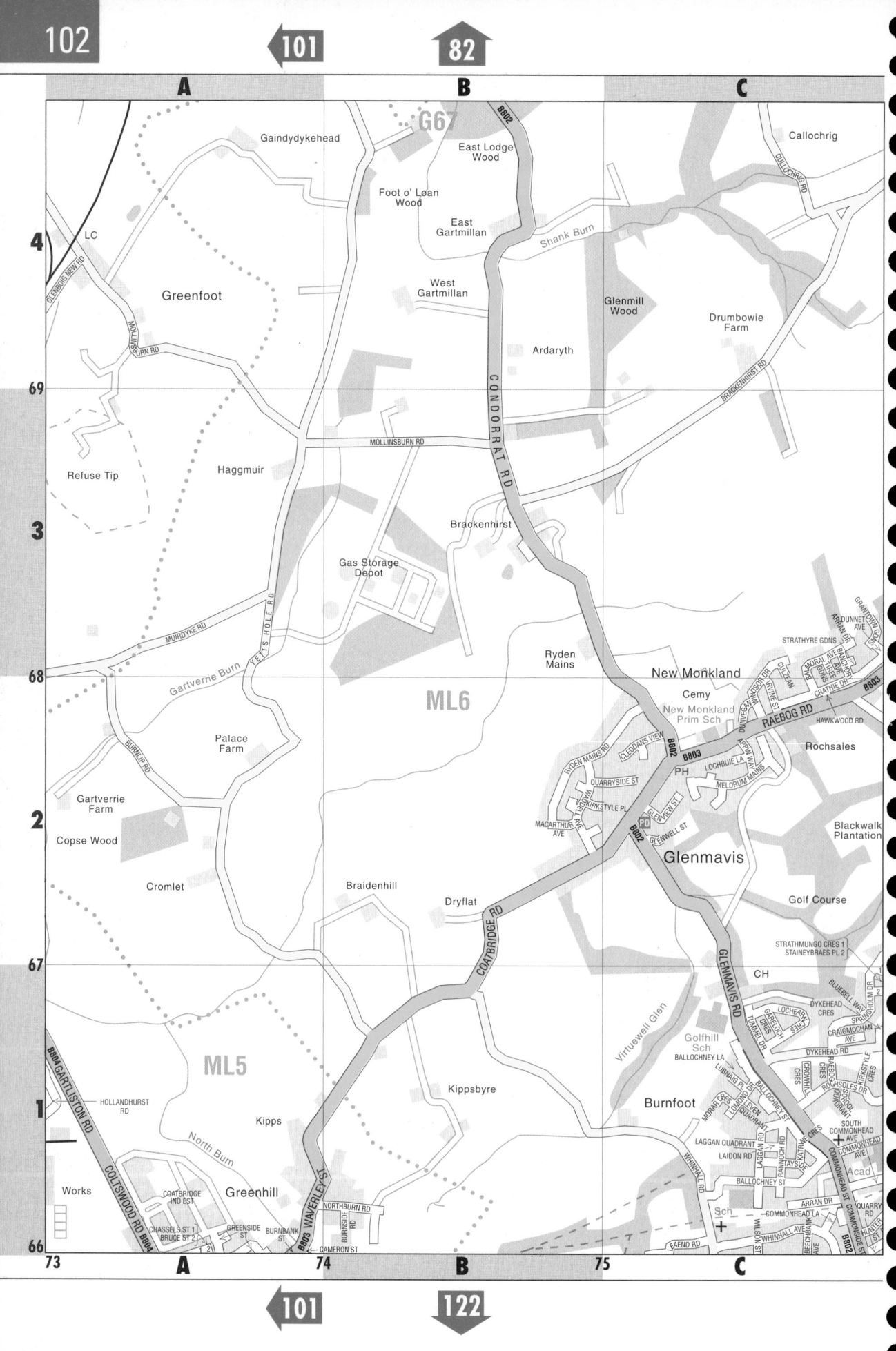
A
B
C
Gaindydykehead
G67
East Lodge Wood
Callochrig
Foot o' Loan Wood
East Gartmillan
LC
Shank Burn
Greenfoot
West Gartmillan
Glenmill Wood
Drumbowie Farm
Ardaryth
CONDORRAT RD
BRACKENHIRST RD
MOLLINSBURN RD
Refuse Tip
Haggmuir
Brackenhirst
Gas Storage Depot
MUIRDYKE RD
YETTS HOLE RD
Ryden Mains
New Monkland
Cemy
New Monkland Prim Sch
Gartverrie Burn
ML6
RAEBOG RD
Rochsales
Palace Farm
PH
Gartverrie Farm
Copse Wood
Blackwalk Plantation
Glenmavis
Cromlet
Braidenhill
Dryflat
Golf Course
COATBRIDGE RD
GLENMAVIS RD
CH
Virtuewell Glen
Golfhill Sch
ML5
Kippsbyre
Burnfoot
Kipps
North Burn
Works
Greenhill
WAVERLEY ST
GARTLISTON RD
COLTSWOOD RD
Acad
Sch
4
69
3
68
2
67
1
66
73
74
75

101
122

83 104

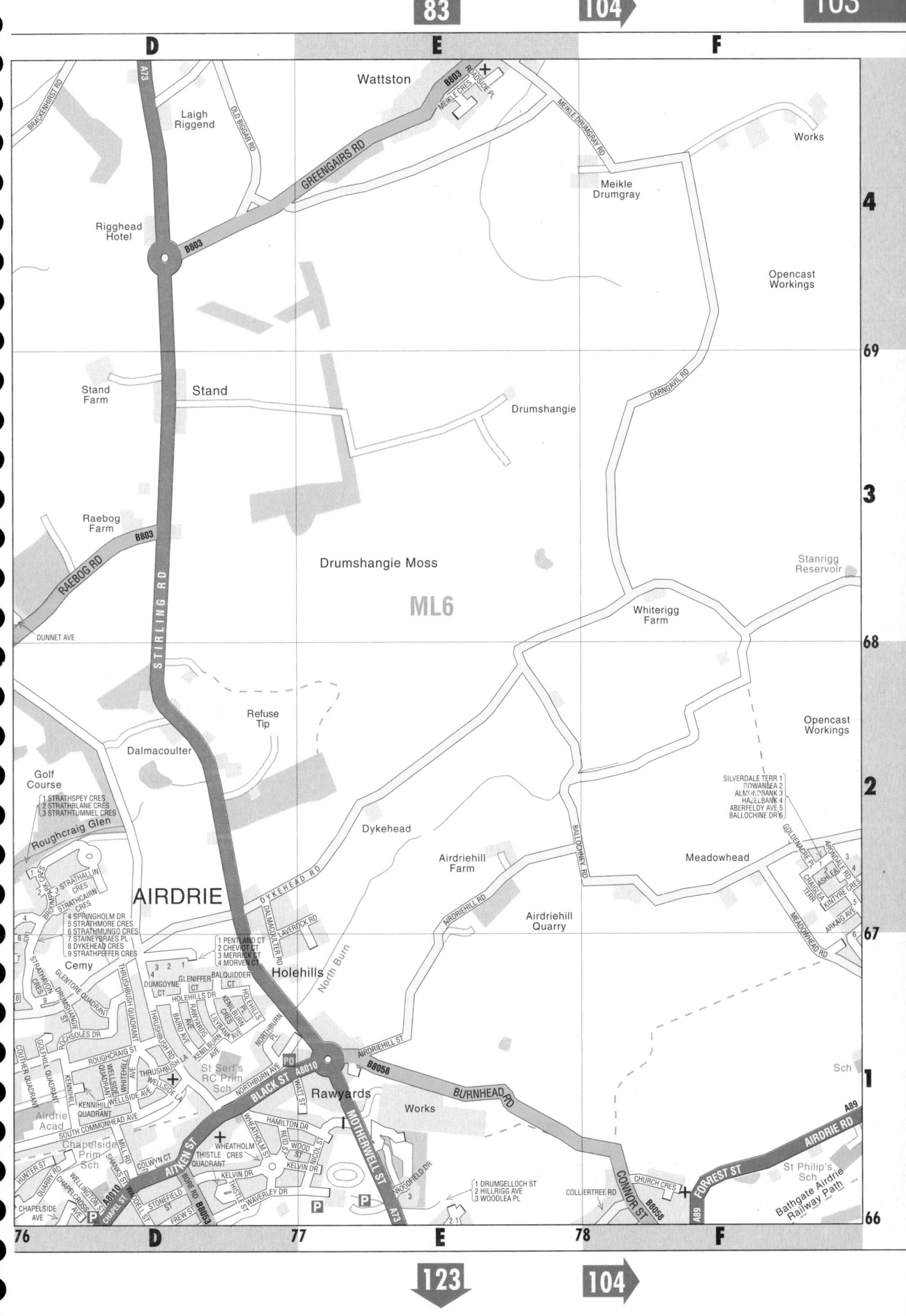
D
E
F
Wattston
Laigh Riggend
Rigghead Hotel
GREENGAIRS RD
B803
A73
Meikle Drumgray
Works
Opencast Workings
Stand Farm
Stand
Drumshangie
Raebog Farm
RAEBOG RD
STIRLING RD
Drumshangie Moss
ML6
Whiterigg Farm
Stanrigg Reservoir
DARNGAVIL RD
Refuse Tip
Dalmacoulter
Golf Course
Roughcraig Glen
Dykehead
Airdriehill Farm
Meadowhead
AIRDRIE
Airdriehill Quarry
Holehills
North Burn
Cemy
Rawyards
Works
BURNHEAD RD
B8058
MOTHERWELL ST
BLACK ST
A8010
AITKEN ST
CONNOR ST
FORREST ST
AIRDRIE RD
A89
St Philip's Sch
Bathgate Airdrie Railway Path
Airdrie Acad
Chapelside Prim Sch
St Serf's RC Prim Sch
Sch
DUNNET AVE
1 STRATHSPEY CRES
2 STRATHBLANE CRES
3 STRATHTUMMEL CRES
4 SPRINGHOLM DR
5 STRATHMORE CRES
6 STRATHMUNGO CRES
7 STAINEYBRAES PL
8 DYKEHEAD CRES
9 STRATHPEFFER CRES
1 PENTLAND CT
2 CHEVIOT CT
3 MERRICK CT
4 MORVEN CT
SILVERDALE TERR 1
ROWANLEA 2
HAZELBANK 4
ABERFELDY AVE 5
BALLOCHINE DR 6
1 DRUMGELLOCH ST
2 HILLRIGG AVE
3 WOODLEA PL
4
69
3
68
2
67
1
66
76
77
78

103
84

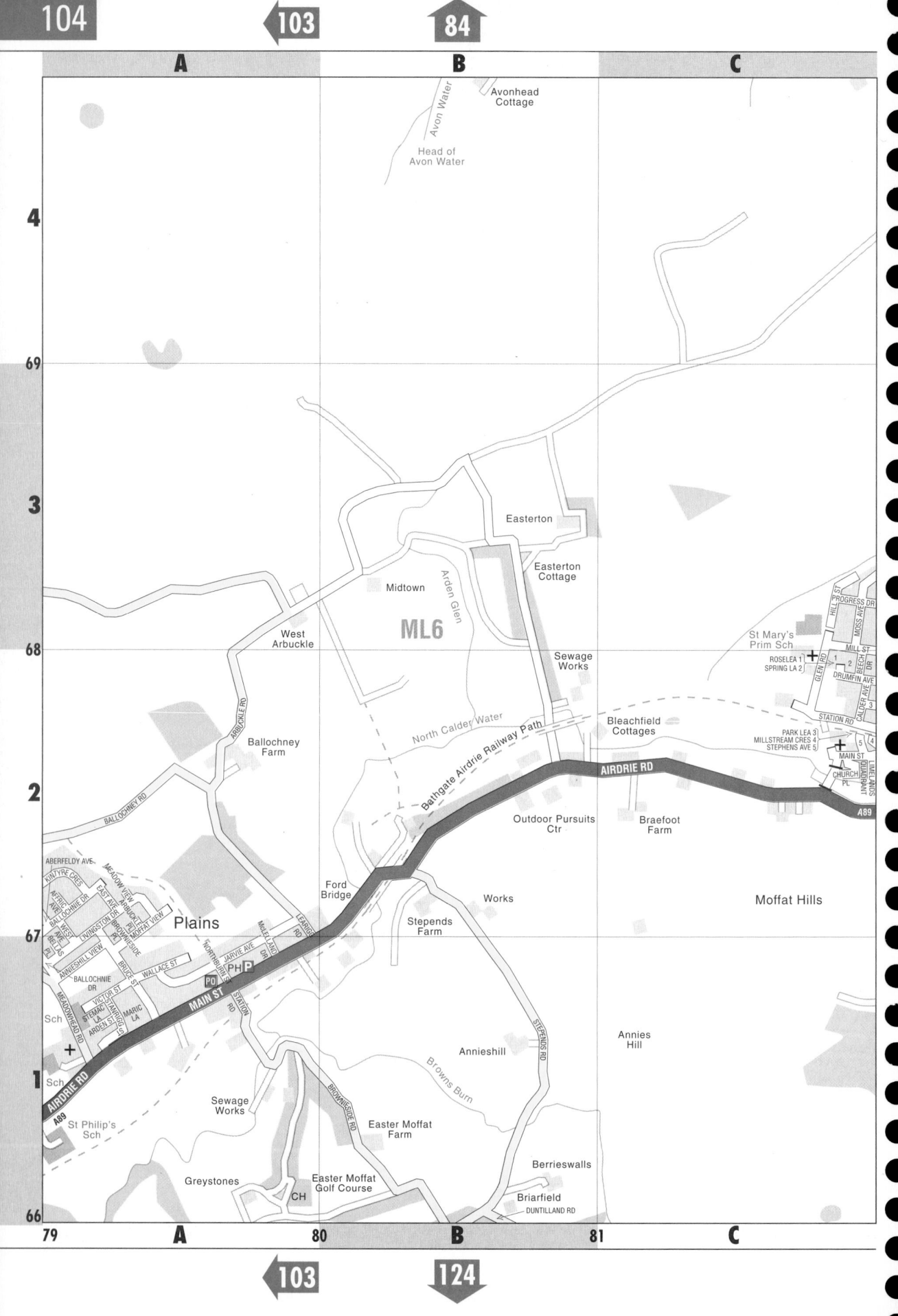
A
B
C
4
69
3
68
2
67
1
66
79
80
81
Avonhead Cottage
Avon Water
Head of Avon Water
Easterton
Easterton Cottage
Midtown
Arden Glen
ML6
West Arbuckle
Sewage Works
St Mary's Prim Sch
HILL ST
PROGRESS DR
MOSS AVE
MILL ST
GLEN RD
BEECH DR
DRUMFIN AVE
CALDER AVE
ROSELEA 1
SPRING LA 2
STATION RD
North Calder Water
Bleachfield Cottages
PARK LEA 3
MILLSTREAM CRES 4
STEPHENS AVE 5
MAIN ST
CHURCH PL
QUADRANT
LIMELANDS
Ballochney Farm
ARBUCKLE RD
Bathgate Airdrie Railway Path
AIRDRIE RD
A89
BALLOCHNEY RD
Outdoor Pursuits Ctr
Braefoot Farm
ABERFELDY AVE
KINTYRE CRES
MEADOW VIEW
AFRIC AVE
BALLOCHNIE DR
EAST AVE
ARBUCKLE PL
MOFFAT VIEW
WEST AVE
BELLAS PL
LIVINGSTON DR
BROWNIESIDE PL
Plains
Ford Bridge
Works
Moffat Hills
Stepends Farm
LEARIGG RD
McLELLAND DR
ANNIESHILL VIEW
JARVIE AVE
NORTHBURN ST
BALLOCHNIE DR
BRUCE ST
WALLACE ST
PH
P
PO
MAIN ST
MEADOWHEAD RD
VICTOR ST
STEMAC LA
STANRIGG ST
ARDEN ST
MARIC LA
STATION RD
Sch
STEPENDS RD
Annies Hill
Annieshill
Browns Burn
Sewage Works
St Philip's Sch
BROWNIESIDE RD
Easter Moffat Farm
Berrieswalls
Greystones
Easter Moffat Golf Course
CH
Briarfield
DUNTILLAND RD

103
124

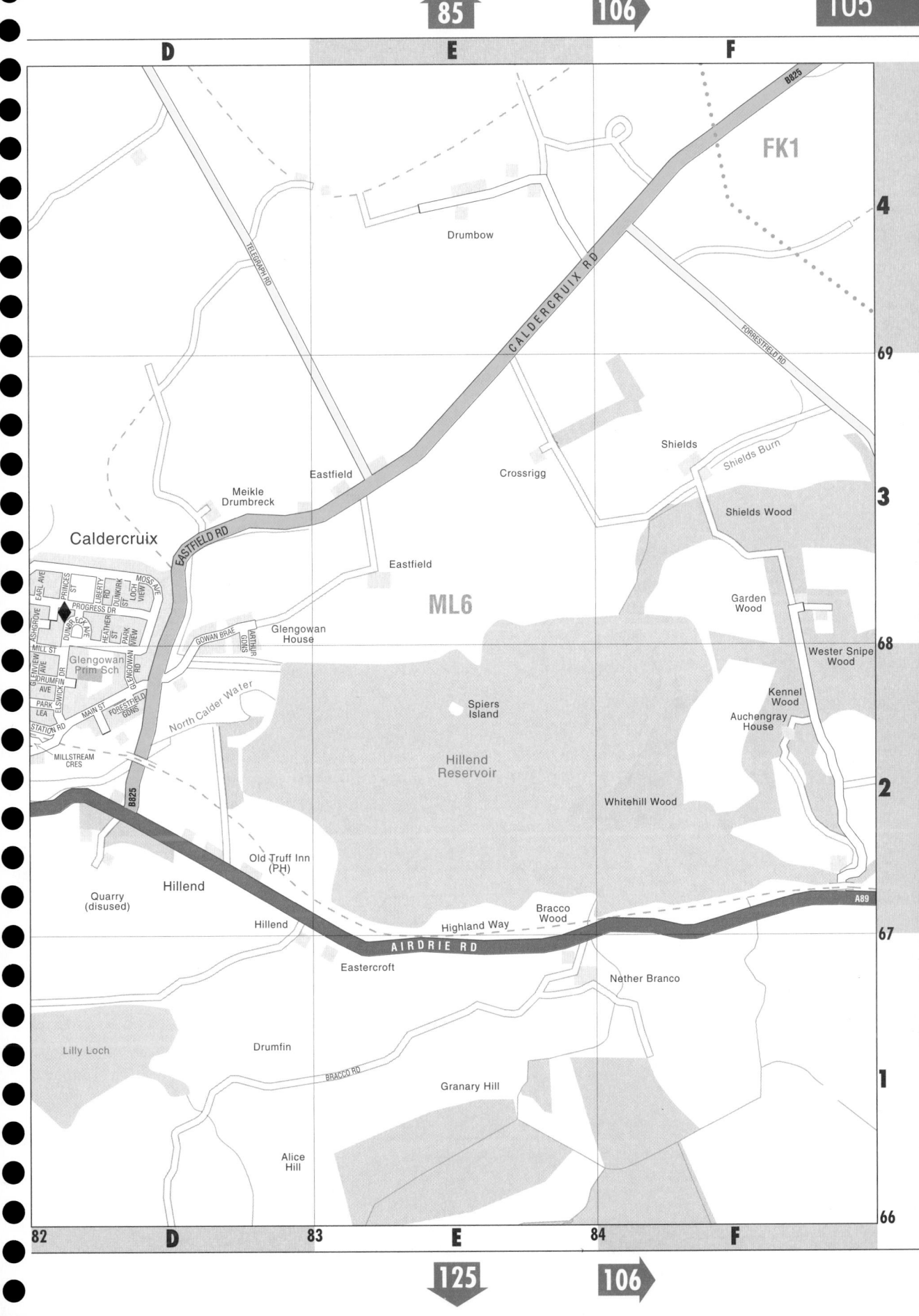

D E F

B825

FK1

4

Drumbow

TELEGRAPH RD

CALDERCRUIX RD

FORRESTFIELD RD

69

Shields

Shields Burn

3

Eastfield

Crossrigg

Meikle
Drumbreck

Shields Wood

EASTFIELD RD

Caldercruix

Eastfield

ML6

Garden
Wood

EARL AVE
PRINCES ST
LIBERTY RD
DUNKIRK RD
LOCH VIEW
MOSS AVE
ASHGROVE
HEATHER ST
PARK VIEW
DUNBAR ECT
PROGRESS DR

GOWAN BRAE

ARTHUR GDNS

Glengowan
House

Wester Snipe
Wood

68

MILL ST

Glengowan
Prim Sch

GLENGOWAN RD

North Calder Water

Spiers
Island

Kennel
Wood

GLENVIEW AVE
GLDRUMFIN AVE
ELSWICK DR
MAIN ST
FORESTFIELD GDNS

Auchengray
House

PARK
LEA
STATION RD

Hillend
Reservoir

MILLSTREAM
CRES

B825

Whitehill Wood

2

Old Truff Inn
(PH)

A89

Quarry
(disused)

Hillend

Bracco
Wood

Hillend

Highland Way

67

Eastercroft

AIRDRIE RD

Nether Branco

Lilly Loch

Drumfin

BRACCO RD

Granary Hill

1

Alice
Hill

66

105
86

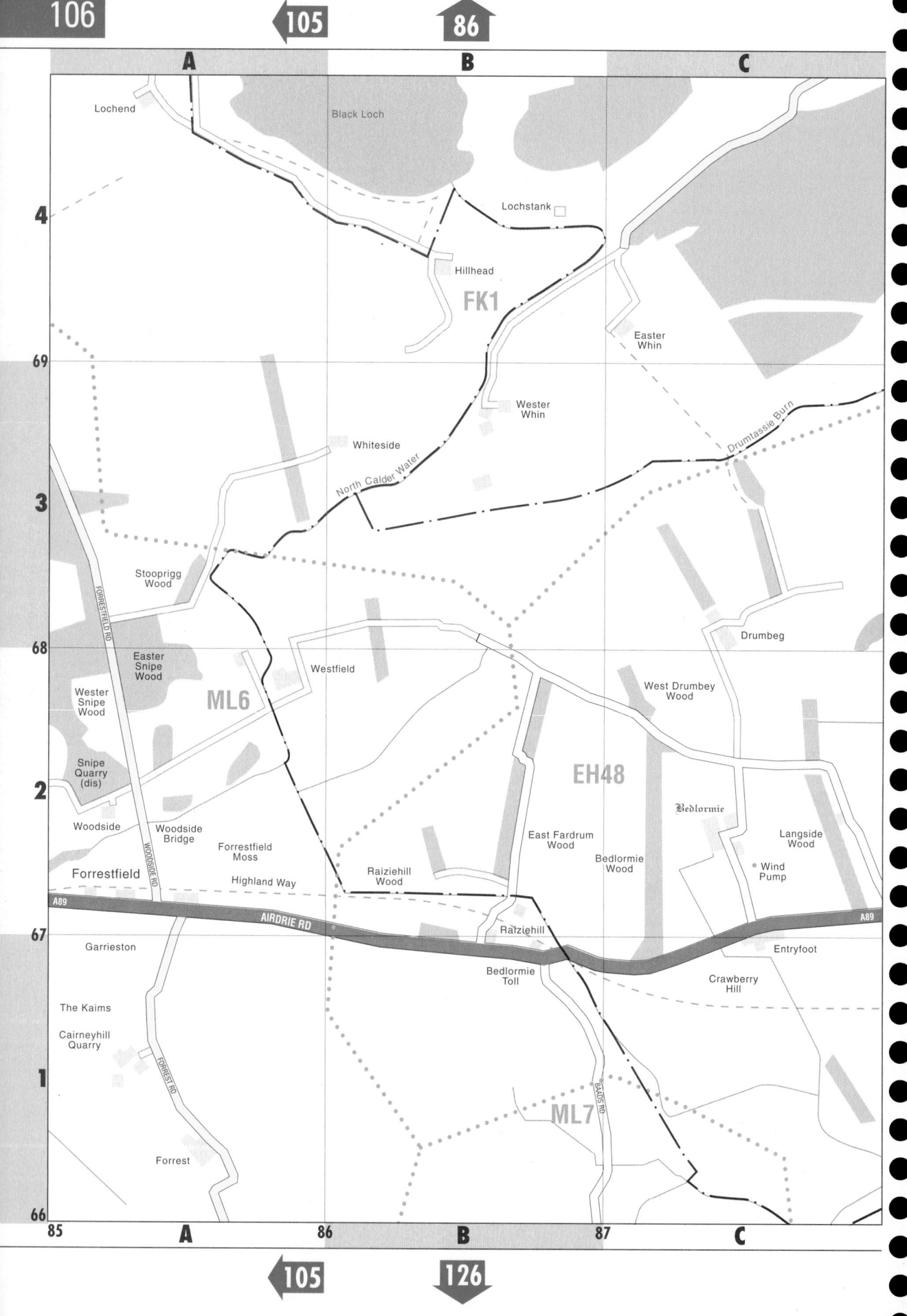
A
B
C
Lochend
Black Loch
Lochstank
Hillhead
FK1
Easter
Whin
Wester
Whin
Whiteside
North Calder Water
Drumtassie Burn
Stooprigg
Wood
FORRESTFIELD RD
Drumbeg
Easter
Snipe
Wood
Westfield
Wester
Snipe
Wood
ML6
West Drumbey
Wood
EH48
Snipe
Quarry
(dis)
Bedlormie
Woodside
Woodside
Bridge
Forrestfield
Moss
East Fardrum
Wood
Langside
Wood
Bedlormie
Wood
Wind
Pump
Forrestfield
Highland Way
Raiziehill
Wood
WOODSIDE RD
A89
AIRDRIE RD
Raiziehill
A89
Garrieston
Entryfoot
Bedlormie
Toll
Crawberry
Hill
The Kaims
Cairneyhill
Quarry
FORREST RD
BAADS RD
ML7
Forrest
4
69
3
68
2
67
1
66
85
86
87
A
B
C

105
126

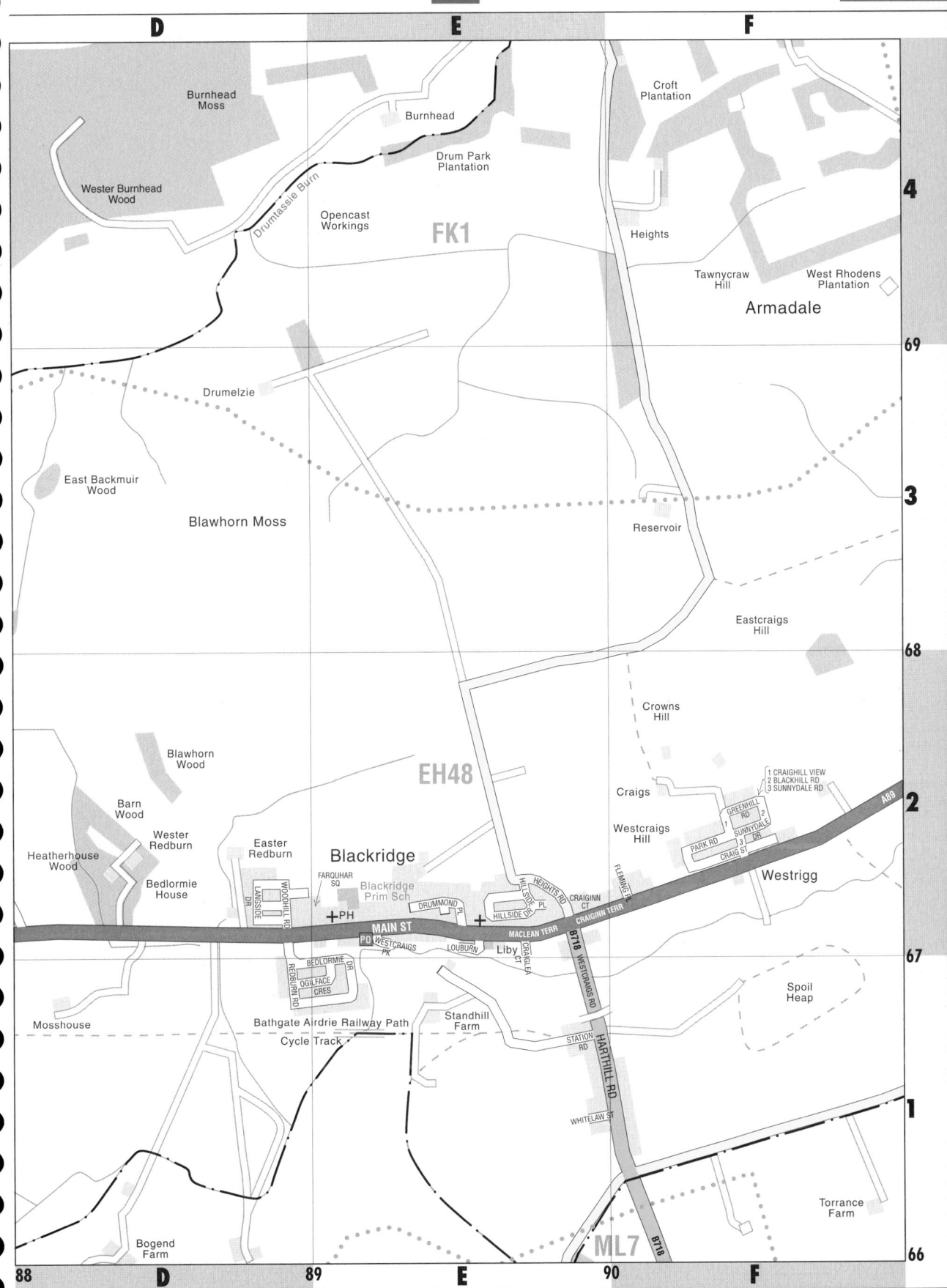

Burnhead
Moss

Burnhead

Wester Burnhead
Wood

Drum Park
Plantation

Croft
Plantation

Opencast
Workings

Drumtassie Burn

FK1

Heights

4

Tawnycraw
Hill

West Rhodens
Plantation

Armadale

69

Drumelzie

East Backmuir
Wood

Blawhorn Moss

Reservoir

3

Eastcraigs
Hill

68

Crowns
Hill

Blawhorn
Wood

EH48

Craigs

1 CRAIGHILL VIEW
2 BLACKHILL RD
3 SUNNYDALE RD

Barn
Wood

Heatherhouse
Wood

Wester
Redburn

Bedlormie
House

Easter
Redburn

Blackridge

FARQUHAR
SQ

Blackridge
Prim Sch

DRUMMOND PL

LANGSIDE DR

WOODHILL RD

+PH

HILLSIDE RD

HILLSIDE ST

HEIGHTS PL

CRAIGINN
CT

Westcraigs
Hill

GREENHILL
RD

SUNNYDALE
DR

PARK RD

CRAIG ST

A89

2

Westrigg

+

MAIN ST

PO

WESTCRAIGS
PK

REDBURN RD

BEDLORMIE DR

OGILFACE
CRES

WESTCRAIGS PK

LOUBURN

Liby

MACLEAN TERR

CRAIGLEA CT

CRAIGINN TERR

FLEMING PL

B718 WESTCRAIGS RD

67

Mosshouse

Bathgate Airdrie Railway Path

Cycle Track

Standhill
Farm

STATION
RD

HARTHILL RD

Spoil
Heap

WHITELAW ST

1

Bogend
Farm

ML7

B718

Torrance
Farm

66

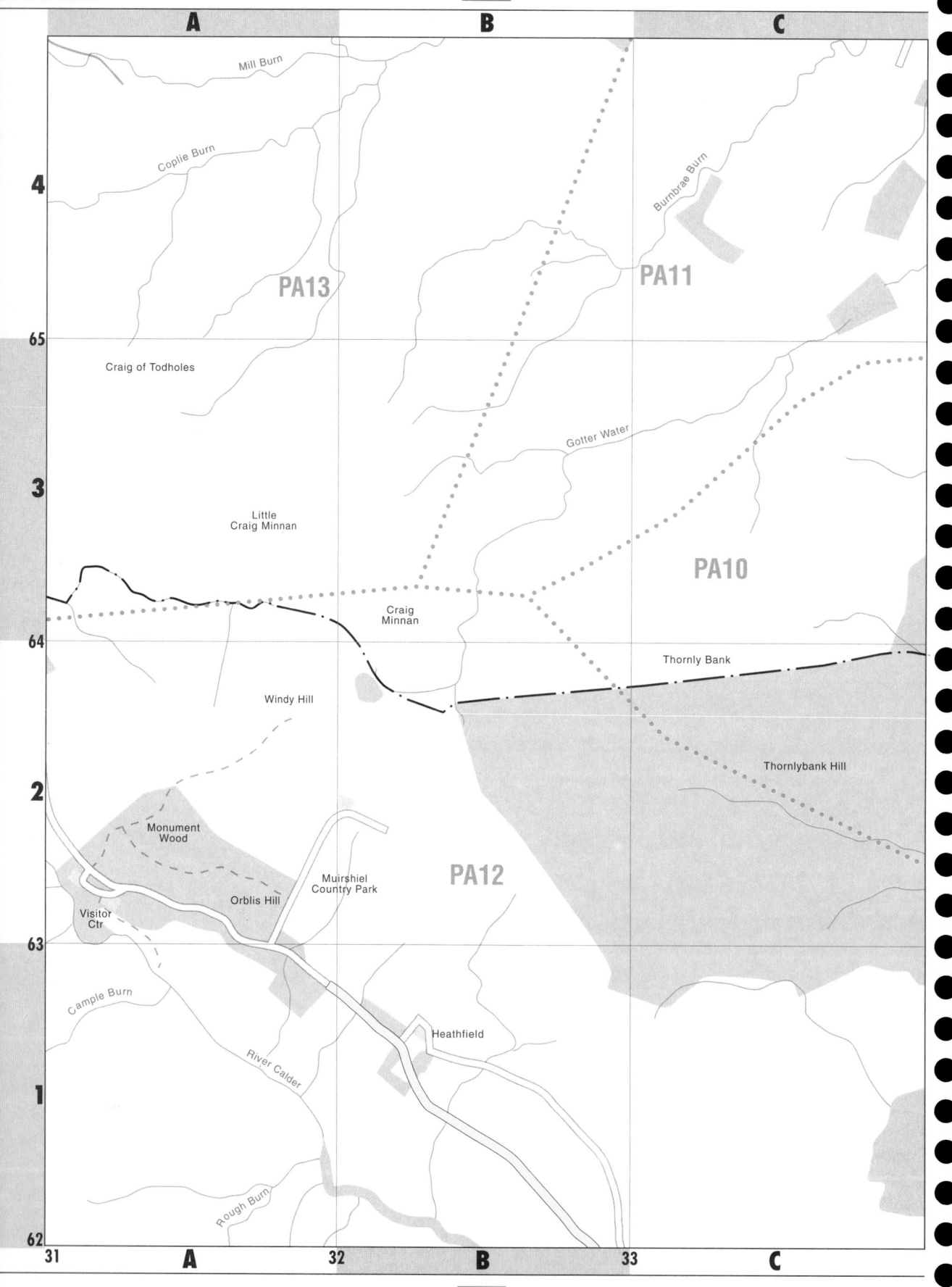

A   B   C

Mill Burn

Coplie Burn

4

PA13   PA11

Burnbrae Burn

65

Craig of Todholes

Gotter Water

3

Little
Craig Minnan   PA10

Craig
Minnan   Thornly Bank

64

Windy Hill

Thornlybank Hill

2

Monument
Wood   PA12

Muirshiel
Country Park
Orblis Hill

Visitor
Ctr

63

Cample Burn

River Calder   Heathfield

1

62

31   32   33
A   B   C

89
110

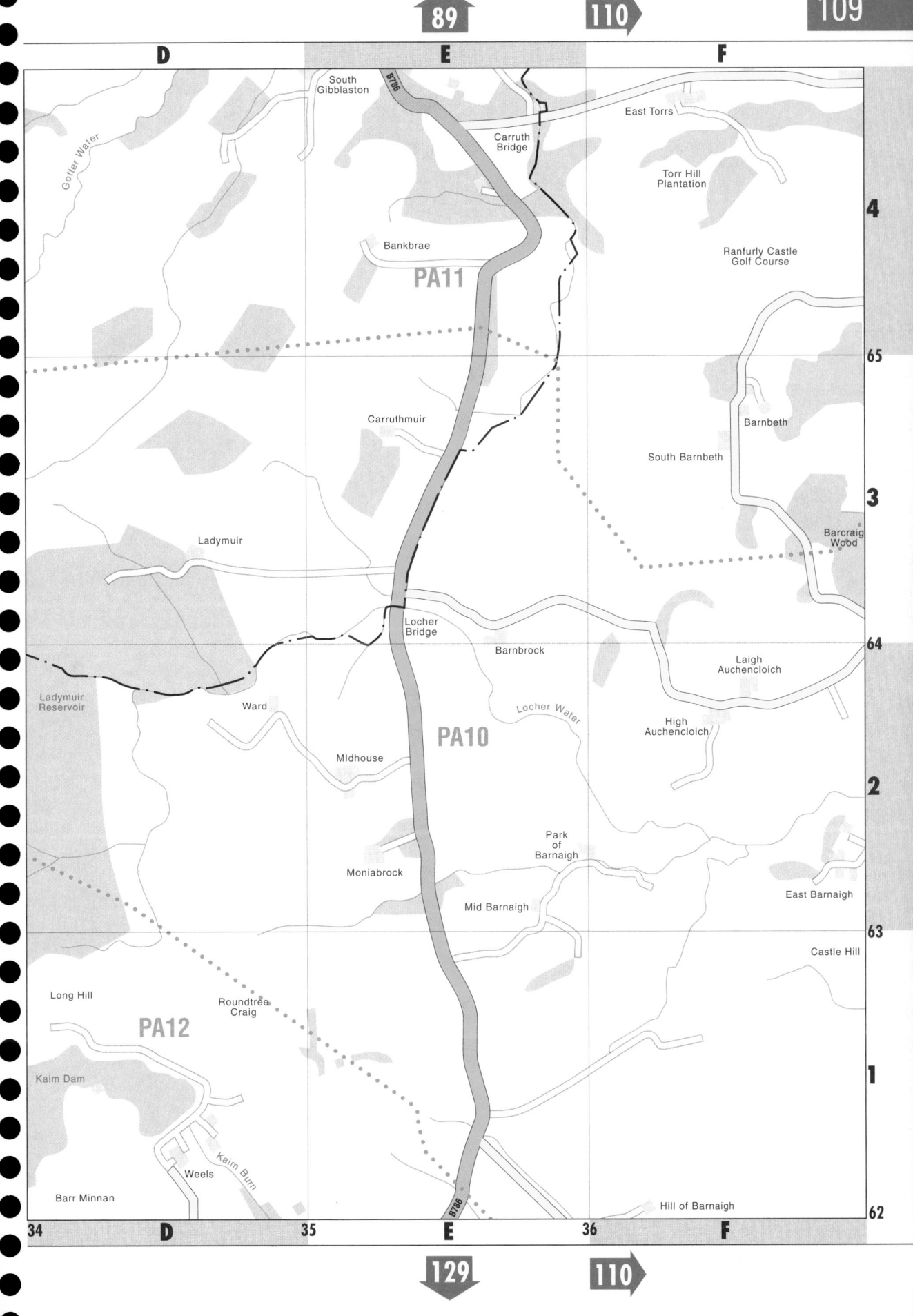
D
E
F
South Gibblaston
B786
East Torrs
Carruth Bridge
Gotter Water
Torr Hill Plantation
4
Bankbrae
Ranfurly Castle Golf Course
PA11
65
Carruthmuir
Barnbeth
South Barnbeth
3
Ladymuir
Barcraig Wood
Locher Bridge
64
Barnbrock
Laigh Auchencloich
Ladymuir Reservoir
Ward
Locher Water
High Auchencloich
PA10
MIdhouse
2
Park of Barnaigh
Moniabrock
Mid Barnaigh
East Barnaigh
63
Castle Hill
Long Hill
Roundtree Craig
PA12
1
Kaim Dam
Kaim Burn
Weels
Barr Minnan
B786
Hill of Barnaigh
62
34
D
35
E
36
F

129
110

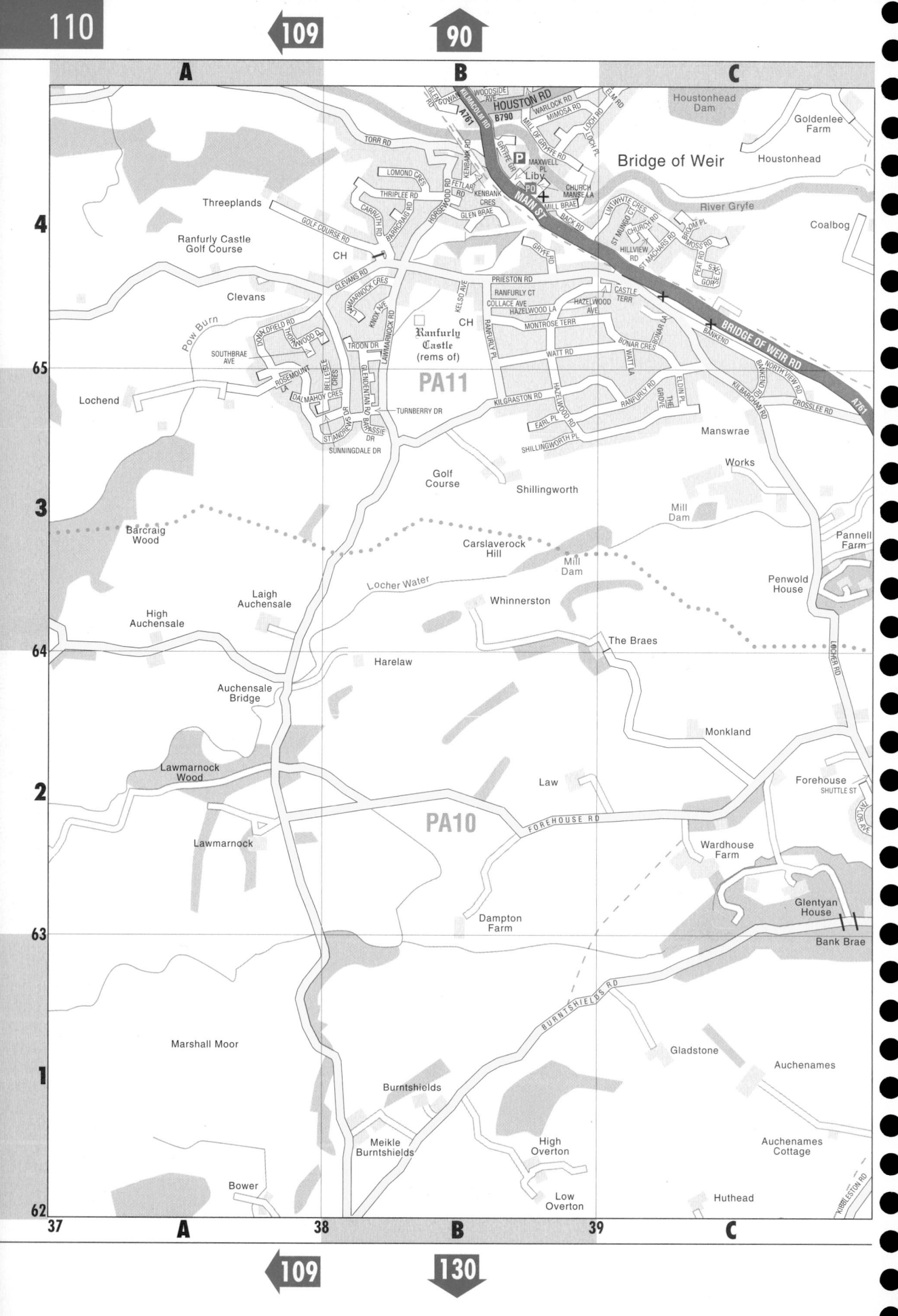
109
90
A
B
C
Houstonhead Dam
Goldenlee Farm
Bridge of Weir
Houstonhead
River Gryfe
Coalbog
HOUSTON RD
WOODSIDE AVE
WARLOCK RD
MIMOSA RD
ELM RD
LOCH RD
LOCH PL
KILMALCOLM RD
A761
B790
MILL OF GRYFFE RD
MAXWELL PL
Liby
PO
CHURCH MANSE LA
MILL BRAE
BACK RD
MAIN ST
GRYFFE GR
TORR RD
LOMOND CRES
THRIPLEE RD
KENBANK RD
FETLAR RD
KENBANK CRES
GLEN BRAE
HORSEWOOD RD
CARRUTH RD
BARRCRAIG RD
Threeplands
GOLF COURSE RD
Ranfurly Castle Golf Course
CH
CLEVANS RD
Clevans
Pow Burn
LAWMARNOCK CRES
KNOX AVE
LAWMARNOCK RD
TROON DR
Ranfurly Castle (rems of)
KELSO AVE
PRIESTON RD
RANFURLY CT
COLLACE AVE
HAZELWOOD LA
HAZELWOOD AVE
CASTLE TERR
MONTROSE TERR
RANFURLY PL
BONAR CRES
BONAR LA
WATT RD
WATT LA
GRYFFE RD
LINTWHITE CRES
ST MUNGO CT
CHURCH RD
ST MACHARS RD
HILLVIEW RD
BROOM PL
MOSS RD
PEAT RD
GORSE
BANKEND
BRIDGE OF WEIR RD
NORTH VIEW RD
BANKEND RD
KILBARCHAN RD
CROSSLEE RD
SOUTHBRAE AVE
ROSEMOUNT LA
DALMAHOY CRES
BELLEISLE CRES
GLENDENTAN RD
TURNBERRY DR
ST ANDREWS DR
GLENEAGLES DR
SUNNINGDALE DR
PA11
KILGRASTON RD
HAZELWOOD RD
RANFURLY RD
THE GROVE
ELDIN PL
EARL PL
SHILLINGWORTH PL
Lochend
Manswrae
Works
Golf Course
Shillingworth
Mill Dam
Barcraig Wood
Carslaverock Hill
Pannell Farm
Penwold House
Locher Water
Laigh Auchensale
High Auchensale
Whinnerston
The Braes
Harelaw
LOCHER RD
Auchensale Bridge
Monkland
Lawmarnock Wood
Law
Forehouse
SHUTTLE ST
TAYLOR AVE
FOREHOUSE RD
PA10
Lawmarnock
Wardhouse Farm
Glentyan House
Dampton Farm
Bank Brae
BURNTSHIELDS RD
Marshall Moor
Gladstone
Auchenames
Burntshields
Meikle Burntshields
High Overton
Auchenames Cottage
Bower
Low Overton
Huthead
KIBBLESTON RD
4
65
3
64
2
63
1
62
37
38
39
130

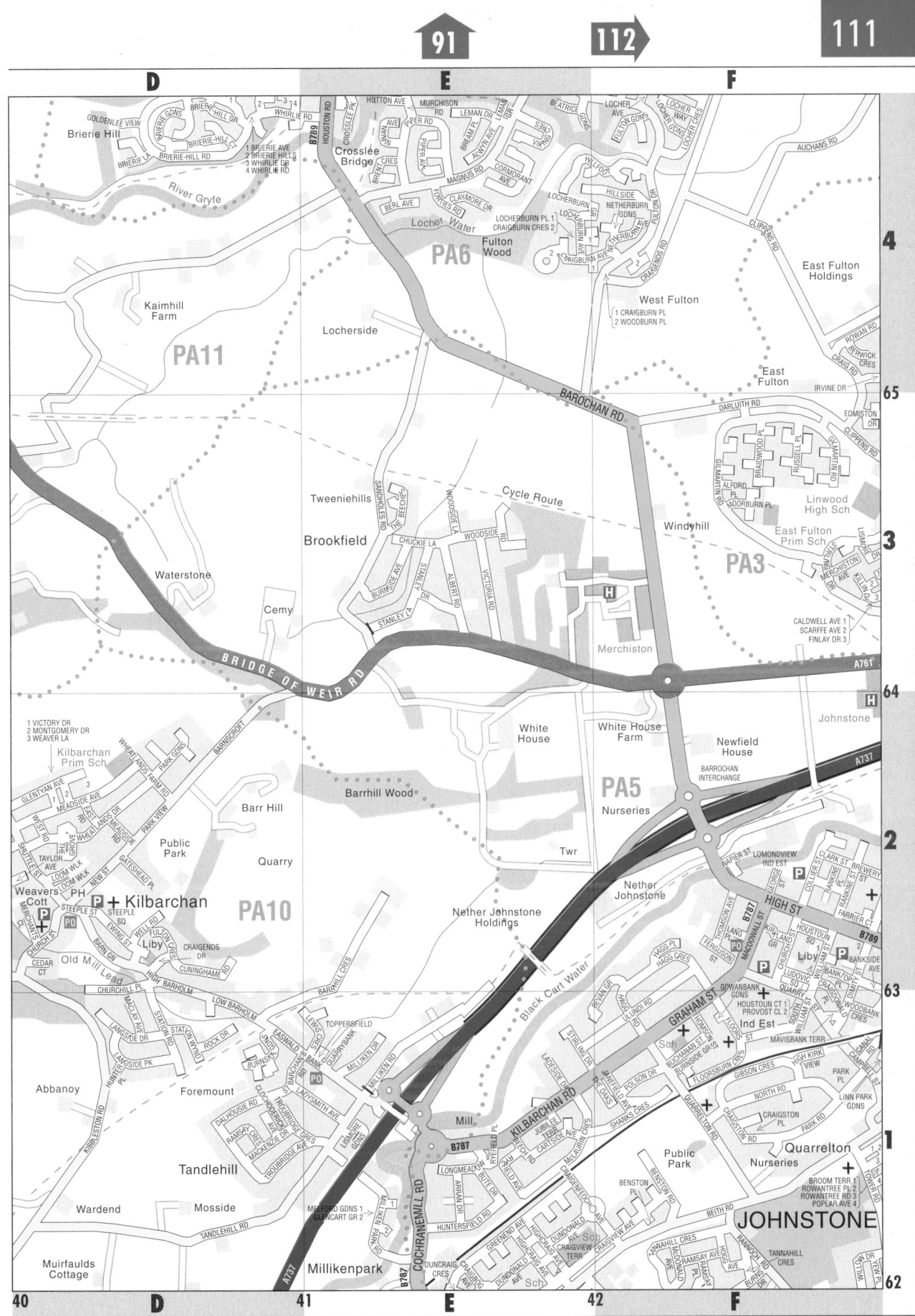

111
92

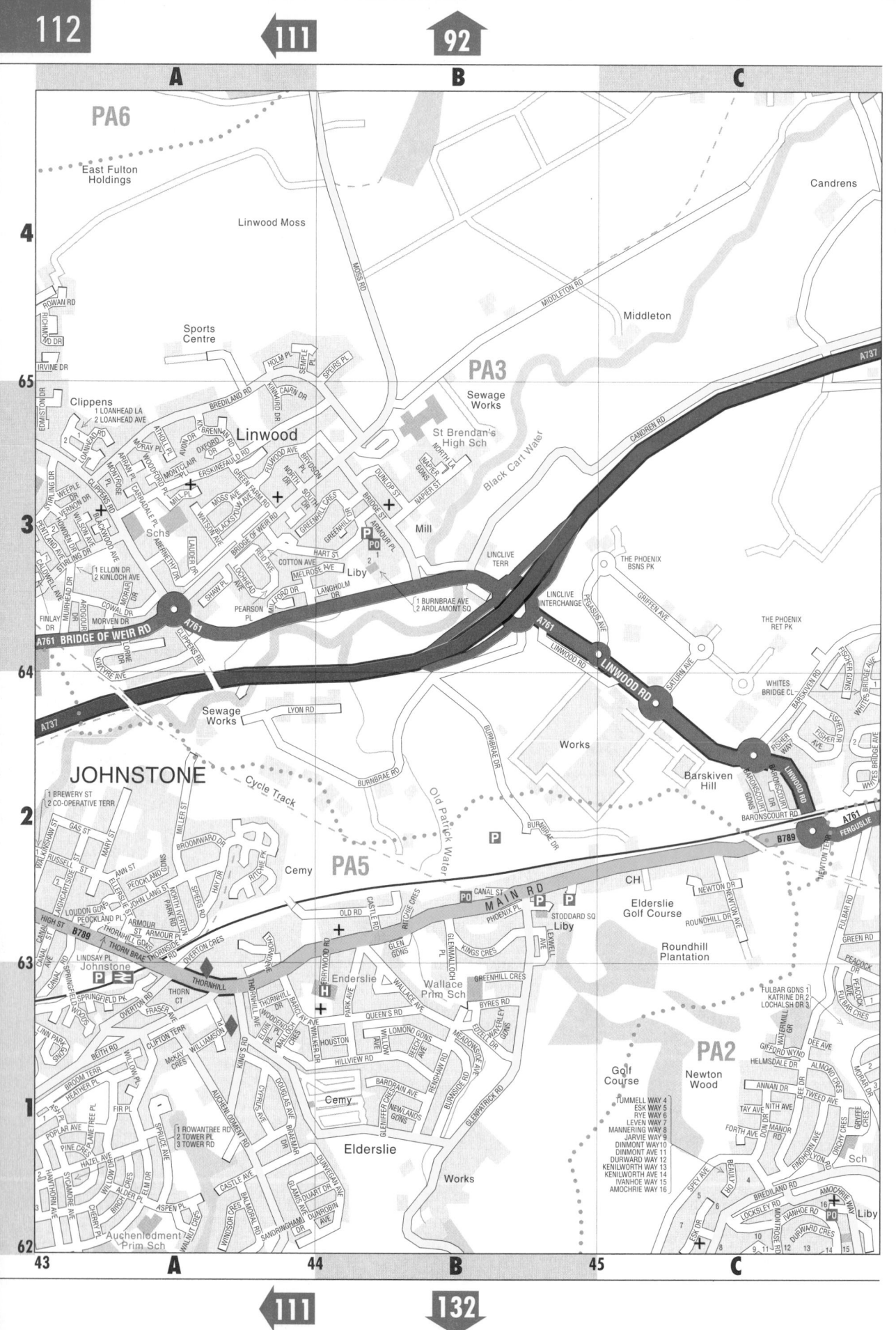
PA6
East Fulton Holdings
Linwood Moss
Candrens
Middleton
Sports Centre
PA3
Sewage Works
Clippens
Linwood
St Brendan's High Sch
Black Cart Water
Mill
Schs
Liby
LINCLIVE TERR
LINCLIVE INTERCHANGE
THE PHOENIX BSNS PK
THE PHOENIX RET PK
A761 BRIDGE OF WEIR RD
A737
A761
LINWOOD RD
Sewage Works
Works
Barskiven Hill
JOHNSTONE
Cycle Track
Old Patrick Water
Cemy
PA5
CH
Elderslie Golf Course
Roundhill Plantation
MAIN RD
B789
A761 FERGUSLIE
Johnstone
Enderslie
Wallace Prim Sch
Golf Course
PA2
Newton Wood
Cemy
Elderslie
Works
Auchenlodment Prim Sch
Sch
Liby
1 LOANHEAD LA
2 LOANHEAD AVE
1 ELLON DR
2 KINLOCH AVE
1 BURNBRAE AVE
2 ARDLAMONT SQ
1 BREWERY ST
2 CO-OPERATIVE TERR
1 ROWANTREE RD
2 TOWER PL
3 TOWER RD
FULBAR GDNS 1
KATRINE DR 2
LOCHALSH DR 3
TUMMELL WAY 4
ESK WAY 5
RYE WAY 6
LEVEN WAY 7
MANNERING WAY 8
JARVIE WAY 9
DINMONT WAY 10
DINMONT AVE 11
DURWARD WAY 12
KENILWORTH AVE 13
KENILWORTH AVE 14
IVANHOE WAY 15
AMOCHRIE WAY 16
A B C
4 65 3 64 2 63 1 62
43 44 45

111
132

93

114

D E F

Glasgow Airport

Boghead

St James' Park

Gockston

Shortroods

Liby

Hotel

Sewage Works

Ind Est

Laigh Park

White Cart Water

Pavilions

East Candren Cottage

PA3

Paisley St James

Craigielea Prim Sch

St Fergus's RC Prim Sch

Ind Est

St Mirren Pk (St Mirren FC)

Coll Annexe

Reid Kerr Coll

Ferguslie Park

Crem

Cemy

Ferguslie Gardens

Mus

TA Ctr

Univ Annexe

University of Paisley

Art Gall

Abbey

Muni Bldgs

Cnty Bldgs

L Ctr

St Martin's H Sch

Millarston

St Mary's Prim Sch

Castlehead H Sch

Castlehead

Paisley Canal

Saucel Hill

Recn Gd

Paisley Maternity

Royal Alexandra

PA2

PAISLEY

Loundsdale

Meikleriggs

Brodie Park

Carriagehill

Potterhill

Lochfield

Works

M8 A726 A737 A741 A761 B7050 B775 B774

BARNSFORD RD

GREENOCK RD

CALEDONIA ST

UNDERWOOD RD

GEORGE ST

CANAL ST

FERGUSLIE

MAXWELLTON ST

CAUSEYSIDE ST

NEILSTON RD

MOREDUN RD

RENFREW RD

GLASGOW RD

LONEND

MILL ST

4 3 2 1

65 64 63 62

46 47 48

D E F

133

114

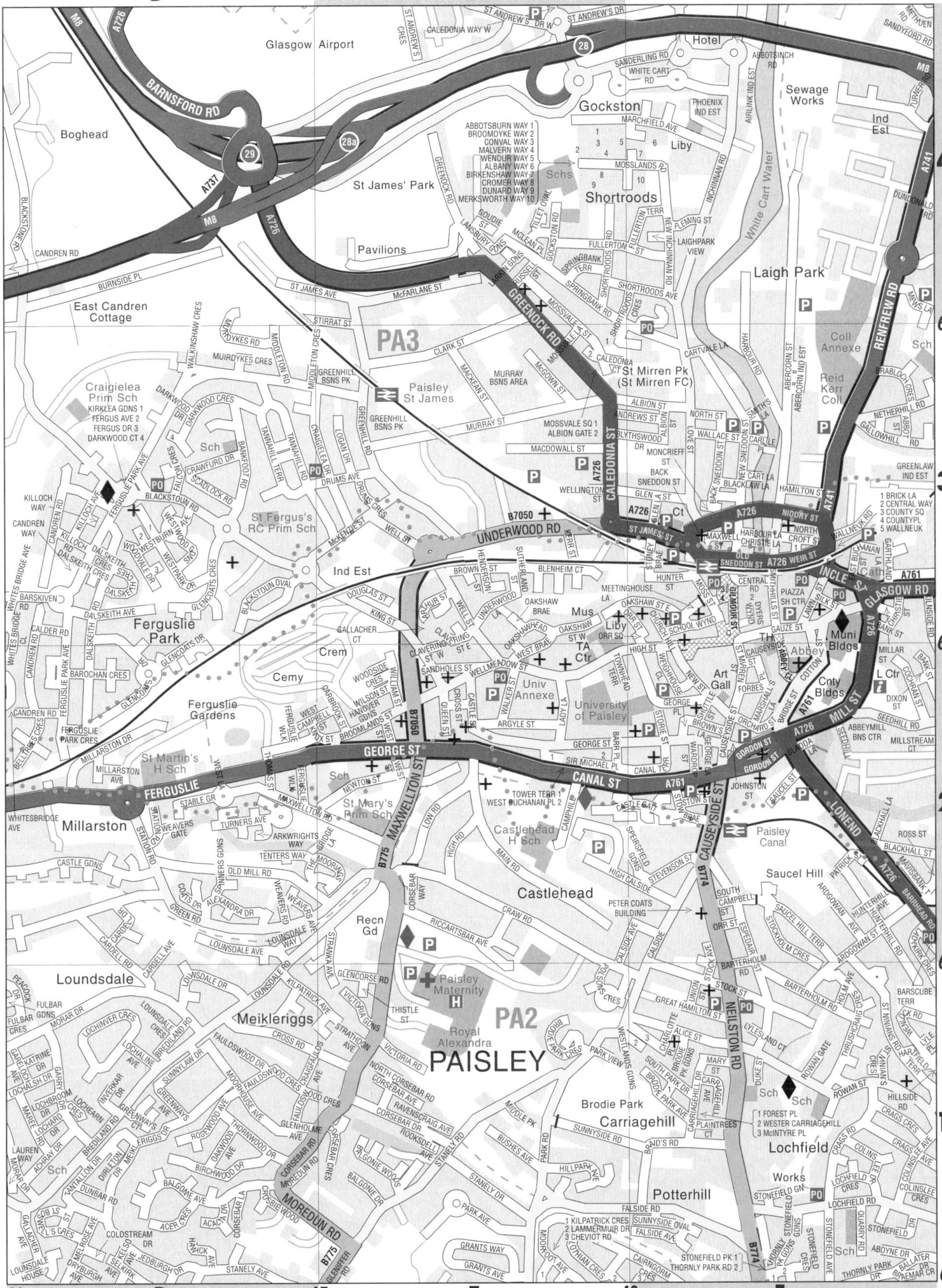

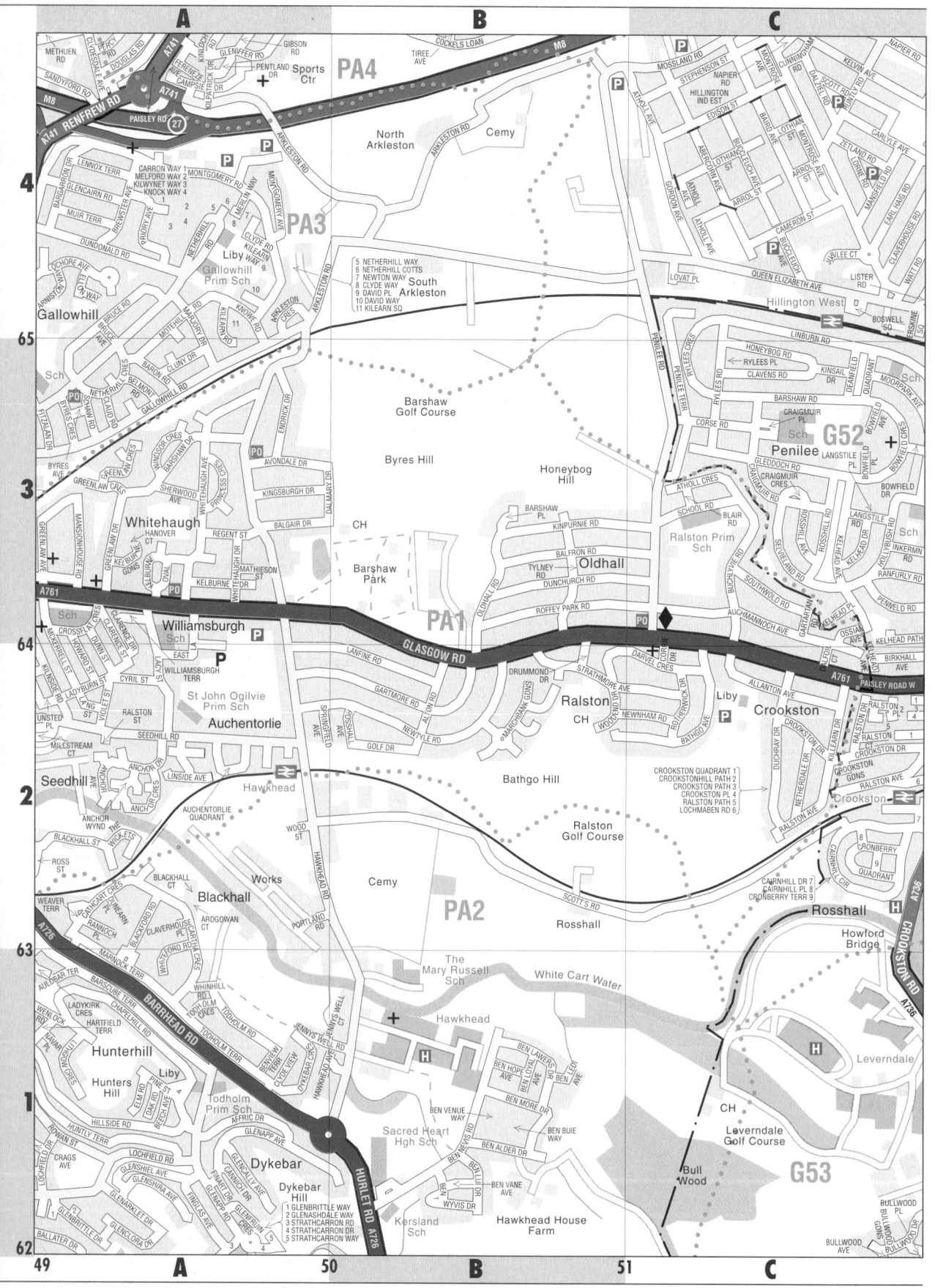
A
B
C
PA4
PA3
PA1
PA2
G52
G53
M8
A741
RENFREW RD
PAISLEY RD
27
Sports Ctr
North Arkleston
Cemy
ARKLESTON RD
COCKELS LOAN
TIREE AVE
MOSSLAND RD
STEPHENSON ST
NAPIER RD
HILLINGTON IND EST
EDISON ST
MONTROSE AVE
CUNNINGHAM RD
KELVIN AVE
NAPIER RD
LOTHIAN ST
ARROL ST
CAMERON ST
QUEEN ELIZABETH AVE
LOVAT PL
JUBILEE CT
LISTER RD
Hillington West
BOSWELL SQ
LINBURN RD
HONEYBOG RD
RYLEES PL
CLAVENS RD
KINSAIL DR
BARSHAW RD
CRAIGMUIR PL
CORSE RD
Penilee
LANGSTILE PL
BOWFIELD DR
ATHOLL CRES
SCHOOL RD
BLAIR RD
Ralston Prim Sch
PENILEE RD
CARRON WAY 1
MELFORD WAY 2
KILWYNET WAY 3
KNOCK WAY 4
LENNOX TERR
GLENCAIRN RD
MUIR TERR
DUNDONALD RD
MONTGOMERY RD
MERLIN WAY
Liby
Gallowhill Prim Sch
Gallowhill
5 NETHERHILL WAY
6 NETHERHILL COTTS
7 NEWTON WAY
8 CLYDE WAY
9 DAVID PL
10 DAVID WAY
11 KILEARN SQ
South Arkleston
Sch
GALLOWHILL RD
Barshaw Golf Course
Byres Hill
Honeybog Hill
AVONDALE DR
KINGSBURGH DR
BALGAIR DR
DALMARY DR
CH
Barshaw Park
Whitehaugh
GREENLAW AVE
MANSIONHOUSE RD
HANOVER CT
REGENT ST
MATHIESON ST
KELBURNE DR
KINPURNIE RD
BALFRON RD
TYLNEY RD
Oldhall
DUNCHURCH RD
ROFFEY PARK RD
OLDHALL RD
A761
GLASGOW RD
PAISLEY ROAD W
Williamsburgh
WILLIAMSBURGH TERR
CYRIL ST
St John Ogilvie Prim Sch
Auchentorlie
SEEDHILL RD
LANFINE RD
GARTMORE RD
NEWTYLE RD
GOLF DR
DRUMMOND DR
STRATHMORE AVE
DARVEL CRES
Ralston
NEWNHAM RD
BATHGO AVE
ALLANTON AVE
Crookston
AUCHMANNOCH AVE
SOUTHWOLD RD
KELHEAD PATH
BIRKHALL AVE
Seedhill
Hawkhead
LINSIDE AVE
AUCHENTORLIE QUADRANT
Bathgo Hill
CROOKSTON QUADRANT 1
CROOKSTONHILL PATH 2
CROOKSTON PATH 3
CROOKSTON PL 4
RALSTON PATH 5
LOCHMABEN RD 6
Ralston Golf Course
RALSTON AVE
CRONBERRY QUADRANT
CAIRNHILL DR 7
CAIRNHILL PL 8
CRONBERRY TERR 9
BLACKHALL ST
Blackhall
Works
Cemy
SCOTT'S RD
Rosshall
HAWKHEAD RD
PORTLAND RD
A726
BARRHEAD RD
The Mary Russell Sch
White Cart Water
Howford Bridge
CROOKSTON RD
A736
Hunterhill
Hunters Hill
Liby
Todholm Prim Sch
TODHOLM RD
Hawkhead
H
Leverndale
BEN LAWERS DR
BEN MORE DR
BEN VENUE WAY
BEN BUIE WAY
BEN ALDER DR
BEN VANE AVE
WYVIS DR
Sacred Heart Hgh Sch
Kersland Sch
Hawkhead House Farm
Bull Wood
Leverndale Golf Course
Dykebar
Dykebar Hill
1 GLENBRITTLE WAY
2 GLENASHDALE WAY
3 STRATHCARRON RD
4 STRATHCARRON RD
5 STRATHCARRON WAY
HURLET RD
HILLSIDE RD
LOCHFIELD RD
BALLATER DR
BULLWOOD PL
BULLWOOD GDNS
BULLWOOD AVE
BULLWOOD DR
4
65
3
64
2
63
1
62
49
50
51

95
116

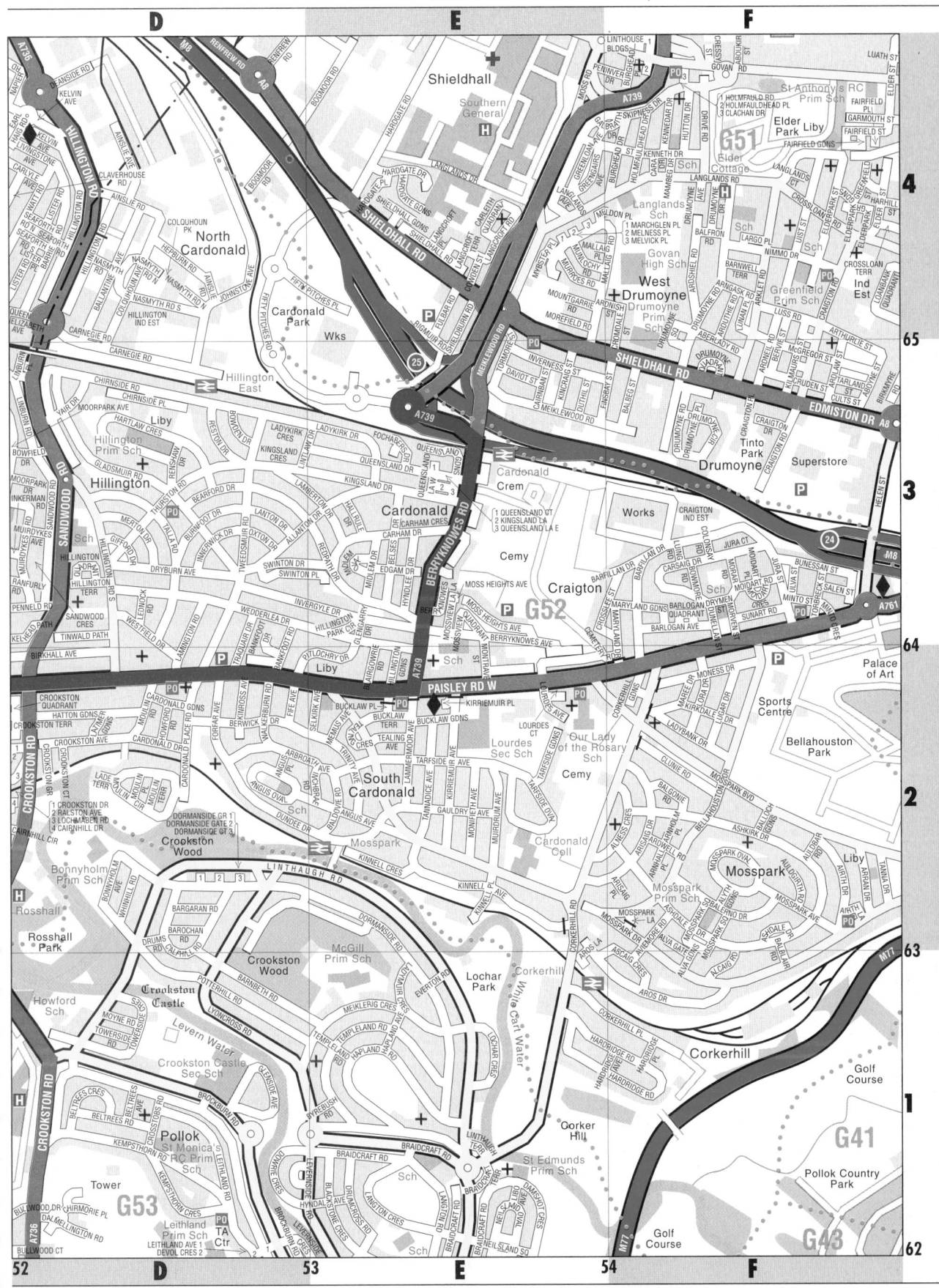
D
E
F
4
65
3
64
2
63
1
62
52
53
54
Shieldhall
Southern General
North Cardonald
Cardonald Park
Wks
Hillington East
Hillington
Hillington Prim Sch
Liby
Cardonald
Cardonald Crem
Cemy
Craigton
Works
Craigton Ind Est
West Drumoyne
Drumoyne Prim Sch
Govan High Sch
Langlands Sch
Elder Park
Elder Cottage
Greenfield Prim Sch
Ind Est
Tinto Park
Drumoyne
Superstore
St Anthony's RC Prim Sch
G51
G52
G53
G41
G43
Palace of Art
Sports Centre
Bellahouston Park
Mosspark
Mosspark Prim Sch
Our Lady of the Rosary Sch
Lourdes Sec Sch
Cardonald Coll
South Cardonald
Mosspark
Crookston Wood
Bonnyholm Prim Sch
Rosshall
Rosshall Park
McGill Prim Sch
Lochar Park
Corkerhill
White Cart Water
Crookston Castle
Levern Water
Crookston Castle Sec Sch
Howford Sch
Pollok
St Monica's RC Prim Sch
Tower
Leithland Prim Sch
TA Ctr
Corker Hill
St Edmunds Prim Sch
Golf Course
Pollok Country Park
SHIELDHALL RD
EDMISTON DR
PAISLEY RD W
BERRYKNOWES RD
HILLINGTON RD
SANDWOOD RD
CROOKSTON RD
LINTHAUGH RD
MOSSPARK BVD
CORKERHILL RD
M8
M77
A8
A739
A736
A761

135
116

115 **96**

For full street detail of the highlighted area see page 240.

A4
1 HARMONY ROW
2 WARDROP ST
3 GARMOUTH GDNS
4 CROSSLOAN TERR
5 ORKNEY PL

7 LETTOCH ST
B3
1 PORTER ST
2 NORTH GOWER ST
3 CLIFFORD PL
4 LANGSHOT ST
5 PLANTATION PARK GDNS

C3
1 EAGLESHAM CT
2 EAGLESHAM PL
3 MIDDLESEX GDNS
4 MILNPARK GDNS
5 LAMBHILL QUADRANT
6 SEAWARD ST

C4
1 CLIFTON PL
2 FITZROY PL
3 WESTMINSTER TERR
4 DERBY TERRACE LA
5 CORUNNA ST
6 STOBCROSS BSNS PK

7 HOULDSWORTH LA
8 CLYDEWAY IND EST
9 FINNIESTON SQ

(Street map of Govan, Ibrox, Bellahouston, Dumbreck, Pollokshields, Crossmyloof, Strathbungo areas of Glasgow. Major features include: Govan, Ibrox Stadium (Rangers FC), Scottish Exhibition & Conference Centre, Finnieston, Prince's Dock, River Clyde, Festival Park, Plantation, Kingston, Anderston, Cranston Hill, Bellahouston Park, Palace of Art, Pollok Country Park, Burrell Collection (Mus), Golf Course, Haggs Castle (Mus), Pollokshields, Maxwell Park, Crossmyloof, Waverley Park, Queen's Park, Strathbungo.)

115 **136**

C1
1 DINMONT PL
2 LOCHSIDE ST
3 WESTCLYFFE ST
4 ABBOT ST
5 SHAWLANDS CROSS
6 NIDDRIE SQ
7 BARBRECK RD

C2
1 ST JOHN'S QUADRANT
2 MAXWELL OVAL
3 LINCLUDEN PATH
4 KNOWHEAD TERR
5 KNOWHEAD GDNS

For full street detail of the highlighted area see pages 240 and 241.

D3
1 LANGBANK ST
2 KILBARCHAN ST
3 COBURG ST
4 HERBERTSON ST
5 S PORTLAND ST
6 BEDFORD LA
7 STIRLINGFAULD PL

97

F3
1 ABERCROMBY SQ
2 MILLROAD GDNS
3 FORBES DR
4 REDAN ST
5 OLYMPIA ST
6 BRIDGETON BSNS CTR

118

F3
7 ABERCROMBY ST
8 GRAIGNESTOCK PL
9 CLAYTHORN CIR
10 MONTEITH PL
F4
1 McINTOSH CT
2 CARDROSS CT
3 SETON TERR
4 OAKLEY TERR
5 CLAYTON TERR
6 BROOMPARK ST
7 BROOMPARK LA
8 BROOMPARK CIR

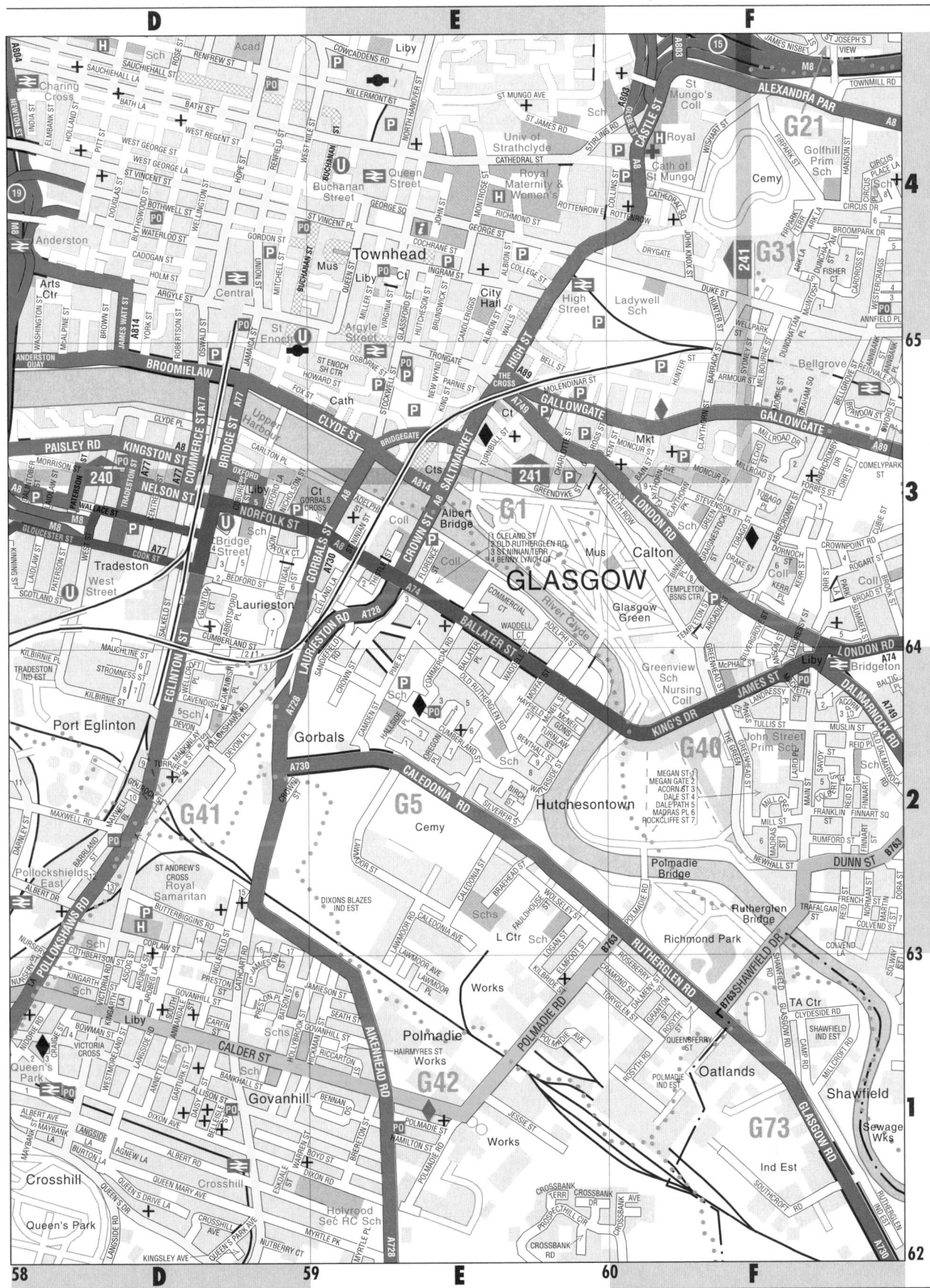
D
E
F
GLASGOW
Charing Cross
Anderston
Arts Ctr
Townhead
Buchanan Street
Queen Street
Univ of Strathclyde
Royal Maternity & Women's
St Mungo's Coll
Cath of St Mungo
Cemy
Golfhill Prim Sch
Central
St Enoch
Argyle Street
City Hall
High Street
Ladywell Sch
Bellgrove
BROOMIELAW
CLYDE ST
GALLOWGATE
PAISLEY RD
KINGSTON ST
NELSON ST
NORFOLK ST
Bridge Street
Tradeston
West Street
Laurieston
Albert Bridge
Mus
Calton
Glasgow Green
River Clyde
BALLATER ST
KING'S DR
JAMES ST
LONDON RD
Bridgeton
Port Eglinton
Gorbals
Hutchesontown
CALEDONIA RD
Cemy
G1
G5
G21
G31
G40
G41
G42
G73
240
241
Pollokshields East
St Andrew's Cross
Royal Samaritan
DIXONS BLAZES IND EST
Polmadie Bridge
Rutherglen Bridge
Richmond Park
RUTHERGLEN RD
Polmadie
Works
Oatlands
Shawfield
Sewage Wks
Ind Est
CALDER ST
Govanhill
Queen's Park
Crosshill
Holyrood Sec RC Sch
AIKENHEAD RD
POLMADIE RD
GLASGOW RD
DUNN ST
TA Ctr
4
3
2
1
65
64
63
62
58
59
60

D1
1 TORRISDALE ST
2 PRINCE EDWARD ST
3 ALLISON PL
4 CHAPMAN ST
5 JAMIESON CT
6 HOLLYBROOK PL
D2
1 SURREY LA
2 SALISBURY ST
3 SURREY ST
4 ABBOTSFORD PL
5 CAVENDISH CT
6 FALFIELD ST
7 FRANCIS ST
8 RITCHIE ST
9 LAUDER ST
10 CARDWELL ST
11 ST ANDREW'S RD
12 MUIRHOUSE ST
13 BUTTERFIELD PL
14 ANNANDALE ST
15 LARKFIELD ST
16 ROBSON GR
17 MORGAN MEWS
E2
1 GILMOUR PL
2 HUTCHINSON TOWN CT
3 CUMBERLAND ARC
4 SANDYFAULDS SQ
5 QUEEN ELIZABETH SQ
6 SANDYFAULDS ST
7 CUMBERLAND PL
8 SNOWDON PL
9 SNOWDON ST

137

118

A   B   C

M8
G21
M8
TOWNMILL RD
ALEXANDRA PAR
A8
Golf Course
Alexandra Park
Alexandra Parade
Kennyhill Sch
CUMBERNAULD RD
G33
EDINBURGH RD   A8
PO
Piershill
4

Dennistoun
Bakery
Duke Street
Carntyne
Liby
CUMBERNAULD RD
MILLERSTON RD

65

Camlachie
BIGGAR ST
G31
Parkhead North Junction
Carntyne
WESTERBURN ST
Gallowgate
GALLOWGATE
THE FORGE SH CTR
SHETTLESTON RD
SHETTLESTON SHEDDINGS
Sports Ctr
A89
3

Acad
Cemy
Mkt
Salamanca St
Parkhead Cross
Celtic Park (Celtic FC)
St Michael's RC Prim Sch
Liby
Thornhill Path
St Mark's Prim RC Sch
Barrowfield
FIELDEN ST

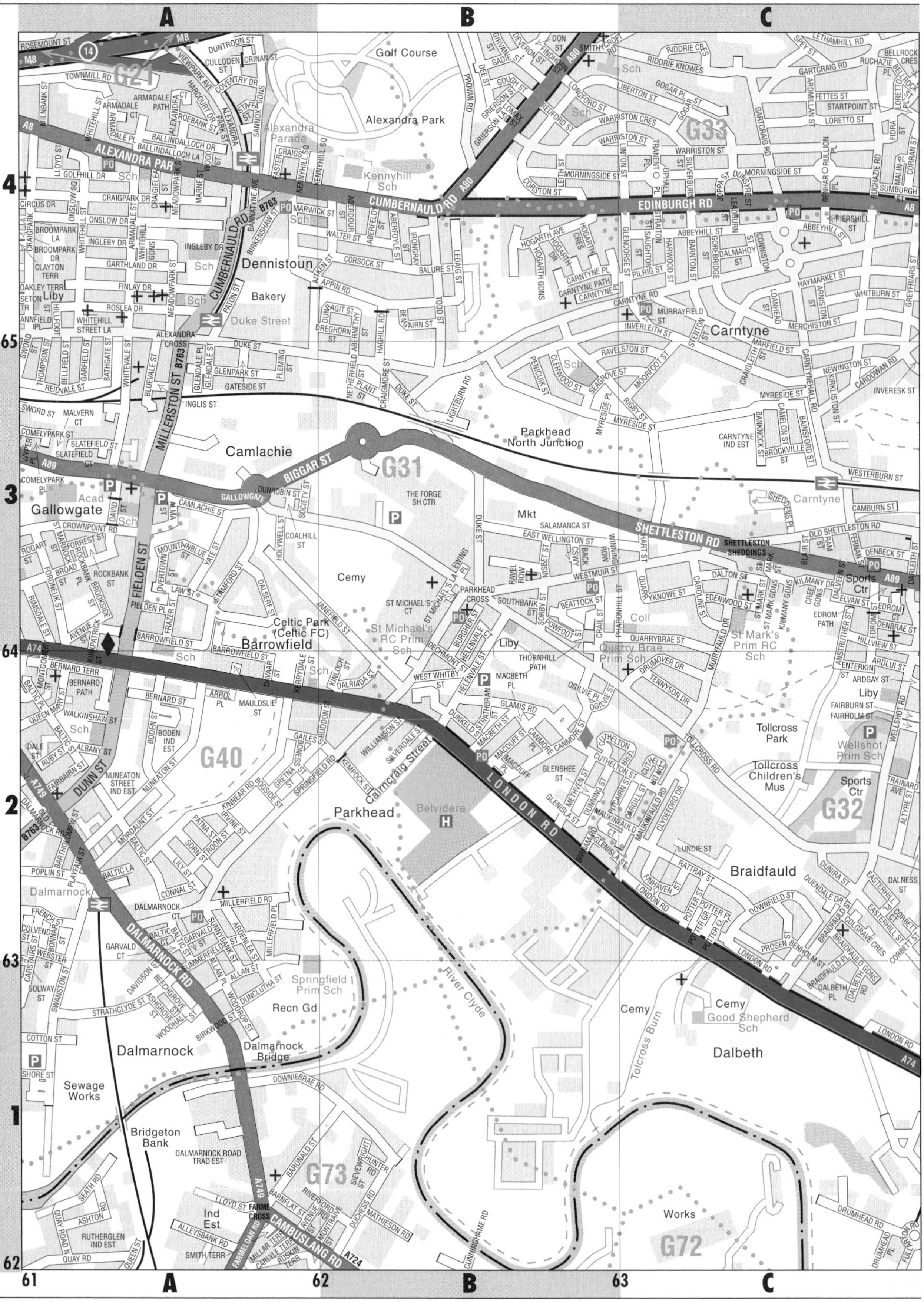

64   A74

Bernard Terr
Bernard Path
Bernard St
Macbeth Pl
Tollcross Park
Wellshot Prim Sch
G40
Boden Ind Est
Cairncraig Street
LONDON RD
Tollcross Children's Mus
Sports Ctr
G32
Braidfauld
DUNN ST
2   A749

Parkhead
Belvidere H
A74
Dalmarnock
DALMARNOCK RD
Springfield Prim Sch
Recn Gd
Dalmarnock Bridge
Cemy
Cemy
Good Shepherd Sch
Dalbeth
LONDON RD

63

Sewage Works
Bridgeton Bank
Dalmarnock Road Trad Est
Tollcross Burn
Works
1

Rutherglen Ind Est
G73
Ind Est
FARME CROSS
CAMBUSLANG RD   A724
G72

62

61   A   62   B   63   C

99
120

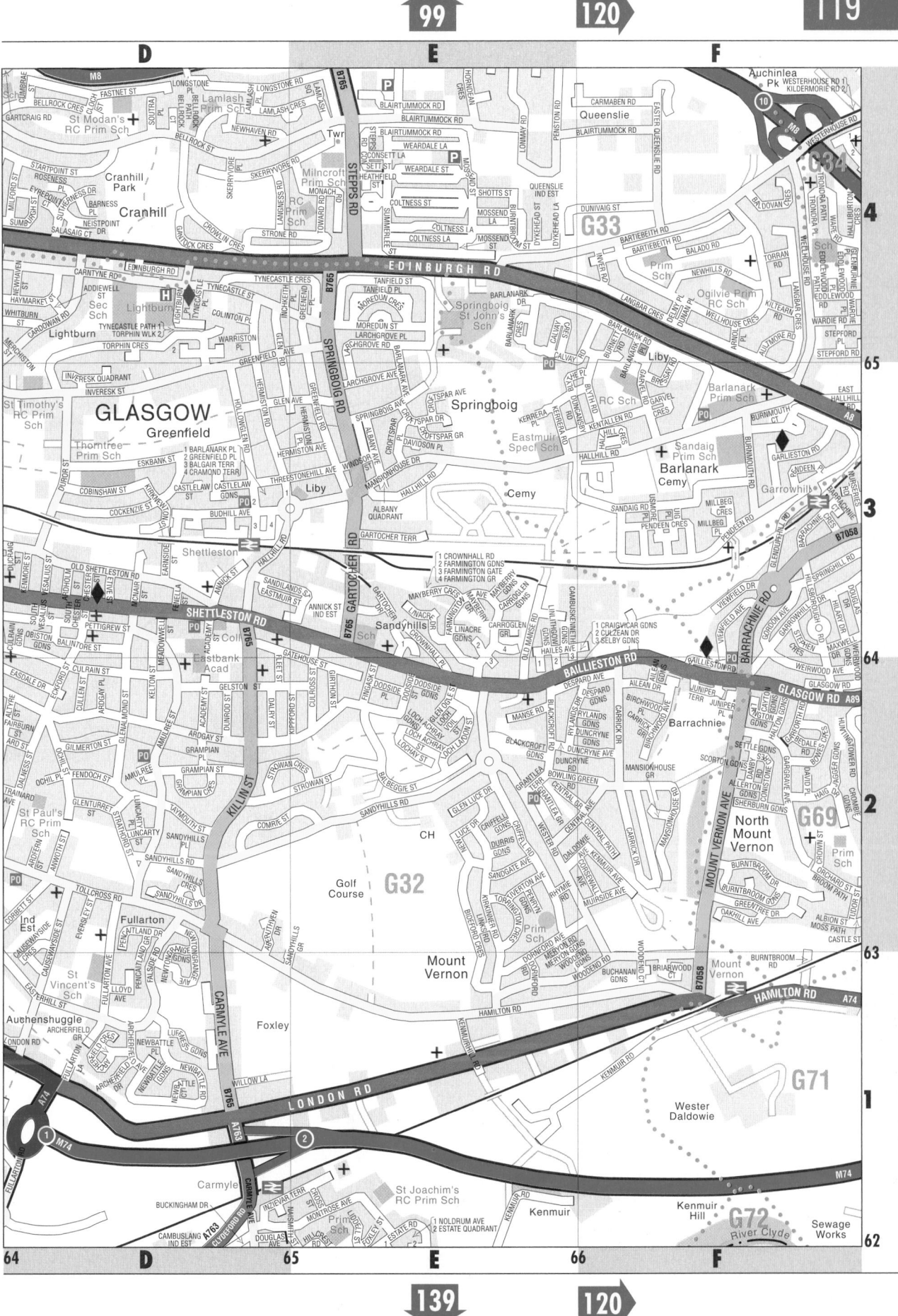
D
E
F
GLASGOW
Greenfield
Cranhill
Cranhill Park
Lightburn
Queenslie
Springboig
Barlanark
Shettleston
Sandyhills
Barrachnie
Garrowhill
North Mount Vernon
Mount Vernon
Fullarton
Auchenshuggle
Foxley
Carmyle
Kenmuir
Kenmuir Hill
Wester Daldowie
Auchinlea Pk
Sewage Works
River Clyde
Golf Course
G32
G33
G34
G69
G71
G72
EDINBURGH RD
SHETTLESTON RD
BAILLIESTON RD
GLASGOW RD
LONDON RD
HAMILTON RD
SPRINGBOIG RD
STEPPS RD
GARTOCHER RD
KILLIN ST
CARMYLE AVE
MOUNT VERNON AVE
BARRACHNIE RD
M8
M74
A8
A74
A89
A763
B765
B7058
St Modan's RC Prim Sch
Lamlash Prim Sch
Milncroft Prim Sch
St Timothy's RC Prim Sch
Thorntree Prim Sch
Eastbank Acad
Eastmuir Spec Sch
Springboig St John's Sch
Ogilvie Prim RC Sch
Barlanark Prim Sch
Sandaig Prim Sch
St Paul's RC Prim Sch
St Vincent's Sch
St Joachim's RC Prim Sch
Cemy
Liby
Coll
Ind Est
4
3
2
1
65
64
63
62
64
65
66

139
120

A   B   C

GLASGOW

G34
G33
G69 Crosshill
G71

Easterhouse
Blairtummock Prim Sch
John Wheatley Coll
Rogerfield Prim Sch
RC Prim Sch
Heatheryknowe
Commonhead
West Maryston
Netherhouse
Rhindmuir
Swinton
Springhill
Garrowhill
Garrowhill Prim Sch
Barrachnie
Baillieston
Muirhead
Ellismuir
Crosshill
Ellismuir Farm
North Calder Water
Newlands Glen
Newlands Farm
Woodhead Farm
Calderbraes Golf Course
Broomhouse
Glasgow Zoo
Calder Bridge
Calderbraes
Birkenshaw
Aitkenhead Prim Sch
Sewage Works
Huntingtower High Sch

EDINBURGH RD
GLASGOW RD
COATBRIDGE RD
GLASGOW AND EDINBURGH RD
HAMILTON RD
OLD EDINBURGH RD
BARRACHNIE RD
BAILLIESTON RD
DALDOWIE RD
MAIN ST
ROUNDKNOWE RD

M8 · M73 · M74 · A8 · A89 · A74 · A752

67   A   68   B   69   C

65 · 64 · 63 · 62 · 4 · 3 · 2 · 1

A3
1 MICKLEHOUSE PL
2 MICKLEHOUSE OVAL
3 MICKLEHOUSE WYND
4 THORNBRIDGE AVE
5 BARONY CT
6 BARONY WYND
7 QUEENSBY AVE
8 BANNERCROSS GDNS
9 BANNERCROSS AVE
10 THORNBRIDGE GDNS
11 HATHERSAGE GDNS

1 BLAIR CRES
2 KELBURNE GDNS
3 ORCHARD ST
4 CALDERWOOD GDNS
5 BROOM PATH
6 MOSS PATH

1 CALDERBRAES AVE
2 CATHKIN RD
3 CATHKIN GDNS
4 DECHMONT RD

WINDSOR PATH 1
PRINCESS DR 2
MELROSE AVE 3
MINSTER WLK 4
CASTLE WAY 5
MONKLAND VIEW CRES 6

ATHOLL TERR 5
BROOMFIELD TERR 6
LAIDLAW GDNS 7
MONROE PL 8
MELROSE GDNS 9

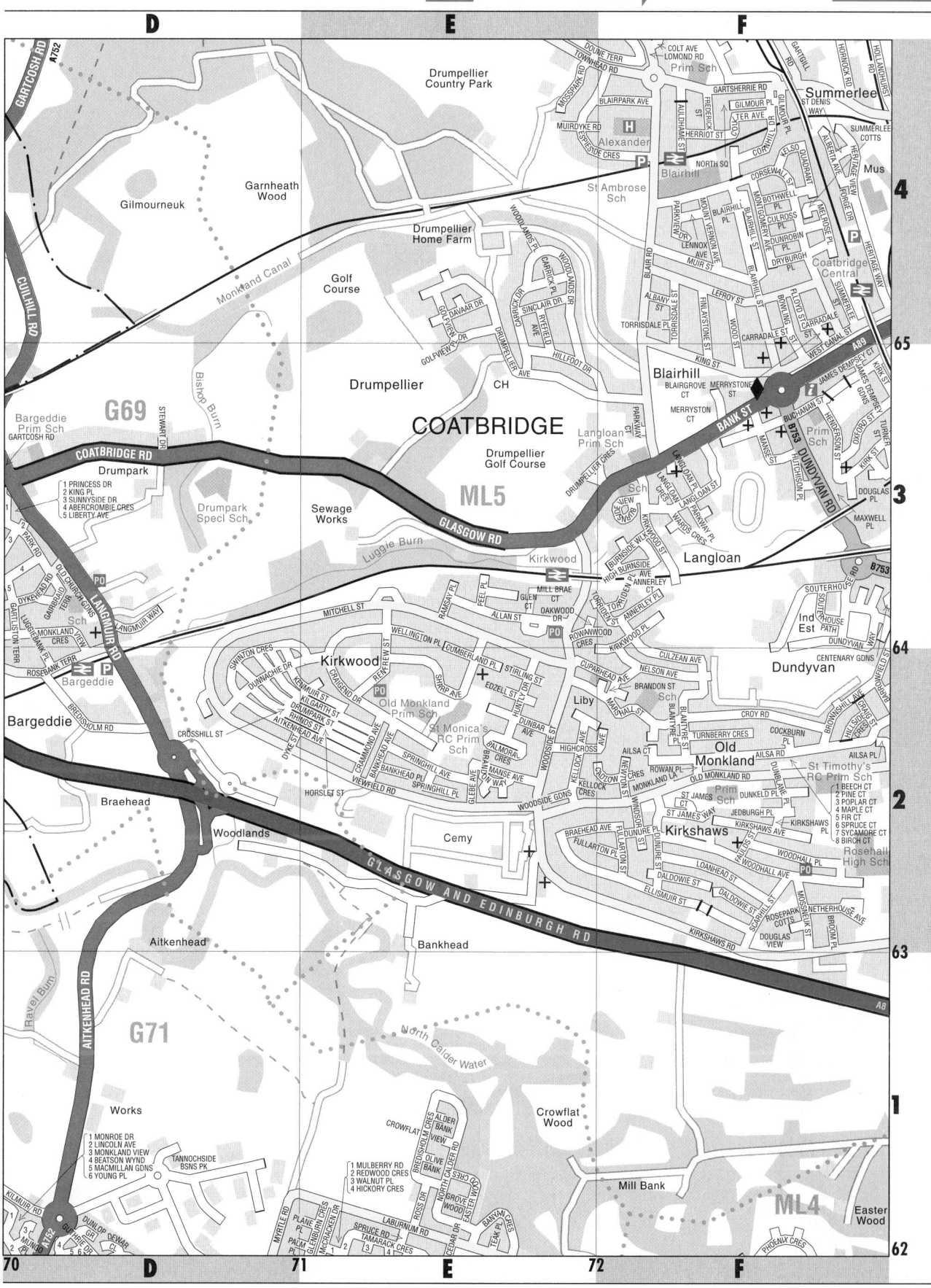

D   E   F

GARTCOSH RD
A752
CUILHILL RD

Gilmourneuk

Garnheath Wood

Drumpellier Country Park

Monkland Canal

Drumpellier Home Farm

Golf Course

Bishop Burn

STEWART DR

G69

Bargeddie Prim Sch
GARTCOSH RD

COATBRIDGE RD

Drumpark

1 PRINCESS DR
2 KING PL
3 SUNNYSIDE DR
4 ABERCROMBIE CRES
5 LIBERTY AVE

Drumpark Specl Sch

Sewage Works

Luggie Burn

Drumpellier

COATBRIDGE

Drumpellier Golf Course

ML5

GLASGOW RD

CH

DOUNE TERR
TOWNHEAD RD
MOSSPARK RD
BLAIRPARK AVE
MUIRDYKE RD
SPRUCESIDE CRES

COLT AVE
LOMOND RD   Prim Sch
GARTSHERRIE RD
GILMOUR PL   GILMOUR ST
FREDERICK   TER AVE
AULDHAME ST
HERRIOT ST

H   NORTH SQ   CORSEWALL ST   KELSO
Alexander
P   Blairhill

St Ambrose Sch

BLAIR RD

WOODLANDS PL
WOODLANDS DR
CARRICK DR
DAVAAR DR
SINCLAIR DR
GOLFHILL DR
GOLFVIEW DR
PYEFIELD AVE
DRUMPELLIER AVE
HILLFOOT DR

ALBANY ST
FINLAYSTONE ST
TORRISDALE ST

Blairhill
BLAIRGROVE CT   Merrystone CT
MERRYSTON CT

BANK ST
B753
BUCHANAN ST

Langloan Prim Sch
DRUMPELLIER CRES
PARKWAY
LANGLOAN CT
LANGLOAN CRES   PARKWAY CT
Sch
LANGLOAN ST   LANGLOAN PARKWAY CT
WARDS CRES
BURNSIDE WY
BURNSIDE ST
HIGH BURNSIDE

ST DENIS WAY
SUMMERLEE
HERITAGE VIEW   COTTS
Mus
Coatbridge Central
P   HERITAGE WAY
WEST CANAL ST   A89
James Dempsey Ct
JAMES DEMPSEY CT
KING ST
Prim   OXFORD ST   TURNER ST
Sch   HENDERSON ST
DOUGLAS ST
MAXWELL PL

Langloan

Kirkwood
MILL BRAE   ANNERLEY   DUNDYVAN RD
GLEN   HIGH BLANTYRE AVE   ANNERLEY PL
CT   OAKWOOD DR   TORIDON RD
ALLAN ST   KIRKWOOD PL
PO   ROWANWOOD CRES   KIRKWOOD PL   DUNDYVAN RD
CRES

B753
SOUTHERHOUSE RD
SOUTHERHOUSE PATH
Ind Est
DUNDYVAN

65

3

64

Bargeddie Prim Sch

LANGMUIR RD
GARTLISTON TERR
MONKLAND VIEW CRES
ROSEBANK TERR
PO
Sch
P
Bargeddie

Bargeddie

Braehead

BREDISHOLM RD

CROSSHILL ST

SWINTON CRES
DUNNACHIE DR
KILGARTH ST
KENMUIR ST
DRUMPARK ST
RHINDS ST
AITKENHEAD AVE
DRAMMOND AVE
DYKE RD
HORSLET ST

Kirkwood
CRAIGEND DR
CRAIGEND ST
VIEWFIELD RD

MITCHELL ST
WELLINGTON PL
RENFREW ST
SHARP AVE
CUMBERLAND PL
STIRLING ST
EDZELL DR
HUNTLY DR
DUNBAR AVE

Old Monkland Prim Sch
St Monica's RC Prim Sch
BALMORAL CRES
BRANDON WY
HIGHCROSS
KELLOCK AVE
CAUTON ST
KELLOCK CRES

Liby
MARSHALL ST
CUPARHEAD AVE
NELSON AVE
CULZEAN AVE
Sch
BRANDON ST
CROY RD
TURNBERRY CRES
NELSON ST
ROWAN ST

CENTENARY GDNS

Dundyvan

BRANNAN HILL CRES
WILSON CRES
AILSA RD
AILSA PL

Old Monkland
OLD MONKLAND RD
ST JAMES PL   DUNKELD RD
ST JAMES WAY   JEDBURGH PL
Prim Sch   WINDSOR ST
BRAEHEAD AVE   DUNURE PL
FULLARTON RD   DUNURE PL   KIRKSHAWS AVE   KIRKSHAWS
FULLARTON ST   Kirkshaws   WOODHALL PL
LOANHEAD AVE   MOSSNEUK RD
DALDOWIE ST   WOODHALL AVE   ROSEPARK COTTS
ELLISMUIR ST   NETHERHOUSE AVE
DALDOWIE ST   BROOM PL
KIRKSHAWS RD   DOUGLAS VIEW

St Timothy's RC Prim Sch
1 BEECH CT
2 PINE CT
3 POPLAR CT
4 MAPLE CT
5 FIR CT
6 SPRUCE CT
7 SYCAMORE CT
8 BIRCH CT
Rosehall High Sch
PO

2

SPRINGHILL AVE
BANKHEAD PL   BANKHEAD
SPRINGHILL PL   GLEBE AVE
WOODSIDE RD   MANSE AVE
WOODSIDE GDNS

Woodlands

Cemy

GLASGOW AND EDINBURGH RD

Aitkenhead

AITKENHEAD RD

Ravel Burn

G71

Works

1 MONROE DR
2 LINCOLN AVE
3 MONKLAND VIEW
4 BEATSON WYND
5 MACMILLAN GDNS
6 YOUNG PL

TANNOCHSIDE BSNS PK

Bankhead

North Calder Water

Crowflat Wood

Mill Bank

ML4

Easter Wood

PHOENIX CRES

63

1

62

KILMUIR RD
MUNGO
A752
GLENHOLME
DUNLOP
DEWAR
GR

MYRTLE RD
PLANE RD
GLENBIRN CRES
MCCRACKEN ST
PALM
SPRUCE ST
TAMARACK CRES

CROWFLAT CRES
BREDISHOLM RD
BREDISHOLM CRES
OLIVE BANK
NORTH CALDER RD
LABURNUM RD
CEDAR RD
ROSS RD

ALDER BANK VIEW
CALDER RD
BROOM WOOD RD
TEAK PL
BANYAN CRES
EASTER RD

1 MULBERRY RD
2 REDWOOD CRES
3 WALNUT PL
4 HICKORY CRES

D   E   F

70   71   72

121
102

A
B
C
4
65
3
64
2
63
1
62
73
74
75
COATBRIDGE
Sunnyside
Dunbeth
Dunbeth Pk
Cliftonville
Mosside
Whinhall
Monklands District General
Coatdyke
Cliftonhill Stad (Albion Rovers FC & Hamilton Academical FC)
Retail Pk
Whifflet
Foundry
Greenend
Sikeside
Barrowfield
Rosehall
Shawhead
Coathill
Carnbroe
Cairnhill
High Palacecraig
Low Palacecraig
Refuse Tips
Sewage Wks
Stank Brae
Fox Covert
Heathery Lea Covert
Orchard Farm
The Mount
Carnbroe Mains Farm
Easter Wood
Ind Est
Works
Wks
ML1
ML4
ML5
ML6
North Calder Water
Monkland Canal (dis)
GLASGOW AND EDINBURGH RD
A8
A89
A725
A8010
B753
B802
B803
B804
B7070
SOUTH CIRCULAR RD
MAIN ST
DEEDES ST
ALEXANDER ST
AITCHISON ST
HIGH ST
COATBANK ST
WHIFFLET ST
DUNBETH RD
SUNNYSIDE RD
LOCKS ST
CALDER ST
DUNDYVAN RD
NORTH RD
St Patrick's High Sch
St Stephen's RC Prim Sch
Sikeside Prim Sch
St Bernard's RC Prim Sch
Shawhead Prim Sch
THE FOUNTAIN BSNS CTR
ROSEHALL IND EST
DEESIDE PL 1
DUNAVON PL 2
GREENLEES GR 3
KIPLAND WLK 4
STRATHMORE PL 5
THORNKIP PL 6
STRATHMORE WLK 7
GLEN LUSS PL 8
GLENSPEAN PL 9
1 BRUCE ST
2 GREENSIDE ST

121
142

103 124

D E F

AIRDRIE

St Margaret's High Sch
Rawyards Park
Drumgelloch
Clarkston
Wester Moffat
Craigneuk
Gartlea
Petersburn
Gartness
Brownsburn
Monkland Bridge
Bowhouse
Moffat Mills
Gimmerscroft
Caldervale High Sch
Dunrobin Prim Sch
Hillhead
Sauchenbog Bridge
Faskine Farm
Calderbank
Corpus Christi RC Prim Sch
Calderbank Prim Sch
Chapelhall Prim & Sec Sch
Chapelhall
St Aloysius RC Prim Sch
Bailside Farm
ML6
ML1

A89 GRAHAM ST
CLARK ST
FORREST ST
MOTHERWELL ST
CARLISLE RD
PETERSBURN RD
BROWNSBURN RD
CALDERBANK RD
CAIRNHILL RD
MAIN ST
WOODHALL MILL RD
BO'NESS RD
BELLSIDE RD
GLASGOW & EDINBURGH RD

1 CAMERON CT
2 GILLIES CT
3 OGILVIE CT
4 FRASER CT
5 ERSKINE CT
6 GORDON CT
7 BRUCE CT

KINGSTON AVE 1
COLSTON PL 2
COLSTON TERR 3
MEADOWSIDE GDNS 4
CASTLE QUADRANT 5
MEADOWSIDE PL 6

CARLISLE LA 7
CEDAR LA 8
LIME CRES 9

FINLAYSON QUADRANT 8
WESTER MOFFAT CRES 9
CRAIGNURE CRES 10
MOORPARK AVE 11

GIMMERSCROFT CRES 1
REAM AVE 2

INVERVALE AVE 3
ARDFERN RD 4
ROUGHRIGG RD 5

MONCRIEFFE RD 1
HOGG RD 2
ABERDEEN RD 3
BURNS RD 4
BURNS LA 5
ROSEBERRY LA 6

LUNAR PATH 1
CHARLES PATH 2
GLEN FRUIN PL 3
GLEN ORCHY PL 4
GLEN SHEE CRES 5
GLEN AFFRIC WAY 6

7 DOUNE CRES
8 DRUMORE AVE

GRAMPIAN CRES 1
CASTLEHILL CRES 2
ROCKLIFFE PATH 3

4 3 65 64 2 63 1 62

76 D 77 E 78 F

143 124

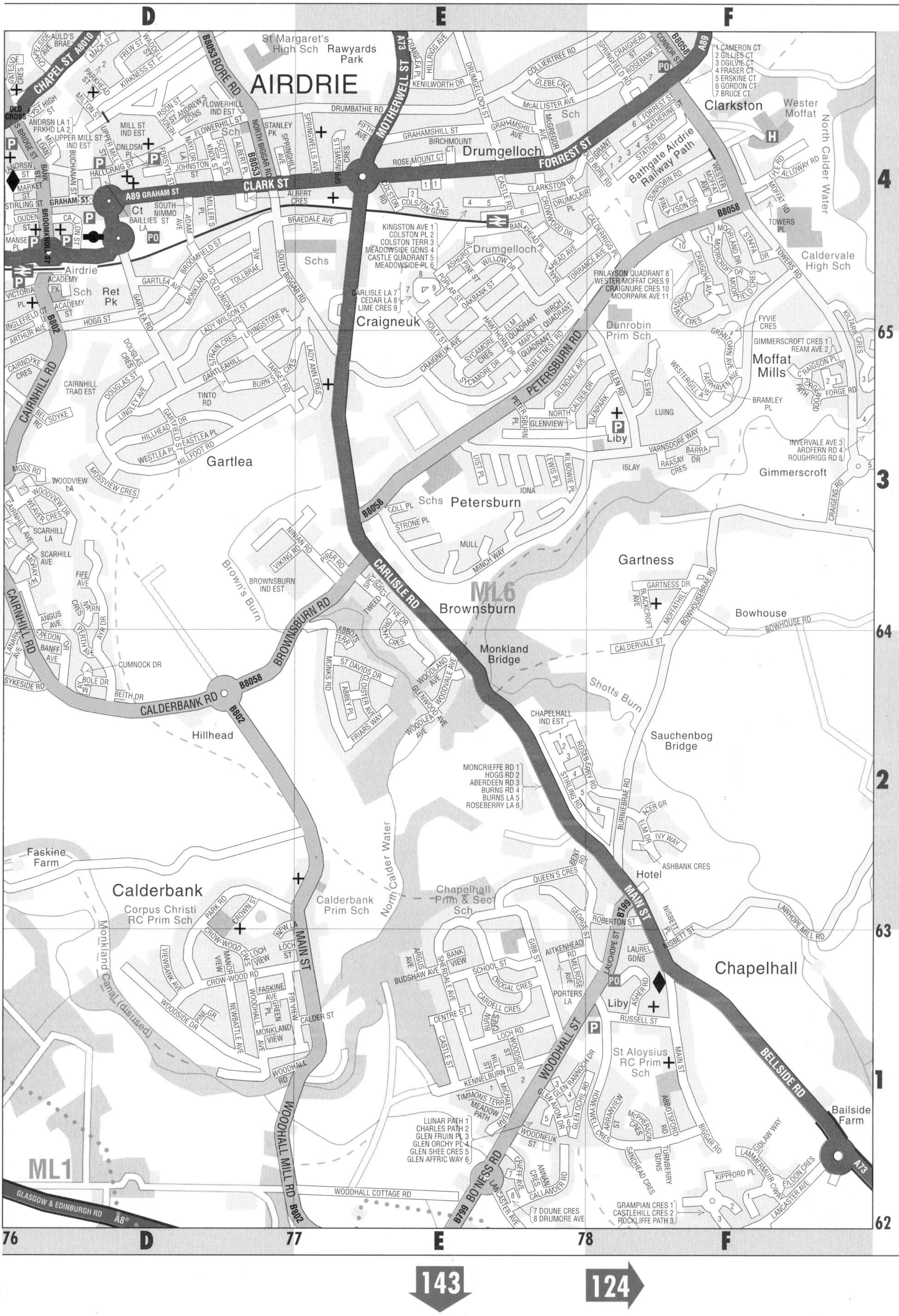

123
104

A **B** **C**

4

BROWNIESIDE RD

STEPENDS RD

Easter Moffat
Golf Course

Lochhill

DUNTILLAND RD

Browns Burn

Wester
Bracco

Springbank Quarry
(disused)

Lady Bell's
Moss

65

BURNWOOD DR
KILTARIE
INVERVALE AVE
ARDFERN RD
ACHNASHEEN RD
BALLOCH RD
DYSART WAY

Burn
Wood

ROUGHRIGG RD

3

BOWHOUSE RD

Clattering Burn

ML6

Roughrigg
Reservoir

64

DUNSISTON RD

Works

Easter
Dunsyston

Craigends

2

Gartness
Farm

GARTNESS RD

Craigends
Moss

Turdees

Blackrig

CRAIGENS RD

Wester
Dunsyston

Langside

63

Bothwellshields

ML1

M8

Longacre

1

Budshaw

BOTHWELLSHIELDS RD

Shotts Burn

Peatpots

SPRINGFIELD RD

B7066

BELSIDE RD
A73

6

M8

GLASGOW AND EDINBURGH RD

WILSONS RD

B7066

ML7

62

79 **A** **80** **B** **81** **C**

D
E
F
4
3
2
1
65
64
63
62
82
83
84
BRACCO RD
Watch Moss
ML6
Black Hill
Torrance
Tipperdavie
Television
Station
Mast
Dun Daugh
Tod Holes
Forrestburn Water
Mountcow
Well Knowe
DUNTILLAND RD
Duntilland Hill
ML7
Duntilland Farm
Duntilland Quarry
M8
Sewage
Works
Kirk O' Shotts
Prim Sch
Shotts Burn
BOGFOOT RD
SCHOOL RD
HIRST RD
B7066
Kirk of
Shotts
Threeprig
Salsburgh
MAIN ST
GIBSON ST
BOGFOOT RD
REID ST
CROSSART
ST
DAVID ST
MUIRHALL TERR
BLACKCROFT TERR
MUIRHEAD GDNS
KIRKVIEW AVE
P
PO
SPRINGFIELD RD
DUNTILLAND AVE
CAMSDALE AVE
CARVALE AVE
LORNE
GDNS
MARGARET AVE 1
SIGHTHILL TERR 2
BERTRAM DR 3
Manse
Glebe
Farm
MANSE RD
NEWMILL AND CANTHILL RD
Roundknowe
Wood
Canthills
Plantation
Riven Loch
Spoil
Tip

125
106

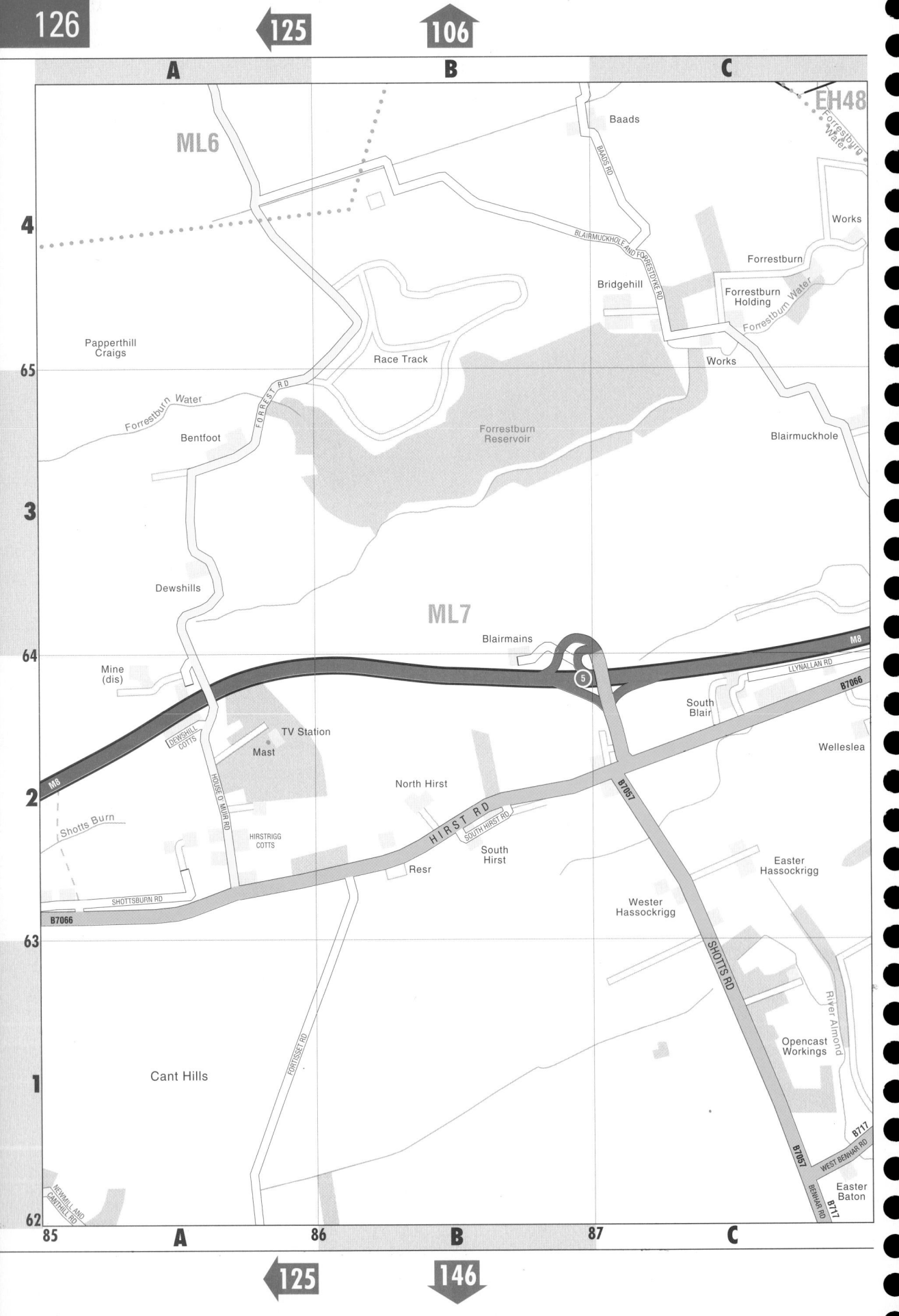
A
B
C
4
65
3
64
2
63
1
62
85
86
87
ML6
ML7
EH48
Baads
BAADS RD
Forrestburn Water
Works
Forrestburn
Forrestburn Holding
Bridgehill
BLAIRMUCKHOLE AND FORRESTDYKE RD
Papperthill Craigs
Race Track
Works
FORREST RD
Forrestburn Water
Bentfoot
Forrestburn Reservoir
Blairmuckhole
Dewshills
Blairmains
M8
Mine (dis)
LYNALLAN RD
B7066
South Blair
5
TV Station
DEWSHILL COTTS
Mast
Welleslea
M8
HOUSE O MUIR RD
North Hirst
B7057
Shotts Burn
HIRST RD
SOUTH HIRST RD
HIRSTRIGG COTTS
South Hirst
Easter Hassockrigg
Resr
SHOTTSBURN RD
Wester Hassockrigg
B7066
SHOTTS RD
River Almond
Opencast Workings
FORTISSET RD
Cant Hills
B717
WEST BENHAR RD
B7057
Easter Baton
NEWMILL AND CANTHILL RD
BENHAR RD
B717

125
146

107

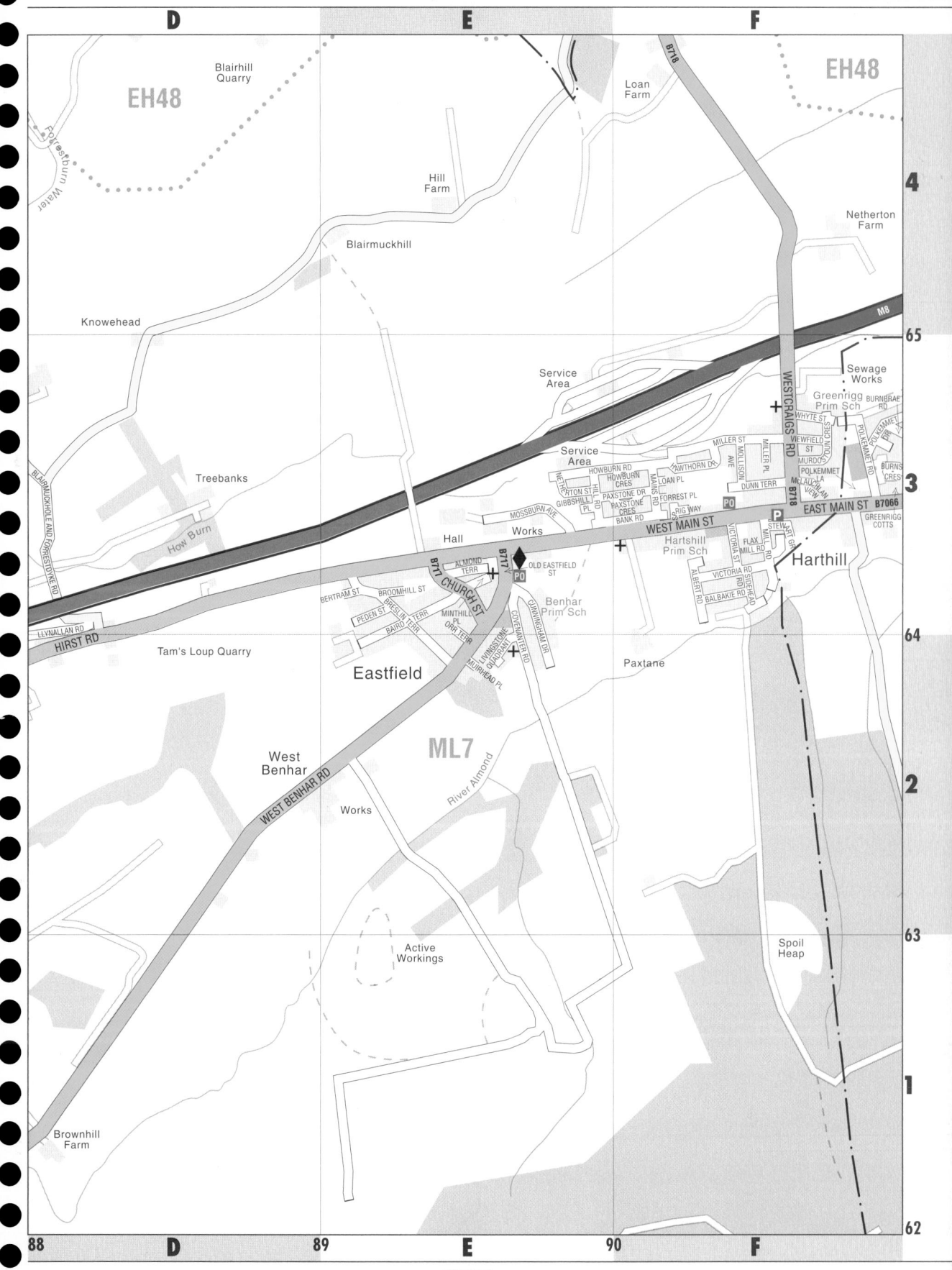

D
E
F
EH48
Blairhill Quarry
Forrestburn Water
Loan Farm
Hill Farm
Netherton Farm
Blairmuckhill
Knowehead
M8
Service Area
Sewage Works
Greenrigg Prim Sch
WESTCRAIGS RD
B718
Treebanks
How Burn
BLAIRMUCKHOLE AND FORRESTDYKE RD
Works
Hall
WEST MAIN ST
EAST MAIN ST
B7066
Hartshill Prim Sch
Harthill
B717
CHURCH ST
OLD EASTFIELD ST
PO
Benhar Prim Sch
LLYNALLAN RD
HIRST RD
Tam's Loup Quarry
Eastfield
Paxtane
ML7
West Benhar
WEST BENHAR RD
River Almond
Works
Active Workings
Spoil Heap
Brownhill Farm
4
65
3
64
2
63
1
62
88
89
90

147

108

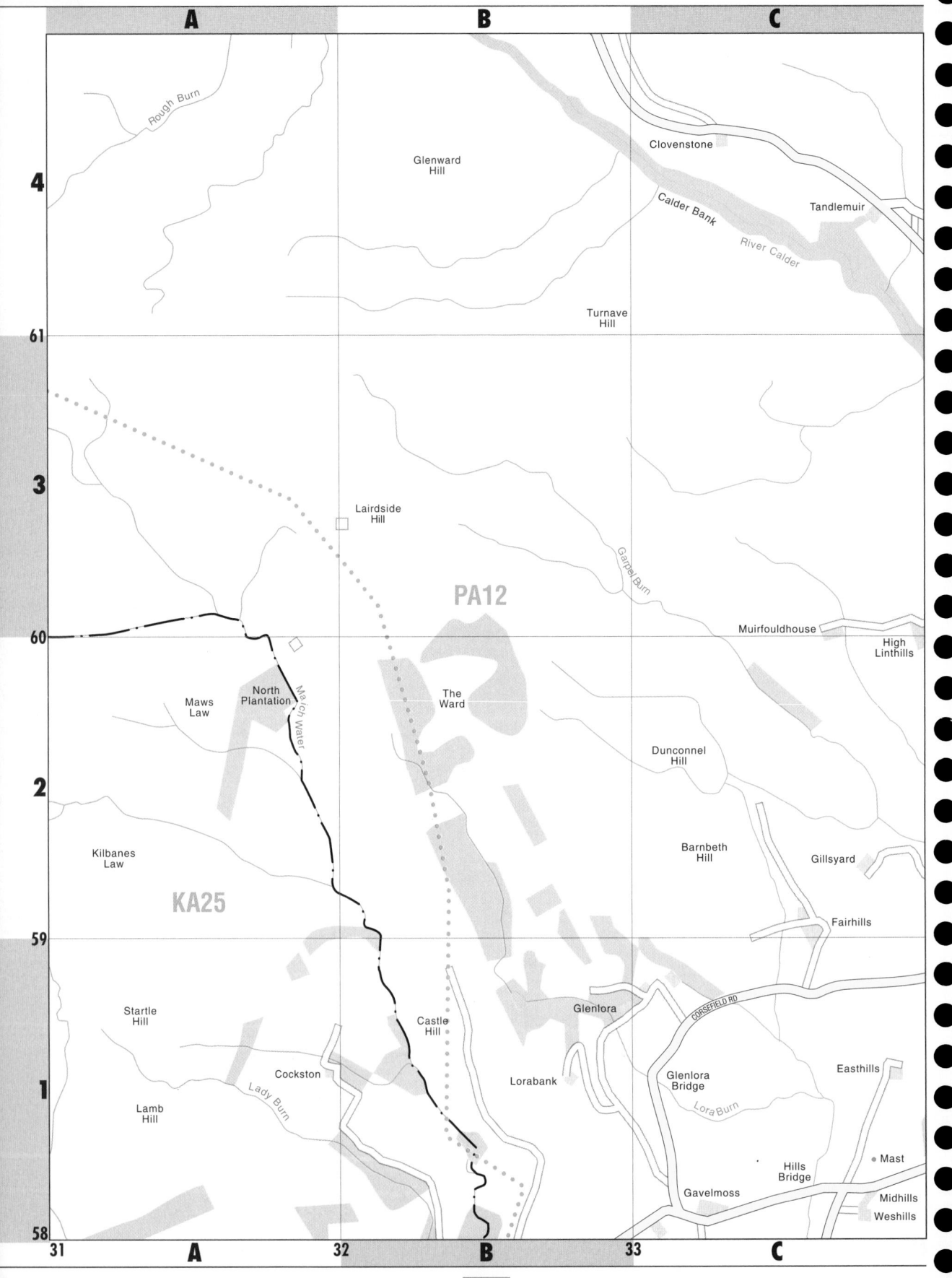

Rough Burn

Glenward
Hill

Clovenstone

Calder Bank

Tandlemuir

River Calder

Turnave
Hill

4

61

Lairdside
Hill

3

PA12

Garpel Burn

Muirfouldhouse

High
Linthills

60

North
Plantation

Maws
Law

March Water

The
Ward

Duconnel
Hill

Kilbanes
Law

Barnbeth
Hill

Gillsyard

2

KA25

Fairhills

59

Glenlora

CORSEFIELD RD

Startle
Hill

Castle
Hill

Lorabank

Glenlora
Bridge

Easthills

Cockston

Lady Burn

Lora Burn

1

Lamb
Hill

Hills
Bridge

• Mast

Gavelmoss

Midhills

Weshills

58

31   A   32   B   33   C

149

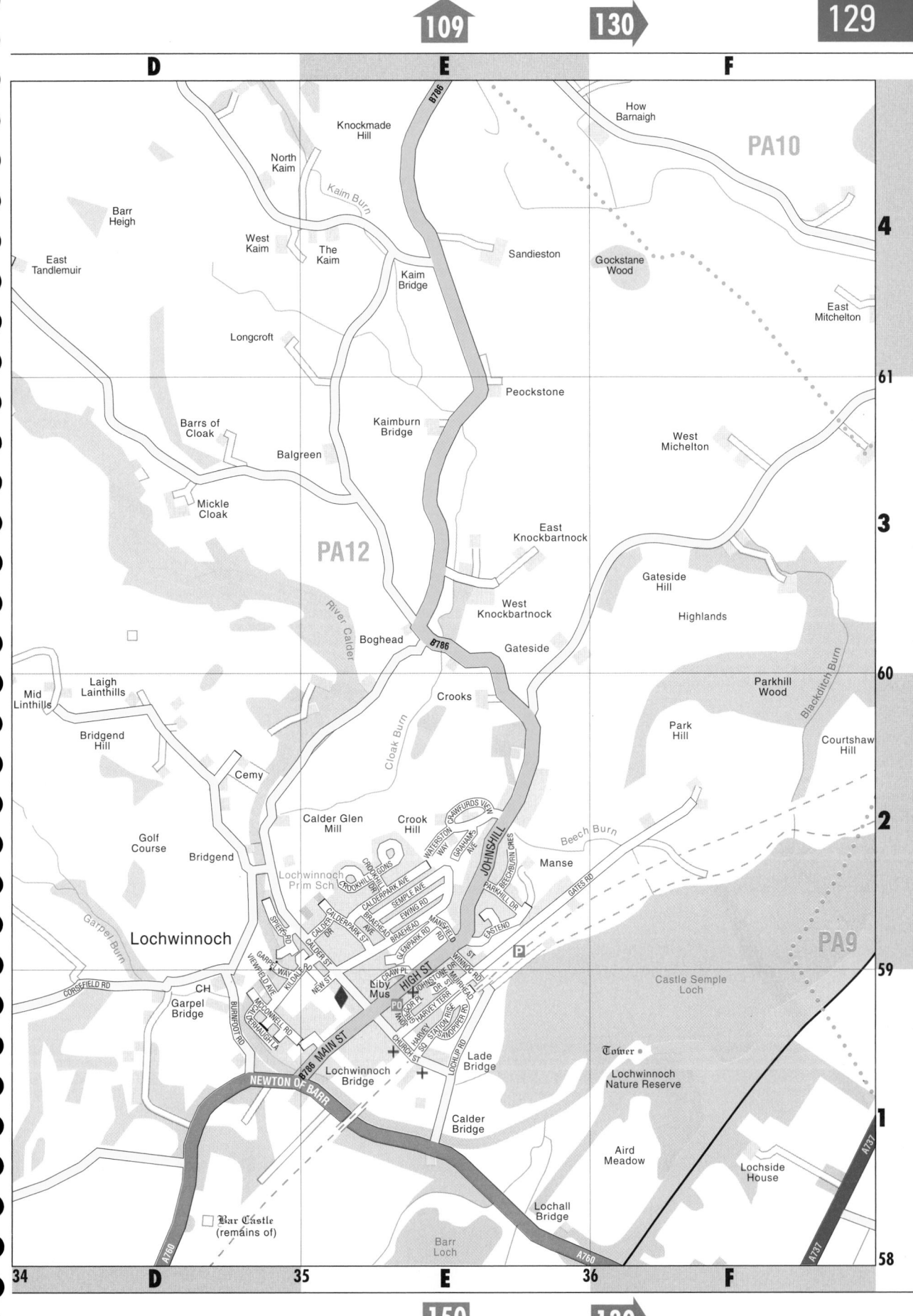

PA10

4

How
Barnaigh

Knockmade
Hill

North
Kaim

Kaim Burn

Gockstane
Wood

Sandieston

East
Mitchelton

Barr
Heigh

West
Kaim

The
Kaim

East
Tandlemuir

Kaim
Bridge

61

Longcroft

B786

Peockstone

Barrs of
Cloak

Kaimburn
Bridge

West
Michelton

Balgreen

3

Mickle
Cloak

PA12

East
Knockbartnock

Gateside
Hill

Highlands

River Calder

Boghead

B786

West
Knockbartnock

Gateside

Parkhill
Wood

Blackditch Burn

60

Mid
Linthills

Laigh
Lainthills

Crooks

Crook
Hill

Park
Hill

Courtshaw
Hill

Bridgend
Hill

Cloak Burn

Cramfurds View

2

Cemy

Calder Glen
Mill

Beech Burn

Golf
Course

Bridgend

Waterston Way

Grahams Ave

Johnshill

Manse

Lochwinnoch
Prim Sch

Cromwell

Crookhill Gdns

Calderpark Ave

Semple Ave

Braehead Ave

Ewing Rd

Braehead Rd

Glenpark Rd

Mansfield

Beechburn Cres

Parkhill Dr

Gates Rd

PA9

Lochwinnoch

Speirs Rd

Calderpark St

Calder Dr

Calder St

New St

High St

Eastend

59

Corssfield Rd

CH

Viewfield Ave

Kildale Wy

Garpel Wy

Craig Pl

Liby
Mus

Johnstone Dr

Muirhead

Winnock Rd

Castle Semple
Loch

Garpel Bridge

Garpel Burn

McConnell Rd

Burnfoot Rd

Lyberaugh La

PO

Harvey
Sq

Harvey Terr

Station Rise

Sandpiper Rd

Lade
Bridge

Tower

B786 MAIN ST

Lochwinnoch
Bridge

Church St

Lochkip Rd

Lochwinnoch
Nature Reserve

NEWTON OF BARR

Calder
Bridge

A737

1

Bar Castle
(remains of)

Lochall
Bridge

A760

Aird
Meadow

Lochside
House

Barr
Loch

A760

A737

A   B   C

Kibbleston

Little
Burntshields
PA10
Passinglinn   Callochant

Clochodrick   Corbet Hill

Crossflat   KIBBLESTON RD

Clochodrick   Crossflat Hill
Bridge
Burnfoot   Drygate

St Bride's Burn   Thirdpart
Bride's Mill   Hall
61   Bridge
                                North
                                Gates   Warbowie

Market   St Brydes   Garthland
Hill   Bridge
Markethill   Howwood
Holdings   STATION RD
                                                              MAYFIELD CRES
                        Shields   Kenmure Hill   HALLSIDE ST BETTY RD B787
3   Holdings   NEW AVE
PA12   Temple   STATION AVE PO
                                                              ELLISTON RD MIDTON RD
                                                              KIRKFIELD WYND B776
                                          East Approach   ELLISTON PL MAIN ST
                                                              EARLSHILL DR GEORGE ST BOWFIELD RD B787
                        Fancy   Black Cart Water LINNISTER CRES Sch
                        Bridge   KENMURE VIEW SEMPLE VIEW
                                          Elliston   Elliston CARSEWOOD AVE HILLFOOT DR
60   Bridge   +
Low Semple   Castle Semple

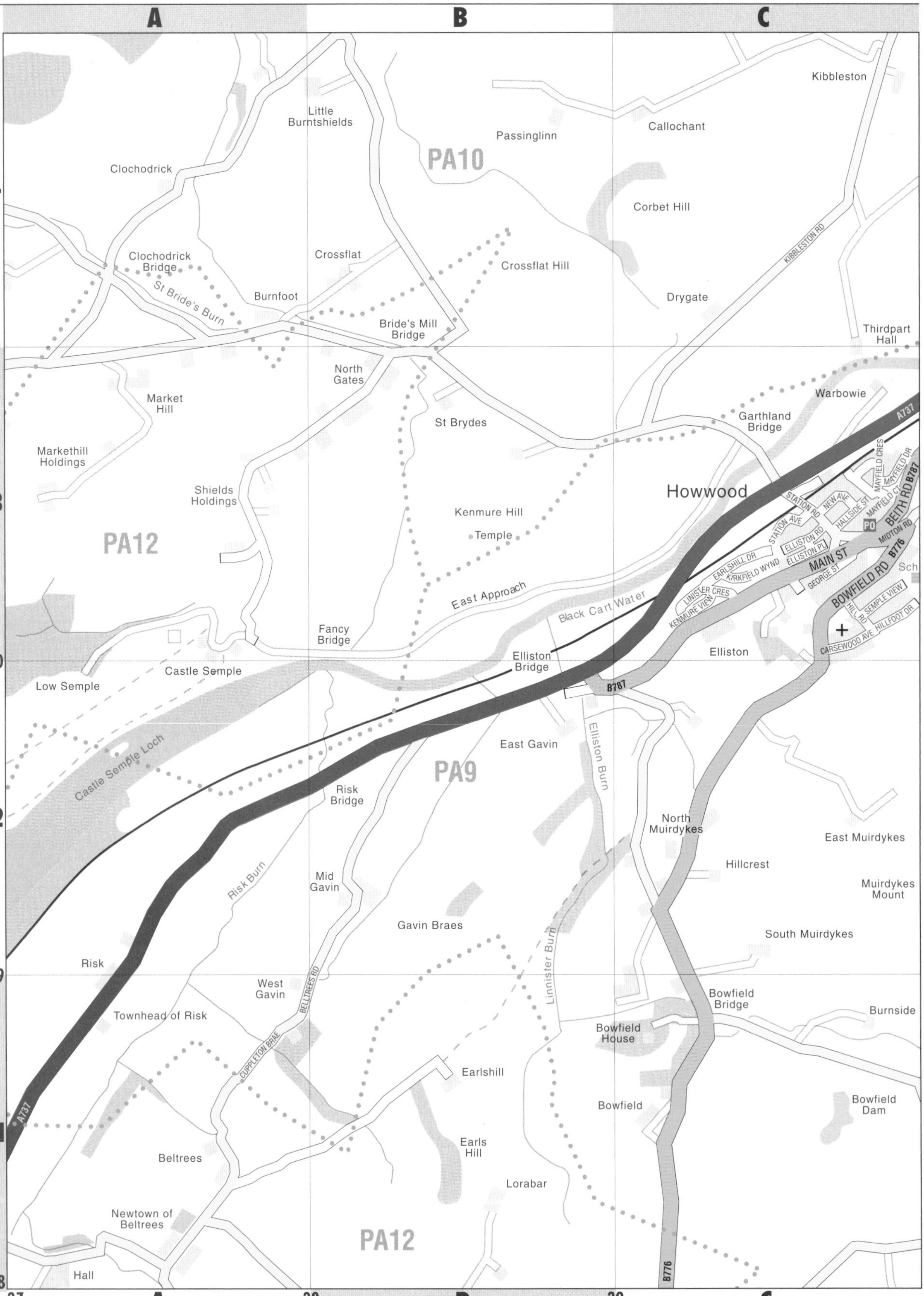

Castle Semple Loch   B787
                                          East Gavin
                                                              North
2   Risk   PA9   Elliston Burn Muirdykes   East Muirdykes
                                Bridge   Hillcrest   Muirdykes
                        Mid   Mount
Risk Burn   Gavin   South Muirdykes
                                          Gavin Braes
                                                              Bowfield
59   Linnister Burn   Bridge   Burnside
                        West   Bowfield
Risk   Gavin   House
Townhead of Risk   BELTREES RD   Bowfield
                        CUPPLETON BRAE   Earlshill   Dam
                                                              Bowfield
1   A737   Earls
                        Beltrees   Hill
                                          Lorabar
Newtown of
Beltrees   **PA12**   B776
58   Hall
37   A   38   B   39   C

D   E   F

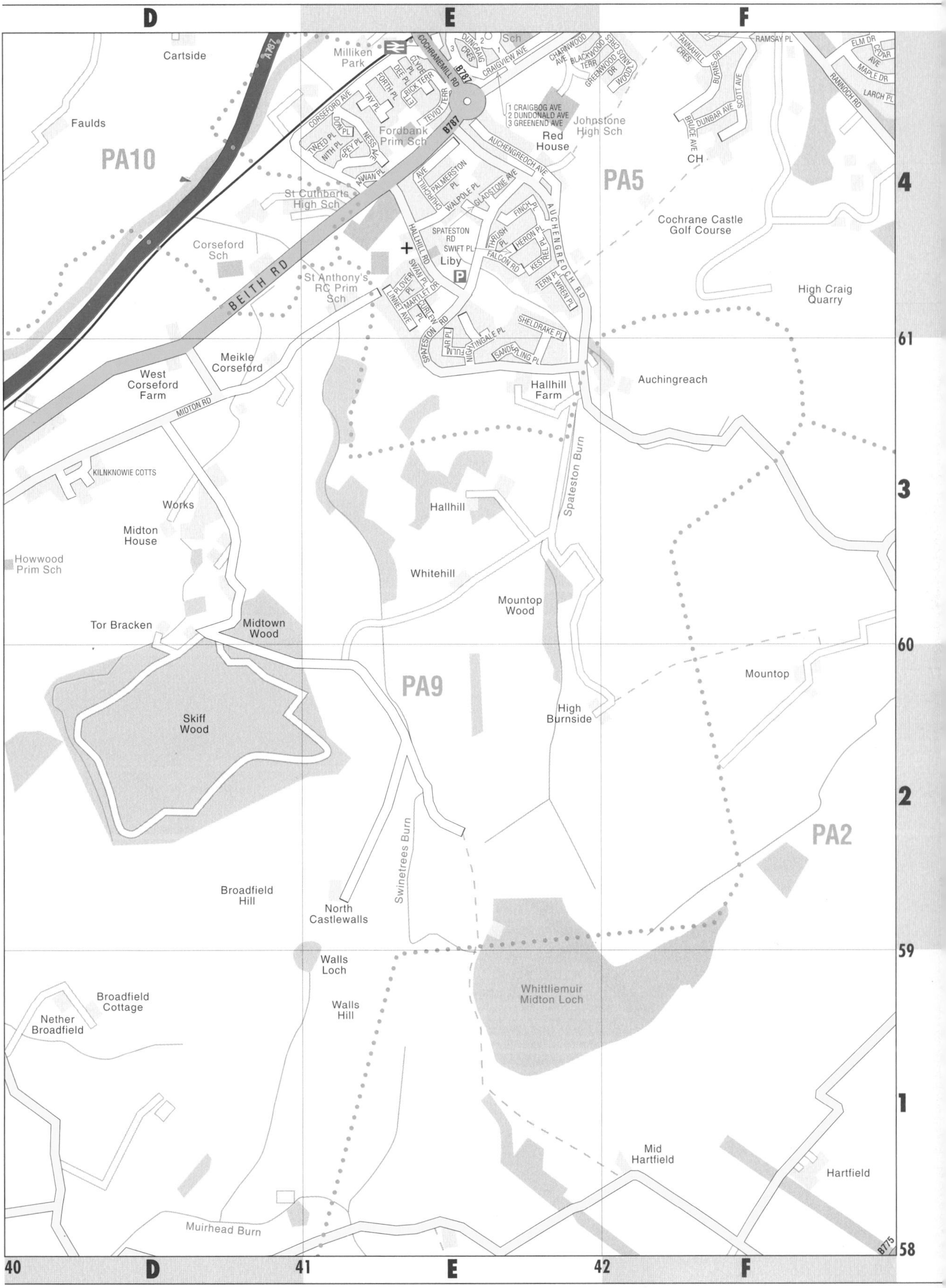

Cartside

Milliken Park

DUNGAIG CRES

CRAIGVIEW AVE

CHARNWOOD AVE
BLACKWOOD TERR
GREENWOOD DR
WOOD

RAMSAY PL

TANNAHILL CRES
BURNS DR
SCOTT AVE
ELM DR
CONR
MAPLE DR
RANNOCH RD
LARCH PL

Faulds

CORSEFORD AVE
TAY PL
WEED PL
DOXY PL
FORTH PL
BRICK TERR
NESS AVE
GREY PL
WITH PL
AWAN PL

PA10

B787

CLYDE TERR
TEVIOT TERR
B787

1 CRAIGBOG AVE
2 DUNDONALD AVE
3 GREENEND AVE

Johnstone High Sch

DUNBAR AVE
BRUCE AVE

Fordbank Prim Sch

Red House

CH

St Cuthbert's High Sch

AUCHENGREOCH AVE

PA5

Corseford Sch

AVE
PALMERSTON PL
WALPOLE PL
THRUSH
FINCH
HERON PL
KESTR

Spateston Rd
Swift Pl
Liby

GLADSTONE INF

Cochrane Castle
Golf Course

St Anthony's RC Prim Sch

HALLHILL RD
SWAN PL
PLOVER PL
LINNET AVE
MARTLET DR
EIDER AVE

FALCON RD
TERN PL
WREN PL

4

High Craig Quarry

SPINSTON RD
FULMAR PL
NIGHTINGALE PL
SHELDRAKE PL
SANDERLING PL

AUCHENGREOCH RD

61

Meikle Corseford

West Corseford Farm

MIDTON RD

Hallhill Farm

Auchingreach

KILNKNOWIE COTTS

Spateston Burn

Works

Hallhill

3

Midton House

Howwood Prim Sch

Whitehill

Tor Bracken

Midtown Wood

Mountop Wood

PA9

60

Mountop

Skiff Wood

High Burnside

2

PA2

Swinetrees Burn

Broadfield Hill

North Castlewalls

Walls Loch

59

Whittliemuir Midton Loch

Broadfield Cottage

Nether Broadfield

Walls Hill

1

Mid Hartfield

Hartfield

Muirhead Burn

B775

58

40   D   41   E   42   F

131
112

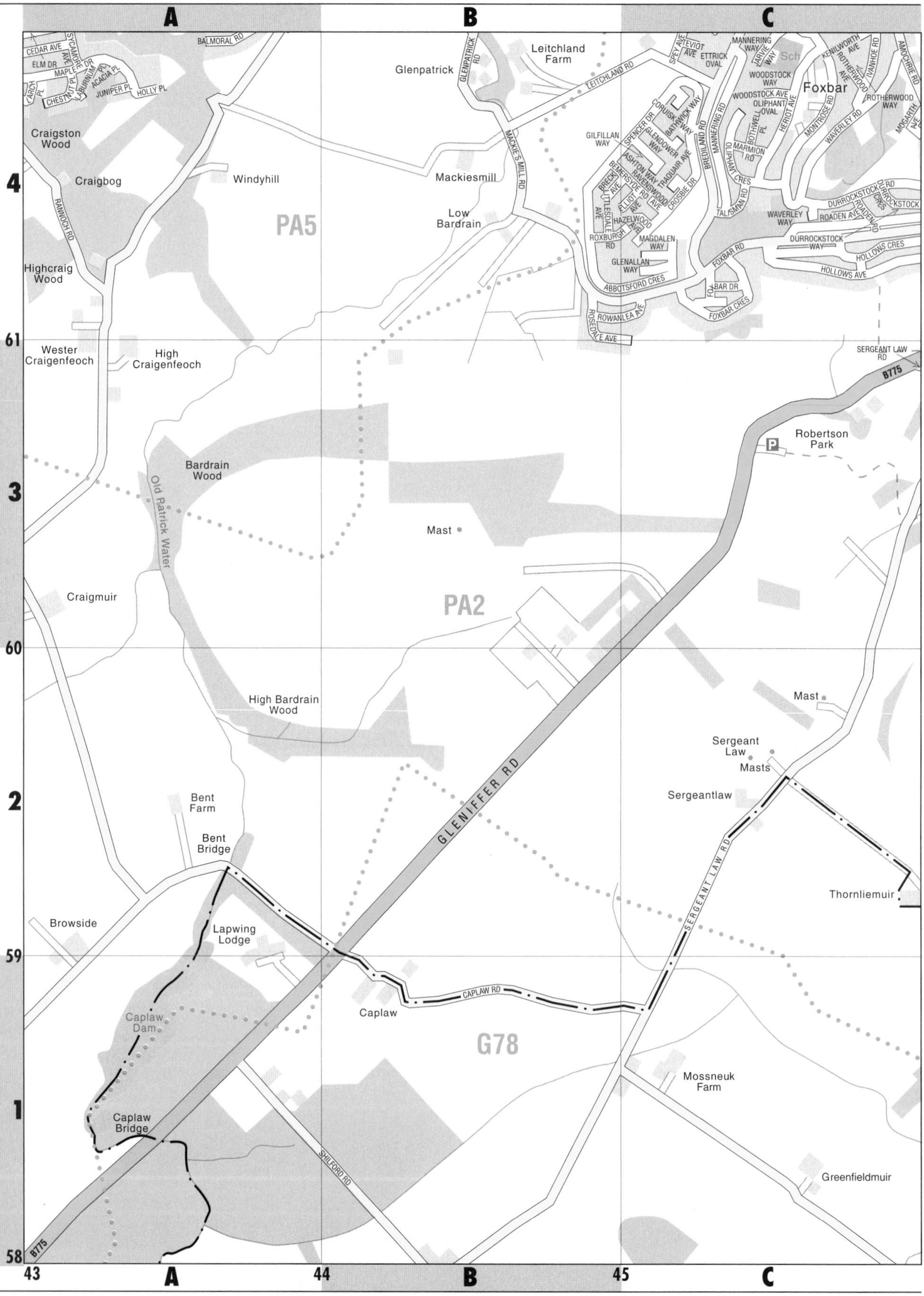

A   B   C

4

Balmoral Rd
CEDAR AVE
SYCAMORE AVE
ELM DR
MAPLE DR
CARR PL
CHESTNUT DR
LABURNUM DR
ACACIA PL
JUNIPER PL
HOLLY PL

Craigston Wood
Craigbog
Windyhill
Glenpatrick
GLENPATRICK RD
Leitchland Farm
LEITCHLAND RD
Mackiesmill
MACKIE'S MILL RD
Low Bardrain

PA5

SPEY AVE
TEVIOT AVE
ETTRICK OVAL
MANNERING WAY
JARVIE WAY
KENILWORTH AVE
IVANHOE RD
ARDMORE RD
Sch
WOODSTOCK WAY
WOODSTOCK AVE
Foxbar
OLIPHANT AVE
ROTHERWOOD AVE
MORGAN RD
CORLISS DR
SPENCER DR
GLENDOWER WAY
BATHWICK WAY
RADGAIR AVE
GILFILLAN WAY
MANNERING RD
MARMION AVE
MONTROSE AVE
WAVERLEY RD
ASHTON WAY
GLENALMOND
CROSSIE DR
BOTHWELL PL
HERIOT AVE
OLIPHANT CRES
BRECKENRIDGE RD
DALSWINTON
ELTIG RD
TALISMAN RD
DURROCKSTOCK RD
DURROCKSTOCK
LITTLESDALE AVE
HAZELWOOD
WAVERLEY WAY
ROADEN AVE
ROXBURGH RD
MAGDALEN WAY
DURROCKSTOCK WAY
HOLLOWS CRES
GLENALLAN WAY
HOLLOWS AVE
ABBOTSFORD CRES
FOXBAR RD
FOXBAR DR
FOXBAR CRES
ROWANLEA AVE
ROSEDALE AVE

61

Wester Craigenfeoch
High Craigenfeoch
Highcraig Wood
SERGEANT LAW RD
B775

3

Old Patrick Water
Bardrain Wood
Mast
Robertson Park
P

Craigmuir
PA2

60

High Bardrain Wood
Mast
Sergeant Law
Masts

2

Bent Farm
GLENIFFER RD
Sergeantlaw
SERGEANT LAW RD
Bent Bridge
Thornliemuir

Browside
Lapwing Lodge

59

Caplaw Dam
Caplaw
CAPLAW RD
G78

1

Caplaw Bridge
Mossneuk Farm
SHILFORD RD
Greenfieldmuir

58
B775

43   A   44   B   45   C

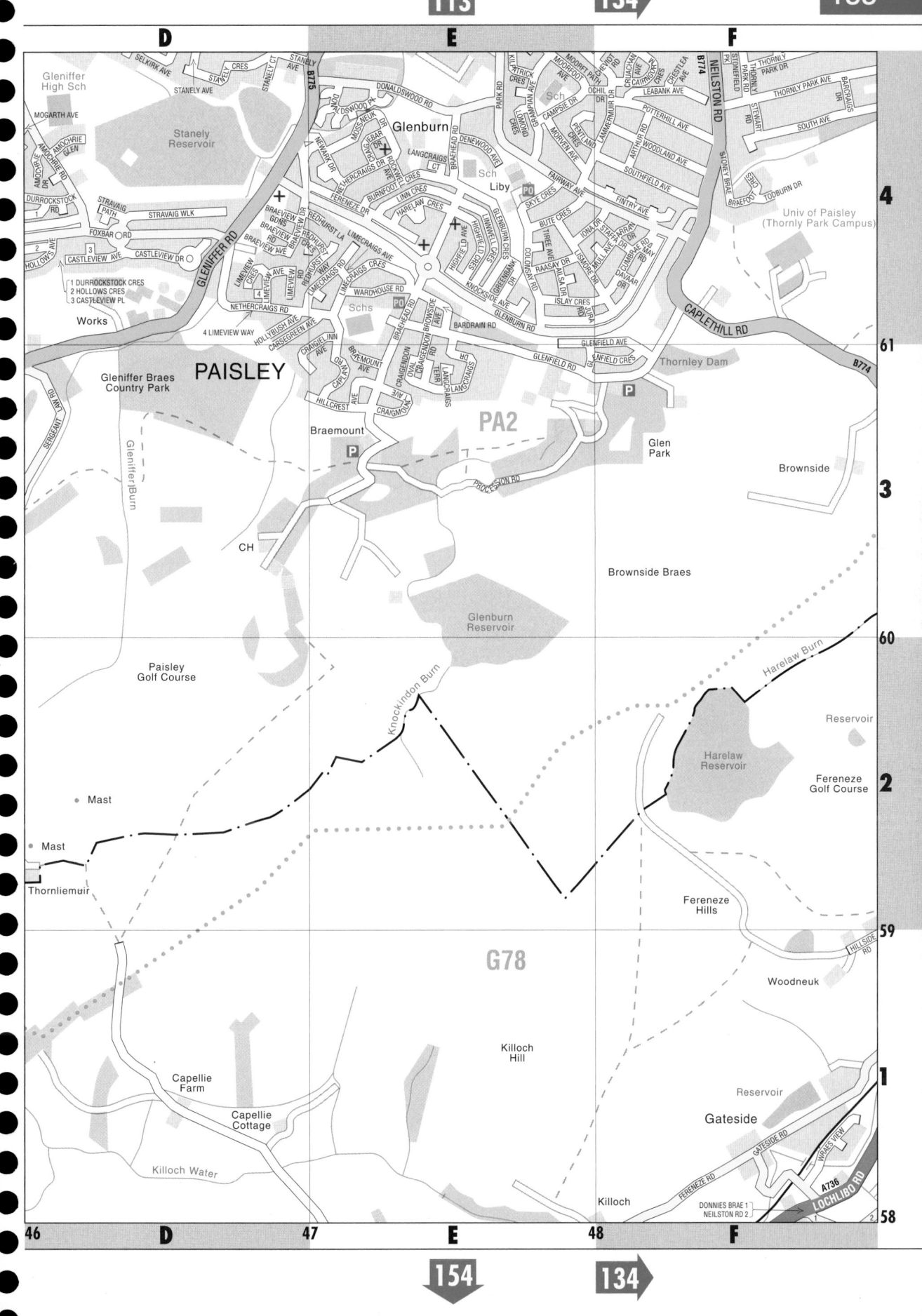

Gleniffer
High Sch

MOGARTH AVE

SELKIRK AVE

STANELY CRES

STANELY CT

STANELY AVE

STANELY AVE

B775

DONALDSWOOD RD

PARK RD

KILPATRICK CRES

MOORPARK PATH

MOORPARK AVE

Sch

Stanely
Reservoir

Glenburn

LANGCRAIGS CT

DONALDSWOOD RD

NEWARK DR

BRAEHEAD RD

DENEWOOD AVE

PARK RD

GRAMPIAN AVE

CAMPSIE DR

OCHIL DR

LEABANK AVE

CRIAGHAM AVE

CAIRNGORM CRES

CRESTLEA

AMOCHRIE
Glen

AMOCHRIE RD

DURROCKSTOCK RD

STRAVAIG
PATH

STRAVAIG WLK

FOXBAR RD

NETHERCRAIGS DR

ROCKWELL AVE

NEWARK DR

BURNFOOT RD

LINN CRES

LANGCRAIGS AVE

FERENEZE DR

REDHURST LA

HAREHAW CRES

HIGHFIELD CRES

LINWELL CRES

GLENBURN CRES

SKYE CRES

BUTE CRES

THREE AVES

FAIRWAY AVE

SOUTHFIELD AVE

FINTRY AVE

POTTERHILL AVE

ARTHUR RD

WOODLAND AVE

PEUTLAND DR

MORVEN AVE

LAMMERMUIR DR

SIDNEY BRAE

B774

NEILSTON RD

STONEFIELD

THORNLY PARK DR

THORNLY PARK AVE

BARCRAIGS DR

STEWART

SOUTH AVE

Univ of Paisley
(Thornly Park Campus)

4

MOGARTH AVE

HOLLOW AVE

CASTLEVIEW AVE

CASTLEVIEW DR

BRAEVIEW GDNS

BRAEVIEW DR

BRAEVIEW AVE

REDHURST CRES

NETHERCRAIGS RD

LIMEVIEW CRES

LIMEVIEW AVE

LIMEVIEW AVE

REDHURST WAY

LIMECRAIGS CRES

WARDHOUSE RD

BRAECAD RD

HIGHFIELD DR

KNOCKSIDE AVE

COLONSAY RD

IONA DR

STAFFA DR

RAASAY DR

LISMORE AVE

ARRAN DR

CUMBRAE RD

MAY DR

DAVAAR DR

ISLAY CRES

BRAEFOOT

TOODBURN DR

TODBURN DR

1 DURROCKSTOCK CRES
2 HOLLOWS CRES
3 CASTLEVIEW PL

Works

PAISLEY

Gleniffer Braes
Country Park

GLENIFFER RD

Gleniffer Burn

SERGEANT LAW RD

4 LIMEVIEW WAY

HOLLYBUSH AVE

CARSEGREEN AVE

CRAIGIELINN AVE

BRAEMOUNT AVE

CRAIGMOUNT AVE

OVAL

LANGCRAIGS TERR

CRAIGENDON RD

BROWNSIDE AVE

BARDRAIN RD

GLENBURN RD

GLENFIELD AVE

GLENFIELD RD

GLENFIELD CRES

Thornley Dam

61

CH

Braemount

HILLCREST AVE

LANGCRAIGS

CRAIGMS

CAPLE LAW AVE

PROCESSION RD

PA2

Glen
Park

Brownside

B774

3

Brownside Braes

Glenburn
Reservoir

Harelaw Burn

60

Paisley
Golf Course

Knockindon Burn

Harelaw
Reservoir

Reservoir

Ferenze
Golf Course

2

Mast

Mast

Thornliemuir

Ferenze
Hills

HILLSIDE RD

59

G78

Woodneuk

Killoch
Hill

Capellie
Farm

Capellie
Cottage

Reservoir

Gateside

1

WRAES VIEW

GATESIDE RD

FERENZE RD

Killoch Water

Killoch

DONNIES BRAE 1
NEILSTON RD 2

A736

LOCHLIBO RD

58

A   B   C

ALLOWAY AVE
BALLATER DR
THORNLY PARK AVE
SOUTH AVE
STRATHCARRON RD
ALLOWAY CRES
GRAHAMSTON PL
Temple Hill
BULLWOOD CT
BULLWOOD AVE   RAESWOOD GDNS
LEVERNDALE IND CTR
MULBEN TER
MULBEN RD
MINMOOR RD

Tod Burn
Dykebar
GRAHAMSTON CRES
GRAHAMSTON CT
Old Cotts
HURLET RD
Tongues Hill
Hurlethill Plantation
FASKIN RD   KINARVIE RD
MULBEN CRES

Shaw Wood
4
H
PA2
OLDBARHILLS TP SITE
Hurlet Hill
Hurlet
KINARVIE TER   KINARVIE PL
KINARVIE GDNS

Hollybush
Oldbar Hills
BARRHEAD RD
A736   A736
KINARVIE CRES

61
GRAHAMSTON RD
Oldbar Burn
West Hurlet House
BARRHEAD RD   A736
HURLET COTTS
NITSHILL RD   A736

B774
Harelaw Burn
Harelaw
Raes Wood
G53
LEVERN RD
PINMORE ST   PINMORE PL
GALSTON ST   DARVEL ST
SEAMILL ST

3
CAPLETHILL RD
Logansraes
Blackbyres
Cemy
Nitshill
Waterside
SEAMILL PATH
WOODHEAD RD
WHITHOPE TER

WNSIDE DR
BROWNSIDE
ROWANPARK DR   GLENIFER DR
LEVEN CT
LINNIE DR   GRAHAMSTON PK
P
B774
B771
SHANKS WAY
SATURLAND RD
Saturland
WHITACRES RD
WENSMOOR RD 1
WHITACRES PATH 2
WILLOWFORD RD

MOSS DR   ACACIA DR
HEATHER ST
CORSEFORD
LOMOND DR
SHELL CRES
SHANKS IND PK
WHITACRES

60
BURNSIDE DR
CH
PAISLEY RD
VICTORIA GDNS
St John's Prim Sch
Crossmill
STEWART ST   STEWART PL
BRIDGEBAR
Bowerwalls
Parkhouse

Cross Arthurlie Sch
QUARRY RD
TREES PARK AVE
VICTORIA RD
COMMERCIAL RD
MURIEL STREET IND EST
WAULKMILL WAY
STEWART CT
Levern Water
PARKHOUSE RD   B773
Redhall

Ferenze Golf Course
CH
BELLFIELD CT
FERENEZE GR
Barrhead
MURIEL ST
MURIEL LA
CARLIBAR GDNS
Carlibar Prim Sch
DOVECOTHALL ST
Dovecothall
DARNLEY RD
Tower Rais
Tower Holm

2
FERENEZE AVE
GRAHAM ST
RUFFLEES AVE
GLASGOW RD
G78
A736
B773
Cowan Park
Barrhead High Sch
Dubbs

HILLSIDE DR
GATESIDE RD
CENTRE WAY
P
NORTH PARK AVE
Sports Ctr
WATER RD
MANSE CT
LYONCROSS CRES
Aurs Burn
DUBBS RD

HILLSIDE AVE
MAXTON AVE
SAUNDERS CT
P
Liby
GLEN ST
MAIN ST
PO
COWAN ST
59
The Centre
Ind Est
ROBERTSON CT
P
Mus
Convent
ST MARYS GDNS
AURSBRIDGE DR
BARRHEAD
Dubbs

West Arthurlie
KELBURN ST
B771
CRAIGHEAD WAY
STORMYLAND WAY
CLOTH ST
SHANKS AVE
ARTHURLIE ST
AURS CRES
PO
GLANDERSTON AVE
AURS RD

1
LOCHLIBO RD
A736
DALMENY DR
KERR ST
BLACKWOOD
SUNNYSIDE WAY
LOMOND ST
Arthurlie
GRAMPIAN WAY
Sch
CAMPBELL DR
KELSO AVE
BROADLIE DR
CRAIGTON AVE
North Brae

Cemy
NEILSTON RD
KIRKTON RD
CAMPSIE AVE
SIDLAW AVE
Sch
AURS GLEN
Auchenback
FENWICK DR
NEWTON AVE
1 OAKBANK DR
2 SPRINGFIELD RD

58
Springhill Prim Sch
PARK AVE
PENTLAND DR
DIVERNIA WAY
NEWTON AVE

49   A   50   B   51   C

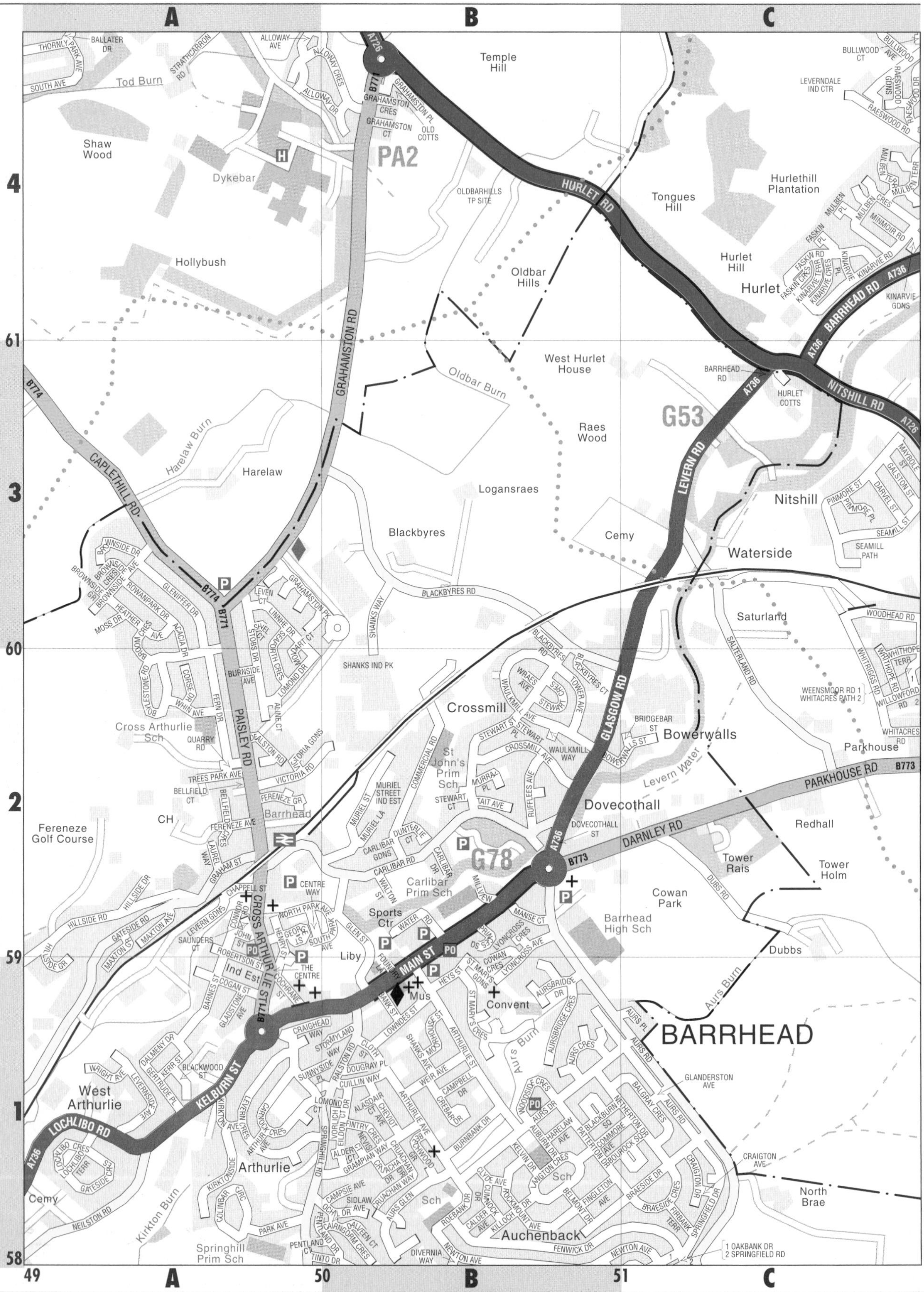

115
136

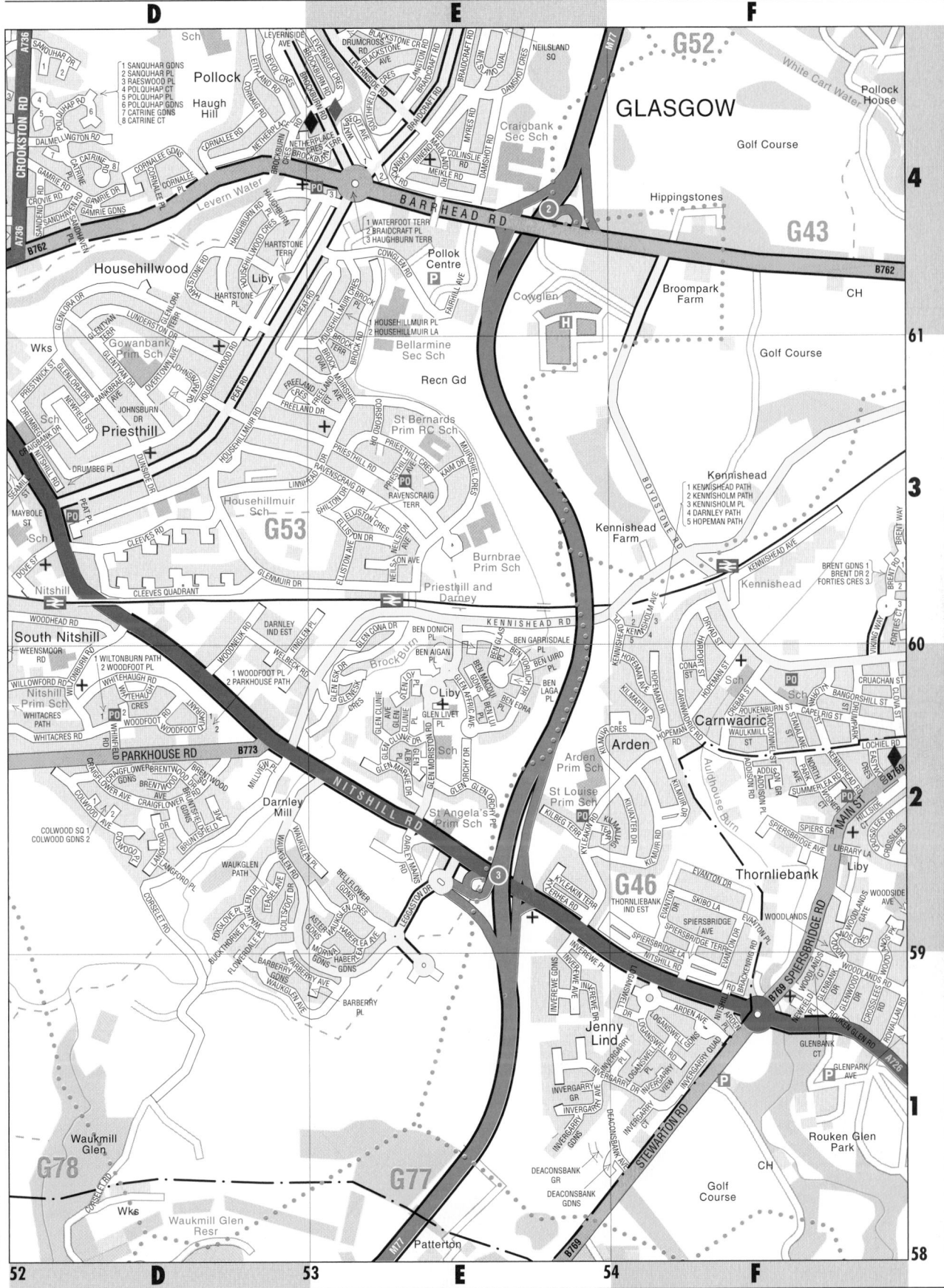
GLASGOW
Pollock
Haugh Hill
Househillwood
Priesthill
South Nitshill
Nitshill
Darnley Mill
Arden
Carnwadric
Kennishead
Thornliebank
Jenny Lind
Patterton
Pollock House
Hippingstones
Broompark Farm
Kennishead Farm
Waukmill Glen
Waukmill Glen Resr
Rouken Glen Park
Golf Course
Pollok Centre
Cowglen
Recn Gd
Craigbank Sec Sch
Bellarmine Sec Sch
St Bernards Prim RC Sch
Burnbrae Prim Sch
Gowanbank Prim Sch
Househillmuir Sch
Nitshill Prim Sch
Arden Prim Sch
St Louise Prim Sch
St Angela's Prim Sch
Priesthill and Darnley
BARRHEAD RD
NITSHILL RD
PARKHOUSE RD
STEWARTON RD
SPIERSBRIDGE RD
MAIN ST
CROOKSTON RD
KENNISHEAD RD
ROUKEN GLEN RD
Levern Water
White Cart Water
Brock Burn
Auldhouse Burn
G52
G43
G53
G46
G78
G77
M77
B762
B773
B769
A736
A726
1 SANQUHAR GDNS
2 SANQUHAR PL
3 RAESWOOD PL
4 POLQUHAP CT
5 POLQUHAP PL
6 POLQUHAP GDNS
7 CATRINE GDNS
8 CATRINE CT
1 WATERFOOT TERR
2 BRAIDCRAFT PL
3 HAUGHBURN TERR
1 HOUSEHILLMUIR PL
2 HOUSEHILLMUIR LA
1 KENNISHEAD PATH
2 KENNISHOLM PATH
3 KENNISHOLM PL
4 DARNLEY PATH
5 HOPEMAN PATH
1 WILTONBURN PATH
2 WOODFOOT PL
1 WOODFOOT PL
2 PARKHOUSE PATH
COLWOOD SQ 1
COLWOOD GDNS 2
BRENT GDNS 1
BRENT DR 2
FORTIES CRES 3
D
E
F
52
53
54
58
59
60
61
1
2
3
4

156
136

135
116

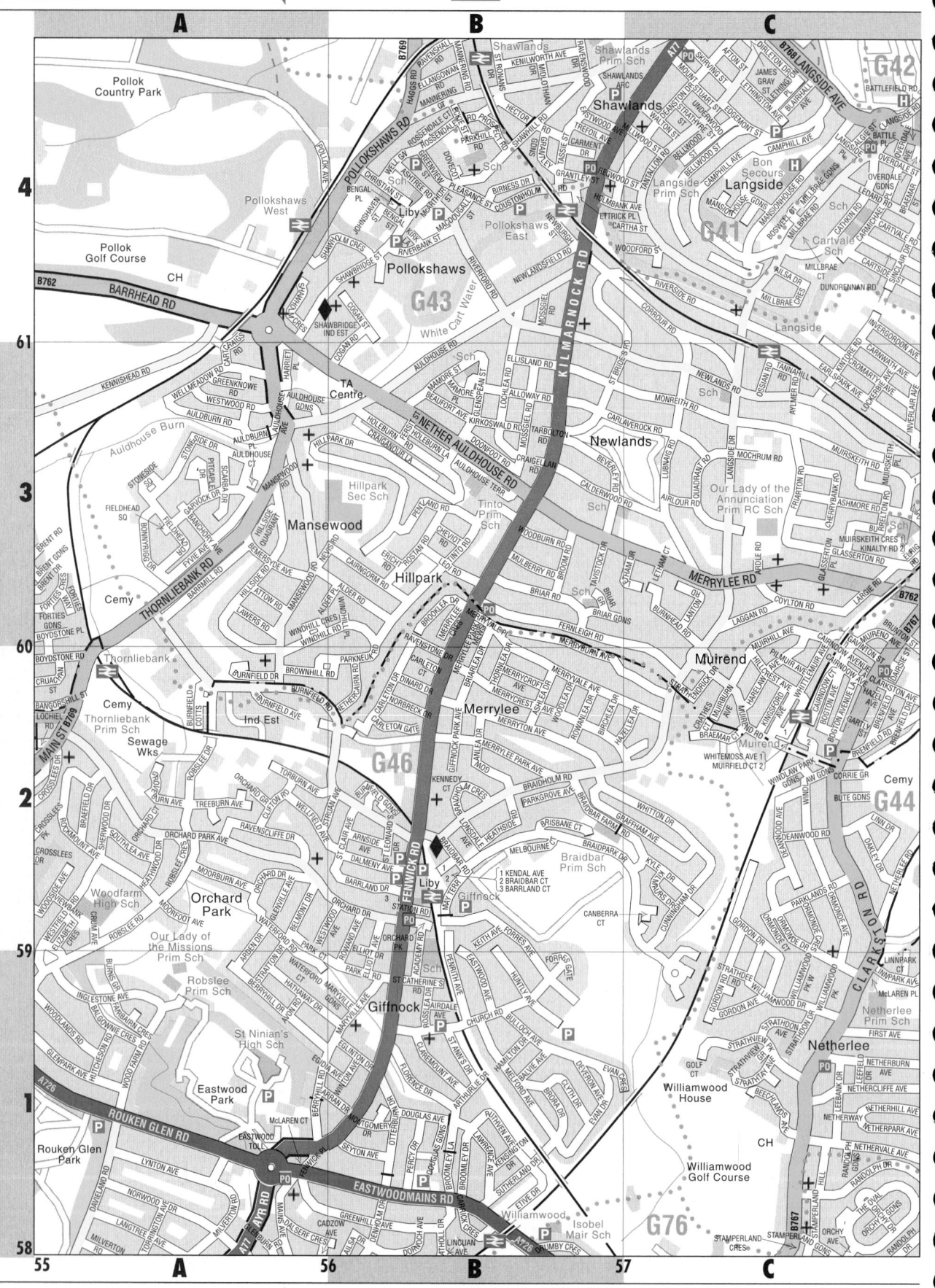
A
B
C
Pollok Country Park
Pollokshaws West
Pollok Golf Course
BARRHEAD RD
POLLOKSHAWS RD
Pollokshaws
Shawlands
Langside
Bon Secours
Langside Prim Sch
Pollokshaws East
KILMARNOCK RD
NETHER AULDHOUSE RD
Newlands
Mansewood
Hillpark
Hillpark Sec Sch
Tinto Prim Sch
Our Lady of the Annunciation Prim RC Sch
MERRYLEE RD
Muirend
Merrylee
THORNLIEBANK RD
Thornliebank
Thornliebank Prim Sch
Sewage Wks
Ind Est
Cemy
Orchard Park
Woodfarm High Sch
Our Lady of the Missions Prim Sch
Robslee Prim Sch
St Ninian's High Sch
Eastwood Park
Rouken Glen Park
ROUKEN GLEN RD
EASTWOODMAINS RD
FENWICK RD
Giffnock
Braidbar Prim Sch
CLARKSTON RD
Netherlee
Netherlee Prim Sch
Williamwood House
Williamwood Golf Course
Isobel Mair Sch
G41
G42
G43
G44
G46
G76
1 KENDAL AVE
2 BRAIDBAR CT
3 BARRLAND CT
WHITEMOSS AVE 1
MUIRFIELD CT 2
4
3
2
1
61
60
59
58
55
56
57

135
157

117
138

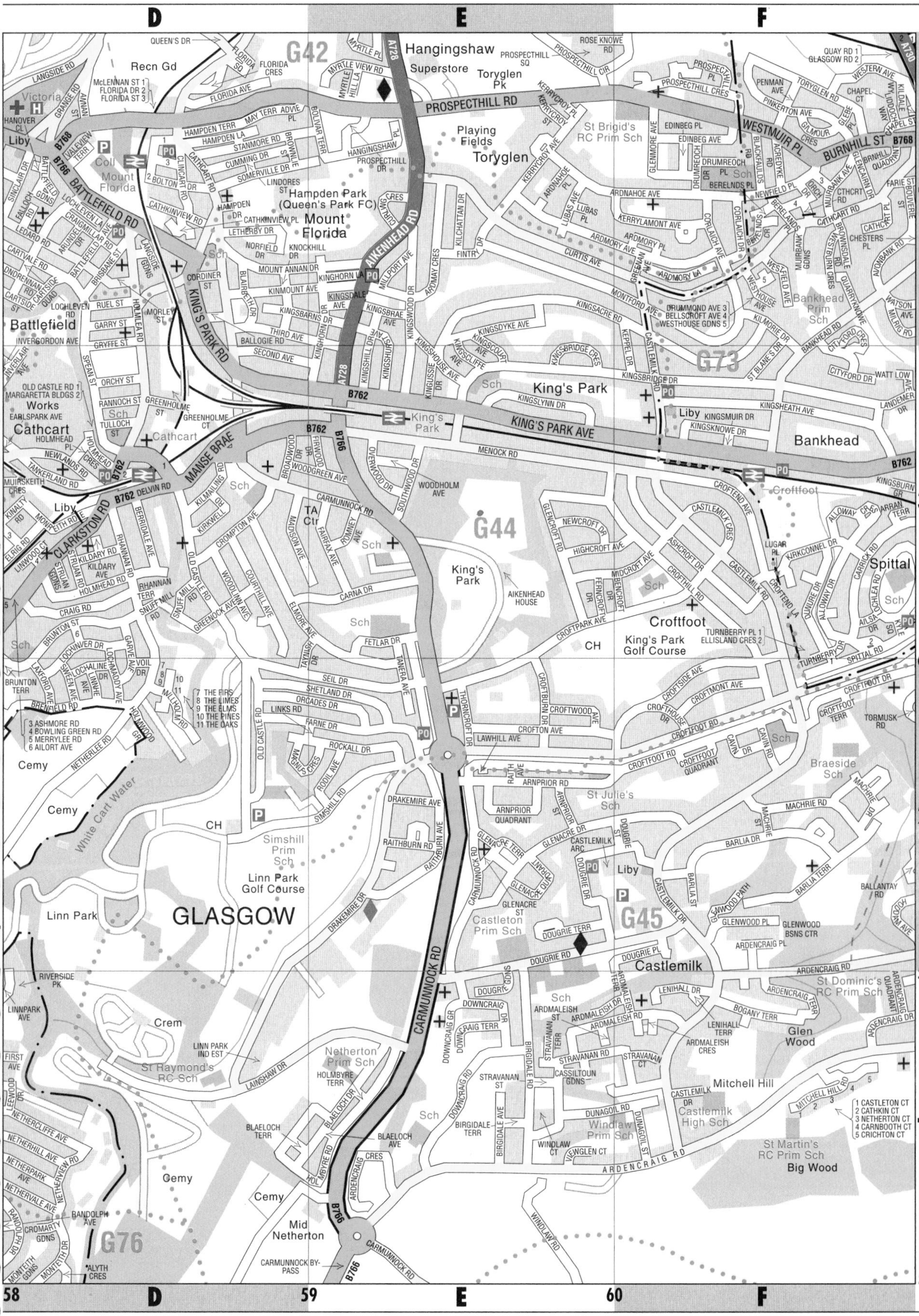

158
138

137
118

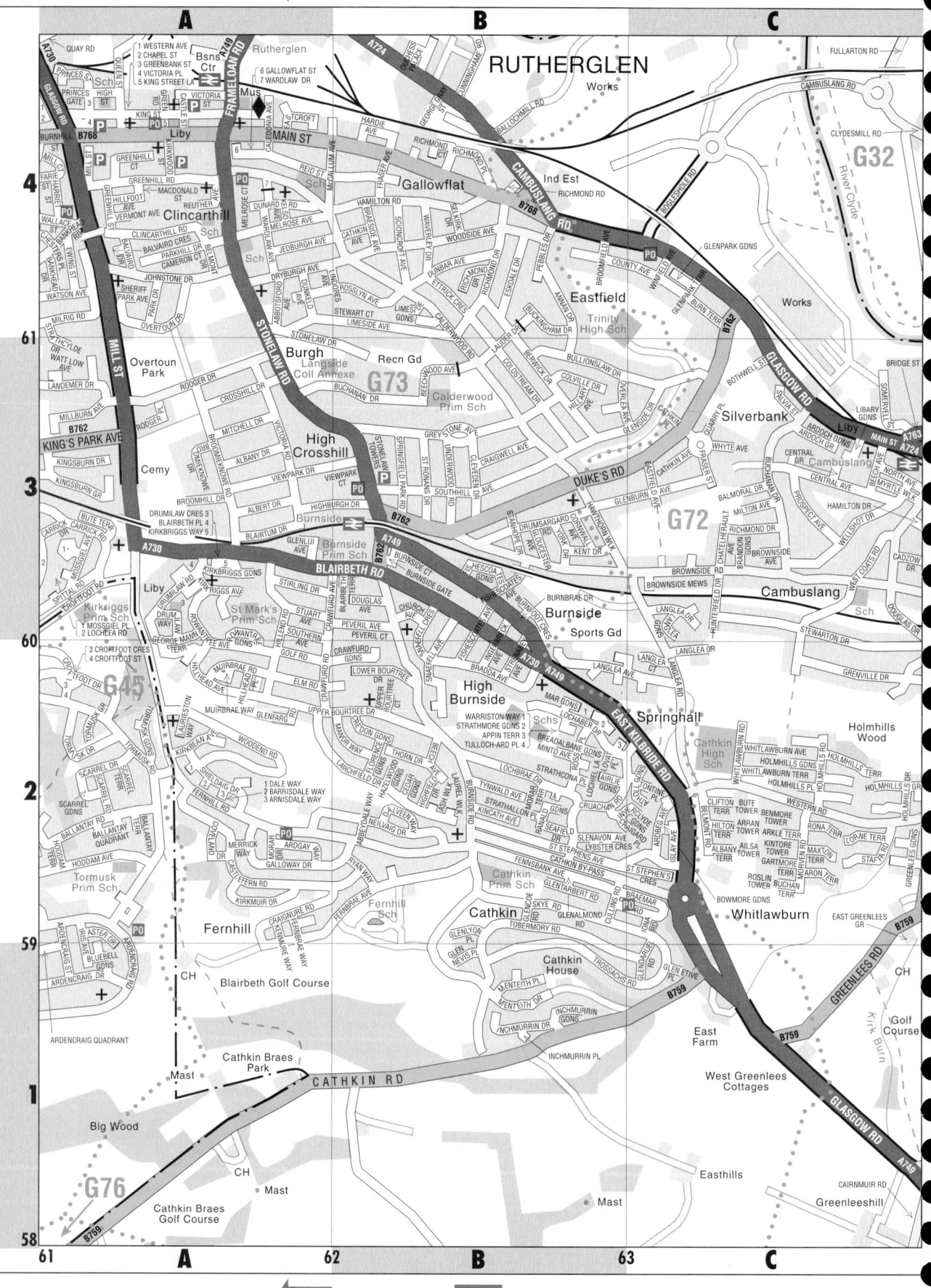
A
B
C
RUTHERGLEN
Rutherglen
Works
Bsns Ctr
Mus
Liby
MAIN ST
Gallowflat
Ind Est
Clincarthill
Sch
G32
River Clyde
Eastfield
Trinity High Sch
Works
Burgh
Langside Coll Annexe
Recn Gd
G73
Calderwood Prim Sch
Overtoun Park
High Crosshill
Silverbank
Cambuslang
Cemy
KING'S PARK AVE
MILL ST
STONELAW RD
FRAMELOAN RD
CAMBUSLANG RD
GLASGOW RD
DUKE'S RD
BLAIRBETH RD
Burnside
Burnside Prim Sch
G72
Kirkriggs Prim Sch
St Mark's Prim Sch
Burnside
Sports Gd
Cambuslang
G45
High Burnside
Springhall
Cathkin High Sch
Holmhills Wood
EAST KILBRIDE RD
Tormusk Prim Sch
Cathkin Prim Sch
Fernhill Sch
Cathkin
Whitlawburn
Fernhill
Blairbeth Golf Course
Cathkin House
East Farm
Golf Course
Kirk Burn
Cathkin Braes Park
Mast
CATHKIN RD
West Greenlees Cottages
Big Wood
G76
CH
Mast
Cathkin Braes Golf Course
Easthills
Mast
Greenleeshill
GREENLEES RD
4
3
2
1
61
60
59
58
61
62
63

137
159

119 140

Carmyle
G32
River Clyde
Newton Farm
Cambuslang Bridge
Newton Bridge
Westburn
Works
James Aiton Prim Sch
Westburn Golf Course
St Charles RC Prim Sch
Cemy
Newton
Spoil Heap
G72
Hallside
Kirkhill
Hallside Prim Sch
Cambuslang
Halfway
Holmhills Farm
Cambuslang Public Park
Wellside
Greenlees
Flemington
Gilbertfield
Dechmont Rifle Ranges
Flemington House
Turnlaw
Helenslea Cottage
Kirkhill Golf Course
Dechmont Hill
Dechmont Lodge
Quarry Wood
MAIN ST
HAMILTON RD
CLYDEFORD RD
BRIDGE ST
GREENLEES RD
NEWTON STATION RD
GLASGOW RD
A763
A724
A749
B759

160 140

139
120

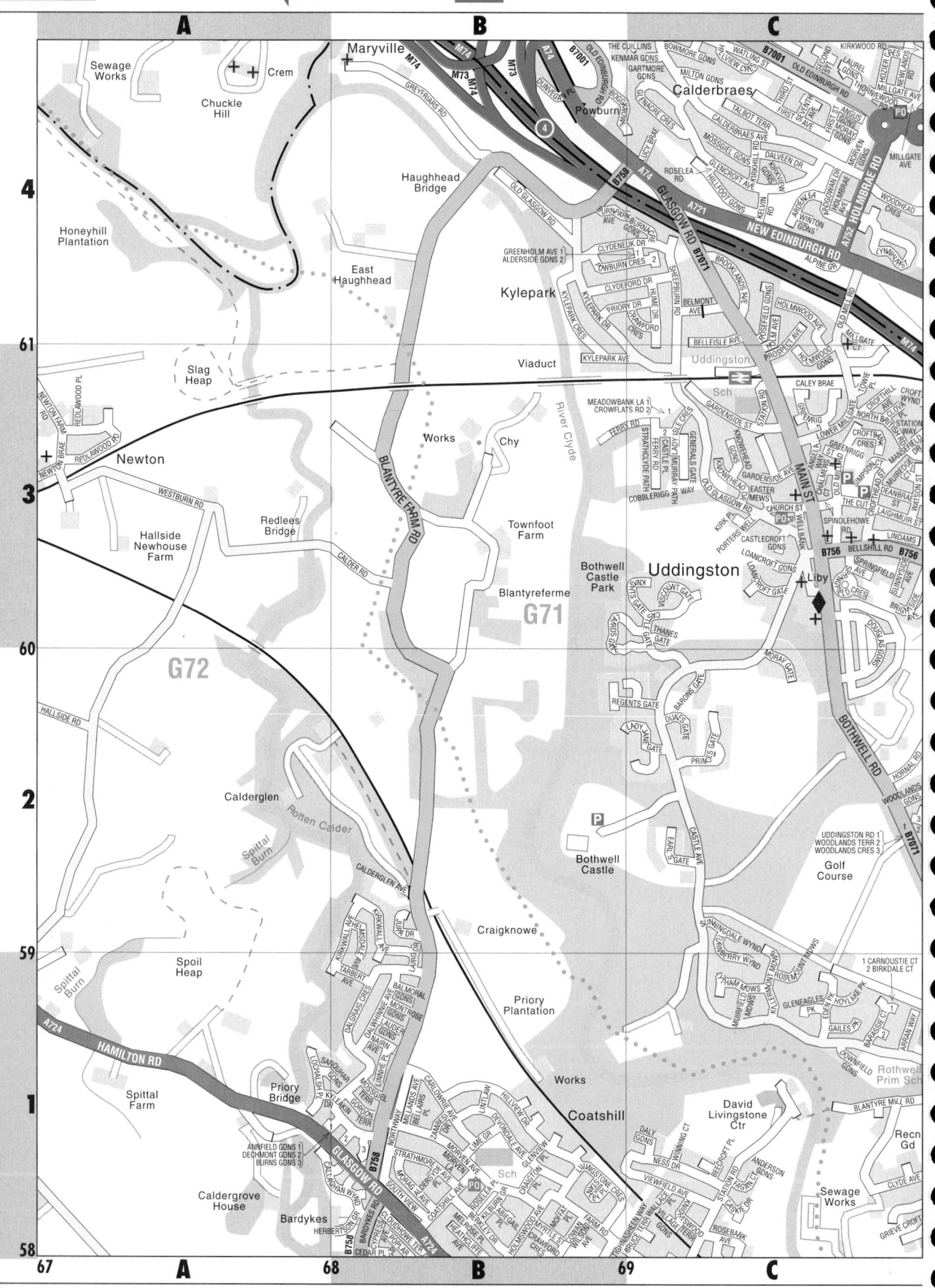
A
B
C
Maryville
Sewage Works
Crem
Chuckle Hill
Haughhead Bridge
Honeyhill Plantation
East Haughhead
Kylepark
Calderbraes
Powburn
NEW EDINBURGH RD
GLASGOW RD
OLD GLASGOW RD
HOLMBRAE RD
Uddingston
Sch
Viaduct
Slag Heap
Newton
WESTBURN RD
Redlees Bridge
Hallside Newhouse Farm
Works
Chy
River Clyde
BLANTYRE FARM RD
Townfoot Farm
Blantyreferme
G71
Bothwell Castle Park
Uddingston
MAIN ST
Liby
BELLSHILL RD
G72
HALLSIDE RD
Calderglen
Rotten Calder
Spittal Burn
Bothwell Castle
CASTLE AVE
Golf Course
BOTHWELL RD
Craigknowe
Spoil Heap
Priory Plantation
HAMILTON RD
Spittal Farm
Priory Bridge
Works
Coatshill
David Livingstone Ctr
Rothwell Prim Sch
Recn Gd
Sewage Works
Caldergrove House
Bardykes
GLASGOW RD
4
61
3
60
2
59
1
58
67
68
69

139
161

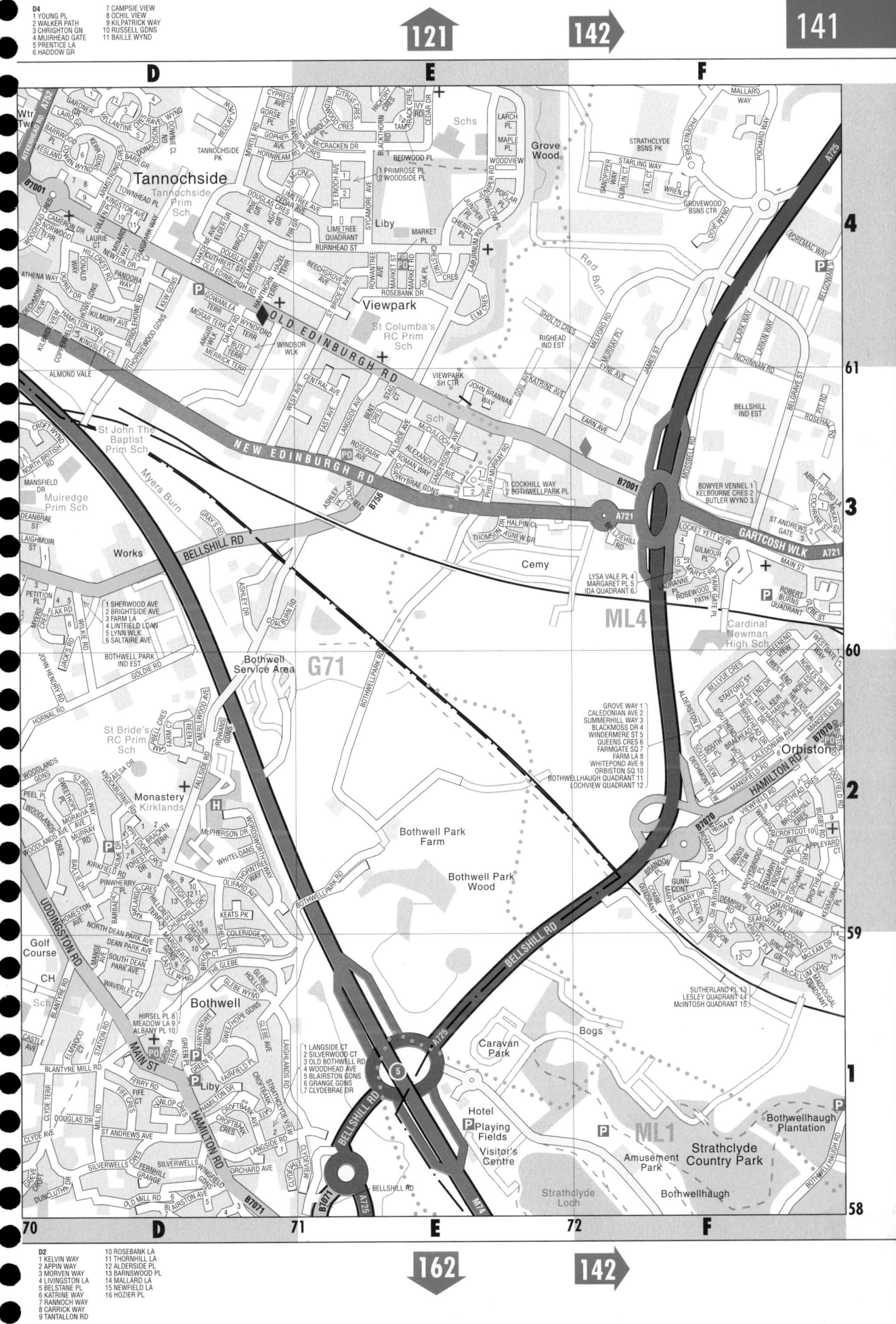

D4
1 YOUNG PL
2 WALKER PATH
3 CRIGHTON GN
4 MUIRHEAD GATE
5 PRENTICE LA
6 HADDOW GR
7 CAMPSIE VIEW
8 OCHIL VIEW
9 KILPATRICK WAY
10 RUSSELL GDNS
11 BAILLE WYND

D2
1 KELVIN WAY
2 APPIN WAY
3 MORVEN WAY
4 LIVINGSTON LA
5 BELSTANE PL
6 KATRINE WAY
7 RANNOCH WAY
8 CARRICK WAY
9 TANTALLON RD
10 ROSEBANK LA
11 THORNHILL LA
12 ALDERSIDE PL
13 BARNSWOOD RD
14 MALLARD GLA
15 NEWFIELD PL
16 HOZIER PL

141 122

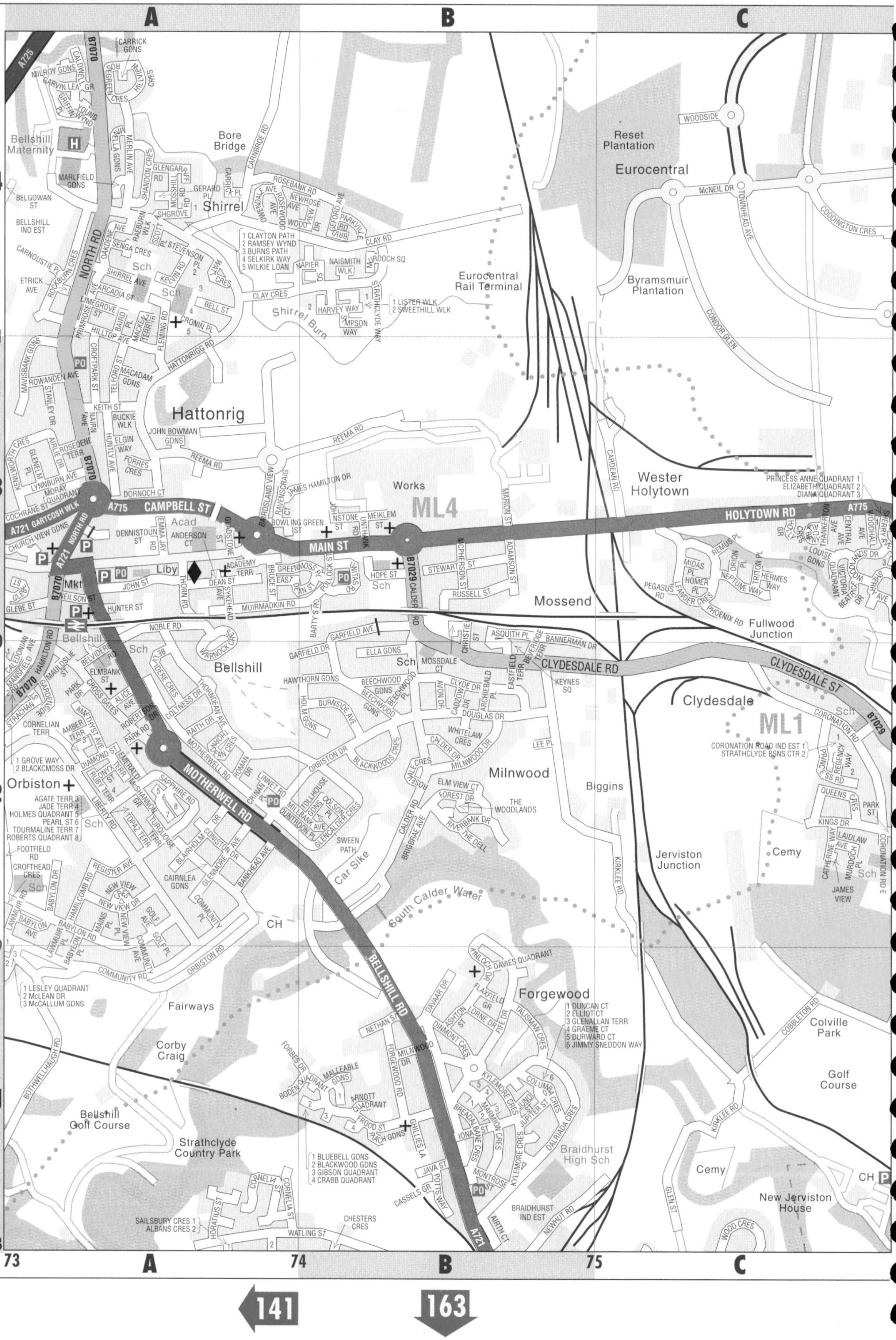

A   B   C

4

Bellshill Maternity H

Bore Bridge

Shirrel

Reset Plantation

Eurocentral

Byramsmuir Plantation

1 CLAYTON PATH
2 RAMSEY WYND
3 BURNS PATH
4 SELKIRK WAY
5 WILKIE LOAN

1 LISTER WLK
2 SWEETHILL WLK

Eurocentral Rail Terminal

Shirrel Burn

61

Hattonrig

Works

ML4

Wester Holytown

PRINCESS ANNE QUADRANT 1
ELIZABETH QUADRANT 2
DIANA QUADRANT 3

3

CAMPBELL ST

Acad

HOLYTOWN RD

MAIN ST

Liby

Mkt

Mossend

Fullwood Junction

60

Bellshill

Bellshill

CLYDESDALE RD

CLYDESDALE ST

Clydesdale

ML1

CORONATION ROAD IND EST 1
STRATHCLYDE BSNS CTR 2

Milnwood

Biggins

THE WOODLANDS

Jerviston Junction

Cemy

2

Orbiston

MOTHERWELL RD

1 GROVE WAY
2 BLACKCMOSS DR

AGATE TERR 3
JADE TERR 4
HOLMES QUADRANT 5
PEARL ST 6
TOURMALINE TERR 7
ROBERTS QUADRANT 8

FOOTFIELD RD
CROFTHEAD CRES

Car Sike

South Calder Water

JAMES VIEW

59

1 LESLEY QUADRANT
2 McLEAN DR
3 McCALLUM GDNS

Fairways

Corby Craig

CH

BELLSHILL RD

Forgewood

1 DUNCAN CT
2 ELLIOT CT
3 GLENALLAN TERR
4 GRAEME CT
5 DURWARD CT
6 JIMMY SNEDDON WAY

Colville Park

Golf Course

1

Bellshill Golf Course

Strathclyde Country Park

1 BLUEBELL GDNS
2 BLACKWOOD GDNS
3 GIBSON QUADRANT
4 CRABB QUADRANT

Braidhurst High Sch

BRAIDHURST IND EST

Cemy

New Jerviston House

CH

58

SAILSBURY CRES 1
ALBANS CRES 2

CHESTERS CRES

WATLING ST

73   A   74   B   75   C

123
144

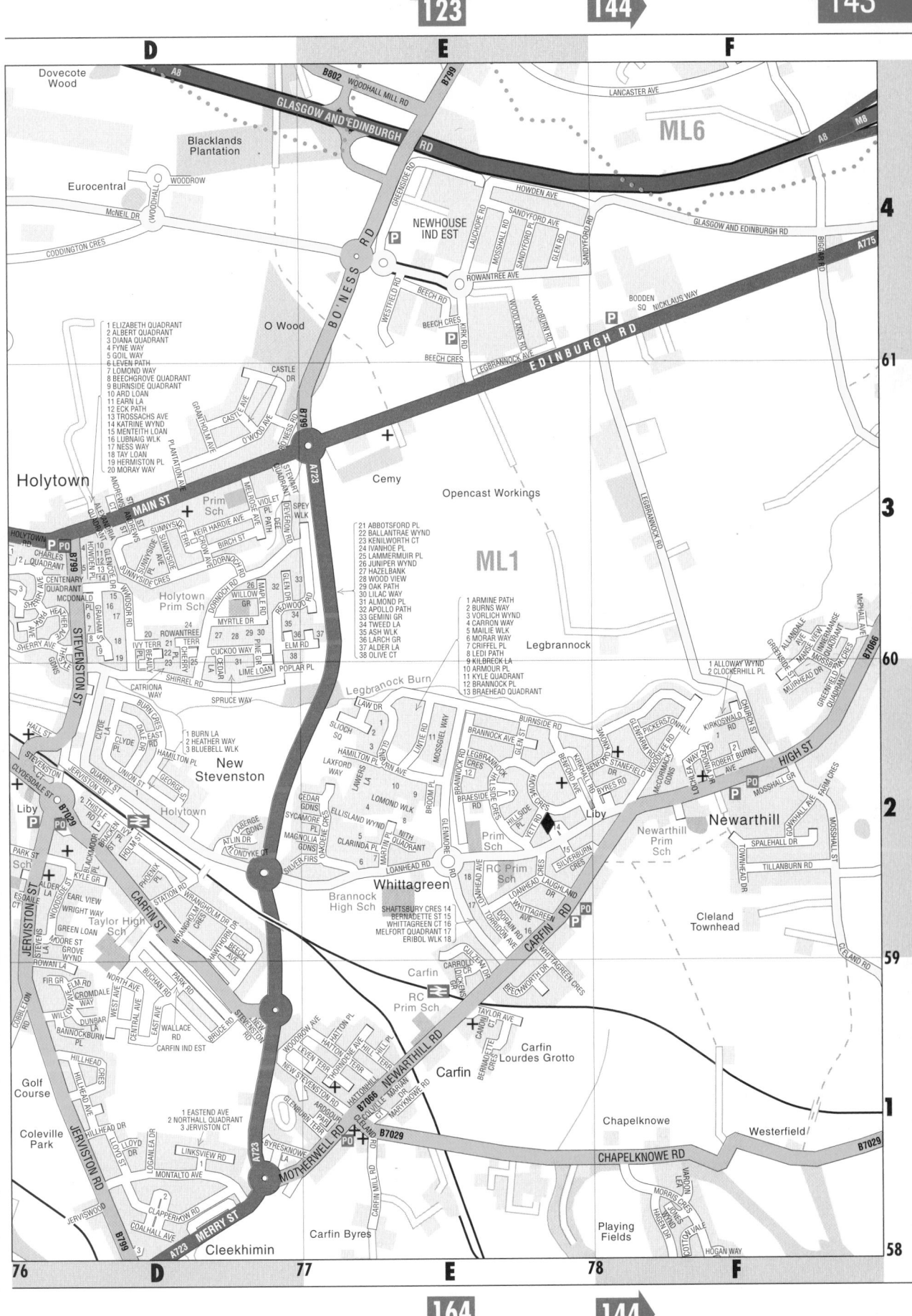
D
E
F
Dovecote Wood
A8
B802
WOODHALL MILL RD
B799
GLASGOW AND EDINBURGH RD
LANCASTER AVE
ML6
M8
Blacklands Plantation
Eurocentral
WOODROW
WOODHALL
McNEIL DR
CODDINGTON CRES
GREENSIDE RD
HOWDEN AVE
SANDYFORD AVE
NEWHOUSE IND EST
LAUCHOPE RD
MOSSHALL RD
SANDYFORD PL
GLEN RD
SANDYFORD RD
GLASGOW AND EDINBURGH RD
BIGGAR RD
A775
4
BO'NESS RD
ROWANTREE AVE
BEECH RD
WESTFIELD RD
BEECH CRES
KIRK RD
WOODLANDS RD
WOODBURN RD
LEGBRANNOCK AVE
BODDEN SQ
NICKLAUS WAY
EDINBURGH RD
O Wood
1 ELIZABETH QUADRANT
2 ALBERT QUADRANT
3 DIANA QUADRANT
4 FYNE WAY
5 GOIL WAY
6 LEVEN PATH
7 LOMOND WAY
8 BEECHGROVE QUADRANT
9 BURNSIDE QUADRANT
10 ARD LOAN
11 EARN LA
12 ECK PATH
13 TROSSACHS AVE
14 KATRINE WYND
15 MENTEITH LOAN
16 LUBNAIG WLK
17 NESS WAY
18 TAY LOAN
19 HERMISTON PL
20 MORAY WAY
CASTLE DR
CASTLE AVE
GRANTHOLM AVE
O WOOD AVE
PLANTATION AVE
61
A723
Cemy
Opencast Workings
Holytown
MAIN ST
Prim Sch
3
HOLYTOWN RD
ML1
LEGBRANNOCK RD
21 ABBOTSFORD PL
22 BALLANTRAE WYND
23 KENILWORTH CT
24 IVANHOE PL
25 LAMMERMUIR PL
26 JUNIPER WYND
27 HAZELBANK
28 WOOD VIEW
29 OAK PATH
30 LILAC WAY
31 ALMOND PL
32 APOLLO PATH
33 GEMINI GR
34 TWEED LA
35 ASH WLK
36 LARCH GR
37 ALDER LA
38 OLIVE CT
Holytown Prim Sch
WINDSOR RD
ROWANTREE
MYRTLE DR
CUCKOO WAY
LIME LOAN
POPLAR PL
ELM RD
SHIRREL RD
STEVENSTON ST
SPRUCE WAY
CATRIONA WAY
1 ARMINE PATH
2 BURNS WAY
3 VORLICH WYND
4 CARRON WAY
5 MAILIE WLK
6 MORAR WAY
7 CRIFFEL PL
8 LEDI PATH
9 KILBRECK LA
10 ARMOUR PL
11 KYLE QUADRANT
12 BRANNOCK PL
13 BRAEHEAD QUADRANT
Legbrannock
Legbranock Burn
1 ALLOWAY WYND
2 CLOCKERHILL PL
60
B7066
1 BURN LA
2 HEATHER WAY
3 BLUEBELL WLK
New Stevenston
HAMILTON PL
UNION ST
QUARRY ST
JERVISTON ST
CLYDESDALE ST
Holytown
Liby
B7029
LAW DR
SLIOCH SQ
HAMILTON PL
LAXFORD WAY
LAWERS LA
LOMOND WLK
ELLISLAND WYND
CLARINDA PL
LOANHEAD RD
MOSSGIEL WAY
BROOM PL
BURNSIDE RD
BRANNOCK AVE
GLEN ST
LEGBRANNOCK CRES
BRAESIDE RD
HILLSIDE CRES
KNOWE CRES
YETT RD
GLENMORE RD
Prim Sch
Liby
STANEFIELD DR
BYRES RD
PICKERSTONHILL
McCORMACK GDNS
KIRKOSWALD RD
CHURCH ST
ROBERT BURNS AVE
HIGH ST
MOSSHALL GR
FARM CRES
Newarthill
Newarthill Prim Sch
SPALEHALL DR
TILLANBURN RD
TOWNHEAD DR
MOSSHALL ST
2
Whittagreen
RC Prim Sch
Brannock High Sch
SHAFTSBURY CRES 14
BERNADETTE ST 15
WHITTAGREEN CT 16
MELFORT QUADRANT 17
ERIBOL WLK 18
LOANHEAD AVE
TORRIDON AVE
WHITTAGREEN AVE
LAUGHLAND DR
CARFIN RD
Cleland Townhead
CLELAND RD
59
Taylor High Sch
CARFIN ST
STATION RD
WRANGHOLM DR
HAWTHORN DR
JERVISTON ST
NORTH AVE
WEST AVE
CENTRAL AVE
EAST AVE
BUCHAN RD
PARK RD
WALLACE RD
CARFIN IND EST
BRUCE RD
NEW STEVENSTON RD
Carfin
RC Prim Sch
TAYLOR AVE
CANON CT
Carfin Lourdes Grotto
WHITTAGREEN CRES
BEECHWORTH DR
Golf Course
HILLHEAD CRES
HILLHEAD AVE
WOODROW AVE
HATTON PL
HORNDENE AVE
NEWARTHILL RD
Carfin
MARYKNOWE RD
B7066
1 EASTEND AVE
2 NORTHALL QUADRANT
3 JERVISTON CT
Coleville Park
JERVISTON RD
LINKSVIEW RD
MONTALTO AVE
MOTHERWELL RD
B7029
Chapelknowe
Westerfield
1
CHAPELKNOWE RD
B7029
CARFIN MILL RD
CLAPPERHOW RD
COALHALL AVE
JERVISWOOD
MERRY ST
A723
Cleekhimin
Carfin Byres
Playing Fields
MORRIS CRES
VARDON LEA
JONES WYND
HAGEN DR
COTTON VALE
HOGAN WAY
58
76
D
77
E
78
F

164
144

143
124

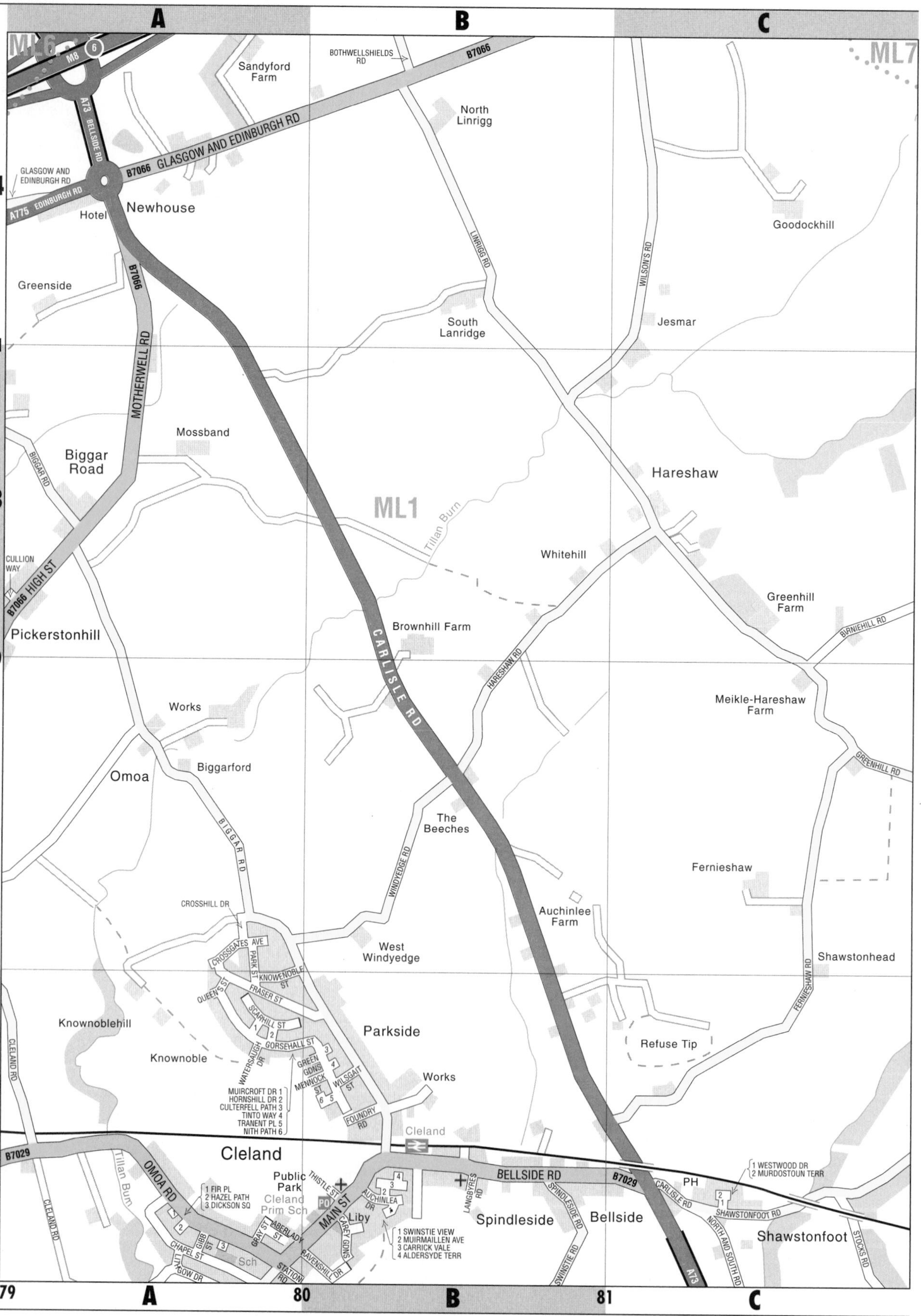

ML6

ML7

A   B   C

Sandyford Farm

BOTHWELLSHIELDS RD

B7066

GLASGOW AND EDINBURGH RD

North Linrigg

GLASGOW AND EDINBURGH RD

A775 EDINBURGH RD

Hotel

Newhouse

4

Goodockhill

Greenside

MOTHERWELL RD

B7066

LINRIGG RD

WILSON'S RD

Jesmar

South Lanridge

61

Mossband

Biggar Road

BIGGAR RD

Hareshaw

3

ML1

Tillan Burn

Whitehill

CULLION WAY

B7066 HIGH ST

Greenhill Farm

BURNIEHILL RD

Pickerstonhill

Brownhill Farm

HARESHAW RD

60

Works

CARLISLE RD

Meikle-Hareshaw Farm

GREENHILL RD

Omoa

Biggarford

BIGGAR RD

The Beeches

2

Fernieshaw

WINDYEDGE RD

Auchinlee Farm

Shawstonhead

FERNIESHAW RD

CROSSHILL DR

West Windyedge

59

CROSSGATES AVE

PARK ST

KNOWNOBLE ST

Parkside

Knownoblehill

QUEEN'S ST

FRASER ST

SCARHILL ST

Refuse Tip

Knownoble

WATERSLOUGH DR

GORSEHALL ST

GREEN GDNS

MENNOCK ST

WILSGAIT ST

Works

MUIRCROFT DR 1
HORNSHILL DR 2
CULTERFELL PATH 3
TINTO WAY 4
TRANENT PL 5
NITH PATH 6

FOUNDRY RD

1

B7029

Cleland

Cleland

BELLSIDE RD

B7029

PH

1 WESTWOOD DR
2 MURDOSTOUN TERR

OMOA RD

Tillan Burn

CLELAND RD

Public Park

Cleland Prim Sch

1 FIR PL
2 HAZEL PATH
3 DICKSON SQ

GRAY ST

THISTLE ST

MAIN ST

LABERLADY

CAREY GDNS

Liby

AUCHINLEA DR

LANGTREE'S RD

Spindleside

SPINDLESIDE RD

SWINSTIE RD

Bellside

CARLISLE RD

SHAWSTONFOOT RD

Shawstonfoot

NORTH AND SOUTH RD

STOCKS RD

A73

1 SWINSTIE VIEW
2 MUIRMAILLEN AVE
3 CARRICK VALE
4 ALDERSYDE TERR

CHAPEL ST

GLASGOW DR

Sch

STATION RD

RAVENSHILL DR

58

79   A   80   B   81   C

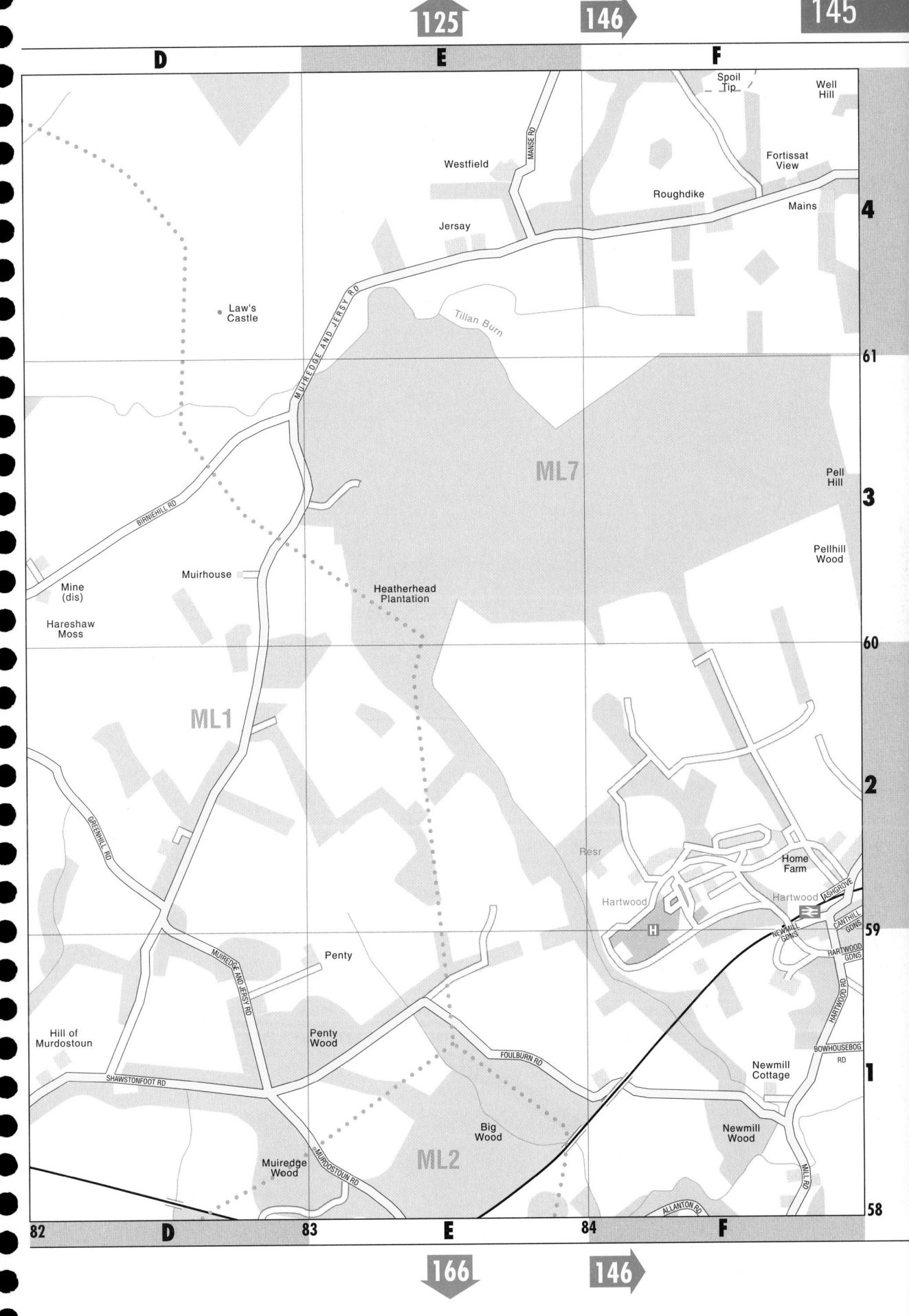

D
E
F

Spoil
Tip
Well
Hill

Westfield

MANSE RD

Fortissat
View

Roughdike

Mains

4

Jersay

MUIREDGE AND JERSY RD

Law's
Castle

Tillan Burn

61

ML7

BIRNIEHILL RD

Pell
Hill

3

Pellhill
Wood

Muirhouse

Heatherhead
Plantation

Mine
(dis)

Hareshaw
Moss

60

ML1

GREENHILL RD

2

Resr

Home
Farm

Hartwood
ASHGROVE

Hartwood

MUIREDGE AND JERSY RD

Penty

CANTHILL
GDNS

H

NEWMILL
GDNS

59

HARTWOOD
GDNS

HARTWOOD RD

Hill of
Murdostoun

Penty
Wood

FOULBURN RD

BOWHOUSEBOG
RD

Newmill
Cottage

1

SHAWSTONFOOT RD

Newmill
Wood

MILL RD

Muiredge
Wood

MURDOSTOUN RD

Big
Wood

ML2

ALLANTON RD

58

82
D
83
E
84
F

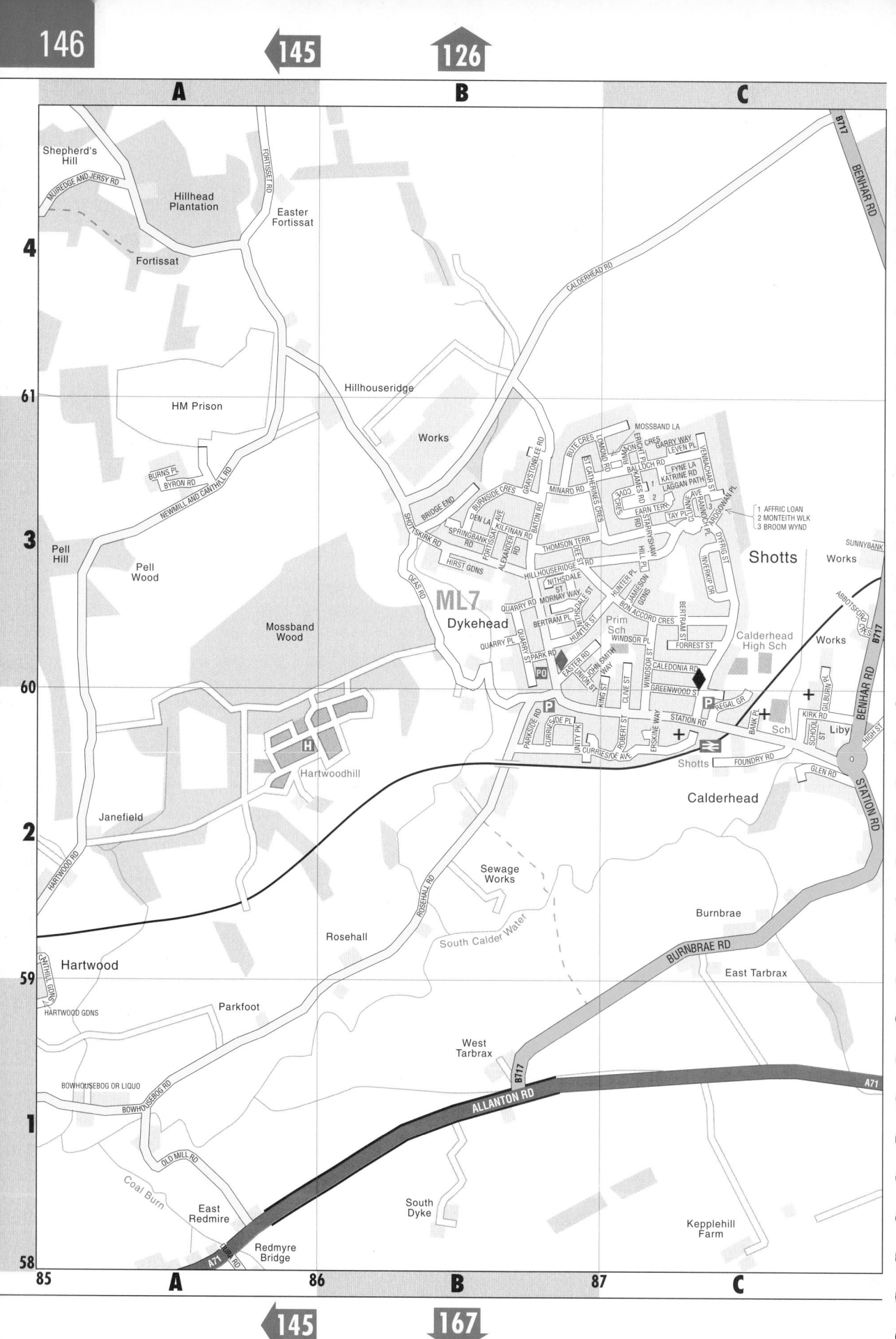

A   B   C

4

61

3

61

60

2

59

1

58

85   A   86   B   87   C

Shepherd's Hill
Hillhead Plantation
Easter Fortissat
Fortissat
MUIREDGE AND JERSY RD
FORTISSE RD

HM Prison
Works
Hillhouseridge

BURNS PL
BYRON RD
NEWMILL AND CANTHILL RD

Pell Hill
Pell Wood

Mossband Wood

ML7
Dykehead

Hartwoodhill

Janefield

Rosehall
Sewage Works
South Calder Water

Hartwood
SNITHILL GDNS
HARTWOOD GDNS
Parkfoot

BOWHOUSEBOG OR LIQUO
BOWHOUSEBOG RD
OLD MILL RD

Coal Burn
East Redmire
Redmyre Bridge
A71
DUBB RD

South Dyke
West Tarbrax
ALLANTON RD
B717

Kepplehill Farm

Burnbrae
East Tarbrax
BURNBRAE RD
A71

Calderhead

Shotts
FOUNDRY RD
GLEN RD
Shotts
STATION RD
BENHAR RD
ABBOTSFORD CRES
HIGH ST
B717

Sunnybank
Works
Works
Liby
Sch
KIRK ST
SCHOOL PL
GILBURN PL
REGAL GR
BANK PL
STATION RD
CALEDONIA RD
GREENWOOD ST
ERSKINE WAY
ROBERT ST
CURRIESIDE AVE
UNITY PK
CURRIESIDE PL
PARKSIDE RD
CLIVE ST
KING ST
JOHN SMITH WAY
WINDSOR PL
WINDSOR ST
FORREST ST
Prim Sch
Calderhead High Sch
BERTRAM ST
INVERKIP DR
DYFRIG ST
ARDGOWAN PL
1 AFFRIC LOAN
2 MONTEITH WLK
3 BROOM WYND
VENNACHAR S
TAY PL
BANNOCH PL
AVE
CRES
EARN TERR
STARRYSHAW
THOMSON TERR
HIRST GDNS
NITHSDALE ST
MORNAY WAY
BERTRAM PL
QUARRY PL
QUARRY RD
PARK RD
EASTER RD
UNION ST
HUNTER ST
HUNTER PL
JAMESON GDNS
BON ACCORD CRES
HUNTSDALE ST
HILLHOUSERIDGE RD
DEN LA
KILFINAN RD
ALEXANDER RD
SPRINGBANK ST
FORTISSAT AVE
BURNSIDE CRES
BRIDGE END
SHOTTSKIRK RD
DEAS RD
GRAYSTONELEE RD
BATON RD
MINARD RD
BUTE CRES
DOMINO RD
RIMMON CRES
EMRYS CRES
ST CATHERINES CRES
BALLOCH RD
KAMES RD
GARRY WAY
LEVEN PL
MOSSBAND LA
FYNE LA
KATRINE RD
LAGGAN PATH
Shotts

PO
P
P
H

D   E   F

Fauldhouse

4

B117

61

BENHAR RD

Golf
Course

CH

Starryshaw
Farm

South Calder Water

3

Spoil
Heap

Stanebent

Cairneyhead

ML7

Torbothie

Stane

STABLE RD

60

GRAY ST
HIGH ST

CHARLES ST
TORBOTHIE RD
HAWTHORN DR
KEVIN DR
CALDER DR
CLYDE DR
SOUTHFIELD RD

Stane
Prim Sch

Torbothie

SOUTHFIELD CRES
SOUTHFIELD

CEMETERY RD

Cemy

+

MANSE RD

NEVIS PL
GARTEN DR

1
2

Cemy

1 ETIVE WLK
2 ULG WAY
3 GAIR WYND
4 BOWMORE WLK
5 TORRIN LOAN
6 SPRINGHILL VIEW
7 DORNIE WYND
8 MORAR WAY
9 COIRE LOAN
10 SUNA PATH
11 SALEN LOAN

CHARLOTTE ST

MAIN ST

SANDYHILL
AV
REDHAWS
RD

1
2

3

LOCHABER
CRES
4
5

TULLOCH RD

APPIN TERR

9
11
10

WYVIS PL

OINICH PL

2

SANDYVALE
PL

Stane

BLINNY CT 1
TARBRAX PATH 2

BRIDGE
PL

KNOLL CROFT RD

NAVAR
GDNS

SHIELD
GDNS

HUNTLY
TERR

LANSDOWNE CRES

MELFORD AVE

LAGGAN AVE

6

SPRINGHILL RD

Springhill

B7010

B7010

59

STANE RD

BELMONT DR
BROWN'S ST
BERRYHILL PL
MULDRON
CT
BEECHMOUNT

ELMWOOD RD

BLACKHALL
ST

LARCHFIELD LA
NORTHFIELD AVE

Works

Springhill

SPRINGHILL AND LEADLOCH RD

B715 HEADLESSCROSS RD B715

Knowton
Farm

Works

Lingore Linn

A71

1

58

88   D   89   E   90   F

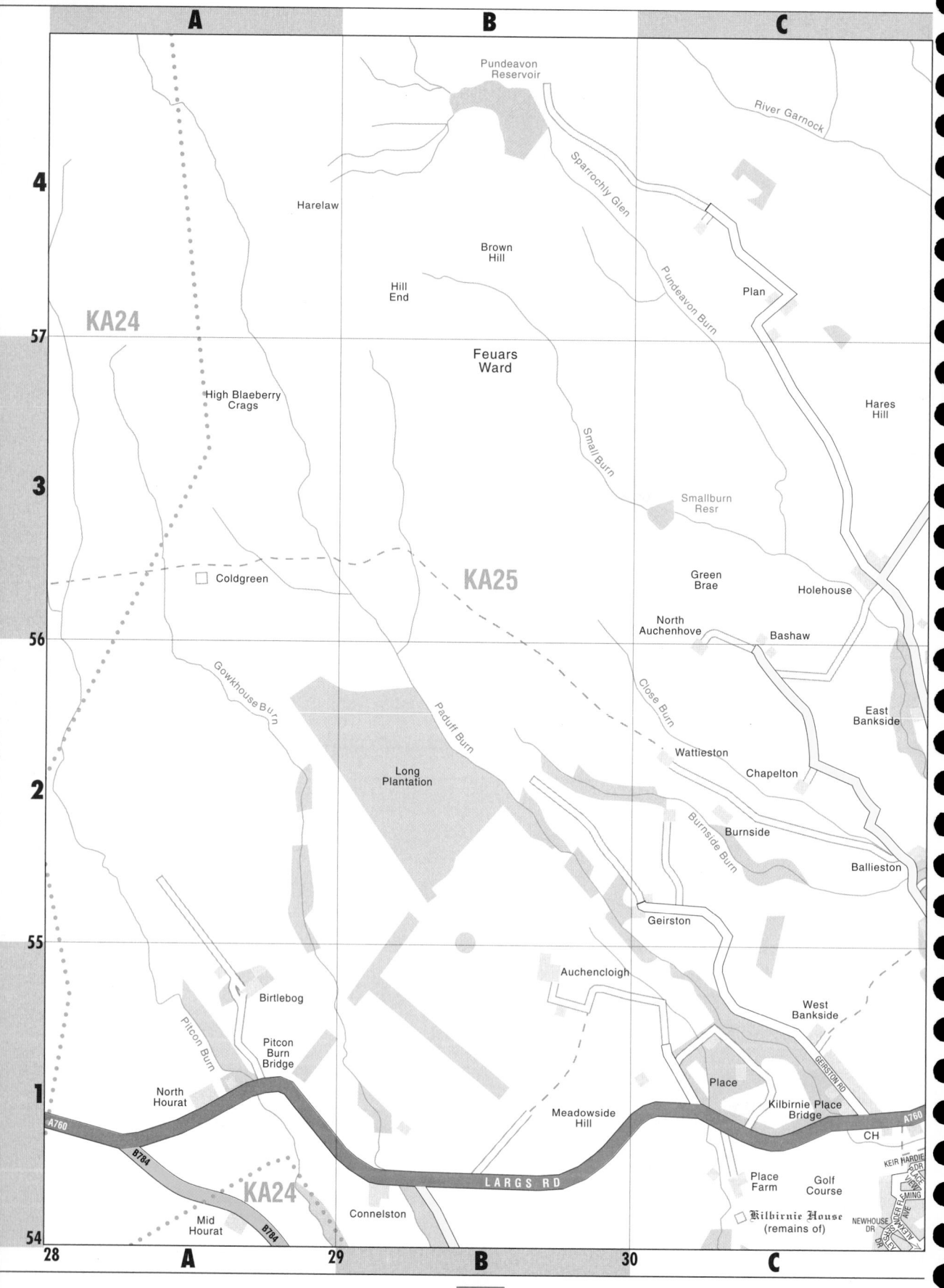

Pundeavon
Reservoir

River Garnock

Sparrochly Glen

Harelaw

Brown
Hill

Pundeavon Burn

Plan

Hill
End

KA24

57

Feuars
Ward

Small Burn

Hares
Hill

High Blaeberry
Crags

3

Smallburn
Resr

Coldgreen

KA25

Green
Brae

Holehouse

North
Auchenhove

Bashaw

56

Gowkhouse Burn

Paduff Burn

Close Burn

East
Bankside

Wattieston

Long
Plantation

Chapelton

2

Burnside Burn

Burnside

Ballieston

Geirston

55

Auchencloigh

West
Bankside

Birtlebog

GEIRSTON RD

Pitcon Burn

Pitcon
Burn
Bridge

Place

Kilbirnie Place
Bridge

1

North
Hourat

A760

Meadowside
Hill

A760

CH

KEIR HARDIE

B784

LARGS RD

Place
Farm

Golf
Course

NEWHOUSE
DR

KA24

Connelston

Kilbirnie House
(remains of)

Mid
Hourat

B784

54

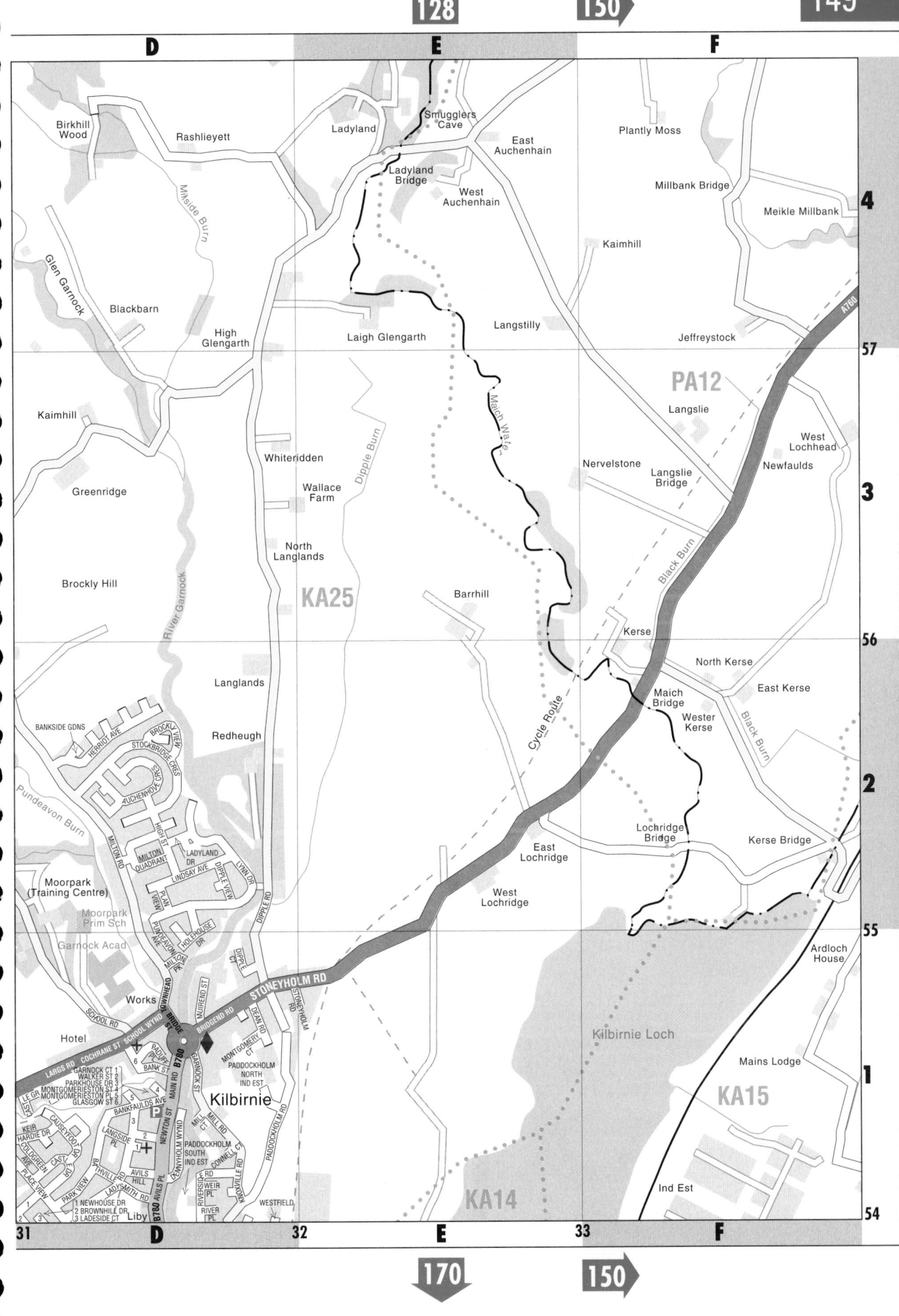

D   E   F

Birkhill Wood
Rashlieyett
Ladyland
Smugglers Cave
East Auchenhain
Plantly Moss
Millbank Bridge
Meikle Millbank

4

Ladyland Bridge
West Auchenhain
Kaimhill

Glen Garnock
Blackbarn
High Glengarth
Laigh Glengarth
Langstilly
Jeffreystock

57

Milside Burn

PA12

Langslie

Kaimhill
Whiteridden
Dipple Burn
Maich Water
Nervelstone
Langslie Bridge
West Lochhead
Newfaulds

3

Greenridge
Wallace Farm
Black Burn

River Garnock
North Langlands
Brockly Hill
KA25
Barrhill

Langlands
Kerse

56

North Kerse
East Kerse

Redheugh
Maich Bridge
Wester Kerse

BANKSIDE GDNS
HERRIOT AVE
BROCKLY VIEW
STOCKBRIDGE CRES
AUCHENHOVE CRES
BROCKLY VIEW

Cycle Route

Pundeavon Burn
LINDSAY AVE
LADYLAND DR
LYNN DR
DIPPLE VIEW
PLAN
PUNDEAVON PK
HOLEHOUSE DR
DIPPLE RD

2

Moorpark (Training Centre)
MILTON RD
MILTON QUADRANT
Lochridge Bridge
Kerse Bridge

Moorpark Prim Sch
Garnock Acad

East Lochridge
West Lochridge

55

Works
STONEYHOLM RD
STONEYHOLM RD
Ardloch House

School Rd
Hotel
MILTON
MILL RD
SCHOOL WYND WINDHEAD
BRIDGE ST
MUIREND ST
BRIDGEND RD
DEAN RD
STONEYHOLM RD
BT80

Kilbirnie Loch

LARGS RD
COCHRANE ST
MAIN RD
GARNOCK ST
BANK ST
1 GARNOCK CT
2 WALKER ST
3 PARKHOUSE DR
4 MONTGOMERIESTON ST
5 MONTGOMERIESTON PL
6 MONTGOMERIESTON
7 GLASGOW ST

Mains Lodge

Montgomery Ct
PADDOCKHOLM NORTH IND EST

1

Le Gr
LADYSMITH RD
NEWTON ST
DALRY RD
PADDOCKHOLM RD
KA15

KEIR HARDIE DR
CAUSE FOOT CT
CO GREEN
CAST
BANKFAULDS AVE
AVILS PL
P
Kilbirnie
MILL RD
PADDOCKHOLM SOUTH IND EST
CONNELL RD
KNOXVILLE RD

BLACK VIEW
PARK VIEW
BATHVILLE RD
AVILS HILL
DALRY RD
WEIR PL
RIVER PL

Ind Est

1 NEWHOUSE DR
2 BROWNHILL DR
3 LADESIDE CT
Liby
WESTFIELD

54

KA14

31   D   32   E   33   F

149
129

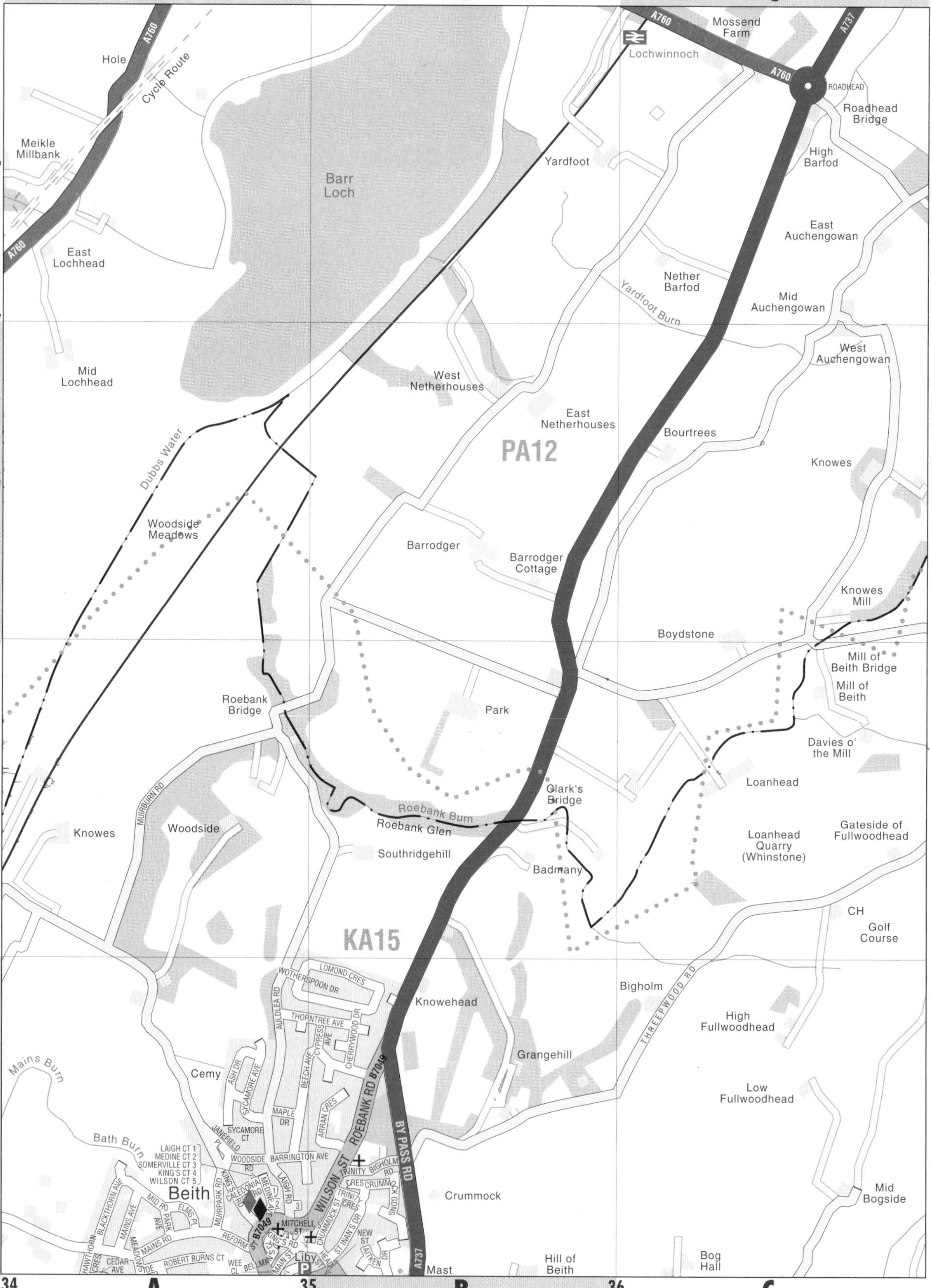

A　　　　B　　　　C

A760

Hole

Cycle Route

Meikle
Millbank

East
Lochhead

A760

Mid
Lochhead

Barr
Loch

Dubbs Water

Woodside
Meadows

Roebank
Bridge

Knowes

Murburn Rd

Woodside

Southridgehill

Roebank Burn
Roebank Glen

KA15

Mains Burn

Cemy

Bath Burn

Ash Dr

Sycamore Ave

Auld Ola Rd

Wotherspoon Dr

Lomond Cres

Thorntree Ave

Beech Ave

Cypress
Ave

Cherrywood Dr

Knowehead

Maple
Dr

Sycamore
Ct

Jamfield
Pl

Arran Cres

Murrah Rd

Hawthorn

Blackthorn Ave

Mains Ave

Mid Rd

Elms Pl

Elms
Ave

Cedar
Ave

Meadowside

Mains Rd

Robert Burns Ct

Caledonia Rd

King's Rd

Woodside
Rd

Barrington Ave

Trinity
Rd

Reform St

Wilson St

Mitchell St

Bigholm
Cres

Crummock
Gdns

Roebank Rd B7049

By Pass Rd

Laigh Ct 1
Medine Ct 2
Somerville Ct 3
King's Ct 4
Wilson Ct 5

Beith

Wee
Cl

Bellman's Cl

Stinan's St

New St

Aitken Dr

Liby
P

Mast

A737

Crummock

Grangehill

Hill of
Beith

Yardfoot

A760

Lochwinnoch

Mossend
Farm

A737

Roadhead

Roadhead
Bridge

High Barfod

East
Auchengowan

Mid
Auchengowan

West
Auchengowan

Knowes

Nether
Barfod

Yardfoot Burn

West
Netherhouses

East
Netherhouses

PA12

Barrodger

Barrodger
Cottage

Bourtrees

Boydstone

Park

Knowes
Mill

Mill of
Beith Bridge

Mill of
Beith

Davies o'
the Mill

Loanhead

Clark's
Bridge

Badmany

Loanhead
Quarry
(Whinstone)

Gateside of
Fullwoodhead

CH

Golf
Course

Bigholm

Threepwood Rd

High
Fullwoodhead

Low
Fullwoodhead

Mid
Bogside

Bog
Hall

4

57

3

56

2

55

1

54

34　　　35　　　36

A　　　　B　　　　C

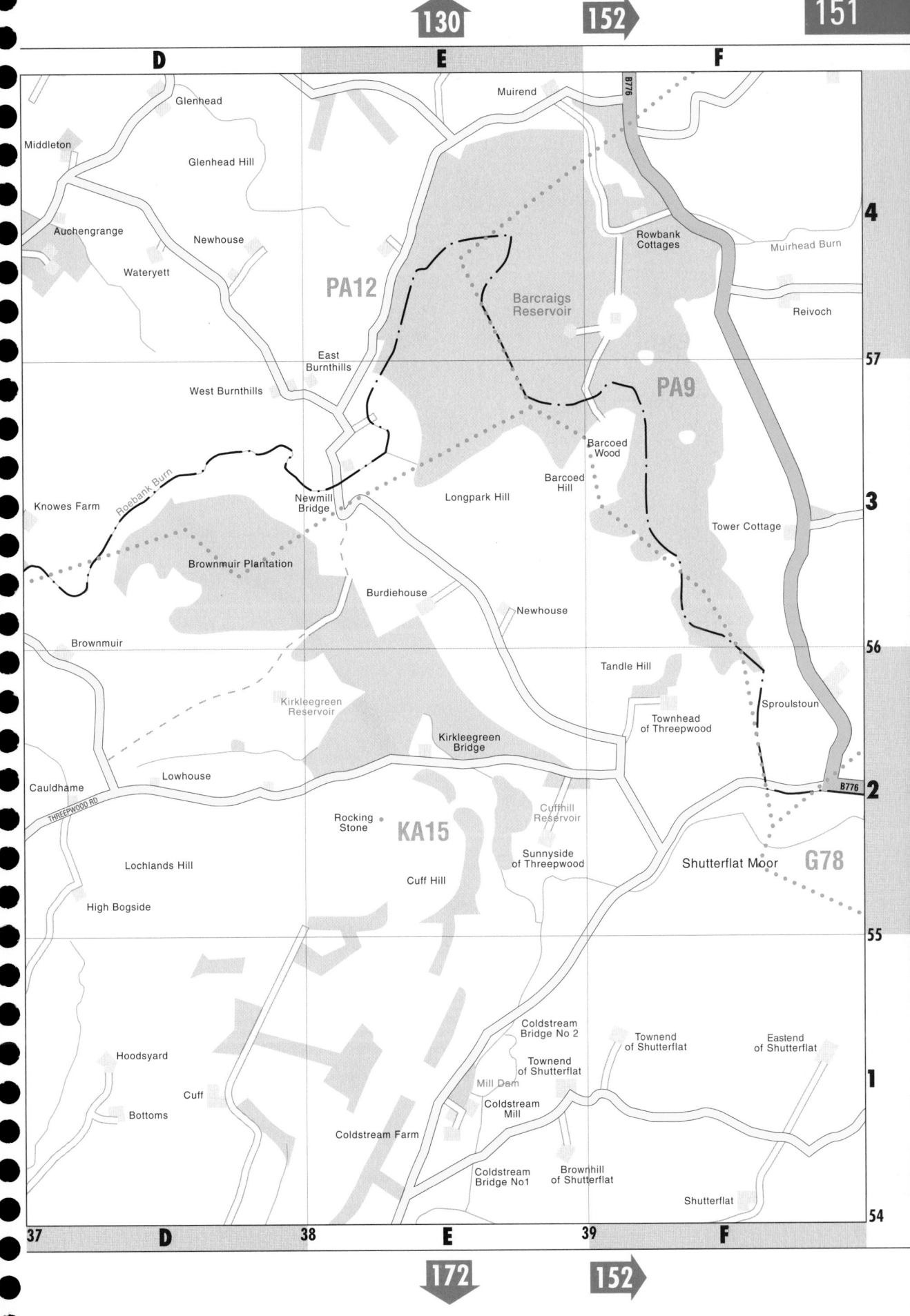

D
E
F

4

57

PA12

Barcraigs
Reservoir

PA9

57

Muirend

B776

Rowbank
Cottages

Muirhead Burn

Reivoch

Glenhead

Middleton

Glenhead Hill

Auchengrange

Newhouse

Wateryett

East
Burnthills

West Burnthills

Barcoed
Wood

Barcoed
Hill

3

Knowes Farm

Roebank Burn

Newmill
Bridge

Longpark Hill

Tower Cottage

Brownmuir Plantation

Burdiehouse

Newhouse

56

Brownmuir

Kirkleegreen
Reservoir

Tandle Hill

Townhead
of Threepwood

Sproulstoun

B776

2

Cauldhame

THREEPWOOD RD

Lowhouse

Kirkleegreen
Bridge

Cuffhill
Reservoir

Rocking
Stone

KA15

Sunnyside
of Threepwood

Shutterflat Moor

G78

Lochlands Hill

Cuff Hill

High Bogside

55

Hoodsyard

Cuff

Bottoms

Coldstream
Bridge No 2

Townend
of Shutterflat

Eastend
of Shutterflat

Townend
of Shutterflat

Mill Dam

1

Coldstream
Mill

Coldstream Farm

Coldstream
Bridge No1

Brownhill
of Shutterflat

Shutterflat

54

A   **B**   **C**

B775

Rashiefield Bridge

PA2

Springside

Old Patrick Water

Plymuir Bridge

4

PA9

Windy Hill

Top of Auchenbathie

Tophouse

Hartfield Moss

Muirhouse Farm

57

Windyhill

3

G78

56

Riglaw

Caldwell Law

Greenside

Caldwell-law Wood

Braco

GLENIFFER RD

Rigfoot Farm

B776

Dunsmore Bridge

Old Barn Farm

2

Bowfield

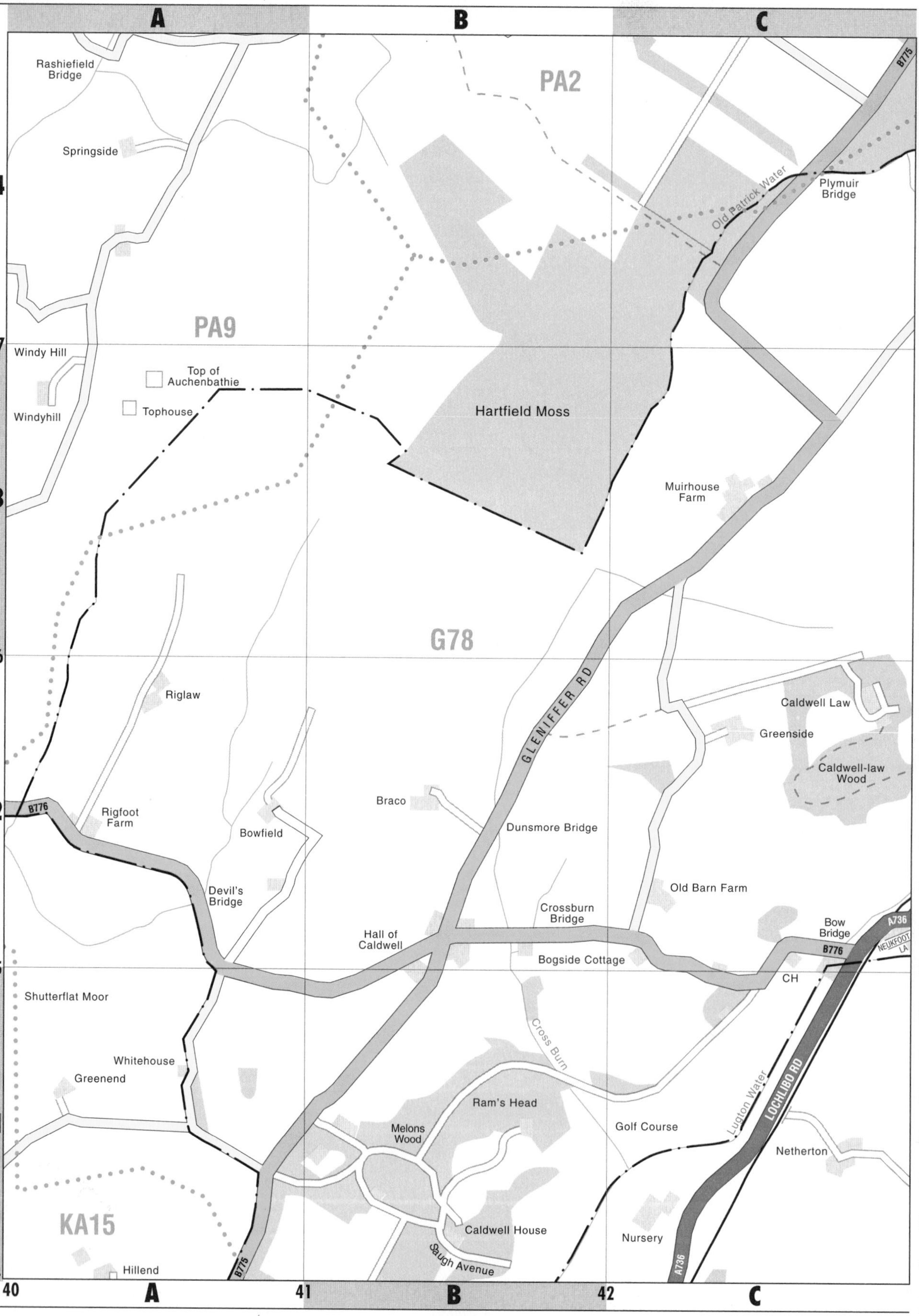

Devil's Bridge

Crossburn Bridge

Bow Bridge

A736

NEUKFOOT LA

Hall of Caldwell

Bogside Cottage

B776

CH

55

Shutterflat Moor

Cross Burn

Lugton Water

LOCHLIBO RD

Whitehouse

Greenend

Ram's Head

Golf Course

Netherton

1

Melons Wood

KA15

Caldwell House

Nursery

A736

Hillend

Saugh Avenue

B775

54

40   **A**   **41**   **B**   **42**   **C**

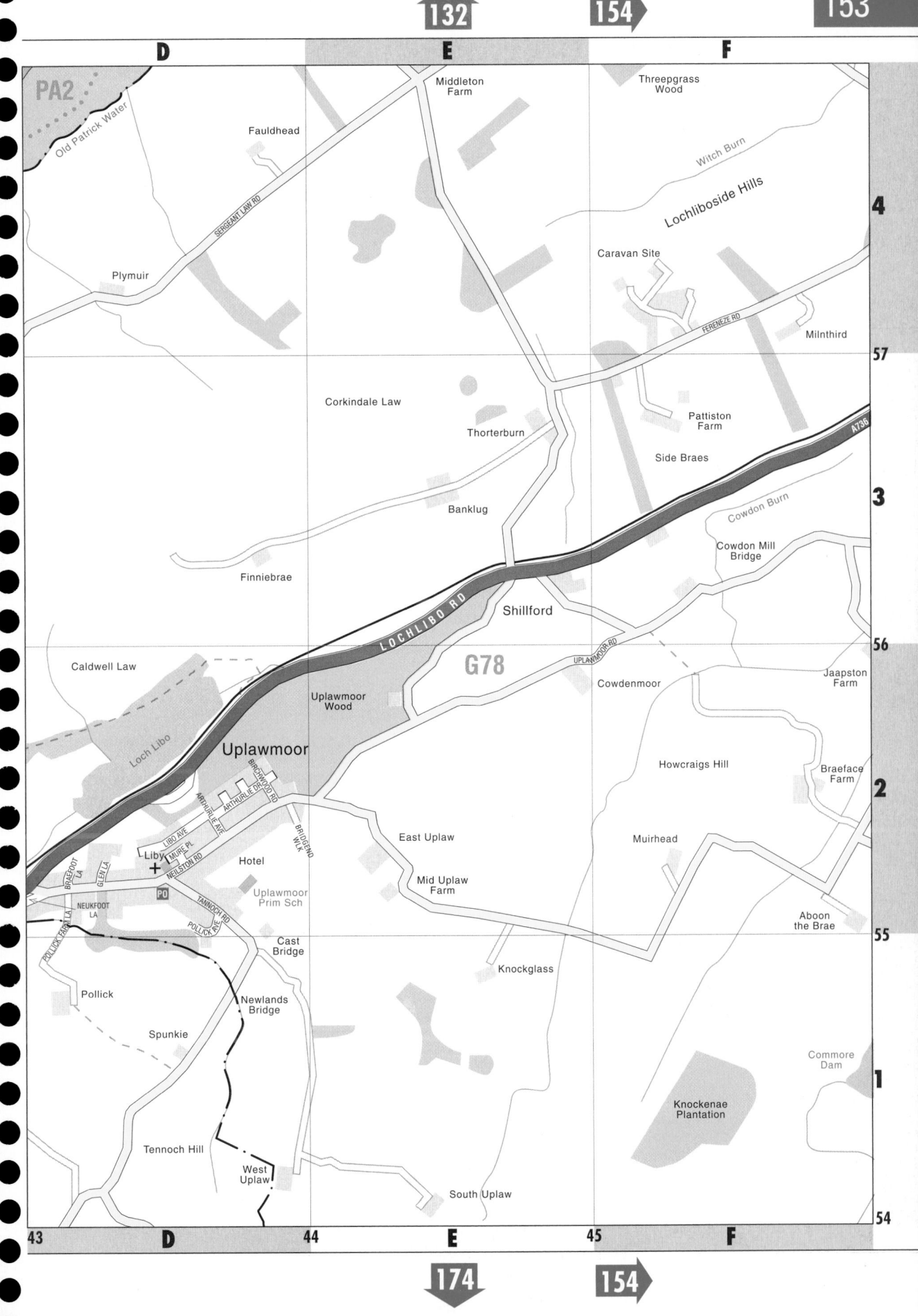

PA2

Old Patrick Water

Fauldhead

Middleton Farm

Threepgrass Wood

Witch Burn

Lochliboside Hills

SERGEANT LAW RD

Plymuir

Caravan Site

FERENEZE RD

Milnthird

Corkindale Law

Thorterburn

Pattiston Farm

Side Braes

A736

Banklug

Cowdon Burn

Finniebrae

Cowdon Mill Bridge

LOCHLIBO RD

Shillford

Caldwell Law

G78

UPLAWMOOR RD

Cowdenmoor

Jaapston Farm

Uplawmoor Wood

Loch Libo

Uplawmoor

Howcraigs Hill

Braeface Farm

BIRCHWOOD RD

ARTHURLIE DR

ARTHURLIE AVE

BRIDGEND WLK

East Uplaw

Muirhead

LIBO AVE

MURE PL

NEILSTON RD

Liby

Hotel

BRAEFOOT LA

GLEN LA

Uplawmoor Prim Sch

Mid Uplaw Farm

Aboon the Brae

PO

NEUKFOOT LA

TANNOCH RD

POLLICK AVE

Cast Bridge

POLLICK CASTLE LA

Pollick

Newlands Bridge

Knockglass

Spunkie

Commore Dam

Tennoch Hill

West Uplaw

South Uplaw

Knockenae Plantation

153
133

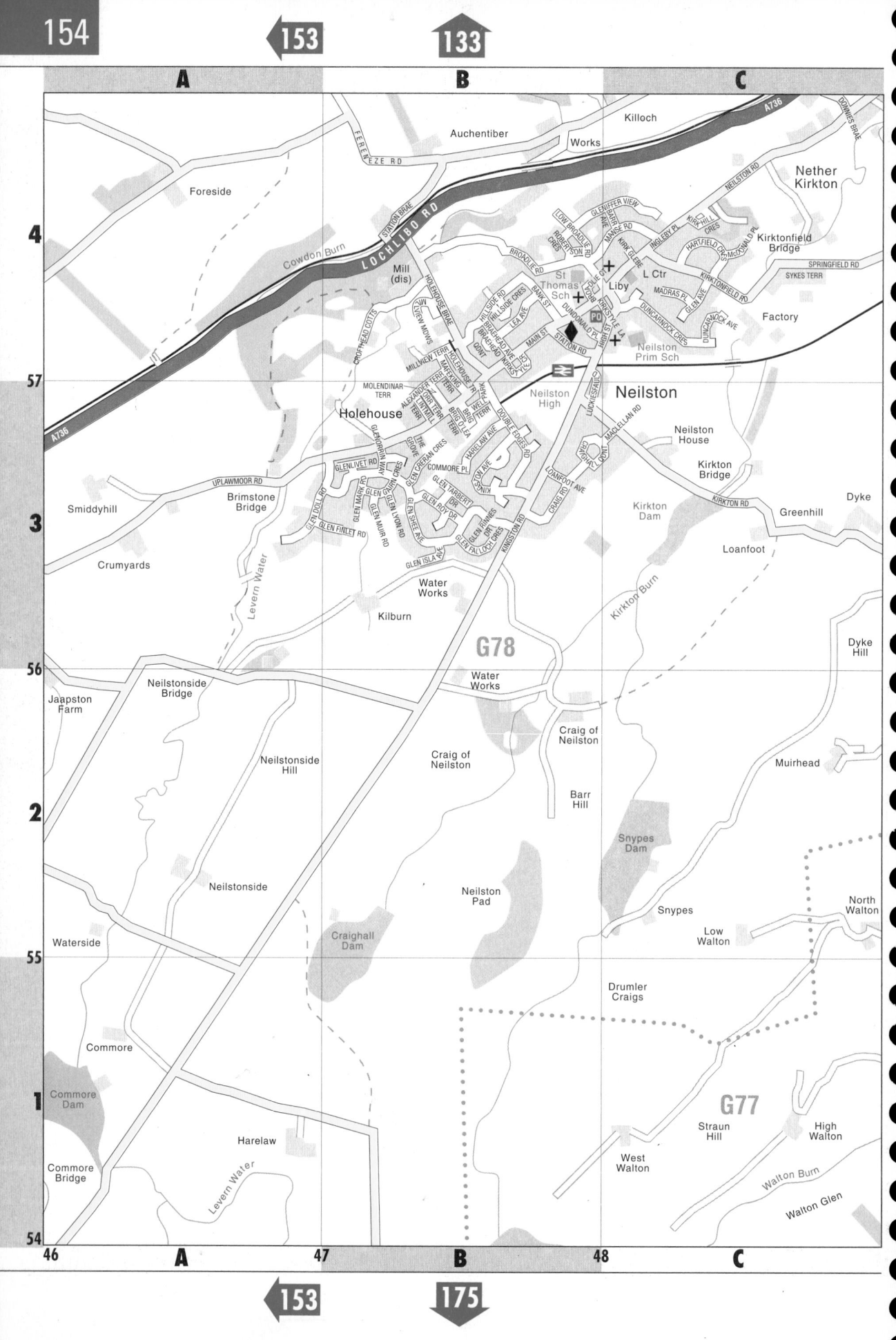
A
B
C
4
57
3
56
2
55
1
54
46
47
48
Auchentiber
Killoch
Works
FERENEZE RD
A736
DONNIES BRAE
Nether
Kirkton
NEILSTON RD
Foreside
STATION BRAE
LOCHLIBO RD
Cowdon Burn
Mill
(dis)
GLENIFFER VIEW
LOW BROADLIE
BARR AVE
MANSE RD
ROBERTSON CRES
BROADLIE RD
KIRK GLEBE
INGLEBY PL
KIRK HILL CRES
HARTFIELD CRES
McDONALD PL
Kirktonfield
Bridge
SPRINGFIELD RD
SYKES TERR
St
Thomas'
Sch
Liby
L Ctr
MADRAS PL
KIRKTONFIELD RD
GLEN AVE
Factory
HOLEHOUSE BRAE
HILLSIDE RD
HILLSIDE CRES
LEA AVE
BANK ST
DUNDONALD PL
PO
KIRKSTYLE LA
DUNCARNOCK CRES
DUNCARNOCK AVE
CROFTHEAD COTTS
MILLVIEW MDWS
BRAEHEAD AVE
BRAEHEAD QDNT
MAIN ST
STATION RD
HIGH ST
Neilston
Prim Sch
MILLVIEW TERR
HOLEHOUSE TERR
MAFEKING TERR
KIRKVIEW
MOLENDINAR
TERR
ALEXANDER TERR
Neilston
High
Neilston
LUCKIESFAULD
Holehouse
ORR TERR
LINTMILL TERR
BRIG O LEA TERR
PARK
WELL TERR
DOUBLE EDGES RD
MACLELLAN RD
Neilston
House
GLENMORRIN WAY
THE GROVE
HARELAW AVE
CRAIGHALL QDNT
Kirkton
Bridge
UPLAWMOOR RD
GLENLIVET RD
GLEN CRERAN CRES
COMMORE PL
LOANFOOT AVE
Dyke
Smiddyhill
Brimstone
Bridge
GLEN GARRY CRES
GLEN MARK RD
GLEN LYON RD
GLEN TARBERT DR
KINGSTON AVE
CRAIG RD
KIRKTON RD
Greenhill
Kirkton
Dam
GLEN DOLL RD
GLEN FINLET RD
GLEN MUIR RD
GLEN SHEE AVE
GLEN ROY DR
GLEN RINNES DR
GLEN FALLOCH CRES
KINGSTON RD
Loanfoot
Crumyards
GLEN ISLA AVE
Levern Water
Water
Works
Kilburn
Kirkton Burn
G78
Dyke
Hill
Jaapston
Farm
Neilstonside
Bridge
Water
Works
Craig of
Neilston
Neilstonside
Hill
Craig of
Neilston
Muirhead
Barr
Hill
Snypes
Dam
Neilstonside
Neilston
Pad
North
Walton
Snypes
Low
Walton
Waterside
Craighall
Dam
Drumler
Craigs
Commore
Commore
Dam
G77
Straun
Hill
High
Walton
Harelaw
West
Walton
Commore
Bridge
Levern Water
Walton Burn
Walton Glen

153
175

134
156
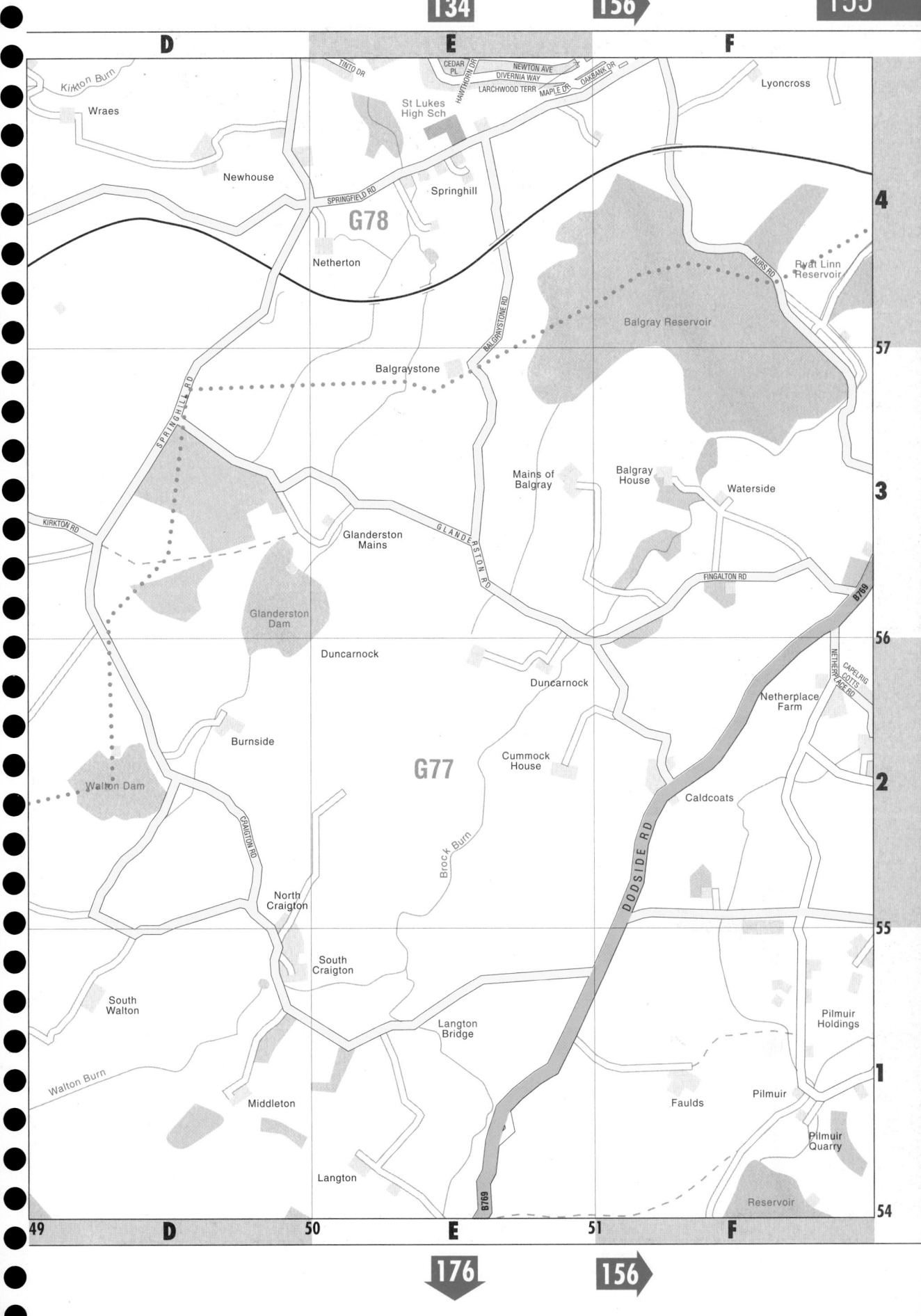
D
E
F
Kirkton Burn
Wraes
Newhouse
TINTO DR
CEDAR PL
HAWTHORN DR
NEWTON AVE
DIVERNIA WAY
LARCHWOOD TERR
MAPLE DR
OAKBANK DR
St Lukes
High Sch
Lyoncross
SPRINGFIELD RD
Springhill
G78
Netherton
AURS RD
Ryat Linn
Reservoir
Balgray Reservoir
BALGRAYSTONE RD
Balgraystone
SPRINGHILL RD
Mains of
Balgray
Balgray
House
Waterside
KIRKTON RD
Glanderston
Mains
GLANDERSTON RD
FINGALTON RD
B769
Glanderston
Dam
Duncarnock
Duncarnock
NETHERPLACE RD
CAPELRIG COTTS
Netherplace
Farm
Burnside
Cummock
House
G77
Walton Dam
Caldcoats
CRAIGTON RD
Brock Burn
DODSIDE RD
North
Craigton
South
Craigton
South
Walton
Pilmuir
Holdings
Langton
Bridge
Walton Burn
Middleton
Faulds
Pilmuir
Pilmuir
Quarry
Langton
B769
Reservoir
4
57
3
56
2
55
1
54
49
50
51
176
156

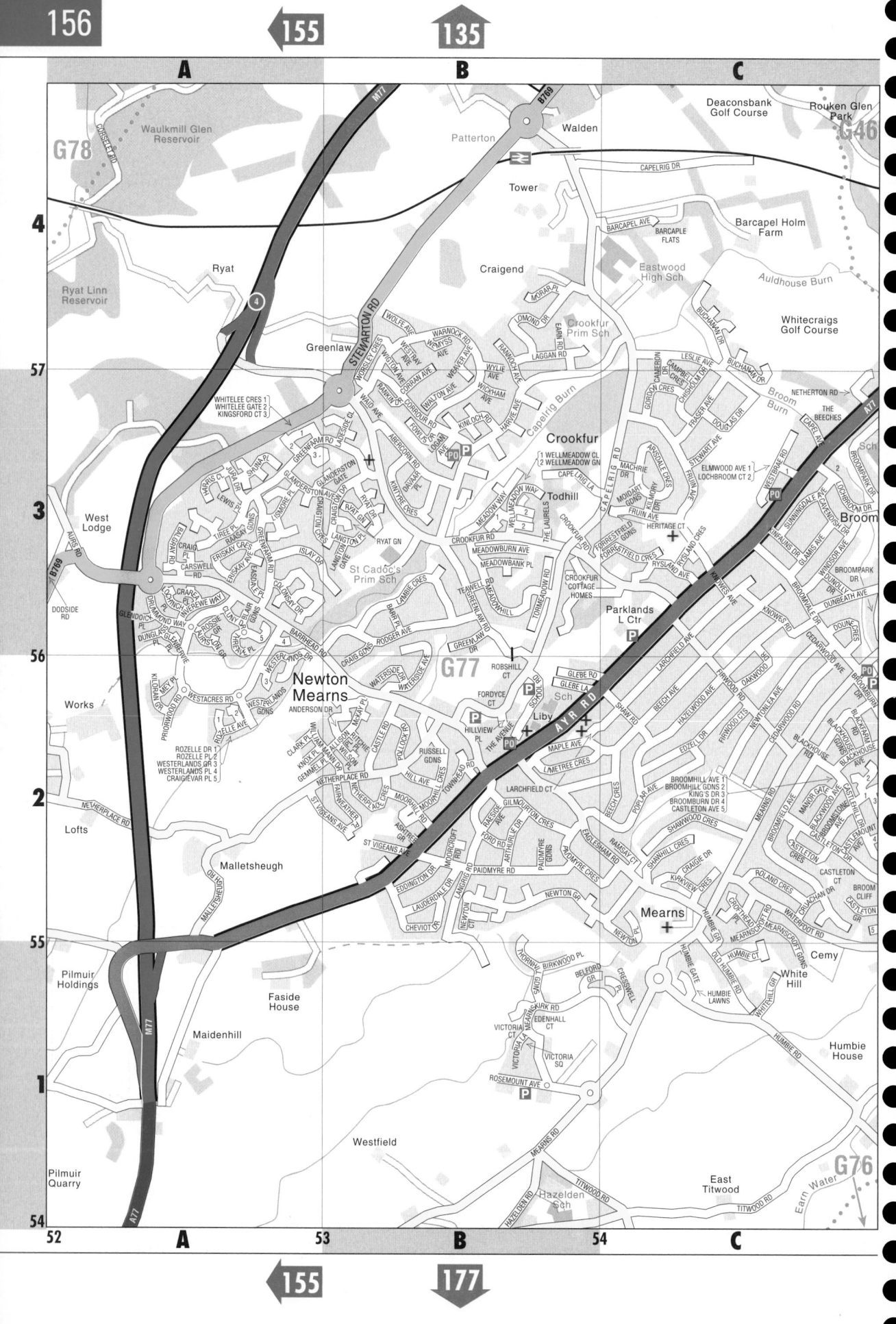
155
135
A
B
C
4
3
2
1
57
56
55
54
52
53
54
G78
G46
G77
G76
Waulkmill Glen Reservoir
Patterton
Walden
Deaconsbank Golf Course
Rouken Glen Park
Tower
CAPELRIG DR
BARCAPEL AVE
BARCAPLE FLATS
Barcapel Holm Farm
Ryat
Ryat Linn Reservoir
Craigend
Eastwood High Sch
Auldhouse Burn
Whitecraigs Golf Course
Crookfur Prim Sch
Greenlaw
STEWARTON RD
Capelrig Burn
Crookfur
Broom Burn
NETHERTON RD
THE BEECHES
West Lodge
Todhill
Broom
St Cadoc's Prim Sch
CROOKFUR RD
MEADOWBURN AVE
MEADOWBANK PL
CROOKFUR COTTAGE HOMES
Parklands L Ctr
BARRHEAD RD
Newton Mearns
AYR RD
Works
Liby
Sch
Lofts
Malletsheugh
Mearns
Cemy
White Hill
Pilmuir Holdings
Faside House
Maidenhill
Humbie House
Westfield
MEARNS RD
East Titwood
TITWOOD RD
Hazelden Sch
Earn Water
Pilmuir Quarry
M77
A77
B769
A
B
C
155
177

136

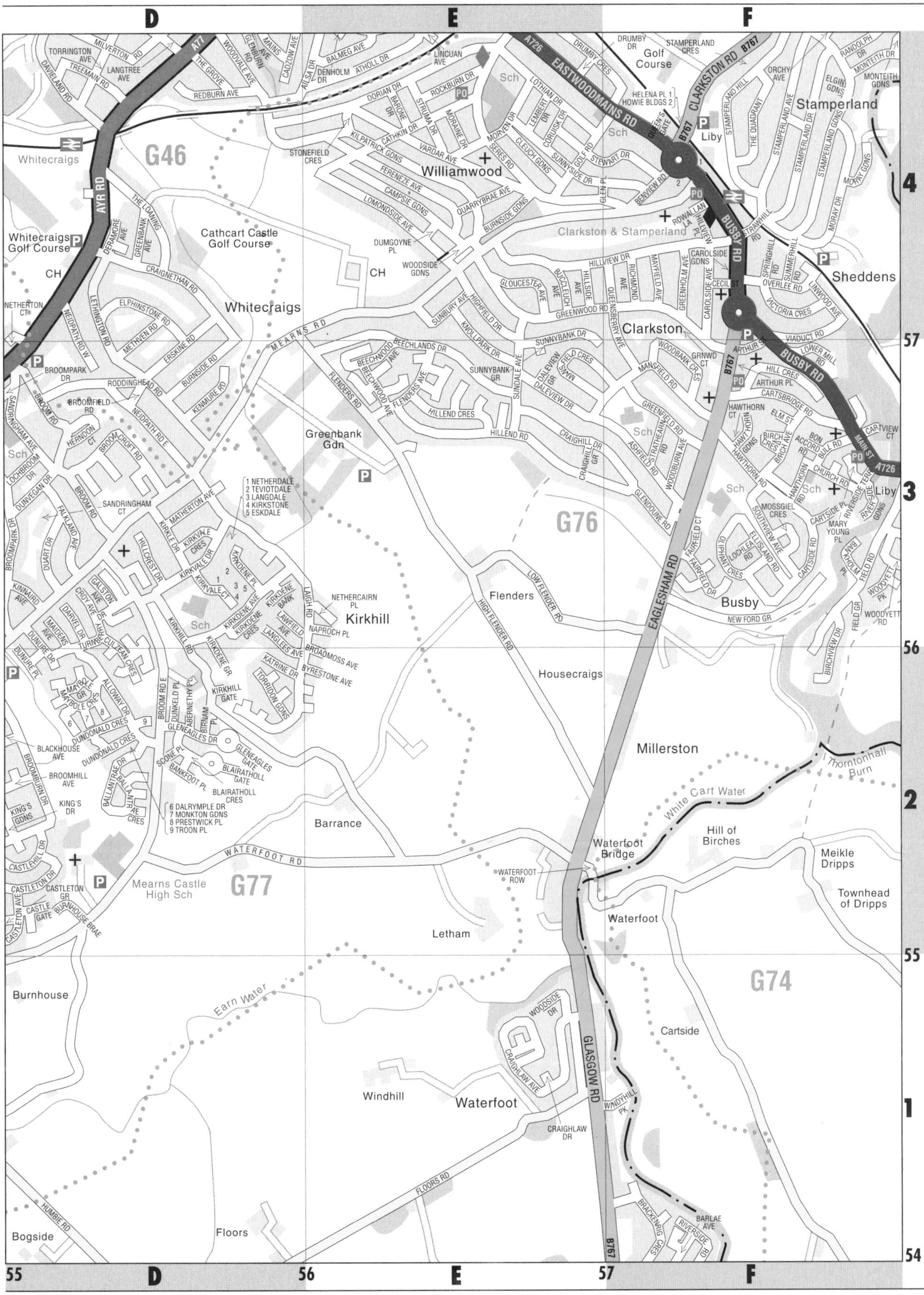
158

D E F

Torrington Ave
Milverton Rd
Treeman Rd
Langtree Ave
Daviel and Rd
A77
The Grove
Woodvale Ave
Glenburn Rd
Mains Ave
Cadzow Ave
Redburn Ave
Ailsa Dr
Denholm Dr
Balmeg Ave
Atholl Dr
Lincuan Ave
Dorian Dr
Rockburn Dr
Barone Dr
Struma Dr
Moraine Dr
Cathkin Dr
Kilpatrick Gdns
Vardar Ave
Stonefield Cres
Ferenze Ave
Campsie Gdns
Lomondside Ave
Williamwood
Quarrybrae Ave
Burnside Gdns
Morven Dr
Seres Rd
Lothian Dr
Lembert Dr
Coruisk Dr
Cleuch Gdns
Sunnyside Dr
Golf Rd
Stewart Dr
Glen Pl
Benview Rd
A726
Eastwoodmains Rd
Drumby Cres
Drumby Dr
Golf Course
Stamperland Cres
Helena Pl
Howie Bldgs
Queen's Gate
B767
Clarkston Rd
Liby
Stamperland Hill
The Quadrant
Orchy Ave
Stamperland Ave
Stamperland Dr
Stamperland Gdns
Elgin Gdns
Randolph Dr
Monteith Dr
Monteith Gdns
Stamperland
Moray Gdns
Moray Dr

Whitecraigs
G46
Ayr Rd
Whitecraigs Golf Course
The Loaming
Deramore Ave
Greenbank Ave
Cathcart Castle Golf Course
Dumgoyne Pl
Woodside Gdns
CH
Rowallan La
Hillview Pl
Clarkston & Stamperland
Busby Rd
Strathill Rd
Springhill Rd
Summerhill Rd
Overlee Rd
Victoria Cres
Linnwood Ave
Sheddens
Craignethan Rd
Netherton Ct
Neidpath Rd W
Lethington Rd
Elphinstone Rd
Methven Rd
Erskine Rd
Whitecraigs
Mearns Rd
Hillview Dr
Gloucester Ave
Buccleuch Ave
Hillside Ave
Queensberry Ave
Richmond Ave
Mayfield Ave
Greenholm Ave
Carolside Gdns
Carolside Ave
Cecil St
Sunbury Ave
Highfield Dr
Knollpark Dr
Greenwood Rd
Clarkston
Sunnybank Dr
Viaduct Rd
Lower Mill Rd
Broompark Dr
Roddinghead Rd
Burnside Rd
Kenmure Rd
Beechlands Dr
Beechwood Ave
Beechwood Dr
Flenders Ave
Sunnybank Gr
Sundale Ave
Daleview Gr
Mansfield Cres
Daleview Dr
Woodbank Cres
Grnwd Ct
Mansfield Rd
Arthur St
Arthur Pl
Hill Cres
Cartsbridge Rd
Sandringham Ave
Broom Rd
Broomfield Rd
Neidpath Rd E
Herndon Ct
Broomcroft Rd
Hillend Cres
Hillend Rd
Flenders Rd
Greenbank Gdn
Craighill Dr
Craighill Gr
Greenfield Rd
Strathearn Rd
Woodburn Ave
Ashfield Rd
Hawthorn Ct
Hawthorn Gdns
Elm St
Birch Cres
Birch Ave
Bon Accord Rd
Bull Rd
Cartview Ct
Main St
Lochbroom Dr
Dunvegan Dr
Sandringham Ct
Matherton Ave
1 Netherdale
2 Teviotdale
3 Langdale
4 Kirkstone
5 Eskdale
Hawthorn Rd
Church Rd
Liby
Broompark Dr
Falkland Ave
Duart Dr
Hillcrest Dr
Kirkle Dr
Kirkvale Cres
Kirkvale Dr
Kirkdene Pl
Sch
G76
Glendoune Rd
Fairfield Ct
Fairfield Dr
Oliphant Cres
Lochlea Rd
Ellisland Rd
Southview Ave
Mossgiel Cres
Cartside Pl
Cartside Rd
Mary Young Pl
Riverside Ter
Riverside Gdns
Kinnaird Ave
Galston Ave
Croy Ave
Kirkvale Ct
Kirkdene Ave
Kirkdene Bank
Kirkdene Cres
Laigh Rd
Nethercairn Pl
Kirkhill
Lawfield Ave
Naproch Pl
Flenders
Low Flender Rd
Eaglesham Rd
Busby
New Ford Gr
Field Gr
Woodyett Pk
Woodyett Rd
Darvel Dr
Maidens Ave
Turnberry Dr
Culzean Cres
Kirkhill Rd
Langlees Ave
Broadmoss Ave
Byrestone Ave
Katrine Dr
Torridon Gdns
High Flender Rd
Housecraigs
Birchview Dr
Dunure Dr
Dunure Pl
Maybole Gr
Alloway Dr
Broom Rd E
Dunkeld Pl
Abernethy Pl
Birnam Pl
Kirkhill Gate
Kirkdene Gr
Dundonald Cres
Dundonald Rd
Gleneagles Dr
Gleneagles Gate
Blackhouse Ave
Broomburn Dr
Scone Pl
Blairatholl Gate
Bankfoot Pl
Blairatholl Cres
Millerston
Thorntonhall Burn
Broomhill Ave
Ballantrae Dr
Ballantrae Cres
6 Dalrymple Dr
7 Monkton Gdns
8 Prestwick Pl
9 Troon Pl
Barrance
White Cart Water
Hill of Birches
King's Gdns
King's Dr
Castlehill Dr
Waterfoot Rd
Waterfoot Bridge
Meikle Dripps
Mearns Castle High Sch
G77
Waterfoot Row
Townhead of Dripps
Castleton Dr
Castleton Gr
Castle Gate
Castleton Ave
Burnhouse Brae
Letham
Waterfoot
G74
Burnhouse
Earn Water
Woodside Dr
Cartside
Glasgow Rd
Craighlaw Ave
Windhill
Waterfoot
Windyhill Pk
Craighlaw Dr
Floors Rd
Humbie Rd
Bogside
Floors
Brackenrig Cres
Barlae Ave
Riverside Rd

4
57
3
56
2
55
1
54

55 D 56 E 57 F

178

158

157
137

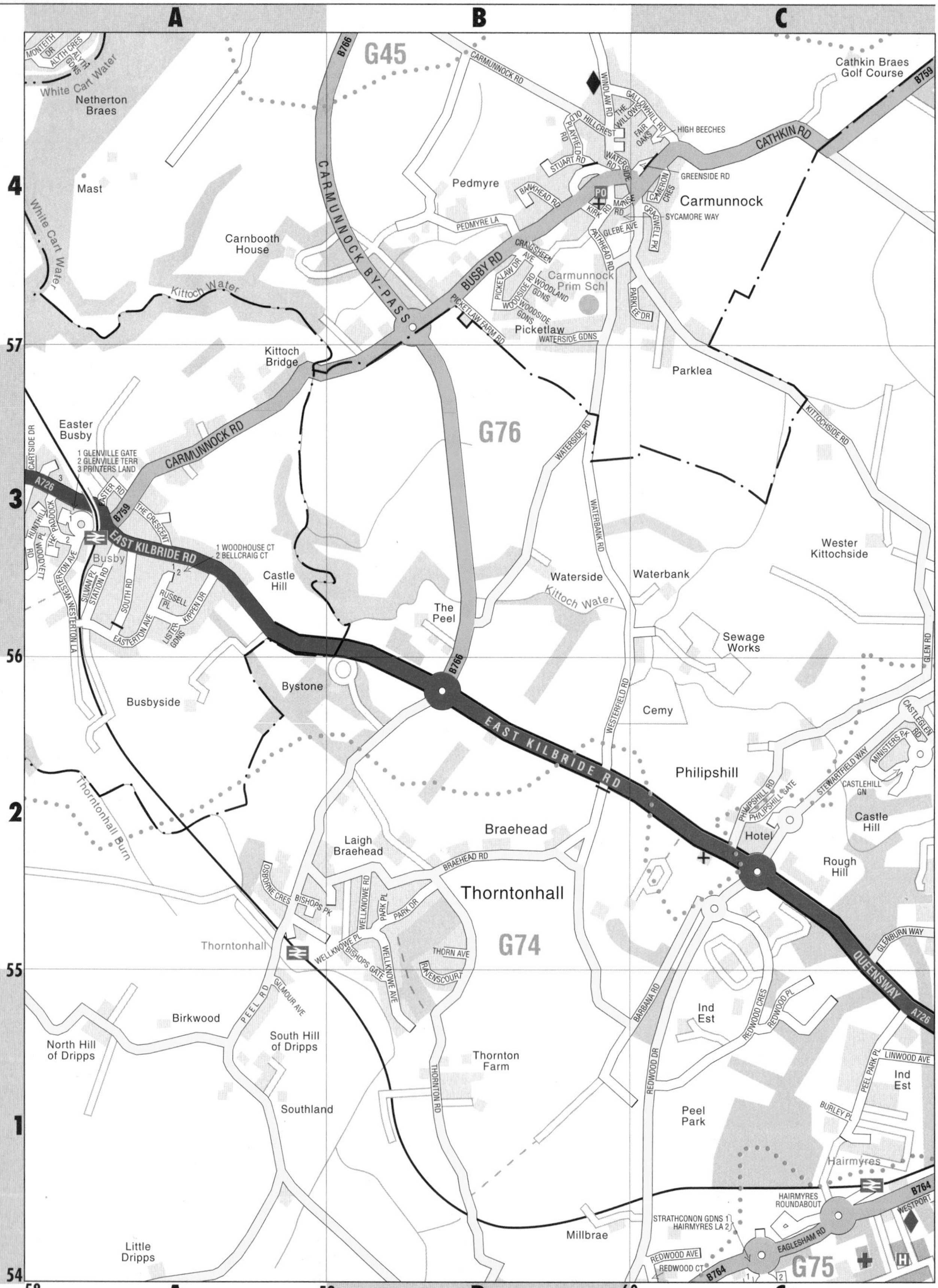

A   B   C

4

White Cart Water

Netherton Braes

MONTEITH DR
ALYTH CRES

B766

G45

CARMUNNOCK RD

Cathkin Braes Golf Course

B759

Mast

Carnbooth House

Pedmyre

HILLCREST
WINDLAW RD
PLATFIELD RD
THE WILLOWS
GALLOWHILL RD
WATERSIDE
High Beeches

CATHKIN RD

Kittoch Water

STUART RD
BARMHEAD RD

MANSE
KIRK
PO

MACE
CAMERON CRES
GREENSIDE RD
Carmunnock

PEDMYRE LA

GLEBE AVE
FAITHEAD RD
CASWELL PKY
SYCAMORE WAY
PARKLEE DR

BUSBY RD
CROSSLEEN AVE

PICKETLAW DR
WOODSIDE RD
WOODLAND GDNS
WOODSIDE GDNS
Carmunnock Prim Sch

CARMUNNOCK BY-PASS

57

Kittoch Bridge

PICKETLAW FARM RD
WATERSIDE GDNS
Picketlaw

Parklea

Easter Busby

CARTSIDE DR
1 GLENVILLE GATE
2 GLENVILLE TERR
3 PRINTERS LAND

CARMUNNOCK RD

B759

G76

WATERSIDE RD

KITTOCHSIDE RD

Wester Kittochside

3

A726
B759
EASTER RD
THE CRESCENT

EAST KILBRIDE RD

1 WOODHOUSE CT
2 BELLCRAIG CT

Castle Hill

The Peel

WATERBANK RD

Waterside

Waterbank

GLEN RD

TRIUMPH RD
WOODCROFT
PADDOCK
SPIERS PL
STATION RD
WESTERTON AVE
WESTERTON LA
Busby

SOUTH RD
RUSSELL PL
LISTER GDNS
EASTCROFT LANE
KYPE DR

1
2

Kittoch Water

Sewage Works

56

Bystone

Busbyside

B766

EAST KILBRIDE RD

Cemy

Philipshill

CASTLEGLEN

CASTLEHILL
GN
MINISTERS PK
STEWARTFIELD WAY
CASTLEHILL WAY

Thorntonhall Burn

Laigh Braehead

Braehead

Hotel

Castle Hill

PHILIPSHILL RD
PHILIPSHILL GATE

Rough Hill

2

Thorntonhall

G74

BRAEHEAD RD

GLENBURN WAY

Thorntonhall

OSBORNE CRES
BISHOPS PK
BISHOPS GATE
WELLKNOWE PL
WELLKNOWE RD
WELLKNOWE AVE
PARK PL
PARK DR
THORN AVE
RAVENSCOURT

WESTERFIELD RD

QUEENSWAY
A726

55

Birkwood

PEEL RD
GILMOUR AVE

South Hill of Dripps

Thornton Farm

THORNTON RD

BARBANA RD

REDWOOD DR
REDWOOD CRES
REDWOOD PL

Ind Est

LINWOOD AVE

Ind Est

North Hill of Dripps

Southland

Peel Park

PEEL PARK PL
BURLEY PL

1

Millbrae

STRATHCONON GDNS 1
HAIRMYRES LA 2
REDWOOD AVE
REDWOOD CT
B764
1
2
EAGLESHAM RD

Hairmyres

HAIRMYRES ROUNDABOUT

B764
WESTPORT

H

G75

Little Dripps

54

58   A   59   B   60   C

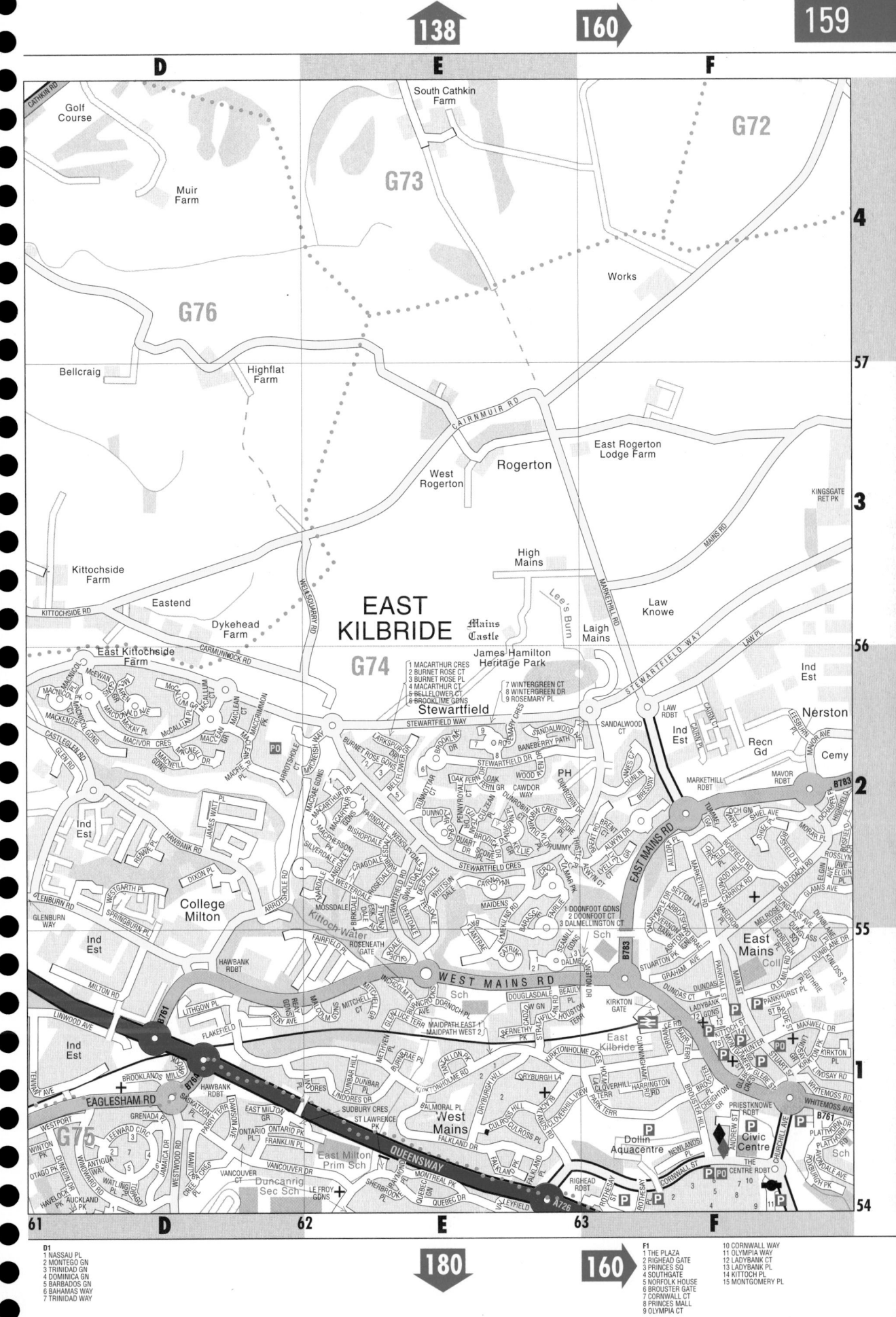

D · E · F

4
57
3
56
2
55
1
54

61 · D · 62 · E · 63 · F

Golf Course
Muir Farm
G73
G72
South Cathkin Farm
Works
G76
Bellcraig
Highflat Farm
CAIRNMUIR RD
West Rogerton
Rogerton
East Rogerton Lodge Farm
KINGSGATE RET PK
MAINS RD
Kittochside Farm
Eastend
KITTOCHSIDE RD
Dykehead Farm
CARMUNNOCK RD
WELLSQUARRY RD
High Mains
Lee's Burn
Laigh Mains
Law Knowe
STEWARTFIELD WAY
LAW PL
East Kittochside Farm
EAST KILBRIDE
G74
Mains Castle
James Hamilton Heritage Park
Ind Est
Nerston
Recn Gd
Cemy
B783
1 MACARTHUR CRES
2 BURNET ROSE CT
3 BURNET ROSE PL
4 MACARTHUR CT
5 BELLFLOWER CT
6 BROOKLIME GDNS
7 WINTERGREEN CT
8 WINTERGREEN DR
9 ROSEMARY PL
Stewartfield
Ind Est
LAW RDBT
MARKETHILL RDBT
MAVOR RDBT
East Mains Coll
College Milton
Kittoch Water
EAST MAINS RD
B783
West Mains Rd
Sch
East Kilbride
Ind Est
HAWBANK RDBT
B761
B764
HAWBANK RDBT
EAGLESHAM RD
G75
QUEENSWAY
A726
West Mains
East Milton Prim Sch
Duncanrig Sec Sch
Dollan Aquacentre
Civic Centre
THE CENTRE RDBT
PRIESTKNOWE RDBT
B761

D1
1 NASSAU PL
2 MONTEGO GN
3 TRINIDAD GN
4 DOMINICA GN
5 BARBADOS GN
6 BAHAMAS WAY
7 TRINIDAD WAY

F1
1 THE PLAZA
2 RIGHEAD GATE
3 PRINCES SQ
4 SOUTHGATE
5 NORFOLK HOUSE
6 BROUSTER GATE
7 CORNWALL CT
8 PRINCES MALL
9 OLYMPIA CT
10 CORNWALL WAY
11 OLYMPIA WAY
12 LADYBANK CT
13 LADYBANK PL
14 KITTOCH PL
15 MONTGOMERY PL

A   B   C

4

Masts

Dechmont
Farm

Crookedshields

Cocks Burn

Nerston
Residential
Sch

Crookedshields Rd

Letterickhills
Cottages

Mid Lettrick
Farm Cottage

Mid
Lettrick

East
Nerston

57

East
Nerston

West
Nerston

Letterickhills

Nerston

Nerston Rd

Golf
Course

Chapelside Rd

Crossbow
House

Kingsgate
Ret Pk

CH

Chapelside

Stoneymeadow Rd

Lee's Burn

Allers

Crossbasket

B7012 Hamilton Rd
A725

3

Stewartfield Way

EAST
KILBRIDE

G72

Law Pl

Mavor Ave

Hamilton Rd

Howard Ave
Howard Ct

A749

A725

Sewage
Works

Mavor Ave

56

Falstaff Dr
Hamlet

Bosworth Rd
Thorndyke
Edmund
Kean
Redgrave
Stratford

Cadell Gdns
Purdie
Morland
Gourlay

Ferguson Pl
Barrie
Wylie
Kenilworth

Basket

Ind Est

Braeview Dr

Albany
Macbeth

Sch
Neville

Warwick

Pembroke

Salisbury

Cambuslang Golf
Allers Annexe

Nerston

Stoneymeadow

A749

A725

The Whirlies
Roundabout

Blackbraes Rd
Orchard

Talbot

Mus
Mowbray

Waverley

Craigneith
Ct

East Mains Rd

Iona Ave

Raeburn Ave

Calderwood

Wingate Pk

Canongate

Cemy

B783

2

Highfield Ave

Stirling Ave

PO

Drummond
Hill

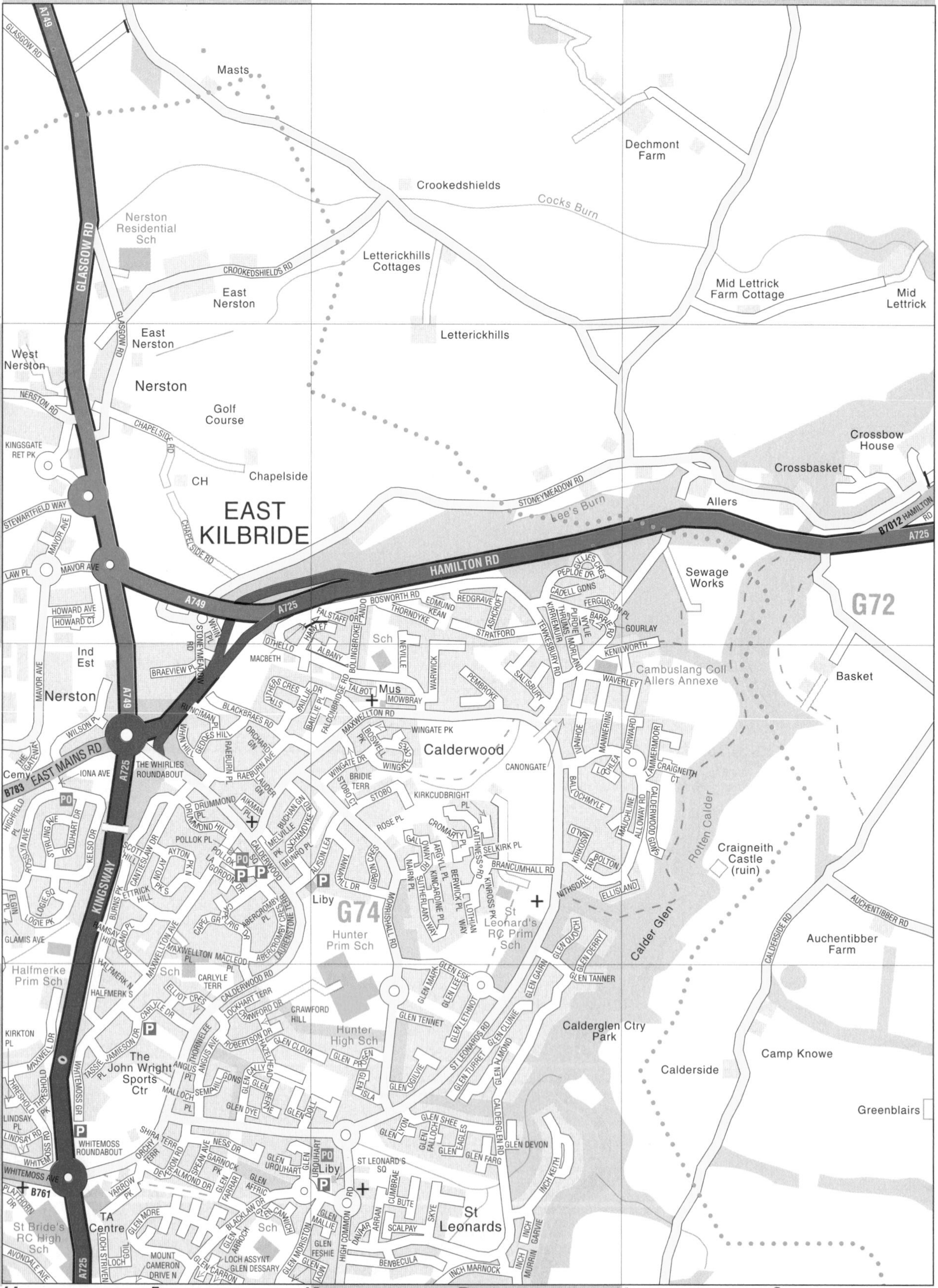

Pollok Pk

Bridie
Terr
Stobo

Rose Pl

Kirkcudbright
Pl

Cromarty

Argyll Rd

Brancumhall Rd

Craigneith
Castle
(ruin)

Rotten Calder

Auchentibber Rd

Kelso Dr

Abercrombie
PO
P

Liby

Selkirk Pl
Berwick Pl
Lothian

Ellisland

P

G74

Morishall Rd

St Leonard's
RC Prim
Sch

Bolton

55

Glamis Ave

Halfmerke
Prim Sch

Halfmerk N

Halfmerk S

Hunter
Prim Sch

Calderwood Rd

Carlyle
Terr

Kirkton
Pl

Crawford
Hill

Hunter
High Sch

Glen Esk

St Leonards Rd

Calderglen Ctry
Park

Auchentibber
Farm

Camp Knowe

Calderside

Greenblairs

Kingsway

Maxwellton Rd

The John Wright
Sports
Ctr

Angus
Gdns

Robertson Dr

Glen Clova

Glen Lyon

Glen Tennet

1

Lindsay
Pl

Whitemoss Ave

Whitemoss
Roundabout

B761

Shira
Terr

Ness Dr

Glen Urquhart

Glen
Dye

Glen
Isla

Glen
Affric

St Leonard's
Sq

Liby
P

Glen Shee

Glen Devon

Glen Farg

Inch Keith

St Bride's
RC High
Sch

TA
Centre

Mount
Cameron
Drive N

Glen More

Glen Carron

Glen Dessary

Loch Assynt

Glen
Mallie

Glen
Feshie

Benbecula

Dinmar

Scalpay

Skye

St
Leonards

Inch Murrin

Inch Marnock

A725

Avondale Ave

54

64   A   65   B   66   C

140
162

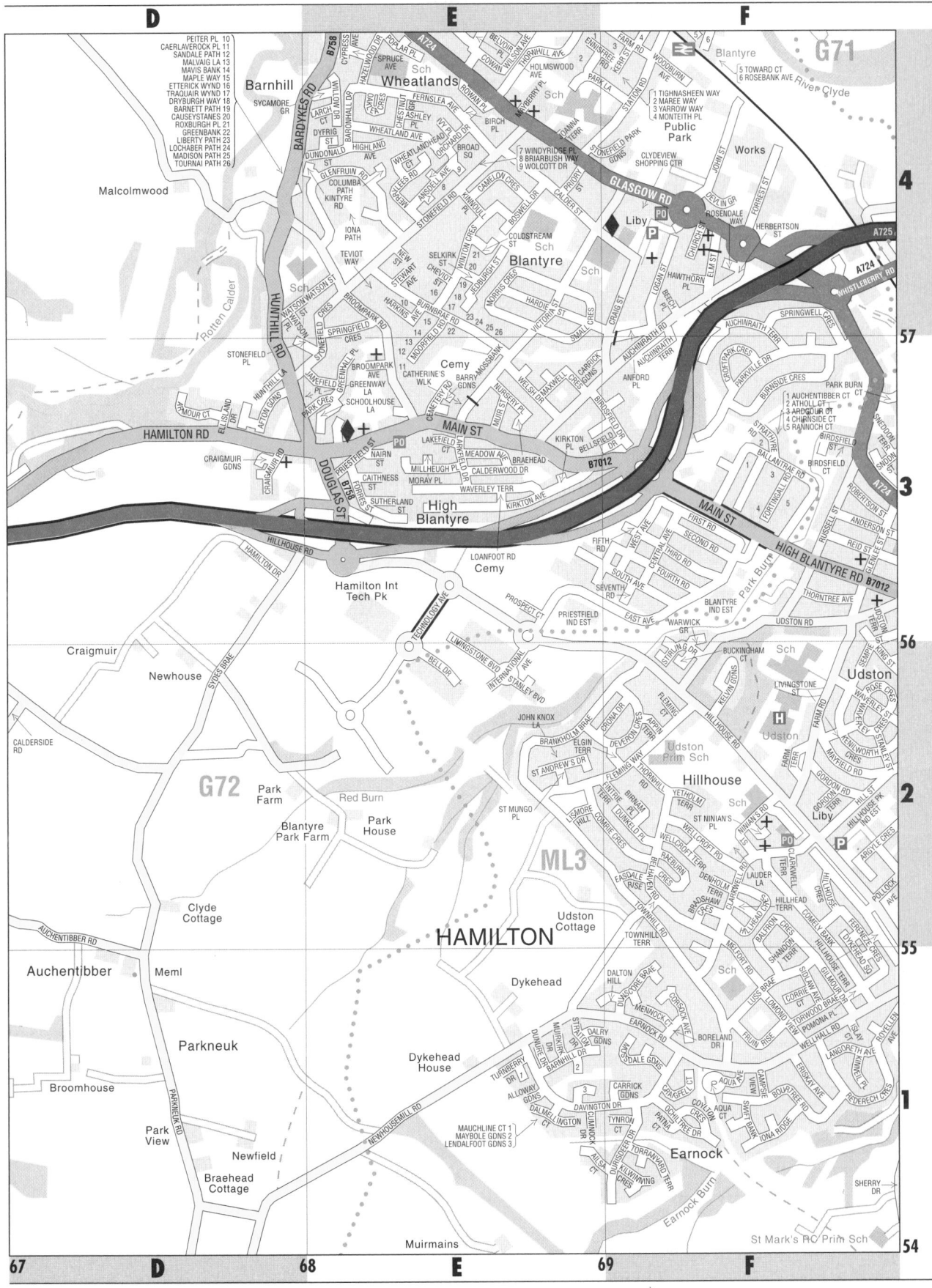
D
E
F
PEITER PL 10
CAERLAVEROCK PL 11
SANDALE PATH 12
MALVAIG LA 13
MAVIS BANK 14
MAPLE WAY 15
ETTERICK WYND 16
TRAQUAIR WYND 17
DRYBURGH WAY 18
BARNETT PATH 19
CAUSEYSTANES 20
ROXBURGH PL 21
GREENBANK 22
LIBERTY PATH 23
LOCHABER PATH 24
MADISON PATH 25
TOURNAI PATH 26
Barnhill
Wheatlands
Malcolmwood
BARDYKES RD
HUNTHILL RD
A724
GLASGOW RD
Blantyre
G71
River Clyde
5 TOWARD CT
6 ROSEBANK AVE
1 TIGHNASHEEN WAY
2 MAREE WAY
3 YARROW WAY
4 MONTEITH PL
Public Park
Works
CLYDEVIEW SHOPPING CTR
7 WINDYRIDGE PL
8 BRIARBUSH WAY
9 WOLCOTT DR
Liby
A725
Rotten Calder
Cemy
HAMILTON RD
MAIN ST
B7012
DOUGLAS ST
B758
High Blantyre
1 AUCHENTIBBER CT
2 ATHOLL CT
3 ARDGOUR CT
4 CHIRNSIDE CT
5 RANNOCH CT
HIGH BLANTYRE RD
HILLHOUSE RD
Hamilton Int Tech Pk
Cemy
PRIESTFIELD IND EST
BLANTYRE IND EST
Park Burn
Craigmuir
Newhouse
CALDERSIDE RD
Udston
Udston Prim Sch
Hillhouse
G72
Park Farm
Red Burn
Blantyre Park Farm
Park House
ML3
Clyde Cottage
Udston Cottage
HAMILTON
AUCHENTIBBER RD
Auchentibber
Meml
Dykehead
Parkneuk
Dykehead House
Broomhouse
NEWHOUSEMILL RD
MAUCHLINE CT 1
MAYBOLE GDNS 2
LENDALFOOT GDNS 3
Park View
Newfield
PARKNEUK RD
Earnock
Braehead Cottage
Earnock Burn
SHERRY DR
Muirmains
St Mark's RC Prim Sch
4
57
3
56
2
55
1
54
67
68
69

182
162

161
141

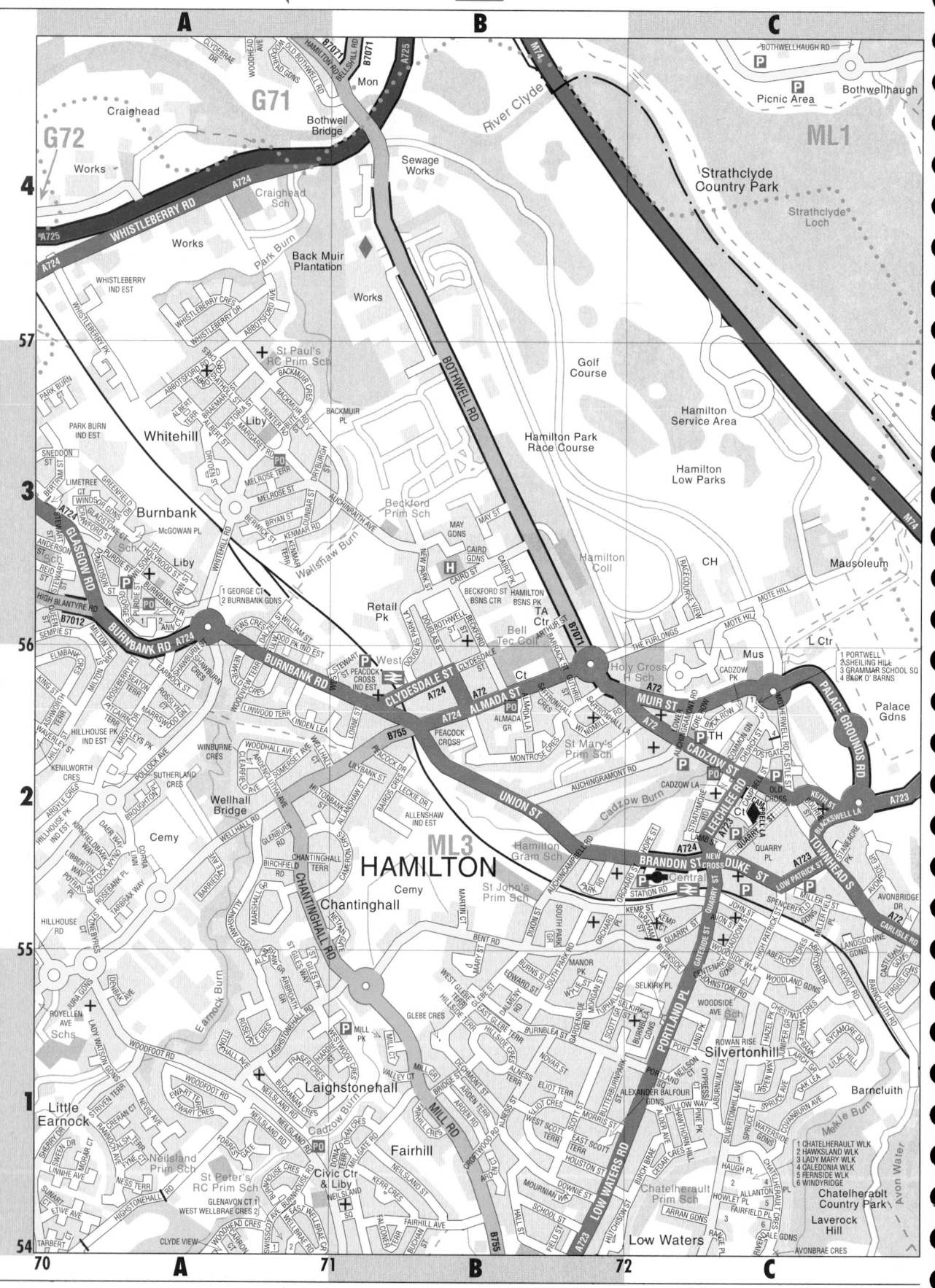

A
B
C
4
57
3
56
2
55
1
54
70
71
72
G72
G71
ML1
ML3
HAMILTON
Craighead
Works
Bothwell Bridge
Mon
River Clyde
Sewage Works
Picnic Area
Bothwellhaugh
BOTHWELLHAUGH RD
Strathclyde Country Park
Strathclyde Loch
Craighead Sch
WHISTLEBERRY RD
Park Burn
Back Muir Plantation
WHISTLEBERRY IND EST
St Paul's RC Prim Sch
Golf Course
Hamilton Service Area
BOTHWELL RD
Hamilton Park Race Course
Hamilton Low Parks
Whitehill
PARK BURN IND EST
Liby
BACKMUIR PL
Burnbank
Beckford Prim Sch
MCGOWAN PL
Wellshaw Burn
Hamilton Coll
CH
Mausoleum
Retail Pk
TA Ctr
Bell Tec Coll
MOTE HILL
THE FURLONGS
L Ctr
HIGH BLANTYRE RD
GLASGOW RD
BURNBANK RD
West
CLYDESDALE ST
ALMADA ST
Holy Cross H Sch
Mus
MUIR ST
PALACE GROUNDS RD
Palace Gdns
1 PORTWELL
2 SHEILING HILL
3 GRAMMAR SCHOOL SQ
4 BACK O' BARNS
HILLHOUSE PK IND EST
PEACOCK CROSS
St Mary's Prim Sch
CADZOW ST
TH
UNION ST
Wellhall Bridge
Cemy
Cadzow Burn
ALLENSHAW IND EST
Hamilton Gram Sch
BRANDON ST
DUKE ST
Central
Old Cross
TOWNHEAD ST
Chantinghall
CHANTINGHALL RD
St John's Prim Sch
LOW PATRICK ST
CARLISLE RD
Earnock Burn
Manor Pk
Silvertonhill
PORTLAND PL
Laighstonehall
Little Earnock
Barncluith
Meikle Burn
Fairhill
MILL RD
Neilsland Prim Sch
St Peter's RC Prim Sch
Civic Ctr & Liby
Chatelherault Prim Sch
LOW WATERS RD
Chatelherault Country Park
Laverock Hill
Avon Water
Low Waters
1 CHATELHERAULT WLK
2 HAWKSLAND WLK
3 LADY MARY WLK
4 CALEDONIA WLK
5 FERNSIDE WLK
6 WINDYRIDGE

161
183

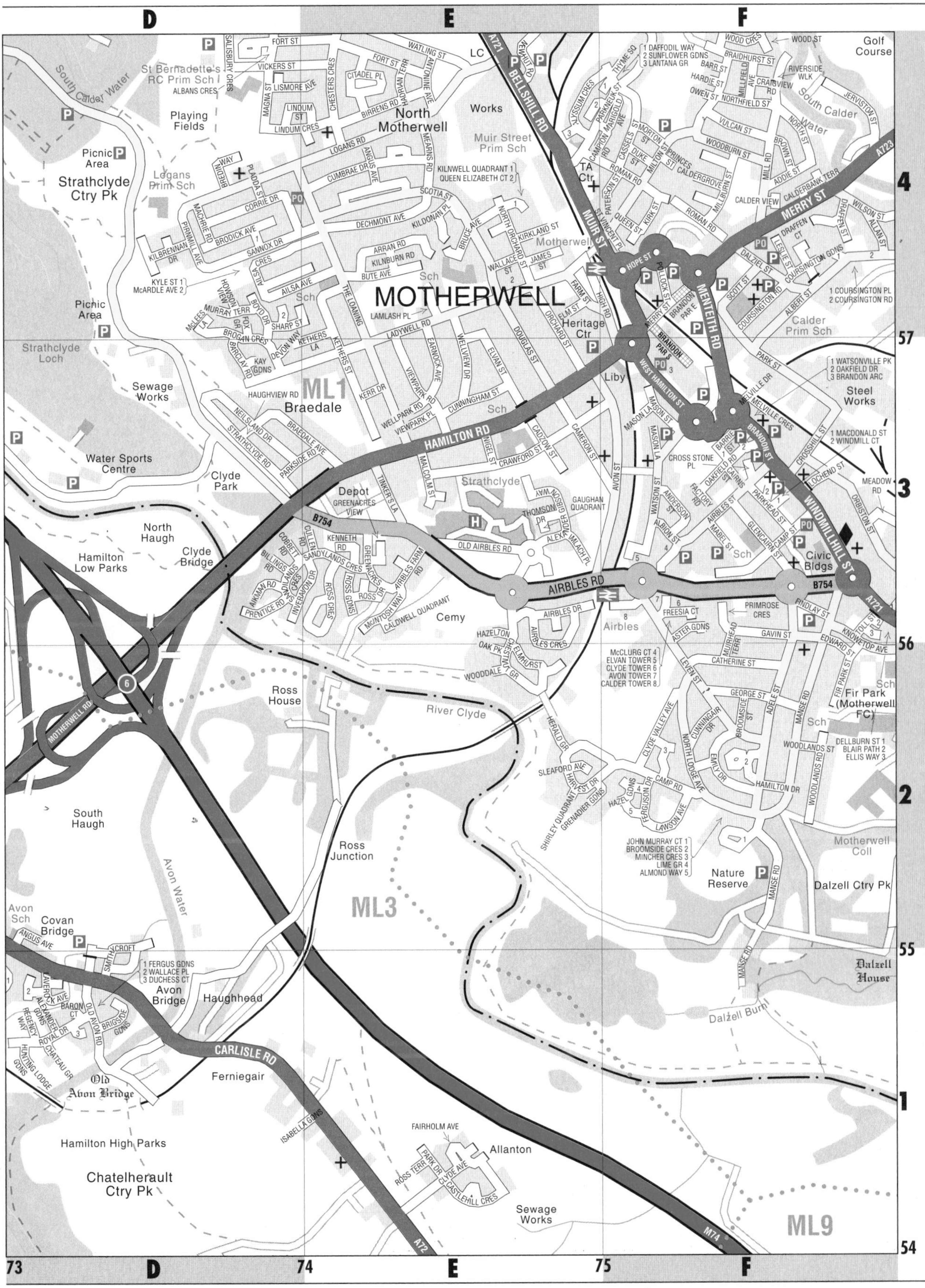
142
164

D E F

Golf Course
St Bernadette's RC Prim Sch
South Calder Water
Playing Fields
Picnic Area
Strathclyde Ctry Pk
Logans Prim Sch
North Motherwell
Works
Muir Street Prim Sch
MOTHERWELL
Motherwell
Heritage Ctr
TA Ctr
Liby
Calder Prim Sch
Steel Works
Strathclyde Loch
Sewage Works
ML1
Braedale
Water Sports Centre
Clyde Park
Depot
North Haugh
Hamilton Low Parks
Clyde Bridge
Strathclyde
Cemy
Airbles
Civic Bldgs
Fir Park (Motherwell FC)
Ross House
River Clyde
South Haugh
Ross Junction
ML3
Avon Water
Nature Reserve
Motherwell Coll
Dalzell Ctry Pk
Dalzell House
Dalzell Burn
Avon Sch
Covan Bridge
Avon Bridge
Haughhead
Old Avon Bridge
Ferniegair
Hamilton High Parks
Chatelherault Ctry Pk
Allanton
Sewage Works
ML9

HAMILTON RD
MUIR ST
BELLSHILL RD
MERRY ST
MENTEITH RD
WINDMILLHILL ST
AIRBLES RD
B754
A721
A723
MOTHERWELL RD
CARLISLE RD
A72
M74

1 DAFFODIL WAY
2 SUNFLOWER GDNS
3 LANTANA GR

KILNWELL QUADRANT 1
QUEEN ELIZABETH CT 2

KYLE ST 1
McARDLE AVE 2

1 COURSINGTON PL
2 COURSINGTON RD

1 WATSONVILLE PK
2 OAKFIELD DR
3 BRANDON ARC

1 MACDONALD ST
2 WINDMILL CT

McCLURG CT 4
ELVAN TOWER 5
CLYDE TOWER 6
AVON TOWER 7
CALDER TOWER 8

DELLBURN ST 1
BLAIR PATH 2
ELLIS WAY 3

JOHN MURRAY CT 1
BROOMSIDE CRES 2
MINCHER CRES 3
LIME GR 4
ALMOND WAY 5

1 FERGUS GDNS
2 WALLACE PL
3 DUCHESS CT

FAIRHOLM AVE

4 3 57 56 2 55 1 54

73 D 74 E 75 F

184
164

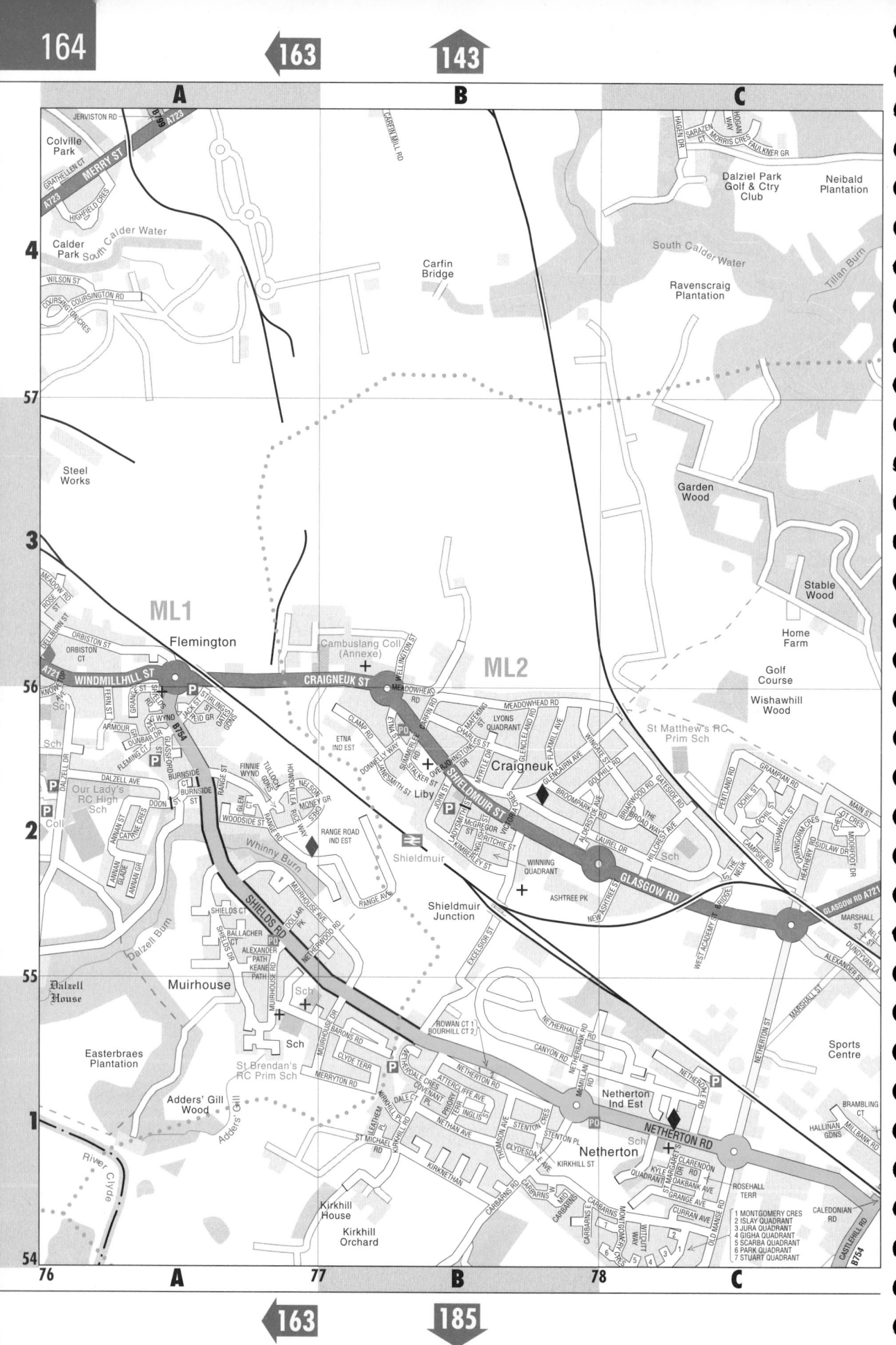
163
143
A
B
C
4
57
3
56
2
55
1
54
76
77
78
JERVISTON RD
B799
A723
Colville Park
MERRY ST
GRATHELLEN CT
HIGHFIELD CRES
Calder Park
South Calder Water
WILSON ST
COURSINGTON RD
COURSINGTON CRES
CARFIN MILL RD
Carfin Bridge
HAGEN DR
SARAZEN CT
HOGAN WAY
MORRIS CRES
FAULKNER GR
Dalziel Park Golf & Ctry Club
Neibald Plantation
Ravenscraig Plantation
Tillan Burn
Steel Works
Garden Wood
Stable Wood
Home Farm
Golf Course
Wishawhill Wood
ML1
ML2
Flemington
MEADOW RD
ROSE ST
BELLBURN ST
ORBISTON ST
ORBISTON CT
A721
WINDMILLHILL ST
KNOWETOP AVE
FERN ST
GRANGE ST
SHIELDS RD
JACK ST
STIRLING ST
REID GR
OATES GDNS
B754
Cambuslang Coll (Annexe)
CRAIGNEUK ST
WELLINGTON ST
MEADOWHEAD RD
MEADOWHEAD RD
CLAMP RD
ETNA IND EST
ETNA ST
SUMMERLEE RD
CARFIN RD
MAFFEKING ST
CHARLES ST
LYONS QUADRANT
GLENCLELAND RD
FLAXMILL AVE
WINGATE ST
GOLFHILL RD
St Matthew's RC Prim Sch
ARMOUR PL
DUNBAR DR
FLEMING CT
GLASSFORD ST
DALZELL AVE
DALZELL DR
BURNSIDE CT
BURNSIDE ST
DOON ST
Our Lady's RC High Sch
Coll
ANNAN ST
CAITHNESS CRES
ANNAN GLADE
ANNAN GR
FINNIE WYND
TULLOCH GDNS
HOWSON LEA
NELSON ST
MONEY GR
RICE WAY
GLEN CT
WOODSIDE ST
RANGE RD
RANGE ST
RANGE ROAD IND EST
Whinny Burn
RANGE AVE
DONNELLY WAY
JANESMITH ST
STALKER ST
OVERJOHNSTONE DR
MYRTLE DR
Liby
Craigneuk
JOHN ST
LADYSMITH ST
McGREGOR ST
ENGLISH ST
RITCHIE ST
KIMBERLEY ST
SHIELDMUIR ST
VICTORIA CRES
GLENCAIRN AVE
BROOMPARK RD
ALDERSYDE AVE
BRIARWOOD RD
THE BROAD WAY
HILLCREST AVE
GATESIDE RD
LAUREL DR
Sch
Shieldmuir
WINNING QUADRANT
ASHTREE PK
NEW ASHTREE ST
GLASGOW RD
THE NEUK
PENTLAND RD
OCHIL ST
WISHAWHILL ST
GRAMPIAN RD
CAIRNGORM CRES
HEATHERY RD
SIDLAW DR
MOORFOOT DR
MAIN ST
CAMPSIE RD
GLASGOW RD A721
MARSHALL ST
ALEXANDER ST
DUNDYVAN LA
Shieldmuir Junction
EXCELSIOR ST
WEST ACADEMY ST
BRIDGE ST
SHIELDS CT
BALLACHER CT
SHIELDS DR
ALEXANDER PATH
KEANE PATH
MUIRHOUSE RD
MUIRHOUSE AVE
DOLLAR PK
NETHERWOOD RD
SHIELDS RD
Dalzell Burn
Dalzell House
Muirhouse
Sch
Sch
MUIRHOUSE DR
BARONS RD
CLYDE TERR
MERRYTON RD
St Brendan's RC Prim Sch
Easterbraes Plantation
Adders' Gill Wood
Adders' Gill
River Clyde
ROWAN CT
BOURHILL CT
NETHERHALL RD
NETHERBANK RD
CANYON RD
McMILLAN RD
NETHERDALE RD
NETHERTON RD
NETHERDALE CRES
COVENANT PL
ATTERCLIFFE AVE
PRIORY TERR
INGLIS ST
DALE CT
NETHAN AVE
LEATHEM PL
KIRKHILL PL
KIRKHILL RD
ST MICHAEL RD
THOMSON AVE
STENTON CRES
STENTON PL
CLYDESDALE AVE
KIRKHILL ST
Netherton Ind Est
NETHERTON RD
Netherton
NETHERTON ST
MARSHALL ST
Sports Centre
BRAMBLING CT
HALLINAN GDNS
MILLBANK RD
KIRKNETHAN
Kirkhill House
Kirkhill Orchard
CARBARNS RD
CARBARNS W
CARBARNS MID
CARBARNS
CARBARNS E
MONTGOMERY CRES
WITCUTT WAY
KYLE QUADRANT
ST MARGARET'S DR
CLARENDON RD
OAKBANK AVE
GRANGE AVE
CURRAN AVE
OLD MANSE RD
ROSEHALL TERR
CALEDONIAN RD
CASTLEHILL RD
B754
1 MONTGOMERY CRES
2 ISLAY QUADRANT
3 JURA QUADRANT
4 GIGHA QUADRANT
5 SCARBA QUADRANT
6 PARK QUADRANT
7 STUART QUADRANT
163
185

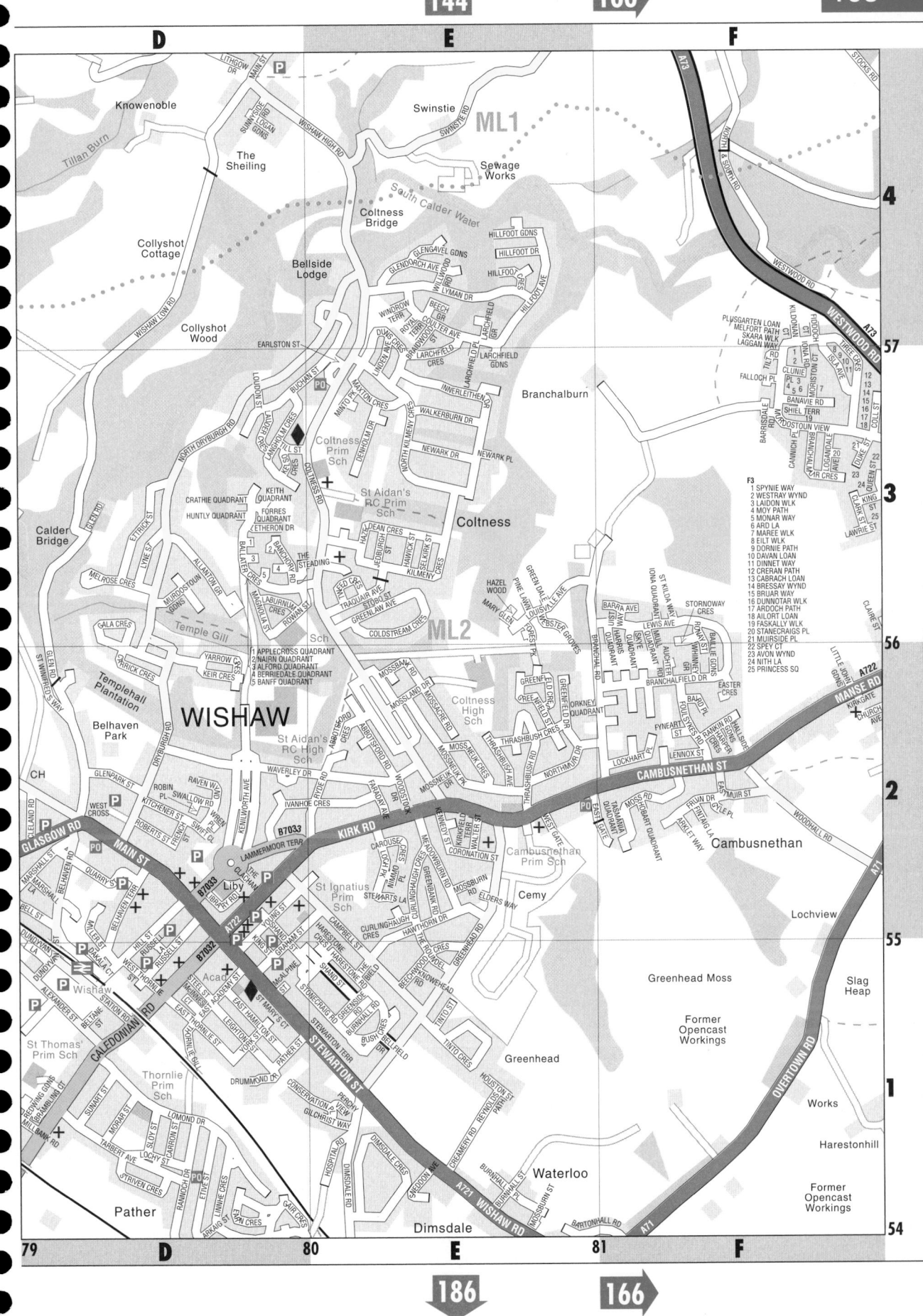
144
166
D
E
F
Knowenoble
Swinstie
ML1
Tillan Burn
The Sheiling
Sewage Works
South Calder Water
Coltness Bridge
Collyshot Cottage
Bellside Lodge
Collyshot Wood
WISHAW LOW RD
WISHAW HIGH RD
MAIN ST
LITHGOW DR
SUNNYSIDE RD
LOGAN GDNS
SWINSTIE RD
HILLFOOT GDNS
HILLFOOT DR
HILLFOOT CRES
HILLFOOT AVE
GLENGAVEL GDNS
GLENDORCH AVE
WILLWOOD RD
LYMAN DR
WINDROW TERR
BEECH GR
ROYAL TERR
COULTER AVE
BRAIDWOOD ST
LARCHFIELD GR
LARCHFIELD CRES
LARCHFIELD PL
LARCHFIELD GDNS
EARLSTON ST
DUNS CRES
LINDEN AVE
INNERLEITHEN DR
Branchalburn
WALKERBURN DR
NEWARK DR
NEWARK PL
NORTH KILMENY CRES
MAXTON CRES
MINTO PK
DENHOLM DR
Coltness Prim Sch
BUCHAN ST
LOUDON ST
LAUDER CRES
LANGHOLM CRES
TILL ST
KELSO CRES
COLTNESS RD
NORTH DRYBURGH RD
St Aidan's RC Prim Sch
Coltness
Calder Bridge
GLEN RD
CRATHIE QUADRANT
KEITH QUADRANT
HUNTLY QUADRANT
FORRES QUADRANT
ETHERON DR
ETTRICK ST
LYNE ST
MELROSE CRES
BANCHORY RD
BALLATER CRES
THE STEADING
DEAN CRES
JEDBURGH ST
HAWICK ST
SELKIRK ST
KILMENY CRES
TWEED CRES
TRAQUAIR AVE
STOBO ST
GREENLAW AVE
COLDSTREAM CRES
ML2
ALLANTON GR
MURDOSTOUN GDNS
LABURNUM CRES
MAGNOLIA ST
ROWAN ST
GALA CRES
Temple Gill
HAZEL WOOD
PINE LAWN
GREEN DALE
LOUISVILLE AVE
MARY GLEN
FOREST PK
WEBSTER GROVES
BRANCHAL RD
BARRA AVE
IONA QUADRANT
ST KILDA WAY
LEWIS AVE
STORNOWAY CRES
HARRIS QUADRANT
SKYE QUADRANT
MULL QUADRANT
AUCHTER GR
WHINNEY GR
RONAY ST
BAILLIE GDNS
BRANCHALFIELD DR
EASTER CRES
CARRICK CRES
YARROW CRES
KEIR CRES
1 APPLECROSS QUADRANT
2 NAIRN QUADRANT
3 ALFORD QUADRANT
4 BERRIEDALE QUADRANT
5 BANFF QUADRANT
Templehall Plantation
Belhaven Park
WISHAW
St Aidan's RC High Sch
MOSSBANK RD
MOSSLAND DR
MOSSACRE RD
MOSSNEUK CRES
MOSSNEUK PK
MOSSNEUK DR
Coltness High Sch
GREENFIELD CRES
GREENFIELD DR
ORKNEY QUADRANT
THRASHBUSH CRES
THRASHBUSH AVE
THRASHBUSH RD
NORTHMUIR DR
FYNEART ST
FOULSYKES RD
BAIRD PL
RANKIN RD
HARPER CRES
HALLSIDE
LENNOX ST
LOCKHART PL
MANSE RD
A722
KIRKGATE
CHURCH AVE
LITTLE JOHN GDNS
CLAIRE ST
CH
GLEN PARK ST
DRYBURGH RD
RAVEN WYND
ROBIN PL
SWALLOW RD
WEST CROSS
KITCHENER ST
WREN PL
ROBERTS ST
FRENCH ST
SWIFT CL
KENILWORTH AVE
WAVERLEY DR
RYDE RD
ABBOTSFORD CRES
ABBOTSFORD RD
FARADAY AVE
WOODSTOCK DR
IVANHOE CRES
B7033
LAMMERMOOR TERR
KIRK RD
CAMBUSNETHAN ST
EAST GATE
TASMANIA QUADRANT
MOSS RD
HOBART QUADRANT
FRUIN DR
GYLE PL
EASTMUIR ST
FINTANG LA
ARKLET WAY
Cambusnethan
WOODHALL RD
GLASGOW RD
CLELAND RD
MARSHALL ST
BELHAVEN RD
MARSHALL LA
QUARRY ST
BELHAVEN TERR
BELL ST
Liby
THE CLACHAN
LIBRARY RD
KENNEDY ST
KIRKFIELD VIEW
WALTER ST
CORONATION ST
CAROUSEL CRES
LOCH PK
NIMMO PL
MEADOWBURN RD
Cambusnethan Prim Sch
WEST GATE
Cemy
ELDERS WAY
MOSSBURN RD
CURLINGHAUGH CRES
GREENBANK RD
STEWARTS LA
St Ignatius Prim Sch
HAWTHORN DR
CAMPBELL ST
YOUNG ST
GRAHAM ST
KING ST
HARESTONE CRES
HARESTONE RD
THE BIELD
THE ROUNDEL
GREENHEAD RD
BEECHWOOD CRES
KNOWEHEAD
Lochview
A71
Greenhead Moss
Slag Heap
Former Opencast Workings
DUNDYVAN LA
DUNDYVAN RD
MILLER ST
DAKOTA CT
HILL ST
RUSSELL ST
RUSSELL LA
WEST THORNLIE ST
Wishaw
STATION RD
ALEXANDER ST
BELTANE ST
Acad
A722
B7032
MCALPINE ST
SHAND ST
STONECRAIG RD
GREENSIDE RD
BURNHALL RD
BUSH CRES
BELLFIELD DR
TINTO ST
TINTO CRES
ST MARY'S CT
EAST HAMILTON ST
EAST ACADEMY ST
STEEL ST
MCINNES CT
LEIGHTON ST
YORK ST
PATHER ST
STEWARTON TERR
EAST THORNLIE ST
THORNLIE GILL
CALEDONIAN RD
St Thomas' Prim Sch
Thornlie Prim Sch
DRUMMOND DR
STEWARTON ST
Greenhead
HOUSTON ST
REYNOLDS ST
PATH ST
CONSERVATION PL
PERCHY VIEW
GILCHRIST WAY
BREDWING GDNS
BRAMBLING CT
MILL BANK RD
SUNART ST
MORAR ST
LOMOND DR
SLOY ST
CARRON ST
TARBERT AVE
LOCHY ST
STRIVEN CRES
RANNOCH DR
ETIVE ST
LINNHE CRES
ARKAIG ST
EWAN CRES
GAIR CRES
HOSPITAL RD
DIMSDALE RD
DIMSDALE CRES
SNEDDON AVE
CREAMERY RD
A721 WISHAW RD
BURNHALL PL
BURNHALL ST
MOSSBURN ST
Waterloo
BARTONHALL RD
Dimsdale
Pather
OVERTOWN RD
Works
Harestonhill
A73
STOCKS RD
HURON & SOUTH RD
WESTWOOD RD
WESTWOOD RD
PLUSGARTEN LOAN
MELFORT PATH
SKARA WLK
LAGGAN WAY
KILDONAN CT
IONA RD
FIDDOCH CT
MORISTON CT
TIREE CRES
ISLA AVE
TILT RD
FALLOCH PL
CLUNIE PL
BANAVIE RD
SHIEL TERR
BARRISDALE RD
WOODSTOUN VIEW
CANNICH PL
BRANCHALMAIR CRES
LOGANDALE AVE
DUKE ST
QUEEN ST
CLARK ST
KING ST
LAWRIE ST
COLL ST
F3
1 SPYNIE WAY
2 WESTRAY WYND
3 LAIDON WLK
4 MOY PATH
5 MONAR WAY
6 ARD LA
7 MAREE WLK
8 EILT WLK
9 DORNIE PATH
10 DAVAN LOAN
11 DINNET WAY
12 CRERAN PATH
13 CABRACH LOAN
14 BRESSAY WYND
15 BRUAR WAY
16 DUNNOTAR WLK
17 ARDOCH PATH
18 AILORT LOAN
19 FASKALLY WLK
20 STANECRAIGS PL
21 MUIRSIDE PL
22 SPEY CT
23 AVON WYND
24 NITH LA
25 PRINCESS SQ
4
57
3
56
2
55
1
54
79
80
81
186
166

165
145

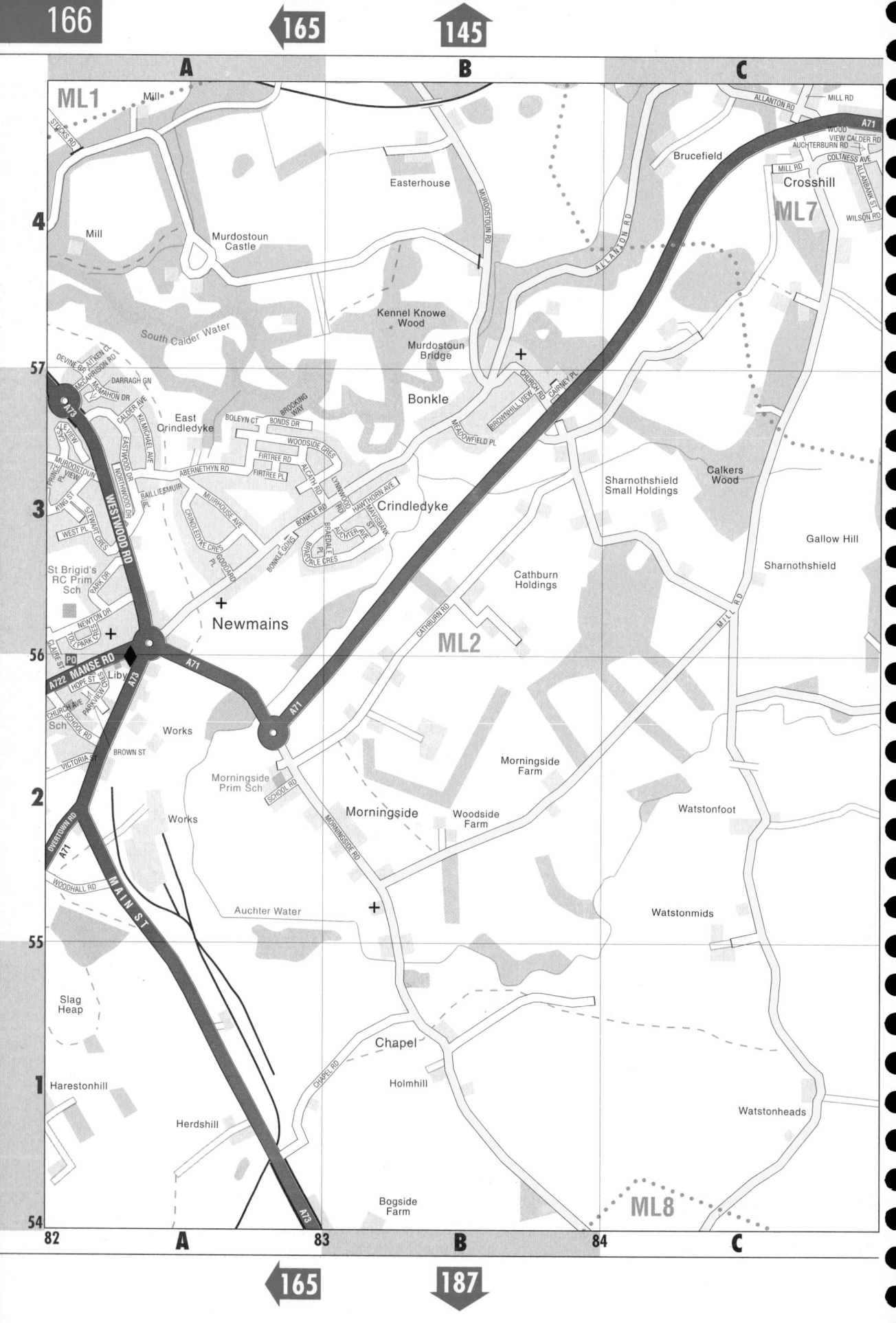
A
B
C
ML1
Mill
Mill
Murdostoun Castle
Easterhouse
Murdostoun Rd
Allanton Rd
Brucefield
Crosshill
ML7
Mill Rd
Allanton Rd
A71
View Calder Rd
Auchterburn Rd
Coltness Ave
Allanbank St
Wilson Rd
Stocks Rd
South Calder Water
Kennel Knowe Wood
Murdostoun Bridge
Bonkle
East Crindledyke
Devine Gr
Aitken Cl
McCarrison Rd
Darragh Gn
McMahon Dr
Calder Ave
Kilmichael Ave
Eastwood Dr
Northwood Dr
Boleyn Ct
Bonds Dr
Brooking Way
Woodside Cres
Firtree Rd
Firtree Pl
Abernethyn Rd
Church Rd
Brownhill View
Cairney Pl
Meadowfield Pl
Alcath Rd
Lynnwood Rd
Hawthorn Ave
Mavisbank St
Crindledyke
Sharnothshield Small Holdings
Calkers Wood
Gallow Hill
Sharnothshield
Murdostoun View
Prince Pl
King St
West Pl
Stewart Cres
Westwood Rd
Bailliesmuir Pl
Muirhouse Ave
Crindledyke Cres
Goddard Pl
Bonkle Rd
Bonkle Gdns
Braedale Pl
Braedale Cres
Auchter Ave
St Brigid's RC Prim Sch
Park Dr
Newton Dr
Park Cres
Claire St
Newmains
Cathburn Holdings
Cathburn Rd
ML2
Mill Rd
A73
A71
A722
Manse Rd
PO
Liby
Hope St
Parkview Cres
Church Ave
School Rd
Sch
Victoria St
Brown St
Works
Morningside Prim Sch
School Rd
Works
Morningside
Morningside Rd
Morningside Farm
Woodside Farm
Watstonfoot
Overtown Rd
A71
Woodhall Rd
Main St
Auchter Water
Watstonmids
Slag Heap
Chapel
Chapel Rd
Holmhill
Harestonhill
Watstonheads
Herdshill
Bogside Farm
ML8
A73
4
57
3
56
2
55
1
54
82
83
84

165
187

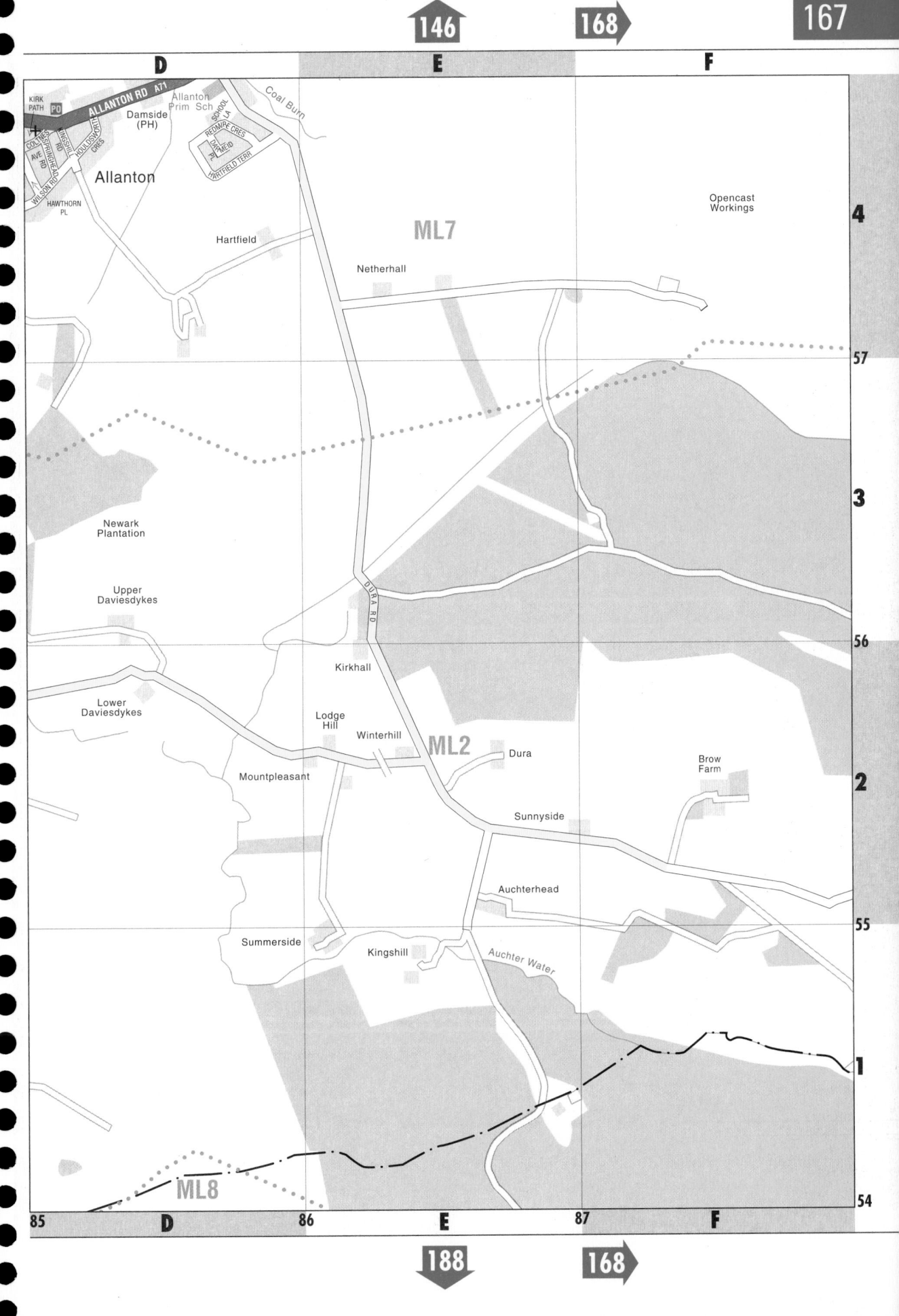
146
168
D
E
F
ALLANTON RD
A71
KIRK PATH
PO
Allanton Prim Sch
Damside (PH)
SCHOOL LA
Coal Burn
REDMIRE CRES
DAMMEID PL
HARTFIELD TERR
COLTNESS AVE
SPRINGHEAD RD
KINGSHILL RD
HOULDSWORTH CRES
WILSON RD
HAWTHORN PL
Allanton
Hartfield
ML7
Opencast Workings
Netherhall
4
57
Newark Plantation
3
Upper Daviesdykes
DURA RD
56
Kirkhall
Lower Daviesdykes
Lodge Hill
Winterhill
ML2
Dura
Brow Farm
Mountpleasant
2
Sunnyside
Auchterhead
55
Summerside
Kingshill
Auchter Water
1
ML8
54
85
86
87
188
168

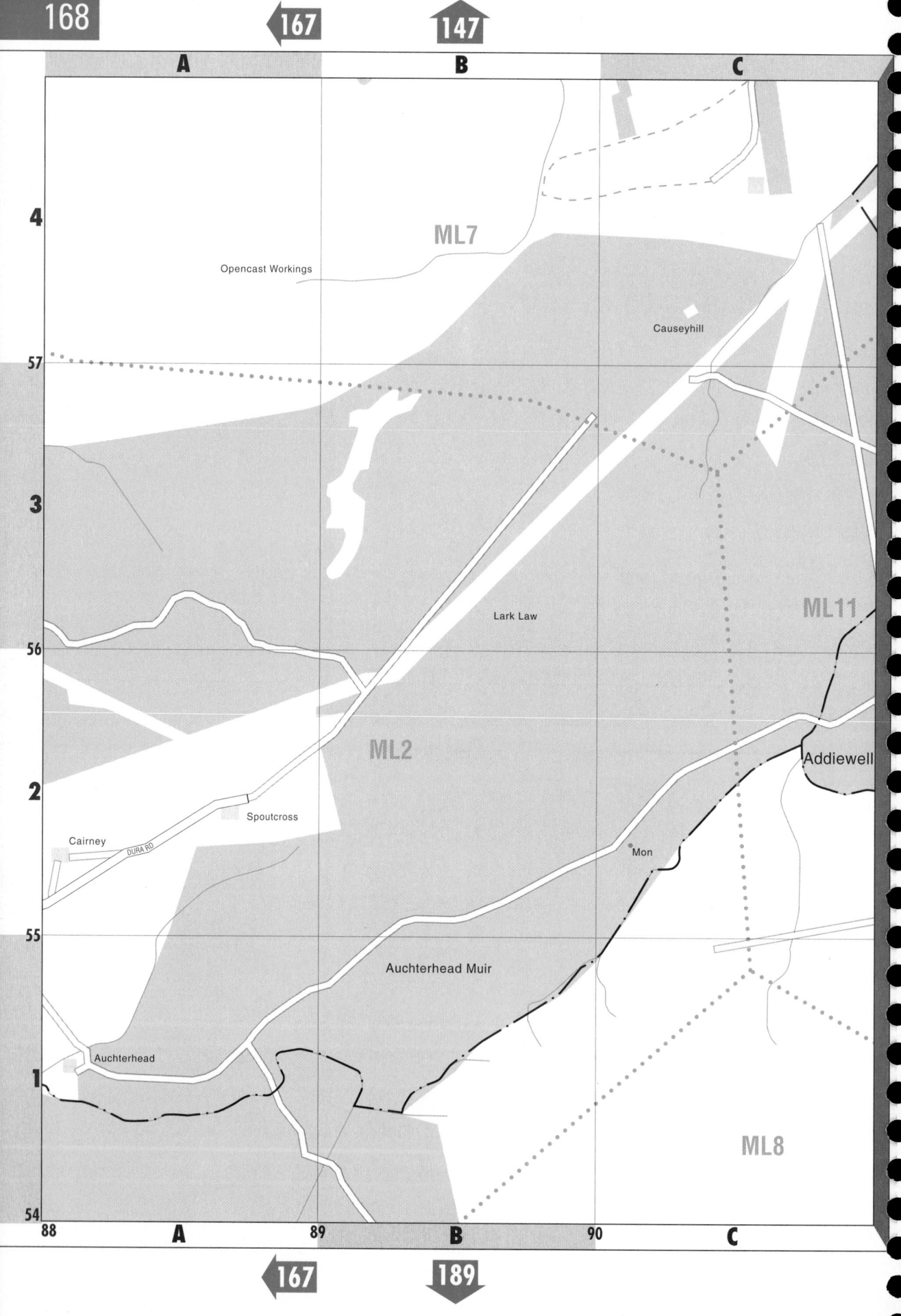

A　　　　　　B　　　　　　C

4

ML7

Opencast Workings

57

ML7

Causeyhill

3

Lark Law

ML11

56

ML2

2

Cairney　DURA RD　Spoutcross

Mon

Addiewell

55

Auchterhead Muir

1

Auchterhead

ML8

54

88　　　　A　　　　89　　　　B　　　　90　　　　C

148
170

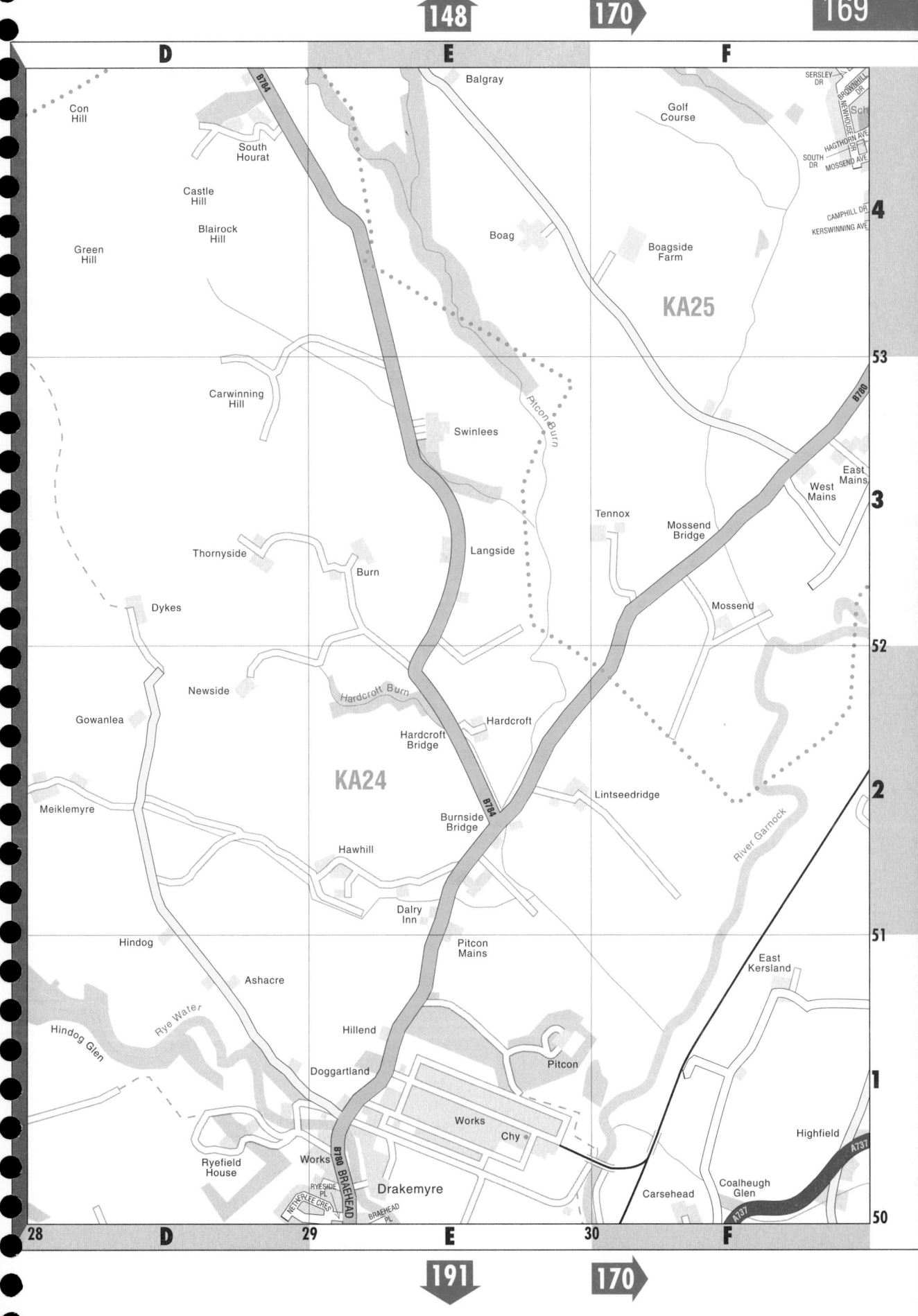
D
E
F
Con Hill
South Hourat
Castle Hill
Blairock Hill
Green Hill
Balgray
Golf Course
Boag
Boagside Farm
KA25
Carwinning Hill
Swinlees
Pitcon Burn
East Mains
West Mains
Tennox
Mossend Bridge
Thornyside
Langside
Burn
Dykes
Mossend
Newside
Hardcroft Burn
Gowanlea
Hardcroft
Hardcroft Bridge
KA24
Lintseedridge
Meiklemyre
Burnside Bridge
River Garnock
Hawhill
Dalry Inn
Hindog
Pitcon Mains
East Kersland
Ashacre
Rye Water
Hindog Glen
Hillend
Pitcon
Doggartland
Works
Chy
Highfield
Ryefield House
Works
Drakemyre
Carsehead
Coalheugh Glen
B784
B780
B780 BRAEHEAD
A737
RYESIDE PL
NETHERLEE CRES
BRAEHEAD PL
SERSLEY DR
BROWNHILL DR
NEWHOUSE DR
Sch
HAGTHORN AVE
SOUTH DR
MOSSEND AVE
CAMPHILL DR
KERSWINNING AVE
4
53
3
52
2
51
1
50
28
29
30

191
170

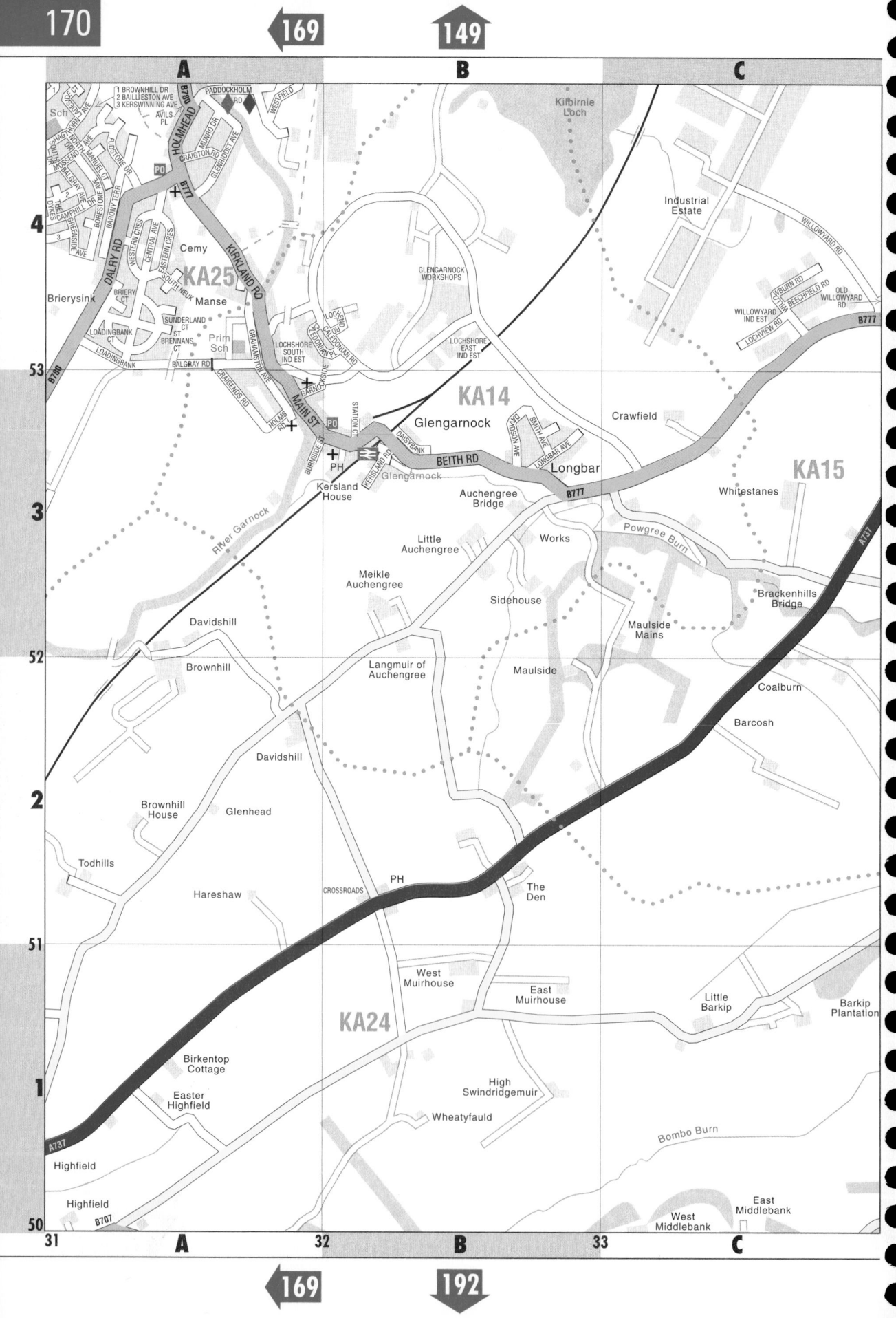
A
B
C
4
3
2
1
53
52
51
50
31
32
33
Kilbirnie Loch
Industrial Estate
WILLOWYARD RD
WILLOWYARD IND EST
OLD WILLOWYARD RD
LOCHVIEW RD
B777
Cemy
KA25
KIRKLAND RD
Brierysink
Manse
Prim Sch
GLENGARNOCK WORKSHOPS
LOCHSHORE SOUTH IND EST
LOCHSHORE EAST IND EST
KA14
Glengarnock
Crawfield
MAIN ST
BEITH RD
Longbar
PH
Kersland House
Auchengree Bridge
KA15
Whitestanes
River Garnock
Powgree Burn
Works
Little Auchengree
Meikle Auchengree
Sidehouse
Brackenhills Bridge
Davidshill
Maulside Mains
Brownhill
Langmuir of Auchengree
Maulside
Coalburn
Barcosh
Davidshill
Brownhill House
Glenhead
Todhills
Hareshaw
CROSSROADS
PH
The Den
West Muirhouse
East Muirhouse
Little Barkip
Barkip Plantation
KA24
Birkentop Cottage
Easter Highfield
High Swindridgemuir
Wheatyfauld
A737
Bombo Burn
Highfield
Highfield
B707
West Middlebank
East Middlebank

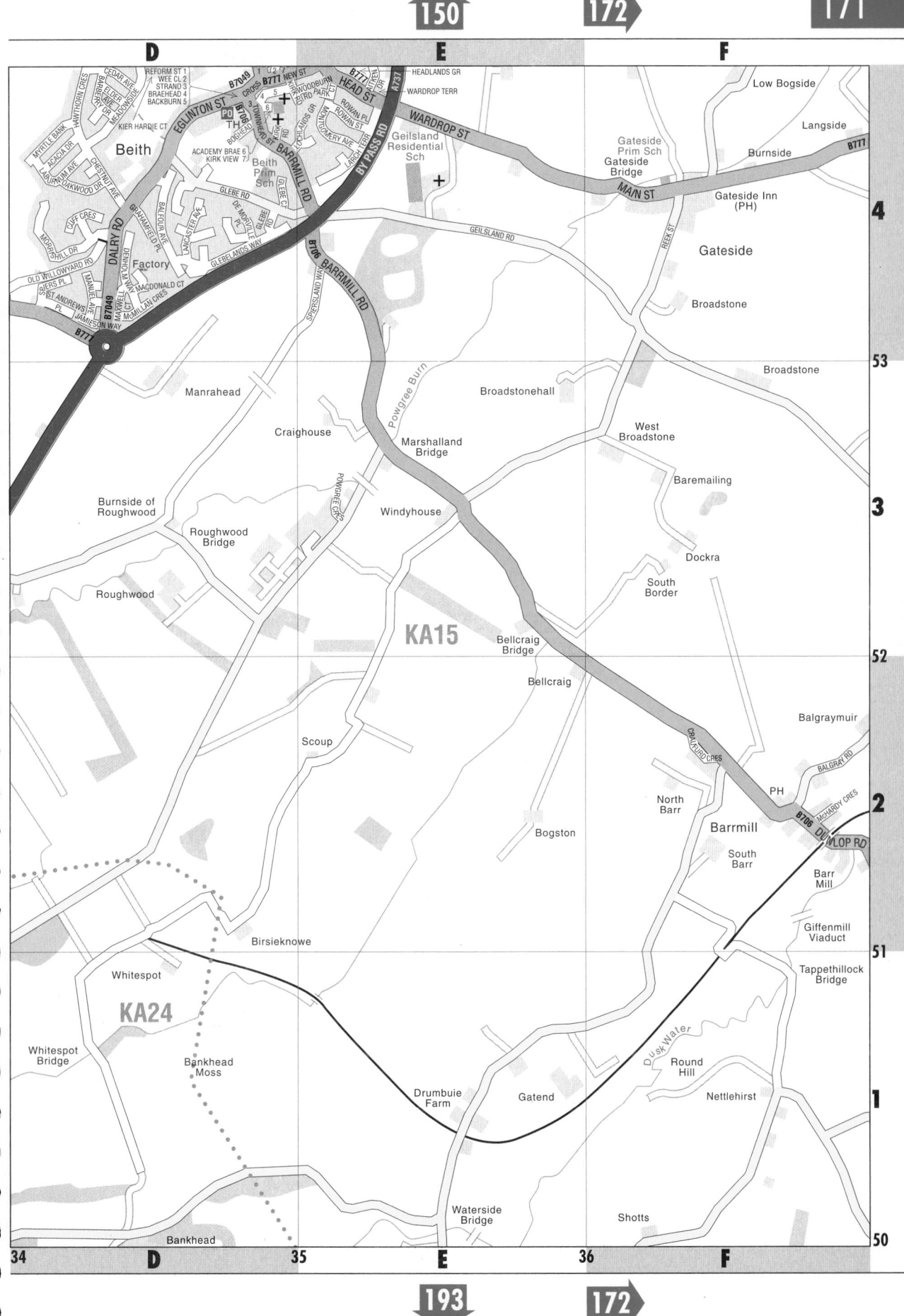

150
172
D
E
F
Beith
EGLINTON ST
HEAD ST
WARDROP ST
BY PASS RD
BARRMILL RD
DALRY RD
GLEBE RD
GEILSLAND RD
MAIN ST
REEK ST
HEADLANDS GR
WARDROP TERR
REFORM ST 1
WEE CL 2
STRAND 3
BRAEHEAD 4
BACKBURN 5
ACADEMY BRAE 6
KIRK VIEW 7
KIER HARDIE CT
Geilsland Residential Sch
Beith Prim Sch
Factory
Gateside Prim Sch
Gateside Bridge
Gateside Inn (PH)
Gateside
Low Bogside
Langside
Burnside
Broadstone
Broadstonehall
Manrahead
Craighouse
Powgree Burn
Marshalland Bridge
West Broadstone
Baremailing
Burnside of Roughwood
Roughwood Bridge
Windyhouse
Dockra
South Border
Roughwood
KA15
Bellcraig Bridge
Bellcraig
Balgraymuir
Scoup
PH
North Barr
Barrmill
DUNLOP RD
Bogston
South Barr
Barr Mill
Giffenmill Viaduct
Birsieknowe
Tappethillock Bridge
Whitespot
KA24
Whitespot Bridge
Bankhead Moss
Dusk Water
Round Hill
Drumbuie Farm
Gatend
Nettlehirst
Waterside Bridge
Shotts
Bankhead
B777
B7049
B706
A737
53
52
51
50
4
3
2
1
34
35
36
193
172

A   B   C

Lyonshields

Overton

Gillies Hill

Washingstone

B777

Overton Bridge

Washingstone Bridge

Over Hessilhead

Blaelochside

Lochend Bridge

Lochend

B777

4

Trearne Quarry

Blaelochhead

Blae Loch

53

Crookhill

Gatehead

Hessilhead

Bungle Burn

Quarry (dis)

Dusk Water

Balgray Cottage

Tandleview

BALGRAY RD

Warehouses

Highgate Bridge

Middleton

3

KA15

Wester Highgate

Easter Highgate

A736

52

Tandlehill Bridge

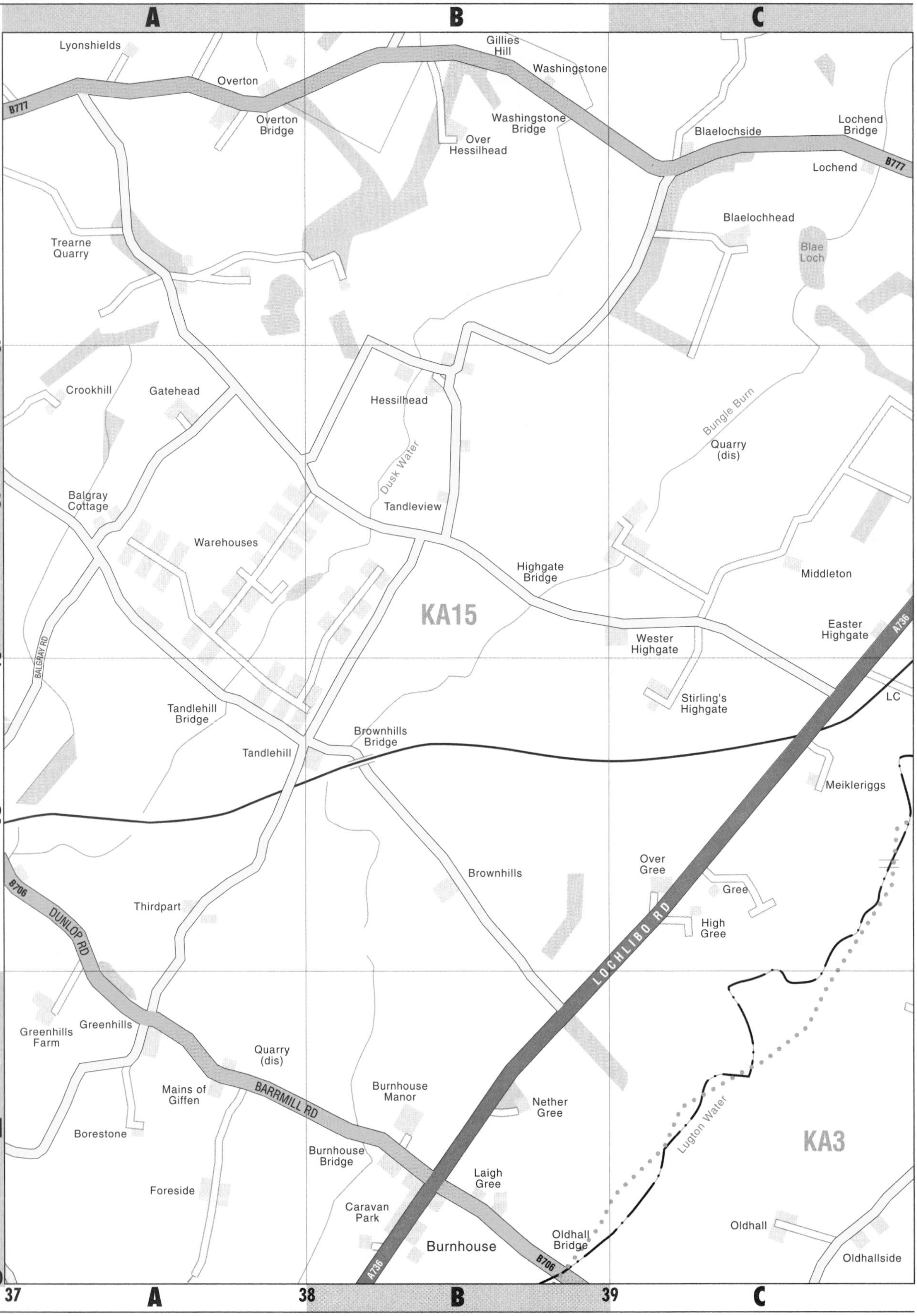

Stirling's Highgate

LC

Tandlehill

Brownhills Bridge

Meikleriggs

2

B706

DUNLOP RD

Thirdpart

Brownhills

Over Gree

Gree

LOCHLIBO RD

High Gree

51

Greenhills Farm

Greenhills

Quarry (dis)

Lugton Water

KA3

Mains of Giffen

BARRMILL RD

Burnhouse Manor

Nether Gree

Borestone

1

Burnhouse Bridge

Laigh Gree

Foreside

Caravan Park

Oldhall Bridge

Oldhall

A736

Burnhouse

B706

Oldhallside

50

37   A   38   B   39   C

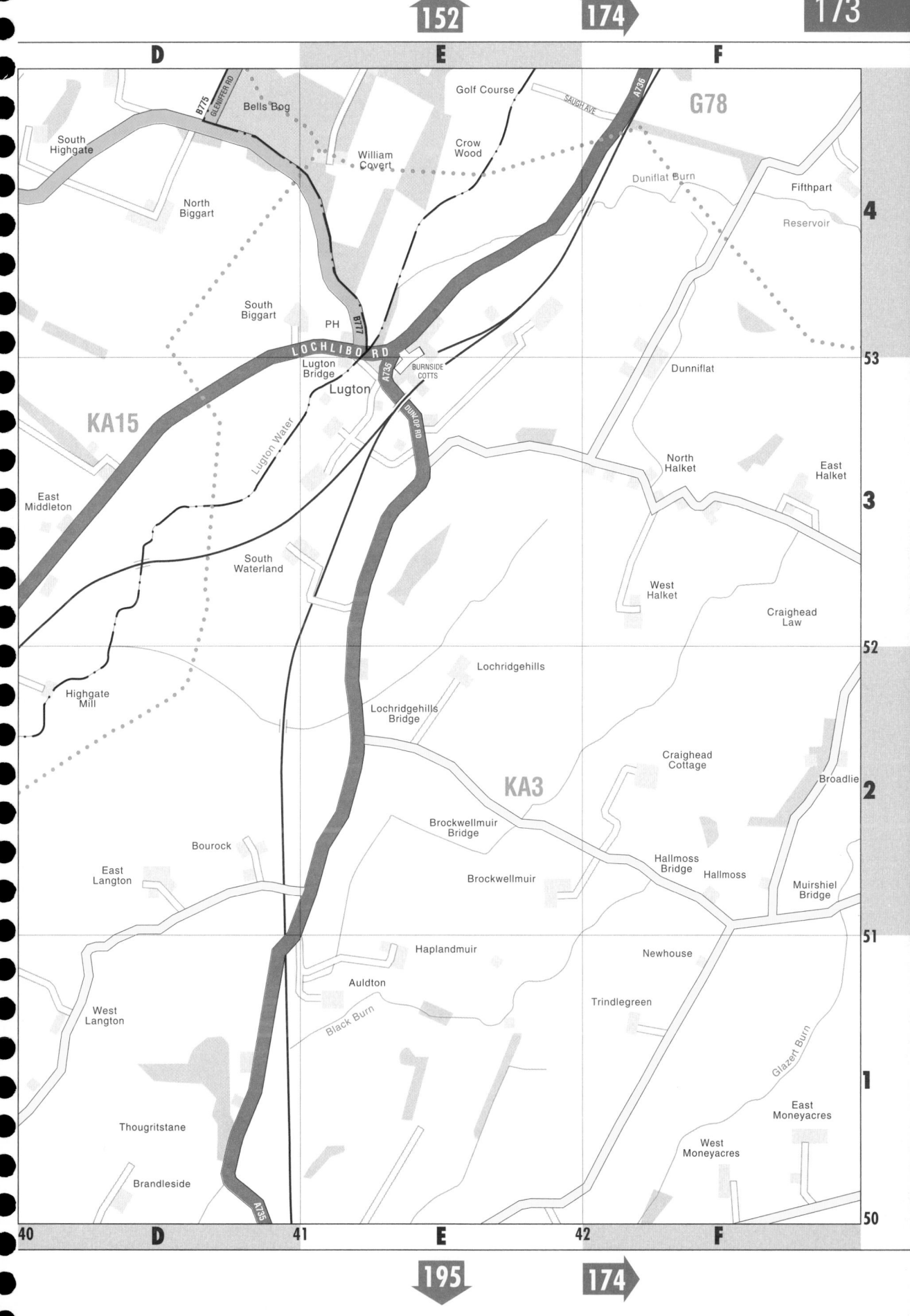

D
E
F

152

174

Golf Course
SAUGH AVE
A736
G78

B775
GLENIFFER RD
Bells Bog

South Highgate

William Covert

Crow Wood

Duniflat Burn

Fifthpart

North Biggart

Reservoir

4

South Biggart

PH

B777

LOCHLIBO RD

Dunniflat

53

Lugton Bridge

A735

BURNSIDE COTTS

Lugton

KA15

DUNLOP RD

North Halket

East Halket

Lugton Water

East Middleton

West Halket

3

South Waterland

Craighead Law

Highgate Mill

Lochridgehills

52

Lochridgehills Bridge

Craighead Cottage

Broadlie

KA3

2

Brockwellmuir Bridge

Hallmoss Bridge

Hallmoss

Muirshiel Bridge

Bourock

East Langton

Brockwellmuir

51

Haplandmuir

Newhouse

Auldton

Trindlegreen

West Langton

Black Burn

Glazert Burn

1

Thougritstane

West Moneyacres

East Moneyacres

Brandleside

A735

50

40
D
41
E
42
F

A　　　　　　　B　　　　　　　C

Linnhead

4

Knockmade
Plantation

Knockmade
Moss

Drumgrain
Plantation

Glebe
Knowe

G78

53

Crummies
Law

Long
Craigs

Dareduff
Hill

Townhead of
Grange

Glazert Burn

3

Fingart

Townend of
Grange

Mid Grange
Farm

Over
Carswell

West
Carswell

Hazelbank
Farm

52

Carswell
Bridge

Southgrange

KA3

Craignaught Quarry
(Whinstone)

2

Craignaught
Farm

East Muirshiel
Farm

Gabroc
Hill

Muirshiel

The
Totherick

51

Tailend

Clerkland Burn

Greensland

1

Newmill
House

Newmill
Bridge

Mill

50

Fullwood

Townend of
Fullwood

43　　　　　A　　　　　44　　　　　B　　　　　45　　　　　C

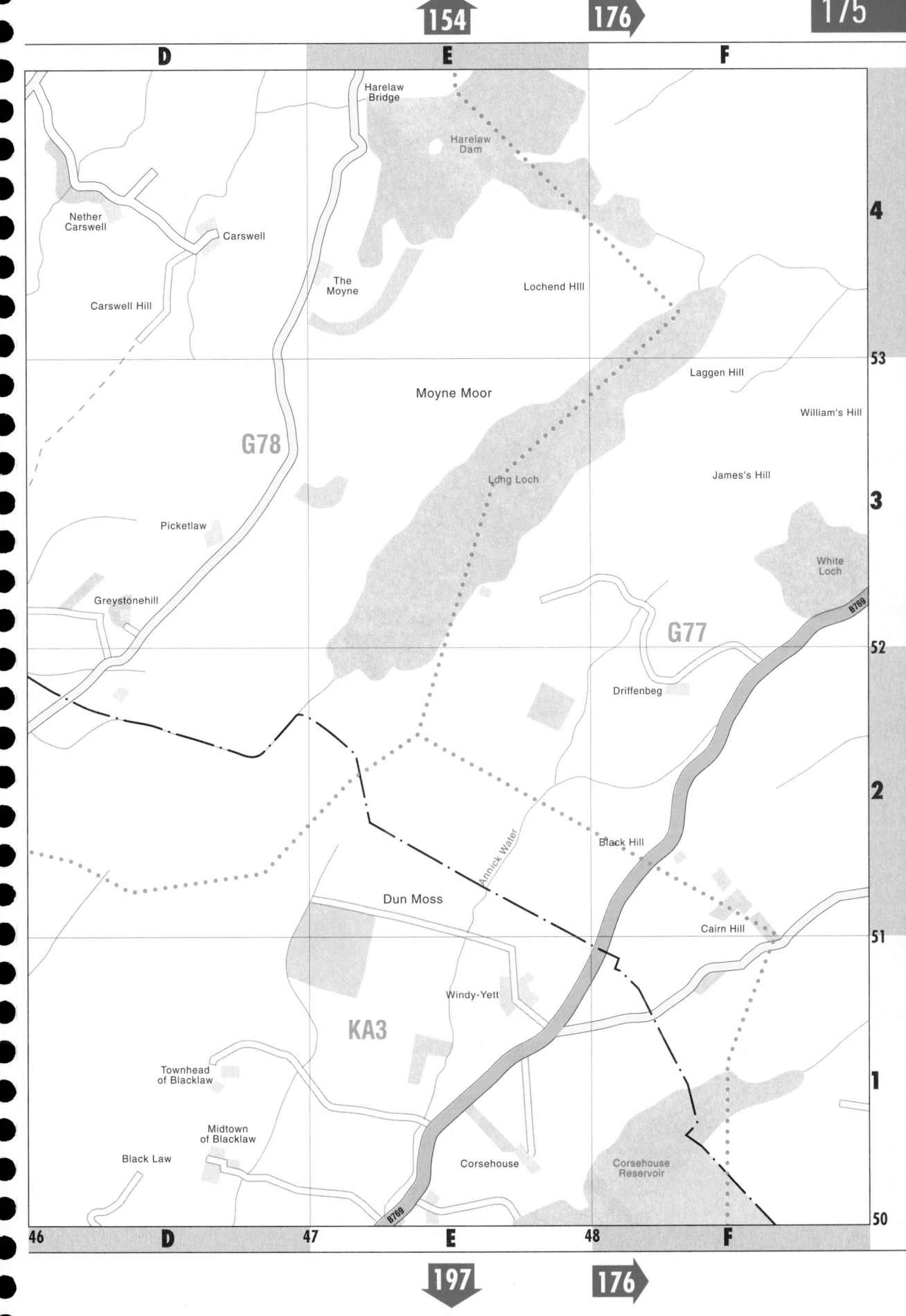

Harelaw Bridge

Harelaw Dam

Lochend Hill

Nether Carswell

Carswell

The Moyne

Carswell Hill

Moyne Moor

Laggen Hill

William's Hill

G78

James's Hill

Long Loch

Picketlaw

White Loch

Greystonehill

G77

Driffenbeg

B769

Annick Water

Black Hill

Dun Moss

Cairn Hill

KA3

Windy-Yett

Townhead of Blacklaw

Midtown of Blacklaw

Black Law

Corsehouse

Corsehouse Reservoir

B769

A | B | C

4

Reservoir (covered)

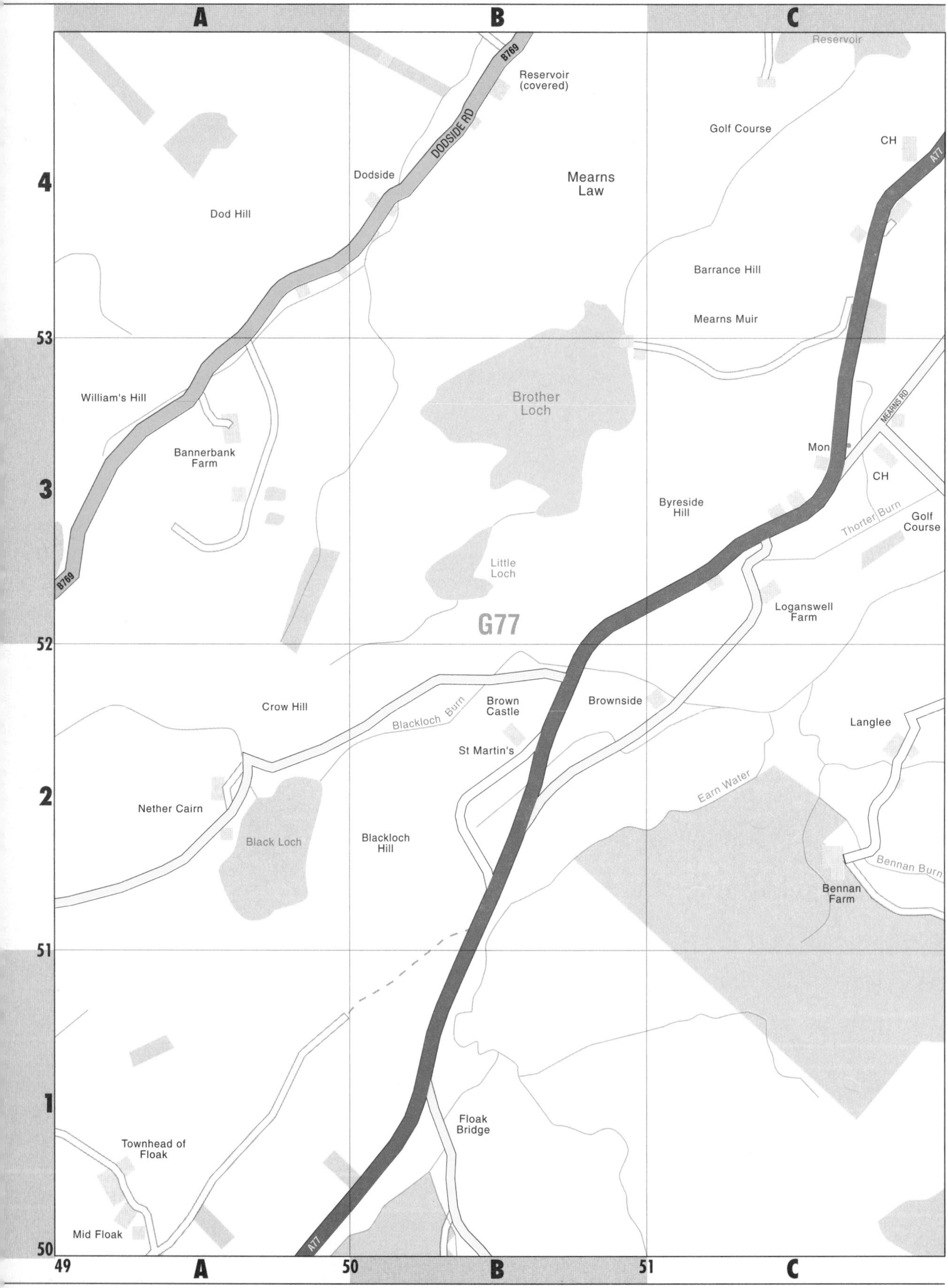

DODSIDE RD

B769

Dodside

Dod Hill

Mearns Law

Golf Course

CH

A77

Barrance Hill

Mearns Muir

53

William's Hill

Brother Loch

Mon

CH

MEARNS RD

3

Bannerbank Farm

Byreside Hill

Thorter Burn

Golf Course

Little Loch

Loganswell Farm

B769

G77

52

Crow Hill

Blackloch Burn

Brown Castle

Brownside

Langlee

St Martin's

Earn Water

2

Nether Cairn

Black Loch

Blackloch Hill

Bennan Burn

Bennan Farm

51

1

Townhead of Floak

Floak Bridge

A77

Mid Floak

50

49 | A | 50 | B | 51 | C

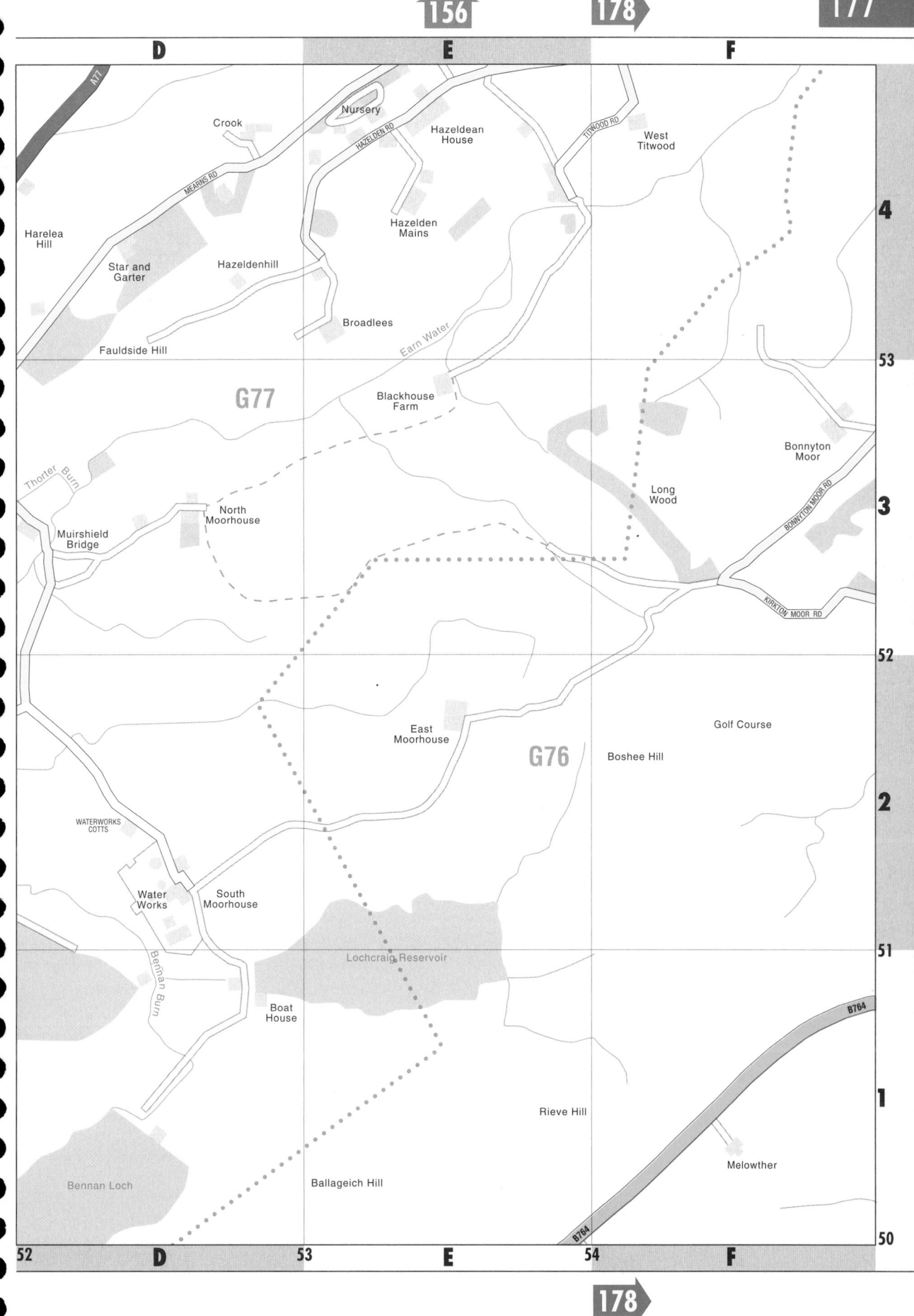
D
E
F
A77
Crook
Nursery
HAZELDEN RD
Hazeldean House
TITWOOD RD
West Titwood
MEARNS RD
Harelea Hill
Hazelden Mains
4
Star and Garter
Hazeldenhill
Broadlees
Earn Water
Fauldside Hill
53
G77
Blackhouse Farm
Bonnyton Moor
Thorter Burn
Long Wood
BONNYTON MOOR RD
3
Muirshield Bridge
North Moorhouse
KIRKTON MOOR RD
52
Golf Course
East Moorhouse
G76
Boshee Hill
2
WATERWORKS COTTS
Water Works
South Moorhouse
51
Lochcraig Reservoir
Bennan Burn
Boat House
B764
1
Rieve Hill
Melowther
Bennan Loch
Ballageich Hill
B764
50
52
D
53
E
54
F

177
157

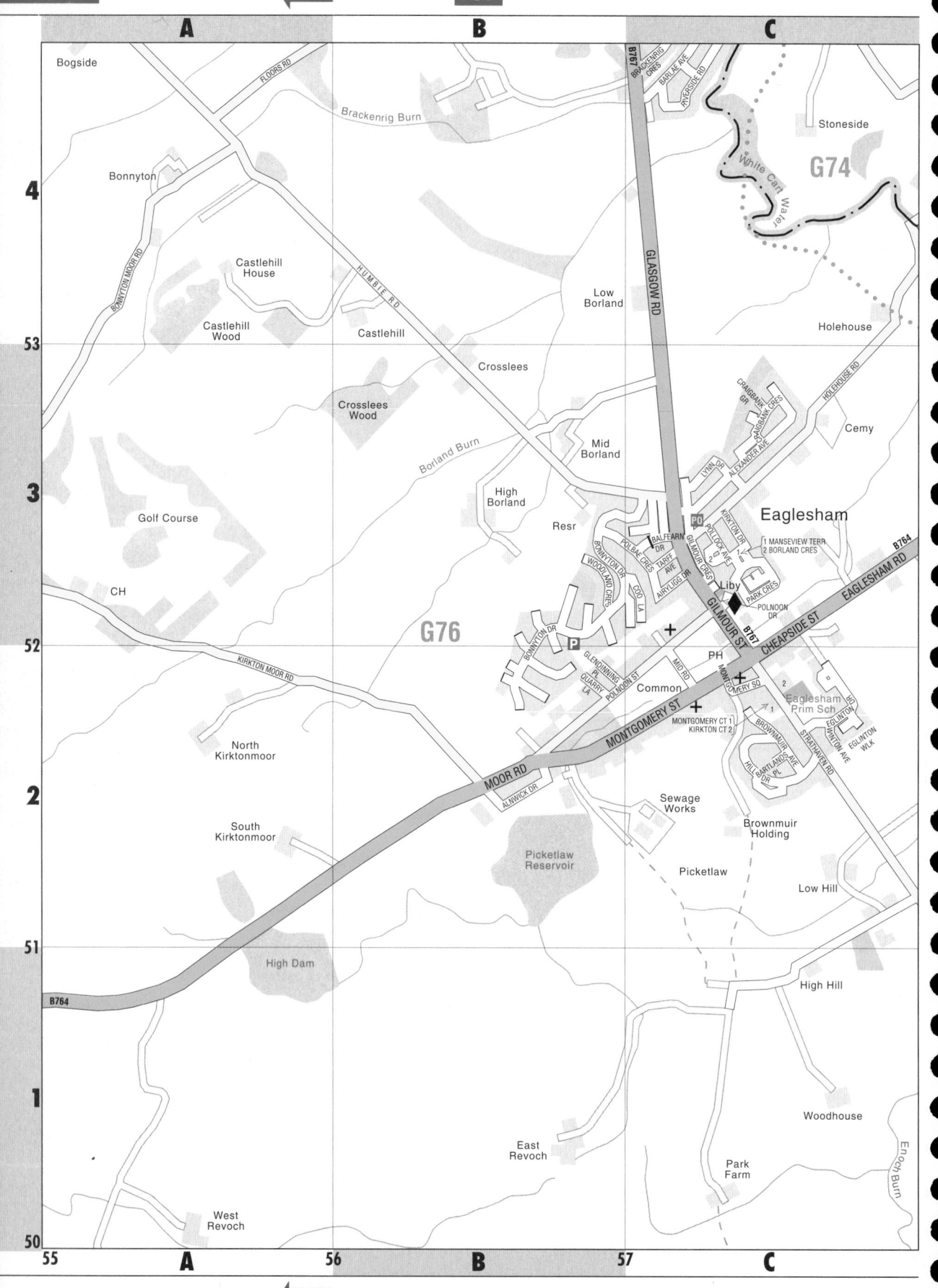
A
B
C
Bogside
FLOORS RD
Brackenrig Burn
B767
BRACKENRIG CRES
BARLAE AVE
RIVERSIDE RD
Stoneside
White Cart Water
G74
Bonnyton
4
BONNYTON MOOR RD
HUMBIE RD
Castlehill House
Castlehill Wood
Castlehill
Low Borland
GLASGOW RD
Holehouse
53
Crosslees
Crosslees Wood
CRAIGBANK GR
CRAIGBANK CRES
HOLEHOUSE RD
Cemy
Borland Burn
Mid Borland
ALEXANDER AVE
LYNN DR
3
High Borland
Golf Course
Resr
PO
Eaglesham
KIRKTON DR
1 MANSEVIEW TERR
2 BORLAND CRES
B764
EAGLESHAM RD
BALFEARN DR
POLBAE CRES
TARFF AVE
GILMOUR CRES
POLLOCK AVE
BONNYTON DR
WOODLAND CRES
WOODLAND DR
COO LA
AIRYLIGG DR
Liby
PARK CRES
POLNOON DR
CH
G76
GILMOUR ST
B767
CHEAPSIDE ST
BONNYTON DR
P
52
KIRKTON MOOR RD
GLENDINNING PL
QUARRY LA
POLNOON ST
MID RD
PH
MONTGOMERY SQ
Common
Eaglesham Prim Sch
EGLINTON DR
MONTGOMERY ST
MONTGOMERY CT 1
KIRKTON CT 2
BROWNMUIR AVE
STRATHAVEN RD
WINTON AVE
EGLINTON WLK
North Kirktonmoor
MOOR RD
HILL DR
BARTLANDS PL
2
ALNWICK DR
Sewage Works
South Kirktonmoor
Brownmuir Holding
Picketlaw Reservoir
Picketlaw
Low Hill
51
High Dam
High Hill
B764
1
Woodhouse
East Revoch
Park Farm
Enoch Burn
West Revoch
50
55
56
57

158
180

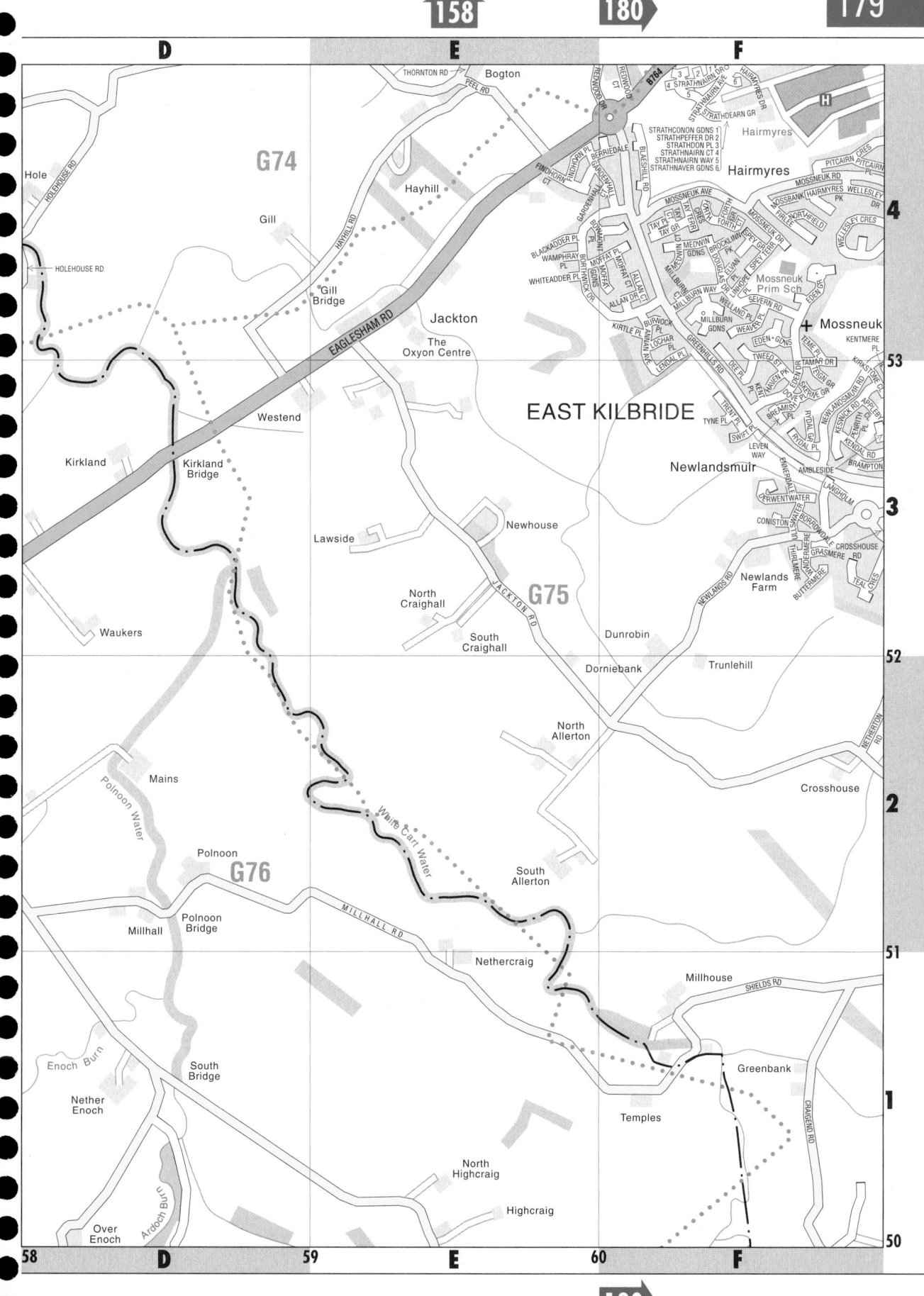
D
E
F
G74
G75
G76
EAST KILBRIDE
Bogton
Hairmyres
Hole
Hayhill
Gill
Gill
Bridge
Jackton
The
Oxyon Centre
Mossneuk
Mossneuk
Prim Sch
Westend
Kirkland
Kirkland
Bridge
Newlandsmuir
Newhouse
Lawside
North
Craighall
South
Craighall
Waukers
Dunrobin
Dorniebank
Trunlehill
Newlands
Farm
North
Allerton
Mains
Crosshouse
Polnoon
Polnoon Water
White Cart Water
South
Allerton
Millhall
Polnoon
Bridge
Nethercraig
Millhouse
Greenbank
Enoch Burn
South
Bridge
Nether
Enoch
Temples
North
Highcraig
Highcraig
Over
Enoch
Ardoch Burn
EAGLESHAM RD
MILLHALL RD
JACKTON RD
SHIELDS RD
HOLEHOUSE RD
HAYHILL RD
NEWLANDS RD
CRAIGEND RD
THORNTON RD
PEEL RD
B764
4
3
2
1
53
52
51
50
58
59
60

180

B4
1 ALBERTA CRES
2 BARKLY TERR
3 BUNBURY TERR
4 LETHBRIDGE PL
5 ALBERTA PL
6 CALGARY PL
7 MELBOURNE GN
8 SYDNEY PL
9 COOLGARDIE PL
10 COOLGARDIE GN
11 STEPHENSON PL
12 STEPHENSON SQ

C4
1 THE PLAZA
2 SOUTHGATE
3 THE OLYMPIA
4 OLYMPIA ARC
5 DENHOLM GN
6 SINCLAIR PK
7 MUIRHOUSE LA
8 HENRY BELL GN
9 FREELAND LA
10 TELFORD TERR
11 SYMINGTON SQ
12 TODHILLS
13 SHEILDHILL
14 SOMERVILLE LA
15 SOMERVILLE TERR
16 HEATHER GR
17 THE MURRAY SQ
18 CULLEN LA
19 STRATHCONA LA

Westwood

Canberra Prim Sch

Newlandsmuir

South Park Prim Sch

Greenhills

EAST KILBRIDE

The Murray

Nat Engineering Lab

Heathery Knowe Prim Sch

St Louise's RC Prim Sch

G75

Greenhills Prim Sch

St Andrew's RC High Sch

Whitehills

Playing Fields

Ind Est

Kittoch Water

GREENHILLS RD

Crosshouse Prim Sch

Liby

Ballerup High Sch

St Vincent's RC Prim Sch

Lindsayfield

1 MOORFOOT GDNS
2 GRAMPIAN DR
3 OCHIL CT
4 INVERCLOY CT
5 PIRNMILL AVE
6 MACHRIE GN
7 CORRIE GDNS
8 TORBEG GDNS
9 KILMORY CT
10 PENRIOCH DR
11 MERKLAND WAY
12 BENNAN PL

Lockhartshields

South Shields

Dykeneuk

Shieldbrae

Shieldburn

Bent Hall

Auldhouse Prim Sch

Crosshill

Golf Course

CH

Langlands

Golf Course

Ind Est

KELVIN SOUTH BSNS PK

Wr Twr

Auldhouse

Causeyhead

Burnhouse

Claddengreen

QUEENSWAY

A726

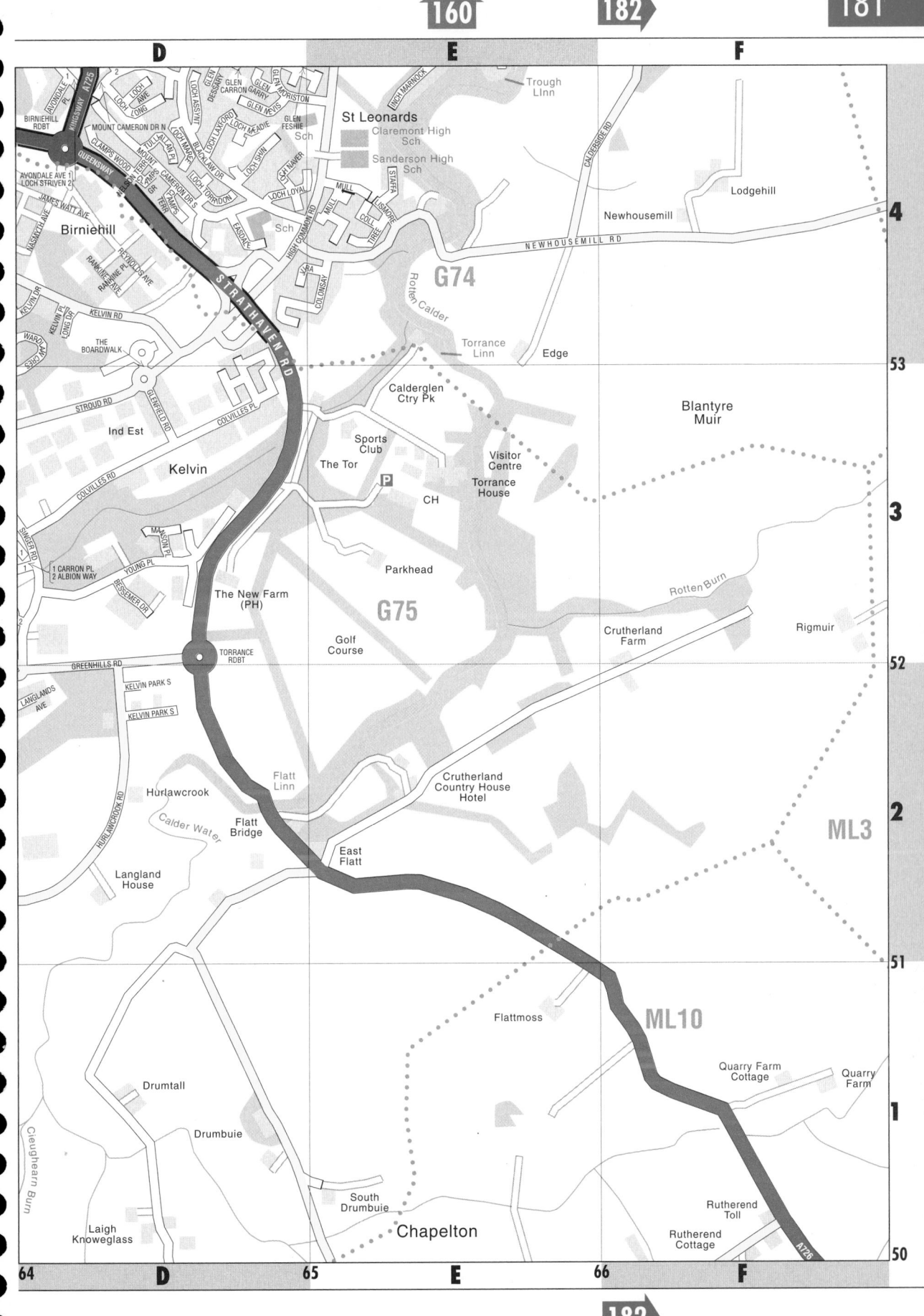

D   E   F

AVONDALE PL
A725
KINGSWAY
BIRNIEHILL RDBT
Birniehill
AVONDALE AVE 1
LOCH STRIVEN 2
JAMES WATT AVE
NASMYTH AVE
KELVIN DR
KELVIN PL
LONG CALY
WATT AVE
REYNOLDS AVE
RANKINE AVE
RANKINE AVE
THE BOARDWALK
STROUD RD
GLENFIELD RD
Ind Est
Kelvin
COLVILLES RD
COLVILLES RD
COLVILLES PL
SINGER RD
1 CARRON PL
2 ALBION WAY
MANSON PL
YOUNG PL
BESSEMER DR
The New Farm (PH)
GREENHILLS RD
TORRANCE RDBT
LANGLANDS AVE
KELVIN PARK S
KELVIN PARK S
HURLANCROOK RD
Hurlawcrook
Calder Water
Langland House
Drumtall
Drumbuie
Cieughearn Burn
Laigh Knoweglass
South Drumbuie
Chapelton

CLAMPS WOOD
MOUNT CAMERON DR N
MOUNT CAMERON DR S
CAMPS TERR
EASTALL
MOUNT
TULLALLAN PL
DESSERT
GLEN CARRON
GARRY
GLEN NEVIS
GLEN FESHIE
LOCH AWE
LOCH LONG
LOCH ASSYNT
LOCH MEADIE
GLEN MORISTON
BLANTYRE DR
LOCH LAXFORD
LOCH SUNN
HIGH COMMON RD
Sch
SRA
COLUMSAY
MULL
MULL
STAFFA
LISMORE
COLL
TIREE
LOCH LOYAL
St Leonards
Claremont High Sch
Sanderson High Sch

STRATHAVEN RD

Rotten Calder
Trough Linn
Torrance Linn
Edge
CALDERSIDE RD
Newhousemill
Lodgehill
NEWHOUSEMILL RD

G74

Calderglen Ctry Pk
Sports Club
The Tor
P
CH
Visitor Centre
Torrance House
Parkhead

G75

Golf Course

Blantyre Muir

Rotten Burn
Crutherland Farm
Rigmuir

Flatt Linn
Flatt Bridge
East Flatt
Crutherland Country House Hotel

ML3

Flattmoss

ML10

Quarry Farm Cottage
Quarry Farm

Rutherend Toll
Rutherend Cottage
A726

4
53
3
52
2
51
1
50

181
161

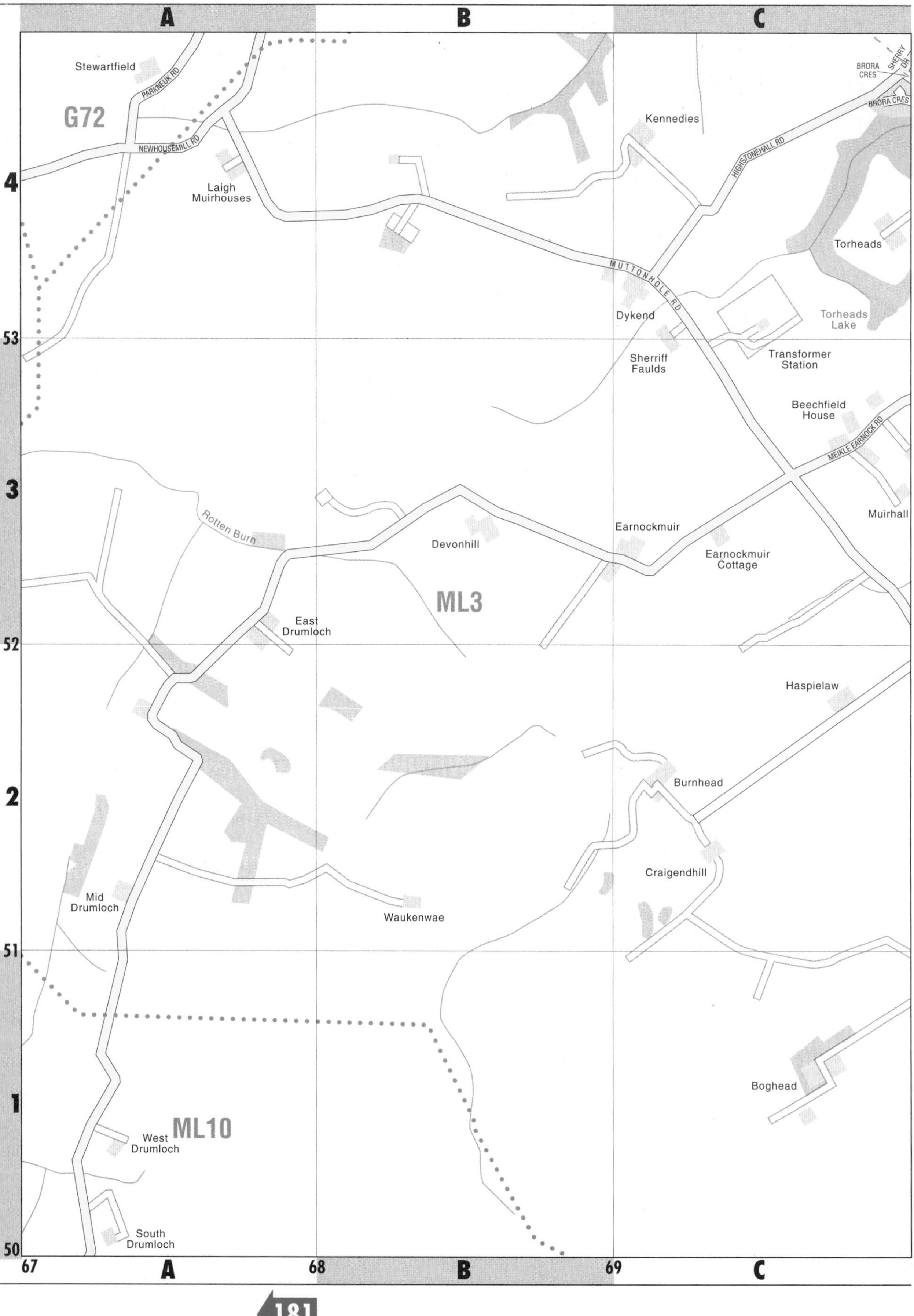

A   **B**   **C**

Stewartfield

PARKNEUK RD

G72

NEWHOUSEMILL RD

Laigh
Muirhouses

4

Kennedies

BRORA
CRES

SHERRY
DR

BRORA CRES

HIGHSTONEHALL RD

MUTTONHOLE RD

Torheads

Dykend

Torheads
Lake

53

Sherriff
Faulds

Transformer
Station

Beechfield
House

MEIKLE EARNOCK RD

3

Rotten Burn

Devonhill

Earnockmuir

Earnockmuir
Cottage

Muirhall

East
Drumloch

ML3

52

Haspielaw

Burnhead

Mid
Drumloch

Craigendhill

2

Waukenwae

51

Boghead

1

West
Drumloch

ML10

South
Drumloch

50

67   **A**   68   **B**   69   **C**

181

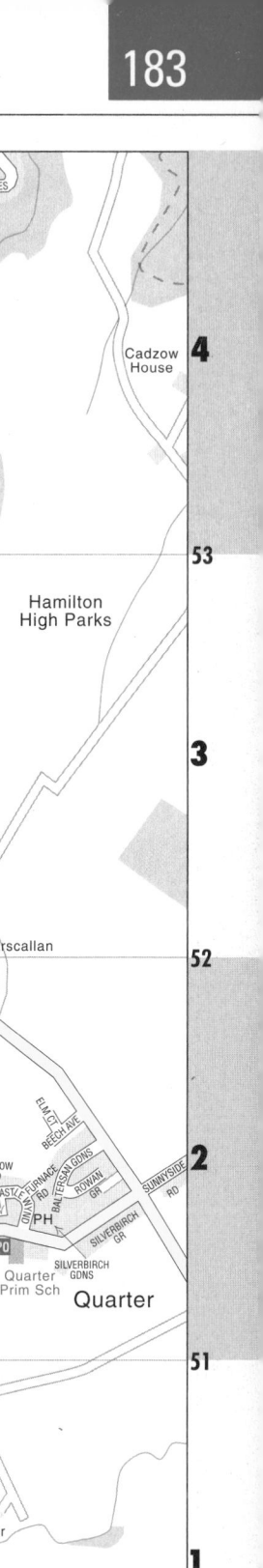

D | E | F

4

Neilsland Park
Woodhead Prim Sch
Woodhead Green
TARBERT CT
TAY GDNS
WEST DR
WELLBRAE RD
GLENDEVON PL
GLENSHEE TERR
GLENLYON CT
GLENCOE PL
BUCHAN ST
MILLGATE
LAUREL BANK
EDGEMONT PK
HOLLANDBUSH GR
ST RONAN'S
Cadzow
BRAESIDE GDNS
CHATELHERAULT CRES
AVONBRAE CRES
Cadzow House

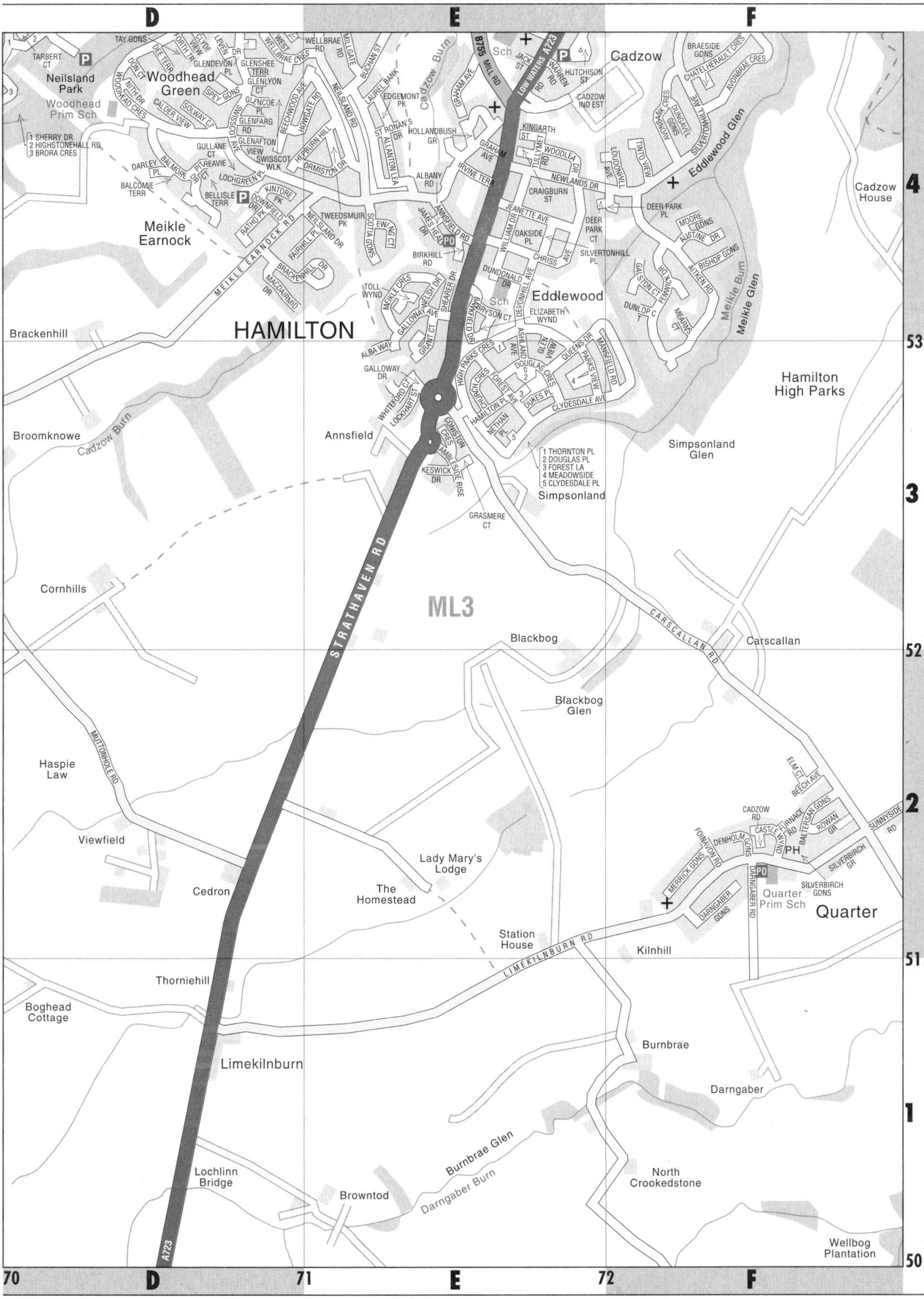

1 SHERRY DR
2 HIGHSTONEHALL RD
3 BRORA CRES

Meikle Earnock
DARLEY PL
BALMORE
GULLANE CT
BELLISLE TERR
RATHO PK
DOWNFIELD RD
KINTORE PK
KIRKREAVIE
LOCHGREEN
FAIRHILL PL

MEIKLE EARNOCK RD

HAMILTON

Brackenhill

53

Broomknowe
Cadzow Burn

Annsfield

Eddlewood
JEANETTE AVE
OAKSIDE PL
CHRISS AVE
DUNDONALD DR
ELIZABETH WYND
DEER PARK
SILVERTONHILL AVE

Hamilton High Parks

Simpsonland Glen

3

Cornhills

ML3

Blackbog

CARSCALLAN RD

Carscallan

52

Blackbog Glen

Haspie Law

MUTTONHOLE RD

2

Viewfield

Cedron

Lady Mary's Lodge

The Homestead

STRATHAVEN RD

CADZOW RD
DENHOLM GDNS
MERRICK GDNS
DARNGABER GDNS
Quarter Prim Sch
SILVERBIRCH GDNS
Quarter
SUNNYSIDE RD

Station House

Kilnhill

51

Thorniehill

Boghead Cottage

Burnbrae

Darngaber

1

Limekilnburn

Lochlinn Bridge

Browntod

Burnbrae Glen
Darngaber Burn

North Crookedstone

Wellbog Plantation

50

A723

183
163

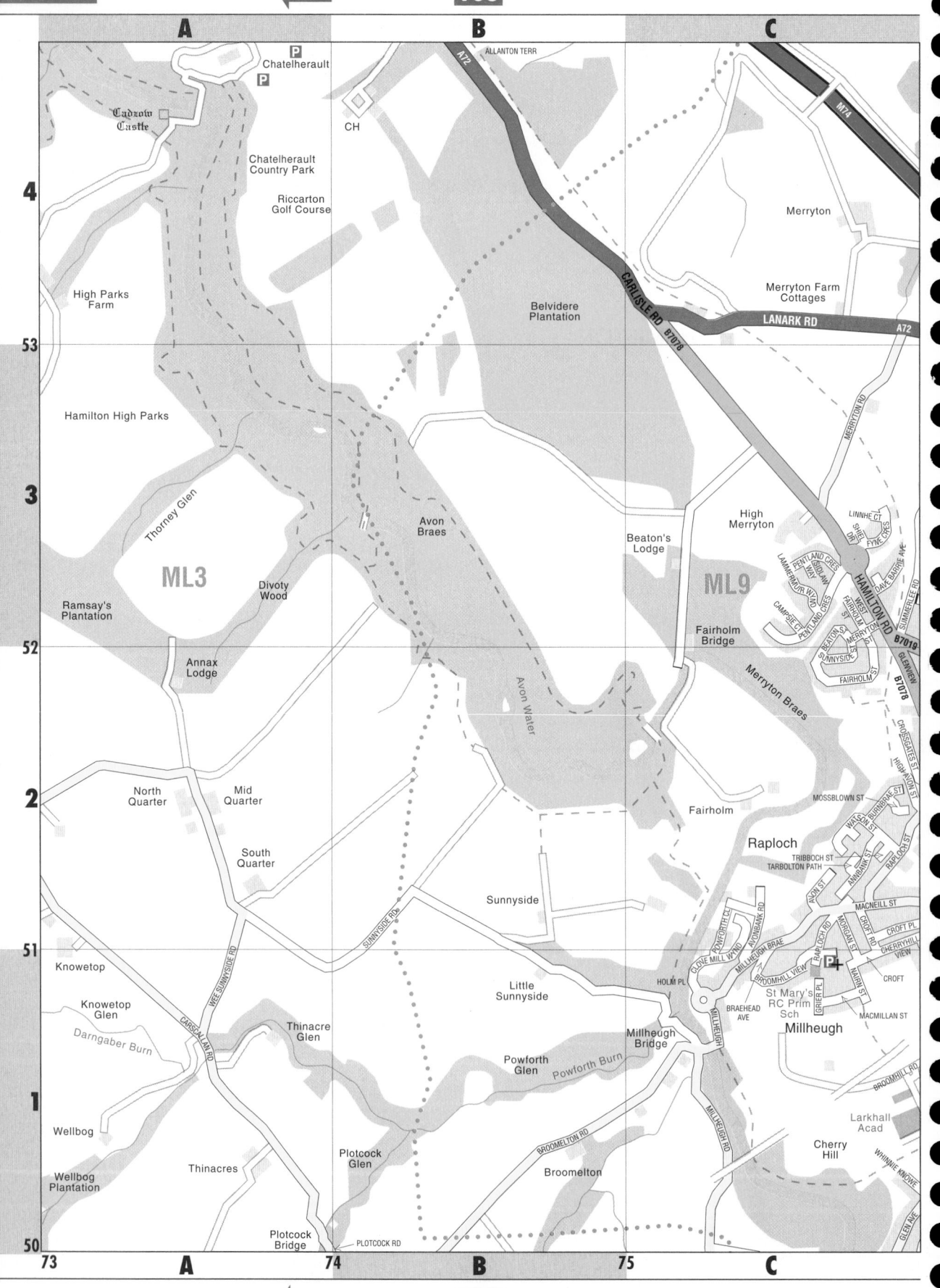
A
B
C
Chatelherault
Cadzow Castle
CH
ALLANTON TERR
A72
M74
Chatelherault Country Park
Riccarton Golf Course
Merryton
High Parks Farm
Merryton Farm Cottages
Belvidere Plantation
CARLISLE RD
LANARK RD
B7078
Hamilton High Parks
MERRYTON RD
Thorney Glen
Avon Braes
High Merryton
Beaton's Lodge
ML3
ML9
Divoty Wood
Ramsay's Plantation
HAMILTON RD
Fairholm Bridge
Annax Lodge
Avon Water
Merryton Braes
GLENVIEW
B7019
North Quarter
Mid Quarter
Fairholm
MOSSBLOWN ST
Raploch
South Quarter
TRIBBOCH ST
TARBOLTON PATH
Sunnyside
SUNNYSIDE RD
MACNEILL ST
Knowetop
Little Sunnyside
HOLM PL
CROFT
St Mary's RC Prim Sch
Knowetop Glen
WEE SUNNYSIDE RD
BRAEHEAD AVE
MACMILLAN ST
Millheugh
Darngaber Burn
CARSCALLAN RD
Thinacre Glen
Millheugh Bridge
Powforth Glen
Powforth Burn
MILLHEUGH
Larkhall Acad
Wellbog
Plotcock Glen
BROOMELTON RD
MILLHEUGH RD
Cherry Hill
WHINNIE KNOWE
Wellbog Plantation
Thinacres
Broomelton
GLEN AVE
Plotcock Bridge
PLOTCOCK RD
4
53
3
52
2
51
1
50
73
74
75

183
198

164
186

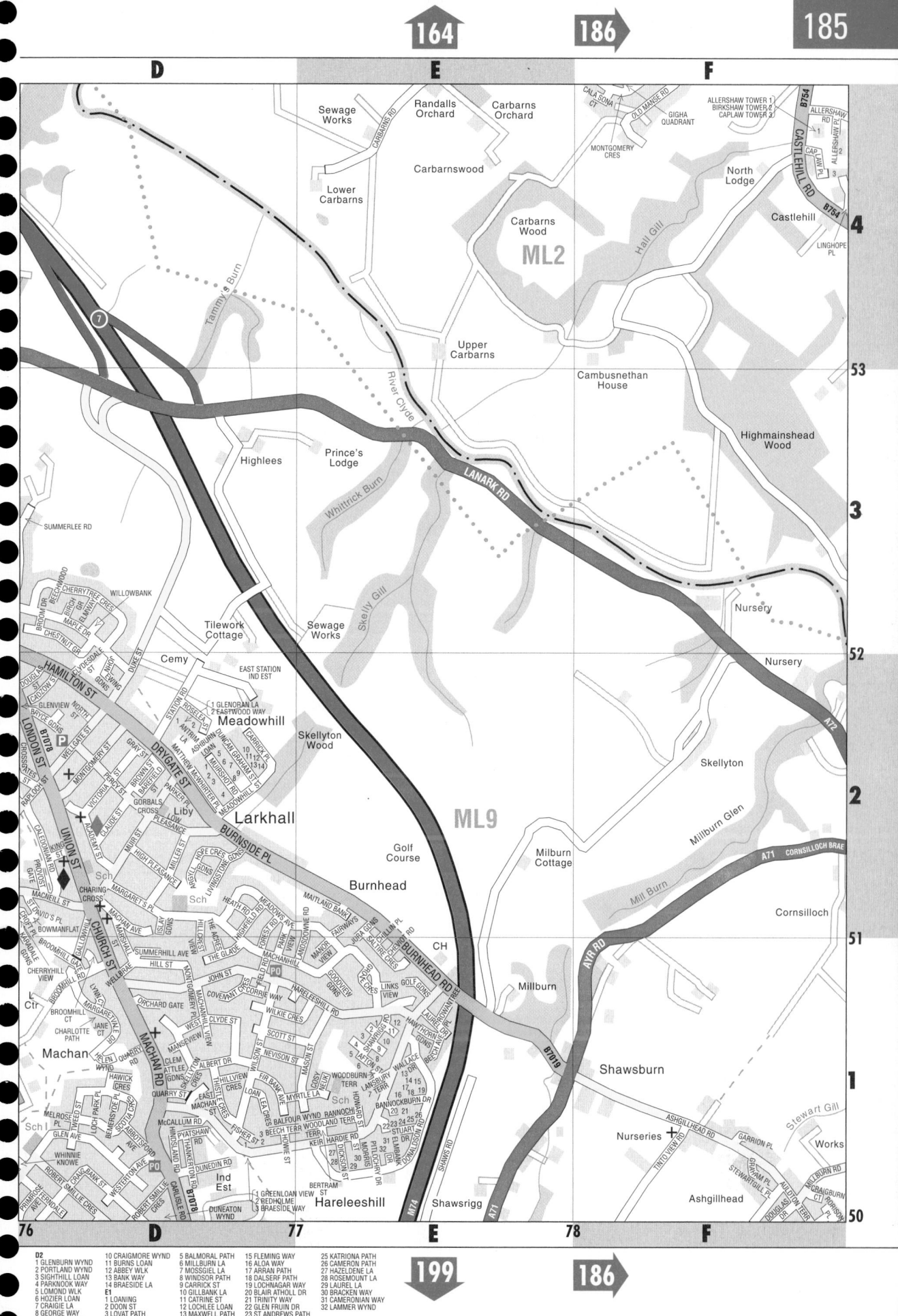

D2
1 GLENBURN WYND
2 PORTLAND WYND
3 SIGHTHILL LOAN
4 PARKNOOK WAY
5 LOMOND WLK
6 HOZIER LOAN
7 CRAIGIE LA
8 GEORGE WAY
9 ALBANY WYND
10 CRAIGMORE WYND
11 BURNS LOAN
12 ABBEY WLK
13 BANK WAY
14 BRAESIDE LA

E1
1 LOANING
2 DOON ST
3 LOVAT PATH
4 ALLOWAY ST
5 BALMORAL PATH
6 MILLBURN LA
7 MOSSGIEL LA
8 WINDSOR PATH
9 CARRICK ST
10 GILLBANK LA
11 CATRINE ST
12 LOCHLEE LOAN
13 MAXWELL PATH
14 BRUCE'S LOAN
15 FLEMING WAY
16 ALOA WAY
17 ARRAN PATH
18 DALSERF PATH
19 LOCHNAGAR WAY
20 BLAIR ATHOLL DR
21 TRINITY WAY
22 GLEN FRUIN DR
23 ST ANDREWS PATH
24 LAWRIE WAY
25 KATRIONA PATH
26 CAMERON PATH
27 HAZELDENE LA
28 ROSEMOUNT LA
29 LAUREL LA
30 BRACKEN WAY
31 CAMERONIAN WAY
32 LAMMER WYND

199
186

A   **B**   **C**

ALLERSHAW RD
LINNHE CRES
ETIVE CRES
NESS ST
HOSPITAL
RANNOCH DR
A721
WELLINGTON PL
A71

Gowkthrapple

BIRKSHAW PL
BIRKSHAW BRAE
GARRION BSNS PK

Waterloo

OVERTOWN RD
WISHAW RD
A721
Gillhead

LINGHOPE PL
Castlehill Prim Sch
SMITH AVE
STANHOPE PL
HEATHFIELD

DIMSDALE RD

Pather Farm

4   B754

CASTLEHILL RD

Clyde Valley High Sch

3 SMITHVIEW
4 GLIDDEN CT
5 GILFILLAN PL
6 McNEIL PL

Overtown Prim Sch

ASH GR 1
HAZEL GR 2
HAWTHORN GR 3
CEDAR GDNS 4
MAULDSLIE DR 5
WOODLANDS AVE 6
ASHHILL

McINNES PL 1
TONER GDNS 2
JESSIE LEE DR
PRIORY GATE
BAILLIE PYFE WAY
KENNEDY GDNS

ASHLEY
COWAN WYN
QUIGLAS ST
HUTCHINSON

BEECH GR
HAZEL GR
HAWTHORN GR

53

BROOKLYN
ROWS RD
ORCHARD ST
BELMONT ST
GREENKNOWE ST

B754

MAIN ST
LISHALY
HOCK
BISHOP'S LADDER
GILL RD
GILL RD
LAW VIEW

1 RHU QUAD
2 BRUCE LOAN

CANFIELD CRES
GREENKNOWE DR
MUIR ST
LAWMUIR RD

Wemysshill

PH
COVENANTERS WAY

GOURLAY DR
OVENDALE PL
GILLBURN ST
CLARION ST

Overtown

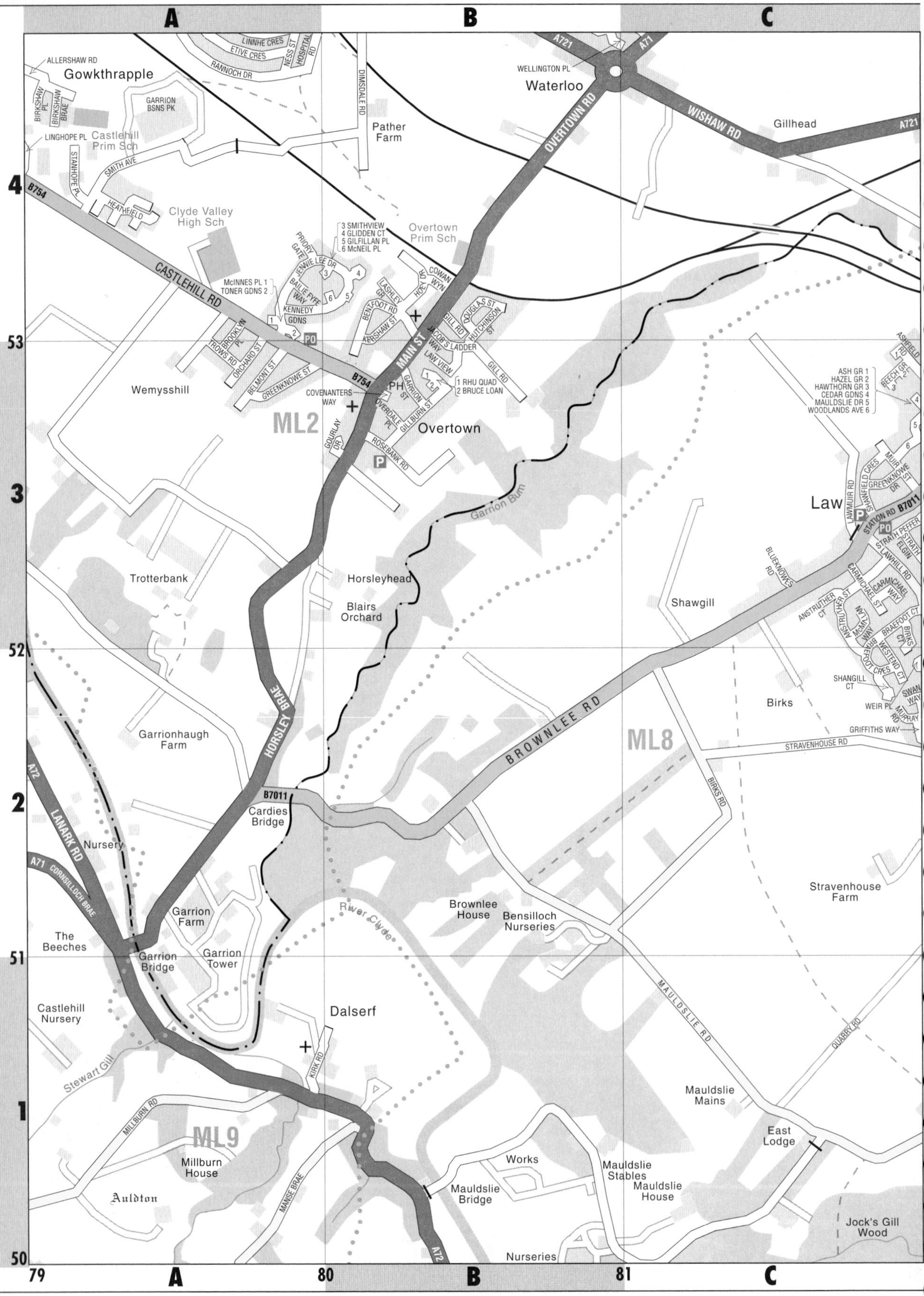

HANFIELD CRES
STATION RD
B7011

Law
P

ML2

P
ROSEBANK RD

Garrion Burn

BLUEKNOWES RD
STRATH PEFFER
STRATH PSTRITH
ELGIN
CARMICHAEL WAY
CANFIELD CT

3

Trotterbank

Horsleyhead

Shawgill

ANSTRUTHER ST
ANSTRUTHER CT
CATHCART ST
CARMICHAEL WAY
MAW
BRAEFOOT CT
BIRKS
WESTEND CT
BRAEFOOT CRES

Blairs Orchard

52

A72

HORSLEY BRAE

Birks

SHANGILL CT
WEIR PL
SWAN WAY
MURRAY
GRIFFITHS WAY

Garrionhaugh Farm

BROWNLEE RD

ML8

STRAVENHOUSE RD

A72
LANARK RD
A71
CORNSILLOCH BRAE

2

Nursery

B7011
Cardies Bridge

BIRKS RD
MAULDSLIE RD

Stravenhouse Farm

The Beeches

Garrion Farm

River Clyde

Brownlee House

Bensilloch Nurseries

51

Castlehill Nursery

Garrion Bridge
Garrion Tower

Dalserf

KIRK RD

MAULDSLIE RD

Mauldslie Mains

QUARRY RD

East Lodge

Stewart Gill

+

1

MILLBURN RD

ML9

Millburn House

MANSE BRAE

Works

Mauldslie Stables
Mauldslie House

Jock's Gill Wood

Auldton

Mauldslie Bridge

A72

Nurseries

50

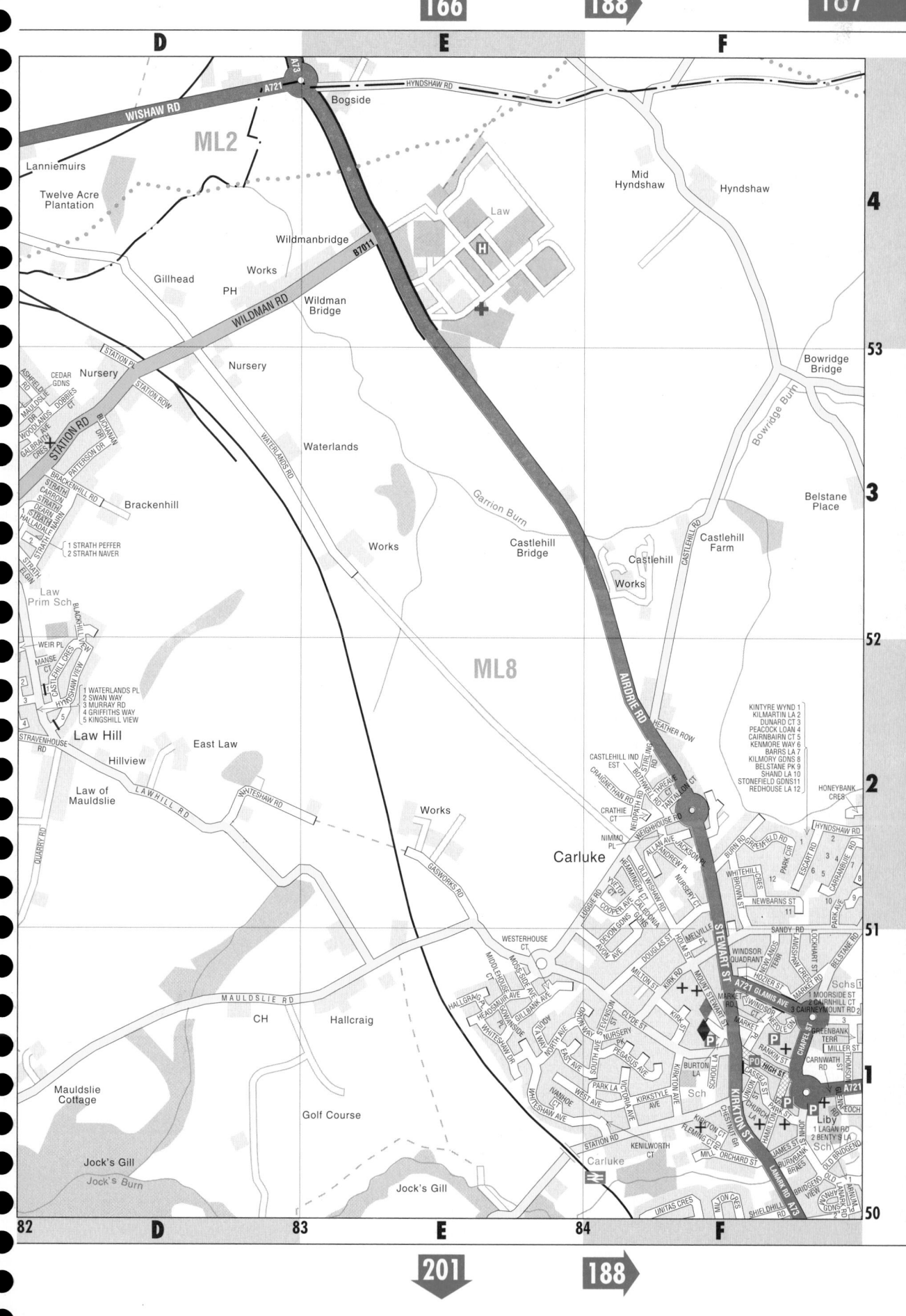

D
E
F

WISHAW RD
A721
Bogside
HYNDSHAW RD
Hyndshaw
ML2
Mid Hyndshaw
Hyndshaw
Lanniemuirs
4
Twelve Acre Plantation
Wildmanbridge
Law
H
Works
Gillhead
Wildman Bridge
PH
WILDMAN RD
B7011
Bowridge Bridge
53
STATION PL
Nursery
Nursery
CEDAR GDNS
STATION ROW
Bowridge Burn
ASHIESLIE DR
WOODLANDS AVE
DOBBIE'S
BUCHANAN
MAULDSLIE
GALBRAITH CRES
STATION RD
PATERSON DR
WATERLANDS RD
Waterlands
Belstane Place
3
STRATH BRAN RD
STRATH CARRON
STRATH EARN
Brackenhill
STRATH HALLADALE
Castlehill RD
Castlehill Farm
1 STRATH PEFFER
2 STRATH NAVER
Garrion Burn
STRATH ELGIN
Works
Castlehill Bridge
Castlehill Works
Law Prim Sch
52
1 WATERLANDS PL
2 SWAN WAY
3 MURRAY RD
4 GRIFFITHS WAY
5 KINGSHILL VIEW
WEIR PL
MANSE
CASTLEHILL CRES
BLACKHILL VIEW
HYNDSHAW VIEW
ML8
KINTYRE WYND 1
KILMARTIN LA 2
DUNARD CT 3
PEACOCK LOAN 4
CAIRNBAIRN CT 5
KENMORE WAY 6
BARRS LA 7
KILMORY GDNS 8
BELSTANE PK 9
SHAND LA 10
STONEFIELD GDNS 11
REDHOUSE LA 12
Law Hill
STRAVENHOUSE RD
AIRDRIE RD
HEATHER ROW
HONEYBANK CRES
2
Hillview
LAWHILL RD
East Law
CASTLEHILL IND EST
HYNDSHAW RD
Law of Mauldslie
WHITESHAW RD
CRAIGNETHAN RD
CRATHIE CT
CRAIGIE CT
TANTALLON CT
WHITEHILL
BURN RD
BREMVIELD RD
PARK CIR
ESCART RD
CAIRNGRUE RD
PARK AVE
QUARRY RD
Works
GASWORKS RD
NIMMO PL
NEIDPATH RD
BOTHWELL RD
STIRLING CT
WEIGHHOUSE RD
ALLAN AVE
JACKSON RD
HENNING AVE
OLD WOOD RD
NURSERY CT
BROWN'S
NEWBARNS ST
PARK AVE
Carluke
WESTERHOUSE CT
MIDDLEHOUSE CT
MOSS SIDE AVE
HEADSMUIR AVE
COWANSIDE AVE
GILLBANK AVE
WHITESHAW DR
LOGIE CT
COOPER'S AVE
DEVON GDNS
GLEN AVE
DOUGLAS ST
MELVILLE LCT
MILTON ST
STEWART ST
A721 GLAMIS AVE
WINDSOR QUADRANT
SANDY RD
LANGSHAW CRES
LOCKHART RD
BELSTANE RD
51
Schs
1 MOORSIDE ST
2 CARNHILL CT
3 CAIRNEYMOUNT RD
GREENBANK TERR
MILLER ST
MAULDSLIE RD
CH
Hallcraig
HALLGRAIG
STEVENSON ST
CLYDE ST
KIRK RD
NORTH AVE
SPEY WAY
NURSERY
EAST AVE
AVON AVE
SOUTH AVE
PEGASUS AVE
KIRKSTYLE AVE
MARKET PL
MOUNT STEWART ST
WINDSOR ST
MARKET
RANKIN ST
CHAPEL ST
CARNWATH RD
THOMSON ST
HIGH ST
P
1
Mauldslie Cottage
NAMHOE LCT
WEST AVE
PARK LA
VICTORIA AVE
KIRKSTYLE LA
BURTON LA
Sch
CASSELS ST
CHURCH ST
KIRKTON GR
KIRKTON LA
FLEMING CT
KIRTON ST
PARK ST
JAMES ST
Liby
1 LAGAN RD
2 BENTY'S LA
MILL RD
ORCHARD ST
LANARK RD
BURNBANK BRAES
OLD BRIDGEND
Golf Course
KENILWORTH CT
STATION RD
Carluke
Jock's Gill
Jock's Burn
Jock's Gill
UNITAS CRES
MILTON CRES
SHIELDHILL
A73
SHAND LA
50

82
D
83
E
84
F

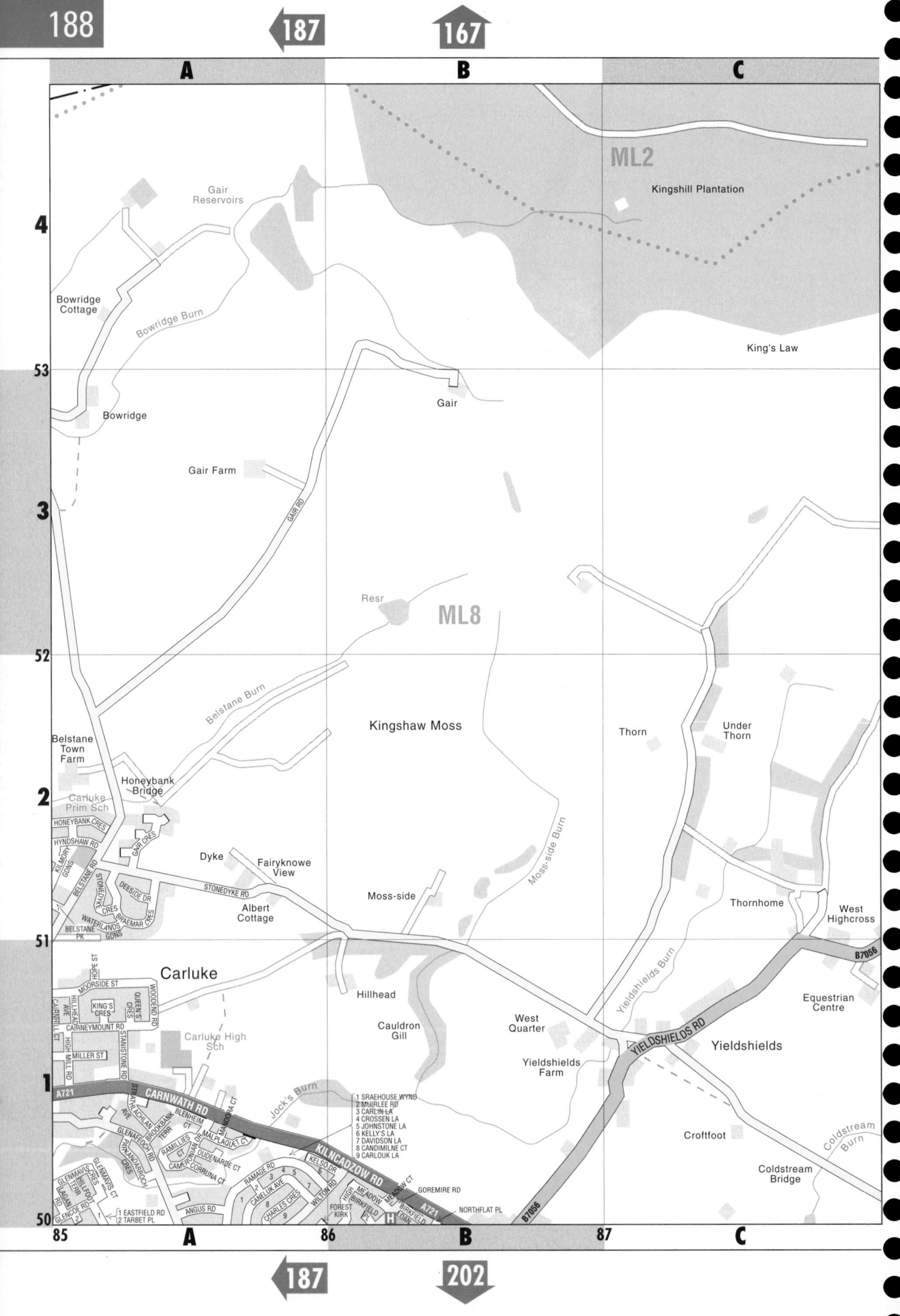

A   B   C

ML2

Kingshill Plantation

King's Law

4

Gair Reservoirs

Bowridge Cottage

Bowridge Burn

53

Bowridge

Gair

Gair Farm

GAIR RD

3

Resr

ML8

52

Belstane Burn

Kingshaw Moss

Thorn

Under Thorn

Belstane Town Farm

Honeybank Bridge

Carluke Prim Sch

HONEYBANK CRES

HYNDSHAW RD

GAIR CRES

Dyke

Fairyknowe View

Moss-side Burn

2

KILMORY GDNS

BELSTANE RD

STONEDYKE CRES

DEESIDE DR

BRAEMAR CRES

STONEDYKE RD

Moss-side

Thornhome

West Highcross

WATERLANDS GDNS

BELSTANE PK

Albert Cottage

51

Hillhead

Yieldshields Burn

YIELDSHIELDS RD

B7056

Equestrian Centre

Carluke

MOORSIDE ST

KING'S CRES

QUEEN'S CRES

WOODEND RD

CAIRNEYMOUNT RD

STANISTONE RD

Carluke High Sch

Cauldron Gill

West Quarter

Yieldshields

HILLHEAD AVE

HIGH MILL RD

MILLER ST

Yieldshields Farm

Croftfoot

Coldstream Burn

1

A721

CARNWATH RD

Jock's Burn

1 SRAEHOUSE WYND
2 MUIRLEE RD
3 CARLIN LA
4 CROSSEN LA
5 JOHNSTONE LA
6 KELLY'S LA
7 DAVIDSON LA
8 CANDIMILNE CT
9 CARLOUK LA

Coldstream Bridge

STRATHACHLAM BROOKBANK BLENHEIM TERR

GLENAFEOCH RD

RAMILLIES CT

OUDENARDE CT

MALPLAQUET CT

CORRUNA CT

KILNCADZOW RD

RAMAGE RD

KELSO DR

WILTON RD

GOREMIRE RD

A721

B7056

NORTHFLAT PL

GLENMAVIS CRES

GLANNARIS CT

HILLFOOT

LOGAN

GLENCOE RD

1 EASTFIELD RD
2 TARBET PL

ANGUS RD

CHARLES CRES

CAMELUK AVE

FOREST KIRK

MEADOW

HIGH MEADOW CT

BIRKFIELD

50

85   A   86   B   87   C

168

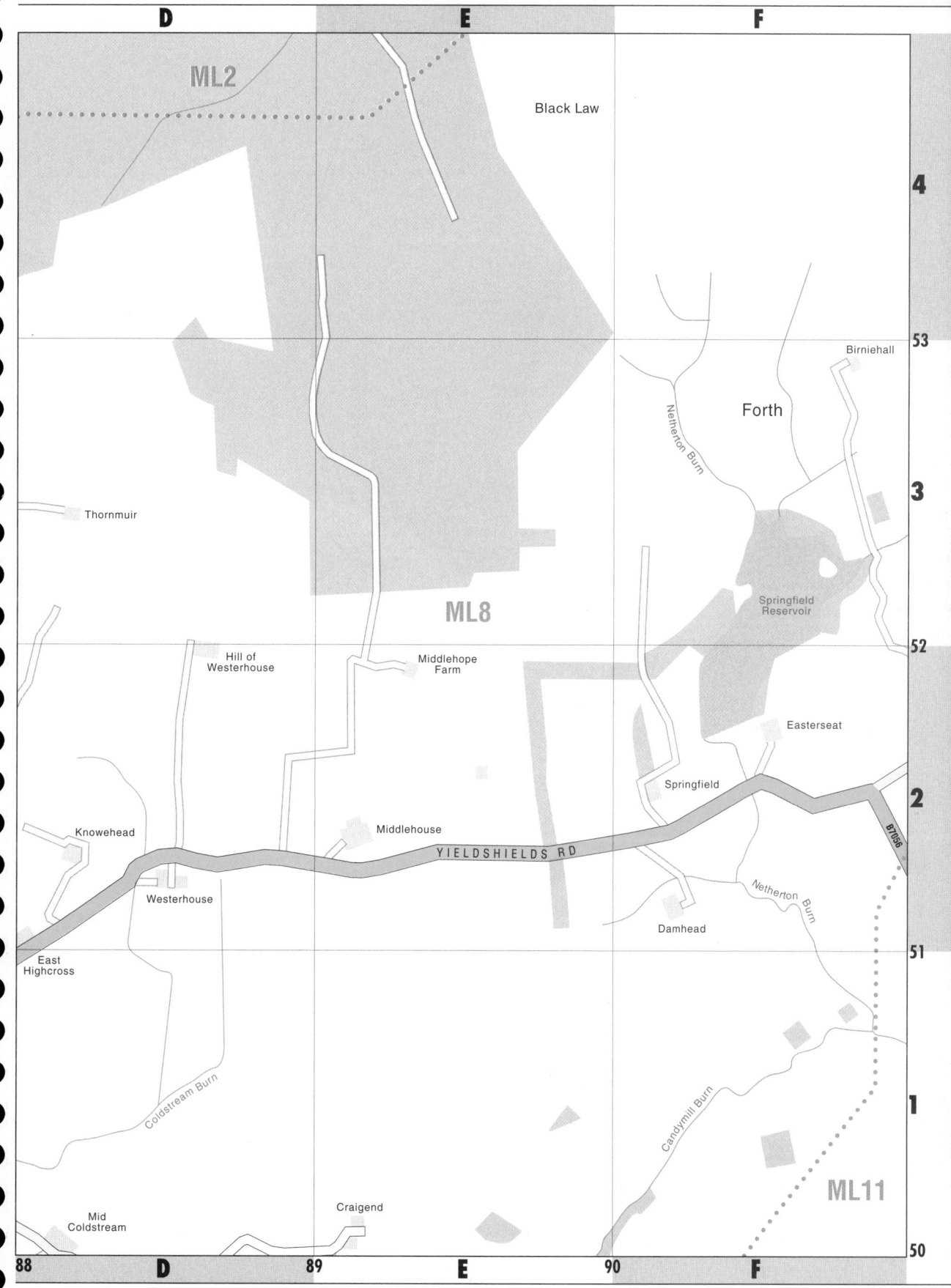

D
E
F
ML2
Black Law
4
53
Birniehall
Forth
Netherton Burn
3
Thornmuir
Springfield Reservoir
ML8
52
Hill of Westerhouse
Middlehope Farm
Easterseat
Springfield
2
Knowehead
Middlehouse
YIELDSHIELDS RD
B7056
Westerhouse
Netherton Burn
Damhead
East Highcross
51
1
Coldstream Burn
Candymill Burn
ML11
Mid Coldstream
Craigend
50
88
D
89
E
90
F

203

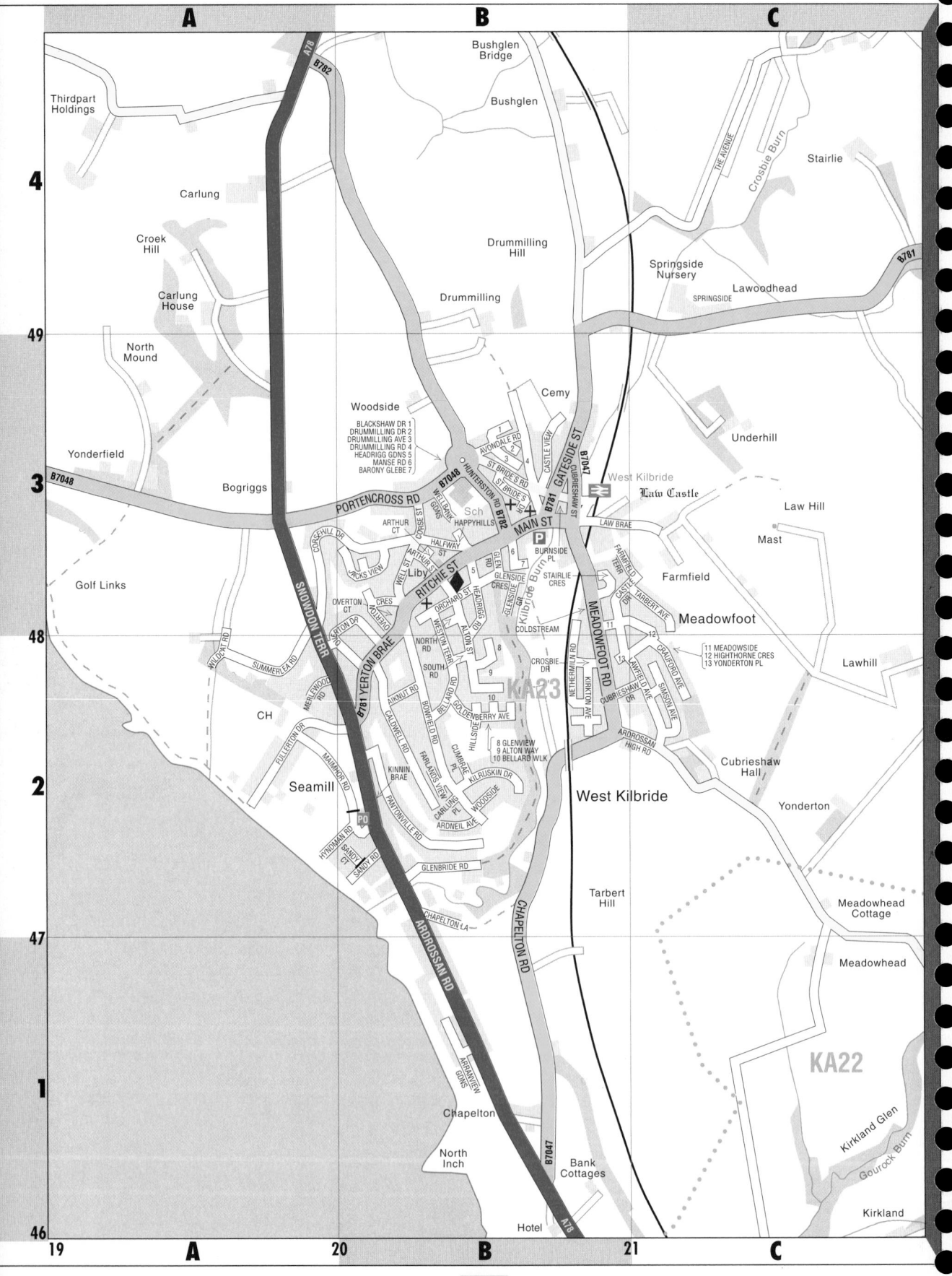

A
B
C
Bushglen Bridge
Bushglen
Thirdpart Holdings
Carlung
Croek Hill
Carlung House
North Mound
Drummilling Hill
Drummilling
Springside Nursery
Lawoodhead
SPRINGSIDE
Stairlie
Crosbie Burn
THE AVENUE
B781
B782
A78
Woodside
Cemy
Underhill
Yonderfield
Bogriggs
B7048
PORTENCROSS RD
West Kilbride
Law Castle
Law Hill
Mast
Golf Links
Farmfield
Meadowfoot
BLACKSHAW DR 1
DRUMMILLING DR 2
DRUMMILLING AVE 3
DRUMMILLING RD 4
HEADRIGG GDNS 5
MANSE RD 6
BARONY GLEBE 7
AVONDALE RD
CASTLE VIEW
GATESIDE ST
B7047
CUBRIESHAW ST
HUNTERSTON RD
ST BRIDE'S RD
Sch
HAPPYHILLS
MAIN ST
RITCHIE ST
LAW BRAE
BURNSIDE PL
STAIRLIE CRES
COLDSTREAM
Kilbride Burn
MEADOWFOOT RD
FARMFIELD TERR
CASTLE DR
TARBERT AVE
11 MEADOWSIDE
12 HIGHTHORNE CRES
13 YONDERTON PL
CRAUFORD AVE
Lawhill
SNOWDON TERR
Liby
ARTHUR CT
CORSEHILL DR
JACKS VIEW
WELL ST
ARTHUR ST
HALFWAY ST
OVERTON CT
OVERTON CRES
B781 YERTON BRAE
ORCHARD ST
HEADRIGG RD
ALTON ST
WESTON TERR
NORTH RD
SOUTH RD
GLENSIDE CRES
GLENSIDE GR
CROSBIE DR
NETHERMILN RD
KIRKTON AVE
CUBRIESHAW DR
LAWFIELD AVE
SIMSON AVE
KA23
WILDCAT RD
SUMMERLEA RD
MERLEWOOD RD
CH
AIKNUT RD
BOWFIELD RD
BELLARD RD
GOLDENBERRY AVE
HILLSIDE
8 GLENVIEW
9 ALTON WAY
10 BELLARD WLK
ARDROSSAN HIGH RD
Cubrieshaw Hall
FULLERTON DR
MAIMHOR RD
Seamill
CALDWELL RD
KINNIN BRAE
FARLANDS VIEW
CUMBRAE PL
KILRUSKIN DR
West Kilbride
Yonderton
PO
HYNDMAN RD
SANDY CT
SANDY RD
PANTONVILLE RD
CARLUNG PL
ARDNEIL AVE
WOODSIDE
GLENBRIDE RD
Tarbert Hill
Meadowhead Cottage
CHAPELTON LA
CHAPELTON RD
ARDROSSAN RD
Meadowhead
ARRANVIEW GDNS
KA22
Chapelton
North Inch
Bank Cottages
Kirkland Glen
Gourock Burn
Kirkland
Hotel
4
49
3
48
2
47
1
46
19
20
21

204

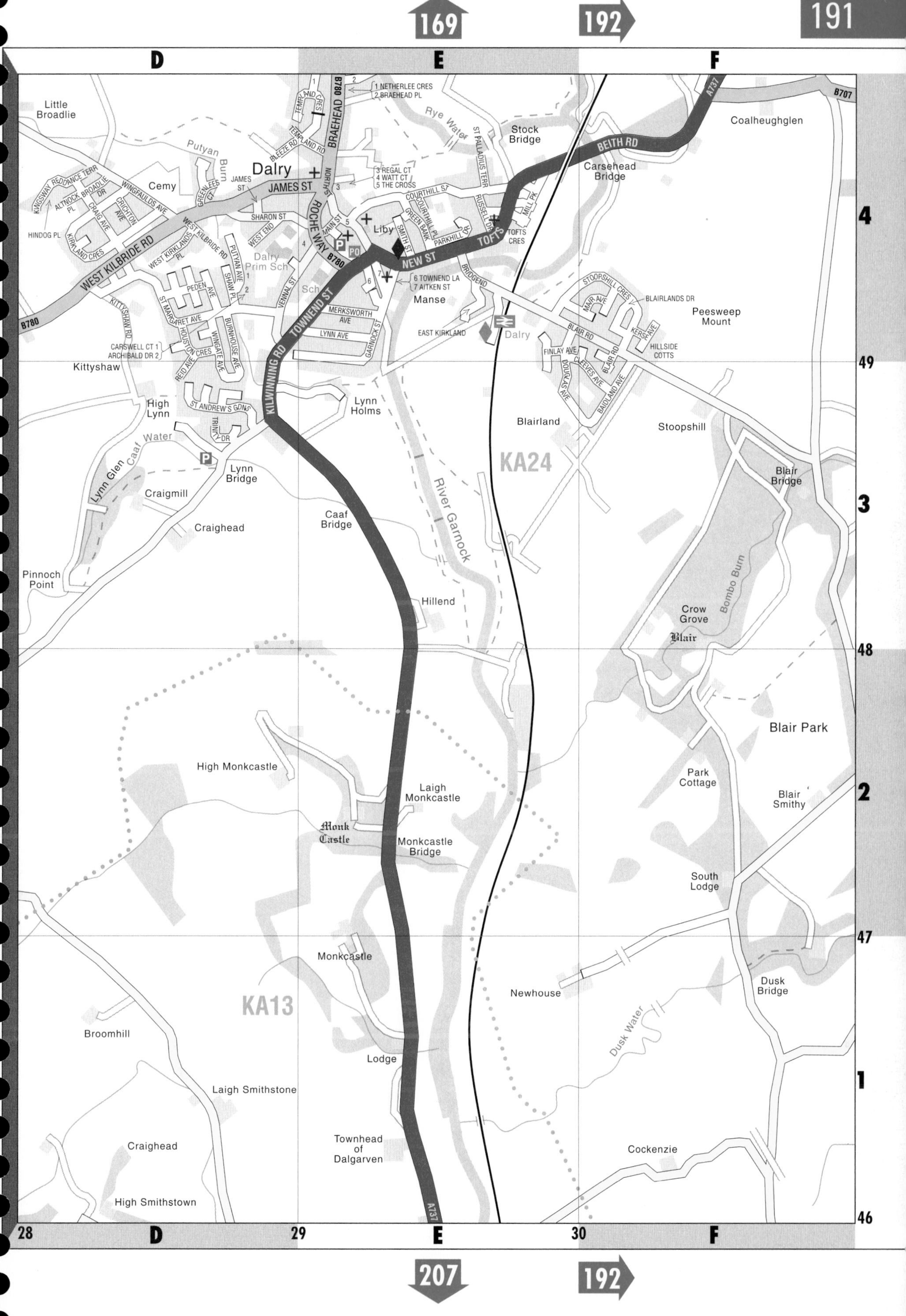

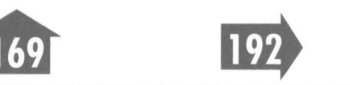
D   E   F

4   **3**   **2**   **1**

49   48   47   46

Little Broadlie

Putyan Burn

Cemy

KINGSWAY
REDANCE TERR
ALTNOCK PL
BROADLIE DR
CRAIG AVE
CRICHTON AVE
WINGFAULDS AVE
GREENLEES
JAMES ST

Dalry

JAMES ST
SHARON ST
WEST END

HINDOG PL
KIRKLAND CRES

WEST KILBRIDE RD

B780

WEST KILBRIDE RD
KITTYSHAW RD
WEST KIRKLANDS PL
PUTYAN AVE
SHAW PL
PEDEN AVE
ST MARYS AVE
MARGARET AVE
HOUSTON CRES
BURNHOUSE AVE
WINGATE AVE
REID AVE
ST ANDREW'S GDNS
TRINITY DR

CARSWELL CT 1
ARCHIBALD DR 2

Kittyshaw

High Lynn

Lynn Glen

Caaf Water

Craigmill

Craighead

Pinnoch Point

BRAEHEAD B780
TEMPLAND CRES
NORTH ST
BLAEZE RD
TEMPLAND RD

1
2
3
5
6
7

ROCHE WAY
B780
MAIN ST
SMITH ST
GREEN BANK
VERNAL ST
GARNOCK ST
MERKSWORTH AVE
LYNN AVE

KILWINNING RD
TOWNEND ST

Sch

Dalry Prim Sch

+ + +

Liby
PO
P

NEW ST

Manse

Lynn Holms

Lynn Bridge

P

Caaf Bridge

Hillend

High Monkcastle

Laigh Monkcastle

Monk Castle

Monkcastle Bridge

Monkcastle

Lodge

Broomhill

Craighead

Laigh Smithstone

High Smithstown

Townhead of Dalgarven

A737

KA13

1 NETHERLEE CRES
2 BRAEHEAD PL

Rye Water

ST PALLADIUS TERR

Stock Bridge

3 REGAL CT
4 WATT CT
5 THE CROSS

COURTHILL PL
COURTHILL ST
RUSSELL AVE
PARKHILL ST

TOFTS
TOFTS CRES

BRIDGEND
6 TOWNEND LA
7 AITKEN ST

East Kirkland

⊞ Dalry

BEITH RD

Carsehead Bridge

A737

Coalheughglen

B707

STOORSHILL CRES
MUIR AVE
KERSE AVE
BLAIRLANDS DR

BLAIR RD
FINLAY AVE
DOUGLAS AVE
CLEEVES AVE
BAIDLAND AVE

HILLSIDE COTTS

Peesweep Mount

Blairland

Stoopshill

Blair Bridge

KA24

River Garnock

Bombo Burn

Crow Grove

Blair

Blair Park

Park Cottage

Blair Smithy

South Lodge

Newhouse

Dusk Water

Cockenzie

Dusk Bridge

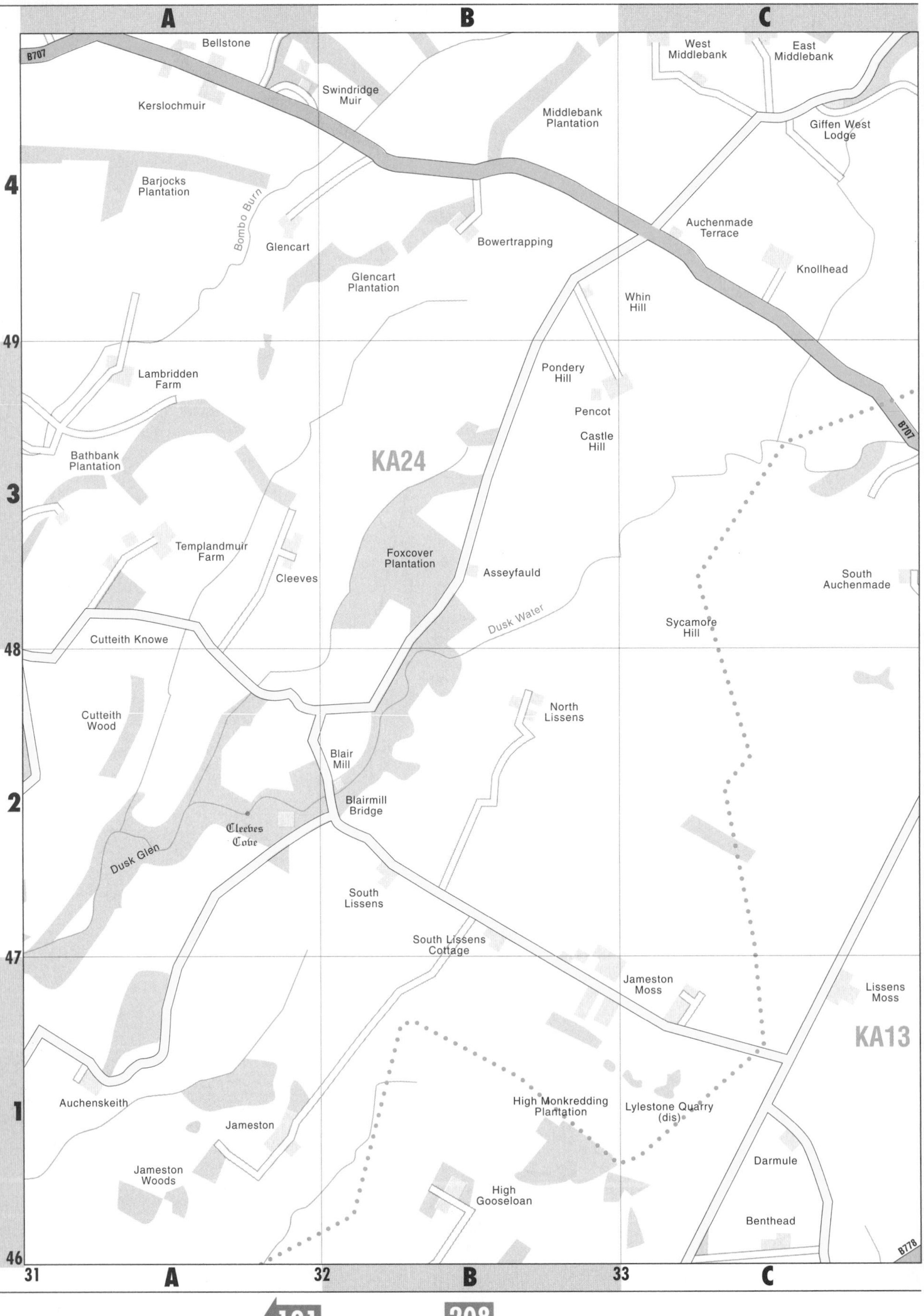

A
B
C

B707

Bellstone

Swindridge
Muir

Middlebank
Plantation

West
Middlebank

East
Middlebank

Kerslochmuir

Giffen West
Lodge

4

Barjocks
Plantation

Bombo Burn

Glencart

Bowertrapping

Auchenmade
Terrace

Knollhead

Glencart
Plantation

Whin
Hill

49

Lambridden
Farm

Pondery
Hill

Pencot

B707

Bathbank
Plantation

KA24

Castle
Hill

3

Templandmuir
Farm

Foxcover
Plantation

South
Auchenmade

Cleeves

Asseyfauld

Dusk Water

Sycamore
Hill

Cutteith Knowe

48

Cutteith
Wood

North
Lissens

Blair
Mill

2

Blairmill
Bridge

Dusk Glen

Cleeves
Cove

South
Lissens

47

South Lissens
Cottage

Jameston
Moss

Lissens
Moss

KA13

Auchenskeith

High Monkredding
Plantation

Lylestone Quarry
(dis)

1

Jameston

Jameston
Woods

High
Gooseloan

Darmule

Benthead

B778

46

31
A
32
B
33
C

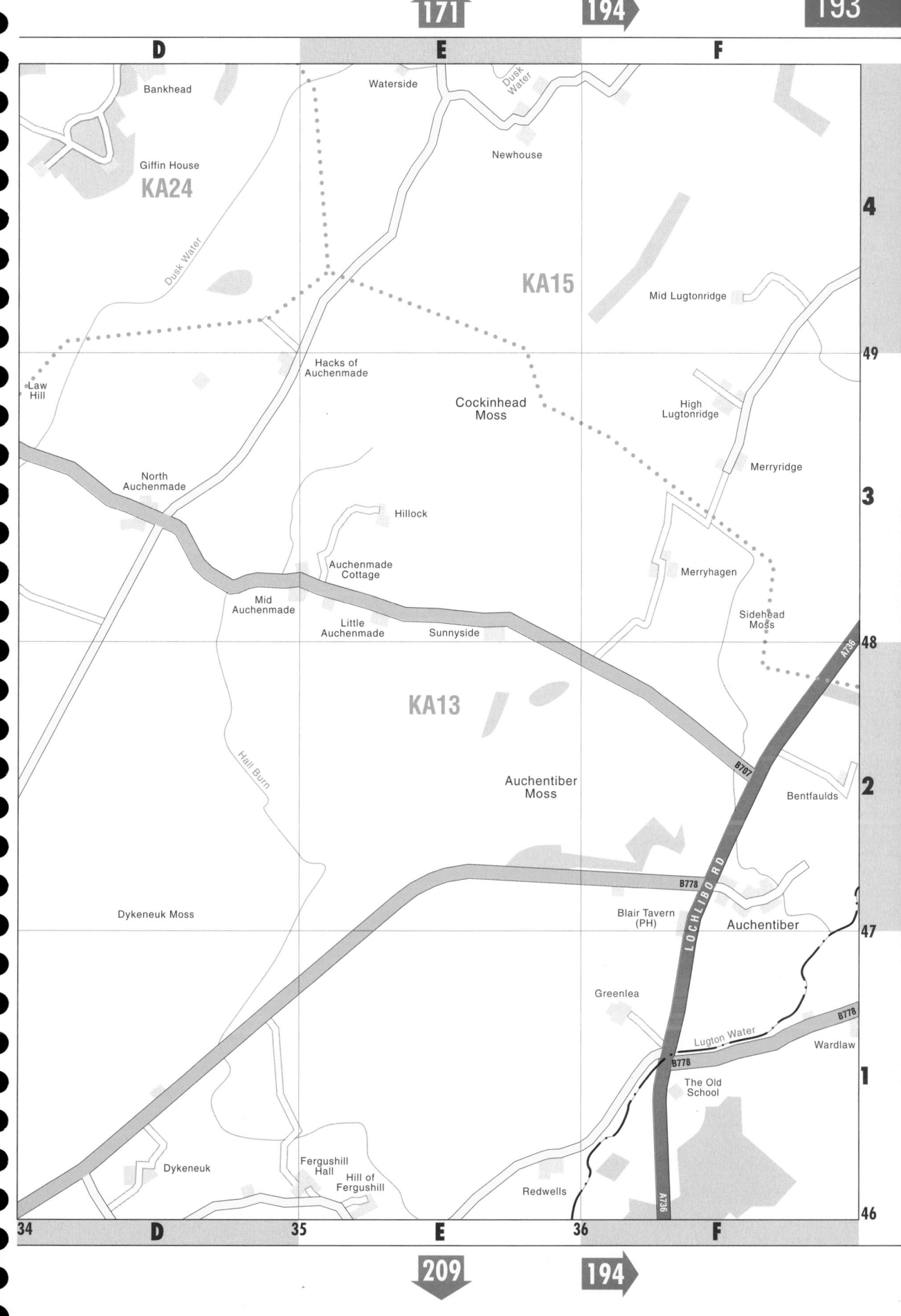
171
194
D
E
F
Bankhead
Waterside
Dusk Water
Newhouse
Giffin House
KA24
4
Dusk Water
KA15
Mid Lugtonridge
49
Law Hill
Hacks of Auchenmade
Cockinhead Moss
High Lugtonridge
Merryridge
North Auchenmade
3
Hillock
Auchenmade Cottage
Merryhagen
Mid Auchenmade
Little Auchenmade
Sunnyside
Sidehead Moss
48
A736
KA13
Hall Burn
B707
Auchentiber Moss
2
Bentfaulds
B778
LOCHLIBO RD
Dykeneuk Moss
Blair Tavern (PH)
Auchentiber
47
Greenlea
B778
Lugton Water
Wardlaw
B778
1
The Old School
Dykeneuk
Fergushill Hall
Hill of Fergushill
Redwells
A736
46
34
D
35
E
36
F
209
194

193
172

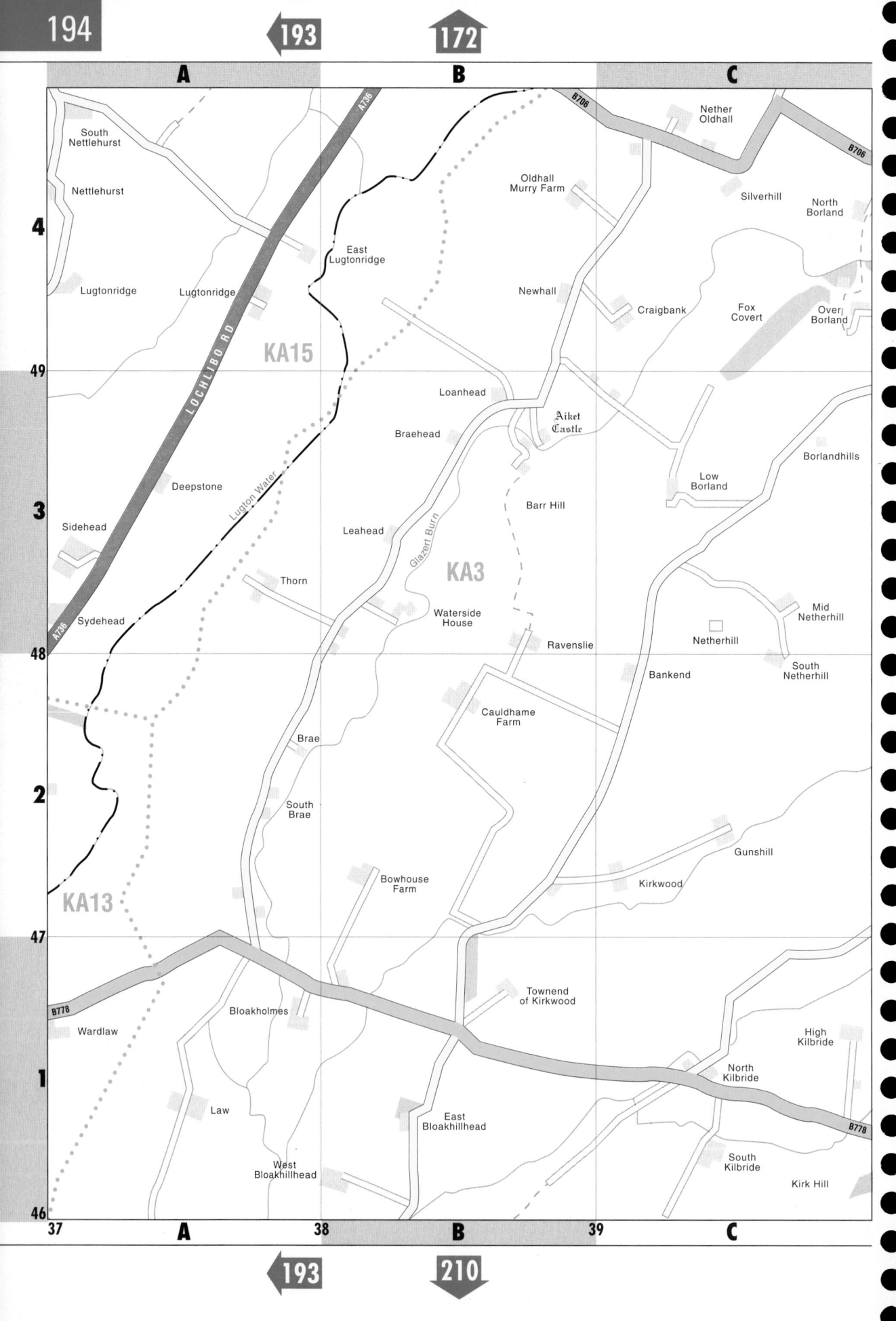
A
B
C
South Nettlehurst
Nettlehurst
Lugtonridge
Lugtonridge
East Lugtonridge
A736
LOCHLIBO RD
KA15
Oldhall Murry Farm
Nether Oldhall
B706
Silverhill
North Borland
Newhall
Craigbank
Fox Covert
Over Borland
Loanhead
Braehead
Aiket Castle
Borlandhills
Deepstone
Low Borland
Barr Hill
Lugton Water
Sidehead
Leahead
Glazert Burn
KA3
Thorn
Mid Netherhill
Sydehead
Waterside House
Netherhill
Ravenslie
South Netherhill
Bankend
Cauldhame Farm
Brae
South Brae
Gunshill
Bowhouse Farm
Kirkwood
KA13
Townend of Kirkwood
B778
Bloakholmes
Wardlaw
High Kilbride
North Kilbride
Law
East Bloakhillhead
West Bloakhillhead
South Kilbride
Kirk Hill
4
49
3
48
2
47
1
46
37
38
39

193
210

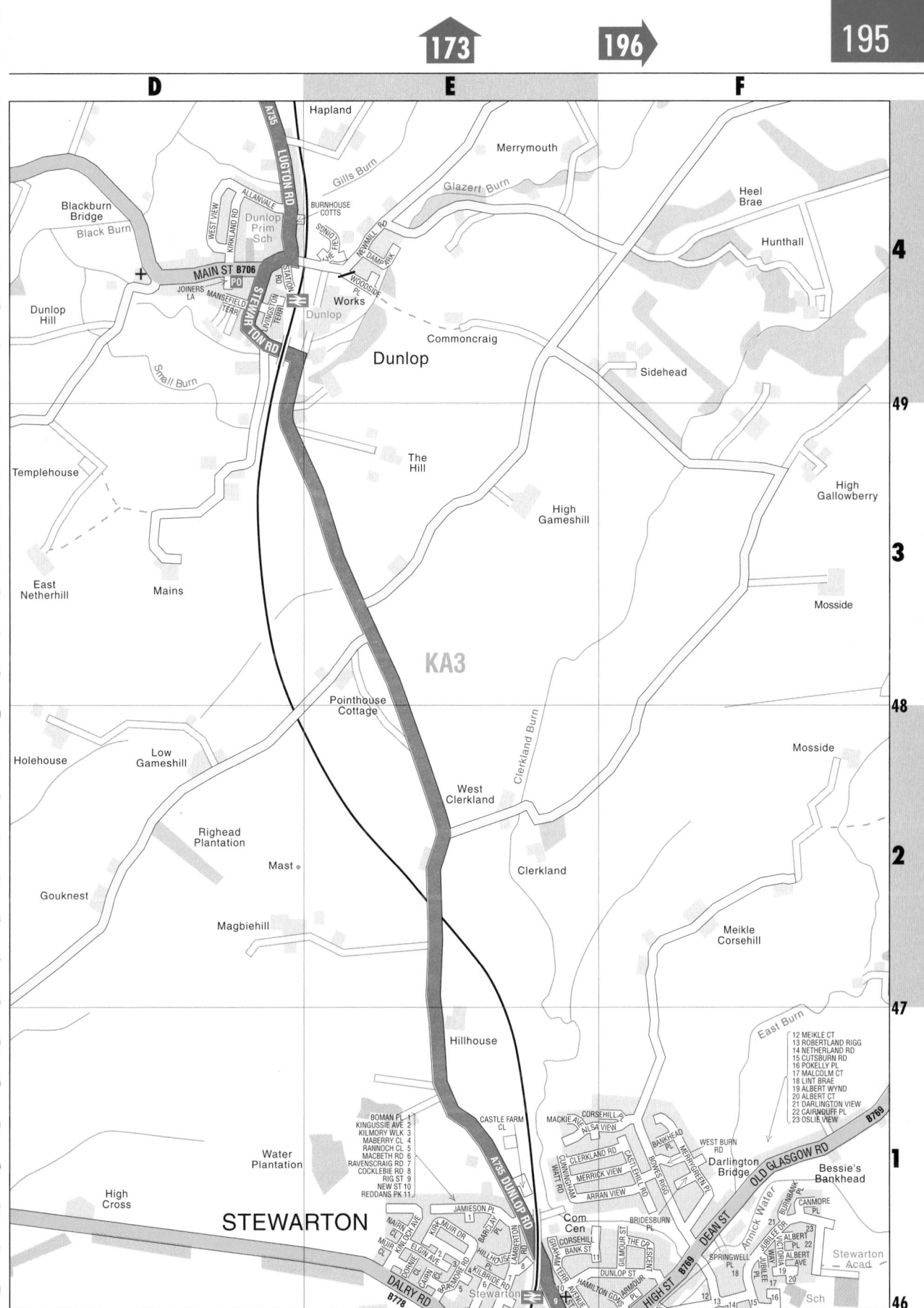

D   E   F

4

49

3

KA3

48

2

47

1

46

40   D   41   E   42   F

Hapland
Merrymouth
Glazert Burn
Heel Brae
Hunthall

LUGTON RD A735
Gills Burn
BURNHOUSE COTTS
Blackburn Bridge
Black Burn
WEST VIEW
KIRKLAND RD
ALLANVALE
Dunlop Prim Sch
NEWMILL RD
DAMPSYK
WOODSIDE PL
Works
Commoncraig
Sidehead

MAIN ST B706
PO
JOINERS LA
MANSEFIELD TERR
STEWARTON RD
STATION RD
LIVINGSTON
THE FIELD
Dunlop

Dunlop Hill
Small Burn

Templehouse

The Hill
High Gameshill
High Gallowberry

East Netherhill
Mains

Mosside

Pointhouse Cottage

Holehouse
Low Gameshill

West Clerkland
Clerkland Burn
Mosside

Righead Plantation
Mast
Clerkland

Gouknest
Meikle Corsehill

Magbiehill

East Burn

Hillhouse

12 MEIKLE CT
13 ROBERTLAND RIGG
14 NETHERLAND RD
15 CUTSBURN RD
16 POKELLY PL
17 MALCOLM CT
18 LINT BRAE
19 ALBERT WYND
20 ALBERT CT
21 DARLINGTON VIEW
22 CAIRNDUFF PL
23 OSLIE VIEW

BOMAN PL 1
KINGUSSIE AVE 2
KILMORY WLK 3
MABERRY CL 4
RANNOCH CL 5
MACBETH RD 6
RAVENSCRAIG RD 7
COCKLEBIE RD 8
RIG ST 9
NEW ST 10
REDDANS PK 11

CASTLE FARM CL
MACKIE AVE
CORSEHILL
NISLA VIEW
Bankhead PL
WEST BURN RD
B769
Darlington Bridge
Bessie's Bankhead

Water Plantation

A735 DUNLOP RD
JAMIESON PL
CLERKLAND RD
MERRICK VIEW
ARRAN VIEW
CASTEHILL RD
BONES RIGG
MERRYGREEN PL
Annick Water
CANMORE PL

High Cross

STEWARTON

NAIRN CL
DUNLOP AVE
ELGIN AVE
KIRK MUIR DR
BARCLAY
HILLHOUSE RD
LAMBERTON RD
BRAMORE RD
KILBRIDE RD
Com Cen
CORSEHILL BANK ST
GILMOUR ST
THE CRESCENT
BRIDESBURN PL
DEAN ST
SPRINGWELL
ALBERT PL
JUBILEE PL
VICTORIA PL
ALBERT AVE
Stewarton Acad
Sch

MUIR CL
DOBIE CL
CAIRN
ARMOUR
HAMILTON GDNS
DUNLOP MOUNT
HIGH ST B769
B769

DALRY RD
B778
Stewarton

195
174

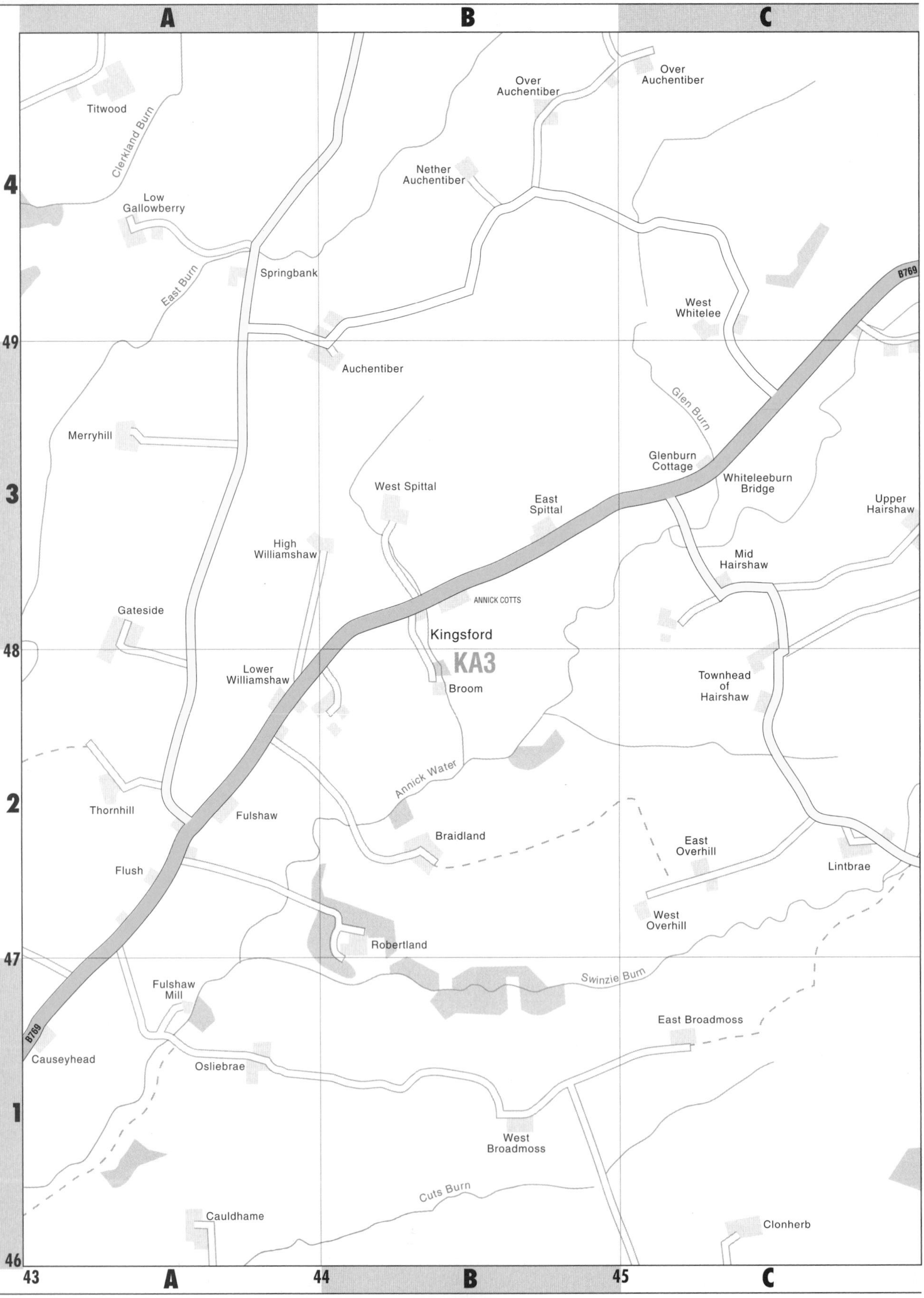

A **B** **C**

Titwood

Clerkland Burn

Low
Gallowberry

East Burn

Springbank

Over
Auchentiber

Over
Auchentiber

Nether
Auchentiber

B769

West
Whitelee

4

49

Auchentiber

Merryhill

Glen Burn

Glenburn
Cottage

Whiteleeburn
Bridge

Upper
Hairshaw

West Spittal

East
Spittal

Mid
Hairshaw

3

High
Williamshaw

ANNICK COTTS

Gateside

Kingsford

48

Lower
Williamshaw

KA3

Broom

Townhead
of
Hairshaw

Annick Water

East
Overhill

2

Thornhill

Fulshaw

Braidland

West
Overhill

Lintbrae

Flush

Robertland

47

Swinzie Burn

Fulshaw
Mill

East Broadmoss

B769

Causeyhead

Osliebrae

1

West
Broadmoss

Cuts Burn

Cauldhame

Clonherb

46

43 **A** 44 **B** 45 **C**

175

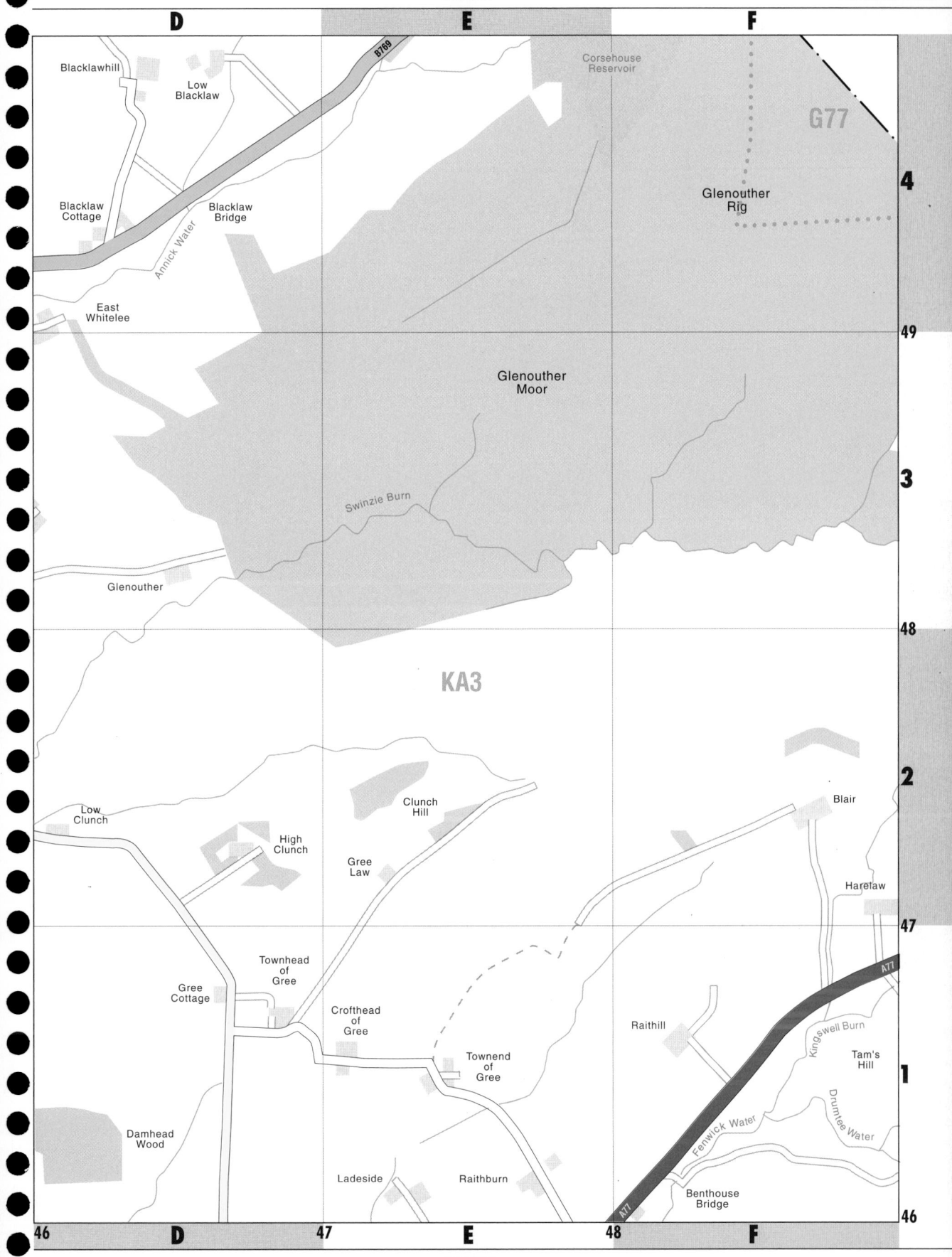

D
E
F
Blacklawhill
Low Blacklaw
B769
Corsehouse Reservoir
G77
Blacklaw Cottage
Blacklaw Bridge
Annick Water
Glenouther Rig
East Whitelee
Glenouther Moor
Swinzie Burn
Glenouther
KA3
Low Clunch
Clunch Hill
High Clunch
Gree Law
Blair
Harelaw
Townhead of Gree
Gree Cottage
Crofthead of Gree
Raithill
A77
Kingswell Burn
Tam's Hill
Townend of Gree
Drumtee Water
Fenwick Water
Damhead Wood
Ladeside
Raithburn
Benthouse Bridge
4
49
3
48
2
47
1
46
46
47
48

213

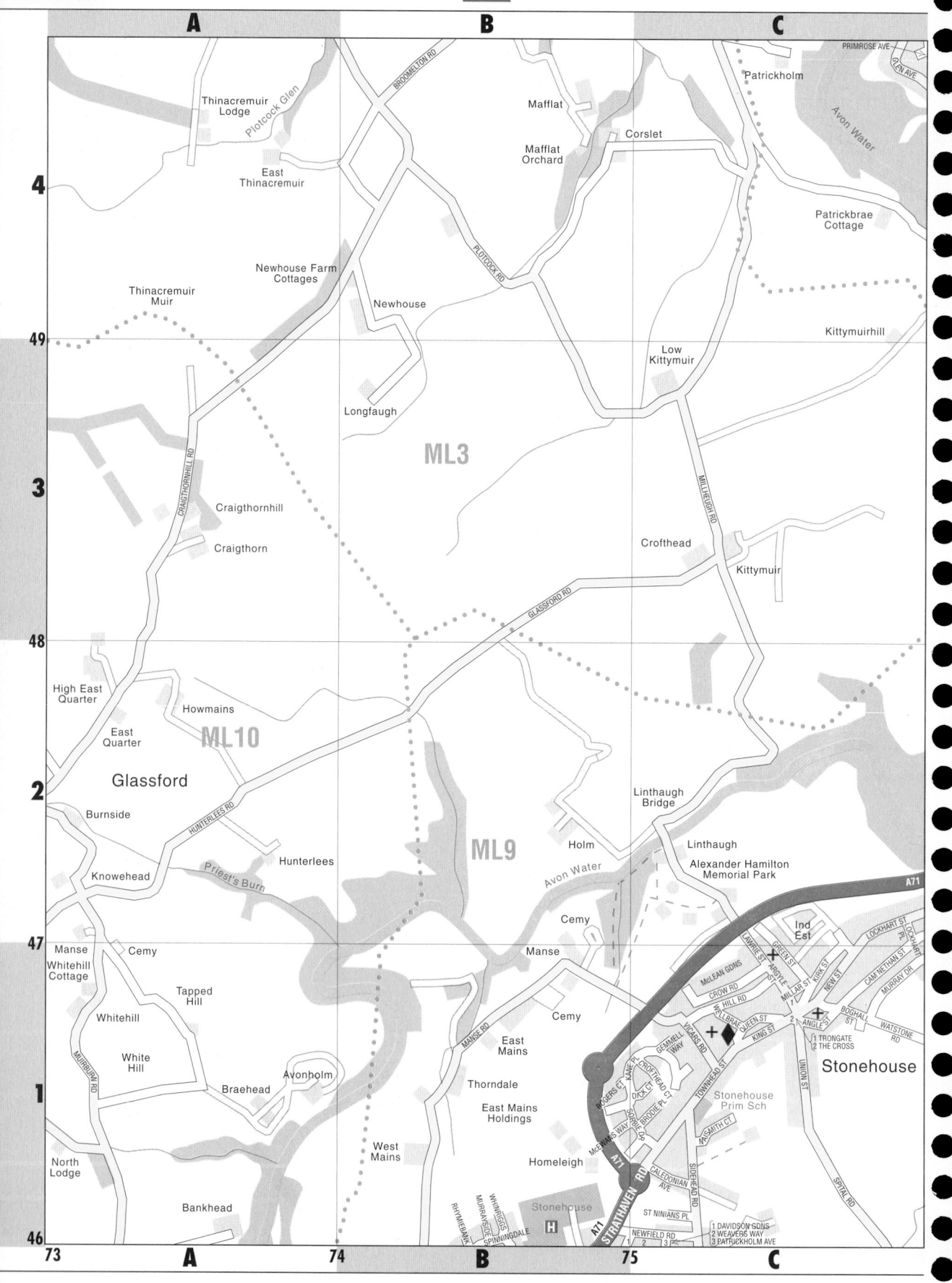

A   B   C

PRIMROSE AVE

Thinacremuir Lodge

Plotcock Glen

Patrickholm

Mafflat

Avon Water

East Thinacremuir

Corslet

Mafflat Orchard

Patrickbrae Cottage

4

Newhouse Farm Cottages

Thinacremuir Muir

Newhouse

Kittymuirhill

49

Low Kittymuir

Longfaugh

ML3

Craigthornhill

Crofthead

3

Craigthorn

Kittymuir

High East Quarter

48

East Quarter

Howmains

ML10

Linthaugh Bridge

Glassford

Holm

Linthaugh

ML9

Alexander Hamilton Memorial Park

2

Burnside

Hunterlees

Avon Water

Knowehead

Priest's Burn

A71

Ind Est

Cemy

Manse

LOCKHART ST

47

Manse

Cemy

McLean GDNS

Whitehill Cottage

Cemy

CROW RD

HILL RD

MILLAR ST

NEW ST

CAM NETHAN ST

MURRAY DR

BOGHALL ST

WATSTONE RD

Tapped Hill

East Mains

Stonehouse

Whitehill

WELLBRAE

KING ST

UNION ST

White Hill

Thorndale

Stonehouse Prim Sch

1 TRONGATE
2 THE CROSS

1

Braehead

Avonholm

East Mains Holdings

SIDEHEAD RD

SPITAL RD

North Lodge

West Mains

Homeleigh

CALEDONIAN AVE

Bankhead

Stonehouse

NEWFIELD RD

ST NINIANS PL

1 DAVIDSON GDNS
2 WEAVERS WAY
3 PATRICKHOLM AVE

H

46

73   A   74   B   75   C

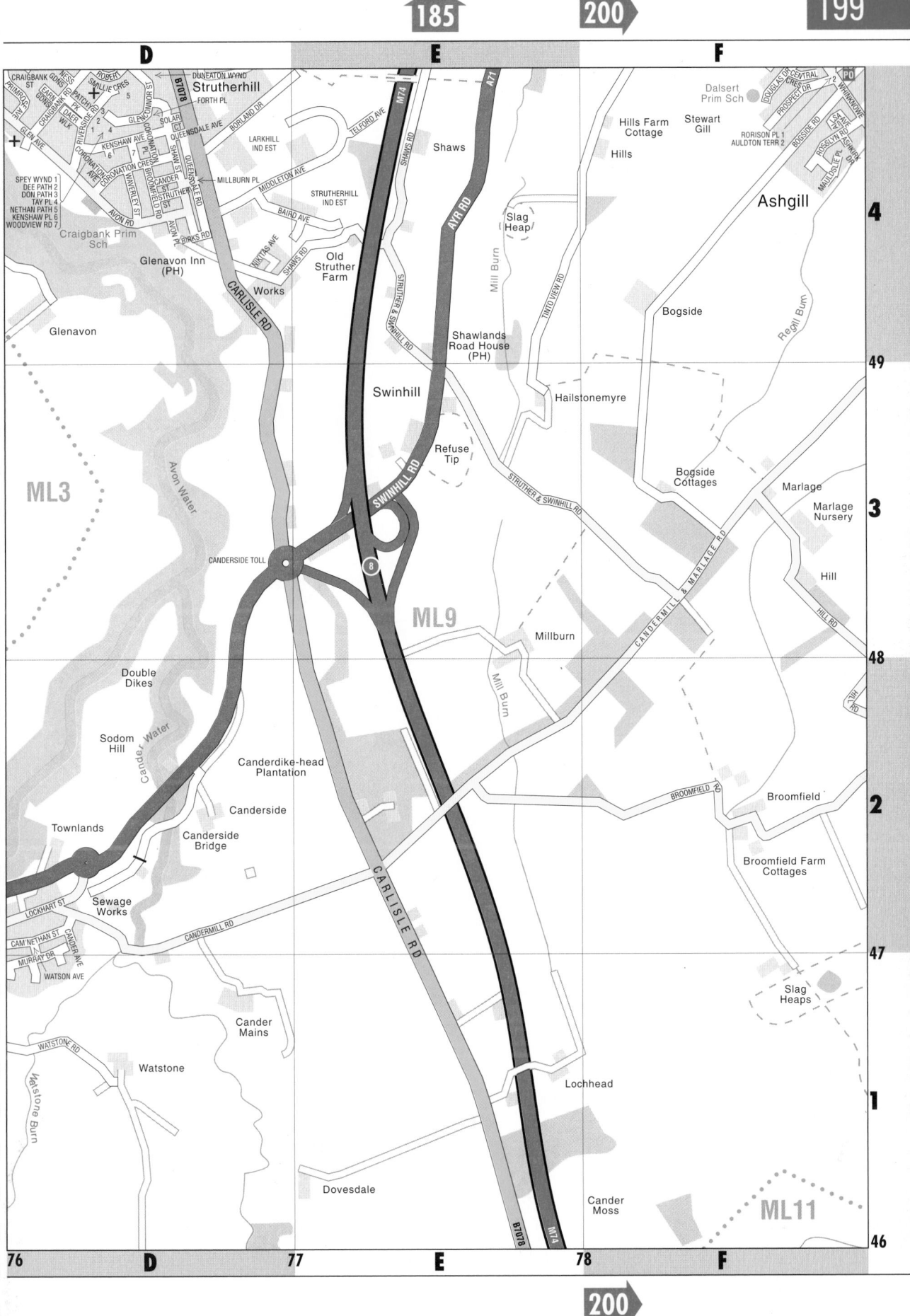

D E F

DUNEATON WYND
FORTH PL
Strutherhill
B7078
CRAIGBANK GDNS
CRAIGBANK ST
NESS RD
ROBERT
SMILLIE CRES
PATCHED
5
SOLAR
PRIMROSE AVE
GLEN AVE
CART RD
GLEN AVE
RIVERSIDE
GLEN
DEE
OAK
WALK
KENSHAW AVE
CORONATION PL
STRUTHER
CANDER
ST
QUEENSDALE AVE
BORLAND DR
TELFORD AVE

SPEY WYND 1
DEE PATH 2
DON PATH 3
TAY PL 4
NETHAN PATH 5
KENSHAW PL 6
WOODVIEW RD 7

CORONATION AVE
WATERLEY ST
CORONATION CRES
BROOMFIELD ST
AVON RD
MILLBURN PL
MIDDLETON AVE

LARKHILL
IND EST

STRUTHERHILL
IND EST

Shaws

+

Craigbank Prim
Sch

Glenavon Inn
(PH)

KENSHAW AVE
AVON RD
QUEENSDALE RD
ST BIRKS RD
VICKTAS AVE
SHAWS RD
BAIRD AVE

Works

Old
Struther
Farm

Glenavon

CARLISLE RD

M74

SHAWS RD

AYR RD

A71

Hills Farm
Cottage

Hills

Dalsert
Prim Sch

PO

DOUGLAS DR CENTRAL
PROSPECT DR
BOGSIDE RD
WHINCROFT
MIDDLDSE DE PL

Stewart
Gill

RORISON PL 1
AULDTON TERR 2

ROSSLYN ASHWIK

Ashgill

4

ML3

Avon Water

Slag
Heap

Mill Burn

STRUTHER & SWINHILL RD

Shawlands
Road House
(PH)

Swinhill

SWINHILL RD

Refuse
Tip

TINTO VIEW RD

Bogside

Regil Burn

Hailstonemyre

Bogside
Cottages

STRUTHER & SWINHILL RD

49

Marlage

Marlage
Nursery

HILL RD

3

CANDERSIDE TOLL

8

ML9

Millburn

Mill Burn

CANDERMILL & MARLAGE RD

Hill

48

Double
Dikes

Sodom
Hill

Cander Water

Canderdike-head
Plantation

Canderside

Townlands

Canderside
Bridge

BROOMFIELD DR

Broomfield

2

Broomfield Farm
Cottages

HILL RD

LOCKHART ST
Sewage
Works
CAM'NETHAN ST
MURRAY DR
CANDER AVE
WATSON AVE
CANDERMILL RD

CARLISLE RD

47

WATSTONE RD

Watstone

Watstone Burn

Cander
Mains

Slag
Heaps

B7078

M74

Lochhead

1

Dovesdale

Cander
Moss

ML11

46

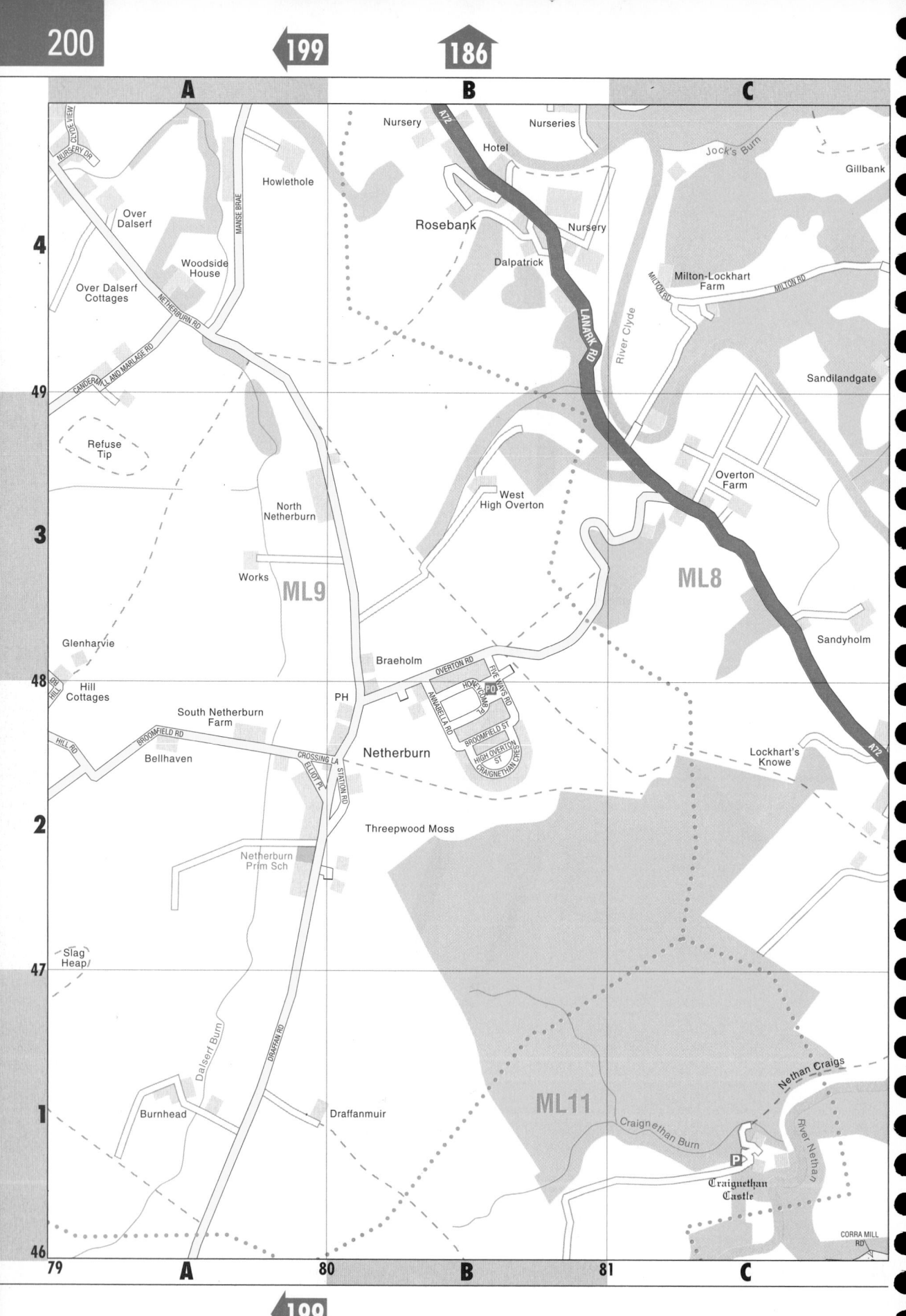

A   B   C

Nursery

Nurseries

Hotel

Gillbank

Jock's Burn

Howlethole

Over Dalserf

Rosebank

Nursery

Milton-Lockhart Farm

MILTON RD

Dalpatrick

MILTON RD

Woodside House

MANSE BRAE

Over Dalserf Cottages

NETHERBURN RD

LANARK RD

River Clyde

Sandilandgate

CANDERS... LAND MARRIAGE RD

HILL DR

4

49

Refuse Tip

Overton Farm

North Netherburn

West High Overton

ML8

3

Works

ML9

Sandyholm

Glenharvie

Braeholm

OVERTON RD

FIVE WAYS RD

48

Hill Cottages

PH

PO

ANNABELL RD

HIGH... GROUND PL

Lockhart's Knowe

A72

South Netherburn Farm

BROOMFIELD RD

CROSSING LA

Netherburn

BROOMFIELD ST

HILL RD

Bellhaven

ELLIOT PL

STATION RD

HIGH OVERTON ST

CRAIGNETHAN CRES

2

Threepwood Moss

Netherburn Prim Sch

47

Slag Heap

Nethan Craigs

Dalserf Burn

DRAFFAN RD

ML11

Craignethan Burn

River Nethan

1

Burnhead

Draffanmuir

P

Craignethan Castle

CORRA MILL RD

46

79   A   80   B   81   C

D E F

UNITAS CRES
GLENBURN TERR
SHIELDHILL RD
BENTY'S LA
A73
OLD LANARK RD
ARRAN GDNS
VIOLET GDNS
UNITAS CRES 1
MILTON CRES 2
SPRINGFIELD CRES 3
JASMINE WAY
PRIMROSE WAY
COLUMBINE WAY
WISTERIA LA
LARKSPUR WAY
LOCH PARK AVE
HYACINTH WAY
JONQUIL WAY
CARTLAND AVE
ISLAY GDNS
ST LUKE'S AVE
LAVENDER LA
BLUEBELL WAY
MARIGOLD WAY
JURA GDNS
STATION RD
Under Shieldhill
RAES RD
Miltonhead (birthplace of General Roy)
MILTON RD
Miltonhead Farm
South Hillhead
Wellriggs
Meadowhead
Townhead Burn
Townhead
Oldhill
BUSHELHEAD RD
LANARK RD
Waygateshawhead
Tower
Waygateshaw
Maregill Burn
Bushelhead
HARESTANES IND EST
Braidwood
B7056
ML8
Braidwood House
Gills
LOCHKNOWE ST
HARESTANES RD
MONKS LA
LOCH AVE
BEANSHIELDS RD
Orchard Knowe
Braidwood Prim Sch
1 HALL BAR GDNS
2 OSWALD GDNS
Threepwood
Poplarglen
MID-LOAN ST
PO
BRAIDWOOD RD
Yett Holm
Woodheads Road
Linnside
River Clyde
Woodhall
Swinsy Hill
Orchard House
Hallbar Tower
AUCHENGLEN RD
Nethanfoot
Millwood
WOODHALL RD
NETHAN GLEN
DARK BRIG RD
HOLM RD
1 JAMES WILSON PL
2 NETHANFOOT BRIG RD
Lodge
Newpark
Hamper Hill
River Nethan
Hotel
SMUGGLERS BRIG RD
HOLM CREST
Mashock Burn
Derwent Wood
Birkhill
BIRKHILL RD
MASHOCK PATH
CARFIN DR
BLAIR RD
B7056
GRAHAM RD
DEWAR WLK
CROSSCLYDE VIEW
Auchenglen
Crossford
PL
FOREST
TAIT WLK
ML11
Auchenglen Hill
NEMPHLAR MOOR RD
Clyde Valley Country Estate
Aaronshill Wood
Blair Cottage
Burned Wood
A72

4 49 3 48 2 47 1 46

82 D 83 E 84 F

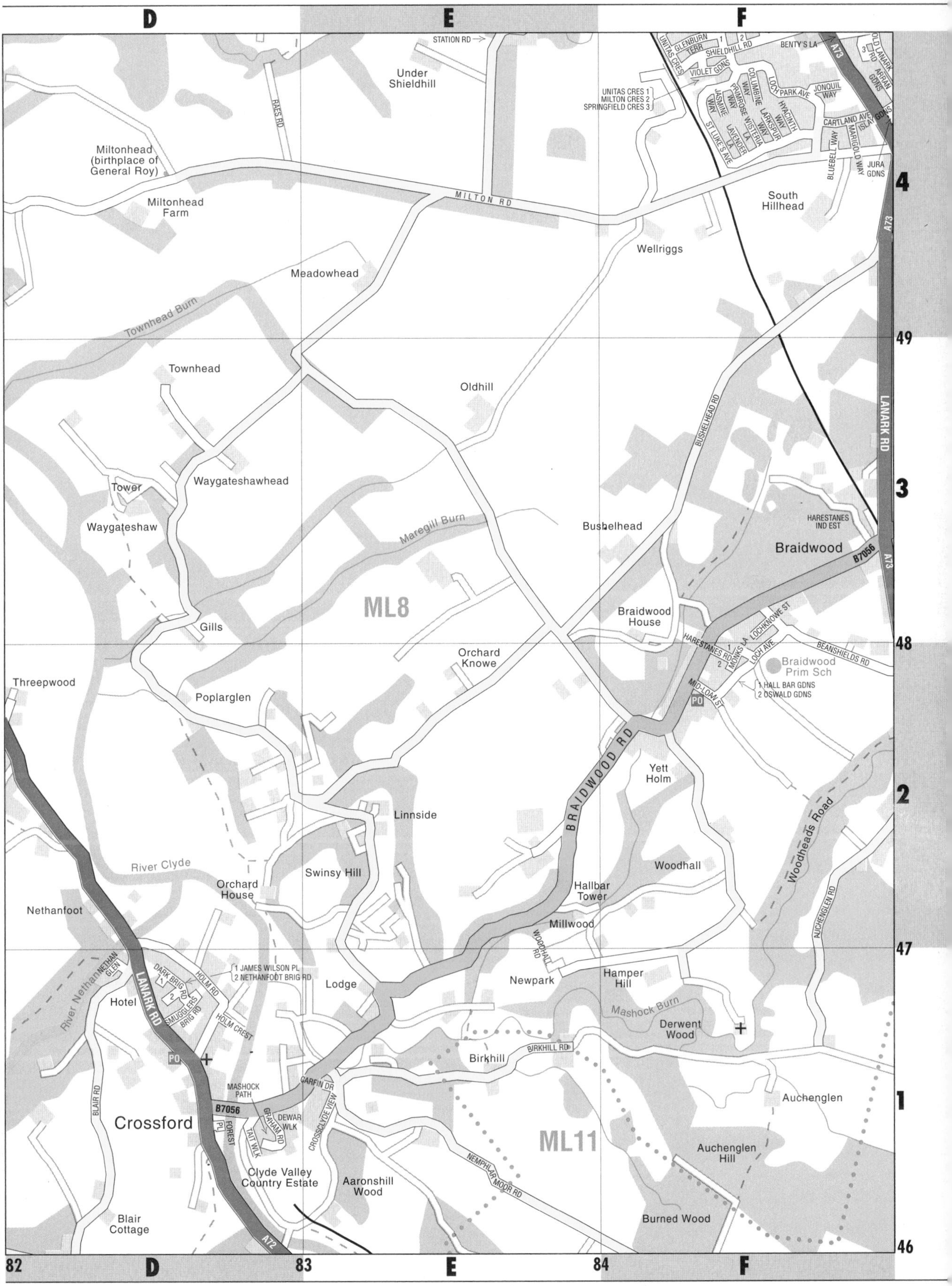

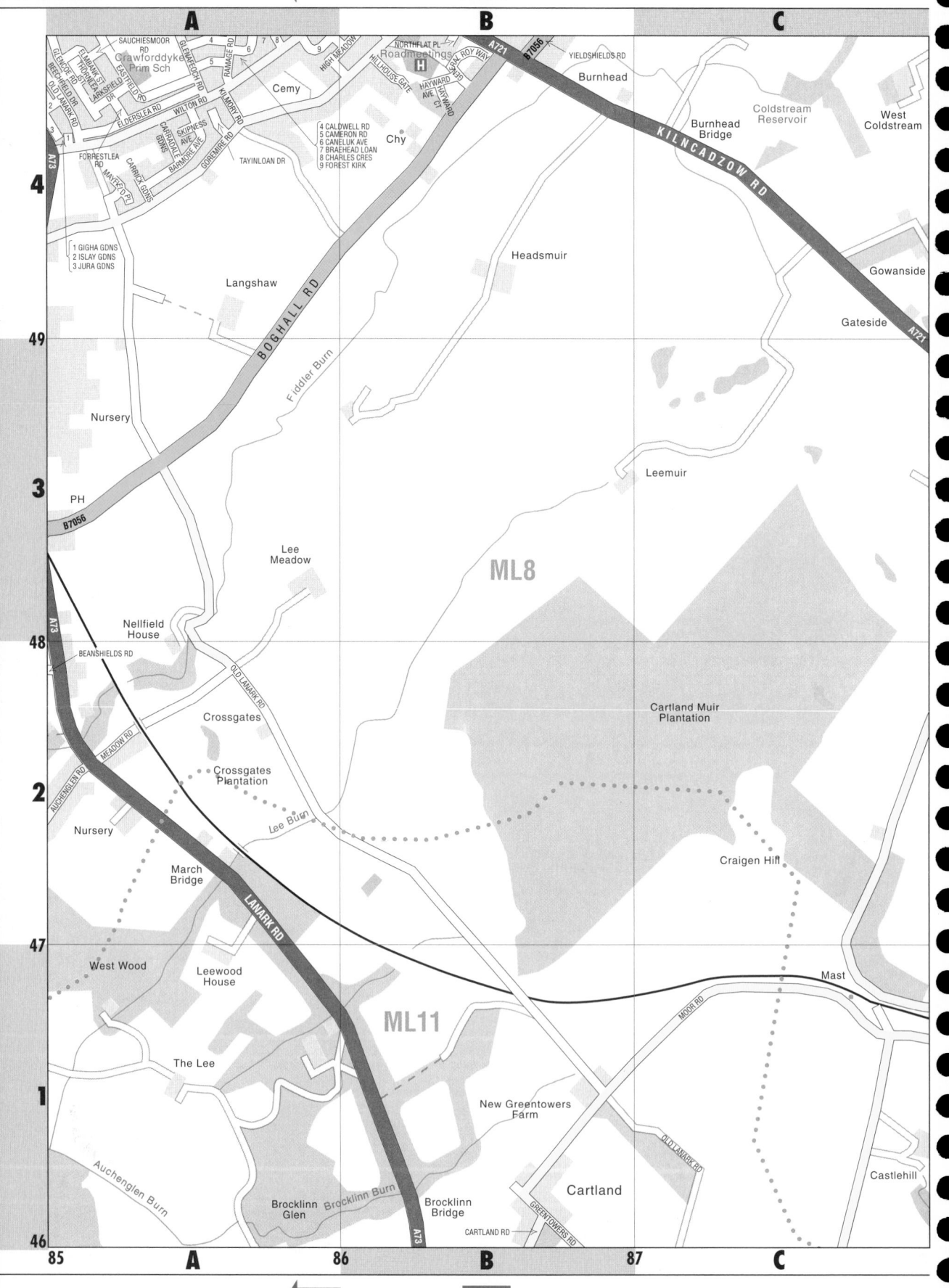

A   B   C

4

49

3

48

2

47

1

46

85   A   86   B   87   C

Crawforddyke Prim Sch
SAUCHIESMOOR RD
ELMBANK ST
THORNIE...
GLENCROE DR
BEECH HILL DR
OLD LANARK RD
ARNSFIELD RD
EASTFIELD RD
GLENAFEORD RD
RAMAGE RD
WILTON RD
KILMORY RD
ELDERSLEA RD
SKIPNESS AVE
CARRADALE GDNS
BARMORE AVE
COREMIRE RD
CARRICK GDNS
MANTFOR PL
FORRESTLEA RD
Cemy
High Meadow
HILLHOUSE GATE
Roadmeatings
NORTHFLAT PL
H
HAYWARD AVE
HAYWARD CT
ROY WAY
A721
B7056
YIELDSHIELDS RD
Burnhead
Burnhead Bridge
Coldstream Reservoir
West Coldstream
KILNCADZOW RD
A721
Gowanside
Gateside

4 CALDWELL RD
5 CAMERON RD
6 CANELUK AVE
7 BRAEHEAD LOAN
8 CHARLES CRES
9 FOREST KIRK
Chy
TAYINLOAN DR

1 GIGHA GDNS
2 ISLAY GDNS
3 JURA GDNS

Langshaw
Headsmuir

BOGHALL RD

Fiddler Burn

A73

Nursery

Leemuir

PH
B7056

ML8

Lee Meadow

A73

Nellfield House
BEANSHIELDS RD

OLD LANARK RD

Crossgates

Cartland Muir Plantation

Crossgates Plantation

AUCHENGLEN RD
MEADOW RD

Lee Burn

Craigen Hill

Nursery

March Bridge

LANARK RD

West Wood

Leewood House

Mast

MOOR RD

ML11

The Lee

New Greentowers Farm

OLD LANARK RD

Castlehill

Cartland

Auchenglen Burn

Brocklinn Glen
Brocklinn Burn
Brocklinn Bridge
A73
CARTLAND RD
GREENTOWERS RD

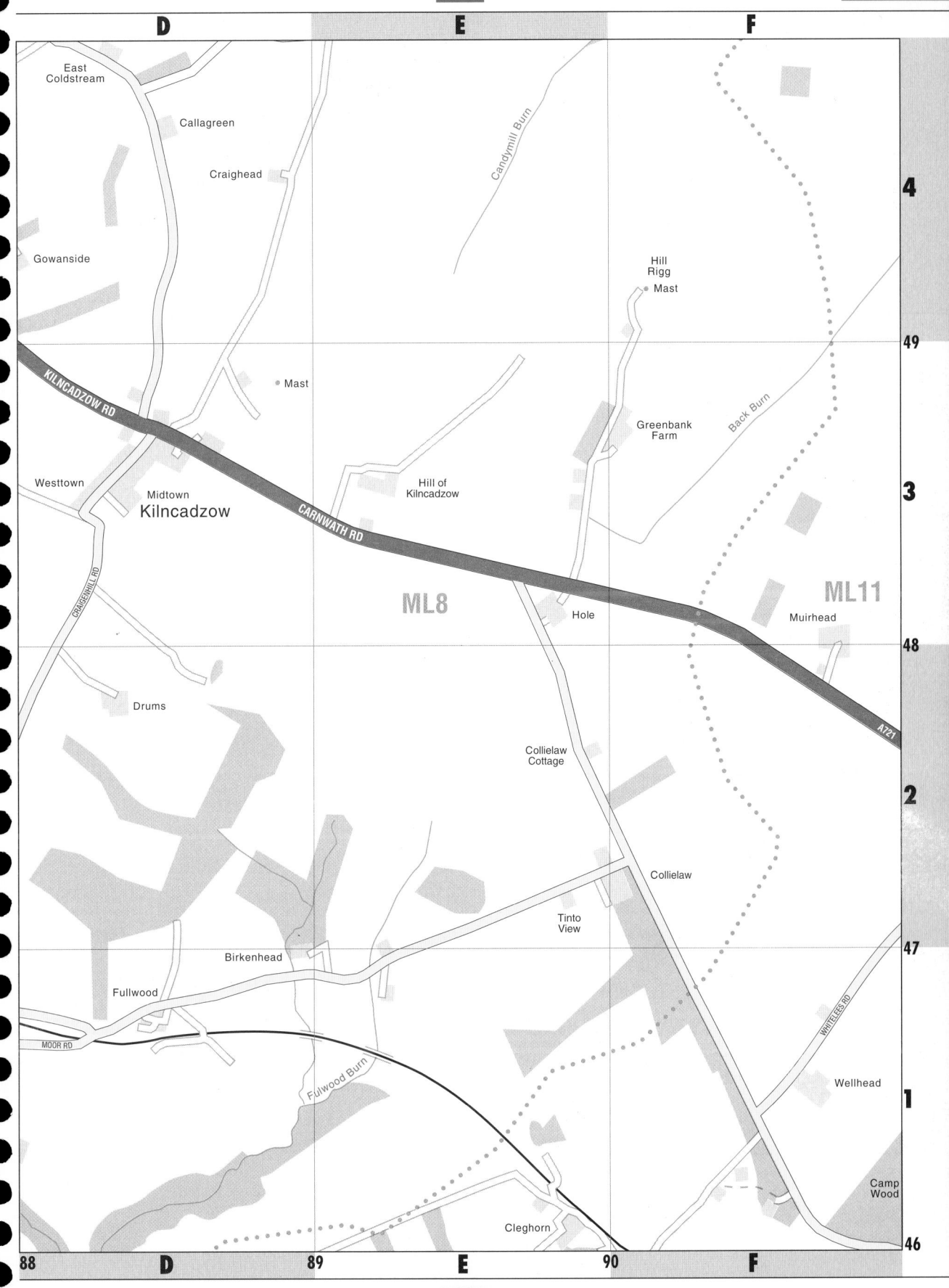

East Coldstream
Callagreen
Craighead
Gowanside
KILNCADZOW RD
Westtown
Midtown
Kilncadzow
CRAIGHILL RD
Drums
MOOR RD
Fullwood
Birkenhead
Fullwood Burn
Candymill Burn
Mast
Hill of Kilncadzow
CARNWATH RD
ML8
Hole
Collielaw Cottage
Collielaw
Tinto View
Cleghorn
Hill Rigg
Mast
Greenbank Farm
Back Burn
Muirhead
ML11
A721
WHITELEES RD
Wellhead
Camp Wood

D   E   F

4
49
3
48
2
47
1
46

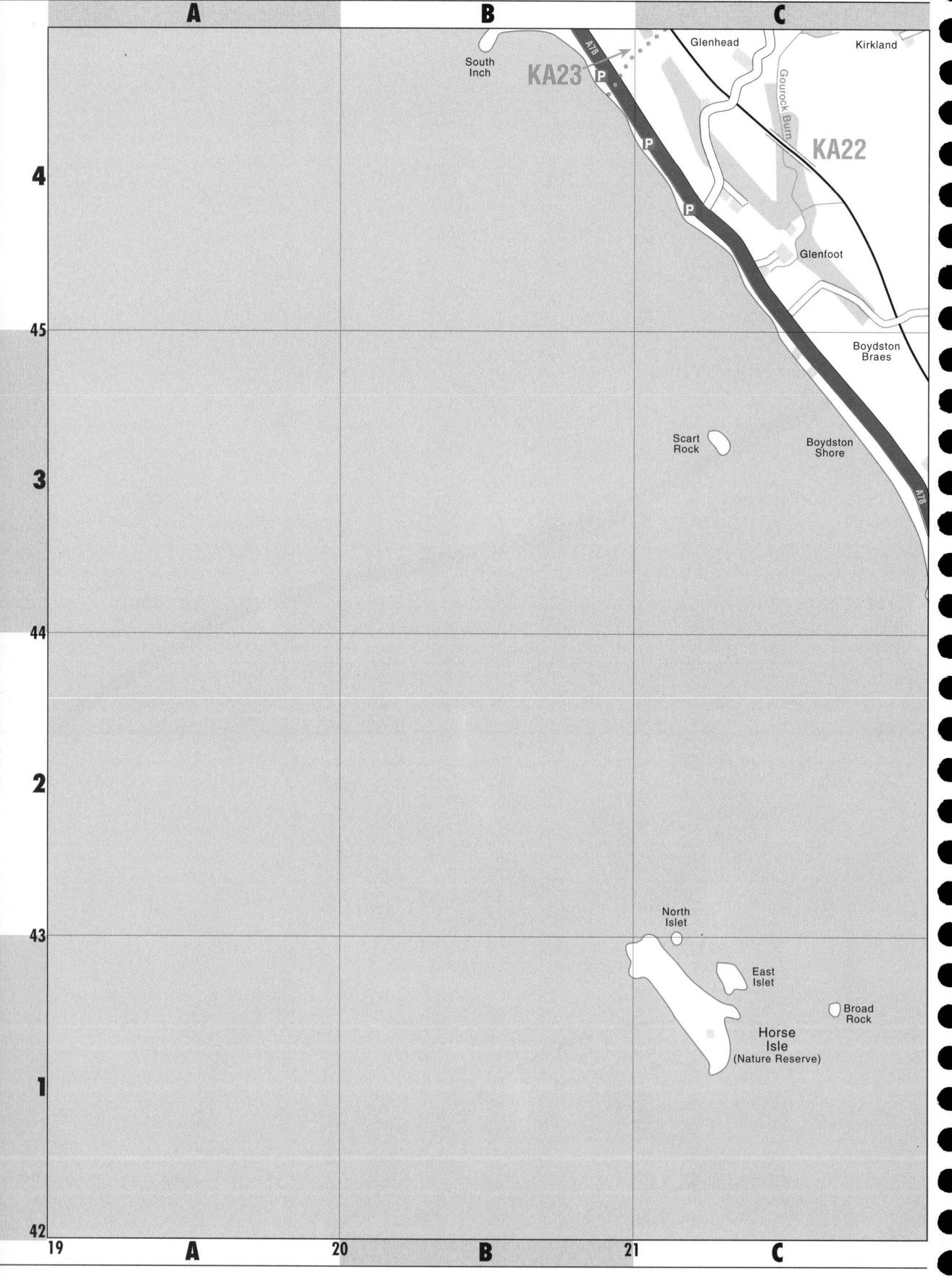

South Inch

KA23

Glenhead

Kirkland

Gourock Burn

KA22

Glenfoot

Boydston Braes

Scart Rock

Boydston Shore

North Islet

East Islet

Broad Rock

Horse Isle
(Nature Reserve)

D E F

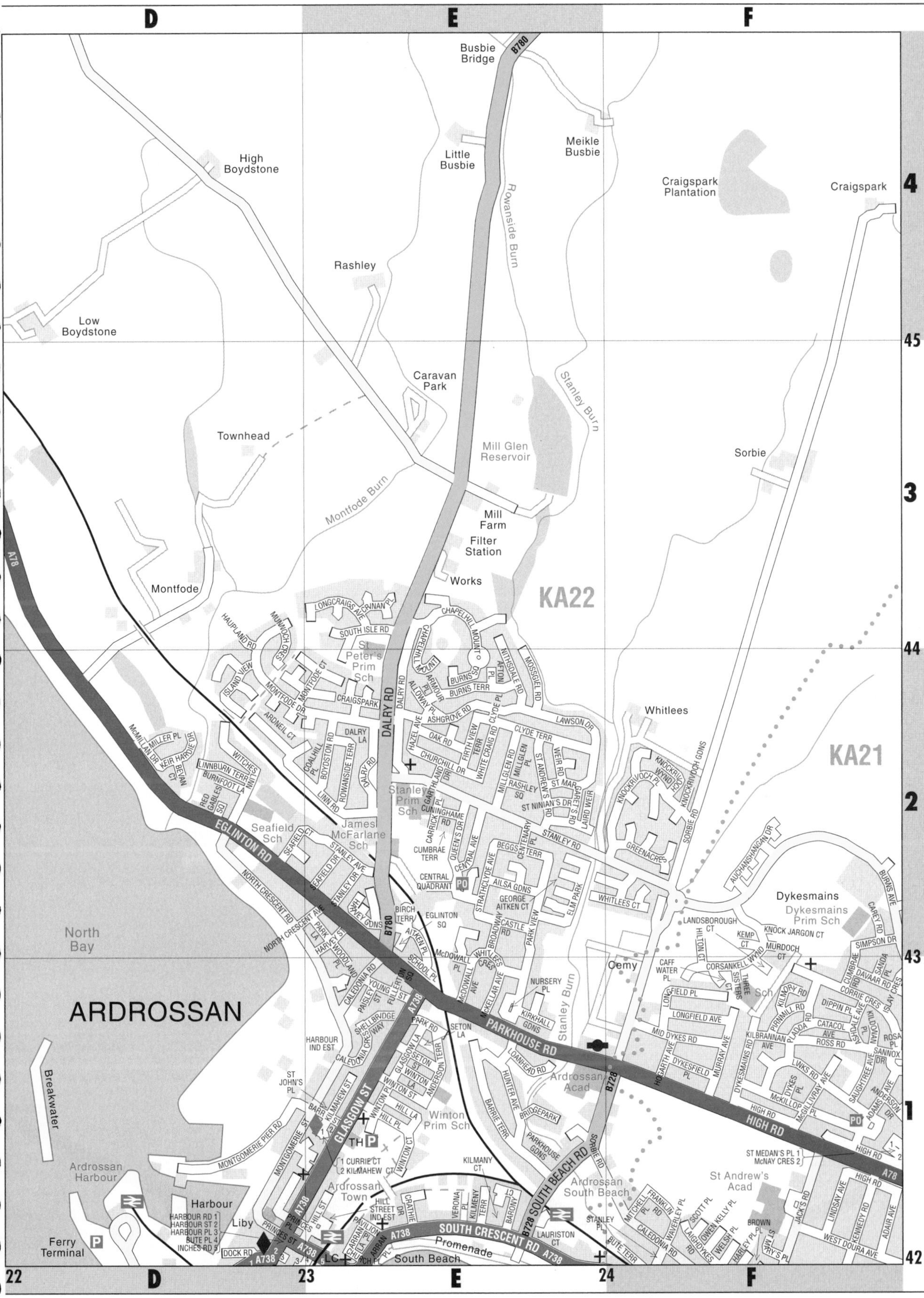

4

45

3

High Boydstone

Little Busbie

Busbie Bridge

Meikle Busbie

Craigspark Plantation

Craigspark

Rashley

B780

Rowanside Burn

Stanley Burn

Sorbie

Low Boydstone

Townhead

Caravan Park

Montfode Burn

Mill Glen Reservoir

Mill Farm Filter Station

Works

KA22

A78

Montfode

LONGCRAIGS AVE

CRINAN

South Isle Rd

Craigspark

St Peter's Prim Sch

CHAPELHILL RD

CHAPELHILL MOUNT

ARMOUR

BURNS RD

BURNS TERR

AFTON

MOSSGIEL RD

AITKENSIDE RD

DALRY RD

Whitlees

KA21

44

2

ISLAND VIEW

HAUPLAND RD

MONTGOMERY CRES

MONTFODE DR

MONTFODE CT

ARDNEIL CT

DALRY LA

DALRY RD

HAZEL AVE

ALLOWAY PL

ASHGROVE RD

DAK RD

FIRTH VIEW

WHITE CRAIG RD

GARTH AVE

CLYDE TERR

LAWSON DR

WEIR RD

KNOCKRIVOCH PL

KNOCKRIVOCH GDNS

AUCHANSKEANGAN DR

BURNS AVE

CRAIGHALL

WITCHES

CHALMILL RD

BOYDSTON RD

ROWANSIDE TERR

LINN RD

CHURCHILL DR

MILLER PL

KEIR HARDIE RD

MCLAND DR

RED GABLES CT

BRIAN CT

BURNFOOT LA

LINNBURN TERR

Seafield Sch

SEAFIELD CT

STANLEY AVE

SEAFIELD RD

STANLEY DR

James McFarlane Sch

Stanley Prim Sch

CUNINGHAME RD

CARRICK RD

QUEEN'S DR

CUMBRAE TERR

CENTRAL AVE

MILLER RD

MILL GLEN PL

RASHLEY SQ

ST ANDREW'S

ST MARN

ST NINIAN'S DR

ST B'S RD

STANLEY RD

BEGGS TERR

KNOCKRIVOCH WYND

SORBIE RD

GREENACRES

EGLINTON RD

North Crescent Rd

NORTH CRESCENT RD

HARVEY GDNS

BIRCH TERR

AITKEN ST

McDOWALL

WHITLEES CRES

STRATHCLYDE AVE

GEORGE AITKEN CT

BROADWAY

CASTLE

PARK VIEW

ELM PARK

WHITLEES CT

Landsborough Ct

KEMP CT

CORSANKELL WYND

MURDOCH CT

Dykesmains

Dykesmains Prim Sch

SIMPSON DR

DAVAAR RD

SANDA

North Bay

CALEDONIA RD

PAISLEY RD

YOUNG ST

SCHOOL RD

B780

NURSERY PL

Stanley Burn

Cemy

CAFF WATER PL

LONGFIELD PL

LONGFIELD AVE

MID DYKES RD

THREE SISTERS Sch

KILNORY RD

PIRNMILL

PLADDA

CATACOL

DIPPIN PL

CORRIE CRES

ROSA

CUMBRAE AVE

ROSS RD

SANNOX DR

43

1

ARDROSSAN

Breakwater

Ardrossan Harbour

Ferry Terminal

Harbour

P

MONTGOMERIE PIER RD

ST JOHN'S PL

HARBOUR IND EST

SHELLBRIDGE WAY

CALEDONIA DR

BARR KILMAHEW ST

GLASGOW ST

MONTGOMERIE ST

HILL ST

BARRIE TERR

Winton Prim Sch

KIRKHALL GDNS

XAGLAR AVE

PARKHOUSE RD

B728

LOANGEAD RD

HUNTER AVE

BRIDGEPARK

MIDEARTH AVE

DYKESFIELD PL

Ardrossan Acad

MURRAY AVE

KILBRANNAN AVE

DYKESMAINS RD

McKILLOP

LWAS RD

MCPH LIVRAY AVE

ANDERSON

ROSS RD

B728 SOUTH BEACH RD

High Rd

HIGH RD

SAUGHTREE AVE

PO

A78

TH P

1 CURRIE CT

2 KILMAHEW CT

Ardrossan Town

1 & 2

HILL STREET WEST

WINTON ST

SETON LA

SETON ST

BUTE PL

WINTON CT

KILMANY CT

Parkhouse Gdns

Ardrossan South Beach

St Medan's Pl 1

McNay Cres 2

St Andrew's Acad

JACK'S RD

KILBIRNIE PL

Liby

P

HARBOUR RD 1

HARBOUR ST 2

HARBOUR PL 3

BUTE PL 4

INCHES RD 5

DOCK RD

A738

PRINCES ST

HILL ST

PAVILION

BARRA

A738

LC

South Beach

SOUTH CRESCENT RD A738

Promenade

VERONA

KILMANY TERR

BARTON

LAURISTON CT

STANLEY PL

BUTE TERR

CALEDONIA

FRANKLIN PL

MITCHELL

SCOTT PL

OWEN KELLY PL

WELSH PL

BROWN

HARVEY'S PL

WEST DOURA AVE

ADAIR AVE

KENNEDY RD

LINDSAY AVE

42

205

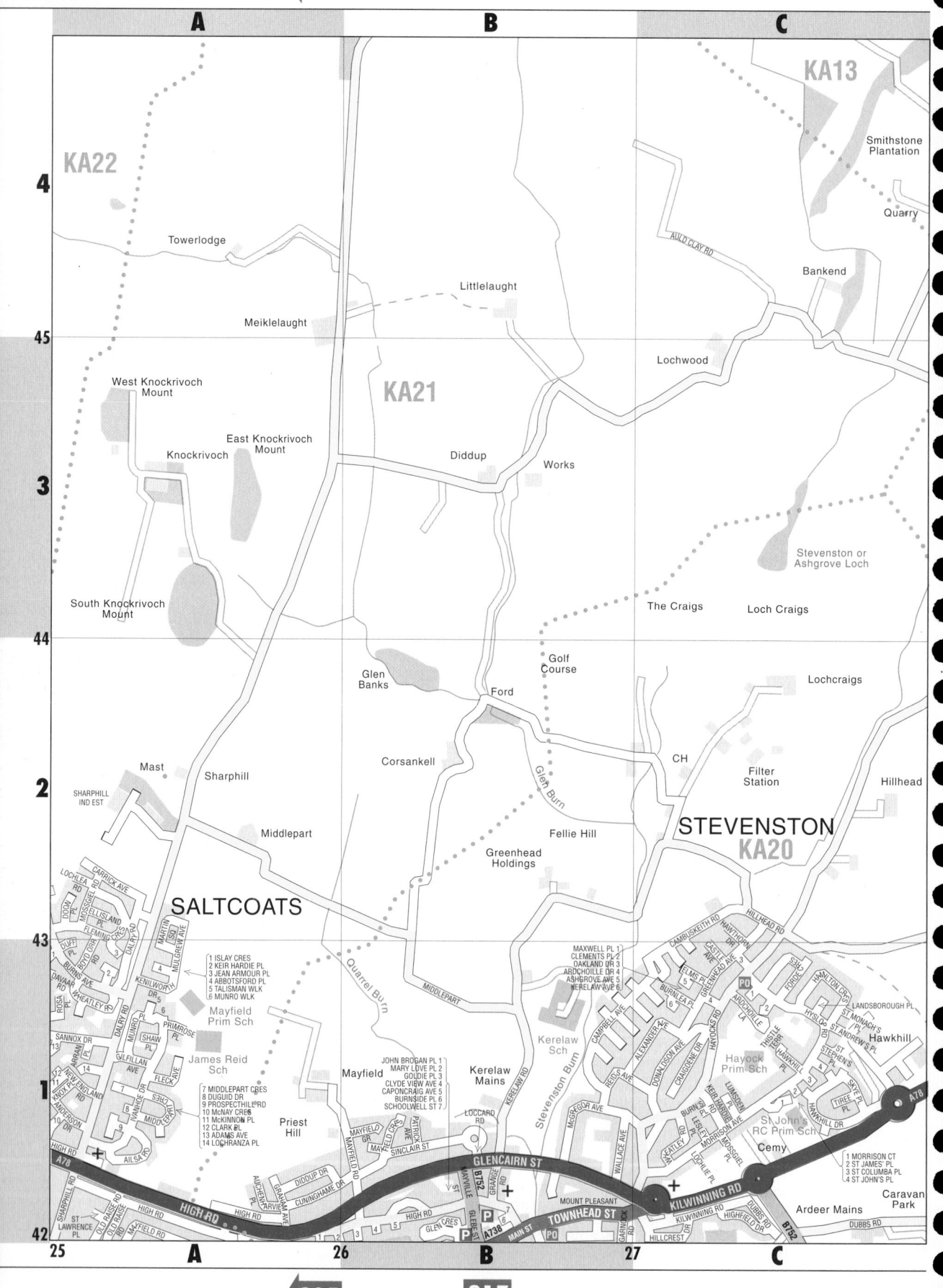

A
B
C
KA22
KA21
KA13
KA20
Towerlodge
Littlelaught
Meiklelaught
Smithstone Plantation
Quarry
Bankend
Lochwood
West Knockrivoch Mount
East Knockrivoch Mount
Knockrivoch
Diddup
Works
South Knockrivoch Mount
Stevenston or Ashgrove Loch
The Craigs
Loch Craigs
Golf Course
Glen Banks
Ford
Lochcraigs
Mast
Sharphill
Corsankell
CH
Filter Station
Hillhead
SHARPHILL IND EST
Middlepart
Glen Burn
Fellie Hill
STEVENSTON
Greenhead Holdings
SALTCOATS
Quarrel Burn
Mayfield Prim Sch
James Reid Sch
Kerelaw Sch
Stevenston Burn
Hayock Prim Sch
Hawkhill
Mayfield
Kerelaw Mains
Priest Hill
St John's RC Prim Sch
Cemy
Caravan Park
Ardeer Mains
HIGH RD
GLENCAIRN ST
KILWINNING RD
TOWNHEAD ST
MIDDLEPART
AULD CLAY RD
1 ISLAY CRES
2 KEIR HARDIE PL
3 JEAN ARMOUR PL
4 ABBOTSFORD PL
5 TALISMAN WLK
6 MUNRO WLK
7 MIDDLEPART CRES
8 DUGUID DR
9 PROSPECTHILL RD
10 McNAY CRES
11 McKINNON PL
12 CLARK PL
13 ADAMS AVE
14 LOCHRANZA PL
JOHN BROGAN PL 1
MARY LOVE PL 2
GOLDIE PL 3
CLYDE VIEW AVE 4
CAPONCRAIG AVE 5
BURNSIDE PL 6
SCHOOLWELL ST 7
MAXWELL PL 1
CLEMENTS PL 2
OAKLAND DR 3
ARDCHOILLE DR 4
ASHGROVE AVE 5
KERELAW AVE 6
1 MORRISON CT
2 ST JAMES' PL
3 ST COLUMBA PL
4 ST JOHN'S PL
LANDSBOROUGH PL
A78
A738
B752
PO
25
26
27
42
43
44
45
1
2
3
4

205
217

191
208

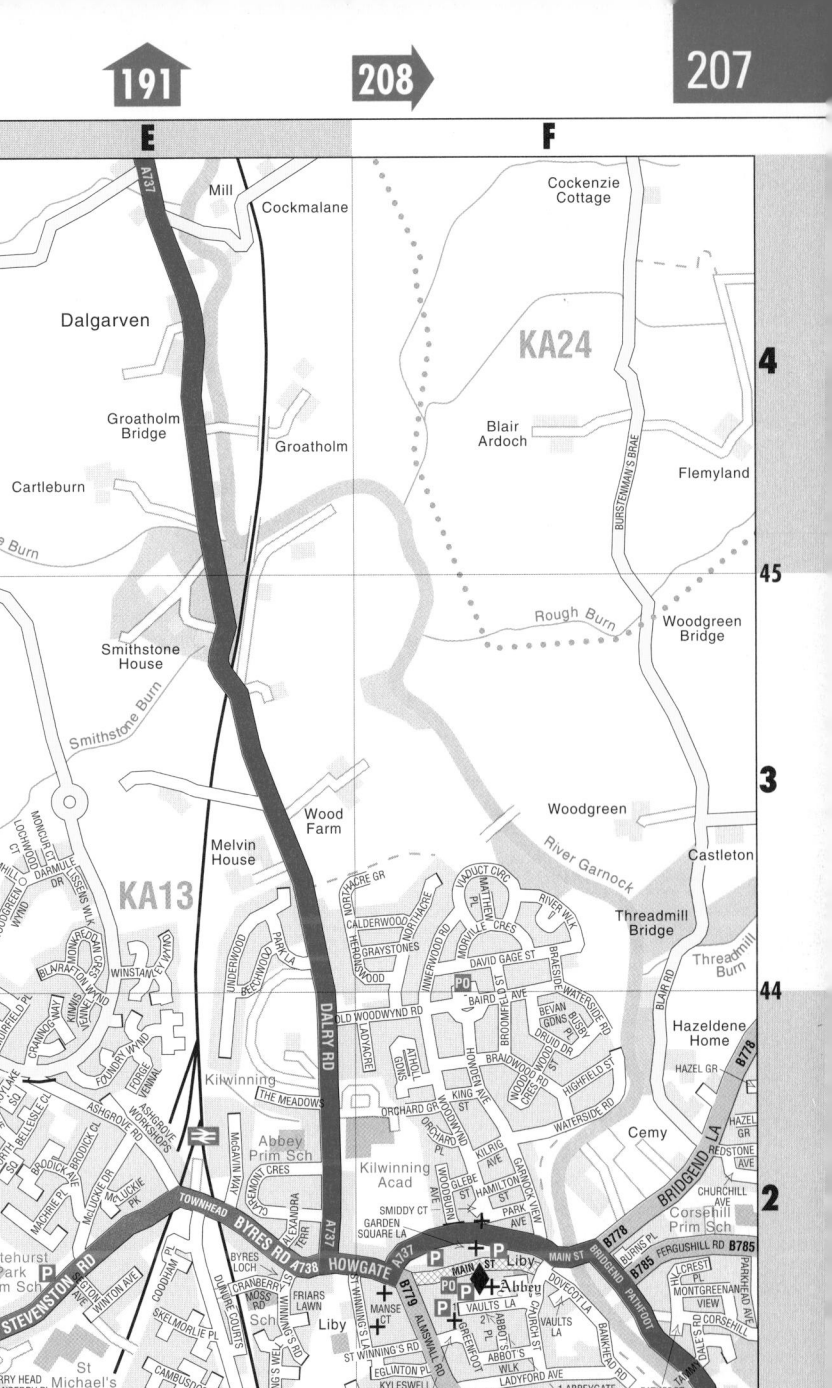
D
E
F
High Smithstone
Smithstone Terr
Dalgarven
Mill
Cockmalane
Cockenzie Cottage
KA24
Blair Ardoch
Groatholm Bridge
Groatholm
Gateside
Cartleburn
Cartle Burn
KA21
Flemyland
Burstenman's Brae
Ashgrove Mount
Smithstone House
Rough Burn
Woodgreen Bridge
Auchenkist
Smithstone Burn
Woodgreen
River Garnock
Castleton
Wood Farm
Melvin House
High Whitehirst
Whitehirst
KA13
Threadmill Bridge
Threadmill Burn
Whitehirst Park
Mine (dis)
Hazeldene Home
Kilwinning
Dalry Rd
Cemy
Abbey Prim Sch
Kilwinning Acad
Bridgend La
Corsehill Prim Sch
Whitehirst Park
Whitehirst Park Prim Sch
Stevenston Rd
Byres Rd
Howgate
Main St
Liby
Abbey
KA20
Castle Hill
Castlehill
St Michael's Acad
St Luke's Prim Sch
Muirside
Pennyburn Prim Sch
Blacklands Prim Sch
KILWINNING
Blacklands
Nethermains Rd
Irvine Rd
Dirrans
West Byrehill Ind Est
Byrehill Ave
Dubbs Junction
Ancumor Farm
Broom
Todhill Farm Training Home
Penny Burn
Byrehill Rd
Dubbs Rd
A737
A738
A78
B779
B778
B785
4
45
3
44
2
43
1
42
28
29
30

218
208

207
192

A **B** **C**

KA24

Barneyhill
Plantation

Laigh
Gooseloan

Lylestone
Farm

Clonbeith
(remains of)

Rough Burn

Monkredding

LYLESTONE
TERR

Lylestone
Cottage

Sevenacres
Wood

4

45

Outer
Ardoch

Monkreddan
Kennels

Hullerhill

Threadmill Burn

Sevenacres
Mains

Sevenacres
Mill

Ardoch

Crofthead

Bannoch Burn

3

KA13

Bannoch

High Moncur

Burrowland

B778

44

Redston

Bannoch
Bridge

Corsehillmuir
Plantation

Mid Moncur

Windyhall

North
Fergushill

Nursery

HAZEL GR

REDSTONE
AVE

CHURCHILL
AVE

McGAVIN
AVE

Sch

BANNOCH GDNS

KEIR HARD

FIVE ROADS

BANNOCH PL

BANNOCH RD

Broomhill

Lugton Water

2

B785 FERGUSHILL RD

MONTGOMERIE TERR

QUEEN'S
PL

LOVE
ST

QUEEN
ST

MONCUR RD

HUNTER
PL

WEIRSTON RD

South
Fergushill

CORSEHILL

PARKHEAD AVE

BANNOCH RD

Eglinton
Kennels

43

Benslie
Fauld

Eglinton
Country Park

Benslie Wood

Weirston

Chapelholms
Wood

North
Millburn

1

A737 IRVINE RD

WOODMILL

Ladyha' Park

KA12

Eglinton
Castle
(remains of)

B785

KA11

Kilwinning
Gates

Millburn
Lodge

Auchenwinsey

1 KELVIN AVE
2 WATERCUT RD

Factory

42

31 **A** **32** **B** **33** **C**

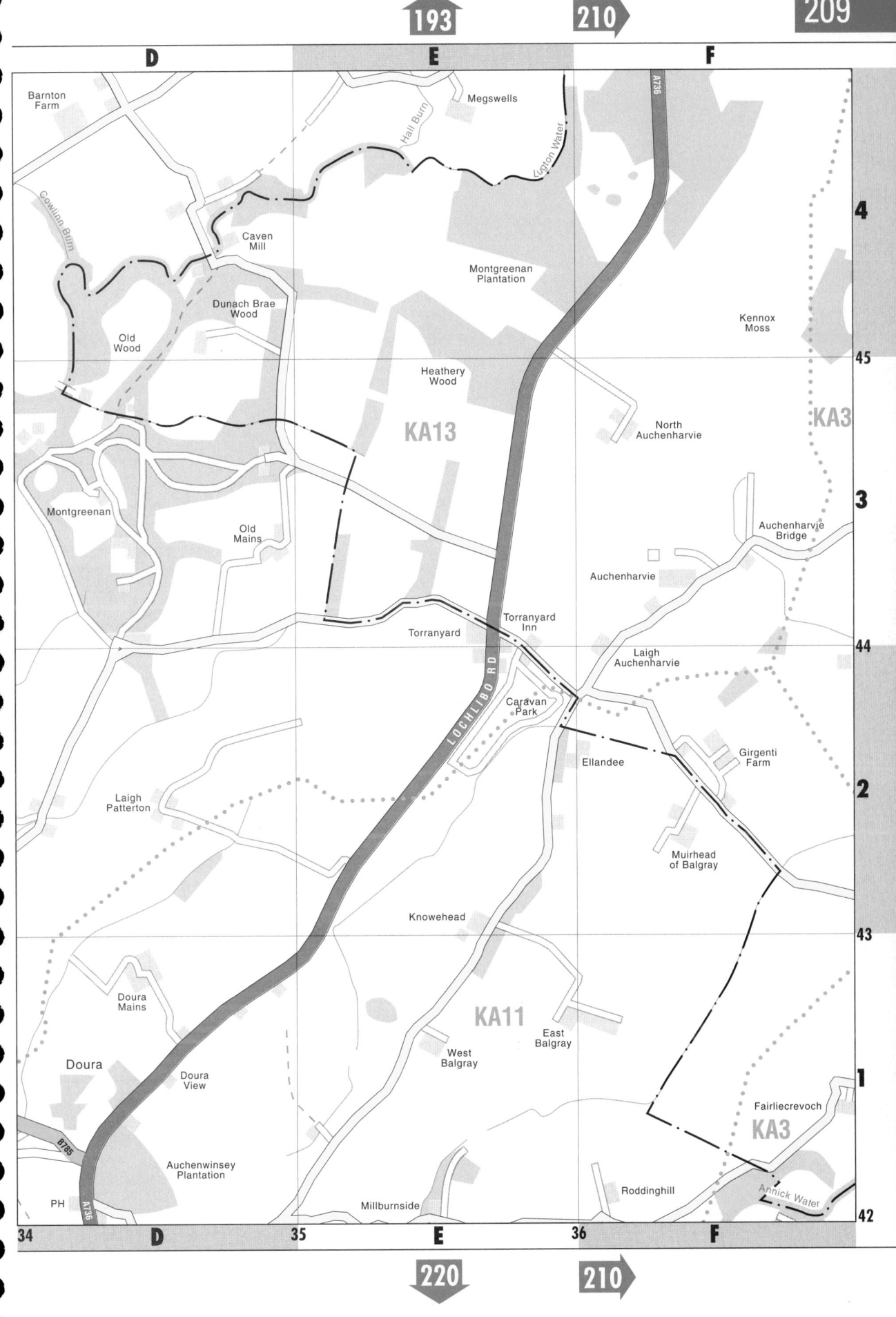
D
E
F
Barnton Farm
Megswells
Hall Burn
Lugton Water
A736
Cowlinn Burn
Caven Mill
Montgreenan Plantation
Dunach Brae Wood
Old Wood
Kennox Moss
Heathery Wood
North Auchenharvie
KA13
KA3
Montgreenan
Old Mains
Auchenharvie Bridge
Auchenharvie
Torranyard Inn
Torranyard
Laigh Auchenharvie
LOCHLIBO RD
Caravan Park
Ellandee
Girgenti Farm
Laigh Patterton
Muirhead of Balgray
Knowehead
Doura Mains
KA11
East Balgray
West Balgray
Doura
Doura View
Fairliecrevoch
KA3
B785
Auchenwinsey Plantation
PH
A736
Millburnside
Roddinghill
Annick Water
4
45
3
44
2
43
1
42
34
35
36
D
E
F

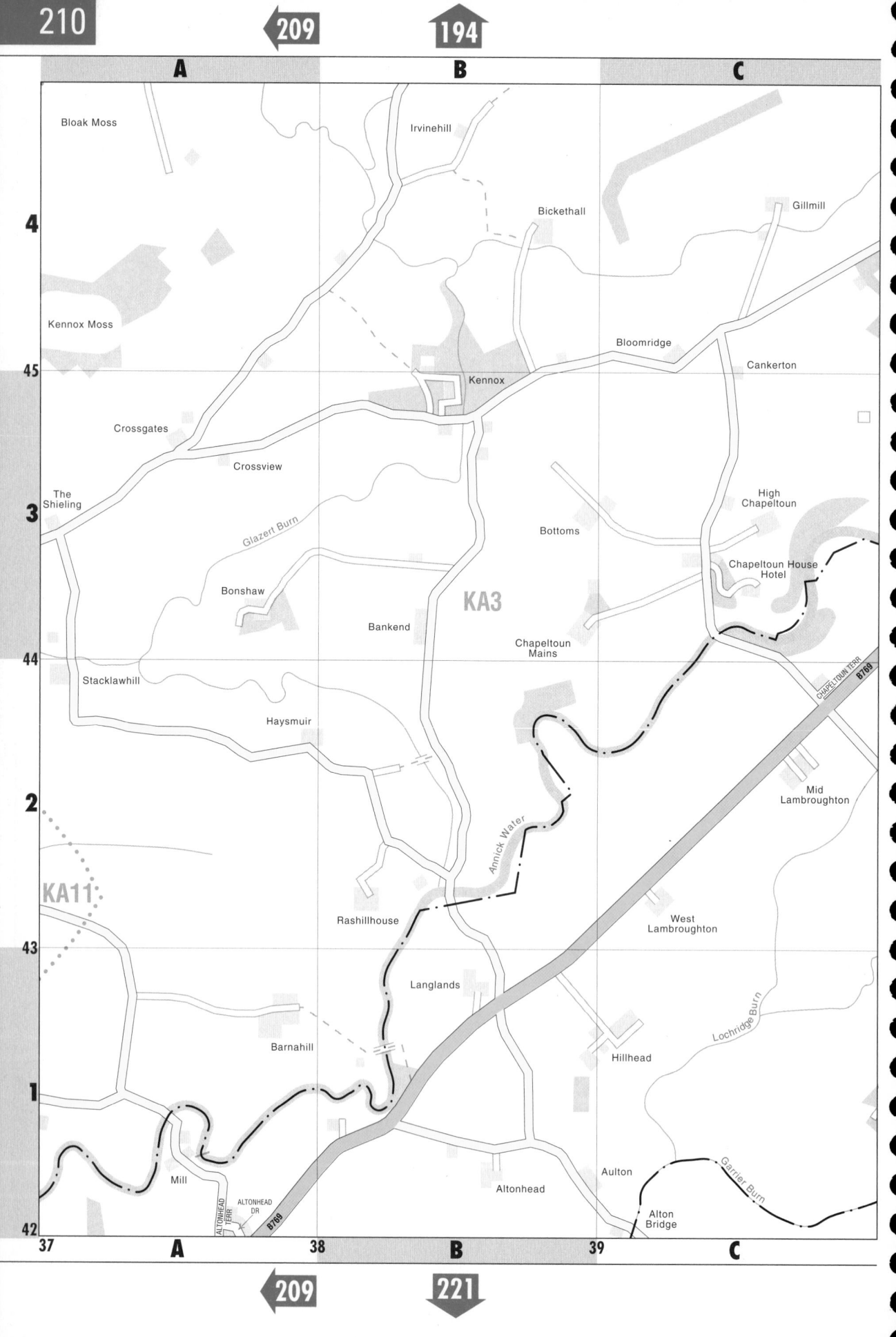

A **B** **C**

Bloak Moss

Irvinehill

Bickethall

Gillmill

4

Kennox Moss

Bloomridge

Cankerton

45

Crossgates

Crossview

High
Chapeltoun

The
Shieling

Glazert Burn

Bottoms

Chapeltoun House
Hotel

3

Bonshaw

KA3

Bankend

Chapeltoun
Mains

44

Stacklawhill

Haysmuir

Mid
Lambroughton

2

KA11

Annick Water

West
Lambroughton

Rashillhouse

43

Langlands

Lochridge Burn

Barnahill

Hillhead

1

Mill

Aulton

Garrier Burn

ALTONHEAD TERR

ALTONHEAD
DR

B769

Altonhead

Alton
Bridge

42

37 **A** **38** **B** **39** **C**

195
212

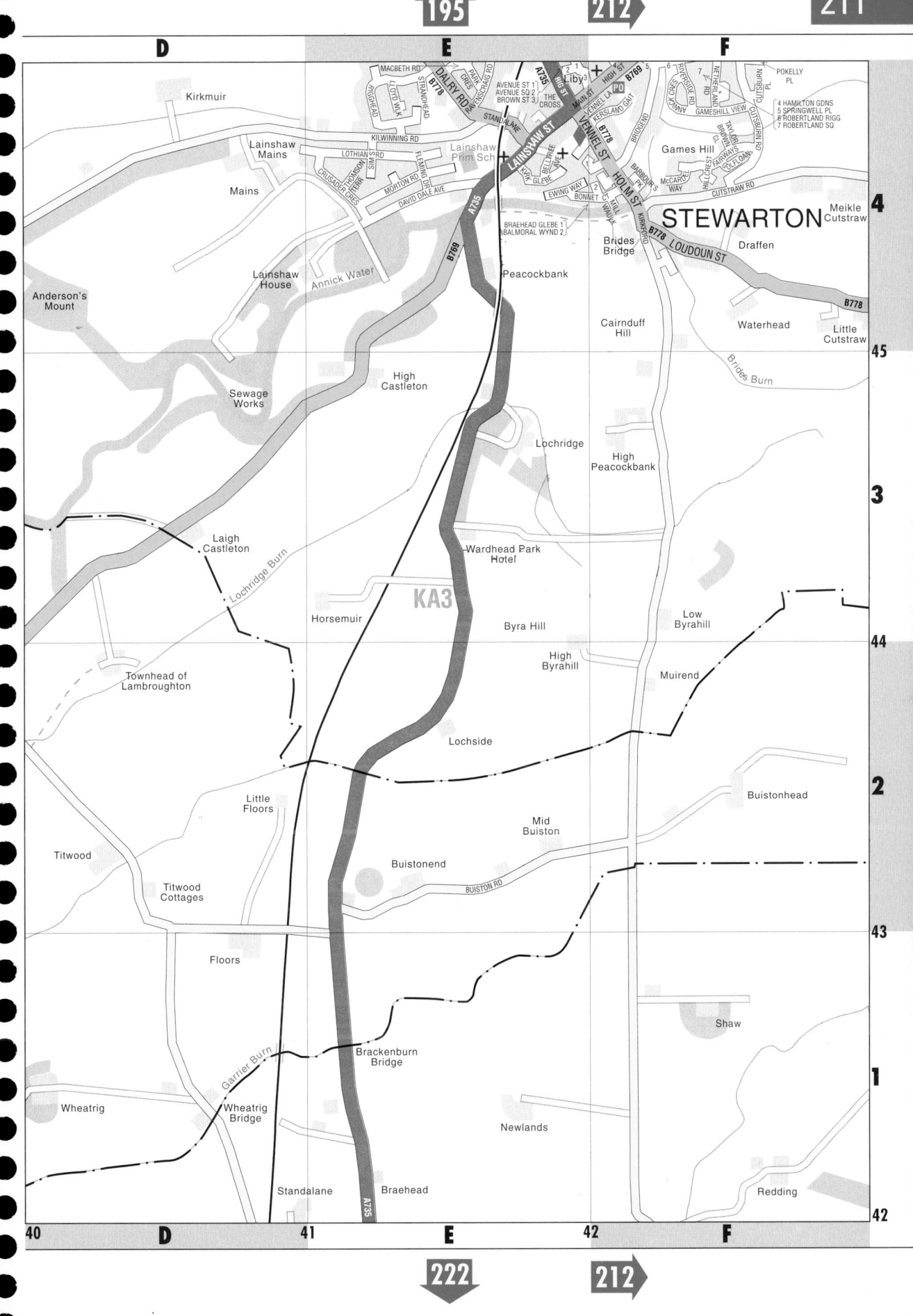
D
E
F
Kirkmuir
MACBETH RD
DALRY RD
B778
PARK CRES
RAVENSCRAIG RD
STRANDHEAD
LLOYD WLK
RIGGHEAD
AVENUE ST 1
AVENUE SQ 2
BROWN ST 3
THE CROSS
A735
RIG ST
Liby
HIGH ST
B769
MAIN ST
VENNEL LA
PO
KERSLAND GAIT
STANDALANE
KILWINNING RD
LAINSHAW ST
Lainshaw Mains
LOTHIAN RD
SIMS ST
FLEMING DR
Lainshaw Prim Sch
BELLTREE AVE
KYLE GLEBE
VENNEL ST
B778
BRIDGEND
RIVERSIDE RD
ANNICK CRES
NETHERLAND RD
GAMESHILL VIEW
CUTSBURN PL
CUTSBURN RD
POKELLY PL
4 HAMILTON GDNS
5 SPRINGWELL PL
6 ROBERTLAND RIGG
7 ROBERTLAND SQ
Games Hill
TAYLOR BROWN CL
FAIRWAYS
POLFLOAN
HILLCREST
McCARDEL WAY
BARBOUR'S PK
CUTSTRAW RD
Mains
THOMSON TERR
CRUSADER CRES
MORTON RD
DAVID DALE AVE
EWING WAY
BONNET CT
MILL WALK
HOLM ST
KIRKFORD
Meikle Cutstraw
STEWARTON
4
BRAEHEAD GLEBE 1
BALMORAL WYND 2
Brides Bridge
B778
LOUDOUN ST
Draffen
Lainshaw House
Annick Water
B769
Peacockbank
Anderson's Mount
Cairnduff Hill
Waterhead
B778
Little Cutstraw
45
Brides Burn
High Castleton
Sewage Works
Lochridge
High Peacockbank
3
Laigh Castleton
Wardhead Park Hotel
Lochridge Burn
KA3
Horsemuir
Byra Hill
Low Byrahill
44
Townhead of Lambroughton
High Byrahill
Muirend
Lochside
2
Buistonhead
Little Floors
Mid Buiston
Titwood
Buistonend
BUISTON RD
Titwood Cottages
43
Floors
Shaw
Garrier Burn
Brackenburn Bridge
1
Wheatrig
Wheatrig Bridge
Newlands
Standalane
Braehead
A735
Redding
42
40
D
41
E
42
F

222
212

A | B | C

Cuts Burn

The Spott

Bogside

West Pokelly

East Pokelly

Darclaboch

Balgray Mill

4

Pokelly Hall

Balgray Mill Burn

B778

Little Cutstraw

45

Thorn

Burnfoot

Burnfoot Reservoir

Blair Hill

Gardrumhill

Poriskon

Over Lochridge

3

Oldhall

Gainford Reservoir

High Gainford

Gainford Bridge

Glaister

44

High Todhill

Low Gainford

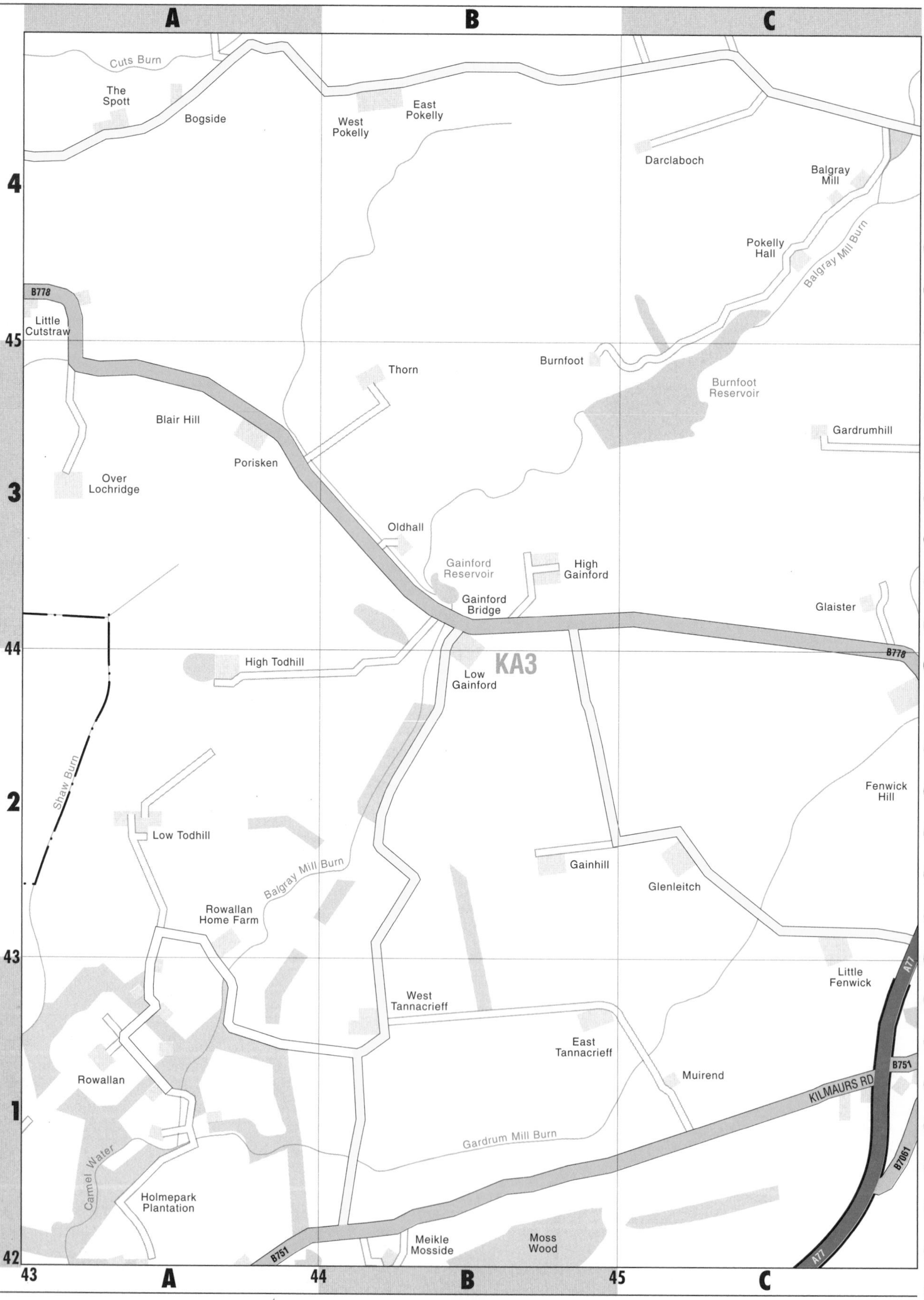

KA3

B778

Shaw Burn

Fenwick Hill

2

Low Todhill

Balgray Mill Burn

Gainhill

Glenleitch

Rowallan Home Farm

43

Little Fenwick

A77

West Tannacrieff

East Tannacrieff

Muirend

Rowallan

KILMAURS RD

B751

1

Gardrum Mill Burn

B7061

Carmel Water

Holmepark Plantation

B751

Meikle Mosside

Moss Wood

A77

42

43 | A | 44 | B | 45 | C

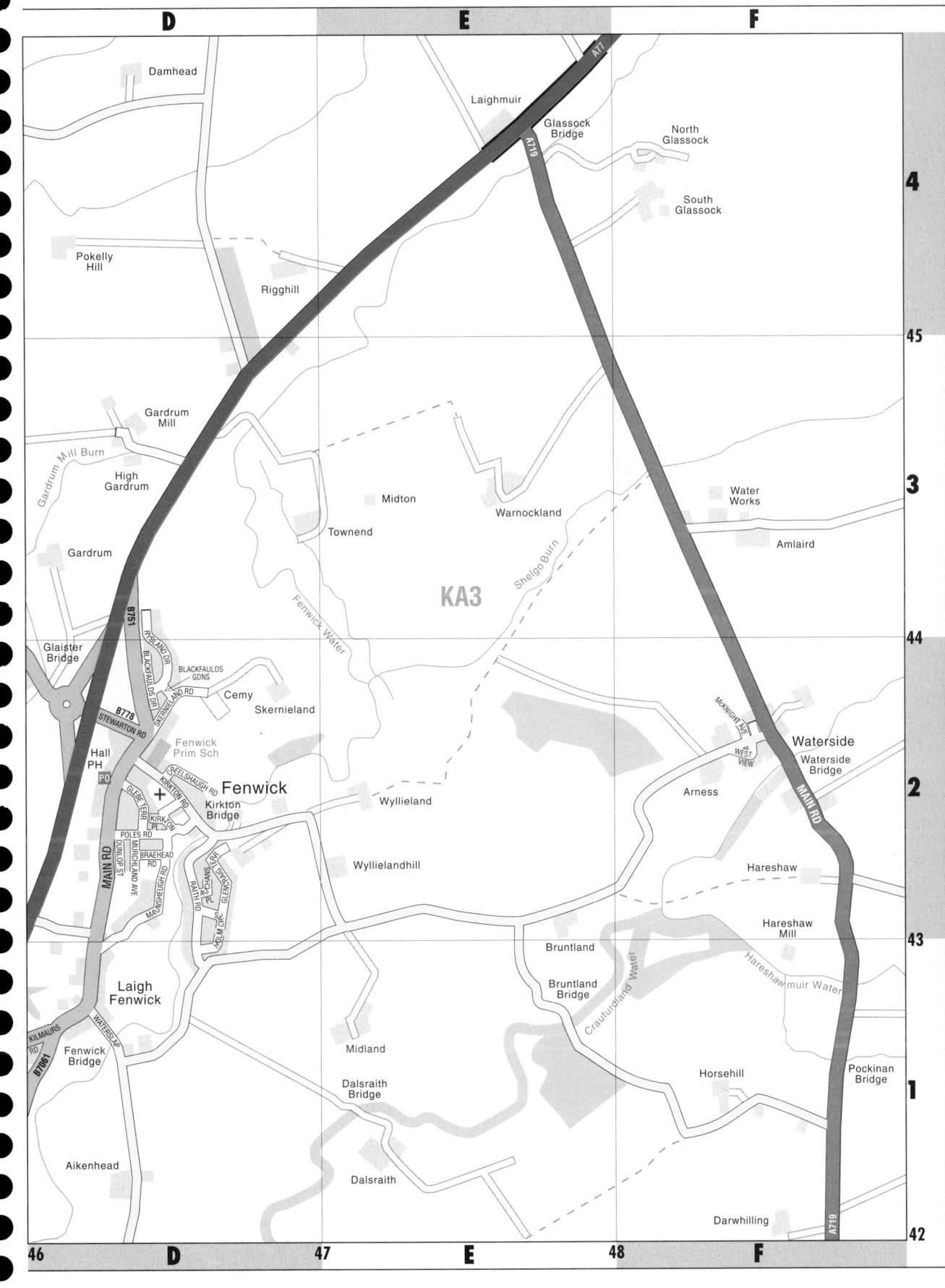

D   E   F

Damhead

Laighmuir

Glassock
Bridge

North
Glassock

A77

A719

South
Glassock

4

Pokelly
Hill

Rigghill

45

Gardrum
Mill

Gardrum Mill Burn

High
Gardrum

Midton

Warnockland

Water
Works

3

Townend

Shelgo Burn

Amlaird

Gardrum

KA3

Fenwick Water

B751

Glaister
Bridge

BLACKFAULDS
GDNS

Cemy

Skernieland

44

RYSLAND DR

BLACKFAULDS DR

SKERNIELAND RD

B778
STEWARTON RD

Fenwick
Prim Sch

McKNIGHT AVE

WEST
VIEW

Waterside

Waterside
Bridge

Hall
PH
PO

Fenwick

Kirkton
Bridge

Wyllieland

Arness

MAIN RD

2

REELSHAUGH RD

KIRKTON RD

GLEBE TERR

KIRK LN

MIRCHLAND AVE

Wyllielandhill

Hareshaw

POLES RD

BRAEHEAD
RD

DUNLOP ST

MANSEHGH RD

RAITH RD

GLENCAIRN TERR

CHANS CRES

KILM CRES

Hareshaw
Mill

MAIN RD

Bruntland

43

Laigh
Fenwick

WATERSLAP

Bruntland
Bridge

Craufurdland Water

Hareshawmuir Water

KILMAURS
RD

B7061

Fenwick
Bridge

Midland

Horsehill

Pockinan
Bridge

1

Aikenhead

Dalsraith
Bridge

Dalsraith

Darwhilling

A719

42

46   D   47   E   48   F

202

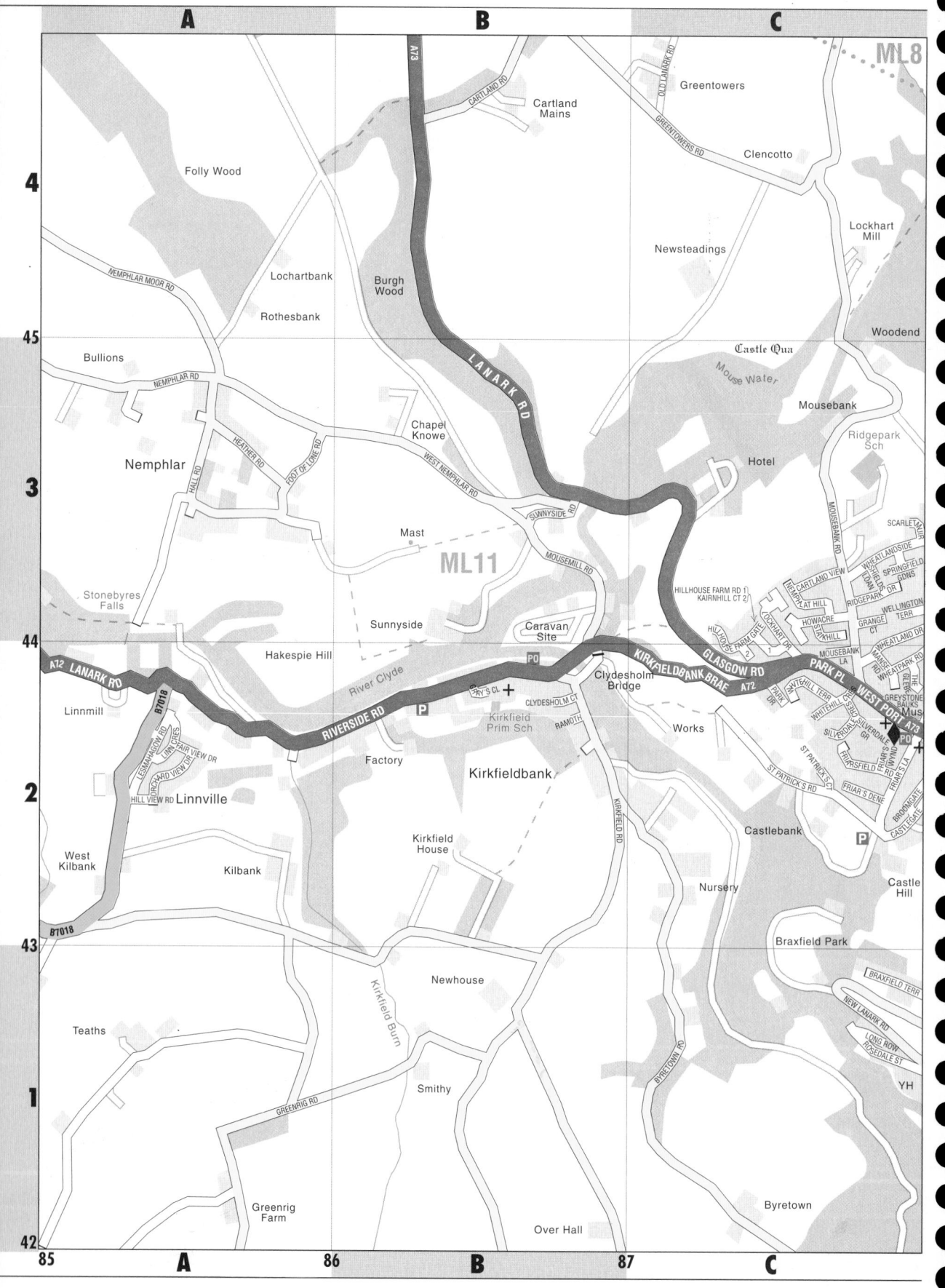
A
B
C
ML8
Greentowers
Cartland Mains
CARTLAND RD
OLD LANARK RD
GREENTOWERS RD
Clencotto
A73
Folly Wood
Lockhart Mill
Newsteadings
NEMPHLAR MOOR RD
Lochartbank
Burgh Wood
Rothesbank
Woodend
Castle Qua
Mouse Water
Bullions
NEMPHLAR RD
LANARK RD
Mousebank
Ridgepark Sch
Chapel Knowe
Hotel
HEATHER RD
FOOT OF LONE RD
Nemphlar
HALL RD
WEST NEMPHLAR RD
MOUSEBANK RD
SUNNYSIDE RD
Mast
ML11
MOUSEMILL RD
Stonebyres Falls
HILLHOUSE FARM RD
KAIRNHILL CT
Sunnyside
Caravan Site
Hakespie Hill
A72 LANARK RD
River Clyde
PO
KIRKFIELDBANK BRAE
GLASGOW RD
PARK PL
WEST PORT
Clydesholm Bridge
Linnmill
B7018
RIVERSIDE RD
CLYDESHOLM CT
Kirkfield Prim Sch
RAMOTH
Works
Factory
Kirkfieldbank
LESMAHAGOW RD
LINN CRES
FAIR VIEW DR
ORCHARD VIEW DR
HILL VIEW RD
Linnville
KIRKFIELD RD
ST PATRICK'S RD
FRIAR'S DENE
Castlebank
Kirkfield House
West Kilbank
Kilbank
Nursery
Castle Hill
Braxfield Park
BRAXFIELD TERR
NEW LANARK RD
LONG ROW
ROSEDALE ST
Newhouse
Teaths
Kirkfield Burn
Smithy
BYRETOWN RD
YH
GREENRIG RD
Greenrig Farm
Byretown
Over Hall
4
45
3
44
2
43
1
42
85
86
87

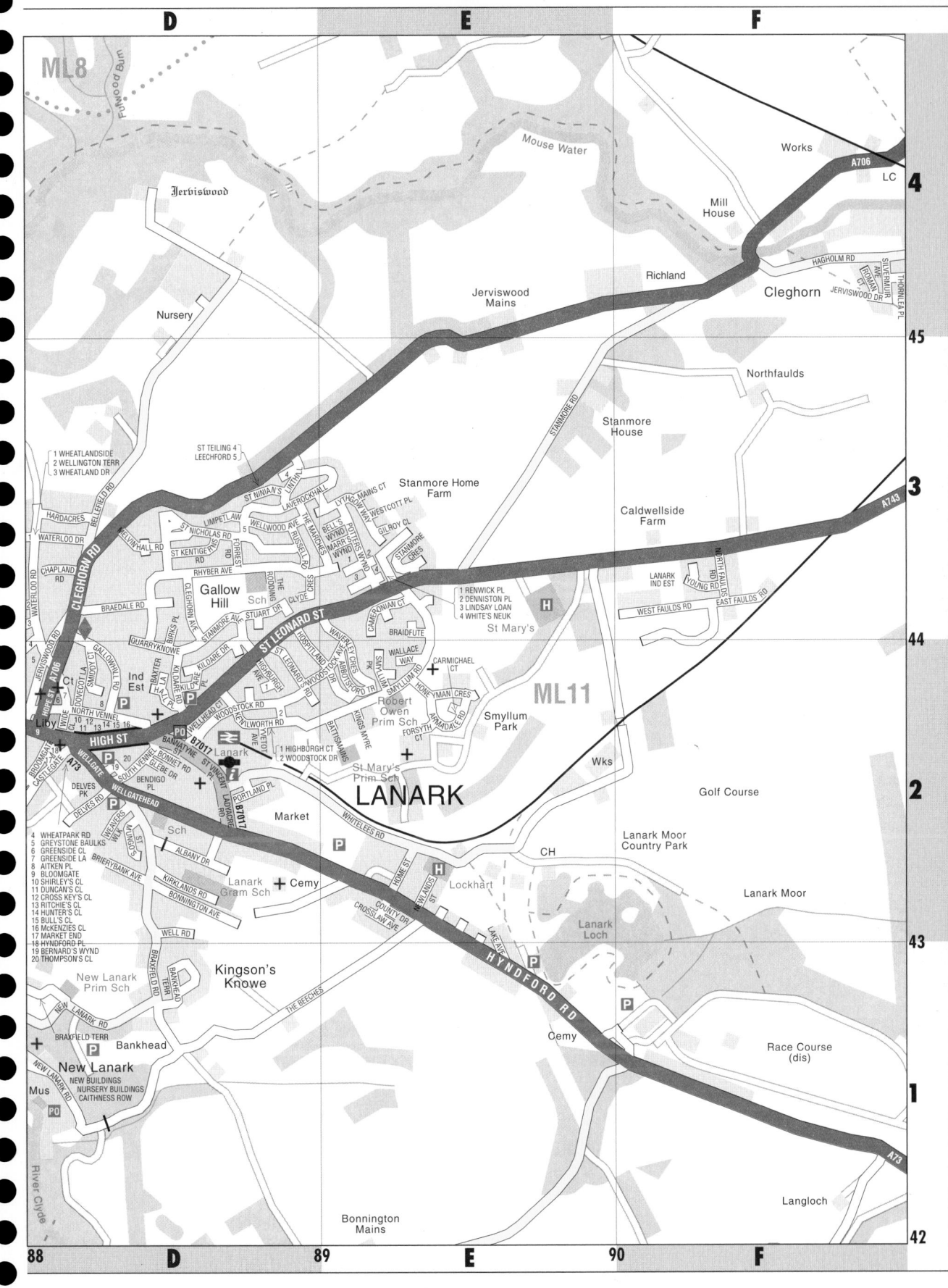
203
D
E
F
ML8
Fullwood Burn
Mouse Water
Works
A706
LC
Jerviswood
Mill House
Richland
Cleghorn
HAGHOLM RD
JERVISWOOD DR
Jerviswood Mains
Nursery
Northfaulds
Stanmore House
STANMORE RD
Stanmore Home Farm
Caldwellside Farm
A743
LANARK IND EST
YOUNG RD
NORTH FAULDS RD
WEST FAULDS RD
EAST FAULDS RD
1 WHEATLANDSIDE
2 WELLINGTON TERR
3 WHEATLAND DR
ST TEILING 4
LEECHFORD 5
HARDACRES
WATERLOO DR
CHAPLAND RD
CLEGHORN RD
Gallow Hill
Sch
1 RENWICK PL
2 DENNISTON PL
3 LINDSAY LOAN
4 WHITE'S NEUK
St Mary's
ST LEONARD ST
Ind Est
ML11
Smyllum Park
Robert Owen Prim Sch
HIGH ST
Liby
Lanark
1 HIGHBURGH CT
2 WOODSTOCK DR
St Mary's Prim Sch
LANARK
Wks
Golf Course
Market
WHITELEES RD
Lanark Moor Country Park
CH
Lockhart
Lanark Moor
Lanark Gram Sch
Cemy
Lanark Loch
4 WHEATPARK RD
5 GREYSTONE BAULKS
6 GREENSIDE CL
7 GREENSIDE LA
8 AITKEN PL
9 BLOOMGATE
10 SHIRLEY'S CL
11 DUNCAN'S CL
12 CROSS KEY'S CL
13 RITCHIE'S CL
14 HUNTER'S CL
15 BULL'S CL
16 McKENZIES CL
17 MARKET END
18 HYNDFORD PL
19 BERNARD'S WYND
20 THOMPSON'S CL
HYNDFORD RD
New Lanark Prim Sch
Kingson's Knowe
THE BEECHES
Bankhead
New Lanark
NEW BUILDINGS
NURSERY BUILDINGS
CAITHNESS ROW
Mus
Cemy
Race Course (dis)
A73
River Clyde
Langloch
Bonnington Mains
88
89
90
42
43
44
45
1
2
3
4

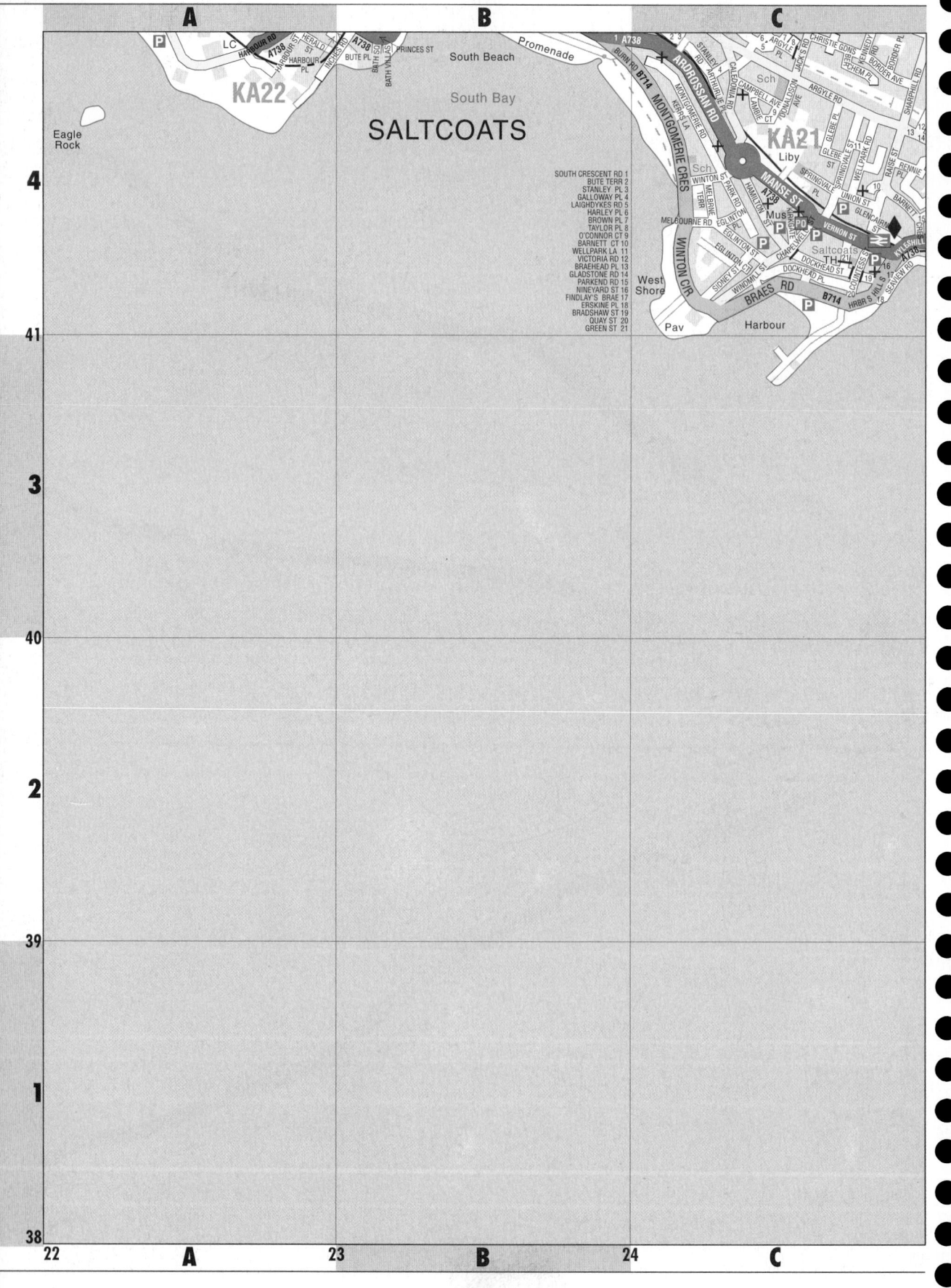

SALTCOATS

Eagle
Rock

KA22

South Beach

South Bay

KA21
Liby

SOUTH CRESCENT RD 1
BUTE TERR 2
STANLEY PL 3
GALLOWAY PL 4
LAIGHDYKES RD 5
HARLEY PL 6
BROWN PL 7
TAYLOR PL 8
O'CONNOR CT 9
BARNETT CT 10
WELLPARK LA 11
VICTORIA RD 12
BRAEHEAD PL 13
GLADSTONE RD 14
PARKEND RD 15
NINEYARD ST 16
FINDLAY'S BRAE 17
ERSKINE PL 18
BRADSHAW ST 19
QUAY ST 20
GREEN ST 21

West
Shore

Pav

Harbour

206
218

D
E
F
STEVENSTON
Auchenharvie
Auchenharvie Acad
Park
Golf Course
KA21
KA20
Saltcoats Campbell
CH
Caravan Park
Caravan Park
Liby
Cemy
Glencairn Prim Sch
Ardeer Park
Stevenston
Ardeer Prim Sch
East Shore
Beach Park
STEVENSTON IND EST
PORTLAND PLACE IND EST
MOORPARK IND EST
SALTCOATS RD
BOGLEMART ST A738
CANAL ST
CALEDONIAN RD
B752
SANDYLANDS PROM
1 THOMAS CAMPBELL ST
2 McISAAC RD
3 PARKEND GDNS
4 CANAL CT
5 PARKEND AVE
4
41
3
40
2
39
1
38
25
26
27

218

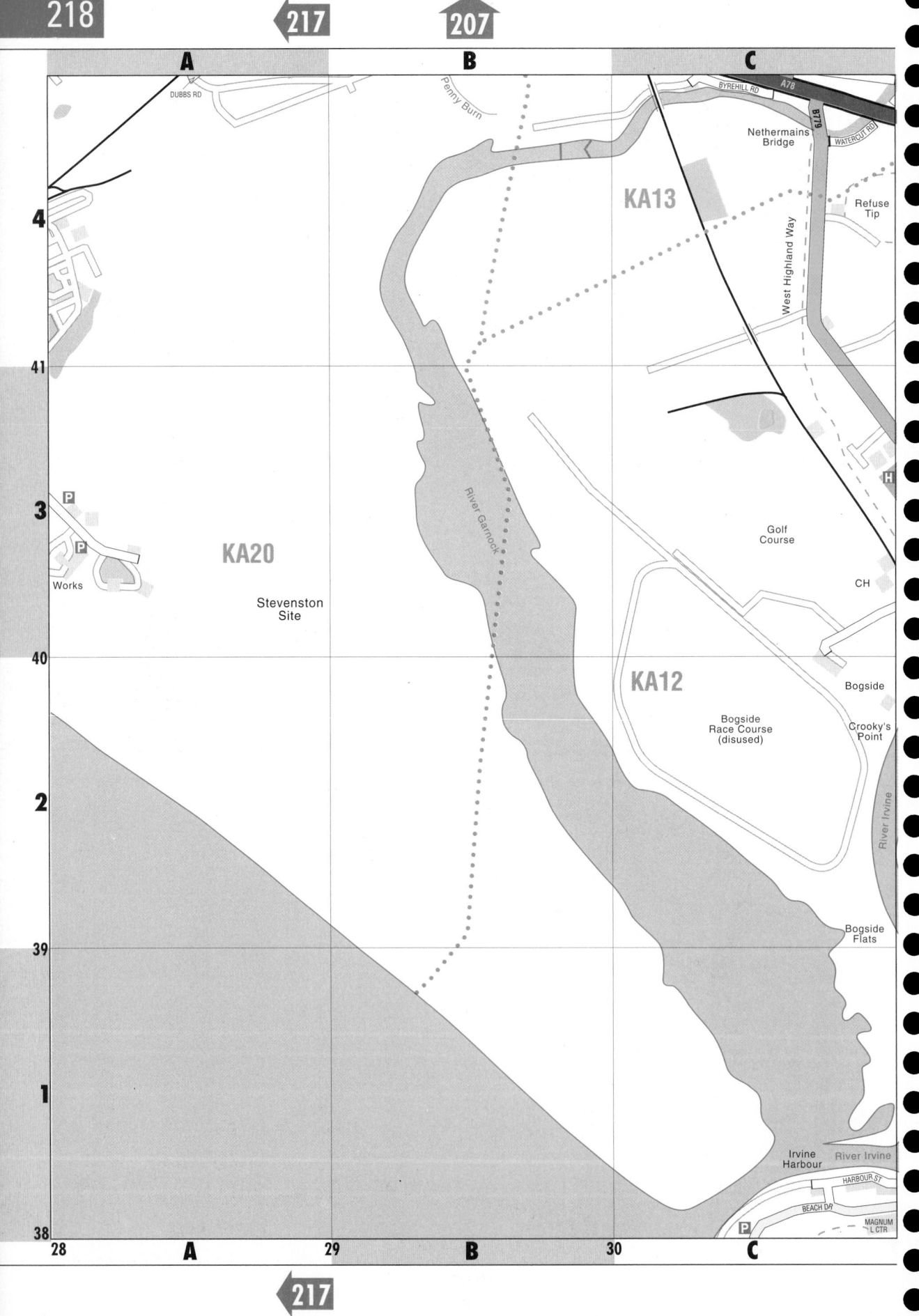

DUBBS RD

Penny Burn

BYREHILL RD
A78
B779
Nethermains
Bridge
WATERCUT RD

KA13

Refuse
Tip

West Highland Way

4

41

River Garnock

P

KA20

P

Works

Stevenston
Site

3

Golf
Course

CH

H

40

KA12

Bogside

Bogside
Race Course
(disused)

Crooky's
Point

2

River Irvine

39

Bogside
Flats

1

Irvine
Harbour
River Irvine
HARBOUR ST

BEACH DR

P

MAGNUM
L CTR

38

208 220

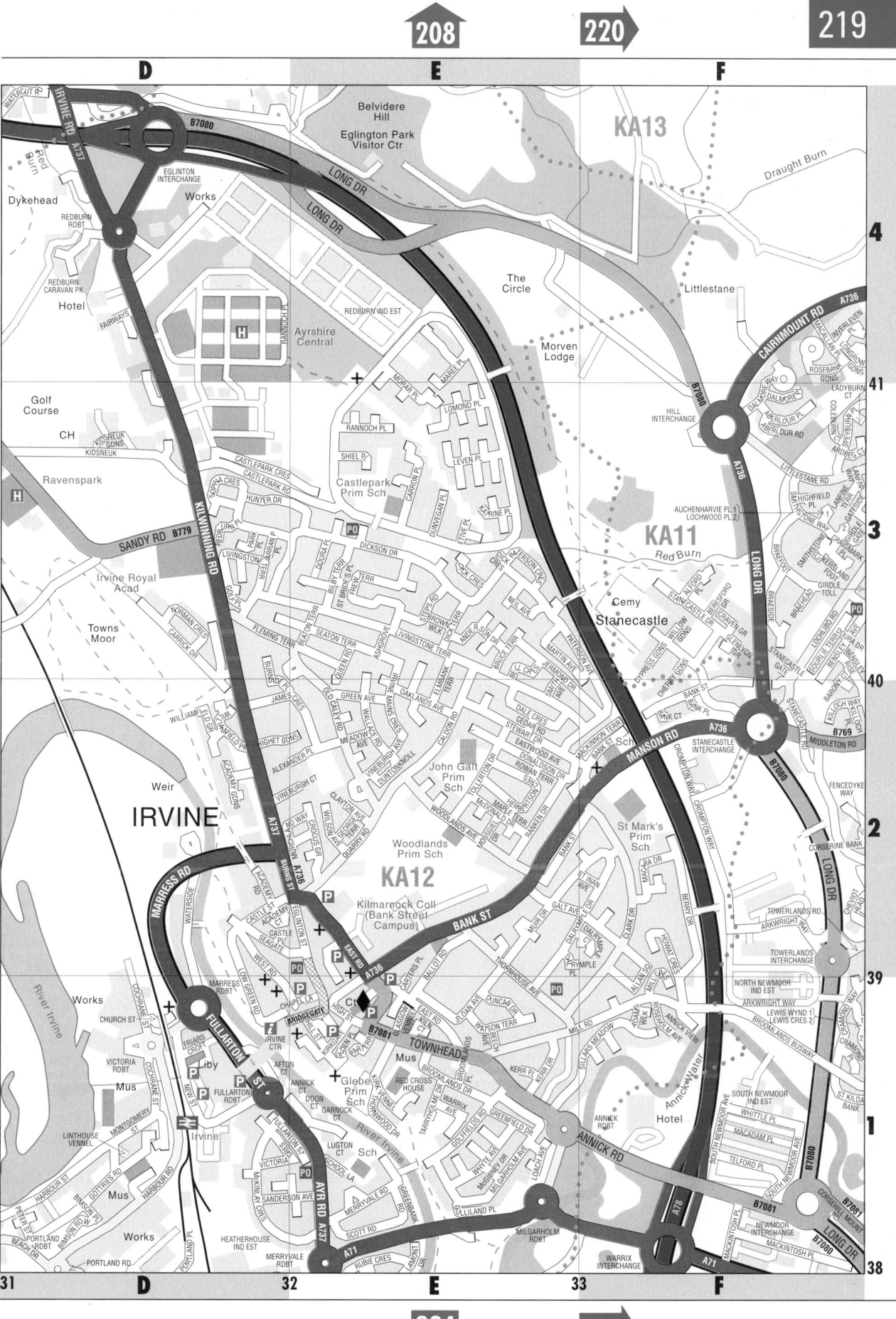
IRVINE
KA12
KA11
KA13
Belvidere Hill
Eglington Park Visitor Ctr
Ayrshire Central
Dykehead
Golf Course
Ravenspark
Irvine Royal Acad
Towns Moor
Weir
The Circle
Littlestane
Morven Lodge
Stanecastle
Castlepark Prim Sch
John Galt Prim Sch
Woodlands Prim Sch
St Mark's Prim Sch
Kilmarnock Coll (Bank Street Campus)
Glebe Prim Sch
River Irvine
Annick Water
Draught Burn
Red Burn
KILWINNING RD
LONG DR
MANSON RD
BANK ST
TOWNHEAD
ANNICK RD
MARRESS RD
FULLARTON ST
AYR RD
SANDY RD
IRVINE RD
EGLINTON INTERCHANGE
HILL INTERCHANGE
STANECASTLE INTERCHANGE
TOWERLANDS INTERCHANGE
NEWMOOR INTERCHANGE
WARRIX INTERCHANGE
MILGARHOLM RDBT
MERRYVALE RDBT
MARRESS RDBT
FULLARTON RDBT
VICTORIA RDBT
ANNICK RDBT
PORTLAND RDBT
REDBURN RDBT
REDBURN IND EST
NORTH NEWMOOR IND EST
SOUTH NEWMOOR IND EST
HEATHERHOUSE IND EST

224 220

219
209

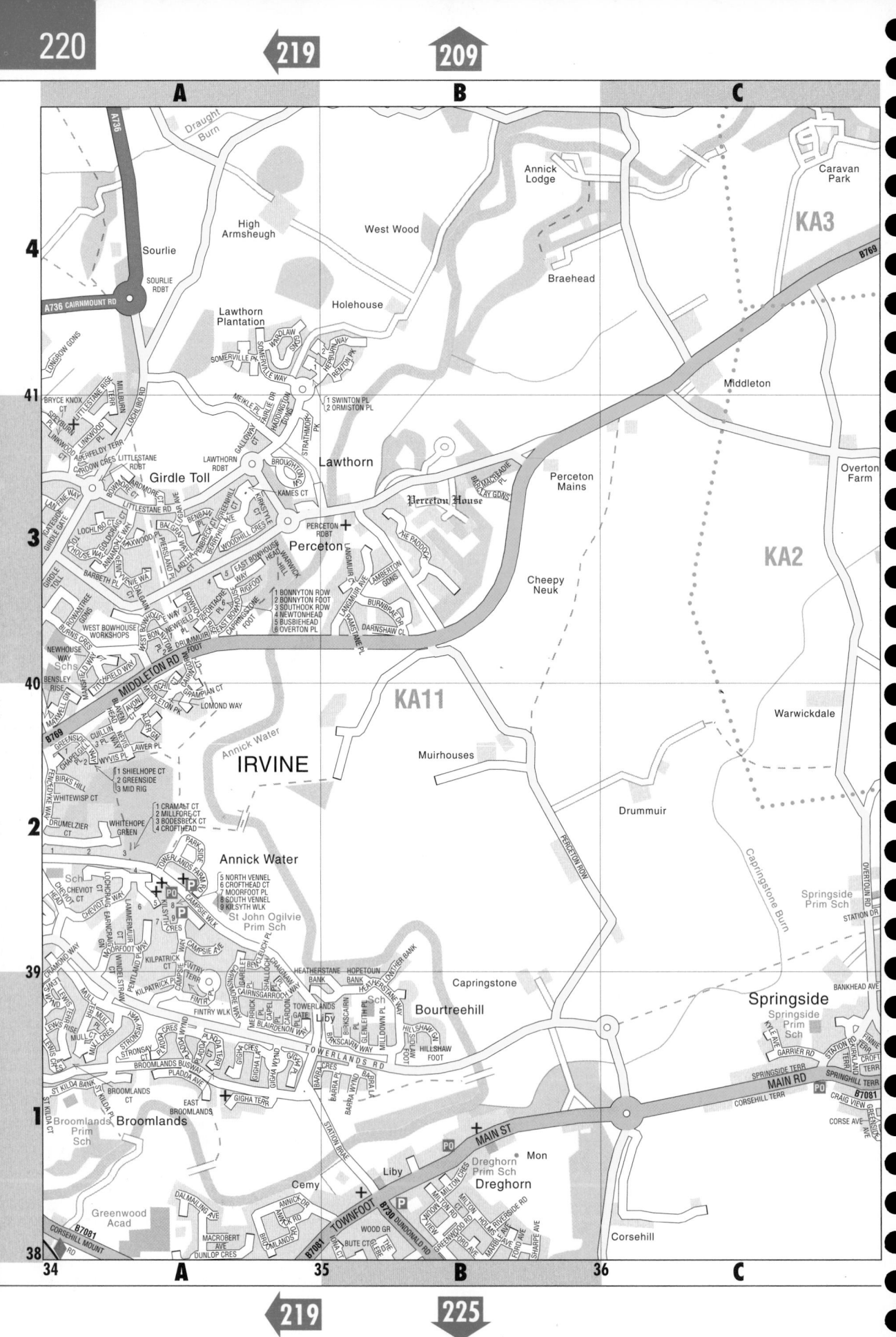
A
B
C
4
3
2
1
41
40
39
38
34
35
36
Draught Burn
A736
Sourlie
SOURLIE RDBT
A736 CAIRNMOUNT RD
High Armsheugh
West Wood
Annick Lodge
Caravan Park
KA3
B769
Braehead
Holehouse
Lawthorn Plantation
Middleton
Lawthorn
Girdle Toll
Perceton Mains
Overton Farm
Perceton House
Perceton
PERCETON RDBT
KA2
Cheepy Neuk
MIDDLETON RD
KA11
Warwickdale
Annick Water
IRVINE
Muirhouses
Drummuir
PERCETON ROW
Annick Water
Capringstone Burn
Springside Prim Sch
St John Ogilvie Prim Sch
Capringstone
Springside
Bourtreehill
TOWERLANDS RD
MAIN RD
B7081
Broomlands Prim Sch
Broomlands
MAIN ST
Dreghorn Prim Sch
Mon
Dreghorn
Liby
Cemy
Greenwood Acad
TOWNFOOT
B730 DUNDONALD RD
Corsehill
CORSEHILL MOUNT

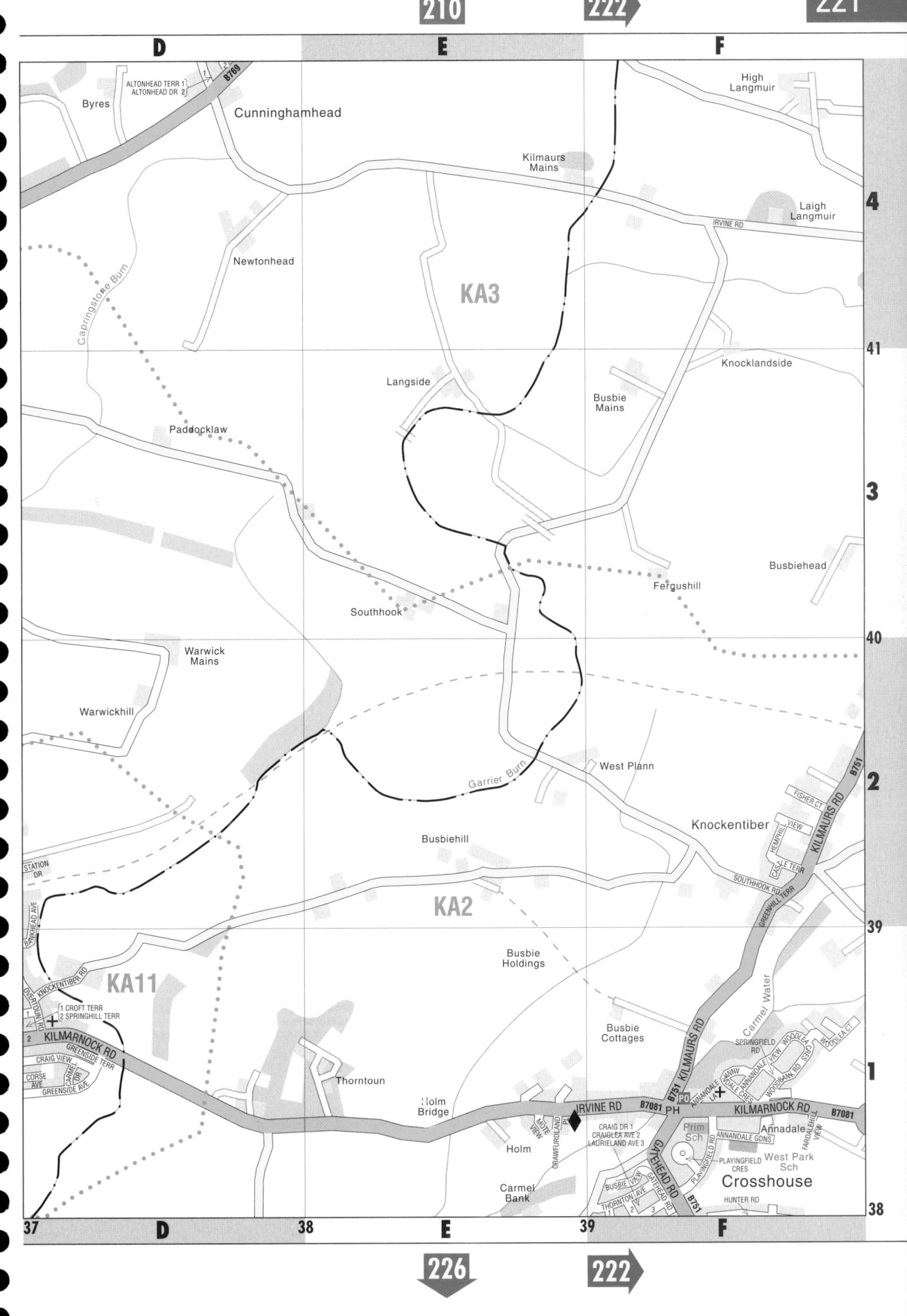

B7769

ALTONHEAD TERR 1
ALTONHEAD DR 2

Byres

Cunninghamhead

High Langmuir

Kilmaurs Mains

IRVINE RD

Laigh Langmuir

4

Newtonhead

KA3

Capringstone Burn

41

Knocklandside

Langside

Busbie Mains

Paddocklaw

3

Busbiehead

Fergushill

Southhook

Warwick Mains

40

Warwickhill

West Plann

Garrier Burn

2

Knockentiber

FISHER CT

KILMAURS RD

B751

HEMPHILL VIEW

CASTLE TERR

SOUTHHOOK RD

GREENHILL TERR

STATION DR

Busbiehill

BOWHEAD AVE

KA2

39

Busbie Holdings

Carmel Water

SPRINGFIELD RD

KA11

KNOCKENTIBER RD

1 CROFT TERR
2 SPRINGHILL TERR

Busbie Cottages

ANNANDALE VIEW

WOODPARK RD

ROYALE CRES

MINN CRES

ROYALE CT

OVERTOUN RD

2   KILMARNOCK RD

GREENSIDE TERR

CRAIG VIEW

CORSE AVE

CARMEL DR

GREENSIDE AVE

Thorntoun

Busbie View

THORNTON AVE

Holm Bridge

Holm

CRAWFURDLAND

MOTE VIEW

IRVINE RD   B7081   PH

CRAIG DR 1
CRAIGLEA AVE 2
LAURIELAND AVE 3

GATEHEAD RD

Prim Sch

ANNANDALE GDNS

PLAYINGFIELD CRES

KILMARNOCK RD   B7081

Annadale

FARDALEHILL VIEW

West Park Sch

1

Carmel Bank

Crosshouse

HUNTER RD

38

221 211

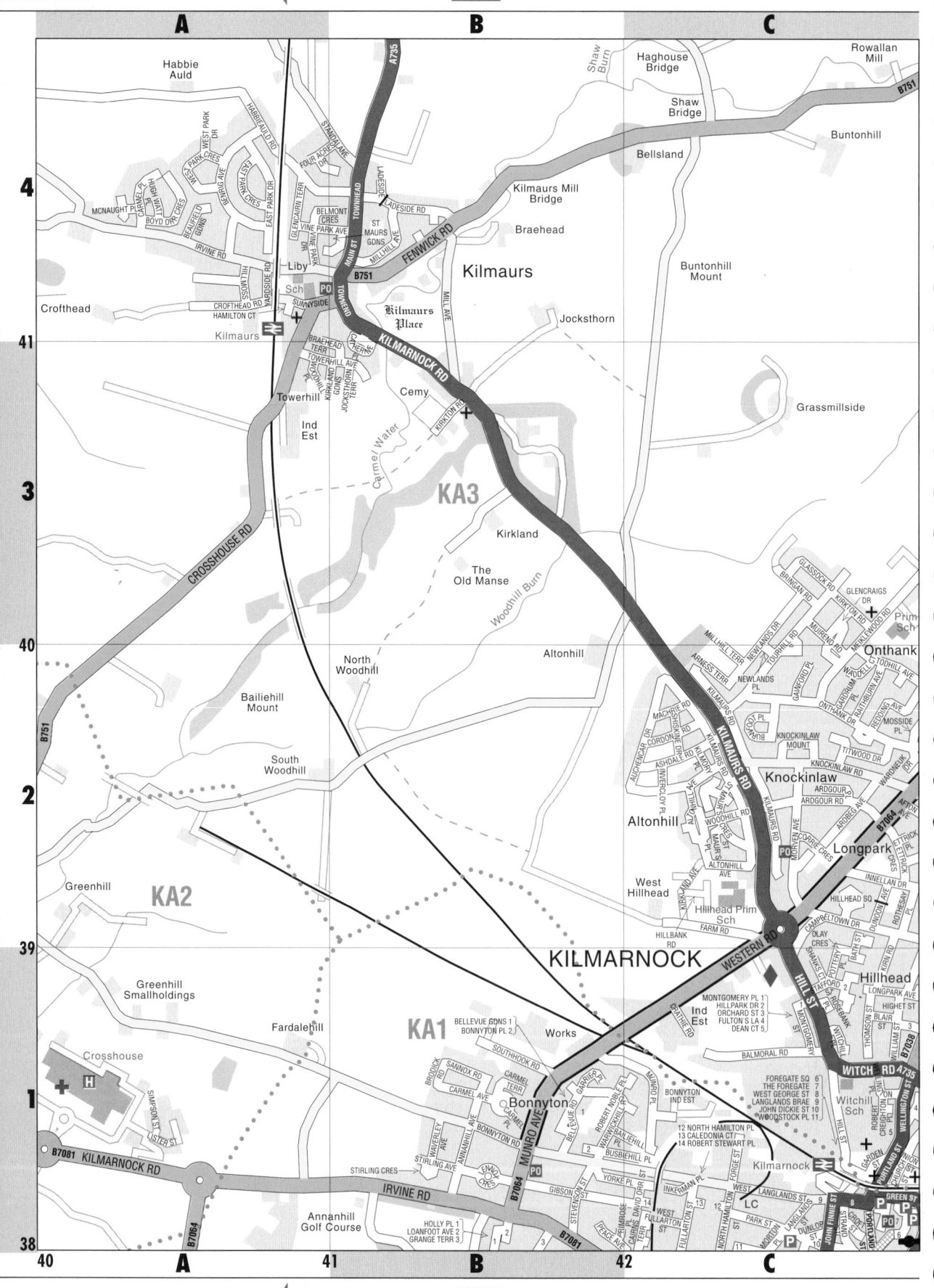
A
B
C
4
3
2
1
41
40
39
38
40
41
42
Habbie Auld
Haghouse Bridge
Rowallan Mill
Shaw Bridge
Shaw Burn
Bellsland
Buntonhill
Kilmaurs Mill Bridge
Braehead
Kilmaurs
Liby
Crofthead
Kilmaurs Place
Jocksthorn
Buntonhill Mount
Towerhill
Ind Est
Cemy
Grassmillside
KA3
Kirkland
The Old Manse
Carmel Water
Woodhill Burn
Altonhill
North Woodhill
Bailiehill Mount
South Woodhill
Onthank
Knockinlaw
Longpark
Altonhill
West Hillhead
Hillhead Prim Sch
KA2
Greenhill
KILMARNOCK
Greenhill Smallholdings
Fardalehill
KA1
Works
Ind Est
Hillhead
Crosshouse
Bonnyton
Witchill Sch
Kilmarnock
Annanhill Golf Course
CROSSHOUSE RD
KILMARNOCK RD
KILMAURS RD
WESTERN RD
HILL ST
IRVINE RD
MUNRO AVE
FENWICK RD
WITCH RD
A735
B751
B7064
B7081
B7038
BELLEVUE GDNS 1
BONNYTON PL 2
MONTGOMERY PL 1
HILLPARK DR 2
ORCHARD ST 3
FULTON'S LA 4
DEAN CT 5
FOREGATE SQ 6
THE FOREGATE 7
WEST GEORGE ST 8
LANGLANDS BRAE 9
JOHN DICKIE ST 10
WOODSTOCK PL 11
12 NORTH HAMILTON PL
13 CALEDONIA CT
14 ROBERT STEWART PL
HOLLY PL 1
LOANFOOT AVE 2
GRANGE TERR 3

221 227

212

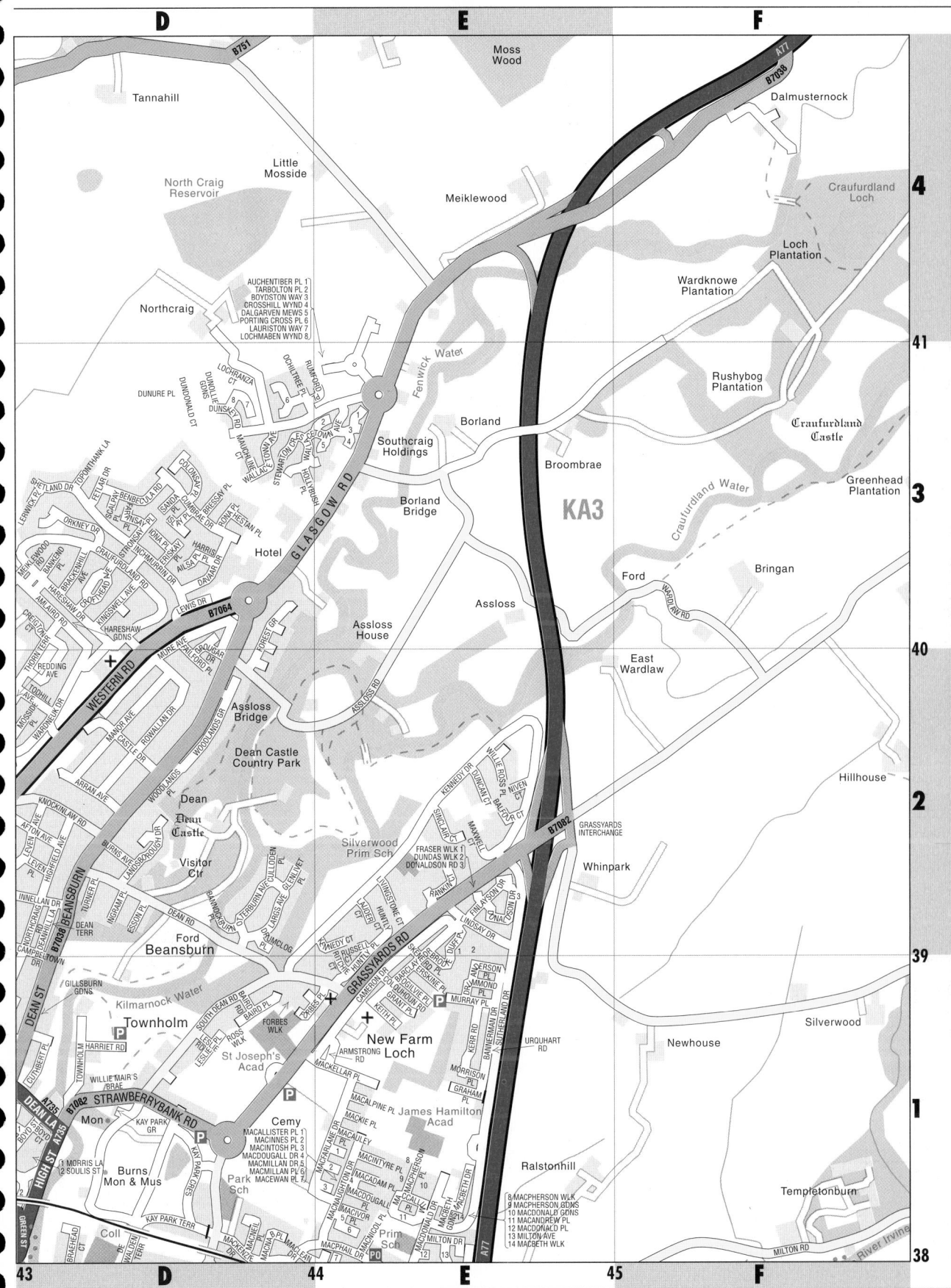

D
E
F
4
41
3
40
2
39
1
38
43
44
45
Moss Wood
Tannahill
Dalmusternock
Little Mosside
North Craig Reservoir
Meiklewood
Craufurdland Loch
Loch Plantation
Wardknowe Plantation
Northcraig
AUCHENTIBER PL 1
TARBOLTON PL 2
BOYDSTON WAY 3
CROSSHILL WYND 4
DALGARVEN MEWS 5
PORTING CROSS PL 6
LAURISTON WAY 7
LOCHMABEN WYND 8
Fenwick Water
Rushybog Plantation
Borland
Craufurdland Castle
Southcraig Holdings
Broombrae
Greenhead Plantation
Craufurdland Water
Borland Bridge
KA3
GLASGOW RD
Hotel
Bringan
Ford
WARDLAW RD
Assloss
Assloss House
East Wardlaw
WESTERN RD
ASSLOSS RD
Assloss Bridge
Dean Castle Country Park
Hillhouse
Dean
Dean Castle
Visitor Ctr
Silverwood Prim Sch
GRASSYARDS INTERCHANGE
Whinpark
FRASER WLK 1
DUNDAS WLK 2
DONALDSON RD 3
BEANSBURN
Ford
Beansburn
GRASSYARDS RD
Kilmarnock Water
Townholm
New Farm Loch
URQUHART RD
Newhouse
Silverwood
St Joseph's Acad
James Hamilton Acad
STRAWBERRYBANK RD
Cemy
Mon
MACALLISTER PL 1
MACINNES PL 2
MACINTOSH PL 3
MACDOUGALL DR 4
MACMILLAN DR 5
MACMILLAN PL 6
MACEWAN PL 7
1 MORRIS LA
2 SOULIS ST
Burns Mon & Mus
Park Sch
Ralstonhill
8 MACPHERSON WLK
9 MACPHERSON GDNS
10 MACDONALD GDNS
11 MACANDREW PL
12 MACDONALD PL
13 MILTON AVE
14 MACBETH WLK
Templetonburn
KAY PARK TERR
Coll
Prim Sch
MILTON DR
MILTON RD
River Irvine
A77
B7038
B751
B7064
B7082
A735
HIGH ST
DEAN ST
DEAN LA

228

219

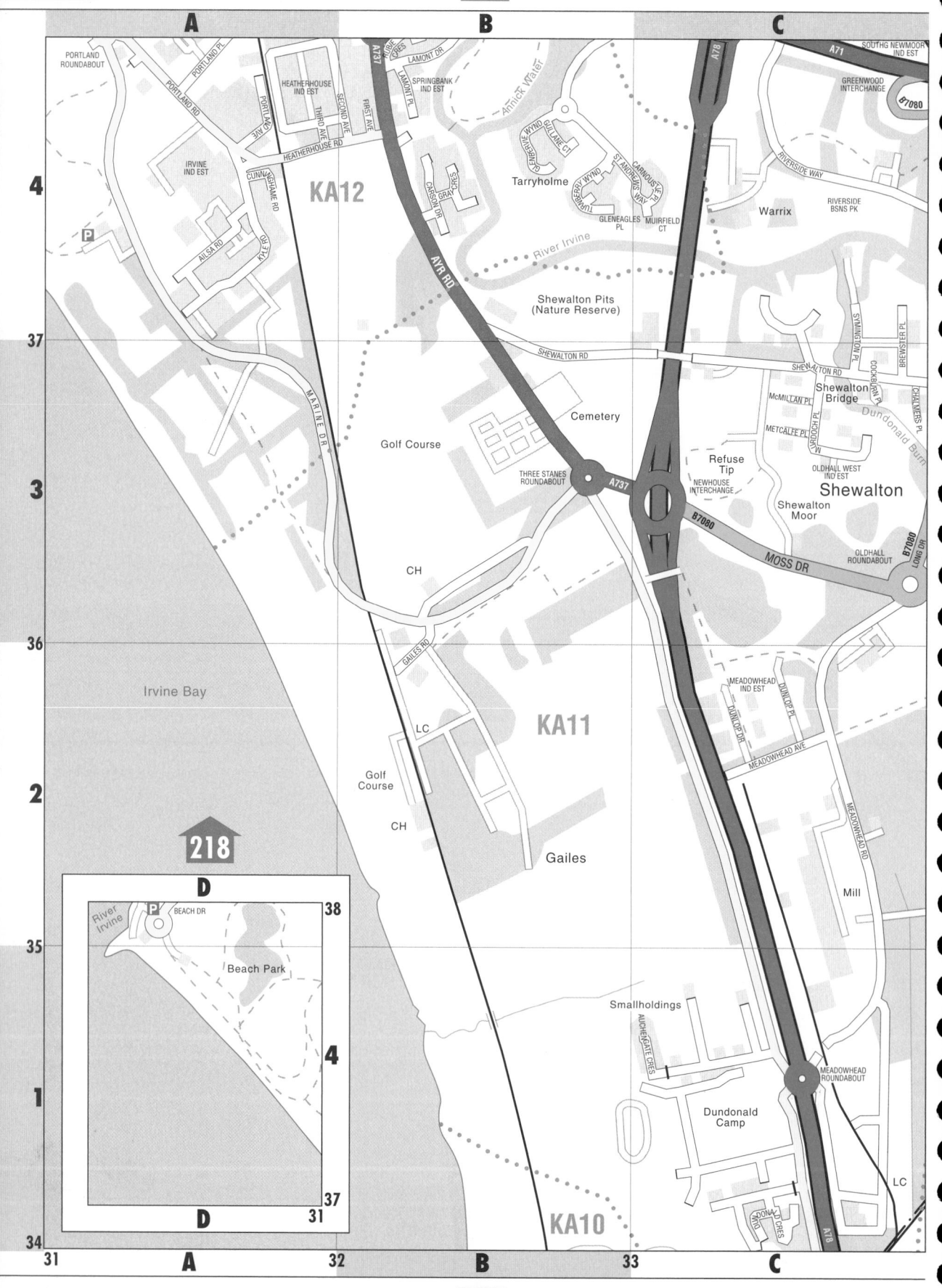
A
B
C
4
3
2
1
37
36
35
34
31
32
33
PORTLAND ROUNDABOUT
PORTLAND PL
PORTLAND RD
HEATHERHOUSE IND EST
SPRINGBANK IND EST
LAMONT DR
LAMONT PL
HEATHERHOUSE RD
THIRD AVE
SECOND AVE
FIRST AVE
IRVINE IND EST
CUNNINGHAME RD
KA12
CARSON DR
GRAY CRES
Annick Water
Tarryholme
GULLANE CT
ST ANDREWS WAY
CARNOUSTIE PL
TURNBERRY WYND
GLENEAGLES PL
MUIRFIELD CT
AILSA RD
KYLE RD
AYR RD
River Irvine
Shewalton Pits
(Nature Reserve)
A737
A78
A71
SOUTHG NEWMOOR IND EST
GREENWOOD INTERCHANGE
B7080
RIVERSIDE WAY
RIVERSIDE BSNS PK
Warrix
SHEWALTON RD
SYMINGTON PL
BREWSTER PL
COCKBURN PL
CHALMERS PL
Shewalton Bridge
McMILLAN PL
METCALFE PL
MURDOCH PL
Dundonald Burn
Cemetery
Refuse Tip
NEWHOUSE INTERCHANGE
OLDHALL WEST IND EST
Shewalton
Shewalton Moor
MOSS DR
OLDHALL ROUNDABOUT
LONG DR
MARINE DR
Golf Course
THREE STANES ROUNDABOUT
CH
GAILES RD
Irvine Bay
MEADOWHEAD IND EST
DUNLOP PL
DUNLOP DR
KA11
LC
MEADOWHEAD AVE
MEADOWHEAD RD
Golf Course
CH
Gailes
Mill
D
River Irvine
BEACH DR
38
Beach Park
4
37
31
Smallholdings
AUCHENGATE CRES
MEADOWHEAD ROUNDABOUT
Dundonald Camp
KA10
MACDONALD CRES
LC

218

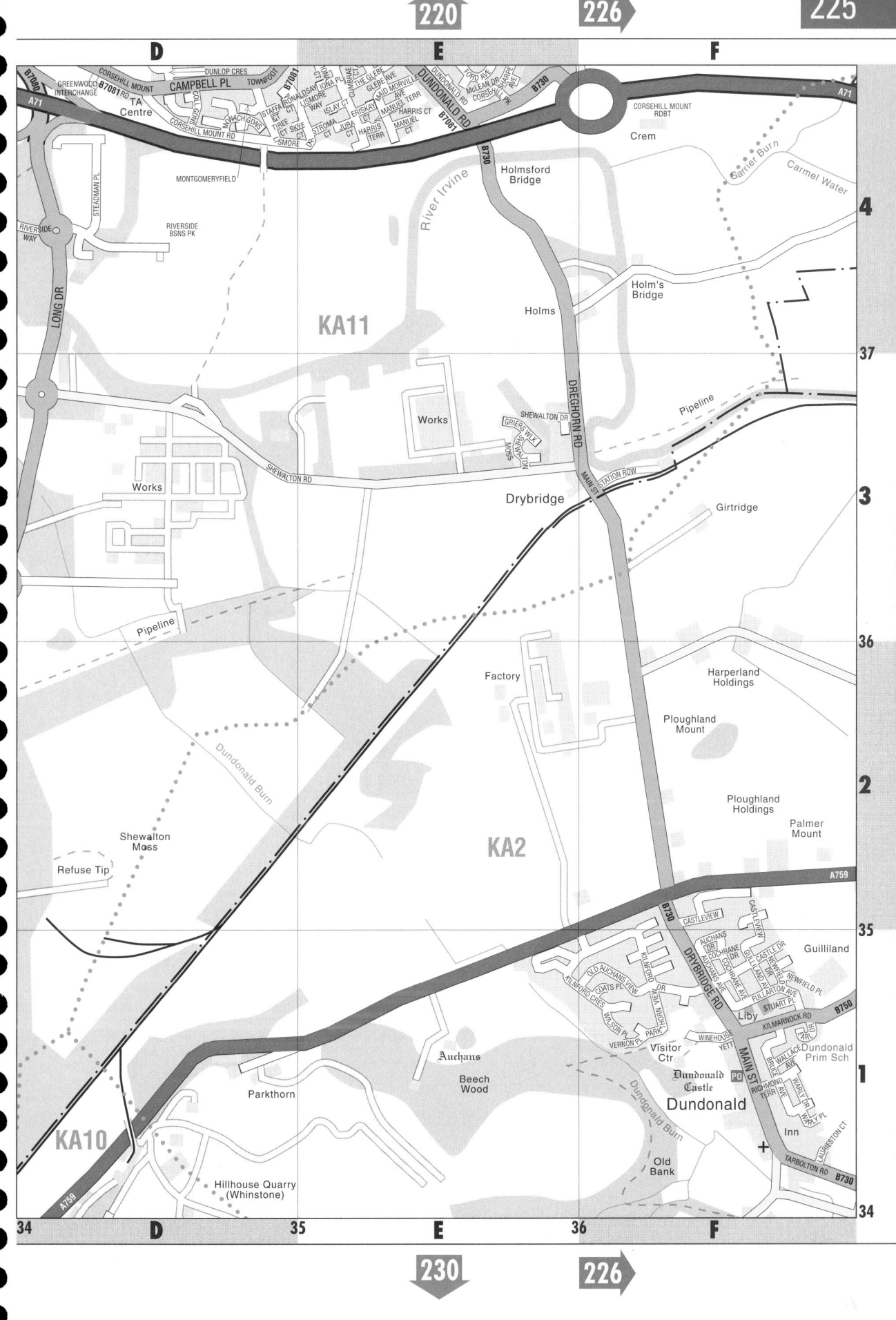

220
226

D   E   F

B7080
GREENWOOD INTERCHANGE
B7081 RD
CORSEHILL MOUNT
DUNLOP CRES
CAMPBELL PL
TOWNFOOT
DONALDSAY
IONA PL
CUMBRAE
THE GLEBE
GLEBE AVE
MID MORVILLE
FORD AVE
McLEAN DR
CORSEHILL PK
SHARPE AVE
B730
A71
TA Centre
COL GORDON CT
CORSEHILL MOUNT RD
MONACH GDNS
STAFFA CT
TIREE CT
ISLAY CT
ERISKAY
STROMA CT
JUBA CT
HARRIS TERR
MANUEL TERR
MANUEL CT
HARRIS CT
DUNDONALD RD
B7081
CREM
CORSEHILL MOUNT RDBT
Crem
LSMORE
LSMORE WAY
SKYE
SKXE
Garnet Burn
Carmel Water
A71

MONTGOMERYFIELD
River Irvine
Holmsford Bridge
B730
4

STEADMAN PL
RIVERSIDE WAY
RIVERSIDE BSNS PK
Holm's Bridge
37

LONG DR
KA11
Holms
Works
SHEWALTON DR
GRIERS WLK
SHEWALTON MOSS
DREGHORN RD
STATION ROW
MAIN ST
Pipeline
3

Works
SHEWALTON RD
Drybridge
Girtridge
Pipeline
36

Factory
Harperland Holdings
Ploughland Mount

Dundonald Burn
KA2
Ploughland Holdings
Palmer Mount
2

Shewalton Moss
A759
35

Refuse Tip
B730
CASTLEVIEW
CASTLEVIEW
AUCHANS DR
A COCHRANE DR
CASTLE DR
GUILL CASTLE DR
NEWFIELD PL
Guilliland

KILNFORD CRES
OLD AUCHANS VIEW
KILNFORD DR
MAIN NICHOL
AUCHANS DR
A COCHRANE AVE
FULLARTON AVE
STUART PL
KILMARNOCK RD
B750
DRYBRIDGE RD
Liby
COATS PL
WILSON PL
PARK
WINEHOUSE
VERNON PL
YETT
Visitor Ctr
MAIN ST
Dundonald Prim Sch
RICHMOND TERR
WALLACE AVE
WARLY PL
WARLY AVE
BRUCE AVE
1

Auchans
Beech Wood
Dundonald Castle
PO
Dundonald
Inn
LAURESTON CT
Parkthorn

KA10
Old Bank
TARBOLTON RD
B730
A759
Hillhouse Quarry (Whinstone)
34

34   D   35   E   36   F   34

230
226

225 221

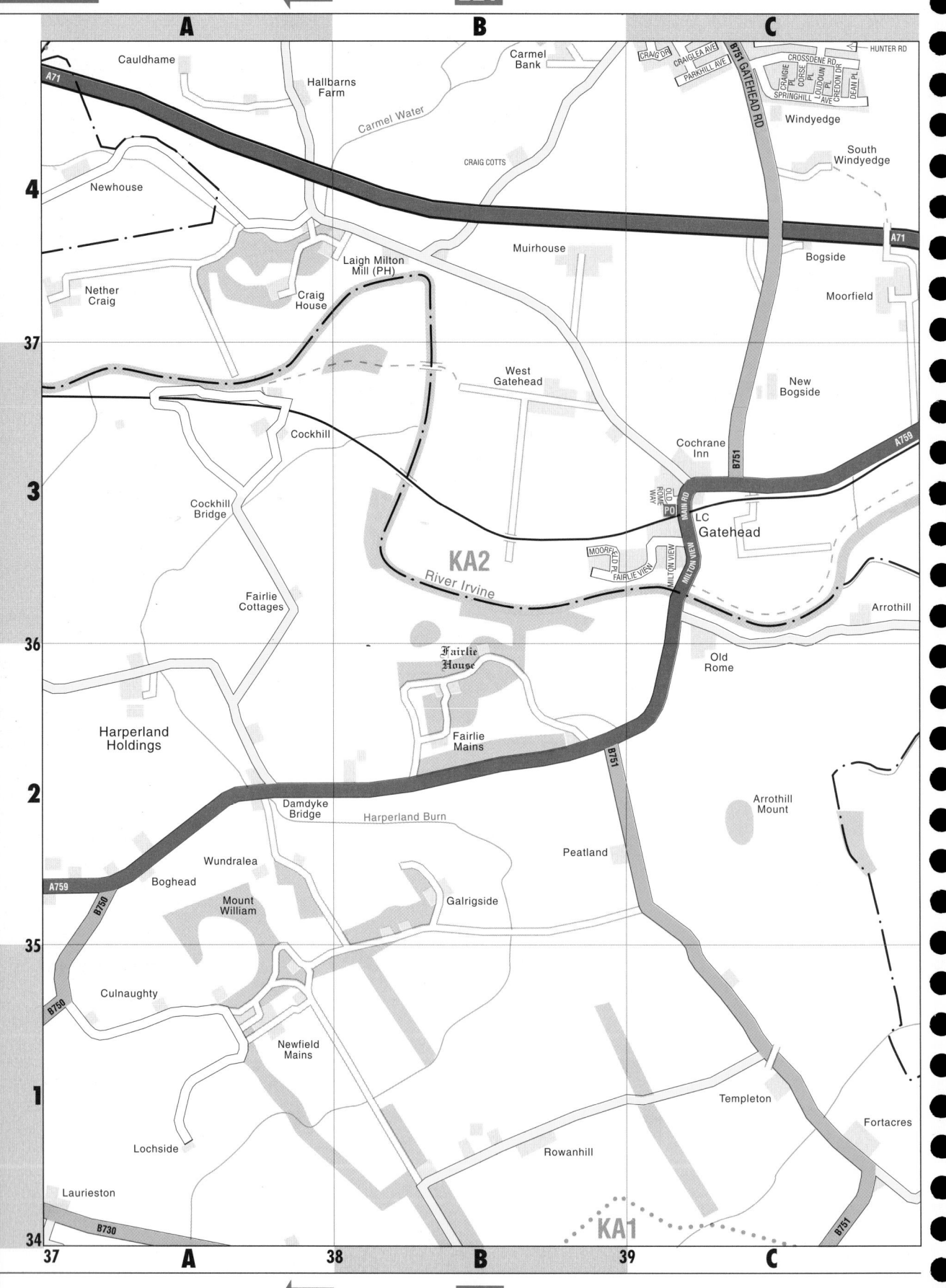
A
B
C
Cauldhame
Carmel Bank
Hallbarns Farm
Carmel Water
CRAIG DR
CRAIGLEA AVE
PARKHILL AVE
B751 GATEHEAD RD
CROSSDENE RD
HUNTER RD
CRAIGIE PL
CORSE PL
LOUDOUN AVE
CREDON DR
DEAN PL
SPRINGHILL
Windyedge
South Windyedge
A71
CRAIG COTTS
Newhouse
4
Muirhouse
Laigh Milton Mill (PH)
Bogside
Nether Craig
Craig House
Moorfield
37
West Gatehead
New Bogside
Cockhill
Cochrane Inn
A759
B751
3
Cockhill Bridge
OLD ROME WAY
MAIN RD
PO
LC
Gatehead
KA2
MOORFIELD PL
FAIRLIE VIEW
MILTON VIEW
River Irvine
Fairlie Cottages
Arrothill
36
Fairlie House
Old Rome
Harperland Holdings
Fairlie Mains
2
Damdyke Bridge
Harperland Burn
Arrothill Mount
Peatland
Wundralea
Boghead
Mount William
Galrigside
B750
35
Culnaughty
Newfield Mains
1
Templeton
Fortacres
Lochside
Rowanhill
Laurieston
B730
KA1
34
37
38
39

225 231

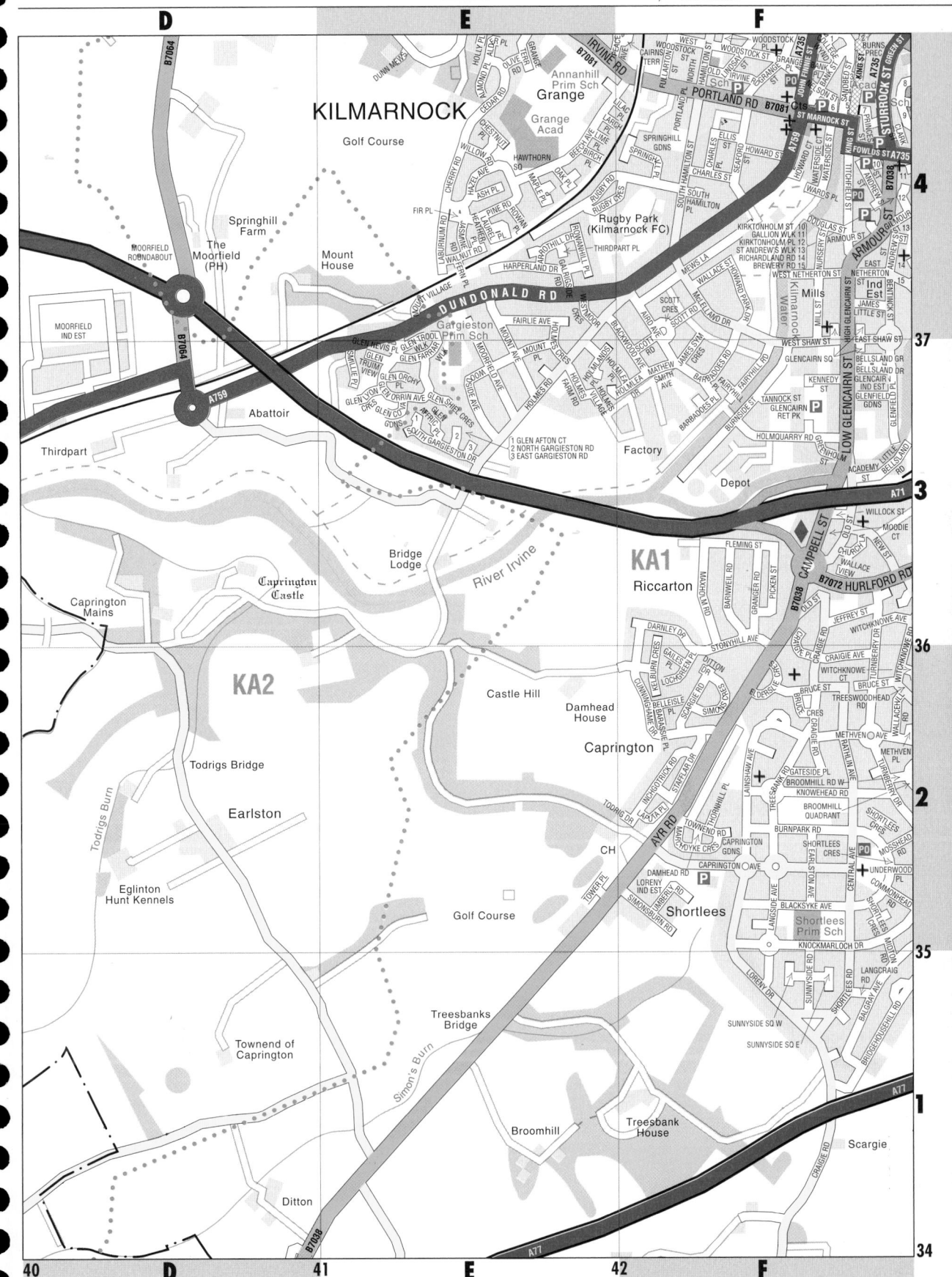

F4
1 LOW CHURCH LA
2 THE CROSS
3 SANDBED LA
4 WATER LA
5 BRIDGE LA
6 ST MARNOCK PL
7 QUEEN ST
8 BRAESIDE ST
9 RENNIE ST

KILMARNOCK

Golf Course

Grange

Springhill Farm

The Moorfield (PH)

Moorfield ROUNDABOUT

Moorfield IND EST

Mount House

Rugby Park (Kilmarnock FC)

DUNDONALD RD

Gargieston Prim Sch

Abattoir

Thirdpart

1 GLEN AFTON CT
2 NORTH GARGIESTON RD
3 EAST GARGIESTON RD

Factory

Depot

Bridge Lodge

River Irvine

Caprington Castle

Caprington Mains

KA2

KA1

Riccarton

KILMARNOCK WATER

Castle Hill

Damhead House

Caprington

Todrigs Bridge

Earlston

Eglinton Hunt Kennels

Golf Course

Townend of Caprington

Treesbanks Bridge

Shortlees

Shortlees Prim Sch

Ditton

Broomhill

Treesbank House

Scargie

227
223

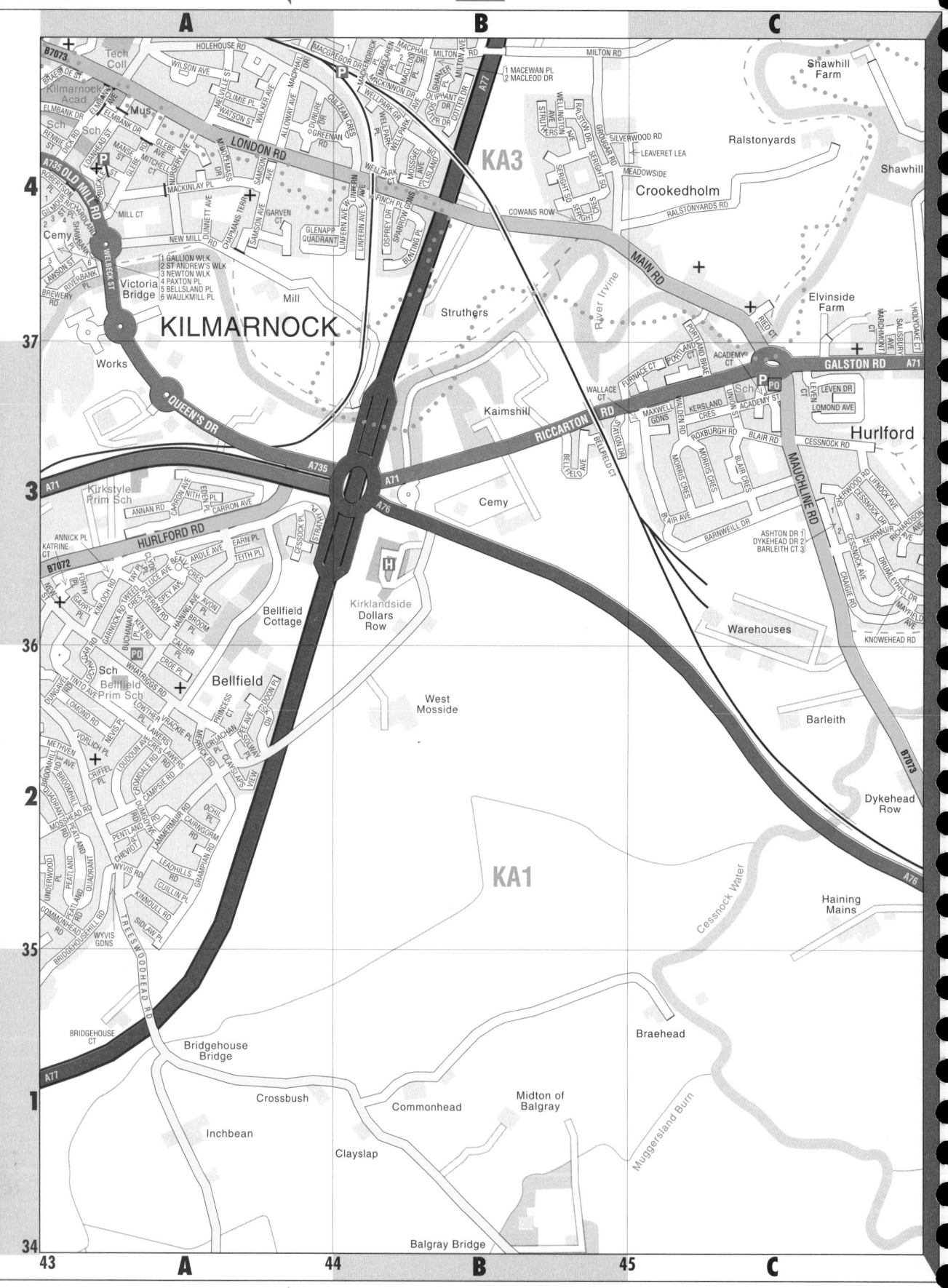
A
B
C
KILMARNOCK
KA3
KA1
Crookedholm
Hurlford
Ralstonyards
Shawhill Farm
Shawhill
Elvinside Farm
Struthers
Kaimshill
Cemy
Mill
Works
Victoria Bridge
Kirklandside
Dollars Row
Bellfield Cottage
Bellfield
West Mosside
Warehouses
Barleith
Dykehead Row
Haining Mains
Braehead
Bridgehouse Bridge
Crossbush
Commonhead
Midton of Balgray
Inchbean
Clayslap
Balgray Bridge
River Irvine
Cessnock Water
Muggersland Burn
LONDON RD
QUEEN'S DR
HURLFORD RD
RICCARTON RD
MAIN RD
GALSTON RD
MAUCHLINE RD
TREESWOODHEAD RD
A71
A76
A77
A735
B7073
B7072
43
44
45
34
35
36
37
1
2
3
4

227

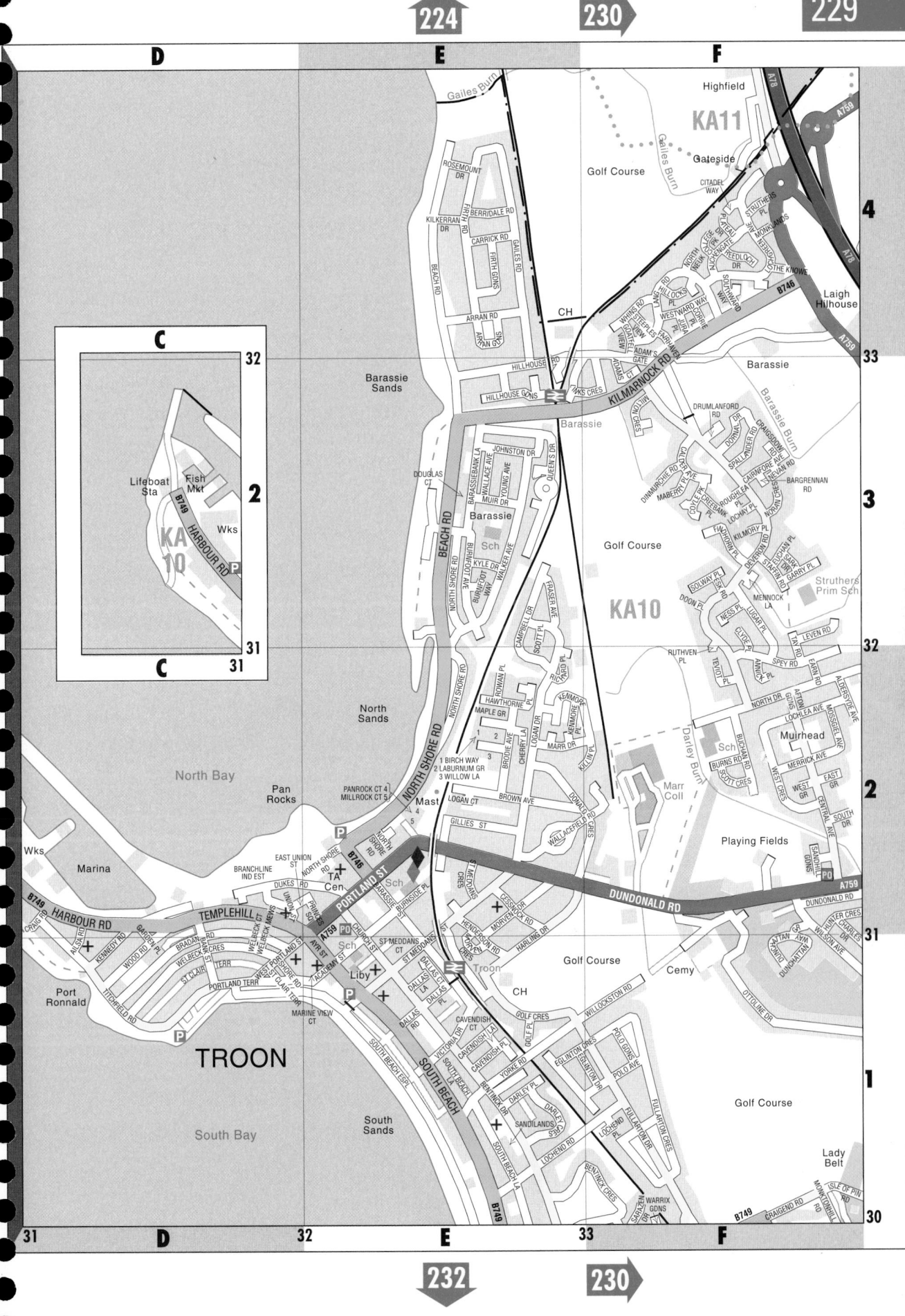
224
230
D
E
F
Highfield
KA11
Gailes Burn
Gateside
Golf Course
CITADEL WAY
ROSEMOUNT DR
KILKERRAN DR
BERRIDALE RD
FIRTH RD
CARRICK RD
FIRTH GDNS
GAILES RD
BEACH RD
ARRAN RD
ARRAN GDNS
CH
B746
Laigh Hilhouse
A78
A759
4
33
Barassie
Barassie Sands
HILLHOUSE RD
HILLHOUSE GDNS
LINKS CRES
KILMARNOCK RD
ADAMS CT
ADAM'S GATE
FAIRHAVEN
MILTON CRES
WESTWARD WAY
WHINS RD
STEEPLES
GOATFELL VIEW
JURA PL
CORRIE PL
SOUTHWARD WAY
HILLOCKS PL
NORTH NEUK
LANG RD
AUCHENGATE
REEDLOCH DR
STRUTHERS PL
MONKLANDS
THE KNOWE
DRUMLANFORD RD
DORNAL DR
SPALLANDER RD
CRAIGSDOW RD
CAIRNFORE AVE
NEVAN RD
BARGRENNAN RD
CALDER AVE
DINMURCHIE RD
MABERRY PL
COYLE PK
CREEBANK PL
ROUGHLEA PL
LOCHAY PL
NORAN CRES
KILMORY PL
FINDHORN PL
DEVERON RD
STAFFIN RD
SARK DR
GARRY PL
Struthers Prim Sch
C
32
2
31
Lifeboat Sta
Fish Mkt
B749
HARBOUR RD
Wks
KA 10
P
DOUGLAS CT
JOHNSTON DR
BARASSIEBANK LA
WALLACE AVE
YOUNG AVE
MUIR DR
QUEEN'S DR
Barassie
Sch
KYLE DR
BURNFOOT AVE
BURNFOOT WAY
WALKER AVE
NORTH SHORE RD
Golf Course
FRASER AVE
CAMPBELL DR
SCOTT PL
KA10
SOLWAY PL
ESK RD
DOON PL
NESS PL
LUGAR PL
CLYDE PL
MENNOCK LA
LEVEN RD
TAY RD
RUTHVEN PL
TEVIOT PL
ANNICK PL
SPEY RD
EARN RD
3
North Sands
RICHARD PL
ROWAN PL
HAWTHORNE PL
MAPLE GR
KENMORE
KENMORE PL
BRODIE AVE
CHERRY LA
LOGAN DR
MARR DR
KILLIN PL
1 BIRCH WAY
2 LABURNUM GR
3 WILLOW LA
NORTH DR
AFTON GDNS
LOCHLEA AVE
MOSSGIEL AVE
ALDERSYDE AVE
Muirhead
Darley Burn
Sch
BUCHAN RD
BURNS RD
SCOTT CRES
MERRICK AVE
WEST CRES
WEST GR
EAST GR
CENTRAL AVE
SOUTH DR
Marr Coll
North Bay
Pan Rocks
PANROCK CT 4
MILLROCK CT 5
Mast
LOGAN CT
BROWN AVE
DONALD CRES
GILLIES ST
WALLACEFIELD RD
Playing Fields
SANDHILL GDNS
PO
A759
Wks
Marina
BRANCHLINE IND EST
EAST UNION ST
NORTH SHORE RD
TA Cen
PORTLAND ST
Sch
BURNSIDE PL
BARASSIE ST
ST MEDDANS CRES
CESSNOCK RD
MORVEN DR
DUNDONALD RD
DUKES RD
UNION ST
PRINCES SQ
TEMPLEHILL
HARBOUR RD
CRAIG RD
AILSA RD
KENNEDY RD
GARDEN PL
WOOD RD
BRADAN RD
BANK ST
WELBECK CRES
WELBECK CT
WELBECK MEWS
WEST PORTLAND ST
AYR ST
CHURCH ST
ST MEDDANS CT
ST MEDDANS ST
HENDERSON RD
HARLING DR
Golf Course
Cemy
HUNTER CRES
CHARLES DR
WILSON AVE
DUNCHATTAN GR
DUNCHATTAN WAY
ST CLAIR TERR
PORTLAND TERR
SHORE RD
ACADEMY ST
Liby
DALLAS CT
DALLAS LA
DALLAS PL
Troon
31
CH
WILLOCKSTON RD
OTTOLINE DR
Port Ronnald
TITCHFIELD RD
MARINE VIEW CT
DALLAS RD
CAVENDISH CT
CAVENDISH LA
CAVENDISH PL
VICTORIA DR
GOLF CRES
GOLF PL
EGLINTON CRES
EGLINTON DR
POLO GDNS
POLO AVE
TROON
SOUTH BEACH ESP
SOUTH BEACH
SOUTH BEACH LA
YORKE RD
BENTINCK DR
DARLEY PL
DARLEY CRES
SANDILANDS
FULLARTON DR
FULLARTON CRES
LOCHEND PL
LOCHEND RD
1
Golf Course
South Bay
South Sands
BENTINCK CRES
WARRIX GDNS
SARAZEN DR
B749
CRAIGEND RD
MONKTONHILL RD
ISLE OF PIN RD
Lady Belt
30
31
D
32
E
33
F

232
230

229 225

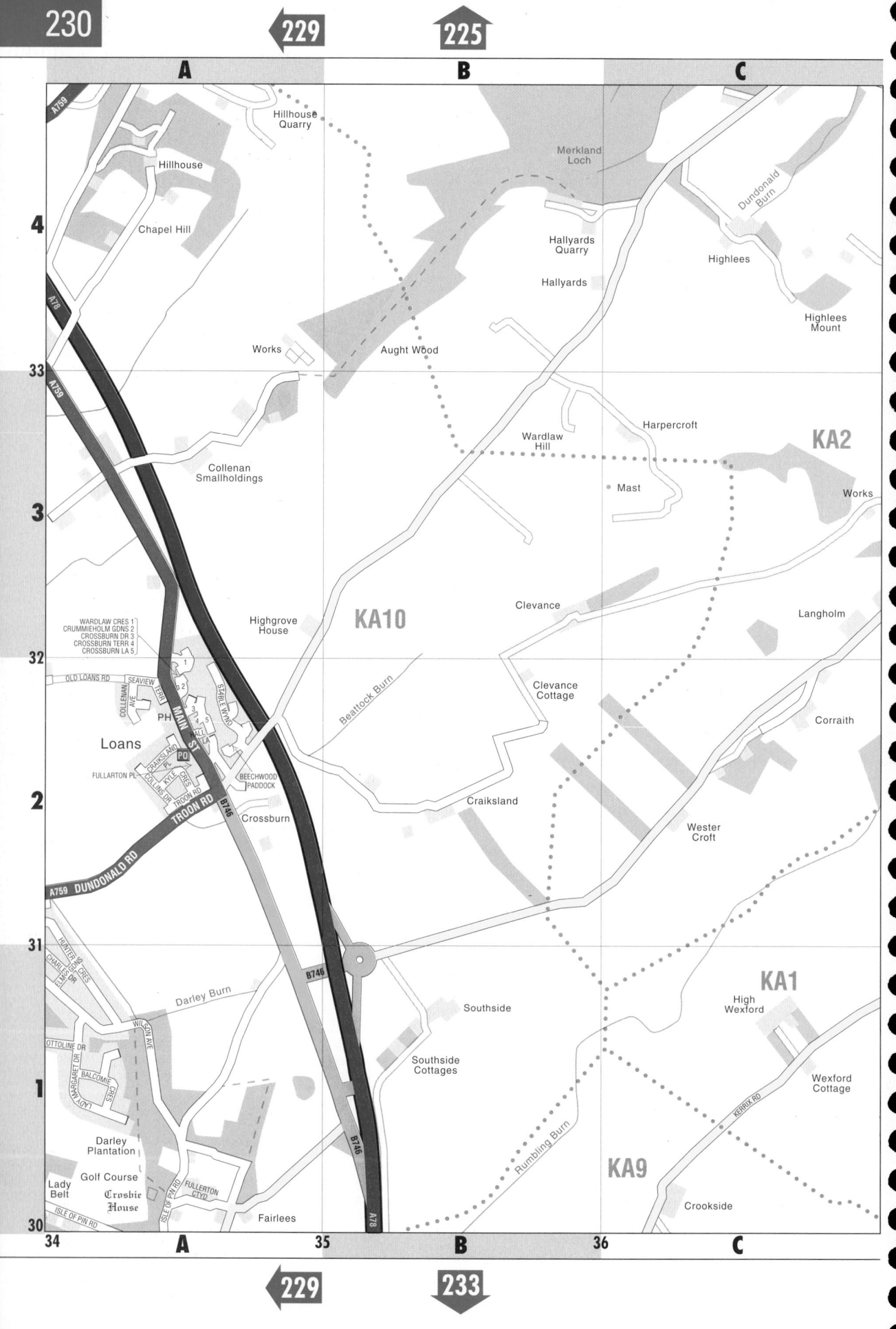
A
B
C
4
33
3
32
2
31
1
30
34
35
36
Hillhouse Quarry
Hillhouse
Chapel Hill
Merkland Loch
Hallyards Quarry
Hallyards
Dundonald Burn
Highlees
Highlees Mount
Works
Aught Wood
Collenan Smallholdings
Wardlaw Hill
Harpercroft
KA2
Mast
Works
KA10
Highgrove House
Clevance
Langholm
Clevance Cottage
Corraith
Beattock Burn
Loans
Craiksland
Wester Croft
Crossburn
WARDLAW CRES 1
CRUMMIEHOLM GDNS 2
CROSSBURN DR 3
CROSSBURN TERR 4
CROSSBURN LA 5
OLD LOANS RD
SEAVIEW TERR
COLLENAN AVE
STABLE WYND
MAIN ST
PH
PO
CRAIKSLAND PL
FULLARTON PL
COLLINS DR
KYLE CRES
TROON RD
BEECHWOOD PADDOCK
B746
A759 DUNDONALD RD
A759
A78
Darley Burn
Southside
Southside Cottages
KA1
High Wexford
Wexford Cottage
KERRIX RD
Rumbling Burn
KA9
Crookside
HUNTER CRES
CHARLES GDNS
ELMS DR
OTTOLINE DR
WILSON AVE
LADY MARGARET DR
BALCOMIE CRES
Darley Plantation
Golf Course
Lady Belt
Crosbie House
ISLE OF PIN RD
FULLERTON CTYD
Fairlees

229 233

226

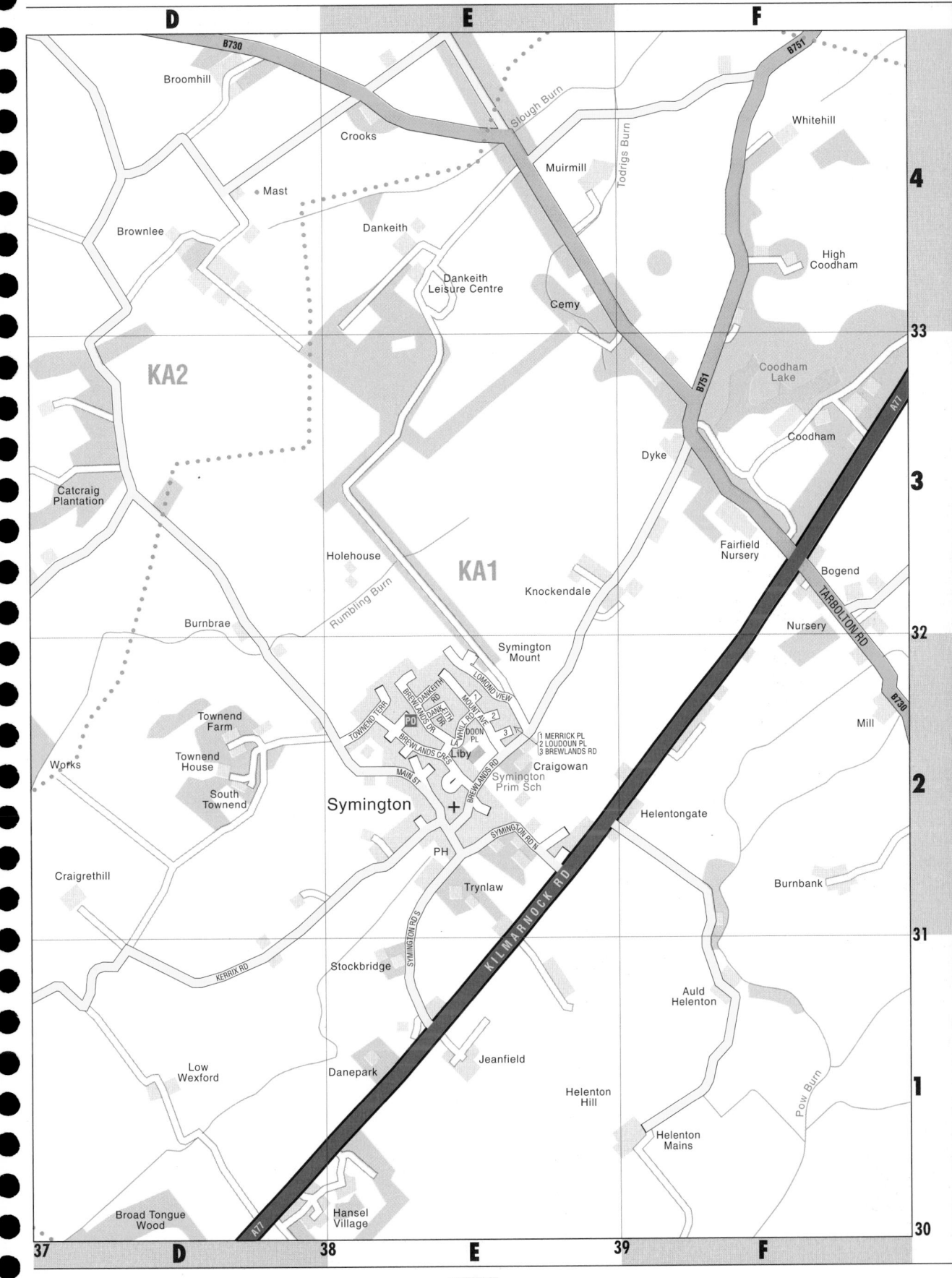

D
E
F
B730
B751
Broomhill
Crooks
Slough Burn
Whitehill
Muirmill
Todrigs Burn
Mast
Dankeith
Brownlee
High Coodham
Dankeith Leisure Centre
Cemy
KA2
Coodham Lake
B751
A77
Coodham
Dyke
Catcraig Plantation
Holehouse
KA1
Fairfield Nursery
Bogend
Rumbling Burn
Knockendale
TARBOLTON RD
Burnbrae
Nursery
Symington Mount
LOMOND VIEW
B730
Townend Farm
TOWNEND TERR
BREWLANDS DR
DANKEITH RD
DANKEITH DR
MOUNT AVE
WHIN RD
DOON PL
Mill
PO
BREWLANDS CRES
1 MERRICK PL
2 LOUDOUN PL
3 BREWLANDS RD
Townend House
Works
Liby
Craigowan
MAIN ST
BREWLANDS RD
Symington Prim Sch
South Townend
Symington
Helentongate
SYMINGTON RD N
PH
Craigrethill
KILMARNOCK RD
Trynlaw
Burnbank
SYMINGTON RD S
KERRIX RD
Stockbridge
Auld Helenton
Jeanfield
Low Wexford
Danepark
Helenton Hill
Pow Burn
Helenton Mains
Broad Tongue Wood
Hansel Village
A77
4
33
3
32
2
31
1
30
37
38
39

234

229

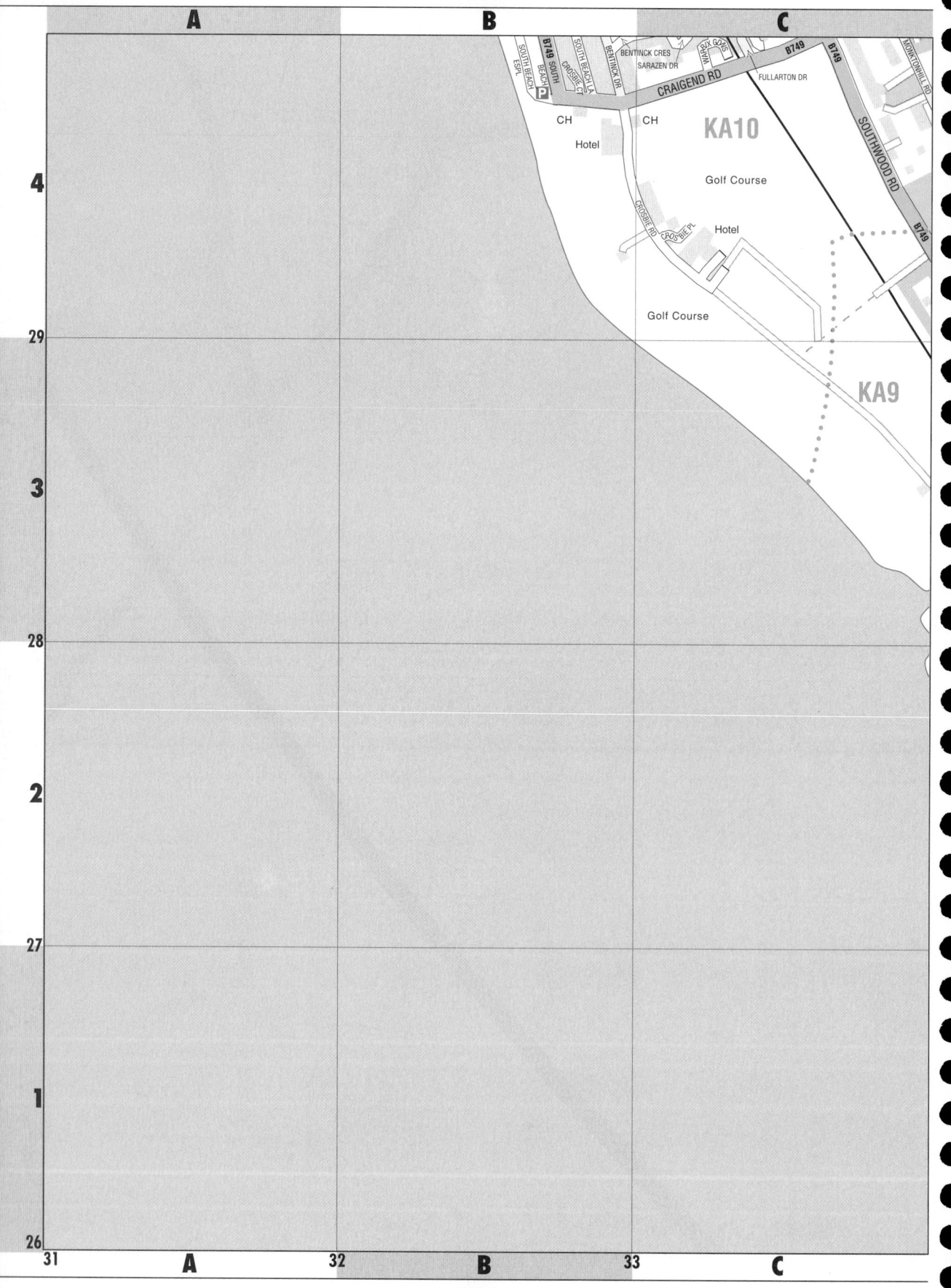

KA10

KA9

Golf Course

Golf Course

Hotel

Hotel

CH

CH

CRAIGEND RD

FULLARTON DR

SARAZEN DR

BENTINCK CRES

SOUTHWOOD RD

MONKTONHILL RD

B749

230 234

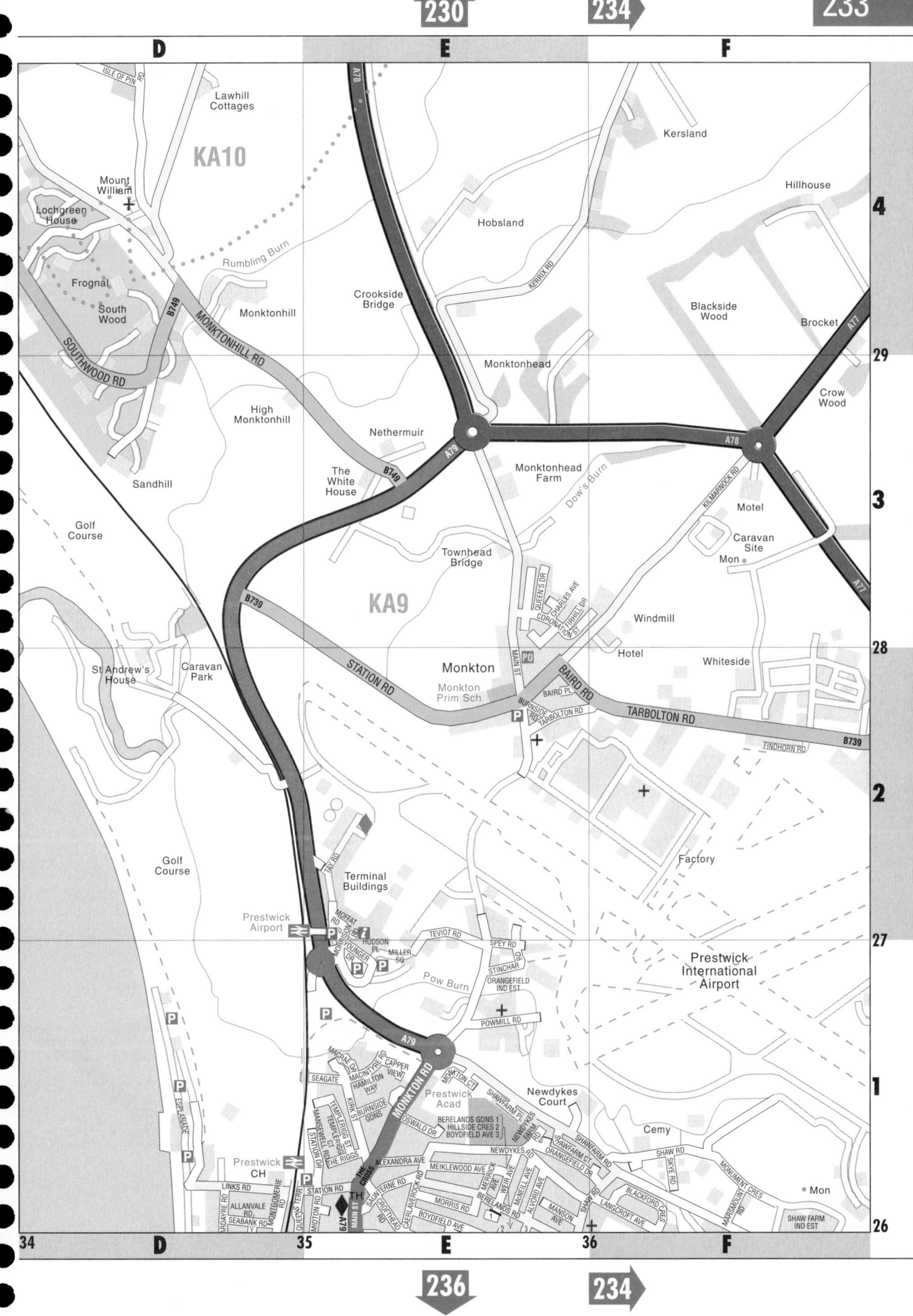
D
E
F
KA10
KA9
Lawhill Cottages
Kersland
Hillhouse
Mount William
Lochgreen House
Hobsland
Rumbling Burn
Frognal
South Wood
Monktonhill
Crookside Bridge
Blackside Wood
Brocket
MONKTONHILL RD
SOUTHWOOD RD
B749
KERRIX RD
A78
A77
A79
Monktonhead
Crow Wood
High Monktonhill
Nethermuir
The White House
Monktonhead Farm
Dow's Burn
KILMARNOCK RD
Motel
Caravan Site
Mon
Sandhill
Golf Course
Townhead Bridge
Windmill
B739
STATION RD
QUEEN'S DR
CHARLES AVE
CORONATION ST
FIRHILL DR
St Andrew's House
Caravan Park
Monkton
Monkton Prim Sch
MAIN ST
PO
BAIRD RD
BAIRD PL
BURNSIDE RD
TARBOLTON RD
TARBOLTON RD
Hotel
Whiteside
FINDHORN RD
Factory
Golf Course
TAY RD
Terminal Buildings
Prestwick Airport
MOFFAT RD
MORRISON RD
YOUNGER DR
HUDSON PL
MILLER SQ
TEVIOT RD
SPEY RD
STINCHAR RD
ORANGEFIELD IND EST
Pow Burn
POWMILL RD
Prestwick International Airport
MACRAE DR
MACINTYRE RD
CAPPER VIEW
HAMILTON WAY
SEAGATE
KIRK ST
BURNSIDE GDNS
MONKTON RD
MONKTON CT
Prestwick Acad
SHAWFARM PL
Newdykes Court
ESPLANADE
TEMPLERIGG ST
TEMPLERIGG CT
MANSEWELL RD
STATION DR
THE RIGGS
OSWALD DR
BERELANDS GDNS 1
HILLSIDE CRES 2
BOYDFIELD AVE 3
NEWDYKES FARM
NEWDYKES RD
SHAWFARM CT
ORANGEFIELD DR
SHAWFARM RD
Cemy
SHAW RD
SKYE RD
MONUMENT CRES
Prestwick CH
ALEXANDRA AVE
MEIKLEWOOD AVE
MERRICK AVE
WEIR AVE
McNEILL AVE
ALVORD AVE
LINKS RD
MONTGOMERIE RD
STATION RD
TH
THE CROSS
SAUTERNE RD
CAERLAVEROCK RD
MORRIS RD
BERELANDS RD
MANSON AVE
SHAW RD
BLACKFORD CRES
LANGCROFT AVE
MARSMOUNT RD
Mon
SHAW FARM IND EST
ARDAYRE RD
ALLANVALE RD
SEABANK RD
QUEEN'S TERR
MIDTON RD
MAIN ST
CROFTHEAD RD
BOYDFIELD AVE
4
29
3
28
2
27
1
26
34
35
36

236 234

A

B

C

Langlands

Pow
Bridge

KA1

Baillieston

Rose Cottage

Underwood
Mains

Baillieston
Glen

4

Rosemount

Lodge

Underwood

Underwood
Glen

Adamton
Mains

Low
Wardneuk

Underwood Burn

29

High
Wardneuk

Pow Burn

Tarbolton

3

Woodside

KA9

Bogside

KA5

28

ADAMTON
EST

Mid
Foulton

Little
Foulton

B739

Brieryside

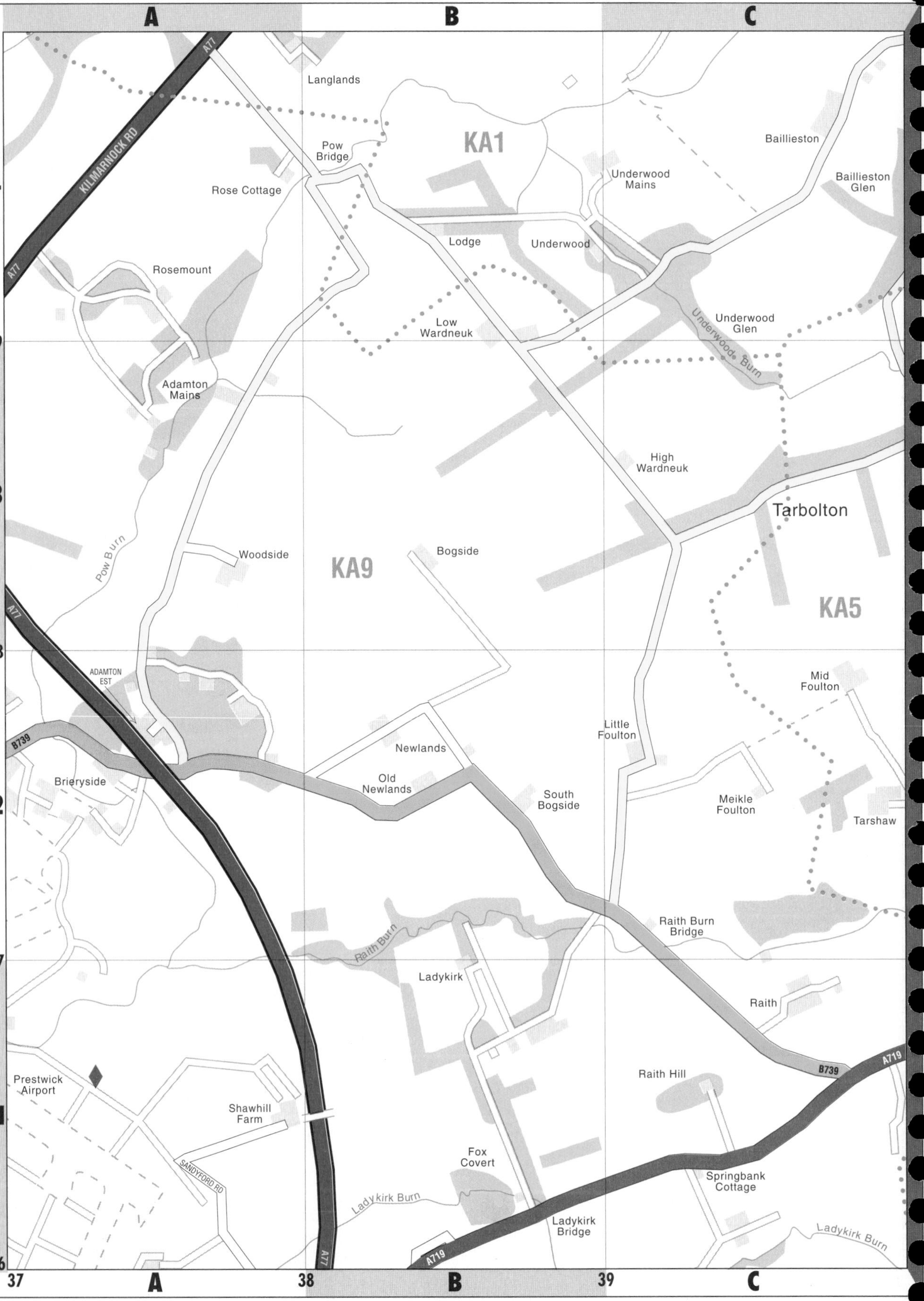

Newlands

Meikle
Foulton

Tarshaw

2

Old
Newlands

South
Bogside

Raith Burn
Bridge

Raith Burn

27

Ladykirk

Raith

Raith Hill

B739

A719

Prestwick
Airport

Shawhill
Farm

1

SANDYFORD RD

Fox
Covert

Springbank
Cottage

Ladykirk Burn

Ladykirk
Bridge

Ladykirk Burn

A77

A719

26

37

A

38

B

39

C

KILMARNOCK RD

A77

A77

D
E
F

4

25

3

24

2

23

North
Breakwater

SHORE RD

KA8

Dock

WAGGON RD

GRIFFIN DOCK RD

OSWALD LA

SPUR RD

YORK ST

TAYLOR
ST

GREEN ST LA

GREEN STREET LA

GREEN ST

SALTFIELD
LA

YORK STREET LA

BSNS PK

BACK PEEBLES ST

PEEBLES ST

NEW RD

CROWN ST

SALTPANS
RD

LIMEKILN RD

WEIR RD

ELMBANK ST

GLEBE CRES

GLEBE RD

HALLS
VENNAL

DAMSIDE

PO

ALLISON
ST

KING ST

A719

South
Pier

Ayr Harbour

BRUCE CRES 1
CATHCART ST 2
ST JOHN ST 3
ACADEMY ST 4
BOAT VENNAL 5
HARBOUR ST 6
SANDGATE 7

NORTH HARBOUR ST

SOUTH HARBOUR ST

River Ayr

B748

NORTH
IND EST

GARDEN
CT

Lily

6

1

ESPLANADE

SOUTH BEACH RD

Citadel
L Ctr

AYR
KA7

SEABANK RD

P

AILSA
PL

ARRAN TERR

QUEEN'S TERRACE LA

CROMWELL RD

MONTGOMERIE TERR

EGLINTON PL

EGLINTON TERR

Ayr
Acad

CITADEL
PL

B748

GEORGE
ST

TH

HIGH ST

NEW BRIDGE ST

A713

AYR
Bitts

RIVER TERR

STRATHAYR
PL

OLD BRIDGE ST

A79

A719 RIVER TERR

P

Ct

7

22

31
D
32
E
33
F

235
233

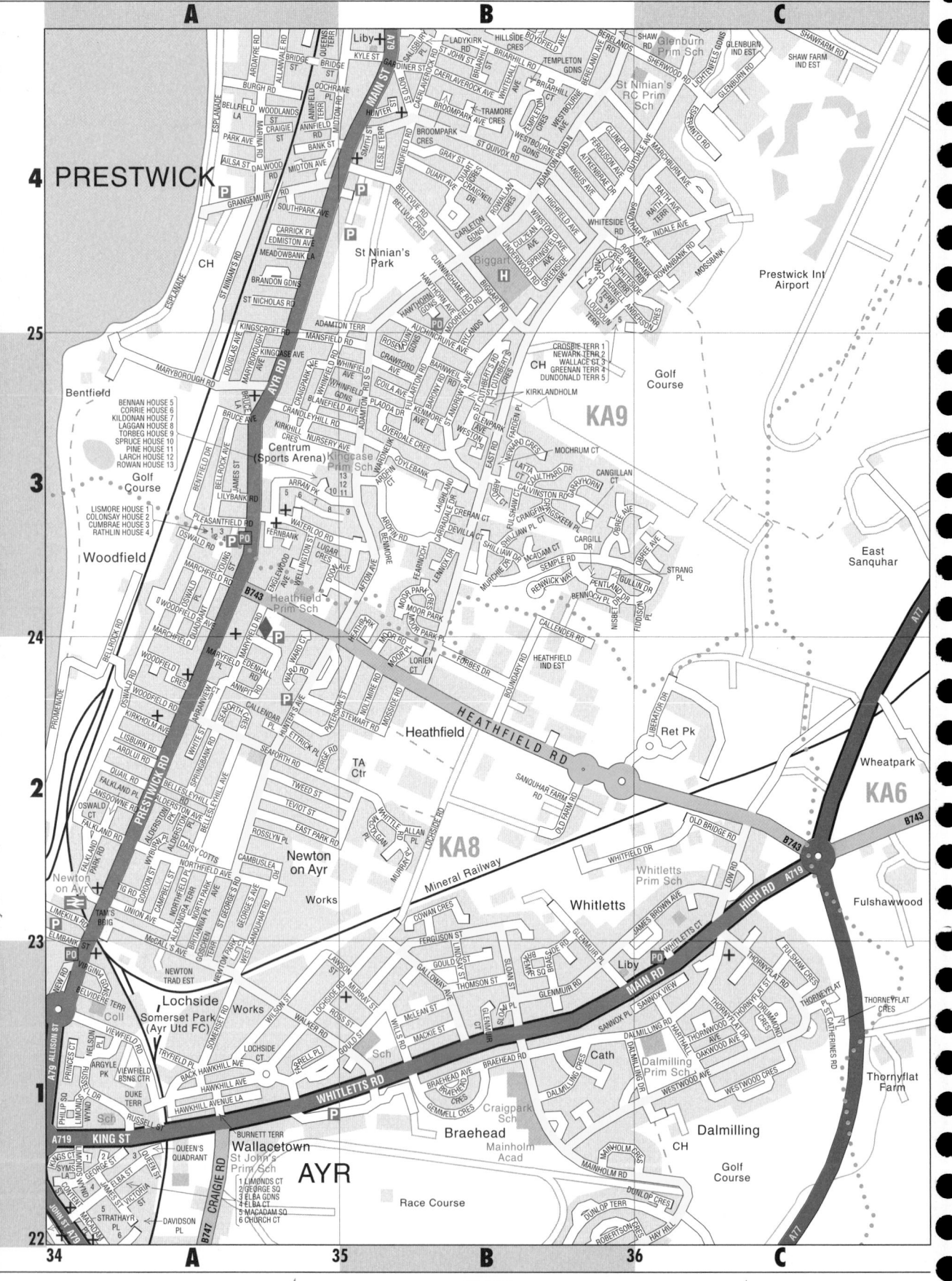
A
B
C
PRESTWICK
4
25
3
24
2
23
1
22
34
35
36
Liby
A79
MAIN ST
KYLE ST
BRIDGE ST
QUEENS TERR
ARDAYRE RD
ALLANVALE RD
BURGH RD
COCHRANE PL
BELLFIELD LA
WOODLANDS ST
CRAIGIE ST
ANNFIELD RD
PARK AVE
BANK ST
AILSA ST
DALWOOD RD
MIDTON AVE
MIDTON RD
SMITH ST
LESLIE TERR
HUNTER ST
GRANGEMUIR RD
SOUTHPARK AVE
CARRICK PL
EDMISTON AVE
MEADOWBANK LA
BRANDON GDNS
ST NICHOLAS RD
ST NINIAN'S RD
ESPLANADE
CH
LADYKIRK RD
ST JOHN ST
BRIARHILL ST
HILLSIDE CRES
BOYDFIELD AVE
CAERLAVEROCK AVE
CAERLAVEROCK RD
BROOMPARK AVE
BROOMPARK CRES
TRAMORE CRES
ST QUIVOX RD
GRAY ST
DUART AVE
DUART CRES
CRAIGNEIL DR
ROWALLAN CRES
CARLETON GDNS
WESTBOURNE GDNS
WESTBOURNE AVE
TEMPLETON GDNS
TEMPLETON CRES
BRIARHILL CT
BERELANDS RD
BERELAND AVE
SHAW RD
Glenburn Prim Sch
GLENBURN IND EST
GLENBURN RD
SHAW FARM IND EST
SHAWFARM RD
SHERWOOD RD
LICHTENFELS GDNS
ESPERANTO RD
St Ninian's RC Prim Sch
ADAMTON ROAD N
CLUNE DR
FERGUSON AVE
AITKENBRAE DR
OUTDALE AVE
MARCHBURN AVE
RAITH AVE
RAITH TERR
INDALE AVE
ROWANBANK RD
MOSSBANK
WHITESIDE RD
SANDILANDS AVE
ANGUS AVE
HIGHFIELD AVE
WINSTON AVE
CULZEAN AVE
SPRINGFIELD AVE
GREENSIDE AVE
UNDERWOOD RD
Biggart
H
BIGGART RD
St Ninian's Park
BELLEVUE RD
BELLEVUE CRES
CUNNINGHAME RD
HAWTHORN AVE
HAWTHORN GDNS
MOORFIELD RD
PO
AUCHINCRUIVE AVE
RYLANDS
CARNELL CRES
CARNELL TERR
LOUDOUN TERR
ANDERSON CRES
Prestwick Int Airport
ADAMTON TERR
KINGSCROFT RD
MANSFIELD RD
DOUGLAS AVE
MARYBOROUGH AVE
KINGCASE AVE
MARYBOROUGH RD
AYR RD
ROSEVALE
COILA AVE
CRAWFORD AVE
BARNWEIL RD
WHINFIELD AVE
WHINFIELD GDNS
WHINFIELD RD
CRAIGPARK AVE
BLANEFIELD AVE
CRANDLEYHILL RD
NURSERY AVE
KIRKHILL CRES
ADAMTON RD S
PLADDA DR
FULLARTON RD
BARONY RD
KENMORE AVE
ST ANDREW'S AVE
ST CUTHBERT'S RD
ST CUTHBERT'S CRES
CROSBIE TERR 1
NEWARK TERR 2
WALLACE CT 3
GREENAN TERR 4
DUNDONALD TERR 5
CH
KIRKLANDHOLM
Golf Course
KA9
Bentfield
BENNAN HOUSE 5
CORRIE HOUSE 6
KILDONAN HOUSE 7
LAGGAN HOUSE 8
TORBEG HOUSE 9
SPRUCE HOUSE 10
PINE HOUSE 11
LARCH HOUSE 12
ROWAN HOUSE 13
BRUCE AVE
Centrum (Sports Arena)
Kingcase Prim Sch
OVERDALE CRES
GLENPARK AVE
WESTON AVE
EAST RD
FARDEN PL
NEWARK CRES
MOCHRUM CT
Golf Course
BENTFIELD DR
BELLROCK AVE
JAMES ST
LILYBANK RD
ARRAN PK
COYLEBANK
ARDFIN CT
WARDNEUK DR
LATTA CT
COULTHARD DR
CANGILLAN CT
GARRYHORN
ABBOT CT
CALVINSTON RD
CRAIGFIN CT
CRAIGSKEEN PL
LISMORE HOUSE 1
COLONSAY HOUSE 2
CUMBRAE HOUSE 3
RATHLIN HOUSE 4
PLEASANTFIELD RD
OSWALD RD
WATERLOO RD
FERNBANK
WELLINGTON ST
LUGAR CRES
DOON AVE
AFTON AVE
ARDFIN RD
BENMORE
CARRADALE DR
CRERAN CT
DEVILLA CT
LAIGHLAND
FULSHAW CT
SHILLIAW PL
SHILLIAW CT
CARGILL DR
OBREE AVE
Woodfield
YOUNG ST
MARCHFIELD RD
ENGLEWOOD AVE
FEARNOCH
LENNOX DR
MURCHIE DR
McADAM CT
SEMPLE RD
RENWICK WAY
PENTLAND DR
GULLIN DR
STRANG PL
East Sanquhar
OSWALD PL
WOODFIELD AVE
QUADRANT
B743
Heathfield Prim Sch
MOOR PARK CRES
MOOR PARK
MOOR PARK PL
HEATHPARK
MOOR RD
MOOR PL
LORIEN CT
BENNOCH PL
NISBET DR
FIDDISON PL
CALLENDER RD
FORBES DR
HEATHFIELD IND EST
BELLROCK RD
MARCHFIELD
MARYFIELD RD
MARYFIELD PL
EDENHALL RD
WOODFIELD CRES
ANNPIT RD
WARD CT
WARD RD
P
WOODFIELD RD
KIRKHOLM AVE
ARRANVIEW
SEAFORTH CRES
CALLENDAR PL
HUNTER'S AVE
ETTRICK PL
PATERSON ST
STEWART RD
NOLMIRE RD
MOSSIDE RD
BOUNDARY RD
PROMENADE
LISBURN RD
ARDLUI RD
QUAIL RD
FALKLAND PL
LANSDOWNE RD
OSWALD CT
FALKLAND RD
PRESTWICK RD
WHITE ST
SPRINGBANK RD
BELLESLEYHILL RD
BELLESLEYHILL AVE
SEAFORTH RD
FORGE RD
Heathfield
HEATHFIELD RD
TA Ctr
TWEED ST
TEVIOT ST
EAST PARK RD
ROSSLYN PL
WHITTLE RD
McCOLGAN PL
ALLAN PL
MURRAY PL
LOCHSIDE RD
KA8
SANQUHAR FARM RD
OLD FARM RD
LIBERATOR DR
Ret Pk
Wheatpark
KA6
B743
A77
ALDERSTON PL
ALDERSTON AVE
WYBURN PL
DAISY COTTS
NORTHFIELD AVE
NORTHFIELD PL
NORTH PARK AVE
CAMBUSLEA RD
Newton on Ayr
Mineral Railway
OLD BRIDGE RD
WHITFIELD DR
Whitletts Prim Sch
LOW RD
A719
HIGH RD
Fulshawwood
FALKLAND PARK RD
Newton on Ayr
GORDON ST
CAMPBELL ST
ALEXANDRA TERR
BRITANNIA PL
ST GEORGE'S RD
ST GEORGE'S AVE
WEST SANQUHAR RD
UNION AVE
McCALL'S AVE
Works
COWAN CRES
FERGUSON ST
LINDSAY ST
GOULD ST
THOMSON ST
SLOAN ST
GLENMUIR PL
Whitletts
JAMES BROWN AVE
WHITLETTS CT
LIMEKILN RD
TAM'S BRIG
ELMBANK ST
NEWTON TRAD EST
NEWTON PARK CT
GOSCHEN TERR
LAWSON ST
GALLOWAY AVE
GLENMUIR RD
Liby
MAIN RD
FULSHAW CRES
THORNYFLAT RD
THORNYFLAT ST
THORNYFLAT DR
THORNYFLAT CRES
THORNYFLAT PL
ST CATHERINES RD
NEW RD
VIRGINIA GDNS
BELVIDERE TERR
Coll
Lochside
Somerset Park (Ayr Utd FC)
SOMERSET RD
Works
WILSON ST
LOCHSIDE RD
MURRAY ST
ROSS ST
WALKER RD
McLEAN ST
MACKIE ST
GLENMUIR CT
SLOAN PL
SANNOX VIEW
SANNOX PL
DALMILLING RD
HARTHALL
THORNWOOD AVE
OAKWOOD AVE
DRUMMOND CRES
Cath
Dalmilling Prim Sch
DALMILLING CRES
DALMILLING DR
WESTWOOD AVE
WESTWOOD CRES
Thornyflat Farm
ALLISON ST
PRINCES CT
NELSON PL
VIEWFIELD RD
ARGYLE PK
VIEWFIELD BSNS CTR
DUKE TERR
TRYFIELD PL
BACK HAWKHILL AVE
HAWKHILL AVE
HAWKHILL AVENUE LA
LOCHSIDE CT
FARRELL PL
GOULD ST
WILLS RD
Sch
WHITLETTS RD
BRAEHEAD AVE
BRAEHEAD CRES
BRAEHEAD RD
GEMMELL CRES
Craigpark Sch
Braehead
Mainholm Acad
Dalmilling
CH
RUSSELL ST
PHILIP SQ
LIMONDS WYND
Sch
A719
KING ST
BURNETT TERR
QUEEN'S QUADRANT
Wallacetown
St John's Prim Sch
CRAIGIE RD
B747
AYR
1 LIMONDS CT
2 GEORGE SQ
3 ELBA GDNS
4 ELBA CT
5 MACADAM SQ
6 CHURCH CT
KINGS CT
SYMS LA
GEORGE ST
ELBA ST
JAMES ST
VICTORIA ST
QUEEN ST
STRATHAYR PL
DAVIDSON PL
JOHN ST
A79
Race Course
MAINHOLM CRES
MAINHOLM RD
DUNLOP CRES
DUNLOP TERR
ROBERTSON CRES
HAY HILL
Golf Course

235
239

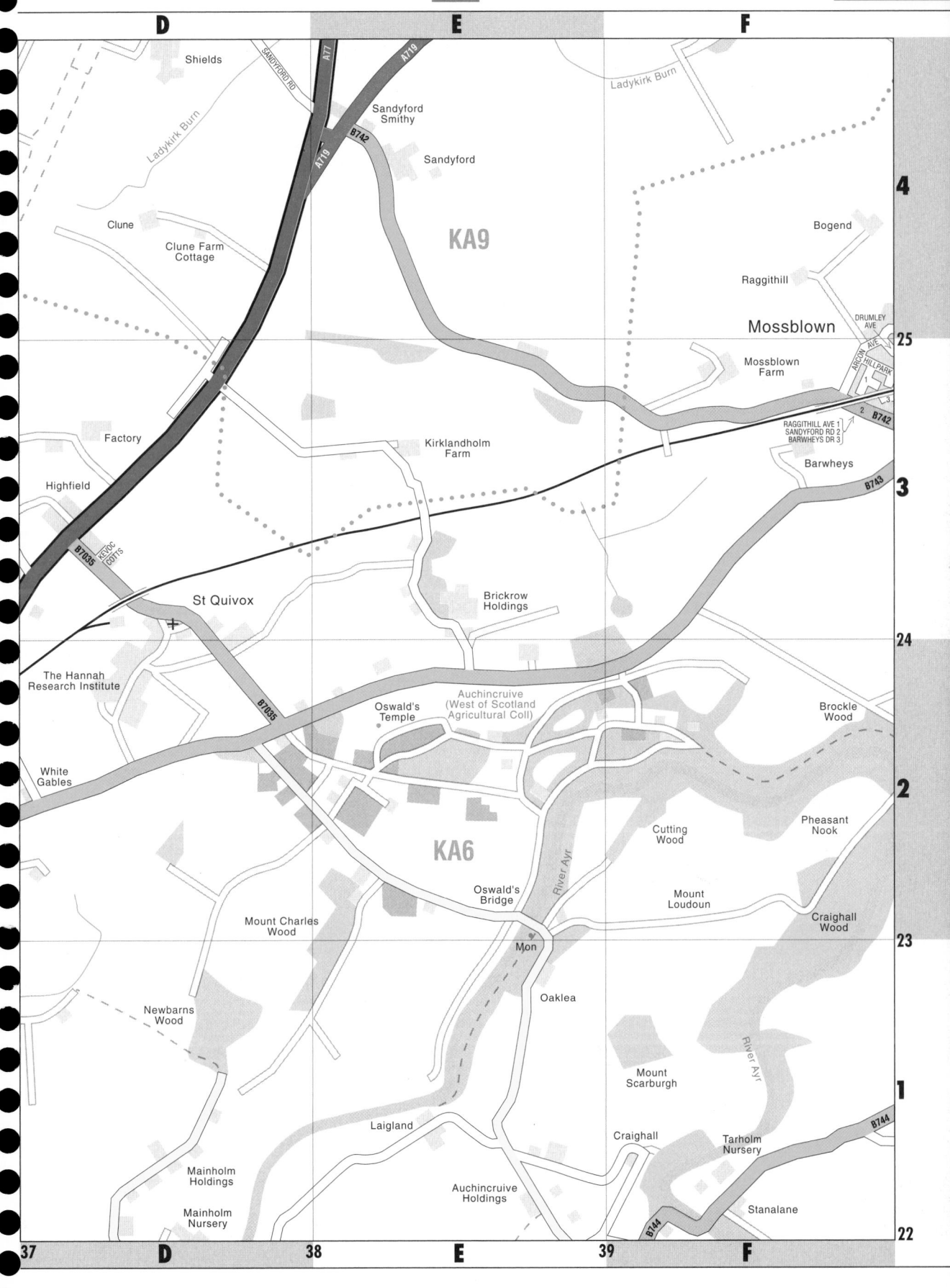
D
E
F
Shields
SANDYFORD RD
A77
A719
Sandyford Smithy
B742
Sandyford
Ladykirk Burn
Clune
Clune Farm Cottage
KA9
Bogend
Raggithill
Mossblown
DRUMLEY AVE
ARCON AVE
HILLPARK
Mossblown Farm
RAGGITHILL AVE 1
SANDYFORD RD 2
BARWHEYS DR 3
Factory
Kirklandholm Farm
Barwheys
B743
Highfield
B7035
KEVOC COTTS
St Quivox
Brickrow Holdings
The Hannah Research Institute
Auchincruive (West of Scotland Agricultural Coll)
Oswald's Temple
Brockle Wood
White Gables
Pheasant Nook
Cutting Wood
KA6
River Ayr
Oswald's Bridge
Mount Loudoun
Craighall Wood
Mount Charles Wood
Mon
Oaklea
Newbarns Wood
Mount Scarburgh
Laigland
Craighall
Tarholm Nursery
B744
Mainholm Holdings
Auchincruive Holdings
Stanalane
Mainholm Nursery
4
25
3
24
2
23
1
22
37
38
39

235

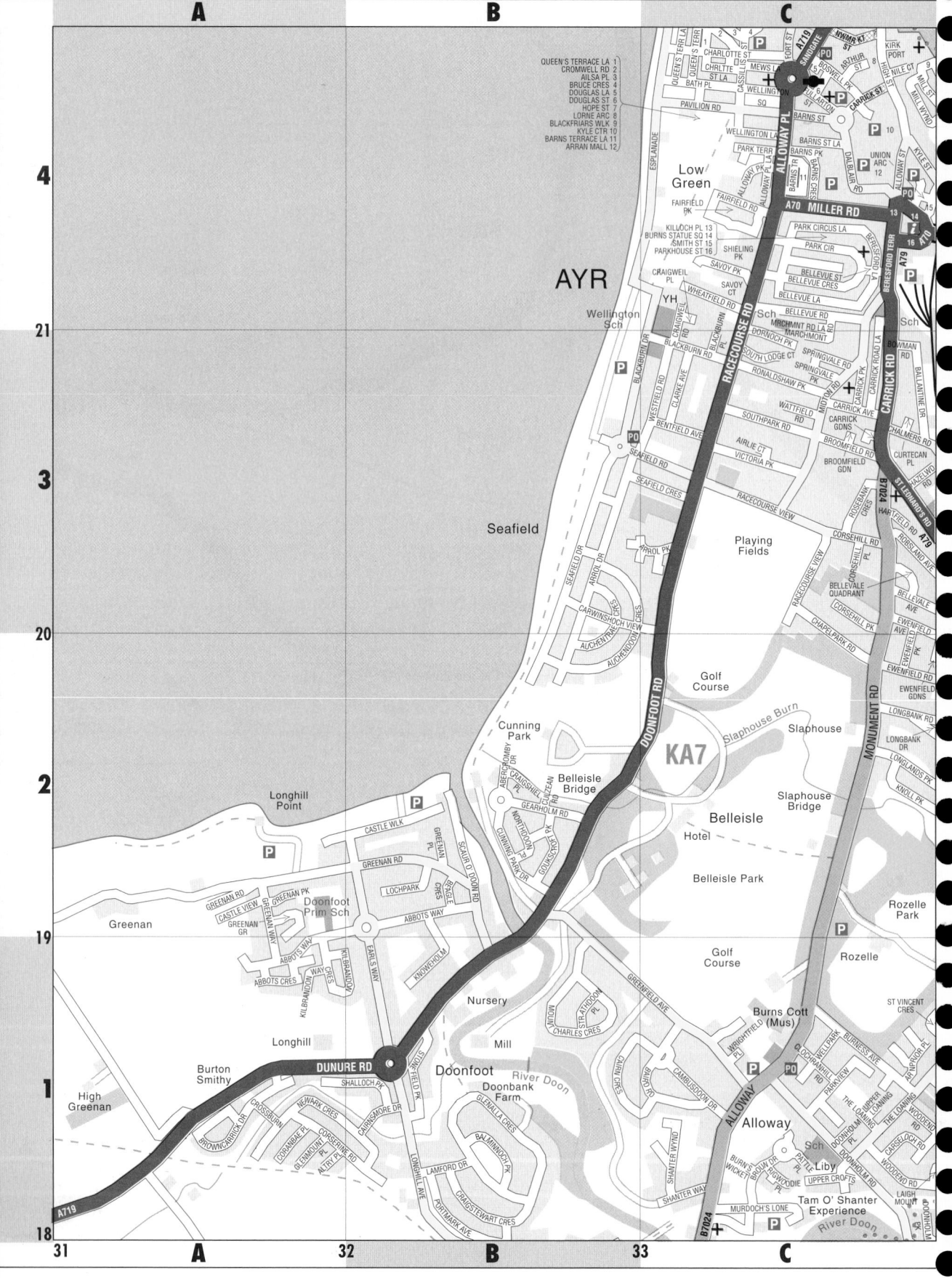

AYR
Low Green
Seafield
Cunning Park
Belleisle Bridge
Longhill Point
Greenan
Doonfoot Prim Sch
Longhill
Burton Smithy
High Greenan
Doonfoot
Doonbank Farm
Nursery
Mill
River Doon
Golf Course
Playing Fields
KA7
Slaphouse Burn
Slaphouse
Slaphouse Bridge
Belleisle
Hotel
Belleisle Park
Rozelle Park
Rozelle
Burns Cott (Mus)
Alloway
Tam O' Shanter Experience
Wellington Sch
DUNURE RD
DOONFOOT RD
RACECOURSE RD
ALLOWAY PL
MILLER RD
CARRICK RD
MONUMENT RD
ALLOWAY
QUEEN'S TERRACE LA 1
CROMWELL RD 2
AILSA PL 3
BRUCE CRES 4
DOUGLAS LA 5
DOUGLAS ST 6
HOPE ST 7
LORNE ARC 8
BLACKFRIARS WLK 9
KYLE CTR 10
BARNS TERRACE LA 11
ARRAN MALL 12
KILLOCH PL 13
BURNS STATUE SQ 14
SMITH ST 15
PARKHOUSE ST 16

236
239

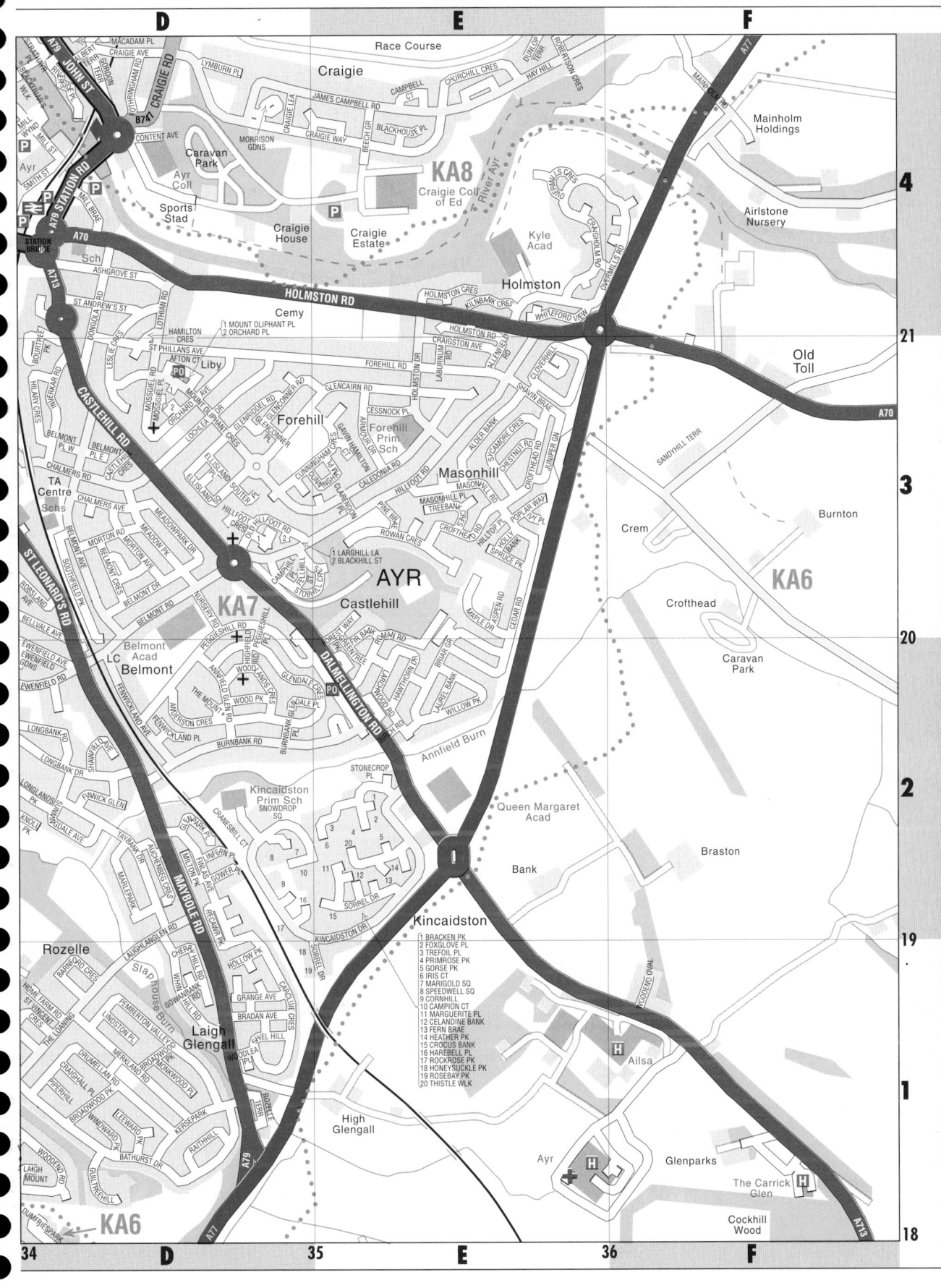
D
E
F
Race Course
Craigie
A79 JOHN ST
MACADAM PL
CRAIGIE AVE
ALBERT TERR
GORDON TERR
FOTHRINGHAM RD
CRAIGIE RD
B747
LYMBURN PL
DUNLOP TERR
ROBERTSON CRES
HAY HILL
CHURCHILL CRES
CAMPBELL CT
JAMES CAMPBELL RD
CRAIGIE LEA
BLACKHOUSE PL
CRAIGIE WAY
BEECH GR
MORRISON GDNS
CONTENT AVE
Caravan Park
Ayr Coll
KA8
Craigie Coll of Ed
River Ayr
MAINHOLM RD
A77
Mainholm Holdings
4
Airlstone Nursery
OVERMILLS CRES
CRAIGHOLM RD
OVERMILLS RD
Kyle Acad
Holmston
MILL WYND
MILL ST
Ayr
SMITH ST
A79 STATION RD
MILL BRAE
Sports Stad
Craigie House
Craigie Estate
STATION BRIDGE
A70
Sch
ASHGROVE ST
A713
HOLMSTON RD
HOLMSTON CRES
KILNBANK CRES
WHITEFORD VIEW
ST ANDREW'S ST
DONGOLA RD
LOTHIAN RD
Cemy
1 MOUNT OLIPHANT PL
2 ORCHARD PL
HAMILTON CRES
HOLMSTON RD
CRAIGSTON AVE
ALLENFIELD RD
21
Old Toll
BOURTREE PK
LESLIE CRES
ST PHILLANS AVE
AFTON CT
PO
Liby
FOREHILL RD
HOLMSTON DR
LABURNUM RD
CLOVERHILL
SHAVIN BRAE
A70
HILARY CRES
WERKAR RD
MOSSGIEL RD
MOSSGIEL PL
ORCHARD AVE
MOUNT OLIPHANT CRES
LOCHLEA DR
GLENRIDDEL RD
GLENCONNER RD
GLENCAIRN RD
Forehill
CESSNOCK PL
ARMOUR DR
Forehill Prim Sch
ALDER BANK
SYCAMORE CRES
CHESTNUT RD
CROFTHEAD RD
JUNIPER GN
SANDYHILL TERR
CASTLEHILL RD
BELMONT PL W
BELMONT PL E
CASTLEHILL CRES
GLENCONNER PL
ELLISLAND PL
ELLISLAND
SOUTER PL
CUNNINGHAM CT
GAVIN HAMILTON
CALEDONIA RD
HILLFOOT RD
Masonhill
MASONHILL RD
MASONHILL PL
TREEBANK CRES
CHALMERS RD
TA Centre
Schs
CHALMERS AVE
MEADOWPARK DR
CLARENDON PL
3
Burnton
Crem
HILLFOOT CRES
OLD HILLFOOT RD
PINE BRAE
ROWAN CRES
CROFTHEAD
HILLTOP PL
HOLLY BANK
POPLAR WAY
SPRUCE PK
MORTON RD
MEADOW PK
BELMONT CRES
MORTON AVE
ST LEONARD'S RD
1 LARGHILL LA
2 BLACKHILL ST
CAMPHILL
FELLHILL ST
STOBHILL CRES
AYR
KA6
Crofthead
ROBSLAND AVE
SOUTHFIELD PK
BELMONT AVE
BELMONT DR
BELMONT RD
NURSERY RD
KA7
Castlehill
ASPEN RD
MAPLE DR
CEDAR RD
BELLVALE AVE
PEGGIESHILL RD
PEGGIESHILL PL
FOREST WAY
GREENTREE
FIR BANK
ROWAN RD
BRIAR GR
20
EWENFIELD AVE
EWENFIELD GDNS
LC
Belmont Acad
Belmont
HIGHFIELD RD
WOODLANDS CRES
DALMELLINGTON RD
LARCHWOOD RD
HAWTHORN DR
LAUREL BANK
WILLOW PK
Caravan Park
EWENFIELD RD
ANNFIELD GLEN RD
THE MOUNT
WOOD PK
GLENDALE CRES
DALE PL
FENWICKLAND AVE
ANDERSON CRES
FENWICKLAND PL
BURNBANK RD
BURNBANK GLEN PL
BIRCH RD
LONGBANK RD
SHAWFIELD AVE
Annfield Burn
LONGBANK DR
STONECROP PL
2
LONGLANDS PK
FINWICK GLEN
Kincaidston Prim Sch
SNOWDROP SQ
Queen Margaret Acad
KNOLL PK
AIRDALE AVE
TAYBANK DR
GLEN PARK PL
CRANESBILL CT
MILTON PK
AUCHENBEG CRES
MAYBOLE RD
LINFERN PL
FINLAS AVE
GOWER PL
MARLEPARK
REGAWR PK
Braston
Bank
SORREL DR
KINCAIDSTON DR
Kincaidston
1 BRACKEN PK
2 FOXGLOVE PL
3 TREFOIL PL
4 PRIMROSE PK
5 GORSE PK
6 IRIS CT
7 MARIGOLD SQ
8 SPEEDWELL SQ
9 CORNHILL
10 CAMPION CT
11 MARGUERITE PL
12 CELANDINE BANK
13 FERN BRAE
14 HEATHER PK
15 CROCUS BANK
16 HAREBELL PL
17 ROCKROSE PK
18 HONEYSUCKLE PK
19 ROSEBAY PK
20 THISTLE WLK
Rozelle
LAUGHLANGLEN RD
CHERRY HILL RD
HOLLOW PK
BARNFORD CRES
Slaphouse Burn
WHIN HILL RD
GOWANBANK
19
WOODEND OVAL
HOME FARM RD
ST VINCENT CRES
THE LOANING
PEMBERTON VALLEY
LINDSTON PL
GRANGE AVE
BRADAN AVE
CARCLUIE CRES
Laigh Glengall
SHIEL HILL
WOODLEA PL
MERKLAND RD
BROADWOOD PK
MONKWOOD PL
DRUMELLAN RD
CRAIGHALL PL
PIPERHILL
BROADWOOD PK
Ailsa
1
ROZELLE TERR
High Glengall
WINDWARD PL
LEEWARD PK
KERSEPARK
RAITHHILL
BATHURST DR
Ayr
Glenparks
LAIGH MOUNT
WOODEND RD
GUILTREEHILL
A79
The Carrick Glen
DUMFRIESPARK
KA6
A77
Cockhill Wood
A713
18
34
35
36

96 96 97

Scale: 7 inches to 1 mile

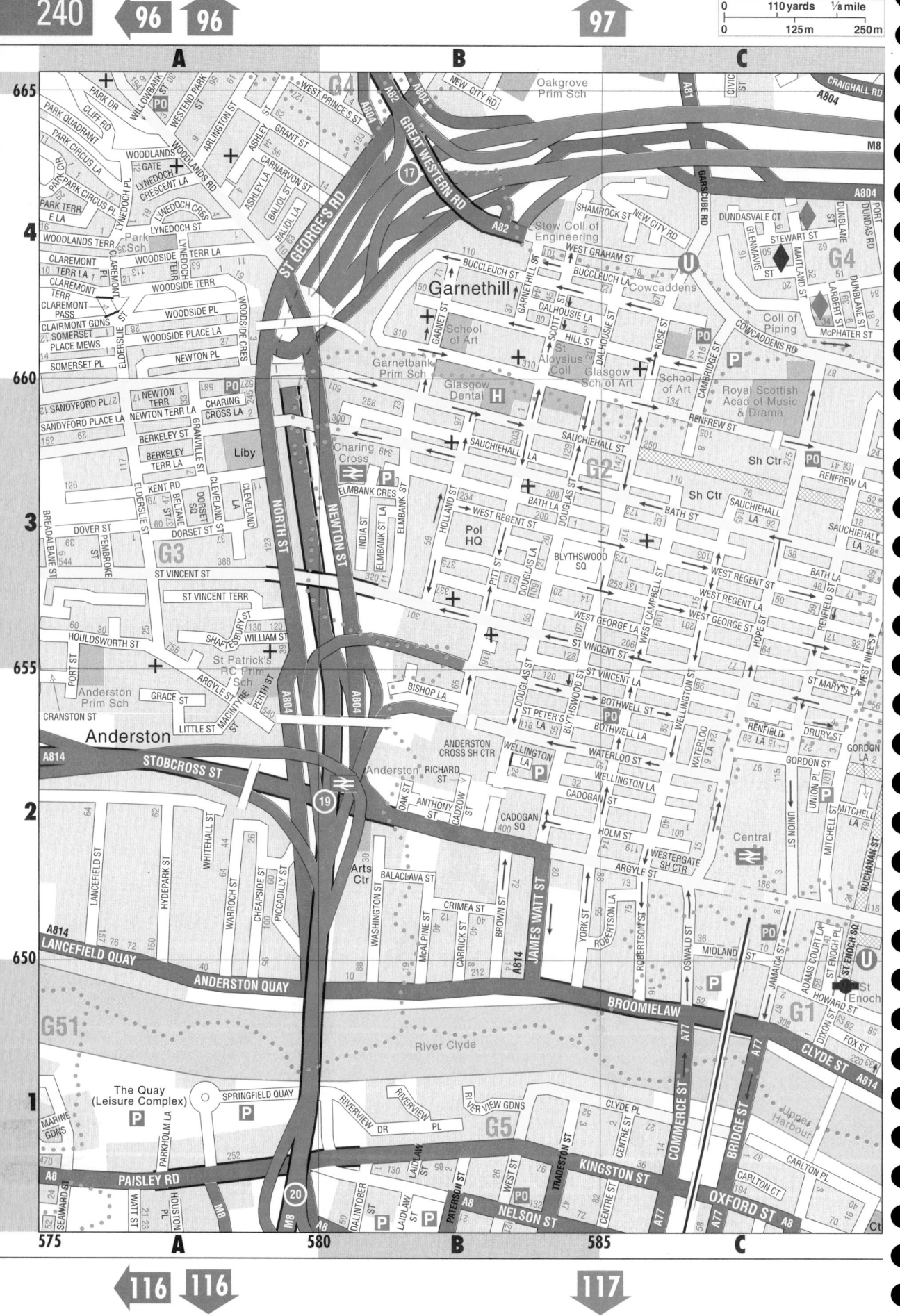
Garnethill
Anderston
Cowcaddens
River Clyde
Charing Cross
Central
St Enoch
Glasgow Sch of Art
Royal Scottish Acad of Music & Drama
Glasgow Dental
Stow Coll of Engineering
School of Art
St Aloysius Coll
Coll of Piping
Garnetbank Prim Sch
Oakgrove Prim Sch
St Patrick's RC Prim Sch
Anderston Prim Sch
Park Sch
Pol HQ
Liby
Sh Ctr
Anderston Cross Sh Ctr
Westergate Sh Ctr
Arts Ctr
The Quay (Leisure Complex)
Upper Harbour
St George's Rd
Great Western Rd
North St
Newton St
Sauchiehall St
Bath St
West Regent St
West George St
St Vincent St
Bothwell St
Waterloo St
Argyle St
Stobcross St
Broomielaw
Clyde St
Lancefield Quay
Anderston Quay
Paisley Rd
Kingston St
Nelson St
Oxford St
James Watt St
Hope St
Renfield St
Union St
Buchanan St
Commerce St
Bridge St
Cowcaddens Rd
Renfrew St
Woodlands Rd
Garscube Rd
Blythswood Sq
Cadogan Sq
Springfield Quay
Tradeston St
Washington St
Robertson St
Oswald St
Jamaica St
Midland St
Holm St
Cadogan St
Wellington St
West Nile St
St Enoch Sq
Howard St
Garnet St
Dalhousie St
Rose St
Cambridge St
West Graham St
Buccleuch St
Hill St
Douglas St
West Campbell St
Pitt St
Holland St
Elmbank St
India St
St Vincent Terr
Houldsworth St
Elderslie St
Granville St
Berkeley St
Newton Pl
Woodside Pl
Woodside Terr
Claremont Terr
Lynedoch St
Park Circus Pl
Park Quadrant
Kent Rd
Dover St
Breadalbane St
Pembroke St
Cleveland St
Dorset St
Lancefield St
Hydepark St
Whitehall St
Warroch St
Cheapside St
Piccadilly St
McAlpine St
Carrick St
Brown St
Crimea St
Balaclava St
York St
Clyde Pl
Centre St
Riverview Dr
Riverview Pl
River View Gdns
Marine Gdns
Parkholm La
Houston Pl
Watt St
Seaward St
Dalintober St
Laidlaw St
Paterson St
West St
Carlton Pl
Carlton Ct
Fox St
Dixon St
Mitchell St
Gordon St
Drury St
St Mary's La
Adams Court La
Craighall Rd
Port Dundas Rd
Dundasvale Ct
Stewart St
Maitland St
Dunblane St
McPhater St
Civic St
New City Rd
Shamrock St
A804 A82 A81 M8 A814 A8 A77

116 116 117

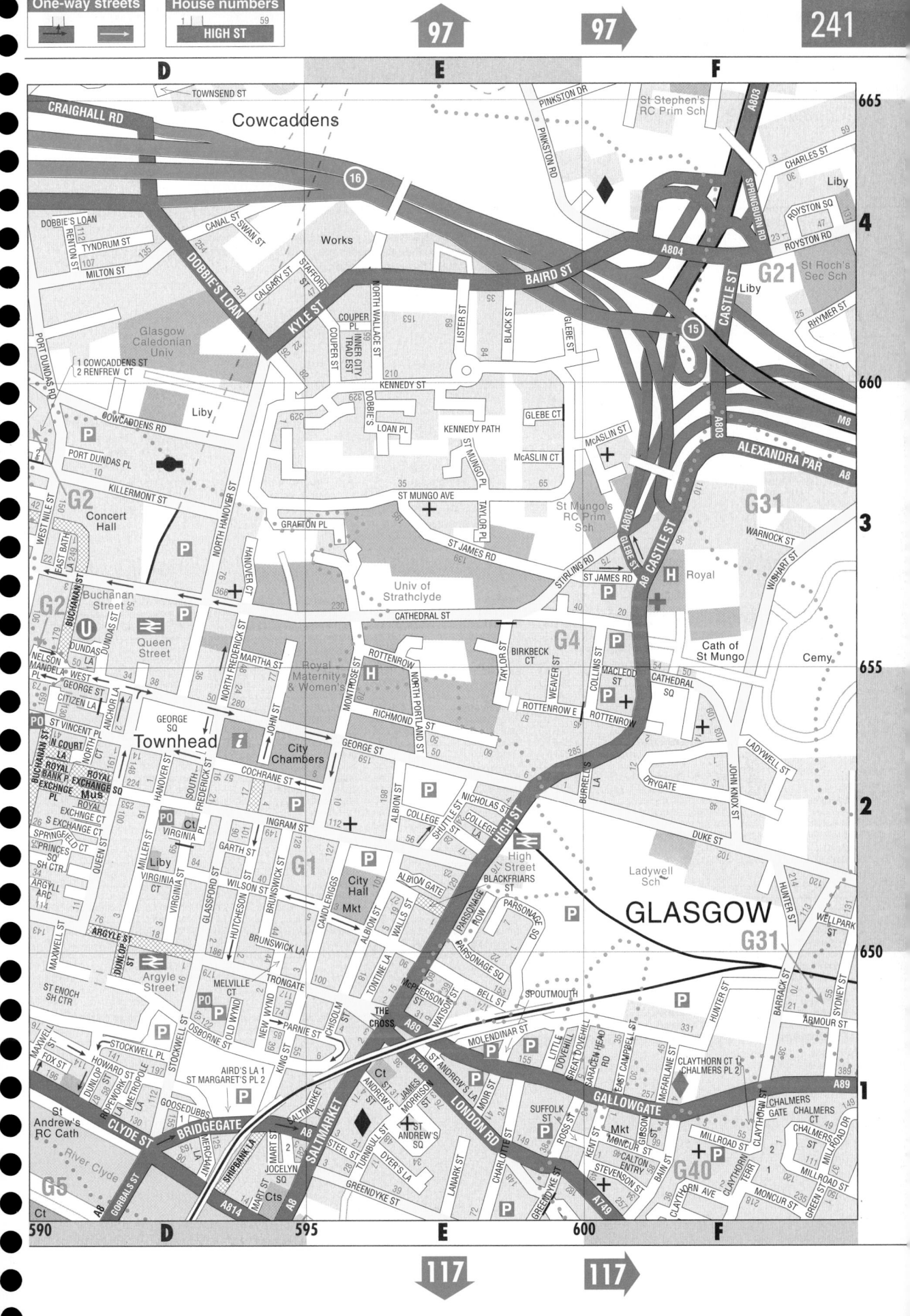
One-way streets
House numbers
HIGH ST
97
117
Cowcaddens
Townhead
GLASGOW
Glasgow Caledonian Univ
Univ of Strathclyde
Royal Maternity & Women's
City Chambers
City Hall
Cath of St Mungo
Concert Hall
Queen Street
Argyle Street
High Street
St Andrew's RC Cath
River Clyde
CRAIGHALL RD
DOBBIE'S LOAN
KYLE ST
BAIRD ST
CASTLE ST
ALEXANDRA PAR
CATHEDRAL ST
GEORGE ST
HIGH ST
DUKE ST
GALLOWGATE
LONDON RD
SALTMARKET
CLYDE ST
BRIDGEGATE
ARGYLE ST
INGRAM ST
NORTH HANOVER ST
BUCHANAN ST
665
660
655
650
4
3
2
1
590
595
600
D
E
F

Index

Street names are listed alphabetically and show the locality, the Postcode District, the page number and a reference to the square in which the name falls on the map page

Cumberland Pl **7** Glasgow G5 ..... **117** E2

Full street name This may have been abbreviated on the map	**Location Number** If present, this indicates the street's position on a congested area of the map instead of the name

Town, village or locality in which the street falls.

Postcode District for the street name

Page number of the map on which the street name appears

Grid square in which the centre of the street falls

Schools, hospitals, sports centres, railway stations, shopping centres, industrial estates, public amenities and other places of interest are also listed. These are highlighted in

Abbreviations used in the index

App	Approach	Cl	Close	Espl	Esplanade
Arc	Arcade	Comm	Common	Est	Estate
Ave	Avenue	Cnr	Corner	Gdns	Gardens
Bvd	Boulevard	Cotts	Cottages	Gn	Green
Bldgs	Buildings	Ct	Court	Gr	Grove
Bsns Pk	Business Park	Ctyd	Courtyard	Hts	Heights
Bsns Ctr	Business Centre	Cres	Crescent	Ho	House
Bglws	Bungalows	Dr	Drive	Ind Est	Industrial Estate
Cswy	Causeway	Dro	Drove	Intc	Interchange
Ctr	Centre	E	East	Junc	Junction
Circ	Circle	Emb	Embankment	La	Lane
Cir	Circus	Ent	Enterprise	Mans	Mansions

Mdw	Meadows	S	South
N	North	Sq	Square
Orch	Orchard	Strs	Stairs
Par	Parade	Stps	Steps
Pk	Park	St	Street, Saint
Pas	Passage	Terr	Terrace
Pl	Place	Tk	Track
Prec	Precinct	Trad Est	Trading Estate
Prom	Promenade	Wlk	Walk
Ret Pk	Retail Park	W	West
Rd	Road	Yd	Yard
Rdbt	Roundabout		

Town and village index

Baird St Coatbridge ML5 122 A4
Falkirk FK1 41 E3
Glasgow G4 241 E4
Baird Terr ML7 127 E3
Bairds Cres ML3 162 B2
Bairdsland View ML4 142 A3
Bairns Ford Ave FK2 42 A4
Bairns Ford Ct FK2 42 A4
Bairns Ford Dr FK2 42 A4
Baker St Glasgow G41 116 C1
Greenock PA15 46 A2
Stirling FK8 7 D4
Bakewell Rd G69 120 A3
Balaclava St G2, G3 240 B2
Balado Rd G33 119 F4
Balbakie Rd ML7 127 F3
Balbeg St G51 115 F3
Balbeggie St G32 119 E2
Balblair Rd G52 115 F1
Balcarres Ave G12 96 B3
Balcastle Gdns G65 36 A1
Balcastle Rd Kilsyth G65 36 A1
Slamannan FK1 86 A3
Balcomie Cres KA10 230 A1
Balcomie St G33 99 D1
Balcomie Terr ML3 183 D4
Balcurvie Rd G34 100 A1
Baldernock Prim Sch G64 56 A1
Baldernock Rd G62 55 E1
Baldinnie Rd G34 120 A4
Baldorran Cres G68 61 D2
Baldovan Cres G33 119 F4
Baldovie Rd G52 115 E2
Baldragon Rd G34 100 B1
Baldric Rd G13 95 E3
Baldwin Ave G13 95 E4
Balerno Dr G52 115 F2
Balfearn Dr G76 178 C3
Balfleurs St G62 55 D1
Balfluig St G34 99 F1
Balfour Ave KA15 171 D4
Balfour Cres Larbert FK5 23 E1
Plean FK7 12 B2
Balfour Ct KA3 223 E2
Balfour St Alloa FK10 10 B4
Bannockburn FK7 7 E1
Bonnybridge FK4 39 F3
Glasgow G20 96 B3
Port Glasgow PA14 47 D1
Stirling FK8 1 C1
Balfour Terr G75 180 C4
Balfour Wynd ML9 185 E1
Balfron Cres ML3 161 F2
Balfron Rd Glasgow G51 115 F4
Greenock PA15 46 B1
Paisley PA1 114 B3
Balgair Dr PA1 114 A3
Balgair St G22 97 D2
Balgair Terr G32 119 D3
Balglass St G22 97 D3
Balgonie Ave PA2 113 D1
Balgonie Dr PA2 113 E1
Balgonie Rd G52 115 F2
Balgonie Woods PA2 113 E1
Balgownie Cres G46 136 A1
Balgray Ave Kilbirnie KA25 170 A4
Kilmarnock KA1 227 F1
Balgray Cres G78 134 C1
Balgray Rd Barrmill KA15 172 A3
Glengarnock KA14 170 A4
Newton Mearns G77 156 A3
Balgray Way KA11 220 A3
Balgraybank St G21 98 A2
Balgrayhill Rd G21 97 F3
Balgraystone Rd G77, G78 155 E4
Balintore St G32 119 D3
Baliol La G3 240 A4
Baliol St G3 240 A4
Baljaffray Prim Sch G61 75 E4
Baljaffray Rd G61 75 D4
Ballachalairy Yett G63 30 B2
Ballacher Ct ML1 164 A2
Ballagan Pl G62 54 B1
Ballaig Ave G61 75 E3
Ballaig Cres G33 99 E3
Ballantay Quadrant G45 138 A2
Ballantay Rd G45 138 A2
Ballantay Terr G45 138 A2
Ballantine Ave G52 115 D4
Ballantine Dr KA7 238 C3
Ballantrae G74 159 E1
Ballantrae Cres G77 157 D2
Ballantrae Dr G77 157 D2
Ballantrae Rd G72 161 F3
Ballater Cres ML2 165 D3
Ballater Dr Bearsden G61 76 A1
Inchinnan PA4 93 E4
Paisley PA2 114 A1
Stirling FK9 2 B2
Ballater Pl G5 117 E2
Ballater St G5 117 E2
Ballater Way ML5 101 E3
Ballayne Dr G69 81 D2
Ballengeich Pass FK8 2 A1
Ballengeich Rd FK8 1 C1
Ballentrae Wynd ML1 143 D3
Ballerup High Sch G75 180 A2
Ballerup Terr G75 180 C3
Ballewan Cres G63 31 D2
Ballindalloch Dr G31 118 A4
Ballindalloch La G31 118 A4
Ballinkier Ave FK4 38 C2
Balloch Castle G83 19 E1
Balloch Castle Ctry Pk G83 19 E1
Balloch Gdns G52 115 F2
Balloch Holdings G68 61 D1
Balloch Rd Airdrie ML6 124 A3
Balloch G83 27 E4
Cumbernauld G68 61 E1
Greenock PA15 46 A1
Shotts ML7 146 C3
Balloch Rdbt G68 61 D1
Balloch Sta G83 27 F4
Balloch View G67 61 F1
Ballochmill Rd G73 138 B4
Ballochmyle G74 160 B2
Ballochney La ML6 102 C1
Ballochney Rd ML6 103 F2
Ballochney St ML6 102 C1
Ballochnie Dr ML6 104 A2
Ballogie Rd G44 137 D4
Ballot Rd KA12 219 E2
Balmalloch Prim Sch G65 36 B1
Balmalloch Rd G65 36 B1
Balmartin Rd G23 76 B1
Balmedie PA8 73 D1
Balmeg Ave G46 157 E4
Balmerino Pl G64 98 B4
Balminnoch Pk KA7 238 B1
Balmoral Ave ML6 102 C3
Balmoral Cres
Coatbridge ML5 121 E2
Inchinnan PA4 93 F3
Balmoral Dr Bearsden G61 76 A1
Cambuslang G72 138 C3
Falkirk FK1 41 F2
Glasgow G32 139 D4
Balmoral Gdns
Blantyre G72 140 B1
Uddingston G71 120 C1
Balmoral Path 5 ML9 185 E1
Balmoral Pl
East Kilbride G74 159 E1
Gourock PA19 43 F3
Stenhousemuir FK5 23 F2
Stirling FK8 7 D4
Balmoral Rd Elderslie PA5 112 A1
Kilmarnock KA3 222 C1
Balmoral St Falkirk FK1 41 F2
Glasgow G14 95 D2
Balmoral Wynd KA3 211 F4
Balmore Ct PA13 89 E4
Balmore Dr ML3 183 D4
Balmore Ind Est G22 97 D4
Balmore Pl G22 97 D3
Balmore Rd Balmore G64 77 F4
Glasgow G22 97 D3
Greenock PA15 46 B1
Balmore Sq G22 97 D3
Balmuildy Prim Sch G64 77 F2
Balmuildy Rd G64 77 E3
Balmulzier Rd FK1 86 A4
Balornock Prim Sch G21 98 A2
Balornock Rd G21 98 A3
Balquhatstone Cres FK1 86 A3
Balquhidderock FK7 7 E2
Balquidder Ct ML6 103 D1
Balrossie Dr PA13 89 D4
Balrossie Sch PA13 89 D4
Balruddery Pl G64 98 B4
Balshagray Ave G11,G14 95 F2
Balshagray Cres G14 95 F1
Balshagray Dr G11 95 F2
Balshagray La G11 95 F2
Balshagray Pl G11 95 F2
Baltersan Gdns ML3 183 F2
Baltic Ct G40 118 A2
Baltic La G40 118 A2
Baltic Pl G40 117 F2
Baltic St G40 118 A2
Balure Cres FK7 8 B2
Balure St G31 118 B4
Balvaird Cres G73 138 A4
Balvaird Dr G73 138 A4
Balvenie St ML5 122 A2
Balveny St G33 99 E1
Balvicar Dr G42 116 C1
Balvicar St G42 116 C1
Balvie Ave Glasgow G15 75 D1
Glasgow, Giffnock G46 136 B1
Balvie Cres G62 54 C1
Balvie Rd G62 54 C1
Banavie Rd Glasgow G11 96 A2
Wishaw ML2 165 F3
Banchory Ave
Glasgow G43 136 A3
Glenmavis ML6 102 C3
Inchinnan PA4 93 E4
Banchory Cres G61 76 A1
Banchory Pl FK10 4 B2
Banchory Prim Sch FK10 4 B2
Banchory Rd ML2 165 D3
Bandeath Ind Est FK7 9 D3
Bandeath Rd FK7 8 B2
Baneberry Path G74 159 E2
Banff Ave ML6 123 D2
Banff Pl East Kilbride G75 180 B4
Greenock PA16 44 B3
Banff Quadrant ML2 165 D3
Banff Rd PA16 44 B3
Banff St G33 99 D1
Bangorshill St G46 135 F2
Bank Ave G62 55 D2
Bank Ct KA12 219 F2
Bank Pk G75 180 B4
Bank Pl Irvine KA12 219 F2
Kilmarnock KA1 227 F4
Shotts ML7 146 C2
Bank Rd Glasgow G32 139 E4
Harthill ML7 127 F3
Bank St Airdrie ML6 123 D4
Alexandria G83 27 F3
Alloa FK10 10 A3
Barrhead G78 134 B1
Cambuslang G72 139 D3
Coatbridge ML5 121 F3
Falkirk FK1 42 A3
Glasgow G12 96 C1
Greenock PA15 45 F2
Irvine KA12 219 E2
Kilbirnie KA25 149 D1
Kilmarnock KA1 227 F4
Neilston G78 154 B4
Paisley PA1 113 F3
Prestwick KA9 236 A4
Slamannan FK1 86 A3
Stirling FK8 7 D4
Troon KA10 229 D1
Bank View ML6 123 E1
Bank Way 13 ML9 185 D2
Bankbrae Ave G53 135 D3
Bankend PA11 110 C4
Bankend Pl KA3 223 D3
Bankend Rd
Bridge Of W PA11 110 C3
Dumbarton G82 49 F2
Bankend St G33 99 D1
Bankfaulds Ave KA25 149 D1
Bankfield Dr ML3 183 E4
Bankfoot Dr G52 115 D2
Bankfoot Pl G77 157 D2
Bankfoot Rd Glasgow G52 115 D2
Paisley PA3 113 D3
Bankglen Rd G15 75 D2
Bankhall St G42 117 D1
Bankhead Ave Airdrie ML6 123 E4
Bellshill ML4 142 A2
Coatbridge ML5 121 E2
Glasgow G13 95 D3
Springside KA11 221 D1
Bankhead Cres FK4 39 E3
Bankhead Dr G73 138 A4
Bankhead Pl Airdrie ML6 123 E4
Coatbridge ML5 121 E2
Stewarton KA3 195 F1
Bankhead Prim Sch
Glasgow G13 95 D3
Glasgow, Bankhead G73 137 F4
Bankhead Rd
Carmunnock G76 158 B4
Fishcross FK10 5 E2
Kilwinning KA13 207 F2
Kirkintilloch G66 80 A4
Rutherglen G73 137 F4
Bankhead Terr ML11 215 D1
Bankholm Pl G76 157 F3
Bankier Prim Sch FK4 38 C2
Bankier Rd FK4 38 C2
Bankier Terr FK4 38 C2
Banknock St G32 118 C3
Banks Rd G66 58 B1
Bankside FK2 42 B4
Bankside Ave PA5 111 F2
Bankside Ct FK6 21 F1
Bankside Gdns KA25 149 D2
Bankside Ind Est FK2 42 B4
Banktop Pl PA5 111 F2
Bankview Cres G66 79 D4
Bankview Dr G66 79 D4
Bannachra Cres G83 27 E3
Bannachra Dr G84 16 A1
Bannatyne Ave G31 118 A4
Bannatyne St ML11 215 D2
Banner Dr G13 75 E1
Banner Rd G13 75 E1
Bannercross Ave 9 G69 120 A3
Bannercross Dr G69 120 A3
Bannercross Gdns 8 G69 120 A3
Bannerman Dr
Bellshill ML4 142 B3
Kilmarnock KA3 223 E1
Bannerman High Sch G69 120 A2
Bannerman Pl G81 74 A1
Bannoch Gdns KA13 208 A2
Bannoch Pl KA13 208 A2
Bannoch Rd KA13 208 A2
Bannock Rd FK7 8 B2
Bannockburn Dr ML9 185 E1
Bannockburn High Sch FK7 7 E1
Bannockburn Hospl FK7 11 F4
Bannockburn Pl KA3 223 D2
Bannockburn Prim Sch FK7 7 F1
Bannockburn Rd
Cowie FK7 12 B4
Stirling FK7 7 E2
Bannockburn St PA16 45 E2
Bannockburn Station Rd FK7 8 A2
Bantaskin Prim Sch FK1 41 F2
Bantaskin St G20 96 B4
Bantaskine Dr FK1 41 F2
Bantaskine Gdns FK1 41 F2
Bantaskine St FK1 41 F2
Banton Pl Bonnybridge FK4 40 A2
Glasgow G33 120 A4
Banton Prim Sch G65 37 F2
Banton Rd G65 37 E1
Banyan Cres G71 121 E1
Bar Hill Pl G65 60 A4
Barassie G74 159 E2
Barassie Cres G68 61 F3
Barassie Ct G72 140 C1
Barassie Dr PA11 110 B3
Barassie Pl KA1 227 F2
Barassie Prim Sch KA10 229 E3
Barassie St KA10 229 E2
Barassie Sta KA10 229 E3
Barassiebank La KA10 229 E3
Barbados Pl KA1 227 F3
Barbadoes Rd KA1 227 F3
Barbados Gn 5 G75 159 D1
Barbae Pl G71 141 D2
Barbana Rd G74 158 C1
Barbegs Cres G65 60 C2
Barberry Ave G53 135 D1
Barberry Dr KA15 171 D4
Barberry Gdns G53 135 D1
Barberry Pl G53 135 E1
Barbeth Gdns G67 82 A3
Barbeth Pl Cumbernauld G67 82 A3
Irvine KA11 220 A3
Barbeth Rd G67 82 A3
Barbeth Way G67 82 A3
Barbour Ave FK7 7 E2
Barbour's Pk KA3 211 F4
Barbreck Rd 7 G42 116 C1
Barcaldine Ave G69 80 A1
Barcapel Ave G77 156 C4
Barcaple Flats G77 156 C4
Barclaven Rd PA13 89 F4
Barclay Ave PA5 112 A1
Barclay Ct G60 73 D3
Barclay Dr Helensburgh G84 16 B2
Kilmarnock KA3 223 E1
Barclay Gdns KA11 220 B3
Barclay Pl KA3 195 E1
Barclay Rd ML1 163 D3
Barclay Sq PA4 94 A1
Barclay St Glasgow G21 97 F3
Old Kilpatrick G60 73 D3
Barcraigs Dr PA2 133 F4
Bard Ave G13 95 D4
Bardowie St G22 97 D2
Bardrain Ave PA5 112 B1
Bardrain Rd PA2 133 E4
Bardrainney Ave PA14 68 C4
Bardrill Dr G64 77 F1
Bardykes Rd G72 161 D4
Barefield St ML9 185 D2
Barfillan Dr G52 115 F3
Bargaran Rd G53 115 D2
Bargarran Prim Sch PA8 72 C1
Bargarran Rd PA8 72 C2
Bargarron Dr PA3 114 A4
Barge Ct G84 15 E3
Bargeddie Prim Sch ML5 121 D3
Bargeddie St G33 98 B1
Bargeddie Sta G69 121 D2
Bargeny KA13 207 D1
Bargrennan Rd KA10 229 F3
Barhill La G65 59 F2
Barhill Rd PA8 73 D1
Barhill Terr G65 60 A2
Barholm Sq G33 99 E1
Barke Rd G67 62 A2
Barkin Ct FK1 42 A1
Barkly Terr 2 G75 180 B4
Barlae Ave G76 178 C4
Barlanark Ave G32 119 E3
Barlanark Cres G33 119 E4
Barlanark Dr G33 119 E4
Barlanark Pl Glasgow G33 119 F4
Glasgow, Greenfield G32 119 D3
Barlanark Prim Sch G33 119 F3
Barlanark Rd G33 119 F4
Barlandfauld St G65 60 C4
Barleith Ct KA1 228 C3
Barleyhill FK4 40 A3
Barlia Dr G45 137 F2
Barlia St G45 137 F2
Barlia Terr G45 137 F2
Barloan Cres G82 50 A3
Barloan Pl G82 50 A3
Barloch Ave G62 55 D1
Barloch Rd G62 55 D1
Barloch St G22 97 E2
Barlogan Ave G52 115 F3
Barlogan Quadrant G52 115 F3
Barmore Ave ML8 202 A4
Barmouth Ave PA19 44 C3
Barmulloch Prim Sch G21 98 B2
Barmulloch Rd G21 98 A2
Barn Gn PA10 111 D2
Barn Rd FK8 7 D4
Barnard Gdns G64 78 A2
Barnbeth Rd G53 115 D1
Barncluith Rd ML3 162 C1
Barnego Rd FK6 21 E2
Barnes Rd G20 97 D3
Barnes St G78 134 A1
Barness Pl G33 119 D4
Barnett Cres KA21 216 C4
Barnett Ct KA21 216 C4
Barnett Path G72 161 E4
Barnflat St G73 118 A1
Barnford Cres KA7 239 D1
Barnhill Dr Hamilton ML3 161 E1
Tullibody FK10 4 B1
Barnhill Rd G82 50 B2
Barnhill St PA15 46 B2
Barnhill Sta G21 98 A2
Barnkirk Ave G15 75 D2
Barns Cres KA7 238 C4
Barns Pk KA7 238 C4
Barns St Ayr KA7 238 C4
Clydebank G81 94 B4
Barns Street La KA7 238 C4
Barns Terr KA7 238 C4
Barns Terrace La KA7 238 C4
Barnscroft PA10 111 D2
Barnsdale Rd FK7 7 D2
Barnsford Ave PA4 93 D2
Barnsford Rd PA4 93 D2
Barnswood Pl 13 G71 141 D2
Barnton La FK1 42 A2
Barnton St Glasgow G32 118 C4
Stirling FK8 7 D4
Barnweil Rd
Kilmarnock KA1 227 F3
Prestwick KA9 236 B3
Barnweill Dr KA1 228 C3
Barnwell Rd FK9 2 B2
Barnwell Terr G51 115 F4
Barochan Cres PA3 113 D2
Barochan Rd Bishopton PA6 71 D1
Glasgow G53 115 D2
Houston PA6 91 D3
Baron Ct ML3 163 D1
Baron Rd PA3 114 A3
Baron St PA4 94 B1
Baronald Dr G12 96 A3
Baronald Gate G12 96 A3
Baronald St G73 118 A1
Barone Dr G76 157 E4
Baronhall Dr G72 161 E4
Baronhill G67 62 A3
Barons Gate G71 140 C2
Barons Rd ML1 164 B1
Baronscourt Dr PA3 112 C2
Baronscourt Gdns PA3 112 C2
Baronscourt Rd PA3 112 C2
Barony Ct Ardrossan KA22 205 E1
5 Glasgow G69 120 A3
Irvine KA11 219 F3
Barony Dr G69 120 A3
Barony Gdns G69 120 A3
Barony Glebe KA23 190 B3
Barony Pl G68 60 C1
Barony Rd KA9 236 B3
Barony Terr KA25 170 A4
Barony Wynd 6 G69 120 A3
Barr Ave G78 154 C4
Barr Cres G81 74 A3
Barr Gr G71 141 D4
Barr Pl
Newton Mearns G77 156 B3
Paisley PA1 113 E2
Barr St Ardrossan KA22 205 E1
Glasgow G20 97 D2
Motherwell ML1 163 F4
Barr Terr G74 159 F1
Barr's Brae Kilmacolm PA13 69 E1
Port Glasgow PA14 68 B4
Barra Ave Renfrew PA4 94 B1
Wishaw ML2 165 F3
Barra Cres Irvine KA11 220 B1
Old Kilpatrick G60 73 E3
Barra Dr ML6 123 F3
Barra Gdns G60 73 E3
Barra La KA11 220 B1
Barra Pl Irvine KA11 220 B1
Stenhousemuir FK5 24 A2
Barra Rd G60 73 E3
Barra St G20 96 B4
Barra Wynd KA11 220 B1
Barrachnie Cres G69 119 F3
Barrachnie Ct G69 119 F3
Barrachnie Rd G69 119 F3
Barrack St Glasgow G4 241 F1
Hamilton ML3 162 B2
Barraston Rd G64 57 D1
Barrcraig Rd PA11 110 B4
Barrhead High Sch G78 134 B2
Barrhead Rd Glasgow G53 135 E4
Newton Mearns G77 156 A3
Paisley PA2 114 A1
Barrhead Sta G78 134 A2
Barrhill Cres PA10 111 E2
Barrhill Ct G66 80 A4
Barrhill Rd Erskine PA8 93 D4
Gourock PA19 44 B4
Kirkintilloch G66 80 A4
Barrie Quadrant G81 74 A2
Barrie Rd East Kilbride G74 160 B3
Glasgow G52 115 D4
Stenhousemuir FK5 23 F2
Barrie St ML1 163 F3
Barrie Terr KA22 205 E1
Barriedale Ave ML3 162 A2
Barrington Ave KA15 150 A1
Barrington Dr G4 96 C1
Barrisdale Rd Glasgow G20 96 B4
Wishaw ML2 165 F3
Barrisdale Way G73 138 A2
Barrland Ct G46 136 B2
Barrland Dr G46 136 B2
Barrland St G41 117 D2
Barrmill Rd Beith KA15 171 E4
Burnhouse KA15 172 A1
Glasgow G43 136 A3
Barrochan Intc PA5 111 F2
Barrochan Rd PA5, PA6 111 F3
Barrowfield Sch G40 118 A3
Barrowfield St G40 118 A3
Barrs Brae La PA14 47 E1
Barrs Cres G82 48 A4
Barrs Ct G82 26 A1
Barrs La ML8 187 F2
Barrs Terr G82 48 A4
Barrwood Pl G71 141 D4
Barrwood St G33 98 C1
Barry Gdns G72 161 E3
Barsail Prim Sch PA8 93 E4
Barscube Ave PA14 68 C4
Barscube Terr PA2 114 A1
Barshaw Dr PA1 114 A3
Barshaw Pl PA1 114 B3
Barshaw Rd G52 114 C3
Barskiven Rd PA3 112 C2
Barterholm Rd PA2 113 F1

Binniehill Rd
Cumbernauld G68 .... 61 E1
Slamannan FK1 .... 85 F2
Binns Rd G33 .... 99 E1
Birch Ave Clarkston G76 .... 157 F3
Stirling FK8 .... 6 C3
Birch Brae ML3 .... 162 C1
Birch Cotts G84 .... 16 B1
Birch Cres Clarkston G76 .... 157 F3
Johnstone PA5 .... 112 A1
Birch Ct ML5 .... 121 F2
Birch Dr Cambuslang G72 .... 139 E3
Kirkintilloch G66 .... 79 E3
Birch Gr Larkhall ML9 .... 185 D3
Uddingston G71 .... 141 D4
Birch Knowe G64 .... 98 A4
Birch Pl Blantyre G72 .... 161 E4
Cambuslang G72 .... 139 F2
Kilmarnock KA1 .... 227 E4
Birch Quadrant ML6 .... 123 E4
Birch Rd Ayr KA7 .... 239 E2
Clydebank G81 .... 74 A3
Cumbernauld G67 .... 62 C2
Dumbarton G82 .... 49 F2
Birch St Glasgow G5 .... 117 E2
Motherwell ML1 .... 143 D3
Birch Terr KA22 .... 205 E2
Birch View G61 .... 76 A3
Birch Way KA10 .... 229 E2
Birchfield Dr G14 .... 95 D2
Birchfield Rd ML3 .... 162 A2
Birchgrove PA6 .... 91 E1
Birchlea Dr G46 .... 136 B2
Birchmount Ct ML6 .... 123 E4
Birchview Dr G76 .... 157 F2
Birchwood FK10 .... 5 E1
Birchwood Ave G32 .... 119 F2
Birchwood Dr PA2 .... 113 D1
Birchwood Pl G32 .... 119 F2
Birchwood Rd G78 .... 153 D2
Birdsfield Ct G72 .... 161 F3
Birdsfield Dr G72 .... 161 F3
Birdsfield St ML3 .... 161 F3
Birdston Rd Glasgow G21 .... 98 B3
Milton Of C G65 .... 58 B2
Birgidale Ave G45 .... 137 E1
Birgidale Rd G45 .... 137 E1
Birgidale Terr G45 .... 137 E1
Birkbeck Ct G4 .... 241 E3
Birkdale G74 .... 159 E2
Birkdale Cl KA13 .... 207 E2
Birkdale Ct G72 .... 140 C1
Birken Rd G66 .... 79 F2
Birkenburn Rd G67 .... 62 C3
Birkenshaw Rd G69, ML5 .... 81 F1
Birkenshaw St G31 .... 118 A4
Birkenshaw Way PA3 .... 113 F4
Birkfield Loan ML8 .... 188 B1
Birkfield Pl ML8 .... 188 B1
Birkhall Ave Glasgow G52 .... 115 D2
Inchinnan PA4 .... 93 E4
Birkhall Dr G61 .... 75 F1
Birkhill Ave G64 .... 78 A1
Birkhill Gdns G64 .... 78 A1
Birkhill Rd
Crossford ML11 .... 201 E1
Hamilton ML3 .... 183 E4
Stirling FK7 .... 6 C3
Birkmyre Ave PA14 .... 47 D1
Birkmyre Rd G51 .... 115 F3
Birks Ct ML8 .... 186 C3
Birks Hill KA11 .... 220 A2
Birks Pl ML11 .... 215 D3
Birks Rd Larkhall ML9 .... 199 D4
Law ML8 .... 186 C2
Birkscairn Pl KA11 .... 220 B1
Birkscairn Way KA11 .... 220 B1
Birkshaw Brae ML2 .... 186 A4
Birkshaw Pl ML2 .... 186 A4
Birkshaw Tower ML2 .... 185 F4
Birkwood Pl G77 .... 156 B1
Birkwood St G40 .... 118 A1
Birmingham Rd PA4 .... 94 A1
Birnam Ave G64 .... 78 A1
Birnam Cres G61 .... 76 A3
Birnam Ct FK2 .... 24 B1
Birnam Gdns G64 .... 78 A1
Birnam Pl Hamilton ML3 .... 161 F2
Newton Mearns G77 .... 157 D2
Birnam Rd G31 .... 118 B2
Birness Dr G43 .... 136 B4
Birnie Ct G21 .... 98 B2
Birnie Rd G21 .... 98 B2
Birniehill Rd ML1 .... 145 D3
Birniehill Rdbt G74 .... 181 D4
Birniewell Rd FK1 .... 86 A3
Birnock Ave PA4 .... 94 C1
Birrell Rd G62 .... 54 C2
Birrens Rd ML1 .... 163 E4
Birsay Rd G22 .... 97 D4
Bishop Gdns
Bishopbriggs G64 .... 77 F1
Hamilton ML3 .... 183 F4
Bishop La G2 .... 240 B2
Bishop Loch Prim Sch
G34 .... 100 B1
Bishopbriggs High Sch
G64 .... 78 A1
Bishopbriggs Sta G64 .... 78 A1
Bishopdale G74 .... 159 E2
Bishopmill Pl G21 .... 98 B2
Bishopmill Rd G21 .... 98 B2
Bishops Gate G74 .... 158 B2
Bishops Pk G74 .... 158 A2
Bishopsgate Dr G21 .... 97 F4
Bishopsgate Gdns G21 .... 97 F4
Bishopsgate Pl 10 G21 .... 97 F4
Bishopsgate Rd G21 .... 97 F4
Bishopton Prim Sch PA7 .... 72 A2
Bishopton Sta PA7 .... 72 A1
Bishpobriggs Ind Est G21 .... 98 A4
Bissett Cres G81 .... 73 F3
Black O' Hill Rdbt G68 .... 61 D1
Black St Airdrie ML6 .... 103 D1
Glasgow G4 .... 241 E4
Blackadder Pl G75 .... 179 E4
Blackbog Rd ML6 .... 82 C1
Blackbraes Rd G74 .... 160 A2
Blackburn Cres
Dumbarton G82 .... 49 E2
Kirkintilloch G66 .... 80 A4
Blackburn Dr KA7 .... 238 C3
Blackburn Pl KA7 .... 238 C3
Blackburn Rd KA7 .... 238 C3
Blackburn Sq G78 .... 134 B1
Blackburn St G51 .... 116 C3
Blackbyres Ct G78 .... 134 B2
Blackbyres Rd G78 .... 134 B3
Blackcraig Ave G15 .... 75 D2
Blackcroft Ave ML6 .... 123 F3
Blackcroft Gdns G32 .... 119 E2
Blackcroft Rd G32 .... 119 E2
Blackcroft Terr ML7 .... 125 D1
Blackdyke Rd G66 .... 79 F4
Blackfarm Rd G77 .... 156 C2
Blackfaulds Dr KA3 .... 213 D2
Blackfaulds Gdns KA3 .... 213 D2
Blackfaulds Rd G73 .... 137 F4
Blackford Cres KA9 .... 233 F1
Blackford Rd PA2 .... 114 A2
Blackfriars Prim Sch G5 .... 117 E2
Blackfriars St G1 .... 241 E2
Blackfriars Wlk KA7 .... 238 C4
Blackhall Ct PA2 .... 114 A2
Blackhall La PA1 .... 113 F2
Blackhall St Paisley PA1 .... 114 A2
Shotts ML7 .... 147 D2
Blackhill Dr G84 .... 16 B2
Blackhill Pl G33 .... 98 B1
Blackhill Rd
Blackridge EH48 .... 107 F2
Glasgow G23 .... 76 C1
Blackhill St KA7 .... 239 D3
Blackhill View ML8 .... 187 D2
Blackhouse Ave G77 .... 156 C2
Blackhouse Gdns G77 .... 156 C2
Blackhouse Pl KA8 .... 239 E4
Blackhouse Rd G77 .... 156 C2
Blackie St G3 .... 96 B1
Blacklands Ave KA13 .... 207 F1
Blacklands Cres KA13 .... 207 F1
Blacklands Pl G66 .... 79 F2
Blacklands Prim Sch
KA13 .... 207 E1
Blacklands Rd G74 .... 159 E1
Blacklaw Dr G74 .... 181 D4
Blacklaw La PA3 .... 113 F3
Blacklaw Prim Sch G74 .... 160 A1
Blackmill Cres FK2 .... 24 A2
Blackmoor Pl ML1 .... 143 D2
Blackmoss Dr ML4 .... 142 A2
Blackmuir Pl FK10 .... 4 B2
Blackness St ML5 .... 122 A2
Blackridge Prim Sch
EH48 .... 107 E2
Blackshaw Dr KA23 .... 190 B3
Blackstone Ave G53 .... 135 E4
Blackstone Cres G53 .... 115 E1
Blackstone Rd PA3 .... 113 D4
Blackstoun Ave PA3 .... 112 A3
Blackstoun Oval PA3 .... 113 D3
Blackstoun Rd PA3 .... 113 D3
Blackswell La ML3 .... 162 C2
Blacksyke Ave KA1 .... 227 F2
Blackthorn Ave
Beith KA15 .... 150 A1
Kirkintilloch G66 .... 79 D3
Blackthorn Gr G66 .... 79 D3
Blackthorn Rd
Cumbernauld G67 .... 62 C2
Uddingston G71 .... 141 E4
Blackthorn St G22 .... 97 F3
Blacktongue Farm Rd
ML6 .... 83 F1
Blackwood G75 .... 180 B3
Blackwood Ave
Kilmarnock KA1 .... 227 F3
Linwood PA3 .... 112 A3
Newton Mearns G77 .... 156 C2
Blackwood Gdns ML1 .... 142 B1
Blackwood Rd
Cumbernauld G68 .... 60 C1
Milngavie G62 .... 54 C2
Blackwood St
Barrhead G78 .... 134 A1
Glasgow G13 .... 95 F4
Blackwood Terr PA5 .... 131 E4
Blackwoods Cres
Bellshill ML4 .... 142 B2
Moodiesburn G69 .... 80 C1
Bladda La PA1 .... 113 F2
Blades Ct G69 .... 101 D3
Bladnoch Dr G15 .... 75 E1
Blaefaulds Cres FK6 .... 39 E4
Blaeloch Ave G45 .... 137 E1
Blaeloch Dr G45 .... 137 E1
Blaeloch Terr G44 .... 137 D1
Blaeshill Rd G75 .... 179 F4
Blair Atholl Dr 20 ML9 .... 185 E1
Blair Ave KA1 .... 228 C3
Blair Cres Glasgow G69 .... 120 A2
Hurlford KA1 .... 228 C3
Blair Dr G65 .... 58 B3
Blair Gdns Gourock PA19 .... 43 F3
Newton Mearns G77 .... 156 A3
Torrance G64 .... 57 D1
Blair House G67 .... 62 A2
Blair Linn View G67 .... 83 D3
Blair Path ML1 .... 163 F3
Blair Rd Coatbridge ML5 .... 121 F4
Crossford ML8 .... 201 D1
Dalry KA24 .... 191 F4
Hurlford KA1 .... 228 C3
Kilwinning KA13 .... 207 F3
Paisley PA1 .... 114 C3
Blair St Glasgow G32 .... 118 C3
Kilmarnock KA3 .... 222 C1
Blair Terr FK5 .... 24 A2
Blairafton Wynd KA13 .... 207 E3
Blairatholl Ave G11 .... 96 A2
Blairatholl Cres G77 .... 157 D2
Blairatholl Gate G77 .... 157 D2
Blairatholl Gdns 11 G11 .... 96 A2
Blairbeth Dr G44 .... 137 D4
Blairbeth Pl G73 .... 138 A3
Blairbeth Rd G73 .... 138 B3
Blairbeth Terr G73 .... 138 B3
Blairdardie Prim Sch G15 .... 75 D1
Blairdardie Rd G13 .... 75 E1
Blairdenan Ave G69 .... 81 D2
Blairdenon Cres FK1 .... 41 F2
Blairdenon Dr Alloa FK10 .... 5 D1
Cumbernauld G68 .... 61 E2
Blairdenon Rd FK12 .... 4 C3
Blairdenon Way KA11 .... 220 A1
Blairforkie Dr FK9 .... 1 C4
Blairgowrie Rd G52 .... 115 E2
Blairgrove Ct ML5 .... 121 F3
Blairhall Ave G41 .... 136 C4
Blairhill Ave G66 .... 80 A3
Blairhill Pl ML5 .... 121 F4
Blairhill St ML5 .... 121 F4
Blairhill Sta ML5 .... 121 F4
Blairholm Dr ML4 .... 142 A2
Blairlands Dr KA24 .... 191 F4
Blairlinn Ind Est G67 .... 82 C3
Blairlinn Rd G67 .... 82 C3
Blairlogie St G33 .... 99 D1
Blairmore Cres PA15 .... 46 B1
Blairmore Rd PA15 .... 46 B1
Blairmuckhole And
Forrestdyke Rd ML7 .... 126 C4
Blairpark Ave ML5 .... 121 F4
Blairquhomrie Cotts G83 .... 20 C1
Blairston Ave G71 .... 141 D1
Blairston Gdns G71 .... 141 D1
Blairtum Dr G73 .... 138 A3
Blairtummock Prim Sch
G34 .... 120 A4
Blairtummock Rd
Glasgow G33 .... 119 E4
Glasgow, Queenslie G33 .... 119 F4
Blake Rd G67 .... 62 A1
Blakely Rd KA21 .... 217 D4
Blane Ave G63 .... 31 D2
Blane Cres G63 .... 31 D2
Blane Dr G62 .... 55 D2
Blane Pl G63 .... 31 D2
Blane St ML5 .... 122 A4
Blanefield Ave KA9 .... 236 B3
Blaneview G33 .... 99 E2
Blantyre Cres G81 .... 73 F4
Blantyre Ct PA8 .... 73 D2
Blantyre Dr PA7 .... 72 A2
Blantyre Farm Rd
G71, G72 .... 140 B3
Blantyre Gdns G68 .... 60 C1
Blantyre High Sch G72 .... 161 E4
Blantyre Ind Est G72 .... 161 F3
Blantyre Mill Rd G71 .... 141 D1
Blantyre Pl ML5 .... 121 F2
Blantyre Rd G71 .... 141 D1
Blantyre St Coatbridge ML5 .... 121 F2
Glasgow G3 .... 96 B1
Blantyre Sta G72 .... 161 F4
Blaven Ct G69 .... 120 B2
Blaven Head KA11 .... 220 A2
Blawarthill Hospl G14 .... 95 D3
Blawarthill St G14 .... 94 C3
Bleachfield Falkirk FK2 .... 42 A3
Milngavie G62 .... 55 D2
Bleeze Rd KA24 .... 191 D4
Blenheim Ave
East Kilbride G75 .... 180 B4
Stepps G33 .... 99 F3
Blenheim Ct Carluke ML8 .... 188 A1
Kilsyth G65 .... 36 C1
Paisley PA1 .... 113 E3
Blenheim Pl FK5 .... 23 F3
Blindwells FK12 .... 4 C3
Blinkbonnie Terr FK1 .... 86 A3
Blinkbonny Rd FK1 .... 41 F2
Blinny Ct ML7 .... 147 D2
Blochairn Rd G21 .... 98 A1
Bloomgate ML11 .... 215 D2
Bluebell Gdns
Glasgow G45 .... 138 A1
Motherwell ML1 .... 142 B1
Bluebell Way Airdrie ML6 .... 102 C1
Carluke ML8 .... 201 F4
Lennoxtown G65 .... 57 F4
Bluebell Wlk ML1 .... 143 D2
Blueknowes Rd ML8 .... 186 C3
Bluevale St G31 .... 118 A3
Blyth Rd G33 .... 119 F3
Blythe Pl G33 .... 119 E3
Blythswood Ave PA4 .... 94 B2
Blythswood Dr PA3 .... 113 F3
Blythswood Ind Est PA4 .... 94 A2
Blythswood Rd PA4 .... 94 B2
Blythswood Sq G2 .... 240 B3
Blythswood St G2 .... 240 B2
Bo'ness Rd Chapelhall ML6 .... 123 E1
Motherwell ML1 .... 143 E4
Boardwalk The G75 .... 181 D4
Boat Vennel KA7 .... 235 F1
Boclair Acad G61 .... 76 B2
Boclair Ave G61 .... 75 F2
Boclair Cres Bearsden G61 .... 76 A2
Bishopbriggs G64 .... 78 A1
Boclair Rd Bearsden G61 .... 76 B3
Bishopbriggs G64 .... 78 A1
Boclair St G13 .... 95 F4
Bodden Sq ML1 .... 143 F4
Boden Ind Est G40 .... 118 A2
Boden Quadrant ML1 .... 142 B1
Boden St G40 .... 118 A2
Bodesbeck Ct KA11 .... 220 A2
Bodmin Gdns G69 .... 80 C2
Bog Rd Banknock FK4 .... 38 C2
Laurieston FK2 .... 42 C2
Bog Rdbt FK2 .... 42 C2
Bog Road Ind Est FK2 .... 42 C2
Bogany Terr G45 .... 137 F1
Bogbain Rd G34 .... 120 A4
Bogend Rd Bannockburn FK7 .... 11 F4
Larbert FK2 .... 23 D4
Torwood FK5 .... 22 C4
Bogfoot Rd ML7 .... 125 D1
Boggknowe G71 .... 140 B4
Boghall Rd Carluke ML8 .... 202 A4
Glasgow G69 .... 120 A2
Boghall St Glasgow G33 .... 99 D1
Stonehouse ML9 .... 198 C1
Boghead KA15 .... 171 D4
Boghead Ave G82 .... 50 A2
Boghead Pk
(Dumbarton FC)
G82 .... 50 A2
Boghead Rd Dumbarton G82 .... 50 A2
Glasgow G21 .... 98 A2
Kirkintilloch G66 .... 79 D3
Bogiewood Rd PA14 .... 47 D1
Bogle St PA15 .... 46 A2
Boglemart St KA20 .... 217 E4
Bogleshole Rd G72 .... 138 C4
Boglestone Ave PA14 .... 68 C4
Boglestone Prim Sch PA14 .... 68 C4
Bogmoor Pl G51 .... 95 E1
Bogmoor Rd G51 .... 115 E4
Bogs View ML4 .... 141 F2
Bogside Rd Ashgill ML9 .... 199 F4
Glasgow G33 .... 99 D3
Kilsyth G65 .... 60 B4
Port Glasgow PA14 .... 68 C4
Bogside St G40 .... 118 A2
Bogston La PA15 .... 46 C1
Bogston Sta PA15 .... 46 C1
Bogstonhill Rd PA6 .... 91 D1
Bogton Ave G44 .... 136 C2
Bogton Avenue La G44 .... 136 C2
Bohun Ct FK7 .... 7 E2
Boleyn Ct ML2 .... 166 A3
Boleyn Rd G41 .... 116 C1
Bolingbroke G74 .... 160 B2
Bolivar Terr G42 .... 137 E4
Bolton Dr G42 .... 137 D4
Bolton Terr G65 .... 57 F4
Boman Pl KA3 .... 195 E1
Bon Accord Cres ML7 .... 146 C3
Bon Accord Rd G76 .... 157 F3
Bon Accord Sq G81 .... 94 A4
Bon Secours Hospl G41 .... 136 C4
Bonar Cres PA11 .... 110 C4
Bonar La PA11 .... 110 C4
Bonar Law Ave G84 .... 16 A1
Bonawe St G20 .... 96 C2
Bonds Dr ML2 .... 166 A3
Boness St G40 .... 118 A2
Bonhill Prim Sch G83 .... 27 F2
Bonhill Rd G82 .... 50 A2
Bonhill St G22 .... 97 D2
Bonkle Gdns ML2 .... 166 A3
Bonkle Rd ML2 .... 166 A3
Bonnar St G40 .... 118 A2
Bonnaughton Rd G61 .... 75 D3
Bonnet Ct KA3 .... 211 F4
Bonnet Rd ML11 .... 215 D2
Bonnhill View G83 .... 27 F2
Bonnington Ave ML11 .... 215 D2
Bonnybridge Hospl FK4 .... 40 B3
Bonnybridge Prim Sch FK4 .... 40 A3
Bonnybridge Rd FK4 .... 39 F3
Bonnyfield Rd FK4 .... 39 F3
Bonnyhill Rd Falkirk FK1 .... 41 D2
High Bonnybridge FK4 .... 40 B2
Bonnyholm Ave G53 .... 115 D2
Bonnyholm Prim Sch G53 .... 115 D2
Bonnyrigg Dr G43 .... 136 A3
Bonnyside Rd FK4 .... 40 A3
Bonnyton Dr G76 .... 178 B3
Bonnyton Foot KA11 .... 220 A3
Bonnyton Ind Est KA1 .... 222 C1
Bonnyton Moor Rd G76 .... 178 A4
Bonnyton Pl Irvine KA11 .... 220 A3
Kilmarnock KA1 .... 222 B1
Bonnyton Rd KA1 .... 222 B1
Bonnyton Row KA11 .... 220 A3
Bonnyview Gdns FK4 .... 40 A3
Bonnywood Ave FK4 .... 40 A4
Bontine Ave G82 .... 49 E2
Bonyton Ave G13 .... 94 C3
Boon Dr G15 .... 75 D1
Booth Pl FK1 .... 42 A2
Boquhanran Pl G81 .... 74 A2
Boquhanran Rd G81 .... 74 A2
Borden La G13 .... 95 F3
Borden Rd G13 .... 95 F3
Border Ave KA21 .... 216 C4
Border Pl KA21 .... 216 C4
Border St PA15 .... 46 B2
Border Way G66 .... 79 F4
Bore Rd ML6 .... 123 D4
Boreland Dr Glasgow G13 .... 95 D3
Hamilton ML3 .... 161 F1
Boreland Pl G13 .... 95 D3
Borestone Ave KA25 .... 170 A4
Borestone Cres FK7 .... 7 D2
Borestone Ct FK7 .... 7 D1
Borestone Pl FK7 .... 7 D1
Borestone Prim Sch FK7 .... 7 D1
Borgie Cres G72 .... 139 D3
Borland Cres G76 .... 178 C3
Borland Dr ML9 .... 199 D4
Borland Rd G61 .... 76 A2
Borron St G4 .... 97 E2
Borrowdale G75 .... 179 F3
Borrowlea Rd FK7 .... 7 E4
Borrowmeadow Rd FK7 .... 7 F4
Borthwick Dr G75 .... 179 E4
Borthwick St G33 .... 99 D1
Bosfield Cnr G74 .... 159 F2
Bosfield Pl G74 .... 159 F2
Bosfield Rd G74 .... 159 F2
Boston Dr G84 .... 16 C2
Boswell Ct G42 .... 136 C4
Boswell Dr G72 .... 161 E4
Boswell Pk Ayr KA7 .... 238 C4
East Kilbride G74 .... 160 B2
Boswell Sq G52 .... 114 C4
Bosworth Rd G74 .... 160 A3
Botanic Cres G20 .... 96 B2
Botanic Crescent La G20 .... 96 B2
Bothkennar Prim Sch FK2 .... 24 C2
Bothkennar Rd FK2 .... 24 C2
Bothlin Dr G33 .... 99 E3
Bothlyn Ave G66 .... 79 F4
Bothlyn Cres G69 .... 100 C4
Bothlyn Rd G69 .... 100 B4
Bothwell Castle G72 .... 140 B2
Bothwell La Glasgow G2 .... 240 C2
4 Glasgow, Kelvingrove G12 .... 96 C1
Bothwell Park Ind Est G71 .... 141 D2
Bothwell Park Sch G71 .... 141 E3
Bothwell Pl Coatbridge ML5 .... 121 F4
Paisley PA2 .... 132 C4
Bothwell Prim Sch G71 .... 141 D1
Bothwell Rd Bothwell G71 .... 140 C2
Carluke ML8 .... 187 F2
Hamilton ML3 .... 162 B3
Bothwell St
Cambuslang G72 .... 138 C3
Glasgow G2 .... 240 C2
Hamilton ML3 .... 162 B3
Bothwellhaugh Quadrant
ML4 .... 141 F2
Bothwellhaugh Rd ML4 .... 142 A1
Bothwellpark Pl ML4 .... 141 E3
Bothwellpark Rd G71 .... 141 E2
Bothwellshields Rd ML1 .... 124 B1
Boturich Dr G83 .... 19 F1
Boundary Rd KA8 .... 236 B2
Bourhill Ct ML2 .... 164 B1
Bourne Cres PA4 .... 93 E4
Bourne Ct PA4 .... 93 E4
Bourne St ML3 .... 162 C2
Bournemouth Rd PA19 .... 44 C3
Bourock Sq G78 .... 134 C1
Bourtree Pk KA7 .... 239 D4
Bourtree Rd ML3 .... 161 F1
Bouverie St Glasgow G14 .... 94 C3
Port Glasgow PA14 .... 47 E1
Rutherglen G73 .... 137 F4
Bow Rd PA16 .... 45 E2
Bow St FK8 .... 7 D4
Bowden Dr G52 .... 115 D3
Bowden Pk G75 .... 180 B4
Bower St G12 .... 96 C2
Bowerwalls St G78 .... 134 C2
Bowes Cres G69 .... 119 F2
Bowes Rigg KA3 .... 195 F1
Bowfield Ave G52 .... 114 C3
Bowfield Cres G52 .... 114 C3
Bowfield Dr G52 .... 115 D3
Bowfield Pl G52 .... 114 C3
Bowfield Rd Howwood PA9 .... 130 C3
West Kilbride KA23 .... 190 B2
Bowhouse Gdns FK10 .... 10 A3
Bowhouse Rd Airdrie ML6 .... 123 F3
Alloa FK10 .... 10 A3
Bowhouse Rise KA11 .... 220 A3
Bowhousebog or Liquo
ML7 .... 146 A1
Bowhousebog Rd ML7 .... 146 A1
Bowhousebrae Rd ML6 .... 123 F3
Bowie Rd G83 .... 27 F3
Bowie St G82 .... 49 F2
Bowling Green La 22 G14 .... 95 E2
Bowling Green Rd
Chryston G69 .... 100 B4
Glasgow G44 .... 137 D3
Glasgow, Barrachnie G32 .... 119 E2
23 Glasgow, Whiteinch G14 .... 95 E2
Bowling Green St ML4 .... 142 A3
Bowling Green View G72 .... 139 F2
Bowling St ML5 .... 121 F4
Bowling Sta G60 .... 72 B4
Bowman Rd KA7 .... 238 C3
Bowman St G42 .... 117 D1
Bowmanflat ML9 .... 185 D2
Bowmont Gdns 15 G12 .... 96 B2
Bowmont Hill G64 .... 78 A2
Bowmont Pl
Cambuslang G72 .... 139 E3
East Kilbride G75 .... 179 E4
Bowmont Terr G12 .... 96 B2
Bowmore Ct KA11 .... 220 A3

Broomhill Pl Denny FK6 21 E2
Glasgow G11 95 F1
Stirling FK7 6 C3
Broomhill Prim Sch G11 95 F2
Broomhill Prim Sch Annexe G14 95 F2
Broomhill Quadrant KA1 228 A2
Broomhill Rd
Bonnybridge FK4 40 A2
Larkhall ML9 185 D1
Broomhill Rd E KA1 228 A2
Broomhill Rd W KA1 227 F2
Broomhill St
Greenock PA15 45 F2
Harthill ML7 127 E3
Broomhill Terr G11 95 F1
Broomhill View ML9 184 C1
Broomhill Way PA15 45 F2
Broomieknowe FK10 4 B2
Broomieknowe Dr G73 138 A3
Broomieknowe Rd G73 138 A3
Broomielaw G1, G2 240 C1
Broomknoll St ML6 123 D4
Broomknowe G68 61 E2
Broomknowe Rd PA13 89 E4
Broomknowes Ave G66 79 F2
Broomknowes Rd G21 98 A2
Broomlands Ave PA8 93 F4
Broomlands Busway KA11 220 A1
Broomlands Cres PA8 93 F4
Broomlands Ct KA11 220 A1
Broomlands Dr KA12 219 E1
Broomlands Gdns PA8 93 E4
Broomlands Pl KA12 219 E1
Broomlands Prim Sch KA11 220 A1
Broomlands Rd
Cumbernauld G67 83 D4
Irvine KA11 220 A1
Broomlands St PA1 113 E2
Broomlands Way PA8 93 F4
Broomlea Cres PA4 93 E4
Broomlea Sch G11 95 F1
Broomlee Rd G67 82 C3
Broomley Cres G83 27 E4
Broomley Dr G46 136 B1
Broomley La G46 136 B1
Broomloan Ct G51 116 A3
Broomloan Pl G51 116 A3
Broomloan Rd G51 116 A3
Broompark Ave
Blantyre G72 161 E3
Prestwick KA9 236 B4
Broompark Cir 8 G31 117 F4
Broompark Cres
Airdrie ML6 103 D2
Prestwick KA9 236 B4
Broompark Dr
Glasgow G31 117 F4
Inchinnan PA4 93 E4
Newton Mearns G77 157 D3
Broompark Gdns FK6 21 F1
Broompark La 7 G31 117 F4
Broompark Rd
Blantyre G72 161 E4
Wishaw ML2 164 B2
Broompark St 6 G31 117 F4
Broomridge Rd FK7 7 E2
Broomside Cres ML1 163 F2
Broomside Pl FK5 23 E1
Broomside Rd FK4 40 A2
Broomside St ML1 163 F2
Broomstone Ave G77 156 C2
Broomton Rd G21 98 B4
Broomvale Dr G77 156 C3
Broomward Dr PA5 112 A2
Brora Dr Bearsden G61 76 A2
Glasgow G46 136 B1
Renfrew PA4 94 C2
Brora Gdns G64 78 A1
Brora Rd G64 78 A1
Brora St G33 98 B1
Brosdale Ct FK1 42 A1
Brougham St PA16 45 F4
Broughton G75 180 C3
Broughton Dr G23 96 C4
Broughton Gdns G23 76 C1
Broughton Gn KA11 220 A3
Broughton Pl
Coatbridge ML5 122 A2
Hamilton ML3 162 A2
Broughton Rd G23 76 C1
Broun Dr KA7 238 C1
Brouster Gate 6 G74 159 F1
Brouster Hill G74 159 F1
Brouster Pl G74 159 F1
Brown Ave Alloa FK10 4 C1
Clydebank G81 94 C4
Dumbarton G82 50 B2
Stirling FK9 2 A1
Troon KA10 229 E2
Brown Pl Cambuslang G72 139 D3
Saltcoats KA21 205 F1
Brown Rd G67 61 F1
Brown St Balloch G83 28 A4
Carluke ML8 187 F2
Coatbridge ML5 122 A3
Falkirk FK1 41 E3
Glasgow G2 240 B2
Greenock PA15 46 B2
Larkhall ML9 185 D2
Motherwell ML1 163 F4
Paisley PA1 113 E3
Port Glasgow PA14 47 D1
Brown St continued
Renfrew PA4 94 A2
Shotts ML7 147 D2
Stewarton KA3 211 E4
Wishaw ML2 166 A2
Brown Wlk KA12 219 E3
Brown's La PA1 113 F2
Browncarrick Dr KA7 238 A1
Brownhill Dr KA25 169 F4
Brownhill Rd G43 136 A2
Brownhill View ML2 166 B3
Brownieside Pl ML6 104 A2
Brownieside Rd ML6 104 B1
Brownlee Rd ML8 186 B2
Brownlie St G42 137 D4
Brownmuir Ave G76 178 C2
Brownsburn Ind Est ML6 123 D3
Brownsburn Rd ML6 123 E3
Brownsdale Rd G73 137 F4
Brownsfield Cres PA4 93 D3
Brownsfield Rd PA4 93 D3
Brownshill Ave ML5 121 F2
Brownside Ave
Barrhead G78 134 A3
Cambuslang G72 138 C3
Brownside Cres G78 134 A3
Brownside Dr
Barrhead G78 134 A3
Glasgow G13 94 C3
Brownside Gr G78 134 A3
Brownside Mews G72 138 C3
Brownside Rd G72 138 C3
Browside Ave PA2 133 E4
Bruar Way 15 ML2 165 F3
Bruart Ave FK5 23 F2
Bruce Ave
Dundonald KA2 225 F1
Johnstone PA5 131 F4
Motherwell ML1 163 E4
Paisley PA3 114 A4
Prestwick KA9 236 A3
Bruce Cres Ayr KA7 238 C4
Falkirk FK2 24 A2
Kilmarnock KA1 227 F2
Plean FK7 12 B2
Bruce Ct ML6 123 F4
Bruce Dr Fallin FK7 8 B3
Stenhousemuir FK5 23 F2
Bruce La KA9 236 A3
Bruce Loan ML2 186 B3
Bruce Pl G75 180 C4
Bruce Rd Bishopton PA7 72 A2
Glasgow G41 116 C2
Motherwell ML1 143 D1
Paisley PA3 114 A4
Renfrew PA4 94 A1
Bruce St Alloa FK10 10 B4
Bannockburn FK7 7 F1
Bellshill ML4 142 A3
Clydebank G81 74 A1
Coatbridge ML5 122 A4
Dumbarton G82 50 A1
Falkirk FK2 42 B3
Greenock PA15 45 F3
Kilmarnock KA1 227 F2
Plains ML6 104 A1
Plean FK7 12 B2
Port Glasgow PA14 47 E1
Stirling FK8 2 A1
Bruce Terr Blantyre G72 140 C1
Cambusbarron FK7 6 B3
East Kilbride G75 180 C4
Irvine KA12 219 E3
Bruce View FK7 7 D1
Bruce's Loan 14 ML9 185 E1
Brucefield Pl G34 120 B4
Brucehill Rd G82 49 E2
Brunel Way G75 180 C4
Brunstane Rd G34 100 A1
Brunswick La G1 241 D2
Brunswick St G1 241 D2
Brunton St G44 137 D3
Brunton Terr G44 137 D2
Bruntsfield Ave
Glasgow G53 135 D2
Kilwinning KA13 207 D2
Bruntsfield Gdns G53 135 D2
Bryan St ML3 162 A3
Bryce Ave FK2 24 A1
Bryce Gdns ML9 185 D2
Bryce Knox Ct KA11 220 A3
Bryce Pl G75 180 B3
Brydson Pl PA3 112 A3
Brymner St PA15 46 A3
Bryon Ct G71 141 D1
Bryony The FK10 4 A1
Bryson Ct ML1 183 E4
Bryson St Clydebank G81 74 C4
Falkirk FK2 42 A3
Bryson Street Ind Est FK2 42 A3
Buccleuch Ave
Clarkston G76 157 E4
Paisley G52 114 C4
Buccleuch Dr G61 75 F4
Buccleuch La G3 240 B4
Buccleuch St G3 240 B4
Buccleugh St PA15 45 F3
Buchan Gn G74 160 A2
Buchan Rd
Motherwell ML1 143 D1
Troon KA10 229 F2
Buchan St Hamilton ML3 183 E4
Wishaw ML2 165 D3
Buchan Terr G72 138 C2
Buchanan Ave
Balloch G83 28 A4
Bishopton PA7 72 A2
Buchanan Bsns Pk G33 99 F3
Buchanan Cres
Bishopbriggs G64 98 B4
Hamilton ML3 162 A1
Buchanan Ct Falkirk FK2 42 A4
Stepps G33 99 F3
Buchanan Dr Bearsden G61 76 A2
Bishopbriggs G64 98 B4
Kirkintilloch G66 79 E2
Law ML8 187 D3
Newton Mearns G77 156 C4
Rutherglen G73, G72 138 C3
Rutherglen, Burgh G73, G72 138 B3
Stirling FK9 2 A2
Buchanan Gdns G32 119 F1
Buchanan Gr G69 120 A3
Buchanan Pl
Kilmarnock KA1 228 A3
Torrance G64 57 D1
Buchanan Rd G84 17 D1
Buchanan St Airdrie ML6 123 D4
Coatbridge ML5 121 F3
Dumbarton G82 50 A1
Glasgow G1 240 C2
Glasgow, Baillieston G69 120 A2
Greenock PA16 45 D2
Johnstone PA5 111 F1
Milngavie G62 55 D1
Buchanan Street Underground Sta G1 241 D3
Buchandyke Rd G74 160 A2
Buchlyvie Gdns G64 97 F4
Buchlyvie Rd PA1 114 C3
Buchlyvie St G34 120 A4
Buckie PA8 73 D2
Buckie Wlk ML4 142 A3
Buckingham Ct ML3 161 F2
Buckingham Dr
Glasgow G32 139 D4
Rutherglen G73 138 B4
Buckingham St G12 96 B2
Buckingham Terr G12 96 B2
Bucklaw Gdns G52 115 E2
Bucklaw Pl G52 115 E2
Bucklaw Terr G52 115 E2
Buckley St G22 97 E3
Bucksburn Rd G21 98 B2
Buckthorne Pl G53 135 D2
Buddon St G40 118 B2
Budhill Ave G32 119 D3
Budshaw Ave ML6 123 E1
Buiston Rd KA3 211 E2
Bull Rd G76 157 F3
Bull's Cl ML11 215 D2
Bulldale Rd G14 94 C3
Bulldale St G14 94 C3
Bullionslaw Dr G73 138 B3
Bulloch Ave G46 136 B1
Bulloch Cres FK6 21 E1
Bullwood Ave G53 134 C4
Bullwood Ct G53 115 D1
Bullwood Dr G53 114 C1
Bullwood Gdns G53 114 C1
Bullwood Pl G53 114 C1
Bunbury Terr 3 G75 180 B4
Bunessan St G52 115 F3
Bungalows The FK5 23 D1
Bunhouse Rd G3 96 B1
Buntine Cres FK7 7 D2
Bunting Pl KA1 228 B4
Burbank G62 55 D1
Burbank Terr PA14 68 B4
Burgh Hall La G11 96 A1
Burgh Hall St G11 96 A1
Burgh La 4 G12 96 B2
Burgh Mews FK10 10 A3
Burgh Prim Sch G73 138 A4
Burgh Rd KA9 236 A4
Burgh Wlk PA19 44 C4
Burghead Dr G51 115 F4
Burghead Pl G51 115 F4
Burgher St G31 118 B3
Burghmuir Ind Est FK8 7 D3
Burghmuir Rd FK7 7 D3
Burleigh Rd G71 141 D2
Burleigh St Coatbridge ML5 122 A2
Glasgow G51 116 A4
Burleigh Way FK10 10 B3
Burley Pl G74 158 C1
Burlington Ave G12 96 A3
Burmola St G22 97 D2
Burn Cres Chapelhall ML6 123 E1
Motherwell ML1 143 D2
Burn Dr FK7 7 E2
Burn La ML1 143 D2
Burn Rd Carluke ML8 187 F2
Saltcoats KA21 216 B4
Burn St G83 27 F2
Burn Street La G83 27 F2
Burn Terr G72 138 C4
Burn View G67 62 B2
Burn's Cres ML6 123 D3
Burn's Pl KA20 206 C1
Burn's Wicket KA7 238 C1
Burnacre Gdns G71 140 C4
Burnbank Braes ML8 187 F1
Burnbank Ctr ML3 162 A3
Burnbank Dr G78 134 B1
Burnbank Gdns ML3 162 A3
Burnbank Pl Ayr KA7 239 D2
2 Glasgow G20 97 D1
Stewarton KA3 195 F1
Burnbank Quadrant ML6 122 C4
Burnbank Rd Ayr KA7 239 D2
Falkirk FK2 42 A4
Hamilton ML3 162 A2
Burnbank St Airdrie ML6 122 C4
Coatbridge ML5 122 A4
Stevenston KA20 217 E4
Burnbank Terr
3 Glasgow G20 97 D1
Kilsyth G65 36 B1
Burnblea Gdns ML3 162 C1
Burnblea St ML3 162 B1
Burnbrae Alloa FK10 10 B4
Clydebank G81 74 A3
Twechar G65 59 F2
Burnbrae Ave
Bearsden G61 76 A4
Linwood PA3 112 B3
Moodiesburn G69 81 D1
Burnbrae Dr
Elderslie PA3, PA5 112 B2
Perceton KA11 220 B3
Rutherglen G73 138 B3
Burnbrae Gdns Alva FK12 5 D3
Falkirk FK1 42 A3
Burnbrae Pl G74 159 E1
Burnbrae Prim Sch G53 135 E3
Burnbrae Rd Blantyre G72 161 E4
Chryston G69, G66 80 A2
Elderslie PA3 112 B2
Falkirk FK1 42 A3
Harthill ML7 127 F3
Kirkintilloch G69, G66 80 A4
Kirkintilloch, Auchinloch G66 79 F1
Shotts ML7 146 C2
Burnbrae St Clydebank G81 74 B4
Glasgow G21 98 A2
Larkhall ML9 184 C2
Burncleuch Ave G72 139 D2
Burncrooks Ave
Bearsden G61 75 E4
East Kilbride G74 159 E1
Burncrooks Ct G81 73 F3
Burndale La PA13 89 E4
Burndyke Ct G51 116 B4
Burndyke Sq G51 116 B4
Burnee FK10 5 F2
Burness Ave KA7 238 C1
Burnet Rose Ct G74 159 E2
Burnet Rose Gdns G74 159 E2
Burnet Rose Pl G74 159 E2
Burnett Rd G33 119 F4
Burnett Terr KA8 236 A1
Burnfield Ave G46 136 A2
Burnfield Cotts G46 136 A2
Burnfield Dr G43 136 A2
Burnfield Gdns G46 136 B2
Burnfield Pl FK2 42 B4
Burnfield Rd G43 136 A2
Burnfoot G82 48 A4
Burnfoot Ave KA10 229 E3
Burnfoot Cres Paisley PA2 133 E4
Rutherglen G73 138 B3
Burnfoot Dr G52 115 D3
Burnfoot La
Ardrossan KA22 205 D2
1 Falkirk FK1 42 A2
Burnfoot Pl KA3 222 C2
Burnfoot Rd Airdrie ML6 122 C4
Lochwinnoch PA12 129 D1
Burnfoot Way KA10 229 E3
Burngreen G65 60 B4
Burngreen Terr G67 62 A3
Burnhall Pl ML2 165 E1
Burnhall Rd ML2 165 E1
Burnhall St ML2 165 E1
Burnham Rd G14 95 D2
Burnhaven PA8 73 D1
Burnhead La Falkirk FK1 42 B2
Port Glasgow PA14 68 B4
Burnhead Prim Sch G71 141 E4
Burnhead Rd Airdrie ML6 103 E1
Cumbernauld G68 61 E1
Glasgow G43 136 C3
Larbert FK5 23 E2
Larkhall ML9 185 E1
Port Glasgow PA14 68 B4
Burnhead St
Greenock PA15 46 A1
Uddingston G71 141 E4
Burnhill Quadrant G73 137 F4
Burnhill St G73 137 F4
Burnhouse Ave
Cumbernauld G68 61 D1
Dalry KA24 191 D4
Burnhouse Brae G77 157 D2
Burnhouse Cotts KA3 195 D4
Burnhouse Cres ML3 162 A1
Burnhouse Rd
East Kilbride G75 180 A1
Hamilton ML3 162 A1
Burnhouse St G20 96 B3
Burniebrae ML6 122 C4
Burniebrae Rd ML6 123 F2
Burnlea Cres PA6 91 D2
Burnlea Pl KA20 206 C1
Burnlip Rd ML6 102 A2
Burnmouth Ct G33 119 F3
Burnmouth Pl G61 76 A3
Burnmouth Rd G33 119 F3
Burnock Pl G75 179 F4
Burnpark Ave G71 140 B4
Burnpark Rd KA1 227 F2
Burns Ave Bishopton PA7 72 A2
Kilmarnock KA3 223 D2
Saltcoats KA21 205 F2
Burns Cott (Mus) KA7 238 C1
Burns Cres Harthill ML7 127 F3
Irvine KA11 220 A3
Laurieston FK2 42 C2
Burns Ct G66 59 D1
Burns Dr Johnstone PA5 131 F4
Kirkintilloch G66 59 D1
Burns Gdns G72 140 B1
Burns Gr G46 136 A1
Burns La ML6 123 E2
Burns Loan 11 ML9 185 D2
Burns Path ML4 142 A4
Burns Pk G74 160 A2
Burns Pl Kilwinning KA13 207 F2
Shotts ML7 146 A3
Burns Prec KA1 227 F4
Burns Rd Chapelhall ML6 123 F2
Cumbernauld G67 62 A1
Greenock PA16 44 B2
Kirkintilloch G66 59 D1
Troon KA10 229 F2
Burns Sq Ardrossan KA22 205 E2
Greenock PA16 44 B2
Burns St Alexandria G83 27 F4
Clydebank G81 73 F2
Hamilton ML3 162 B1
Irvine KA12 219 D2
Renton G82 27 E1
Stirling FK8 2 A1
Burns Statue Sq KA7 238 C4
Burns Terr
Ardrossan KA22 205 E2
Cowie FK7 12 B4
Burns Way ML1 143 E2
Burnside G61 75 E4
Burnside Ave
Barrhead G78 134 A2
Bellshill ML4 142 B2
Brookfield PA5 111 E3
Calderbank ML6 123 D1
Kirkintilloch G66 79 D4
Port Glasgow PA14 68 C4
Burnside Cotts KA3 173 E3
Burnside Cres Balloch G83 27 F4
Clydebank G81 74 A4
Hamilton G72 161 F3
Plean FK7 12 B2
Shotts ML7 146 B3
Burnside Ct Bearsden G61 75 E4
Motherwell ML1 164 A2
Rutherglen G73 138 B3
Burnside Gate G73 138 B3
Burnside Gdns
Clarkston G76 157 E4
Johnstone PA10 111 D1
Prestwick KA9 233 E1
Burnside Gr PA5 111 F1
Burnside Ind Est G65 60 B4
Burnside La ML3 162 C1
Burnside Pl Dumbarton G82 50 A1
Falkirk FK2 24 A2
Irvine KA12 219 D2
Larkhall ML9 185 D2
Paisley PA3 113 D4
Stevenston KA20 206 B1
Troon KA10 229 E2
West Kilbride KA23 190 B3
Burnside Prim Sch G73 138 A3
Burnside Quadrant ML1 143 D3
Burnside Rd Elderslie PA5 112 B1
Glenmavis ML6 102 B1
Gourock PA19 44 C3
Menstrie FK11 3 F3
Monkton KA9 233 E2
Motherwell ML1 143 E2
Rutherglen G46 157 D3
Rutherglen, High Burnside G73 138 B2
Burnside St Alloa FK10 5 E1
Dumbarton G82 50 A1
Glengarnock KA14 170 A3
Kilmarnock KA1 227 F3
Motherwell ML1 164 A2
Stirling FK7 7 E3
Burnside Sta G73 138 B3
Burnside Terr FK1 41 F3
Burnside View ML5 121 F3
Burnside Wlk ML5 121 F3
Burntbroom Dr G69 119 F2
Burntbroom Gdns G69 119 F2
Burntbroom Rd G69 119 F1
Burntbroom St G33 119 E4
Burntshields Rd PA10 110 B1
Burnwood Dr ML6 124 A3
Burra Gdns G64 78 B1
Burrell Collection (Mus) G43 116 A1
Burrell Ct G41 116 B1
Burrell's La G4 241 F2
Burrelton Rd G43 136 C3
Burstenman's Brae KA13, KA24 207 F4
Burton La Carluke ML8 187 F1
Glasgow G42 117 D1
Busbie View KA2 221 F1
Busbiehead KA11 220 A3
Busbiehill Pl KA1 222 B1
Busby District Prim Sch G76 157 F3
Busby Pl KA13 207 F2
Busby Rd Bellshill ML4 141 F2
Carmunnock G76 158 B4
Clarkston G76 157 F3
Busby Sta G76 158 A3
Bush Cres ML2 165 E1
Bushelhead Rd ML8 201 F3
Bushes Ave PA2 113 E1
Bushes Prim Sch PA2 133 E4
Busheyhill St G72 139 D3
Bute G74 160 B1
Bute Ave Motherwell ML1 163 E4
Port Glasgow PA14 69 D4
Renfrew PA4 94 B1
Bute Cres Bearsden G61 75 F1
Old Kilpatrick G60 73 E3
Paisley PA2 133 E4
Shotts ML7 146 B3

Catrine St 11 ML9 185 E1
Catriona Way ML1 143 D2
Catter Gdns G62 54 C2
Cauldhame Cres FK7 6 B3
Cauldstream Pl G62 54 C1
Causeway The FK9 2 B3
Causewayhead Rd FK9 2 B2
Causewayside Cres G32 119 D2
Causewayside St G32 119 D1
Causeyfoot Dr KA25 149 D1
Causeyside St PA1 113 F2
Causeystanes G72 161 E4
Cavendish Ct
5 Glasgow G5 117 D2
Troon KA10 229 E1
Cavendish Dr G77 156 C3
Cavendish La KA10 229 E1
Cavendish Pl Glasgow G5 117 D2
Troon KA10 229 E1
Cavendish St G5 117 D2
Cavin Dr G45 137 F2
Cavin Rd G45 137 F2
Cawder Ct G68 61 E3
Cawder Gdns FK9 1 C4
Cawder Pl G68 61 F3
Cawder Rd Bridge Of A FK9 1 C4
Cumbernauld G68 61 F3
Cawder View G68 61 F3
Cawder Way G68 61 F3
Cawdor Cres Bishopton PA7 72 A1
Greenock PA16 45 D2
Cawdor Pl PA16 45 D2
Cawdor Way G74 159 E2
Cayton Gdns G69 119 F2
Cecil St Clarkston G76 157 F4
Coatbridge ML5 122 A3
Glasgow G12 96 B2
Stirling FK7 7 D3
Cedar Ave Beith KA15 171 D4
Clydebank G81 73 E2
Johnstone PA5 132 A4
Stirling FK8 6 C3
Uddingston G71 141 D4
Cedar Cres Greenock PA15 46 C1
Hamilton ML3 162 C1
Cedar Ct Cambuslang G72 139 F2
East Kilbride G75 180 B3
Glasgow G20 97 D1
Kilbarchan PA10 111 D2
Cedar Dr East Kilbride G75 180 B3
Kirkintilloch G66 79 E3
Milton Of C G65 58 B3
Uddingston G71 141 E4
Cedar Gdns Law ML8 186 C3
Motherwell ML1 143 E2
Rutherglen G73 138 B2
Cedar Gr Cardross G82 48 A4
Stenhousemuir FK5 23 E1
Cedar La Airdrie ML6 123 E4
Motherwell ML1 143 D2
Cedar Pl Barrhead G78 155 E4
Blantyre G72 140 B1
East Kilbride G75 180 B3
Gourock PA19 44 B3
Cedar Rd Ayr KA7 239 E3
Banknock FK4 38 C1
Bishopbriggs G64 98 A4
Cumbernauld G67 62 B2
Irvine KA12 219 E2
Kilmarnock KA1 227 E4
Cedar St G20 97 D1
Cedar Wlk G64 98 A4
Cedars The FK10 4 A1
Cedarwood Ave G77 156 C3
Cedarwood Rd G77 156 C2
Cedric Pl G13 95 E4
Cedric Rd G13 95 E4
Celandine Bank KA7 239 E2
Celtic Pk (Celtic FC) G40 118 A3
Celtic St G20 96 B4
Cemetery Rd Blantyre G72 161 E3
Glasgow G52 115 F2
Shotts ML7 147 D2
Centenary Ave ML6 122 B4
Centenary Ct G81 74 A1
Centenary Gdns
Coatbridge ML5 122 A3
Hamilton ML3 162 C1
Centenary Pl KA22 205 E2
Centenary Quadrant ML1 143 D3
Central Ave
Ardrossan KA22 205 E2
Cambuslang G72 138 C3
Clydebank G81 74 A1
Glasgow G11 95 F1
Glasgow, North Mount Vernon G32 119 F2
Hamilton G72 161 F3
Kilbirnie KA25 170 A4
Kilmarnock KA1 227 F2
Motherwell ML1 143 D1
Motherwell, Holytown ML1 142 C3
Troon KA10 229 F2
Uddingston G71 141 E3
Central Bvd FK5 23 D2
Central Cres ML9 199 F4
Central Dr FK5 23 F2
Central Gr
Cambuslang G72 138 C3
Glasgow G32 119 E2
Central Park Ave FK5 23 D2
Central Park Bsns Pk FK5 23 D2
Central Path G32 119 F2
Central Quadrant KA22 205 E2
Central Rd PA1 113 F3
Central Ret Pk FK1 42 B3
Central Sta Glasgow G2 240 C2
Hamilton ML3 162 C2
Central Way
Cumbernauld G67 61 F1
Paisley PA1 113 F3
Centre Rdbt The G74 159 F1
Centre St Chapelhall ML6 123 E1
Glasgow G5 117 D3
Glenboig ML5 101 E3
Centre The G78 134 A1
Centre Way G78 134 A2
Centrum (Sports Arena) KA9 236 A3
Ceres Gdns G64 78 B1
Cessnock Ave KA1 228 C3
Cessnock Dr KA1 228 C3
Cessnock Pl Ayr KA7 239 E3
Cambuslang G72 139 E3
Cessnock Rd Hurlford KA1 228 C3
Millerston G33 99 D2
Troon KA10 229 E2
Cessnock St G51 116 B3
Cessnock Underground Sta G51 116 B3
Cessock Pl KA1 228 A3
Chacefield St FK4 40 A3
Chacefield Wood FK6 39 F4
Chalmers Ave KA7 239 D3
Chalmers Cres G75 180 C4
Chalmers Ct G40 241 F1
Chalmers Dr G75 180 C4
Chalmers Gate G40 241 F1
Chalmers Pl Glasgow G40 241 F1
Irvine KA11 224 C3
Chalmers Rd KA7 239 D3
Chalmers St Clydebank G81 74 A1
Glasgow G40 241 F1
Gourock PA19 44 C4
Chalmerston Rd FK9 1 A2
Chalton Rd FK9 2 A4
Chamberlain La G13 95 F3
Chamberlain Rd G13 95 F3
Chambers Dr FK2 24 A1
Chamfron Gdns FK7 7 F2
Chancellor St G11 96 B1
Chantinghall Rd ML3 162 A2
Chantinghall Terr ML3 162 A2
Chapel Cres FK2 24 A2
Chapel Ct G73 137 F4
Chapel Dr FK5 23 F2
Chapel La Falkirk FK1 42 A3
Irvine KA12 219 E1
Chapel Rd Clydebank G81 74 A3
Houston PA6 91 D2
Wishaw ML2 166 B1
Chapel St Airdrie ML6 123 D4
Carluke ML8 187 F1
Cleland ML1 144 A1
Glasgow G20 96 C3
Gourock PA19 44 C4
Greenock PA15 46 A2
Lennoxtown G65 57 E4
Rutherglen G73 137 F4
Chapel Street Ind Est G20 96 C3
Chapelacre Gr G84 16 C1
Chapelcross Ave ML6 103 D1
Chapelgill Pl KA11 220 A2
Chapelgreen Prim Sch G65 59 F4
Chapelhall Ind Est ML6 123 E2
Chapelhall Prim & Sec Sch ML6 123 E1
Chapelhill Mount KA22 205 E3
Chapelhill Rd PA2 114 A1
Chapelknowe Rd ML1 143 F1
Chapelpark Rd KA7 238 C2
Chapelside Ave ML6 123 D4
Chapelside Prim Sch ML6 103 D1
Chapelside Rd G74 160 A3
Chapelton Ave
Bearsden G61 75 F2
Dumbarton G82 50 A3
Chapelton Gdns
Bearsden G61 75 F2
Dumbarton G82 50 A3
Chapelton La KA23 190 B2
Chapelton Rd
Cumbernauld G67 82 B3
West Kilbride KA23 190 B1
Chapelton St Glasgow G22 97 D3
Port Glasgow PA14 47 D1
Chapeltoun Terr KA3 210 C2
Chapelwell St KA21 216 C4
Chapland Rd ML11 215 D3
Chaplet Ave G13 95 E4
Chapman Ave ML5 101 E3
Chapman St 4 G42 117 D1
Chapmans Terr KA1 228 A4
Chappell St G78 134 A2
Charing Cross ML9 185 D2
Charing Cross La G3 240 A3
Charing Cross Sta G2 240 B3
Charles Ave Bridge Of A FK9 2 A3
Monkton KA9 233 E3
Renfrew PA4 94 B2
Charles Cres Carluke ML8 188 A1
Kirkintilloch G66 79 E2
Charles Dr Larbert FK5 41 E4
Troon KA10 229 F1
Charles Path ML6 123 E1
Charles Pl Greenock PA15 45 F3
Kilmarnock KA1 227 F4
Charles Quadrant ML1 143 D3
Charles Rodger Pl FK9 2 A3
Charles St Alloa FK10 9 F4
Glasgow G21 97 F1
Kilmarnock KA1 227 F4
Kilsyth G65 36 B1
Shotts ML7 147 D2
Stirling FK8 7 D3
Wishaw ML2 164 B2
Charleson Row G65 60 C2
Charlotte Ave G64 78 A4
Charlotte Hill Ct FK5 23 D2
Charlotte Path ML9 185 D1
Charlotte Pl PA2 113 F1
Charlotte St Ayr KA7 238 C4
Dumbarton G82 49 E2
Glasgow G1 241 E1
Helensburgh G84 16 C1
Shotts ML7 147 D2
Charlotte Street La KA7 238 C4
Charnwood Ave PA5 131 E4
Charter St FK7 7 D2
Chartershall Rd FK7 7 D1
Chartwell Rd PA7 72 A2
Chassels St ML5 122 A4
Chateau Gr ML3 163 D1
Chatelherault Ave G72 138 C3
Chatelherault Cres ML3 162 C1
Chatelherault Prim Sch ML3 162 C1
Chatelherault Wlk ML3 162 C1
Chatham G75 180 B4
Chattan Ave FK9 2 A2
Chattan Ind Est FK4 40 B2
Chatton St G23 76 B1
Cheapside St
Eaglesham G76 178 C3
Glasgow G3 240 A2
Chelmsford Dr G12 96 A3
Cherry Bank G66 79 D3
Cherry Cres G81 74 A2
Cherry Gdns KA11 219 F3
Cherry Hill Rd KA7 239 D1
Cherry La Banknock FK4 38 C1
Troon KA10 229 E2
Cherry Pl Bishopbriggs G64 98 A4
Johnstone PA5 112 A1
Milton Of C G65 58 A2
Motherwell ML1 143 D3
Uddingston G71 141 E4
Cherry Rd KA1 227 E4
Cherrybank Rd G43 136 C3
Cherrybank Wlk ML6 122 B4
Cherryhill View ML9 184 C2
Cherrytree Cres ML9 185 D3
Cherrytree Dr G72 139 F2
Cherrywood Dr KA15 150 B1
Cherrywood Rd PA5 112 B1
Chester Rd PA16 44 C2
Chester St G32 119 D3
Chesterfield Ave G12 96 A3
Chesters Cres ML1 163 E4
Chesters Pl G73 138 A4
Chesters Rd G61 75 E2
Chestnut Ave Beith KA15 171 D4
Bishopton PA7 71 F3
Cumbernauld G67 62 C3
Chestnut Cres Denny FK6 21 E2
East Kilbride G75 180 B3
Hamilton ML3 162 C1
Uddingston G71 141 E4
Chestnut Ct
Cumbernauld G67 62 C3
Milton Of C G65 58 A3
Chestnut Dr Clydebank G81 74 A3
Kirkintilloch G66 79 D3
Chestnut Gr Blantyre G72 161 E4
Carluke ML8 187 F1
Glenboig ML5 101 E3
Larkhall ML9 185 D3
Motherwell ML1 163 E2
Stenhousemuir FK5 23 F2
Chestnut La G62 54 C1
Chestnut Pl
Cumbernauld G67 62 C3
Johnstone PA5 132 A4
Kilmarnock KA1 227 E4
Chestnut Rd KA7 239 E3
Chestnut St G22 97 E3
Cheviot Ave G78 134 B1
Cheviot Cres
East Kilbride G75 180 A2
Wishaw ML2 164 C2
Cheviot Ct Airdrie ML6 103 D1
Irvine KA11 220 A2
Cheviot Dr G77 156 B2
Cheviot Gdns G61 75 E4
Cheviot Head KA11 219 F2
Cheviot Pl KA1 228 A2
Cheviot Rd Glasgow G43 136 B3
Hamilton ML3 162 C1
Larkhall ML9 185 E1
Paisley PA2 113 F1
Cheviot St G72 161 E4
Cheviot Way KA11 220 A2
Chillin Pl ML9 185 E1
Chirmorie Pl G53 115 D1
Chirnside Ct G72 161 F3
Chirnside Pl G52 115 D3
Chirnside Rd G52 115 D3
Chirnsyde Prim Sch G22 97 E3
Chisholm Ave
Bishopton PA7 72 B2
Stirling FK9 2 A2
Chisholm Dr G77 156 C3
Chisholm St ML5 122 A4
Chislom St G1 241 E1
Chrighton Gn 3 G71 141 D4
Chriss Ave ML3 183 E4
Christ the King Prim Sch ML1 143 D3
Christchurch Pl G75 180 A4
Christian St G43 136 B4
Christie Gdns KA21 216 C4
Christie La PA3 113 F3
Christie Park Prim Sch G83 27 E3
Christie Pl G72 139 D3
Christie St Bellshill ML4 142 B3
Paisley PA1 113 F3
Christie Terr FK5 23 F2
Christopher St G21 98 A1
Chromars Pl PA15 45 F2
Chryston Prim Sch G69 100 B4
Chryston Rd Chryston G69 100 B4
Kirkintilloch G69, G66 80 B3
Chryston Sec Sch G69 100 B4
Chuckie La PA5 111 E3
Church Ave Cardross G82 48 A4
Rutherglen G73 138 B3
Stepps G33 99 E3
Wishaw ML2 166 A2
Church Cres Airdrie ML6 103 F1
Hamilton ML3 183 E3
Church Ct Ayr KA8 236 A1
Dumbarton G82 49 F2
Church Dr G66 79 E3
Church Gr FK10 5 E1
Church Hill PA1 113 F3
Church La Carluke ML8 187 F1
Coatbridge ML5 122 A4
Denny FK6 21 E2
Kilmarnock KA1 227 F3
Kilsyth G65 60 B4
Church Manse La PA11 110 B4
Church Pl Ardrossan KA22 205 E1
Caldercruix ML6 104 C2
Falkirk FK2 42 A3
Old Kilpatrick G60 73 D3
Rhu G84 15 E2
Church Rd
Bridge Of W PA11 110 C4
California FK1 66 C3
Clarkston G76 157 F3
Glasgow G46 136 B1
Muirhead G69 100 B4
Quarriers Village PA11 89 F1
Rhu G84 15 E3
Wishaw ML2 166 B3
Church St Alexandria G83 27 F2
Alloa FK10 10 A3
Blantyre G72 161 F4
Clydebank G81 74 A2
Coatbridge ML5 122 A4
Dumbarton G82 49 F2
Falkirk FK2 24 B1
Glasgow G11 96 B1
Glasgow, Muirhead G69 120 B2
Gourock PA19 44 C4
Hamilton ML3 162 C2
Harthill ML7 127 E3
High Bonnybridge FK4 40 B2
Irvine KA12 219 D1
Johnstone PA5 111 F2
Kilbarchan PA10 111 D2
Kilmarnock KA3 222 C1
Kilsyth G65 60 B4
Kilwinning KA13 207 F2
Larkhall ML9 185 D1
Lochwinnoch PA12 129 E1
Motherwell ML1 143 F2
Port Glasgow PA14 47 E1
Stenhousemuir FK5 23 F2
Troon KA10 229 E1
Uddingston G71 140 C3
Church View
Cambuslang G72 139 D4
Coatbridge ML5 122 A4
Church View Ct G65 33 E1
Church View Gdns ML4 142 A3
Church Wlk FK6 21 F1
Churchill Ave
East Kilbride G74 159 F1
Johnstone PA5 131 E4
Kilwinning KA13 208 A2
Churchill Cres Ayr KA8 239 E4
Bothwell G71 141 D2
Churchill Dr
Ardrossan KA22 205 E2
Bishopton PA7 72 A2
Bridge Of A FK9 2 A3
Glasgow G11 96 A2
Churchill Pl PA10 111 D2
Churchill Rd PA13 89 E4
Churchill Sq G84 17 D1
Churchill St FK10 9 F4
Churchill Way G64 77 F1
Circus Dr G31 117 F4
Circus Pl G31 117 F4
Circus Place La G31 117 F4
Citadel L Ctr KA7 235 F1
Citadel Pl Ayr KA7 235 F1
Motherwell ML1 163 E4
Citadel Way KA10 229 F4
Citizen La G1 241 D2
Citrus Cres G71 141 E4
Cityford Cres G73 137 F4
Cityford Dr G73 137 F3
Civic St G4 97 D1
Civic Way G66 79 E4
Clachan Dr G51 115 F4
Clachan Rd G84 15 D2
Clachan The ML2 165 D2
Clackmannan Coll of F Ed FK10 10 A4
Clackmannan Rd FK10 10 B3
Claddens Pl G66 79 F2
Claddens Quadrant G22 97 E3
Claddens St G22 97 D3
Claddoch Cotts G82 25 E3
Cladence Gr G75 180 C3
Clair Rd G64 78 B1
Claire St ML2 166 A3
Clairinch Gdns 1 PA4 94 B1
Clairmont Gdns G3 240 A4
Clamp Rd ML2 164 B2
Clamps Gr G74 181 D4
Clamps Terr G74 181 D4
Clamps Wood G74 181 D4
Clanranald Pl FK1 41 F1
Clanrye Dr ML5 122 A2
Clapperhow Rd ML1 143 D1
Clare St G21 98 A1
Claremont FK10 9 F4
Claremont Ave G66 79 D4
Claremont Cres KA13 207 E2
Claremont Dr
Bridge Of A FK9 2 B4
Milngavie G62 55 D1
Claremont Gdns G62 55 D1
Claremont High Sch G74 181 E4
Claremont Ind Est FK10 10 A3
Claremont Pass G3 240 A4
Claremont Pl Glasgow G3 96 C1
Glasgow G3 240 A4
Claremont Prim Sch FK10 9 F4
Claremont St
Bonnybridge FK4 39 F3
Glasgow G3 116 C4
Claremont Terr G3 240 A4
Claremont Terrace La G3 240 A4
Claremount Ave G46 136 B1
Clarence Dr Glasgow G11 96 A2
Paisley PA1 114 A2
Clarence Gdns G11 96 A2
Clarence La G12 96 A2
Clarence St Clydebank G81 74 B2
Greenock PA15 45 F3
Paisley PA1 114 A3
Clarendon Pl Ayr KA7 239 E3
9 Glasgow G20 97 D1
Stirling FK8 7 D4
Clarendon Rd Stirling FK8 7 D4
Wishaw ML2 164 C1
Clarendon St G20 97 D1
Clarinda Ave FK1 41 D3
Clarinda Cres G66 59 D1
Clarinda Pl ML1 143 E2
Clarion Cres G13 95 D4
Clarion Rd G13 95 D4
Clark Cres KA20 217 E4
Clark Dr KA12 219 F2
Clark Pl
Newton Mearns G77 156 A2
Saltcoats KA21 206 A1
Torrance G64 78 B4
Clark St Airdrie ML6 123 D4
Bannockburn FK7 7 D1
Clydebank G81 73 F2
Johnstone PA5 111 F2
Kilmarnock KA1 227 F4
Paisley PA3 113 E3
Renfrew PA4 94 A2
Wishaw ML2 165 F3
Clark Way ML4 141 F4
Clarke Ave KA7 238 C3
Clarkston Ave G44 136 C2
Clarkston Dr ML6 123 E4
Clarkston Prim Sch ML6 123 E4
Clarkston Rd G44 136 C2
Clarkston & Stamperland Sta G76 157 F4
Clarkwell Rd ML3 161 F2
Clarkwell Terr ML3 161 F2
Clathic Ave G61 76 A2
Claud Rd PA3 114 A3
Claude Ave G72 139 F2
Claude St ML9 185 D2
Clavens Rd G52 114 C3
Claverhouse Pl PA2 114 A2
Claverhouse Rd G52 114 C4
Clavering St E PA1 113 E3
Clavering St W PA1 113 E2
Clay Cres Bellshill ML4 142 B4
Kilmarnock KA3 222 C1
Clay Rd ML4 142 B4
Claycrofts Pl FK7 7 D3
Clayhouse Rd G33 99 F2
Claymore Dr Houston PA6 111 E4
Stirling FK7 7 E2
Claypotts Pl G33 99 D1
Claypotts Rd G33 99 D1
Clayslaps Rd G3 96 B1
Clayslaps View KA1 228 A2
Claythorn Ave G40 241 F1
Claythorn Cir 9 G40 117 F3
Claythorn Ct G40 241 F1
Claythorn Pk G40 117 F3
Claythorn St G40 241 F1
Claythorn Terr G40 241 F1
Clayton Ave KA12 219 E2
Clayton Path ML4 142 A4
Clayton Terr 5 G31 117 F4
Clearfield Ave ML3 162 A2
Cleaves The FK10 4 A1
Cleddans Cres G81 74 B3
Cleddans Rd Clydebank G81 74 B3
Kirkintilloch G66 58 C1
Cleddans View
Clydebank G81 74 B2
Glenmavis ML6 102 C2
Cleddens Ct G64 78 A1
Cleeves Ave KA24 191 F3
Cleeves Quadrant G53 135 D3
Cleeves Rd G53 135 D3
Cleghorn Ave ML11 215 D3
Cleghorn Rd ML11 215 D3
Cleghorn St G22 97 D2
Cleish Ave G61 75 E4
Cleland La G5 117 E3
Cleland Pl G74 160 A2

Corpach Pl G34 100 B1
Corporation St FK1 42 B2
Corpus Christi RC Prim Sch
Airdrie ML6 123 D2
Glasgow G13 95 E3
Corra Linn ML3 162 A2
Corran Ave G77 156 B3
Corran St G33 118 C4
Correen Gdns G61 75 D4
Corrie Ave FK5 23 F2
Corrie Brae G65 36 B1
Corrie Cres
Kilmarnock KA3 222 C2
Saltcoats KA21 205 F1
Corrie Ct ML3 161 F1
Corrie Dr Motherwell ML1 163 D4
Paisley PA1 114 C2
Corrie Gdns G75 180 A2
Corrie Gr G44 136 C2
Corrie House KA9 236 A3
Corrie Pl Falkirk FK1 41 E2
Helensburgh G84 16 C2
Kirkintilloch G66 79 F2
Troon KA10 229 F4
Corrie Rd G65 36 B1
Corrie View G68 81 F4
Corrie Way ML9 185 D1
Corrour Rd Glasgow G43 136 C4
Newton Mearns G77 156 B3
Corruna Ct ML8 188 A1
Corsankell Wynd KA21 205 F1
Corse Ave KA11 221 D1
Corse Dr G78 134 A2
Corse Pl KA2 226 C4
Corse Rd G52 114 C3
Corse St KA23 190 B3
Corsebar Ave PA2 113 E1
Corsebar Cres PA2 113 E1
Corsebar Dr PA2 113 E1
Corsebar La PA2 113 D1
Corsebar Rd PA2 113 D1
Corsebar Way PA2 113 E2
Corsefield Rd PA12 128 C1
Corseford Ave PA5 131 E4
Corseford Sch PA10 131 D4
Corsehill KA13 208 A2
Corsehill Dr KA23 190 A3
Corsehill Mount Rd KA11 225 D4
Corsehill Mount Rdbt
KA11 225 E4
Corsehill Pk Ayr KA7 238 C3
Irvine KA11 225 E4
Corsehill Pl Ayr KA7 238 C3
Glasgow G34 120 B4
Stewarton KA3 195 F1
Corsehill Prim Sch KA13 207 F2
Corsehill Rd KA7 238 C3
Corsehill St G34 120 B4
Corsehill Terr KA11 220 C1
Corsehillbank St KA3 195 E1
Corselet Rd G53 135 D2
Corserine Bank KA11 219 F2
Corserine Rd KA7 238 A1
Corsewall Ave G32 119 F2
Corsewall St ML5 121 F4
Corsford Dr G53 135 E3
Corsliehill Rd PA6 90 C4
Corsock Ave ML3 161 F1
Corsock St G31 118 B4
Corston St G33 118 B4
Cortachy Ave FK2 24 A2
Cortachy Pl G64 78 B1
Coruisk Dr G76 157 E4
Corunna St [5] G3 116 C4
Coshneuk Rd G33 99 D2
Cosy Neuk ML9 185 E1
Cottage Cres FK1 41 F3
Cottar St G20 96 C4
Cotter Dr KA3 228 B4
Cotton Ave PA3 112 A3
Cotton St Glasgow G40 118 A1
Paisley PA1 113 F2
Cotton Vale ML1 143 F1
Coulport Pl G84 16 A1
Coulter Ave
Coatbridge ML5 121 F4
Wishaw ML2 165 E4
Coulthard Dr KA9 236 B3
Countess St KA21 216 C4
County Ave G72 138 C4
County Dr ML11 215 E2
County Hospl FK10 10 A4
County Pl PA1 113 F3
County Sq PA1 113 F3
Couper Pl G4 241 E4
Couper St G4 241 E4
Coursington Cres ML1 164 A4
Coursington Gdns ML1 163 F4
Coursington Pl ML1 163 F4
Coursington Rd ML1 164 A4
Court Hill G84 15 D2
Court Rd PA14 47 E1
Courthill Alva FK12 5 D4
Bearsden G61 75 E3
Courthill Ave G44 137 D3
Courthill Cres G65 60 C4
Courthill Pl KA24 191 E4
Courthill St KA24 191 E4
Courtrai Ave G84 16 A1
Coustonholm Rd G43 136 B4
Couther Quadrant ML6 103 D1
Covanburn Ave ML3 162 C1
Cove Cres ML7 146 C3
Cove Pl G84 16 A1
Cove Rd PA19 44 C4
Coveland Dr G73 138 A2
Covenant Cres ML9 185 D1
Covenant Pl ML2 164 B1
Covenanter Rd ML7 127 E2
Covenanters Way ML2 186 B3
Coventry Dr G31 118 A4
Cow Wynd FK1 42 A2
Cowal Cres Gourock PA19 44 A3
Kirkintilloch G66 59 D1
Cowal Dr PA3 112 A3
Cowal St G20 96 B4
Cowal View PA19 44 A3
Cowan Cres Ayr KA8 236 B2
Barrhead G78 134 B2
Cowan La G12 96 C1
Cowan Rd G68 61 E1
Cowan St Bonnybridge FK4 40 A3
Glasgow G12 96 C1
Cowan Wilson Ave G72 161 E4
Cowan Wynd
Uddingston G71 141 D4
Wishaw ML2 186 B4
Cowane St FK8 7 D4
Cowans Row KA3 228 B4
Cowcaddens Rd G3 97 D1
Cowcaddens St G2 241 D3
Cowcaddens Underground
Sta G4 240 C4
Cowden Dr G64 78 A2
Cowden St G51 115 E4
Cowdenhill Cir G13 95 E4
Cowdenhill Pl G13 95 E4
Cowdenhill Rd G13 95 E4
Cowdray Cres PA4 94 B2
Cowgate G66 79 E4
Cowglen Hospl G53 135 E4
Cowglen Rd G53 135 E4
Cowie Prim Sch FK7 12 B4
Cowie Rd FK7 12 A4
Cowiehall Rd FK7 12 B4
Cowlairs Ind Est G22 97 E3
Cowlairs Rd [6] G21 97 F2
Coxdale Ave G66 79 D4
Coxhill St G21 97 E2
Coxithill Rd FK7 7 D2
Coxton Pl G33 99 E1
Coyle Pk KA10 229 F3
Coylebank KA9 236 B3
Coylton Cres ML3 161 F1
Coylton Rd G43 136 C3
Crabb Quadrant ML1 142 B1
Cragdale G74 159 E2
Craggan Dr G14 95 D3
Crags Ave PA2 113 F1
Crags Cres PA2 113 F1
Crags Rd PA2 113 F1
Cragwell Pk G76 158 C4
Craig Ave Alexandria G83 27 E4
Dalry KA24 191 D4
Craig Cotts KA2 226 B4
Craig Cres Kirkintilloch G66 80 A4
Stirling FK9 2 B2
Craig Ct FK9 2 A3
Craig Dr KA2 226 C4
Craig Gdns G77 156 B3
Craig Hill G75 180 B4
Craig Leith Rd FK7 7 E3
Craig Pl G77 156 A3
Craig Rd Glasgow G44 137 D3
Linwood PA3 111 F4
Neilston G78 154 B3
Troon KA10 229 D2
Craig St Airdrie ML6 122 C4
Blackridge EH48 107 F2
Blantyre G72 161 F4
Coatbridge ML5 121 F2
Craig View KA11 221 D1
Craigallian Ave
Cambuslang G72 139 E2
Milngavie G62 55 D2
Craiganour La G43 136 B3
Craigard Pl G73 138 B2
Craigash Quadrant G62 54 C2
Craigash Rd G62 54 C2
Craigbank FK10 5 E1
Craigbank Cres G76 178 C3
Craigbank Dr G53 135 D3
Craigbank Gr G76 178 C3
Craigbank Prim Sch
Alloa FK10 5 E1
Larkhall ML9 199 D4
Craigbank Rd ML9 199 D4
Craigbank Sch KA21 216 C4
Craigbank Sec Sch G53 135 E4
Craigbank St ML9 185 D1
Craigbanzo St G81 74 B4
Craigbarnet Ave G64 78 A4
Craigbarnet Cres G33 99 D2
Craigbarnet Rd G62 54 B1
Craigbet Ave PA11 89 F1
Craigbet Cres PA11 89 F1
Craigbet Pl PA11 89 F1
Craigbo Ave G23 76 B1
Craigbo Ct G23 96 B4
Craigbo Dr G23 76 B1
Craigbo Pl G23 96 B4
Craigbo Rd G23 76 B1
Craigbo St G23 76 B1
Craigbog Ave PA5 131 E4
Craigburn Ave PA6 111 E4
Craigburn Cres PA6 111 E4
Craigburn Ct Ashgill ML9 185 F1
Falkirk FK1 41 F1
Craigburn Pl PA6 111 F4
Craigburn St ML3 183 E4
Craigdene Dr KA20 206 C1
Craigdhu Ave Airdrie ML6 123 F4
Milngavie G62 54 C1
Craigdhu Prim Sch G62 75 F4
Craigdhu Rd Bearsden G61 75 F4
Milngavie G62 54 C1
Craigdonald Pl PA5 111 F2
Craigellan Rd G43 136 B3
Craigelvan Ave G67 81 F3
Craigelvan Ct G67 81 F3
Craigelvan Dr G67 81 F3
Craigelvan Gdns G67 81 F3
Craigelvan Gr G67 81 F3
Craigelvan Pl G67 81 F3
Craigelvan View G67 81 F3
Craigenbay Cres G66 79 F3
Craigenbay Rd G66 79 F3
Craigenbay St G21 98 A2
Craigencart Ct G81 73 F3
Craigend Cres G62 54 C1
Craigend Dr ML5 121 E2
Craigend Dr W G62 54 C1
Craigend Pl G13 95 F3
Craigend Rd
Cumbernauld G67 81 F3
East Kilbride G75 179 F1
Stirling FK7 7 D2
Troon KA10 232 C4
Craigend St G13 95 F3
Craigend View G67 81 F3
Craigend Visitor Ctr G62 54 C4
Craigendmuir Rd G33 99 F2
Craigendmuir St G33 98 B1
Craigendon Oval PA2 133 E3
Craigendon Rd PA2 133 E3
Craigendoran Ave G84 25 C4
Craigendoran Sta G84 25 C4
Craigends Ave PA11 89 F2
Craigends Dr PA10 111 D2
Craigends Pl PA11 89 F2
Craigends Rd
Glengarnock KA14 170 A3
Houston PA6 111 F4
Craigenfeoch Ave PA5 111 E1
Craigenhill Rd ML8 203 D3
Craigenlay Ave G63 31 E2
Craigens Rd ML1,ML6 124 B2
Craigfaulds Ave PA2 113 D1
Craigfell Ct ML3 161 F1
Craigfern Dr G63 31 E2
Craigfin Ct KA9 236 B3
Craigflower Ave G53 135 D2
Craigflower Gdns G53 135 D2
Craigflower Rd G53 135 D2
Craigford Dr FK7 7 E1
Craigforth Cres FK8 1 C1
Craighalbert Rd G68 61 E2
Craighalbert Rdbt G68 61 E2
Craighalbert Way G68 61 E2
Craighall Pl KA7 239 D1
Craighall Quadrant G78 154 B3
Craighall Rd G4 97 D1
Craighall St FK8 1 C1
Craighaw St G81 74 B4
Craighead Ave Glasgow G33 98 B2
Milton Of C G65 58 B3
Craighead Dr G62 54 B1
Craighead Prim Sch G65 58 B3
Craighead Rd
Bishopton PA7 72 A1
Milton Of C G65 58 B3
Craighead Sch ML3 162 A4
Craighead St ML6 123 F4
Craighead Way G78 134 A1
Craighill Dr G76 157 E3
Craighill Gr G76 157 E3
Craighill View EH48 107 F2
Craighirst Dr G81 74 A4
Craighirst Rd G62 54 B1
Craighlaw Ave G76 157 E1
Craighlaw Dr G76 157 E1
Craigholm Rd KA7 239 E4
Craigholme PA6 91 E1
Craigholme Sch G41 116 B2
Craighorn FK11 4 A3
Craighorn Dr FK1 41 F1
Craighorn Rd FK12 4 C3
Craighouse St G33 99 D1
Craighton Gdns G65 57 F4
Craigie Ave Ayr KA8 239 D4
Kilmarnock KA1 227 F2
Craigie Coll of Ed KA8 239 E4
Craigie Ct FK5 23 D1
Craigie Dr G77 156 C2
Craigie La [7] ML9 185 D2
Craigie Lea KA8 239 D4
Craigie Pk G66 79 F3
Craigie Pl Crosshouse KA2 226 C4
Kilmarnock KA1 227 F2
Craigie Rd Ayr KA8 236 A1
Hurlford KA1 228 C3
Kilmarnock KA1 227 F1
Kilmarnock, Riccarton KA1 227 F2
Craigie St Glasgow G42 117 D1
Prestwick KA9 236 A4
Craigie Way KA8 239 E4
Craigiebar Dr PA2 133 E4
Craigieburn Gdns G20 96 A4
Craigieburn Rd G67 61 F1
Craigiehall Ave PA8 93 D4
Craigiehall Cres PA8 93 D4
Craigiehall Pl G51 116 B3
Craigiehall St G51 116 C3
Craigiehall Way PA8 93 D4
Craigieknowes St PA15 46 B2
Craigielea Cres G62 54 C1
Craigielea Ct PA4 94 B2
Craigielea Dr PA3 113 E3
Craigielea Pk PA4 94 B2
Craigielea Prim Sch PA3 113 D3
Craigielea Rd
Clydebank G81 73 F4
Renfrew PA4 94 B2
Craigielea St G31 118 A4
Craigielinn Ave PA2 133 E4
Craigievar Ave FK2 24 A2
Craigievar Pl G77 156 A3
Craigievar St G33 99 F1
Craiginn Ct EH48 107 E2
Craiginn Terr EH48 107 E2
Craiglea Ave KA2 226 C4
Craiglea Ct EH48 107 E2
Craiglea Pl ML6 123 E4
Craiglea Terr ML6 103 F2
Craiglee G75 180 C3
Craigleith FK10 5 F2
Craigleith Ave FK1 41 F1
Craigleith St G32 118 C3
Craiglinn Park Rd G68 61 D1
Craiglinn Rdbt G68 61 D1
Craiglockhart St G33 99 E1
Craiglomond Gdns G83 27 E4
Craiglynn Gdns G83 27 F4
Craigmaddie Gdns G64 78 A4
Craigmaddie Rd G64 56 A1
Craigmaddie Terrace La [17]
G3 96 C1
Craigmark Pl KA11 219 F3
Craigmarloch Ave G64 78 A4
Craigmarloch Rdbt G68 61 E2
Craigmarloch View G63 31 D2
Craigmillar Ave G62 55 D2
Craigmillar Pl FK5 23 F2
Craigmillar Rd G42 137 D4
Craigmochan Ave ML6 102 C1
Craigmont Dr G20 96 C3
Craigmont St G20 96 C3
Craigmore Rd G61 75 D4
Craigmore St G31 118 B3
Craigmore Wynd [10] ML9 185 D2
Craigmount Ave PA2 133 E3
Craigmount St G66 79 E4
Craigmuir Cres G52 114 C3
Craigmuir Gdns G72 161 D3
Craigmuir Pl G52 114 C3
Craigmuir Rd
Blantyre G72 161 D3
Glasgow G52 114 C3
Craigmuschat Rd PA19 44 C4
Craignaw Pl KA11 220 A1
Craigneil Dr KA9 236 B4
Craigneil St G33 99 F1
Craigneith Ct G74 160 C2
Craignethan Castle ML9 200 C1
Craignethan Cres ML9 200 B2
Craignethan Rd
Carluke ML8 187 F2
Rutherglen G46 157 D4
Craigneuk Ave ML6 123 E3
Craigneuk St ML1 164 B3
Craignure Cres ML6 123 F4
Craignure Rd G73 138 A2
Craigomus Cres FK11 3 F3
Craigpark G31 118 A4
Craigpark Ave KA9 236 A3
Craigpark Dr G31 118 A4
Craigpark Sch KA8 236 B1
Craigpark St G81 74 B4
Craigpark Way G71 141 D4
Craigs Ave G81 74 B3
Craigs Pl KA21 217 D4
Craigs The PA16 45 E4
Craigsdow Rd KA10 229 F3
Craigsheen Ave G76 158 B4
Craigshiel Pl KA7 238 B2
Craigside Ct G68 81 F4
Craigside Rd G68 81 F4
Craigskeen Pl KA9 236 B3
Craigson Pl ML6 123 F3
Craigspark KA22 205 E2
Craigstewart Cres KA7 238 B1
Craigston Ave KA7 239 E3
Craigston Pl PA5 111 F1
Craigston Rd PA5 111 F1
Craigstone View G65 60 C4
Craigthornhill Rd ML10 198 A3
Craigton Ave
Barrhead G78 134 C1
Milngavie G62 54 C1
Craigton Cotts G62 54 B3
Craigton Cres Alva FK12 4 C3
Newton Mearns G77 156 A3
Craigton Dr Barrhead G78 134 C1
Glasgow G51 115 F3
Newton Mearns G77 156 B3
Craigton Gdns G62 54 C1
Craigton Ind Est G52 115 F3
Craigton Pl Blantyre G72 140 B1
Glasgow G51 115 F3
Craigton Prim Sch G52 115 F3
Craigton Rd Glasgow G51 115 F4
Kilbirnie KA25 170 A4
Milngavie G62 54 C2
Neilston G77 155 D2
Craigton St G81 74 B4
Craigvale Cres ML6 123 F4
Craigvicar Gdns G32 119 E2
Craigview FK10 5 E1
Craigview Ave PA5 111 F1
Craigview Rd ML1 163 F4
Craigview Terr PA5 111 E1
Craigward FK10 10 A3
Craigweil Pl KA7 238 C4
Craigweil Rd KA7 238 C4
Craigwell Ave G73 138 B3
Craiksland Pl KA10 230 A2
Crail St G31 118 B3
Cramalt Ct KA11 220 A2
Crammond Ave ML5 121 E2
Cramond Ave PA4 94 C1
Cramond Ct FK1 42 A1
Cramond Pl KA11 219 F1
Cramond St G5 117 F1
Cramond Terr G32 119 D3
Cramond Way KA11 219 F1
Cranberry Moss Rd
Kilwinning KA13 207 E1
Kilwinning KA13 207 E2
Cranberry Rd KA13 207 D1
Cranborne Rd G12 96 A3
Cranbrooke Dr G20 96 B4
Crandleyhill Rd KA9 236 A3
Cranesbill Ct KA7 239 D2
Crannog Rd G82 50 C1
Crannog Way KA13 207 E2
Cranston St G3 240 A2
Cranworth La G12 96 B2
Cranworth St G12 96 B2
Crarae Ave G61 75 F1
Crathes Ave FK5 24 A2
Crathes Ct G44 136 C2
Crathie Ct ML8 187 F2
Crathie Dr Ardrossan KA22 205 E1
Denny FK6 21 E2
Glasgow G11 96 A1
Glenmavis ML6 102 C2
Crathie Quadrant ML2 165 D3
Crathie Rd KA3 222 C1
Crauford Ave KA23 190 C2
Craufurd Cres KA15 171 F2
Craufurdland Rd KA3 223 D3
Craven Gr KA11 219 F3
Craw Pl PA12 129 E1
Craw Rd PA2 113 E2
Crawberry Rd PA15 46 A1
Crawford Ave
Kirkintilloch G66 79 F2
Prestwick KA9 236 B3
Crawford Cres
Blantyre G72 140 B1
Uddingston G71 140 C4
Crawford Dr
East Kilbride G74 160 A1
Glasgow G15 75 D1
Helensburgh G84 16 C2
Crawford Hill G74 160 A1
Crawford Rd Houston PA6 91 E1
Milngavie G62 54 C2
Crawford Sq FK2 14 B2
Crawford St Glasgow G11 96 A1
Hamilton ML3 162 A3
Motherwell ML1 163 E3
Port Glasgow PA14 47 E1
Crawforddyke Prim Sch
ML8 202 A4
Crawfurd Ave G73 138 A3
Crawfurd Dr PA3 113 D3
Crawfurd Gdns G73 138 B2
Crawfurd Rd G73 138 A2
Crawfurd St PA15 45 F3
Crawfurdland Pl KA2 221 E1
Crawfurds View PA12 129 E2
Crawhin Gdns PA15 45 E2
Crawriggs Ave G66 79 E3
Creamery Rd ML2 165 E1
Crebar Dr G78 134 B1
Crebar St G46 135 F2
Credon Dr Airdrie ML6 123 D2
Crosshouse KA2 226 C4
Credon Gdns G73 138 B2
Cree Ave G64 78 B1
Cree Gdns G32 118 C3
Cree Pl G75 159 D1
Creebank Pl KA10 229 F3
Creelshaugh Rd KA3 213 D2
Creighton Gr G74 159 F1
Creigton Ct KA3 223 D3
Creinch Dr G83 19 F1
Creran Ct Hamilton ML3 162 A1
Prestwick KA9 236 B3
Creran Dr Denny FK6 39 E3
Renfrew PA4 94 A2
Creran Path [12] ML2 165 F3
Crescent Rd G13 95 D3
Crescent St PA15 46 A2
Crescent The
Clarkston G76 158 A3
Clydebank G81 73 F2
Longriggend ML6 84 B1
Stewarton KA3 195 F1
Cresswell La G12 96 B2
Cresswell Pl G77 156 C1
Cresswell St [5] G12 96 B2
Cressy St G51 115 F4
Crest Ave G13 95 D4
Crestlea Ave PA2 133 F4
Creteil Ct FK1 42 B2
Creveul Ct G83 27 F3
Crichton Ave KA24 191 D4
Crichton Ct G45 137 F1
Crichton Pl G21 97 F2
Crichton St Coatbridge ML5 122 A4
Glasgow G21 97 F2
Cricketfield La PA6 91 D2
Crieff Ave ML6 123 E1
Criffel Pl Kilmarnock KA1 228 A2
Motherwell ML1 143 E2
Criffell Gdns G32 119 E2
Criffell Rd G32 119 E2
Crimea St G2 240 B2
Crimond Pl Kilsyth G65 36 A1
Shieldhill FK1 66 C4
Crinan Cres ML5 101 E1
Crinan Gdns G64 78 B1
Crinan Pl Ardrossan KA22 205 E3
Bellshill ML4 142 A2
Coatbridge ML5 101 E1

Dalreoch Sta G82 49 F2
Dalriada Cres ML1 142 B1
Dalriada Dr G64 78 B4
Dalriada Rd PA16 44 B2
Dalriada St G40 118 B2
Dalry Gdns ML3 161 E1
Dalry La KA22 205 E2
Dalry Prim Sch KA24 191 D4
Dalry Rd Ardrossan KA22 205 E2
Beith KA15 171 D4
Kilbirnie KA25 170 A4
Kilwinning KA13 207 E2
Saltcoats KA21 206 A1
Stewarton KA3 195 E1
Uddingston G71 141 D4
Dalry St G32 119 D2
Dalry Sta KA24 191 E4
Dalrymple Ct Irvine KA12 219 F2
Kirkintilloch G66 79 E4
Dalrymple Dr
East Kilbride G74 159 F1
Irvine KA12 219 F2
Newton Mearns G77 157 D2
Dalrymple Pl KA12 219 E2
Dalrymple St PA15 46 A3
Dalserf Cres G46 136 A1
Dalserf Path 18 ML9 185 E1
Dalserf St G31 118 A3
Dalsert Prim Sch ML9 199 F4
Dalsetter Ave G15 75 D1
Dalsetter Pl G15 75 D1
Dalshannon Pl G67 82 A4
Dalshannon Rd G67 82 A4
Dalshannon View G67 82 A4
Dalshannon Way G67 82 A4
Dalsholm Rd G20 96 A4
Dalskeith Ave PA3 113 D3
Dalskeith Cres PA3 113 D3
Dalskeith Rd PA3 113 D3
Dalswinton St G34 120 B4
Dalton Ave G81 74 C1
Dalton Hill ML3 161 F1
Dalton St G31 118 C3
Dalvait Gdns G83 27 F4
Dalvait Rd G83 27 F4
Dalveen Ct G78 134 B1
Dalveen Dr G71 140 C4
Dalveen Quadrant ML5 122 B3
Dalveen St G32 118 C3
Dalveen Way G73 138 B2
Dalwhinnie Ave G72 140 B1
Dalwood Rd KA9 236 A4
Daly Gdns G72 140 C1
Dalzell Ave ML1 164 A2
Dalzell Ctry Pk ML1 163 F2
Dalzell Dr ML1 164 A2
Dalziel Dr G41 116 B2
Dalziel High Sch ML1 163 E3
Dalziel Rd G52 114 C4
Dalziel St Hamilton ML3 162 A3
Motherwell ML1 163 F4
Damhead Rd KA1 227 F2
Dampark KA3 195 E4
Damshot Cres G53 115 E1
Damshot Rd G53 135 E4
Damside KA8 235 F1
Danby Rd G69 119 F2
Danes Ave 1 G14 95 E2
Danes Cres G14 95 D3
Danes Dr G14 95 E2
Danes La N 3 G14 95 E2
Danes La S G14 95 E2
Daniel McLaughlin Pl G66 58 C1
Dankeith Dr KA1 231 E2
Dankeith Rd KA1 231 E2
Darg Rd KA20 217 E4
Dargarvel Ave G41 116 A2
Dargavel Ave PA7 72 A2
Dargavel Rd Bishopton PA7 72 B1
Erskine PA8 72 C1
Dark Brig Rd ML8 201 D1
Darkwood Cres PA3 113 D3
Darkwood Ct PA3 113 D3
Darkwood Dr PA3 113 D3
Darleith Rd Alexandria G83 27 F3
Cardross G82 26 A1
Darleith St G32 118 C3
Darley Cres KA10 229 E1
Darley Mains Rd G53 135 E2
Darley Pl Hamilton ML3 183 D4
Troon KA10 229 E1
Darley Rd G68 61 F3
Darlington View KA3 195 F1
Darluith Rd PA3 111 F3
Darmeid Pl ML7 167 D4
Darmule Dr KA13 207 E3
Darnaway Ave G33 99 E1
Darnaway Dr G33 99 E1
Darnaway St G33 99 E1
Darndaff Rd PA15 46 A1
Darngaber Gdns ML3 183 F2
Darngaber Rd ML3 183 F2
Darngavil Rd ML6 103 F3
Darnick St G21 98 A1
Darnley Cres G64 77 F2
Darnley Dr KA1 227 F3
Darnley Gdns G41 116 C1
Darnley Ind Est G53 135 D3
Darnley Path G46 135 F3
Darnley Pl G41 116 C1
Darnley Prim Sch No 1
G53 135 E2
Darnley Rd Barrhead G78 134 C2
Glasgow G41 116 C1
Darnley St Glasgow G41 116 C2
Stirling FK8 7 D4
Darnshaw Cl KA11 220 B3
Darrach Dr FK6 21 D1
Darragh Gn ML2 166 A3
Darroch Ave PA19 44 C4
Darroch Dr Erskine PA8 72 C2
Gourock PA19 44 C4
Darroch Way G67 62 A2
Dartford St G22 97 D2
Dartmouth Ave PA19 44 C3
Darvel Cres PA1 114 C2
Darvel Dr G77 157 D3
Darvel St G53 134 C3
Darwin Pl G81 73 E2
Darwin Rd G75 180 B4
Dava St G51 116 A4
Davaar G74 160 B1
Davaar Dr Coatbridge ML5 121 E4
Kilmarnock KA3 223 D3
Motherwell ML1 142 B1
Paisley PA2 133 F4
Davaar Pl G77 156 B3
Davaar Rd Greenock PA16 44 B2
Renfrew PA4 94 B1
Saltcoats KA21 205 F1
Davaar St G40 118 A2
Davan Loan 10 ML2 165 F3
Davarr Pl FK1 41 E2
Dave Barrie Ave ML9 184 C3
Daventry Dr G12 96 A3
Davey St PA16 45 E3
David Dale Ave KA3 211 E4
David Gage St KA13 207 F3
David Livingstone Ctr G72 140 C1
David Livingstone Meml
Prim Sch G72 140 B1
David Orr St KA1 222 C1
David Pl Glasgow G69 119 F2
Paisley PA3 114 A4
David St Coatbridge ML5 122 B4
Glasgow G40 118 A3
Salsburgh ML7 125 D1
David Way PA3 114 A4
David's Cres KA13 207 E1
David's Loan FK2 24 B1
Davidson Ave KA14 170 B3
Davidson Cres G65 59 F2
Davidson Dr PA19 44 C4
Davidson Gdns G14 95 F2
Davidson La ML8 188 A1
Davidson Pl Ayr KA8 236 A1
Glasgow G32 119 E3
Davidson Quadrant G81 73 F4
Davidson Rd G83 27 F4
Davidson St Airdrie ML6 122 C4
Bannockburn FK7 7 E1
Clydebank G81 94 C4
Coatbridge ML5 122 A2
Glasgow G40 118 A2
Davidston Pl G66 79 F2
Davieland Rd G46 136 A1
Davies Dr G83 27 F3
Davies Quadrant ML1 142 B1
Davington Dr ML3 161 E1
Daviot St G51 115 E3
Dawsholm Ind Est G20 96 A4
Dawson Ave Alloa FK10 9 F4
East Kilbride G75 159 D1
Dawson Park Sch FK2 24 A1
Dawson Pl G4 97 D2
Dawson Rd G4 97 D2
Dawson St FK2 42 A4
De Morville Pl KA15 171 D4
De Walden Terr KA3 223 D1
Deacons Rd G65 60 C4
Deaconsbank Ave G46 135 F1
Deaconsbank Gdns G46 135 E1
Deaconsbank Gr G46 135 E1
Dealston Rd G78 134 A2
Dean Castle Ctry Pk KA3 223 D2
Dean Cres Chryston G69 80 B1
Hamilton ML3 162 B1
Stirling FK8 2 B1
Dean Ct KA3 222 C1
Dean La KA3 223 D1
Dean Park Ave G71 141 D1
Dean Park Dr G72 139 E2
Dean Park Rd PA4 94 C1
Dean Pl KA2 226 C4
Dean Rd Kilbirnie KA25 149 D1
Kilmarnock KA3 223 D2
Dean St Bellshill ML4 142 A3
Clydebank G81 74 B1
Kilmarnock KA3 223 D1
Stewarton KA3 195 F1
Dean Terr KA3 223 D2
Deanbank Sch ML5 101 E1
Deanbrae St G71 140 C3
Deanfield Quadrant G52 114 C3
Deanhill La KA3 223 D2
Deans Ave G72 139 E2
Deanside Rd G52 115 D4
Deanston Dr G41 136 C4
Deanstone Pl ML5 122 B2
Deanstone Wlk ML5 122 B1
Deanwood Ave G44 136 C2
Deanwood Rd G44 136 C2
Deas Rd ML7 146 B3
Dechmont G75 180 B3
Dechmont Ave
Cambuslang G72 139 E2
Motherwell ML1 163 E4
Dechmont Cotts G72 139 F2
Dechmont Gdns G72 140 B1
Dechmont Pl G72 139 E2
Dechmont Rd G71 120 C1
Dechmont St Glasgow G31 118 B2
Hamilton ML3 162 B1
Dechmont View
Bellshill ML4 141 F2
Uddingston G71 141 D4
Dee Ave Kilmarnock KA1 228 A2
Paisley PA2 112 C1
Renfrew PA4 94 C2
Dee Dr PA2 112 C1
Dee Path Larkhall ML9 199 D4
Motherwell ML1 143 D3
Dee Pl East Kilbride G75 179 F3
Johnstone PA5 131 E4
Dee St Coatbridge ML5 101 E1
Glasgow G33 118 B4
Greenock PA16 45 D3
Shotts ML7 146 B3
Dee Terr ML3 183 D4
Deedes St ML6 122 B3
Deep Dale G74 159 E2
Deepdene Rd Bearsden G61 75 E1
Chryston G69 80 C1
Deer Park Ave KA20 217 F4
Deer Park Ct ML3 183 E4
Deer Park Pl ML3 183 F4
Deerdykes Ct N G68 81 F3
Deerdykes Ct S G68 81 F3
Deerdykes Pl G68 81 F3
Deerdykes Rd G68 81 F3
Deerdykes Rdbt G68 81 E3
Deerdykes View G68 81 E3
Deerpark FK10 5 F1
Deerpark Prim Sch FK10 5 F1
Deeside Dr ML8 188 A2
Deeside Pl ML5 122 B2
Delfie Dr PA16 45 D2
Delhi Ave G81 73 E2
Dell The ML4 142 B2
Dellburn St ML1 164 A3
Dellingburn St PA15 46 A2
Delny Pl G33 119 F4
Delph Rd FK10 4 B1
Delphwood Cres FK10 4 B1
Delves Pk ML11 215 D2
Delves Rd ML11 215 D2
Delvin Rd G44 137 D3
Dempsey Rd ML4 141 F2
Dempster St PA15 45 F2
Den La ML7 146 B3
Denbak Ave ML3 162 A1
Denbeck St G32 118 C3
Denbrae St G32 118 C3
Denewood Ave PA2 133 E4
Denham St G22 97 D2
Denholm Cres G75 180 C4
Denholm Dr Glasgow G46 136 B1
Wishaw ML2 165 E3
Denholm Gdns
Greenock PA16 45 E3
Quarter ML3 183 F2
Denholm Gn 5 G75 180 C4
Denholm St PA16 45 E3
Denholm Terr
Greenock PA16 45 E3
Hamilton ML3 161 F2
Denholm Way KA15 171 D4
Denmark St G22 97 E2
Denmilne Gdns G34 120 B4
Denmilne Path G34 120 B4
Denmilne Rd G34 120 B4
Denmilne St G34 120 B4
Denniston Pl ML11 215 E3
Dennistoun Cres G84 25 D4
Dennistoun Rd PA14 70 B4
Dennistoun St ML4 142 A3
Denny High Sch FK6 39 F4
Denny Prim Sch FK6 21 E1
Denny Rd
Dennyloanhead FK4 39 F3
Larbert FK5 23 D1
Dennyholm Wynd KA25 149 D1
Denovan Rd FK6 21 F2
Dentdale G74 159 E2
Deramore Ave G46 157 D4
Derby St G3 116 C4
Derby Terrace La 4 G3 116 C4
Deroran Pl FK8 6 C3
Derrywood Rd G65 58 B3
Dervaig Gdns ML6 84 B2
Derwent Ave FK1 41 F2
Derwent Dr ML5 101 E1
Derwent St G22 97 D2
Derwentwater G75 179 F3
Despard Ave G32 119 F2
Despard Gdns G32 119 F2
Deveron Ave G46 136 B1
Deveron Cres ML3 161 F2
Deveron Rd Bearsden G61 75 E1
East Kilbride G74 160 A1
Kilmarnock KA1 228 A3
Motherwell ML1 143 D3
Troon KA10 229 F3
Deveron St Coatbridge ML5 101 E1
Glasgow G33 98 B1
Devilla Ct KA9 236 B3
Devine Gr ML2 166 A3
Devlin Gr G72 161 F4
Devol Ave PA14 47 D1
Devol Cres G53 135 D4
Devol Rd PA14 68 B3
Devon Ct FK10 4 A1
Devon Dr Bishopton PA7 72 B2
Tullibody FK10 4 C2
Devon Gdns
Bishopbriggs G64 77 F2
Carluke ML8 187 F1
Devon Pl Glasgow G41 117 D2
Tullibody FK10 4 A1
Devon Rd Alloa FK10 10 B3
Greenock PA16 44 B2
Devon St G5 117 D2
Devon Village FK10 5 F2
Devon Way ML1 163 D3
Devon Wlk G68 81 F4
Devonbank FK10 5 F2
Devondale Ave G72 140 B1
Devonhill Ave ML3 183 E4
Devonport Pk G75 180 A4
Devonshire Gardens La 2
G12 96 A2
Devonshire Gdns 1 G12 96 A2
Devonshire Terr G12 96 A2
Devonshire Terrace La
G12 96 A2
Devonview Pl ML6 122 C3
Devonview Sch ML6 122 C3
Devonview St ML6 122 C3
Devonway FK10 10 C3
Dewar Cl G71 121 D1
Dewar Wlk ML8 201 D1
Dewshill Cotts ML7 126 A2
Dhuhill Dr E G84 16 C2
Diamond St ML4 142 A2
Diana Ave G13 95 D4
Diana Quadrant ML1 143 D3
Diana Vernon Ct G84 25 C4
Dick Cres KA12 219 E3
Dick Ct ML9 198 C1
Dick Institute Mus KA1 228 A4
Dick Quad G82 48 A4
Dick Rd KA1 228 A4
Dick St G20 96 C2
Dick Terr KA12 219 E3
Dickburn Cres FK4 39 F3
Dickens Ave G81 74 A2
Dickens Gr ML1 143 E1
Dickies Wells FK12 5 E4
Dicks Pk G75 180 B4
Dickson Dr KA12 219 E3
Dickson Sq ML1 144 A1
Dickson St ML9 185 E1
Diddup Dr KA20 206 A1
Differ Ave G65 59 F1
Dillichip Cl G83 27 F1
Dillichip Gdns G83 27 F2
Dillichip Loan G83 27 F2
Dillichip Terr G83 27 F2
Dilwara Ave G14 95 F1
Dimity St PA5 111 F2
Dimsdale Cres ML2 165 E1
Dimsdale Rd ML2 165 E1
Dinard Dr G46 136 B2
Dinart St G33 98 B1
Dinduff St G34 100 B1
Dingwall Dr PA16 44 C2
Dinmont Ave PA2 112 C1
Dinmont Cres ML1 142 B1
Dinmont Pl 1 G41 116 C1
Dinmont Rd G41 116 B1
Dinmont Way PA2 112 C1
Dinmurchie Rd KA10 229 F3
Dinnet Way 11 ML2 165 F3
Dinwiddie St G21 98 B1
Dinyra Pl ML5 101 E3
Dippin Pl KA21 205 F1
Dipple Ct KA25 149 D1
Dipple Pl G15 75 D1
Dipple Rd KA25 149 D2
Dipple View KA25 149 D2
Dirleton Dr Glasgow G41 136 C4
Paisley PA2 113 D1
Dirleton Gate G61 75 E1
Dirleton Gdns FK10 9 F4
Dirleton La FK10 9 F3
Dirrans Terr KA13 207 F1
Ditton Dr KA1 227 F2
Divernia Way G78 155 E4
Diverswell FK10 5 E1
Divert Rd PA19 44 B3
Divert Wlk PA19 44 B3
Dixon Ave Dumbarton G82 49 F2
Glasgow G42 117 D1
Dixon Dr G82 49 E1
Dixon Pl G74 159 D2
Dixon Rd Glasgow G42 117 E1
Helensburgh G84 16 C2
Dixon St Coatbridge ML5 122 A2
Glasgow G1 240 C1
Hamilton ML3 162 B2
Paisley PA1 113 F2
Dixons Blazes Ind Est
G42, G5 117 E2
Dobbie Ave FK5 23 E1
Dobbie's Loan G4 241 D4
Dobbie's Loan Pl G4 241 E3
Dobbies Ct ML8 187 D3
Dochart Ave PA4 94 C1
Dochart Dr ML5 101 E1
Dochart Pl FK1 42 B1
Dochart St G33 98 C1
Dock Breast PA15 46 A3
Dock Rd KA22 205 D1
Dock St Clydebank G81 94 B4
Falkirk FK2 24 B1
Dockhead Pl KA21 216 C4
Dockhead St KA21 216 C4
Dodhill Pl G13 95 D3
Dodside Gdns G32 119 E2
Dodside Pl G32 119 E2
Dodside Rd G77 155 F2
Dodside St G32 119 E2
Dolan St G69 120 A3
Dollar Ave FK2 42 A4
Dollar Gdns FK2 42 A4
Dollar Ind Est FK1 42 A3
Dollar Pk ML1 164 A2
Dollar Terr G20 96 B4
Dollin Aquacentre G74 159 F1
Dolphin Rd G41 116 B1
Dominica Gn 4 G75 159 D1
Don Ave PA4 94 C1
Don Ct ML3 183 D4
Don Dr PA2 112 C1
Don Path ML9 199 D4
Don Pl PA5 131 E4
Don St Glasgow G33 98 B1
Greenock PA16 45 E3
Donald Cres KA10 229 E2
Donald Terr ML3 162 B1
Donald Way G71 141 D4
Donald's Ct PA15 46 A3
Donaldfield Rd PA11 110 A4
Donaldson Ave Kilsyth G65 60 C4
Saltcoats KA21 216 C4
Stevenston KA20 206 C1
Donaldson Cres G66 79 E4
Donaldson Dr Irvine KA12 219 E2
Kilmarnock KA3 223 E2
Renfrew PA4 94 B2
Donaldson Gn G71 141 D4
Donaldson Pl Airdrie ML6 123 D4
Cambusbarron FK7 6 B3
Kirkintilloch G66 79 E4
Donaldson Rd
Kilmarnock KA3 223 E2
Larkhall ML9 185 E1
Donaldson St
Hamilton ML3 162 A3
Kirkintilloch G66 79 E4
Donaldswood Pk PA2 133 E4
Donaldswood Rd PA2 133 E4
Doncaster St G20 97 D2
Dongola Rd KA7 239 D4
Donnelly Way ML2 164 B2
Donnies Brae G78 154 C4
Doo'cot Brae FK10 10 A4
Doon Ave KA9 236 A3
Doon Cres G61 75 E2
Doon Ct KA12 219 E1
Doon Pl Kilmarnock KA1 228 A2
Kirkintilloch G66 58 C1
Saltcoats KA21 206 A2
Symington KA1 231 E2
Troon KA10 229 F3
Doon Rd G66 59 D1
Doon Side G67 62 A1
Doon St Clydebank G81 74 B2
2 Larkhall ML9 185 E1
Motherwell ML1 164 A2
Doon Way G66 59 D1
Doonfoot Ct G74 159 E1
Doonfoot Gdns G74 159 E1
Doonfoot Prim Sch KA7 238 A2
Doonfoot Rd Ayr KA7 238 C2
Glasgow G43 136 B3
Doonholm Pl KA7 238 C1
Doonholm Rd KA7 238 C1
Dora St G40 117 F2
Dorain Rd ML1 143 E2
Dorchester Ave G12 96 A3
Dorchester Ct G12 96 A3
Dorchester Pl G12 96 A3
Dorian Dr G76 157 E4
Dorlin Rd G33 99 F3
Dormanside Ct G53 115 D2
Dormanside Gate G53 115 D2
Dormanside Gr G53 115 D2
Dormanside Rd G53 115 E2
Dornal Ave G13 94 C4
Dornal Dr KA10 229 F3
Dornford Ave G32 119 E2
Dornford Rd G32 119 E1
Dornie Cl KA3 195 E1
Dornie Dr G32 139 D4
Dornie Path 9 ML2 165 F3
Dornie Wynd ML7 147 D2
Dornoch Ave G46 136 B1
Dornoch Ct Bellshill ML4 142 A3
Kilwinning KA13 207 D2
Dornoch Pk KA7 238 C3
Dornoch Pl
Bishopbriggs G64 78 B1
Chryston G69 80 B1
East Kilbride G74 159 E1
Dornoch Rd Bearsden G61 75 E1
Motherwell ML1 143 D3
Dornoch St G40 117 F3
Dornoch Way Airdrie ML6 122 C3
Cumbernauld G68 62 A3
Dorrator Rd FK1 41 F3
Dorset Rd PA16 44 C2
Dorset Sq G3 240 A3
Dorset St G3 240 A3
Dosk Ave G13 94 C4
Dosk Pl G13 94 C4
Double Edges Rd G78 154 B3
Dougalston Ave G62 55 D1
Dougalston Cres G62 55 D1
Dougalston Gdns N G62 55 D1
Dougalston Gdns S G62 55 D1
Dougalston Rd G23 76 C1
Douglas Acad G62 54 B2
Douglas Ave Dalry KA24 191 E3
Elderslie PA5 112 A1
Glasgow G46 136 B1
Glasgow, Carmyle G32 119 D1
Kirkintilloch G66 79 E3
Langbank PA14 70 B4
Prestwick KA9 236 A3
Rutherglen G73 138 B3
Douglas Cres Airdrie ML6 123 D3
Bishopton PA7 72 C2
Hamilton ML3 183 E3
Uddingston G71 141 D4
Douglas Ct Kirkintilloch G66 79 E3
Troon KA10 229 E3

Ferry Loan G83 27 F3
Ferry Orch FK9 2 B1
Ferry Rd Bishopton PA7 72 A2
Bothwell G71 141 D1
Cardross G82 48 A3
Glasgow G3 96 A1
Renfrew PA4 94 B3
Rosneath G84 15 D2
South Alloa FK7 9 F2
Stirling FK9 2 B1
Uddingston G71 140 C3
Ferryden Ct G14 95 F1
Ferryden St G14 95 F1
Fersit St G43 136 B3
Fetlar Dr Glasgow G44 137 E3
Kilmarnock KA3 223 D3
Fetlar Rd PA11 110 B4
Fettercairn Ave G15 74 C2
Fettercairn Gdns G64 78 B1
Fettes St G33 118 C4
Fiddison Pl KA9 236 C3
Fiddoch Ct ML2 165 F4
Fidra St G33 118 C4
Field Gr G76 157 F3
Field Rd Clarkston G76 157 F3
Clydebank G81 74 B4
Larkhall ML9 185 D1
Field St ML3 162 B1
Fielden Pl G40 118 A3
Fielden St G40 118 A3
Fieldhead Dr G43 136 A3
Fieldhead Sq G43 136 A3
Fieldings The KA3 195 E4
Fields La PA6 91 D2
Fife Ave Airdrie ML6 123 D3
Glasgow G52 115 D2
Fife Cres G71 141 D1
Fife Ct G71 141 D1
Fife Dr Greenock PA16 44 B3
Motherwell ML1 142 B1
Fife Rd PA16 44 B3
Fife Way G64 98 B4
Fifth Ave Airdrie ML6 123 E4
Glasgow G12 95 F3
Millerston G33 99 D3
Renfrew PA4 94 B1
Fifth Rd G72 161 F3
Fifty Pitches Pl G52, G51 115 E4
Fifty Pitches Rd G52 115 D4
Finart Dr PA2 114 A1
Finaven Gdns G61 75 D4
Finch Dr G13 95 D4
Finch Pl Johnstone PA5 131 E4
Kilmarnock KA1 228 B4
Finch Rd PA16 45 D3
Findhorn PA8 73 D1
Findhorn Ave Paisley PA2 112 C1
Renfrew PA4 94 C2
Findhorn Ct G75 179 E4
Findhorn Pl
East Kilbride G75 179 E4
Falkirk FK1 42 B1
Troon KA10 229 F3
Findhorn Rd KA9 233 F2
Findhorn St G33 118 B4
Findlay St Kilsyth G65 60 B4
Motherwell ML1 163 F3
Findlay's Brae KA21 216 C4
Findochty PA8 73 D2
Findochty St G33 99 F1
Fingal La G20 96 B4
Fingal St G20 96 B4
Fingalton Rd G77 155 F3
Fingask St G32 119 E2
Finglas Ave PA2 114 A1
Finglen Gdns G62 54 C1
Finglen Pl G53 135 D3
Fingleton Ave G78 134 B1
Finhaven St G32 118 C2
Finistere Ave FK1 42 A2
Finlarig Ct FK5 23 F2
Finlarig St G34 120 B4
Finlas Ave KA7 239 D2
Finlas St G22 97 E2
Finlay Ave KA24 191 E4
Finlay Dr Glasgow G31 118 A4
Linwood PA3 111 F3
Finlay Rise G62 76 B4
Finlayson Dr Airdrie ML6 123 F4
Kilmarnock KA3 223 E2
Finlayson Quadrant ML6 123 F4
Finlaystone PA14 69 F4
Finlaystone Cres PA13 69 E1
Finlaystone Rd
Kilmacolm PA13 69 E2
Port Glasgow PA14 69 D4
Finlaystone St ML5 121 F4
Finnart Cres PA19 44 B3
Finnart Rd PA16 45 E3
Finnart Sq G40 117 F2
Finnart St Glasgow G40 117 F2
Greenock PA16 45 E3
Finneston La PA15 46 A2
Finneston St PA15 46 A2
Finneston Way PA15 46 A2
Finnick Glen KA7 239 D2
Finnie Terr Gourock PA19 44 B3
Springside KA11 220 C1
Finnie Wynd ML1 164 A2
Finnieston Sq 9 G3 116 C4
Finnieston St G3 116 C4
Finsbay St G51 115 F3
Fintaig La ML2 165 F2
Fintrie Terr ML3 161 F2
Fintry Ave PA2 133 F4
Fintry Cres
Barrhead G78 134 B1
Bishopbriggs G64 78 B1
Fintry Dr G44 137 E4
Fintry Gdns G61 75 E4
Fintry Pl
East Kilbride G75 180 A2
Irvine KA11 220 A1
Fintry Rd PA15 46 A1
Fintry Terr KA11 220 A2
Fintry Wlk KA11 220 A1
Fir Bank KA7 239 E3
Fir Bank Ave ML9 185 D1
Fir Ct Cambuslang G72 139 F2
Coatbridge ML5 121 F2
Fir Dr G75 180 A3
Fir Gr G71 141 E4
Fir La FK5 23 E1
Fir Park St ML1 163 F2
Fir Pk
(Motherwell FC) ML1 163 F2
Fir Pl Cambuslang G72 139 E3
Cleland ML1 144 A1
Glasgow G69 120 A2
Johnstone PA5 112 A1
Kilmarnock KA1 227 E4
Fir St PA15 46 C1
Fir Terr PA19 44 B3
Fir View ML6 123 D1
Firbank Ave G64 78 A4
Firbank Terr G78 134 C1
Firdon Cres G15 75 D1
Firhill Ave ML6 122 C3
Firhill Dr KA9 233 E3
Firhill Pk
(Partick Thistle FC) G20 97 D2
Firhill Rd G20 97 D2
Firhill St G20 97 D2
Firlee G75 179 F4
Firpark Rd G64 98 A4
Firpark Sch ML1 163 F2
Firpark St G31 117 F4
Firpark Terr
Cambusbarron FK7 6 B3
Glasgow G31 117 F4
Firs Cres FK7 7 E1
Firs Entry FK7 7 E1
Firs Pk
(East Stirlingshire FC)
FK2 42 B3
Firs Rd FK10 4 B1
Firs St FK2 42 B3
Firs The Bannockburn FK7 7 E1
Glasgow G44 137 D2
First Ave Alexandria G83 27 F3
Bearsden G61 76 A2
Dumbarton G82 50 B1
Glasgow G44 136 C1
Irvine KA12 224 B4
Kirkintilloch G66 79 E1
Millerston G33 99 D2
Renfrew PA4 94 B1
Uddingston G71 140 C4
First Gdns G41 116 A2
First Rd G72 161 F3
First St G71 140 C4
First Terr G81 74 A2
Firth Cres PA19 44 B3
Firth Gdns KA10 229 E4
Firth Rd KA10 229 E4
Firth View Terr KA22 205 E2
Firthview Terr G82 49 E2
Firtree Pl ML2 166 A3
Firtree Rd ML2 166 A3
Firwood Cts G77 156 C2
Firwood Dr G44 137 E3
Firwood Rd G77 156 C2
Fischer Gdns PA3 112 C3
Fishcross Prim Sch FK10 5 E2
Fisher Ave Kilsyth G65 60 B4
Paisley PA3 112 C2
Fisher Cres G81 74 A3
Fisher Ct Glasgow G31 117 F4
Knockentiber KA2 221 F2
Fisher Dr PA3 112 C2
Fisher Pl G84 17 D1
Fisher St ML9 185 D1
Fisher Way PA3 112 C2
Fishers Rd PA4 94 B3
Fisherwood Rd G83 27 F4
Fishescoates Ave G73 138 B3
Fishescoates Gdns G73 138 B3
Fitzalan Dr PA3 114 A3
Fitzalan Rd PA4 94 A1
Fitzroy La G3 116 C4
Fitzroy Pl 2 G3 116 C4
Five Roads KA13 208 A2
Five Ways Rd ML9 200 B2
Flakefield G74 159 D1
Flanders St G81 74 B4
Flatterton La PA16 44 B1
Flatterton Rd PA16 44 B1
Flax Mill Rd ML7 127 F3
Flax Rd G71 141 D3
Flaxfield Gr ML1 142 B1
Flaxmill Ave ML2 164 B2
Fleck Ave KA21 206 A1
Fleet Ave PA4 94 C1
Fleet St G32 119 D2
Fleming Ave
Chryston G69 100 B4
Clydebank G81 94 B4
Fleming Cres KA21 206 A2
Fleming Ct Carluke ML8 187 F1
Clydebank G81 74 A1
Hamilton ML3 161 F2
Motherwell ML1 164 A2
Fleming Dr
Stenhousemuir FK5 24 A2
Stewarton KA3 211 E4
Fleming Gdns FK1 41 F3
Fleming Pl Blackridge EH48 107 F2
East Kilbride G75 180 C4
Fleming Rd Bellshill ML4 142 A4
Bishopton PA7 72 A2
Cumbernauld G67 61 F1
Houston PA6 91 D1
Fleming St Glasgow G31 118 A3
Kilmarnock KA1 227 F3
Paisley PA3 113 F4
Fleming Terr KA12 219 D3
Fleming Way Hamilton ML3 161 F2
15 Larkhall ML9 185 E1
Flemington Ind Est G72 139 F2
Flemington St G21 97 F2
Flenders Ave G76 157 E3
Flenders Rd G76 157 E3
Fletcher Ave PA19 44 C4
Fleurs Ave G41 116 A2
Fleurs Rd G41 116 A2
Flinders Pl G75 180 A4
Flint Cres FK7 12 B4
Flint Mill La PA15 46 A1
Flloyd St ML5 121 F4
Floors Rd G76 157 E1
Floors St PA5 111 F1
Floorsburn Cres PA5 111 F1
Flora Gdns G64 78 B1
Florence Dr Glasgow G46 136 B1
Kilmacolm PA13 89 D4
Florence Gdns G73 138 B2
Florence St Glasgow G5 117 E3
Greenock PA16 45 D2
Florida Ave G42 137 D4
Florida Cres G42 137 D4
Florida Dr G42 137 D4
Florida Gdns G69 120 A3
Florida Sq G42 137 D4
Florida St G42 137 D4
Florish Rd PA8 93 F4
Flowerdale Pl G53 135 D2
Flowerhill Ind Est ML6 123 D4
Flowerhill St ML6 123 D4
Flures Ave PA8 93 F4
Flures Cres PA8 93 F4
Flures Dr PA8 93 F4
Flures Pl PA8 93 F4
Fochabers Dr G52 115 E3
Fogo Pl G20 96 B3
Foinavon Rd ML3 183 F2
Foot Of Lone Rd ML11 214 A3
Footfield Rd ML4 141 F2
Forbes Cres FK5 23 E1
Forbes Ct FK2 42 C3
Forbes Dr Ayr KA8 236 B2
3 Glasgow G40 117 F3
Motherwell ML1 142 B1
Forbes Pl Kilmarnock KA3 223 D1
Paisley PA1 113 F2
Forbes Rd FK1 42 B2
Forbes St Alloa FK10 9 F3
Glasgow G40 117 F3
Forbes Wlk KA3 223 D1
Ford Ave KA11 225 E4
Ford Rd Bonnybridge FK4 40 A3
Glasgow G12 96 B2
Newton Mearns G77 156 B2
Fordbank Prim Sch PA5 131 E4
Forde Cres KA20 206 C1
Fordneuk St G40 118 A3
Fordoun St G34 120 B4
Fordyce Ct G77 156 B2
Fordyce St G11 96 B1
Fore Row ML3 162 C2
Fore St Glasgow G14 95 E2
Port Glasgow PA14 47 E1
Forebraes FK10 10 A4
Foregate Sq KA1 222 C1
Foregate The KA1 222 C1
Forehill Prim Sch KA7 239 E3
Forehill Rd KA7 239 E3
Forehouse Rd PA10 110 B2
Foremount Terrace La
18 G12 96 B2
Forest Ave ML3 183 E3
Forest Dr Bearsden G61 75 D4
Bellshill ML4 142 B2
Bothwell G71 141 D2
Forest Gdns G66 79 D2
Forest Gr KA3 223 D3
Forest Kirk ML8 202 A4
Forest La ML3 183 E3
Forest Pk ML2 165 E3
Forest Pl Crossford ML8 201 D1
Kirkintilloch G66 79 D2
Paisley PA2 113 F1
Forest Rd Cumbernauld G67 62 C3
Larkhall ML9 185 D2
Forest View G67 62 B2
Forest Walks G65 57 D3
Forest Way KA7 239 E3
Forester Gr FK10 4 C1
Forestfield Gdns ML6 105 D2
Foresthall Cres G21 98 A2
Foresthall Dr G21 98 A2
Forfar Ave G52 115 D2
Forfar Cres G64 98 B4
Forfar Rd PA16 44 C2
Forgan Gdns G64 98 B4
Forge Dr ML5 121 F4
Forge Pl G21 98 A1
Forge Rd Airdrie ML6 123 F3
Ayr KA8 236 A2
Forge Sh Ctr The G31 118 B3
Forge St Glasgow G21 98 A1
Kilmarnock KA1 222 C1
Forge Vennal KA13 207 E2
Forgewood Path ML6 123 F3
Forgewood Rd ML1 142 B1
Forglen Cres FK9 2 A3
Forglen Rd FK9 2 A3
Forglen St G34 100 A1
Formby Dr G23 76 B1
Forres Ave G46 136 B2
Forres Cres ML4 142 A3
Forres Gate G46 136 B1
Forres Quadrant ML2 165 D3
Forres St Blantyre G72 161 E3
Glasgow G23 76 C1
Forrest Gate ML3 162 A1
Forrest Pl ML7 127 F3
Forrest Rd
Forrestfield ML6 106 A1
Lanark ML11 215 D3
Salsburgh ML7 126 A3
Stirling FK8 2 A1
Forrest St Airdrie ML6 123 E4
Blantyre G72 161 F4
Glasgow G40 118 A3
Shotts ML7 146 C3
Forrester Ct 1 G64 97 F4
Forrester Pl FK2 14 B2
Forrestfield Cres G77 156 C3
Forrestfield Gdns G77 156 C3
Forrestfield Rd ML6 106 A3
Forrestfield St G21 98 A1
Forrestlea Rd ML8 202 A4
Forsa Ct G75 180 B2
Forsyth Ct ML11 215 E2
Forsyth Gr PA16 45 E3
Forsyth St Airdrie ML6 123 D4
Greenock PA16 45 E3
Fort Matilda Pl PA16 45 D4
Fort Matilda Sta PA16 45 D4
Fort Matilda Terr PA16 45 D4
Fort St Ayr KA7 235 F1
Motherwell ML1 163 E4
Fortacre Pl KA11 220 A3
Forteviot Ave G69 120 B3
Forteviot Pl G69 120 B3
Forth Ave Larbert FK5 23 D2
Paisley PA2 112 C1
Forth Cres Alloa FK10 10 B3
East Kilbride G75 179 F4
Stirling FK8 7 E4
Forth Ct East Kilbride G75 179 F4
Stirling FK8 2 A1
Forth Gr G75 179 F4
Forth Pk FK9 2 A3
Forth Pl Johnstone PA5 131 E4
Kilmarnock KA1 228 A3
Larkhall ML9 199 D4
Forth Rd Bearsden G61 75 E1
Torrance G64 78 A4
Forth St Cambus FK10 9 D4
Clydebank G81 94 B4
Fallin FK7 8 B2
Glasgow G41 116 C2
Greenock PA16 45 D3
Stirling FK8 2 A1
Forth Terr ML3 183 D4
Forth View FK8 2 A1
Forthbank Ind Est FK10 10 A2
Forthbank
(Stirling Albion FC) FK7 7 F4
Forthvale FK11 4 A3
Forthview FK7 7 F1
Forthview Ct FK1 41 F1
Forties Cres G46 136 A3
Forties Gdns G46 136 A3
Forties Rd PA6 111 E4
Forties Way G46 136 A3
Fortieth Ave G75 180 C3
Fortingale Ave G12 96 B3
Fortingale Pl G12 96 B3
Fortingall Rd G72 161 F3
Fortissat Ave ML7 146 B3
Fortisset Rd ML7 126 A1
Fortrose St G11 96 A1
Fortuna Ct FK1 42 B2
Forum Sh Ctr The PA15 45 F3
Fossil Gr G66 59 D1
Foswell Pl G15 74 C3
Fotheringay La G41 116 B1
Fotheringay Rd G41 116 C1
Fothringham Rd KA8 239 D4
Foulburn Rd ML7 145 E1
Foulis La G13 95 F3
Foulis St G13 95 F3
Foulsykes Rd ML2 165 F2
Foundry La G78 134 B1
Foundry Loan FK5 23 D1
Foundry Rd
Bonnybridge FK4 40 A3
Cleland ML1 144 B1
Shotts ML7 146 C2
Foundry St FK2 42 A4
Foundry Wynd KA13 207 E2
Fountain Ave PA4 93 D2
Fountain Bsns Ctr The
ML5 122 A3
Fountain Cres PA4 93 E3
Fountain Dr PA4 93 E2
Fountain Rd FK9 2 A4
Fountainwell Ave G21 97 E2
Fountainwell Dr G21 97 E1
Fountainwell Pl G21 97 E2
Fountainwell Rd G21 97 E1
Fountainwell Sq G21 97 F1
Fountainwell Terr G21 97 F1
Four Acres Dr KA3 222 A4
Four Windings PA6 91 D1
Fourth Ave Dumbarton G82 50 B1
Kirkintilloch G66 79 E1
Millerston G33 99 D3
Renfrew PA4 94 B1
Fourth Gdns G41 116 A2
Fourth Rd G72 161 F3
Fourth St G71 120 C1
Fowlds St KA1 227 F4
Fowlis Dr G77 156 B3
Fox Gr ML1 163 D4
Fox St Glasgow G1 240 C1
Greenock PA16 45 E4
Foxbar Cres PA2 132 C4
Foxbar Dr Glasgow G13 95 D3
Paisley PA2 132 C4
Foxbar Rd PA2 132 C4
Foxes Gr G66 79 F3
Foxglove Pl Ayr KA7 239 E2
Glasgow G53 135 D2
Foxhills Pl G23 76 C1
Foxley St G32 119 E1
Foyers Terr G21 98 A2
Franchi Dr FK5 23 F3
Francis St 7 G5 117 D2
Frankfield Rd G33 99 F3
Frankfield St G33 98 C1
Frankfort St G41 116 C1
Franklin Pl G75 159 D1
Franklin Rd KA21 205 F1
Franklin St G40 117 F2
Fraser Ave Bishopton PA7 72 A2
Dumbarton G82 50 B2
Johnstone PA5 112 A1
Newton Mearns G77 156 C3
Rutherglen G73 138 B4
Troon KA10 229 E3
Fraser Cres ML3 162 A1
Fraser Ct ML6 123 F4
Fraser Gdns G66 79 D4
Fraser Pl FK9 2 A2
Fraser St Cambuslang G72 138 C3
Cleland ML1 144 A1
Fraser Wlk KA3 223 E2
Frazer Ave G84 16 A2
Frazer St G40 118 A3
Frederick St ML5 121 F4
Freeland Cres G53 135 D3
Freeland Ct G53 135 E3
Freeland Dr
Bridge Of W PA11 90 B1
Glasgow G53 135 D3
Inchinnan PA4 93 E3
Freeland La 9 G75 180 C4
Freeland Pl G66 79 E4
Freeland Rd PA8 93 D4
Freelands Cres G60 73 E3
Freelands Ct G81 73 E2
Freelands Rd G60 73 E2
Freesia Ct ML1 163 F3
French St Clydebank G81 73 F2
Glasgow G40 117 F2
Renfrew PA4 94 A1
Wishaw ML2 165 D2
Freuchie St G34 120 A4
Frew Terr KA12 219 E3
Friar Ave G64 78 A2
Friar's Dene ML11 214 C2
Friar's La ML11 214 C2
Friar's Wynd ML11 214 C2
Friars Croft Irvine KA12 219 D1
Kirkintilloch G66 79 F4
Friars Lawn KA13 207 E2
Friars Pl G13 95 E4
Friars St FK8 7 D4
Friars Way ML6 123 E2
Friarscourt Ave G13 95 E4
Friarscourt Rd G69 80 A1
Friarsfield Rd ML11 214 C2
Friarton Rd G43 136 C3
Friendship Gdns FK2 24 B2
Friendship Way PA4 94 B1
Frobisher Ave FK1 41 F2
Frobisher Pl G84 17 D1
Frood St ML1 142 B1
Fruin Ave G77 156 C3
Fruin Dr ML2 165 F2
Fruin Rd G15 74 C1
Fruin Rise ML3 161 F1
Fruin St G22 97 E2
Fudstone Dr KA25 170 A4
Fulbar Ave PA4 94 B2
Fulbar Cres PA2 112 C1
Fulbar Ct PA4 94 B2
Fulbar Gdns PA2 112 C1
Fulbar La PA4 94 B2
Fulbar Rd Glasgow G51 115 E4
Paisley PA2 112 C2
Fulbar St PA4 94 B2
Fullarton Ave
Dundonald KA2 225 F1
Glasgow G32 119 D1
Fullarton Cres KA10 229 F1
Fullarton Dr KA10 229 F1
Fullarton La G32 119 D1
Fullarton Pl
Coatbridge ML5 121 F2
Stevenston KA20 217 E4
Troon KA10 230 A2
Fullarton Rd
Cumbernauld G68 61 F3
Glasgow G32 119 D1
Prestwick KA9 236 B3
Fullarton Rdbt KA12 219 D1
Fullarton St Ayr KA7 238 C4
Coatbridge ML5 121 F2
Irvine KA12 219 D1
Kilmarnock KA1 222 C1
Fullers Gate G81 74 B4
Fullerton Ctyd KA10 230 A1
Fullerton Dr KA23 190 A2

Fullerton La PA15 46 C2
Fullerton Sq KA22 205 E1
Fullerton St PA3 113 E4
Fullerton Terr PA3 113 F4
Fulmar Ct 4 G64 97 F4
Fulmar Pk G74 159 E2
Fulmar Pl PA5 131 E3
Fulshaw Cres KA8 236 C1
Fulshaw Ct KA9 236 B3
Fulton Cres PA10 111 D2
Fulton Dr PA6 111 F4
Fulton Gdns PA6 111 F4
Fulton Rd G62 55 D1
Fulton St G13 95 F4
Fulton's La KA3 222 C1
Fulwood Ave Glasgow G13 94 C4
  Linwood PA3 112 A3
Fulwood Pk Ind Est ML3 162 A2
Fulwood Pl G13 94 C4
Furlongs The ML3 162 C3
Furnace Ct KA1 228 C3
Furnace Rd ML3 183 F2
Fyfe Park Terr PA14 47 F1
Fyfe Shore Rd PA14 47 F1
Fyffe Park Rd PA14 47 F1
Fyne Ave ML4 141 F3
Fyne Cres ML9 184 C3
Fyne Ct ML3 162 A1
Fyne La ML7 146 C3
Fyne Way ML1 143 D3
Fyneart St ML2 165 F2
Fynloch Pl G81 73 F4
Fyvie Ave G43 136 A3
Fyvie Cres ML6 123 F3

Gaberston Ave FK10 10 B4
Gabriel St PA15 46 A1
Gadburn Sch G21 98 B3
Gadie Ave PA4 94 C1
Gadie St G33 118 B4
Gadloch Ave G66 79 E1
Gadloch Gdns G66 79 E2
Gadloch St G22 97 E3
Gadloch View G66 79 E1
Gadsburn Ct G21 98 B3
Gadshill St G21 97 F1
Gael St PA16 45 E2
Gagarin Terr KA13 207 F1
Gailes Pk G72 140 C1
Gailes Pl KA1 227 F2
Gailes Rd
  Cumbernauld G68 61 F3
  Irvine KA11 224 B2
  Troon KA10 229 E4
Gailes St G40 118 A2
Gain Rd G67, ML5 82 A1
Gain & Shankburn Rd
  G67 82 B1
Gainburn Cres G67 81 F3
Gainburn Ct G67 81 F3
Gainburn Gdns G67 81 F3
Gainburn Pl G67 81 F3
Gainburn View G67 82 A3
Gainford Pl KA3 222 C2
Gainside Rd ML5 101 E3
Gair Cres Carluke ML8 188 A2
  Wishaw ML2 165 D1
Gair Rd ML8 188 A3
Gair Wynd ML7 147 D2
Gairbraid Ave G20 96 B3
Gairbraid Ct G20 96 B3
Gairbraid Pl G20 96 B3
Gairbraid Terr G69 121 D3
Gairdoch Dr FK2 24 B2
Gairdoch St FK2 42 A4
Gairloch Gdns G66 59 D1
Gaitskell Ave G83 27 E4
Gala Ave PA4 94 C1
Gala Cres ML2 165 D3
Gala St G33 98 C1
Galbraith Cres ML8 187 D3
Galbraith Dr Glasgow G51 115 F4
  Milngavie G62 75 F4
Galdenoch St G33 99 D1
Gallacher Ave PA2 113 D1
Gallacher Cres G83 19 F1
Gallacher Ct PA1 113 E3
Gallacher Way G82 27 E1
Gallahill Ave PA14 69 D4
Gallamuir Dr FK7 12 B2
Gallamuir Rd FK7 12 B3
Gallan Ave G23 76 C1
Gallion Wlk KA1 227 F4
Galloway Ave Ayr KA8 236 B1
  Hamilton ML3 183 E4
Galloway Ct Falkirk FK1 42 A3
  Irvine KA11 220 A3
Galloway Dr Hamilton ML3 183 E3
  Rutherglen G73 138 A2
Galloway Pl KA21 216 C4
Galloway Rd Airdrie ML6 122 C2
  East Kilbride G74 160 B2
Galloway St Falkirk FK1 42 A3
  Glasgow G21 97 F3
Gallowflat St G73 138 A4
Gallowgate G1, G4, G40 117 F3
Gallowhill ML9 185 D1
Gallowhill Ave G66 79 E3
Gallowhill Gr G66 79 E4
Gallowhill Prim Sch PA3 114 A4
Gallowhill Rd
  Carmunnock G76 158 C4
  Kirkintilloch G66 79 E3
  Lanark ML11 215 D2
  Paisley PA3 114 A3
Galrigside Rd KA1 227 E4
Galston Ave G77 157 D3
Galston Ct ML3 183 F4
Galston Rd KA1 228 C3
Galston Sq KA22 205 E1
Galston St G53 134 C3
Galt Ave KA12 219 E2
Galt Pl G75 180 B4
Galt St PA15 46 B2
Gambeson Cres FK7 7 E2
Gameshill View KA3 211 F4
Gamrie Dr G53 135 D4
Gamrie Gdns G53 135 D4
Gamrie Rd G53 135 D4
Gannochy Dr G64 78 B1
Gantock Cres G33 119 D4
Ganton Ct KA13 207 D2
Garden Ct KA8 235 F1
Garden Pl KA10 229 D2
Garden Square La KA13 207 F2
Garden Square Wlk ML6 122 B4
Garden St Ayr KA8 235 F1
  Falkirk FK1 42 B3
  Kilmarnock KA3 222 C1
Garden Terr FK1 42 B3
Garden Veteran's Cotts
  PA8 72 C3
Gardenhall G75 179 F4
Gardenhall Ct G75 179 F4
Gardenside ML4 142 A2
Gardenside Ave
  Glasgow G32 139 D4
  Uddingston G71 140 C3
Gardenside Cres G32 139 D4
Gardenside Pl G32 139 D4
Gardenside Rd ML3 162 B1
Gardenside St G71 140 C3
Gardiner St KA9 236 B4
Gardner Gr G71 141 D4
Gardner St G11 96 A1
Gardrum Gdns FK1 66 B4
Gardrum Pl KA3 222 C2
Gardyne St G34 100 A1
Gare Rd G84 15 D2
Garelet Pl KA11 220 A1
Gareloch Ave PA2 113 D1
Gareloch Cl PA15 46 A1
Gareloch Cres ML6 102 C1
Gareloch La PA14 68 B4
Gareloch Rd
  Greenock PA15 46 A2
  Port Glasgow PA14 68 C4
  Rhu G84 15 F2
Garfield Ave ML4 142 B3
Garfield Dr ML4 142 B2
Garfield St G31 118 A3
Garforth Rd G69 119 F2
Gargieston Prim Sch KA2 227 E3
Gargrave Ave G69 119 F2
Garion Dr G13 95 D3
Garlieston Rd G33 119 F3
Garmouth Ct 3 G51 116 A4
Garmouth Gdns 4 G51 116 A4
Garmouth St G51 115 F4
Garnet St G3 240 B4
Garnetbank Prim Sch G3 240 B4
Garnethill St G3 240 B4
Garngaber Ave G66 79 E3
Garngaber Ct G66 79 F3
Garngrew Rd FK4 38 C2
Garnhall Farm Rd G68 62 C4
Garnie Ave PA8 93 E4
Garnie La PA8 93 E4
Garnie Oval PA8 73 E1
Garnie Pl PA8 73 E1
Garnieland Rd PA8 73 E1
Garnkirk La G33 99 F3
Garnock Acad KA25 149 D1
Garnock Ct Irvine KA12 219 E1
  Kilbirnie KA25 149 D1
Garnock Pk G74 160 A1
Garnock Rd
  Kilmarnock KA1 228 A3
  Stevenston KA20 217 E4
Garnock St Dalry KA24 191 E4
  Glasgow G21 97 F1
  Kilbirnie KA25 149 D1
Garnock View KA13 207 F2
Garnockside KA14 170 A3
Garpel Way PA12 129 D1
Garrallan KA13 207 E1
Garraway Rd G84 16 C1
Garrel Gr G65 36 B1
Garrell Ave G65 36 B1
Garrell Pl G65 60 B4
Garrell Rd G65 60 B4
Garrell Way
  Cumbernauld G67 61 F1
  Kilsyth G65 60 B4
Garrier Pl KA1 222 B1
Garrier Rd KA11 220 C1
Garrioch Cres 3 G20 96 B3
Garrioch Dr G20 96 B3
Garrioch Gate 17 G20 96 B3
Garrioch Quadrant 4 G20 96 B3
Garrioch Rd G20 96 B3
Garriochmill Rd G20 96 C2
Garrion Bsns Pk ML2 186 A4
Garrion Pl ML9 185 F1
Garrion St ML2 186 B3
Garrison Pl FK1 42 A3
Garrowhill Dr G69 119 F3
Garrowhill Halt G33 119 F3
Garrowhill Prim Sch G69 120 A3
Garry Ave G61 76 A1
Garry Dr PA2 113 D1
Garry Pl Falkirk FK1 42 B1
  Kilmarnock KA1 228 A3
  Troon KA10 229 F3
Garry St G44 137 D4
Garry Way ML7 146 C3
Garryhorn KA9 236 B3
Garscadden Prim Sch G13 94 C4
Garscadden Rd G15 75 D1
Garscadden Rd S
  Glasgow G15 94 C4
  Glasgow G13 95 D4
Garscadden Sta G14 95 D3
Garscadden View G81 74 B2
Garscube Cross G4 97 D1
Garscube Rd G4, G20 97 D1
Garshake Ave G82 50 B3
Garshake Rd G82 50 B3
Garshake Terr G82 50 B3
Gartartan Rd PA1 114 C3
Gartcarron Hill G68 61 E2
Gartcloss Rd ML5 101 E1
Gartclush Gdns FK7 11 F4
Gartconnell Dr G61 75 F3
Gartconnell Gdns G61 75 F3
Gartconnell Rd G61 75 F3
Gartconner Ave G66 80 A4
Gartconner Prim Sch G66 80 A4
Gartcosh Prim Sch G69 100 C2
Gartcosh Rd ML5 101 D1
Gartcosh Wlk ML4 141 F3
Gartcows Ave FK1 42 A2
Gartcows Cres FK1 42 A2
Gartcows Dr FK1 42 A2
Gartcows Gdns FK1 41 F2
Gartcows Pl FK1 42 A2
Gartcows Rd FK1 42 A2
Gartcraig Rd G33 118 C4
Garten Dr ML7 147 D2
Gartferry Ave G69 80 C1
Gartferry Rd G69 80 C1
Gartferry St G21 98 A2
Gartfield St ML6 123 D3
Gartgill Rd ML5 101 F1
Garth St G1 241 D2
Garthamloch
  Prim Sch G33 99 E1
Garthamlock Rd G33 99 F1
Garthamlock Sec Sch G34 99 F1
Garthill Gdns FK1 42 A2
Garthill La FK1 42 A2
Garthland Dr
  Ardrossan KA22 205 E2
  Glasgow G31 118 A4
Garthland La PA1 113 F3
Gartlea Ave ML6 123 D4
Gartlea Rd ML6 123 D4
Gartleahill ML6 123 D3
Gartliston Rd ML5 101 F2
Gartliston Terr G69 121 D3
Gartloch Rd G69, G33 100 B2
Gartly St G44 136 C2
Gartmore Gdns G71 140 C4
Gartmore La G69 81 D1
Gartmore Rd PA1 114 B2
Gartmore Terr G72 138 C2
Gartmorn Rd FK10 5 E1
Gartnavel General Hospl
  G12 96 A2
Gartnavel Royal Hospl G12 96 A2
Gartness Dr ML6 123 F3
Gartness Rd ML6 124 A2
Gartocher Dr G32 119 E3
Gartocher Rd G32 119 E3
Gartocher Terr G32 119 E3
Gartons Rd G21 98 B2
Gartsherrie Ave ML5 101 F3
Gartsherrie Ind Est ML5 101 F1
Gartsherrie Prim Sch
  ML5 121 F4
Gartsherrie Rd ML5 121 F4
Gartshore Cres G65 59 F1
Gartshore Gdns G68 60 C1
Garturk St Coatbridge ML5 122 A2
  Glasgow G42 117 D1
Garvald Ct G40 118 A2
Garvald La FK6 21 E1
Garvald Rd FK6 39 E4
Garvald St Glasgow G40 118 A2
  Greenock PA15 46 B2
Garvally Cres FK10 10 A4
Garve Ave G44 137 D3
Garvel Cres G33 119 F3
Garvel Dr PA15 45 E2
Garvel Pl G62 54 B1
Garvel Rd Glasgow G33 119 F3
  Milngavie G62 54 C1
Garvel Sch for the Deaf
  PA16 44 C3
Garven Ct KA1 228 A4
Garven Rd KA20 217 F3
Garvie Ave PA19 44 C3
Garvin Lea ML4 142 A4
Garvock Dr Glasgow G43 136 A3
  Greenock PA15 45 E2
Garwhitter Dr G62 55 D1
Gas St PA5 112 A2
Gascoyne G75 180 B4
Gask House Sch G64 97 F4
Gask Pl G13 94 C4
Gaskin Path G33 99 F3
Gasworks Rd ML8 187 E2
Gatehead Rd KA2 221 F1
Gatehouse St G32 119 E2
Gates Rd PA12 129 E2
Gateshead Pl PA10 111 D2
Gateside KA11 219 F3
Gateside Ave
  Bonnybridge FK4 40 B3
  Cambuslang G72 139 E3
  Greenock PA16 45 D2
  Kilsyth G65 60 A4
Gateside Cres
  Airdrie ML6 123 D4
  Barrhead G78 134 A1
Gateside Gdns PA16 45 D2
Gateside Gr PA16 45 D2
Gateside Pk G65 60 A4
Gateside Pl KA1 227 F2
Gateside Prim Sch KA15 171 F4
Gateside Rd
  Barrhead G78 134 A1
  Stirling FK7 7 D2
  Wishaw ML2 164 C2
Gateside Sch for the Deaf
  PA2 133 E4
Gateside St Glasgow G31 118 A3
  Hamilton ML3 162 C2
  West Kilbride KA23 190 B3
Gateway The G74 160 A2
Gaughan Quadrant ML1 163 E3
Gauldry Ave G52 115 E2
Gauze St PA1 113 F3
Gavell Rd G65 60 A4
Gavin Hamilton Ct KA7 239 E3
Gavin St ML1 163 F3
Gavin's Mill Rd G62 55 D1
Gavinburn Gdns G60 73 D4
Gavinburn Pl G60 73 D4
Gavinburn Sch G60 72 C4
Gavinburn St G60 73 D4
Gavins Rd Alloa FK10 4 C1
  Clydebank G81 74 A3
Gavinton St G44 136 C3
Gayne Dr ML5 101 E3
Gean Ct G67 62 C2
Gean Rd FK10 9 F4
Gearholm Rd KA7 238 B2
Geary St G23 76 B1
Geddes Hill G74 160 A2
Geddes Rd G21 98 B4
Geelong Gdns G65 33 E1
Geils Ave G82 50 B1
Geils Quadrant G82 50 B2
Geilsland Rd KA15 171 E4
Geilsland Residential Sch
  KA15 171 E4
Geilston Pk G82 48 A4
Geirston Rd KA25 148 C1
Gelston St G32 119 D2
Gemini Gr ML1 143 D3
Gemmel Pl G77 156 B2
Gemmell Cres KA8 236 B1
Gemmell Way ML9 198 C1
General Roy Way ML8 202 B4
Generals Gate G71 140 C3
Gentle Row G81 73 F3
George Aitken Ct KA22 205 E2
George Ave G81 74 B2
George Cres G81 74 B2
George Ct ML3 162 A3
George Gray St G73 138 B4
George La PA1 113 F2
George Mann Terr G73 138 A2
George Pl PA1 113 F2
George Rd PA19 44 C3
George Reith Ave G12 95 F3
George Sq Ayr KA8 236 A1
  Glasgow G2 241 D2
  Greenock PA15 45 F3
George St Airdrie ML6 122 C4
  Alexandria G83 27 F2
  Alva FK12 5 D3
  Ayr KA8 236 A1
  Barrhead G78 134 A2
  Chapelhall ML6 123 E2
  Falkirk FK2 42 A3
  Glasgow G1 241 E2
  Glasgow, Biallieston G69 120 A2
  Hamilton ML3 162 A3
  Helensburgh G84 16 C1
  Howwood PA9 130 C3
  Johnstone PA5 111 F2
  Larbert FK5 23 E2
  Laurieston FK2 42 C2
  Motherwell ML1 163 F2
  Motherwell, New Stevenston
  ML1 143 D2
  Paisley PA1 113 E2
  Stevenston KA20 217 E4
George Street La G83 27 F2
George Terr KA12 219 E2
George Way 8 ML9 185 D2
George's Ave KA8 236 A2
Gerald Terr FK5 23 F2
Gerard Pl ML4 142 A4
Gertrude Pl G78 134 A1
Ghillies La ML1 142 B1
Gibb St Chapelhall ML6 123 E1
  Cleland ML1 144 A1
Gibbdun Pl FK6 39 F4
Gibbon Cres G74 160 B2
Gibbshill Pl ML7 127 E3
Gibshill Rd PA15 46 C1
Gibson Ave G82 50 A2
Gibson Cres PA5 111 F1
Gibson La PA13 69 E1
Gibson Quadrant ML1 142 B1
Gibson Rd PA4 94 A1
Gibson St Dumbarton G82 50 A2
  Glasgow G4 241 F1
  Glasgow, Kelvingrove G12 96 C1
  Greenock PA15 46 C1
  Kilmarnock KA1 222 B1
  Salsburgh ML7 125 D1
Gibsongray St FK2 42 A4
Giffen Rd KA21 217 D4
Giffnock Park Ave G46 136 B2
Giffnock Prim Sch G46 136 B1
Giffnock Sta G46 136 B2
Gifford Dr G52 115 D3
Gifford Wynd PA2 112 C1
Gigha Cres KA11 220 A1
Gigha Gdns ML8 202 A4
Gigha La KA11 220 A1
Gigha Pl KA11 220 A1
Gigha Quadrant ML2 164 C1
Gigha Terr KA11 220 A1
Gigha Wynd KA11 220 A1
Gilbert St G3 116 B4
Gilbertfield Path G33 99 D1
Gilbertfield Pl G33 99 D1
Gilbertfield Rd G72 139 F2
Gilbertfield St G33 99 D1
Gilburn Pl ML7 146 C2
Gilchrist Dr FK1 41 F2
Gilchrist St ML5 122 A4
Gilchrist Way ML2 165 E1
Gilderdale G74 159 E1
Gilfillan Ave KA21 206 A1
Gilfillan Pl Falkirk FK2 24 B1
  Overtown ML2 186 B4
Gilfillan Way PA2 132 C4
Gilhill St G20 96 B4
Gill Pk FK6 21 F1
Gill Rd ML2 186 B3
Gillbank Ave ML8 187 E1
Gillbank La 10 ML9 185 E1
Gillburn Rd PA13 89 E4
Gillburn St ML2 186 B3
Gillespie Dr G84 16 B2
Gillespie Pl FK7 7 D1
Gillespie Terr FK7 12 B1
Gillies Cres G74 160 B3
Gillies Ct ML6 123 F4
Gillies Dr FK7 7 E2
Gillies Hill FK7 6 B3
Gillies La G69 120 B2
Gillies St KA10 229 E2
Gillsburn Gdns KA3 223 D1
Gilmartin Rd PA3 111 F3
Gilmerton St G32 119 D2
Gilmour Ave
  Clydebank G81 74 A3
  Thorntonhall G74 158 A1
Gilmour Cres
  Eaglesham G76 178 C3
  Rutherglen G73 137 F4
Gilmour Dr ML3 161 F1
Gilmour Pl Bellshill ML4 141 F3
  Coatbridge ML5 121 F4
  1 Glasgow G5 117 E2
Gilmour St Alexandria G83 27 E3
  Clydebank G81 74 B2
  Eaglesham G76 178 C3
  Greenock PA15 46 B1
  Kilmarnock KA1 228 A4
  Paisley PA1 113 F3
  Stewarton KA3 195 F1
Gilmourton Cres G77 156 B2
Gilroy Cl ML11 215 E3
Gilsay Ct FK1 42 B1
Gilshochill Sta G23 96 C4
Gimmerscroft Cres ML6 123 F3
Girdle Gate KA11 219 F3
Girdle Toll KA11 220 A3
Girthon St G32 119 E2
Girvan St G33 118 B4
Glade The ML9 185 D1
Gladney Ave G13 94 C4
Gladsmuir Rd G52 115 D3
Gladstone Ave
  Barrhead G78 134 A1
  Johnstone PA5 131 E4
Gladstone Ct ML3 162 A3
Gladstone Pl FK8 7 D3
Gladstone Rd
  Saltcoats KA21 217 D4
  Stenhousemuir FK5 23 E2
Gladstone St
  Bellshill ML4 142 A3
  Clydebank G81 73 F1
  11 Glasgow G4 97 D1
Glaive Ave FK7 7 E2
Glaive Rd G13 75 E1
Glamis Ave Carluke ML8 187 F1
  East Kilbride G74 159 F2
  Elderslie PA5 112 A1
  Newton Mearns G77 156 C3
Glamis Dr PA16 45 D3
Glamis Gdns G64 78 A2
Glamis Pl PA16 45 D3
Glamis Rd G31 118 B2
Glanderston Ave
  Barrhead G78 134 C1
  Newton Mearns G77 156 A3
Glanderston Ct G13 95 D4
Glanderston Dr G13 95 D4
Glanderston Gate G77 156 A3
Glanderston Rd G77 155 E3
Glasgow Acad G12 96 C2
Glasgow Bot Gdns G12 96 B2
Glasgow Caledonian Univ
  G4 241 D4
Glasgow Caledonian
  Univ Park Campus G3 96 C1
Glasgow Coll of
  Building & Printing G5 117 E3
Glasgow Coll of
  Building & Printing
  (Annexe) G31 118 C3
Glasgow Coll of
  Building & Printing
  (David Dale Bldg) G40 117 F3
Glasgow Coll of
  Building & Printing
  (Bridgeton Annexe) G40 117 F3
Glasgow Dental Hospl G2 240 B3

Glenpark Ave
Glasgow G46 ... 136 A1
Prestwick KA9 ... 236 B3
Glenpark Dr PA14 ... 47 D1
Glenpark Gdns G72 ... 138 C4
Glenpark Pl KA7 ... 239 D2
Glenpark Rd PA12 ... 129 E2
Glenpark St Glasgow G31 ... 118 A3
Wishaw ML2 ... 165 D2
Glenpark Terr G72 ... 138 C4
Glenpath G82 ... 50 B2
Glenpatrick Rd PA5 ... 112 B1
Glenraith Path G33 ... 99 D2
Glenraith Rd G33 ... 99 D1
Glenraith Sq G33 ... 99 D2
Glenraith Wlk G33 ... 99 E2
Glenriddel Rd KA7 ... 239 D3
Glenriddet Ave KA25 ... 170 A4
Glenshee St G31 ... 118 B2
Glenshee Terr ML3 ... 183 D4
Glenshiel Ave PA2 ... 114 A1
Glenshira Ave PA2 ... 114 A1
Glenside Ave G53 ... 115 D1
Glenside Cres KA23 ... 190 B3
Glenside Dr G73 ... 138 C3
Glenside Gr KA23 ... 190 B3
Glenside Rd
Dumbarton G82 ... 50 B3
Port Glasgow PA14 ... 68 B4
Glenspean Pl ML5 ... 122 B3
Glenspean Sch G43 ... 136 B3
Glenspean St G43 ... 136 B3
Glentanar Pl G22 ... 97 D4
Glentanar Rd G22 ... 97 D4
Glentarbert Rd G73 ... 138 B2
Glentore Quadrant ML6 ... 103 D1
Glentrool Gdns
Glasgow G22 ... 97 E2
Moodiesburn G69 ... 81 D2
Glenturret St G32 ... 119 D2
Glentyan Ave PA10 ... 111 D2
Glentyan Dr G53 ... 135 D3
Glentyan Terr G53 ... 135 D4
Glentye Gdns FK1 ... 41 F1
Glenview Airdrie ML6 ... 123 E3
Denny FK6 ... 21 D2
Kirkintilloch G66 ... 79 E4
Larkhall ML9 ... 184 C2
Menstrie FK11 ... 4 A3
West Kilbride KA23 ... 190 B2
Glenview Ave Banknock FK4 ... 38 C2
Caldercruix ML6 ... 105 D2
Glenview Cres G69 ... 81 D2
Glenview Dr FK1 ... 41 F1
Glenview Pl G72 ... 140 B1
Glenview St ML6 ... 102 C2
Glenview Terr PA15 ... 45 E2
Glenville Ave G46 ... 136 A2
Glenville Gate G76 ... 158 A3
Glenville Terr G76 ... 158 A3
Glenward Ave G65 ... 57 F4
Glenwell St ML6 ... 102 C2
Glenwinnel Rd FK12 ... 4 C4
Glenwood Ave ML6 ... 123 E2
Glenwood Bsns Ctr G45 ... 137 F2
Glenwood Ct G14 ... 79 D3
Glenwood Dr G46 ... 135 F1
Glenwood Gdns G66 ... 79 D3
Glenwood Path G45 ... 137 F2
Glenwood Pl Glasgow G45 ... 137 F2
Kirkintilloch G66 ... 79 D3
Glenwood Rd G66 ... 79 D3
Glenyards Rd FK4 ... 40 A1
Glidden Ct ML2 ... 186 B4
Glorat Ave G65 ... 57 F4
Gloucester Ave
Clarkston G76 ... 157 E4
Rutherglen G73 ... 138 B3
Gloucester St G5 ... 117 D3
Glowrorum Dr FK6 ... 39 F4
Glynwed Ct FK2 ... 42 B4
Goatfell View KA10 ... 229 F4
Gockston Rd PA3 ... 113 E4
Goddard Pl ML2 ... 166 A3
Godfrey Ave FK6 ... 21 E1
Godfrey Cres FK5 ... 23 E1
Gogar Loan FK9 ... 3 E3
Gogar Pl Glasgow G33 ... 118 C4
Stirling FK7 ... 7 E1
Gogar St G33 ... 118 C4
Goil Ave ML4 ... 141 E3
Goil Way ML1 ... 143 D3
Goldberry Ave G14 ... 95 D3
Goldcraig Ct KA11 ... 220 A3
Goldenacre Pl ML6 ... 103 F2
Goldenberry Ave KA23 ... 190 B2
Goldenhill Prim Sch G81 ... 74 A3
Goldenlee View PA6 ... 111 D4
Goldie Pl KA20 ... 206 B1
Goldie Rd G71 ... 141 D2
Golf Ave Bellshill ML4 ... 142 A2
Stevenston KA20 ... 217 F3
Golf Course Rd Balmore G64 ... 77 F4
Bridge Of W PA11 ... 110 B4
Golf Cres KA10 ... 229 E1
Golf Ct G44 ... 136 C1
Golf Dr Clydebank G15 ... 74 C1
Paisley PA1 ... 114 B2
Port Glasgow PA14 ... 68 B4
Golf Gdns ML9 ... 185 E1
Golf Pl Bellshill ML4 ... 142 A2
Greenock PA16 ... 45 E4
Helensburgh G84 ... 17 D1
Irvine KA12 ... 219 D3
Troon KA10 ... 229 E1
Golf Rd Bishopton PA7 ... 72 A2
Clarkston G76 ... 157 E4
Gourock PA19 ... 44 B3
Rutherglen G73 ... 138 A2
Golf View G81 ... 73 F2
Golffields Rd KA12 ... 219 E1
Golfhill Dr Alexandria G83 ... 27 F3
Glasgow G31 ... 118 A4
Helensburgh G84 ... 16 C1
Golfhill Prim Sch G31 ... 117 F4
Golfhill Quadrant ML6 ... 103 D1
Golfhill Rd ML2 ... 164 C2
Golfhill Sch ML6 ... 102 C1
Golfloan KA3 ... 211 F4
Golfview G61 ... 75 E3
Golfview Dr ML5 ... 121 E4
Golfview Pl ML5 ... 121 E3
Golspie Ave ML6 ... 122 C2
Golspie St G51 ... 116 A4
Good Shepherd Sch G32 ... 118 C1
Goodview Gdns ML9 ... 185 E1
Goosecroft Rd FK8 ... 7 D4
Goosedubbs G1 ... 241 D1
Gooseholm Cres G82 ... 50 A3
Gooseholm Rd G82 ... 50 A3
Gopher Ave G71 ... 141 D4
Gorbals Cross
Glasgow G5 ... 117 E3
Larkhall ML9 ... 185 D2
Gorbals St G1, G5 ... 117 E3
Gordon Ave Bishopton PA7 ... 72 A2
Glasgow G69 ... 119 F3
Glasgow, Netherlee G44 ... 136 C1
Paisley G52 ... 114 C4
Gordon Cres
Bridge Of A FK9 ... 2 A4
Newton Mearns G77 ... 156 C3
Stirling FK8 ... 1 C1
Gordon Ct ML6 ... 123 F4
Gordon Dr Alloa FK10 ... 10 B4
East Kilbride G74 ... 160 A2
Glasgow G44 ... 136 C2
Gordon La G1 ... 240 C2
Gordon Pl Bellshill ML4 ... 141 F1
Falkirk FK1 ... 41 F3
Gordon Rd Glasgow G44 ... 136 C1
Hamilton ML3 ... 161 F2
Gordon St Ayr KA8 ... 236 A2
Glasgow G1 ... 240 C2
Greenock PA15 ... 45 F2
Paisley PA1 ... 113 F2
Gordon Terr Ayr KA8 ... 239 D4
Blantyre G72 ... 140 B1
Hamilton ML3 ... 161 F2
Gorebridge St G32 ... 118 C4
Goremire Rd ML8 ... 202 A4
Gorget Ave G13 ... 75 E1
Gorget Pl G13 ... 75 E1
Gorget Quadrant G13 ... 75 D1
Gorrie St FK6 ... 21 E1
Gorse Cres PA11 ... 110 C4
Gorse Pk KA7 ... 239 E2
Gorse Pl G71 ... 141 D4
Gorsehall St ML1 ... 144 A1
Gorsewood G64 ... 77 F1
Gorstan Pl G20 ... 96 B3
Gorstan St G23 ... 96 B4
Goschen Terr KA8 ... 236 A1
Gosford La G14 ... 95 D2
Gottries Rd KA12 ... 219 D1
Goudie St PA3 ... 113 E4
Gough St G33 ... 118 B4
Goukscroft Pk KA7 ... 238 B2
Gould St KA8 ... 236 B1
Gourlay G74 ... 160 B3
Gourlay Dr ML2 ... 186 B3
Gourlay St Glasgow G21 ... 97 E2
1 Glasgow, Springburn G21 ... 97 F2
Gourock High Sch PA19 ... 44 B4
Gourock Prim Sch PA19 ... 44 C4
Gourock St G5 ... 117 D2
Gourock Sta PA19 ... 44 C4
Govan Dr G83 ... 27 E3
Govan High Sch G51 ... 115 F4
Govan Rd Glasgow G51 ... 115 F4
Glasgow, Plantation G51 ... 116 B3
Govan Underground Sta
G51 ... 116 A4
Govanhill St G42 ... 117 D1
Gowan Ave FK2 ... 42 A3
Gowan Brae ML6 ... 105 D3
Gowan La FK2 ... 42 A3
Gowanbank Gdns PA5 ... 111 F1
Gowanbank Prim Sch G53 ... 135 D3
Gowanbank Rd KA7 ... 239 D1
Gowanbrae G66 ... 79 E3
Gowanhill Gdns FK8 ... 1 C1
Gowanlea Ave G15 ... 75 D1
Gowanlea Dr
Glasgow G46 ... 136 B2
Slamannan FK1 ... 86 A3
Gowanlea Terr G71 ... 141 D4
Gowanside Pl ML8 ... 187 E1
Gower Pl KA7 ... 239 D2
Gower St G41 ... 116 B2
Gower Terr G41 ... 116 B3
Gowkhall Ave ML1 ... 143 F2
Gowkhouse Rd PA13 ... 89 F4
Goyle Ave G15 ... 75 E2
Grace Ave G69 ... 120 C3
Grace St G3 ... 240 A2
Gracie Cres FK7 ... 8 B2
Gradlon Pl FK1 ... 42 A2
Graeme Ct ML1 ... 142 B1
Graeme High Sch FK1 ... 42 B2
Graeme Pl FK1 ... 41 F2
Graffham Ave G46 ... 136 C2
Grafton Pl G1 ... 241 D3
Graham Ave
Cambuslang G72 ... 139 E3
Clydebank G81 ... 74 A2
East Kilbride G74 ... 159 F1
Hamilton ML3 ... 183 E4
Larbert FK5 ... 23 D2
Stirling FK9 ... 2 B2
Graham Cres G82 ... 48 A4
Graham Dr G62 ... 54 C1
Graham Pl Ashgill ML9 ... 185 F1
Helensburgh G84 ... 17 D1
Kilmarnock KA3 ... 223 E1
Kilsyth G65 ... 36 B1
Graham Rd Crossford ML8 ... 201 D1
Dumbarton G82 ... 49 E2
Graham Sq G31 ... 117 F3
Graham St Airdrie ML6 ... 123 D4
Barrhead G78 ... 134 A2
Bridge Of A FK9 ... 2 A4
Greenock PA16 ... 45 E3
Hamilton ML3 ... 162 C2
Johnstone PA5 ... 111 F1
Motherwell ML1 ... 143 D3
Wishaw ML2 ... 165 D1
Graham Terr Airth FK2 ... 14 B2
Bishopbriggs G64 ... 98 A4
Stewarton KA3 ... 195 E1
Grahamfield Pl KA15 ... 171 D4
Grahams Ave PA12 ... 129 E2
Grahams Rd FK2 ... 42 A3
Grahamsdyke Cres FK4 ... 40 A2
Grahamsdyke Rd
Bonnybridge FK4 ... 40 A2
Kirkintilloch G66 ... 58 C1
Grahamsdyke St FK2 ... 42 C2
Grahamshill Ave ML6 ... 123 E4
Grahamshill St ML6 ... 123 E4
Grahamston Ave KA14 ... 170 A4
Grahamston Cres PA2 ... 134 B4
Grahamston Ct PA2 ... 134 B4
Grahamston Pk G78 ... 134 A3
Grahamston Pl PA2 ... 134 B4
Grahamston Rd G78, PA2 ... 134 B3
Grahamston Sta FK1 ... 42 A3
Graigleith View FK10 ... 4 B2
Graignestock Pl 8 G40 ... 117 F3
Graignestock St G40 ... 117 F3
Graigside Pl G68 ... 81 F4
Grainger Rd G64 ... 78 B1
Grammar School Sq ML3 ... 162 C2
Grampian Ave PA2 ... 133 E4
Grampian Cres
Chapelhall ML6 ... 123 F1
Glasgow G32 ... 119 D2
Grampian Ct KA11 ... 220 A2
Grampian Dr G75 ... 180 A2
Grampian Pl G32 ... 119 D2
Grampian Rd
Kilmarnock KA1 ... 228 A2
Port Glasgow PA14 ... 69 D3
Stirling FK7 ... 6 C3
Wishaw ML2 ... 164 C2
Grampian St G32 ... 119 D2
Grampian Way
Barrhead G78 ... 134 B1
Bearsden G61 ... 75 D4
Cumbernauld G68 ... 61 D1
Gran St G81 ... 94 C4
Granary Rd FK2 ... 42 A4
Granary Sq FK2 ... 42 A4
Granby La G12 ... 96 B2
Grandtuly Dr G12 ... 96 B3
Grange Acad KA1 ... 227 E4
Grange Ave Ayr KA7 ... 239 D1
Falkirk FK2 ... 42 B3
Milngavie G62 ... 55 D1
Wishaw ML2 ... 164 C1
Grange Ct ML11 ... 214 C3
Grange Dr FK2 ... 42 B3
Grange Gdns Bothwell G71 ... 141 D1
Bridge Of A FK9 ... 2 B4
Grange Pl Alexandria G83 ... 27 F3
Kilmarnock KA1 ... 227 F4
Grange Rd Alloa FK10 ... 9 F3
Bearsden G61 ... 75 F3
Bridge Of A FK9 ... 2 B3
Glasgow G42 ... 137 D4
Stevenston KA20 ... 206 B1
Grange St Kilmarnock KA1 ... 227 F4
Motherwell ML1 ... 164 A2
Grange Terr KA1 ... 227 E4
Grangemouth Rd FK2 ... 42 C3
Grangemuir Rd KA9 ... 236 A4
Grangeneuk Gdns G68 ... 61 E1
Granger Rd Balloch G83 ... 27 F4
Kilmarnock KA1 ... 227 F3
Grangeview FK5 ... 23 F1
Grant Cres G82 ... 27 E1
Grant Ct Airdrie ML6 ... 123 F4
Hamilton ML3 ... 183 E4
Grant Pl Coatbridge ML5 ... 122 B2
Kilmarnock KA3 ... 223 E1
Stirling FK9 ... 2 A2
Grant St Alloa FK10 ... 9 F3
Glasgow G3 ... 240 A4
Greenock PA15 ... 46 B2
Helensburgh G84 ... 16 B1
Grantholm Ave ML1 ... 143 D3
Grantlea Gr G32 ... 119 E2
Grantlea Terr G32 ... 119 E2
Grantley Gdns G41 ... 136 B4
Grantley St G41 ... 136 B4
Grantoften Path G75 ... 180 C3
Granton St G5 ... 117 F1
Grantown Ave ML6 ... 123 F3
Grantown Gdns ML6 ... 102 C3
Grants Ave PA2 ... 113 E1
Grants Way PA2 ... 113 E1
Granville St Clydebank G81 ... 74 A2
Glasgow G3 ... 240 A3
Helensburgh G84 ... 16 C1
Grasmere G75 ... 179 F3
Grasmere Ct ML3 ... 183 E3
Grassyards Intc KA3 ... 223 E2
Grassyards Rd KA3 ... 223 E1
Grathellen Ct ML1 ... 164 A4
Gray Cres KA12 ... 224 B4
Gray Dr G61 ... 75 F2
Gray St Alexandria G83 ... 27 F3
Cleland ML1 ... 144 A1
Glasgow G3 ... 96 C1
Greenock PA15 ... 46 A2
Kirkintilloch G66 ... 80 A4
Larkhall ML9 ... 185 D2
Prestwick KA9 ... 236 B4
Shotts ML7 ... 147 D2
Gray's Cl ML11 ... 214 B2
Gray's Rd G71 ... 141 D3
Grayshill Rd G68 ... 81 F3
Graystale Rd FK7 ... 7 D2
Graystonelee Rd ML7 ... 146 B3
Graystones KA13 ... 207 F3
Great Dovehill G1, G4 ... 241 E1
Great George La 6 G12 ... 96 B2
Great George St G12 ... 96 B2
Great Hamilton St PA2 ... 113 F1
Great Kelvin La G12 ... 96 C1
Great Western Rd
Clydebank G15, G13 ... 74 B2
Glasgow G12 ... 96 B2
Great Western Terr 33
G12 ... 96 B2
Great Western Terrace La 32
G12 ... 96 B2
Green Ave KA12 ... 219 E2
Green Bank KA24 ... 191 E4
Green Bank Rd G68 ... 61 E1
Green Dale ML2 ... 165 E3
Green Farm Rd PA3 ... 112 A3
Green Gdns ML1 ... 144 B1
Green Loan ML1 ... 143 D2
Green Pl Bothwell G71 ... 141 D1
Calderbank ML6 ... 123 D1
Green Rd Paisley PA2 ... 113 D2
Rutherglen G73 ... 138 A4
Green St Ayr KA8 ... 235 F1
Bothwell G71 ... 141 D1
Clydebank G81 ... 74 A2
Glasgow G40 ... 117 F3
Saltcoats KA21 ... 216 C4
Stonehouse ML9 ... 198 C1
Green Street La KA8 ... 235 F1
Green Street La Bsns Pk
KA8 ... 235 F1
Green The Alva FK12 ... 5 D4
Glasgow G40 ... 117 F2
Greenacre Ct FK7 ... 7 F1
Greenacre Pl FK7 ... 7 F1
Greenacres
Ardrossan KA22 ... 205 F2
Motherwell ML1 ... 163 E3
Greenacres View ML1 ... 163 E3
Greenan Ave G42 ... 137 F4
Greenan Gr KA7 ... 238 A2
Greenan Pk KA7 ... 238 A2
Greenan Pl KA7 ... 238 B2
Greenan Rd Ayr KA7 ... 238 B2
Kilmarnock KA3 ... 228 A4
Greenan Terr KA9 ... 236 B4
Greenan Way KA7 ... 238 A2
Greenbank G72 ... 161 E4
Greenbank Ave G46 ... 157 D4
Greenbank Dr PA2 ... 133 E4
Greenbank Gdn G76 ... 157 E3
Greenbank Pl FK1 ... 41 E2
Greenbank Rd
Falkirk FK1 ... 41 E2
Irvine KA12 ... 219 E1
Wishaw ML2 ... 165 E2
Greenbank St G73 ... 138 A4
Greenbank Terr ML8 ... 187 F1
Greencraig Ave FK1 ... 66 B3
Greendyke St G1 ... 241 E1
Greenend Ave PA5 ... 111 E1
Greenend Pl G32 ... 119 E4
Greenend View ML4 ... 141 F3
Greenfarm Rd G77 ... 156 A3
Greenfaulds Cres G67 ... 83 D4
Greenfaulds Rd
Cumbernauld G67 ... 82 C4
Cumbernauld G67 ... 83 D4
Greenfaulds Sta G67 ... 82 C4
Greenfield Ave Ayr KA7 ... 238 B1
Glasgow G32 ... 119 D4
Greenfield Cres ML2 ... 165 E2
Greenfield Dr Irvine KA12 ... 219 E1
Wishaw ML2 ... 165 E2
Greenfield Pl G32 ... 119 D3
Greenfield Prim Sch G51 ... 115 F4
Greenfield Quadrant ML1 ... 143 F2
Greenfield Rd
Carluke ML8 ... 187 F2
Clarkston G76 ... 157 F3
Glasgow G32 ... 119 E3
Hamilton ML3 ... 162 A3
Greenfield St Alloa FK10 ... 10 A4
Bonnybridge FK4 ... 40 A3
Glasgow G51 ... 115 F4
Wishaw ML2 ... 165 E2
Greenfields High Sch G67 ... 82 B4
Greenfoot KA13 ... 207 F2
Greengairs Ave G51 ... 115 E4
Greengairs Prim Sch ML6 ... 83 F1
Greengairs Rd ML6 ... 83 F1
Greenhall Pl G72 ... 161 E3
Greenhead FK12 ... 5 D3
Greenhead Ave
Dumbarton G82 ... 50 A2
Stevenston KA20 ... 206 C1
Greenhead Gdns G82 ... 50 A2
Greenhead Rd
Bearsden G61 ... 75 F2
Dumbarton G82 ... 50 B2
Inchinnan PA4 ... 93 E3
Lennoxtown G65 ... 57 F4
Wishaw ML2 ... 165 E1
Greenhead St G40 ... 117 F2
Greenhill G64 ... 98 B4
Greenhill Ave
Gartcosh G69 ... 100 C4
Glasgow G46 ... 136 B1
Greenhill Bsns Pk PA3 ... 113 E3
Greenhill Cres
Elderslie PA3, PA5 ... 112 B1
Linwood PA3, PA5 ... 112 B3
Greenhill Ct
Bonnybridge FK4 ... 40 A1
Irvine KA11 ... 220 A3
Rutherglen G73 ... 138 A4
Greenhill Dr PA3 ... 112 B3
Greenhill Prim Sch ML5 ... 122 A4
Greenhill Rd
Blackridge EH48 ... 107 F2
Bonnybridge FK4 ... 40 A2
Cleland ML1 ... 144 C2
Paisley PA3 ... 113 E3
Rutherglen G73 ... 138 A4
Greenhill St G73 ... 138 A4
Greenhill Terr KA2 ... 221 F2
Greenhills Cres G75 ... 180 A3
Greenhills Prim Sch G75 ... 180 B3
Greenhills Rd G75 ... 180 B3
Greenholm Ave
Clarkston G76 ... 157 F4
Uddingston G71 ... 140 C4
Greenholm St KA1 ... 227 F3
Greenholme Ct G44 ... 137 D3
Greenholme St G44 ... 137 D3
Greenhorn's Well Ave FK1 ... 41 F2
Greenhorn's Well Cres
FK1 ... 41 F2
Greenhorn's Well Dr FK1 ... 41 F2
Greenknowe Dr ML8 ... 186 C3
Greenknowe Rd G43 ... 136 A3
Greenknowe St ML2 ... 186 A3
Greenlaw Ave Paisley PA1 ... 114 A3
Wishaw ML2 ... 165 E3
Greenlaw Cres PA1 ... 114 A3
Greenlaw Dr
Newton Mearns G77 ... 156 B3
Paisley PA1 ... 114 A3
Greenlaw Ind Est PA3 ... 113 F3
Greenlaw Rd Glasgow G14 ... 94 C3
Newton Mearns G77 ... 156 B3
Greenlea Rd G69 ... 100 A4
Greenlea St G13 ... 95 F3
Greenlees Ct KA24 ... 191 D4
Greenlees Gdns G72 ... 138 C2
Greenlees Gr ML5 ... 122 B3
Greenlees Pk G72 ... 139 D2
Greenlees Rd G72 ... 139 D2
Greenloan Ave G51 ... 115 E4
Greenloan View ML9 ... 185 D1
Greenmoss Pl ML4 ... 142 B3
Greenmount G22 ... 97 D4
Greenmount Dr FK1 ... 66 B3
Greenock Acad PA16 ... 45 E4
Greenock Ave G44 ... 137 D3
Greenock Central Sta PA15 ... 46 A2
Greenock High Sch PA16 ... 44 B1
Greenock Rd Bishopton PA7 ... 71 E3
Greenock PA15 ... 46 C1
Inchinnan PA4 ... 93 E3
Langbank PA14 ... 70 B4
Paisley PA3 ... 113 E4
Port Glasgow PA14 ... 47 E1
Greenock West Sta PA15 ... 45 F3
Greenrig G71 ... 140 C3
Greenrig Rd ML11 ... 214 A1
Greenrig St G33 ... 98 B2
Greenrigg Cotts ML7 ... 127 F3
Greenrigg Prim Sch ML7 ... 127 F3
Greenrigg Rd G67 ... 62 A1
Greenrigg St G71 ... 140 C3
Greens Ave G69 ... 79 E4
Greens Cres G66 ... 79 E4
Greens Rd G67 ... 82 C3
Greenshields Rd G69 ... 120 A3
Greenside KA11 ... 220 A2
Greenside Ave
Kilbirnie KA25 ... 170 A4
Prestwick KA9 ... 236 B4
Springside KA11 ... 221 D1
Greenside Cl ML11 ... 215 D2
Greenside Cres G33 ... 98 C2
Greenside La ML11 ... 215 D2
Greenside Pl G61 ... 75 E4
Greenside Rd
Carmunnock G76 ... 158 C4
Clydebank G81 ... 74 A4
Motherwell ML1 ... 143 E4
Wishaw ML2 ... 165 E1
Greenside St Alloa FK10 ... 10 A3
Glasgow G33 ... 98 C2
Motherwell ML1 ... 143 F2
Greenside Terr KA11 ... 221 D1
Greenside Way KA11 ... 220 A2
Greentowers Rd ML11 ... 214 C4
Greentree Dr G69 ... 119 F2
Greentree Pk KA7 ... 239 E2
Greenview Prim Sch G40 ... 117 F2
Greenview St G43 ... 136 B4
Greenville Ct FK1 ... 41 F2
Greenway La G72 ... 161 E3

Hobden St G21 ...... 98 A2
Hoddam Ave G45 ...... 138 A2
Hoddam Terr G45 ...... 138 A2
Hodge St FK1 ...... 42 A2
Hoey Dr ML2 ...... 186 B4
Hogan Ct G81 ...... 73 F3
Hogan Way ML1 ...... 143 F1
Hogarth Ave Glasgow G32 ... 118 B4
Saltcoats KA21 ...... 205 F1
Hogarth Cres G32 ...... 118 B4
Hogarth Ct G83 ...... 27 F3
Hogarth Dr G32 ...... 118 B4
Hogarth Gdns G32 ...... 118 B4
Hogg Ave PA5 ...... 111 F1
Hogg Rd ML6 ...... 123 E2
Hogg St ML6 ...... 123 D4
Hogganfield St G33 ...... 98 B1
Holbourne Pl FK11 ...... 4 A4
Hole Farm Rd PA16 ...... 45 E2
Holeburn La G43 ...... 136 B3
Holeburn Rd G43 ...... 136 B3
Holehills Dr ML6 ...... 103 D1
Holehills Pl ML6 ...... 103 D1
Holehouse Brae G78 ...... 154 B4
Holehouse Dr Glasgow G13 .. 95 D3
Kilbirnie KA25 ...... 149 D2
Holehouse Rd
Eaglesham G76 ...... 178 C3
East Kilbride G74 ...... 179 D4
Kilmarnock KA3 ...... 228 A4
Holehouse Terr G78 ...... 154 B4
Holland St G2 ...... 240 B3
Hollandbush Ave FK4 ...... 38 C2
Hollandbush Cres FK4 ...... 38 C2
Hollandbush Gr ML3 ...... 183 E4
Hollandhurst Rd ML5 ...... 101 F1
Hollinwell Rd G23 ...... 76 B1
Hollow Pk KA7 ...... 239 D1
Hollowglen Rd G32 ...... 119 D3
Hollows Ave PA2 ...... 132 C4
Hollows Cres PA2 ...... 132 C4
Holly Ave Milton Of C G65 ...... 58 A3
Stenhousemuir FK5 ...... 23 F2
Holly Bank KA7 ...... 239 E3
Holly Dr Dumbarton G82 ...... 49 D3
Glasgow G21 ...... 98 A2
Holly Gr Banknock FK4 ...... 38 C1
Bellshill ML4 ...... 142 C3
Holly Pl Johnstone PA5 ...... 132 A4
Kilmarnock KA1 ...... 222 B1
Holly St Airdrie ML6 ...... 123 E3
Clydebank G81 ...... 74 A2
Hollybank Pl G72 ...... 139 D2
Hollybank St G21 ...... 98 A1
Hollybrook Pl 6 G42 ...... 117 D1
Hollybrook Sch G42 ...... 117 D1
Hollybrook St G42 ...... 117 D1
Hollybush Ave PA2 ...... 133 D4
Hollybush Pl KA3 ...... 223 D3
Hollybush Rd G52 ...... 114 C3
Hollymount G61 ...... 75 F1
Holm Ave Paisley PA2 ...... 113 F1
Uddingston G71 ...... 140 C4
Holm Cres KA3 ...... 213 D2
Holm Crest ML8 ...... 201 D1
Holm Gdns ML4 ...... 142 B2
Holm La G74 ...... 159 F1
Holm Pl Larkhall ML9 ...... 184 C1
Linwood PA3 ...... 112 A4
Holm Rd ML8 ...... 201 D1
Holm St Carluke ML8 ...... 187 F1
Glasgow G2 ...... 240 C2
Motherwell ML1 ...... 143 D2
Stewarton KA3 ...... 211 F4
Holmbank Ave G41 ...... 136 B4
Holmbrae Ave G71 ...... 140 C4
Holmbrae Rd G71 ...... 140 C4
Holmbyre Rd G45 ...... 137 E1
Holmbyre Terr G45 ...... 137 E1
Holmes Ave PA4 ...... 94 B1
Holmes Cres KA1 ...... 227 E3
Holmes Farm Rd KA1 ...... 227 E3
Holmes Quadrant ML4 ...... 142 A2
Holmes Rd KA1 ...... 227 E3
Holmes Village KA1 ...... 227 E3
Holmfauld Rd G51 ...... 95 F1
Holmfauldhead Dr G51 ...... 115 F4
Holmfauldhead Pl G51 ...... 115 F4
Holmfield G66 ...... 79 F4
Holmhead KA25 ...... 170 A4
Holmhead Cres G44 ...... 137 D3
Holmhead Pl G44 ...... 137 D3
Holmhead Rd G44 ...... 137 D3
Holmhill Ave G72 ...... 139 D2
Holmhills Dr G72 ...... 138 C2
Holmhills Gdns G72 ...... 138 C2
Holmhills Gr G72 ...... 138 C2
Holmhills Pl G72 ...... 138 C2
Holmhills Rd G72 ...... 138 C2
Holmhills Terr G72 ...... 138 C2
Holmlands Pl KA1 ...... 227 E3
Holmlea Dr KA1 ...... 227 F3
Holmlea Pl KA1 ...... 227 F3
Holmlea Prim Sch G44 ...... 137 D3
Holmlea Rd G44 ...... 137 D4
Holmpark PA7 ...... 72 A2
Holmquarry Rd KA1 ...... 227 F3
Holms Ave KA11 ...... 220 B1
Holms Cres PA8 ...... 72 C1
Holms Pl G69 ...... 100 C4
Holms Rd KA14 ...... 170 A3
Holmscroft Ave PA15 ...... 45 F2
Holmscroft St PA15 ...... 45 F3
Holmscroft Way PA15 ...... 45 F2
Holmston Cres KA7 ...... 239 E4
Holmston Dr KA7 ...... 239 E3
Holmston Prim Sch KA7 ...... 239 D4
Holmston Rd KA7 ...... 239 E4
Holmswood Ave G72 ...... 140 B1
Holmwood Ave G71 ...... 140 C4
Holmwood Gdns G71 ...... 140 C3
Holmwood Gr G44 ...... 137 D2
Holton Cres FK10 ...... 5 E1
Holton Sq FK10 ...... 5 E1
Holy Cross High Sch ML3 ...... 162 C2
Holy Cross Prim RC Sch
G42 ...... 117 D1
Holy Cross Prim Sch G65 ...... 60 C2
Holy Cross RC Prim Sch
PA16 ...... 45 D3
Holy Family Prim Sch G66 .. 79 D3
Holy Family RC Prim Sch
Bellshill ML4 ...... 142 B3
Port Glasgow PA14 ...... 69 D4
Holy Trinity Episcopal
Prim Sch FK8 ...... 7 D4
Holyknowe Cres G65 ...... 57 F4
Holyknowe Rd G65 ...... 57 F4
Holyoake Ct KA1 ...... 228 C4
Holyrood Cres G20 ...... 96 C1
Holyrood Pl FK5 ...... 23 F2
Holyrood Quadrant 9 G20 .. 96 C1
Holyrood Sec RC Sch G42 ...... 117 E1
Holyrood St ML3 ...... 162 A3
Holytown Prim Sch ML1 ...... 143 D3
Holytown Rd ML4 ...... 142 C3
Holytown Sta ML1 ...... 143 D2
Holywell St G31 ...... 118 A3
Home Farm Cotts FK6 ...... 39 F3
Home Farm Rd KA7 ...... 239 D1
Home St ML11 ...... 215 E2
Homer Pl ML4 ...... 142 C3
Homesteads The FK8 ...... 6 B4
Homeston Ave G71 ...... 141 D2
Homoeopathic Hospl G12 ...... 96 A3
Honeybank Cres ML8 ...... 188 A2
Honeybog Rd G52 ...... 114 C3
Honeycomb Pl ML9 ...... 200 B2
Honeyman Cres ML11 ...... 215 E2
Honeysuckle La G83 ...... 27 F4
Honeysuckle Pk KA7 ...... 239 D1
Honeywell Cres ML6 ...... 123 F1
Hood Ct G84 ...... 16 A1
Hood St Clydebank G81 ...... 74 B1
Greenock PA15 ...... 45 F3
Hookney Terr FK6 ...... 21 E1
Hope Ave PA11 ...... 89 F1
Hope Cres ML9 ...... 185 D2
Hope St Ayr KA7 ...... 238 C4
Bellshill ML4 ...... 142 B3
Carluke ML8 ...... 188 A1
Falkirk FK1 ...... 42 A3
Glasgow G2 ...... 240 C3
Greenock PA15 ...... 45 F2
Hamilton ML3 ...... 162 C2
Helensburgh G84 ...... 25 C4
Lanark ML11 ...... 215 D2
Motherwell ML1 ...... 163 F4
Stirling FK8 ...... 1 C1
Wishaw ML2 ...... 166 A2
Hopefield Ave G12 ...... 96 B3
Hopehill Gdns G20 ...... 97 D2
Hopehill Rd G20 ...... 97 D2
Hopeman PA8 ...... 73 D2
Hopeman Ave G46 ...... 135 F2
Hopeman Dr G46 ...... 135 F2
Hopeman Path G46 ...... 135 F3
Hopeman Rd G46 ...... 135 F2
Hopeman St G46 ...... 135 F2
Hopepark Terr FK6 ...... 39 F3
Hopetoun Bank KA11 ...... 220 B1
Hopetoun Dr FK9 ...... 2 A4
Hopetoun Pl G23 ...... 76 C1
Hopetoun Terr G21 ...... 98 A2
Hopkin's Brae G66 ...... 58 B1
Horatius St ML1 ...... 142 A1
Hornal Rd Bothwell G71 ...... 141 D2
Uddingston G71 ...... 140 C2
Hornbeam Dr G81 ...... 74 A2
Hornbeam Rd
Cumbernauld G67 ...... 62 C3
Uddingston G71 ...... 141 D4
Horndean Cres G33 ...... 99 E1
Horndean Ct G64 ...... 78 A2
Horne St G22 ...... 97 F3
Hornock Rd ML5 ...... 101 F1
Hornshill Dr ML1 ...... 144 A1
Hornshill Farm Rd G33 ...... 99 F3
Hornshill St G21 ...... 98 A2
Horsbrugh Ave G65 ...... 36 B1
Horsburgh St G33 ...... 99 E1
Horse Shoe Rd G61 ...... 75 F2
Horsewood Rd PA11 ...... 110 B4
Horslet St ML5 ...... 121 E2
Horslethill Rd G12 ...... 96 B2
Horsley Brae ML2 ...... 186 A2
Horton Pl G84 ...... 17 D2
Hospital Rd ML2 ...... 186 A4
Hospital St ML5 ...... 122 A2
Hospitland Dr ML11 ...... 215 E2
Hotspur St G20 ...... 96 C2
Houldsworth Cres ML7 ...... 167 D4
Houldsworth La 7 G3 ...... 116 C4
Houldsworth St G3 ...... 240 A3
House O' Muir Rd ML7 ...... 126 A2
Househillmuir Cres G53 ...... 135 E4
Househillmuir La G53 ...... 135 E4
Househillmuir Pl G53 ...... 135 E4
Househillmuir Rd G53 ...... 135 D3
Househillmuir Sch G53 ...... 135 D3
Househillwood Cres G53 .. 135 D4
Househillwood Rd G53 ...... 135 D3
Housel Ave G13 ...... 95 D4
Houston Cres KA24 ...... 191 D4
Houston Pl Elderslie PA5 ...... 112 B1
Glasgow G5 ...... 116 C3
Houston Rd
Bridge Of W PA11 ...... 90 B1
Houston PA6 ...... 91 D1
Inchinnan PA3, PA4, PA6 ...... 92 B2
Kilmacolm PA13 ...... 89 F4
Houston St Glasgow G5 ...... 116 C3
Greenock PA16 ...... 45 F3
Hamilton ML3 ...... 162 B1
Renfrew PA4 ...... 94 B2
Wishaw ML2 ...... 165 E1
Houston Terr G74 ...... 159 E1
Houstonfield Quadrant
PA6 ...... 91 D1
Houstonfield Rd PA6 ...... 91 D1
Houstoun Ct PA5 ...... 111 F2
Houstoun Sq PA5 ...... 111 F2
Howacre ML11 ...... 214 C3
Howard Ave G74 ...... 160 A3
Howard Ct
East Kilbride G74 ...... 160 A3
Kilmarnock KA1 ...... 227 F4
Howard Park Dr KA1 ...... 227 F4
Howard St Falkirk FK1 ...... 41 F2
Glasgow G1 ...... 241 D1
Kilmarnock KA1 ...... 227 F4
Larkhall ML9 ...... 185 E1
Paisley PA1 ...... 114 A2
Howat Cres KA12 ...... 219 F2
Howat St G51 ...... 116 A4
Howatshaws Rd G82 ...... 50 A3
Howburn Cres ML7 ...... 127 F3
Howburn Rd ML7 ...... 127 E3
Howden Ave
Kilwinning KA13 ...... 207 F2
Motherwell ML1 ...... 143 E4
Howden Dr PA3 ...... 112 A3
Howden Pl ML1 ...... 143 D3
Howe Gdns G71 ...... 141 D4
Howe Rd G65 ...... 60 B4
Howes St ML5 ...... 122 A2
Howetown FK10 ...... 5 E2
Howford Rd G52 ...... 115 D2
Howford Sch G53 ...... 115 D1
Howgate KA13 ...... 207 E2
Howgate Ave G15 ...... 74 C2
Howgate Rd ML3 ...... 183 E4
Howgate Sh Ctr 7 FK1 ...... 42 A2
Howie Bldgs G76 ...... 157 F4
Howie Cres G84 ...... 15 D2
Howie St ML9 ...... 185 D1
Howie's Pl FK1 ...... 41 D2
Howieshill Ave G72 ...... 139 D3
Howieshill Rd G72 ...... 139 D3
Howlands Rd FK7 ...... 7 D2
Howlet Pl ML3 ...... 162 C1
Howletnest Rd ML6 ...... 123 E3
Howson Lea ML1 ...... 164 A2
Howson View ML1 ...... 163 D4
Howth Dr G13 ...... 95 F4
Howth Terr G13 ...... 95 F4
Howwood Prim Sch PA9 ...... 131 D3
Hoylake Pk G72 ...... 140 C1
Hoylake Pl G23 ...... 76 C1
Hoylake Sq KA13 ...... 207 E2
Hozier Cres G71 ...... 140 C4
Hozier Loan 6 ML9 ...... 185 D2
Hozier Pl 16 G71 ...... 141 D2
Hozier St Carluke ML8 ...... 187 F1
Coatbridge ML5 ...... 122 A2
Hudson Pl KA9 ...... 233 E1
Hudson Terr G75 ...... 180 B4
Hudson Way G75 ...... 180 B4
Hudspeth Ct G83 ...... 27 E4
Hugh Murray Dr G72 ...... 139 E3
Hugh Watt Pl KA3 ...... 222 A4
Hughenden Dr G12 ...... 96 A2
Hughenden Gdns G12 ...... 96 A2
Hughenden La G12 ...... 96 A2
Hughenden Rd G12 ...... 96 A2
Hugo St G20 ...... 96 C3
Hulks Rd ML6 ...... 83 E2
Humbie Ct G77 ...... 156 C1
Humbie Gate G77 ...... 156 C1
Humbie Gr G77 ...... 156 C2
Humbie Lawns G77 ...... 156 C1
Humbie Rd Eaglesham G76 .. 178 B4
Newton Mearns G77 ...... 156 C1
Hume Cres FK9 ...... 2 A3
Hume Ct FK9 ...... 2 A3
Hume Dr Bothwell G71 ...... 141 D2
Uddingston G71 ...... 140 C4
Hume Pl G75 ...... 180 B4
Hume Rd G67 ...... 62 A2
Hume St G81 ...... 74 A1
Hunt Hill G68 ...... 60 B1
Hunter Ave KA22 ...... 205 E1
Hunter Cres KA10 ...... 230 A1
Hunter Dr KA12 ...... 219 D3
Hunter Gdns Bonnybridge FK4 40 A3
Denny FK6 ...... 21 E1
Hunter High Sch G74 ...... 160 B1
Hunter Pl Kilbarchan PA10 .. 111 D1
Kilwinning KA13 ...... 208 A2
Milngavie G62 ...... 54 C1
Shotts ML7 ...... 146 C3
Stenhousemuir FK2 ...... 24 A2
Hunter Prim Sch G74 ...... 160 B2
Hunter Rd Crosshouse KA2 .. 221 F1
Hamilton ML3 ...... 162 A3
Milngavie G62 ...... 54 C1
Rutherglen G73 ...... 118 B1
Hunter St Airdrie ML6 ...... 103 D1
Bellshill ML4 ...... 142 A3
East Kilbride G74 ...... 159 F1
Glasgow G4 ...... 241 F2
Paisley PA1 ...... 113 F3
Prestwick KA9 ...... 236 B4
Shotts ML7 ...... 146 B3
Hunter's Ave Ayr KA8 ...... 236 A2
Dumbarton G82 ...... 50 B2
Hunter's Cl ML11 ...... 215 D2
Hunterfield Dr G72 ...... 138 C3
Hunterhill Ave PA2 ...... 113 F2
Hunterhill Rd PA2 ...... 113 F2
Hunterian Mus G12 ...... 96 B1
Hunterlees Rd ML10 ...... 198 A2
Hunters Hill Ct G22 ...... 97 F3
Hunters Pl PA15 ...... 45 F3
Huntersfield Rd PA5 ...... 111 E1
Huntershill Rd 3 G64 ...... 97 F4
Huntershill St G22 ...... 97 F3
Hunterston Rd KA23 ...... 190 B3
Hunthill La G72 ...... 161 D3
Hunthill Pl G76 ...... 158 A3
Hunthill Rd G72 ...... 161 D4
Hunting Lodge Gdns ML3 . 163 D1
Huntingdon Rd G21 ...... 97 F1
Huntingdon Sq G21 ...... 97 F1
Huntingtower Rd G69 ...... 119 F2
Huntley Cres FK8 ...... 1 C1
Huntly Ave Bellshill ML4 ...... 142 A3
Glasgow G46 ...... 136 B1
Huntly Ct Bishopbriggs G64 .... 98 A4
Kilmarnock KA3 ...... 223 E2
Huntly Dr Bearsden G61 ...... 75 F4
Cambuslang G72 ...... 139 D2
Coatbridge ML5 ...... 121 E2
Greenock PA16 ...... 44 C2
Huntly Gdns G12 ...... 96 B2
Huntly Path G69 ...... 81 D1
Huntly Pl Kilmarnock KA3 ...... 223 E1
Port Glasgow PA14 ...... 47 D1
Huntly Quadrant ML2 ...... 165 D3
Huntly Rd Glasgow G12 ...... 96 B2
Paisley G52 ...... 114 C4
Huntly Terr Paisley PA2 ...... 114 A1
Port Glasgow PA14 ...... 47 D1
Shotts ML7 ...... 147 D2
Hurlawcrook Rd G75 ...... 180 C1
Hurlet Cotts G53 ...... 134 C3
Hurlet Rd PA2, G53 ...... 134 B4
Hurlford Ave G13 ...... 94 C4
Hurlford Rd KA1 ...... 228 A3
Hurly Hawkin G64 ...... 98 B4
Hurworth St FK1 ...... 41 F2
Hutcheson Rd G46 ...... 136 A1
Hutcheson St G1 ...... 241 D2
Hutchesons' Gram Sch
Glasgow G42 ...... 117 D1
Glasgow, Crossmyloof G41 .. 116 C1
Hutchinson Pl G72 ...... 139 F2
Hutchinson St ML2 ...... 186 B4
Hutchinson Town Ct 2
G5 ...... 117 E2
Hutchison Dr G61 ...... 76 A1
Hutchison Pl ML5 ...... 121 F3
Hutchison St ML3 ...... 162 B1
Hutton Ave PA6 ...... 111 E4
Hutton Dr G51 ...... 115 F4
Hutton Pk FK10 ...... 10 B4
Huxley St G20 ...... 96 C3
Hyacinth Way ML8 ...... 201 F4
Hydepark St G3 ...... 240 A2
Hyndal Ave G53 ...... 115 E1
Hyndford Pl ML11 ...... 215 D2
Hyndford Rd ML11 ...... 215 E1
Hyndland Ave G11 ...... 96 A1
Hyndland Prim Sch G11 ...... 96 A1
Hyndland Rd G12 ...... 96 A2
Hyndland Sec Sch G12 ...... 96 A2
Hyndland St G11 ...... 96 B1
Hyndland Sta G12 ...... 96 A2
Hyndlee Dr G52 ...... 115 E3
Hyndman Rd KA23 ...... 190 B2
Hyndshaw Rd Carluke ML8 . 188 A2
Law ML2 ...... 187 E4
Hyndshaw View ML8 ...... 187 D2
Hyslop Pl G81 ...... 74 A2
Hyslop Rd KA20 ...... 206 C1
Hyslop St ML6 ...... 122 C4

Iain Dr G61 ...... 75 E3
Iain Rd G61 ...... 75 E3
Ian Smith Ct G81 ...... 94 B4
IBM Sta PA16 ...... 44 B1
Ibrox Ind Est G51 ...... 116 B3
Ibrox Prim Sch G51 ...... 116 A3
Ibrox St G51 ...... 116 B3
Ibrox Sta G51 ...... 116 A3
Ibrox Stad (Rangers FC)
G51 ...... 116 A3
Ibrox Terr G51 ...... 116 A3
Ibroxholm Ave G51 ...... 116 A3
Ibroxholm Oval G51 ...... 116 A3
Ibroxholm Pl G51 ...... 116 A3
Ida Quadrant ML4 ...... 141 F3
Iddesleigh Ave G62 ...... 55 D1
Ilay Ave G61 ...... 96 A4
Ilay Ct G61 ...... 96 A4
Ilay Rd G61 ...... 96 A4
Imlach Pl ML1 ...... 163 E3
Imperial Dr ML6 ...... 122 C3
Inch Garve G74 ...... 160 B1
Inch Keith G74 ...... 160 B1
Inch Marnock G74 ...... 160 B1
Inch Murrin G74 ...... 160 B1
Inchbrae Rd G52 ...... 115 E2
Inchcnock Ave G69 ...... 101 D3
Inchcolm Gdns G69 ...... 81 D2
Inchcolm Pl G74 ...... 159 E1
Inchconnachan Ave G83 ...... 19 F1
Inchcruin Pl G15 ...... 74 C2
Inches Rd KA22 ...... 216 A4
Inchfad Dr G15 ...... 74 C2
Inchfad Pl G15 ...... 74 C2
Inchfad Rd G83 ...... 19 F1
Inchgotrick Rd KA1 ...... 227 F2
Inchgower Gr G84 ...... 15 E3
Inchgreen St PA14 ...... 46 C1
Inchholm La G11 ...... 95 F1
Inchholm St G11 ...... 95 F1
Inchinnan Bsns Pk PA4 ...... 93 D2
Inchinnan Ind Est PA4 ...... 93 D3
Inchinnan Prim Sch PA4 ...... 93 E4
Inchinnan Rd Bellshill ML4 .. 141 F4
Paisley PA3 ...... 113 F4
Renfrew PA4 ...... 94 A2
Inchkeith Pl Falkirk FK1 ...... 42 A1
Glasgow G32 ...... 119 D4
Inchlaggan Pl G15 ...... 74 C2
Inchlee St G14 ...... 95 F2
Inchlonaig Dr G83 ...... 19 F1
Inchmoan Pl G15 ...... 74 C2
Inchmurrin Ave G66 ...... 80 A4
Inchmurrin Cres G83 ...... 19 F1
Inchmurrin Dr
Kilmarnock KA3 ...... 223 D3
Rutherglen G73 ...... 138 B1
Inchmurrin Gdns G73 ...... 138 B1
Inchmurrin Pl G73 ...... 138 B1
Inchna FK11 ...... 4 A3
Inchneuk Rd ML5 ...... 101 F3
Inchoch St G33 ...... 99 F1
Inchrory Pl G15 ...... 74 C2
Inchwood Ct G68 ...... 82 A4
Inchwood Pl G68 ...... 81 F4
Inchwood Rd G68 ...... 82 A4
Incle St PA1 ...... 113 F3
Indale Ave KA9 ...... 236 C4
India Dr PA4 ...... 93 E3
India St Alexandria G83 ...... 27 F3
Glasgow G2 ...... 240 B3
Industry St G66 ...... 79 E4
Inga St G20 ...... 96 C4
Ingerbreck Ave G73 ...... 138 B2
Ingleby Dr G31 ...... 118 A4
Ingleby Pl G78 ...... 154 C4
Inglefield Ct ML6 ...... 123 D4
Inglefield St G42 ...... 117 D1
Ingleneuk Ave G33 ...... 99 D3
Ingleside G66 ...... 79 E3
Ingleston Ave FK6 ...... 21 E3
Ingleston St PA15 ...... 46 A2
Inglestone Ave G46 ...... 136 A1
Inglewood FK10 ...... 9 F4
Inglewood Cres G75 ...... 180 A4
Inglewood Rd FK10 ...... 9 F4
Inglis Dr FK2 ...... 24 B1
Inglis Pl G75 ...... 180 C4
Inglis St Glasgow G31 ...... 118 A3
Wishaw ML2 ...... 164 B1
Ingliston Dr PA7 ...... 71 F2
Ingram Pl KA3 ...... 223 D2
Ingram St G1 ...... 241 D2
Inishail Rd G33 ...... 99 E1
Inkerman Pl KA1 ...... 222 C1
Inkerman Rd G52 ...... 114 C3
Innellan Dr KA3 ...... 222 C2
Inner City Trad Est G4 ...... 241 E4
Innerleithen Dr ML2 ...... 165 E3
Innermanse Quadrant
ML1 ...... 143 F3
Innerpeffray Dr FK2 ...... 24 A2
Innerwick Dr G52 ...... 115 D3
Innerwood Rd KA13 ...... 207 F3
Innes Ct G74 ...... 159 F2
International Ave ML3 ...... 161 E2
Inver Ct FK2 ...... 24 B1
Inver Rd G33 ...... 119 F4
Inverallan Ct FK9 ...... 1 C4
Inverallan Dr FK9 ...... 1 C4
Inverallan Rd FK9 ...... 1 C4
Inveraray Dr G64 ...... 78 A2
Inverary Dr FK5 ...... 23 F3
Inveravon Dr ML1 ...... 163 E3
Inverbervie PA8 ...... 73 D1
Invercanny Dr G15 ...... 75 D2
Invercanny Pl G15 ...... 75 D2
Invercargill G75 ...... 180 A4
Invercloy Ct G75 ...... 180 A2
Invercloy Pl KA3 ...... 222 C2
Inverclyde Gdns G73 ...... 138 C2
Inverclyde Royal Hospl
PA16 ...... 44 C2
Invercree Wlk ML5 ...... 101 E3
Inveresk Pl ML5 ...... 122 A4
Inveresk Quadrant G32 ...... 119 D3
Inveresk St G32 ...... 119 D3
Inverewe Ave G46 ...... 135 E1
Inverewe Dr G46 ...... 135 E1
Inverewe Gdns G46 ...... 135 E1
Inverewe Pl G46 ...... 135 E2
Inverewe Way G77 ...... 156 A3
Invergarry Ave G46 ...... 135 E1
Invergarry Ct G46 ...... 135 F1
Invergarry Dr G46 ...... 135 F1
Invergarry Gdns G46 ...... 135 E1
Invergarry Gr G46 ...... 135 E1
Invergarry Pl G46 ...... 135 F1
Invergarry Quad G46 ...... 135 F1
Invergarry View G46 ...... 135 F1
Inverglas Ave PA4 ...... 94 C1
Invergordon Ave G43 ...... 136 C4
Invergyle Dr G52 ...... 115 E3
Inverkar Dr PA2 ...... 113 D1
Inverkar Rd KA7 ...... 239 D3
Inverkip Dr ML7 ...... 146 C3
Inverkip Rd Gourock PA16 ...... 44 B1
Greenock PA16 ...... 45 E2
Inverkip St PA15 ...... 45 F3
Inverlair Ave G43 ...... 136 C3

Lestrange Terr FK12 ... 5 D4
Letham Cotts FK2 ... 24 B4
Letham Ct G43 ... 136 C3
Letham Dr Bishopbriggs G64 . 98 B4
Glasgow G43 ... 136 C3
Letham Grange G68 ... 62 A3
Letham Oval G64 ... 98 B4
Letham Terrs FK2 ... 14 B1
Lethamhill Cres G33 ... 98 C1
Lethamhill Pl G33 ... 98 C1
Lethamhill Rd G33 ... 98 C1
Lethbridge Pl 4 G75 ... 180 B4
Letherby Dr G44 ... 137 D4
Letheron Dr ML2 ... 165 D3
Lethington Ave G41 ... 136 C4
Lethington Pl G41 ... 136 C4
Lethington Rd G46 ... 157 D4
Letterfearn Rd G23 ... 76 C1
Letterickhills Cres G72 ... 139 F2
Lettoch St 7 G51 ... 116 A4
Levanne Gdns PA19 ... 43 F3
Levanne Pl PA19 ... 43 F3
Leven Ave Bishopbriggs G64 .. 78 A1
Kilmarnock KA3 ... 223 D2
Leven Ct Alloa FK10 ... 10 B3
Barrhead G78 ... 134 A3
Dumbarton G82 ... 49 F2
Hurlford KA1 ... 228 C3
Leven Dr Bearsden G61 ... 75 F2
Hamilton ML3 ... 183 D4
Hurlford KA1 ... 228 C3
Leven Path ML1 ... 143 D3
Leven Pl Erskine PA8 ... 72 C1
Greenock PA15 ... 46 B1
Irvine KA12 ... 219 E3
Kilmarnock KA3 ... 223 D2
Shotts ML7 ... 146 C3
Leven Quadrant ML6 ... 102 C1
Leven Rd Coatbridge ML5 ... 101 E1
Greenock PA15 ... 46 B1
Langbank PA14 ... 70 B4
Troon KA10 ... 229 F3
Leven Sq PA4 ... 94 A2
Leven St Alexandria G83 ... 27 F2
Dumbarton G82 ... 50 A2
Falkirk FK2 ... 42 A4
Glasgow G41 ... 116 C2
Motherwell ML1 ... 163 F2
Renton G82 ... 49 E4
Leven Terr ML1 ... 143 E1
Leven Valley Ent Pk G82 ... 49 E2
Leven Way
East Kilbride G75 ... 179 F3
Paisley PA2 ... 112 C1
Levenbank Gdns G83 ... 27 F4
Levencroft Mews G83 ... 27 F2
Levenford Terr G82 ... 49 F2
Levengrove Ct G82 ... 49 F2
Levengrove Terr G82 ... 49 F2
Levenhowe Pl G83 ... 27 F4
Levenhowe Rd G83 ... 27 F4
Levenvale Prim Sch G83 ... 27 E4
Lever Rd G84 ... 16 C2
Levern Cres G78 ... 134 A1
Levern Gdns G78 ... 134 A2
Levern Prim Sch G53 ... 135 D3
Levern Rd G53 ... 134 C3
Leverndale Hospl
Glasgow G53 ... 115 D1
Paisley G53 ... 114 C1
Leverndale Ind Ctr G53 ... 134 C4
Levernside Ave
Barrhead G78 ... 134 A1
Glasgow G53 ... 135 E4
Levernside Cres G53 ... 135 E4
Levernside Rd G53 ... 135 E4
Lewis Ave Renfrew PA4 ... 94 B1
Wishaw ML2 ... 165 F3
Lewis Cres Irvine KA11 ... 219 F1
Johnstone PA10 ... 111 E1
Old Kilpatrick G60 ... 73 E3
Lewis Ct Alloa FK10 ... 10 A3
Falkirk FK1 ... 42 A1
Lewis Dr Kilmarnock KA3 ... 223 D3
Old Kilpatrick G60 ... 73 D3
Lewis Gdns Bearsden G61 ... 75 D3
Old Kilpatrick G60 ... 73 E3
Lewis Gr G60 ... 73 E3
Lewis Pl Airdrie ML6 ... 123 E3
Newton Mearns G77 ... 156 A3
Old Kilpatrick G60 ... 73 E3
Lewis Rd Greenock PA16 ... 45 E2
Port Glasgow PA14 ... 69 D4
Lewis Rise KA11 ... 220 A1
Lewis Terr KA11 ... 220 A1
Lewis Wynd KA11 ... 220 A1
Lewiston Dr G23 ... 76 B1
Lewiston Pl G23 ... 76 B1
Lewiston Rd G23 ... 76 B1
Lexwell Rd PA2 ... 112 C1
Leyden Ct G20 ... 96 C3
Leyden Gdns G20 ... 96 C3
Leyden St G20 ... 96 C3
Leys Pk ML3 ... 162 A2
Leys The G64 ... 78 A1
Libary Gdns G72 ... 138 C3
Libberton Way ML3 ... 162 A2
Liberator Dr KA8 ... 236 C2
Liberton St G33 ... 118 C4
Liberty Ave G69 ... 121 D3
Liberty Path G72 ... 161 E4
Liberty Rd Bellshill ML4 ... 142 A2
Caldercruix ML6 ... 105 D3
Libo Ave Glasgow G53 ... 115 E1
Uplawmoor G78 ... 153 D2
Libo Pl PA8 ... 72 C1
Library La G46 ... 135 F2
Library Rd ML2 ... 165 D2
Lichtenfels Gdns KA9 ... 236 C4
Lickprivick Rd G75 ... 180 A3
Liddel Rd G67 ... 61 F1
Liddell Gr G75 ... 180 B4
Liddell St G32 ... 119 E1
Liddells Ct G64 ... 98 A4
Liddesdale Pl G22 ... 97 F4
Liddesdale Rd G22 ... 97 E4
Liddesdale Sq G22 ... 97 F4
Liddesdale Terr G22 ... 97 F4
Liddlesdale Pass G22 ... 97 E4
Liddoch Way G73 ... 137 F4
Liff Gdns G64 ... 98 B4
Liff Pl G34 ... 100 B1
Lifnock Ave KA1 ... 228 C3
Lightburn Hospl G32 ... 119 D4
Lightburn Pl G32 ... 119 D4
Lightburn Rd
Cambuslang G72 ... 139 F2
Glasgow G31 ... 118 B3
Lilac Ave Clydebank G81 ... 73 E3
Cumbernauld G67 ... 62 C3
Lilac Cres G71 ... 141 E4
Lilac Ct G67 ... 62 C3
Lilac Gdns G64 ... 98 A4
Lilac Hill Cumbernauld G67 ... 62 C3
Hamilton ML3 ... 162 C1
Lilac Pl Cumbernauld G67 ... 62 C3
Kilmarnock KA1 ... 227 F4
Lilac Way ML1 ... 143 D3
Lilac Wynd G72 ... 139 F2
Lillyburn Pl G15 ... 74 C3
Lily St G40 ... 118 A2
Lilybank Ave Airdrie ML6 ... 103 D1
Cambuslang G72 ... 139 E2
Muirhead G69 ... 100 B4
Lilybank Ct FK10 ... 5 E1
Lilybank Gardens La G12 ... 96 B1
Lilybank Gdns G12 ... 96 B1
Lilybank La G12 ... 96 B1
Lilybank Rd
Port Glasgow PA14 ... 47 D1
Prestwick KA9 ... 236 A3
Lilybank Sch PA14 ... 47 D1
Lilybank St ML3 ... 162 B2
Lilybank Terr G12 ... 96 B1
Lilybank Terrace La G12 ... 96 B1
Lime Cres Airdrie ML6 ... 123 E4
Cumbernauld G67 ... 62 C2
Lime Gr Blantyre G72 ... 140 B1
Kirkintilloch G66 ... 79 E3
Larbert FK5 ... 23 E1
Motherwell ML1 ... 163 F2
Lime La 24 G14 ... 95 E2
Lime Loan ML1 ... 143 D2
Lime Pl KA1 ... 227 E4
Lime Rd Dumbarton G82 ... 49 F2
Falkirk FK1 ... 41 D2
Lime St Glasgow G14 ... 95 E2
Greenock PA15 ... 45 F2
Limecraigs Ave PA2 ... 133 E4
Limecraigs Cres PA2 ... 133 E4
Limecraigs Rd PA2 ... 133 E4
Limegrove St ML4 ... 142 A4
Limekiln Rd Ayr KA8 ... 236 A2
Stevenston KA20 ... 217 F4
Limekilnburn Rd ML3 ... 183 E2
Limekilns Rd G67 ... 82 C3
Limekilns St G81 ... 74 B4
Limelands Quadrant
ML6 ... 104 C2
Limerigg Prim Sch FK1 ... 86 B1
Limes The G44 ... 137 D2
Limeside Ave G73 ... 138 B4
Limeside Gdns G73 ... 138 B4
Limetree Ave G71 ... 141 E4
Limetree Cres G77 ... 156 B2
Limetree Ct ML3 ... 162 A3
Limetree Dr G81 ... 74 A2
Limetree Quadrant G71 ... 141 E4
Limetree Wlk G65 ... 58 A2
Limeview Ave PA2 ... 133 D4
Limeview Cres PA2 ... 133 D4
Limeview Rd PA2 ... 133 D4
Limeview Way PA2 ... 133 D4
Limonds Ct KA8 ... 236 A1
Limonds Wynd KA8 ... 236 A1
Limpetlaw ML11 ... 215 D3
Linacre Dr G32 ... 119 E3
Linacre Gdns G32 ... 119 E3
Linburn Pl G52 ... 115 D3
Linburn Rd Erskine PA8 ... 72 C1
Glasgow G52 ... 114 C3
Linburn Sch G52 ... 114 C3
Linclive Intc PA3 ... 112 B3
Linclive Terr PA3 ... 112 B3
Lincluden Path 3 G41 ... 116 C2
Lincoln Ave Glasgow G13 ... 95 E3
Uddingston G71 ... 120 C1
Lincoln Rd PA16 ... 44 B2
Lincuan Ave G46 ... 157 E4
Lindams G71 ... 140 C3
Linden Ave Denny FK6 ... 21 E2
Stirling FK7 ... 7 E3
Wishaw ML2 ... 165 E3
Linden Dr Banknock FK4 ... 38 C1
Clydebank G81 ... 74 A3
Linden Lea Hamilton ML3 ... 162 A2
Milton Of C G65 ... 58 A3
Linden Pl G13 ... 95 F4
Linden St G13 ... 95 F4
Linden Way G13 ... 95 F4
Lindores Ave G73 ... 138 B4
Lindores Dr G74 ... 159 E1
Lindores Pl G74 ... 159 E1
Lindores St G42 ... 137 D4
Lindrick Dr G23 ... 76 C1
Lindsay Ave Kilbirnie KA25 . 149 D2
Saltcoats KA21 ... 205 F1
Lindsay Dr Glasgow G12 ... 96 A3
Kilmarnock KA3 ... 223 E2
Stirling FK9 ... 2 A2
Lindsay Gdns G83 ... 27 F3
Lindsay Gr G74 ... 159 F1
Lindsay Loan ML11 ... 215 E3
Lindsay Pl
East Kilbride G74 ... 160 A1
Glasgow G12 ... 96 A3
Johnstone PA5 ... 112 A2
Kirkintilloch G66 ... 79 E2
Lindsay Quadrant G83 ... 28 A4
Lindsay Rd G74 ... 159 F1
Lindsay St Ayr KA8 ... 236 B1
Kilmarnock KA1 ... 227 F4
Lindsay Terr G65 ... 57 F4
Lindsaybeg Rd G69 ... 80 A1
Lindsayfield Ave G75 ... 180 B2
Lindsayfield Rd G75 ... 180 A2
Lindston Pl KA7 ... 239 D1
Lindum Cres ML1 ... 163 D4
Lindum St ML1 ... 163 D4
Lineside Wlk G84 ... 15 F3
Linfern Ave KA1 ... 228 B4
Linfern Ave E KA1 ... 228 B4
Linfern Ave W KA1 ... 228 B4
Linfern Pl KA7 ... 239 D2
Linfern Rd G12 ... 96 B2
Linghope Pl ML2 ... 185 F4
Lingley Ave ML6 ... 123 D3
Linhope Pl G75 ... 179 F4
Linister Cres PA9 ... 130 C3
Links Cres KA10 ... 229 F3
Links Rd Glasgow G44 ... 137 E2
Glasgow, Mount Vernon G32 119 E2
Prestwick KA9 ... 233 D1
Saltcoats KA21 ... 205 F1
Links The G68 ... 62 A3
Links View ML9 ... 185 E1
Linksview Rd ML1 ... 143 D1
Linkwood Ave G15 ... 74 C2
Linkwood Cres G15 ... 75 D2
Linkwood Ct KA11 ... 220 A3
Linkwood Dr G15 ... 75 D2
Linkwood Pl Clydebank G15 .. 74 C2
Irvine KA11 ... 220 A3
Linlithgow Gdns G32 ... 119 E3
Linlithgow Pl FK5 ... 23 F2
Linn Cres
Kirkfieldbank ML11 ... 214 A2
Paisley PA2 ... 133 E4
Linn Dr G44 ... 136 C2
Linn Gdns G68 ... 61 D1
Linn Glen G65 ... 57 F4
Linn Park Gdns PA5 ... 112 A1
Linn Park Ind Est G45 ... 137 D1
Linn Rd KA22 ... 205 E2
Linnburn Terr KA22 ... 205 D2
Linnet Ave PA5 ... 131 E4
Linnet Pl G13 ... 94 C4
Linnet Rd Bellshill ML4 ... 142 A2
Greenock PA16 ... 45 D2
Linnhe Ave
Bishopbriggs G64 ... 78 A1
Glasgow G44 ... 137 D2
Hamilton ML3 ... 162 A1
Linnhe Cres ML2 ... 165 D1
Linnhe Ct ML9 ... 184 C3
Linnhe Dr G78 ... 134 A3
Linnhe Pl Blantyre G72 ... 140 B1
Erskine PA8 ... 72 C1
Linnhead Dr G53 ... 135 E3
Linnhead Pl G14 ... 95 D2
Linnpark Ave G44 ... 136 C1
Linnpark Ct G44 ... 136 C1
Linnvale Prim Sch G81 ... 74 B1
Linnwell Cres PA2 ... 133 E4
Linrigg Rd ML1 ... 144 B4
Linside Ave PA1 ... 114 A2
Lint Brae KA3 ... 195 F1
Lint Riggs FK1 ... 42 A3
Lintfield Loan G71 ... 141 D3
Linthaugh Rd G53 ... 115 E2
Linthaugh Terr G53 ... 115 E1
Linthill ML11 ... 215 D3
Linthouse Bldgs G51 ... 115 F4
Linthouse Rd G51 ... 95 F1
Linthouse Vennel KA12 ... 219 D1
Lintie Rd ML1 ... 143 E2
Lintlaw G72 ... 140 B1
Lintlaw Dr G52 ... 115 D3
Lintmill Terr G78 ... 154 B3
Linton St G33 ... 118 C4
Lintwhite Cres PA11 ... 110 C4
Linwood Ave
Clarkston G76 ... 157 F4
East Kilbride G74 ... 159 D1
Linwood Ct G44 ... 137 D3
Linwood High Sch PA3 ... 111 F3
Linwood Rd PA3 ... 112 C2
Linwood Terr ML3 ... 162 A2
Lion Bank G66 ... 58 B1
Lionthorn Rd FK1 ... 41 F1
Lipney FK11 ... 4 A3
Lisburn Rd KA8 ... 236 A2
Lismore G74 ... 181 E4
Lismore Ave
Motherwell ML1 ... 163 D4
Port Glasgow PA14 ... 69 D4
Renfrew PA4 ... 94 B1
Lismore Ct FK1 ... 42 A1
Lismore Dr Irvine KA11 ... 225 D4
Linwood PA3 ... 111 F3
Paisley PA2 ... 133 E4
Lismore Gdns PA10 ... 111 E1
Lismore Hill ML3 ... 161 E2
Lismore House KA9 ... 236 A3
Lismore Pl
Moodiesburn G69 ... 81 D2
Newton Mearns G77 ... 156 A3
Lismore Rd G12 ... 96 A3
Lismore Way KA11 ... 225 E4
Lissens Wlk KA13 ... 207 E3
Lister Ct FK9 ... 2 A3
Lister Gdns G76 ... 158 A3
Lister Pl G52 ... 115 D4
Lister Rd G52 ... 115 D4
Lister St Crosshouse KA2 ... 222 A1
Glasgow G4 ... 241 E4
Lister Wlk ML4 ... 142 B4
Lithgow Ave
Kirkintilloch G66 ... 79 F4
Langbank PA14 ... 70 A4
Lithgow Cres PA2 ... 114 A1
Lithgow Dr ML1 ... 144 A1
Lithgow Pl G74 ... 159 D1
Little Bellsland Rd KA1 ... 228 A3
Little Denny Rd FK6 ... 21 E1
Little Dovehill G1 ... 241 E1
Little John Gdns ML2 ... 165 F2
Little St G3 ... 240 A2
Littlehill Prim Sch G33 ... 98 B2
Littlehill St G21 ... 98 A2
Littleholm Pl G81 ... 73 F2
Littlemill Ave G68 ... 60 C1
Littlesdale Ave PA2 ... 132 B4
Littlestane Rd KA11 ... 220 A3
Littlestane Rdbt KA11 ... 220 A3
Littlestane Rise KA11 ... 220 A3
Littleston Gdns PA8 ... 72 C1
Littleton Dr G23 ... 76 B1
Littleton St G23 ... 76 B1
Livilands Ct FK8 ... 7 D3
Livilands Gate FK8 ... 7 D3
Livilands La FK8 ... 7 D3
Livingston Dr ML6 ... 104 A2
Livingston La 4 G71 ... 141 D2
Livingston Terr KA3 ... 195 D4
Livingstone Ave G52 ... 115 D4
Livingstone Bvd ML3 ... 161 E2
Livingstone Cres
Blantyre G72 ... 140 B1
East Kilbride G75 ... 180 B4
Falkirk FK2 ... 42 C3
Livingstone Ct KA3 ... 223 E2
Livingstone Dr
East Kilbride G75 ... 180 C4
Laurieston FK2 ... 42 C1
Livingstone Gdns ML9 ... 185 D2
Livingstone Pk G65 ... 36 B1
Livingstone Pl ML6 ... 123 D4
Livingstone Quadrant
ML7 ... 127 E2
Livingstone St
Clydebank G81 ... 74 B1
Hamilton ML3 ... 161 F2
Livingstone Terr KA12 ... 219 E3
Livinstone Pk G65 ... 36 A1
Lloyd Ave G32 ... 119 D1
Lloyd Dr ML1 ... 143 D1
Lloyd St Glasgow G31 ... 118 A4
Motherwell ML1 ... 143 D1
Rutherglen G73 ... 118 A1
Lloyd Wlk KA3 ... 211 E4
Lloyds St ML5 ... 122 A2
Llynallan Rd ML7 ... 127 D3
Loach Ave KA12 ... 219 E1
Loadingbank KA25 ... 170 A4
Loadingbank Ct KA25 ... 170 A4
Loan Lea Cres ML9 ... 185 D1
Loan Pl ML7 ... 127 F3
Loan The G62 ... 54 B2
Loanbank Quadrant G51 ... 115 F4
Loancroft Ave G69 ... 120 B2
Loancroft Gate G71 ... 140 C3
Loancroft Gdns G71 ... 140 C3
Loancroft Pl G69 ... 120 A2
Loanend Cotts G72 ... 139 F1
Loanfoot Ave Glasgow G13 ... 95 D4
Kilmarnock KA1 ... 222 B1
Neilston G78 ... 154 B3
Loanfoot Gdns FK7 ... 12 B2
Loanfoot Rd G72 ... 161 E3
Loanhead Ave
Dennyloanhead FK4 ... 39 E3
Linwood PA3 ... 112 A3
Motherwell ML1 ... 143 E2
Renfrew PA4 ... 94 B2
Loanhead Cres ML1 ... 143 E2
Loanhead La PA3 ... 112 A3
Loanhead Prim Sch KA1 ... 228 A4
Loanhead Rd
Ardrossan KA22 ... 205 E1
Linwood PA3 ... 112 A3
Motherwell ML1 ... 143 E2
Loanhead St
Coatbridge ML5 ... 121 F2
Glasgow G32 ... 118 C4
Kilmarnock KA1 ... 228 A4
Loaning 1 ML9 ... 185 E1
Loaning The Ayr KA7 ... 239 D1
Kirkintilloch G66 ... 79 E4
Motherwell ML1 ... 163 E4
Rutherglen G46 ... 157 D4
Loaninghead Dr G82 ... 50 A3
Lobnitz Ave PA4 ... 94 B2
Loccard Rd KA20 ... 206 B1
Loch Achray Gdns G32 ... 119 E2
Loch Achray St G32 ... 119 E2
Loch Assynt G74 ... 181 D4
Loch Ave ML8 ... 201 F2
Loch Awe G74 ... 181 D4
Loch Dr G84 ... 16 A1
Loch Goil G74 ... 160 A1
Loch Laidon St G32 ... 119 E2
Loch Laxford G74 ... 181 D4
Loch Lea G66 ... 58 C1
Loch Long G74 ... 181 D4
Loch Loyal G74 ... 181 D4
Loch Maree G74 ... 181 D4
Loch Meadie G74 ... 181 D4
Loch Naver G74 ... 181 D4
Loch Park Ave ML8 ... 201 F4
Loch Park Pl ML9 ... 185 D1
Loch Pk ML2 ... 165 E2
Loch Pl PA11 ... 110 B4
Loch Prim Sch G73 ... 138 B2
Loch Rd Bridge Of W PA11 ... 110 B4
Chapelhall ML6 ... 123 E1
Kirkintilloch G66 ... 79 F4
Milngavie G62 ... 55 D2
Stepps G33 ... 99 E2
Loch Shin G74 ... 181 D4
Loch St ML6 ... 123 D1
Loch Striven G74 ... 160 A1
Loch Torridon G74 ... 181 D4
Loch View
Calderbank ML6 ... 123 D1
Caldercruix ML6 ... 105 D3
Loch Voil St G32 ... 119 E2
Lochaber Cres ML7 ... 147 D2
Lochaber Dr
Rutherglen G73 ... 138 B2
Stenhousemuir FK5 ... 23 F2
Lochaber Path G72 ... 161 E4
Lochaber Pl G74 ... 159 F2
Lochaber Rd G61 ... 76 A1
Lochaber Wlk G65 ... 58 B4
Lochaline Ave PA2 ... 113 D1
Lochaline Dr G44 ... 137 D2
Lochalsh Cres G65 ... 58 B4
Lochalsh Dr PA2 ... 113 D1
Lochalsh Pl G72 ... 140 A1
Lochans The G84 ... 15 D2
Lochar Cres G53 ... 115 E1
Lochar Pl G75 ... 179 F4
Lochard Dr PA2 ... 113 D1
Lochay Pl KA10 ... 229 F3
Lochay St G32 ... 119 E2
Lochbrae FK10 ... 5 E1
Lochbrae Dr G73 ... 138 B2
Lochbridge Rd G34 ... 120 A4
Lochbroom Ct G77 ... 156 C3
Lochbroom Dr
Newton Mearns G77 ... 156 C3
Paisley PA2 ... 113 D1
Lochbuie La ML6 ... 102 C2
Lochburn Cres G20 ... 96 C4
Lochburn Pass G20 ... 96 C4
Lochburn Rd G20 ... 96 C4
Lochcraig Ct KA11 ... 220 A2
Lochdochart Rd G34 ... 120 B4
Lochearn Cres
Airdrie ML6 ... 102 C1
Paisley PA2 ... 113 D1
Lochearnhead Rd G33 ... 99 E3
Lochend Ave G69 ... 100 C4
Lochend Cotts G83 ... 20 C2
Lochend Cres G61 ... 75 E2
Lochend Dr G61 ... 75 F2
Lochend Pl KA10 ... 229 F1
Lochend Rd Bearsden G61 ... 75 F2
Coatbridge ML5 ... 101 D1
Glasgow G34, G69 ... 100 B1
Glengarnock KA14 ... 170 B4
Troon KA10 ... 229 E1
Lochend Sec Sch G34 ... 100 B1
Lochend St ML1 ... 163 F3
Locher Ave PA6 ... 91 F1
Locher Cres PA6 ... 111 F4
Locher Gdns PA6 ... 111 F4
Locher Rd PA10 ... 110 C2
Locher Way PA6 ... 111 F4
Locherburn Ave PA6 ... 111 E4
Locherburn Gr PA6 ... 111 E4
Locherburn Pl PA6 ... 111 E4
Lochfauld Rd G23 ... 77 D1
Lochfield Cres PA2 ... 113 F1
Lochfield Dr PA2 ... 114 A1
Lochfield Prim Sch PA2 ... 113 F1
Lochfield Rd PA2 ... 114 A1
Lochgilp St G20 ... 96 B4
Lochgoin Ave G15 ... 74 C2
Lochgoin Prim Sch G15 ... 74 C2
Lochgreen Ave KA10 ... 229 F4
Lochgreen Hospl FK1 ... 41 F1
Lochgreen Pl
Coatbridge ML5 ... 101 E1
Hamilton ML3 ... 183 D4
Kilmarnock KA1 ... 227 F2
Lochgreen Rd FK1 ... 41 F1
Lochgreen St G33 ... 98 B2
Lochhead Ave Denny FK6 ... 21 F1
Linwood PA3 ... 112 A3
Lochiel Dr G65 ... 58 B3
Lochiel La G73 ... 138 B2
Lochiel Rd G46 ... 135 F2
Lochinch Pl G77 ... 156 A3
Lochinvar Pl FK4 ... 40 B2
Lochinvar Rd G67 ... 82 C4
Lochinver Cres PA2 ... 113 D1
Lochinver Dr G44 ... 137 D3
Lochinver Gr G72 ... 139 D3
Lochknowe St ML8 ... 201 F3
Lochlands Gr KA15 ... 171 E4
Lochlands Ind Est FK5 ... 41 D4
Lochlea G74 ... 160 B2
Lochlea Ave Clydebank G81 ... 74 B2
Troon KA10 ... 229 F2
Lochlea Dr KA7 ... 239 D3

Lochlea Rd Clarkston G76 ... 157 F3
Cumbernauld G67 ... 62 B2
Glasgow G43 ... 136 B3
Rutherglen G73 ... 137 F3
Saltcoats KA21 ... 206 A2
Lochlea Way ML1 ... 143 F2
Lochlee Loan 12 ML9 ... 185 E1
Lochleven La G42 ... 137 D4
Lochleven Rd G42 ... 137 D4
Lochlibo Ave G13 ... 94 C4
Lochlibo Cres G78 ... 134 A1
Lochlibo Ct KA11 ... 220 A3
Lochlibo Rd Barrhead G78 ... 134 A1
Burnhouse KA15 ... 172 C2
Irvine KA11, KA13 ... 209 E2
Lugton G78 ... 152 C1
Neilston G78 ... 154 C4
Lochlibo Terr G78 ... 134 A1
Lochlie Pl KA20 ... 206 C1
Lochlip Rd PA12 ... 129 E1
Lochmaben Dr FK5 ... 23 F2
Lochmaben Rd G52 ... 114 C2
Lochmaben Wynd KA3 ... 223 D3
Lochmaddy Ave G44 ... 137 D2
Lochnagar Dr G61 ... 75 D4
Lochnagar Rd KA1 ... 228 A2
Lochnagar Way 19 ML9 ... 185 E1
Lochore Ave PA3 ... 114 A4
Lochpark KA7 ... 238 B2
Lochpark Pl FK6 ... 21 F1
Lochranza Ct KA3 ... 223 D3
Lochranza Dr
East Kilbride G75 ... 180 A2
Helensburgh G84 ... 16 C1
Lochranza La G75 ... 180 B2
Lochranza Pl KA21 ... 206 A1
Lochridge Pl FK6 ... 21 E1
Lochshore East Ind Est
KA14 ... 170 B4
Lochshore South Ind Est
KA25 ... 170 A4
Lochside Bearsden G61 ... 75 F2
Gartcosh G69 ... 100 C3
Lochside Ct KA8 ... 236 A1
Lochside Rd Ayr KA8 ... 236 A1
Slamannan FK1 ... 86 B1
Lochside St 2 G41 ... 116 C1
Lochview Ave PA19 ... 45 D4
Lochview Cres G33 ... 98 C2
Lochview Dr G33 ... 98 C2
Lochview Gdns G33 ... 98 C2
Lochview Pl G33 ... 98 C2
Lochview Quadrant ML4 ... 141 F2
Lochview Rd Bearsden G61 ... 75 F2
Beith KA15 ... 170 C4
Coatbridge ML5 ... 101 E1
Port Glasgow PA14 ... 47 D1
Lochview Terr G69 ... 100 C3
Lochwinnoch Prim Sch
PA12 ... 129 E2
Lochwinnoch Rd PA13 ... 89 E4
Lochwinnoch Sta PA12 ... 150 C4
Lochwood Ct KA13 ... 207 E3
Lochwood Loan G69 ... 81 D2
Lochwood Pl KA11 ... 219 F3
Lochwood St G33 ... 98 C1
Lochy Ave PA4 ... 94 C1
Lochy Gdns G64 ... 78 A1
Lochy Pl PA8 ... 72 C1
Lochy St ML2 ... 165 D1
Lock Sixteen FK1 ... 41 E3
Lockerbie Ave G43 ... 136 C3
Locket Yett View ML4 ... 141 F3
Lockhart Ave G72 ... 139 E3
Lockhart Dr
Cambuslang G72 ... 139 E3
Lanark ML11 ... 214 C3
Lockhart Hospl ML11 ... 215 E2
Lockhart Pl Stonehouse ML9 ... 198 C2
Wishaw ML2 ... 165 F2
Lockhart St Carluke ML8 ... 187 F1
Glasgow G21 ... 98 A1
Hamilton ML3 ... 183 E3
Stonehouse ML9 ... 199 D2
Lockhart Terr G74 ... 160 A1
Locks St ML5 ... 122 B3
Locksley Ave
Cumbernauld G67 ... 82 C4
Glasgow G13 ... 95 E4
Locksley Cres G67 ... 82 C3
Locksley Ct G67 ... 82 C3
Locksley Pl G67 ... 82 C3
Locksley Rd
Cumbernauld G67 ... 82 C3
Paisley PA2 ... 112 C1
Lodge Cres PA13 ... 89 F4
Lodge Dr FK5 ... 23 F1
Lodge Gdns PA13 ... 69 F1
Lodge Gr PA13 ... 69 F1
Lodge Pk PA13 ... 69 F1
Logan Ave G77 ... 156 B3
Logan Ct KA10 ... 229 E2
Logan Dr Cumbernauld G68 ... 61 E2
Paisley PA3 ... 113 E3
Troon KA10 ... 229 E2
Logan Gdns ML1 ... 165 D4
Logan St Blantyre G72 ... 161 F4
Glasgow G5 ... 117 E2
Logan Tower G72 ... 139 F2
Logandale Ave ML2 ... 165 F3
Loganlea Dr ML1 ... 143 D1
Logans Prim Sch ML1 ... 163 D4
Logans Rd ML1 ... 163 E4
Loganswell Dr G46 ... 135 F1
Loganswell Gdns G46 ... 135 F1
Loganswell Pl G46 ... 135 F1
Loganswell Rd G46 ... 135 F1
Logie Dr FK5 ... 23 D2
Logie La FK9 ... 2 B4
Logie Pk G74 ... 160 A2
Logie Rd FK9 ... 2 B2
Logie Sq G74 ... 160 A2
Lomax St G33 ... 118 B4
Lomond G75 ... 180 C3
Lomond Ave Hurlford KA1 ... 228 C3
Port Glasgow PA14 ... 68 C4
Renfrew PA4 ... 94 A1
Lomond Cres Alexandria G83 ... 27 E4
Beith KA15 ... 150 B1
Bridge Of W PA11 ... 110 B4
Cumbernauld G67 ... 82 B4
Paisley PA2 ... 133 E4
Stenhousemuir FK5 ... 23 F2
Stirling FK9 ... 2 A2
Lomond Ct Alloa FK10 ... 10 B3
Barrhead G78 ... 134 B1
Cumbernauld G67 ... 82 B4
Dumbarton G82 ... 49 F2
Helensburgh G84 ... 16 C1
Lomond Dr Airdrie ML6 ... 102 C1
Alexandria G83 ... 27 E4
Bannockburn FK7 ... 7 F1
Barrhead G78 ... 134 A2
Bishopbriggs G64 ... 78 A2
Bothwell G71 ... 141 D2
Cumbernauld G67 ... 82 A4
Dumbarton G82 ... 50 A3
Falkirk FK2 ... 24 B1
Newton Mearns G77 ... 156 B4
Wishaw ML2 ... 165 D1
Lomond Gdns PA5 ... 112 B1
Lomond Gr G67 ... 82 B4
Lomond Ind Est G83 ... 27 F3
Lomond Pl Coatbridge ML5 ... 101 F1
Cumbernauld G67 ... 82 A4
Erskine PA8 ... 72 C1
Irvine KA12 ... 219 E3
Stepps G33 ... 99 F2
Lomond Prim Sch G84 ... 16 B1
Lomond Rd Alexandria G83 ... 27 E4
Balloch G83 ... 27 F4
Bearsden G61 ... 75 F1
Coatbridge ML5 ... 101 E1
Greenock PA15 ... 46 A2
Kilmarnock KA1 ... 228 A2
Kirkintilloch G66 ... 79 E3
Shotts ML7 ... 146 C3
Uddingston G71 ... 120 C1
Lomond Sec Sch G84 ... 16 B1
Lomond St Alloa FK10 ... 4 C1
Glasgow G22 ... 97 D3
Helensburgh G84 ... 16 C1
Lomond View
Cumbernauld G67 ... 82 B4
Hamilton ML3 ... 161 F1
Symington KA1 ... 231 E2
Lomond Way Denny FK6 ... 39 E3
Irvine KA11 ... 220 A2
Motherwell ML1 ... 143 D3
Lomond Wlk
5 Larkhall ML9 ... 185 D2
Motherwell ML1 ... 143 E2
Lomondside Ave G76 ... 157 E4
Lomondview Ind Est PA5 ... 111 F2
London Rd
Glasgow G31, G32, G40 ... 118 C1
Kilmarnock KA3 ... 228 A4
London Road Prim Sch
G40 ... 118 A2
London St Larkhall ML9 ... 185 D2
Renfrew PA4 ... 94 B3
Lonend PA1 ... 113 F2
Loney Cres FK6 ... 39 F4
Long Calderwood Prim Sch
G74 ... 160 B2
Long Crags View G82 ... 50 B3
Long Dr East Kilbride G75 ... 181 D4
Irvine KA11 ... 219 F3
Long Row Glasgow G69 ... 120 B3
Lanark ML11 ... 214 C1
Menstrie FK11 ... 4 A4
Longay Pl G22 ... 97 E4
Longay St G22 ... 97 E4
Longbank Dr KA7 ... 239 D2
Longbank Rd KA7 ... 239 D2
Longbar Ave KA14 ... 170 B3
Longcraigs Ave KA22 ... 205 E3
Longcroft Dr PA4 ... 94 B2
Longdales Ave FK2 ... 42 A4
Longdales Ct FK2 ... 42 A4
Longdales Pl FK2 ... 42 A4
Longdales Rd FK2 ... 42 A4
Longden St G81 ... 94 B4
Longdyke Pl FK2 ... 24 B2
Longfield Ave KA21 ... 205 F1
Longfield Pl KA21 ... 205 F1
Longford Ave KA13 ... 207 F1
Longford St G33 ... 118 B4
Longhill Ave KA7 ... 238 B1
Longlands Pk KA7 ... 238 C2
Longlands Prim Sch G67 ... 82 C4
Longlee G69 ... 120 A2
Longmeadow PA5 ... 111 E1
Longpark Ave KA3 ... 222 C1
Longriggend Rd ML6 ... 85 E1
Longrow Gdns KA11 ... 219 F4
Longstone Pl G33 ... 119 D4
Longstone Rd G33 ... 119 D4
Longwill Terr G67 ... 62 A2
Lonmay Rd G33 ... 119 E4
Lonsdale Ave G46 ... 136 B2
Loom Wlk PA10 ... 111 D2
Lora Dr G52 ... 115 F2
Loreny Dr KA1 ... 227 F1
Loreny Ind Est KA1 ... 227 F2
Loretto Pl G33 ... 118 C4
Loretto St G33 ... 118 C4
Lorien Ct KA8 ... 236 B2
Lorimar Pl FK2 ... 24 A1
Lorimer Cres G75 ... 180 B4
Lorn Ave G69 ... 100 B4
Lorn Dr G83 ... 19 F1
Lorn Pl G66 ... 59 E1
Lorne Arc KA7 ... 238 C4
Lorne Cres G64 ... 78 B1
Lorne Dr Linwood PA3 ... 112 A3
Motherwell ML1 ... 142 B1
Lorne Gdns Laurieston FK2 ... 42 C2
Salsburgh ML7 ... 125 D1
Lorne Pl ML5 ... 122 B3
Lorne Rd Larbert FK5 ... 23 E1
Paisley G52 ... 114 C4
Lorne St Glasgow G51 ... 116 B3
Hamilton ML3 ... 162 B2
Helensburgh G84 ... 16 B1
Lorne Street Prim Sch G51 ... 116 B3
Lorne Terr G72 ... 138 C2
Lornshill Acad FK10 ... 4 C1
Lornshill Cres FK10 ... 9 F4
Lorraine Gardens La 25 G12 ... 96 B2
Lorraine Gdns 24 G12 ... 96 B2
Lorraine Rd 23 G12 ... 96 B2
Lorraine Way G83 ... 27 F1
Loskin Dr G22 ... 97 D4
Losshill FK11 ... 4 A3
Lossie Cres PA4 ... 94 C1
Lossie St G33 ... 98 B1
Lothian Cres Paisley PA2 ... 113 E1
Stirling FK9 ... 2 B2
Lothian Dr G76 ... 157 E4
Lothian Gdns 3 G20 ... 96 C2
Lothian Rd Ayr KA7 ... 239 D4
Greenock PA16 ... 44 B2
Stewarton KA3 ... 211 E4
Lothian St G52 ... 114 C4
Lothian Way G74 ... 160 B2
Louburn EH48 ... 107 E2
Louden Hill Rd G33 ... 98 C3
Louden St ML6 ... 123 D4
Loudens Wlk FK6 ... 21 E3
Loudon G75 ... 180 C3
Loudon Gdns PA5 ... 112 A2
Loudon Rd G33 ... 99 D2
Loudon St ML2 ... 165 D3
Loudon Terr G61 ... 75 E4
Loudonhill Ave ML3 ... 183 F4
Loudoun Ave KA1 ... 228 A2
Loudoun Cres KA13 ... 207 D2
Loudoun Pl Crosshouse KA2 ... 226 C4
Symington KA1 ... 231 E2
Loudoun St KA3 ... 211 F4
Loudoun Terr KA9 ... 236 B4
Loudoun-Montgomery
Prim Sch KA12 ... 219 E1
Louise Gdns ML1 ... 142 C3
Louisville Ave ML2 ... 165 E3
Lounsdale Ave PA2 ... 113 D2
Lounsdale Cres PA2 ... 113 D1
Lounsdale Dr PA2 ... 113 D1
Lounsdale House PA2 ... 113 D1
Lounsdale Pl G14 ... 95 D2
Lounsdale Rd PA2 ... 113 D1
Lounsdale Way PA2 ... 113 D2
Lourdes Ave G52 ... 115 E2
Lourdes Ct G52 ... 115 E2
Lourdes Prim RC Sch G52 ... 115 E3
Lourdes Sec Sch G52 ... 115 E2
Lovat Ave G61 ... 75 F4
Lovat Dr G66 ... 79 D4
Lovat Path 3 ML9 ... 185 E1
Lovat Pl Paisley G52 ... 114 C4
Rutherglen G73 ... 138 B2
Love Ave PA11 ... 89 F1
Love St Kilwinning KA13 ... 208 A2
Paisley PA3 ... 113 F3
Lovers Loan FK12 ... 5 D4
Lovers Wlk FK8 ... 2 A1
Low Barholm PA10 ... 111 D1
Low Broadlie Rd G78 ... 154 B4
Low Church La 1 KA1 ... 227 F4
Low Craigends G65 ... 60 C4
Low Cres G81 ... 94 C4
Low Flender Rd G76 ... 157 E3
Low Glencairn St KA1 ... 227 F3
Low Green Rd KA12 ... 219 D1
Low Moss Ind Est G64 ... 78 A2
Low Parksail PA8 ... 93 E4
Low Patrick St ML3 ... 162 C2
Low Pleasance ML9 ... 185 D2
Low Rd Ayr KA8 ... 236 C2
Paisley PA2 ... 113 E2
Low Waters Rd ML3 ... 162 B1
Lower Auchingramont Rd
ML3 ... 162 C2
Lower Bourtree Dr G73 ... 138 B2
Lower Bouverie St PA14 ... 47 E1
Lower Bridge St FK8 ... 2 A1
Lower Castlehill FK8 ... 2 A1
Lower Mill Rd G76 ... 157 F3
Lower Millgate G71 ... 140 C3
Lower Stoneymollan Rd
G83 ... 27 E4
Lower Sutherland Cres
G84 ... 16 A2
Lowndes St G78 ... 134 B1
Lowther Ave G61 ... 75 E4
Lowther Bank KA11 ... 220 B1
Lowther Pl KA1 ... 228 A2
Lowther Terr 35 G12 ... 96 B2
Loyal Ave PA8 ... 72 C1
Loyal Gdns G61 ... 75 D4
Loyal Pl PA8 ... 72 C1
Loyne Dr PA4 ... 94 C1
Luath St G51 ... 116 A4
Lubas Ave G42 ... 137 E4
Lubas Pl G42 ... 137 E4
Lubnaig Dr PA8 ... 72 C1
Lubnaig Gdns G61 ... 75 E4
Lubnaig Pl ML6 ... 102 C1
Lubnaig Rd G43 ... 136 C3
Lubnaig Wlk ML1 ... 143 D3
Luce Ave KA1 ... 228 A3
Luckenhill Dr ML6 ... 84 B2
Luckiesfauld G78 ... 154 B3
Luckingsford Ave PA4 ... 93 E4
Luckingsford Dr PA4 ... 93 E4
Luckingsford Rd PA4 ... 93 E4
Lucy Brae G71 ... 140 C4
Ludgate FK10 ... 10 A3
Ludovic Sq PA5 ... 111 F2
Luffness Gdns G32 ... 119 D1
Lugar Ave KA11 ... 220 A3
Lugar Cres KA9 ... 236 A3
Lugar Dr G52 ... 115 F2
Lugar Pl Glasgow G44 ... 137 F3
Troon KA10 ... 229 F3
Lugar St ML5 ... 122 A4
Luggie Rd ML8 ... 187 F2
Luggie View G67 ... 82 A4
Luggiebank Pl G69 ... 121 D2
Luggiebank Rd
Kirkintilloch G66 ... 79 E4
Kirkintilloch, Eastside G66 ... 58 B1
Lugton Ct KA12 ... 219 E1
Lugton Rd KA3 ... 195 D4
Luing ML6 ... 123 F3
Luing Rd G52 ... 115 F3
Lumloch St G21 ... 98 A2
Lumsden La G3 ... 96 B1
Lumsden Pl KA20 ... 206 C1
Lumsden St G3 ... 96 B1
Lunan Dr G64 ... 98 B4
Lunan Pl G51 ... 115 F4
Lunar Path ML6 ... 123 E1
Luncarty Pl G32 ... 119 D2
Luncarty St G32 ... 119 D2
Lunderston Dr G53 ... 135 D4
Lundholm Rd KA20 ... 217 F4
Lundie Gdns G64 ... 98 B4
Lundie St G32 ... 118 C2
Lurg St PA14 ... 68 B4
Luss Ave PA15 ... 46 A1
Luss Brae ML3 ... 161 F1
Luss Pl PA15 ... 46 A1
Luss Rd Alexandria G83 ... 27 E4
Glasgow G51 ... 115 F4
Helensburgh G84 ... 17 D3
Lusset Glen G60 ... 73 D3
Lusset Rd G60 ... 73 D3
Lusshill Terr G71 ... 120 A1
Lybster Cres G73 ... 138 B2
Lychgate Rd FK10 ... 4 A1
Lye Brae G67 ... 62 A1
Lyell Ct G74 ... 159 F2
Lyell Gr G74 ... 159 F2
Lyle Cres PA7 ... 72 A2
Lyle Gr PA16 ... 45 D4
Lyle Pl Greenock PA16 ... 45 D4
Paisley PA2 ... 113 F1
Lyle Rd Airdrie ML6 ... 123 F4
Greenock PA16 ... 45 D4
Kilmacolm PA13 ... 89 E4
Lyle Sq G62 ... 54 C1
Lyle St PA15 ... 45 F2
Lylefoot Cres PA16 ... 45 D4
Lylefoot Pl PA16 ... 45 D4
Lylesland Ct PA2 ... 113 F1
Lylestone Terr KA13 ... 208 B4
Lyman Dr ML2 ... 165 E4
Lymburn Pl KA8 ... 239 D4
Lymburn St G3 ... 116 B4
Lymekilns Rd G74 ... 159 E2
Lyndale Pl G20 ... 96 B4
Lyndale Rd G20 ... 96 B4
Lyndhurst Gardens La
G20 ... 96 C2
Lyndhurst Gdns G20 ... 96 C2
Lyne Croft G64 ... 78 A2
Lyne St ML2 ... 165 D3
Lynedoch Cres G3 ... 240 A4
Lynedoch Crescent La G3 ... 96 C1
Lynedoch Ind Est PA15 ... 46 A2
Lynedoch Pl G3 ... 240 A4
Lynedoch St Glasgow G3 ... 240 A4
Greenock PA15 ... 45 F2
Lynedoch Terr G3 ... 240 A4
Lynmouth Pl PA19 ... 44 C3
Lynn Ave KA24 ... 191 E4
Lynn Ct ML9 ... 185 D1
Lynn Dr Eaglesham G76 ... 178 C3
Kilbirnie KA25 ... 149 D2
Milngavie G62 ... 55 E1
Lynn Wlk Balloch G83 ... 27 F4
Bothwell G71 ... 141 D3
Lynnburn Ave ML4 ... 142 A3
Lynne Dr G23 ... 76 C1
Lynnhurst G71 ... 140 C4
Lynnwood Rd ML2 ... 166 B3
Lynton Ave G46 ... 136 A1
Lyon Cres FK9 ... 2 A3
Lyon Rd Erskine PA8 ... 72 C1
Linwood PA5 ... 112 A2
Paisley PA2 ... 112 C1
Lyoncross Ave G78 ... 134 B2
Lyoncross Cres G78 ... 134 B2
Lyoncross Rd G53 ... 115 D1
Lyons Quadrant ML2 ... 164 B2
Lysa Vale Pl ML4 ... 141 F3
Lysander Way 9 PA4 ... 94 B1
Lytham Dr G23 ... 76 C1
Lytham Mdws G72 ... 140 C1
Lythgow Way ML11 ... 215 E3
Lyttelton G75 ... 180 A4
Mabel St ML1 ... 163 F3
Maberry Cl KA3 ... 195 E1
Maberry Pl KA10 ... 229 F3
Macadam Gdns ML4 ... 142 A3
Macadam Pl Ayr KA8 ... 236 A1
East Kilbride G75 ... 180 C4
Falkirk FK1 ... 41 E3
Irvine KA11 ... 219 F1
Kilmarnock KA3 ... 223 E1
Macadam Sq KA8 ... 236 A1
Macallan Pl KA11 ... 219 F4
Macallister Pl KA3 ... 223 E1
Macalpine Pl KA3 ... 223 E1
Macandrew Pl KA3 ... 223 E1
Macara Dr KA12 ... 219 F2
Macarthur Ave ML6 ... 102 B2
Macarthur Cres G74 ... 159 E2
Macarthur Ct G74 ... 159 E2
Macarthur Dr G74 ... 159 E2
Macarthur Gdns G74 ... 159 E2
Macaulay Pl G84 ... 16 A1
Macauley Pl KA3 ... 223 E1
Macbeth G74 ... 160 A3
Macbeth Dr KA3 ... 223 E1
Macbeth Gdns KA3 ... 223 E1
Macbeth Pl G31 ... 118 B2
Macbeth Rd Greenock PA16 ... 45 D3
Stewarton KA3 ... 211 E4
Macbeth St G31 ... 118 B2
Macbeth Wlk KA3 ... 223 E1
Maccabe Gdns G65 ... 57 F4
Maccallum Pl KA3 ... 223 E1
Maccrimmon Pk G74 ... 159 D2
Macdairmid Dr ML3 ... 183 D4
Macdonald Ave G74 ... 159 D2
Macdonald Cres G65 ... 60 A2
Macdonald Ct KA15 ... 171 D4
Macdonald Dr
Kilmarnock KA3 ... 223 E1
Stirling FK7 ... 7 D2
Macdonald Gdns KA3 ... 223 E1
Macdonald Gr ML4 ... 141 F1
Macdonald Pl KA3 ... 223 E1
Macdonald St
Motherwell ML1 ... 163 F3
Rutherglen G73 ... 138 A4
Macdonald Wlk G83 ... 27 F4
Macdougal Quadrant ML4 ... 141 F1
Macdougall Dr KA3 ... 223 E1
Macdougall St Glasgow G43 ... 136 B4
Greenock PA15 ... 46 B2
Macdowall St
Johnstone PA5 ... 111 F2
Paisley PA3 ... 113 E3
Macduff PA8 ... 73 D1
Macduff Pl G31 ... 118 B2
Macduff St G31 ... 118 B2
Mace Ct FK7 ... 7 E2
Mace Rd G13 ... 75 E1
Macewan Pl KA3 ... 228 B4
Macfarlane Cres FK1 ... 42 A3
Macfarlane Dr KA3 ... 223 E1
Macfarlane Rd G61 ... 76 A2
Macfie Pl G74 ... 159 D2
Macgregor Dr KA3 ... 228 B4
Machan Ave ML9 ... 185 D2
Machan Rd ML9 ... 185 D1
Machanhill ML9 ... 185 D1
Machanhill Prim Sch ML9 ... 185 D2
Machanhill View ML9 ... 185 D1
Machrie Ct FK1 ... 41 E2
Machrie Dr Glasgow G45 ... 137 F2
Helensburgh G84 ... 16 C2
Newton Mearns G77 ... 156 C3
Machrie Gn G75 ... 180 A2
Machrie Pl KA13 ... 207 E2
Machrie Rd Glasgow G45 ... 137 F2
Kilmarnock KA3 ... 222 C2
Motherwell ML1 ... 163 D4
Machrie St G45 ... 137 F2
Macinnes Pl KA3 ... 223 E1
Macintosh Pl
East Kilbride G75 ... 180 B4
Falkirk FK1 ... 42 A1
Kilmarnock KA3 ... 223 E1
Macintyre Pl KA3 ... 223 E1
Macintyre Rd KA9 ... 233 E1
Macintyre St G3 ... 240 A2
Macivor Cres G74 ... 159 D2
Macivor Pl KA3 ... 223 E1
Mack St ML6 ... 123 D4
Mackean St PA3 ... 113 E3
Mackeith St G40 ... 117 F2
Mackellar Pl KA3 ... 223 E1
Mackendrick Pl KA3 ... 228 B4
Mackenzie Dr
Johnstone PA10 ... 111 D1
Kilmarnock KA3 ... 223 D1
Mackenzie Gdns G74 ... 159 D2
Mackenzie Pl FK1 ... 42 A1
Mackenzie St PA15 ... 46 B2
Mackenzie Terr ML4 ... 142 A4
Mackie Ave
Port Glasgow PA14 ... 47 D1
Stewarton KA3 ... 195 E1
Mackie Pl KA3 ... 223 E1
Mackie St KA8 ... 236 B1
Mackie's Mill Rd PA5 ... 132 B4
Mackinlay Pl KA1 ... 228 A4
Mackinlay St G5 ... 117 D2
Mackinnon Dr KA3 ... 228 B4
Mackinnon Terr KA12 ... 219 F2
Mackintosh Pl KA11 ... 219 F1

Maclachlan Ave FK6 .... 21 E1
Maclachlan Pl G84 .... 16 C2
Maclachlan Rd G84 .... 16 C2
Maclaren Pl KA3 .... 228 B4
Maclaren Terr FK2 .... 24 A1
Maclay Ave PA10 .... 111 D1
Maclean Cres FK12 .... 5 E4
Maclean Ct
East Kilbride G74 .... 159 D2
Stirling FK7 .... 7 E2
Maclean Dr KA3 .... 223 D1
Maclean Gr G74 .... 159 D2
Maclean Pl G74 .... 159 D2
Maclean Sq G51 .... 116 C3
Maclean St Clydebank G81 .... 94 C4
Glasgow G51 .... 116 B3
Maclean Terr EH48 .... 107 E2
Maclehose Rd G67 .... 62 B2
Maclellan Rd G78 .... 154 C3
Maclellan St G41 .... 116 B3
Macleod Cres G84 .... 16 A2
Macleod Dr
Helensburgh G84 .... 16 B2
Kilmarnock KA3 .... 228 B4
Macleod Pl
East Kilbride G74 .... 160 A2
Kilmarnock KA3 .... 228 B4
Macleod St G4 .... 241 F2
Macmillan Dr Gourock PA19 . 44 B3
Kilmarnock KA3 .... 223 E1
Macmillan Gdns G71 .... 121 D1
Macmillan Pl KA3 .... 223 E1
Macmillan St ML9 .... 184 C1
Macnab Pl KA3 .... 223 D1
Macnaughton Dr KA3 .... 223 E1
Macneil Pl KA3 .... 223 D1
Macneill Dr G74 .... 159 D2
Macneill Gdns G74 .... 159 D2
Macneill St ML9 .... 184 C2
Macneish Way G74 .... 159 E2
Macnicol Ct G74 .... 159 D2
Macnicol Pk G74 .... 159 D2
Macnicol Pl
East Kilbride G74 .... 159 D2
Kilmarnock KA3 .... 223 E1
Macphail Dr KA3 .... 223 E1
Macpherson Gdns KA3 .... 223 E1
Macpherson Pk G74 .... 159 E2
Macpherson Pl Falkirk FK1 ... 41 F1
Kilmarnock KA3 .... 223 E1
Macpherson Wlk KA3 .... 223 E1
Macphie Rd G82 .... 50 B2
Macrae Dr KA9 .... 233 E1
Macrae Gdns G74 .... 159 E2
Macreadie Pl KA11 .... 220 B3
Macrimmon Pl G75 .... 180 C4
Macrobert Ave KA11 .... 220 A1
Mactaggart Rd G67 .... 82 C4
Madeira La PA16 .... 45 E4
Madeira St PA16 .... 45 E4
Madill Pl FK5 .... 23 F2
Madison Ave G44 .... 137 D3
Madison Path G72 .... 161 E4
Madras Pl Glasgow G40 .... 117 F2
Neilston G78 .... 154 C4
Madras St G40 .... 117 F2
Mafeking St Glasgow G51 .. 116 A3
Wishaw ML2 .... 164 B2
Mafeking Terr G78 .... 154 B4
Magdalen Way PA2 .... 132 C4
Maggie Wood's Loan FK1 .. 41 F3
Magna St ML1 .... 163 D4
Magnolia Dr G72 .... 139 F2
Magnolia Gdns ML1 .... 143 E2
Magnolia Pl G71 .... 141 E4
Magnolia St ML2 .... 165 D3
Magnum L Ctr KA12 .... 218 C1
Magnus Cres G44 .... 137 D2
Magnus Rd PA6 .... 111 E4
Mahon Ct G69 .... 80 C1
Maid Morville Ave KA11 .... 225 E4
Maidens G74 .... 159 E2
Maidens Ave G77 .... 157 D3
Maidland Rd G53 .... 135 E4
Maidpath East G74 .... 159 E1
Maidpath West G74 .... 159 E1
Mailerbeg Gdns G69 .... 80 C2
Mailie Wlk ML1 .... 143 E2
Mailing Ave G64 .... 78 B1
Mailings Rd G65 .... 37 F2
Maimhor Rd KA23 .... 190 B2
Main Rd Ayr KA8 .... 236 C1
Cardross G82 .... 48 A4
Crookedholm KA3 .... 228 C4
Cumbernauld G67 .... 82 A4
Elderslie PA5 .... 112 B2
Fenwick KA3 .... 213 D2
Gatehead KA2 .... 226 C3
Kilbirnie KA25 .... 149 D1
Langbank PA14 .... 70 B4
Paisley PA2 .... 113 E2
Rosneath G84 .... 15 D2
Springside KA11 .... 220 C1
Waterside KA3 .... 213 F2
Main St Airth FK2 .... 14 B2
Alexandria G83 .... 27 F2
Alexandria, Dalmonach G83 .... 27 F3
Alloa FK10 .... 5 E1
Ayr KA8 .... 235 F1
Balloch G83 .... 19 F1
Bannockburn FK7 .... 7 E1
Banton G65 .... 37 E2
Barrhead G78 .... 134 B1
Beith KA15 .... 150 A1
Bellshill ML4 .... 142 A3
Main St continued
Blackridge EH48 .... 107 E2
Blantyre G72 .... 161 E3
Bonnybridge FK4 .... 40 A3
Bothwell G71 .... 141 D1
Bridge Of W PA11 .... 110 B4
Calderbank ML6 .... 123 E1
Caldercruix ML6 .... 105 D2
California FK1 .... 66 C3
Cambus FK10 .... 9 D4
Cambuslang G72 .... 139 D3
Chapelhall ML6 .... 123 F2
Chryston G69 .... 80 B1
Clarkston G76 .... 157 F3
Cleland ML1 .... 144 B1
Coatbridge ML5 .... 122 B3
Cowie FK7 .... 12 B4
Cumbernauld G67 .... 62 A3
Dalry KA24 .... 191 E4
Drybridge KA11 .... 225 E3
Drybridge, Dundonald KA11, KA2 .... 225 F1
Dunlop KA3 .... 195 D4
East Kilbride G74 .... 159 F1
Falkirk FK1 .... 41 F3
Falkirk, Bainsford FK2 .... 42 A4
Falkirk, Carronshore FK2 .... 24 B2
Fallin FK7 .... 8 C2
Gateside KA15 .... 171 F4
Glasgow G40 .... 117 F2
Glasgow, Muirhead G69 .... 120 B2
Glasgow, Thornliebank G46 .. 135 F2
Glenboig ML5 .... 101 F3
Glengarnock KA14 .... 170 A3
Greenock PA15 .... 46 B2
Hamilton G72 .... 161 F3
Houston PA6 .... 91 D1
Howwood PA9 .... 130 C3
Irvine KA11 .... 220 B1
Kilmaurs KA3 .... 222 B4
Kilsyth G65 .... 60 B4
Kilwinning KA13 .... 207 F2
Larbert FK5 .... 23 E1
Lennoxtown G65 .... 57 E4
Lochwinnoch PA12 .... 129 E1
Longriggend ML6 .... 85 D1
Milngavie G62 .... 76 A4
Monkton KA9 .... 233 E2
Motherwell ML1 .... 143 D3
Neilston G78 .... 154 B4
Overtown ML2 .... 186 B3
Plains ML6 .... 104 A1
Plean FK7 .... 12 B2
Prestwick KA9 .... 236 B4
Rutherglen G73 .... 138 A4
Salsburgh ML7 .... 125 D1
Shieldhill FK1 .... 66 B3
Shotts ML7 .... 147 D2
Slamannan FK1 .... 86 A4
Stenhousemuir FK5 .... 23 F1
Stevenston KA20 .... 206 B1
Stewarton KA3 .... 211 E4
Stirling FK7 .... 6 B3
Stirling, St Ninians FK7 .... 7 D2
Symington KA1 .... 231 E2
Torrance G64 .... 78 A4
Troon KA10 .... 230 A2
Tullibody FK10 .... 4 A1
Twechar G65 .... 59 F2
Uddingston G71 .... 140 C3
West Kilbride KA23 .... 190 B3
Wishaw ML2 .... 165 D2
Wishaw, Newmains ML2 .... 166 A2
Main St E FK11 .... 4 A3
Main St W FK11 .... 3 F3
Mainhead Terr G67 .... 62 A3
Mainhill Ave G69 .... 120 B3
Mainhill Dr G69 .... 120 B3
Mainhill Pl G69 .... 120 B3
Mainhill Rd G69 .... 120 C3
Mainholm Acad KA8 .... 236 B1
Mainholm Cres KA8 .... 236 B1
Mainholm Rd Ayr KA8 .... 239 F4
Ayr, Braehead KA8 .... 236 B1
Mains Ave Beith KA15 .... 150 A1
Glasgow G46 .... 136 A1
Helensburgh G84 .... 16 A2
Mains Ct ML11 .... 215 E3
Mains Dr PA8 .... 73 E1
Mains Hill PA8 .... 73 D1
Mains Pl ML4 .... 142 A2
Mains Rd Beith KA15 .... 150 A1
East Kilbride G74 .... 159 F3
Harthill ML7 .... 127 F3
Mains River PA8 .... 73 E1
Mains Wood PA8 .... 73 E1
Mainscroft PA8 .... 73 E1
Mainshill Ave PA8 .... 73 D1
Mainshill Gdns PA8 .... 73 D1
Mair Ave KA24 .... 191 F4
Mair St G51 .... 116 C3
Maitland Ave FK7 .... 7 E1
Maitland Bank ML9 .... 185 E2
Maitland Cres FK7 .... 7 D2
Maitland Ct G84 .... 16 B1
Maitland Dr G64 .... 57 D1
Maitland Pl PA4 .... 94 A1
Maitland St Glasgow G4 .... 240 C4
Helensburgh G84 .... 16 B1
Majors Loan FK1 .... 42 A2
Majors Pl FK1 .... 42 A2
Malcolm Ct KA3 .... 195 F1
Malcolm Dr FK5 .... 23 F2
Malcolm Gdns G74 .... 159 E1
Malcolm Pl G84 .... 17 D1
Malcolm St ML1 .... 163 E3
Malin Pl G33 .... 118 C4
Mallaig Pl G51 .... 115 E4
Mallaig Rd Glasgow G51 .... 115 F4
Port Glasgow PA14 .... 68 C4
Mallaig Terr PA16 .... 44 C2
Mallard Cres
East Kilbride G75 .... 180 A3
Greenock PA16 .... 45 D3
Mallard La
14 Bothwell G71 .... 141 D2
Greenock PA16 .... 45 D3
Mallard Pl G75 .... 180 A3
Mallard Rd G81 .... 74 A3
Mallard Terr G75 .... 180 A3
Mallard Way ML4 .... 141 F4
Malleable Gdns ML1 .... 142 B1
Malletsheugh Rd G77 .... 156 A2
Malloch Cres PA5 .... 112 A1
Malloch Pl G74 .... 160 A1
Malloch St G20 .... 96 C3
Malov Ct G75 .... 180 C3
Malplaquet Ct ML8 .... 188 A1
Maltbarns St G20 .... 97 D2
Malvaig La G72 .... 161 E3
Malvern Ct G31 .... 118 A3
Malvern Way PA3 .... 113 E4
Mambeg Dr G51 .... 115 F4
Mamore Pl G43 .... 136 B3
Mamore St G43 .... 136 B3
Mamre Dr FK1 .... 66 C3
Manchester Dr G12 .... 96 A3
Mandela Ave FK2 .... 42 B4
Mandora Ct ML8 .... 188 A1
Manitoba Cres G75 .... 159 D1
Mannering G74 .... 160 B2
Mannering Ct G41 .... 136 B4
Mannering Rd
Glasgow G41 .... 136 B4
Paisley PA2 .... 132 C4
Mannering Way PA2 .... 112 C1
Mannfield Ave FK4 .... 39 F2
Mannofield G61 .... 75 E2
Manor Ave KA3 .... 223 D2
Manor Cres Gourock PA19 .... 44 C4
Tullibody FK10 .... 4 A1
Manor Dr ML6 .... 122 C4
Manor Gate G77 .... 156 C2
Manor Loan FK11 .... 3 D2
Manor Pk ML3 .... 162 B1
Manor Powis Cotts FK11 .... 3 D2
Manor Rd Clydebank G15 .... 74 C1
Gartcosh G69 .... 100 C3
Glasgow G14 .... 95 F2
Paisley PA2 .... 112 C1
Manor St FK1 .... 42 A2
Manor View
Calderbank ML6 .... 123 D1
Larkhall ML9 .... 185 E1
Manor Way G73 .... 138 B2
Manresa Pl 14 G4 .... 97 D1
Manse Ave Bearsden G61 .... 75 F3
Bothwell G71 .... 141 D1
Coatbridge ML5 .... 121 E2
Manse Brae Dalserf ML9 .... 200 A4
Glasgow G44 .... 137 D3
Rhu G84 .... 15 E3
Manse Cres Houston PA6 .... 91 D1
Stirling FK7 .... 7 D2
Manse Ct Barrhead G78 .... 134 B2
Kilsyth G65 .... 60 B4
Kilwinning KA13 .... 207 F2
Law ML8 .... 187 D2
Manse Dr G83 .... 27 F4
Manse Gdns G83 .... 27 F4
Manse Pl Airdrie ML6 .... 123 D4
Bannockburn FK7 .... 7 F1
Falkirk FK1 .... 42 A2
Slamannan FK1 .... 86 A4
Manse Rd Bearsden G61 .... 75 F3
Bowling G60 .... 72 B4
Carmunnock G76 .... 158 B4
Coatbridge G69 .... 120 C3
Glasgow G32 .... 119 E2
Kilsyth G65 .... 60 C4
Lanark ML11 .... 214 C2
Motherwell ML1 .... 163 F2
Neilston G78 .... 154 C4
Salsburgh ML7 .... 125 E1
Shotts ML7 .... 147 D2
Stonehouse ML9 .... 198 B1
West Kilbride KA23 .... 190 B3
Wishaw ML2 .... 166 A2
Manse St Coatbridge ML5 .... 121 F3
Kilmacolm PA13 .... 89 F4
Kilmarnock KA1 .... 228 A4
Renfrew PA4 .... 94 B2
Saltcoats KA21 .... 216 C4
Manse View ML1 .... 143 F3
Mansefield Ave G72 .... 139 D2
Mansefield Cres G60 .... 73 D3
Mansefield Dr G71 .... 140 C3
Mansefield Rd G76 .... 157 E3
Mansefield Terr KA3 .... 195 D4
Mansel St G21 .... 98 A3
Manseview ML9 .... 185 D1
Manseview Terr G76 .... 178 C3
Mansewood Ct G69 .... 120 B2
Mansewood Dr G82 .... 50 A3
Mansewood Rd G43 .... 136 A3
Mansfield Ave FK10 .... 5 E1
Mansfield Cres G76 .... 157 E3
Mansfield Rd Bellshill ML4 .. 141 F2
Clarkston G76 .... 157 F3
Lochwinnoch PA12 .... 129 E2
Paisley G52 .... 114 C4
Prestwick KA9 .... 236 A3
Quarter ML3 .... 183 F3
Mansfield St G11 .... 96 B1
Mansfield Way KA11 .... 220 A3
Mansion Ave PA14 .... 69 D4
Mansion Ct G72 .... 139 D3
Mansion St
Cambuslang G72 .... 139 D3
Glasgow G22 .... 97 E3
Mansionhouse Ave G32 .... 139 E4
Mansionhouse Dr G32 .... 119 E3
Mansionhouse Gdns G41 . 136 C4
Mansionhouse Gr G32 .... 119 F2
Mansionhouse Rd
Falkirk FK1 .... 41 E3
Glasgow G32 .... 119 F2
Glasgow, Langside G41 .... 136 C4
Paisley PA1 .... 114 A3
Manson Ave KA9 .... 233 E1
Manson Pl G75 .... 181 D3
Manson Rd KA12 .... 219 F2
Manuel Ave KA15 .... 171 D4
Manuel Ct Irvine KA11 .... 225 E4
Kilbirnie KA25 .... 170 A4
Manuel Terr KA11 .... 225 E4
Maple Ave Dumbarton G82 .... 49 D3
Milton Of C G65 .... 58 A3
Newton Mearns G77 .... 156 B2
Stenhousemuir FK5 .... 23 F2
Maple Bank ML3 .... 162 C1
Maple Cres G72 .... 139 F2
Maple Ct Alloa FK10 .... 10 A3
Coatbridge ML5 .... 121 F2
Cumbernauld G67 .... 62 C3
Maple Dr Ayr KA7 .... 239 E3
Barrhead G78 .... 155 E4
Beith KA15 .... 150 A1
Clydebank G81 .... 74 A3
Johnstone PA5 .... 132 A4
Kirkintilloch G66 .... 79 D3
Larkhall ML9 .... 185 D3
Maple Gr East Kilbride G75 .. 180 A3
Troon KA10 .... 229 E2
Maple Pl Banknock FK4 .... 38 C1
Denny FK6 .... 21 E2
East Kilbride G75 .... 180 A3
Kilmarnock KA1 .... 227 E4
Uddingston G71 .... 141 E4
Maple Quadrant ML6 .... 123 E3
Maple Rd Cumbernauld G67 .... 62 C3
Glasgow G41 .... 116 A2
Greenock PA16 .... 45 D2
Motherwell ML1 .... 143 D3
Maple Terr
East Kilbride G75 .... 180 A3
Irvine KA12 .... 219 E2
Maple Way G72 .... 161 E4
Mar Ave PA7 .... 72 A2
Mar Dr G61 .... 75 F4
Mar Gdns G73 .... 138 B2
Mar Pl Alloa FK10 .... 10 A4
Alloa, New Sauchie FK10 .... 5 E1
Stirling FK8 .... 7 D4
Mar St FK10 .... 10 A3
Marble Ave KA11 .... 220 B1
March St G41 .... 116 C1
Marchbank Gdns PA1 .... 114 B2
Marchburn Ave KA9 .... 236 C4
Marchdyke Cres KA1 .... 227 F2
Marches The Lanark ML11 . 215 D3
Stirling FK8 .... 7 D4
Marchfield G64 .... 77 F2
Marchfield Ave PA3 .... 113 F4
Marchfield Quadrant KA8 .... 236 A3
Marchfield Rd KA8 .... 236 A3
Marchglen FK13 .... 5 F3
Marchglen Pl G51 .... 115 E4
Marchmont Ct KA1 .... 228 C4
Marchmont Gdns G64 .... 77 F1
Marchmont Rd KA7 .... 238 C3
Marchmont Road La KA7 . 238 C3
Marchmont Terr 12 G12 .... 96 B2
Marchside Ct FK10 .... 5 E1
Mardale G74 .... 159 E2
Maree Ct FK10 .... 10 B3
Maree Dr Cumbernauld G67 .... 82 A4
Glasgow G52 .... 115 F2
Maree Gdns G64 .... 78 A1
Maree Pl KA12 .... 219 E4
Maree Rd PA2 .... 113 D1
Maree Way G72 .... 161 E4
Maree Wlk 7 ML2 .... 165 F3
Marfield St G32 .... 118 C3
Margaret Ave Haggs FK4 .... 39 D2
Salsburgh ML7 .... 125 D1
Margaret Ct FK6 .... 21 F1
Margaret Dr Alexandria G83 .. 27 E3
Bonnybridge FK4 .... 40 A3
Margaret Pl ML4 .... 141 F3
Margaret Rd
Bannockburn FK7 .... 7 E1
Hamilton ML3 .... 162 A3
Margaret St
Coatbridge ML5 .... 122 A2
Gourock PA19 .... 44 C4
Greenock PA16 .... 45 E4
Margaret Terr FK5 .... 23 F2
Margaret's Pl ML9 .... 185 D2
Margaretta Bldgs G44 .... 137 D3
Margaretvale Dr ML9 .... 185 D1
Marguerite Ave G66 .... 79 E3
Marguerite Dr G66 .... 79 E3
Marguerite Gdns
Bothwell G71 .... 141 D1
Kirkintilloch G66 .... 79 E3
Marguerite Gr G66 .... 79 E3
Marguerite Pl Ayr KA7 .... 239 E2
Milton Of C G65 .... 58 A3
Marian Dr ML1 .... 143 E1
Marigold Ave ML1 .... 163 F4
Marigold Sq KA7 .... 239 D2
Marigold Way ML8 .... 201 F4
Marina Ct ML4 .... 141 F2
Marina Rd KA9 .... 236 A4
Marine Cres G51 .... 116 C3
Marine Dr KA12 .... 224 A3
Marine Gdns G51 .... 240 A1
Marine View Ct KA10 .... 229 E1
Mariner Ave FK1 .... 41 D3
Mariner Dr FK1 .... 41 D3
Mariner Gdns FK1 .... 41 E3
Mariner Rd FK1 .... 41 E3
Mariner St FK1 .... 41 D3
Marion St ML4 .... 142 B3
Mariscat Rd G41 .... 116 C1
Marjory Dr PA3 .... 114 A4
Marjory Rd PA4 .... 94 A1
Market Cl G65 .... 60 B4
Market End ML11 .... 215 D2
Market Pl Carluke ML8 .... 187 F1
Kilmacolm PA13 .... 89 E4
Kilsyth G65 .... 60 B4
Uddingston G71 .... 141 E4
Market Rd Carluke ML8 .... 187 F1
Kirkintilloch G66 .... 80 A4
Uddingston G71 .... 141 E4
Market Sq G65 .... 60 B4
Market St Airdrie ML6 .... 123 D4
Kilsyth G65 .... 60 B4
Uddingston G71 .... 141 E4
Markethill Rd
East Kilbride G74 .... 159 F3
East Kilbride, East Mains G74 .... 159 F2
Markethill Rdbt G74 .... 159 F2
Markinch Rd PA14 .... 68 C3
Marlborough Ave G11 .... 95 F2
Marlborough Dr FK9 .... 2 B2
Marlborough La N G11 .... 95 F2
Marlborough La S G11 .... 95 F2
Marlborough Pk G75 .... 180 A4
Marldon La G11 .... 95 F2
Marlepark KA7 .... 239 D2
Marley Way G65 .... 58 A3
Marlfield Gdns ML4 .... 142 A4
Marloch Ave PA14 .... 69 D3
Marlow St G41 .... 116 C3
Marlow Terr G41 .... 116 C2
Marmion Ave G84 .... 25 D4
Marmion Cres ML1 .... 142 B1
Marmion Dr G66 .... 79 F4
Marmion Pl G67 .... 82 C4
Marmion Rd
Cumbernauld G67 .... 82 C4
Paisley PA2 .... 132 C4
Marmion St FK2 .... 42 A4
Marne St G31 .... 118 A4
Marnoch Dr ML5 .... 101 E3
Marnoch Way G69 .... 80 C1
Marnock Terr PA2 .... 114 A1
Marr Coll KA10 .... 229 F2
Marr Dr KA10 .... 229 E2
Marr's Wynd ML11 .... 215 E3
Marress Rd KA12 .... 219 D2
Marress Rdbt KA12 .... 219 D1
Marrswood Gn ML3 .... 162 A2
Marrwood Ave G66 .... 80 A3
Mars Rd PA16 .... 44 B1
Marschal Ct FK7 .... 7 E2
Marshall Gr ML3 .... 162 A2
Marshall La ML2 .... 165 D2
Marshall St Coatbridge ML5 . 121 F2
Larkhall ML9 .... 185 D1
Wishaw ML2 .... 164 C1
Marshall's La PA1 .... 113 F2
Marshill FK10 .... 10 A3
Marsmount Rd KA9 .... 233 F1
Mart St G1 .... 241 D1
Martha St G1 .... 241 D3
Martin Ave Balloch G83 .... 28 A4
Irvine KA12 .... 219 E3
Martin Cres G69 .... 120 B3
Martin Ct ML3 .... 162 B2
Martin Pl ML1 .... 143 E2
Martin Sq KA21 .... 206 A1
Martin St Coatbridge ML5 .... 122 B4
Glasgow G40 .... 117 F2
Martinside G75 .... 180 C3
Martlet Dr PA5 .... 131 E4
Martyn St ML6 .... 122 C3
Martyrs Pl G64 .... 98 A4
Marwick St G31 .... 118 A4
Mary Dr ML4 .... 141 F2
Mary Glen ML2 .... 165 E3
Mary Love Pl KA20 .... 206 A1
Mary Rae Rd ML4 .... 141 F2
Mary Russell Sch The PA2 .... 114 B1
Mary Sq G69 .... 120 C3
Mary St Greenock PA16 .... 45 E2
Hamilton ML3 .... 162 B1
Johnstone PA5 .... 112 A2
Laurieston FK2 .... 42 C2
Paisley PA2 .... 113 F1
Port Glasgow PA14 .... 47 D1
Mary Stevenson Dr FK10 .. 10 A4
Mary Street Rdbt FK2 .... 42 C2
Mary Young Pl G76 .... 157 F3
Maryborough Ave KA9 .... 236 A3
Maryborough Rd KA9 .... 236 A3
Maryfield Pl Ayr KA8 .... 236 A2
Falkirk FK1 .... 41 D2
Maryfield Rd KA8 .... 236 A2
Maryhill Prim Sch G20 .... 96 B4
Maryhill Rd Bearsden G61 .... 76 A1
Glasgow G20 .... 96 B3
Maryhill Sta G20 .... 96 B4
Maryknowe Rd ML1 .... 143 E1
Maryland Dr G52 .... 115 F3
Maryland Gdns G52 .... 115 F3
Maryland Rd G82 .... 50 B3

Marypark Rd PA14 70 A4
Maryston St G33 98 B1
Maryville Ave G46 136 B1
Maryville Gdns G46 136 B1
Maryville View G71 120 B1
Marywood Sq G41 116 C1
Mashock Path ML8 201 D1
Mason La ML1 163 F3
Mason St Larkhall ML9 185 E1
Motherwell ML1 163 F3
Masonfield Ave G68 61 E1
Masonhill Pl KA7 239 E3
Masonhill Rd KA7 239 E3
Masterton St G21 97 E2
Mather Terr FK2 42 C2
Matherton Ave G77 157 D3
Matheson Wlk G83 27 F4
Mathew Smith Ave KA1 227 F3
Mathie Cres PA19 44 C3
Mathieson Rd G73 118 B1
Mathieson St PA1 114 A3
Matilda Rd G41 116 C2
Matthew McWhirter Pl
ML9 185 D2
Matthew Pl KA13 207 F3
Mauchline G74 160 C2
Mauchline Ave G66 59 D1
Mauchline Ct
Hamilton ML3 161 E1
Kilmarnock KA3 223 D3
Kirkintilloch G66 59 D1
Mauchline La PA16 44 C2
Mauchline Rd KA1 228 C3
Mauchline St G5 117 D2
Mauchline Terr PA16 44 C2
Maukinfauld Ct G32 118 B2
Maukinfauld Rd G32 118 C2
Mauldslie Dr ML8 187 D3
Mauldslie Pl ML9 199 F4
Mauldslie Rd Carluke ML8 187 D1
Law ML8 186 C1
Mauldslie St Bellshill ML4 142 A2
Coatbridge ML5 122 A3
Glasgow G40 118 A2
Maule Dr G11 96 A1
Maunsheugh Rd KA3 213 D2
Maurice Ave FK7 7 E2
Mavis Bank
Bishopbriggs G64 97 F4
Blantyre G72 161 E4
Mavis Rd PA16 45 D2
Mavisbank Ave FK1 66 B3
Mavisbank Gdns
Bellshill ML4 142 A3
Glasgow G51 116 C3
Mavisbank Rd G51 116 B3
Mavisbank Sch ML6 122 C4
Mavisbank St Airdrie ML6 122 C4
Wishaw ML2 166 B3
Mavisbank Terr
Johnstone PA5 111 F1
Paisley PA1 113 F2
Mavor Ave G74 160 A2
Mavor Rdbt G74 159 F2
Maxholm Rd KA1 227 F3
Maxton Ave G78 134 A2
Maxton Cres Alva FK12 5 E4
Wishaw ML2 165 E3
Maxton Gr G78 134 A2
Maxton Terr G72 138 C2
Maxwell Ave Bearsden G61 75 F1
Glasgow G69 120 A3
Glasgow, Pollockshields G41 116 C2
Maxwell Cres G72 161 E3
Maxwell Ct Beith KA15 171 D4
Kilmarnock KA3 223 E2
Maxwell Dr Erskine PA8 72 C2
Glasgow G69 120 A3
Glasgow, Pollockshields G41 116 B2
Maxwell Gdns Glasgow G41 116 B2
Hurlford KA1 228 C3
Maxwell Gn KA11 220 A2
Maxwell Gr G41 116 B2
Maxwell La G41 116 C2
Maxwell Oval 2 G41 116 C2
Maxwell Park Sta G41 116 B1
Maxwell Path 13 ML9 185 E1
Maxwell Pl
Bridge Of W PA11 110 B4
Coatbridge ML5 121 F3
Glasgow G41 117 D2
Kilsyth G65 36 B1
Stevenston KA20 206 C1
Stirling FK8 7 D4
Maxwell Rd Bishopton PA7 72 A2
Glasgow G41 117 D2
Maxwell St Clydebank G81 73 F2
Glasgow G1 241 D1
Glasgow G1 241 D2
Glasgow, Biallieston G69 120 A2
Paisley PA3 113 F3
Port Glasgow PA14 47 F1
Maxwell Terr G41 116 C2
Maxwellton Ave G74 160 A2
Maxwellton Pl G74 160 A2
Maxwellton Rd
East Kilbride G74 160 B2
Paisley PA1 113 D2
Port Glasgow PA14 68 C3
Maxwellton St PA1 113 E2
Maxwelton Prim Sch G74 160 A2
Maxwelton Rd G33 98 B1
Maxwood Pl KA11 220 A3
May Gdns ML3 162 B3
May Rd PA2 133 F4
May St ML3 162 B3
May Terr Glasgow G42 137 D4
Glasgow, Merrylee G46 136 B2
Maybank La G42 117 D1
Maybank St G42 117 D1
Mayberry Cres G32 119 E3
Mayberry Gdns G32 119 E3
Mayberry Gr G32 119 E3
Mayberry Pl G72 161 E4
Maybole Cres G77 157 D2
Maybole Dr ML6 123 D2
Maybole Gdns ML3 161 E1
Maybole Gr G77 157 D2
Maybole Pl ML5 122 B2
Maybole Rd Ayr KA7 239 D2
Port Glasgow PA14 68 C3
Maybole St G53 134 C3
Mayfield Ave Clarkston G76 157 F4
Hurlford KA1 228 C3
Mayfield Cres
Howwood PA9 130 C3
Stevenston KA20 206 B1
Mayfield Ct Howwood PA9 130 C3
Stirling FK7 7 D2
Mayfield Dr Howwood PA9 130 C3
Longcroft FK4 39 D2
Mayfield Gr KA20 206 B1
Mayfield Mews FK1 41 F2
Mayfield Pl Carluke ML8 202 A4
Saltcoats KA21 217 D4
Mayfield Prim Sch KA21 206 A1
Mayfield Rd Hamilton ML3 161 F2
Saltcoats KA21 217 D4
Stevenston KA20 206 B1
Mayfield St Glasgow G20 96 C3
Stirling FK7 7 D2
Mayne Ave FK9 2 A3
Mayville St KA20 206 B1
McAdam Ct KA9 236 B3
McAlister Rd G83 27 F3
McAlley Ct FK9 1 C4
McAllister Ave ML6 123 E4
McAllister Ct FK7 7 E1
McAlpine St Glasgow G2 240 B2
Wishaw ML2 165 D1
McArdle Ave ML1 163 D4
McArthur Pk G66 79 E4
McArthur St G43 136 B4
McAslin Ct G4 241 E3
McAslin St G4 241 F3
McAuslan Pl G84 16 C1
McBride Ave G66 79 E4
McCall's Ave KA8 236 A1
McCallum Ave G73 138 A4
McCallum Cres PA19 44 C4
McCallum Ct G74 159 D2
McCallum Gdns ML4 141 F1
McCallum Gr G74 159 D2
McCallum Pl G74 159 D2
McCallum Rd ML9 185 D1
McCardel Way KA3 211 F4
McCarrison Rd ML2 166 A3
McCash Pl G66 79 E4
McClue Ave PA4 94 A2
McClue Rd PA4 94 B2
McClurg Ct ML1 163 F3
McColgan Pl KA8 236 B2
McColl Ave G83 27 E3
McColl Pl G83 27 E3
McConnell Rd PA12 129 D1
McCormack Gdns ML1 143 F2
McCracken Ave PA4 94 A1
McCracken Dr G71 141 E4
McCreery St G81 94 B4
McCulloch Ave G71 141 E3
McCulloch La G83 27 E4
McCulloch St G41 116 C2
McDonald Ave PA5 111 F1
McDonald Cres G81 94 B4
McDonald Dr KA12 219 E2
McDonald Pl
Motherwell ML1 143 D3
Neilston G78 154 C4
McDowall Ave KA22 205 E1
McDowall Pl KA22 205 E1
McEwan Dr G84 16 C2
McEwan Gdns G74 159 D2
McEwan Wlk G83 27 F3
McEwans Way ML9 198 B1
McFarlane Rd G83 28 A4
McFarlane St Glasgow G4 241 F1
Paisley PA3 113 E4
McGavin Ave KA13 208 A2
McGavin Way KA13 207 E2
McGhee St G81 74 A2
McGibney Dr KA12 219 E1
McGill Prim Sch G53 115 E1
McGillivray Ave KA21 205 F1
McGowan Pl ML3 162 A3
McGown St PA3 113 E3
McGregor Ave Airdrie ML6 123 E4
Balloch G83 28 A4
Renfrew PA4 94 A1
Stevenston KA20 206 B1
McGregor Dr G82 50 B2
Mcgregor Path ML5 101 E3
McGregor Rd G67 61 F1
McGregor St Clydebank G81 94 B4
Glasgow G51 115 F3
Wishaw ML2 164 B2
McGrigor Rd Milngavie G62 54 C2
Stirling FK7 7 D2
McHardy Cres KA15 171 F2
McInnes Ct ML2 165 D1
McInnes Pl ML2 186 A4
McInnes St G83 28 A4
McIntosh Ct 1 G31 117 F4
McIntosh Quadrant ML4 141 F1
McIntosh St G31 117 F4
McIntosh Way ML1 163 E3
McIntyre Pl PA2 113 F1
McIntyre Terr G72 139 D3
McInver St G72 139 F3
McIsaac Rd KA21 217 D4
McKay Cres PA5 112 A1
McKay Gr ML4 141 F3
McKay Pl East Kilbride G74 159 D2
Newton Mearns G77 156 B2
McKechnie St G51 116 A4
McKell Ct FK1 42 A2
McKellar Ave KA22 205 E1
McKenna Dr ML6 122 C4
McKenzie Ave G81 74 A2
McKenzie Dr G83 19 F1
McKenzie St PA3 113 E3
McKenzie's Cl ML11 215 D2
McKerrell St PA1 114 A3
McKillop Pl KA21 205 F1
McKim Wlk G82 49 E4
McKinlay Ave G83 20 A1
McKinlay Cres Alloa FK10 10 B4
Irvine KA12 219 D1
Mckinnon Pl KA21 206 A1
McKnight Ave KA3 213 F2
McLachlan Ave FK7 7 D1
McLachlan St FK5 23 E1
McLaren Ave PA4 94 B1
McLaren Cres G20 96 C4
McLaren Ct Glasgow G46 136 A1
Stenhousemuir FK5 23 E1
McLaren Gdns G20 96 C4
McLaren Gr G74 159 D2
McLaren Pl G44 136 C1
McLaren Terr FK7 7 D2
McLauchlan View ML7 127 F3
McLaurin Cres PA5 111 E1
McLean Cres G83 19 F1
McLean Dr Bellshill ML4 141 F1
Irvine KA11 225 E4
McLean Gdns ML9 198 C1
McLean Mus PA16 45 F3
McLean Pl PA3 113 E4
McLean St KA8 236 B1
McLees La ML1 163 D4
McLelland Dr
Kilmarnock KA1 227 F4
Plains ML6 104 A1
McLennan St G42 137 D4
McLeod Rd G82 50 B2
McLeod St PA15 46 B2
McLuckie Dr KA13 207 E2
McLuckie Pk KA13 207 E2
McMahon Dr ML2 166 A3
McMillan Cres KA15 171 D4
McMillan Dr KA22 205 D2
McMillan Pl KA11 224 C3
McMillan Rd ML2 164 B1
McMillan Way ML8 186 C3
McNair St G32 119 D3
McNaught Pl
Kilmaurs KA3 222 A4
Renton G82 27 E1
McNay Cres KA21 206 A1
McNeil Ave G81 74 C1
McNeil Dr ML1 143 D4
McNeil Gdns G5 117 E2
McNeil Pl ML2 186 B4
McNeil St G5 117 E2
McNeill Ave KA9 233 E1
McPhail Ave ML1 143 F3
McPhail St Glasgow G40 117 F2
Greenock PA15 46 B2
McPhater St G4 240 C4
McPherson Cres ML6 123 F1
McPherson Dr
Bothwell G71 141 D2
Gourock PA19 44 B4
Stirling FK8 2 A1
McPherson La G83 27 E4
McPherson St
Bellshill ML4 142 B3
Glasgow G1 241 E1
McShannon Gr ML4 142 A2
McTaggart Ave FK6 21 F1
McVean Pl FK4 39 D2
Meadow Ave Blantyre G72 161 E3
Irvine KA12 219 E2
Meadow Ct Carluke ML8 188 B1
Dumbarton G82 49 F3
Meadow Gn FK10 5 D1
Meadow La Bothwell G71 141 D1
Renfrew PA4 94 B3
Meadow Path ML6 123 E1
Meadow Pk Alva FK12 5 D3
Ayr KA7 239 D3
Meadow Pl FK8 2 B1
Meadow Rd
Braidwood ML8 202 A2
Dumbarton G82 50 A2
Glasgow G11 96 A1
Motherwell ML1 164 A3
Meadow St Coatbridge ML5 122 A2
Falkirk FK1 42 B2
Meadow View
Cumbernauld G67 62 B2
Plains ML6 104 A2
Meadow Way G77 156 B3
Meadow Wlk ML5 122 A3
Meadowbank La
Prestwick KA9 236 A4
Uddingston G71 140 C3
Meadowbank Pl G77 156 B3
Meadowbank St G82 49 F2
Meadowburn G64 78 A2
Meadowburn Ave
Kirkintilloch G66 79 F3
Newton Mearns G77 156 B3
Meadowburn Prim Sch
G64 78 A2
Meadowburn Rd ML2 165 E2
Meadowfield Pl ML2 166 B3
Meadowfoot Rd KA23 190 B2
Meadowforth Rd FK7 7 E4
Meadowhead Ave
Chryston G69 80 C1
Irvine KA11 224 C2
Meadowhead Ind Est
KA11 224 C3
Meadowhead Rd
Irvine KA11 224 C2
Plains ML6 103 F1
Wishaw ML2 164 B2
Meadowhead Rdbt KA11 224 C1
Meadowhill G77 156 B3
Meadowhill St ML9 185 D2
Meadowland Rd FK9 2 A3
Meadowpark Dr KA7 239 D3
Meadowpark St G31 118 A4
Meadows Ave ML9 185 D2
Meadows The Houston PA6 91 F1
Kilwinning KA13 207 E2
Meadowside Beith KA15 171 D4
Crookedholm KA3 228 C4
Hamilton ML3 183 E3
West Kilbride KA23 190 B3
Meadowside Ave PA5 112 B1
Meadowside Gdns ML6 123 E4
Meadowside Ind Est PA4 94 B3
Meadowside Pl ML6 123 E4
Meadowside Rd G65 59 F4
Meadowside St
Glasgow G11 96 A1
Renfrew PA4 94 B3
Meadowwell St G32 119 D3
Meadside Ave PA10 111 D2
Meadside Rd PA10 111 D2
Mealkirk St G81 74 B4
Mearns Castle High Sch
G77 157 D2
Mearns Ct ML3 183 F4
Mearns Prim Sch G77 156 B2
Mearns Rd Motherwell ML1 163 E4
Newton Mearns G77 156 B1
Mearns St PA15 45 F2
Mearns Way G64 78 B1
Mearnscroft Gdns G77 156 C2
Mearnscroft Rd G77 156 C2
Mearnskirk Rd G77 156 B1
Medine Ave KA15 150 A1
Medine Ct KA15 150 A1
Medlar Ct G72 139 F2
Medlar Rd G67 62 B1
Medrox Gdns G67 81 F3
Medwin Ct G75 179 F4
Medwin Gdns G75 179 F4
Medwin St G72 139 F3
Medwyn Pl FK10 9 F3
Medwyn St G14 95 E2
Meek Pl G72 139 D3
Meeks Rd FK2 42 A3
Meetinghouse La PA1 113 F3
Megan St G40 117 F2
Meikle Ave PA4 94 B1
Meikle Bin Brae G65 57 F4
Meikle Cres
Greengairs ML6 103 E4
Hamilton ML3 183 E4
Meikle Ct KA3 195 F1
Meikle Drumgray Rd ML6 103 F4
Meikle Earnock Rd ML3 183 D4
Meikle Pl KA11 220 A3
Meikle Rd G53 135 E4
Meiklehill Ct G66 58 C1
Meiklehill Rd G66 58 C1
Meiklem St ML4 142 B3
Meiklerig Cres G53 115 E1
Meikleriggs Dr PA2 113 D1
Meiklewood Ave KA9 233 E1
Meiklewood Rd
Glasgow G51 115 E3
Kilmarnock KA3 222 C3
Melbourne Ave
Clydebank G81 73 E3
East Kilbride G75 180 B4
Melbourne Ct G46 136 B2
Melbourne Gn 7 G75 180 B4
Melbourne Rd KA21 216 C4
Melbourne St G31 117 F3
Melbourne Terr KA21 216 C4
Meldon Pl G51 115 E4
Meldrum Gdns G41 116 B1
Meldrum Mains ML6 102 C2
Meldrum St G81 94 B4
Melford Ave Glasgow G46 136 B1
Kirkintilloch G66 79 D4
Shotts ML7 147 D2
Melford Gdns PA10 111 E1
Melford Rd ML4 141 F4
Melford Way PA3 114 A4
Melfort Ave Clydebank G81 74 B2
Glasgow G41 116 A2
Melfort Dr FK7 7 D2
Melfort Path ML2 165 F4
Melfort Quadrant ML1 143 E2
Melfort Rd ML3 161 F1
Mellerstain Dr G14 94 C3
Mellock Gdns FK1 41 F1
Melness Pl G51 115 E4
Melrose Ave
Chapelhall ML6 123 E1
Coatbridge G69 120 C3
Linwood PA3 112 A3
Motherwell ML1 143 D3
Paisley PA2 113 D1
Rutherglen G73 138 A4
Melrose Cres ML2 165 D3
Melrose Ct G73 138 A4
Melrose Gdns Glasgow G20 96 C2
Twechar G65 59 F2
Uddingston G71 120 C1
Melrose Pl Blantyre G72 140 B1
Coatbridge ML5 121 F4
10 Falkirk FK1 42 A2
Larkhall ML9 185 D1
Melrose Prim Sch G67 82 C4
Melrose Rd
Cumbernauld G67 82 C4
Port Glasgow PA14 68 C4
Melrose St 6 Glasgow G4 97 D1
Hamilton ML3 162 A3
Melrose Terr
East Kilbride G74 159 F2
Hamilton ML3 162 A3
Melvaig Pl G20 96 B3
Melvick Pl G51 115 E4
Melville Cres ML1 163 F3
Melville Ct G1 241 D1
Melville Dr ML1 163 F3
Melville Gdns G64 78 A1
Melville Pk G74 160 A2
Melville Pl Bridge Of A FK9 2 A4
Carluke ML8 187 F1
Melville St Falkirk FK1 42 A3
Glasgow G41 116 C2
Kilmarnock KA3 228 A4
Melville Terr FK8 7 D3
Melvinhall Rd ML11 215 D3
Memel St G21 97 F3
Memus Ave G52 115 E2
Mennock Ct ML3 161 F1
Mennock Dr G64 78 A2
Mennock La KA10 229 F3
Mennock St ML1 144 B1
Menock Rd G44 137 E3
Menstrie Castle FK11 3 F3
Menstrie Pl FK11 4 A3
Menstrie Prim Sch FK11 4 A3
Menteith Ave G64 78 A1
Menteith Ct FK10 10 B3
Menteith Dr G73 138 B1
Menteith Gdns G61 75 E4
Menteith Loan ML1 143 D3
Menteith Pl G73 138 B1
Menteith Rd
Motherwell ML1 163 F4
Stirling FK9 2 A2
Menzies Dr Glasgow G21 98 A3
Stirling FK8 2 A1
Menzies Pl G21 98 A3
Menzies Rd G21 98 A3
Merchant La G1 241 D1
Merchants Cl PA10 111 D2
Merchiston Ave Falkirk FK2 42 A4
Linwood PA3 111 F3
Merchiston Gdns FK2 42 A3
Merchiston Hospl PA5 111 F3
Merchiston Ind Est FK2 42 B4
Merchiston Rd Falkirk FK2 42 A4
Falkirk, Grahamston FK2 42 A3
Merchiston St G32 118 C4
Merchiston Terr FK2 42 A4
Mercury La PA16 44 B2
Meredith Dr FK5 23 F2
Merino Rd PA15 45 F2
Merkins Ave G82 50 A3
Merkland Ct Glasgow G11 96 A1
Kirkintilloch G66 59 D1
Merkland Dr Falkirk FK1 42 C1
Kirkintilloch G66 80 A4
Merkland Pl G66 59 D1
Merkland Rd Ayr KA7 239 D1
Coatbridge ML5 101 E1
Merkland Sch G66 58 C1
Merkland St G11 96 A1
Merkland Way G75 180 B2
Merksworth Ave KA24 191 E4
Merksworth High Sch PA3 113 E4
Merksworth Way PA1 113 F4
Merlewood Rd KA23 190 A2
Merlin Ave Bellshill ML4 142 A4
Greenock PA16 45 D3
Merlin La PA16 45 D3
Merlin Way PA3 114 A4
Merlinford Ave PA4 94 C2
Merlinford Cres PA4 94 C2
Merlinford Dr PA4 94 C2
Merlinford Way PA4 94 C2
Merrick Ave
Prestwick KA9 233 E1
Troon KA10 229 F2
Merrick Ct ML6 103 D1
Merrick Gdns Bearsden G61 75 E4
Glasgow G51 116 A3
Quarter ML3 183 F2
Merrick Pl Irvine KA11 220 A1
Symington KA1 231 E2
Merrick Rd KA1 228 A2
Merrick Terr G71 141 D4
Merrick View KA3 195 F1
Merrick Way G73 138 A2
Merry St ML1 163 F4
Merryburn Ave G46 136 B2
Merrycrest Ave G46 136 B2
Merrycroft Ave G46 136 B2
Merryflats G65 59 F2
Merrygreen Pl KA3 195 F1
Merryland Pl G51 116 B4
Merryland St G51 116 B4
Merrylee Ave PA14 68 C4
Merrylee Cres G46 136 B3
Merrylee Park Ave G46 136 B2
Merrylee Park Mews G46 136 B3

Montgomery Pl
15 East Kilbride G74 159 F1
Kilmarnock KA3 222 C1
Larkhall ML9 185 D1
Montgomery Rd PA3 114 A4
Montgomery Sq G76 178 C2
Montgomery St
Cambuslang G72 139 F3
Eaglesham G76 178 C2
East Kilbride G74 159 F1
Falkirk FK2 42 C3
Glasgow G40 118 A2
Irvine KA12 219 D1
Kilmarnock KA3 222 C1
Larkhall ML9 185 D2
Montgomery Terr G65 58 B3
Montgomery Way FK9 2 A2
Montgomery Well FK2 24 A1
Montgomeryfield KA11 225 D4
Montgreenan View KA13 207 F2
Montraive St G73 118 B1
Montrave St G52 115 E2
Montreal Pk G75 159 E1
Montrose Ave
Glasgow G32 119 E1
Paisley G52 114 C4
Port Glasgow PA14 68 C3
Montrose Cres ML3 162 B2
Montrose Dr G61 75 F4
Montrose Gdns
Blantyre G72 140 B1
Kilsyth G65 36 B1
Milngavie G62 55 D2
Montrose Pl PA3 112 A3
Montrose Rd Paisley PA2 132 C4
Stirling FK9 2 B2
Montrose St Clydebank G81 74 B1
Glasgow G1 241 E2
Motherwell ML1 142 B1
Montrose Terr
Bishopbriggs G64 98 B4
Bridge Of W PA11 110 B4
Montrose Way FK4 39 E3
Monument Cres KA9 233 F1
Monument Rd KA7 238 C2
Monymusk Gdns G64 78 B1
Monymusk Pl G15 74 C3
Moodie Ct KA1 227 F3
Moodiesburn St G33 98 C1
Moor Park Cres KA9 236 B3
Moor Park Pl KA9 236 B3
Moor Pk KA9 236 B3
Moor Pl KA8 236 B2
Moor Rd Ayr KA8 236 B3
Cartland ML11 202 C1
Eaglesham G76 178 B2
Milngavie G62 55 D1
Strathblane G63 31 E1
Moorburn Ave G46 136 A2
Moorburn Pl PA3 111 F3
Moorcroft Dr ML6 123 F4
Moorcroft Rd G77 156 B2
Moore Dr Bearsden G61 75 F2
Helensburgh G84 25 D4
Moore Gdns ML3 183 F4
Moore St Glasgow G31 117 F3
Motherwell ML1 143 D2
Moorfield Ave
Kilmarnock KA1 227 E3
Port Glasgow PA14 68 B4
Moorfield Cres ML6 123 F4
Moorfield Ind Est KA2 227 D4
Moorfield La PA19 44 B3
Moorfield Pl KA2 226 B3
Moorfield Rd Blantyre G72 161 E3
Gourock PA19 44 B4
Prestwick KA9 236 B4
Moorfield Rdbt KA1 227 D4
Moorfoot G64 78 B1
Moorfoot Ave
Glasgow G46 136 A2
Paisley PA2 113 E1
Moorfoot Dr Gourock PA19 44 B3
Wishaw ML2 164 C2
Moorfoot Gdns G75 180 A2
Moorfoot Path PA2 133 E4
Moorfoot Pl KA11 220 A2
Moorfoot Prim Sch PA19 44 B3
Moorfoot St G32 118 C3
Moorfoot Way
Bearsden G61 75 E4
Irvine KA11 220 A2
Moorhill Cres G77 156 B2
Moorhill Rd G77 156 B2
Moorhouse Ave
Glasgow G13 94 C3
Paisley PA2 113 D1
Moorhouse St G78 134 B1
Moorland Dr ML6 123 F4
Moorpark Ave Airdrie ML6 123 F4
Muirhead G69 100 B4
Moorpark Dr G52 115 D3
Moorpark Ind Est KA20 217 E4
Moorpark Pl KA20 217 E4
Moorpark Prim Sch
Kilbirnie KA25 149 D2
Renfrew PA4 94 A1
Moorpark Rd E KA20 217 E4
Moorpark Rd W KA20 217 E4
Moorpark Sq PA4 94 A1
Moorside St ML8 188 A1
Morag Ave G72 140 B1
Moraine Ave G15 75 D1
Moraine Cir G15 75 D1
Moraine Dr Clarkston G76 157 E4
Glasgow G15 75 D1
Moraine Pl G15 75 D1
Morar Ave G81 74 A2
Morar Cres Airdrie ML6 102 C1
Bishopbriggs G64 77 F1
Bishopton PA7 72 B1
Clydebank G81 74 A2
Coatbridge ML5 101 E1
Morar Ct Clydebank G81 74 A2
Cumbernauld G67 82 A4
Hamilton ML3 162 A1
Morar Dr Bearsden G61 76 A2
Clydebank G81 74 A2
Cumbernauld G67 82 A4
Falkirk FK2 24 B1
Linwood PA3 112 A3
Paisley PA2 113 D1
Rutherglen G73 138 A2
Morar Pl East Kilbride G74 159 F2
Irvine KA12 219 E3
Newton Mearns G77 156 B4
Renfrew PA4 94 A2
Morar Rd Clydebank G81 74 A2
Glasgow G52 115 F3
Port Glasgow PA14 68 C4
Morar St ML2 165 D1
Morar Terr Rutherglen G73 138 B2
Uddingston G71 141 D4
Morar Way Motherwell ML1 143 E2
Shotts ML7 147 D2
Moravia Ave G71 141 D2
Moray Ave ML6 123 D3
Moray Dr Clarkston G76 157 F4
Torrance G64 57 D1
Moray Gate G71 140 C2
Moray Gdns Clarkston G76 157 F4
Cumbernauld G68 61 F3
Uddingston G71 140 C4
Moray Pl Bishopbriggs G64 78 B1
Blantyre G72 161 E3
Chryston G69 100 B4
Glasgow G41 116 C1
Kirkintilloch G66 59 D1
Linwood PA3 112 A3
Moray Quadrant ML4 142 A3
Moray Rd PA14 47 E1
Moray Way ML1 143 D3
Mordaunt St G40 118 A2
Moredun Cres G32 119 E4
Moredun Rd PA2 113 D1
Moredun St G32 119 E4
Morefield Rd G51 115 E4
Morgan Ct FK7 7 E2
Morgan Mews 17 G42 117 D2
Morgan St Hamilton ML3 162 B1
Larkhall ML9 184 C2
Morina Gdns G53 135 E2
Morion Rd G13 95 E4
Moriston Ct ML2 165 F3
Morland G74 160 B2
Morley Cres FK7 7 D2
Morley St G42 137 D4
Morna La G14 95 F1
Mornay Way ML7 146 B3
Morningside Prim Sch
ML2 166 A2
Morningside Rd ML2 166 B2
Morningside St G33 118 C4
Morrin Path G21 97 F2
Morrin St G21 97 F2
Morris Cres Blantyre G72 161 E4
Hurlford KA1 228 C3
Motherwell ML1 143 F1
Morris La KA3 223 D1
Morris Moodie Ave KA20 217 F4
Morris Rd KA9 233 E1
Morris St Greenock PA15 46 B2
Hamilton ML3 162 B1
Larkhall ML9 185 E1
Morris Terr FK8 7 D4
Morrishall Rd G74 160 B2
Morrishill Dr KA15 171 D4
Morrison Ave
Bonnybridge FK4 39 F3
Stevenston KA20 206 C1
Morrison Ct KA20 206 C1
Morrison Dr
Bannockburn FK7 7 E1
Lennoxtown G65 57 F4
Morrison Gdns Ayr KA8 239 D4
Torrance G64 78 B4
Morrison Pl KA3 223 E1
Morrison Quadrant G81 74 C1
Morrison Rd KA9 233 E2
Morrison St Clydebank G81 73 F3
Glasgow G5 240 B1
Morriston Cres PA4 94 C1
Morriston Park Dr G72 139 D3
Morriston St G72 139 D3
Morten Gdns G41 116 B1
Morton Ave KA7 239 D3
Morton Pl KA1 222 C1
Morton Rd Ayr KA7 239 D3
Stewarton KA3 211 E4
Morton St ML1 163 F4
Morven Ave
Bishopbriggs G64 78 B1
Blantyre G72 140 B1
Kilmarnock KA3 222 C2
Paisley PA2 133 E4
Morven Cres KA10 229 E1
Morven Ct Airdrie ML6 103 D1
Falkirk FK1 42 B1
Morven Dr Clarkston G76 157 E4
Linwood PA3 112 A3
Troon KA10 229 E2
Morven Gait PA8 93 F4
Morven Gdns G71 140 C4
Morven La G72 140 B1
Morven Rd Bearsden G61 75 F3
Cambuslang G72 138 C2
Morven St Coatbridge ML5 122 A4
Glasgow G52 115 F3
Morven Way 3 G71 141 D2
Morville Cres KA13 207 F3
Mosesfield St G21 97 F3
Moss Ave Caldercruix ML6 105 D3
Linwood PA3 112 A3
Moss Dr Barrhead G78 134 A3
Erskine PA8 93 D4
Irvine KA11 224 C3
Moss Heights Ave G52 115 E3
Moss Knowe G67 62 B1
Moss Path G69 119 F2
Moss Rd Airdrie ML6 123 D3
Bridge Of W PA11 110 C4
Cumbernauld G67 62 C2
East Kilbride G75 180 B2
Fallin FK7 8 B2
Glasgow G51 115 E4
Helensburgh G82 25 E2
Kilmacolm PA13 89 E4
Kirkintilloch G66 80 A4
Kirkintilloch, High Gallowhill
G66 79 D3
Linwood PA3 112 B4
Muirhead G69 100 B4
Port Glasgow PA14 68 C4
Wishaw ML2 165 F2
Moss Side Ave ML6 122 C4
Moss St PA1 113 F3
Moss-Side Ave ML8 187 E1
Moss-Side Rd G41 116 C1
Mossacre Rd ML2 165 E2
Mossband La ML7 146 C3
Mossbank Blantyre G72 161 E3
East Kilbride G75 179 F4
Prestwick KA9 236 C4
Mossbank Ave G33 98 C2
Mossbank Cres ML1 143 F2
Mossbank Dr G33 98 C2
Mossbank Rd ML2 165 E2
Mossbell Rd ML4 141 F3
Mossblown St ML9 184 C2
Mossburn Ave Balloch G83 19 F1
Harthill ML7 127 E3
Mossburn Rd ML2 165 E2
Mossburn St ML2 165 E1
Mosscastle Rd Glasgow G33 99 E1
Slamannan FK1 86 A4
Mossdale G74 159 E2
Mossdale Ct ML4 142 B3
Mossdale Gdns ML3 161 F1
Mossend Ave
Helensburgh G84 16 C1
Kilbirnie KA25 170 A4
Mossend La G33 119 E4
Mossend Pl G84 16 C1
Mossend St G33 119 E4
Mossgiel G75 180 A4
Mossgiel Ave Cowie FK7 12 B4
Kilmarnock KA3 228 B4
Rutherglen G73 138 A3
Stirling FK8 2 A1
Troon KA10 229 F2
Mossgiel Cres G76 157 F3
Mossgiel Dr Clydebank G81 74 B2
Irvine KA12 219 E2
Mossgiel Gdns
Kirkintilloch G66 58 C1
Uddingston G71 140 C4
Mossgiel La 7 ML9 185 E1
Mossgiel Pl Ayr KA7 239 D3
Rutherglen G73 138 A3
Stevenston KA20 206 C1
Mossgiel Rd
Ardrossan KA22 205 E2
Ayr KA7 239 D3
Cumbernauld G67 62 A1
Glasgow G43 136 B3
Glasgow G43 136 B4
Saltcoats KA21 206 A2
Mossgiel St FK1 41 D3
Mossgiel Terr G72 140 B1
Mossgiel Way ML1 143 E2
Mosshall Gr ML1 143 F2
Mosshall Rd ML1 143 E4
Mosshall St ML1 143 F2
Mosshead Prim Sch G61 75 F4
Mosshead Rd
Bearsden G61 76 A4
Kilmarnock KA1 228 A2
Mosshill Rd ML4 142 A4
Mosshouse FK7 6 C2
Mosside Pl KA3 222 C2
Mosside Rd KA8 236 B2
Mossland Dr ML2 165 E2
Mossland Rd G52 114 C4
Mosslands Rd PA1 113 F4
Mosslingal G75 180 C3
Mossmulloch G75 180 C3
Mossneuk Ave G75 179 F4
Mossneuk Cres ML2 165 E2
Mossneuk Dr
East Kilbride G75 179 F4
Paisley PA2 133 E4
Wishaw ML2 165 E2
Mossneuk Pk ML2 165 E2
Mossneuk Prim Sch G75 179 F4
Mossneuk Rd G75 180 A4
Mossneuk St ML5 121 F2
Mosspark Ave
Glasgow G52 115 F2
Milngavie G62 55 D2
Mosspark Bvd G52 115 F2
Mosspark Dr G52 115 F2
Mosspark La G52 115 F2
Mosspark Oval G52 115 F2
Mosspark Prim Sch G52 115 F2
Mosspark Rd
Coatbridge ML5 121 E4
Milngavie G62 55 D2
Mosspark Sq G52 115 F2
Mosspark Sta G52 115 E2
Mossvale Cres G33 99 E1
Mossvale La PA3 113 E3
Mossvale Path G33 99 E2
Mossvale Rd G33 99 E1
Mossvale Sq Glasgow G33 99 D1
Paisley PA3 113 E3
Mossvale St PA3 113 E4
Mossvale Terr G69 81 D2
Mossvale Way G33 99 E1
Mossvale Wlk G33 99 E1
Mossview Cres ML6 123 D3
Mossview La G52 115 E3
Mossview Quadrant G52 115 E3
Mossview Rd G33 99 F3
Mosswell Rd G62 55 D2
Mossyde Ave PA14 69 D4
Mossywood Ct G68 81 F4
Mossywood Pl G68 81 F4
Mossywood Rd G68 81 F4
Mote Hill ML3 162 C3
Mote View KA2 221 E1
Motehill Rd PA3 114 A4
Motherwell Coll ML1 163 F2
Motherwell Heritage Ctr
ML1 163 E4
Motherwell Rd
Bellshill ML4 142 A2
Hamilton ML3 163 D2
Motherwell ML1 144 A3
Motherwell, Carfin ML1 143 E1
Motherwell St ML6 123 E4
Motherwell Sta ML1 163 E4
Moulin Cir G52 115 D2
Moulin Pl G52 115 D2
Moulin Rd G52 115 D2
Moulin Terr G52 115 D2
Mount Annan Dr G44 137 D4
Mount Ave Kilmarnock KA1 227 E3
Symington KA1 231 E2
Mount Cameron Dr N
G74 181 D4
Mount Cameron Dr S
G74 181 D4
Mount Cameron Prim Sch
G74 181 D4
Mount Carmel Prim Sch
KA3 222 C3
Mount Charles Cres KA7 238 B1
Mount Florida Prim Sch
G42 137 D4
Mount Florida Sta G42 137 D4
Mount Harriet Ave G33 99 F3
Mount Harriet Dr G33 99 F3
Mount Hope FK9 2 B4
Mount Oliphant FK7 12 B4
Mount Oliphant Cres KA7 239 D3
Mount Oliphant Pl KA7 239 D3
Mount Pl KA1 227 E3
Mount Pleasant Cres G65 58 A3
Mount Pleasant Dr G60 73 D3
Mount Pleasant St PA15 45 F2
Mount St G20 96 C2
Mount Stewart St ML8 187 F1
Mount Stuart St G41 136 C4
Mount The KA7 239 D2
Mount Vernon Ave
Coatbridge ML5 121 F4
Glasgow G32 119 F2
Mount Vernon Prim Sch
G32 119 E2
Mount Vernon Sta G32 119 F1
Mount View KA11 220 B1
Mount Village KA1 227 E4
Mount William FK10 5 F1
Mountainblue St G31 118 A3
Mountblow Rd G81 73 E3
Mountblow Sch G81 73 F3
Mountgarrie Rd G51 115 E4
Mountherrick G75 180 C3
Mournian Way ML3 162 B1
Mousebank La ML11 214 C2
Mousebank Rd ML11 214 C3
Mousemill Rd ML11 214 B3
Mowbray G74 160 B2
Mowbray Ave G69 100 C3
Mowbray Ct FK7 7 E2
Moy Path 4 ML2 165 F3
Moyne Rd G53 115 D1
Muckcroft Rd G69 80 B2
Mudale Ct FK1 42 B1
Mugdock Ctry Pk G62 55 D3
Mugdock Rd G62 55 D2
Muir Cl KA3 195 E1
Muir Cres G83 27 E4
Muir Dr Irvine KA12 219 E2
Stevenston KA20 217 E4
Troon KA10 229 E3
Muir Drive Cotts KA20 217 E4
Muir Rd G82 50 B3
Muir St Alexandria G83 27 E4
Bishopbriggs G64 78 A1
Blantyre G72 161 E3
Coatbridge ML5 121 F4
Hamilton ML3 162 C2
Larkhall ML9 185 D2
Law ML8 186 C3
Motherwell ML1 163 E4
Renfrew PA4 94 B2
Stenhousemuir FK5 23 E1
Muir Street Prim Sch
ML1 163 E4
Muir Terr PA3 114 A4
Muiralehouse Rd FK7 11 F4
Muirbank Ave G73 137 F4
Muirbank Gdns G73 137 F4
Muirbrae Rd G73 138 A2
Muirbrae Way G73 138 A2
Muirburn Ave G44 136 C2
Muirburn Rd Beith KA15 150 A2
Stonehouse ML10 198 A1
Muircroft Dr ML1 144 A1
Muirdrum Ave G52 115 E2
Muirdyke Ave FK2 24 B2
Muirdyke Rd
Coatbridge ML6 102 A3
Coatbridge, Drumpellier ML5 121 E4
Muirdykes Ave
Glasgow G52 115 D3
Port Glasgow PA14 68 B4
Muirdykes Cres PA3 113 D3
Muirdykes Rd
Glasgow G52 115 D3
Paisley PA3 113 D3
Muiredge Ct G71 140 C3
Muiredge & Jersy Rd
Cleland ML1 145 D1
Shotts ML7, ML1 145 E4
Muiredge Prim Sch G71 141 D3
Muiredge Terr G69 120 A2
Muirend Ave G44 136 C3
Muirend Rd Cardross G82 48 A4
Glasgow G44 136 C2
Kilmarnock KA3 222 C3
Stirling FK7 7 D3
Muirend St KA25 149 D1
Muirend Sta G44 136 C2
Muirfield Cres G23 76 C1
Muirfield Ct Glasgow G44 136 C2
Irvine KA12 224 C4
Muirfield Mdws G72 140 C1
Muirfield Pl KA13 207 E2
Muirfield Rd
Cumbernauld G68 62 A3
Stenhousemuir FK5 23 F1
Muirhall Pl FK5 23 E2
Muirhall Rd FK5 23 E2
Muirhall Terr ML7 125 D1
Muirhead Ave FK2 42 A4
Muirhead Cotts G66 80 A4
Muirhead Dr Linwood PA3 112 A3
Motherwell ML1 143 F2
Muirhead Gate 4 G71 141 D4
Muirhead Gdns
Glasgow G69 120 B2
Salsburgh ML7 125 D1
Muirhead Pl ML7 127 E2
Muirhead Prim Sch KA10 229 F2
Muirhead Rd Glasgow G69 120 A2
Stenhousemuir FK5 23 F2
Muirhead St
Kirkintilloch G66 79 E4
Lochwinnoch PA12 129 E1
Muirhead Terr ML1 163 F2
Muirhead Way G64 78 B1
Muirhead-Braehead Rdbt
G67 62 A2
Muirhill Ave G44 136 C3
Muirhill Cres G13 95 D4
Muirhouse Ave
Motherwell ML1 164 A2
Wishaw ML2 166 A3
Muirhouse Dr ML1 164 B1
Muirhouse La 7 G75 180 C4
Muirhouse Pk G61 75 E4
Muirhouse Prim Sch ML1 164 A1
Muirhouse Rd ML1 164 A1
Muirhouse St 12 G41 117 D2
Muirkirk Dr Glasgow G13 95 F4
Hamilton ML3 161 E1
Muirlee Rd ML8 188 A1
Muirlees Cres G62 54 C1
Muirmadkin Rd ML4 142 A3
Muirmaillen Ave ML1 144 B1
Muirpark Ave PA4 94 B1
Muirpark Dr
Bishopbriggs G64 98 A4
Shieldhill FK1 66 B3
Muirpark Gdns FK10 4 C2
Muirpark Rd KA15 150 A1
Muirpark St G11 96 A1
Muirshiel Ave G53 135 E3
Muirshiel Cres G53 135 E3
Muirshiel Ctry Pk PA12 108 A2
Muirshiel La PA14 68 B4
Muirshiel Rd PA14 68 B4
Muirshot Rd ML9 185 D2
Muirside Ave Glasgow G32 119 F2
Kirkintilloch G66 80 A4
Muirside Ct KA13 207 E1
Muirside Pl
Kilwinning KA13 207 E1
21 Wishaw ML2 165 F3
Muirside Rd Glasgow G69 120 A2
Kilwinning KA13 207 E1
Tullibody FK10 4 B2
Muirside St G69 120 A2
Muirskeith Cres G44 137 D3
Muirskeith Pl G43 136 C3
Muirskeith Rd G43 136 C3
Muirton Dr G64 77 F2
Muirton Rd FK7 7 F3
Muirton Rdbt FK7 7 F4
Muiryfauld Dr G31 118 C3
Muiryhall St ML5 122 A4
Muiryhall St E ML5 122 B4
Mulben Cres G53 134 C4
Mulben Pl G53 134 C4
Mulben Terr G53 134 C4

Peel Rd G76 158 A1
Peel St Cardross G82 48 A4
Glasgow G11 96 A1
Peel View G81 74 B2
Pegasus Ave Carluke ML8 187 F1
Paisley PA3 112 C3
Pegasus Rd ML4 142 C3
Peggieshill Pl KA7 239 D3
Peggieshill Rd KA7 239 D3
Peile La PA16 45 E3
Peile St PA16 45 E3
Peiter Pl G72 161 E4
Pelstream Ave FK7 7 D2
Pemberton Valley KA7 239 D1
Pembroke G74 160 B2
Pembroke Rd PA16 44 B2
Pembroke St Glasgow G3 240 A3
Larbert FK5 23 E2
Penbreck Ct KA11 220 A3
Pencaitland Dr G32 119 D2
Pencaitland Gr G32 119 D2
Pencaitland Pl G23 76 C1
Pendeen Cres G33 119 F3
Pendeen Pl G33 119 F3
Pendeen Rd G33 119 F3
Penders La FK1 42 A3
Pendicle Cres G61 75 E2
Pendicle Rd G61 75 F2
Pendreich Way FK9 2 A2
Penfold Cres G75 180 B4
Penicuik St G32 118 B3
Penilee Rd PA1 114 C3
Penilee Sec Sch G52 114 C3
Penilee Terr G52 114 C3
Peninver Dr G51 115 F4
Penman Ave G73 137 F4
Pennan PA8 73 D2
Pennan Pl G14 95 D3
Penneld Rd G52 114 C3
Penniecroft Ave G82 50 B3
Pennyburn Prim Sch
KA13 207 E1
Pennyburn Rd KA13 207 E1
Pennyfern Dr PA16 45 D2
Pennyfern Rd PA16 45 D2
Pennyroyal Ct G74 159 E2
Pennyvenie Way KA11 220 A3
Penrioch Dr G75 180 B2
Penrith Ave G46 136 B1
Penrith Dr G12 96 A3
Penrith Pl G75 179 F3
Penryn Gdns G32 119 E2
Penston Rd G33 119 E4
Pentland Ave Linwood PA3 112 A3
Port Glasgow PA14 68 C3
Pentland Cres
Larkhall ML9 184 C3
Paisley PA2 133 E4
Pentland Ct Airdrie ML6 103 D1
Barrhead G78 134 B1
Pentland Dr Barrhead G78 134 B1
Bishopbriggs G64 78 B1
Prestwick KA9 236 B3
Renfrew PA4 114 A4
Pentland Pl Bearsden G61 75 D4
Irvine KA11 220 A2
Pentland Rd Chryston G69 100 B4
East Kilbride G75 180 A2
Glasgow G43 136 B3
Kilmarnock KA1 228 A2
Wishaw ML2 164 C2
Penzance Way G69 80 C1
Peockland Gdns PA5 112 A2
Peockland Pl PA5 112 A2
People's Palace (Mus)
G40 117 F3
Peploe Dr G74 160 B3
Perceton Rdbt KA11 220 A3
Perceton Row KA11 220 B2
Perchy View ML2 165 E1
Percy Dr G46 136 B1
Percy Rd PA4 94 A1
Percy St Glasgow G51 116 B3
Larkhall ML9 185 D2
Perran Gdns G69 80 C1
Perray Ave G82 49 D3
Perrays Dr G82 49 D2
Perth Ave ML6 123 D2
Perth Cres G81 73 E3
Perth St G3 240 A2
Peter Coats Building PA2 113 F2
Peter D.Stirling Rd G66 58 B1
Peter St KA12 219 D1
Peters Ave G83 20 A1
Petersburn Pl ML6 123 E3
Petersburn Prim Sch ML6 123 E3
Petersburn Rd ML6 123 E3
Petershill Ct G21 98 B2
Petershill Dr G21 98 B2
Petershill Pl G21 98 A2
Petershill Rd G21 98 A2
Peterson Dr G13 94 C4
Peterson Gdns G13 94 C4
Peterswell Brae FK7 7 F1
Petition Pl G71 141 D3
Pettigrew St G32 119 D3
Peveril Ave Glasgow G41 116 B1
Rutherglen G73 138 B3
Peveril Ct G73 138 B3
Pharonhill St G31 118 B3
Philip Dr FK5 23 E1
Philip Murray Rd ML4 141 E3
Philip Sq KA8 236 A1
Philip St FK2 42 A4
Philipshill Gate G74 158 C2
Philipshill Rd G76 158 C2
Phoenix Bsns Pk The PA3 112 C3
Phoenix Cres ML4 141 F4
Phoenix Pl Elderslie PA5 112 B2
Motherwell ML1 143 D2
Phoenix Rd ML4 142 C3
Phoenix Ret Pk The PA3 112 C3
Piazza Sh Ctr PA1 113 F3
Piccadilly St G3 240 A2
Picken St KA1 227 F3
Pickerstonhill ML1 143 F2
Picketlaw Dr G76 158 B4
Picketlaw Farm Rd G76 158 B4
Pier Rd Balloch G83 19 E1
Rhu G84 15 F2
Piershill St G32 118 C4
Piersland Pl KA11 220 A3
Pike Rd FK7 7 E2
Pikeman Rd G13 95 E4
Pilmuir Ave G44 136 C2
Pilrig St G32 118 C4
Pilton Rd G15 75 D2
Pine Ave G72 139 F2
Pine Brae KA7 239 E3
Pine Cl G67 62 C2
Pine Cres Cumbernauld G67 62 C2
East Kilbride G75 180 A3
Johnstone PA5 112 A1
Pine Ct Coatbridge ML5 121 F2
Cumbernauld G67 62 C2
East Kilbride G75 180 B3
Pine Gr Alloa FK10 10 B3
Calderbank ML6 123 D1
Cumbernauld G67 62 C2
Motherwell ML1 143 D3
Uddingston G71 141 D4
Pine House KA9 236 A3
Pine Lawn ML2 165 E3
Pine Pk ML3 162 C1
Pine Pl Cumbernauld G67 62 C2
Glasgow G5 117 E2
Pine Rd Clydebank G81 73 E2
Cumbernauld G67 62 C2
Dumbarton G82 49 F2
Kilmarnock KA1 227 E4
Pine St Airdrie ML6 123 E4
Greenock PA15 45 F2
Lennoxtown G65 57 F4
Paisley PA2 114 A1
Pine Wlk FK5 23 E1
Pineapple The FK2 14 A3
Pinelands G64 78 A2
Pines The G44 137 D2
Pinewood Ave G66 79 D3
Pinewood Ct
Dumbarton G82 50 B3
Kirkintilloch G66 79 D3
Pinewood Pl G66 79 D3
Pinewood Prim Sch G15 75 E2
Pinkerton Ave G73 137 F4
Pinkerton La PA4 94 B1
Pinkston Dr G21 97 F1
Pinkston Rd G21, G4 241 E4
Pinmore KA13 207 E1
Pinmore Pl G53 134 C3
Pinmore St G53 134 C3
Pinwherry Dr G33 98 C3
Pinwherry Pl G71 141 D2
Piper Ave PA6 111 E4
Piper Rd Airdrie ML6 123 E3
Houston PA6 111 E4
Piperhill KA7 239 D1
Pirleyhill Dr FK1 66 B3
Pirleyhill Gdns FK1 42 A1
Pirnhall Rd FK7 11 D4
Pirnie Pl G65 60 B4
Pirnmill Ave
East Kilbride G75 180 A2
Motherwell ML1 163 D4
Pirnmill Pl G84 16 C1
Pirnmill Rd KA21 205 F1
Pit Rd Bellshill ML4 141 F3
Kirkintilloch G66 80 B4
Pitcairn Cres G75 179 F4
Pitcairn Gr G75 180 A4
Pitcairn Pl G75 179 F4
Pitcairn St G31 118 C2
Pitcairn Terr ML3 162 A2
Pitcaple Dr G43 136 A3
Pitfairn Rd FK10 5 F2
Pitlochry Dr Glasgow G52 115 E2
Larkhall ML9 185 E1
Pitmedden Rd G64 78 B1
Pitmilly Rd G15 75 E2
Pitreavie Ct ML3 183 D4
Pitreavie Pl G33 99 E1
Pitt St G2 240 B3
Pitt Terr FK8 7 D3
Place Of Bonhill G82 27 E2
Place View KA25 149 D1
Pladda Ave Irvine KA11 220 A1
Port Glasgow PA14 69 D4
Pladda Cres KA11 220 A1
Pladda Ct KA11 220 A1
Pladda Dr KA9 236 B3
Pladda Rd Renfrew PA4 94 B1
Saltcoats KA21 205 F1
Pladda St ML1 163 D4
Pladda Terr KA11 220 A1
Pladda Way G84 16 C1
Pladda Wynd KA11 220 A1
Plains Prim Sch ML6 104 A1
Plaintrees Ct PA2 113 F1
Plan View KA25 149 D2
Plane Pl G71 121 E1
Planetree Pl PA5 112 A1
Planetree Rd G81 74 A3
Plant St G31 118 B3
Plantation Ave ML1 143 D3
Plantation Park Gdns 5
G51 116 B3
Plantation Sq G51 116 C3
Plateau Dr KA10 229 F4
Platthorn Dr G74 159 F1
Platthorn Rd G74 159 F1
Players Rd FK7 7 E4
Playfair St G40 118 A2
Playingfield Cres KA2 221 F1
Playingfield Rd KA2 221 F1
Plaza The 1 G74 159 F1
Pleaknowe Cres G69 80 C1
Pleamuir Pl G68 61 E1
Plean Ctry Pk FK7 12 A1
Plean St G14 95 D3
Pleasance FK1 42 A2
Pleasance Ct 13 FK2 42 A2
Pleasance Gdns FK1 42 A2
Pleasance Rd FK2 42 A2
Pleasance Sq 12 FK1 42 A2
Pleasance St G43 136 B4
Pleasantfield Rd KA9 236 A3
Pleasantside Ave PA14 69 D4
Plotcock Rd ML3 198 B4
Plover Dr G75 180 A3
Plover Pl PA5 131 E4
Plusgarten Loan ML2 165 F4
Plymouth Ave PA19 44 C3
Pochard Way ML4 141 F4
Poet's View G66 79 F4
Poindfauld Terr G82 50 A2
Pointhouse Rd G3 116 B4
Pokelly Pl KA3 195 F1
Polbae Cres G76 178 C3
Poles Rd KA3 213 D2
Polkemmet Dr ML7 127 F3
Polkemmet La ML7 127 F3
Polkemmet Rd ML7 127 F3
Pollick Ave G78 153 D2
Pollick Farm La G78 153 D1
Pollock Ave
Eaglesham G76 178 C3
Hamilton ML3 162 A2
Pollock Cres KA13 207 F1
Pollock House G43 135 F4
Pollock Rd Bearsden G61 76 A2
Newton Mearns G77 156 B2
Pollock St Bellshill ML4 142 B3
Motherwell ML1 163 F4
Pollockshields East Sta
G41 117 D2
Pollok Ave G43 136 A4
Pollok Ctry Pk G43 116 A1
Pollok Dr G64 77 F1
Pollok La G74 160 A2
Pollok Pl G74 160 A2
Pollokshaws East Sta
G43 136 B4
Pollokshaws Rd G41 117 D2
Pollokshaws West Sta
G43 136 A4
Pollokshields Prim Sch
G41 116 C2
Pollokshields Prim Sch
Annexe (Infs) G41 116 C2
Pollokshields West Sta
G41 116 C1
Polmadie Ave G5 117 E1
Polmadie Ind Est G5 117 F1
Polmadie Rd G42, G5 117 E1
Polmadie St G42 117 E1
Polmaise Ave FK7 7 D2
Polmaise Cres FK7 8 B3
Polmaise Ct FK7 7 D2
Polmaise Rd
Cambusbarron FK7 6 C2
Stirling FK7 6 C3
Polnoon Ave G13 95 D3
Polnoon Dr G76 178 C3
Polnoon St G76 178 B2
Polo Ave KA10 229 F1
Polo Gdns KA10 229 F1
Polquhap Ct G53 135 D4
Polquhap Gdns G53 135 D4
Polquhap Pl G53 135 D4
Polson Dr PA5 111 F1
Polsons Cres PA2 113 E1
Polwarth La G12 96 A2
Polwarth St G12 96 A2
Pomona Pl ML3 161 F1
Pompee Rd FK10 5 D1
Poplar Ave Bishopton PA7 72 A1
Glasgow G11 95 F2
Johnstone PA5 112 A1
Newton Mearns G77 156 C2
Poplar Cres PA7 72 A1
Poplar Ct ML5 121 F2
Poplar Dr Clydebank G81 73 F3
Kirkintilloch G66 79 D3
Milton Of C G65 58 B3
Poplar Gdns G75 180 B3
Poplar Pl Blantyre G72 140 B1
Gourock PA19 44 B3
Motherwell ML1 143 D2
Uddingston G71 141 E4
Poplar Rd G82 49 F2
Poplar St Airdrie ML6 123 E4
Greenock PA15 46 C1
Poplar Way Ayr KA7 239 E3
Cambuslang G72 139 F2
Poplars The Bearsden G61 75 E4
Tullibody FK10 4 A1
Poplin St G40 118 A2
Porchester St G33 99 E1
Port Dundas Ind Est G4 97 E1
Port Dundas Pl G2 241 D3
Port Dundas Rd G4 241 D4
Port Glasgow High Sch
PA14 69 D3
Port Glasgow Ind Est PA14 68 C4
Port Glasgow Rd
Greenock PA15 46 C2
Kilmacolm PA13 69 D1
Port Glasgow Sta PA14 47 E1
Port St Glasgow G3 240 A2
Stirling FK8 7 D4
Portal Rd G13 95 E4
Portdownie FK1 41 E3
Portencross Rd KA23 190 B3
Porter St 1 G51 116 B3
Porterfield Rd
Kilmacolm PA13 89 F4
Renfrew PA4 94 A2
Porters La ML6 123 E1
Porters Well G71 140 C3
Portessie PA8 73 D1
Porthlethen PA8 73 D1
Porting Cross Pl KA3 223 D3
Portland Ave KA12 224 A4
Portland Brae KA1 228 C3
Portland Ct KA1 228 C3
Portland Pk ML3 162 C1
Portland Pl Hamilton ML3 162 C1
Irvine KA12 224 A4
Kilmarnock KA1 227 F4
Lanark ML11 215 D2
Stevenston KA20 217 E4
Portland Place Ind Est
KA20 217 E4
Portland Rd
Cumbernauld G68 61 F3
Irvine KA12 224 A4
Kilmarnock KA1 227 F4
Paisley PA2 114 A2
Portland Rdbt KA12 219 D1
Portland Sq ML3 162 C1
Portland St
Coatbridge ML5 122 A4
Kilmarnock KA1 222 C1
Troon KA10 229 E2
Portland Terr KA10 229 D1
Portland Wynd 2 ML9 185 D2
Portman St G41 116 C3
Portmark Ave KA7 238 B1
Portmarnock Dr G23 96 C4
Porton Pl PA7 72 A2
Portpatrick Rd G60 72 C4
Portreath Rd G69 80 C2
Portree Terr PA16 44 C2
Portsmouth Dr PA19 44 C3
Portsoy PA8 73 D1
Portsoy Ave G13 94 C4
Portsoy Pl G13 94 C4
Portugal St G5 117 D3
Portwell ML3 162 C2
Possil Cross G22 97 E2
Possil Rd G4 97 D2
Possilpark & Parkhouse
Sta G22 97 D3
Postgate ML3 162 C2
Posthill FK10 5 E1
Potassels Rd G69 100 B4
Potrail Pl ML3 162 A2
Potter Cl G32 118 C2
Potter Gr G32 118 C2
Potter Pl Glasgow G32 118 C2
Skinflats FK2 24 C2
Potter St G32 118 C2
Potterhill Ave PA2 133 F4
Potterhill Rd G53 115 D1
Potters Wynd ML11 215 E3
Pottery Pl KA3 222 C1
Pottery St PA15 46 C2
Pottis Rd FK7 7 E2
Potts Way ML1 142 B1
Powbrone G75 180 C3
Powburn Cres G71 140 B4
Powfoot St G31 118 B3
Powforth Cl ML9 184 C2
Powgree Cres KA15 171 E3
Powmill Rd KA9 233 E1
Powrie St G33 99 E2
Prentice La 5 G71 141 D4
Prentice Rd ML1 163 D3
President Kennedy Dr
FK7 12 B2
Preston Pl Glasgow G42 117 D1
Gourock PA19 44 B4
Preston St G42 117 D1
Prestonfield G62 54 C1
Prestonfield Ave KA13 207 D2
Prestwick Acad KA9 233 E1
Prestwick Airport Sta
KA9 233 D2
Prestwick Ct G68 61 F2
Prestwick Int Airport
KA9 233 F1
Prestwick Pl G77 157 D2
Prestwick Rd KA8 236 A2
Prestwick St G53 135 D3
Prestwick Sta KA9 233 D1
Pretoria Ct G75 180 A2
Pretoria Rd FK5 23 D1
Priestfield Ind Est G72 161 E3
Priestfield St G72 161 E3
Priesthill Ave G53 135 E3
Priesthill Cres G53 135 E3
Priesthill & Darney Sta
G53 135 E3
Priesthill Rd G53 135 E3
Priestknowe Rdbt G74 159 F1
Prieston Rd PA11 110 B4
Primrose Ave
Bellshill ML4 142 A4
Larkhall ML9 199 D4
Primrose Cres ML1 163 F3
Primrose Ct 21 G14 95 E2
Primrose Pk KA7 239 E2
Primrose Pl Alloa FK10 10 A3
Cumbernauld G67 82 A3
Kilmarnock KA1 222 B1
Saltcoats KA21 206 A1
Uddingston G71 141 E4
Primrose St Alloa FK10 10 A4
Bonnybridge FK4 40 A3
Glasgow G14 95 E2
Primrose Way ML8 201 F4
Prince Albert Rd G12 96 B2
Prince Albert Terr G84 16 B1
Prince Edward St 2 G42 117 D1
Prince of Wales Gdns G20 96 B4
Prince Pl ML2 166 A3
Prince's Gdns G12 96 A2
Prince's Pl 20 G12 96 B2
Prince's Terr G12 96 B2
Princes Ct KA8 236 A1
Princes Gate Bothwell G71 140 C2
Rutherglen G73 138 A4
Princes Mall 8 G74 159 F1
Princes Pk PA8 72 C2
Princes Pl KA22 205 D1
Princes Sq Barrhead G78 134 B2
3 East Kilbride G74 159 F1
Troon KA10 229 E2
Princes Square Shop Ctr
G1 241 D2
Princes St
Ardrossan KA22 205 D1
Caldercruix ML6 105 D3
California FK1 66 C3
Falkirk FK1 42 A3
Greenock PA15 45 F3
Kilmarnock KA1 227 F4
Motherwell ML1 163 F4
Port Glasgow PA14 47 E1
Rutherglen G73 138 A4
Stirling FK8 7 D4
Princes St E G84 16 C1
Princess Anne Quadrant
ML1 142 C3
Princess Cres PA1 114 A3
Princess Ct
Helensburgh G84 16 B1
Kilmarnock KA1 228 A2
Princess Dr G69 121 D3
Princess Rd ML1 142 C2
Princess Sq 25 ML2 165 F3
Princess St FK4 40 A3
Princess Way G84 15 D2
Printers Land G76 158 A3
Priorwood Rd G77 156 A2
Priory Ave PA3 114 A4
Priory Dr G71 140 B4
Priory Gate ML2 186 A4
Priory Pl Cumbernauld G68 60 C1
Glasgow G13 95 E4
Priory Rd G13 95 E4
Priory St G72 161 E4
Priory Terr ML2 164 B1
Procession Rd PA2 133 E3
Professors' Sq G12 96 B1
Progress Dr ML6 105 D3
Promenade KA8 236 A2
Prosen St G32 118 C2
Prospect Ave
Cambuslang G72 138 C3
Uddingston G71 140 C4
Prospect Ct G72 161 E3
Prospect Dr ML9 199 F4
Prospect Rd
Cumbernauld G68 61 E3
Glasgow G41 136 B4
Prospect St FK1 41 F3
Prospecthill Cir G42 117 E1
Prospecthill Cres G42 137 F4
Prospecthill Dr G42 137 E4
Prospecthill Pl
Glasgow G42 137 F4
Greenock PA15 45 F2
Prospecthill Rd Falkirk FK1 42 A1
Glasgow G42 137 E4
Saltcoats KA21 206 A1
Prospecthill Sq G42 137 E4
Prospecthill St PA15 45 F2
Provan Hall G34 99 F1
Provan Rd G33 118 B4
Provand Hall Cres G69 120 A2
Provanhall Prim Sch G34 100 A1
Provanhill St G21 97 F1
Provanmill Rd G33 98 C1
Provost Cl PA5 111 F2
Provost Driver Ct PA4 94 C1
Provost Gate ML9 185 D2
Provost Hunter Ave FK12 5 E4
Pullar Ave FK9 2 A3
Pullar Ct FK9 2 A3
Pundeavon Ave KA25 149 D2
Purdie G74 160 B3
Purdie St ML3 162 A3
Purdon St G11 96 A1
Putyan Ave KA24 191 D4
Pyatshaw Rd ML9 185 D1
Quadrant Rd G43 136 C3
Quadrant The G76 157 F4
Quail Rd KA8 236 A2
Quakerfield FK7 7 F1
Quarrelton Rd PA5 111 F1
Quarrier St PA15 46 B2
Quarrolhall Cres FK2 24 A2
Quarry Ave G72 139 F2
Quarry Brae Prim Sch
G31 118 B3

Richmond Dr
Bishopbriggs G64 78 A2
Linwood PA3 112 A4
Rutherglen G73, G72 138 B4
Rutherglen, Cambuslang G73, G72 138 C3
Richmond Gdns G69 100 A4
Richmond Gr G73 138 B4
Richmond Park Sch G5 117 E2
Richmond Pl G73 138 B4
Richmond Rd G73 138 B4
Richmond St Clydebank G81 74 B1
Glasgow G1 241 E2
Richmond Terr KA2 225 F1
Riddell St Clydebank G81 74 B2
Coatbridge ML5 122 B4
Riddon Ave G81 94 C4
Riddon Pl G13 94 C4
Riddrie Cres G33 118 C4
Riddrie Knowes G33 118 C4
Riddrievale Ct G33 98 C1
Riddrievale St G33 98 C1
Ridgepark Dr ML11 214 C3
Ridgepark Sch ML11 214 C3
Ried Ct KA3 228 C4
Rig St KA3 211 E4
Rigby St G32 118 C3
Rigfoot KA11 220 A3
Righead KA3 211 E4
Rigghead Ave G67 62 A3
Riggs The Milngavie G62 55 D2
Prestwick KA9 233 E1
Riggside Rd G33 99 E1
Righead Gate 2 G74 159 F1
Righead Ind Est ML4 141 E4
Righead Rdbt G75 159 E1
Riglands Way PA4 94 B2
Riglaw Pl G13 95 D4
Rigmuir Rd G51 115 E3
Rigwoodie Pl KA7 238 C1
Rimmon Cres ML7 146 C3
Rimsdale St G40 118 A3
Ring Rd FK10 10 A4
Ringford St G21 97 F2
Ripon Dr G12 96 A3
Risk St Clydebank G81 73 F2
Dumbarton G82 49 F2
Ristol Rd G13 95 D3
Ritchie Cres PA5 112 B2
Ritchie Ct KA3 223 E1
Ritchie Pk PA5 112 A2
Ritchie Pl G77 156 B2
Ritchie St 8 Glasgow G5 117 D2
West Kilbride KA23 190 B3
Wishaw ML2 164 B2
Ritchie's Cl ML11 215 D2
River Pl KA25 149 D1
River Rd G32 139 D4
River St Ayr KA8 235 F1
Falkirk FK2 24 A1
River Terr KA8 235 F1
River View Cres G82 48 A4
River Wlk KA13 207 F3
Riverbank Dr ML4 142 B2
Riverbank Pl KA1 228 A4
Riverbank St G43 136 B4
Riverbank View FK8 7 E4
Riverdale Gdns ML3 162 C1
Riverford Rd Glasgow G43 136 B4
Rutherglen G73 118 B1
Riversdale La G14 95 D2
Riverside Balloch G83 27 F4
Houston PA6 91 E1
Milngavie G62 55 D1
Riverside Bsns Pk KA11 224 C4
Riverside Dr FK8 2 B1
Riverside Gdns G76 157 F3
Riverside La G82 49 F2
Riverside Pk G44 137 D1
Riverside Pl Ayr KA8 239 D4
Cambuslang G72 139 F3
Riverside Prim Sch FK8 2 A1
Riverside Rd
Eaglesham G76 178 C4
Glasgow G43 136 C4
Greenock PA15 46 A2
Irvine KA11 220 B1
Kilbirnie KA25 149 D1
Kirkfieldbank ML11 214 B2
Larkhall ML9 199 D4
Stewarton KA3 211 F4
Riverside Terr G76 157 F3
Riverside View FK10 10 A2
Riverside Way KA11 224 C4
Riverside Wlk ML1 163 F4
Riverton Dr G75 180 A4
Riverview Dr G5 240 B1
Riverview Gdns G5 240 B1
Riverview Pl G5 240 B1
Roaden Ave PA2 132 C4
Roaden Rd PA2 132 C4
Roadhead PA12 150 C4
Roadmeetings Hospl ML8 202 B4
Roadside G67 62 A3
Roadside Pl ML6 103 E4
Robb Terr G66 80 A3
Robert Bruce Ct FK5 23 D1
Robert Burns Ave
Clydebank G81 74 B2
Motherwell ML1 143 F2
Robert Burns Ct KA15 150 A1
Robert Burns Quadrant ML4 141 F3
Robert Creighton Pl KA3 222 C1
Robert Dick Ct FK10 4 B1
Robert Gilson Gdns ML5 122 A3
Robert Hardie Ct FK5 23 E1
Robert Kinmond Ave FK10 4 B1
Robert Knox Ave FK10 4 B1
Robert Noble Pl KA1 222 B1
Robert Owen Prim Sch ML11 215 E2
Robert Smillie Cres ML9 185 D1
Robert Smillie Memorial Prim Sch ML9 185 D1
Robert St Glasgow G51 116 A4
Port Glasgow PA14 47 F1
Shotts ML7 146 C2
Robert Stewart Pl KA1 222 C1
Robert Templeton Dr G72 139 D3
Robert W Service Ct KA13 207 F1
Robertland Rigg KA3 195 F1
Robertland Sq KA3 211 F4
Roberton Ave G41 116 B1
Roberton St ML6 123 F2
Roberts Quadrant ML4 142 A2
Roberts St Clydebank G81 73 F2
Wishaw ML2 165 D2
Robertson Ave FK4 40 A3
Robertson Cres Ayr KA8 236 B1
Neilston G78 154 B4
Saltcoats KA21 217 D4
Robertson Dr Bellshill ML4 142 A2
East Kilbride G74 160 A1
Robertson La G2 240 C2
Robertson Pl
Kilmarnock KA1 228 A4
Stirling FK7 7 D2
Robertson St Airdrie ML6 122 C4
Alva FK12 5 D4
Barrhead G78 134 A1
Glasgow G1, G2 240 C2
Greenock PA16 45 F3
Hamilton ML3 161 F3
Robertson Terr G69 120 B3
Robin Pl ML2 165 D2
Robin Rd PA16 45 D3
Robin Way G32 139 E4
Robroyston Ave G33 98 C2
Robroyston Rd
Bishopbriggs G64 78 C1
Glasgow G33 98 B2
Glasgow G33 98 C2
Glasgow, Robroyston G33 98 C3
Kirkintilloch G66 79 D2
Robshill Ct G77 156 B2
Robsland Ave KA7 238 C3
Robslee Cres G46 136 A2
Robslee Dr G46 136 A2
Robslee Prim Sch G46 136 A1
Robslee Rd G46 136 A2
Robson Gr 16 G42 117 D2
Rochdale Pl G66 79 E4
Roche Way KA24 191 E4
Rochsoles Dr ML6 103 D1
Rochsolloch Farm Cotts ML6 122 C4
Rochsolloch Prim Sch ML6 122 C3
Rochsolloch Rd ML6 122 B3
Rock Dr PA10 111 D1
Rock St G4 97 D2
Rockall Dr G44 137 E2
Rockbank Pl Clydebank G81 74 B3
Glasgow G40 118 A3
Rockbank St G40 118 A3
Rockburn Cres ML4 142 A4
Rockburn Dr G76 157 E4
Rockcliffe St G40 117 F2
Rockfield Pl G21 98 B3
Rockfield Rd G21 98 B3
Rockhampton Ave G75 180 A4
Rockliffe Path ML6 123 F1
Rockmount Ave
Barrhead G78 134 B1
Glasgow G46 136 A2
Rockpark Ct KA21 217 D4
Rockrose Pk KA7 239 D2
Rockwell Ave PA2 133 E4
Rodding The ML11 215 D3
Roddinghead Rd G46 157 D3
Rodger Ave G77 156 B3
Rodger Dr G73 138 A3
Rodger Pl G73 138 A3
Rodil Ave G44 137 E2
Rodney Pl G84 17 D1
Rodney Rd PA19 44 C3
Rodney St G4 97 D1
Roebank Dr G78 134 B1
Roebank Rd KA15 150 B1
Roebank St G31 118 A4
Roffey Park Rd PA1 114 B3
Rogart St G40 117 F3
Rogerfield Prim Sch G34 120 B4
Rogerfield Rd G34 120 B4
Rogers Ct ML9 198 B1
Rokeby La G12 96 C2
Roland Cres G77 156 C2
Roman Ave Bearsden G61 75 F3
Glasgow G15 75 D1
Roman Cres G60 72 C4
Roman Ct Bearsden G61 75 F3
Cleghorn ML11 215 F4
Roman Dr Bearsden G61 75 F3
Bellshill ML4 142 A2
Falkirk FK1 41 E3
Roman Gdns G61 75 F3
Roman Hill Rd G81 74 A4
Roman Pl ML4 141 F2
Roman Rd Ayr KA7 239 E3
Bearsden G61 75 F3
Bonnybridge FK4 40 A2
Clydebank G81 74 A3
Kirkintilloch G66 79 D4
Motherwell ML1 163 F4
Roman Way G71 141 E3
Romney Ave G44 137 E3
Rona Ave PA14 69 D4
Rona Pl KA3 223 D3
Rona St G21 98 A1
Rona Terr G72 138 C2
Ronades Rd FK2 42 A4
Ronald Cres FK5 23 D1
Ronald Pl FK8 7 D4
Ronaldsay Ct KA11 225 D4
Ronaldsay Dr G64 78 B1
Ronaldsay Pl G67 82 B4
Ronaldsay St G22 97 E4
Ronaldshaw Pk KA7 238 C3
Ronay St Glasgow G22 97 E4
Wishaw ML2 165 F3
Rook Rd PA16 45 D3
Rooksdell Ave PA2 113 E1
Ropework La G1 241 D1
Rorison Pl ML9 185 F1
Rosa Burn Ave G75 180 A2
Rosa Pl KA21 206 A1
Rose Cres Gourock PA19 44 B3
Hamilton ML3 161 F2
Rose Dale G64 98 A4
Rose Knowe Rd G42 137 E4
Rose Mount Ct ML6 123 E4
Rose Pl G74 160 B2
Rose St Alloa FK10 4 C1
Bonnybridge FK4 40 A3
Cumbernauld G67 82 A3
Glasgow G3 240 C4
Greenock PA16 45 E2
Kirkintilloch G66 79 E4
Motherwell ML1 164 A3
Rose Terr Denny FK6 21 E1
Stenhousemuir FK5 23 F2
Rosebank FK10 5 E1
Rosebank Ave
Blantyre G72 140 C1
Falkirk FK1 41 F3
Kirkintilloch G66 79 F4
Rosebank Cres KA7 238 C3
Rosebank Dr
Cambuslang G72 139 E2
Uddingston G71 141 E4
Rosebank Gdns Alloa FK10 10 B4
Irvine KA11 219 F4
Rosebank La 10 G71 141 D2
Rosebank Pl Falkirk FK1 41 F3
Hamilton ML3 162 A2
Kilmarnock KA3 222 C1
Rosebank Rd Bellshill ML4 142 A4
Wishaw ML2 186 B3
Rosebank Sch KA7 239 D3
Rosebank St ML6 123 F4
Rosebank Terr
Bargeddie G69 121 D2
Kilmacolm PA13 89 E4
Rosebay Pk KA7 239 D1
Roseberry La ML6 123 F2
Roseberry Pl ML3 162 A2
Roseberry Rd ML6 123 F2
Roseberry St G5 117 F1
Rosebery Pl FK8 2 A1
Roseburn Ct G67 62 C3
Rosedale G74 159 E2
Rosedale Ave PA2 132 B4
Rosedale Dr G69 120 A2
Rosedale Gdns
Glasgow G20 96 B4
Helensburgh G84 16 C1
Rosedale St ML11 214 C1
Rosedene Terr ML4 142 A3
Rosefield Gdns G71 140 C4
Rosegreen Cres ML4 142 A4
Rosehall Ave ML5 122 A2
Rosehall High Sch ML5 121 F2
Rosehall Ind Est ML5 122 A2
Rosehall Rd Bellshill ML4 141 F3
Shotts ML7 146 B2
Rosehall Terr Falkirk FK1 42 A2
Wishaw ML2 164 C1
Rosehill Dr G67 82 A3
Rosehill Rd G64 78 B4
Roseholm Ave KA12 219 F1
Roselea ML6 104 C2
Roselea Dr G62 55 D2
Roselea Gdns G13 95 F4
Roselea Pl G72 140 B1
Roselea Rd G71 140 C4
Roselea St ML9 185 D2
Rosemary Cres G74 159 E2
Rosemary Pl G74 159 E2
Rosemead Terr FK1 66 C3
Rosemount
Cumbernauld G68 61 F3
Kilwinning KA13 207 E1
Rosemount Ave G77 156 B1
Rosemount Dr KA10 229 E4
Rosemount Gdns KA9 236 B3
Rosemount La
Bridge Of W PA11 110 A3
28 Larkhall ML9 185 E1
Rosemount Mdws G72 140 C1
Rosemount Pl PA19 44 A3
Rosemount St G21 97 F1
Rosendale Way G72 161 F4
Roseneath Dr G84 16 A1
Roseneath Gate G74 159 E1
Roseneath Prim Sch G84 15 D2
Roseneath St PA16 45 E4
Roseness Pl G33 119 D4
Rosepark Ave G71 141 E3
Rosepark Cotts ML5 121 F2
Rosevale Cres
Bellshill ML4 142 B2
Hamilton ML3 162 A1
Rosevale Rd G61 75 F2
Rosevale Sch G22 97 E4
Rosevale St G11 96 A1
Rosewood Ave
Bellshill ML4 142 A4
Paisley PA2 113 D1
Rosewood Path ML4 141 F3
Rosewood St G13 95 F4
Roslea Dr G31 118 A4
Roslin Ct PA13 89 E4
Roslin St PA15 45 F3
Roslin Tower G72 138 C2
Roslyn Dr G69 120 C3
Rosneath Rd
Port Glasgow PA14 68 B4
Rosneath G84 15 D1
Rosneath St G51 116 A4
Ross Ave Kirkintilloch G66 79 F4
Renfrew PA4 94 A1
Ross Cres Falkirk FK1 41 E3
Motherwell ML1 163 E3
Ross Ct FK7 7 D2
Ross Dr Airdrie ML6 122 C2
Motherwell ML1 163 E3
Uddingston G71 121 E1
Ross Gdns ML1 163 E3
Ross Hall Pl PA4 94 B2
Ross Pl G73 138 B2
Ross Rd KA21 205 F1
Ross St Ayr KA8 236 B1
Coatbridge ML5 122 A4
Glasgow G40 241 E1
Paisley PA1 114 A2
Ross Terr ML3 163 E1
Ross Wlk KA3 223 D1
Rossbank Rd PA14 47 D1
Rossendale Ct G43 136 B4
Rossendale Rd G43 136 B4
Rosshall Ave PA1 114 B2
Rosshall Hospl G52 115 D2
Rosshill Ave G52 114 C3
Rosshill Rd G52 114 C3
Rossie Cres G64 98 B4
Rossie Gr G77 156 A3
Rossland Cres PA7 72 A2
Rossland Pl PA7 72 B1
Rosslea Dr G46 136 B1
Rosslyn Ave
East Kilbride G74 160 A2
Rutherglen G73 138 B4
Rosslyn Ct ML3 162 A2
Rosslyn Pl KA8 236 A2
Rosslyn Rd Ashgill ML9 199 F4
Bearsden G61 75 D3
Rosslyn Terr 33 G12 96 B2
Rossvail Sch FK1 41 E3
Rostan Rd G43 136 B3
Rosyth Rd G5 117 F1
Rosyth St G5 117 F1
Rotherwick Dr PA1 114 C2
Rotherwood Ave
Glasgow G13 75 E1
Paisley PA2 132 C4
Rotherwood La G13 75 E1
Rotherwood Pl G13 95 E4
Rotherwood Way PA2 132 C4
Rothes Dr G23 96 B4
Rothes Pl G23 76 B1
Rothesay Cres ML5 122 A2
Rothesay Pl
Coatbridge ML5 122 A2
East Kilbride G74 159 F1
Kilmarnock KA3 222 C2
Rothesay Rd PA16 44 C2
Rothesay St G74 180 C4
Rottenrow Glasgow G4 241 E3
Glasgow G4 241 F2
Rottenrow E G4 241 E2
Roughburn Rd FK9 2 A3
Roughcraig St ML6 103 D1
Roughlands Cres FK2 24 A2
Roughlands Dr FK2 24 A2
Roughlea Pl KA10 229 F3
Roughrigg Rd ML6 124 B3
Rouken Glen Pk G46 135 F1
Rouken Glen Rd G46 136 A1
Roukenburn St G46 135 F2
Round Riding Rd G82 50 A2
Roundel The Falkirk FK2 42 B4
Wishaw ML2 165 E1
Roundelwood FK10 5 D1
Roundhill Dr PA5 112 C2
Roundhouse FK7 12 B4
Roundknowe Rd G71 120 B1
Rowallan KA13 207 E1
Rowallan Cres KA9 236 B4
Rowallan Dr
Bannockburn FK7 11 F4
Kilmarnock KA3 223 D2
Rowallan Gdns G11 96 A2
Rowallan La Clarkston G76 157 F4
Glasgow G11 96 A2
Rowallan Rd G46 135 F1
Rowallan St G84 16 A2
Rowallan Terr G33 99 D2
Rowan Ave Milton Of C G65 58 B3
Renfrew PA4 94 B2
Rowan Cres Ayr KA7 239 E3
Falkirk FK1 41 D2
Kirkintilloch G66 79 E3
Rowan Ct Bannockburn FK7 7 F1
Wishaw ML2 164 B1
Rowan Dr Banknock FK4 38 C1
Bearsden G61 76 A4
Clydebank G81 73 F2
Dumbarton G82 49 D2
Rowan Gate PA2 113 F1
Rowan Gdns G41 116 A2
Rowan Gr ML3 183 F2
Rowan House KA9 236 A3
Rowan La ML1 143 D1
Rowan Pl Beith KA15 171 E4
Blantyre G72 161 E4
Cambuslang G72 139 E3
Coatbridge ML5 121 F2
Kilmarnock KA1 227 E4
Troon KA10 229 E2
Rowan Rd Cumbernauld G67 62 B2
Glasgow G41 116 A2
Linwood PA3 111 F4
Rowan Rise ML3 162 C1
Rowan St Beith KA15 171 E4
Greenock PA16 45 E3
Paisley PA2 113 F1
Wishaw ML2 165 D3
Rowan Terr KA12 219 E2
Rowanbank Pl ML6 122 B4
Rowanbank Rd KA9 236 C4
Rowand Ave G46 136 B2
Rowandale Ave G69 120 A2
Rowanden Ave ML4 142 A3
Rowanhill Pl KA1 227 E4
Rowanlea ML6 103 F2
Rowanlea Ave PA2 132 C4
Rowanlea Dr G46 136 B2
Rowanpark Dr G78 134 A3
Rowans Gdns G71 141 D2
Rowans The Alloa FK10 5 E1
Bishopbriggs G64 77 F1
Rowanside Terr KA22 205 E2
Rowantree Ave
Motherwell ML1 143 E4
Rutherglen G73 138 A3
Uddingston G71 141 E4
Rowantree Gdns
Irvine KA11 220 A3
Rutherglen G73 138 A3
Rowantree Pl
Johnstone PA5 111 F1
Larkhall ML9 185 E1
Lennoxtown G65 57 F4
Rowantree Rd PA5 112 A1
Rowantree Terr
Lennoxtown G65 57 F4
Motherwell ML1 143 D3
Rowantreehill Rd PA13 89 F4
Rowanwood Cres ML5 121 E3
Rowena Ave G13 75 E1
Rowmore Quays G84 15 F2
Roxburgh Ave PA15 45 F2
Roxburgh Dr Bearsden G61 75 F4
Coatbridge ML5 122 B2
Roxburgh Pk G74 159 F1
Roxburgh Pl Blantyre G72 161 E4
Stenhousemuir FK5 23 F2
Roxburgh Rd Hurlford KA1 228 C3
Paisley PA2 132 B4
Roxburgh St Glasgow G12 96 B2
Greenock PA15 45 F2
Roxburgh Way PA15 45 F2
Roy St G21 97 E2
Roy Young Ave G83 28 A4
Royal Alexandra Hospl PA2 113 E1
Royal Bank Pl G1 241 D2
Royal Cres G3 116 C4
Royal Dr ML3 163 D1
Royal Exchange Ct G1 241 D2
Royal Exchange Sq G1 241 D2
Royal Gdns FK8 7 D4
Royal Hospl (For Sick Children) G3 96 B1
Royal Inch Terr PA4 94 B3
Royal Infmy G4 241 F3
Royal Maternity & Women's Hospl G1 241 E2
Royal Samaritan Hospl For Women G42 117 D2
Royal Scottish Acad of Music & Drama G3 240 C3
Royal Scottish National Hospl The FK5 22 C2
Royal St PA19 44 C4
Royal Terr Glasgow G3 96 C1
Wishaw ML2 165 E4
Royal Terrace La G3 96 C1
Royellen Ave ML3 161 F1
Royston Rd G21, G33 98 B2
Royston Sq G21 241 F4
Roystonhill G21 97 F1
Rozelle KA7 238 C1
Rozelle Ave Glasgow G15 75 D2
Newton Mearns G77 156 A2
Rozelle Dr G77 156 A2
Rozelle Pl G77 156 A2
Rozelle Terr KA7 239 D1
Rubie Cres KA12 219 E1
Rubislaw Dr G61 75 F2
Ruby St G40 118 A2
Ruchazie Pl G33 118 C4
Ruchazie Prim Sch G33 99 D1
Ruchazie Rd G32 118 C4
Ruchill Hospl (Infectious diseases) G20 97 D3
Ruchill Pl G20 96 C3
Ruchill Prim Sch G20 96 C3
Ruchill St G20 96 C3
Rue End St PA15 46 A2
Ruel St G44 137 D4
Rufflees Ave G78 134 B2
Rugby Ave G13 95 D4
Rugby Cres KA1 227 E4
Rugby Pk (Kilmarnock FC) KA1 227 F4

Rugby Rd KA1 227 E4
Rulley View FK6 21 E2
Rullion Pl G33 118 C4
Rumford Pl KA3 223 E3
Rumford St G40 117 F2
Rumlie The FK1 86 A3
Runciman Pl G74 160 A2
Rundell Dr G65 58 B3
Rupert St G4 96 C1
Rushyhill St G21 98 A2
Ruskie Rd FK9 2 A2
Ruskin La G12 96 C2
Ruskin Pl Glasgow G12 96 C2
Kilsyth G65 60 B4
Ruskin Sq G64 78 A1
Ruskin Terr Glasgow G12 96 C2
Rutherglen G73 118 A1
Russel St FK2 42 A3
Russell Colt St ML5 122 A4
Russell Ct KA3 223 E2
Russell Dr Alexandria G83 27 E4
Ayr KA8 236 A1
Bearsden G61 75 F3
Dalry KA24 191 E4
Russell Gdns
Newton Mearns G77 156 B2
[10] Uddingston G71 141 D4
Russell La ML2 165 D1
Russell Pl Clarkston G76 158 A3
East Kilbride G75 180 B4
Linwood PA3 111 F3
Russell Rd Clydebank G81 73 F4
Lanark ML11 215 D3
Russell St Ayr KA8 236 A1
Bellshill ML4 142 B3
Chapelhall ML6 123 F1
Hamilton ML3 161 F3
Johnstone PA5 112 A2
Paisley PA3 113 E4
Wishaw ML2 165 D1
Rutherford Ave
Bearsden G61 75 D4
Kirkintilloch G66 80 A3
Rutherford Ct
Bridge Of A FK9 2 A4
Clydebank G81 74 A1
Rutherford Grange G66 79 E3
Rutherford La G75 180 C4
Rutherford Sq G75 180 C4
Rutherglen Ind Est G73 118 A1
Rutherglen Rd G5 117 F1
Rutherglen Sta G73 138 A4
Ruthven Ave G46 136 B1
Ruthven La [8] Glasgow G12 96 B2
Glenboig ML5 101 E3
Ruthven Pl
Bishopbriggs G64 98 B4
Troon KA10 229 F2
Ruthven St G12 96 B2
Rutland Cres G51 116 C3
Rutland Pl G51 116 C3
Ryan Rd G64 78 A1
Ryan Way G73 138 B2
Ryat Dr G77 156 B3
Ryat Gn G77 156 B3
Ryatt Linn PA8 72 C1
Rydal Gr G75 179 F3
Rydal Pl G75 179 F3
Ryde Rd ML2 165 E2
Ryden Mains Rd ML6 102 B2
Rye Cres G21 98 A3
Rye Rd G21 98 B3
Rye Way PA2 112 C1
Ryebank Rd G21 98 B3
Ryecroft Dr G69 120 A3
Ryedale Pl G15 75 D2
Ryefield Ave
Coatbridge ML5 121 E4
Johnstone PA5 111 E1
Ryefield Pl PA5 111 E1
Ryefield Rd G21 98 A3
Ryehill Pl G21 98 B3
Ryehill Rd G21 98 B2
Ryemount Rd G21 98 B3
Ryeside Pl KA24 169 E1
Ryeside Rd G21 98 A2
Rylands KA9 236 B3
Rylands Dr G32 119 E2
Rylands Gdns G32 119 F2
Rylees Cres G52 114 C3
Rylees Pl G52 114 C3
Rylees Rd G52 114 C3
Rysland Ave G77 156 C3
Rysland Cres G77 156 C3
Ryvoan Dr KA3 213 D2
Ryvra Rd G13 95 E3

Sachelcourt Ave PA7 72 A1
Sackville Ave G13 95 F3
Sackville La G13 95 F3
Sacred Heart High Sch
PA2 114 B1
Sacred Heart Prim Sch
Cumbernauld G67 62 A1
Gourock PA16 44 C2
Sacred Heart RC Prim Sch
Bellshill ML4 142 A2
Glasgow G40 117 F2
Saddell Rd G15 75 D2
Saffronhall Cres ML3 162 B2
Saffronhall La ML3 162 B2
Sainford Cres FK2 24 A1
St Abb's Dr PA2 113 D1
St Agatha's Prim Sch G66 80 A4
St Agnes' Prim Sch G23 96 C4
St Aidan's RC High Sch
ML2 165 D2
St Aidan's RC Prim Sch
ML2 165 E3
St Aidan's RC Sch G31 118 B3
St Albert's RC Prim Sch
G41 116 C2
St Aloysius Coll G3 240 B4
St Aloysius' Prim Sch G22 97 F3
St Aloysius RC Prim Sch
ML6 123 F1
St Ambrose Sch ML5 121 F4
St Ambrose's Prim RC Sch
G22 97 F4
St Andrew St PA15 46 A2
St Andrew's Acad KA21 205 F1
St Andrew's Ave
Bishopbriggs G64 77 F1
Prestwick KA9 236 B3
St Andrew's Brae G82 50 A3
St Andrew's Coll G61 75 E4
St Andrew's Cres
Dumbarton G82 50 A3
Paisley PA3 113 E4
St Andrew's Cross G41 117 D2
St Andrew's Ct FK5 23 D2
St Andrew's Dr Airth FK2 14 A4
Glasgow G41 116 B2
Hamilton ML3 161 E2
Paisley PA3 113 E4
St Andrew's Dr W PA3 93 E1
St Andrew's Gdns
Airdrie ML6 123 D4
Dalry KA24 191 D3
St Andrew's High Sch G81 94 B4
St Andrew's La G1 241 E1
St Andrew's Pl KA20 206 C1
St Andrew's Prim Sch
Airdrie ML6 102 C1
Falkirk FK1 42 B2
St Andrew's RC Cath G1 241 D1
St Andrew's RC High Sch
G75 180 B3
St Andrew's RC Prim Sch
G61 75 E3
St Andrew's Rd
Ardrossan KA22 205 E2
Glasgow G41 116 C2
Renfrew PA4 94 B1
St Andrew's Sec Sch G32 119 D4
St Andrew's Sq G1 241 E1
St Andrew's St Ayr KA7 239 D4
Glasgow G1 241 E1
Kilmarnock KA1 227 F4
St Andrew's Wlk KA1 227 F4
St Andrews Ave G71 141 D1
St Andrews Cres G41 116 C2
St Andrews Ct
East Kilbride G75 180 B3
Motherwell ML1 143 D3
St Andrews Dr
Bridge Of W PA11 110 B3
Cumbernauld G68 62 A3
Gourock PA19 44 A3
St Andrews Gate ML4 141 F3
St Andrews La
Alexandria G83 27 F2
Gourock PA19 44 A3
St Andrews Path [23] ML9 185 E1
St Andrews Pl Beith KA15 171 D4
[11] Falkirk FK1 42 A2
Kilsyth G65 36 B1
St Andrews St ML1 143 D3
St Andrews Way KA12 224 C4
St Andrews Wynd G84 16 C2
St Angela's Prim Sch G53 135 E2
St Ann's Dr G46 136 B1
St Anne's Cres FK7 7 F1
St Anne's Prim RC Sch
G40 118 A3
St Anne's Prim Sch PA8 93 E4
St Annes Pl PA8 93 E4
St Annes Wynd PA8 93 E4
St Anthony's Prim Sch
KA21 205 F1
St Anthony's RC Prim Sch
Glasgow G51 115 F4
Johnstone PA5 131 E4
Rutherglen G73 138 B2
St Athanasius' RC Prim Sch
ML8 187 F1
St Augustine's Prim RC Sch
G22 97 E4
St Augustine's RC Prim Sch
ML5 121 F3
St Barbara's RC
Prim & Sec Sch G69 100 B4
St Barchan's Rd PA10 111 D1
St Bartholomew's Prim Sch
G45 137 F2
St Bartholomew's
RC Prim Sch ML5 101 E1
St Benedict's Prim RC Sch
G34 100 A1
St Bernadette's
RC Prim Sch
Motherwell ML1 163 D4
Tullibody FK10 4 A1
St Bernard's RC Prim Sch
ML5 122 A2
St Bernards Prim RC Sch
G53 135 D3
St Blane's Dr G73 137 F3
St Blane's RC Prim Sch
G72 161 E4
St Blanes Prim Sch G23 76 B1
St Bonaventure's Prim RC Sch
G5 117 E2
St Boswell's Cres PA2 113 D1
St Boswells Dr ML5 122 B2
St Brendan's High Sch
PA3 112 B3
St Brendan's Prim Sch
G13 94 C4
St Brendan's RC Prim Sch
ML1 164 A1
St Brennans Ct KA25 170 A4
St Bride's Ave G71 141 E4
St Bride's Dr KA23 190 B3
St Bride's Pl KA12 219 E3
St Bride's RC High Sch
G74 160 A1
St Bride's RC Prim Sch
G71 141 D2
St Bride's Rd Glasgow G43 136 B3
West Kilbride KA23 190 B3
St Bride's Sec Sch G72 139 D3
St Brides Way G71 141 D2
St Bridget's Prim Sch
G69 120 A3
St Bridget's RC Prim Sch
KA25 170 A4
St Brigid's RC Prim Sch
Glasgow G42 137 E4
Wishaw ML2 166 A3
St Bryde St G74 159 F1
St Cadoc's Prim Sch G77 156 B3
St Cadoc's Sch G72 139 E2
St Catherine's Prim Sch
PA3 113 F3
St Catherine's RC Prim Sch
G21 98 B3
St Catherine's Rd G46 136 B1
St Catherines Cres ML7 146 C3
St Catherines Rd KA8 236 C1
St Charles Prim Sch PA2 113 F1
St Charles RC Prim Sch
G72 139 F3
St Charles's Prim Sch G20 96 C2
St Clair Ave G46 136 B2
St Clair Terr KA10 229 D1
St Clare's Prim RC Sch
G15 75 D2
St Clare's RC Prim Sch
G34 120 B4
St Columba Dr G66 79 F4
St Columba Pl KA20 206 C1
St Columba's High Sch
Clydebank G81 74 B2
Greenock PA16 45 D3
St Columba's Prim Sch
PA13 89 E4
St Columba's RC Prim Sch
Kilmarnock KA1 228 A4
Uddingston G71 141 E4
St Columbkille's
RC Prim Sch G73 138 A4
St Constantine's
Prim RC Sch G51 115 F4
St Conval's Prim RC Sch
G43 136 B4
St Crispin's Pl FK1 42 A2
St Cuthbert's Cres KA9 236 B3
St Cuthbert's Prim RC Sch
G22 97 D2
St Cuthbert's RC Prim Sch
ML3 162 A3
St Cuthbert's Rd KA9 236 B3
St Cuthberts High Sch
PA5 131 E4
St Cyrus Gdns G64 78 B1
St Cyrus Rd G64 78 B1
St David's Ct FK5 23 D1
St David's Pl ML9 185 D2
St David's RC Prim Sch
PA5 111 E1
St David's RC Sch ML6 104 A1
St Davids Dr ML6 123 E2
St Denis Way ML5 121 F4
St Denis's Prim Sch G31 118 A4
St Dominic's RC Prim Sch
Airdrie ML6 123 E3
Glasgow G45 137 F1
St Edmunds Gr G62 55 D2
St Edmunds Prim Sch G53 115 E1
St Edward's Prim Sch ML6 123 E4
St Elizabeth Seton RC
Prim Sch G33 119 E4
St Elizabeth's RC Prim Sch
ML3 183 E4
St Enoch Ave G71 141 E4
St Enoch Pl G1 240 C2
St Enoch Sh Ctr G1 241 D1
St Enoch Sq G1 240 C2
St Enoch Underground Sta
G1 240 C2
St Eunan's Prim Sch G81 74 B1
St Fergus's RC Prim Sch
PA3 113 D3
St Fillan's Prim Sch G44 137 D3
St Fillan's RC Prim Sch
PA6 91 D1
St Fillans Dr PA6 91 D1
St Fillans Rd G33 99 E3
St Flanan Rd G66 59 E1
St Flannan's Prim Sch G66 58 C1
St Francis of Assisi
Prim Sch
Cumbernauld G68 82 A4
Glasgow G69 119 F2
St Francis Prim RC Sch G5 117 E2
St Francis Prim Sch PA14 68 C4
St Francis Private Prim Sch
G43 136 B3
St Francis' RC Prim Sch
FK2 42 A3
St Francis Xavier Coll ML5 122 B2
St Gabriel's Prim Sch G71 141 E4
St Gabriel's RC Prim Sch
PA16 44 B2
St George's Cross [10] G3 97 D1
St George's Cross
Underground Sta G3 97 D1
St George's Ct FK5 23 D1
St George's Pl [8] G20 97 D1
St George's Prim RC Sch
G52 114 C3
St George's RC Prim Sch
ML4 142 A4
St George's Rd Ayr KA8 236 A2
Glasgow G3 240 B4
St Gerard's Sec Sch G51 116 A4
St Germains G61 75 F2
St Gilbert's RC Prim Sch
G21 98 B2
St Giles Pk ML3 162 A1
St Giles Sq FK1 41 D3
St Giles Way Falkirk FK1 41 D3
Hamilton ML3 162 A1
St Gregory's Prim RC Sch
G20 96 B3
St Helen's Prim Sch
Bishopbriggs G64 78 B1
Cumbernauld G67 82 A4
St Helena Cres G81 74 B3
St Hilary's RC Prim Sch
G74 181 D4
St Ignatius Prim Sch ML2 165 D2
St Inan Ave KA12 219 F2
St Inan's Dr KA15 150 B1
St Ives Rd G69 80 C2
St Jame's RC Sch ML5 121 F2
St James Ave PA3 113 D4
St James Ct ML5 121 F2
St James' Orch FK9 2 B1
St James' Pl KA20 206 C1
St James' Prim Sch G40 117 F3
St James Prim Sch PA3 113 E4
St James' RC Prim Sch
PA4 94 B2
St James Rd G4 241 E3
St James' St PA3 113 F3
St James Terr PA13 89 E4
St James Way ML5 121 F2
St Jerome's RC Prim Sch
G51 115 F4
St Joachim's RC Prim Sch
G32 119 E1
St Joan of Arc RC Sch G22 97 D4
St Joan's Cres KA13 207 F1
St John Bosco Prim Sch
PA8 72 C1
St John Maxwell Prim Sch
G43 136 B4
St John Ogilvie Prim Sch
Irvine KA11 220 A2
Paisley PA1 114 A2
St John St Ayr KA7 235 F1
Coatbridge ML5 122 A4
Prestwick KA9 236 B4
Stirling FK8 7 D4
St John The Baptist
Prim Sch G71 141 D3
St John's Ave FK2 42 B3
St John's Ct G41 116 C2
St John's Gate FK6 21 E1
St John's Gdns FK6 21 E1
St John's Gr FK6 21 E1
St John's Pl KA22 205 E1
St John's Pl KA20 206 C1
St John's Prim RC Sch G5 117 D3
St John's Prim Sch KA8 236 A1
St John's Prim Sch
Barrhead G78 134 B2
Hamilton ML3 162 B2
St John's Quadrant [1]
G41 116 C2
St John's RC Prim Sch
PA14 47 D1
St John's Rd Glasgow G41 116 C2
Gourock PA19 44 C4
St Joseph's Acad KA3 223 D1
St Joseph's Ct G21 97 F1
St Joseph's Pl G21 97 F1
St Joseph's Prim Sch
Bonnybridge FK4 40 A2
Clarkston G76 157 F3
Clydebank G81 74 B4
Cumbernauld G67 82 C4
Glasgow G4 97 D1
Milngavie G62 54 C1
St Joseph's Prim Sch G69 99 F3
St Joseph's RC Prim Sch
G72 161 E4
St Joseph's RC Prim Sch
PA16 45 D2
St Joseph's Sch ML5 101 E4
St Joseph's View G21 97 F1
St Josephs Prim Sch G84 16 C1
St Jude's Prim RC Sch
G33 119 F3
St Julie's Sch G44 137 E2
St Kenneth Dr G51 115 F4
St Kenneth's Prim RC Sch
G74 159 E1
St Kenneth's RC Prim Sch
PA15 46 B1
St Kentigerns Rd ML11 215 D3
St Kessogs RC Prim Sch
G83 27 F4
St Kevin's RC Prim Sch
ML5 121 D3
St Kevin's Sch G21 97 F1
St Kilda Bank KA11 220 A1
St Kilda Ct KA11 220 A1
St Kilda Dr G14 95 F2
St Kilda Pl KA11 220 A1
St Kilda Way ML2 165 F3
St Laurence Cres FK1 86 A3
St Lawrence Pk G75 159 E1
St Lawrence Pl KA21 206 A1
St Lawrence Prim Sch
PA15 46 A2
St Lawrence St PA15 46 A2
St Leonard St ML11 215 D3
St Leonard's Dr G46 136 B2
St Leonard's RC Prim Sch
G74 160 B2
St Leonard's Rd Ayr KA7 239 D3
Lanark ML11 215 D2
St Leonard's Sec RC Sch
G34 100 B1
St Leonard's Sq G74 160 B1
St Leonards Rd G74 160 B1
St Leonards Wlk ML5 122 B2
St Louise Prim Sch G46 135 E2
St Louise's RC Prim Sch
G75 180 C3
St Lucy's Prim Sch G67 62 C2
St Luke's Ave ML8 201 F4
St Luke's Prim Sch KA13 207 D1
St Lukes High Sch G78 155 E4
St Machan's RC Prim Sch
G65 33 E1
St Machan's Way G65 33 E1
St Machars Rd PA11 110 C4
St Margaret Ave KA24 191 D4
St Margaret Mary RC
Sec Sch G45 137 E1
St Margaret Mary's RC
Prim Sch G45 137 E1
St Margaret's Ave G65 37 F2
St Margaret's Dr ML2 164 C1
St Margaret's High Sch
ML6 123 D4
St Margaret's Pl G1 241 D1
St Margaret's Prim Sch
PA5 111 F1
St Margaret's RC Prim Sch
FK7 12 B4
St Margaret's Rd KA22 205 E2
St Mark Gdns G32 118 C3
St Mark St G32 118 C3
St Mark's Prim RC Sch
G31 118 C3
St Mark's Prim Sch
Glasgow G73 138 A3
Irvine KA12 219 F2
St Mark's RC Prim Sch
Barrhead G78 134 B1
Hamilton ML3 161 F1
St Marnock Pl [6] KA1 227 F4
St Marnock St
Glasgow G40 118 A3
Kilmarnock KA1 227 F4
St Marnock's RC Prim Sch
G53 115 E1
St Marnock's RC Prim Sch
Annexe G53 115 E1
St Martha's RC Prim Sch
G21 98 A3
St Martin's High Sch PA1 113 D2
St Martin's Prim Sch G83 27 F2
St Martin's RC Prim Sch
G45 137 F1
St Mary's Convent Sch
G31 117 F4
St Mary's Cres G78 134 B1
St Mary's Ct ML2 165 D1
St Mary's Hospl ML11 215 E3
St Mary's La G2 240 C2
St Mary's (Maryhill) Prim
RC Sch G20 96 B4
St Mary's Pl KA21 205 F1
St Mary's Prim Sch G83 27 F3
St Mary's Prim Sch ML6 104 C3
St Mary's Prim Sch
Cumbernauld G67 61 F1
Hamilton ML3 162 B2
Lanark ML11 215 E2
Paisley PA1 113 E2
St Mary's RC Prim Sch
Bannockburn FK7 7 E1
Cleland ML1 144 A1
Coatbridge ML5 122 A3
St Mary's RC Prim Sch
ML9 184 C1
St Mary's RC Prim Sch FK8 1 C1
St Mary's RC Sch G81 74 A3
St Mary's RC Sec Sch PA16 45 F3
St Mary's Rd Bellshill ML4 141 F3
Bishopbriggs G64 77 F1
St Mary's Sec Sch PA16 45 F3
St Mary's Way G82 49 F2
St Mary's Wynd FK8 7 D4
St Marys Gdns G78 134 B1
St Mathew's Prim Sch G64 78 A1
St Matthew's Prim Sch
KA3 223 E1
St Matthew's RC Prim Sch
ML2 164 C2
St Maur's Cres KA3 222 C2
St Maur's Pl KA3 222 C2
St Maurice's Rdbt G68 61 D1
St Maurices High Sch G68 82 A4
St Maurs Gdns KA3 222 B4
St Medan's Pl KA21 205 F1
St Meddans Cres KA10 229 E2
St Meddans Ct KA10 229 E1
St Meddans St KA10 229 E1
St Michael Dr G84 16 C1
St Michael Rd ML2 164 B1

Tower St Alloa FK10 10 A4
Glasgow G41 116 C3
Tower Terr PA1 113 E2
Tower View FK10 5 F1
Towerhill Ave KA3 222 B3
Towerhill Rd G13 75 E1
Towerlands Farm Rd KA11 220 A2
Towerlands Gate KA11 220 A1
Towerlands Intc KA11 219 F2
Towerlands Prim Sch KA11 220 B1
Towerlands Rd KA11 220 B1
Towers Ct FK2 42 A3
Towers Pl Airdrie ML6 123 F4
Stirling FK9 2 B2
Towers Rd ML6 123 F4
Towerside Cres G53 115 D1
Towerside Rd G53 115 D1
Towie Pl 10 Glasgow G20 96 B3
Uddingston G71 140 C3
Town Burn FK7 6 C2
Town House St FK6 21 F1
Townend KA3 222 B4
Townend La KA24 191 E4
Townend Rd
Dumbarton G82 50 A3
Kilmarnock KA1 227 F2
Townend St KA24 191 E4
Townend Terr KA1 231 E2
Townfoot KA11 220 B1
Townhead Irvine KA12 219 E1
Kilbirnie KA25 149 D1
Kilmaurs KA3 222 B4
Kilwinning KA13 207 E2
Kirkintilloch G66 79 E4
Townhead Ave ML1 142 C4
Townhead Dr ML1 143 F2
Townhead Pl G71 141 D4
Townhead Prim Sch ML5 101 E1
Townhead Rd
Coatbridge ML5 101 E1
Helensburgh G84 17 D1
Newton Mearns G77 156 B2
Saltcoats KA21 217 D4
Townhead St
Beith KA15 171 D4
Hamilton ML3 162 C2
Kilsyth G65 60 B4
Stevenston KA20 206 B1
Stonehouse ML9 198 C1
Townhead Terr PA1 113 E2
Townhill Prim Sch ML3 161 F1
Townhill Rd ML3 161 F2
Townhill Terr ML3 161 F2
Townholm KA3 223 D1
Townmill Rd G31 118 A4
Townsend St G4 97 E1
Tradeston Ind Est G5 117 D2
Tradeston St G5 240 B1
Trafalgar St Clydebank G81 73 F1
Glasgow G40 117 F2
Greenock PA15 45 F2
Trainard Ave G32 118 C2
Tramore Cres KA9 236 B4
Tranent Pl Cleland ML1 144 B1
Glasgow G33 118 C4
Traquair Ave Paisley PA2 132 C4
Wishaw ML2 165 E3
Traquair Dr G52 115 D3
Traquair Wynd G72 161 E4
Treebank Cres KA7 239 E3
Treeburn Ave G46 136 A2
Treemain Rd G46 157 D4
Trees Park Ave G78 134 A2
Treesbank KA13 207 E1
Treesbank Rd KA1 227 F2
Treeswoodhead Rd KA1 228 A1
Trefoil Ave G41 136 B4
Trefoil Pl KA7 239 E2
Trelawney Terr KA20 217 F3
Trent Pl G75 179 F3
Trent St ML5 101 E1
Tresta Rd G23 96 C4
Tribboch St ML9 184 C2
Trident Way PA4 94 B1
Trinidad Gn 3 G75 159 D1
Trinidad Way 7 G74 159 D1
Trinity Ave G52 115 E2
Trinity Cres KA15 150 B1
Trinity Dr Cambuslang G72 139 E2
Dalry KA24 191 D3
Trinity High Sch
Renfrew PA4 94 B2
Rutherglen G73 138 B4
Trinity Way 21 ML9 185 E1
Trinley Rd G13 75 E1
Triton Pl ML4 142 C3
Tron Ct FK10 4 A1
Trondra Path G34 119 F4
Trondra Pl G34 119 F4
Trongate Glasgow G1 241 D1
Stonehouse ML9 198 C1
Troon Ave G75 180 A3
Troon Ct G75 180 A3
Troon Dr PA11 110 B4
Troon Gdns G68 61 F3
Troon Pl G77 157 D2
Troon Prim Sch KA10 229 E2
Troon Rd KA10 230 A2
Troon St G40 118 A2
Troon Sta KA10 229 E1
Trossachs Ave ML1 143 D3
Trossachs Ct G20 97 D2
Trossachs Rd G73 138 B1
Trossachs St G20 97 D2
Troubridge Ave PA10 111 D1
Troubridge Cres PA10 111 D1
Trows Rd ML2 186 A3
Truce Rd G13 95 D4
Truro Ave G69 80 C2
Tryfield Pl KA8 236 A1
Tryst Rd Cumbernauld G67 61 F1
Cumbernauld, Carbrain G67 62 A1
Stenhousemuir FK5 23 E2
Tudhope Cres G83 27 E4
Tudor La S G14 95 F2
Tudor Rd G14 95 F2
Tudor St G69 119 F2
Tulliallan Pl
East Kilbride G74 181 D4
Stenhousemuir FK5 24 A2
Tullibody Rd FK10 4 C1
Tullichewan Cres G83 27 E4
Tullichewan Dr G83 27 E4
Tullichewan Rd G83 27 E4
Tulligarth Pk FK10 10 A4
Tullis St G40 117 F2
Tulloch Gdns ML1 164 A2
Tulloch Rd ML7 147 D2
Tulloch St G44 137 D3
Tulloch-Ard Pl G73 138 B2
Tullymet Rd ML3 183 E4
Tummel Dr ML6 102 C1
Tummel Gn G74 159 F2
Tummel Pl FK5 23 F2
Tummel St G33 98 C1
Tummell Way PA2 112 C1
Tunnel St G3 116 C4
Tuphall Rd ML3 162 B1
Turnberry Ave
5 Glasgow G11 96 A2
Gourock PA19 44 A3
Turnberry Cres ML5 121 F2
Turnberry Ct KA13 207 D2
Turnberry Dr
Bridge Of W PA11 110 B3
Hamilton ML3 161 E1
Kilmarnock KA1 227 F2
Newton Mearns G77 157 D3
Rutherglen G73 137 F3
Turnberry Gdns
Chapelhall ML6 123 F1
Cumbernauld G68 61 F3
Turnberry Pl
East Kilbride G75 180 A3
Rutherglen G73 137 F2
Turnberry Rd G11 96 A2
Turnberry Wynd
Bothwell G72 140 C1
Irvine KA12 224 B4
Turnbull Ave G83 27 E2
Turnbull Cres G83 27 E2
Turnbull High Sch G64 77 F1
Turnbull St G1 241 E1
Turner Pl KA3 223 D2
Turner Rd Glasgow G21 97 F1
Paisley PA3 113 F4
Turner St ML5 121 F3
Turners Ave PA2 113 D2
Turnhill Ave PA8 93 D4
Turnhill Cres PA8 93 D4
Turnhill Dr PA8 93 D4
Turnhill Gdns PA8 93 D4
Turningshaw Rd PA6 91 F3
Turnlaw G75 180 B3
Turnlaw Rd G72 139 D1
Turnlaw St G5 117 E2
Turnyland Mdws PA8 93 D4
Turnyland Way PA8 93 D4
Turquoise Terr ML4 142 A2
Turret Cres G13 95 E4
Turret Ct FK10 10 B3
Turret Rd G13 95 E4
Turriff St G5 117 D2
Twain Ave FK5 24 A2
Twechar Prim Sch G65 60 A2
Tweed Ave PA2 112 C1
Tweed Cres Glasgow G33 98 C1
Kilmarnock KA1 228 A3
Renfrew PA4 94 C1
Wishaw ML2 165 E3
Tweed Ct ML6 123 E3
Tweed Dr G61 75 E2
Tweed La ML1 143 D3
Tweed Pl PA5 131 E4
Tweed St Ayr KA8 236 A2
Coatbridge ML5 122 A2
East Kilbride G75 179 F4
Greenock PA16 45 D3
Larkhall ML9 185 D1
Tweedmuir Pl ML5 122 B2
Tweedsmuir G64 78 B1
Tweedsmuir Cres G61 75 F4
Tweedsmuir Pk ML3 183 E4
Tweedsmuir Rd G52 115 D3
Tweedvale Ave G14 94 C3
Tweedvale Pl G14 94 C3
Twinlaw St G34 100 B1
Tylney Rd PA1 114 B3
Tyndrum Rd G61 76 A3
Tyndrum St G4 241 D4
Tyne Pl G75 179 F3
Tynecastle Cres G32 119 D4
Tynecastle Path G32 119 D4
Tynecastle Pl G32 119 D4
Tynecastle St G32 119 D4
Tynron Ct ML3 161 F1
Tynwald Ave G73 138 B2

U.P. La G65 60 B4
U.P. Rd G65 60 B4
Uddingston Gram Sch G71 140 C3
Uddingston Rd G71 141 D2
Uddingston Sta G71 140 C3
Udston Hospl ML3 161 F3
Udston Prim Sch ML3 161 F2
Udston Rd ML3 161 F3
Udston Terr ML3 161 F3
Uig Pl G33 119 F3
Uist Ave PA14 69 D4
Uist Cres G33 99 F2
Uist Dr G66 80 A4
Uist Pl ML6 123 E3
Uist St G51 115 F4
Uist Way ML2 165 F3
Ulg Way ML7 147 D2
Ullswater G75 179 F3
Ulundi Rd PA5 111 F1
Ulva St G52 115 F3
Umberly Rd KA1 227 F2
Underwood KA13 207 E3
Underwood Cotts FK7 6 B3
Underwood La PA1 113 E3
Underwood Pl KA1 227 F2
Underwood Rd
Cambusbarron FK7 6 B3
Paisley PA3 113 E3
Prestwick KA9 236 B4
Rutherglen G73 138 B3
Underwood St G41 136 C4
Union Arc KA7 238 C4
Union Ave KA8 236 A2
Union Pl Glasgow G1 240 C2
Larbert FK5 23 D1
Union Rd FK1 41 E3
Union St Alexandria G83 27 F2
Alloa FK10 10 A3
Bridge Of A FK9 2 A4
Carluke ML8 187 F1
Falkirk FK2 42 A4
Glasgow G1 240 C2
Greenock PA16 45 F3
Hamilton ML3 162 B2
Hurlford KA1 228 C3
Kilmarnock KA3 222 C1
Kirkintilloch G66 79 E4
Larkhall ML9 185 D2
Motherwell ML1 143 D2
Paisley PA2 113 F1
Saltcoats KA21 216 C4
Shotts ML7 146 B3
Stenhousemuir FK5 23 F2
Stirling FK8 2 A1
Stonehouse ML9 198 C1
Troon KA10 229 D2
Union Street La G83 27 F2
Unitas Cres ML8 187 F1
Unitas Rd ML4 142 B3
Unity Pk ML7 146 B2
Unity Pl G4 97 D1
Univ of Paisley (Thornly Park Campus) PA2 133 F4
Univ of Stirling (Dept of Nursing & Midwifery, ForthValley Campus) FK1 42 A2
Univ of Strathclyde G1, G4 241 E3
Univ Veterinary Hospl (Univ of Glasgow) G61 96 A4
Universal Rd FK2 42 C4
University Ave G12 96 B1
University Gdns G12 96 B1
University of Glasgow G20 76 A1
University of Paisley PA1 113 E2
University of Stirling FK9 2 B3
University Pl G12 96 B1
University Rd W FK9 2 B3
Unsted Pl PA1 114 A2
Unthank Rd ML4 142 B3
Uphall Pl G33 118 C4
Upland La 2 G14 95 E2
Upland Rd G14 95 E2
Uplawmoor Prim Sch G78 153 D2
Uplawmoor Rd G78 153 F2
Upper Adelaide St G84 16 C1
Upper Arthur St G83 27 E2
Upper Bourtree Ct G73 138 B2
Upper Bourtree Dr G73 138 B2
Upper Bridge St
Alexandria G83 27 E2
Stirling FK8 2 A1
Upper Cartsburn St PA15 46 A2
Upper Castlehill FK8 7 D4
Upper Colquhoun St G84 16 B2
Upper Craigs FK8 7 D4
Upper Crofts KA7 238 C1
Upper Glenburn Rd G61 75 E3
Upper Glenfinlas St G84 16 C1
Upper Hall Rd G84 15 E3
Upper Loaning KA7 238 C1
Upper Mill St ML6 123 D4
Upper Mill Street Ind Est ML6 123 D4
Upper Newmarket St FK1 42 A3
Upper Smollett St G83 27 E2
Upper Stoneymollan Rd G83 27 E4
Upper Sutherland Cres G84 16 A2
Upper Sutherland St G84 16 A2
Upper Torwoodhill Rd G84 15 F2
Ure Cres FK4 40 A3
Urquhart Cres PA4 94 B1
Urquhart Dr
East Kilbride G74 160 A2
Gourock PA19 43 F3
Urquhart Pl G84 16 B2
Urquhart Rd KA3 223 E1
Urrdale Rd G41 116 A3
Usmore Pl G33 119 F3

Vaila Pl G23 97 D4
Vaila St G23 96 C4
Vale Gr FK9 1 C3
Vale of Leven Acad G83 27 E2
Vale of Leven Hospl (General) G83 27 E3
Vale of Leven Ind Est G82 27 F1
Vale Pl FK6 21 F2
Valentine Cres G71 141 D4
Valetta Pl G81 73 E2
Valeview FK5 23 E1
Valeview Terr
Dumbarton G82 50 A3
Glasgow G42 137 D4
Vallantine Cres G71 141 D4
Vallay St G22 97 E4
Valley Ct ML3 162 B1
Valley View G72 139 E3
Valleybank G65 37 E2
Valleyfield
East Kilbride G75 159 E1
Milton Of C G65 58 A3
Valleyfield Dr G68 60 C1
Valleyfield Pl FK7 7 E3
Valleyfield St 2 G21 97 F2
Valleyview Dr FK2 42 A4
Valleyview Pl FK2 42 A4
Vancouver Ct G75 159 D1
Vancouver Dr G75 159 D1
Vancouver La
17 Glasgow G14 95 E2
8 Glasgow G14 95 E2
Vancouver Pl G81 73 E2
Vancouver Rd G14 95 E2
Vanguard St G81 74 B1
Vanguard Way PA4 94 B1
Vardar Ave G76 157 E4
Vardon Lea ML1 143 F1
Varna La G14 95 F2
Varna Rd G14 95 F2
Varnsdorf Way ML6 123 F3
Vasart Pl G20 96 C2
Vaults La KA13 207 F2
Veir Terr G82 49 F2
Veitch Pl G65 57 E4
Veitches Ct G81 74 A3
Vennachar St ML7 146 C3
Vennacher Rd PA4 94 A2
Vennal St KA24 191 D4
Vennard Gdns G41 116 C1
Vennel La KA3 211 F4
Vennel St KA3 211 F4
Vennel The FK6 21 F1
Vermont Ave G73 138 A4
Vermont St G41 116 C3
Vernon Bank G74 159 F2
Vernon Dr PA3 112 A3
Vernon Pl KA2 225 F1
Vernon St KA21 216 C4
Verona Ave G14 95 E2
Verona Gdns 4 G14 95 E2
Verona La G14 95 E2
Verona Pl KA22 205 E1
Vesalius St G32 119 D3
Viaduct Circ KA13 207 F3
Viaduct Rd G76 157 F4
Vicar St FK1 42 A3
Vicarfield St G51 116 A4
Vicarland Pl G72 139 D2
Vicarland Rd G72 139 D3
Vicars Rd ML9 198 C1
Vicars Wlk G72 139 D3
Vickers St ML1 163 D4
Victor St ML6 104 A1
Victoria Ave ML8 187 F1
Victoria Cir G12 96 B2
Victoria Cres Airdrie ML6 122 C3
Clarkston G76 157 F4
Irvine KA12 219 E1
Kilsyth G65 60 A4
Wishaw ML2 164 B2
Victoria Crescent La G12 96 B2
Victoria Crescent Pl
16 G12 96 B2
Victoria Crescent Rd G12 96 B2
Victoria Cross G42 117 D1
Victoria Ct G77 156 B1
Victoria Dr KA10 229 E1
Victoria Dr E PA4 94 B1
Victoria Dr W PA4 94 A2
Victoria Drive Sec Sch G14 95 D2
Victoria Gdns Airdrie ML6 122 C4
Barrhead G78 134 A2
Kilmacolm PA13 69 E1
Paisley PA3 113 E1
Victoria Infmy
Glasgow G42 137 D4
Helensburgh G84 16 C1
Victoria La G77 156 B1
Victoria Meml Cottage Hospl G65 60 A4
Victoria Park Cnr G14 95 E2
Victoria Park Dr N G14 95 F2
Victoria Park Dr S G14 95 F2
Victoria Park Gdns N G11 95 F2
Victoria Park Gdns S G11 95 F2
Victoria Park La N G14 95 E2
Victoria Park La S G14 95 E2
Victoria Park Sch ML8 187 F1
Victoria Park St 27 G14 95 E2
Victoria Pk Ayr KA7 238 C3
Glasgow G14 95 F2
Kilsyth G65 60 A4
Victoria Pl Airdrie ML6 122 C3
Bellshill ML4 141 F2
Kilsyth G65 60 B4
Milngavie G62 55 D1
Rutherglen G73 138 A4
Stirling FK8 7 D4
Victoria Prim Sch
Airdrie ML6 122 C4
Falkirk FK2 42 B3
Glasgow G42 117 D1
Victoria Quadrant ML1 142 C3
Victoria Rd Barrhead G78 134 A2
Brookfield PA5 111 E3
Cumbernauld G68 61 E3
Falkirk FK2 42 B3
Glasgow G42 117 D2
Gourock PA19 44 B4
Harthill ML7 127 F3
Helensburgh G84 16 C1
Kirkintilloch G66 79 E2
Larbert FK5 23 D1
Paisley PA2 113 E1
Rutherglen G73 138 A3
Saltcoats KA21 217 D4
Stepps G33 99 E3
Stirling FK8 7 D4
Victoria Rdbt KA12 219 D1
Victoria Sq
Newton Mearns G77 156 B1
Stirling FK8 7 D4
Victoria St Alexandria G83 27 F2
Alloa FK10 10 A4
Ayr KA8 236 A1
Blantyre G72 161 E4
Dumbarton G82 50 A2
Hamilton ML3 162 A3
Harthill ML7 127 F3
Kirkintilloch G66 79 E4
Larkhall ML9 185 D2
Rutherglen G73 138 A4
Wishaw ML2 166 A2
Victoria Terr
Cumbernauld G68 61 E3
Menstrie FK11 4 A4
Victoria Way KA3 195 F1
Victory Dr PA10 111 D2
Victory Way G69 120 A2
Viewbank G46 136 A2
Viewbank Ave ML6 123 D1
Viewbank St ML5 101 F3
Viewfield ML6 122 C4
Viewfield Ave
Bishopbriggs G64 97 F4
Blantyre G72 140 C1
Glasgow G69 119 F3
Kirkintilloch G66 79 E3
Lochwinnoch PA12 129 D1
Milton Of C G65 58 A3
Viewfield Bsns Ctr KA8 236 A1
Viewfield Dr Alva FK12 4 C3
Bishopbriggs G64 97 F4
Glasgow G69 119 F3
Viewfield La G12 96 C1
Viewfield Rd Ayr KA8 236 A1
Banknock FK4 38 B2
Bellshill ML4 141 F2
Bishopbriggs G64 97 F4
Coatbridge ML5 121 E2
Viewfield St Harthill ML7 127 F3
Stirling FK8 7 D4
Viewglen Ct G45 137 E1
Viewmount Dr G20 96 B4
Viewpark G62 55 D1
Viewpark Ave G31 118 A4
Viewpark Ct G73 138 B3
Viewpark Dr G73 138 A3
Viewpark Gdns PA4 94 A1
Viewpark Pl ML1 163 E3
Viewpark Rd ML1 163 E3
Viewpark Sh Ctr G71 141 E3
Viewpoint Pl G21 97 F3
Viewpoint Rd G21 97 F3
Viking Cres PA6 111 E4
Viking Rd ML6 123 D3
Viking Terr G75 180 C3
Viking Way Glasgow G46 135 F3
Renfrew PA4 94 B1
Villa Bank FK6 21 F1
Villafield Ave G64 78 A2
Villafield Dr G64 78 A2
Villafield Loan G64 78 A2
Village Gdns G72 140 C1
Village Rd G72 139 F2
Vine Park Ave KA3 222 A4
Vine Park Dr KA3 222 A4
Vine St G11 96 A1
Vineburgh Ave KA12 219 E2
Vineburgh Ct KA12 219 D2
Vinicombe La 3 G12 96 B2
Vinicombe St G12 96 B2
Vintner St G4 97 E1
Viola Pl G64 78 B4
Violet Gdns ML8 201 F4
Violet Pl ML1 143 D3
Violet St PA1 114 A2
Virginia Ct G1 241 D2
Virginia Gdns Ayr KA8 236 A1
Milngavie G62 76 B4
Virginia Pl G1 241 D2
Virginia St Glasgow G1 241 D2
Greenock PA15 46 A2
Viscount Ave PA4 94 B1
Viscount Gate G71 140 C3
Vivian Ave G62 54 C1
Voil Dr G44 137 D2
Voil Rd FK9 2 A2
Vorlich Ct G78 134 B1
Vorlich Dr FK1 66 C4

Vorlich Gdns G61 75 E4
Vorlich Pl Kilmarnock KA1 228 A2
Stirling FK9 2 A2
Vorlich Wynd ML1 143 E2
Vrackie Pl KA1 228 A2
Vulcan St 5 Glasgow G21 97 F2
Motherwell ML1 163 F4

Waddell Ave ML6 102 B2
Waddell Ct Glasgow G5 117 E3
Kilmarnock KA3 222 C2
Waddell St Airdrie ML6 103 D1
Falkirk FK2 24 B1
Glasgow G5 117 E2
Waggon Rd Ayr KA8 235 F1
Falkirk FK2 42 A4
Waid Ave G77 156 B3
Waldemar Rd G13 95 E4
Walden Rd KA1 228 C3
Waldo St 3 G13 95 F4
Walk The FK10 10 A3
Walker Ave
Kilmarnock KA3 228 A4
Troon KA10 229 E3
Walker Ct G11 96 A1
Walker Dr
Dennyloanhead FK4 39 E3
Elderslie PA5 112 B1
Walker Path 2 G71 141 D4
Walker Rd KA8 236 A1
Walker St Glasgow G11 96 A1
Greenock PA16 45 E3
Kilbirnie KA25 149 D1
Paisley PA1 113 E2
Walkerburn Dr ML2 165 E3
Walkerburn Rd G52 115 D2
Walkinshaw Cres PA3 113 D3
Walkinshaw Rd PA4 93 E2
Walkinshaw St
Glasgow G40 118 A2
Johnstone PA5 112 A2
Wall Gdns FK1 41 E3
Wall St FK1 41 E3
Wallace Ave Bishopton PA7 72 A2
Dundonald KA2 225 F1
Elderslie PA5 112 B1
Stevenston KA20 206 B1
Troon KA10 229 E3
Wallace Cres Denny FK6 21 E1
Plean FK7 12 B2
Wallace Ct
Kilmarnock KA1 228 C3
Prestwick KA9 236 B4
Stirling FK8 2 A1
Wallace Dr ML9 185 E1
Wallace Gdns Stirling FK9 2 B2
Torrance G64 57 D1
Wallace High Sch FK9 2 A2
Wallace Monument FK9 2 C2
Wallace Pl Blantyre G72 140 C1
Cambusbarron FK7 6 B3
Falkirk FK2 42 B3
Fallin FK7 8 B2
Greenock PA15 45 F3
Hamilton ML3 163 D1
Wallace Prim Sch PA5 112 B1
Wallace Rd Irvine KA12 219 E2
Motherwell ML1 143 D1
Renfrew PA4 94 A1
Wallace St Alloa FK10 10 B4
Bannockburn FK7 7 F1
Clydebank G81 74 A1
Coatbridge ML5 122 A3
Dumbarton G82 50 A2
Falkirk FK2 42 B3
Glasgow G5 117 D3
Greenock PA16 45 E2
Kilmarnock KA1 227 F4
Motherwell ML1 163 E4
Paisley PA3 113 F3
Plains ML6 104 A1
Port Glasgow PA14 47 F1
Rutherglen G73 138 A4
Stirling FK8 2 A1
Wallace View
Kilmarnock KA1 227 F3
Shieldhill FK1 66 B4
Tullibody FK10 4 B2
Wallace Way ML11 215 E2
Wallacefield Rd KA10 229 E2
Wallacehill Rd KA1 227 F2
Wallacetown Ave KA3 223 D3
Wallacewell Cres G21 98 A3
Wallacewell Pl G21 98 A3
Wallacewell Quadrant G21 98 B3
Wallacewell Rd G21 98 B3
Wallbrae Rd G67 83 D4
Wallneuk Rd PA1 113 F3
Walls St G1 241 E2
Wallstale Rd FK7 7 D2
Walmer Cres G51 116 B3
Walnut Cres Glasgow G22 97 E3
Johnstone PA5 112 A1
Walnut Ct G65 58 A3
Walnut Dr G66 79 D3
Walnut Pl Glasgow G22 97 E3
Uddingston G71 121 E1
Walnut Rd Glasgow G22 97 E3
Kilmarnock KA1 227 E4
Walpole Pl PA5 131 E4
Walter St Glasgow G31 118 B4
Wishaw ML2 165 E2
Walton Ave G77 156 B3
Walton St Barrhead G78 134 B2
Glasgow G41 136 C4
Wamba Ave G13 95 F4
Wamphray Pl G75 179 E4
Wandilla Ave G81 74 B1
Wanlock St G51 116 A4
Ward Ct KA8 236 A2
Ward Rd KA8 236 A2
Ward St FK10 10 A3
Warden Rd G13 95 E4
Wardend Rd G64 57 D1
Wardhill Rd G21 98 A3
Wardhouse Rd PA2 133 E4
Wardie Pl G33 119 F4
Wardie Rd G34 120 A4
Wardlaw Ave G73 138 A4
Wardlaw Cres
East Kilbride G75 181 D4
Troon KA10 230 A2
Wardlaw Dr G73 138 A4
Wardlaw Gdns KA11 220 A4
Wardlaw Pl FK2 24 B1
Wardlaw Rd Bearsden G61 75 F1
Kilmarnock KA3 223 F3
Wardneuk KA9 236 B3
Wardneuk Dr KA3 223 D2
Wardpark Ct G67 62 B3
Wardpark East Ind Est
G68 62 C4
Wardpark North Ind Est
G68 62 B4
Wardpark Pl G67 62 B3
Wardpark Rd G67 62 B3
Wardpark South Ind Est
G67 62 B3
Wardrop Pl G74 159 F2
Wardrop St Beith KA15 171 E4
2 Glasgow G51 116 A4
Paisley PA1 113 F2
Wardrop Terr KA15 171 E4
Wards Cres ML5 121 F3
Wards Pl KA1 227 F4
Ware Rd G34 120 A4
Warilda Ave G81 74 B1
Warlock Dr PA11 90 B1
Warlock Rd PA11 90 B2
Warly Dr KA2 225 F1
Warly Pl KA2 225 F1
Warner St KA20 217 E4
Warnock Cres ML4 142 A2
Warnock Rd G77 156 B4
Warnock St G31 241 F3
Warren Rd ML3 183 E4
Warren St G42 117 D1
Warren Wlk G65 57 F4
Warriston Cres G33 118 C4
Warriston Pl G32 119 D4
Warriston St G33 118 C4
Warriston Way G73 138 B2
Warrix Ave KA12 219 E1
Warrix Gdns KA10 232 C4
Warrix Intc KA11 219 F1
Warroch St G3 240 A2
Warwick G74 160 B2
Warwick Gr ML3 161 F3
Warwick Hill KA11 220 A3
Warwick Rd PA16 44 C2
Warwickhill Rd KA1 222 B1
Washington Rd G66 79 D4
Washington St G3 240 B2
Watchmeal Cres G81 74 B4
Water La 4 KA1 227 F4
Water Rd G78 134 B2
Water Row G51 116 A4
Water St PA14 47 E1
Waterbank Rd G76 158 B3
Watercut Rd KA13 219 D4
Waterfoot Ave G53 135 E4
Waterfoot Rd G76, G77 157 D2
Waterfoot Row G76 157 E2
Waterfoot Terr G53 135 E4
Waterford Ct G46 136 A1
Waterford Rd G46 136 A2
Waterlands Gdns ML8 188 A2
Waterlands Pl ML8 187 D2
Waterlands Rd ML8 187 D3
Waterloo Dr ML11 215 D3
Waterloo Gdns G66 58 B1
Waterloo La G2 240 C2
Waterloo Rd Lanark ML11 215 D3
Prestwick KA9 236 A3
Waterloo St G2 240 C2
Watermill Ave G66 79 E2
Watermill Gr PA2 112 C1
Watersaugh Dr ML1 144 A1
Watersedge Ct G84 15 E2
Waterside KA12 219 D2
Waterside Ave G77 156 B2
Waterside Ct KA1 227 F4
Waterside Dr G77 156 B2
Waterside Gdns
Carmunnock G76 158 B4
Hamilton ML3 162 C1
Waterside Rd
Carmunnock G76 158 B3
Kilwinning KA13 207 F2
Kirkintilloch G66 79 F4
Waterside St Glasgow G5 117 E2
Kilmarnock KA1 227 F4
Waterslap KA3 213 D1
Waterston Way PA12 129 E2
Waterworks Cotts G77 177 D2
Wateryetts Dr PA13 69 E1
Watling Ave FK1 41 E3
Watling Dr FK1 41 E3
Watling Gdns FK1 41 E3
Watling Pl G75 159 D1
Watling St Falkirk FK1 41 E3
Motherwell ML1 142 B1
Uddingston G71 140 C4
Watson Ave Linwood PA3 112 A3
Rutherglen G73 138 A4
Stonehouse ML9 199 D2
Watson Cres G65 60 C4
Watson Pl Blantyre G72 161 D4
Dennyloanhead FK4 39 E2
Watson St Blantyre G72 161 E4
Falkirk FK2 42 A3
Glasgow G1 241 E1
Kilmarnock KA3 228 A4
Larkhall ML9 184 C2
Motherwell ML1 163 F3
Uddingston G71 140 C3
Watson Terr KA12 219 E1
Watsonville Pk ML1 163 F3
Watstone Rd ML9 199 D1
Watt Cres ML4 142 A4
Watt Ct KA24 191 E4
Watt Gdns FK1 41 F3
Watt La PA11 110 C4
Watt Low Ave G73 137 F3
Watt Pl Greenock PA15 46 A3
Milngavie G62 54 C2
Watt Rd Bridge Of W PA11 110 B4
Glasgow G52 115 D4
Watt St Airdrie ML6 103 E1
Glasgow G5 116 C3
Greenock PA16 45 F3
Wattfield Rd KA7 238 C3
Waukglen Ave G53 135 D1
Waukglen Cres G53 135 E2
Waukglen Dr G53 135 D2
Waukglen Path G53 135 D2
Waukglen Pl G53 135 D2
Waukglen Rd G53 135 D2
Waulking Mill Rd G81 74 B4
Waulkmill Ave G78 134 B2
Waulkmill Pl KA1 228 A4
Waulkmill St G46 135 F2
Waulkmill Way G78 134 B2
Waverley G74 160 B2
Waverley Ave
Helensburgh G84 25 D4
Kilmarnock KA1 222 B1
Waverley Cres
Cumbernauld G67 82 B4
Hamilton ML3 161 F2
High Bonnybridge FK4 40 A2
Kirkintilloch G66 79 E4
Lanark ML11 215 E2
Stirling FK8 2 B1
Waverley Ct Bothwell G71 141 D1
Helensburgh G84 16 B1
Waverley Dr Airdrie ML6 103 D1
Rutherglen G73 138 B4
Wishaw ML2 165 D2
Waverley Gdns
Elderslie PA5 112 B1
Glasgow G41 116 C1
Waverley Pl KA21 205 F1
Waverley Rd Paisley PA2 132 C4
Stenhousemuir FK5 23 E1
Waverley St
Coatbridge ML5 102 A1
Falkirk FK2 42 A4
Glasgow G41 116 C1
Greenock PA16 45 E2
Hamilton ML3 161 F2
Larkhall ML9 199 D4
Waverley Terr
Blantyre G72 161 E3
Dumbarton G82 49 D2
Stenhousemuir FK5 23 E1
Waverley Way PA2 132 C4
Weardale La G33 119 E4
Weardale St G33 119 E4
Weaver Ave G77 156 B4
Weaver Cres ML6 123 D3
Weaver La PA10 111 D2
Weaver Pl G75 179 F4
Weaver Row FK7 7 D2
Weaver St Ayr KA8 235 F1
Glasgow G4 241 E2
Weaver Terr PA2 114 A2
Weavers Ave PA2 113 D2
Weavers Cott PA10 111 D2
Weavers Gate PA1 113 D2
Weavers Rd PA2 113 D2
Weavers Way ML9 198 C1
Weavers Wlk ML11 215 D2
Webster Ave FK2 24 A2
Webster Groves ML2 165 E3
Webster St Clydebank G81 94 C4
Glasgow G40 118 A2
Wedderlea Dr G52 115 D3
Wee Cl KA15 171 D4
Wee Row FK2 42 A3
Wee Sunnyside Rd ML3 184 A1
Weensmoor Rd G53 134 C2
Weeple Dr PA3 112 A3
Weighhouse Cl PA1 113 F2
Weighhouse Rd ML8 187 F2
Weir Ave Barrhead G78 134 B1
Prestwick KA9 233 E1
Weir Dr FK7 8 B2
Weir Pl Greenock PA15 46 B2
Kilbirnie KA25 149 D1
Law ML8 186 C2
Weir Rd Ardrossan KA22 205 E2
Ayr KA8 235 F2
Weir St Coatbridge ML5 122 A4
Falkirk FK1 42 B3
Greenock PA15 46 B1
Paisley PA3 113 F3
Stirling FK8 1 C1
Weirston Rd KA13 208 A2
Weirwood Ave G69 120 A3
Weirwood Gdns G69 119 F2
Welbeck Cres KA10 229 D1
Welbeck Ct KA10 229 D1
Welbeck Mews KA10 229 D1
Welbeck Rd G53 135 D2
Welbeck St
Greenock PA16 45 E4
Kilmarnock KA1 228 A4
Weldon Pl G65 60 C2
Welfare Ave G72 139 E2
Well Gn G43 136 B4
Well La G65 57 E4
Well Rd Bridge Of A FK9 2 A4
Kilbarchan PA10 111 D2
Lanark ML11 215 D2
Well St Paisley PA1 113 E3
West Kilbride KA23 190 B3
Welland Pl G75 179 F4
Wellbank Gdns KA23 190 B3
Wellbank Pl G71 140 C3
Wellbrae Larkhall ML9 185 D1
Stonehouse ML9 198 C1
Wellbrae Rd ML3 162 A1
Wellbrae Terr G69 80 C1
Wellcroft Pl G5 117 D2
Wellcroft Rd ML3 161 F2
Wellcroft Terr ML3 161 F2
Wellesley Cres G75 179 F4
Wellesley Dr G75 179 F4
Wellfield Ave G46 136 A2
Wellfield St G21 97 F2
Wellgate ML11 215 D2
Wellgate Dr FK9 2 B4
Wellgate St ML9 185 D2
Wellgatehead ML11 215 D2
Wellgreen Pl FK8 7 D3
Wellhall Ct ML3 162 A2
Wellhall Rd ML3 162 A2
Wellhead Ct ML11 215 D2
Wellhouse Cres G33 119 F4
Wellhouse Prim Sch G33 119 F4
Wellhouse Rd G33 119 F4
Wellington G75 180 A4
Wellington Ave KA3 228 B4
Wellington La Ayr KA7 238 C4
Glasgow G2 240 C2
Wellington Pl
Clydebank G81 73 E2
Coatbridge ML5 121 E3
Kilmarnock KA3 222 C1
Wishaw ML2 186 B4
Wellington Rd G64 78 A2
Wellington Sch KA7 238 C4
Wellington Sq KA7 238 C4
Wellington St Airdrie ML6 103 D1
Glasgow G2 240 C2
Greenock PA15 45 F2
Kilmarnock KA3 222 C1
Paisley PA3 113 E3
Prestwick KA9 236 A3
Wishaw ML2 164 B3
Wellington Terr ML11 214 C3
Wellington Way
Greenock PA15 45 F2
5 Renfrew PA4 94 B1
Wellknowe Ave G74 158 B1
Wellknowe Pl G74 158 B2
Wellknowe Rd G74 158 B2
Wellmeadow Annexe
(Univ Paisley) PA1 113 E2
Wellmeadow Cl G77 156 B3
Wellmeadow Gn G77 156 B3
Wellmeadow Rd G43 136 A3
Wellmeadow St PA1 113 E2
Wellmeadow Way G77 156 B3
Wellpark KA7 238 C1
Wellpark Ave KA3 228 B4
Wellpark Bldgs PA15 46 A2
Wellpark Cres FK7 6 C2
Wellpark Ct KA3 228 B4
Wellpark Gr KA3 228 B4
Wellpark La KA21 216 C4
Wellpark Pl KA3 228 B4
Wellpark Rd Banknock FK4 38 B1
Motherwell ML1 163 E3
Saltcoats KA21 216 C4
Wellpark St G31 241 F2
Wellpark Terr
Bonnybridge FK4 40 A3
Neilston G78 154 B3
Wells St G81 73 F2
Wellshot Dr G72 138 C3
Wellshot Prim Sch G32 118 C2
Wellshot Rd G32 118 C2
Wellside Ave ML6 103 D1
Wellside Dr G72 139 E2
Wellside La ML6 103 D1
Wellside Pl FK1 42 A3
Wellside Quadrant ML6 103 D1
Wellsquarry Rd G74 159 E3
Wellview Dr ML1 163 E3
Wellwood KA13 207 E1
Wellwood Ave ML11 215 D3
Wellwynd ML6 122 C4
Wellyard La PA16 44 B2
Wellyard Way PA16 44 B1
Wellyard Wynd PA16 44 B1
Welsh Dr Blantyre G72 161 E3
Hamilton ML3 183 E4
Welsh Gdns FK9 2 A4
Welsh Pl KA21 205 F1
Wemyss Ave G77 156 B4
Wemyss Bay St PA15 45 F2
Wemyss Dr G68 60 C1
Wendur Way PA3 113 E4
Wenlock Rd PA2 113 F1
Wensleydale G74 159 E2
Wentworth Dr G23 76 C1
Wentworth Sq KA13 207 E2
Wesley St ML6 122 C4
West Abercromby St G84 16 B2
West Academy St ML2 164 C2
West Ave Carluke ML8 187 F1
Hamilton G72 161 F3
Motherwell ML1 143 D1
Plains ML6 104 A2
Renfrew PA4 94 B2
Stepps G33 99 E3
Uddingston G71 141 E3
West Balgrochan Rd G64 57 D1
West Barmoss Ave PA14 68 C4
West Benhar Rd ML7 127 D2
West Blackhall St PA15 45 F3
West Boreland Rd FK6 21 E1
West Bowhouse Way
KA11 220 A3
West Bowhouse
Workshops KA11 220 A3
West Brae PA1 113 E2
West Bridge St FK1 42 A3
West Bridgend G82 49 F2
West Buchanan Pl PA2 113 E2
West Burn Rd KA3 195 F1
West Burn St PA15 45 F3
West Burnside St G65 60 B4
West Byrehill Ind Est
KA13 207 D1
West Campbell St
Glasgow G2 240 C3
Paisley PA1 113 D2
West Canal St ML5 121 F4
West Carmuirs Loan FK5 40 C3
West Chapelton Ave G61 75 F2
West Chapelton Cres G61 75 F2
West Chapelton Dr G61 75 F2
West Chapelton La G61 75 F2
West Clyde St
Helensburgh G84 16 B1
Larkhall ML9 185 D1
West Coats Prim Sch G72 138 C3
West Coats Rd G72 138 C3
West Cres KA10 229 F2
West Cross ML2 165 D2
West Ct G81 73 F2
West Dhuhill Dr G84 16 B2
West Doura Ave KA21 205 F1
West Doura Way KA13 207 E2
West Dr Airdrie ML6 123 F3
Larbert FK5 23 E1
West End KA24 191 D4
West End Dr ML4 141 F2
West End Gdns FK10 10 A3
West End Pl ML4 141 F2
West Fairholm St ML9 184 C3
West Faulds Rd ML11 215 F3
West Fullarton St KA1 222 C1
West Gate ML2 165 E2
West George La G2 240 C3
West George St
Coatbridge ML5 122 A4
Glasgow G2 240 C3
Kilmarnock KA1 222 C1
West Glebe Terr ML3 162 B1
West Glen Gdns PA13 69 F1
West Glen Rd
Kilmacolm PA13 69 F1
Kilmalcolm PA13 70 A1
West Gr KA10 229 F2
West Graham St G4 97 D1
West Greenhill Pl G3 116 C4
West Hamilton St ML1 163 F3
West High St G66 58 B1
West James St FK12 5 D3
West Johnstone St FK12 5 D3
West Kilbride Prim Sch
KA23 190 B3
West Kilbride Rd KA24 191 D4
West Kilbride Sta KA23 190 B3
West King St G84 16 A1
West Kirk St ML6 122 C4
West Kirklands Pl KA24 191 D4
West La PA1 113 D2
West Langlands St KA1 222 C1
West Lennox Dr G84 16 B2
West Link Rd FK9 2 B3
West Lodge Gdns FK10 9 F4
West Lodge Rd PA4 94 A2
West Main St ML7 127 F3
West Mains Ind Est FK3 42 C4
West Mains Rd
East Kilbride G74 159 E1
Falkirk FK3 42 C4
West Montrose St G84 16 B1
West Murrayfield FK7 7 E1
West Nemphlar Rd ML11 214 B3
West Netherton St KA1 227 F4
West Nile St G1 241 D3
West Park Cres KA3 222 A4
West Park Dr KA3 222 A4
West Park Sch KA2 221 F1
West Pl ML2 166 A3
West Port ML11 214 C2
West Portland St KA10 229 D1
West Porton Pl PA7 71 F2
West Prim Sch PA2 113 E2
West Prince's St G4 96 C1
West Princes St G84 16 B1
West Quay PA14 47 E1
West Rd Irvine KA12 219 D2
Kilbarchan PA10 111 D2
Port Glasgow PA14 68 C4
Torrance G64 57 D1
West Regent La G2 240 C3
West Regent St G2 240 C3
West Rossdhu Dr G84 16 B2
West Row G63 31 D2
West Sanquhar Rd KA8 236 A2

West Scott Terr ML3 ... 162 B1
West Shaw St
Greenock PA15 ... 45 F3
Kilmarnock KA1 ... 227 F3
West St Clydebank G81 ... 94 C4
Glasgow G5 ... 117 D3
Paisley PA1 ... 113 E2
West Sta ML3 ... 162 B2
West Stewart St
Greenock PA15 ... 45 F3
Hamilton ML3 ... 162 B2
West Stirling St FK12 ... 4 C4
West Street Underground Sta G5 ... 117 D3
West Thomson St G81 ... 74 A2
West Thornlie St ML2 ... 165 D1
West Vennel FK10 ... 10 A3
West View Dunlop KA3 ... 195 D4
Waterside KA3 ... 213 F2
West Wellbrae Cres ML3 .. 183 D4
West Whitby St G31 ... 118 B2
West Woodside Ave PA14 .. 68 C3
West Woodstock St KA1 ... 227 F4
Westacres Rd G77 ... 156 A2
Westbank Ct 7 G12 ... 96 C1
Westbank La G12 ... 96 C1
Westbank Quadrant G12 ... 96 C1
Westborne Gdns G84 ... 16 B1
Westbourn Bldgs PA15 ... 45 F3
Westbourne Ave KA9 ... 236 B4
Westbourne Cres G61 ... 75 E3
Westbourne Dr G61 ... 75 E3
Westbourne Gardens La 26 G12 ... 96 B2
Westbourne Gdns KA9 ... 236 B4
Westbourne Gdns N 27 G12 ... 96 B2
Westbourne Gdns S G12 ... 96 B2
Westbourne Gdns W 28 G12 ... 96 B2
Westbourne Rd G12 ... 96 A2
Westbourne Terrace La N 29 G12 ... 96 B2
Westbourne Terrace La S 3 G12 ... 96 A2
Westbrae Dr G14, G13, ... 95 F2
Westbrae Rd G77 ... 156 C3
Westburn Ave
Cambuslang G72 ... 139 E3
Falkirk FK1 ... 41 F2
Paisley PA3 ... 113 D3
Westburn Cres
Clydebank G81 ... 74 A4
Rutherglen G73 ... 137 F4
Westburn Farm Rd G72 ... 139 D3
Westburn Rd
Cambuslang G72 ... 140 A3
Cambuslang, Westburn G72 . 139 E3
Westcliff G82 ... 49 D2
Westclyffe St 3 G41 ... 116 C1
Westcott Pl ML11 ... 215 E3
Westcraigs Pk EH48 ... 107 E2
Westcraigs Rd
Blackridge EH48 ... 107 E2
Harthill ML7 ... 127 F3
Westend G61 ... 76 A1
Westend Ct ML8 ... 186 C2
Westend Park St G3 ... 240 A4
Westend Ret Pk G11 ... 96 A1
Wester Carriagehill PA2 ... 113 F1
Wester Cleddans Prim Sch G64 ... 78 A1
Wester Cleddens Rd G64 ... 78 B1
Wester Common Dr G22 ... 97 D2
Wester Common Prim Sch G22 ... 97 D2
Wester Common Rd G22 ... 97 D2
Wester Mavisbank Ave ML6 ... 122 C4
Wester Moffat Ave ML6 ... 123 F4
Wester Moffat Cres ML6 .. 123 F4
Wester Moffat Hospl ML6 . 123 F4
Wester Myvot Rd G67 ... 82 A2
Wester Rd G32 ... 119 E2
Westerburn St G32 ... 118 C3
Westercraigs G31 ... 117 F4
Westerdale G74 ... 159 E2
Westerfield Rd G76 ... 158 B2
Westergate Sh Ctr G2 ... 240 C2
Westergill Ave ML6 ... 123 F3
Westerglen Rd FK1 ... 42 A1
Westergreens Ave G66 ... 79 E3
Westerhill Rd G64 ... 78 B2
Westerhouse Ct ML8 ... 187 E1
Westerhouse Rd G34 ... 120 A4
Westerkirk Dr G23 ... 76 C1
Westerlands Dr
Newton Mearns G77 ... 156 A2
Stirling FK8 ... 7 D3
Westerlands Gdns G77 ... 156 A2
Westerlands Gr G77 ... 156 A2
Westerlands Pl G77 ... 156 A3
Westerlea Ct FK9 ... 2 A3
Westerlea Dr FK9 ... 2 A3
Westermains Ave G66 ... 79 D4
Western Ave Falkirk FK2 ... 42 A3
Rutherglen G73 ... 137 F4
Western Cres KA25 ... 170 A4
Western Infmy G11 ... 96 B1
Western Isles Rd G60 ... 73 E3
Western Rd
Cambuslang G72 ... 138 C2
Kilmarnock KA3 ... 223 D2
Westerton Cowie FK7 ... 12 B4
Lennoxtown G65 ... 57 F4
Westerton Ave
Bearsden G61 ... 95 F4
Clarkston G76 ... 158 A3
Larkhall ML9 ... 185 D1
Westerton Dr FK9 ... 2 A4
Westerton La G76 ... 158 A3
Westerton Prim Sch G61 ... 75 F2
Westerton Sta G61 ... 75 F1
Westerton Terr FK2 ... 24 B2
Westfield Dumbarton G82 ... 49 E2
Kilbirnie KA25 ... 170 A4
Westfield Ave G73 ... 137 F4
Westfield Cres G61 ... 75 F1
Westfield Dr Bearsden G61 ... 75 F1
Cumbernauld G68 ... 81 F4
Glasgow G52 ... 115 D3
Greenock PA16 ... 45 E4
Kilmacolm PA13 ... 89 D4
Westfield Ind Area G68 ... 81 F3
Westfield Pl
Cumbernauld G68 ... 81 E3
Denny FK6 ... 21 F1
Westfield Prim Sch G68 ... 81 F4
Westfield Rd Ayr KA7 ... 238 C3
Cumbernauld G68 ... 81 F4
Glasgow G46 ... 136 A2
Kilsyth G65 ... 36 A1
Motherwell ML1 ... 143 E4
Port Glasgow PA14 ... 68 C4
Westfield Rdbt FK2 ... 42 C3
Westfield St FK2 ... 42 C3
Westfields G64 ... 77 F2
Westgarth Pl G74 ... 159 D2
Westgate Way ML4 ... 141 F2
Westhouse Ave G73 ... 137 F4
Westhouse Gdns G73 ... 137 F4
Westland Dr G14 ... 95 E2
Westland Drive La 28 G14 ... 95 E2
Westlands Gdns PA2 ... 113 E1
Westlea Pl ML6 ... 123 D3
Westminster Pl FK5 ... 23 F2
Westminster Terr 3 G3 ... 116 C4
Westmoor Cres KA1 ... 227 E4
Westmoreland St G42 ... 117 D1
Westmorland Rd PA16 ... 44 C2
Westmuir Pl G73 ... 137 F4
Westmuir St G31 ... 118 B3
Weston Pl KA9 ... 236 B3
Weston Terr KA23 ... 190 B3
Westpark Ct KA20 ... 217 E4
Westpark Dr PA3 ... 113 D3
Westport G75 ... 159 D1
Westport St G65 ... 60 B4
Westray Ave
Newton Mearns G77 ... 156 B4
Port Glasgow PA14 ... 69 D3
Westray Cir G22 ... 97 E3
Westray Ct G67 ... 82 C4
Westray Pl
Bishopbriggs G64 ... 78 B1
Glasgow G22 ... 97 E4
Westray Rd G67 ... 82 C4
Westray Sq G22 ... 97 E4
Westray St G22 ... 97 E4
Westray Terr FK1 ... 42 B1
Westray Wynd 2 ML2 ... 165 F3
Westside Gdns G11 ... 96 B1
Westview Cres FK10 ... 4 B1
Westward Way KA10 ... 229 F4
Westwood Ave Ayr KA8 ... 236 C1
Glasgow G46 ... 136 A2
Westwood Cres Ayr KA8 ... 236 C1
Hamilton ML3 ... 162 B1
Westwood Dr ML1 ... 144 C1
Westwood Gdns PA3 ... 113 D3
Westwood Hill G75 ... 180 A4
Westwood Quadrant G81 ... 74 B1
Westwood Rd
East Kilbride G75 ... 180 A4
Glasgow G43 ... 136 A3
Wishaw ML2 ... 166 A3
Westwood Sq G75 ... 180 A4
Weymouth Cres PA19 ... 44 C3
Weymouth Dr G12 ... 96 A3
Whamflet Ave G34 ... 120 B4
Whangie The G63 ... 29 D3
Wharry Rd FK12 ... 4 C4
Whatriggs Rd KA1 ... 228 A2
Wheatfield Rd Ayr KA7 ... 238 C4
Bearsden G61 ... 75 E1
Wheatholm Cres ML6 ... 103 D1
Wheatholm St ML6 ... 103 D1
Wheatland Ave G72 ... 161 E4
Wheatland Dr ML11 ... 214 C3
Wheatlandhead Ct G72 ... 161 E4
Wheatlands Ave FK4 ... 40 A3
Wheatlands Dr PA10 ... 111 D2
Wheatlands Farm Rd PA10 ... 111 D2
Wheatlandside ML11 ... 214 C3
Wheatley Cres G65 ... 60 B4
Wheatley Loan G64 ... 98 B4
Wheatley Rd
Saltcoats KA21 ... 206 A1
Stevenston KA20 ... 206 C1
Wheatpark Rd ML11 ... 214 C2
Whifflet Ct ML5 ... 122 A3
Whifflet St ML5 ... 122 A2
Whifflet Sta ML5 ... 122 A3
Whin Ave G78 ... 134 A2
Whin Hill G74 ... 160 A2
Whin Hill Rd KA7 ... 239 D1
Whin Loan G65 ... 59 E4
Whin Pl G74 ... 160 A3
Whin St G81 ... 74 A2
Whinfell Dr G75 ... 180 A3
Whinfell Gdns G75 ... 180 A3
Whinfield Ave KA9 ... 236 B3
Whinfield Gdns KA9 ... 236 A3
Whinfield Rd Glasgow G53 . 135 D2
Prestwick KA9 ... 236 A3
Whinhall Ave ML6 ... 102 C1
Whinhall Rd ML6 ... 102 C1
Whinhill Cres PA15 ... 46 A1
Whinhill Rd Glasgow G53 ... 115 D2
Greenock PA15 ... 46 A2
Paisley PA2 ... 114 A1
Whinhill Sta PA15 ... 46 A2
Whinknowe ML9 ... 199 F4
Whinney Gr ML2 ... 165 F2
Whinnie Knowe ML9 ... 184 C1
Whinpark Ave ML4 ... 141 F2
Whinriggs ML9 ... 198 B1
Whins of Milton Sch FK7 ... 7 D1
Whins Rd Alloa FK10 ... 10 B4
Glasgow G41 ... 116 B1
Stirling FK7 ... 7 D1
Troon KA10 ... 229 F4
Whinwell Rd FK8 ... 2 A1
Whirlie Dr PA6 ... 111 D4
Whirlie Rd PA6 ... 91 D1
Whirlies Rdbt The G74 ... 160 A2
Whirlow Gdns G69 ... 120 A3
Whirlow Rd G69 ... 120 A3
Whistleberry Cres ML3 ... 162 A4
Whistleberry Dr ML3 ... 162 A4
Whistleberry Ind Est ML3 . 162 A4
Whistleberry Pk ML3 ... 162 A4
Whistleberry Rd ML3 ... 162 A4
Whistlefield Ct G61 ... 75 F2
Whitacres Path G53 ... 135 D2
Whitacres Rd G53 ... 135 D2
Whitburn St G32 ... 118 C4
White Ave G82 ... 50 A2
White Cart Rd PA3 ... 113 F4
White Craig Rd KA22 ... 205 E2
White St Ayr KA8 ... 236 A2
Clydebank G81 ... 94 B4
Glasgow G11 ... 96 B1
Whiteadder Pl G75 ... 179 E4
Whitecraigs Pl G23 ... 96 C4
Whitecraigs Sta G46 ... 157 D4
Whitecrook Prim Sch G81 .. 74 B1
Whitecrook St G81 ... 74 B1
Whitefield Ave G72 ... 139 D2
Whitefield Rd G51 ... 116 B3
Whitefield Terr G65 ... 33 E1
Whiteford Ave G82 ... 50 B3
Whiteford Cres G82 ... 50 B3
Whiteford Ct ML3 ... 183 E3
Whiteford Pl G82 ... 50 B3
Whiteford Rd PA2 ... 114 A1
Whiteford View KA7 ... 239 E4
Whitegates Pl FK1 ... 41 E2
Whitehall Ave KA9 ... 236 B4
Whitehall St G3 ... 240 A2
Whitehaugh Ave PA1 ... 114 A3
Whitehaugh Cres G53 ... 135 D2
Whitehaugh Dr PA1 ... 114 A3
Whitehaugh Rd G53 ... 135 D2
Whitehill Ave Airdrie ML6 .. 103 D1
Cumbernauld G68 ... 61 E1
Kirkintilloch G66 ... 58 C1
Stepps G33 ... 99 E3
Whitehill Cres
Carluke ML8 ... 187 F2
Clydebank G81 ... 74 C4
Kirkintilloch G66 ... 58 C1
Lanark ML11 ... 214 C2
Whitehill Farm Rd G33 ... 99 E3
Whitehill Gdns G31 ... 118 A4
Whitehill Gr G77 ... 156 C1
Whitehill Pl FK8 ... 7 D3
Whitehill Rd Bearsden G61 ... 75 E2
Hamilton ML3 ... 162 A3
Whitehill Sec Sch G31 ... 118 A4
Whitehill St G31 ... 118 A4
Whitehill Street La G31 ... 118 A4
Whitehill Terr ML11 ... 214 C2
Whitehills PA8 ... 73 D1
Whitehills Dr G75 ... 180 C4
Whitehills Pl G75 ... 180 C4
Whitehills Terr G75 ... 180 C4
Whitehirst Park Rd KA13 .. 207 D2
Whitehope Green KA11 ... 220 A2
Whitehorse Wlk G75 ... 180 A4
Whitehouse Rd FK7 ... 7 E4
Whitehurst G61 ... 75 E3
Whitehurst Park Prim Sch KA13 ... 207 E2
Whiteinch Prim Sch G14 ... 95 E2
Whitekirk Pl G15 ... 75 D1
Whitelaw Ave ML5 ... 101 F3
Whitelaw Cres ML4 ... 142 B2
Whitelaw St
Blackridge EH48 ... 107 E1
Glasgow G20 ... 96 B4
Whitelaw Terr G65 ... 59 F2
Whitelea Ave PA13 ... 89 E4
Whitelea Cres PA13 ... 89 E4
Whitelea Rd PA13 ... 89 E4
Whitelee G75 ... 180 B3
Whitelee Cres G77 ... 156 A3
Whitelee Gate G77 ... 156 A3
Whitelees Prim Sch G67 ... 62 C3
Whitelees Rd
Cumbernauld G67 ... 62 C3
Greenock PA15 ... 46 C1
Lanark ML11 ... 203 F1
Lanark ML11 ... 215 E2
Whitelees Rdbt G67 ... 62 C3
Whiteloans G71 ... 141 D2
Whitemoss Ave
East Kilbride G74 ... 159 F1
Glasgow G44 ... 136 C2
Whitemoss Gr G74 ... 160 A1
Whitemoss Rdbt G74 ... 160 A1
Whitepond Ave ML4 ... 141 F2
Whites Bridge Ave
Paisley PA2 ... 112 C2
Paisley PA3 ... 113 D3
Whites Bridge Cl PA3 ... 113 D3
Whites' Loan ML11 ... 215 E3
Whiteshaw Ave ML8 ... 187 E1
Whiteshaw Dr ML8 ... 187 E1
Whiteshaw Rd ML8 ... 187 D2
Whiteside Rd KA9 ... 236 B4
Whiteside Terr KA9 ... 236 B4
Whitestone Ave G68 ... 61 D1
Whitevale St G31 ... 118 A4
Whitewisp Ct KA11 ... 220 A2
Whitfield Dr KA8 ... 236 B2
Whithope Rd G53 ... 134 C2
Whithope Terr G53 ... 134 C2
Whithorn Cres G69 ... 80 C2
Whitlawburn Ave G72 ... 138 C2
Whitlawburn Rd G72 ... 138 C2
Whitlawburn Terr G72 ... 138 C2
Whitlees Cres KA22 ... 205 E2
Whitlees Ct KA22 ... 205 F2
Whitletts Ct KA8 ... 236 C1
Whitletts Prim Sch KA8 ... 236 C2
Whitletts Rd KA8 ... 236 B1
Whitriggs Rd G53 ... 134 C2
Whitslade Pl G34 ... 99 F1
Whitslade St G34 ... 100 A1
Whitsun Dale G74 ... 159 E2
Whittagreen Ave ML1 ... 143 E2
Whittagreen Cres ML1 ... 143 E1
Whittagreen Ct ML1 ... 143 E2
Whittingehame Dr G12 ... 96 A3
Whittingehame La G12 ... 95 F3
Whittington St ML5 ... 122 A3
Whittle Pl KA11 ... 219 F1
Whittle Rd KA8 ... 236 B2
Whittlemuir Ave G44 ... 136 C2
Whitton Dr G46 ... 136 C2
Whitton St G20 ... 96 B4
Whitworth Dr G81 ... 74 A1
Whitworth St G20 ... 97 D3
Whyte Ave
Cambuslang G72 ... 138 C3
Irvine KA12 ... 219 E1
Whyte Cnr G82 ... 50 C1
Whyte St ML7 ... 127 F3
Wick Ave ML6 ... 122 C2
Wickets The PA1 ... 114 A2
Wickham Ave G77 ... 156 B3
Wide Cl ML11 ... 215 D2
Wigton Ave G77 ... 156 B4
Wigtoun Pl G67 ... 62 A2
Wildcat Rd KA23 ... 190 A2
Wilderness The FK2 ... 14 B2
Wildman Rd ML8 ... 187 D4
Wilfred Ave G13 ... 95 E4
Wilkie Cres ML9 ... 185 D1
Wilkie Loan ML4 ... 142 A4
Wilkie Rd G71 ... 141 D3
William Booth Pl FK7 ... 7 D2
William Dr ML3 ... 183 E4
William Mann Dr G77 ... 156 B2
William St Clydebank G81 ... 74 A3
Coatbridge ML5 ... 122 A3
Glasgow G3 ... 240 A3
Greenock PA15 ... 46 A3
Hamilton ML3 ... 162 A3
Helensburgh G84 ... 16 B1
Johnstone PA5 ... 111 F2
Kilmarnock KA3 ... 222 C1
Kilsyth G65 ... 60 B4
Paisley PA1 ... 113 E2
Port Glasgow PA14 ... 47 D1
Williamfield Ave FK7 ... 7 D2
Williamfield Gr KA12 ... 219 D2
Williamfield Pk KA12 ... 219 D2
Williamsburgh Prim Sch PA1 ... 114 A3
Williamsburgh Terr PA1 ... 114 A3
Williamson Ave
Dumbarton G82 ... 50 A2
Falkirk FK2 ... 24 A1
Williamson Dr G84 ... 16 C2
Williamson Pl Falkirk FK2 ... 42 B4
Johnstone PA5 ... 112 A1
Williamson St
Clydebank G81 ... 74 A2
Falkirk FK1 ... 42 A2
Glasgow G31 ... 118 B2
Williamwood Dr G44 ... 136 C1
Williamwood High Sch G76 ... 157 E4
Williamwood Pk G44 ... 136 C1
Williamwood Pk W G44 ... 136 C1
Williamwood Sta G46 ... 136 B1
Willie Mair's Brae KA3 ... 223 D1
Willie Ross Pl KA3 ... 223 E2
Willison's La PA14 ... 47 E1
Willock Pl G20 ... 96 C4
Willock St KA1 ... 227 F3
Willockston Rd KA10 ... 229 F1
Willoughby Dr G13 ... 95 F3
Willoughby La G13 ... 95 F3
Willow Ave
Bishopbriggs G64 ... 98 A4
Elderslie PA5 ... 112 B1
Kirkintilloch G66 ... 79 E3
Willow Cres ML5 ... 122 A2
Willow Ct G75 ... 180 A3
Willow Dr Airdrie ML6 ... 123 E4
Banknock FK4 ... 38 C1
Blantyre G72 ... 161 E4
Johnstone PA5 ... 112 A1
Milton Of C G65 ... 58 B3
Willow Gdns KA11 ... 219 F3
Willow Gr ML1 ... 143 D3
Willow La Glasgow G32 ... 119 D1
Troon KA10 ... 229 E2
Willow Pk KA7 ... 239 E2
Willow Pl Johnstone PA5 ... 112 A1
Uddingston G71 ... 141 E4
Willow Rd KA1 ... 227 E4
Willow St G13 ... 95 F4
Willow Way ML3 ... 162 C1
Willowbank ML9 ... 185 D3
Willowbank Cres 8 G3 ... 96 C1
Willowbank Gdns G66 ... 79 E4
Willowbank Prim Sch G3 ... 96 C1
Willowbank Sch ML5 ... 121 F3
Willowbank St G3 ... 240 A4
Willowburn Rd KA15 ... 170 C4
Willowdale Cres G69 ... 120 A2
Willowdale Gdns G69 ... 120 A2
Willowford Rd G53 ... 135 D2
Willows The
Carmunnock G76 ... 158 C4
Tullibody FK10 ... 4 A1
Willowyard Ind Est KA15 ... 170 C4
Willowyard Rd KA15 ... 170 C4
Wills Rd KA8 ... 236 B1
Willwood Rd ML2 ... 165 E4
Wilmot Rd G13 ... 95 E3
Wilsgait St ML1 ... 144 B1
Wilson Ave Denny FK6 ... 21 E1
Falkirk FK1 ... 41 E3
Irvine KA12 ... 219 E2
Kilmarnock KA3 ... 228 A4
Linwood PA3 ... 112 A3
Troon KA10 ... 230 A1
Wilson Ct KA15 ... 150 A1
Wilson Dr
Bannockburn FK7 ... 7 E1
Falkirk FK1 ... 41 E3
Wilson Gdns FK1 ... 41 E3
Wilson Pl Dundonald KA2 ... 225 F1
East Kilbride G74 ... 160 A2
High Bonnybridge FK4 ... 40 B2
Newton Mearns G77 ... 156 B2
Wilson Rd Falkirk FK1 ... 41 E3
Shotts ML7 ... 167 D4
Wilson St Airdrie ML6 ... 122 C4
Alexandria G83 ... 27 F3
Ayr KA8 ... 236 A1
Beith KA15 ... 150 B1
Coatbridge ML5 ... 122 B4
Glasgow G1 ... 241 D2
Hamilton ML3 ... 162 A3
Larkhall ML9 ... 185 D1
Motherwell ML1 ... 163 F4
Paisley PA1 ... 113 E2
Port Glasgow PA14 ... 47 E1
Renfrew PA4 ... 94 B2
Wilson's Rd ML1 ... 144 C4
Wilton Crescent La G20 ... 96 C2
Wilton Dr G20 ... 96 C2
Wilton Rd ML8 ... 202 A4
Wilton St Coatbridge ML5 ... 101 E1
Glasgow G20 ... 96 C2
Wiltonburn Path G53 ... 135 D2
Wiltonburn Rd G53 ... 135 D2
Wilverton Rd G13 ... 95 F4
Winburne Cres ML3 ... 162 A2
Winchester Ave FK6 ... 21 F2
Winchester Avenue Ind Est FK6 ... 21 F2
Winchester Dr G12 ... 96 A3
Windelstraw Ct KA11 ... 220 A2
Winderemere St ML4 ... 141 F2
Windermere G75 ... 179 F3
Windhill Cres G43 ... 136 A3
Windhill Pl G43 ... 136 B3
Windhill Rd G43 ... 136 B3
Windlaw Ct G45 ... 137 E1
Windlaw Gdns G44 ... 136 C2
Windlaw Park Gdns G44 ... 136 C2
Windlaw Prim Sch G45 ... 137 F1
Windlaw Rd
Carmunnock G76 ... 158 B4
Glasgow G45 ... 137 E1
Windmill Ct ML1 ... 163 F3
Windmill Rd ML3 ... 162 B2
Windmill St KA21 ... 216 C4
Windmillhill St ML1 ... 163 F3
Windrow Terr ML2 ... 165 E4
Windsor Ave Falkirk FK1 ... 41 F2
Newton Mearns G77 ... 156 C3
Windsor Cres
Clydebank G81 ... 74 A2
Elderslie PA5 ... 112 A1
Falkirk FK1 ... 41 F2
Paisley PA1 ... 114 A3
Windsor Ct ML8 ... 187 F1
Windsor Dr Denny FK6 ... 21 E2
Falkirk FK1 ... 41 F2
Glenmavis ML6 ... 102 C2
Windsor Gdns Alloa FK10 ... 9 F4
Falkirk FK1 ... 41 F2
Hamilton ML3 ... 162 A3
Windsor Path 8 ML9 ... 185 E1
Windsor Pl Shotts ML7 ... 146 C3
Stirling FK8 ... 7 D4
Windsor Quadrant ML8 ... 187 F1
Windsor Rd Falkirk FK1 ... 41 F2
Motherwell ML1 ... 143 D3
Renfrew PA4 ... 94 B1
Windsor St
Coatbridge ML5 ... 121 F2
Glasgow G32 ... 119 E3
4 Glasgow, Woodside G20 ... 97 D1
Menstrie FK11 ... 3 F3
Shotts ML7 ... 146 C3
Windsor Terr G20 ... 97 D1
Windsor Wlk G71 ... 141 D4

STREET ATLASES
ORDER FORM

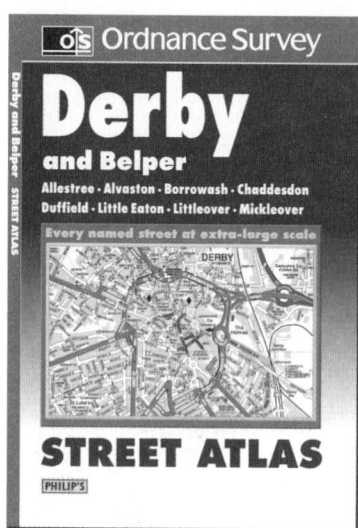

os Ordnance Survey

Derby
and Belper
Allestree · Alvaston · Borrowash · Chaddesden
Duffield · Little Eaton · Littleover · Mickleover

Every named street at extra-large scale

STREET ATLAS
PHILIP'S

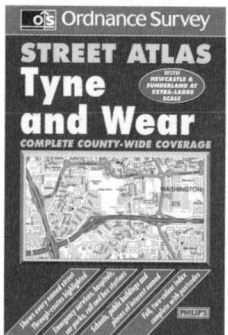

os Ordnance Survey

STREET ATLAS
Tyne and Wear
COMPLETE COUNTY-WIDE COVERAGE

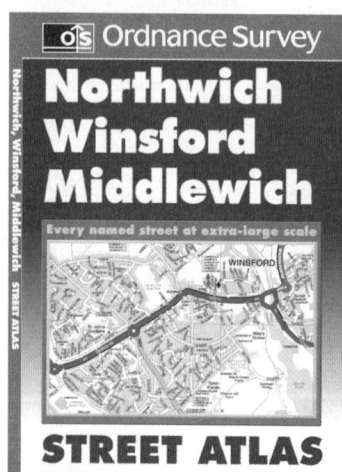

os Ordnance Survey

Northwich
Winsford
Middlewich

Every named street at extra-large scale

STREET ATLAS
PHILIP'S

PHILIP'S

The Street Atlases are available from all good bookshops or by mail order direct from the publisher. Orders can be made in the following ways. **By phone** Ring our special Credit Card Hotline on **01933 443863** during office hours (9am to 5pm) or leave a message on the answering machine, quoting your full credit card number plus expiry date and your full name and address. **By post or fax** Fill out the order form below (you may photocopy it) and post it to: **Philip's Direct, 27 Sanders Road, Wellingborough, Northants NN8 4NL** or fax it to: **01933 443849**. Before placing an order by post, by fax or on the answering machine, please telephone to check availability and prices.

COLOUR LOCAL ATLASES

	PAPERBACK	
	Quantity @ £3.50 each	£ Total
CANNOCK, LICHFIELD, RUGELEY	☐ 0 540 07625 2 ➤	☐
DERBY AND BELPER	☐ 0 540 07608 2 ➤	☐
NORTHWICH, WINSFORD, MIDDLEWICH	☐ 0 540 07589 2 ➤	☐
PEAK DISTRICT TOWNS	☐ 0 540 07609 0 ➤	☐
STAFFORD, STONE, UTTOXETER	☐ 0 540 07626 0 ➤	☐
WARRINGTON, WIDNES, RUNCORN	☐ 0 540 07588 4 ➤	☐

COLOUR REGIONAL ATLASES

	HARDBACK	SPIRAL	POCKET	£ Total
	Quantity @ £10.99 each	Quantity @ £8.99 each	Quantity @ £5.99 each	
BERKSHIRE	☐ 0 540 06170 0	☐ 0 540 06172 7	☐ 0 540 06173 5 ➤	☐
	Quantity @ £10.99 each	Quantity @ £8.99 each	Quantity @ £4.99 each	£ Total
MERSEYSIDE	☐ 0 540 06480 7	☐ 0 540 06481 5	☐ 0 540 06482 3 ➤	☐
	Quantity @ £12.99 each	Quantity @ £9.99 each	Quantity @ £4.99 each	£ Total
DURHAM	☐ 0 540 06365 7	☐ 0 540 06366 5	☐ 0 540 06367 3 ➤	☐
EAST KENT	☐ 0 540 07483 7	☐ 0 540 07276 1	☐ 0 540 07287 7 ➤	☐
WEST KENT	☐ 0 540 07366 0	☐ 0 540 07367 9	☐ 0 540 07369 5 ➤	☐
EAST SUSSEX	☐ 0 540 07306 7	☐ 0 540 07307 5	☐ 0 540 07312 1 ➤	☐
WEST SUSSEX	☐ 0 540 07319 9	☐ 0 540 07323 7	☐ 0 540 07327 X ➤	☐
	Quantity @ £12.99 each	Quantity @ £9.99 each	Quantity @ £5.50 each	£ Total
GREATER MANCHESTER	☐ 0 540 06485 8	☐ 0 540 06486 6	☐ 0 540 06487 4 ➤	☐
TYNE AND WEAR	☐ 0 540 06370 3	☐ 0 540 06371 1	☐ 0 540 06372 X ➤	☐
	Quantity @ £12.99 each	Quantity @ £9.99 each	Quantity @ £5.99 each	£ Total
BIRMINGHAM & WEST MIDLANDS	☐ 0 540 07603 1	☐ 0 540 07604 X	☐ 0 540 07605 8 ➤	☐
BUCKINGHAMSHIRE	☐ 0 540 07466 7	☐ 0 540 07467 5	☐ 0 540 07468 3 ➤	☐
CHESHIRE	☐ 0 540 07507 8	☐ 0 540 07508 6	☐ 0 540 07509 4 ➤	☐
DERBYSHIRE	☐ 0 540 07531 0	☐ 0 540 07532 9	☐ 0 540 07533 7 ➤	☐
EDINBURGH & East Central Scotland	☐ 0 540 07653 8	☐ 0 540 07654 6	☐ 0 540 07656 2 ➤	☐

STREET ATLASES
ORDER FORM

Ordnance Survey

COLOUR REGIONAL ATLASES

	HARDBACK Quantity @ £12.99 each	SPIRAL Quantity @ £9.99 each	POCKET Quantity @ £5.99 each	£ Total
GLASGOW & West Central Scotland	☐ 0 540 07648 1	☐ 0 540 07649 X	☐ 0 540 07651 1	➤ ☐
NORTH HAMPSHIRE	☐ 0 540 07471 3	☐ 0 540 07472 1	☐ 0 540 07473 X	➤ ☐
SOUTH HAMPSHIRE	☐ 0 540 07476 4	☐ 0 540 07477 2	☐ 0 540 07478 0	➤ ☐
HERTFORDSHIRE	☐ 0 540 06174 3	☐ 0 540 06175 1	☐ 0 540 06176 X	➤ ☐
OXFORDSHIRE	☐ 0 540 07512 4	☐ 0 540 07513 2	☐ 0 540 07514 0	➤ ☐
SURREY	☐ 0 540 06435 1	☐ 0 540 06436 X	☐ 0 540 06438 6	➤ ☐
WARWICKSHIRE	☐ 0 540 07560 4	☐ 0 540 07561 2	☐ 0 540 07562 0	➤ ☐
SOUTH YORKSHIRE	☐ 0 540 06330 4	☐ 0 540 06331 2	☐ 0 540 06332 0	➤ ☐
WEST YORKSHIRE	☐ 0 540 06329 0	☐ 0 540 06327 4	☐ 0 540 06328 2	➤ ☐
	Quantity @ £14.99 each	Quantity @ £9.99 each	Quantity @ £5.99 each	£ Total
LANCASHIRE	☐ 0 540 06440 8	☐ 0 540 06441 6	☐ 0 540 06443 2	➤ ☐
NOTTINGHAMSHIRE	☐ 0 540 07541 8	☐ 0 540 075426 6	☐ 0 540 07543 4	➤ ☐
STAFFORDSHIRE	☐ 0 540 07549 3	☐ 0 540 07550 7	☐ 0 540 07551 5	➤ ☐

BLACK AND WHITE REGIONAL ATLASES

	HARDBACK Quantity @ £11.99 each	SOFTBACK Quantity @ £8.99 each	POCKET Quantity @ £3.99 each	£ Total
BRISTOL AND AVON	☐ 0 540 06140 9	☐ 0 540 06141 7	☐ 0 540 06142 5	➤ ☐
	Quantity @ £12.99 each	Quantity @ £9.99 each	Quantity @ £4.99 each	£ Total
CARDIFF, SWANSEA & GLAMORGAN	☐ 0 540 06186 7	☐ 0 540 06187 5	☐ 0 540 06207 3	➤ ☐
EAST ESSEX	☐ 0 540 05848 3	☐ 0 540 05866 1	☐ 0 540 05850 5	➤ ☐
WEST ESSEX	☐ 0 540 05849 1	☐ 0 540 05867 X	☐ 0 540 05851 3	➤ ☐

Post to: Philip's Direct, 27 Sanders Road, Wellingborough, Northants NN8 4NL

◆ Free postage and packing

◆ All available titles will normally be dispatched within 5 working days of receipt of order but please allow up to 28 days for delivery

☐ Please tick this box if you do not wish your name to be used by other carefully selected organisations that may wish to send you information about other products and services

Registered Office: Michelin House, 81 Fulham Road, London SW3 6RB

Registered in England number: 3597451

I enclose a cheque / postal order, for a **total** of ☐
made payable to *Octopus Publishing Group Ltd*, or please debit my

☐ Access   ☐ American Express   ☐ Visa   ☐ Diners

account by ☐

Account no
☐☐☐☐☐ ☐☐☐☐ ☐☐☐☐ ☐☐☐☐

Expiry date ☐☐ ☐☐

Signature...

Name..

Address...

....

....

....POSTCODE

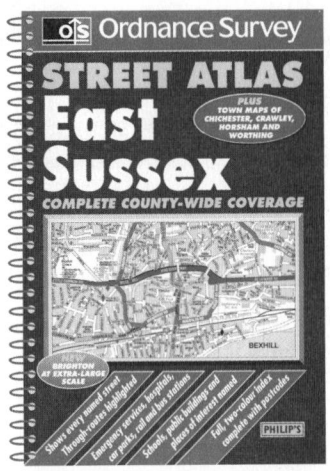

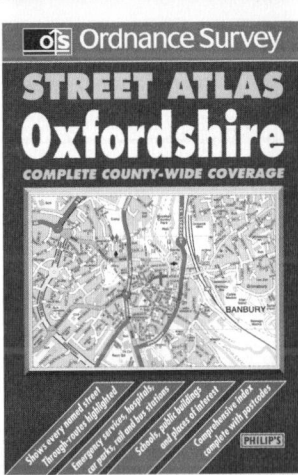

PHILIP'S

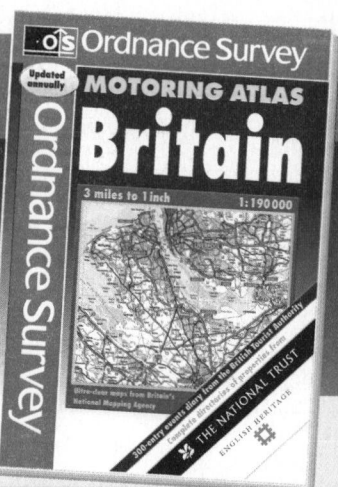

Adobe® InDesign® CS4

Level 1

Adobe® InDesign® CS4: Level 1

Part Number: 084048
Course Edition: 1.0

NOTICES

HELP US IMPROVE OUR COURSEWARE

Your comments are important to us. Please contact us at Element K Press LLC, 1-800-478-7788, 500 Canal View Boulevard, Rochester, NY 14623, Attention: Product Planning, or through our Web site at **http://support.elementkcourseware.com**.

Adobe® InDesign® CS4: Level 1

About This Course

You are starting to familiarize yourself with print layouts and designs using Adobe InDesign. You want to learn about the tools and features available to you in Adobe InDesign CS4. In this course, you will work with some of the tools and features to create eye-catching printed documents using InDesign CS4.

Adobe InDesign CS4 provides you with many time-saving tools for the creation of high-quality printable documents. By reviewing and applying some of the tools and features InDesign CS4 provides, you will be able to use that information to better assist you when working with printable documents.

Course Description

Target Student

This course is intended for students who want to explore the basic tools and features of InDesign for creating professional page layouts and designs.

Course Prerequisites

Before taking this course, students should be familiar with the functions of their computer's operating system such as creating folders, launching programs, copying and pasting objects, formatting text, and retrieving and saving files. Familiarity with other Adobe software applications is helpful, but not required.

How to Use This Book

As a Learning Guide

Each lesson covers one broad topic or set of related topics. Lessons are arranged in order of increasing proficiency with *Adobe® InDesign® CS4*; skills you acquire in one lesson are used and developed in subsequent lessons. For this reason, you should work through the lessons in sequence.

Each lesson is organized into results-oriented topics. Topics include all the relevant and supporting information you need to master *Adobe® InDesign® CS4*, and activities allow you to apply this information to practical hands-on examples.

You get to try out each new skill on a specially prepared sample file. This saves you typing time and allows you to concentrate on the skill at hand. Through the use of sample files, hands-on activities, illustrations that give you feedback at crucial steps, and supporting background information, this book provides you with the foundation and structure to learn *Adobe® InDesign® CS4* quickly and easily.

As a Review Tool

Any method of instruction is only as effective as the time and effort you are willing to invest in it. In addition, some of the information that you learn in class may not be important to you immediately, but it may become important later on. For this reason, we encourage you to spend some time reviewing the topics and activities after the course. For additional challenge when reviewing activities, try the "What You Do" column before looking at the "How You Do It" column.

As a Reference

The organization and layout of the book make it easy to use as a learning tool and as an after-class reference. You can use this book as a first source for definitions of terms, background information on given topics, and summaries of procedures.

Course Icons

Icon	Description
	A **Caution Note** makes students aware of potential negative consequences of an action, setting, or decision that are not easily known.
	Display Slide provides a prompt to the instructor to display a specific slide. Display Slides are included in the Instructor Guide only.
	An **Instructor Note** is a comment to the instructor regarding delivery, classroom strategy, classroom tools, exceptions, and other special considerations. Instructor Notes are included in the Instructor Guide only.
	Notes Page indicates a page that has been left intentionally blank for students to write on.
	A **Student Note** provides additional information, guidance, or hints about a topic or task.
	A **Version Note** indicates information necessary for a specific version of software.

Course Objectives

In this course, you will utilize Adobe InDesign CS4 to create and deliver eye-catching printed documents.

You will:

- explore the various elements of the Adobe InDesign interface.
- design documents.
- enhance documents.
- work with page elements.
- manage objects.
- work with tables.
- finalize documents.

Course Requirements

Hardware

- An Intel® Pentium® 4, Intel Centrino®, Intel Xeon®, or Intel Core™ Duo (or compatible) processor
- 256 MB of RAM (512 MB recommended)
- 1.8 GB of available hard disk space (additional free space required during installation)
- A color monitor with a 16-bit or greater video card
- A monitor with 1024 x 768 monitor resolution
- A CD-ROM drive
- Internet or phone connection required for product activation

Software

- Adobe® InDesign® CS4
- Adobe® Reader® 7.0

Class Setup

1. Install Windows XP Professional on the C drive using the following parameters:
   a. Accept the license agreement.
   b. Create a 4 GB partition on the C drive.
   c. Format the C partition to NTFS.
   d. Select the appropriate regional and language settings.
   e. Enter the appropriate name and organization for your environment.
   f. Enter the product key.
   g. For each student computer, configure the settings:
      - Name of computer: Computer# (where # is a unique integer representing the student computer)

- Administrator password: *password*
- Select your time zone
- Select the **Typical** network configuration

2. Install Service Pack 2 for Windows XP.

3. Run a standard installation of the Adobe® InDesign® CS4 software from the CD-ROM.

   a. In the **Adobe InDesign CS4 Installer: License Agreement** window, select a language and click **Accept.**

   b. In the **Adobe InDesign CS4 Installer: Options** window, select the installation options and click **Next.**

   c. In the **Adobe InDesign CS4 Installer: Installation Location** window, verify the location for installing the software and click **Next.**

   d. In the **Adobe InDesign CS4 Installer: Summary** window, read the Summary report and click **Install.**

   e. In the **Adobe InDesign CS4 Installer: Done** window, click **Finish.**

4. Install Adobe® Reader® 7.0 accepting all default settings.

5. On the course CD-ROM, run the 084048dd.exe self-extracting file located within. This will install a folder named 084048Data on your C drive. This folder contains all the data files that you will use to complete this course. Solution files are also provided in this folder. These files may help you find a possible solution if you are unable to proceed at any point during the course. If you would like to view the final output or solution of an activity, navigate to the respective lesson or solution folder.

6. In addition to the specific setup procedures needed for this class to run properly, you should also check the Element K Press product support website at http://support.elementkcourseware.com for more information. Any updates about this course will be posted there.

List of Additional Files

Printed with each activity is a list of files students open to complete that activity. Many activities also require additional files that students do not open, but are needed to support the file(s) students are working with. These supporting files are included with the student data files on the course CD-ROM or data disk. Do not delete these files.

1 | Exploring the InDesign Environment

Lesson Time: 20 minutes

Lesson Objectives:

In this lesson, you will explore the various elements of the Adobe InDesign interface.

You will:

- Explore the InDesign interface.
- Customize the interface.
- Explore the navigation controls.
- Set general and interface preferences.

Introduction

You are a graphic designer using InDesign for the first time. As with any new application, you need to get familiar with the components of the application window in order to ensure efficient work. In this lesson, you will explore the InDesign interface, customize its components, and save the settings as a workspace.

Accessing InDesign user interface and its elements will be difficult when you are not familiar with it. Getting to know the InDesign user interface and understanding the functionality of its different components enable you to tailor the interface according to your project requirements and to work efficiently. You can also utilize the customized interface for other similar projects.

TOPIC A

Explore the InDesign Interface

Before you start working with InDesign CS4, you need to familiarize yourself with its basic interface components. In this topic, you will explore the InDesign environment.

While working on new software, you could potentially spend a significant amount of time searching for specific options in the work environment. You can prevent this by familiarizing yourself with the user interface elements. This will help you achieve the desired output when you eventually begin using the software.

Adobe InDesign CS4

Adobe InDesign CS4 is a robust and easy-to-use layout application that designers use to produce documents such as newsletters, brochures, mailers, magazines, and newspapers. Although you can add text and create some graphic elements within InDesign CS4, you will typically use other applications to type large quantities of text and to create, edit, and adjust images. You will then use InDesign CS4 to combine text and graphics into unique layouts that meet your project needs.

The Welcome Screen

The **Welcome Screen** is displayed when the InDesign application is launched. The buttons on the screen help you tour the application and also open, create, and share documents.

Section	Description
Open a Recent Item	Displays a set of recently opened files in the InDesign application. You can also click the **Open** button, navigate to the desired folder, and open a file.
Create New	Allows you to create a new InDesign document and also create books and libraries. You can also create a document based on an existing template.
Community	Helps you view user guides, videos, tutorials, articles, forums, blogs, and customer support of other Adobe software. It gives you access to all community help.
Getting Started	Helps you view the **Getting Started** page in the Help window.
New Features	Helps you view the **What's new** page in the Help window.
Resources	Helps you view the **Resources** page in the Help window.

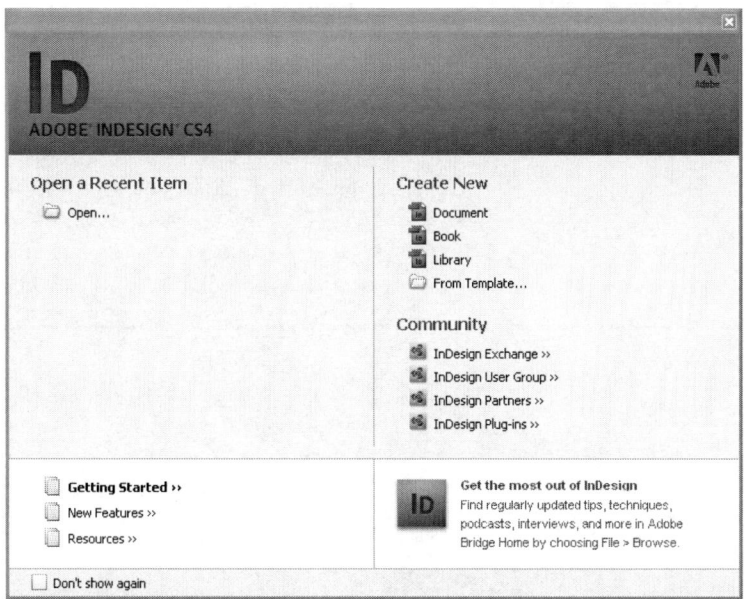

Figure 1-1: The Welcome Screen helps you open, create, and share documents.

The InDesign Window

The InDesign window includes a number of components that can be used to create professional-looking documents with graphics and text. It is widely used to create brochures, newsletters, magazines, cover pages, and so on.

Window Element	Description
The Menu bar	Organizes InDesign commands under menus. Contains menus such as **File, Edit, Layout, Type, Object, Table, View, Window,** and **Help.**
The Application bar	Allows you to view level adjustments, and settings such as rulers, guides, and baseline grids. You can also turn on bleed, preview, and slug modes. The **Zoom Level** drop-down list displays the different levels of zoom.
The Tools panel	Contains tools for drawing and modifying objects.
The Control panel	Helps you quickly access options, commands, and panels related to the objects or items selected in a document. The **Control** panel is docked to the top of the document window by default.
Panels	Allows you to perform different operations. These panels change according to the workspace selected. Panels are collectively called a dock as they are docked at the right edge of the application window. By clicking the **Expand Panel** button, every panel in the dock can be expanded. Two or more panels are grouped together to form a panel group.

Window Element	Description
The document window	Displays the area where the layout can be created and the navigation buttons, at the bottom of the page, that can be used to navigate between the pages in a document. It also displays the pasteboard that allows you to create, add, and edit objects. Anything placed on the pasteboard will not be included when the document is sent to print; however, it will be saved as part of the document.

Figure 1-2: The InDesign window and its elements.

The Tools Panel

The **Tools** panel contains tools for creating and modifying text, graphics, lines, and other page elements. The **Tools** panel contains four major sections.

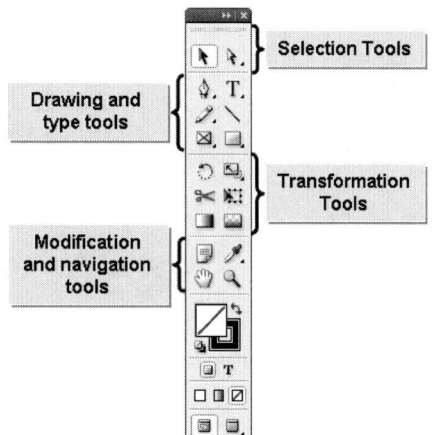

Figure 1-3: The Tools panel displaying different tools.

The following table displays the various sections in the **Tools** panel.

Section	Description
Selection tools	Comprises the **Selection** and **Direct Selection** tools. The **Selection** tool allows you to select and drag an object. The **Direct Selection** tool enables you to edit anchor points and adjust path segments.
Drawing and Type tools	Comprises the **Pen, Pencil, Line, Rectangle Frame,** and **Rectangle** tools. The **Pen** tool flyout allows you to draw straight and curved paths. You can draw free-form paths using the **Pencil** tool flyout. The **Line** tool allows you to draw lines, arcs, spirals, and grids. You can draw shapes with ease using the **Rectangle** and **Rectangle Frame** tools. Using the tools in the **Type** tool flyout, you can type text vertically or on a path.
Transformation tools	Comprises tools such as **Rotate, Scale, Scissors, Free Transform, Gradient Swatch,** and **Gradient Feather.** These tools allow you to modify the size and shape of an object.
Modification and Navigation tools	Comprises the **Note, Eyedropper, Hand,** and **Zoom** tools. They help you to pan and zoom in a document.

ACTIVITY 1-1

Exploring the InDesign Environment

Data Files:

House.indd

Scenario:

You are working for the OGC Real Estate company. Your company released a new list of pictures of attractive houses that can be used for an advertisement in a property magazine. You decided to use the Adobe InDesign CS4 software for creating the advertisement. Since, you are a novice user of InDesign, you want to explore the environment of the application and get to know the different interface elements.

What You Do	How You Do It
1. Explore the interface elements in the InDesign application window.	a. Choose **Start→All Programs→Adobe InDesign CS4.**
	b. On the **Welcome Screen,** in the **Create New** section, observe the available new document profiles.
	c. In the **Open a Recent Item** section, click **Open.**
	d. In the **Open a File** dialog box, navigate to the C:\084048Data\Exploring the InDesign Environment folder.
	e. Select **House.indd** and click **Open.**
	f. In the **Tools** panel, move the mouse pointer over the first tool and observe the tooltip.
	g. To the right of the application window, click the **Expand Panels** button to view the details of the panel.

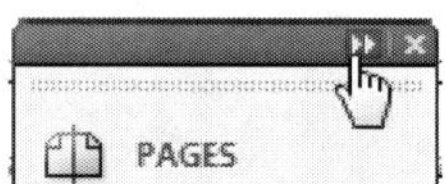

h. Click the **Collapse to Icons** button.

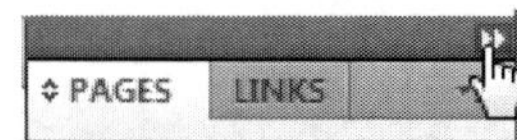

---

2. Control document views using the Application bar.

a. On the Application bar, click **Screen Mode,** and select **Bleed.**

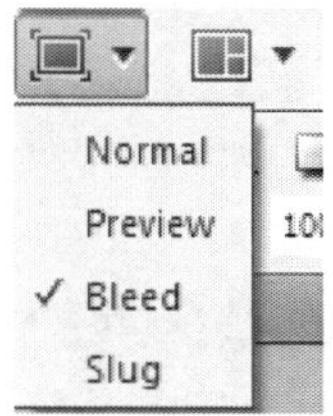

b. Observe that the page view is set outside the document area.

c. Click **Arrange Documents,** and select **New Window.**

d. Observe that the same document is opened in another window.

e. Click **Arrange Documents** again and select **Consolidate All,** which is the option in the first row first column.

f. Observe that both the documents are consolidated as tabs.

g. Click **Arrange Documents** again and select **2-Up,** which is the first option in the second row.

h. Observe that both the documents are arranged side by side.

i. Choose **File→Close** to close the House.indd:2 file.

j. Choose **File→Close** to close the House.indd file.

... interact with window

TOPIC B

Customize the Interface

You explored the Adobe InDesign interface. You may now find the need to set up the InDesign interface so that it has a consistent look and feel that meets your production needs. In this topic, you will customize the interface.

By customizing the workspace, you can make sure that InDesign consistently opens in a window layout that is comfortable for your production needs. This consistency of the application's layout enables you to work more efficiently because you will always know where certain window elements will be when you open an existing file or create a new file.

Predefined Workspaces

A *workspace* is a group of settings that specifies how the panels and buttons are displayed in the environment. You can reset, create, or delete a workspace. The default workspace of Adobe InDesign CS4 is **Essentials.** The panel locations, keyboard shortcuts, and menus can be customized and these settings can be used for future reference when saved as a workspace.

Predefined Workspace	Description
Essentials	Displays the essential panels required for working on an artboard. This is the default workspace.
Printing and Proofing	Displays components required for viewing the proof of the page design and for previewing the color separation before printing.
Typography	Displays components required for changing the text design and modifying the text glyph used on the artboard.

The Keyboard Shortcuts Dialog Box

The **Keyboard Shortcuts** dialog box is used to create a shortcut set for the various commands in the Adobe InDesign application. This enables you to work quickly on documents using the keyboard. You can also use the default shortcut sets of InDesign, QuarkXPress 4.0, or Page Maker 7.0. You can create, save, delete, or preview a shortcut set that you have created.

Component	Description
Set	A drop-down list that displays the built-in keyboard shortcut for PageMaker 7.0 and QuarkXPress 4.0 and also the default keyboard shortcut for InDesign. When a new set of shortcuts are created, they are added as options in the drop-down list.
Product Area	A drop-down list that displays a list of all the menus.

you have to create a new set to add shortcut.

Component	Description
Commands	A section that lists the various commands present on the menu that is currently selected in the **Product Area** drop-down list.
Current Shortcuts	A section that displays the shortcut key for the currently selected command.
New Shortcut	A text box where the new keyboard shortcut can be entered.
New Set	A button that opens the **New Set** dialog box. You can include a name for the newly created set of shortcut keys.
Show Set	A button that opens a text file that displays the shortcut set for all the commands.
Delete Set	A button that is used to delete a customized keyboard shortcut set.
Save	A button that is used to save the changes made to the keyboard shortcut.

The Menu Customization Dialog Box

The **Menu Customization** dialog box is used to hide commands to simplify the user interface. Colors can also be applied to commands for easier identification or to mark preferred commands for specific workflows or tasks. The application menu and the context and panel menus can be customized and included in the workspaces saved. *edit > menus*

The Customize Control Panel Dialog Box

The **Customize Control Panel** dialog box is used to hide or add options in the **Control** panel to simplify the user interface. The **Control** panel offers quick access to options for the selected objects. The **Customize Control Panel** dialog box reduces cluttering of options in the **Control** panel, thereby making it easy for the user to work with the page elements. The dialog box consists of controls for object, character, paragraph, tables, and quick apply.

Enable dynamic text auto correct > preferences.

How to Customize the Interface

Procedure Reference: Customize the Interface

To customize the interface:

1. Open the Adobe InDesign application.
2. If necessary, select a workspace layout.
   - On the Application bar, click the workspace switcher and select a workspace.
   - Or, choose **Window→Workspace Layout** and choose a workspace.
3. Customize the panels.
   - Hide a panel.
     a. If necessary, select the panel.
     b. In the desired panel group, from the panel options menu, choose **Close.**
     c. If necessary, from the **Window** menu, choose the panel name to restore the panel.
   - Dock a panel.
     a. If necessary, from the **Window** menu, choose a panel name to display it.
     b. Click and drag the panel to a location at the edge of the workspace to dock the panel.
     c. If necessary, click and drag the panel to a location within the workspace to undock the panel.
   - Group panels.
     a. If necessary, from the **Window** menu, choose a panel to display it.
     b. Click and drag the panel to a panel or panel group to group the panel, or click and drag the tab bar of the panel group to a panel or panel group to group the panel group.
   - Stack panels.
     a. If necessary, click and drag the panel from the dock into the workspace to set it as a floating panel.
     b. Click and drag the panel to be stacked to the drop zone at the top or bottom of a floating panel.
     c. Click and drag the panel above or below a panel to rearrange the panel.
   - Collapse panels to icons.
     a. On the title bar of the panel groups, click the **Collapse to Icons** button to display the panels as icons with labels.
     b. Click and drag the left edge of the panel to reduce the width and display only icons.
     c. If necessary, on the title bar of the panel groups, click the **Expand Panels** button to expand the panels.
4. If necessary, specify the general preferences.
5. Save the customized workspace.
   a. Open the **New Workspace** dialog box.
      - On the Application bar, click the workspace switcher and select **New Workspace.**

- Or, choose **Window→Workspace Layout→New Workspace.**

b.   In the **Name** text box, type a name for the workspace.

c.   In the **Capture** section, check the check boxes to save a custom workspace.

- Check the **Panel Locations** check box to save the location of the panels to the workspace.

- Check the **Menu Customization** check box to save the customized menus to the workspace.

6.   If necessary, delete a workspace layout.

a.   Open the **Manage Workspaces** dialog box.

- On the Application bar, click the workspace switcher and select **Manage Workspaces.**

- Or, choose **Window→Workspace Layout→Manage Workspaces.**

b.   In the **Manage Workspaces** dialog box, select a workspace layout and click **Delete.**

Procedure Reference: Customize the Context and Panel Menus

To customize the context and panel menus:

1.   Open the Adobe InDesign CS4 application.

2.   Choose **Edit→Menus.**

3.   In the **Menu Customization** dialog box, in the list box, in the **Application Menu Command** column, expand a menu category to display its subcategories.

4.   From the **Category** drop-down list, select **Context & Panel Menus.**

5.   In the list box, in the **Application Menu Command** column, expand a menu category to display its subcategories.

6.   If necessary, in the **Visibility** column, click the eye icon next to a menu command to remove the menu command from the menu command list.

7.   If necessary, in the **Color** column, click **None** next to a menu command to display the drop-down list and from the drop-down list, select a color to make the menu command appear in that color.

8.   Click **OK.**

Procedure Reference: Customize the Application Menu Commands

To customize the application menu commands:

1.   Open the Adobe InDesign CS4 application.

2.   Choose **Edit→Menus.**

3.   In the **Menu Customization** dialog box, in the list box, in the **Application Menu Command** column, expand a menu category to display its subcategories.

4.   In the **Visibility** column, click the eye icon next to a menu command to remove the menu command from the menu command list.

5.   In the **Color** column, click **None** next to a menu command to display the drop-down list and from the drop-down list, select a color to make the menu command appear in that color.

6.   Click **OK.**

Procedure Reference: Customize the Control Panel

To customize the **Control** panel:

1. From the **Control** panel options menu, choose **Customize.**

2. In the **Customize Control Panel** dialog box, expand a menu and uncheck the check boxes to remove the option from the **Control** panel.

3. Click **OK.**

Procedure Reference: Customize the Keyboard Shortcuts

To customize the keyboard shortcuts:

1. Choose **Edit→Keyboard Shortcuts.**

2. In the **Keyboard Shortcuts** dialog box, from the **Set** drop-down list, select a shortcut set.

3. From the **Product Area** drop-down list, select a menu command.

4. In the **Commands** list box, select the command for which you desire to change the shortcut key.

5. In the **New Shortcut** text box, type a shortcut and click **New Set.**

6. In the **New Set** dialog box, in the **Name** text box, type a name and click **OK.**

7. If necessary, click **Delete Set** and in the **Adobe InDesign** message box, click **Yes** to delete a set.

8. In the **Keyboard Shortcuts** dialog box, click **OK.**

ACTIVITY 1-2

Customizing the Workspace

Scenario:

You acquainted yourself with the various components of the InDesign application. You realize that there are many panels and options that are not required in the interface. Therefore, you decide to remove the unnecessary panels and hide options that make your workspace look cluttered. You also want to make sure that the customized workspace is available for future use.

What You Do	How You Do It
1. View the predefined workspace.	a. On the **Welcome Screen,** check the **Don't show again** check box and close the **Welcome Screen.**
	b. On the Application bar, observe **Essentials,** which is the default workspace, and click the workspace switcher.
	c. Observe the various predefined workspaces.
	d. Select **Typography.**
	e. Observe the changes in the panel arrangements.
2. Rearrange the panels.	a. Choose **Window→Object & Layout→ Align.**
	b. Click and drag the **ALIGN** panel group to below the **CHARACTER STYLES** panel until a blue line appears between the document window and the panel groups.
	c. In the left pane, click the **Expand Panels** button to expand the panels.
	d. Choose **Window→Links.**
	e. Click and drag the **LINKS** panel to the right of the **SWATCHES** panel in the **LAYERS** panel group.

3.	Hide the unnecessary panels.	a. Observe that both the **HYPERLINKS** and **EFFECTS** panels are available along with the **STORY** panel.
		b. Right-click the **STORY** panel and choose **Close Tab Group** to close the panel group.
		c. In the **ALIGN** panel group, right-click the **PATHFINDER** panel and choose **Close.**
		d. Click the **Collapse to Icons** button.
4.	Customize the menu commands.	a. Click **File** to view the commands.
		b. Choose **Edit→Menus.**
		c. In the **Menu Customization** dialog box, from the **Category** drop-down list, verify that **Applications Menus** is selected.
		d. In the **Application Menu Command** list box, expand **File.**
		e. In the **Check In** row, click the eye icon, 👁 to turn off the visibility.
		f. In the **Save** row, click **None** and from the drop-down list, select **Red.**
		g. Click **OK** to close the **Menu Customization** dialog box.
		h. Click **File** to view the commands.
		i. Observe that the **Save** command appears in red, and click **File** to hide the menu.
5.	Save the custom workspace.	a. Choose **Window→Workspace→New Workspace.**
		b. In the **New Workspace** dialog box, in the **Name** text box, type _My Workspace_
		c. Verify that the **Panel Locations** and **Menu Customization** check boxes are checked, and click **OK.**

TOPIC C

Explore the Navigation Controls

You customized the interface for easy use of the interface elements. Now, you may want to familiarize yourself with the navigation controls for easy navigation within a document. In this topic, you will explore the different navigation controls in InDesign.

In ancient days, while travelling in a ship, the captain of the ship would hold the navigation map that controlled the direction the ship took to reach its destination. Similarly, in InDesign it is necessary that the user is aware of the various navigation controls so that he or she can use the application more effectively without wasting much time navigating within the document.

Navigation Controls

Navigation controls provide options for navigating within a document in InDesign. These options are available at the bottom-left portion of the layout window. If there is more than one page in a document, the navigation arrows, **First Page, Previous Page, Next Page,** and **Last Page** are enabled.

Zoom Tools

The zoom tools are used to increase or decrease the magnification of the page. The **Zoom Level** drop-down list on the Application bar allows you to select or set the zoom percentage of the document page. On the **View** menu, the **Zoom In** command allows you to have an enlarged view of the contents in a document, and the **Zoom Out** command allows you to decrease the magnification and view the contents.

The **Fit Page in Window** command allows you to view a single page of the spread in the window area and the **Fit Spread in Window** command allows you to view the entire spread in the window area. The **Actual Size** command allows you to view a page with 100 percent zoom level and the **Entire Pasteboard** command allows you to view all the pages of a document in the window area.

How to Explore the Navigation Controls

Procedure Reference: Zoom Objects

To zoom objects:

1. Open an InDesign file.

2. If necessary, in the **Tools** panel, double-click the **Hand** tool to fit the page in the document window.

3. Zoom the objects.

    ●   Zoom the objects using the commands on **View** menu.

    ●   Zoom the objects using the **Zoom** tool.

        a. In the **Tools** panel, select the **Zoom** tool.

        b. Click at a location on the page or click the page where you need to magnify an area, and drag to view the objects more clearly.

    ●   On the Application bar, from the **Zoom Level** drop-down list, select a zoom level to view the objects.

Procedure Reference: Navigate Through a Page Using the Hand Tool

To navigate through a page using the **Hand** tool:

1. In the **Tools** panel, select the **Hand** tool.

2. Click a location on the page and drag it to the left, right, up, or down to view a portion of the page.

ACTIVITY 1-3
Exploring the Navigation Controls

Data Files:

House.indd

Before You Begin:

From the C:\084048Data\Exploring the InDesign Environment folder, open the House.indd file.

Scenario:

While creating a layout, you may need to focus on a particular area minutely. Before you begin your work, it will be useful if you know how to move and view that area at different magnification levels.

What You Do	**How You Do It**
1. Magnify the text in the image box using the **Zoom** tool.	a. In the **Tools** panel, select the **Zoom** tool.
	b. Observe that the mouse pointer changes to a magnifying glass, when moved over the document window.
	c. Click the text at the bottom of the image two times to view the text clearly.
	d. Hold down **Alt** and observe that the magnifying glass with the Plus Sign (+), changes to a Minus Sign (-), denoting that the **Zoom Out** tool is active.
	e. Click the page.
	f. On the Application bar, in the **Zoom Level** text box, observe that the zoom percentage is 200.
	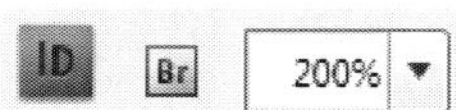
	g. Click in the **Zoom Level** text box, type *80%* and then press **Enter.**

2.	Magnify a specific region in the document.	a.	Choose **View→Fit Page in Window.**
		b.	Observe that the page fits in the document window.
		c.	On the page, click and drag around the text "Our Global."
		d.	Observe that the area is magnified and the text can be viewed more closely now.
3.	Navigate within the image using the **Hand** tool.	a.	In the **Tools** panel, select the **Hand** tool.
		b.	Using the **Hand** tool, view the remaining text.
		c.	Choose **File→Close.**

TOPIC D

Set General and Interface Preferences

You customized the workspace. Now, you want to specify the settings for the InDesign application and the documents that are created using the application. In this topic, you will set general and interface preferences.

Setting general and interface preferences allows you to establish a consistent look and feel for various file elements so that every time you open a new file, you will not have to reset common attributes and settings that you need across multiple files.

The Preferences Dialog Box

The various options in the **Preferences** dialog box are used to set the preferences that determine the way in which the InDesign documents are managed.

The following are the options in the **Preferences** dialog box.

Option	Enables You To
General	Define how documents will handle page numbering, and how fonts will be downloaded and embedded in a document. It also allows you to reset all warning dialog boxes so that they will display again, even if you have already checked the **Don't Show Again** check box.
Interface	Change the **Tools** panel layout, collapse expanded panel icons when clicked away from it, and define the time that will elapse before a tooltip is displayed.
Units & Increments	Set the ruler units and the keyboard increments. You can choose the ruler origin and also set the measurement system.
Spelling	Set the options to display spelling mistakes or words that InDesign does not recognize in the document. You can also set different colors for different spelling errors.
Autocorrect	Automatically correct misspelled words and capitalization errors. You can enable or disable **Autocorrect** and set any number of misspelled words and their equivalent corrections.

How to Set General and Interface Preferences

Procedure Reference: Set General and Interface Preferences

To set general and interface preferences:

1. Choose **Edit→Preferences→General** to display the **Preferences** dialog box.

2. Set the **General** preferences.

   - In the **Page Numbering** section, from the **View** drop-down list, select an option to determine the way InDesign assigns numbers to document pages.

   - In the **Font Downloading and Embedding** section, in the **Always subset fonts with glyph counts greater than** text box, type a number to set the maximum threshold to trigger font subsetting.

   - In the **When Scaling** section, select an option to determine the appearance of scaled text in panels.

   - In the **Scripting** section, check the **Enable Attached Scripts** check box to allow the use of scripts in the application.

   - Click **Reset All Warnings Dialogs** to display all warning messages.

3. In the left pane, select **Interface** and set the interface preferences.

   - In the **Cursor Options** section, from the **Tool Tips** drop-down list, select an option to set the way tooltips are displayed.

   - Check the **Show Thumbnails on Place** check box to display a thumbnail view of the file you are going to place in the document.

   - In the **Panels** section, from the **Floating Tools Panel** drop-down list, select an option to determine the way the **Tools** panel is displayed.

   - Check the **Auto-Collapse Icon Panels** check box to automatically collapse the panels when clicked outside it.

4. Click **OK.**

ACTIVITY 1-4

Setting the General and Interface Preferences

Scenario:
You are creating an advertisement for OGC properties. Therefore, you decide to set up a layout for the advertisement. Before you set up the layout, you want to organize the settings, so that forthcoming documents that will be based on this document do not have a cluttered workspace.

What You Do	How You Do It
1. Specify the general and interface preferences.	a. Hover the mouse pointer over the tools in the **Tools** panel and observe that the tooltips are displayed slowly.
	b. Choose **Edit→Preferences→Interface.**
	c. In the **Preferences** dialog box, in the **Interface** section, in the **Cursor Options** section, from the **Tool Tips** drop-down list, select **Fast.**
	d. In the **Panels** section, from the **Floating Tools Panel** drop-down list, select **Double Column.**
2. Change the unit of measurement.	a. In the **Preferences** dialog box, select the **Units & Increments** category.
	b. In the **Ruler Units** section, from the **Horizontal** drop-down list, select **Inches.**
	c. From the **Vertical** drop-down list, select **Inches.**
	d. Click **OK** to apply the changes.
	e. Observe that the **Tools** panel that appeared as a single column of tools now appears in a double column.
	f. In the **Tools** panel, move the mouse pointer over the tools and observe that the tooltips are appearing faster.

Lesson 1 Follow-up

In this lesson, you familiarized yourself with the InDesign environment. Familiarizing yourself with the InDesign environment prior to production will enable you to use the application more efficiently to create well-designed documents.

1. **Which of InDesign's tools and panels do you think you will use often? Why?**

2. **Which InDesign tools will help you in creating visually enhanced illustrations and drawings?**

2 | Designing Documents

Lesson Time: 45 minutes

Lesson Objectives:

In this lesson, you will design documents.

You will:

- Create a document.
- Add text.
- Add graphics.
- Convert other application files to InDesign files.

Introduction

You explored various features and elements of the InDesign environment and customized the interface to suit your needs. Now, you may want to develop a document. In this lesson, you will design documents.

The core component of any illustration or drawing is its shape. To create an art form, a graphic designer will first begin by drawing the basic shapes and lines. A document must have a good balance of images and text, because a surplus of text is surely bound to intimidate the reader. However, by inserting graphical objects related to the content, you can rekindle the interest and hold the attention of the reader by enhancing the aesthetic value of the document and giving it a consistent and creative look.

TOPIC A

Create a Document

You explored the InDesign environment and customized it to suit your work requirements. Now, you have to create a document that will be used for a new project. In this topic, you will create a document.

The ever-changing business requirements demand creation of new documents with appropriate layouts. Adobe® InDesign® CS4 not only helps you create documents by specifying the document attributes, but it also provides the flexibility of modifying the structure of the documents.

The New Document Dialog Box

The **New Document** dialog box has a number of components that can be used to create new documents in InDesign.

Component	Description
Document Preset	A drop-down list that allows you to enter a name for the customized document that you want to create.
Number of Pages	A text box that allows you to enter the number of pages in a document.
Page Size	A drop-down list that enables you to select the page type and specify the width and height of the page. You can set the orientation of the page to either **Portrait** or **Landscape.**
Columns	A section that allows you to specify the number of columns in the **Number** spin box and specify the space between the columns in the **Gutter** spin box.
Margins	A section that allows you to specify the top, bottom, inside, and outside margins in a document.
Bleed and Slug	A section that allows you to specify the area for text or graphics that go beyond the edge of a page and leave no margin, is called the bleed. A section that allows you to specify the area used to store some non-print information, such as a title, date, and so on, in order to identify a document is called the slug.
Save Preset	A button that allows you to save a preset.
Fewer Options	A button that enables you to hide the **Bleed and Slug** section in the **New Document** dialog box.

How to Create a Document

Procedure Reference: Create a Document Preset

To create a document preset:

1. Open the Adobe InDesign application.
2. Display the **New Document Preset** dialog box.
    a. Choose **File→Document Presets→Define.**
    b. In the **Document Presets** dialog box, click **New.**
3. In the **New Document Preset** dialog box, in the **Document Preset** text box, type a name for the preset.
4. Adjust the presets to the desired values.
    ● In the **Number of Pages** text box, type the number of pages for a document.
    ● Check the **Facing Pages** check box to make the left and right pages face each other in a two-page spread.
    ● Check the **Master Text Frame** check box to place an empty text frame on the document's default master page.
    ● In the **Page Size** section, specify the size, width, height, and orientation of the page.
    ● In the **Columns** section, set the number of columns and specify the gutter value for the document.
    ● In the **Margins** section, set the size of the top, bottom, inside, and outside margins for the document.
    ● In the **Bleed and Slug** section, specify the size of the top, bottom, inside, and outside bleed and slug for the document.
5. Click **OK** to close the **New Document Preset** dialog box.

Procedure Reference: Create a Document

To create a document:

1. Choose **File→New→Document** to display the **New Document** dialog box.
2. From the **Document Preset** drop-down list, select a preset.
3. If necessary, adjust the document presets.
4. Click **OK** to view a new document with the preset settings.
5. If necessary, alter a document's layout.
    a. Choose **File→Document Setup.**
    b. Adjust the document setup using the **Number of Pages, Page Size,** and **Orientation** options.
    c. Click **OK.**
6. Choose **File→Save** to save the document.

ACTIVITY 2-1

Creating a Document

Scenario:

Being a layout designer, you are assigned the task of developing the structure of a brochure for the OGC Real Estate company. You realize that there are no predefined document layouts that meet your requirements. In order to suit the specification of the company's magazine, you decide to create a document based on your preferences and make it available for use at a later point.

What You Do	How You Do It
1. Create a document that will be used to develop the brochure.	a. Choose **File→New→Document.**
	b. In the **New Document** dialog box, observe that **[Default]** is displayed in the **Document Preset** text box.
	c. In the **Number of Pages** text box, type *4* and press **Tab.**
	d. Observe that **[Custom]** is displayed in the **Document Preset** text box indicating that custom settings are being applied.
	e. Verify that the **Facing Pages** check box is checked.
	f. In the **Page Size** section, from the drop-down list, select **Letter.**
	g. Verify that **Portrait** is selected in the **Orientation** section.
	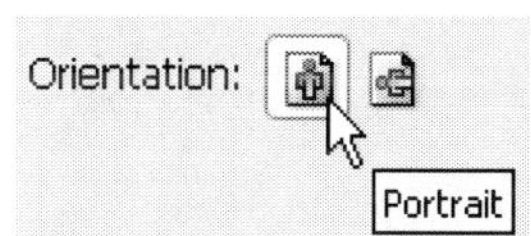
	h. In the **Columns** section, in the **Number** text box, double-click, type *3* and then press **Tab.**
	i. In the **Gutter** text box, type *0.25* and press **Tab.**
	j. Click **More Options.**
	k. In the **Bleed and Slug** section, in the **Bleed** section, in the **Top** text box, click before the value, hold down **Shift,** click at the end of the value and then type *0.5*

l. Click the **Make all settings the same** but-
    ton to make all the four settings the same.

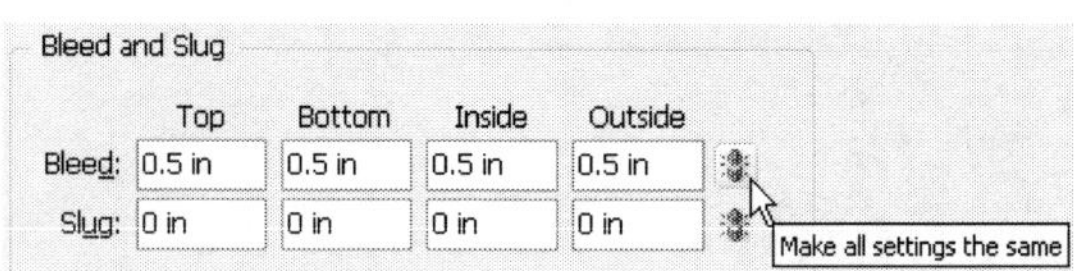

2. Save the current setting as a preset
    so that it is available for future use.

    a. Click **Save Preset.**

    b. In the **Save Preset** dialog box, in the
        Save Preset As text box, type *OGC
        Magazine* and click **OK.**

    c. Observe that in the **New Document** dia-
        log box, the name in the **Document
        Preset** text box is changed to **OGC Maga-
        zine.**

    d. Click **OK** to save the current setting as a
        preset.

    e. Choose **File→Save.**

    f. In the **Save As** dialog box, navigate to the
        C:\084048Data\Designing Documents
        folder.

    g. In the **File name** text box, click, type
        Property Finder.indd and then click
        Save.

TOPIC B

Add Text

You created a document. You may now want to place text in the document to make it informative. In this topic, you will add text to the document.

Text can be in the form of words, sentences, or paragraphs. Though they form a major chunk in brochures and other printed documents, text in documents takes different forms when it is associated with images. One of the reasons for using InDesign is to create a visually attractive and informative document. The placement of text in a document plays a significant role in adding attributes to the aesthetic presentation of the document.

Text Frames

A *text frame* is used to include text in a document. It determines the flow of text in a layout, and is generally rectangular with handles that can be used to resize the frame. You can place a text frame at any location in a document. The *Type tool*, which is located in the **Tools** panel, allows you to type text in a text frame or select text from it. You can also use the various options in InDesign to increase or decrease the space between the text and text frame, and change the color.

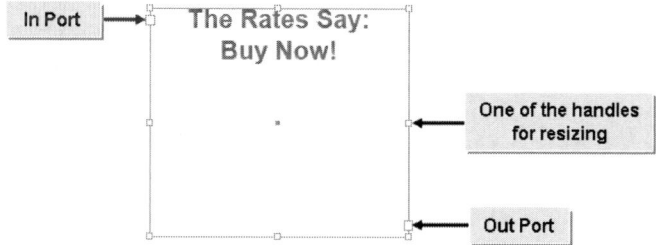

Figure 2-1: A text frame with text.

The Control Panel

The **Control** panel helps you quickly access options, commands, and panels related to the objects or items selected in the document. By default, the **Control** panel is docked at the top of the document window. However, you can dock it at the bottom of the window, convert it to a floating panel, or hide it altogether.

The Text Frame Options Dialog Box

The **Text Frame Options** dialog box has the **General** and **Baseline Options** tabs that contain options for specifying the different settings for a text frame.

The following are the components of the **Text Frame Options** dialog box.

Component	*Description*
Columns	A section that enables you to specify the number of columns, width of each column, and spacing between each column. The **Fixed Column Width** check box allows you to change the number of columns without changing its width while resizing a text frame.
Inset Spacing	A section that enables you to specify the margin distance between the text and the text frame from the top, bottom, left, and right. The **Make all settings the same** button allows you to apply the same value to all the sides.
Vertical Justification	A section that enables you to align or distribute lines of text in the text frame along its vertical line.
Ignore Text Wrap	A check box that enables you to ignore text wrap in a text frame. It is useful when you want one text frame to wrap around an image, but you may want a different text frame to appear within the image.
Preview	A check box that enables you to preview the text and baseline grid in a text frame.
First Baseline	A section that enables you to specify the first baseline of character in the selected text frame. The **Offset** drop-down list allows you to specify and distribute the font character of the text in the text frame in different ways. The **Min** spin box allows you to determine a minimum value for the selected baseline offset.
Baseline Grid	A section that enables you to specify and adjust the leading for body text in a document and also determine the consistency in the location of text elements on a page in different ways.

The Place Dialog Box

The **Place** dialog box is used to place text and graphical objects in a document.

Component	Description
Look in	A drop-down list that enables you to navigate to a specific folder in order to select files.
File name	A text box that enables you to view the name of the selected file.
Files of type	A drop-down list that enables you to select the type of files you want to open.
Show Import Options	A check box that enables you to view the import options for the file type that is selected.
Replace Selected item	A check box that enables you to replace the already existing content in the frame with the imported file.
Preview	A check box that enables you to preview text or a graphic file.

Text Import Options

There are a number of options available while importing text into documents that are created using different applications. Based on the file type of the file that is being imported, the text importing options change.

File Type	Description
TXT	You can use the import options available to set the computer language, the platform, and the type of dictionary. You can also specify extra paragraph returns and apply formatting.
RTF	You can use the import options available to specify the settings for removing and preserving styles for text and tables. You can either import paragraph and character styles automatically or customize the style by mapping the RTF style and the InDesign style.
XLS	You can use the import options available to specify the worksheet of the XLS file. You can define the cell range of the sheet to be imported, specify the view options, and the formatting of the table, table style, and cells. You can also specify the number of decimal places for the data in the spreadsheet and retain the inline graphics from the Excel document in InDesign.

File Type	Description
DOC	You can use the import options available to specify the settings for removing and preserving styles for text and tables. You can either import paragraph and character styles automatically or customize the style by mapping the DOC style and the InDesign style.

The Multiple File Place Feature

You can import multiple files at the same time by using the **Place** dialog box or dragging multiple files from a folder into an InDesign document. The thumbnail preview of the files imported and the number of files imported are indicated next to the loaded text or graphic icon. You can use the arrow keys on the keyboard to page through the files, and the **Esc** key to unload a file from the loaded text or graphics icon.

Rulers

Definition:

A *ruler* is an on-screen measuring device that is used to measure the vertical and horizontal position of page elements in a document. Rulers are used to draw, align, or size objects more accurately. The position at which the zeros of both the horizontal and vertical rulers intersect is called zero out. You can also hide the rulers.

Example:

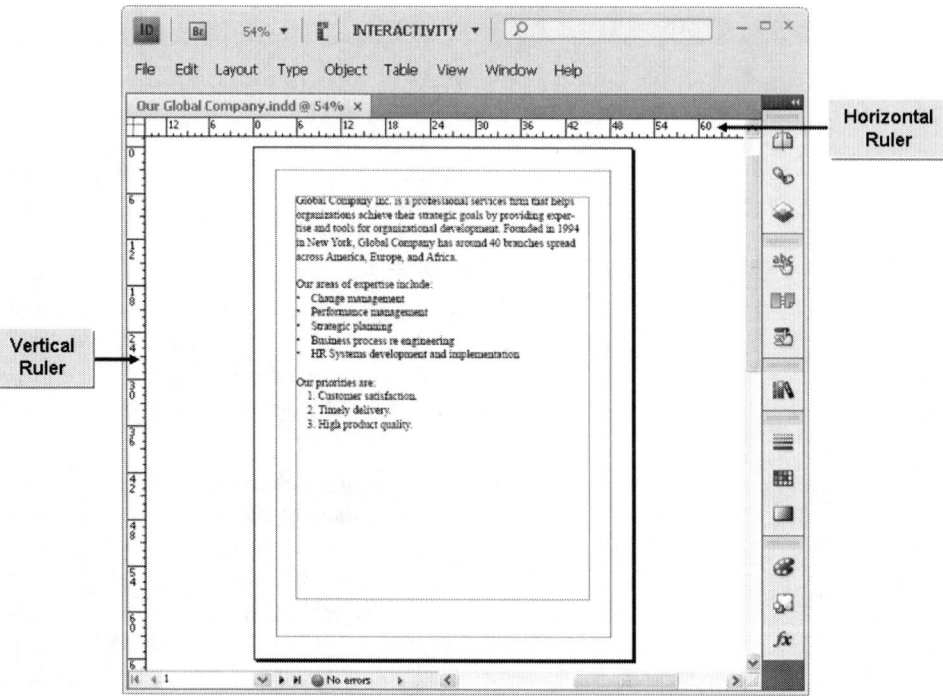

The Text Flow Feature

The text flow feature allows you to flow text from one text frame to another. It is useful in case of long articles when you can link a text frame. There are different methods in which text can flow.

Method	*Used To*
Manual text flow	Flow text to a text frame at a time. If the loaded text does not fit into the text frame, you will need to reload it again in order to flow it in another text frame.
Semi-automatic text flow	Flow text to a text frame at a time in which you need not load text again if the loaded text does not fit in the text frame. You will need to hold down **Alt** when the text is loaded and click in a frame so as to flow text. The text remains loaded till the entire text flows in the document.
Automatic text flow	Flow text in text frames. You will need to hold down **Shift** when the text is loaded and click in a column or in a text frame so as to create frames or pages for the loaded text to flow.
Smart text reflow	Flow text in text frames automatically. The text remains loaded and creates frames or pages for the loaded text automatically until the entire text flows into the document.
Fixed page autoflow	Flow text in text frames automatically. You will need to press **Shift+Alt** when the text is loaded and click in the desired location so as to create only frames, not pages, in a document. If no text frame is available in the document, the extra text remains loaded.

How to Add Text

Procedure Reference: Create a Text Frame

To create a text frame:

1. Open an InDesign document.
2. From the page selection drop-down list, select a page.
3. In the **Tools** panel, select the **Type** tool.
4. Click a location in the document.
5. Click at a location in the document and drag to create a text frame of the desired size using the horizontal and vertical rulers.
6. If necessary, in the **Control** panel, specify the desired settings using the **X, Y, W,** and **H** text boxes.

Procedure Reference: Specify the Settings for a Text Frame

To specify the settings for a text frame:

1. Select a text frame.
2. Choose **Object→Text Frame Options,** and in the **Text Frame Options** dialog box, specify the settings for the text frame.
   - On the **General** tab, specify the settings.
     - In the **Columns** section, specify the values in the **Number, Width,** and **Gutter** text boxes.
     - Check the **Fixed Column Width** check box.
     - In the **Inset Spacing** section, specify the values in the **Top, Bottom, Left,** and **Right** text boxes.
     - In the **Vertical Justification** section, from the **Align** drop-down list, select an option.
     - In the **Vertical Justification** section, specify the value in the **Paragraph Spacing Limit** text box.
     - Check the **Ignore Text Wrap** check box.
     - Check the **Preview** check box.
   - On the **Baseline Options** tab, specify the settings.
     - In the **First Baseline** section, select an option from the **Offset** drop-down list and specify the value in the **Min** text box to select a minimum value for the baseline offset.
     - In the **Baseline Grid** section, check the **User Custom Baseline Grid** check box to use the baseline grid for this specific frame and not for the entire document.
     - Specify the value in the **Start** and **Increment Every** text boxes, and select an option from the **Relative To** or **Color** drop-down list.
     - Check the **Preview** check box.
3. Click **OK** to apply the settings to the text frame.

Procedure Reference: Add Text to a Text Frame

To add text to the text frame:

1. In the **Tools** panel, select the **Type** tool.

2. Add text to the text frame.

    ● Place the mouse pointer in the text frame and type the text.

    ● Place the text from a file.

        a. In the **Tools** panel, select the **Selection** tool and select the text frame where you want to place the file.

        b. Choose **File→Place** to open the **Place** dialog box.

        c. Select a file.

        d. If necessary, check the **Show Import Options** check box.

        e. Click **Open.**

        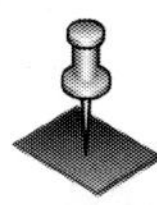 If you had checked the **Show Import Options** check box, you will need to specify the settings in the dialog box that is displayed and click **OK.**

    ● Copy and paste text.

        a. In the **Tools** panel, select the **Selection** tool and select the text in the text frame that you want to copy.

        b. Choose **Edit→Copy.**

        c. Place the cursor where you want to paste the text.

        d. Choose **Edit→Paste.**

ACTIVITY 2-2

Adding Text

Data Files:

Property Finder.indd, OGC Property Finder.rtf

Before You Begin:

The Property Finder.indd file is open.

Scenario:

After creating a customized document based on the specified requirement of the magazine, you decide to include some text in the monthly magazine. Having placed the text in a text frame, you realize that the text frame size is smaller than the amount of text that needs to be included, and the extra text in the text frame needs to be placed in another text frame of the document.

What You Do	How You Do It
1. Create text frames at the desired location.	a. At the bottom-left of the document window, from the page selection drop-down list, select **2**. 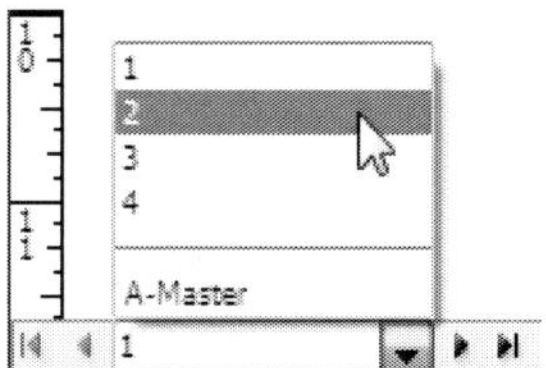 b. In the **Tools** panel, select the **Type** tool. c. Observe that the mouse pointer changes to an I-beam. d. Scroll to the left to view the pasteboard. e. On the pasteboard of page 2, click and drag from the point of intersection of the -8-inch mark on the horizontal ruler and the 0-inch mark on the vertical ruler to the point of intersection of the -4-inch mark on the horizontal ruler and the 2-inch mark on the vertical ruler to create a rectangular text frame. *ignore* f. Click and drag from the point of intersection of the -8-inch mark on the horizontal ruler and the 4-inch mark on the vertical ruler to the point of intersection of the -4-inch mark on the horizontal ruler and the 6-inch mark on the vertical ruler to create another rectangular text frame on the pasteboard. *ignore* g. In the **Tools** panel, select the **Selection** tool and select the first text frame. h. In the **Control** panel, in the **X** text box, click before the value, hold down **Shift**, click at the end of the value, type **3.85** and then press **Tab**. i. In the **Y** text box, type **0.92** and press **Tab**. j. In the **W** text box, type **5.4** and press **Tab**. In the **H** text box, type **1.5** and then press **Enter**. k. Select the second text frame.

l. In the **Control** panel, in the **X** text box, click before the value, hold down **Shift,** click at the end of the value, type *5.55* and then press **Tab.**

m. In the **Y** text box, type *6.8* and press **Tab.**

n. In the **W** text box, type *4.9* and press **Tab.** In the **H** text box, type *2* and then press **Enter.**

2. Specify the settings for the columns of the first text frame.

a. Select the first text frame.

b. Choose **Object→Text Frame Options.**

c. In the **Text Frame Options** dialog box, on the **General** tab, in the **Columns** section, in the **Number** text box, verify that **1** is displayed and press **Tab** two times.

d. In the **Gutter** text box, type *0.25* and click **OK.**

3. Add text to the text frame.

a. On the Application bar, from the **Zoom Level** drop-down list, select **150%.**

b. In the **Tools** panel, select the **Type** tool.

c. Click in the first text frame and type *"A man travels the world over in search of what he needs and returns home to find it." - George Moore*

d. Scroll down and to the right to view the second text frame fully.

e. In the **Tools** panel, select the **Selection** tool and select the second text frame.

f. Choose **File→Place.**

g. In the **Place** dialog box, select **OGC Property Finder.rtf.**

h. Check the **Show Import Options** check box and click **Open.**

i. In the **RTF Import Options (OGC Property Finder.rtf)** dialog box, in the **Formatting** section, select the **Remove Styles and Formatting from Text and Tables** option.

j. Verify that the **Preserve Local Overrides** check box is unchecked and click **OK.**

4. Flow text into another text frame.

    a. Click the out port that has the red plus sign in the text frame.

    b. Observe that the mouse pointer changes to a loaded text icon.

    c. Click at the top-left corner of the first column on the third page.

    d. Choose **File→Save.**

TOPIC C
Add Graphic

You added text to a document. You may now want to enhance the document by placing graphics. In this topic, you will add graphics to the document.

There is always a need to use a broad range of InDesign's fundamental features for designing documents so that you can create eye-catching and substantive content. Placing graphics according to requirement enables you to attach appealing attributes to the document.

Graphic Frames

A *graphic frame* is a container or placeholder for images. It has eight handles to control and define the vertical and horizontal dimensions of the frame. When you create a graphic frame using the **Rectangle Frame, Ellipse Frame,** or **Polygon Frame** tool, the diagonal lines in the frame denote that they should be replaced by an image.

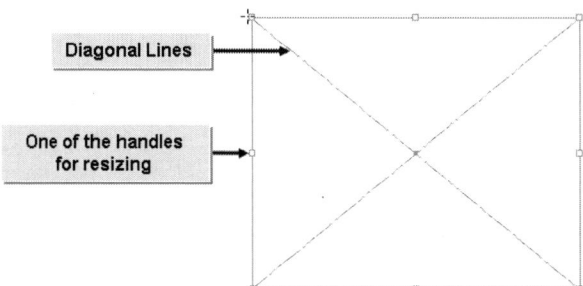

Image Import Options

There are a number of options available while importing images into documents that are created using different applications. The image import options in InDesign are based on the file type that is being imported.

File Type	Description
EPS (Encapsulated PostScript)	You can use the import options available to convert the desired path to a clipping path in Photoshop before you save it as an EPS file. You can preserve or remove the Open PrePress Interface (OPI) link and create a proxy low-resolution bitmap representation of an image by specifying the desired settings.
BMP (Bitmap)	You can use the import options available to use the desired color management. You can create a transparent mask on the image and import a clipping path so that you can choose an image and modify its path without any change in the graphic frame. You can also use the same options for PSD, TIFF, GIF, and JPG files.

File Type	Description
PNG (Portable Network Graphics)	You can use the import options available to apply different settings to PNG files. You can also specify the various color and image setting options.
PDF (Portable Document Format)	You can use the import options available to specify the page or range of pages you want to import or preview, apply transparent background to the page if desired, control visibility layers in a layered PDF file, and select the specific option for cropping the placed PDF file.
INDD (InDesign)	You can use the import options available to specify the page or a range of pages, control visibility layers, and select the desired option for cropping the file.

Text Wrap

Text wrap refers to the different settings that allow text to flow around another object in various ways. When text wrap is applied to an object, InDesign creates a boundary around that object and it repels text. Text can be wrapped to the right, left, or to the largest side of the object. Text can also be wrapped in various wrap shapes. A *rectangular text wrap* allows you to wrap text around the squared edges of a rectangular frame. A *contour text wrap* allows you to wrap text in the shape of the selected frame. You can apply specific text wrap settings using the **TEXT WRAP** panel.

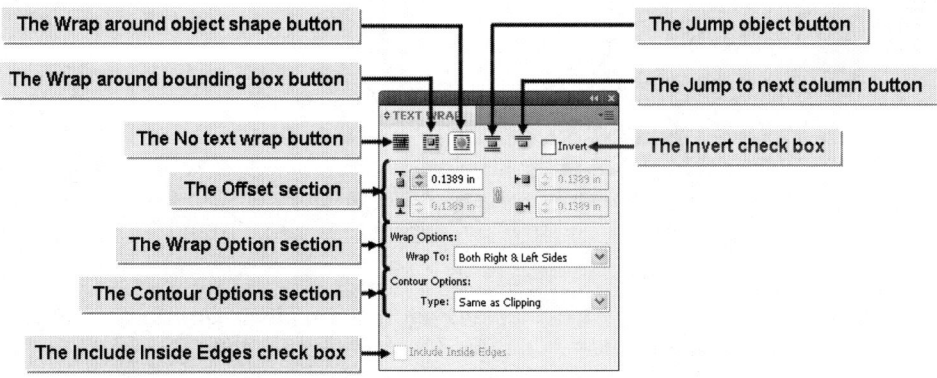

Figure 2-2: Text wrap settings.

You can apply the specific text wrap settings using the **TEXT WRAP** panel.

Component	Description
No text wrap	A button that allows you to flow text behind the object without any wrapping.
Wrap around bounding box	A button that allows you to create a rectangular wrap so that text flows around that rectangle.

Component	Description
Wrap around object shape	A button that allows you to flow text around the contours of the selected object.
Jump object	A button that allows you to flow text to the next available space, such as left, right, top, and bottom of the frame.
Jump to next column	A button that allows you to flow text to the immediate column or text frame.
Invert	A check box that allows you to flow text to wrap inside an object. This option is generally selected when you want text to flow with the shape of the object.
Offset	A section that allows you to specify the top, bottom, left, and right offset values to move the wrap away from the frame or within the frame.
Make all settings the same	A button that allows you to specify the same values for all settings in the offset section.
Wrap Options	A section that allows you to specify the sides to which you want to apply the text wrap.
Contour Options	A section that allows you to specify the type of edges and connecting points during the wrapping process.
Include Inside Edges	A check box that allows you to include and wrap even the inside edge area between text and object.

The INFO Panel

The **INFO** panel displays information about the selected objects. It displays information about the width, height, size, and rotation of the selected objects. It deals with the horizontal and vertical positions of the cursor, the distance an object or tool has moved from its starting position, the degree of rotation, and the width and height in current units. In addition, this panel provides an effective control over word counts, number of paragraphs and lines, and so on when a text file is selected.

When you select a graphic file, the panel displays information about the file type, actual and effective pixels per inch, color profile, and so on. You can use the **INFO** panel to find hidden information about a document, and you cannot use this panel to edit or enter values.

The LINKS Panel

The *LINKS panel* tracks and displays all the images and external files that are used to create a primary InDesign file. When a linked file is double-clicked, the **Link Info** section displays information such as the name of the linked file, date, time, size, type, path, and so on of the file on the hard disk. The **LINKS** panel also provides information on updates when you modify an InDesign file placed within the primary InDesign document.

The **LINKS** panel has a number of components that help you track and display information about images.

Component	Description
Name	A section that allows you to view additional file information such as the name of a file, file type, and so on.
Page	A section that helps you view the page number where the image is located in a document.
Link Info	A section that allows you to view information, such as the name of the file, file type, page number of the file, creation date, time, size, type, location, and so on, about the selected file.
Buttons	A section that has a number of buttons that can be used to show or hide the **Link Info** section, view the total number of links, relink all the missing links, select and view a linked graphic, update all the links in a document, and edit the original graphics using the default or a different application.
Next or Previous	An arrow in the **Link Info** section that allows you to select the previous or next link from the list of links displayed.
Panel options menu	A menu that allows you to relink the image or folder, update links, select the specific links, edit images using the default or different applications, and so on.

The Controlling Image Quality Feature

The image quality feature deals with the resolution feature of an image. You can import various types of graphic file formats such as JPEG, GIF, TIFF, BMP, and EPS. Each graphic file has its own image quality based on its pixel number, color separation, and degree of image resolution. Though higher resolution gives a clearer image, the quality of the image is distorted with the increase in size because the size of pixels increases.

Display Performance

Display performance of an image refers to the pixel dimension of an image that controls the resolution of images in a document. There are three types of display settings: Fast Display, Typical Display, and High Quality Display. You can determine the display settings either for the entire document or for specific graphics so that these options do not affect the print quality or exported output. You can use the **Allow Object-Level Display** command to preserve the same display performance of all the images or specify different display performance settings for different images. The **Clear Object-Level Display** command is used to remove the display setting for all the images in a document.

Setting	*Description*
Fast Display	Allows you to display an image at low resolution. This helps you move through numerous pages of a document quickly that contains lots of images and transparency effects.
Typical Display	Allows you to display an image at balanced image resolution for identifying and positioning it. It is the default option that enables you to strike a balance between image quality and display performance of an image.
High Quality Display	Allows you to display a raster image or vector graphic at high resolution. You cannot move through numerous pages of a document quickly.

How to Add Graphic

Procedure Reference: Place Images in a Document

To place images in a document:

1. Select a page where you want to place the graphic.
2. In the **Tools** panel, select the **Rectangle Frame** tool and draw a graphic frame.
3. Choose **File→Place.**

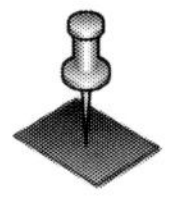

> In the **Place** dialog box, check the **Show Import Options** check box to display the import options dialog box.

4. Navigate to the specific file, select the images and then click **Open.**
5. Place the graphic at a location in the frame.
6. If necessary, specify the settings using the **Control** panel.
    a. In the **Tools** panel, select the **Selection** tool.
    b. Select the image and specify the settings using the **Control** panel.
        *   In the **X** text box, specify a value to set the horizontal coordinates.
        *   In the **Y** text box, specify a value to set the vertical coordinates.
        *   In the **W** text box, specify a value for the width.

- In the **H** text box, specify a value for the height.
7. Choose **File→Save** to save the document and close the file.

Procedure Reference: Check File Information

To check file information:

1. Select the page from which you want to check file information.
2. Choose **Window→Info.**
3. Select the **Selection** tool and select an image.
4. In the **INFO** panel, observe the X and Y coordinates, height, width, file type, and the color space of the selected image.
5. If necessary, choose **Window→Links** and observe the link information and other details of the file.

Procedure Reference: Control the Display Performance

To control the display performance:

1. Select the image.
2. Choose **View→Display Performance** or **Object→Display Performance** and then choose a command.
   - Choose **Fast Display** to view low-quality images with a fast display.
   - Choose **Typical Display** to view medium-quality images.
   - Choose **High Quality Display** to view high-quality images.
3. Choose **File→Save** to save the document and close the file.

Procedure Reference: Wrap Text

To wrap text:

1. Select an image.
2. Choose **Window→Text Wrap.**
3. In the **TEXT WRAP** panel, specify the settings for the text wrap.
   - Click the **No text wrap** button if you do not desire to have a text wrap.
   - Click the **Wrap around bounding box** button to create a rectangular wrapping.
   - Click the **Wrap around object shape** button to wrap text around an object of any shape.
   - Click the **Jump object** button to wrap text around objects on parallel sides only.
   - Click the **Jump to next column** button to move the text around the object to the next column or to the text frame.
   - Specify the offset value in the **Top Offset, Bottom Offset, Left Offset,** and **Right Offset** text boxes to wrap the text accordingly.
   - In the **Wrap Options** section, from the **Wrap To** drop-down list, select the desired wrap options.
   - In the **Contour Options** section, from the **Type** drop-down list, select the desired contour options.
   - Check the **Include Inside edges** check box to wrap text inside the selected object.

ACTIVITY 2-3

Adding Graphics

Data Files:

Property Finder.indd

Before You Begin:

The Property Finder.indd file is open.

Scenario:

After placing text in the brochure, you decide to include graphics so as to make the document attractive. You feel that the graphics when placed would catch the attention of the readers. You may feel it necessary to place the graphics at the desired locations in the brochure and check the file information of the document. Finally, you want to change the display performance settings of the images so as to get the desired quality of image.

What You Do	How You Do It
1. Create a graphic frame.	a. Choose **View→Fit Page in Window.**
	b. From the page selection drop-down list, select **2.**
	c. In the **Tools** panel, select the **Rectangle Frame** tool.
	d. Click in the pasteboard.
	e. In the **Rectangle** dialog box, in the **Width** text box, type *0.35* and press **Tab.**
	f. In the **Height** text box, type *5.75* and click **OK.**
	g. In the **Control** panel, in the **X** text box, click before the value, hold down **Shift,** click at the end of the value, type *8.325* and then press **Tab.**
	h. In the **Y** text box, type *8.375* and press **Enter.**

2. Place the images in the desired location in the brochure.

   a. Choose **File→Place.**

   b. In the **Place** dialog box, uncheck the **Show Import Options** check box.

   c. Select **Image 01.jpg,** hold down **Shift,** and select **Image 08.jpg.**

   d. Click **Open.**

   e. Observe that the mouse pointer changes to a graphic loaded icon.

   f. Scroll to the extreme left of the document.

   g. Click at the point of intersection of the -8-inch mark on the horizontal ruler and the 0-inch mark on the vertical ruler to place the first graphic on the pasteboard.

   h. Place the next three images on the pasteboard of page 2.

   i. Scroll to the extreme right of the document.

   j. Similarly, place the fifth, sixth, seventh, and eighth images on the third page.

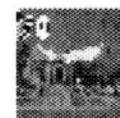

3. Arrange the images on the second and third pages of the brochure.

a. Scroll to the extreme left of the document.

b. Select the **Selection** tool and select the first image on the pasteboard.

c. In the **Control** panel, specify the values in the **X** and **Y** text boxes as *4.25* and *3* respectively, and in the **W** and **H** text boxes as *7.5* and *5* respectively.

d. Select the second image on the pasteboard.

e. In the **Control** panel, specify the values in the **X** and **Y** text boxes as *1.67* and *6.8* respectively.

f. Select the third image and specify the values in the **X** and **Y** text boxes as *2.25* and *9.3* respectively.

g. Select the fourth image and specify the values in the **X** and **Y** text boxes as *6.2* and *9.3,* respectively.

h. Position the fifth, sixth, seventh, and eighth images in the appropriate location.
   - Fifth image—X: 14.05, Y: 2.14.
   - Sixth image—X: 12.47, Y: 5.5.
   - Seventh image—X: 15.02, Y: 5.5.
   - Eighth image—X: 14.05, Y: 8.55.

4. Check file information and display performance.

a. From the page selection drop-down list, select **2.**

b. Choose **Window→Info** to display the **INFO** panel.

c. Select the first image on the second page.

d. In the **INFO** panel, observe the height, width, file type, and the color space of the selected image.

e. Expand the **LINKS** panel.

f. In the **LINKS** panel, in the **Link Info** section, observe the path of the file where it has been imported from and also other file information.

g. In the **LINKS** panel, click the **Collapse to Icons** button to hide the panel.

h. Click and drag the **INFO** panel to below the **SWATCHES** panel to dock the **INFO** panel.

i. Choose **View→Display Performance.**

j. Verify that **Typical Display** is chosen.

k. Click **View** to hide the menu.

l. Save the file.

TOPIC D

Convert Other Application Files to InDesign

You added text and graphics to an InDesign document. Until now, you worked with only InDesign documents, but there may be instances when you need to convert other application files to InDesign files. In this topic, you will convert other application files to InDesign files.

There may be occasions where you may receive a newsletter created using Adobe PageMaker and you may want to format the document and enhance the layout. However, you do not have Adobe PageMaker® installed on your system. InDesign provides options that enable the conversion of other application files to InDesign files.

How to Convert Other Application Files to InDesign

Procedure Reference: Open a PageMaker File in the InDesign Application

To open a PageMaker file in the InDesign application:

1. Open the InDesign application.
2. Choose **File→Open.**
3. In the **Open a File** dialog box, navigate to the folder where the file is located.
4. If necessary, from the **Files of Type** drop-down list, select a PageMaker file.
5. Select the PageMaker file that you want to open and click **Open.**
6. In the **Warnings** message box, click **Close.**
7. Choose **File→Save.**
8. If necessary, in the **Save As** dialog box, navigate to the folder where the PageMaker file is, and type a file name in the **File name** text box.
9. Click **Save** and close the file.

Procedure Reference: Place a PageMaker File as an InDesign Document

To place a PageMaker file as an InDesign document:

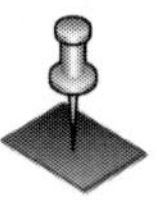 Only files from Adobe PageMaker 6.0 or later versions and QuarkXpress 3.3 or 4.1x formats can be converted to the InDesign file format.

1. Navigate to the page where you want to place a PageMaker file as an InDesign document.
2. Choose **File→Place.**
3. In the **Place** dialog box, navigate to the folder where the PageMaker file is.
4. Select a file and click **Open.**
5. Place the graphic loaded mouse pointer at a location on the page.
6. Save and close the file.

ACTIVITY 2-4

Converting Other Application Files to InDesign

Data Files:

Property Finder.indd, Property Finder Cover.pmd

Before You Begin:

The Property Finder.indd file is open.

Scenario:

One of your colleagues created a cover page for the brochure using the PageMaker application and asked you to include that content in the brochure. You do not have the PageMaker application installed on your system and therefore, you decide to open the PageMaker file first and save it as an InDesign document to facilitate the placing and modification of the file in the InDesign application.

What You Do	How You Do It
1. Open the PageMaker file in the InDesign application.	a. Choose **File→Open.**
	b. In the **Open a File** dialog box, navigate to the C:\084048Data\Designing Documents\ Property Finder Cover folder.
	c. Select **Property Finder Cover.pmd** and click **Open.**
	d. In the **Warnings** message box, click **Close.**
	e. Choose **File→Save.**
	f. If necessary, in the **Save as** dialog box, from the **Save in** drop-down list, navigate to the C:\084048Data\Designing Documents folder.
	g. In the **Save As** dialog box, in the **File name** text box, type *Property Finder Cover.indd*
	h. In the **Save as type** drop-down list, verify that **InDesign CS4 document** is selected and click **Save** to save the document as an InDesign file.
	i. Close the Property Finder Cover.indd file.

2. Place the cover page in the brochure.

a. From the page selection drop-down list, select **1.**

b. Choose **File→Place.**

c. Scroll down, select **Property Finder Cover.indd,** and then click **Open.**

d. Click at the top-left corner of the page to place the image.

e. Click outside the document to deselect the graphic frame of the cover page.

f. Save and close the file.

Lesson 2 Follow-up

In this lesson, you designed documents with images and text to hold the attention of the reader. Designing documents helps you employ numerous InDesign's features that provide a presentable look and substantive information to the content.

1. **What are the advantages of designing documents?**

2. **What are the advantages of using InDesign in designing documents? How useful is it in making your document more professional?**

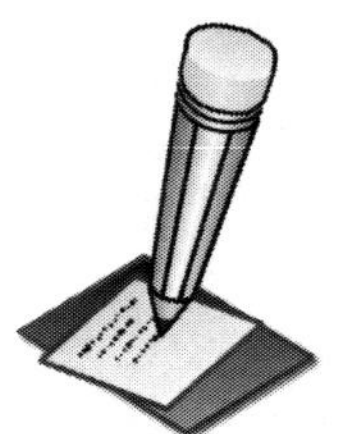

3 | Enhancing Documents

Lesson Time: 55 minutes

Lesson Objectives:

In this lesson, you will enhance documents.

You will:

- Format characters and paragraphs.
- Apply color, swatches, and gradients.
- Apply fills and strokes.
- Create and apply styles.

Introduction

You added text and graphics and designed a basic InDesign document. You now want to further improve the quality of the document. In this lesson, you will enhance documents.

Enhancing InDesign documents will help you capture and maintain your audience's attention. You can enhance the look and feel of the documents by formatting text and adding color.

TOPIC A
Format Characters and Paragraphs

Now that you applied fills, gradients, and strokes, you can begin to enhance text and paragraphs. To make a selection stand out from the remaining text or to meet a stylistic requirement to enhance your document, formatting is the solution. In this topic, you will format characters and paragraphs in a document.

Formatting paragraphs allows you to space, shape, and define the look and feel of paragraphs so that you can create appealing and useful documents. Well-formatted characters can draw readers' attention through a document, making it easier for the reader to access the information he or she needs.

Leading

Definition:

Leading is the measurement of space between the baseline of one line and the baseline of the next. By default, the text in a document uses *auto leading*. Auto leading is a predefined setting that creates a leading value at 120 percent of the largest type size on a line. When more than one leading value is applied to a line, the largest value determines the leading of that line.

Example:

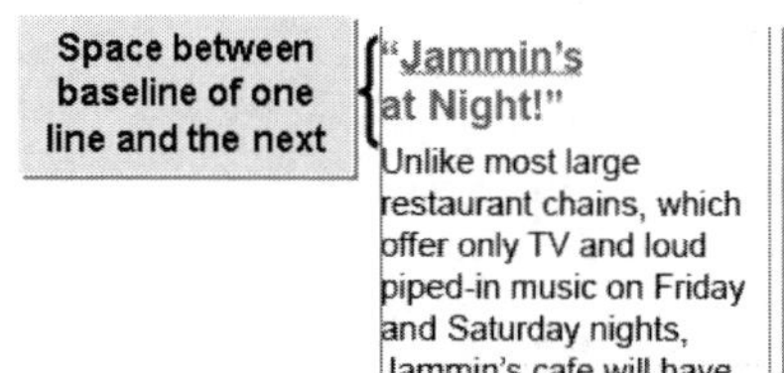

Character Formatting Attributes

Character formatting attributes are specified for a character and can be added to a style. When a character style is created, attributes that are different from the format of the selected text become part of the style. All formatting attributes of the selected text may not be included in a character style. Therefore, when you create a character style and apply it to text, few changes such as in the font family and size are made; all other character attributes are ignored.

Special Characters and Glyphs

InDesign allows you to type special characters and glyphs that are not on the keyboard. Special characters include symbols such as the copyright symbol, the registered trademark symbol, or a bullet character. Glyphs are alternate forms of a specific character. For example, in a given font, each uppercase letter may be available in varying forms, such as a lowercase version. The **GLYPHS** panel can be used to locate a glyph in a specific font, view recently used glyphs, add glyph sets, and sort glyphs.

OpenType Fonts

OpenType fonts contain many characters, including fractions, small caps, superscript and subscript characters, swashes, and many more, that are not available in other font types. Each OpenType font has one file that can be used for both Windows and Macintosh. When you apply an OpenType font to text, you can select from the following OpenType attributes.

- Ligatures, which are typographic characters used in place of specific letter pairs, such as "fi" and "fl."

- Fractions, which are typographic characters used in place of fractions typed as multiple characters.

- Ordinals, which are numbers such as 1st and 2nd, in which the letters are formatted as superscript.

- Swashes, which are alternate characters for capital letters, typically with ornamental, curving serifs.

Different options are available for different fonts. Options not available for the font you selected are enclosed in brackets.

Paragraph Formatting Options

There are different paragraph formatting options such as alignment buttons, indents, paragraph spacing, drop cap controls, and keep options.

Option	*Used To*
Alignment buttons	Align text with the left, right, or both edges of a text frame. You can align text using the various alignment buttons in the **PARAGRAPH** panel.
Indents	Move text inward from the left and right edges of the frame. You can set indents using the **Left Indent, First Line Left Indent, Right Indent,** and **Last Line Right Indent** text boxes in the **PARAGRAPH** panel.
Paragraph spacing	Add space before or after paragraphs by using paragraph spacing instead of typing an extra paragraph break between paragraphs. The amount of space between paragraphs can be controlled by using the **Space Before** or **Space After** text boxes in the **PARAGRAPH** panel.
Drop cap controls	Position the baseline of the first letter or word one or more lines below the baseline of the first line of the paragraph. The number of lines below which the baseline of the selected characters should be placed can be specified.
Keep options	Specify the number of lines that need to be kept together in a paragraph. This helps prevent individual lines of a paragraph from standing alone at either the top or bottom of a column.

Hanging Indents

You will typically format bulleted and numbered paragraphs to line up as hanging indents. In a hanging indent, the first line of a paragraph is positioned to the left of the other lines in the paragraph. A hanging indent is used to line up bulleted or numbered paragraphs so that the main text lines up to the right of the bullet or number.

Optical Margin Alignment

Punctuation marks and certain letters such as "W" and "A" can make the left or right edge of a text frame appear misaligned. The punctuation marks and the edges of letters can be made to hang outside the text margins by checking the **Optical Margin Alignment** check box in the **STORY** panel.

Rules

Definition:

Rules are lines that appear either above or below paragraphs. They are used to separate the heading and the body text of a document. Rules move with a paragraph similar to the way text flows within a frame. You can format a rule's weight, type, color, offset, and indents. The width of a rule is determined by the column width.

Example:

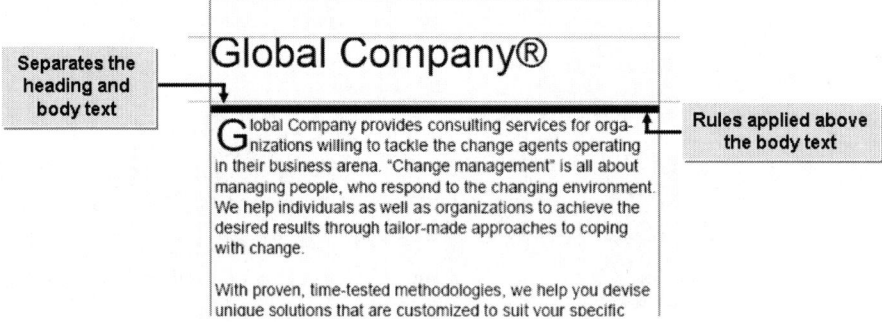

Lists

Definition:

Lists are used to present information separately from the surrounding text. InDesign allows you to create two types of lists: a *bulleted list,* which is used to denote a group of equally significant items, and a *numbered list,* which is used to denote a ranking or sequence that must be followed to achieve the desired outcome. Advanced hierarchical sequences can also be created using the numbered list.

Example:

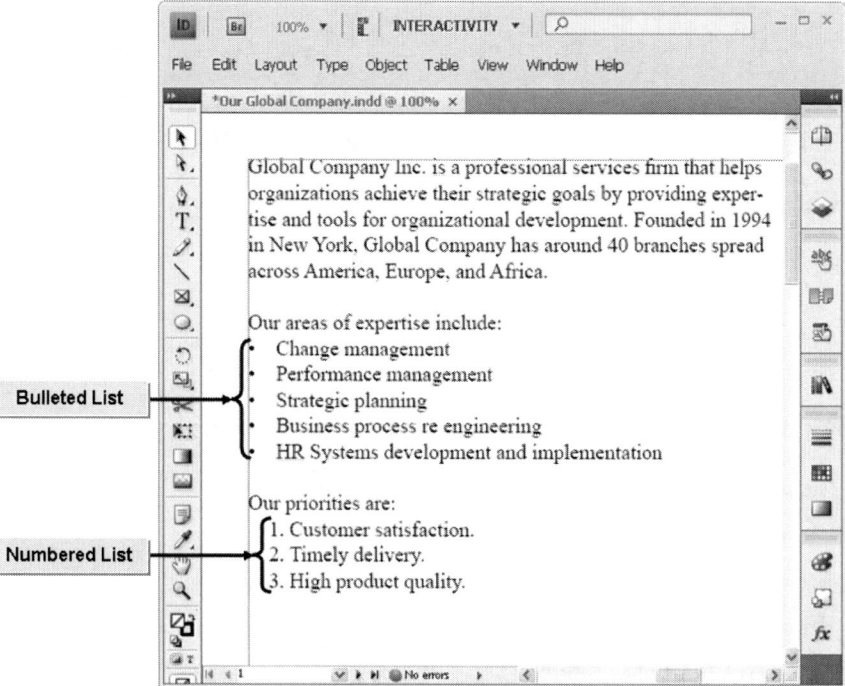

The Bullets and Numbering Dialog Box

The **Bullets and Numbering** dialog box allows you to create bulleted and numbered lists. The type of list to be created or applied to text in a document can be chosen from the **List Type** drop-down list. The type of bullet character, format of the numbering list, and position of the bullets and numbers can be specified.

How to Format Characters and Paragraphs

Procedure Reference: Format Characters

To format characters:

1. Select the **Type** tool and place the insertion point in a text frame.
2. Select the text.
    - Click at the beginning of the text, hold down **Shift,** and click at the end of the text.
    - Choose **Edit→Select All** to select the entire content in a document.
3. In the **Control** panel, specify the settings.

 Options in the **Control** panel include: **Font Size, Leading, Kerning, Tracking, Vertical Scale, Baseline Shift, Horizontal Scale, Skew,** and **Language.**

4. If necessary, set the font type and size using the menu command.
    - Choose **Type→Font** and then choose a font.
    - Choose **Type→Size** and then choose a font size.

Procedure Reference: Insert Special Characters

To insert special characters:

1. In the **Tools** panel, select the **Type** tool.
2. Place the insertion point where you would like to add the special character.
3. Choose **Type→Insert Special Character** and then choose a special character.

Procedure Reference: Add Glyphs

To add a glyph:

1. In the **Tools** panel, select the **Type** tool.
2. Place the insertion point where you would like the glyph added.
3. Choose **Window→Type & Tables→Glyphs.**
4. In the **Glyphs** panel, double-click a glyph to add it to the document.

Procedure Reference: Format Paragraphs

To format paragraphs:

1. Select a paragraph.
2. Choose **Window→Type & Tables→Paragraph.**
3. In the **PARAGRAPH** panel, adjust the options.

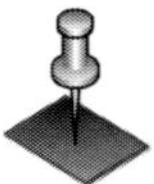

 Options in the **PARAGRAPH** panel include: **Left Indent, First Line Left Indent, Space Before, Drop Cap Number of Lines, Right Indent, Last Line Right Indent, Space After,** and **Drop Cap One or More Characters.**

Procedure Reference: Set Paragraph Rules

To set paragraph rules:

1. Select a paragraph.
2. Choose **Window→Type & Tables→Paragraph.**
3. From the **PARAGRAPH** panel options menu, choose **Paragraph Rules.**
4. In the **Paragraph Rules** dialog box, adjust the values as necessary.
   - In the **Weight** text box, type a value for the stroke thickness.
   - From the **Color** drop-down list, select a rule color.
   - In the **Left Indent** text box, type a left indent value to align text to the left.
   - From the **Type** drop-down list, select a type of rule.
   - In the **Tint** text box, type a value for the color tint.
   - In the **Offset** text box, type an offset value.
   - In the **Right Indent** text box, type a right indent value to align text to the right.

Procedure Reference: Add Bulleted and Numbered Lists

To add bulleted and numbered lists:

1. Select the text.
2. In the **PARAGRAPH** panel, from the **PARAGRAPH** panel options menu, choose **Bullets and Numbering.**

3. Add a bulleted list.

    a. In the **Bullets and Numbering** dialog box, from the **List Type** drop-down list, select **Bullets.**

    b. In the **Bullet Character** section, select a bullet type.

    c. In the **Bullet or Number Position** section, set the position of the bullets and text in the document.

    d. Click **OK.**

4. If necessary, add a numbered list.

    a. In the **Bullets and Numbering** dialog box, from the **List Type** drop-down list, select **Numbers.**

    b. In the **Numbering Style** section, set the style of the numbers.

    c. In the **Bullet or Number Position** section, set the position of the numbers and text in the document.

    d. Click **OK.**

ACTIVITY 3-1

Formatting Characters and Paragraphs

Data Files:

Property Finder.indd

Before You Begin:

1. From the C:\084048Data\Enhancing Documents folder, open the Property Finder.indd file.

2. From the **Zoom Level** drop-down list, select **100%.**

Scenario:

While reviewing the brochure you created, and after adding an additional page to your document, you want to change the quotation marks and headings' formats to be consistent. You also want to change the color of the headings on each page, and adjust the spacing between each quote and name. Additionally, you want to add special characters to the text so as to highlight the important content.

What You Do	How You Do It
1. Apply character formatting to the text "The Rates Say: Buy Now!"	a. Click the **Next Page** button to navigate to page 2. 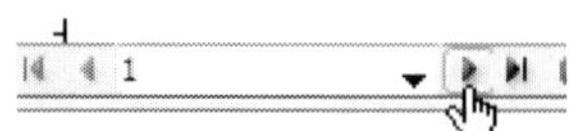
	b. Select the **Type** tool.
	c. Click before the text "The Rates Say: Buy Now!," hold down **Shift,** and click after the text.
	d. Expand the **CHARACTER** panel.
	e. In the **CHARACTER** panel, from the font style drop-down list, select **Bold.**
	f. In the **Font Size** text box, select the value, type *20* and then press **Enter.**
	g. From the **Horizontal Scale** drop-down list, select **75%.**
	h. Collapse the **CHARACTER** panel.

2. Insert the trademark and the phone symbols.

    a. Click the **Last Page** button to navigate to page 4.

    b. Scroll down to the bottom of the document.

    c. Click after the text "OGC Properties" that is below the text "To Contact."

    d. Choose **Type→Insert Special Character→Symbols→Trademark Symbol.**

    e. Select the text "Call us."

    f. Choose **Type→Glyphs.**

    g. In the **GLYPHS** panel, in the font drop-down list, scroll down and select **Wingdings.**

    h. In the symbols list box, double-click the phone symbol in the first row. ☎

    i. Collapse the **GLYPHS** panel.

3. Apply paragraph formatting.

    a. Navigate to page 2 and click the text "The Rates Say: Buy Now!"

    b. Expand the **PARAGRAPH** panel.

    c. In the **PARAGRAPH** panel, in the **Space After** text box, select the value, type *0.084* and then press **Enter.**

    d. Place the insertion point at the start of the paragraph below the heading text "The Rates Say: Buy Now!"

    e. In the **Drop Cap Number of Lines** text box, double-click, type *2* and then press **Enter.**

    f. Verify that in the **Drop Cap One or More Characters** text box, **1** is displayed.

    g. In the **Space After** text box, select the value, type *0.084* and then press **Enter.**

4. Create a bullet list.

a. Navigate to page 3 and scroll up the page.

b. Click before the text "Relocation Team" that is below the heading "Experts at Your Service," hold down **Shift,** and then click after the last list item.

c. From the **PARAGRAPH** panel options menu, choose **Bullets and Numbering.**

d. In the **Bullets and Numbering** dialog box, check the **Preview** check box.

e. From the **List Type** drop-down list, select **Bullets.**

f. In the **Bullet Character** section, select the fourth character.

g. Click the right arrow to the right of the **Text After** drop-down list,

and select **Em Space.**

h. In the **Bullets or Number Position** section, in the **Left Indent** text box, select the value, type *0.325* and then press **Tab.**

i. In the **First Line Indent** text box, type *0.325* and press **Tab.**

j. Verify that **1** is displayed in the **Tab Position** text box, and click **OK.**

k. Deselect the text.

l. Click below the bullet list to deselect the text.

m. Observe that the text has been converted to a bulleted list.

n. Collapse the **PARAGRAPH** panel.

o. Save the file as *My Property Finder.indd*

TOPIC B

Apply Color, Swatches, and Gradients

You created documents and added text and graphics. Now, you may want to apply colors and modify color schemes applied to text and graphics in the documents to enhance their look and feel. In this topic, you will apply colors, swatches, and gradients.

Applying color to text and graphics is a powerful way to make them stand apart, adding visual interest while pointing out significant information to the reader.

Process Colors

Process colors are defined by combining different colors to produce the required shade. There are three basic color models: RGB, CMYK, and LAB.

Color Model	How it Works
RGB	Defines colors by their red, green, and blue components. RGB is typically used for defining colors displayed on screen because these are the phosphor colors used in monitors.
CMYK	Defines colors by their cyan, magenta, yellow, and black components. CMYK is typically used to define colors for printing because these are the ink colors used in most printers and presses.
LAB	Defines colors by a luminance (brightness) component and by two chromatic components (green-to-red balance and blue-to-yellow balance). LAB color is typically used for displaying colors on a monitor and for color-management software because it has a wide gamut and is not defined based on any specific device.

Process Colors and Printing

The RGB and LAB color models can create much brighter colors than can be printed with CMYK inks because the CMYK color model has a narrower gamut or range of reproducible colors. If you are choosing colors that will only be viewed on screen, such as for documents created for distribution on the Internet, then you can safely use these models. However, for printing, you should generally use CMYK. If you select a LAB or RGB color that is not reproducible by the CMYK color model for printing, the **COLOR** panel displays an exclamation point, representing an out-of-gamut warning. You can click the exclamation point to revert the color to the closest CMYK approximation.

Spot Color

Unlike a process color, a *spot color* is printed from one premixed ink, and can reproduce colors that are outside the gamut of process colors. They are generally used to replicate a color, such as a color used in a company's logo, accurately and consistently. Ordinarily, you will select spot colors from a printed swatch book, such as the PANTONE Formula Guide. This will give you an exact idea as to how the color will look on print.

Spot Colors and Printing

Because the printing inks are independent of the color model you use to choose a color, you can define a color using the CMYK or RGB color model, but specify that it gets printed as a spot color. In general, it's not a good idea to define spot colors using the screen as a reference because the monitor, even if calibrated, will often inaccurately represent the true ink color.

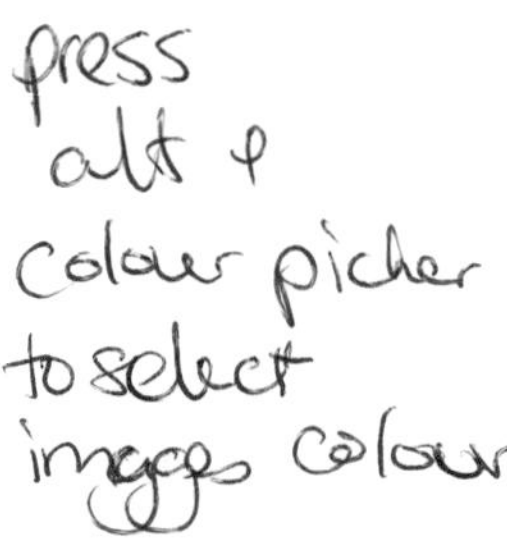

press alt & colour picker to select images colour .

The COLOR Panel

The **COLOR** panel is used to define colors using one of the three process color models: RGB, CMYK, or LAB. The colors defined using the **COLOR** panel can be added to the **SWATCHES** panel. The **COLOR** panel is used to apply color to grayscale and bitmap images and strokes. This panel is useful when unnamed colors need to be mixed.

The Color Picker

InDesign's **Color Picker** enables you to choose colors precisely and easily while simultaneously displaying the settings in RGB, LAB, and CMYK values. These settings describe a color through the various color modes. To pick and mix colors, you can select them using the color spectrum, or specify colors numerically.

Component	Description
Previous color	Displays the last color selected in the color spectrum.
Current color	Displays the color currently represented in the color spectrum.
Color spectrum	Allows selecting color and viewing from a range established by the color slider.
Color slider triangles	Controls precision color selection in the color slider by sliding the triangles up or down.
Color sliders	Controls the viewable color range in the color spectrum. Allows precision color selection and viewing by using the color slider triangles.

Swatches

Definition:

A *swatch* is a stored color definition that can be applied to any element that requires color. Swatches provide consistent and flexible color definitions that allow you to define a color once and reuse it throughout a document. When you redefine a swatch color, the elements to which you applied the color will change to match the new color.

Example:

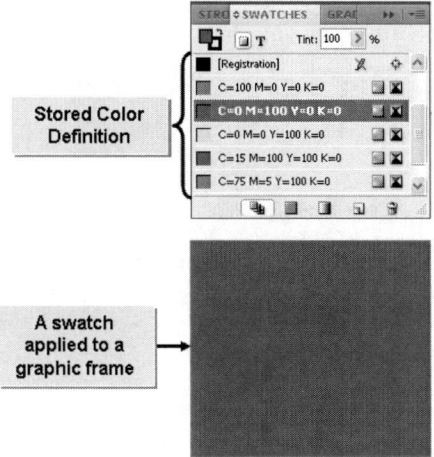

Stored Color Definition

A swatch applied to a graphic frame

The SWATCHES Panel

The **SWATCHES** panel is used to create colors, gradients, and tints, and control all colors and gradients in a document. When you use a color or gradient from the **SWATCHES** panel for a fill or stroke applied to objects in a document, the applied color is highlighted in the **SWATCHES** panel. Using this panel, you can edit, duplicate, delete, import, or save swatches from other InDesign documents. The display of swatches can also be customized in this panel.

Tint Swatches

Tints are lighter variations of colors that you define as swatches. For consistency and flexibility, you can define specific tint percentages as swatches. You can easily modify either the original color swatch on which the tint is based or the tint itself, and all the items in the document that use the tint will reflect that change.

Mixing Inks

A mixed ink is a mixture of two spot colors or a spot color with one or more process colors. Mixing inks allows you to print a number of colors with few inks. You can create a single mixed ink or a mixed ink group. A mixed ink group is used to generate multiple swatches at one time, and contains a series of colors created from incremental percentages of different spot and process colors. You can convert mixed inks to process colors to reduce the cost of printing. A minimum of one spot color should be added to the **SWATCHES** panel before creating a mixed ink.

Gradients

Definition:

A *gradient* is a combination of background colors that move from a scale of light to dark. Gradients can be created and displayed either linearly or radially. By adding gradients, you can give depth to an object or type.

Example:

Color fades from light to dark

How to Apply Color, Swatches, and Gradients

Procedure Reference: Apply Colors to Objects

To apply colors to objects:

1. Select the desired object to apply color.
2. Choose **Window→Color.**
3. From the **COLOR** panel options menu, choose a color model.
4. In the **Tools** panel, select the **Selection** tool and an object.
5. In the **COLOR** panel, click the **Fill** icon.
6. Select a color using the **COLOR** panel.
   - In the **CMYK Spectrum,** click a color.
   - Type the color percentages in the text boxes to adjust the colors.

Procedure Reference: Save Colors as Swatches

To save a color as a swatch:

1. Select the solid-colored object.
2. Choose **Window→Swatches.**
3. From the **SWATCHES** panel options menu, choose **New Color Swatch.**
4. If necessary, in the **New Color Swatch** dialog box, uncheck the **Name with Color Value** check box to enter a name for the swatch.
5. In the **Swatch Name** text box, type a name and click **OK** to save the selected object color as a swatch.

Procedure Reference: Apply Swatches

To apply a swatch:

1. Select an object to which you want to apply a swatch.
2. Choose **Window→Swatches.**
3. In the **SWATCHES** panel, select a swatch to apply the swatch color to the object.

Procedure Reference: Create Gradients

To create gradients:

1. Select an object to which you want to apply a gradient.

2. Choose **Window→Swatches.**

3. From the **SWATCHES** panel options menu, choose **New Gradient Swatch.**

4. In the **New Gradient Swatch** dialog box, in the **Swatch Name** text box, type a name for the swatch.

5. From the **Type** drop-down list, select either **Radial** or **Linear.**

6. From the **Stop Color** drop-down list, select a color type.

7. On the **Gradient Ramp** slider, click the ending color stop to define the ending color of the gradient.

8. Select a color and click **OK.**

ACTIVITY 3-2

Applying Color, Swatches, and Gradients

Data Files:

My Property Finder.indd

Before You Begin:

The My Property Finder.indd file is open.

Scenario:

You ask one of your colleague to have a look at the brochure you created. He suggests that you add some color to the brochure to make it more attractive. You are familiar with the company's colors and you want to follow the same color pattern for the brochure. You want to make sure that the colors chosen are available to you at a later point so that you can apply them easily to the other pages of the document.

What You Do	How You Do It
1. Create a color swatch.	a. Expand the **SWATCHES** panel.
	b. From the **SWATCHES** panel options menu, choose **New Color Swatch.**
	c. In the **New Color Swatch** dialog box, uncheck the **Name with Color Value** check box to enable the **Swatch Name** text box, and in the **Swatch Name** text box, type *Orange*
	d. In the **Color Type** and **Color Mode** drop-down lists, verify that **Process** and **CMYK** are selected, respectively.
	e. In the **Magenta** text box, double-click, type *40* and then press **Tab.**
	f. In the **Yellow** text box, type *100* and then press **Tab.**
	g. In the **Black** text box, type *0*
	h. Click **OK.**

2. Create a gradient swatch and modify it.

a. From the **SWATCHES** panel options menu, choose **New Gradient Swatch.**

b. In the **New Gradient Swatch** dialog box, in the **Swatch Name** text box, type *Orange Gradient*

c. From the **Type** drop-down list, select **Radial.**

d. On the **Gradient Ramp** slider, click the ending color stop to view the swatches available in the color box.

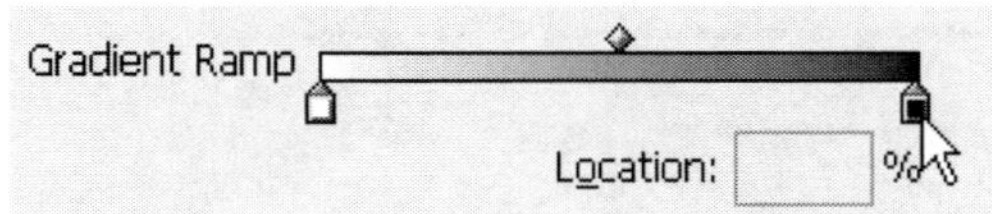

e. In the **Stop Color** section, in the color list box, scroll down, select **Orange** and then click **OK.**

f. Navigate to page 4 and scroll down.

g. Select the **Selection** tool and click in the blank space to the right of the fourth image.

h. In the **SWATCHES** panel, scroll down and select **Orange Gradient.**

i. Observe that a darker shade appears on both ends of the graphic frame.

j. From the **SWATCHES** panel options menu, choose **Swatch Options.**

k. In the **Gradient Options** dialog box, from the **Type** drop-down list, select **Linear** and click **OK.**

l. Observe the gradient.

3. Apply color to text.

a. Navigate to page 2 and select the **Type** tool.

b. Select the drop cap letter "M" from the first paragraph below the heading "The Rates Say: Buy Now!"

c. In the **SWATCHES** panel, in the color list box, select **Red.**

d. Click in the pasteboard of page 2 to deselect and view the color applied to text.

e. Save the file.

TOPIC C
Apply Fills and Strokes

You applied colors and modified color schemes used in documents. Now, you would like to add various textures to graphical elements; this is another method to highlight the contents of a document. In this topic, you will apply fills and strokes.

Not every graphic needs to be filled with a solid color. Some graphics need a border that isn't a simple line but rather a dotted line. Knowing how to apply fills, gradients, and strokes allows you to manipulate graphic elements to fit your production needs.

Fills

Definition:

A *fill* is a background color used within a graphic or text placeholder. A fill can be a solid color or a gradient.

Example:

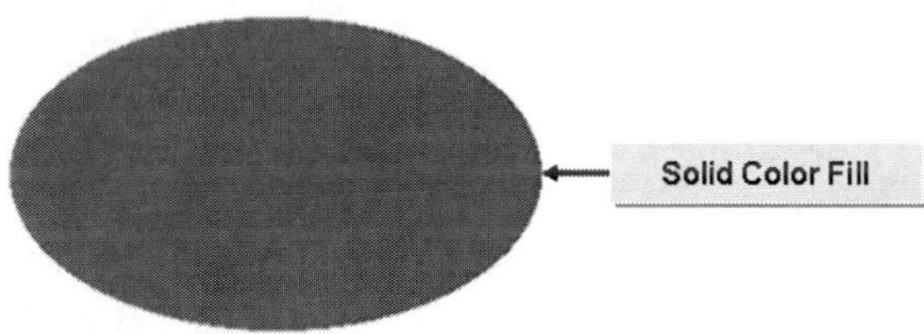

Strokes

Definition:

A *stroke* is the line that acts as a boundary for the outer perimeter of a graphic or text frame. Strokes can take many shapes, including solid or dashed lines, wavy lines, slanted lines, and dots. You can control the weight and appearance of a stroke.

Example:

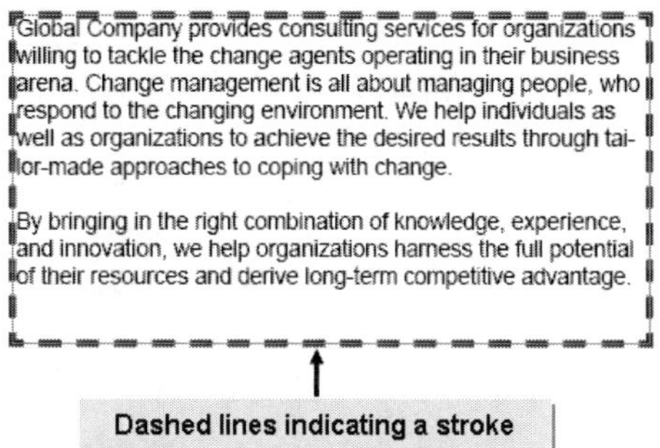

The STROKE Panel

The **STROKE** panel is used to apply stroke to an object. You can use this panel to specify the width and appearance of the stroke. You can also specify the stroke style, width, start and end shapes, and position relative to the object's path.

How to Apply Fills and Strokes

Procedure Reference: Apply Fill

To apply fill:

1. Select the text or graphic frame to which you want to apply the fill.
2. Choose **Window→Color.**
3. In the **COLOR** panel, select **Fill.**
4. In the **T** text box, type the percentage of tint or drag the slider to the desired value.

Procedure Reference: Apply Strokes

To apply strokes:

1. Select the text or graphic frame.
2. Choose **Window→Stroke.**
3. In the **STROKE** panel, select the stroke options.
    *   In the **Weight** text box, type a value to specify the weight of the stroke.
    *   In the **Miter Limit** text box, type a value to specify the limit of point length to stroke width.
    *   In the **Cap** section, select a cap style.
        *   Click the **Butt Cap** button to create squared ends of an open path.
        *   Click the **Round Cap** button to create semicircular ends that extend beyond the endpoints by half the stroke width.
        *   Click the **Projecting Cap** button to create squared ends that extend beyond the endpoints by half the stroke width.
    *   In the **Join** section, select a join style.
        *   Click the **Miter Join** button when the miter's length is within the miter limit to create pointed corners that extend beyond the endpoint.
        *   Click the **Round Join** button to create rounded corners that extend beyond the endpoints by half the stroke width.
        *   Click the **Bevel Join** button to create squared corners about the endpoints.
    *   In the **Align Stroke** section, select the desired align stroke option to specify the position of the stroke in relevance to its path.
    *   From the **Type** drop-down list, select a stroke type.
    *   From the **Start** drop-down list, select the desired beginning of a path.
    *   From the **End** drop-down list, select the desired end of a path.
    *   From the **Gap Color** drop-down list, select the color that appears in the space between lines, dashes or dots in a patterned stroke.
    *   In the **Gap Tint** slider, drag the slider to specify the percentage of tint to be applied.

ACTIVITY 3-3

Applying Fills and Strokes

Data Files:

My Property Finder.indd

Before You Begin:

1. The My Property Finder.indd file is open.

2. Choose **View→Fit Page in Window.**

Scenario:

You look at a few other brochures created for the OGC Real Estate company and notice that they use strokes in order to enhance the visual appeal of the documents. You decide to highlight the address of the company included in the document using strokes that are stylish. You believe this will enhance the visual appeal of the brochure and also make it consistent with the other brochures that have been created for your company.

What You Do	How You Do It
1. Fill the graphic frame with color.	a. Select the **Selection** tool and select the rectangle appearing at the right edge of the page.

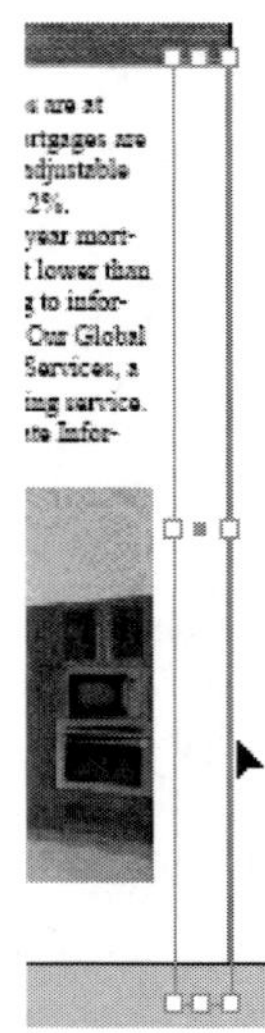

	b. In the **SWATCHES** panel, in the color list box, scroll down and select **Orange.**
	c. Choose **Window→Color.**
	d. In the **COLOR** panel, in the **T** text box, type *60* and press **Enter.**
	e. Close the **COLOR** panel.
2. Apply strokes.	a. Navigate to page 4 and expand the **STROKE** panel.
	b. Select the image at the bottom of the page.
	c. In the **STROKE** panel, in the **Weight** text box, select, type *5* and press **Enter.**
	d. From the **Type** drop-down list, select **Thin - Thick.**
	e. From the **Gap Color** drop-down list, select **Red.**
	f. Expand the **SWATCHES** panel.

g. In the **SWATCHES** panel, click the **Stroke** icon.

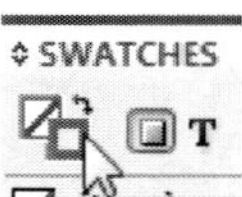

h. Select **Black.**

3. View the stroke applied to the image.

a. Select the **Zoom** tool.

b. Click the selected image twice.

c. Observe that the effect of the stroke style along the corners of the image appears in black and red.

d. On the Application bar, from the **Zoom Level** drop-down list, select **75%.**

e. Save the file.

TOPIC D
Create and Apply Styles

To make a selection stand out from the remaining text, you formatted characters and paragraphs. However, to render readability, you would like to maintain the same look and feel across multiple elements of the same document. In this topic, you will create and apply styles.

When creating official documents, you may want to apply specific design and typographical changes to them. Instead of accessing the options from across different panels, InDesign enables you to produce the desired output by creating styles. Styles help you quickly achieve consistent and customized design and formatting effects.

Styles

Definition:

A *style* is a user-specified factor that can be consistently applied across multiple page elements. You can specify a variety of attributes in a single style. Once created, a style can be applied to any page element that accepts it. Styles can be edited anytime, and objects using a style will reflect the changes made to that style.

Styles that can be applied to specific ranges of text within a paragraph are called *nested styles*. You can apply a sequence of character styles within a paragraph. This sequence can be repeated, and is called nested style looping.

Example:

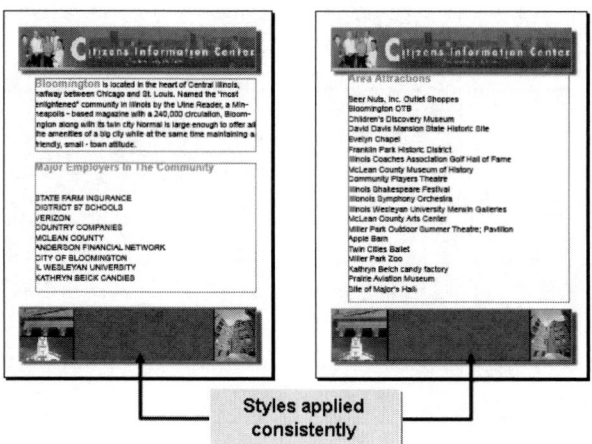

Styles applied consistently

PARAGRAPH STYLE and CHARACTER STYLE Panels

The **PARAGRAPH STYLES** panel and **CHARACTER STYLES** panel provide a collection of formatting attributes that can be created and applied to text. InDesign allows you to import paragraph and character styles from another document into the active document. A set of related styles can be grouped into separate folders in the **PARAGRAPH STYLES** panel and the **CHARACTER STYLES** panel.

Object Style Options

The options in the **OBJECT STYLES** panel are used to create, edit, save, and apply object styles to objects in an InDesign document. The text frame icon in the **OBJECT STYLES** panel marks the default style for text frames, and the graphics frame icon marks the default style for graphic frames and drawn shapes.

Quick Apply

The **Quick Apply** feature prevents you from opening various panels every time you want to apply a style. InDesign gives you the flexibility to quickly and efficiently use any menu commands, styles, or text variables by typing part of the style name in the **Quick Apply** text box. You can narrow down the search to a single category by typing the appropriate prefixes for the menu commands, styles, and text variables.

How to Create and Apply Styles

Procedure Reference: Create a Character Style

To create a character style:

1. Choose **Window→Type & Tables→Character Styles.**
2. Create a new character style.
   - In the **CHARACTER STYLES** panel, select a character style group, right-click, and choose **New Character Style.**
   - Or, from the **CHARACTER STYLES** panel options menu, choose **New Character Style.**
3. In the **New Character Style** dialog box, on the **General** tab, in the **Style Name** text box, type the desired name.
4. If necessary, adjust the other available options that include **Basic Character Formats, Advanced Character Formats, Character Color, Open Type Features, Underline Options,** and **Strikethrough Options.**
5. Click **OK.**
6. Apply a character style.
   a. Select the text.
   b. In the **CHARACTER STYLES** panel, select a style to apply it.

Procedure Reference: Create a Character Style Group

To create a character style group:

1. Choose **Window→Type & Tables→Character Styles.**

2. Create a new style group.

- In the **CHARACTER STYLES** panel, click the **Create new style group** button.
- Or, from the **CHARACTER STYLES** panel options menu, choose **New Style Group** and in the **New Style Group** dialog box, in the **Name** text box, type a name and then click **OK.**

Procedure Reference: Create a Paragraph Style

To create a paragraph style:

1. Choose **Window→Type & Tables→Paragraph Styles.**
2. Create a new paragraph style.

- Select a style group, right-click and then choose **New Paragraph Style.**
- Or, from the **PARAGRAPH STYLES** panel options menu, choose **New Paragraph Style.**

3. In the **New Paragraph Style** dialog box, on the **General** tab, in the **Style Name** text box, type a name.
4. If necessary, adjust the other available options that include **General, Basic Character Formats, Advanced Character Formats, Indents and Spacing, Tabs, Paragraph Rules, Keep Options, Hyphenation, Justification, Drop Caps and Nested Styles, GREP Style, Bullets and Numbering, Character Color, OpenType Features, Underline Options,** and **Strikethrough Options.**
5. Click **OK.**
6. Apply the paragraph style.

- Apply the paragraph style using the **PARAGRAPH STYLES** panel.
   a. Select the text.
   b. In the **PARAGRAPH STYLES** panel, select a style to apply it.
- Apply the paragraph style using the **Quick Apply** command.
   a. Select the text.
   b. Choose **Edit→Quick Apply.**
   c. In the **Quick Apply** dialog box, in the text box, type the name of the style.
   d. Click the style to apply it to the selected text.

Procedure Reference: Create a Paragraph Style Group

To create a paragraph style group:

1. Choose **Window→Type & Tables→Paragraph Styles.**
2. From the **PARAGRAPH STYLES** panel options menu, choose **New Style Group.**
3. In the **New Style Group** dialog box, in the **Name** text box, type a name and click **OK.**

Procedure Reference: Create and Apply an Object Style

To create and apply an object style:

1. Choose **Windows→Object Styles.**
2. From the **OBJECT STYLES** panel options menu, choose **New Object Style.**
3. In the **New Object Style** dialog box, in the **Style Name** text box, type a name.
4. In the **Basic Attributes** section, specify the settings.

5. From the **Effects for** drop-down list, select the part of the object to which you want to apply the effects.

    ● Select **Object** to fill the entire object.

    ● Select **Stroke** to apply the effect to the object.

    ● Select **Fill** to apply the effect to the object.

    ● Select **Text** to apply the effect to the text in a frame.

6. In the list box below the **Effects for** drop-down list, select the effect.

7. In the right pane, set the settings according to the effects chosen from the **Effects for** drop-down list.

8. Click **OK.**

9. In the **OBJECT STYLES** panel, select an object style to apply the style.

Access Menus Using Quick Apply

You can also access menu commands by using the **Quick Apply** command. In the **Quick Apply** dialog box, you can type the name of the command and double-click the command to activate it.

ACTIVITY 3-4

Creating and Applying Styles

Data Files:

My Property Finder.indd

Before You Begin:

The My Property Finder.indd file is open.

Scenario:

You notice that the subheadings within the text of the brochure need to be formatted. You also want to maintain a consistent format for the text and subheadings throughout the document. Instead of formatting the text and subheadings individually, you decide to create a style and apply it to the rest of the document thereby saving time and effort. Also, you received a formatted InDesign document and want to reuse the style instead of creating it.

What You Do	How You Do It
1. Create paragraph styles and apply them to the subheadings.	a. Navigate to page 2 and select the **Type** tool.
	b. Click the heading **"The Rates Say: Buy Now!"**
	c. Expand the **PARAGRAPH STYLES** panel.
	d. From the **PARAGRAPH STYLES** panel options menu, choose **New Paragraph Style.**
	e. In the **New Paragraph Style** dialog box, in the **Style Name** text box, type *Header*
	f. In the left pane, select **Indents and Spacing.**
	g. In the **Space Before** text box, select the value and type *0.25*
	h. In the left pane, select **Character Color.**
	i. In the **Character Color** section, in the color list box, select **Red** and click **OK.**
	j. In the **PARAGRAPH STYLES** panel, in the styles that are listed, select **Header.**
	k. Observe that the color of the text has changed to red.
	l. Navigate to page 3 and click the header text **"Experts at Your Service."**
	m. In the **PARAGRAPH STYLES** panel, in the styles that are listed, select **Header.**

2.	Create paragraph styles and apply them to the paragraphs.	a.	On page 2, click the second paragraph under the heading "The Rates Say: Buy Now!"
		b.	From the **PARAGRAPH STYLES** panel options menu, choose **New Paragraph Style.**
		c.	In the **New Paragraph Style** dialog box, in the **General** section, in the **Style Name** text box, type *Para Indent*
		d.	In the left pane, select **Indents and Spacing.**
		e.	In the **Indents and Spacing** section, in the **First Line Indent** text box, select the value and type *0.25*
		f.	In the **Space After** text box, verify that **0.084 in** is displayed and click **OK.**
		g.	Hold down **Shift** and click at the end of the last paragraph on page 3.
		h.	In the **PARAGRAPH STYLES** panel, in the styles that are listed, select **Para Indent.**
		i.	Click in the pasteboard of page 2 to view the style applied.
3.	Create and apply character styles.	a.	Expand the **CHARACTER STYLES** panel.
		b.	From the **CHARACTER STYLES** panel options menu, choose **New Character Style.**
		c.	In the **New Character Style** dialog box, in the **General** section, in the **Style Name** text box, type *Blue Bold*
		d.	In the left pane, select **Basic Character Formats.**
		e.	In the **Basic Character Formats** section, from the **Font Style** drop-down list, select **Bold.**
		f.	In the left pane, select **Character Color.**
		g.	In the **Character Color** section, from the color list box, select **Blue** and click **OK.**

4. Create and apply object styles.

   a. Navigate to page 4.

   b. Using the **Selection** tool, select the image that is at the bottom of the page.

   c. Choose **Window→Object Styles.**

   d. From the **OBJECT STYLES** panel options menu, choose **New Object Style.**

   e. In the **New Object Style** dialog box, in the **Style Name** text box, type *Border* and click **OK.**

   f. Select the first three images on the page.

   g. In the **Control** panel, click the **Quick Apply** button.

   h. In the **Quick Apply** dialog box, in the list box, select **Border.**

   i. Close the **OBJECT STYLES** panel and collapse the **CHARACTER STYLES** panel.

   j. Save and close the file.

OPTIONAL ACTIVITY 3-5
Modifying Styles

Data Files:

Property Finder.indd

Before You Begin:

Open the Property Finder.indd file.

Scenario:

In a newsletter, you formatted the title text and now the body text and the subheadings within the body require formatting. After some manual formatting in the newsletter, you want to load styles from a different InDesign document and save the formatting in style sheets to use them throughout the newsletter to make your work faster and consistent. You also want to highlight the website address of the company.

What You Do	How You Do It
1. Load styles from another InDesign document and apply them.	a. Expand the **PARAGRAPH STYLE** panel.
	b. From the **PARAGRAPH STYLE** panel options menu, choose **Load All Text Styles.**
	c. In the **Open a file** dialog box, select **Import Style.indd** and click **Open.**
	d. In the **Load Styles** dialog box, click **OK.**
	e. Observe that in the **PARAGRAPH STYLES** panel, more paragraph styles are added.
	f. Using the **Type** tool, click the heading text **"A Corporate Division."**
	g. In the **PARAGRAPH STYLES** panel, in the styles that are listed, select **Div_Head.**
	h. Observe that the paragraph styles are applied.
	i. Select the text under the heading "A Corporate Division" and in the **PARAGRAPH STYLES** panel, in the styles that are listed, select **Div_Para.**
	j. Click the heading text, **"Our New Website"** and in the **PARAGRAPH STYLES** panel, in the styles that are listed, select **Div_Head.**
2. Apply character styles to the text "Buy Now!"	a. Navigate to page 2.
	b. In the heading text "Rates Say: Buy Now!" select the text **"Buy Now!"**
	c. In the **Control** panel, click the **Quick Apply** button, and in the **Quick Apply** dialog box, select **Blue Bold.**
	d. Select the letter **"M"** in the first paragraph under the heading text "The Rates Say: Buy Now!" and apply the same character style.
	e. Deselect the letter "M."
	f. Observe the changes on the page.

3. Modify a style.

   a. Navigate to page 4.

   b. In the **PARAGRAPH STYLES** panel, right-click **Div_Head** and choose **Edit "Div_ Head"**.

   c. In the **Paragraph Style Options** dialog box, in the left pane, click **Character Color.**

   d. In the **Character Color** section, in the color list box, select blue that is above the yellow swatch and click **OK.**

   e. Observe that the changes are made to the styles applied.

4. Apply styles using the **Quick Apply** dialog box.

   a. Under the heading text "Our New Website," in the last line of the paragraph, select the website address "www.ourglobalcompany.com."

   b. In the **Control** panel, click the **Quick Apply** button.

   c. In the **Quick Apply** dialog box, in the text box, type *w*

   d. In the list of paragraph styles that are listed, select **Web_Add.**

   e. Click in the pasteboard of page 4 to view the changes.

   f. Save the file as *My Property Finder.indd*

Lesson 3 Follow-up

In this lesson, you enhanced documents. This allowed you to enrich the look and feel of the documents and make them more appealing to the users.

1. **How will you deploy the various types of styles in your upcoming projects?**

2. **Where can you utilize gradients to emphasize particular graphics in your current project?**

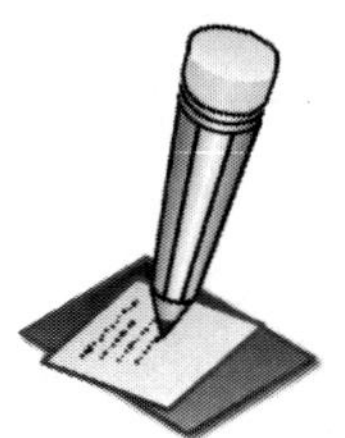

4 Working with Page Elements

Lesson Time: 1 hour(s), 20 minutes

Lesson Objectives:

In this lesson, you will work with page elements.

You will:

- Arrange objects.
- Align objects.
- Manage page elements with layers.
- Set up pages.

Introduction

You created text and graphical elements in documents. You may now want to finalize the layout by formatting and repositioning various objects in the document. In this lesson, you will work with page elements.

Deploying various types of page elements becomes inevitable when you have to create appealing documents. Being able to apply the advanced techniques used to manage these elements will enable you to present content neatly and creatively.

TOPIC A
Arrange Objects

You created and applied styles to achieve consistent formatting. You may now want to arrange objects in the document so that the document is visually appealing and does not look cluttered. In this topic, you will arrange objects.

In advertisements or brochures, different shapes appear along with text. If these objects are disorderly, the reader will lose interest. By understanding the various methods to arrange objects, you can create your own unique project that is appealing to the reader.

Arrangement Commands

The arrangement commands are used to place numerous elements of an object in an ordered manner for efficient utilization. The **Bring to Front** and **Send to Back** commands move an object to the front and back of a stack, respectively. The **Bring Forward** and **Send Backward** commands move an object forward and backward, respectively, one object away from it in a stack.

Stacking Order

Stacking is the process of grouping objects. In a stack, overlapping objects are arranged in the order in which they are created or imported. Each named layer has a separate stack of objects, and the arrangement commands control the order only within each named layer. If there are no named layers, a document will contain just one stack of objects on its single default layer. Objects on masters exist at the back of each named layer. If objects are grouped, the stacking order will change.

Master Page

A master page is created in situations where you need to include common elements on different pages in a document. The elements included on the master page will be incorporated in all document pages to which the master is applied.

How to Arrange Objects

Procedure Reference: Change the Stacking Order

To change the stacking order:

1. Select the object you want to move.
2. Choose **Object→Arrange** and then choose a command.
   - Choose **Bring to Front** to move the object to the front of a stack.
   - Choose **Bring Forward** to move the object forward, past the next object in a stack.
   - Choose **Send Backward** to move the object backward, past the next object in a stack.
   - Choose **Send to Back** to move the object to the back of a stack.

Procedure Reference: Lock the Position of an Object

To lock the position of an object:

1. Select the object you want to lock.
2. Choose **Object→Lock Position.**
3. Save the file.

ACTIVITY 4-1

Arranging Objects

Data Files:

Property Finder.indd

Before You Begin:

1. From the C:\084048Data\Working with Page Elements folder, open the Property Finder.indd file.

2. Navigate to page 2.

Scenario:

After enhancing documents, you decide to review the formatting pattern of the brochure and check the relevance of the enhanced attributes. You review the document, and notice that the graphic frame overlaps with a portion of the text frame. Also, the placement of objects in the brochure are not stacked properly. You feel that the objects need to be organized and arranged appropriately in the brochure.

What You Do	How You Do It
1. Change the stacking order of the objects.	a. Select the text frame of the quote.
	b. From the **Zoom Level** drop-down list, select **150%.**
	c. Choose **Object→Arrange→Bring to Front.**
	d. Expand the **CHARACTER** panel.
	e. In the **CHARACTER** panel, in the font name drop-down list, verify that **Times New Roman** is selected, and in the font style drop-down list, verify that **Regular** is selected.
	f. In the **Font Size** text box, select the value, type *21* and then press **Tab.**
	g. In the **Leading** text box, type *26* and then press **Enter.**

2. Format the text.

a. Select the **Type** tool and double-click before the opening quotation mark of the quote.

b. In the **CHARACTER** panel, in the **Font Size** text box, select the value, type *66* and then press **Enter.**

c. In the **Tracking** text box, double-click, type *-20* and then press **Enter.**

d. In the **Baseline Shift** text box, select the value, type *-25* and then press **Enter.**

e. Apply the same formatting to the closing quotation mark of the quote.

f. Select the hyphen and the text **"George Moore."**

g. In the **CHARACTER** panel, from the **Font Style** drop-down list, select **Italic.**

h. In the **Font Size** text box, select the value, type *18* and then press **Tab.**

i. In the **Leading** text box, type *21* and then press **Enter.**

j. Expand the **PARAGRAPH** panel.

k. In the **PARAGRAPH** panel, click the **Justify with last line aligned right** button, which is the fourth button from the right.

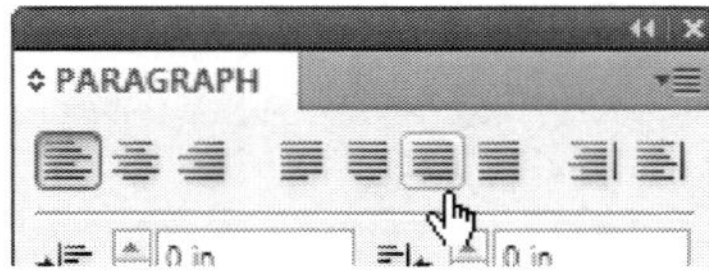

l. Collapse the **PARAGRAPH** panel.

m. Observe that the text "George Moore" is right aligned, and select the **Selection** tool.

n. Verify that the quotation text frame is selected.

o. In the **Control** panel, in the **Y** text box, select the value, type *0.9375* and then press **Enter.**

3. Apply color to the text.

a. Double-click before the open quotation mark.

b. Choose **Edit→Select All**.

c. Expand the **SWATCHES** panel.

d. In the **SWATCHES** panel, verify that the **Fill** icon is activated.

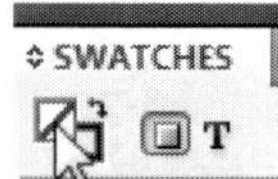

e. In the color list box, scroll up and select **[Paper]**.

f. Deselect the text.

g. Collapse the **SWATCHES** panel.

h. Save the file as *My Property Finder.indd*

TOPIC B

Align Objects

You arranged objects in the document to make it appealing. Now, you may need to alter the way contents or objects are lined up. In this topic, you will align objects.

After applying different formats to data, the alignment of labels and values might not be consistent. Applying consistent alignment to a page gives it a neat and professional appearance, which makes data easier to comprehend.

Guides

Guides indicate the position of margins and other areas of a page. They can be moved and positioned as needed. Guides are visible on the screen to help align elements on document pages.

There are three types of guides. *Page guides* appear only on the page they are created. *Spread guides* appear across all pages of a multiple-page spread. Smart guides make it easier to snap objects to items in a layout. You can set the options for smart guides in the **Preferences** dialog box. By default, smart guides are enabled when the InDesign application is launched.

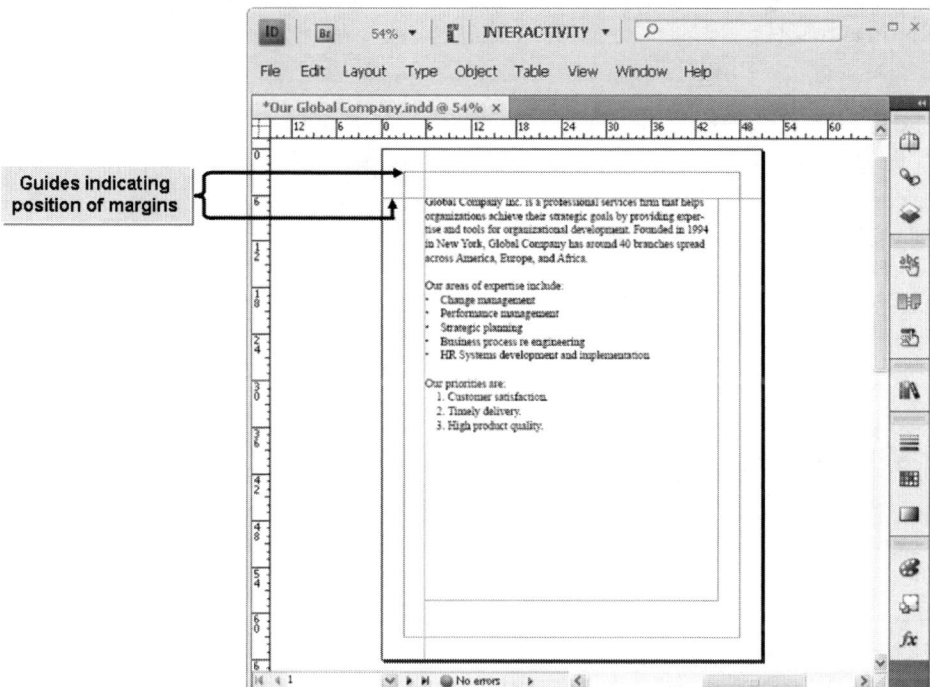

Figure 4-1: Guides indicating the position of margins on a page.

Smart Guides

Smart guides are temporary snap-to guides that help you create, align, edit, and transform objects relative to other objects. You can set the preferences to specify the type of smart guides and feedback.

Grids

A *grid* is an on-screen alignment tool that can be used to align objects or columns of text. Grids are of two types. *Baseline grids* are used to align columns of text. *Document grids* are used to align objects. You can customize the color and spacing increments of both types of grids. Grids cannot be moved or positioned on-screen, nor can they be printed. You can hide or display the grids whenever required.

The ALIGN Panel

The **ALIGN** panel can be used to evenly distribute space between the objects and align objects in relation to one another. You can distribute objects horizontally or vertically along selections, margins, pages, or spreads. However, aligned text paragraphs that are locked using the **Lock** command will not be affected by the settings specified in the **ALIGN** panel.

How to Align Objects

Procedure Reference: Customize the Unit of Measurement and Increments

To customize the unit of measurement and increments:

1. Choose **View→Show Rulers.**
2. Choose **Edit→Preferences→Units & Increments.**
3. In the **Preferences** dialog box, on the **Units & Increments** tab, specify the settings.
   - In the **Ruler Units** section, specify the settings.
     - From the **Origin** drop-down list, select an origin.
     - From the **Horizontal** drop-down list, specify a unit of measurement.
     - From the **Vertical** drop-down list, specify a unit of measurement.
   - In the **Points/Pica Size** section, from the **Points/Pica Size** drop-down list, select either **PostScript (72 pts/inch)** or **Traditional (72.27 pts/inch).**
   - In the **Keyboard Increments** section, specify the settings.
     - In the **Cursor Key** text box, type a value to adjust the movement of the selected objects each time an arrow key is pressed.
     - In the **Size/Leading** text box, type a value to adjust the vertical space between two consecutive lines.
     - In the **Baseline Shift** text box, type a value to adjust the character up or down relative to the baseline of the surrounding text.
     - In the **Kerning/Tracking** text box, type a value to adjust the space between characters and text.
4. Click **OK.**

Procedure Reference: Align Objects Using Guides

To align objects using guides:

1. Click the vertical or horizontal ruler bar and drag it to the location where you want the guide to appear.
2. If necessary, include more guides in the document.
3. Select an image or text.
4. Drag the image or text to a location using the guide.

Procedure Reference: Align Images Using the ALIGN Panel

To align images using the **ALIGN** panel:

1. Choose **Window→Object & Layout→Align** to display the **ALIGN** panel.

2. Select an image to align it.

3. In the **ALIGN** panel, specify the settings for the objects.

   - In the **Align Objects** section, perform the necessary action.

     ■ Click the **Align left edges** button to align the selected objects based on the left edges of the objects.

     ■ Click the **Align horizontal centers** button to align the selected objects based on the horizontal centers of the objects.

     ■ Click the **Align right edges** button to align the selected objects based on the right edges of the objects.

     ■ Click the **Align top edges** button to align the selected objects based on the top edges of the objects.

     ■ Click the **Align vertical centers** button to align the selected objects based on the vertical centers of the objects.

     ■ Click the **Align bottom edges** button to align the selected objects based on the bottom edges of the objects.

   - In the **Distribute Objects** section, specify the settings for distributing objects.

     ■ Select **Distribute top edges** to apply vertical distribution evenly among the top edges of the objects.

     ■ Select **Distribute vertical centers** to apply vertical distribution evenly among the centers of the objects.

     ■ Select **Distribute bottom edges** to apply vertical distribution evenly among the bottom edges of the objects.

     ■ Select **Distribute left edges** to apply horizontal distribution evenly among the left edges of the objects.

     ■ Select **Distribute horizontal centers** to apply horizontal distribution evenly among the centers of the objects.

     ■ Select **Distribute right edges** to apply horizontal distribution evenly among the right edges of the objects.

     ■ Check the **Use Spacing** check box and specify a value in the text box.

   - In the **Distribute Spacing** section, specify the settings for the space between objects.

     ■ Select **Distribute vertical space** to align the vertical spacing among images evenly.

     ■ Select **Distribute horizontal space** to align the horizontal spacing among images evenly.

     ■ Check the **Use Spacing** check box, and in the text box, specify the amount of spacing.

4. Close the **ALIGN** panel.

ACTIVITY 4-2

Aligning Objects

Data Files:

My Property Finder.indd

Before You Begin:

1. The My Property Finder.indd file is open.

2. From the **Zoom Level** drop-down list, select **75%**.

Scenario:

After reviewing the brochure, you notice that the objects in the brochure are not aligned properly. You decide to use rulers and guides to align the objects to give a symmetric look to the document.

What You Do	How You Do It
1. Align the image of the agent on page 4.	a. Navigate to page 4.
	b. Click and drag the vertical ruler to the right edge of the third image from the top.
	c. Scroll down, click and drag the horizontal ruler to the 10.5-inch mark on the vertical ruler.
	d. Select the **Selection** tool.
	e. Click and drag the fourth image and place it so that the bottom and right sides of the image are in alignment with the horizontal and vertical guides.
	f. Click and drag the horizontal ruler to the 2.5-inch mark on the vertical ruler.
	g. Click and drag the first image from the top and place it so that the bottom and right sides of the image are in alignment with the horizontal and vertical guides.
	h. Observe that the images and text are symmetrically aligned.

2. Align the three images located towards the right margin of page 3.

a. Navigate to page 3.

b. Expand the **ALIGN** panel.

c. Select the first image that is located at the top-right of the page.

d. Hold down **Shift,** select the image that is at the bottom-right of the selected image, and select the image at the bottom of the page.

e. In the **ALIGN** panel, in the **Align Objects** section, click the **Align right edges** button.

f. In the **Distribute Spacing** section, click the **Distribute vertical space** button, to evenly distribute available space among the selected images evenly.

g. Click outside the document to deselect the selected images.

h. Observe that all the selected images are aligned along the right edge of the document.

i. Save the file.

TOPIC C
Manage Page Elements with Layers

You aligned objects in documents. Now you need to make sure that the objects do not overlap on a single page. In this topic, you will manage page elements with layers.

Well-designed publications frequently use many overlapping graphic and text elements. The more complex a design, the more difficult it is to select and manipulate what you want without accidentally changing something else. You can alleviate this problem by using layers, which allow you to selectively hide or lock items so that they temporarily cannot be viewed or edited.

Layers

Definition:

Layers are transparent elements of a document that are stacked. You can place graphics and text on layers. Layers can be used to display alternate design ideas for the same layout, because you can hide one transparent sheet and view the other sheets. Individual layers can be edited, relocated, or deleted without affecting other layers.

Example:

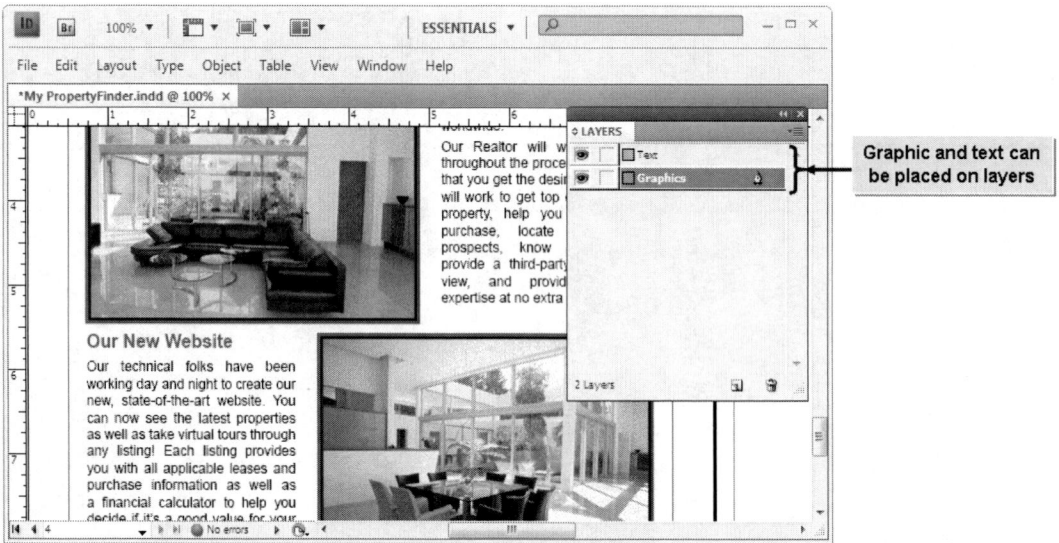

Graphic and text can be placed on layers

The LAYERS Panel

The **LAYERS** panel displays the layers that are used in a document. The layers in this panel are listed with the first layer appearing at the top of the panel. You can create, duplicate, delete, hide, lock, and merge layers, and specify options that determine how layers are displayed and printed. You can change the stacking order of layers and move objects from one layer to another. When a layer is created, the name of the layer by default is **Layer 1.** However, you can change the name of the layer as needed.

Flattening

Flattening is the act of merging the artwork in a document into a single, printable layer. During flattening, InDesign identifies areas where transparent objects overlap other objects and divides the objects into components.

How to Manage Page Elements with Layers

Procedure Reference: Create Layers

To create layers:

1. Choose **Window→Layers.**
2. From the **LAYERS** panel options menu, choose **New Layer** or click the **Create new layer** button, and double-click the created layer to open the **New Layer** dialog box.
3. In the **New Layer** dialog box, specify the settings.
   - In the **Name** text box, type a name.
   - From the **Color** drop-down list, select a color for the layer.
   - Check the **Show Layer** check box to make the layer visible.
   - Check the **Show Guides** check box to display the guides.
   - Check the **Lock Layer** check box to prevent changes to any object in the layer.
   - Check the **Lock Guides** check box to prevent changes to the guides.
   - Check the **Print Layer** check box to make the layer available for print.
   - Check the **Suppress Text Wrap When Layer is Hidden** check box to suppress the text wrap and allow the text in the other layers to flow normally when the layer is hidden.
4. If necessary, rename a layer.
   - In the **LAYERS** panel, double-click the name of the layer and type a name.
   - From the **LAYERS** panel options menu, choose **Layer Options for "<Layer Name>"** and in the **Layer Options** dialog box, in the **Name** text box, type a name and click **OK.**
5. If necessary, rearrange the layers by dragging a layer above or below another layer.
6. If necessary, click the **Toggles Visibility** icon to show or hide the layer, or click the **Toggles Lock** icon to lock or unlock a layer.

Procedure Reference: Merge Layers

To merge layers:

1. In the **LAYERS** panel, select a layer.
2. Press **Ctrl** and select the layers to be merged.

3. From the **LAYERS** panel options menu, choose **Merge Layers** to merge the layers.

 You can flatten a document by merging all the layers in the document.

Procedure Reference: Make a Copy of Objects on Layers

To make a copy of objects on layers:

1. In the **Tools** panel, select the **Selection** tool and select the object.
2. Press **Alt** and in the **LAYERS** panel, drag the colored square on the right side of the layer to a layer to make a copy.

ACTIVITY 4-3

Managing Page Elements with Layers

Data Files:

My Property Finder.indd

Before You Begin:

The My Property Finder.indd file is open.

Scenario:

You aligned the image appropriately in the brochure. You notice that, in this document, you need to handle the layout of multiple objects. Now, you decide to create and position a layer based on the needs of the document. In addition, you want to change the name and color of the layer.

What You Do	How You Do It
1. Rename **Layer 1** as *Text* and assign a color.	a. Expand the **LAYERS** panel.
	b. From the **LAYERS** panel options menu, choose **Layer Options for "Layer 1"**.
	c. In the **Layer Options** dialog box, in the **Name** text box, type *Text*
	d. From the **Color** drop-down list, select **Green** and click **OK**.

2. Create two layers and assign colors to them.

   a. From the **LAYERS** panel options menu, choose **New Layer.**

   b. In the **New Layer** dialog box, in the **Name** text box, type *Background*

   c. From the **Color** drop-down list, select **Red** and click **OK.**

   d. In the **LAYERS** panel, click the **Create new layer** button.

   e. Double-click **Layer 3.**

   f. In the **Layer Options** dialog box, in the **Name** text box, type *Images*

   g. From the **Color** drop-down list, select **Magenta** and click **OK.**

   h. Select the **Text** layer and drag it above the **Images** layer.

3. Organize the images in the brochure and place them in the **Images** layer.

    a. Navigate to page 1 and select the cover page image.

    b. In the **LAYERS** panel, observe that the **Text** layer is selected, and that the **Indicates selected items** icon, which is a small green square box that appears beside the pen icon, is displayed indicating that the cover page image is in that layer.

    c. Observe that the graphic frame on which the cover page is placed is in green.

    d. Drag the **Indicates selected items** icon to the **Images** layer.

    e. Observe that the color of the graphic frame has turned to magenta, indicating that the cover page image is transferred to the **Images** layer.

    f. Navigate to page 2 and select the four images.

    g. Drag the **Indicates selected items** icon in the **Text** layer to the **Images** layer.

    h. Similarly, place the images on pages 3 and 4 in the **Images** layer.

4. Organize the background images in the brochure and place them in the **Background** layer.

a. On page 4, select the graphic frame to which the gradient is applied.

b. Drag the **Indicates selected items** icon in the **Text** layer to the **Background** layer.

c. Observe that the color of the graphic frame changes to red, indicating that the background image is moved to the **Background** layer.

d. On page 2, select the graphic frame to which the fill is applied and move it to the **Background** layer.

e. In the **Control** panel, click the top-left reference point.

f. In the **Control** panel, specify the following values:

- X–2.9514
- Y–5.125
- W–5.5417
- H–5.875

5. Lock the **Images** layer.

a. Select the image at the top of page 2.

b. In the **Control** panel, observe that all the options are enabled, indicating that the image is editable.

c. In the **LAYERS** panel, click the box to the right of the eye icon of the **Images** layer.

d. In the **Control** panel, observe that all the options are disabled, indicating that the image is not editable.

e. Save the file.

TOPIC D
Set Up Pages

You managed page elements with layers. Based on the output and rough sketches of the objects on the pages, you need to set up pages to ensure that your work will go smoothly. In this topic, you will set up pages.

Page properties, such as the dimension, background, and orientation, will change for different tasks. You might need a long page to create a brochure, whereas a short page would suffice for a certificate. Setting up the page before working on a task enables you to fit the content on the page perfectly, and enhances the document's appearance and readability.

Master Pages

Definition:

A *master page* is an InDesign document page that contains text and images, which will be reflected on multiple pages of the document. All new documents initially contain only one master page, labeled **A-Master.** Master pages can be edited like any other document page. Any change or edit made to a master page will reflect on every document page that is based on the master. Documents can have one master page or multiple master pages.

Example:

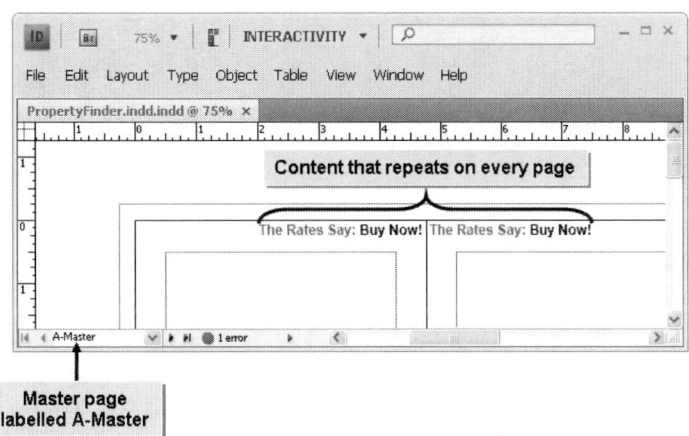

Object Stacking Order

Objects in a single layer have their own stacking order within that layer. Objects in a master page layer appear behind objects assigned to the same layer on the document page.

Text Wrap with Master Page

If you have an object with text wrap on a master page, it will affect only the text frames that are located on that master page. Text on document pages cannot wrap around master page items. You can choose the **Apply to Master Page Only** command from the **TEXT WRAP** panel options menu to wrap text only on the master page. This command functions only if it is manually enabled.

Hierarchical Master Pages

Within an InDesign document, a master page can be created on which other master pages can be based and updated. The master page on which other master pages in this document are based is called the *parent master*. The other master pages in the document are called *child masters*. This hierarchy in master pages helps to keep the design of the InDesign documents up-to-date.

Document Pages

A *document page*, a rectangular area, is used for creating and laying out text and graphical objects. It is made up of master pages and pages. Anything placed on this page can be saved or printed. The immediate area surrounding the document page, called the pasteboard, can be used to create, add, and edit objects. Anything placed on the pasteboard will not be included when the document is sent for printing; however, it will be saved as part of the document. Any change applied to the master page will be reflected in all document pages that are based on that master page. You can insert, duplicate, move, and delete document pages.

The PAGES Panel

The **PAGES** panel displays page thumbnails in various icon sizes for document pages and master pages. It allows you to navigate to pages, and while moving document pages to a new location, the **PAGES** panel automatically scrolls to pages that are out of view. You can also create a document without master pages using the **[None]** option in the **PAGES** panel. The **PAGES** panel is used to create, delete, and apply master pages to pages. In addition, you can also insert, duplicate, move, rotate, rearrange, and delete document pages.

There are different commands on the **PAGES** panel options menu.

Command	Used To
Apply Master to Pages	Apply a master to multiple pages.
Load Master Pages	Import master pages from another InDesign document into the current document.
Override All Master Page Items	Place a copy of a master item on the document page without breaking its link with the master page.
Detach All Objects from Master	Break the link of objects with their master page. The objects must be overridden on the document page before detaching the objects from their master page.

How to Set Up Pages

Procedure Reference: Develop Master Pages

To develop master pages:

1. Choose **Window→Pages.**
2. In the **PAGES** panel, right-click a page and choose **Save as Master** to save the page as a master page.
3. Select and right-click the master page, and then choose **Apply Master to Pages** to apply the master pages to other pages.
4. In the **Apply Master** dialog box, specify the settings.
   - From the **Apply Master** drop-down list, specify a master to apply it to the document.
   - In the **To Pages** text box, type a page number.
5. Click **OK** to set up a master on a page.
6. If necessary, in the **Pages** panel, right-click a page and choose **Override All Master Page Items** to override the master page items.

Procedure Reference: Create Hierarchical Master Pages

To create hierarchical master pages:

1. In the **PAGES** panel, select and right-click a master page, and then choose **Master options for "<name of the master page>-Master"** to create a child master page.
2. In the **Master Options** dialog box, from the **Based on Master** drop-down list, select the master page that will be the parent master page.
3. In the **Number of Pages** text box, type the page numbers.
4. Click **OK** to create a child master page that is based on the parent master page.

Procedure Reference: Set Header and Footer for a Master Page

To set the header and footer for a master page:

1. Choose **Window→Pages.**
2. In the **PAGES** panel, double-click **A-Master** to open the master page.
3. Select a layer in the **LAYERS** panel.
4. If necessary, use the **Reference Point** in the **Control** panel to specify the reference point.
5. Select the **Type** tool and draw a text frame on a page.
6. In the Control panel, set a value in the **X, Y, W,** and **H** text boxes.
7. Type the header or footer text in the document.

8. If necessary, in the **PARAGRAPH STYLES** panel, specify the settings.
   - Select **Basic Paragraph** to specify the document's default style for the text.
   - Select **Para Indent** to give the default space between paragraphs.
   - Select **Header** to format the spacing of the headers.
   - Select **Div_Para** to provide space between words of the entire paragraph.
   - Select **Div_Head** to provide space between words of the heading.
   - Select **RunningFoot Left** to set the footer text on the left.
   - Select **RunningHead Right** to set the header text on the right.
   - Select **RunningHead Left** to set the header text on the left.
   - Select **RunningFoot Right** to set the footer text on the right.

Procedure Reference: Modify a Master Page

To modify a master page:

1. Select the **A-Master** page.
2. From the **PAGES** panel options menu, choose **Master Options for "A-Master"**.
3. In the Master Options dialog box, specify the settings.
   - In the **Prefix** text box, type a prefix.
   - In the **Name** text box, type a name.
   - From the **Based on Master** drop-down list, specify the settings.
   - In the **Number of Pages** text box, type the page numbers.
4. Click **OK** to modify the master page.

ACTIVITY 4-4

Setting Up Pages

Data Files:

My Property Finder.indd

Before You Begin:

The My Property Finder.indd file is open.

Scenario:

You realize that the brochure you are working on has a few elements that should occur repeatedly on every page of the document. You decide to display header and footer information on all the pages of the brochure and format the content.

What You Do	How You Do It
1. Create a text frame and enter the header and footer text on the left master page.	a. Expand the **PAGES** panel.
	b. In the **PAGES** panel, in the **A-Master** section, double-click the left master page to select the left frame.
	c. Observe that **A-Master** is selected from the page selection drop-down list.
	d. Expand the **LAYERS** panel.
	e. In the **LAYERS** panel, select the **Background** layer.
	f. Select the **Type** tool.
	g. Click and drag from the point of intersection of the 1.5-inch mark on the horizontal ruler and the 1-inch mark on the vertical ruler to the point of intersection of the 4.5-inch mark on the horizontal ruler and the 4-inch mark on the vertical ruler to create a rectangular text frame on the left page.
	h. Select the **Selection** tool to display the new text frame.
	i. In the **Control** panel, in the **X** text box, select the value, type *0.5* and then press **Tab.**
	j. In the **Y** text box, type *0.08* and press **Enter.**
	k. Specify the values in the **W** and **H** text boxes as *7.5* and *0.35* respectively.
	l. Press **Page Up** and select the **Type** tool.
	m. Select the text frame located at the top of the page.
	n. Type *The Rates Say: Buy Now!*

2. Apply paragraph styles to the header and footer on the left master page.

a. Expand the **PARAGRAPH STYLES** panel.

b. In the **PARAGRAPH STYLES** panel, scroll down and select **RunningHead Left.**

c. Observe that the text "The Rates Say: Buy Now!" appears in bold format and the color of the text "The Rates Say:" has changed from black to red.

d. Click and drag from the point of intersection of the 1-inch mark on the horizontal ruler and the 1-inch mark on the vertical ruler to the point of intersection of the 4-inch mark on the horizontal ruler and the 3-inch mark on the vertical ruler to create a rectangular text frame on the left page.

e. Select the **Selection** tool to display the new text frame.

f. Specify the values in the **X** and **Y** text boxes as *0.5* and *10.6* respectively and specify the values in the **W** and **H** text boxes as *7.5* and *0.25* respectively.

g. Scroll down and select the **Type** tool.

h. Select the text frame located at the bottom of the page.

i. Choose **Type→Insert Special Character→Markers→Current Page Number.**

j. At the bottom-left corner of the page, observe that the letter "A" appears, indicating the page number.

k. In the **PARAGRAPH STYLES** panel, select **RunningFoot Left.**

l. Observe that the color of the current page number has changed to red.

m. Collapse the **PARAGRAPH STYLES** panel.

3. Add the header and footer to the right master page.

a. Select the **Selection** tool, on the left page, scroll up and select the text frame containing the header text.

b. Choose **Edit→Copy.**

c. In the **PAGES** panel, double-click the right section of the master page to select the right frame.

d. Choose **Edit→Paste.**

e. Specify the values in the **X** and **Y** text boxes as *9* and *0.08* respectively.

f. In the **PARAGRAPH STYLES** panel, select **RunningHead Right.**

g. Copy the text frame that contains the footer text and place it on the right page with **X:** *9* and **Y:** *10.6*

h. In the **PARAGRAPH STYLES** panel, scroll down and select **RunningFoot Right.**

i. Navigate to page 3.

j. Verify that the footer displays the page number as "3."

k. Save the file.

ACTIVITY 4-5

Modifying Master Pages

Data Files:

My Property Finder.indd

Before You Begin:

The My Property Finder.indd file is open.

Scenario:

You included the header and footer information in the brochure and formatted the information. While reviewing the document, you realize that the text is not aligned. You decide to override the settings so that the component alone can be modified as necessary.

What You Do	How You Do It
1. Modify the **A-Master** page.	a. Navigate to the **A-Master** page.
	b. From the **PAGES** panel options menu, choose **Master Options for "A-Master."**
	c. In the **Master Options** dialog box, in the **Name** text box, double-click, type *Article* and then click **OK.**
	d. Observe that in the page selection drop-down list the name of the master page is "A-Article."

2. Create a new master page.

   a. From the **PAGES** panel options menu, choose **New Master.**

   b. In the **New Master** dialog box, in the **Name** text box, double-click and type *Organization*

   c. From the **Based on Master** drop-down list, select **A-Article** and click **OK.**

   d. From the **PAGES** panel options menu, choose **Override All Master Page Items** to create a local copy of the master page without breaking its association with the master page.

   e. Press **Page Up** and scroll to the left of the page.

   f. Select the **Type** tool.

   g. On the **B-Organization** master page, select the text **"The Rate Say: Buy Now!"** in the header text frame.

   h. Type *OGC: A Complete Property Solution*

   i. Similarly, on the right page, change the text "The Rates Say: Buy Now!" to "OGC: A Complete Property Solution."

---

3. Apply master to a page.

   a. Navigate to page 4, and from the **PAGES** panel options menu, choose **Apply Master to Pages.**

   b. In the **Apply Master** dialog box, from the **Apply Master** drop-down list, select **B-Organization.**

   c. In the **To Pages** text box, verify that **4** is selected and click **OK** to apply the master page.

   d. Scroll to the left of the page to view the changes.

---

4. Override the master page item on the body page.

a. Navigate to page 1.

b. In the **LAYERS** panel, in the **Images** layer, click the **Toggle visibility** icon.

c. On page 1, observe that the cover page image is hidden and the master page text "The Rates Say: Buy Now!" is placed at the top-right corner of the page.

d. From the **PAGES** panel options menu, choose **Override All Master Page Items.**

e. Select the **Selection** tool, and at the top-right corner of the page, select the text frame that has the text "The Rates Say: Buy Now!" and press **Delete.**

f. Similarly, remove the footer text frame.

g. In the **LAYERS** panel, in the **Images** layer, click the **Toggle visibility** icon to display the hidden image.

h. Navigate to the **A-Article** page and select the header and footer text frames.

i. Choose **Object→Lock Position.**

j. Save and close the file.

k. Collapse the **LAYERS** panel.

Lesson 4 Follow-up

In this lesson, you worked with page elements. By applying advanced techniques to manage page elements, you will be able to present content neatly and creatively.

1. **In what kind of job situations will using rulers, guides, and grids be helpful to you ?**

2. **How does setting up pages before laying out objects on them help you work efficiently in your job?**

5 | Managing Objects

Lesson Time: 1 hour(s)

Lesson Objectives:

In this lesson, you will manage objects.

You will:

- Transform objects.
- Edit objects.
- Thread text frames.
- Search and replace objects.
- Edit text.

Introduction

You worked with page elements. Now, you may want to manipulate the elements. In this lesson, you will manage objects.

A big part of working with objects such as text frames, graphic frames, shapes, and so forth involves managing, transforming, and editing objects, searching and replacing text, and so on. InDesign is not a drawing application, but it provides various tools for modifying an object's size and shape in a document. This enables you to enhance the quality of InDesign documents, and present an appealing and error-free document to users.

TOPIC A
Transform Objects

You may need to change the shape and size of objects in your InDesign document. In this topic, you will transform objects.

You may have to modify text and graphic elements in a document to meet specific require-ments. By transforming objects, you will be able to modify them to change their shape or position.

Transformation

Definition:

Transformation is a format applied to objects to change their shape or position. While trans-forming, an object can be rotated, moved, sheared, or flipped. You can apply one type of transformation several times to objects. Also, the transformed object can be reverted to its original position or shape.

Example:

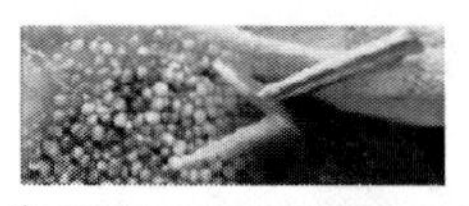

Object's shape changes
after transformation

Object can be reverted
to its original position

Single type of transformation can be applied several times

The TRANSFORM Panel

The *TRANSFORM panel* displays various geometrical information such as position, size, rota-tion, and shear about an object, and allows you to specify values for transformation.

Component	Allows You To
Reference Point locator	Assign and reassign the reference point so that you can change the coordinates for the X and Y axes and the anchor point for rotation and skewing.
Constrain proportions for scaling button	Maintain the object's relative proportions when scaled.
X and **Y** text boxes	Specify the horizontal (X) and vertical (Y) posi-tions of the selected object. These text boxes also allow you to change the position of the selected frame, and view the cursor position when no object is selected.

Component	Allows You To
W and **H** text boxes	Specify the width and height of an object when the object is selected.
Scale X Percentage drop-down list	Specify the value of an object to scale it horizontally in percentage.
Scale Y Percentage drop-down list	Specify the value of an object to scale it vertically in percentage.
Rotation Angle drop-down list	Specify the rotation angle of an object. You can enter a positive angle to rotate the object counter-clockwise, and a negative angle to rotate the object clockwise. You can change the axis of rotation by altering the object's reference point.
Shear X Angle drop-down list	Specify the shear or slant angle of an object, and rotate both objects' axes.
Panel options menu	Use various options so that you can perform transformations, such as scaling, rotating, and flipping. You can include stroke weight, apply total transformation, show the offset of the content, and adjust the stroke weight when scaling.

The Transform Again Commands

The **Transform Again** commands are used to apply the last applied transformation many times on single or multiple objects.

Command	Description
Transform Again	The previous transformation is applied to the selected objects as a group.
Transform Again Individually	The previous transformation is applied to the selected objects one after the other, and not as a group.
Transform Sequence Again	The previous set of sequentially applied transformations is applied to the selected objects as a group.
Transform Sequence Again Individually	The previous set of sequentially applied transformations is applied to the selected objects one after the other, and not as a group.

How to Transform Objects

Procedure Reference: Transform Objects Using the TRANSFORM Panel

To transform objects using the **TRANSFORM** panel:

1. Open an InDesign document.
2. Select an object to transform.
3. Choose **Window→Object & Layout→Transform.**
4. In the **TRANSFORM** panel, specify the reference point for the transformation.
5. If necessary, enter the values in the **X, Y, W, H, Scale X Percentage, Scale Y Rotation Angle, Rotation Angle,** and **Shear X Angle** text boxes for defining the different types of transformation.
6. Press **Enter** to apply the defined transformation.

Procedure Reference: Apply Repetitions of Transformation to Objects

To apply repetitions of transformation to objects:

1. Open an InDesign document.
2. Select an object to transform.
3. Apply transformation to the object.
4. Choose **Object→Transform Again,** and then choose a command to apply to the object.
   - Choose **Transform Again** to repeat the previous single transformation.
   - Choose **Transform Again Individually** to repeat the previous single transformation to each object.
   - Choose **Transform Sequence Again** to repeat the previous sequence of transformations.
   - Choose **Transform Sequence Again Individually** to repeat the previous sequence of transformations to each object.

ACTIVITY 5-1
Transforming Objects

Data Files:

Newsletter.indd

Before You Begin:

From the C:\084048Data\Managing Objects folder, open the Newsletter.indd file.

Scenario:

You are creating a newsletter that will list the different food products of a company. You want to create the final layout of the document and make it look visually appealing.

What You Do	How You Do It
1. Rotate objects using the **Rotate** dialog box.	a. In the **Control** panel, click the center reference point.
	b. On page 1, select the image at the bottom-left corner of the page.
	c. Choose **Object→Transform→Rotate.**
	d. In the **Rotate** dialog box, in the **Angle** text box, type *10* and check the **Preview** check box.
	e. Observe the image at 10 degrees and click **OK.**
2. Rotate objects using the **Transform Again** command.	a. Choose **Object→Transform Again→ Transform Again.**
	b. Observe that the selected object is rotated again by another 10 degrees.
	c. Click outside the page to deselect the image.
	d. Save the file as *My Newsletter.indd*

TOPIC B
Edit Objects

You transformed objects. You may need to modify graphic frames by changing their shapes. In this topic, you will edit objects.

The shape of a graphic frame may not suit the document. By modifying and editing objects, you can create precise shapes for graphics. The correct shape and size of frames give an appealing look to your document, and capture users' attention.

Shapes

Shapes are building blocks for placing text and graphics. The different types of shapes that you can create are rectangle, rounded rectangle, beveled rectangle, inverse rounded rectangle, ellipse, triangle, polygon, and so on. There are various settings that you can specify for creating different shapes for objects. You can create compound shapes using the compound paths, text frames, text outlines, or other shapes.

The Convert Shape Commands

The **Convert Shape** commands allow you to convert one shape to another. The conversion of one frame shape to another enables you to format and modify the different text and graphic frames. You can convert shapes created with the rectangle, ellipse, and polygon tools into either image frames or text frames.

How to Edit Objects

Procedure Reference: Convert a Shape

To convert a shape:

1. Open the InDesign file and select the text frame you want to edit.
2. Choose **Object→Convert Shape** and then choose a command.
    *   Choose **Rectangle** to convert the shape of the existing text frame into a rectangle.
    *   Choose **Rounded Rectangle** to convert the shape of the existing text frame into a rounded rectangle.
    *   Choose **Beveled Rectangle** to convert the shape of the existing text frame into a beveled rectangle.
    *   Choose **Inverse Rounded Rectangle** to convert the shape of the existing text frame into an inverted, rounded rectangle.
    *   Choose **Ellipse** to convert the shape of the existing text frame into an ellipse.
    *   Choose **Triangle** to convert the shape of the existing text frame into a triangle.
    *   Choose **Polygon** to convert the shape of the existing text frame into a polygon based on the settings in the **Polygon Settings** dialog box.
    *   Choose **Line** to convert the shape of the existing text frame into a line.
    *   Choose **Orthogonal Line** to convert the shape of the existing text frame into an orthogonal line.

Procedure Reference: Edit Objects Using Different Applications

To edit objects using different applications:

1.   Open the InDesign file and select the images you want to edit.
2.   Choose **Edit→Edit With** to specify the application you want to use to edit the file.
3.   If no application appears, choose **Other** to navigate to another application.
4.   Edit the object.
5.   Save the edited file.

ACTIVITY 5-2
Editing Objects

Data Files:

My Newsletter.indd

Before You Begin:

The My Newsletter.indd file is open.

Scenario:

You rotated the objects on the page. Now, you notice that some shapes are plain, and the images overlap with the text. You decide to change the shape of the objects, and place text around the images.

What You Do	How You Do It
1. Change the shape of the object to rounded rectangle.	a. Select the text frame with the text "Open at 5 P.M. Daily."
	b. Choose **Object→Convert Shape→ Rounded Rectangle.**
	c. Observe that the object frame is a rounded rectangle.
2. Wrap text around the text frame.	a. Expand the **TEXT WRAP** panel.
	b. In the **TEXT WRAP** panel, click the **Wrap around object shape** button.
	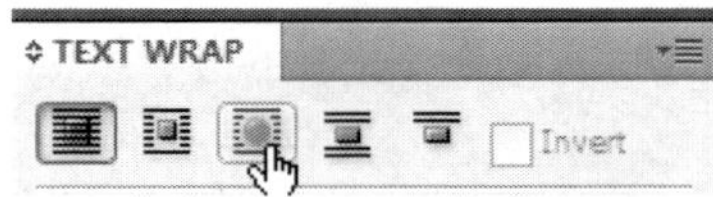
	c. In the **Top Offset** text box, select the value, type *0.084* and then press **Enter.**
3. Wrap text around the graphic frame.	a. Scroll down and select the image at the bottom-left corner of the page.

b. In the **TEXT WRAP** panel, click the **Wrap around bounding box** button.

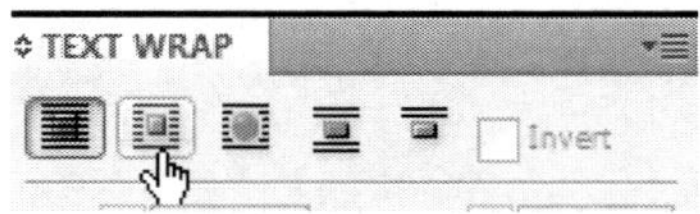

c. In the **Top Offset** text box, select the value, type *0.11* and then press **Enter.**

d. Select the image that is placed at the center of the page.

e. In the **TEXT WRAP** panel, click the **Wrap around bounding box** button.

f. In the **Top Offset** text box, select the value, type *0.084* and then press **Enter.**

g. Verify that in the **Wrap Options** section, in the **Wrap To** drop-down list, the **Both Right & Left Sides** option is selected.

h. Observe that the text around the image flows along the edges of the image.

i. Click outside the page document to deselect the image.

j. Collapse the **TEXT WRAP** panel group.

k. Save the file.

TOPIC C
Thread Text Frames

You edited objects. You want the text to flow from one column to another, or from one page to another, in a document. In this topic, you will thread text frames.

When you work on a document and create text frames, the text you want to place in a text frame could be more than what it can contain. By connecting text within text frames, managing the layout of long text entries in the document becomes easier.

A Story

Definition:

A *story* is an uninterrupted body of text that flows in a text frame. A text frame is a subset of a story. A story may range from one letter of the alphabet to several pages of text. You can either place the text from a story in a single frame or spread the story across several linked frames. These frames need not be adjacent.

Example:

Text Overset

Text overset is a feature for placing unseen text in a text frame. It occurs when the amount of text you want to place in a text frame or cell is more than the size of the text frame or cell. In this case, additional text in the text frame is indicated by a red plus sign (+) in an out port of the text frame. You can accommodate the overset text by resizing the text frame or cell, reducing the font size of the text, or clicking the red plus sign (+). By using the **Selection** tool, you can load the cursor with additional text and place the text in the specified text frame.

Text Threading

Text threading is the act of designating one text frame to receive text that extends beyond the boundaries of another text frame. Each text frame contains an in port and an out port that can be used to make connections with other text frames.

Text Thread Navigation

When a document contains multiple stories, each of which flows within multiple threaded frames, a visual hint that displays the frames that are threaded will be useful. You can also display lines that connect the out ports of frames to the in ports of the next frames.

Text Flow by Using Text Threading

When you place text in a frame that is threaded, text automatically flows to the threaded frames, regardless of the method used for text flow.

Threaded Frame Removal

InDesign allows you to delete a frame from the middle of a threaded story. Deleting a frame does not delete the text it contains. Instead, the text of the deleted or removed text frame flows into the following frame in the thread.

Frame Unthreading

To unthread frames, apply the process that is used to manually thread frames. This allows you to break stories apart whenever the need arises.

How to Thread Text Frames

Procedure Reference: Thread Text

To thread text:

1. Place the text file in the text frame.

2. In the text frame, click the red plus sign at the bottom-right corner of the frame.

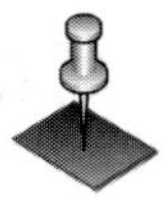

 You can double-click the red plus sign to thread a frame. The threaded frame will be placed directly under the original text frame.

3. Draw a new text frame by clicking and dragging the mouse, or by clicking a location in the document.

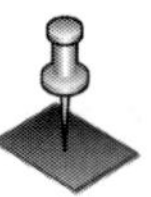

 To thread text to multiple frames, hold down **Shift** and click the red plus sign on the overfilled frame. You can then click anywhere in the document to select the necessary frames.

Procedure Reference: Change Text Threads

To change text threads:

1. In the **Tools** panel, select the **Type** tool and draw a new text frame.

2. In the **Tools** panel, select the **Selection** tool, and then select the text frame to change the thread.

3. Click the out port icon.

4. Click the new frame to change the thread.

Procedure Reference: Flow Overset Text

To flow overset text:

1. Click the out port icon that has the red plus symbol in the text frame.

2. From the page selection drop-down list, select the page that has a text frame.

3. Click the page to place the overflowing text.

Semiautomatic Text Flow

When text flows from one frame to another, it stops at the new frame. An overset symbol appears in the new frame if the entire text does not fit that particular frame. If you want the text to continue flowing, you must click the overset symbol. However, if you hold down **Alt** when you click a frame, the mouse pointer automatically appears again as a loaded text icon.

Automatic Text Flow

If you hold down **Shift** as you click with a loaded text icon to continue text in a new frame, the text will automatically flow into as many additional frames as necessary to display all the text.

Shortcuts for Navigating Among Threaded Frames

You can use shortcuts to navigate among threaded text frames. Select a threaded text frame, then use one of the shortcuts to navigate to the other frames in the story.

Navigation Shortcut	Navigates To
Ctrl+Alt+Page Down	The next frame in the thread.
Ctrl+Alt+Page Up	The previous frame in the thread.
Ctrl+Alt+Shift+Page Up	The first frame in the story.
Ctrl+Alt+Shift+Page Down	The last frame in the story.

ACTIVITY 5-3

Threading Text Frames

Data Files:

My Newsletter.indd

Before You Begin:

The My Newsletter.indd file is open.

Scenario:

You placed text in the newsletter, but the text is overflowing in the text frame. You need to place the text into another text frame, so that all content is visible.

What You Do	How You Do It
1. Link text frames to flow the overset text.	a. Select the last text frame and set the zoom percentage to **150.**
	b. Observe that the out port of the text frame appears with a red plus sign on the last text column of the page. ⊞
	c. Click the out port of the text frame.
	d. Observe that the mouse pointer changes to a loaded icon.
	e. Move the loaded text icon to the text frame on the right and observe that the loaded icon changes to a link icon.
	f. Select the text frame in the last column.
	g. Choose **View→Show Text Threads.**
	h. Scroll down to the bottom of the page and observe that the text frames are threaded from the in port of the text frame to the out port of the next text frame.

2. Break the link to remove unnecessary threading.

   a. Select the blank text frame.

   b. Observe the text threading between the text frame of the last column and the blank text frame at the bottom of the page.

   c. Select the in port of the blank text frame at the bottom-right corner of the page.

   d. Observe that the mouse pointer changes to a link icon.

   e. In the second column of the text frame, click the out port icon.

   f. Choose **View→Hide Text Threads.**

   g. Save the file.

TOPIC D
Search and Replace Objects

You threaded text frames in a document. Scrolling through a document to locate and fix errors can be time consuming. In this topic, you will search and replace content.

If you are working with a document that is not lengthy, it is easy to scroll up or down the page to locate the required text. However, if you are working with a multi-page document, the task of looking for specific portions of text will be painstaking. InDesign enables you to locate every occurrence of the text, object, or special character, and presents you with the opportunity to selectively replace them with the click of a button.

The Find/Change Dialog Box

The **Find/Change** dialog box allows you to specify text, special characters, or objects that you want to find and change in a document. The various tabs help you narrow down your search.

The following are the various tabs in the **Find/Change** dialog box.

Tab	Enables You To
Text	Search and replace specific occurrences of characters, words, groups of words, or formatted text. The additional buttons, such as **Case Sensitive** and **Whole Word,** enable you to efficiently search and replace the textual part of the content. The **More Options** button enables you to specify additional options for formatting text.
GREP	Search and replace alphanumeric strings in lengthy documents. The tab is used for advanced pattern-based searches. Searching for text within quotation marks and phone numbers are some examples of GREP searches.
Glyph	Search and replace glyphs by specifying the font or unicode values of the glyph.
Object	Search and replace formatting effects and attributes in objects and frames.

GREP Expressions

GREP metacharacters can be entered manually or chosen from the **Special Characters for search** and **Special Characters for replace** drop-down lists in the **Find/Change** dialog box. Metacharacters are characters or symbols that help in constructing a GREP expression. To search for a character with a symbolic meaning in GREP, enter **Backslash** before the character. Parentheses can be used to search for grouped words.

How to Search and Replace Objects

Procedure Reference: Search and Replace Text

To search and replace text:

1. Open an InDesign file.
2. Choose **Edit→Find/Change.**
3. In the **Find/Change** dialog box, on the **Text** tab, in the **Find what** text box, type the text.
4. In the **Change to** text box, type the text you want to replace the original text with.
5. If necessary, from the **Search** drop-down list, select an option.
   - Select **Document** to search the whole document.
   - Select **All Documents** to search all open documents.
   - Select **Story** to search in the selected frame.
   - Select **To End of Story** to search from the insertion point to the end of the story.
6. If necessary, click the **Case Sensitive** button to check for the words that have the same casing.
7. Click **Find** to locate the first occurrence of the text.
8. Make the appropriate selection to replace the text.
   - Click **Change** to replace the highlighted text and to continue searching for the next occurrence.
   - Click **Find Next** to leave the highlighted text unchanged and to continue searching for the next occurrence.
9. In the **Adobe InDesign** message box, click **OK.**
10. Click **Done.**

Procedure Reference: Add Glyphs Using the Find/Change Dialog Box

To add glyphs using the **Find/Change** dialog box:

1. Choose **Edit→Find/Change.**
2. In the **Find/Change** dialog box, on the **Text** tab, in the **Find what** text box, type the text.
3. In the **Change to** text box, type the text you want to replace the original text with, click the **Special characters for replace** button, and choose a glyph.
4. Click **Find** to locate the first occurrence of the text.
5. Make the appropriate selection to replace the text with the specified text and glyph.
   - Click **Change** to replace the highlighted text and to continue searching for the next occurrence.
   - Click **Find Next** to leave the highlighted text unchanged and to continue searching for the next occurrence.
6. In the **Adobe InDesign** message box, click **OK.**
7. Click **Done.**

Procedure Reference: Search and Replace Glyphs

To search and replace glyphs:

1. Choose **Edit→Find/Change.**
2. In the **Find/Change** dialog box, select the **Glyph** tab.

3. In the **Find Glyph** section, from the **Font Family** drop-down list, select a font family.

4. From the **Font Style** drop-down list, select a font style.

5. Click the **Glyph** button to display the glyphs in the font family.

6. In the list box, double-click a glyph.

7. In the **Change Glyph** section, from the **Font Family** drop-down list, select a font family.

8. From the **Font Style** drop-down list, select a font style.

9. Click the **Glyph** button to display the glyphs in the font family.

10. In the list box, double-click a glyph that you want to replace.

11. Click **Find** to find the glyph.

12. Click **Change** to replace the glyph.

13. Click **Done.**

ACTIVITY 5-4

Searching and Replacing Objects

Data Files:

My Newsletter.indd

Before You Begin:

The My Newsletter.indd file is open.

Scenario:

The newsletter is near completion, and you find that there are instances of words that you need to change throughout the newsletter. You want to search for these words and replace them with the correct words. You also want to change the formatting of the text New Jammin and the star object.

What You Do	How You Do It
1. Find all occurrences of "Jammin's" and replace with "New Jammin."	a. Choose **View→Fit Page in Window.**
	b. In the first column, observe the heading text, "Jammin's at Night."
	c. Choose **Edit→Find/Change.**
	d. In the **Find/Change** dialog box, on the **Text** tab, in the **Find what** text box, type *Jammin's* and then press **Tab.**
	e. In the **Change to** text box, type *New Jammin* and click **Change All.**
	f. In the **Adobe InDesign** message box, observe the message, and click **OK.**
	g. Observe that the heading text is now "New Jammin," and all occurrences of "Jammin's" is replaced with "New Jammin."
2. Format the headings.	a. In the **Find/Change** dialog box, on the **Text** tab, in the **Find what** text box, double-click, and press **Delete.**
	b. Press **Tab** and then press **Delete.**

c. In the **Find Format** section, click the **Specify attributes to find** button.

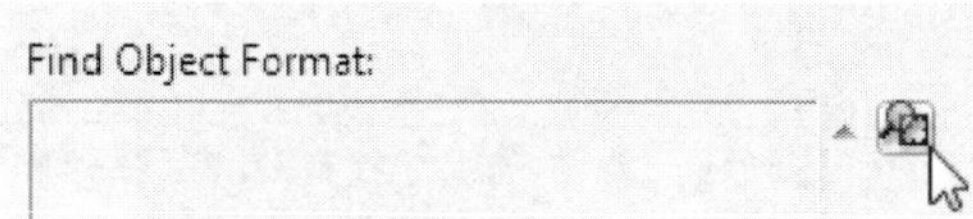

d. In the **Find Format Settings** dialog box, in the left pane, select **Character Color.**

e. In the **Character Color** section, in the color list box, scroll down, select **Red,** and click **OK.**

f. In the **Find/Change** dialog box, in the **Change Format** section, click the **Specify attributes to change** button.

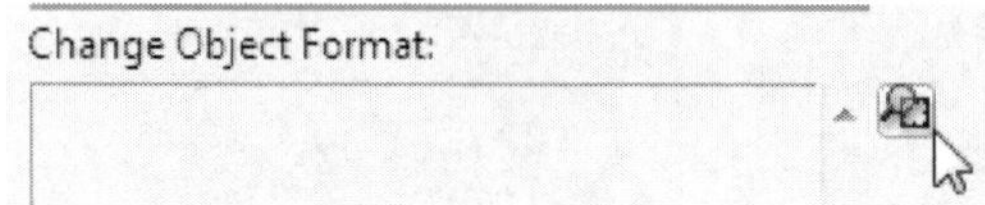

g. In the **Change Format Settings** dialog box, in the left pane, select **Character Color.**

h. In the **Character Color** section, in the color list box, select **Green,** and click **OK.**

i. On the page, in the first text column, click the first paragraph.

j. In the **Find/Change** dialog box, click **Find.**

k. Observe that the **Fill** icon has a red "T" indicating that the text is in red.

l. Observe that the text "New Jammin at Night" is selected, because the search is performed on the basis of formatting.

m. In the **Find/Change** dialog box, click **Change.**

n. Observe that in the **Fill** icon, the color of "T" has changed from red to green, indicating that the text is in green.

o. In the **Find/Change** dialog box, click **Find Next,** and then click **Change/Find** four times to change all similar headings to green.

3. Find and change object formatting for the star object.

a. In the **Find/Change** dialog box, select the **Object** tab.

b. In the **Find Object Format** section, click the **Specify attributes to find** button.

c. In the **Find Object Format Options** dialog box, in the **Basic Attributes** list box, select **Fill.**

d. In the **Fill** section, in the color list box, scroll down, select **Star1** and click **OK.**

e. In the **Find/Change** dialog box, in the **Change Object Format** section, click the **Specify attributes to change** button.

f. In the **Change Object Format Options** dialog box, in the **Basic Attributes** list box, select **Fill.**

g. In the **Fill** section, in the color list box, scroll down, select **Star2,** and then click **OK.**

h. From the **Search** drop-down list, select **Document.**

i. From the **Type** drop-down list, select **All Frames.**

j. Click **Change All.**

k. In the **Adobe InDesign** message box, observe the message, and click **OK.**

l. In the **Find/Change** dialog box, click **Done.**

m. Save the file.

TOPIC E
Edit Text

You searched and replaced objects in your documents. You may need to make changes and corrections to text for grammatical and conceptual accuracy. In this topic, you will edit text.

By editing text that already exists, rather than re-creating text, you can save production time and reduce development costs. InDesign provides various editing tools that you can use to edit text.

The Story Editor

The *Story Editor* is a text-editing tool that allows you to focus on editing text without having to view the text in a formatted layout. Each story appears in a different Story Editor window. A vertical depth ruler indicates the extent to which text fills the frame, and a horizontal line indicates where text exceeds the frame size. When a story is edited, the changes are reflected in the layout window.

Autocorrect

Autocorrect automatically corrects misspelled words and capitalization errors. In the **Autocorrect** section of the **Preferences** dialog box, you can enable or disable **Autocorrect** and set any number of misspelled words and their equivalent corrections. You can add, edit, and remove misspelled words.

Spell Check

Spell check is a feature that enables you to check for spelling errors in documents. The dynamic spell check feature immediately identifies any misspelled words, repeated words, uncapitalized words, or uncapitalized sentences in a document. Under the **Spelling** category, in the **Dynamic Spelling** section of the **Preferences** dialog box, you can enable or disable the dynamic spell check feature. This feature allows you to detect misspelled words by underlining them when you type. The **Underline Color** section allows you to assign a specific color for different types of errors so that you can categorize them for fast editing, and analyze the types of mistakes for quality editing processes.

User Dictionaries

A *user dictionary* is a user-defined list of correctly spelled words that you can use to spell check documents with. Word lists can be imported into user dictionaries using the **Dictionary** dialog box. With the various buttons in the dialog box, you can create, add, remove, and export a user dictionary based on the emerging needs of editing. The **Dictionary** category in the **Preferences** dialog box helps you select the options for adding the exception word list of a user dictionary to a document, and recomposes all the stories when defined settings are changed. You can create a new user dictionary or add an existing user dictionary.

Notes

Notes are briefly written entities or reminders that help you communicate information to a team member working on the same InDesign document or to an editor reviewing the document. The **NOTES** panel allows you to show or hide notes, cycle through the notes created, add notes to an InDesign document, and delete notes from an InDesign document. Notes are indicated with a note anchor in the **Layout** view, and the content of the note is displayed between note bookends in the **Story Editor** view. The user settings such as the user name and color for the note can be set for the notes inserted in a document.

How to Edit Text

Procedure Reference: Edit Text in the Story Editor

To edit text in the **Story Editor:**

1. In the **Tools** panel, select the **Selection** tool, and then select text.
2. Choose **Edit→Edit in Story Editor.**
3. In the **Story Editor** dialog box, edit the text.
4. Close the **Story Editor.**

Procedure Reference: Update InDesign Files

To update InDesign files:

1. Place an InDesign file in the document.
2. Edit the original file.
3. In the **LINKS** panel, place the mouse pointer over the caution icon to display its tooltip.
4. Click the **Update Link** button to update the file.

Procedure Reference: Check Spelling

To check spelling:

1. Choose **Edit→Spelling→Check Spelling.**
2. In the **Check Spelling** dialog box, specify the settings.
   - From the **Add To** drop-down list, select the user dictionary to check the user-defined spell check list of the content.
   - From the **Search** drop-down list, select an option.
     - Select **All Documents** to check the spelling of all the opened documents.
     - Select **Document** to check the spelling of the specified documents.
     - Select **Story** to check the spelling of the text in the selected text frame, threaded text frame, and overset text.
     - Select **To End of Story** to check the spelling of the selected text from the point of insertion to the end of the story.
     - Select **Selection** to check the spelling of only the selected text.

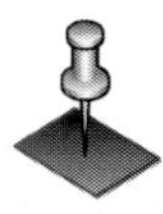 This option is available only when text is selected.

- Click **Change** to change the occurrences of the misspelled words using the **Suggested Corrections** and **Change To** list boxes.

- Click **Ignore All** to ignore all the occurrences of the highlighted words in a document.

- Click **Change All** to change all the occurrences of the misspelled word in a document.

- Click **Dictionary** to open the **Dictionary** dialog box and select the target dictionary and language for checking the spelling.

- Click **Add** to add a word to a dictionary.

- Click **Skip** to reject the suggested change.

3. Click **Done.**

Procedure Reference: Create a User Dictionary

To create a user dictionary:

1. Choose **Edit→Preferences→Dictionary.**

2. If necessary, in the **Preferences** dialog box, from the **Language** drop-down list, select a language.

3. In the **Language** section, click the **New User Dictionary** button.

4. In the **New User Dictionary** dialog box, navigate to the folder in which you want to save the new dictionary.

5. In the **File name** text box, enter a name for the dictionary, and click **Save.**

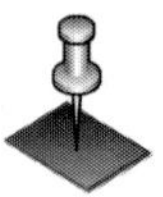

 Dictionary files have a .udc extension.

6. Click **OK.**

7. Add a word to the user dictionary created.

   a. Choose **Edit→Spelling→Dictionary.**

   b. From the **Target** drop-down list, select the dictionary to which you want to add a word.

   c. In the **Dictionary** dialog box, in the **Word** text box, type a word, click **Add,** and then click **Done.**

Procedure Reference: Import a Word List into a User Dictionary

To import a word list into a user dictionary:

1. Choose **Edit→Spelling→Dictionary.**

2. In the **Dictionary** dialog box, from the **Target** drop-down list, select the dictionary to which you want to import the list.

3. If necessary, from the **Language** drop-down list, select a language.

4. Click **Import.**

5. If necessary, in the **Import User Dictionary** dialog box, navigate to the folder to which you want to import the word list.

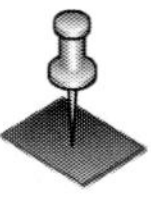

The imported word list must be a text (.txt) file. The words in the word list must be separated by a space, tab, or paragraph return.

6. Select the file that contains the word list you want to import, click **Open** and click **Done.**

Procedure Reference: Enable Autocorrect

To enable **Autocorrect:**

1. Choose **Edit→Preferences→Autocorrect.**
2. In the **Preferences** dialog box, check the **Enable Autocorrect** check box, and click **Add.**
3. In the **Add to Autocorrect List** dialog box, in the **Misspelled Word** text box, type a word.
4. In the **Correction** text box, type the corrected word, and click **OK.**
5. In the **Preferences** dialog box, click **OK.**

ACTIVITY 5-5

Editing Text

Data Files:

My Newsletter.indd

Before You Begin:

The My Newsletter.indd file is open.

Scenario:

You completed the newsletter, and you need to send it to your manager for review. You want to make sure that there are no textual errors. You also want to insert a note for the list of food items before you send the document for review.

What You Do	How You Do It
1. Perform a spell check using the **Dynamic Spelling** command.	a. Choose **Edit→Spelling→Dynamic Spelling.**
	b. From the **Zoom Level** drop-down list, select **100%.**
	c. Observe that all the misspelled words have a red wavy underline.
	d. In the "New Jammin at Night" paragraph, in the second paragraph, double-click the word **"busines."**
	e. Right-click the selected word and from the menu, choose **business.**
	f. Observe that the misspelled word on the page is corrected.
2. Open the **Story Editor** to work with text.	a. On the page, click the first text paragraph.
	b. Choose **Edit→Edit in Story Editor.**
	c. In the **Story Editor,** scroll down the page, and in the left pane, view the information on paragraph styles.

3. Perform spell check.

   a. Choose **Edit→Spelling→Check Spelling.**

   b. In the **Check Spelling** dialog box, in the **Not in Dictionary** text box, verify that **Jammin** is displayed as a misspelled word.

   c. Click **Dictionary** to add the word "Jammin" to the dictionary.

   d. In the **Dictionary** dialog box, verify that in the **Target** text box, **User Dictionary** is selected, in the **Language** text box, **English: USA** is selected, and in the **Dictionary List** drop-down list, **Added Words** is selected.

   e. Click **Add** to add the word to the user dictionary, and then click **Done.**

   f. In the **Check Spelling** dialog box, click **Skip** three times.

   g. Observe that in the **Suggested Corrections** section, the next misspelled word is identified.

   h. In the **Suggested Corrections** list box, select **escalating,** and then click **Change.**

   i. Click **Skip.**

   j. In the **Suggested Corrections** section, select **Chocolate,** and then click **Change** to correct the misspelled word "Choclate."

   k. Click **Skip.**

   l. Observe that the spell check is complete. Click **Done.**

<table>
<tr>
<td>4. Add notes for future reference.</td>
<td>
a. In the Story Editor, click at the end of the text "Our Festival Foods."

b. Choose Type→Notes→Show All Menu Items.

c. Choose New Note.

d. In the Story Editor, in the Notes text box, type Please check whether the list of festival foods meets your expectations.

e. Choose File→Close to close the Story Editor.

f. Scroll to the right of the page.

g. Observe that on the page, an inverse triangle symbol appears after the text "Our Festival Foods" indicating that a note is added at the location.
</td>
</tr>
<tr>
<td>5. View the note in layout view.</td>
<td>
a. Click the text "Our Festival Foods."

b. Choose Type→Notes→Show All Menu Items.

c. Choose Previous Note.

d. Observe that the NOTES panel displays the note that was included.

e. Close the NOTES panel.

f. Save and close the file.
</td>
</tr>
</table>

Lesson 5 Follow-up

In this lesson, you managed objects. This will help you transform and edit objects in different ways so that you have error-free documents.

1. **How are the various techniques of managing objects useful to you?**

2. **What editing methods will you apply to ensure an error-free document?**

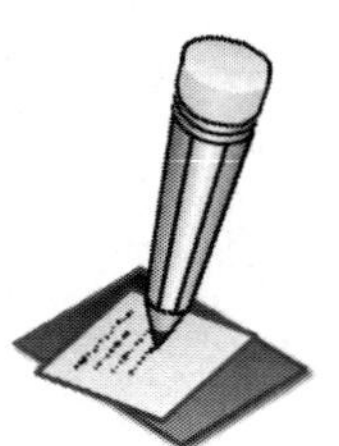

6 | Working with Tables

Lesson Time: 50 minutes

Lesson Objectives:

In this lesson, you will work with tables.

You will:

- Create a table.
- Modify a table structure.
- Format a table.
- Create table and cell styles.

Introduction

You managed objects in InDesign documents. While preparing a document, you need to pay attention to how text is presented on the page. In this lesson, you will work with tables to organize and enhance information in your document.

Sometimes, when data is presented as a list or paragraph, readers may not easily understand the content. When you use tables appropriately, they can significantly improve reader comprehension by enabling you to organize your information and eliminate unnecessary words.

TOPIC A

Create a Table

You entered textual information in a document. However, your document may contain other data that needs to be arranged for easy reading. In this topic, you will create tables to represent data.

When text containing statistical or numerical data is included in a document, the data often gets buried, making it difficult for readers to read and comprehend. Data arranged in columns and rows is easy to understand. Tables will allow you to easily organize complex data, and make information more readily accessible to the reader.

Tables

Definition:

A *table* is a container that enables you to organize text or graphics. Tables consist of boxes called cells. A group of cells arranged vertically is called a column, and a group of cells arranged horizontally is called a row. Header and footer table rows are useful for a table that splits across multiple-threaded text frames, because those rows appear within each threaded text frame. A table may have numerous rows and columns to accommodate data.

Example:

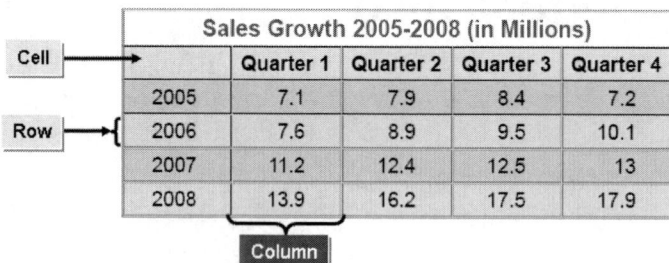

Table Creation Options

You can choose a command from the **Table** menu to create a table. The **Insert Table** command allows you to create a table from scratch. The **Convert Text to Table** command is used to convert text in a document to a table. The **Convert Table to Text** command is used to convert a table in a document to text. Tables can be imported from another application into InDesign documents using the **Place** command.

The Table Options Dialog Box

The **Table Options** dialog box enables you to apply basic formatting to a table. It can also be used to add strokes, fills, headers, and footers to a table.

Tab	Used To
Table Setup	Add rows and columns in a table, apply borders to a table, add spaces before or after a table, and change the order of display of row and column strokes.
Row Strokes	Specify the rows to which strokes need to be applied, and set the weight, type, color, and tint for the row strokes inserted.
Column Strokes	Specify the columns to which strokes need to be applied, and set the weight, type, color, and tint for the column strokes inserted.
Fills	Specify the rows and columns to which fills need to be applied, and set the color and tint for the fills inserted.
Headers and Footers	Add header and footer rows to a table, and specify how they appear in tables.

How to Create a Table

Procedure Reference: Create a Table

To create a table:

1. Create a text frame.
2. Choose **Table→Insert Table.**
3. In the **Insert Table** dialog box, specify the number of rows, columns, header rows, and footer rows.
4. Click **OK.**
5. In the **Tools** panel, select the **Type** tool and type text in the table cells.

Table Navigation Methods

Although you can click to select table cells to enter text, you can also use keyboard keys to navigate within a table.

To Move	Press This Key
One cell to the right	**Tab** or **Right Arrow**
One cell to the left	**Shift+Tab** or **Left Arrow**
Down one row	**Down Arrow**
Up one row	**Up Arrow**

Procedure Reference: Break a Table Across Frames

To break a table across frames:

1. Select the **Selection** tool.
2. Click the red plus sign in the overset frame.
3. Click in a text frame to continue the table.

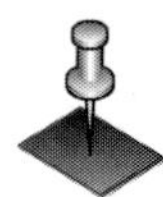

 If you thread text to another frame, the table continues in that frame. Rows move into threaded frames one at a time; you cannot break a single row across multiple frames.

Procedure Reference: Merge Cells

To merge cells:

1. Select the cells you want to merge.
2. Choose **Table→Merge Cells** to merge the cells.

Procedure Reference: Import a Table from Another Application

To import a table from another application:

1. Open the file to which you want to import a table.
2. Choose **File→Place.**
3. In the **Place** dialog box, select the file containing the table you want to import.
4. If necessary, check the **Show Import Options** check box to modify the table before importing it.
5. Click **Open.**
6. If necessary, in the **Import Options** dialog box, specify the settings.
7. Click **OK.**
8. Click the loaded text icon at a location on the page to place the table.
9. Save and close the file.

ACTIVITY 6-1

Creating a Table

Data Files:

Newsletter.indd

Before You Begin:

From the C:\084048Data\Working with Tables folder, open the Newsletter.indd file.

Scenario:

The data in the newsletter, which you created, looks unorganized. You want to arrange and format the sales growth data to capture the reader's attention, and make the data easy to read. So, you decide to place the sales growth information in a table.

What You Do	How You Do It
1. Convert text to a table so that the content appears organized.	a. Scroll to the bottom of the page, and in the table, click before the text "Sales Growth 2005-2008 (in Millions)."
	b. Choose **Edit→Select All.**
	c. Choose **Table→Convert Text to Table.**
	d. In the **Convert Text to Table** dialog box, in the **Column Separator** drop-down list, verify that **Tab** is selected, and in the **Row Separator** drop-down list, **Paragraph** is selected
	e. Click **OK.**
	f. Observe that the data is converted to a table.
	g. In the table, click in the cell that has the text "Sales Growth 2005-2008 (in Millions)."
	h. Choose **Table→Select→Row** to select the first row of the table.
	i. Choose **Table→Merge Cells.**

2. Import a table from a text document.

a. Scroll to the right of the page.

b. To the right of the "Sales Growth 2005-2008 (in Millions)" table, click in the blank text frame.

c. Choose **File→Place.**

d. In the **Place** dialog box, select **Projected Sales Growth.doc** and click **Open** to import the file.

e. Save the file as *My Newsletter.indd*

TOPIC B

Modify a Table Structure

You created a table. As you work with the table, you may find that it contains more rows than required, or that the cell size needs tweaking. In this topic, you will modify a table structure.

You created a table using InDesign. You realize that you need to include additional columns and rows, and move existing information. Creating another table structure and reentering all the existing information will be time consuming. It would be ideal if you could use the existing table and modify its structure to meet the new requirements.

Table Structure Modification Options

You may need to modify the structure of an existing table to include more information or delete unnecessary information from the cells. You can delete and insert rows or columns, and merge or split cells. You can perform all these tasks using the **Table** menu, the **TABLE** panel, or the **TABLE** panel options menu. In addition, you can use the **TABLE** panel to modify the row height and column width, align and rotate text within cells, and set cell inset spacing.

The TABLE Panel

The **TABLE** panel has varied elements that can be used to modify the structure of an existing table and the text that it contains.

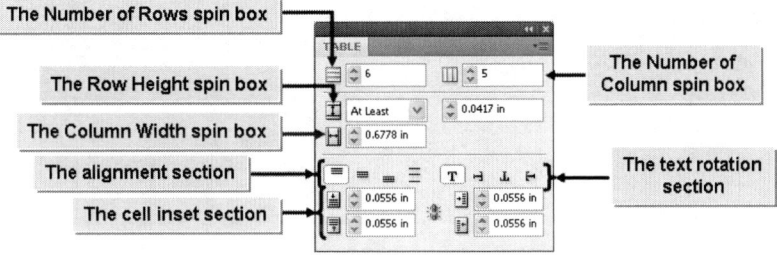

Figure 6-1: The TABLE panel and its components.

The following are the components of the **TABLE** panel.

Component	Description
Number of Rows	A spin box that allows you to specify the number of rows for a table.
Number of Columns	A spin box that allows you to specify the number of columns for a table.
Row Height	A spin box that allows you to modify the height of rows in a table.
Column Width	A spin box that allows you to modify the width of columns in a table.

Component	Description
Alignment	A section that allows you to align text in a cell or table using the **Align top, Align center, Align bottom,** and **Justify vertically** buttons.
Text rotation	A section that allows you to rotate text within cells using the **Rotate text 0°, Rotate text 90°, Rotate text 180°,** and **Rotate text 270°** options.
Cell inset	A section that allows you to specify the top, bottom, left, and right spacing in cells. You can use the **Make all settings the same** button to set the same settings for all cells.

How to Modify a Table Structure

Procedure Reference: Insert Rows or Columns Using the Table Menu

To insert rows or columns using the **Table** menu:

1. In the **Tools** panel, select the **Type** tool, and position the insertion point in a table on the page.
2. Insert columns or rows.
   - Choose **Table→Insert→Row** to open the **Insert Row(s)** dialog box, and then specify the row settings.
   - Choose **Table→Insert→Column** to open the **Insert Column(s)** dialog box, and then specify the column settings.
3. Click **OK** to apply the specified settings.

Table Selection Methods

There are many selection techniques that you can use to select the components of a table.

To Select	Do This
A row or rows	Move the mouse pointer to the left border of the row until the mouse pointer changes to a right-headed arrow, and click to select the column. You can also click and drag to select the row or use the **Go to Row** command on the **Table** menu.
A column or columns	Move the mouse pointer to the top line border of the column until the mouse pointer changes to a down-headed arrow, and click to select the column. You can also click and drag to select the column.
A cell or cells	Click inside a table cell and choose **Table→Select→Cell** to select the cell. Select the **Type** tool and drag it over the cells to select multiple cells.

To Select	Do This
The entire table	Click inside a table and choose **Table→ Select→Table,** or select the **Type** tool and drag it over the table.

Procedure Reference: Modify a Table Using the TABLE Panel

To modify a table using the **TABLE** panel:

1. Place the insertion point in a table.
2. Choose **Window→Type & Tables→Table.**
3. In the **TABLE** panel, specify the settings using the commands on the panel options menu.
4. Save the file.

TABLE Panel Options

There are a number of commands available on the **TABLE** panel options menu that allow you to perform different functions when you work with tables.

Command	Allows You To
Table Options	Open the **Table Options** dialog box, which has options to modify the table dimensions, row and column strokes, fills, and headers and footers.
Cell Options	Open the **Cell Options** dialog box, which has options to modify the cell dimensions, color, tint, strokes, fills, type, and so on.
Insert	Insert rows and columns using the options in the **Insert Row(s)** and **Insert Column(s)** dialog boxes.
Delete	Delete rows, columns, and tables.
Merge Cells	Merge the selected cells in a table.
Unmerge Cells	Remove the merge of the selected cells in a table.
Split Cell Horizontally	Split the selected cell in a table horizontally.
Split Cell Vertically	Split the selected cell in a table vertically.
Convert Rows	Change the selected cell or row as header, footer, and body rows of the table.
Distribute Rows Evenly	Distribute the selected rows in a table evenly.
Distribute Columns Evenly	Distribute the selected columns in a table evenly.
Edit Header	Edit header row in a table.
Edit Footer	Edit footer row in a table.

Procedure Reference: Modify a Table Using the Table Menu

To modify a table using the **Table** menu:

1. Place the insertion point in a table.
2. Choose **Table** and then choose a command to modify the table.
3. Save the file.

Table Menu Commands

There are various **Table** menu commands that can be used to perform different functions. The panel options menu in the **TABLE** panel display the commands that can be used to work with a table.

ACTIVITY 6-2

Modifying a Table Structure

Data Files:

My Newsletter.indd

Before You Begin:

The My Newsletter.indd file is open.

Scenario:

You imported tables from the newsletter. The imported table does not have the desired height and width. You want to modify the table by defining the new height and width values.

What You Do	How You Do It
1. Apply paragraph styles to the table content.	a. At the bottom-right corner of the page, in the table "Projected Sales for 2009-2011 (in Millions)," click before the heading "Projected Sales for 2009-2011 (in Millions)."
	b. Expand the **PARAGRAPH STYLES** panel.
	c. In the **PARAGRAPH STYLES** panel, select **TH.**
	d. Observe that the selected style is applied to the heading "Projected Sales for 2009-2011 (in Millions)."
	e. Move the mouse pointer over the third row, first column, and observe the mouse pointer changing to a dark right arrow. ➡
	f. Click, hold down **Shift** and then click in the last cell of the last row.
	g. In the **PARAGRAPH STYLES** panel, scroll up and select **TB.**
	h. Click in the pasteboard to deselect the **Selection** tool.

2. Adjust the width and height of the table.

   a. Select the row that has the text "Projected Sales for 2009-2011."

   b. Choose **Table→Cell Options→Rows and Columns.**

   c. In the **Cell Options** dialog box, on the **Rows and Columns** tab, from the **Row Height** drop-down list, select **Exactly** and press **Tab.**

   d. Type *0.2072* and press **Tab** two times.

   e. In the **Column Width** text box, type *3.3899* and click **OK.**

   f. Observe that the height of the cell with the text "Projected Sales for 2009-2011 (in Millions)" is adjusted.

   g. In the **Control** panel, in the cell alignment section, click the **Align center** button.

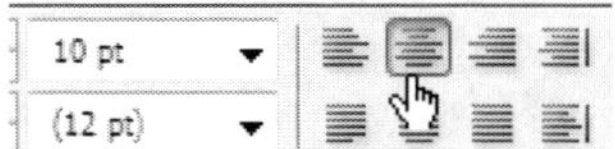

   h. Select the **Selection** tool, and in the **H** text box, type *1.2511* and then press **Enter.**

   i. In the **STROKE** panel, from the **Weight** drop-down list, select **0.5 pt.**

   j. Collapse the **STROKE** panel.

   k. Save the file.

TOPIC C

Format a Table

You modified the structure of table. Once the table's data and structure are established, you need to complete the formatting of the table. In this topic, you will format a table.

As you review the document, you notice a table that is plain, without any formatting. This table looks out of place and does not draw much attention. You know that the right combination of formatting can make the information really stand out.

How to Format a Table

Procedure Reference: Format a Table

To format a table:

1. Place the insertion point in a table.
2. Choose **Table→Table Options→Table Setup.**
3. In the **Table Options** dialog box, specify the settings.
   - On the **Table Setup** tab, adjust the table dimensions, border, and spacing.
   - On the **Row Strokes** tab, set the pattern, color, and tint for lines separating the rows.
   - On the **Column Strokes** tab, set the pattern, color, and tint for lines separating the columns.
   - On the **Fills** tab, set the background color and tint for rows or columns.
   - On the **Headers and Footers** tab, set the options to add headers or footers to a table.
4. Click **OK.**

Procedure Reference: Format Table Cells

To format table cells:

1. Select table cells.
2. Choose **Table→Cell Options→Strokes and Fills.**
3. In the **Cell Options** dialog box, specify the settings.
   - On the **Text** tab, adjust the cell inset spacing, alignment, and text rotation.
   - On the **Strokes and Fills** tab, set the stroke and color for the cells.
   - On the **Rows and Columns** tab, set the row height and column width.
   - On the **Diagonal Lines** tab, insert diagonal lines in the cells.
4. Click **OK.**

ACTIVITY 6-3
Formatting a Table

Data Files:

My Newsletter.indd

Before You Begin:

The My Newsletter.indd file is open.

Scenario:

You modified the table structure in the newsletter. You realize that the table looks very plain. You want to use the options available in InDesign to enhance the look and feel of the table. You decide to apply fills to the cells of the table and then format those cells.

What You Do	How You Do It
1. Apply formatting to the cells below the header.	a. Scroll to the left and double-click in the first row of the table "Sales Growth 2005-2008 (in Millions)."
	b. Choose **Table→Table Options→Table Setup**.
	c. In the **Table Options** dialog box, select the **Fills** tab.
	d. On the **Fills** tab, from the **Alternating Pattern** drop-down list, select **Every Other Row**.
	e. In the **Alternating** section, in the **First** text box, verify that **1** is displayed, and in the **Color** drop-down list, **[Black]** is selected.
	f. In the **Tint** text box, double-click, type *10%* and then press **Tab**.
	g. In the **Skip First** text box, type *1*
	h. Below the **Next** text box, from the **Color** drop-down list, select **Purple**.

i. In the **Tint** text box, double-click, type *30%* and then click **OK.**

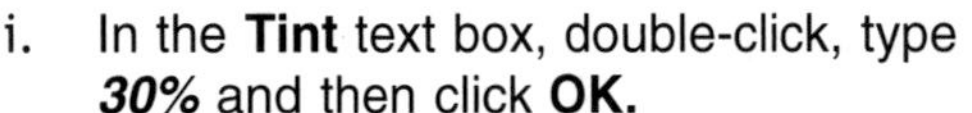

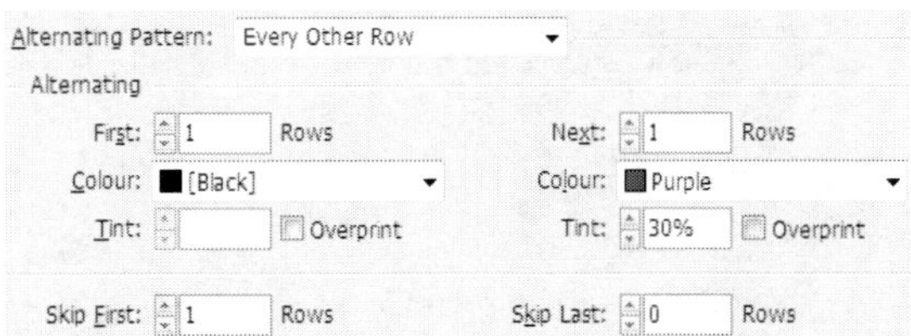

2. Apply formatting to the header row.

a. Choose **Table→Select→Row.**

b. Choose **Table→Cell Options→Strokes and Fills.**

c. In the **Cell Options** dialog box, on the **Stokes and Fills** tab, in the **Cell Fill** section, from the **Color** drop-down list, select **Green.**

d. In the **Tint** text box, double-click, type *30%* and then click **OK.**

e. Deselect the table.

f. Save the file.

TOPIC D
Create Table and Cell Styles

You formatted a table. You want to maintain a consistent look for the tables in a document. In this topic, you will create and apply table and cell styles.

You have a document with many tables. You find it time consuming and tedious to apply the formatting attributes to all the tables in the document. InDesign enables you to select from an existing set of pre-formatted table and cell styles, and then apply them to the tables.

The Cell Options Dialog Box

The **Cell Options** dialog box has various tabs that enable you to include the style name, and format cells accordingly.

Tab	Allows You To
Text	Specify cell settings. You can apply different vertical justifications, and specify offset settings in the cell. This tab also enables you to rotate text and cut the contents of a cell.
Strokes and Fills	Specify different settings for weight, type, and color of strokes in a cell. You can apply a different color and tint percentage for the fill.
Rows and Columns	Specify the row height and column width. You can also specify the different settings for the location of the starting rows in cells.
Diagonal Lines	Select the desired diagonal line using the different buttons available. This tab also enables you to specify the settings for the weight, type, color, tint, and so on for the diagonal lines.

TABLE STYLES and CELL STYLES Panels

The **TABLE STYLES** panel provides a collection of table formatting attributes such as table borders and spacing, row strokes, column strokes, and fills that can be created and applied to a table in a single step. Similarly, the **CELL STYLES** panel provides a collection of cell formatting attributes such as paragraph styles, cell insets, strokes, fills, and diagonal lines. InDesign allows you to create and apply table and cell styles to the tables in documents. You can also import table and cell styles from another document into the active document. A group of related styles can be grouped into folders in the **TABLE STYLES** panel and the **CELL STYLES** panel.

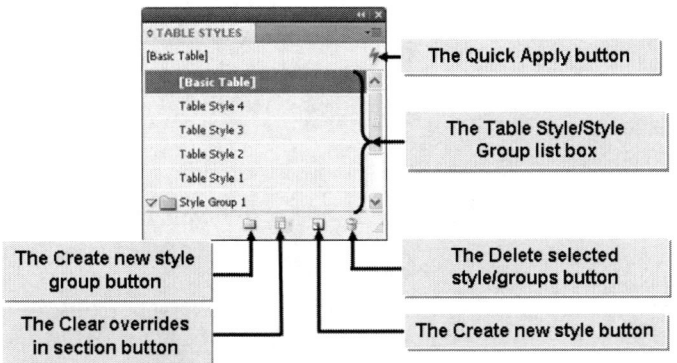

Figure 6-2: *Formatting attributes of the TABLE STYLES panel.*

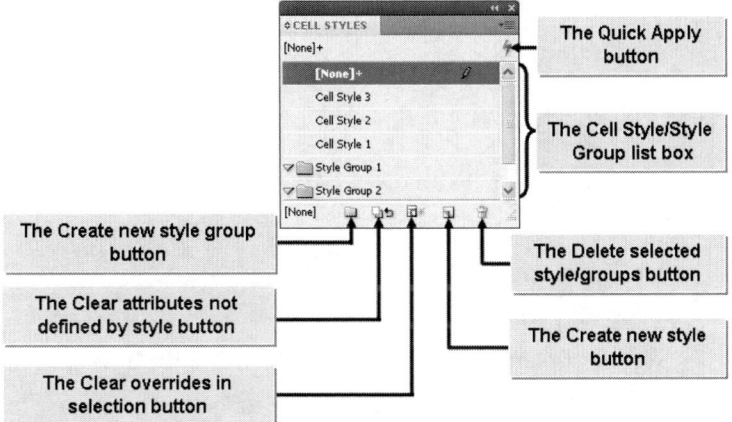

Figure 6-3: *Formatting attributes of the CELL STYLES panel.*

How to Create Table and Cell Styles

Procedure Reference: Create a Table Style

To create a table style:

1. Open an InDesign document.

2. In the **Tools** panel, select the **Type** tool.

3. Click any cell of the table to save its style as a table style.

4. Choose **Window→Type & Tables→Table Styles** to display the **TABLE STYLES** panel.

5. Create a new table style.

   - At the bottom of the **TABLE STYLES** panel, click the **Create new style** button, and then double-click the new style to open the **Table Style Options** dialog box.

   - Or, from the **TABLE STYLES** panel options menu, choose **New Table Style.**

6. In the dialog box that is displayed, in the **General** section, in the **Style Name** text box, type a name.

7. Click **OK.**

8. Select a table.

9. In the **TABLE STYLES** panel, select a table style to apply the style.

Procedure Reference: Create a Cell Style

To create a cell style:

1. Open an InDesign document.
2. In the **Tools** panel, select the **Type** tool.
3. Click any cell of the table to save its style as a cell style.
4. Choose **Window→Type & Tables→Cell Styles** to display the **CELL STYLES** panel.
5. Create a new cell style.
    - At the bottom of the **CELL STYLES** panel, click the **Create new style** button, and then double-click the new cell style to open the **Cell Style Options** dialog box.
    - Or, from the **CELL STYLES** panel options menu, choose **New Cell Style.**
6. In the dialog box that is displayed, in the **General** section, in the **Style Name** text box, type a name.
7. Click **OK.**
8. Click in a cell.
9. In the **CELL STYLES** panel, select a cell style to apply the style.

Procedure Reference: Import a Table or Cell Style

To import a table or cell style:

1. Open the file to which you want to import a style.
2. Choose **Window→Type & Tables→Table Styles.**
3. From the **TABLE STYLES** panel options menu, choose **Load Table and Cell Styles.**
4. In the **Open a File** dialog box, select the file that has the styles you want to import.
5. In the **Load Styles** dialog box, check the styles that you want to import, and click **OK.**
6. If necessary, test the styles on a table.

ACTIVITY 6-4
Creating Table and Cell Styles

Data Files:

My Newsletter.indd

Before You Begin:

The My Newsletter.indd file is open.

Scenario:

After reviewing the layout of a table in the newsletter, your manager suggests that you should use the applied style as a standard style for all company-related tabular information. Also, you want the other tables in the document to have a similar formatting to give a consistent look and feel to the document.

What You Do	How You Do It
1. Save the applied style to the table as a table style.	a. In the table "Sales Growth 2005-2008 (in Millions)," click before the text "Year."
	b. Choose **Window→Type & Tables→Table Styles.**
	c. From the **TABLE STYLES** panel options menu, choose **New Table Style.**
	d. In the **New Table Style** dialog box, under the **General** category, in the **Style Name** text box, type *Growth* and click **OK.**
2. Save the style applied to the cell in the table.	a. Choose **Table→Select→Row.**
	b. Choose **Window→Type & Tables→Cell Styles.**
	c. From the **CELL STYLES** panel options menu, choose **New Cell Style.**
	d. In the **New Cell Style** dialog box, under the **General** category, in the **Style Name** text box, type *Column Header 1* and click **OK.**

3.	Import table and cell styles to apply their styles to another table.	a.	Select the **TABLE STYLES** panel.
		b.	From the **TABLE STYLES** panel options menu, choose **Load Table and Cell Styles.**
		c.	In the **Open a File** dialog box, select **Table Style Import.indd** and click **Open.**
		d.	In the **Load Styles** dialog box, click **Uncheck All.**
		e.	In the **Load Styles** dialog box, check the **Projected** and **Column Header 2** check boxes and then click **OK.**
4.	Apply table and cells styles to another table.	a.	In the table "Projected Sales for 2009-2011 (in Millions)," click before the text "Year."
		b.	In the **TABLE STYLES** panel, select **Projected.**
		c.	Observe that the **Projected** style is applied to the "Projected Sales for 2009-2011 (in Millions)" table.
		d.	Choose **Table→Select→Row.**
		e.	Select the **CELL STYLES** panel.
		f.	In the **CELL STYLES** panel, select **Column Header 2.**
		g.	Deselect the row.
		h.	Close the **CELL STYLES** panel group.
		i.	Save and close the file.

Lesson 6 Follow-up

In this lesson, you worked with tables. Tables can significantly improve reader comprehension by enabling you to organize information clearly.

1. **What are the advantages of creating tables in your document?**

2. **How do table and cell styles help you apply formatting attributes to tables in your document?**

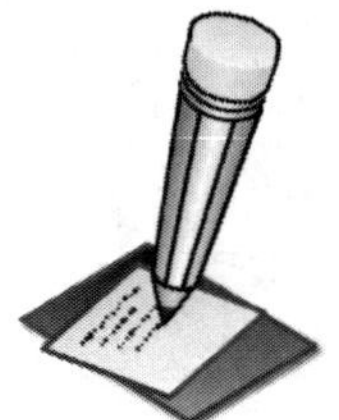

7 | Finalizing Documents

Lesson Time: 45 minutes

Lesson Objectives:

In this lesson, you will finalize documents.

You will:

● Check documents for errors.

● Print a document.

● Package files.

● Export PDF files for commercial printing.

● Prepare PDF files for web distribution.

Introduction

You worked with tables, and completed the development of the InDesign document. Now, you are ready to distribute the document. In this lesson, you will finalize documents.

You can distribute your InDesign document by printing it using a commercial printer or preparing PDFs to make it available to multiple users on different computing systems. Knowing how to prepare and finalize your files for commercial printing will help you create the desired end product efficiently.

TOPIC A
Check Documents for Errors

You completed a document. Now, you want to check if it is ready for printing. In this topic, you will check documents for errors.

Sending an error-ridden document to a printer will only increase costs. You can proof your documents for such errors, prior to sending them to a printer so that your documents are viable, error-free, and printable.

Preflight

Preflight is the process of performing quality checks on a document before printing it. The **Preflight** command checks a document for problems and alerts you to issues you might not have otherwise noticed.

How to Check Documents for Errors

Procedure Reference: Check the Document for Errors

To check the document for errors:

1. Display the **PREFLIGHT** panel.
   - Choose **File→Preflight.**
   - Or, choose **Window→Output→Preflight.**
2. In the **PREFLIGHT** panel, in the **Summary** section, view the errors in the document.
3. Rectify the displayed errors.
   - Change the font used in the document.
     a. In the list box on the left, select **Fonts.**
     b. In the **Fonts** section, check the **Show Problems Only** check box to view the fonts that have problems.
     c. In the list box, if there are fonts listed as missing, incomplete, or protected, change the font in the document.
        A. Click **Find Font.**
        B. In the **Find Font** dialog box, in the **Fonts in Document** list box, select a font to be replaced.
        C. In the **Replace With** section, from the **Font Family** and **Font style** drop-down lists, select a font family and font style, respectively.
        D. Click **Change All** to change the font.
        E. Click **Done.**
   - Repair links.
     a. In the list box on the left, select **Links and Images.**
     b. In the **Links and Images** section, if a message indicating that links are modified is displayed, repair the links.
        - Click **Repair All** to update all the modified files.
        - In the list box, select a link and click **Update** to update the modified file.

4. If necessary, view information about the colors and inks, print settings, and external plug-ins used in the document.

- In the list box on the left, select **Colors and Inks** to display information on the colors and inks used in the document.

- In the list box on the left, select **Print Settings** to display information on the print settings applied to the document.

- In the list box on the left, select **External Plug-ins** to display information on the external plug-ins used in the document.

5. Click **Cancel** to close the **Preflight** dialog box.

Procedure Reference: Relink Images

To relink images:

1. Choose **Window→Links.**

2. In the **LINKS** panel, scroll down and double-click the image you want to relink.

3. In the **Link Information** dialog box, click **Relink.**

4. If necessary, in the **Relink** dialog box, navigate to the folder that contains the image.

5. Select the image file and then click **Open.**

ACTIVITY 7-1

Checking the Document for Errors

Data Files:

Property Finder.indd

Before You Begin:

From the C:\084048Data\Finalizing Documents folder, open the Property Finder.indd file.

Scenario:

You completed the creation of the brochure for the OGC Real Estate company, and want to send the document for printing. Your company has signed an agreement with a new printing vendor, and you need to thoroughly check the fonts and links used in your documents to ensure that you send an error-free document for printing.

What You Do	How You Do It
1. Load a profile before preflight to detect errors.	a. Choose **Window→Output→Preflight.**
	b. From the **PREFLIGHT** panel options menu, choose **Define Profiles.**
	c. In the **Preflight Profiles** dialog box, at the bottom of the left pane, click the **Preflight profile menu** button.
	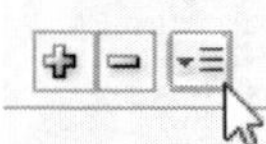
	d. From the drop-down menu, choose **Load Profile.**
	e. In the **Open a File** dialog box, select **Print 4 Color.idpp** and then click **Open.**
	f. In the **Preflight Profiles** dialog box, click **OK.**

2. Use the **PREFLIGHT** panel to view and rectify the errors in the document.

a. In the **PREFLIGHT** panel, verify that the **On** check box is checked.

b. From the **Profile** drop-down list, select **Print 4 Color.**

c. In the **PREFLIGHT** panel, in the **Error** section, observe that a red bullet point indicating an error appears.

d. In the **Error** section, expand **COLOR (1).**

e. Expand **Color space not allowed (1).**

f. Select **'www.ourglobalcompany.com.' (25 chars).**

g. Expand **Info** to view the error and its solution.

h. Double-click **'www.ourglobalcompany.com' (25 chars)** to navigate to page 4.

i. Expand the **SWATCHES** panel, and from the panel options menu, choose **Swatch Options.**

j. In the **Swatch Options** dialog box, from the **Color Mode** drop-down list, scroll up, select **CMYK,** and click **OK.**

k. At the bottom-left corner of the **PREFLIGHT** panel, observe that a green bullet point indicates **No errors.**

l. Collapse the **SWATCHES** panel and close the **PREFLIGHT** panel.

m. Save the file as *My Property Finder.indd*

TOPIC B

Print a Document

You checked documents for errors. Now that there are no errors in the document, you want to distribute hard copies. In this topic, you will print a document.

By printing a document, you make its contents available to all end users who cannot or do not want to access the document electronically.

The Print Dialog Box

The **Print** dialog box has many settings that help you set up print jobs. These settings can be customized and saved as presets.

Print Setting	Description
General	Controls the number of copies and pages, and page sequence, and presents useful options for designers. These options include the ability to print master pages, visible guides, baseline grids, non-printing objects, and blank pages.
Setup	Controls the paper size and orientation and scaling and position of the image on the page, and presents options for printing thumbnails and tiling.
Marks and Bleed	Adds printer marks. You can separately set the bleed distance at each edge.
Output	Creates a composite or color separation. When printing separations, you can control prepress settings such as trapping, screening, and inks.
Graphics	Controls the way in which images and fonts are sent to the printer, and chooses the PostScript level and data format.
Color Management	Achieves accurate color matches between the on screen appearance of the document and the printed version. Color management works by determining the color reproduction characteristics (color space) of each device you use (for example, your monitor and printer), and writing the information about each in a profile.
Advanced	Specifies OPI image replacement settings, substituting low-resolution proxy images for the high-resolution ones for working in InDesign and reducing network traffic, but printing the high-resolution versions. And, controls how InDesign handles gradients and transparency.
Summary	Summarizes the settings you chose in the other categories, and allows you to save the information in a text file that you can keep for future reference.

Commercial Printing

If you need to produce a large number of color pages, a composite printer will not be helpful. Rather, your document should be printed in a press.

Instead of printing directly to a page, you can prepare color separations for the press. Each color separation consists of one color ink. Color separations are typically printed from the computer; they pass from a Raster Image Processor (RIP) to an *imagesetter,* which sends the output to a film instead of paper. Light is then shone through the film to expose a photosensitive material, which is used to create a printing plate. The printing plate is then mounted on the press, and rollers transfer the image from the plate to the paper.

Color Printing

Color printing is produced by using one or more color inks. Depending on the complexity of the document, you may use as few as one, or as many as six or more inks. If the pages contain full-color photographs, the document must be printed with at least four inks—cyan, magenta, yellow, and black (CMYK). This method of printing is also known as process-color or four-color printing.

Composite Printing

Desktop color printers use CMYK colors in the form of inks, dyes, toner, or waxy crayon-like sticks to reproduce all printed colors. Some desktop color printers use additional inks to allow a broader range of colors, but all the printers use CMYK colors. Desktop color printers, and any other printers that create color output directly to a page (such as color copiers), are called composite printers. They combine all the inks directly onto the finished medium. Composite printers are usually used for low print quantities, and for proofs of publications that will be commercially printed.

How to Print a Document

Procedure Reference: Configure Print Settings

To configure print settings:

1. Choose **File→Print.**
2. In the **Print** dialog box, from the **Print Preset** drop-down list, select a print preset.
3. From the **Printer** drop-down list, select a printer.
4. Select a tab to configure print settings.
   - Select the **General** tab to specify the number of pages, the sequence, and the layers to print.
   - Select the **Setup** tab to specify the page size, orientation, and width.
   - Select the **Marks and Bleed** tab to specify the printer marks, bleeds, and slug areas.
   - Select the **Output** tab to specify the color and the inks.
   - Select the **Graphics** tab to specify the settings for graphics.
   - Select the **Color Management** tab to specify the color management options.
   - Select the **Advanced** tab to specify the transparency flattener presets.
5. Click **Print** to print the document.

ACTIVITY 7-2
Printing a Document

Data Files:

My Property Finder.indd

Before You Begin:

The My Property Finder.indd file is open.

Scenario:

Before printing documents, you want to check them by printing a proof with your desktop printer. You want to create a postscript file of your document before you send it for print.

What You Do	How You Do It
1. Configure the print presets.	a. Choose **File→Print Presets→Define.**
	b. In the **Print Presets** dialog box, click **Load.**
	c. In the **Load Print Presets** dialog box, select **Final Proof.prst** and click **Open.**
	d. In the **Print Presets** dialog box, in the **Presets** list box, select **Final Proof** and click **OK.**
2. Save the postscript file for printing.	a. Choose **File→Print.**
	b. In the **Print** dialog box, from the **Print Preset** drop-down list, select **Final Proof.**
	c. Click **Save.**
	d. In the **Save PostScript® File** dialog box, click **Save.**

TOPIC C

Package Files

You printed a proof of a document with a desktop printer. You are satisfied with the output, and decide to ship the document and all its supporting files to a commercial printer. In this topic, you will package files.

Sometimes, a document that you send to a commercial printer may have supporting files. The printer will need the source file and all the supporting files to print the document completely. Sometimes all the files may not reach the printer. This possibility can be eliminated by packaging the files.

Packaging

You can package a primary InDesign file with all its supporting files into one folder. Supporting files include fonts and graphics. Packaging the primary file and its supporting files ensures that your commercial printing vendor gets all necessary files they need to create the printed version of a document.

How to Package Files

Procedure Reference: Package Files

To package files:

1. Choose **File→Package.**
2. In the **Package** dialog box, on the **Summary** page, click **Package.**
3. If necessary, in the **Printing Instructions** dialog box, fill in the company details and other instructions if any.
4. Click **Continue.**
5. In the **Package Publication** dialog box, navigate to a folder, and in the **Folder Name** text box, type a name for the folder.
6. If necessary, in the **Package Publication** dialog box, set the options.
   - Check the **Copy Fonts (Except CJK)** check box to copy the font files to the package folder.
   - Check the **Copy Linked Graphics** check box to copy the linked graphic files to the package folder.
   - Check the **Update Graphic Links In Package** check box to change the graphic links to the package folder location.
   - Check the **Include Fonts and Links From Hidden and Non-Printing Content** check box to package objects on hidden and non-printing layers.
7. Click **Package.**
8. In the **Warning** message box, click **OK.**

ACTIVITY 7-3
Packaging Files

Data Files:

My Property Finder.indd

Before You Begin:

The My Property Finder.indd file is open.

Scenario:

The OGC Real Estate company brochure is error free. You need to send the document to the commercial printer. Before you do that, you want to package all the necessary files and then send it to the printer so that none of the required files are missed.

What You Do	How You Do It
1. Package the file.	a. If necessary, save the file.
	b. Choose **File→Package.**
	c. In the **Package** dialog box, click **Package.**
	d. In the **Printing Instructions** dialog box, in the **Company** text box, click and type *OGC Properties*
	e. In the **Phone** text box, click and type *(617) 555-4438* and then click **Continue.**
	f. In the **Package Publication** dialog box, in the **Folder Name** text box, type *Property Finder Package*
	g. Uncheck the **Copy Fonts (Except CJK)** check box.
	h. Verify that the **Copy Linked Graphics** and **Update Graphic Links In Package** check boxes are checked.
	i. Click **Package.**

2. View the packaged files.

a. In Windows Explorer, navigate to the C:\084048Data\Finalizing Documents\ Property Finder Package folder.

b. Observe that the Instructions.txt report file and the **Links** folder containing all the images are displayed.

c. Double-click the **Instructions.txt** file.

d. Observe that the information about printing instructions for the service provider report is displayed.

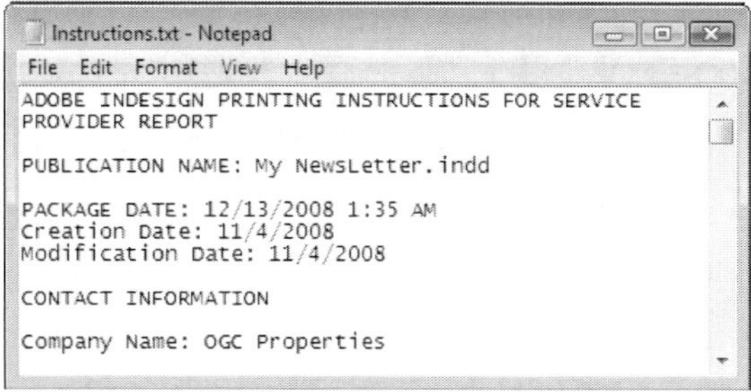

e. Close the Instructions.txt file.

f. Close Windows Explorer.

TOPIC D

Export PDF Files for Commercial Printing

You created a PDF file. You want to send the PDF file to a printer. In this topic, you will export PDF files for printing.

Exporting PDF files for printing allows you to maintain the highest quality type and image resolution for your documents. This makes your printed documents clear, crisp, and easy to read.

How to Export PDF Files for Commercial Printing

Procedure Reference: Export PDF Files for Commercial Printing

To export a PDF file for commercial printing:

1. Open a file.
2. Choose **File→Adobe PDF Presets→Define.**
3. In the **Adobe PDF Presets** dialog box, in the **Presets** section, select an option.
   - Select **[High Quality Print]** for quality printing on desktop printers and proofers.
   - Select **[PDF/X-1a:2001]** and **[PDF/X-3:2002]** to use ISO standards for graphic exchange.
   - Select **[Press Quality]** for high-quality press printing.
   - Select **[Smallest File Size]** for documents that are best suited for on screen display, email, and the Internet.
4. In the **Adobe PDF Presets** dialog box, click **Save As** and select a location to save the file.
5. In the **File name** text box, type a name.
6. Click **Save** to save the PDF.
7. Click **Export** to export the PDF.

Procedure Reference: Create PDF Presets

To create a PDF preset:

1. Open a file.
2. Choose **File→Adobe PDF Presets→Define.**
3. In the **Adobe PDF Presets** dialog box, in the **Presets** section, select a preset.
4. Click **New.**
5. In the **New PDF Export Preset** dialog box, in the **Preset Name** text box, type a name.
6. Modify the required options and click **OK.**
7. In the **Adobe PDF Presets** dialog box, click **Done.**

ACTIVITY 7-4

Export PDF Files for Commercial Printing

Data Files:

My Property Finder.indd

Before You Begin:

The My Property Finder.indd file is open.

Scenario:

The file intended for web distribution also needs to be prepared for printing. You want to create a PDF version of the document that is suitable for printing.

What You Do	How You Do It
1. Export the file as a PDF.	a. Choose **File→Adobe PDF Presets→ [Press Quality]**.
	b. In the **Export** dialog box, in the **File name** text box, type *Property Finder.pdf* and click **Save**.
	c. Verify that in the **Export Adobe PDF** dialog box, in the **Compatibility** drop-down list, **Acrobat 5 (PDF 1.4)** is selected, and then click **Export**.
2. View the PDF file.	a. In Windows Explorer, navigate to the C:\ 084048Data\Finalizing Documents folder.
	b. Double-click **Property Finder.pdf.**
	c. Observe the PDF file and close it, and then close Windows Explorer.

TOPIC E
Prepare PDF Files for Web Distribution

You exported PDF files for printing. Now, you want to prepare these documents so that you can send them to end users via the web. In this topic, you will prepare PDF files for web distribution.

Overly large and inefficiently managed documents can be difficult for viewing and downloading by end users. By preparing your files for web distribution, you can create streamlined, optimized files that are easy to download and view.

Acrobat PDF

Portable Document Format (PDF) provides a versatile way to distribute files, because any computer on any platform can read PDF files with either the free Adobe Reader application or the full Adobe Acrobat application. PDF files can be read through a web browser, and when printed from the browser, they retain the original document's print quality. This format is also used to pass files to commercial printing vendors, because PDF files are usually smaller in size and easier to print than original document files or PostScript files.

Bookmarks

A bookmark is a text entry that appears in the **Bookmarks** panel within Adobe Acrobat or Adobe Reader. Before exporting an InDesign file as a PDF file, the **BOOKMARKS** panel is used to specify bookmarks for the exported PDF file. Users viewing the file in Adobe Acrobat or Adobe Reader can click a specific bookmark to navigate directly to the section they want to view.

PDF Presets

PDF presets are groups of settings that affect the process of creating a PDF. The **New PDF Export Preset** dialog box can be used to modify the settings for a specific setup. PDF presets are saved with InDesign preferences, so that they are available when printing any document.

PDF Presets and Document-Specific Settings

Because PDF presets are designed for use across multiple documents, document-specific settings, such as security settings, cannot be saved in PDF presets.

JDF Integration

While exporting an Adobe PDF file, InDesign can pass information to Acrobat to automatically create a JDF job ticket. Job tickets created with Acrobat 7 Professional or later can be used to automate PDF file creation and preflight, and package final files.

How to Prepare PDF Files for Web Distribution

Procedure Reference: Specify a Bookmark

To specify a bookmark:

1. Choose **Window→Interactive→Bookmarks** to open the **BOOKMARKS** panel.

2. Select an object.

3. From the **BOOKMARKS** panel options menu, choose **New Bookmark** to create a book-mark.

4. Select the bookmark.

5. From the **BOOKMARKS** panel options menu, choose **Rename Bookmark.**

6. In the **Rename Bookmark** dialog box, in the **Name** text box, type a name and click **OK.**

Procedure Reference: Export a PDF Document

To export a PDF document:

1. Choose **File→Export.**

2. In the **Export** dialog box, from the **Save as type** drop-down list, select **Adobe PDF.**

3. Select a location to save the file.

4. In the **File name** text box, type a name and click **Save.**

5. In the **Export Adobe PDF** dialog box, from the **Adobe PDF Preset** drop-down list, select a preset and click **Export.**

ACTIVITY 7-5

Preparing PDF Files for Web Distribution

Data Files:

My Property Finder.indd

Before You Begin:

The My Property Finder.indd file is open.

Scenario:

You decide to make the required changes to the Property Finder document so that it can be distributed over the web. You want to make navigation easier before you export the document as a PDF file.

What You Do	How You Do It
1. Load a PDF preset to optimize the PDF file.	a. Choose **File→Adobe PDF Presets→ Define.**
	b. In the **Adobe PDF Presets** dialog box, click **Load.**
	c. In the **Load PDF Export Presets** dialog box, select **Web PDF.joboptions** and then click **Open.**
	d. In the **Adobe PDF Presets** dialog box, click **Done.**

2. Export a PDF file for web distribution.

    a. Choose **File→Adobe PDF Presets→Web PDF.**

    b. In the **Export** dialog box, in the **File name** text box, type ***Property Finder for Web.pdf*** and click **Save.**

    c. In the **Export Adobe PDF** dialog box, in the **Options** section, verify that the **Embed Page Thumbnails** and **Optimize for Fast Web View** check boxes are checked.

    d. In the **Include** section, verify that the **Bookmarks, Hyperlinks,** and **Interactive Elements** check boxes are checked.

    e. Click **Export.**

    f. In the **Warning** message box, click **OK.**

    g. Save and close the file.

    h. Close the InDesign application.

Lesson 7 Follow-up

In this lesson, you finalized documents and created PDF files. Understanding how to prepare your files for a commercial printer will make it easier for your printer to create the end product you desire, and you can then distribute your work by creating PDF files from the InDesign documents.

1. **How will you prepare your documents for delivery to a commercial printer?**

2. **How will you use PDF files in your current workflow?**

Follow-up

In this course, you worked with some of the tools and features of InDesign CS4 to create eye-catching printed documents. InDesign CS4 provides you with many time-saving tools for the creation of high-quality printable documents.

1. **What are the features of InDesign CS4 that you will use at your workplace?**

2. **For what purposes will you use InDesign CS4 at your workplace?**

3. **How will you use InDesign CS4 to streamline the development of current and future print-based projects?**

What's Next?

Adobe® InDesign® CS4: Level 2 is the next course in this series. The course will teach students how to use the more complex features of InDesign CS4. Other courses that may be of interest include: *Adobe® Photoshop® CS4* and *Adobe® Illustrator® CS4*.

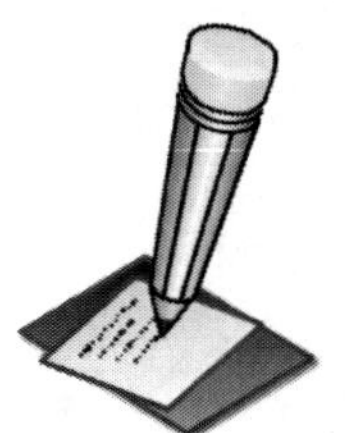

Lesson Labs

Due to classroom setup constraints, some labs cannot be keyed in sequence immediately following their associated lesson. Your instructor will tell you whether your labs can be practiced immediately following the lesson or whether they require separate setup from the main lesson content.

Lesson 1 Lab 1

Exploring the Interface

Data Files:

OGC Travel Guide.indd

Scenario:

You are using the Adobe InDesign application for the first time and you want to familiarize yourself with the interface elements of the application.

1. Display the **Tools** panel in **Double Column** and then change the unit of measurement to **Picas.**

2. Position the **LAYERS, PAGES,** and **LINKS** panels to below the **SWATCHES** panel.

3. Save the settings as *My OGC Workspace.*

4. Navigate to the C:\084048Data\Exploring the InDesign Environment folder and open the OGC Travel Guide.indd file.

5. Using the **Zoom** tool, zoom the text "Get 50% off."

6. Close the file.

Lesson 2 Lab 1

Developing Documents

Data Files:

Import Text 1.txt, Import Text 2.txt, Image 01.eps, Image 02.eps, Image 03.eps, Image 04.eps, Image 05.eps, Image 06.eps, Image 07.eps, Image 08.eps, Image 09.eps, Image 10.eps

Scenario:

You are planning to create a travel guide for the Our Global Company. You decide to develop a document and include text and images in it.

1. Set the top-left reference point, and create a document using the following specifications:
   - **Number of Pages:** *4* inches
   - **Width:** *8.5* inches
   - **Height:** *11* inches
   - **Orientation: Landscape**
   - **Margins:** *0.5* inches
   - **Bleeds:** *0.125* inches

2. On page 1, create a text frame with **X, Y, W,** and **H** as *0.5, 0.5, 10,* and *1.6.* Import text from the Import Text 1.doc file into the text frame.

3. On page 1, create another text frame with **X, Y, W,** and **H** as *4.47, 2.25, 2.23,* and *1.34* and then type ***Chichen Itza-Mexico, Colosseum-Rome, Machu Picchu-Peru, Petra-Jordan, Giza Pyramid Complex-Egypt.***

4. Navigate to page 2, import the text in the Import Text 2.doc file to the page, and flow the text to page 3.

5. For the text frames on pages 2 and 3, specify the number of columns as *2* and gutter as *0.1667* inches.

6. On page 1, place and resize the first five images at the specified location.
   - Image 01.eps:
     - X=0.5
     - Y=2.25
     - W=3.75
     - H=2.625
   - Image 02.eps:
     - X=0.5
     - Y=5.5125
     - W=3.8
     - H=2.4917
   - Image 03.eps: X=3.52 and Y=3.9
   - Image 04.eps:
     - X=6.85
     - Y=2.25
     - W=3.65
     - H=2.6312
   - Image 05.eps:
     - X=6.556
     - Y=5.55
     - W=3.9441
     - H=2.45

7. On page 2, place the sixth and seventh images at the specified location.
   - Image 06.eps: X=2.56 and Y=2.27
   - Image 07.eps: X=7.58 and Y=2.27

8. On page 3, place the eighth and ninth images at the specified location.
   - Image 08.eps: X=13.53 and Y=2.27
   - Image 09.eps: X=18.64 and Y=2.27

9. On page 4, place the last image at the specified location.
   - Image 10.eps: X=2.5 and Y=2.27

10. Save the file as *OGC Travel Guide.indd.*

Lesson 3 Lab 1

Enhancing InDesign Documents

Data Files:

OGC Travel Guide.indd

Before You Begin:

From the C:\084048Data\Enhancing Documents folder, open the OGC Travel Guide.indd file.

Scenario:

You created the document structure and added text and graphics to it. Now, you want to format the text and highlight the title text. You also want to enhance the visual appeal of the document by applying special effects to the text and images in the document.

1. On page 1, set the font, font style, and font size of the first paragraph to **Arial, Bold,** and *18 pt.*

2. Set the font, font style, and font size of the second paragraph to **Times New Roman, Bold Italic,** and *30 pt.* Align the paragraph to the right with the **Space Before** value as *0.1667* inches.

3. Set the font, font style, and font size of the list in the text frame at the bottom of the page to **Times New Roman, Bold,** and *14 pt.* Apply **Bullet** style to the list with the **Left Indent, First Left Indent,** and **Tab Position** values as *0.2083, -0.2083,* and **0.2083** respectively.

4. On page 2, specify the following settings.

   a. Set the font, font style, and font size of the first paragraph to **Arial, Bold,** and *16 pt,* and align it to the left with the **Space Before** and **Space After** values as *6 pt.*

   b. Set the font and font size of the second paragraph to **Arial** and *11 pt.* Align the paragraph to the left with the **Drop Cap Number of Lines** value as *3* and **Drop Cap One or More Characters** as *1.*

   c. Set the font and font size of the third paragraph to **Arial** and *11 pt.* Align the paragraph to the left with the **Space Before** value as *6 pt.*

5. Create a color, *Color01,* with C=0, M=100, Y=100, and K=0, apply it to the images on page 1, and change the stroke to **3 pt.**

6. On pages 2, 3, and 4, change the stroke of the images to **3 pt** and then apply the color black to the stroke.

7. Save the file as *My OGC Travel Guide.indd.*

Lesson 4 Lab 1

Managing Page Elements

Data Files:

OGC Travel Guide.indd

Before You Begin:

From the C:\084048Data\Working with Page Elements folder, open the OGC Travel Guide.indd file.

Scenario:

While enhancing the appearance of an InDesign document, you notice that most of the objects in the file are not appropriately arranged and aligned. You decide to organize the page elements, place objects on respective layers, and apply the attributes of the master pages to all pages of the document.

---

1. Select the image at the center of page 1 and bring it to the front.

---

2. Rename **Layer 1** as *Text* and create two more layers naming them *Images* and *Frames.* Place them in the **Images, Text,** and **Frames** order.

---

3. Place all the images in the **Images** layer.

---

4. On the **A-Master** page, perform the following actions.

   a. Create a text frame with **X, Y, W,** and **H** values as *-0.125, -0.125, 11.125,* and *8.75,* respectively and apply **Color01.**

   b. Copy the text frame, paste it on the right master page with **X** and **Y** values as *11* and *-0.125,* respectively.

   c. Place both the text frames in the **Frames** layer.

---

5. Create a **B-Master** page based on the **A-Master** page and perform the following actions.

   a. Create a text frame with the **X, Y, W,** and **H** values as *-0.125, 0.195, 11.125,* and *6.13,* respectively and apply **Color04.**

   b. Create another text frame with the **X, Y, W,** and **H** values as *0.5, 0.8, 10,* and *0.32,* respectively.

   c. Enter the text *Overview* in the text frame and apply the **Header** paragraph style.

   d. Create a text frame for the footer with the **X, Y, W,** and **H** values as *0.5, 8.17, 10,* and *0.3,* respectively.

   e. Select the footer text frame, insert an auto-page number, and then apply the **Footer** paragraph style.

   f. Group all the objects and copy and paste them on the right master page with the **X** and **Y** values as *11* and *-8,* respectively.

6. Apply the settings of the **A-Master** page to page 1 and the **B-Master** page to pages 2, 3, and 4.

7. On pages 2, 3, and 4, select the text frame and change the coordinates of **Y** to *2.5* and **H** to *5.75* to align the text frame.

8. Save the document as *My OGC Travel Guide.indd.*

Lesson 5 Lab 1

Managing Objects in an InDesign Document

Data Files:

OGC Travel Guide.indd

Before You Begin:

From the C:\084048Data\Managing Objects folder open the OGC Travel Guide.indd file.

Scenario:

The text in your document appears with spelling errors, so you decide to spell check the document. You also want to improve the appearance of the document by modifying text formats.

1. On page 1, rotate the banner at 15 degrees and change its shape to rounded corner.

2. On pages 2, 3, and 4, select the images and wrap them at **0.14** inches from the left.

3. Perform spell check and fix the following spelling errors.

    a. Replace "diffrent" with "different."

    b. Replace "proprty" with "property."

4. Save the file as ***My OGC Travel Guide.indd.***

Lesson 6 Lab 1

Working with Page Elements

Data Files:

OGC Travel Guide.indd

Before You Begin:

From the C:\084048Data\Working with Tables folder open the OGC Travel Guide.indd file.

Scenario:

While creating the brochure, you notice that the text in the document looks unorganized. You decide to present the text as a table and apply various formatting settings to make the tabular data more appealing and readable.

1. At the bottom of page 4, convert the text in the text frame to a table.

2. Apply the following settings to the table.

- For the first row, set the **Alternating Pattern** as **Every Other Row**, color as **Color04**, tint value as **20%,** and **Skip First** value as **1.**
- Apply color as **Color 05 10%** and tint value as **10%** to the next row.
- Apply **Color 05** to the header row.

3. Save the file as ***My OGC Travel Guide.indd.***

Lesson 7 Lab 1

Finalizing InDesign Documents

Data Files:

OGC Travel Guide.indd

Before You Begin:

From the C:\084048Data\Finalizing Documents folder open the OGC Travel Guide.indd file.

Scenario:

Your manager wants you to create a PDF file that will be used for the organization's website, and will also be handed off to a print service provider. Before you send the finalized file to the client, you want to make sure that the output is of the desired quality.

1. Check the document for missing fonts or images. Also, check the color space used in the document.

2. Create a package of the document that includes only images.

3. Export the document as Web.pdf using the **[Smallest File Size]** preset.

4. Export the document as Print.pdf using the **[High Quality Print]** preset.

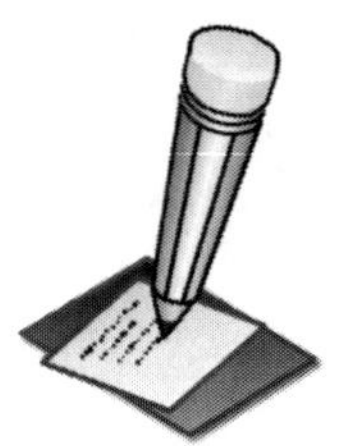

Solutions

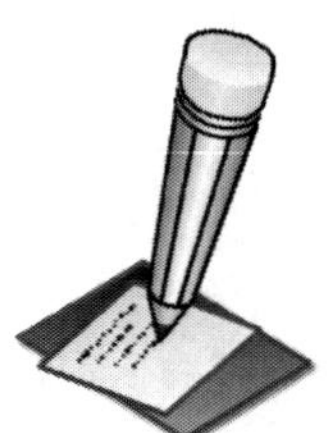

Glossary

Adobe InDesign CS4

An easy-to-use layout application that designers use to produce documents such as newsletters, brochures, mailers, magazines, and newspapers.

auto leading

A predefined setting that creates a leading value at 120 percent of the largest type size on a line.

baseline grid

An on-screen alignment tool that is used to align columns of text.

bulleted list

A list used to denote a group of equally significant items.

child master

The master pages in a document that are based on the parent master page of the same document.

contour text wrap

A type of text wrap that allows you to wrap text in the same shape as the selected frame.

document grid

An on-screen alignment tool that is used to align objects.

document page

An InDesign page that is used for creating and laying out text and graphical objects.

fill

The background color used within the bounds of a graphic placeholder.

flattening

The act of merging the artwork in a document into a single printable layer.

gradient

A combination of background colors that move from a scale of light to dark.

graphic frame

A container or placeholder that is used to place images.

grid

An on-screen alignment tool that is used to align objects or columns of text.

imagesetter

An output device that generates high-resolution output from a computer file, typically for camera-ready content.

layers

Transparent parts of a document that are stacked.

leading

The measurement of space between the baseline of one line and the baseline of the next.

LINKS panel

A panel that has a number of elements that enable you to list and track all the files placed in a document.

lists
Used to present information separately from the surrounding text.

master page
An InDesign document page that contains text and images, which will repeat on multiple pages in the document.

nested style
A style that can be applied to specific ranges of text within a paragraph.

notes
Briefly written entities or reminders that help you communicate information.

numbered list
A list used to denote a ranking or sequence that must be followed to achieve a desired outcome.

page guides
Guides that appear only on the page on which they are created.

parent master
The master page on which other master pages in the document are based.

Preflight
The process of performing a quality check on a document before printing it.

process colors
Colors defined by combining different colors to produce a required shade.

rectangular text wrap
A type of text wrap that allows you to wrap text around the squared edges of a rectangular frame.

ruler
An on-screen measuring device used to measure the vertical and horizontal position of page elements in a document.

rules
Lines that appear either above or below paragraphs and are used to separate the heading and the body text of a document.

shapes
A representation of creating a building block that enables you to place text and graphics.

spot color
Printed from one premixed ink and can reproduce colors that are outside the gamut of process colors.

spread guides
Guides that appear across all pages of a multiple-page spread.

Story Editor
A text-editing tool that allows you to focus on editing text without having to view it in a formatted layout.

story
An uninterrupted body of text that flows in a text frame.

stroke
A line that bounds the outer perimeter of a graphic or text frame.

style
A user-specified look and feel factor that can be consistently applied across multiple page elements.

swatch
A stored color definition that can be applied to any element that requires color.

table
A container used to organize text or graphics in a column and row format.

text frame
Used to include text in a document.

text overset
A feature that has unseen text in a text frame. It occurs when the amount of text you want to place in a text frame or cell is more than the size of the text frame or cell.

text threading
The act of designating one text frame to receive text that extends beyond the boundaries of another text frame.

text wrap

It refers to the different settings that allow text to flow around another object in various ways.

tints

Lighter variations of colors defined as swatches.

TRANSFORM panel

A panel that displays various geometrical information, such as position, size, rotation, and shear, about an object.

transformation

A format applied to objects to change their shape or position.

Type tool

A tool that enables you to add text to a text frame and also to select text.

user dictionary

A customized list of correctly spelled words that you can use to spell check your documents.

workspace

An arrangement of window elements in a document.

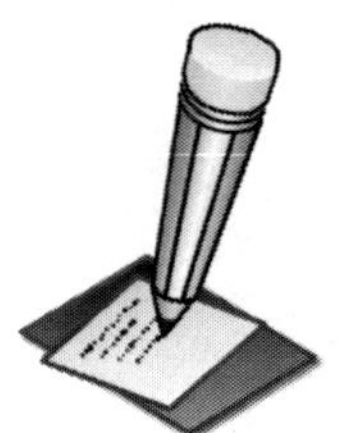

Index

lists, 58

M

masters
  child, 110
  parent, 110

N

nested style, 78
notes, 143
numbered list, 58

P

pages
  document, 110
  master, 109
panels
  ALIGN, 98
  BOOKMARKS, 186
  CELL STYLES, 166
  CHARACTER STYLES, 79
  COLOR, 66
  Control, 9
  GLYPHS, 56
  INFO, 42
  LAYERS, 103
  LINKS, 43
  NOTES, 143
  OBJECT STYLES, 79
  PAGES, 110
  PARAGRAPH STYLES, 79
  STROKE, 74
  SWATCHES, 66
  TABLE, 157
  TABLE STYLES, 166
  Tools, 4
  TRANSFORM, 122

Preflight, 174
process colors, 65

R

ruler, 32
rules, 58

S

shapes, 126
spell check, 142
spot color, 66
story, 130
Story Editor, 142
stroke, 73
style, 78
swatch, 67

T

table, 152
text overset, 131
text threading, 131
tints, 67
tools
  Selection, 131
transformation, 122
Type tool, 29

U

user dictionary, 142

W

Welcome Screen, 2
workspace, 8
wraps
  contour text, 41
  rectangular text, 41
  text, 41